IRISH CONFLICTS OF LAW

Also by the author (with Bryan M.E. McMahon

THE IRISH LAW OF TORTS (1981)
A CASEBOOK ON THE IRISH LAW OF TORTS (1983)

Also by the author (as sole Author)

A CASEBOOK OF IRISH FAMILY LAW

IRISH CONFLICTS OF LAW

by

WILLIAM BINCHY

B.A., B.C.L., LL.M.

Barrister-at-Law, Research Counsellor,
The Law Reform Commission

with a
FOREWORD
by
The Honourable Mr. Justice Brian Walsh

M.A. (N.U.I.), LL.D. (H.C.) (Dublin)

Senior Ordinary Judge of the Supreme Court of Ireland
Judge of the European Court of Human Rights

Butterworth (Ireland) Ltd
1988

Republic of Ireland	Butterworth (Ireland) Ltd
United Kingdom	Butterworth & Co (Publishers) Ltd, 88 Kingsway, LONDON WC2B 6AB and 61A North Castle Street, EDINBURGH EH2 3LJ
Australia	Butterworths Pty Ltd, SYDNEY, MELBOURNE, BRISBANE, ADELAIDE, PERTH, CANBERRA and HOBART
Canada	Butterworths, A division of Reed Inc, TORONTO and VANCOUVER
New Zealand	Butterworths of New Zealand Ltd, WELLINGTON and AUCKLAND
Singapore	Butterworth & Co (Asia) Pte Ltd, SINGAPORE
USA	Butterworths Legal Publishers, ST PAUL, Minnesota, SEATTLE, Washington, BOSTON, Massachusetts, AUSTIN, Texas and D & S Publishers, CLEARWATER, Florida

© Butterworth (Ireland) Ltd 1988

ISBN: Hardback: 0 86205 220 3
       Paperback: 0 86205 221 1

Printed in Great Britain by William Clowes Ltd, Beccles

CONTENTS

		Page
Foreword		vii
Preface		xiii
Acknowledgment		xix
The Constitution		xxi
Table of Statutes		xxiii
Statutes in other Jurisdictions		xxxiii
Table of Cases		xxxv
Bibliography		lxxi

Part 1:	**Preliminary Topics**	1
Chapter 1:	The Historical Background	3
Chapter 2:	Ireland and the Conflict of Laws	22
Chapter 3:	Characterisation	27
Chapter 4:	The "Incidental Question"	31
Chapter 5:	Renvoi	35
Chapter 6:	Domicile and other Connecting Factors	45
Chapter 7:	Proof of Foreign Law	104

Part II:	**Jurisdiction and Related Matters**	121
Chapter 8:	Jurisdiction	123
Chapter 9:	Exclusion of a Foreign Law	192

Part III:	**Family Law and Related Matters**	209
Chapter 10:	Monogamy and Polygamy	211
Chapter 11:	Marriage Validity and Annulment	218
Chapter 12:	Divorce	269
Chapter 13:	Divorce a Mensa et Thoro and Restitution of Conjugal Rights	294
Chapter 14:	Maintenance Entitlements	301
Chapter 15:	Minority	321
Chapter 16:	Legitimacy and Legitimation	347
Chapter 17:	Adoption	368
Chapter 18:	Mental Incompetency	381

Part IV:	**Law of Property**	389
Chapter 19:	Movable and Immovable Property	391
Chapter 20:	Immovables: Jurisdiction	401
Chapter 21:	Immovables: Choice of Law	408
Chapter 22:	Family Property	414
Chapter 23:	Succession	429

Chapter 24:   Administration of Estates   453
Chapter 25:   Bankruptcy   462
Chapter 26:   Companies   482
Chapter 27:   Negotiable Instruments   487
Chapter 28:   Transfer of Choses in Possession   494
Chapter 29:   Assignment of Choses in Action   501
Chapter 30:   Trusts   506

Part V: Law of Obligations   515
Chapter 31:   Contracts   517
Chapter 32:   Torts   567

Part VI: Foreign Judgments and Arbitrations   583
Chapter 33:   Recognition and Enforcement of Foreign Judgments
                and Arbitrations   585

Part VII: Procedure   623
Chapter 34:   Substance and Procedure   625
Chapter 35:   Security for Costs   652

INDEX   671

Foreword

By giving us this first Irish textbook on Private International Law Mr. William Binchy has rendered a signal service to all practitioners and students of Irish law. In recent years it has become apparent that Private International Law was beginning to play a more important part in Irish Law. It is safe to say that prior to the 1960's the subject attracted little attention in legal circles in Ireland. While it has always been part of the Irish common law it was not a necessary subject for qualification as a lawyer. Indeed, generations of lawyers have come and gone without ever having made any real study of Private International Law or ever having much, if any, occasion to consult it. The law reports in Ireland indicate a comparative paucity of cases and judicial decisions on this branch of the law. Such decisions as are to be found, particularly in this century, appear mostly to deal with questions of jurisdiction.

There were certain historical reasons for the apparent neglect in Ireland of Private International Law and particularly for the narrow scope of the case law. There was little litigation in Ireland involving foreign law and most of that which did occur related to English Law. As English law was in most areas almost identical with Irish law, the cases offered little if any scope for Irish lawyers or Judges to engage in examination of foreign law in the full sense of the term. In addition, prior to Ireland's accession to the European Communities, the great bulk of all our foreign trade was conducted with the United Kingdom. Following Ireland's entry into the European Communities the pattern of foreign trade changed very dramatically. More than half of our foreign trade is now with States other than the United Kingdom. The rapid growth of easier travel and greater freedom of movement of peoples between Ireland and other countries has given rise to the necessity of examining anew the problems which will arise in the field of Private International Law.

Some of the English cases which Mr. Binchy cites illustrate that since 1949 English Courts seem to suffer from confusion regarding the name of our State. This is possibly due to the United Kingdom statute, the Ireland Act, 1949, which purported to provide that this State should be "referred to ..... by the name attributed thereto by the law thereof, that is to say, as the Republic of Ireland". It is difficult to understand how such an error could have been made as, of course, the name which Irish law attributes to the State is "Ireland", as it has been for fifty years, by Article 4 of the Constitution and which was so acknowledged by a communiqué from No. 10 Downing St., in 1937. Regrettably some of our statutory semi State bodies seem to be infected with a similar confusion. There is only one State in the world named "Ireland" and references in contracts to the applicable law as "the law of the Republic of Ireland" or "the law of the Irish Republic" are wrong. Whatever justification may exist for English confusion there is none whatever for Irish ignorance. Our semi State bodies and their legal advisers might at least honour the Golden Jubilee of the Constitution of Ireland by learning the correct name of the State upon which they depend.

Family law is one of the areas giving rise to increasing conflict of laws situations due to the greater international mobility of persons. The Law Reform Commission, to which Mr. Binchy in his capacity as a research counsellor has given invaluable service, devoted much time to, and published several reports dealing with, conflict of laws situations in matters of family law. In these areas of law it was the policy of the Commission, insofar as it was possible, to adopt the various Hague Conventions as the basis of an attempt to achieve some degree of uniformity in several fields of family law. The Commission was also motivated by the desire to achieve the adoption of concepts of Private International Law which would pay particular attention to those which existed in other member states of the European Communities, and indeed in the whole of Europe. It was decided that the Hague Conventions formed a very useful basis for this exercise and a good vehicle for introducing uniformity into this field. The fact that Ireland had very little experience and little tradition in the field of Private International Law was an advantage in that those engaged in law reform were not burdened by any preconceptions or wedded to any particular national views about what the rules of Private International Law ought to be, bearing in mind, of course, that nothing inconsistent with the Constitution could be adopted. As will be evident to the readers of this book, among the subjects which the Law Reform Commission studied and in respect of which it published several reports with detailed recommendations for changing the law, were the rival claims of domicile and habitual residence as connecting factors in the conflict of laws, the recognition of foreign divorces and legal separations, and the conflict rules concerning international child abduction.

Regrettably the many reforms urged by the Law Reform Commission have not yet received statutory attention. This inattention is probably due, to a considerable extent, to lack of parliamentary time and lack of resources in personnel in the relevant Government Departments to whom would be committed the preparation of the necessary legislation. But one cannot omit as a factor the power of inertia produced by political apathy or of antipathy on the part of many of those persons who vociferously called for reform in these areas but who, in the event, seemed to be more interested in posing questions than in receiving answers. The only resultant legislation was the Domicile and Recognition of Foreign Divorces Act, 1986 which embodied the Law Reform Commission's recommendation that the rule of the domicile of dependency of a married woman be abolished. It also introduced a change in the law on the recognition of foreign divorces which is calculated to create more problems than it will solve. The latter subject is dealt with on the basis of continuing to recognise domicile as a connecting factor in the conflict of laws. Admittedly at the time it was stated that this measure, for which it was perceived there was some political necessity, was without prejudice to a future consideration of the Commission's recommendations that this concept should be abolished as a connecting factor in favour of habitual residence.

The particular areas of law where habitual residence had already been adopted as a connecting factor in Irish legislation are in the Succession Act, 1965, and the Air Navigation Act, 1973. The many other recommendations of the Law Reform Commission in the field of family law were based on the assumption that the connecting factor would be habitual residence rather than domicile. Habitual residence offers a much more realistic approach than domicile and a much more concrete basis of a close connection with a particular State than the more abstract concept of domicile. In addition, the concept of domicile as we know it is virtually impossible to explain in any State whose legal system is essentially based on the civil law. The majority of our fellow members of the European Communities fall into that category.

Our membership of the European Communities should be the decisive factor in the choice we make. The Judgments Convention of the European Communities is one that Ireland was by the Treaty of Accession bound to accept and one that accepts the principle of ordinary or habitual residence. The United Kingdom legislation which already has been enacted has for the purpose of this convention redefined "domicile" to make it accord with the concept of ordinary or habitual residence. However this convention has not yet come into force in Ireland. Happily it is currently being processed through the Oireachtas. That proposed legislation also redefines "domicile" for the purpose of the Convention in terms of ordinary or habitual residence.

In a quite different field of Private International Law within the European Communities Ireland has agreed to adopt uniform rules regarding contractual obligations. The Convention for this purpose was agreed after more than ten years negotiation and study by a Working Party comprised of the representatives of all the then ten members of the European Community. The Working Party had originally also included in its work the subject of obligations arising from tort but after a couple of years this was abandoned because of the complexity of the subject and because it became clear that there was no hope of agreement between the member States on this topic. This Convention, the Rome Convention, 1980, was intended to be a sister convention to the Judgments Convention and to come into force at the same time. Unfortunately the necessary legislation for this has not yet been prepared. This is not a Convention which the State is obliged under the Treaty of Accession to accept but it is nevertheless one which the State did sign and agreed to accept. This Convention, which fixes uniform rules of Private International Law in respect of contractual obligations, will be a new venture in Irish Law and will be of very considerable importance in view of our great increase in trading with other member States of the European Community and with States outside the Community. Both that Convention and the Judgments Convention will also mark a new departure so far as aids to interpretation in Court are concerned. The explanatory report prepared in relation to the Judgments Convention may be relied upon in court and the court may take it into account in interpreting the Convention. This valuable report by Mr. P. Jenard will be of great assistance. In addition the Courts may also consider the Schlosser Report. Mr. Jenard was Chairman of the Working Party which drew up the Judgments Convention. Professor Schlosser was not a member of that group and his report deals with the 1978 Accession Convention. The proposed legislation to bring the Convention to force makes provision for these aids to interpretation. So far as the Rome Convention, 1980 is concerned, similar legislation will provide that the explanatory report concerning that Convention may also be used in Court. This report will be of particular value because it was drawn up by the late Professor Giuliano of the University of Milan and his co-rapporteur, Professor Lagarde of the University of Paris, who were both members of the Working Party. Its particular value lies in the fact that the report itself was considered in every detail by the Working Party contemporaneously with the Convention. This report, both as to form and content, is the result of the agreement of all the representatives of the States taking part in the negotiations. Thus, in this particular branch of Private International Law, the Irish Courts will enjoy not only the benefits of the uniform rules in force in every other member State in the European

Communities but also the advantage of being aided by the explanatory report which simultaneously will be in use in the Courts of all the other member States of the Communities.

Another area of Private International law in which Ireland has been active has been the Hague Permanent Conference on Private International Law, which comprises very many countries outside Europe as well as in Europe. Ireland became a member of this Permanent Conference in 1955 and from the 1960s onwards was represented on virtually every special committee and in the Plenary Sessions of the Conference. The Irish delegates played an active and prominent part in discussions at the various Plenary Sessions, as the records of those meetings testify. Not a great deal of interest was aroused in Ireland by these discussions. The first systematic effort to incorporate them in Irish Law was by the Law Reform Commission, in the area of family law. As one would expect, Mr. Binchy's chapters on the recognition of foreign marriages and the recognition of foreign divorces are of very considerable interest. Readers will be particularly interested to note the careful analysis of the effects of the Constitution on the rules of Private International Law and particularly the effect of Article 41, Section 3 of the Constitution. It may well be, as he suggests, that the full conflict of laws implications of Section 3, subsection 3, have not yet been wholly appreciated by our judicial decisions which deal with it. However it must be realised that, even if there were no constitutional ban on enacting legislation permitting the dissolution of marriage, the serious and complex issues that arise in the area of recognition of foreign marriages and foreign divorces would still exist unless and until there is some effort at achieving a degree of uniformity in the complex rules of the various countries. In their own modest way the Law Reform Commission proposals were designed to make a contribution to this end. The thirty or so pious couples who had their marriages celebrated in Lourdes required the passing of the Marriages Act, 1972 to validate them in Irish law might perhaps fail to appreciate the irony of the fact that a Communist State, the German Democratic Republic, would have recognised the marriages as being valid.

The question of the recognition of common law marriages had always been an unclear one but was made even more so by the the the decision in the *Millis* case, which was patently wrong because of a misunderstanding of what the relevant Canon Law had been. The close connection between the basis of a common law marriage and the Canon Law cannot be overlooked, in particular in view of the fact that the decree of the Council of Trent which outlawed clandestine marriages, only took effect as and from when it was promulgated in each diocese. In Ireland that occurred at different times in the various dioceses between the middle of the 17th century and the first quarter of the 19th century. It was never promulgated in England. The observations of Gavan Duffy J. in *Cook v. Carroll* to the effect that there are some areas, in particular those dealing with religion, in which the common law in Ireland and the common law in England may not coincide should not be overlooked. In other words:- is the common law to be determined as it stood before the Reformation or as it was expounded after the Reformation? The relevance of this in the field of the Irish rules of conflict of laws is that it may be a determining factor in deciding whether some particular form of marriage abroad would be recognised in Ireland as a common law marriage.

As Mr. Binchy rightly stresses, the conflict of laws rules are part of the common law of Ireland save insofar as they have been varied or introduced by statute. Up to now law students and teachers alike have been greatly impeded by the absence of any Irish textbook on this subject. The subject has had to be studied with the aid of foreign textbooks which made little or no reference to Irish cases and no reference whatever to particular Irish legal situations and how they could affect or be affected by a foreign element in litigation. Mr. Binchy's book fills this gap within the Irish legal context. For this he will earn the well deserved gratitude of Irish practitioners and students and also the esteem and gratitude of scholars of Private International Law throughout the world. This book is another outstanding contribution by Mr. Binchy to Irish legal scholarship. Contemporary Irish lawyers are indeed fortunate to have him in their midst.

Brian Walsh
The Supreme Court
August, 1987.

PREFACE

The Irish conflict of laws is a fascinating subject. In view of the historical background and contemporary social realities, no student could be content with identifying "black letter" rules of law. Inevitably, policy issues demand resolution. Throughout the book, I have sought to identify some of the more important of these issues and to indicate possible avenues for a solution. A prior task, however, was to locate the law on the subject. I was pleased to find that there is a substantial body of case-law, some of it already widely known, but other parts of it a good deal less prominent.

In analysing the Irish material, I have sought to place it in a wider international context. My reliance on the work of scholars in other jurisdictions will be immediately obvious.

This book began as a joint venture, with Joseph Brosnan, B.L. When he had completed two long chapters, on Jurisdiction and Judgments, Joseph was appointed Assistant Secretary at the Department of Justice, and had to withdraw. He was good enough to let me use these chapters, for which I am most grateful.

I have stated the law on the basis of materials available to me at the beginning of February. In one or two instances, where this did not greatly interfere with the proofs, I was able to include brief references in the text to somewhat later developments.

From the law's inexorable progress over the past few months, a number of judicial and legislative developments are worthy of particular note. In *C.M. v. T.M.*, High Ct., 23 February 1987 (1986-500P), Egan, J. addressed the question of the effect on family maintenance entitlements of recognition of a foreign divorce. He considered himself "compelled" (on the authority of *T. v. T.*, [1983] I.R. 29 and *L.B. v. H.B.*, [1980] I.L.R.M. 257) to conclude that, on the granting of a foreign divorce absolute to a husband, based on his domicile alone, a wife would have no right to claim maintenance under the *Family Law (Maintenance of Spouses and Children) Act 1976* either on her own behalf or on behalf of her children. He observed that there was "consolation" in the fact that the wife would still seem able to apply for maintenance for her children under section 11 of the *Guardianship of Infants Act 1964*. As regards proceedings under section 12 of the *Married Women's Status Act 1957*, it appeared to Egan, J. that a claim would lie only in respect of assets of the husband within the jurisdiction as he did not consider that the Act could have extra-territorial effect. He reserved final judgment of this point, however, for the trial judge who would be hearing subsequent proceedings in the case before him.

In *Kutchera v. Buckingham International Holdings Ltd.*, High Ct., 27 February 1987 (1986-11642P), the plaintiff, a South-African, resident in London, sued a Public Company incorporated in Alberta, on foot of a loan agreement, seeking, *inter alia*, a declaration that he was entitled to nominate four directors to the board as well as to have certain shares allotted to him. A clause in the loan agreement provided that all aspects of it should be construed and governed by the "law of the Republic of Ireland". The judgment gives no indication of any connection between the parties and Ireland. Carroll, J. discussed, but did not expressly resolve, the important question as to the limits on the freedom of parties to submit the contract to any law of their choosing. The case can best be understood as one in which the Court declined to exercise jurisdiction on the basis that Ireland was not the *forum conveniens*. However, one part of the Judge's disposition of the case merits quotation:

> "The proper law of a contract determines its essential validity. The provisions of the contract sought to be enforced here are concerned with the internal management and control of a public company. The essential validity of the contract depends on whether the company was entitled to enter into and is bound by the contract or not. In my opinion Irish law could not be applied to decide whether the Defendant had the capacity to enter into the contract and whether it was binding and legal. The Defendant, being a creature of statute, only has such powers as have been conferred on it by the laws of the place where it was incorporated. Therefore, it is Canadian or Alberta law which must be considered to determine whether the contract is valid and enforceable. This is saying, in other words, that Canadian law must be applied to determine the essential validity of the contract.
>
> Apart from Clause 10, Clause 1(d) provides in effect that the legal requirements of Canadian law should be complied with in order to give the agreement full effect. The Plaintiff submitted that this was the incorporation of some provisions of foreign law as a term of the contract as distinct from the choice of Irish law as the proper law of the contract and therefore that Canadian law could be applied as a term of the contract to determine the capacity of the Defendant to enter into the contract and the legality of the obligations thereby created. But that is in effect saying that Canadian law is to be the proper law of the contract, thus contradicting Clause 10. To decide whether the obligations are created or not is to determine the essential validity of a contract."

This passage raises a difficulty in suggesting that "Canadian" law would have to be applied to determine the essential validity of the contract merely because the defendant was a company incorporated in Alberta. Carroll, J. mentions no obstacle under the law of Alberta to the defendant's capacity to enter into a loan agreement or to choose Irish law as the proper law of that agreement. The judgment would appear to deny any freedom to parties, one of which is a company, to choose a law other than of the place of incorporation of the company. The judgment also appears to identify incorporation with the selection of the proper law. According to the conventional view, there is a difference between these two processes: cf. *infra*, pp. 523-524. The case is perceptively analysed by Mr A.V. Gill in 5 Ir. L. Times (n.s.) 114 (1987).

In re Fleming Deceased, High Ct., 16 March 1987, is a case teeming with conflicts issues. Gannon, J. held that the annulment in Nevada in 1968 of a marriage of a man then domiciled in England should not be recognised here and that, accordingly, his subsequent marriage (to the same person) in 1977 had not the effect (under section 85(1) of the *Succession Act 1965*) of revoking a will made by him in 1971. The precise basis of non-recognition is not entirely clear. It seems that Gannon, J. considered that recognition should be based on the domicile or residence of the respondent in the country where the decree is made. He did not refer to the position under the law of England or California (which was, it seems, the wife's *lex domicilii*); thus we still have no explicit judicial resolution of the question whether a decree recognised as valid in the country of the domicile of one party should be recognised here: cf. *infra*, p. 260. The case contains a thorough analysis of the issue of the testator's somicile, which is worthy of close attention.

Several decisions mentioned in the text have now been reported; they include *K.E.D. (otherwise K.C.) v. M.C.*, [1987] I.L.R.M. 189 (referred to in the text *sub nom. K.C. v. M.C.*), *S.E.E. Co. Ltd. v. Public Lighting Services Ltd*, [1987] I.L.R.M. 255, *Sachs v. Standard Chartered Bank*, [1987] I.L.R.M. 297 and *Conlan v. Mohamed*, [1987] I.L.R.M. 1972.

In the wake of the fall of the previous Government, a Bill seeking to give effect in our law to the EEC Judgments Convention was introduced in the Seanad and has now passed all stages. It is drafted in very similar terms to the earlier Bill: cf. *infra*, p. 182. A fairly important modification, however, is contained in section 6, which provides that lump sum maintenance payments are to be enforced as if they were High Court Judgments and which empowers the Master, on the application of the maintenance creditor, to declare that arrears of maintenance which had accumulated before the issue of an enforcement order are to be capable of enforcement as if they were a High Court judgment.

In relation to Article 5(1) of the Convention (cf. *infra*, pp. 184-185), the ruling of the European Court of Justice in *Shenavai v. Kreischer*, (case 266/85), 15 January 1987, should be noted, The Court held that, in determining the place of performance within the meaning of Article 5(1), the obligation to be taken into consideration in an action for the recovery of fees, by an architect commissioned to prepare plans for the building of houses, is the contractual obligation actually forming the basis of the legal proceedings. The Court took the view that contracts of employment have certain special characteristics compared with other contracts, even those relating to the provision of services, since contracts of employment create a long-term relationship located at the place where the business is carried out, that place determining the application of mandatory provisions of law and collective agreements. In the absence of these special characteristics, the Court held, the identification of the obligation characterising the contract was not necessary and might create uncertainty.

The massive work on the Convention by Peter Kaye (*Civil Jurisdiction and Enforcement of Foreign Judgments*), published last May, is worthy of particular attention.

On the important question of the range of constitutional protection to those with little or no ties to the State (cf. *infra*, pp. 332-337) the Supreme Court, in *Sanders v. Midwestern Health Board*, 23 June 1987, rejected the appeal by English parents against an order by Hamilton P. for the return to England of their children, whom they had brought into the jurisdiction in breach of orders of the English High Court. Finlay, C.J., giving the decision of the Court, is reported (Irish Times, 24 June 1987, p. 8) as having said that the Court could not accept that the parents, who had no connection with this country, had conferred on themselves and their children constitutional rights under Articles 40 and 41. As a general principle, the comity of courts had accepted that matters relating to children should be determined by a court of the jurisdiction where the children ordinarily resided and where it was intended that they be brought up. He did not find any exceptional circumstances which would prevent him from departing from the general principle.

During legal argument before the judgment, Henchy, J. is reported as having said that, when the English court orders were made, neither the parents nor the children had acquired rights under our Constitution. He asked how it was possible to acquire these rights when they had kidnapped the three children and brought them to Ireland. Finlay, C.J., and Hederman, J. stressed the fact that the parties had consented to the order that their children be put in care.

In view of the urgency of the case the Court did not reserve judgment. It would be unwise to read too much into the observations during legal argument. The Court did not have to address the broader questions as to the limits of constitutional protection. All that the case decides is that foreign parents, with no connection with this country, who consent to their children being taken from them may not invoke Articles 40 and 41 when they "kidnap" the children in breach of an order of the court of the country of their ordinary residence and bring them here. The more difficult issues have yet to be resolved, as, for example, where the parents have acted perfectly legally and where they reasonably apprehend that their children will be subjected to an intervention (by a foreign state or individual) which is not permitted by our Constitution. Recent High Court decisions (notably *Pok Sun Shun v. Ireland* [1986] I.L.R.M. 593 (High Ct., Costello, J., 1985) and *Osheku v. Ireland*, [1987] I.L.R.M. 330 (High Ct., Gannon, J., 1986)) analysing the constitutional implications of legislation dealing with aliens do not resolve this issue. In none of these cases did the court hold that the Constitution excluded aliens from the protection of Articles 41 and 42 (though in *Pok Sun Shun*, at p. 597, Costello, J. left the point open). Clearly the fact that the legislative control of aliens is constitutional involves no necessary conclusion that aliens with little or no connection with Ireland are excluded from the protection of these Articles.

Some recent publications should be noted. *Doing Business in Ireland*, edited by Patrick Ussher, is a mine of information on several aspects of the law. Of particular relevance are the contributions by David Clarke and Max Abrahamson (ch. 16, *Litigation and Arbitration*) and by William Duncan (choice of law in contract). I had advance access to Gerard Hogan's contribution, and was able to incorporate references to it in the text.

The first round of analysis of the Supreme Court decision in *Grehan* has now taken place. I was able to record Mr A.V. Gill's contribution (5 Ir. L. Times (n.s.) 3 (1987)) in the text *infra*, pp. 579-580). Mr Gabriel McGann, B.L. has since produced a stimulating appraisal of the implications of the case, in 81 Gaz. of Incorp. L. Soc. of Ireland 109 (1987). Practitioners would be well advised to take note of what it has to say.

The Hague Convention on the Law Applicable to Trusts and their Recognition has been the subject of recent analysis in England (Hayton, 36 Int. & Comp. L.Q. 260 (1987)) and the United States (Gaillard & Trautman, 35 Amer. J. of Comp. L. 307 (1987)).

I owe a debt of gratitude to several people. First I must thank Mr Justice Brian Walsh for his help and encouragement during the preparation of the text. His very broad international experience, at The Hague, Brussels and Strasbourg, gives him a unique insight into the subject. I am very grateful to him for having provided a foreword.

I received a great deal of help and detailed advice from Gerard Hogan of Trinity College and David Morgan of University College, Cork, each of whom read the manuscript in its entirety and made many suggestions for improvement. They also brought to my attention a number of decisions, from Ireland and abroad.

Caoimhín Ó hUiginn, of the Department of Justice, read the chapters on Jurisdiction and Judgments, and gave me the benefit of his considerable expertise on the EEC Judgments Convention. Mr Gerard Lee, S.C. gave me some very useful information in relation to guardianship of infants. Ms Peggy McQuinn of the Supreme Court Office, and Ms Margaret Byrne, Librarian, of the Law Society, could not have been more helpful in locating unreported judgments. Mr Jonathan Armstrong, Librarian, King's Inns Library and Mr Nigel Cochrane, Assistant Librarian, patiently unearthed some very old materials. I should also record the helpful advice and support of my colleagues, Charles Lysaght, B.L., and Frank Ryan, B.L. Mr Gary Lynch gave me very considerable help, for which I am most grateful. Mr Harold Slawik, of St. Paul, Minnesota, could not have been of greater assistance, at very short notice.

The Arthur Cox Foundation provided financial support in the preparation of the text; I am grateful to the Trustees of the Foundation for their generous assistance.

WILLIAM BINCHY
7 July 1987

THE ARTHUR COX FOUNDATION

Arthur Cox, solicitor, classical scholar and former President of the Incorporated Law Society of Ireland, was asssociated with the setting up of many Irish Companies, not least the E.S.B. He was a specialist in company law and was a member of the Company Law Reform Committee which sat from 1951 and reported to the Government in 1958, ultimately giving rise to the Companies Act, 1963. When he decided to retire from practice as a solicitor in 1961 a number of his clients, professional colleagues and other friends, in recognition of his outstanding contribution to Ireland and his profession, thought that a fund should be established as a tribute to him which fund would subsidise the publication of legal text books. There was a generous response to this appeal.

After his retirement he studied for the priesthood and was ordained in 1963. He went to Zambia to do missionary work. He died there in 1965 as a result of a car accident.

The Foundation was established to honour Arthur Cox and was for many years administered by Mr. Justice John Kenny in conjunction with the Law Society. In paying tribute to the memory of Arthur Cox it is appropriate that tribute should also be paid to Mr. Justice John Kenny, who died on 25 March, 1987. John Kenny was a close personal friend of Arthur Cox and, like Arthur Cox, graced with distinction his own barristers' profession, as a chancery practitioner, and both the High Court and Supreme Court, as a judge. John Kenny was the encouraging force behind the publication of a number of Irish legal textbooks. Without his quiet drive and enthusiasm there would have been no Foundation. To both Arthur Cox and John Kenny we pay tribute.

The Law Society, as the continuing trustee of the Foundation, is pleased to have been able to assist in the publication of Mr. William Binchy's book.

David R. Pigot,
President,
The Incorporated Law Society of Ireland.
July, 1987

xix

THE CONSTITUTION

Generally 25, 26, 78, 80, 82, 203, 224, 229, 271
272, 273, 274, 275, 276, 277, 278, 279, 280
282, 288, 297, 320, 334, 335, 336, 337, 338
339, 341, 356, 379, 380, 470, 471, 473, 608, 630, 631
Article 2 ....278, 356
Article 3 ....278, 356
Article 29.1 206
Article 29.3 ....173, 175, 206
Article 40 ....335, 338
Article 40.1 80
Article 40.3 81
Article 41 ....25, 34, 81, 239, 271, 272, 273, 274, 275
276, 277, 278, 282, 293, 335, 336, 337, 338, 339
Article 41.1 ....321, 322, 337
Article 41.3 ....237, 274, 635
Article 41.3.1° 279
Article 41.3.2° 271
Article 41.3.3° 26, 34, 237, 238, 239
271, 272, 273, 274, 275, 276, 277, 278
Article 42 ....321-322, 332, 335, 336
Article 42.5 322
Article 43 ....81, 335
Article 44 335
Article 50 279

TABLE OF STATUTES

Pre-Union Statutes of the Irish Parliament

Statute of Frauds 1695 (7 Will. 3, c.12) 539, 631
Marriages Act 1745 (19 Geo. 2, c.13) 219

Post-Union Statutes

Ecclesiastical Courts Act 1813
                    s.1 297
                    s.3 297
Lotteries Act 1823
                    s.41 520
Marriages Confirmation Act 1823 (4 Geo. 4, c.91) 116
Gaming Act 1835 (5 & 6 Will. 4, c.41)
                    s.1 552
Marriage Act 1835 (5 & 6 Will. 4 & 1 Vict., c.26) 219
Wills Act 1837 (7 Will. 4 & 1 Vict., c.26)
                    s.27 451
Charitable Donations and Bequests (Ireland) Act 1844
                    s.15 511
                    s.16 508
Fatal Accidents Act 1846 (9 & 10 Vict., c.93) 639
Petty Sessions (Ireland) Act 1851 203
Income Tax Act 1853
                    s.2 483
                    Schedule D 483
Bills of Sale (Ireland) Act 1854 499
Common Law Procedure Amendment Act (Ireland) 1856
                    s.14 133
Foreign Tribunals Evidence Act 1856 (19 & 20 Vict., c.113)
                   634-636
                    s.1 ....634, 636
                    s.2 634
                    s.5 635
Irish Bankrupt and Insolvent Act 1857 (20 & 21 Vict., c.60)
                    ....463, 477
                    s.31 464
                    s.90 ....463, 464
                    s.127 463
                    s.178 464
                    s.267 465
                    s.268 465
                    s.353 463
                    s.409 463

Probates and Letters of Administration Act (Ireland) 1857 (29 & 21 Vict., c.79)
    s.5 ....454, 457
    s.6 454
    s.94 457
Landlord and Tenant Law Amendment Act 1860
    s.4 631
Offences Against the Person Act 1861 (24 & 25 Vict., c.114)
    s.55 346
    s.56 346
Wills Act 1861 (24 & 25 Vict., c.114) 39, 40, 432
    s.1 432
Companies Act 1862 (25 & 26 Vict., c.89)
    s.199 485
Judgments Extension Act 1868 (31 & 32 Vict., c.54)
    ....498, 499, 610, 661
    s.1 610
Legitimacy Declaration Act (Ireland) 1868 (31 & 32 Vict., c.54)
    ....355-357, 367
    s.1 355-357
    s.6 356
    s.7 ....356, 367
    s.8 ....356, 367
    s.9 ....356, 367
Extradition Act 1870
    s.24 634
Matrimonial Causes and Marriage Law (Ireland)
Amendment Act 1870 269
    s.13 ....293, 294
Lunacy Regulation (Ireland) Act 1871 ....380, 382
    s.68 382
    s.91 386
    s.96 382
Bankruptcy (Ireland) Amendment Act 1872 (35 & 36 Vict., c.58)
    ....463, 472, 473, 474, 477
    s.5 464
    s.17 464
    s.21, para.1 463
    s.21, para.2 463
    s.21, para.3 463
    s.58 480
    s.70 ....477, 478
    s.71 ....202, 203, 469, 471-477
Debtors Act (Ireland) 1872 463-464
Trade Union Act Amendment Act 1876
    s.6 24
Supreme Court of Judicature (Ireland) Act 1877 401
    s.27(5) 162, 163
    s.28(8) 153
    s.38(10) 312
Fugitive Offenders Act 1881 23
Bills of Exchange Act 1882 (45 & 46 Vict., c.61)
    s.2 487
    s.4(1) 489
    s.4(2) 489
    s.49(5) 490
    s.50(2) 490
    s.50(2), para.(a) 490
    s.50(2), para.(b) 490

s.50(2), para.(c) 490
s.51(2) 490
s.51(9) 491

s.72 487-493
s.72(1) 487, 488
s.72(2) 488-490

s.72(3) 491
s.72(4) 491
s.72(5) 492
s.89(1) 492

Married Women's Property Act 1882 (45 & 46 Vict., c.75)
s.17 ....427, 428
Settled Land Act 1882 (45 & 46 Vict., c.38) 393-396
s.22(5) 393, 395
Married Women (Maintenance in Case of Desertion) Act 1886
....301, 315
s.1 313
Deeds of Arrangement Act 1887 (50 & 51 Vict., c.57) 463
Factors Act 1889 (52 & 53 Vict., c.45) 497
s.9 497
Interpretation Act 1889 (52 & 53 Vict., c.63)
s.18(2) 384
Preferential Payments in Bankruptcy (Ireland) Act 1889 463
Deeds of Arrangement Act 1890 463
Intestates Estates Act 1890 (53 & 54 Vict., c.29) 440
s.1 441
s.2 441
Lunacy Act 1890 (53 & 54 Vict., c.5)
s.107 ....382, 383
s.110 ....383, 384
s.116(1)(e) 382
s.131 383
s.131(2) 383
s.131(3) 383
s.131(4) 382, 383
Local Registration of Title (Ireland) Act 1891 470
Colonial Probates Act 1892 (55 & 56 Vict., c.6) 457
Foreign Marriages Act 1892 (55 & 56 Vict., c.23) 230
s.11 230
s.21(6) 230
s.22 230
s.11 460
Sale of Goods Act 1893 (56 & 57 Vict., c.71) 497, 532
s.1 498
s.4 631
s.9 498
s.12 ....523, 532, 533
s.13 ....523, 532, 533
s.14 ....523, 532, 533
s.15 ....523, 532, 533
s.25(2) 497, 498
s.55 523
s.55A 532
s.61(6) 523, 532
Moneylenders Act 1900 (63 & 64 Vict., c.51) 519, 520, 528, 546
s.6 546

Irish Land Act 1903
s.16 395
s.34 395
Public Trustee Act 1906 511
Trade Disputes Act 1906 (6 Edw.7, c.47)
s.4(1) 24
Probation of Offenders Act 1907
s.1(3) 186
s.1(4) 186
Children Act 1908
s.99 186
Companies (Consolidation) Act 1908 (8 Edw.7, c.69)
s.180(1) 610
s.278 667
Bankruptcy (Scotland) Act 1913 (3 & 4 Geo.5, c.20)
s.97(3) 471
Forgery Act 1913
s.4(1) 203
Bankruptcy Act 1914 (4 & 5 Geo.5, c.59) 468, 470, 472, 477
s.2 472
s.18(1) 470
s.53(1) 468
s.121 478
s.122 ....472, 473, 475, 476
s.T167 ....468, 470
Administration of Justice Act 1920 (10 & 11 Geo.5,c.81) 610
Government of Ireland Act 1920 661
Maintenance Orders (Facilities for Enforcement) Act 1920 (10 & 11 Geo. 5, c.33)
....309, 310
s.1 309
s.2 309
s.3 309
s.3(4) 309
s.4 309
s.10 ....309, 319

Post-Independence Statutes

Adaptation of Enactments Act 1922 (No.2) 22, 23, 661
s.3 ....22-24, 231, 310, 472, 475, 487
Irish Free State Constitution Act 1922
First Schedule, Art. 3 42
Courts of Justice Act 1924 (No.10)
s.79 183
Illegitimate Children (Affiliation Orders) Act 1930 (No.17)
....315-317
s.2(1) 311
s.2(2) 318, 319
s.3 314
s.3(2) 319
Public Charitable Hospitals (Temporary Provisions) Act 1930
(No.12) 547
s.3(3) 547
Legitimacy Act 1931 (No.13) 49, 357-367, 371
s.1 367
s.1(1) 49, 352, 360, 361
s.2 367
s.2(1) 366, 367

s.2(1A) 366, 367
s.3 363-365
s.3(1) 365
s.3(2) 365
s.3(3) 365
s.3(4) 365
s.4 ....360, 365
s.8 ....361, 363, 366, 367
s.8(1) 352, 361, 363
s.8(2) 361, 366
s.9(2) 355
s.10(2) 363
s.11 367
Schedule 371
Public Hospitals Act 1933 (No. 18) 655
Aliens Act 1935 (No.14) 102
s.5(5)(c) 102, 103
Air Navigation and Transport Act 1936 (No.40) 160
Courts of Justice Act 1936 (No.48)
s.3 ....610, 662
Schedule 1, Part I 610, 662
Constitution (Consequential Provisions) Act 1937 (No.40)
s.2 ....310, 356
Interpretation Act 1937 (No.38)
s.20(1) 314
Enforcement of Court Orders Act 1940 (No.23)
s.8 315
Adoption Act 1952 (No.25) 375
s.3 370
s.10 ....370, 371
s.11(1) 370
s.11(4) 370
s.11(5) 370
s.40 ....345, 346
Arbitration Act 1954 (No.26) 616
Part V 618, 619
s.12 621
s.12(1) 525
s.39(3) 622
s.41 617-619
s.54(4) 618
s.55(1) 618
s.55(2) 618
s.56(1) 618
s.56(2) 618, 620
s.57(1) 619
s.58 618
s.59 616
First Schedule 618, 619
Second Schedule 618
Gaming and Lotteries Act 1956 (No.2) 552
s.36 552
Irish Nationality and Citizenship Act 1956 (No.26)
s.6(1) 96
s.6(2) 96
s.6(3) 96
s.6(4) 96
s.7(2) 96

Married Women's Status Act 1957 (No.5)

s.12 ....216, 407, 427-428

Statute of Limitations 1957 (No.6) 641

s.12(2) 639

s.24 639

s.35 639

s.38 639

s.39 639

s.41 639

Administration of Estates Act 1959 (No.8)

s.15 457

s.16 454

s.29 454

Courts (Supplemental Provisions) Act 1961 (No.39)

s.9 381

s.9(4) 381

Third Schedule 183

Civil Liability Act 1961 (No.41) 582

Part IV 216, 454, 639

s.11(3) 320

s.31 639

s.34(1) 582

s.49(1) 644

Charities Act 1961 (No.17)

s.4 508

Copyright Act 1963 (No.10)

s.7(5)(a) 98

Companies Act 1963 (No.33) 128, 611

Part X 485

s.99(1) 498

s.99(2) 498

s.345(4)(a) 485

s.345(7) 485

s.352(1)(c) 128

s.356(1) 128

s.356(2) 128

s.390 ....667, 668

s.399(5)(a) 485

Adoption Act 1964 (No.2) 375

s.2(1) 371

s.5 370

s.5(2) 370, 375

s.5(3) 370

Guardianship of Infants Act 1964 (No.7) 302

s.2 322

s.2(3) 322

s.3 ....323, 327

s.5 321

s.6 340

s.10(1) 322

s.11 322

s.11(1) 322

s.11(2)(a) 322

s.11(2)(b) 323

s.11(4) 323

s.11(5) 322

s.17(2) 530

Land Act 1965 (No.2) 530

Succession Act 1965 (No.27) 65, 79, 216, 238, 429, 447, 450, 453, 585

              Part VIII 98, 433, 434, 450, 456, 457

              Part IX 437

              s.5 434

              s.6 454

              s.8 457

              s.10(1) 457

              s.13 457

              s.27(1) 455

              s.27(3) 455

              s.27(4) 455

              s.29 ....454, 455

              s.31 455

              s.45 453

              s.46 453

              s.47 453

              s.48 453

              s.50 453

              s.55 453

              s.57 453

              s.58 453

              s.59 453

              s.60 453

              s.61 453

              s.64 453

              s.65 453

              s.67(1) 435

              s.67(2) 435

              s.67(3) 354

              s.73(1) 354, 429

              s.82 434

              s.85 452

              s.85(1) 447, 449

              s.85(2) 447

              s.93 451

              s.102 450

              s.102(1) 433, 434, 447, 450

              s.102(2) 447

              s.102(3) 433

              s.102(4) 50, 433

              s.103 433

              s.104(1) 450

              s.104(2) 450

              s.106(1) 434

              s.106(2) 434

              s.107(1) 443, 445

              s.107(2) 434

              s.109(2) 437

              s.110 366

              s.111(1) 435

              s.111(2) 435

              s.117 ....42, 366, 435, 436, 437, 438, 439

              s.117(1) 354

              s.117(6) 639

Diplomatic Relations and Immunities Act 1967 (No.8) 178,

                                        179, 180, 181

              Article 5(j) 636

s.5(1) 178
s.6(1) 180
ss.7-25 180
ss.26-36 181
ss.39-45 178
First Schedule 178
Second Schedule 180
Third Schedule 180
Fourth Schedule 180
Fifth Schedule 180

Income Tax Act 1967 (No.6)
    s.76 101
    s.199 101

Courts Act 1971 (No.36)
    s.12 302
    s.20 ....358, 366

European Communities Act 1972 (No.27)
    s.2 181

Marriages Act 1972 (No.30)
    s.2 223-227

Air Navigation and Transport Act 1973 (No.29)
    s.11(4) 98
    s.11(5) 98

Adoption Act 1974 (No.24) 375
    s.5 370

Maintenance Orders Act 1974 (No.16) 290, 310-317
                                         610, 611, 614
    s.3(1) 310-312, 315, 319
    s.3(2) 311, 312
    s.4 ....310, 315
    s.6(1) 312
    s.6(4) 312
    s.6(5) 312
    s.6(6)(a) 312
    s.6(6)(b) 312
    s.7 312
    s.7(2) 313
    s.7(3) 312, 313
    s.7(4) 313
    s.8(1) 313
    s.8(2) 313
    s.8(3) 313
    s.9 ....212, 213, 290, 314, 319
    s.10 313
    s.11(1) 314
    s.11(2) 314
    s.12 ....314, 653
    s.13(2) 312
    s.13(4) 312
    s.13(5) 312
    s.14(1) 314
    s.14(2)(a) 315
    s.14(2)(b) 315
    s.14(3) 315
    s.14(4) 315
    s.14(5) 315
    s.14(6) 315
    s.14(7) 315

s.14(8) 315
s.14(8)(b) 315
s.14(8)(c) 315
s.14(9) 315
s.16 ....313, 314
s.17(1) 316, 319
s.17(2) 316
s.17(3)(a) 316
s.17(3)(b) 316
s.18 316
s.19(1) 316
s.19(2) 316
s.19(3) 312
s.19(3)(i) 316
s.19(3)(ii) 316
s.19(3)(ii) 316
s.20 317
s.21(1) 317
s.21(2) 317
s.22 317
s.22(1) 317
Capital Gains Tax Act 1975 (No.20)
s.4(1) 101
Building Societies Act 1976 (No.38)
s.23(3) 453
Family Law (Maintenance of Spouses and Children) Act 1976
(No.11) 81, 285, 292, 302, 303, 314, 316, 317
Part III 315
s.3(1) 315
s.5 ....304, 314
s.6 303
s.6(1)(a) 304
s.6(1)(b) 303, 304
s.8 ....311, 550
s.10(1)(a)(iii)(II) 315
s.23 302
s.28(1)(b) 318, 319
Family Home Protection Act 1976 (No.27) 81, 216, 282, 292
s.1(1) 216
s.4 216
Consumer Information Act 1978 (No.1)
s.17(3) 186
Arbitration Act 1980 (No.7) 162, 616, 619-622
Part III 159, 619
Part IV 159, 619, 621
s.2(1) 621
s.4 525
s.5 ....621, 622
s.5(1) 622
s.5(2) 622
s.6(1) 619, 620
s.6(2) 619, 620
s.7(2) 620
s.8 620
s.9(1) 620
s.9(2)(d) 621
s.9(2)(e) 621
s.9(3) 621

s.9(4) 621
s.11 616
s.16(2) 621
s.17 629
Second Schedule 619

Sale of Goods and Supply of Services Act 1980 (No.16)
....532, 545
s.23 ....523, 545
s.26 ....524, 533
s.27 ....524, 533
s.28 ....524, 533
s.29 ....524, 533
s.31 ....524, 533
s.36 ....524, 533, 545
s.39 ....524, 533
s.40 ....524, 533
s.41 524
s.42 ....533, 545

Courts Act 1981 (No.11)
s.4 454
s.12 232
s.28 644

Family Law Act 1981 (No.22)
s.2 ....532, 552
s.2(1) 545

Air Navigation (Eurocontrol) Act 1983 (No.38)
s.2 199

Age of Majority Act 1985 (No.2) 90, 539
s.1 377
s.2 ....50, 90, 539
s.2(1) 431
s.6 322

Domicile and Recognition of Foreign Divorces Act 1986 26
78, 84, 278, 281-284
s.1 ....41, 46, 78
s.1(1) 78
s.1(2) 78
s.2 ....46, 78, 79, 82
s.3 ....46, 78, 79
s.4 ....46, 82, 84, 88, 89, 351
s.4(1) 87, 88
s.4(1)(a) 89
s.4(1)(b) 89
s.4(2) 89, 90
s.4(3) 87
s.4(4) 84
s.5 281-284
s.5(1) 214, 281-283
s.5(2) 49, 282, 283
s.5(3) 49, 282, 283
s.5(4) 281, 283, 284, 304
s.5(6) 284
s.7 78

Irish Nationality and Citizenship Act 1986
s.3 96
s.4 96
s.5 96
s.6 96

STATUTES IN OTHER JURISDICTIONS

Northern Ireland

Legitimacy Act (Northern Ireland) 1928
  s.1(1) 48
Statute Law (Repeals) Act 1981
  sl.(1), Sched.1, Part 1 .... 471, 476

Britain

Carriage of Goods by Sea Act 1871 523
Guardianship of Infants Act 1925
  s.1 331
Adoption of Children (Scotland) Act 1930 369
Companies Act 1948 530
Ireland Act 1949
  s.2(1) 475
  s.3(2) 475
Arbitration 1950 .... 528, 529
Variation of Trusts Act 1958 510
Wills Act 1963
  s.1 98
  s.2(1)(a) 433
Adoption Act 1968
  s.4(3) 376
Divorce Reform 1969 303
Recognition of Divorces and Legal Separations Act 1971
  s.3 98
  s.7 264
  s.8(2) 287
Maintenance Orders (Reciprocal Enforcement) Act 1972
  Part I 310
Domicile and Matrimonial Proceedings Act 1973
  Parts 1-5 49
  s.1(2) 79
  s.5 98
Children Act 1975
  Schedule 1 376
  Schedule 1, para.3(1) 85
  para.4(1) 85
Adoption Act 1976
  s.39 85
Administration of Justice Act 1977
  s.4 491
Matrimonial Homes and Property Act 1981
  s.3 216

Civil Jurisdiction and Judgments Act 1982
s.30 402
s.45(3) 188
Insolvency Act 1985 462
Insolvency Act 1986 462
s.426 472

New Zealand

Insolvency Act 1967
s.135 474

Domicile Act 1976
s.5(1) 78
s.7 76
s.10 50
s.12 77

Australia

Domicile Act 1982
s.7 76

New South Wales

Domicile Act 1979
s.6 76

TABLE OF CASES

Page

A. v. A., 19 L.R. Ir. 403 (1897) 242
A. v. H., High Court, D'Arcy, J., 1978 333
A. (Infants), Re. [1970] Ch. 665; [1970] 3 W.L.R. 142; 114 S.J. 415; [1970]
  3 All E.R. 184 327
A.B. v. A.G., I.R. 4 Eq. 56 (1869) 356, 357
Abate v. Abate, [1961] P. 29, [1961] 1 All E.R. 569; 259
Abbot-Smith v. Governors of University of Toronto, 45 D.L.R. (2d) 672 (1964) 148
Abernethy v. Greer, 36 I.L.T.R. 63 (1902) 328
Abidin Daver, The, [1981] A.C. 557; 166, 167, 168
Achillopoulos, In re, [1928] Ch. 433, 97 L.J. Ch. 246; 139 L.T. 62 ....458, 459
A.C.L. v. R.L. High Court, Barron, J., 8 October 1982 287
Adams v. Clutterbuck, 10 Q.B.D. 403; 52 L.J.Q.B. 607; 48 L.T. 614; 31 W.R. 723
  (1883) 411
Adams v. Davison, 6 Ir. Jur. (N.S.) 390 (1861); 146
Adams Deceased, Re; Bank of Ireland Trustee Co. v. Adams, [1967] I.R. 424; 43, 44
  46, 50, 63, 64, 66, 68, 69, 70, 72, 73, 75, 90, 111, 430, 431, 432, 434, 437, 442,
  443, 444
Adams v. Mavro, 17 I.C.L.R. 686 (1866) 144
Adastra Aviation v. Airports, [1964] N.Z.L.R. 393 148
Adcock v. Aarons, 5 W.A.R. 140 (1903) 141
Addison v. Addison, [1955] N. Ir. 1 ....242, 243, 294
Addison v. Brown, [1954] 1 W.L.R. 779; 98 S.J. 338; [1954] 2 All E.R. 213; 617
Adelaide Electric Supply Co. Ltd., v. Prudential Assurance Co., [1934] A.C. 122; 103
  L.J. Ch. 85; 150 L.T. 281; 50 T.L.R. 147; 77 S.J. 913 543
Adelman v. Adelman, [1948] 1 W.W.R. 1071 (Alta) 252
Agnew v. Usher, 14 Q.B.D. 78 (1884) 137
Ah Yin v. Christie, 4 Comm. L.R. 1428 (1907) 54
Ainslie v. Ainslie, 39 C.L.R. 381; 27 S.R.N.S.W. 524; [1927] Argus L.R. 301 297, 602
Alaska Packers Ass. v. Industrial Accident Commission, 294 U.S. 532 (1935) 16
Alaska Trainship Corp. v. Canadian Merchant Service Guild, 41 D.L.R. (3d) 116 (1973) ..195
Alberta v. Cook, [1926] A.C. 444 47
Alcock v. Smith, [1892] 1 Ch. 238; 61 L.J. Ch. 161; 66 L.T. 126; 8 T.L.R. 222; 36
  S.J. 199 ....489, 490, 495
Aldrich v. A.G., [1968] P. 281; [1968] 2 W.L.R. 413; [1968] 1 All E.R. 345 356, 454
Aldridge v. Aldridge, 1954 S.C. 58; 1954 S.L.T. 84 251
Alexander v. Burke, 22 L.R. (Ir.) 443 (1887) 88
Ali v. Ali, [1968] P. 564; [1966] 2 W.L.R. 620; [1966] 1 All E.R. 664; 214
Alison's Trusts, Re, 31 L.T. 638; 23 W.R. 226 (1874) 219
Allain v. Chambers, 8 Ir. C.L.R. vii (1858) 656
Allan's Trustees, 24 R. 718; 34 S.L.R. 532; 4 S.L.T. 361 (1897) 513
Allard v. Charbonneau, [1953] 2 D.L.R. 442; [1953] O.W.N. 381 640
Allen, In re, [1945] 2 All E.R. 264 ....439, 440
Aloulaff v. Oppenheimer, 10 Q.B.D. 295 (1882) 607

Amanat-Khan v. Fredian Travel Inc., (No. 2), 36 O.R. (2d) 17 (1982) 175
Ambrose v. Ambrose (otherwise Harnish or Hornish), 25 D.L.R. (2d) 1 (1961) 222, 234
Amin Rasheed Shipping Corporation v. Kuwait Insurance Co. [1984] A.C. 50 ..557
Anchor Line (Henderson Brothers) Ltd., Re, [1937] Ch. 483; 105 L.J. Ch. 330; 155
    L.T. 100; 80 S.J. 572; [1936] 2 All E.R. 941 413
Anderson v. Eric Anderson Radio & T.V. Pty. Ltd., 114 C.L.R. 20 (1965) 582
Anderson v. Nobels Explosive Co., 12 O.L.R. 644 (1906) 149
Andros, Re, 24 Ch. D. 637 (1883) 369
Anghinelli v. Anghinelli, [1918] P. 247; 87 L.J.P. 176; 119 L.T. 227: 34 T.L.R. 438;
    62 S.J. 548; 295
Annesley, Re; Davidson v. Annesley, [1926] Ch. 692; 95 L.J. Ch. 404; 135 L.T. 508;
    42 T.L.R. 584 ....41, 44, 50, 68, 90, 444
Anning v. Anning, 4 C.L.R. 1049 (1907) 503
Anstruther v. Adair, (1834) 2 My. & K. 513 417
Anstruther v. Chalmer, 2 Sim. 1; 4 L.J. (o.s.) Ch. 123 (1826) 444
Anthony v. Shea, 86 I.L.T.R. 29 (1951) 552
Anziani, Re. [1930] 1 Ch. 407; 99 L.J. Ch. 215; 142 L.T. 570 ....495, 502, 503
Apicella v. Scala, 66 I.L.T.R. 33 (1931) 546, 549
Apollinaris Co's Trade Marks, In re, [1891] 1 Ch. 1; 63 L.T. 502; 39 W.R. 309 658
Apt v. Apt, [1948] P. 83; [1948] L.J.R. 539; 177 L.T. 620; 63 T.L.R. 618; [1947]
    2 All E.R. 677 240
Archer v. Preston, 1 Eq. Cas. Abr. 133; 21 E.R. 938 404
Archie Colpitts Ltd. v. Graimmer, 83 D.L.R. (3d) 281 (1978) 104
Ardagh, In the Estate of, [1914] 1 I.R. 5 511
Arglasse v. Muschamp, 1 Vern. 75 (1682) 404
Armitage v. A.G., [1906] P. 135 ....131, 262, 272, 284
Armstrong v. Armstrong, 21 D.L.R. (3d) 140 82
Armytage v. Armytage, [1898] P. 178; 67 L.J.P. 90; 78 L.T. 689; 14 T.L.R. 480 295, 296
Arum, The [1921] P. 12; 90 L.J.P. 166; 37 T.L.R. 38 580
Ashworth v. White, I.R. 5 C.L. 520 (1871) 663
Askew, Re [1930] 2 Ch. 259; 99 L.J. Ch. 466; 143 L.J. 616 ....15, 362, 366
Assunzione, The, [1954] P. 150; [1954] 2 W.L.R. 234; 98 S.J. 107; [1954] 1 All
    E.R. 278; [1953] 2 Lloyd's Rep. 716 ....527, 529
Aston v. London & North-Western Ryan Co., I.R. 1 C.L. 604 (1867) 146
Atkins & Co. Ltd., v. Thompson, 56 I.L.T.R. 107 (1922) 141
Atkinson, In bonis, I.R. 7 Eq. 219 (1873) 629
Atlantic Star, The; Atlantic Star (Owners) v. Bona Spes (Owners), [1974] A.C. 436
    ....161, 166
Attenee, The, 11 Ll. L. Rep. 6 (1922) 162
Atteridge v. Executors of Lord Audley, 15 Ir. L.R. 90 (1842) 132
Attorney-General for Alberta v. Cook, [1926] A.C. 444 81
Attorney-General v. Campbell, L.R. 4 H.L. 524 (1872) 507
Attorney-General v. Drapers' Co. [1894] 1 I.R. 185 ....136, 138, 409
Attorney-General v. Higgins, 2 H. & N. 339; 157 E.R. 140 (1857) 399
Attorney-General v. Jewish Colonisation Association, [1901] 1 K.B. 123 484
Attorney-General (ex rel. Johnston) v. The Irish Society, 26 I.L.T.R. 56 (1892) .136
Attorney-General v. Kent, 1 H. & C. 12; 158 E.R. 782 (1862) 66
Augustus v. Permanent Trustee Co. (Canberra) Ltd., [1971] A.L.R. 661; 45 A.L.J.R.
    365 510
Australian Assets Co. Ltd. v. Higginson, 18 L.R. (N.S.W.) Eq. 189 125
Auten v. Auten, (1954) 308 N.Y. 155; 124 N.E. (2d) 99 (C.A.) 541, 577
Aylward v. Jones, 18 I.L.T.R. 111 (1884) 629
Azoff-Don Commercial Bank, Re, [1954] Ch. 315; [1954] 2 W.L.R. 654; 98 S.J.
    252; [1954] 1 All E.R. 947 485
B- a Lunatic, In re, 1 Ir. Eq. Rep. 181 (1839) 381, 382, 386
B.P. Exploration Co. (Libya) Ltd. v. Hunt [1976] 3 All E.R. 879, [1976] 1 W.L.R.
    788 ....139, 141, 650
B. (S) (an Infant), Re, [1968] Ch. 204; [1967] 3 W.L.R. 1438 372

Babcock v. Jackson, 12 N.Y. 2d 473 577
Baccus S.R.L. v. Servicio Nacional Del Trigo, [1957] 1 Q.B. 174, 175
Baelz v. A.G. for Ontario, [1930] A.C. 161 504
Bagot v. Bagot, 1 L.R. (Ir.) 1 633
Bailey v. Welphy, I.R. 4 C.L. 243 (1869) 610
Bain v. Whitehaven and Furness Junction, (1850) 3 H.L. Cas. 1 632
Baindail v. Baindail, [1946] P. 122 369
Baker v. Baker, 49 Man. R. 163 83
Balfour v. Scott, (1793) 6 Bro. P.C. 550 429
Ballantine v. Golding, (1784) Cooke, Bankrupt Laws, 8th ed. 481
Ballinrobe and Claremorris Light Railway Co. & Kenny, Ex parte, [1913] 1 I.R. 519 398
Balshaw v. Balshaw, 1967 S.C. 63 251
Bamgbose v. Daniel, [1955] A.C. 107 217
Banco Ambrosiano S.P.A. (in compulsory voluntary liquidation) v. Ansbacher & Co.
   Ltd., High Ct., Murphy, J., 19 July 1985 (1984-585P) 662, 663, 664, 667
Banco de Bilbao v. Sando, [1938] 2 All E.R. 253 178
Banco de Portugal v. Waddell, (1880) 5 App. Cas. 161 468
Banco de Vizcaya v. Don Alfonso de Borbon y Austria, [1935] 1 K.B. 140 195
Banco Nacional de Cuba v. Sabbationo, 376 U.S. 398 (1964) 171
Banfield v. Chester, 94 L.J.K.B. 805, 59 I.L.T.R. 118 (1925) 610, 661
Bank of Africa Ltd. v. Cohen, [1909] 2 Ch. 129 ....410, 413, 431
Bank of Australasia v. Harding, (1850) 9 C.B. 661; 19 L.J.C.P. 345 587
Bank of Australasia v. Nias, (1851) 16 Q.B. 717; 20 L.J.Q.B. 284 603
Bank of Egypt Ltd., In re, [1913] 1 I.R. 502 610
Bank voor Handel en Scheepvaart N.V. v. Slatford, [1953] 1 Q.B. 248 204, 206, 495
Bank of Ireland Trustee Co. Ltd. v. Adams, 452 (High Ct., Budd, J.) 72
Bankes, Re, [1902] 2 Ch. 333 ....423, 427, 510
Banku Polskiego v. Mulder & Co., [1942] 1 K.B. 497 491
Bannantyne v. Barrington, 9 Ir. Ch. Rep. 406 (1858) 519, 545
Bannon v. Macaire, 7 L.R. Ir. 211 (1881) 457
Banque des Merchands de Moscou v. Kindersley, [1951] 4 D.L.R. 485
Barber v. Mexican Land Co., (1899) 16 T.L.R. 127, 44 S.J. 145 504
Barclay's Bank International v. Levin Bros. (Bradford) Ltd., [1977] Q.B. 270 491, 651
Barcroft's Trusts, In re, 32 I.L.T.R. 35 (1897) 511
Bardford v. Bardford, [1918] P. 140 107
Bariatenski (Princess), Re, 1 Ph. 375, 13 L.J. Ch. 69 (1843) 94, 382
Barker v. Damer, 1 Salk. 81, 91 E.R. 76 (1691) 401
Baron de Bode's Case, 8 Q.B. 208; 115 E.R. 854 (1845) 110
Barretto v. Young, [1900] 2 Ch. 339 450
Barrie's Estate, Re, 240 Iowa 431; 35 N.W. 2d 658 (1949) 448
Barton v. Deputy Commissioner of Taxation, 48 A.L.J.R. 463 (1974) 463
Baschet v. London Illustrated Standard Co., [1900] 1 Ch. 73, 81 L.T. 509 638
Bata v. Bata, [1948] W.N. 366 (1948) 148
Bateman v. Bateman, [1901] P. 136 299
Bateman v. Sneyd, 2 I.C.L.R. 376 (1852) 668
Bater v. Bater, [1906] P. 209 ....284, 605
Bath v. British & Malayan Trustees Ltd., 90 W.N. (Part I) (N.S.W.) 44 (1969) 199, 456
Battersby v. Rochfort, 2 Jones & La Touche 431 (1845) 465
Baxter v. Morgan, 6 Taunt 377, 128 E.R. 1081 (1815) 653
Bayer v. Connell Bros. & Co. [1977] 1 I.R. 544 160
Beamish v. Beamish, (1788) cited in 2 Hagg. Con. 83 ....228, 295
Beatty v. Beatty, [1924] 1 K.B. 807 ....105, 113, 603
Beaumont, In re, [1898] 3 Ch. 490 ....85, 90, 92, 94
Beaumont v. Oliveira, L.R. 6 Eq. 534 (1868) 440
Beausang v. Condon, 13 I.C.L.R. app. xxxvii (1862) 668
Beck v. Willard Chocolate Co. Ltd., [1924] 2 D.L.R. 1140 149
Beckett, In re, 5 L.R. Ir. 43 (1880) 653, 660
Beckford v. Kemble, (1822) 1 Sim & St. 7 406

Becquet v. MacCarthy, 2 B. & Ad. 951, 109 E.R. 1396 (1831) 598
Belfast Shipowners Co. (Ltd), In re, [1894] 1 I.R. 321 .....130, 170, 392, 467, 486
Belfast Empire Theatre of Varieties Ltd, In re, [1963] I.R. 41 504
Bell v. Bell, [1922] 2 I.R. 152 ....71, 73, 74, 299
Bell v. Kennedy, L.R. 1 Sc. & Div., 307 (1868) 54, 66, 71, 74, 75
Belyando Shire Council v. Rivers, 2 Q.J.P.R. 47 (1908) 141
Bempde v. Johnstone, 3 Ves. 198, 30 E.R. 967 (1796) 64, 93
Bennett v. Cook, 35 I.L.T.R. 153 (1901) 133, 142
Bentley v. Robinson, 4 Ir. Ch. Rep. 37 (1853) 668
Benton v. Horeau, (1880) Clunet 480 632
Bergerem v. Marsh, (1921) 6 B. & C.R. 195; 91 L.J.K.B. 80; 125 L.T. 630 480
Berinton (otherwise Hewitson) v. Hewitson, 47 D.L.R. (3d) 510 (1974) 280
Berkshire Co. v. Reading Borough Council, [1921] 1 K.B. 787 54
Bernard, Ex parte, 6 Ir. Ch. Rep. 133 (1856) 138
Bernhard v. Harrah's Club, 16 Cal. 3d 313; 128 Cal. Rept. 215, 546 P. 2d 719 (1976) 562
Bernie v. Bernie, [1959] Ir. Jur. Rep. 78 662
Berthiaume v. Dastous, [1930] A.C. 79 ....219, 236
Betham v. Fernie, 4 I.C.L.R. 92 (1854) 148
Bethell, Re, (1888) 38 Ch. D. 220, 57 L.J. Ch. 487 ....213, 348
Bettison's Question, In re, [1956] Ch. 67 (1955) 428
Bevan v. Gillows & Co., 40 I.L.T.R. 251 (1906) 133, 140, 149
Bevand v. Bevand, [1955] 1 D.L.R. 854 251
Bieber & Co. v. Rio Tinto Co., [1918] A.C. 260 113
Biggar v. Biggar, 42 B.C.R. 329 [1930] 2 D.L.R. 940 607
Birch (A Lunatic), In re, 29 L.R. Ir. 274 (1892) 54, 385
Birch v. Birch, [1902] P. 130 607
Birch v. Purtill, [1936] I.R. 122 ....663, 666
Birtwhistle v. Vardill, (1840) 7 Cl. & Fin. 895; 4 Jur. 1076 365
Bischoffsheim, Re; Cassel v. Grant, [1948] Ch. 79 350-352
Black v. Baird, 31 I.L.T. & Sol. J. 8 (1876) 134, 139
Black-Clawson International Ltd. v. Papierwerke Waldhof-Aschaffenburg A.G.,
   [1975] A.C. 591 ....639, 640
Blake v. Blake, 4 Ir. Ch. Rep. 349 (1853) 120
Blanckaert and Willems P.V. P.A. v. Luise Trost, [1981] E.C.R. 819 .....186, 187
Blohn v. Desser, [1962] 2 Q.B. 116; [1961] 3 W.L.R. 719 ....595, 601
Bloomfield v. Serenyi, [1945] 2 All E.R. 646 136
Boate's Estate, In re. 10 Ir. Ch. Rep. 164 (1859) 412, 427, 542
Bodley Head, Ltd. v. Flagon, [1972] 1 W.L.R. 680 541
Boissevain v. Weil, [1950] A.C. 327 552
Boissière v. Brockner & Co., (1889) 6 T.L.R. 85 591
Boldrini v. Boldrini & Martin, [1932] P. 9 55
Bolton, In re, [1920] 2 I.R. 324 ....106, 110, 476
Bonacina, Re, [1912] 2 Ch. 394; 81 L.J. Ch. 674 553
Bonaparte v. Bonaparte, [1892] P. 402 608
Bondholders Securities Corporation v. Manville, [1933] 4 D.L.R. 699 ......488, 640
Bonelli, In the goods of, L.R. 1 P.D. 69 (1875) 107
Bonnet, deceased, In re: Johnston v. Langheld, [1983] I.L.R.M. 359 393, 443, 445
Bonython v. Commonwealth of Australia, [1951] A.C. 201 544
Booth v. Egan, I.R. 9 C.L. 282 (1880) 610
Boss v. O'Connor, I.R. 9 C.L. 478 (1875) 610
Boswell, Re; Baron Talbot de Malahide, dec'd, 86 I.L.T.R. 191 (1950) 511
Bowes, In re; Bates v. Wengel, 22 Times L.R. (1906) 41
Bowden Bros. & Co. v. Imperial Marine & Transport Insurance Co., 5 S.R. (N.S.W.)
   614 (1905) 104
Bowling v. Cox, [1926] A.C. 751 141
Boyd v. Fitt, 14 I.C.L.R. 43 (1863) 643
Boyd v. Lee Guinness, Ltd., [1963] N.I. 49 157
Boyce v. Rusboro, 2 I.C.L.R. 266 (1852) 633

Boyle v. Boyle, I.R. 11 Eq. 433 (1877) 508
Boyle v. Sacker, 39 Ch. D. 249 (1888) 130
Boyle v. Victoria Yukon Trading Co., (1902) 9 B.C.R. 213 602
Boys v. Chaplin, [1971] A.C. 356, [1969] 3 W.L.R. 322; 571, 574, 576, 577, 578,
                                                                                    638, 642
Boyse v. Colclough, 1 K. & J. 123, 69 E.R. 396 (1854) 401
Brabo, The, [1949] A.C. 326 158
Bradfield v. Swanton, [1931] I.R. 446 ....63, 69
Bradford v. Young, (1885) 29 Ch. D. 617; 53 L.T. 407; 33 W.R. 860 .....444, 445
Bradley v. Archibald, [1899] 2 I.R. 108 490
Brailey v. Rhodesia Consolidated Ltd., [1910] 2 Ch. 95 107
Brand v. National Life Assurance Co., [1918] 3 W.W.R. 858; 44 D.L.R. 412 (1918) 164
Brassard v. Smith, [1925] A.C. 371 ....399, 504
Breen v. Breen, [1964] P. 144; [1961] 3 W.L.R. 900 ....236, 276
Bremer v. Freeman, 10 Moo. P.C. 306; 14 E.R. 508 (1857) 39, 432
Brennan v. Lockyer, [1932] I.R. 100 ....133, 134, 136, 139, 140
Breull, Ex parte; In re Bowie, 16 Ch. D. 484 (1880) 101
Brewster v. Brewster, [1945] 3 D.L.R. 541 (B.C.C.A.) 68
Briesemann, In the goods of, [1894] P. 260..455
Bristow v. Sequeville, 5 Ex. 275; 155 E.R. 118 (1850) 107, 488, 616
British Linen Co. v. Drummond, (1830) 10 B. & C. 903; 9 L.J. (o.s.) K.B. 213 640
British Leyland Exports Ltd. v. Brittain Group Sales Ltd, [1982] I.L.R.M. 359 .520
British Marine Assoc. v. Macinnes, 31 Sol. Jo. 95 (1886) 153
British South Africa Co. v. Compania de Moçambique, [1893] A.C. 602 401, 402, 403,
                                                                                    404, 406, 407
British South Africa Co. v. De Beers Consolidated Mines Co. Ltd, [1912] A.C. 52 413
Broadman v. Broadman, 36 S.R. (N.S.W.) 447 (1939) 82
Brook v. Brook, (1861) 9 H.L.C. 193; 4 L.T. 93 ....219, 232, 235, 240, 355
Brooke v. Kavanagh, 21 L.R. Ir. 474 (1889) 666
Brookes v. Harrison, 6 L.R. Ir. 332 (1880) 498, 610
Brooks Associates Inc. v. Basu, [1983] Q.B. 220 505
Brophy, Re, [1959] N.Z.L.R. 1006 375
Brown, a Minor, In re, 8 Ir. Ch. Rep. 172 (1858) 330
Brown, Gow, Wilson v. Beleggings-Societeit N.V., [1961] O.R. 815 193
Brown v. Gracey, 1 D. & R., N.P. Cas. 41n; 171 E.R. 911 (1821) 117
Brown (dec'd), Brown v. Harrison, 35 I.L.T.R. 25 (1900) 508
Browne v. Redmond, II Ir. C.L.R. xxvi (1861) 665, 666
Bruce v. Bruce, (1790) 2 Bos. & Pul. 229; 6 Bro. Parl. Cas. 566; 2 Coop.t. Cott. 510 429
Bruce (Executors of) v. Poe. 4 Ir. L.R. 4 (1841) 132
Brunfiel v. Brunfiel, [1926] 2 D.L.R. 129 369
Bryant v. Bryant, [1981] Fam. L. 85 171
B's Settlement, Re, [1940] Ch. 54 330
Buchanan v. Darragh, 36 I.L.T.R. 9 (1901) 505
Buchanan Ltd. v. McVey, [1954] I.R. 89 192, 196, 197, 199, 201, 202, 206, 208, 474, 551
Bucheridge v. Hall, [1963] 1 Q.B. 614; [1963] 2 W.L.R. 354 319
Buckland v. Buckland (orse Camilleri), [1968] P. 296; [1967] 2 W.L.R. 1506 242, 287
Buerger v. New York Life Assurance Co., 43 Times L.R. 601 (1927) 111, 112
Bull v. Pile, 27 I.L.T.R. 136 161
Bull v. Wallis & Sons, 26 I.L.T.R. 114 (1892) 657, 660
Bullen, In re, [1930] I.R. 82 ....469, 470, 473, 478
Bullock v. Caird, (1875) L.R. 10 Q.B. 276; 44 L.J.Q.B. 124; 647
Burbridge, In re, [1902] 1 Ch. 426 382
Burchell v. Burchell, 58 Ont. L.R. 515 (1926) 193, 195
Burke v. Gt. Southern & Western Ry., 36 I.L.T.R. 51 (1902) 668
Burke v. Irwin, 41 I.L.T.R. 73 (1907) 661
Burke v. Quinlan, 3 Ir. L.R. 310 (1841) 126
Burpee v. Burpee, [1929] 3 D.L.R. 18; 41 B.C.R. 201 591
Burton v. Fisher, Milw. 183 (1828) 64, 67

Bush v. Curran, 9 Ir. C.L.R. xxx (1859) 668
Bushbey, In re, 112 N.Y.S. 262 (1908) 78
Butchart (Deceased) In re: Butchart v. Butchart, [1932] N.Z.L.R. 125 436-438
Butler v. Bianconi, 11 Ir. L.R. 286 (1847) 149
Butler v. Butler, 6 I.C.L.R. 77 (1856) 219
Butler v. Corcoran, 7 I.C.L.R. 276 (1857) 53
Butler v. Freeman, Amb. 301; 27 E.R. 204 (1756) 218
Butson, deceased, In bonis, 9 L.R. Ir. 21 (1882) 65, 457
Buttigeig v. Universal Terminal & Stevedoring Corporation, [1972] V.R. 626 ...150
Byrne v. Limerick Steamship Co. Ltd., [1946] I.R. 138 544
Byrne v. Sherlock, I.C.L.R. App. xxxii (1858) 132

Caffin, Deceased, Re; Bank of Ireland v. Caffin, [1971] I.R. 123 238, 276, 277, 585
Callan, Deceased, Estate of, Owens v. O'Reilly, 39 I.R. L.T. & Sol. J. 372 (1905) 629
Callan v. M'Kenna, [1929] N.I. 1 ....610, 661
Callwood v. Callwood, [1960] A.C. 659 ....105, 110, 422
Cammell v. Cammell, [1965] P. 465 302
Cammell v. Sewell, (1858) 3 H. & N. 617, (1860) 5 H. & N. 728, ...495, 599
Canadian Imperial Bank of Commerce v. Kabat, [1985] N.W.T.R.I. 594
Canadian National Steamships Co. v. Watson, [1939] S.C.R. 11 [1939] 1 D.L.R. 273
....104, 113
Canning v. Donegal Co. Co., [1961] Ir. Jur. Rep. 7 148
Cannon v. Fallon, 52 I.L.T.R. 34 (1918) 141
Canny v. Fox, I.R. 4 Eq. 410 (1870) 392
Cantieri Riuniti Dell'Adriatico Di Monfalcone v. Gdynia Amerijka Linje Zeglugowe
   Spolke Akcyjna, [1939] 4 D.L.R. 491 160
Cap Bon, The, [1967] 1 Lloyd's Rep 543 162
Capelloni & Aquiliui v. Pelkmans, [1986] 1 C.M.L.R. 388.........................615
Capon v. Capon, 42 D.L.R. (2d) 675 (1965) 82, 261
Carden v. Carden, 1 Curt. 558, 163 E.R. 196 (1837) 294
Carl Zeiss Stiftung v. Rayner & Keeler Ltd. (No. 2), [1965] Ch. 596 ......178, 207
Carl Zeiss Stiftung v. Rayner & Keeler Ltd. (No. 3), [1970] Ch. 506 484, 586, 606
Carr v. Fracis Times & Co., [1902] A.C. 176 ....575, 580
Carrick v. Hancock, 12 Times L.R. 59 (1895) 125, 590
Carruthers' Trustees, 24 R. 238 (1896) 513
Carson v. Crozier, 51 I.L.T.R. 38 (1917) 126
Carter v. Carter, [1932] N.Z.L.R. 1104 234
Cartwright v. Ball, 3 I.C.L.R. 31 (1853) 132
Cartwright v. Pettus, 2 Chan. Cas. 214, 22 E.R. 401
Carvell v. Wallace, 9 N.S.R. 165 (1873) 640
Casdagli v. Casdagli, [1919] A.C. 145 66
Casey v. Arnott, 2 C.P.D. 24 (1876) 137
Casey v. Casey [1949] P. 420 113
Castanho v. Brown & Root (U.K.) Ltd., [1981] A.C. 557 ....167, 171
Castree v. Squibb, [1980] 1 W.L.R. 1248 150
Castrique v. Imrie, L.R. 4 H.L. 414 ....106, 599, 600, 604
Catalyst Research Corp. v. Medtronic Inc., 131 D.L.R. (3d) 767 131
Catteral v. Catteral, 1 Rob. Ecc. 580, 163 E.R. 142 228
Caudron v. Air Zaire, [1986] I.L.R.M. 10 ....153, 647
Ceylon v. Reid, [1965] A.C. 720 214
Chapelle v. Chapelle, [1950] P. 134 ....257, 258, 263
Chaplin v. Boys, [1971] A.C. 356 ....573, 577, 578
Chapman v. Cottrel, 3 H. & C. 865 (1865) 487
Charkieh, The, L.R. 4 Adm. & Ecc. 59 (1873) 174, 177
Charlesworth v. Clayton, 10 L.R. Ir. 357 (1882) 668
Charlton v. Morris, [1895] 2 I.R. 541 ....53, 64
Charron v. Montreal Trust Co. [1958] O.R. 597 541

Chartered Mercantile Bank of India, London and China v. Netherlands India Steam
  Navigation Co. Ltd., 10 Q.B.D. 521 (1883) 542
Chatenay v. Brazilian Submarine Telegraph Co., [1891] 1 Q.B. 79 ...143, 542, 543
Cheang Thye Phin v. Tan Ah Loy, [1920] A.C. 369 216
Chemical Bank v. MacCormack, [1983] I.L.R.M. 350 633
Cheni v. Cheni, [1965] P. 85.. 214, 240
Chenoweth v. Summers, [1941] A.L.R. 364 142
Chetti v. Chetti, [1909] P. 67 240
Children's Aid Society of Eastern Manitoba v. Rural Municipality of St. Clements, 6
  W.W.R. (n.s.) 39 (1952) 83
Chomuto Savings Bank, In Re, [1957] I.R. 355 635
Christenson v. Christenson, 45 W.W.R. (N.S.) 47 (1963) 82
Chung Chi Cheung v. R., [1939] A.C. 160 581
City of Dublin Steam Packet Co. v. Cooper, [1899] 2 I.R. 381 159
City of Mecca, The, (1879) 5 P.D. 28; (1881) 5 P.D. 106 ....161, 599, 601
Civil Air Transportation Inc. v. Central Air Transport Corporation, [1953] A.C. 70 207
Clare Co. Council v. Wilson, [1913] 2 I.R. 89 ....137, 141, 184
Clark v. Dickinson, 8 Ir. L.R. 161 (1846) 663, 668
Clarke v. Barber, 6 Times L.R. 256 (1890) 658
Clarke v. Cassells Ltd., Unreported, cited 72 I.L.T.R., at 145 588
Clarke v. Crooker, I.R. 8 C.L. 318 (1874) 661
Clarke v. Doolin, 29 I.L.T.R. 4 (1894) 655
Clarke v. Gardiner, 12 I.C.L.R. 472 (1861) 632
Clarke v. Harper & Robinson, [1938] N.I. 162 ....140, 143, 531
Clarke v. Riordan, 9 I.C.L.R. App. xxiv (1859) 668
Clarkson v. Clarkson, 86 D.L.R. (ed) 694 (1978) 280
Clayton, Re, 43 Times L.R. 659 (1927) 367
Clements v. Gardiner, I.R. 6 C.L. 18 (1871) 658
Clokey v. London & North Western Railway Co., [1905] 2 I.R. 251 ....126, 129
Cloncurry's Estate, In Re, [1932] I.R. 687 ....423, 509
Coast Lines Ltd. v. Hudig and Veder Chartering N.V., [1972] 2 Q.B. 34 529
Cochrane v. Moore, 25 Q.B.D. 57 (1890) 500
Cohane v. Cohane, [1968] I.R. 176 ....662, 665, 667
Cohan v. Rothfield, [1919] 1 K.B. 410 170
Cohn, Re, [1945] Ch. 5 434
Colbert v. Tocumwal Trading Co. Pty Ltd., [1964] V.R. 820 130
Colclough, In bonis, [1902] 2 I.R. 449 455
Collens (deceased) Re; Royal Bank of Canada (London) Ltd. v. Krogh, [1986] 1
  All E.R. 611 437
Collier v. Rivaz, 2 Curt, Ecc. 855, 163 E.R. 608 (1841) 38, 39
Collins v. A.G., 47 T.L.R. 484 (1931) 361, 367
Collins v. Doyle, [1982] I.L.R.M. 495 ....662, 665, 666
Collins v. North British & Mercantile Insurance Co., [1894] 3 Ch. 228 159
Collopy v. O'Shaughnessy, 6 L.R. Ir. 449 (1879) 655, 656
Colonial Bank v. Cady, 15 App. Cas. 267 (1890) 504
Colorado, The, [1923] P. 102 ....113, 648
Colt Industries Inc. v. Sarlie, [1966] 1 All E.R. 673 ....125, 601
Colzani v. Ruwa, [1976] E.C.R. 1831 191
Commercial Bank of South Australia, Re, 33 Ch. D. 174 (1886) 485, 493
Compagnie D'Armement Maritime S.A. v. Compagnie Tunisienne de Navigation
  S.A., [1971] A.C. 572 ....522, 524, 617
Compania Merabello San Nicholas S.A., Re, [1973] Ch. 75 ....485, 486
Compania Mercantil Argentina v. United States Shipping Board, 131 L.T. 388
  (1924) 175, 176
Compton v. Bearcroft, 2 Hag. Con. 444n, 161 E.R. 799 (1769) 218
Conlon v. Mohamed, High Ct., Barron, J., 25 July 1986 ....197, 213-215, 230, 240
Connellan v. Fallon, [1953-54] Ir. Jur. Rep. 43 ....139, 144
Connor, deceased, In bonis, 19 L.R. Ir. 261 (1892) 454, 629

Connor v. Bellamount (Earl of), 2 Atk. 382, 26 E.R. 631 (1742) 518
Connor v. Connor, [1974] 1 N.Z.L.R. 632 ....198, 199
Contsworth v. Willington, 11 Ir. L.R. 54 (1847) 655
Conway v. Wilson, 2 Ir. C.L.R. 47 (1851) 56, 656
Cook v. Gregson, 2 Drew. 286, 61 E.R. 729 (1852) 459
Cooke, In bonis, I.R. 5 Eq. 240 (1871) 629
Cooke's Trusts, Re, [1932] I.R. 687 424
Cooke v. Walsh, [1984] I.L.R.M. 208 ....644, 645
Cooney v. Wilson and Henderson, [1913] 2 I.R. 204 157
Cooper v Cadwalader, 5 Tax Cas. 201 (1904) 101
Cooper v. Cooper, Milw. 373 (1836) 298, 299, 425
Cooper (falsely called Crane) v. Crane, [1891] P. 369 ....242, 253
Cooper v. General Accident Corporation, 36 Ir. L.T.R. 24 (1901) 128
Cooper-King v. Cooper-King, [1900] P. 65 108
Cooper v. Philadelphia Worsted Co. (Lees v. Hocling), 68 N.J. Eq. 622 (1905) .494
Copin v. Adamson, L.R. 1 Ex. D. 17 (1875) 595
Coppin v. Coppin, 2 P. Wms. 291, 24 E.R. 735 (1725) 411
Corballis, deceased, In re, [1929] I.R. 226 ....408, 468, 470
Corbett v. Corbett, [1957] 1 All E.R. 621 ....260, 262
Corcoran, An Infant, Re, 86 I.L.T.R. 6 (1950) 14, 328, 331
Cordova Land Co. Ltd. v. Victor Brothers Inc., [1966] 1 W.L.R. 793 .....149, 150
Cornelius v. Banque Franco-Serbe, [1942] 1 K.B. 29, [1941] 2 All E.R. 728 ..491
Corner v. Irwin, I.R. 8 C.L. 504 (1874) 661
Corscaden v. Stewart, 1 I.L.R. 110 (1839) 656
Courtney, Re; Ex parte Pollard, Mont. & Ch. 239 (1840) 406
Cowan v. Braidwood, 1 Man. & G. 882, 133 E.R. 589 (1840) 608
Cox Ltd. v. *M.V. Fritz Raabe* (Owners of), Sup. Ct., 1 August 1974 161
Crabtree v. Crabtree, 1929 S.L.T. 675 262
Craig, Re, 86 L.J. Ch. 62 (1916) 480
Craigie v. Lewin, 3 Curt. Ecc. 435 (1842) 432
Craignish, Re, [1892] 3 Ch. 180 66
Craik v. Korth, 17 I.L.T.R. 45 (1883) 133
Cranstown v. Johnston, 3 Ves. 170, 30 E.R. 952 (1796) 405
Craven's Estate, Re, [1937] Ch. 423 500
Crawford, Ex parte, 2 Ir. Ch. Rep. 573 (1853) 138
Crawford v. Wright & Butler, 27 I.L.T.R. 75 (1892) 132
Cremer GmbH v. Co-operative Molasses Traders Ltd., [1985] I.L.R.M. 564 619
Crichton's Trust, Re, 24 L.T. (O.S.) 267 (1855) 328
Crick v. Hennessy, [1973] W.A.R. 74 597
Crickmay v. Crickmay, 60 D.L.R. (2d) 734 (1966) 234
Crinion v. Minister for Justice, [1959] Ir. Jur. Rep. 15 490
Cripps Warburg Ltd. v. Cologne Investment Co. Ltd., [1980] I.R. 321 106, 402, 408,
                                                   412, 518, 522, 545, 546, 548
Cristina, The, [1938] A.C. 485 173
Croker v. Hertford, 4 Moo. P.C. 339, 13 E.R. 334 (1844) 432
Crookenden v. Fuller, 1 Sw. & Tr. 441, 164 E.R. 804 (1859) 67
Crowe v. Crowe, [1937] 2 All E.R. 723 284
Crowe v. Kadar, [1968] W.A.R. 122 213
Cruh v. Cruh, [1945] 2 All E.R. 545 55
Crumpton's Judicial Factor v. Finch-Noyes, 1918 S.C. 375 94
Cruse v. Chittum, [1974] 2 All E.R. 940 98
Cuff Knox, In re, 98 I.L.T.R. 141 (1961) 509
Cumming v. Great Northern Ry. Co., 27 I.L.T.R. 74 (1893) 141, 142
Cummings v. Stewart (No. 2), [1913] 1 I.R. 95 543
Cummins & Sons, Carrigaloe Gridiron & Works Co. v. Corry, 29 I.L.T.R. 144 (1895) 161
Cunningham Infants, In re, [1915] 1 I.R. 380 321
Cunnington, In re; Healing v. Webb, [1924] 1 Ch. 68 444

D. v. D., 36 D.L.R. (3d) 17 (1973) 252
Dakota Lumber Co. v. Rinderknecht, 6 Terr. L.R. 210 (1905) 596
Dale v. Hamilton, 5 Hare 369, 67 E.R. 955 (1846) 422
D'Almeida Aranjo Ltd. v. Becker (Sir Frederick) & Co. Ltd., [1953] 2 Q.B. 329 642, 643
Dalmia Dairy Industries Ltd. v. National Bank of Pakistan, [1978] 2 Lloyd's Rep.
 223 ....616, 617
Dalrymple v. Dalrymple, 2 Hag. Con. 54, 161 E.R. 665 (1811) 15, 104, 111, 218, 231, 253
Dalton v. Dalton, [1982] I.L.R.M. 418 ....276, 549
Daly's Settlement, Re, 25 Beav. 456, 53 E.R. 711 (1858) 81
Damen & Zonen v. O'Shea, unreported, High Ct., McMahon, J., 25 May 1977 492, 650,
                                                                              651
Dammert v. Osborn, 140 N.Y. 30, 35 N.E. 407 (1893) 442
D'Arcy Infants, In re, 11 I.C.L.R. 298 (1860) 348, 629
Davidson's Settlement Trusts, Re, L.R. 15 Eq. 383 (1873) 480
Davies v. Lynch, I.R. 4 C.L. 570 (1868) 97
Davis v. Adair, [1895] 1 I.R. 379 ......46, 52, 55, 59, 66, 67, 69, 71, 76, 91, 234
Day, Re, 7 Ir. Jur. N.S. 162 (1862), 7 Ir. Jur. N.S. 309 (1862) 464
Deane & Sandford, I.R. 9 C.L. 228 (1875) 139, 140, 144, 148, 149
De Beéche v. South American Stores Ltd., [1935] A.C. 148 108
De Beers Consolidated Mines Ltd. v. Howe, [1906] A.C. 455 482
De Bernales v. New York Herald, [1893] 2 Q.B. 97 153
De Bonneval v. De Bonneval, 1 Curt. Ecc. 856, 163 E.R. 296 (1838) 38
Debtor (No. 199 of 1922), Re [1922] 2 Ch. 470 465
Debtor (Order in aid) (No. 1 of 1979), Re, [1981] Ch. 384 ....474, 476
De Cavel v. De Cavel (No. 1), [1979] E.C.R. 1065 ....185, 612, 614
Deck v. Deck, 2 Sw. & Tr. 90 (1860) 51
De Cosse Brissac v. Rathbone, 6 H. & N. 301, 158 E.R. 123 (1861) .593, 603, 604
De Fogassieras v. Duport, 11 L.R. Ir. 123 (1881) 105, 392, 393, 430, 432
De Gasquet James v. Mechlenburg-Schwerin, [1914] P. 53 300
De Hossen, In re; Erwin v. De Hossen, [1937] I.R. 467 ....59, 72
Dejardin v. Dejardin, [1932] 2 W.W.R. 237 234
De la Saussaye, In the goods of, L.R. 3 P. & D. 42 (1873) 455
De la Vega v. Vianna, 1 B. & Ald. 284, 109 E.R. 792 (1830) 648
De Lusi's Settlement, Re, 3 L.R. Ir. 232 (1879) 451
De Montaigu v. De Montaigu, [1913] P. 154 81
De Nicols, Re; De Nicols v. Curlier, [1900] A.C. 21 ......416, 420, 421, 422, 440
Denilauler v. Couchet Freres, [1980] E.C.R. 1553 614
Denman v. O'Callaghan, 31 I.L.T.R. 141 (1897) 601, 606, 608
Dennis v. Leinster Paper Co., [1901] 2 I.R. 337 586, 588, 590, 606, 608, 663, 669
Denny v. Denny, 48 I.L.T.R. 150 (1914) 634
Derby & Co. Ltd. v. Larsson, [1976] 1 All E.R. 401 159
De Reneville v. De Reneville, [1948] P. 100 ....131, 233, 246, 252, 254, 259
Deschamps v. Miller, [1908] 1 Ch. 856 ....403, 406
D'Etchegoyen v. D'Etchegoyen, 13 P.D. 132 (1882) 66
Deutsche National Bank v. Paul, [1898] 1 Ch. 283 160
Dever, Ex parte; In re Suse and Sibeth, 18 Q.B.D. 660 (1887) 523
Deverall v. Grant Advertising Inc., [1955] Ch. 111 128
Devine v. Cementation Co. Ltd., [1963] N.I. 65 128
Devos v. Devos, 10 D.L.R. (3d) 603 (1970) 420
De Wolf v. Cox, [1976] E.C.R. 1759 614
Dharamal v. Holmpatrick (Lord), [1935] I.R. 760 106
Diamond v. Bank of London & Montreal Ltd., [1979] 2 W.L.R. 228 148
Dickinson v. Del Solar, [1930] 1 K.B. 376 180
Dicks v. Dicks, [1899] P. 275 299
Didisheim v. London & Westminster Bank, [1900] 2 Ch. 15 ....384, 387
Di Fernando v. Simon Smits & Co. Ltd., [1920] 3 K.B. 409 649
Dillon v. O'Brien, 20 L.R. (Ir.) 300 (1887) 490
Di Mento v. Visalli, [1973] 2 N.S.W.L.R. 199 242

Dimskal Shipping Co. S.A. v. International Transport Workers Federation, [1986]
  2 Lloyd's L. Rep. 165 167
Direct Winters Transport Ltd. v. Duplate Canada Ltd., [1962] O.R. 360 108
Di Rollo v. Di Rollo, 1959 S.C. 75 242
Di Sora v. Philips, 10 H.L.C. 624, 11 E.R. 1168 (1863) 112
Distillers Co. (Biochemicals) Ltd. v. Thompson, [1971] A.C. 458 148
Dobell v. Steamship Rossmore Co., [1895] 2 Q.B. 408 523
Doe, d., Birtwhistle v. Vardill, 2 Cl. & Fin. 571, 6 E.R. 1270 (1835) 364
Dollfus Mieg et Compagnie S.A. v. Bank of England, [1949] 1 All E.R. 946 ...599
Dolphin v. Robins, 7 H.L.C. 390, 11 E.R. 156 (1859) 81
Don v. Lippman, 5 Cl. & Fin. 1, 7 E.R. 303 (1837) 640
Donald Export Trading Ltd. v. Vandevelde PVBA, [1981] Recent L. 353 130
Dongan & Titterington Ltd. v. Economical Housing Co., 41 I.L.T.R. 57 (1907) .668
Donnelly, Re, 28 S.R. (N.S.W.) 34 (1927) 436, 437
Donnelly v. Graham, 24 L.R. (Ir.) 127 (1888) 53, 54, 64
Donohue v. Donohue, 19 L.R. (Ir.) 349 (1887) 91, 106, 328, 431
Donovan v. North German Lloyd Steamship Co., [1933] I.R. 33 ....128, 186
Doohan v. National Coal Board, 1959 S.C. 310 611
Dooley v. Egan, 72 I.L.T.R. 155 (1938) 139
D'Orleans (Duchesse), In the Goods of, 1 Sw. & Tr. 253, 164 E.R. 716 (1859) .457
Dorrance's Estate, In re, 309 Pa. 151, 163 A. 303 (1932) 68
Dost Aly Khan, In bonis, 6 P.D. 6 (1880) 108
Doucet v. Geoghegan, 9 Ch. Div. 441 (1878) 52, 68
Douglas v. Forrest, 4 Bing. 686 (1828) 595
Downing, In bonis, 19 L.R. (Ir.) 233 (1887) 455
Downton v. Royal Trust Co., [1973] S.C.R. 437, 34 D.L.R. (3d) 403 .....289, 290
Dowling v. Jedos Ltd., unreported, Sup. Ct., 30 March 1977 644
Doyle v. Doyle, 52 D.L.R. (3d) 143 (1974) 125
Drapers' Co. v. McCann, 1 L.R. (Ir.) 13 (1878) 138
Drevon v. Drevon, 45 L.J. Ch. 129 (1864) 46
Drost v. Freightlines of Canada Ltd., 2 C.C.L.T. 49 (1976) 150
Druitt v. Druitt, 6 Ir. Ch. Rep. 23 (Brady, L.C., 1852) 633
Duane, Re, [1936] Ir. Jur. Rep. 60 356
Duc D'Aumale, The, [1903] P. 18 159
Duddy, In re, [1935] I.R. 760 ....328, 391, 392, 399
Dues v. Smith, Jac. 544, 37 E.R. 955 (1822) 417
Duff Development Co. v. Kelantin Government, [1924] A.C. 797 173
Duffy v. Chambers, 26 L.R. (Ir.) 100 (1889) 54
Duffy v. Joyce, 25 L.R. (Ir.) 42 (1890) 666, 668
Duke v. Adler, [1932] S.C.R. 732 ....407, 600
Duleep Singh, Re; Ex parte Cross, 6 T.L.R. 385 (1890) 83, 216
Du Moulin v. Druitt, 13 Ir. C.L.R. 212 (1860) 65, 219, 231
Dunbee Ltd. v. Gilman & Co. (Australia) Pty. Ltd., 70 S.R. (N.S.W.) 219, [1968]
  2 Lloyd's Rep. 394 595
Duncan v. Lawson, 41 Ch. D. 394 (1889) 410, 513
Dunlop v. Dunlop Rubber Co. Ltd., [1921] A.C. 367 153
Dunne v. Dunne, [1947] I.R. 227 297
Dunne v. Lewis, 8 Ir. C.L.R. 298 (1860) 633
Durra v. Bank of New South Wales, [1940] V.L.R. 170 142
Dyas, In re, [1932] I.R. 427 ....105, 106, 454, 456

Earl, In bonis, L.R. 1 P. & D. 450 (1867) 455
Earthworks and Quarries Ltd. v. Eastman (F.T.) & Sons Pty. Ltd., [1966] V.R. 24 142
Easterbrook v. Easterbrook, [1944] P. 10 ....244, 255
Ebrard v. Gassier, 28 Ch. Div. 232 (1884) 658
Eccles & Co. v. Louisville & Nashville Railroad Co., [1912] 1 K.B. 135 636
Edelstyn v. Coleman, 72 I.L.T.R. 142 (1938) 587, 589, 597
Edinburgh Parish Council v. Local Bd. for Scotland, [1915] A.C. 717 54

E.E.L. (An Infant), Re, [1938] N.I. 56 270

Effer Spa v. Kantner, Case 38/81, [1982] E.C.R. 825 184

Egan v. Egan, [1928] N.I. 159 ....48, 295

Egan (William) & Sons Ltd. v. Sisk (John & Sons Ltd. [1986] I.L.R.M. 283 ...643

Egerton's Will Trusts, Re [1956] Ch. 593 ....417, 418

Eyre v. Jacob, 14 Gratt. (Va.) 422; 73 AM. Dec. 367 (1858) 420

Egyptian Delta Land & Investment Co., Ltd. v. Todd, [1929] A.C. 1 483

Eiffe v. Caledonian Insurance Co. 5 Ir. L.R. 138 (1842) 132, 142

Elderman Lines v. Read, [1928] 2 K.B. 144 ....170, 607

Eliftheria, The,[1970] P. 94 ....162, 164

Ellinger v. Guinness, Mahon & Co., [1939] 4 All E.R. 16 158

Elliott, deceased, In bonis, 3 L.R. (Ir) 147 (1879) 454

Ellis v. M'Henry, L.R. 6 C.P. 228 (1871) 481, 603

Eloc Electric-Optieck and Communicatie B.V., In re, [1982] 1 Ch. 43 486

Emanuel v. Symon, [1908] 1 K.B. 302 ....595, 596, 598

Embiricos v. Angelo-Austrian Bank, [1905] 1 K.B. 677 ....489, 490

Emory v. Grenough, 3 Ball. 369 (1797) 9

English, Scottish & Australian Bank v. I.R.C., [1932] A.C. 238 ....398, 501

Eolo, The, [1918] 2 I.R. 78 ....174, 176

Erickson v. McFarlane, 42 O.L.R. 32 (1918) 653

Erie Beach Co., v. A.G. for Ontario, [1930] A.C. 161 399

Etler v. Kertesz, 26 D.L.R. (2d) 209 (1960) 551

Ets. A. de Bloos SPRL v. Bouyer, Case 14/76 [1976] E.C.R. 1497 ..185, 186, 187

European Asian Bank A.G. v. Punjab & Sind Bank, [1982] 2 Lloyd's L. Rep. 356 167

Eustace v. Eustace, [1924] P. 45 295

Evans v. Evans, 136 Colo, 6; 314 p. 3d 291 (1957) 86

Evans (Joseph) & Sons v. Stein (John G.) & Co., 7 F. 65, 12 S.L.T. 143 (1904) 148

Evans Marshall & C. Ltd. v. Bertola S.A. [1973] 2 W.L.R. 349 163

Ewin, Re 1 Cr. & J. 151; 148 E.R. 1371 (1830) 494

Ewing v. Orr-Ewing, 9 App. Cas. 34 (1883) 406, 513

Eyre v. Baldwin, 4 O.C.L.R. 270 (1855) 656

Eyre v. National News Proprietary Ltd., [1967] N.Z.L.R. 851 148

Fenton Textile Association Ltd. v. Kraggin, 38 T.L.R. 259 176

Ferguson, deceased, In re [1935] I.R. 21 ....399, 504

Ferguson v. Lomax, 2 Dr. & War. 120 (1842) 412

Ferguson v. Mahon, 11 Af. & El. 179; 113 E.R. 382 (1839) 608

Ferguson's Trust, In re, I.R. 8 Eq. 563 (1874) 90, 106

Fermanagh Co. Co., v. Board of Education of Donegal Presbytery, [1923] 2 I.R. 184 148

Fermanagh Co. Co., v. Farrendon, [1923] 2 I.R. 180 148

Ferranti-Packard Ltd. v. Cushman Rentals Ltd., 26 O.R. (2d) 344 (1979) 175

Fibretex Lte v. Beleir Ltd., 89 I.L.T.R. 141 (1947) 208, 546, 551, 552

Fife Banking Co., Ex parte: In re Little v. Little, 6 Ir. Eq. Rep. 197 588

Finance Act, In re and Deane Deceased, [1936] I.R. 556 ....398, 399

Finlay v. Finlay, 31 L.J.P.M.A. 149 (1862) 626

Finnegan v. Cementation Co. Ltd., [1953] 1 Q.B. 688 460

Finnigan v. London & N.W. Ry. Co., 9 I.L.T.R. 230 (1875) 146

Firebrace v. Firebrace, 4 P.D. 63 (1878) 81

Firestone and Firestone, Re, 90 D.L.R. (3d) 724 (1978) 324

Fitter & Co. v. Tuke, 40 I.L.T.R. 1 (1905) 606

Fitzgerald v. Lowe, 3 Ir. L.R. 259 (1841) 126

Fitzpatrick, Re, [1952] Ch. 86 458

Fitzpatrick v. Dunphy, 1 Ir. C.L.R. 366 (1851) 490

Fitzpatrick v. International Ry., 252 N.Y. 127; 169 N.E. 122; 68 A.L.R. 801
(1929) 627

Fitzpatrick v. Irwan, 35 I.L.T.R. 250 (1901) 129

Fitzpatrick v. Stewart, 51 I.L.T.R 14 (1916) 136, 142

Flanagan, deceased, In bonis, 39 I.L.T.R. 188 (1905) 654

Flash v. Thoresen, 30 I.L.T.R. 116 (1896) 161
Fleming v. Horiman, 44 Times L.R. 315 (1928) 69
Flynn (No. 2), Re, [1969] 2 Ch. 403 587
Flynn v. Buckley, [1980] I.R. 423 22
Flynn v. Eivers, 86 I.L.T.R. 85 ....665, 666
Forbes v. Forbes, Kay 341; 69 E.R. 145 (1854) 83, 219
Forbes v. Simmons, 20 D.L.R. 100; 8 Alta. L.R. 87; 7 W.W.R. 97 (1914) 125, 590
Foresta Romana S.A. v. Georges Mobro, 66 Ll. L. Rep. 139 (1940) 162
Forrest, Re, 54 Sol. J. 737 (1910) 513
Forrest v. Maher, 2 I.C.L.R. 546 (1852) 53
Forster v. Hale, 3 Ves. 696; 30 E.R. 1226 (1798); 5 ves. 308; 31 E.R. 603 (1800) 422
Forsyth v. Forsyth, [1948] P. 125 ....302, 595
Foster v. Driscoll, [1929] 1. K.B. 470 ....198, 551
Foubert v. Turst, 1 Brown Parl. Cas. 129; 1 E.R. 464 (1703) 518
Found, In re; Found v. Seemens, [1924] S.A.S.R. 237 ....436, 438
Fowler v. Vail, 4 O.A.R. 267 (1878) 596
Fracis Times & Co. v. Carr, 82 L.T. 698 (1900) 599
Francke and Rasch, Re [1818] 1 Ch. 470 492
Freeland Ltd. v. Kelly, 84 I.L.T. & Sol. J 660
Freedman v. Opdehyde, [1945] Ir. Jur. Rep. 22 134
Freel v. Trant, 11 Ir. Eq. Rep. 278 (1847) 668
Freeman v. Freeman, 4 Ir. Ch. Rep. 39 (1853) 138
Freke v. Lord Carbery, L.R. 16 Eq. 461 (1873) 392, 393, 408, 411, 513
Fremlin v. Fremlin, 16 C.L.R. 212 (1913) 68
French v. Royal Exchange Assurance Co., 6 Ir. Ch. Rep. 523 (1857) 169
Frew (otherwise Reed) v. Reed, 69 W.W.R. 327; 6 D.L.R. (3d) 617 (1969) 219
Frew v. Stone, 6 Ir. Jur. 267 (1854) 142
Freytag, In bonis, 43 I.L.T.R. 116 (1909) 629
Friedrich Krupp A/G, Re [1917] 2 Ch. 188 551
Frummer v. Hilton Hotels International Inc., 60 Misc. 2d 840; 304 N.Y.S. 2d 335
  (1969) 627
Fry v. Moore, 23 Q.B.D. 395 (1889) 126, 130
Fuld (No. 3) In the Estate of Hartley v. Fuld, [1868] p. 675 ....430, 434, 627
Furlong v. Burns & Co. Ltd., [1964] 2 O.R. 3, 43 D.L.R. (2d) 689 104

G. v. An Bord Uchtála, [1980] I.R. 32 ....336, 337
G. & E. Auto Brokers Ltd. v. Toyota Canada Inc., 25 B.C.L.R. 145; 117 D.L.R.
  (3d) 707 (1980) 164
G. v. G. [1984] I.R. 368 ....107, 243, 290, 305, 308
G.M. deceased, In bonis; F.M. v. T.A.M., 106 I.L.T.R. 82 (1970) 429, 436, 437, 438
Gaffney v. Gaffney, [1975] I.R. 133 14, 65, 68, 79, 80, 238, 276, 277, 282, 284, 286,
                                                     288, 585, 599, 605, 607, 608
Galabrun v. Bruce, Symes & Williams, [1903] 2 I.R. 488 159
Galbraith v. Grimshaw, [1910] A.C. 508 482
Gallen v. Lee, [1938] I.R. 142 130
Gardiner v. Harris, 8 L.R. Ir. 352 (1881) 663
Gardiner v. Haughton, 2 B. & S. 743; 121 E.R. 1247 (1862) 481
Garthwaite v. Garthwaite, [1964] 2 All E.R. 233; [1964] P. 356 .....123, 253, 295
Gasque v. Inland Revenue Commissioners, [1940] 2 K.B. 80 484
Gavin Gibson & Co. Ltd. v. Gibson, [1913] 3 K.B. 379 595
Gdynia Ameryka Linie Zeglugowe v. Boguslawski, [1953] A.C. 11 207
General Steam Navigation Co. v. Guillon, 11 M. & W. 877; 152 E.R. 1061 (1843) 595, 647
Gentili, In bonis, I.R. 9 Eq. 541 (1875) 108, 391, 392, 393, 408, 409, 410, 411, 429,
                                                     430, 454, 455, 456, 494
Georges, Re, 65 Sol. J. 311 (1921) 513
Georges-Picot v. Henderson, [1963] N.Z.L.R. 950 511
Geyer v. Aguilar, 7 Term Rep. 681; 101 E.R. 1196 (1798) 586
Gibbon v. Commerz & Creditbank A/G, [1958] 2 L. Rep. 113 141

Gibbons, In re, A Bankrupt in England. Ex Parte Walter, [1960] Ir. Jur. Rep. 60 202, 471, 473, 478
Gibbs & Son v. Société Industrielle des Métaux, 25 Q.B.D. 399 (1890) 481
Gibson v. Goleman, [1950] I.R. 50 664
Gibson v. Holland, L.R. 1 C.P. 1, (1865) 632
Gieves v. O'Connor, [1924] 2 I.R. 182 ....610, 661
Gill v. Manly, 16 I.L.T.R. 57 (1882) 629
Gillespie v. Cummins, 2 I.L.R. 200 (1840) 132
Gillespie, In re; Ex parte Robarts, 18 Q.B.D. 286 (1886) 493
Gilliland & Son v. Latta, 41 I.L.T.R. 91 (1907) 144
Gillis v. Gillis, I.R. 8 Eq. 597 (1874) 51, 62, 66, 67, 72, 74, 295
Glover v. B.L.N. (No. 2), [1973] I.R. 432 645
Godard v. Gray, L.R. 6 Q.B. 139 (1870) 602, 603, 604
Goldin v. Goldin, 104 D.L.R. (3d) 76 (1979) 279
Goldsbrough, Mort & Co. Ltd. v. Hall, 78 C.L.R. 1 (1949) 542
Goodman's Trusts, Re, 17 Ch. D. 266 (1881) 358, 363, 364, 369
Goudain v. Nadler, [1979] E.C.R. 733; [1979] 3 C.M.L.R. 180 612
Government of India, Ministry of Finance v. Taylor, [1955] A.C. 491 .....199, 459
Golden Trader, The, [1974] 2 All E.R. 686, [1975] Q.B. 348 162
Graham v. Canandaigna Lodge No. 236 of the Independent Order of Oddfellows of the State of New York, 24 O.R. 255 (1893) 431
Graham v. Graham, [1923] P. 31 295
Graham v. Wray, 35 I.L.T.R. 237 (1901) 665
Grant v. Easton, 13 Q.B.D. 302 (1883) 602
Grassi, In re, [1905] 1 Ch. 584 411
Gray v. Formosa, [1963] P. 259 ....46, 77, 257, 258, 259, 262, 608
Gray v. National Trust Co., 8 W.W.R. 1061; 23 D.L.R. 608 (1915) 234
Great Northern Ry. Co. v. Johnson, 254 F. 683 (1918) 221
Greenaway v. A.G., 44 T.L.R. 124 (1927) 367
Grehan v. Medical Incorporated & Valley Pines, [1986] I.L.R.M. 627 21, 133, 147, 151, 573, 578
Grell v. Levy, 16 C.B. (N.S.) 73; 143 E.R. 1052 (1864) 550
Gremson v. Lipman, 58 I.L.T.R. 93 (1924) 661
Grey's Trusts, Re, [1892] 3 Ch. 88 ....359, 365
Grierson, In bonis, 7 L.R. Ir. 589 (1881) 455
Griffin, In bonis, 65 I.L.T.R. 108 (1931) 629
Griffin v. Royal Liver Friendly Society, [1942] Ir. Jur. Rep. 29 523
Griffiths v. Van Raaj, [1986] I.L.R.M. 582 644
Grimwood v. Bartels, 46 L.J. Ch. 788 (1877) 387
Groos, Re; Groos v. Groos, [1915] 1 Ch. 572 435
Grove, Re, 40 Ch. D. 216 (1888) 352, 358, 359
Grove v. Boyle, 26 I.L.T.R. 22 (1892) 132
Guarantee Trust Co. of New York v. Stevens, 28 N.J. 243; 146 A. 2d 97 (1958) 450
Guaranty Trust Co. v. Hannay, [1918] 1 K.B. 43 ....488, 489
Guepratte v. Young, 4 De G. & Sm. 217; 64 E.R. 804 (1851) 427, 510
Guiard v. De Clermont, [1914] 3 K.B. 145 ....591, 593
Guido v. Grainger, Ir. R. 8 C.L. 113 (1874) 668
Guinness v. Armic, 3 Ir. L.R. 165 (1841) 126
Guion v. Heffernan, [1929] I.R. 487 ....654, 656
Gulbenkian v. Gulbenkian, [1937] 4 All E.R. 618 ....71, 83
Gulf Oil Corporation v. Gilbert, 330 U.S. 501 (1947) 165
Gwyn v. Mellen, [1979] 6 W.W.R. 385 ....260, 262
Gyonyor v. Sanjenko, [1971] 5 W.W.R. 381 595

H (Infants), Re, [1966] 1 W.L.R. 381 ....333, 334
Habgood v. Paul, 8 Ir. C.L.R. xxx (1859) 656, 658
Hackett, a Lunatic, In re, 3 Ir. Ch. Rep. 375 (1864) 386
Hadley v. Baxendale, 9 Exch. 341, 156 E.R. 145 (1854) 642

Hagen, The, [1908] P. 189 ....134, 136, 459
Hagerbaum, deceased, In re; Bond v. Pidding, [1933] I.R. 198 ....358, 359, 363
Halcyon Isle, The; Bankers Trust International Ltd. v. Todd Shipyards Corporation
 [1981] A.C. 221 648
Hall v. Australian Capital Territory Electricity Authority, 31 A.L.R. 557 (1980) .150
Halley, The, L.R. 2 P.C. 193 (1868) 572, 573, 574, 580
Halligan v. Halligan, [1896] 1 I.R. 244 306
Hamburger v. Poetting, 47 L.T. 249 (1882) 658
Hamilton v. Foreign & Mercantile Co., 3 Ir. L.T. & Sol. J. 389 (1869) 141
Hamlin v. Hamlin [1985] 2 All E.R. 1037 407
Hamlyn & Co. v. Talisker Distillery [1894] A.C. 202 ....545, 616, 617
Hammond Lane Industries Ltd. v. Ongree Steel Trading Co. Ltd. 99. I.L.T.R. 5 (1956) 524
Handelskimekerij G.J. Bier B.V. v. Mines de Potasse d'Alsace S.A., [1976] E.C.R.
 1735 ....151, 186
Hannon v. Eisler, 13 W.W.R. 565, [1955] D.L.R. 183 86
Hanrahan v. Hanrahan, 19 O.R. 396 (1890) 328
Haque v. Haque, 114 C.L.R. 98 (1985) 391, 392, 396, 397
Harben v. Harben, [1957] 1 All E.R. 379 324
Harding v. Commissioners of Stamps for Queensland [1898] A.C. 769 397
Hardwick Game Farm v. Suffolk Agricultural Poultry Producers Association, [1966]
 1 W.L.R. 287 495
Hardy (N.W.) & Co. Ltd. v. Pound & Co., [1955] 1 Q.B. 499 543
Harley v. Kinnear Moodie & Co. 1964 S.C. 99 610
Harold Meyers Travel Service Ltd. v. Magid, 60 D.L.R. (3d) 42 (1975) 105
Harris, In bonis, L.R. 2 P&D 83 (1870) 455
Harris Investment Ltd. v. Smith, [1934] 1 D.L.R. 748 510
Harris v. Harris, [1930] 1 W.W.R. 173 82
Harris v. Quine, L.R. 4 Q.B. 653 (1869) 606
Harris v. Taylor, [1915] 2. K.B. 580 ....592, 593, 594
Harris' Trustees, 1919 S.C. 432 513
Har-Shefi v. Har-Shefi (No. 2) [1953] P. 220 274
Hartmann v. Konig, 50 Times L.R. 114 (1933) 113
Harwood v. Tenison, 5 Ir. Ch. Rep. 340 (1856) 653
Hassan v. Hassan, Re, 12 O.R. (2d) 432 (1976) 214, 234
Haut v. Haut, 86 D.L.R. (3d) 757 (1978) 74, 280
Haydon v. Haydon, [1937] 4 D.L.R. 617 505
Hayes v. Reid, 12 Ir. L.R. 119 (1848) 161
Hazelton, a Bankrupt, In re, 49 I.L.T.R. 29 (1914) 464
Hearst, deceased, In bonis, 40 I.L.T.R. 198 (1906) 455
Heany v. Malocca [1958] I.R. 111 ....660, 665, 666, 667
Heenan v. Clements, 1 Ir. C.L.R. 44 (1850) 164
Heffernan v. Atkin, 47 I.L.T.R. 245 (1913) 129, 130
Heil v. Lazenby, 12 L.R. Ir. 75 (1883) 668
Helbert Wagg & Co. Ltd's Claim, Re, [1956] Ch. 323 ....204, 206, 522, 551
Hellman's Will, L.R. 2 Eq. 363 431
Hemelryck v. William Lyall Shipbuilding Co., [1921] 1 A.C. 698 139
Henderson v. Henderson, 6 Q.B. 288 (1844) 603, 604
Hennahy v. Hutchins, Stewart's Law Forms, 344 663
Henry v. Geopresco International Ltd., [1976] Q.B. 726 ....592, 593
Hepworth, [1936] Ch. 759 366
Herbert, deceased; In re Estate of; Herbert v. Herbert 25 L.R. Ir. 102 (1890) ...457
Herbert v. Herbert, 3 Phill. Ecc. 58, 161 E.R. 1257 (1819) 219
Hernando, Re; Hernando v. Sawtell, 27 Ch. D. 284 (1884) 431, 451
Hesperides Hotels Ltd. v. Aegean Turkish Holdings Ltd., [1979] A.C. 508 402
Heung Won Lee, Re, 36 D.L.R. (2d) 177 (1962) 419
Hewitt's Settlement, In re; Hewitt v. Hewitt, [1915] 1 Ch. 228 423
Heydon v. Hammond & Murray, 10 Ir. L. Rep. 268 (1848) 127
Heywood v. Heywood, 29 Beav. 9, 54 E.R. 527 (1860) 420

Higgins v. Byrne, 42 I.L.T. 252 (1908) 400, 437, 441
Higgins v. Irish Shipping Ltd. [1944] I.R. 178 161
High Commissioner for India v. Ghosh, [1960] 1 Q.B. 134 ....130, 174
Hill, In re, [1900] I I.R. 349 387
Hill v. William Hill (Park Lane) Ltd., [1949] A.C. 530 552
Hispano Americana Mercantile S.A. v. Central Bank of Nigeria, [1979] 2 Lloyd's
    L. Rep. 277 175
Hodson v. McQueen, 7 Ir. C.L.R. 288 (1857) 658
Hoff, Re, [1942] Ch. 298 366
Hoffman v. Sofaer, [1982] 1 W.L.R. 1350 650
Hogan v. Hogan [1924] 2 I.R. 14 668
Hogg v. Provincial Tax Commission [1941] 4 D.L.R. 501 397
Holden, Re, [1935] W.N. 52 458
Hole Estate, Re, [1948] 2 W.W.R. 754; 56 Man. R. 295; [1948] 4 D.L.R. 419 391
Holthausen, Ex Parte, L.R. 9 ch. App. 722 (1874) 480
Holman v. Johnson, 1 Comp. 341, 98, E.R. 1120 (1775) 9, 198
Holub v. Holub, 71 D.L.R. (3d) 698 (1976) 280
Hood & Co. v. Magee, [1918] 2 I.R. 34 ....53, 482
Hooper v. Hooper, [1959] 1 W.L.R. 1021 227
Hope v. Brewer, 136 N.Y. 126, 32 N.E. 558 (1892) 442
Hope v. Carnegie, L.R. 1 Ch. App. 320 (1866) 513
Hope v. Hope, [1968] N.I. 1 ....86, 324, 326
Hopes v. Hopes, [1949] P. 227 88
Hopton v. M'Carthy, 10 L.R. Ir. 266 (1882) 632
Hoskins v. Matthews, 8 De G.M. & G. 13, 44 E.R. 294 (1856) 62
Houlditch v. Donegal, 2 Cl. & F. 470 603
Houlditch v. Stackpole, 3 Law. Rec. (O.S. 123 (1830) 656
Houston, In re, 1 Russ. 312, 38 E.R. 121 (1826) 382, 386
Hovells v. Hovells, *Irish Times*, 1 August 1962 635
Howard v. Howard, 30 L.R. Ir. 340 (1892) 656
Howe Lewis, Re, 14 D.L.R. (3d) 49 (B.C.C.A. 1970) 222
Howley, deceased, In re; Naughton v. Hagarty, [1940] I.R. 109 511
Hoyles, Re, [1911] 1 Ch. 179 ....391, 397, 411, 600
Huber v. Steiner, Bing N.C. 202, 132, E.R. 80 (1835) 639, 640
Hubert v. Quine, L.R. 4 Q.B. 653 (1869) 639
Hughes v. Hughes, [1958] C.L.Y. 502 297
Hunter v. Potts, 4 Term Rep. 182, 100 E.R. 962 (1791) 467
Huntington v. Attrill, [1893] A.C. 150 ....192, 193, 194, 197
Hurll, Re, [1952] Ch. 722 ....359, 362, 366
Hussein (otherwise Blitz) v. Hussein, [1938] P. 159 ....242, 253
Hutchinson v. Cathcart, 8 Ir. Eq. Rep. 394 (1845) 398, 416, 418, 420, 501, 633
Hutchinson's Executor v. The Master, 1919 A.D. 71 46
Hutter v. Hutter (otherwise Perry), [1944] P. 95 ....244, 253, 255, 295
Hutton v. Dant, [1924] 1 D.L.R. 401 603
Hyde v. Hyde, L.R. 1 P. & D. 130 (1866) 213, 214, 215, 216, 219

I.E. v. W.E., [1985] I.L.R.M. 691 223
Imrie v. Castique, (1860) 8 C.B. (N.S.) 405; (1870) L.R. 4 H.L. 414 599
Industrie, The, [1894] P. 58 543
Industria Tessili Italiana Como v. Dunlop A.G., Case 12/76 [1976] E.C.R. 1473 185
Indyka v. Indyka, [1969] 1 A.C. 633 ....279, 280
Inglis v. Commonwealth Trading Bank of Australia, 20 F.L.R. 30 (1972) 406
Inglis v. Robertson, [1898] A.C. 616 499
Inkerman Brown, In bonis, 36 I.L.T.R. 173 (1902) 629
Inland Revenue Commissioners v. Duchess of Portland, [1982] Ch. 314 79
International Alltex Corporation v. Lawler Creations Ltd., [1965] I.R. 264 591,
                                                                       594, 616, 617
Interview Ltd., In re, [1975] I.R. 382 ....34, 36, 44, 106, 495, 496, 520

Inverclyde (otherwise Tripp) v. Inverclyde, [1931] P. 29 254
Iraqui M.O.D. v. Arcepey Shipping, [1980] 2 W.L.R. 488 646
I.R.C. v. Highland Engineering Ltd., 1975 S.L.T. 203 485
I.R.C. v. Lysaght, [1928] A.C. 234 101
Irish Commercial Society Ltd. v. Plunkett, High Ct., Costello, J., 29 November 1985 667
Irish Leisure Industries Ltd. v. Gaiety Theatre Enterprises Ltd., unreported, High
  Ct., O'Higgins C.J., 12 February 1975 645
Irish Transport & General Workers Union v. Green & Transport & General Workers
  Union, [1936] I.R. 471 ....24, 633
Iveagh v. I.R.C., [1954] Ch. 364 ....424, 509
Iveagh v. Revenue Commissioners, [1930] I.R. 386 ....66, 67
Ivenel v. Schwab, Case 133/81, [1982] E.C.R. 1891 185

Jabbour (F. & K.) v. Custodian of Israeli Absentee's Property of State of Israel,
  [1954] 1 All E.R. 145 502
Jablonowski v. Jablonowski, [1972] 3 O.R. 410; 28 D.L.R. (3d) 440 (1972) 54, 82
Jack v. Noble, 17 I.C.L.R. 381 (1867) 668
Jackson (A Bankrupt in the Republic of Ireland), In re, [1973] N.I. 67 473, 475, 476
Jacobs v. Australian Abrasives Pty. Ltd., [1971] V.R. 92 150
Jacobs v. Beaver, 17 O.L.R. 496 (1908) 607
Jacobs v. Crédit Lyonnais, 12 Q.B.D. 589 (1884) 531, 543, 545, 548
Jacobson v. Carr, 1 Cr. & D. 107 (1837) 663
Jacobson v. Frachon, 138 L.T. 386 (1927) 609
Jaffer v. Williams, 25 T.L.R. 12 (1908) 596
James v. Catherwood, 3 Dow. & Ry. (K.B.) 190 (1823) 488
James v. Despott, 14 L.R. Ir. 71 (1884) 133
James (An Insolvent) In re; (Attorney General-Intervening), [1977] Ch. 41 177, 473
Miller (James) & Partners Ltd. Whitworth Street Estates (Manchester) Ltd., [1970]
  A.C. 583 617
Janson v. Driefontein Consolidated Mines Ltd., [1902] A.C. 484 484
Jarrett v. Wabash Ry. Co., 57 F. 2d 669 (1932) 627
Jay v. Budd, [1898] 1 Q.B. 12 127
Jeannot v. Fuerst, 25 T.L.R. 424 (1909) 602
Jeffrey v. Jeffrey, 81 I.L.T.R. 22 (1946) 133, 134
Jeffrey v. Taggart, 6 M. & S. 126; 105 E.R. 1190 (1817) 504
Jenner v. Sun Oil Co., [1952] O.R. 240; [1952] 2 D.L.R. 526 148
Johnson, Re, [1903] 1 Ch. 821 ....35, 40, 41, 43, 365
Johnson (falsely called Cooke) v. Cooke, [1898] 1 I.R. 130 ....65, 250, 251, 252
Johnson v. Hazan, 43 N.B.R. 154 (1912) 219
Johnson v. Taylor Bros., [1920] A.C. 144 134
Johnstone v. Beattie, 10 Cl. & Fin. 42; 8 E.R. 657 ....83, 328
Johnstone v. Bucknall, [1898] 2 I.R. 499 610
Jones v. Evans, 35 I.L.T.R. 237n (1901) 665
Jones, In the Estate of, 192 Iowa 78; 182 N.W. 227; 16 A.L.R. 1286 (1921) 76
Jones v. Oceanic Steam Navigation Co., [1924] 2 K.B. 730 545
Jones v. Smith, 56 O.L.R. 550 [1925] 599
Jones Trusts, In re, 20 Ont. L.R. 457 (1910) 511
Joyce, In re; Corbet v. Fagan, [1946] I.R. 277 ....56, 57, 58, 72, 74, 75, 94
Joyce v. Director of Public Prosecutions, [1946] A.C. 347 324
Joynt v. M'Crum, [1899] I.R. 217 ....153, 157
Jugoslavenska Oceanska Plovidba v. Castle Investment Co. Inc. [1974] Q.B. 292 649
Julian, In re; Julian v. Goodbody, [1936] I.R. 126 654
Junior Books Ltd. v. Veitchi, [1983] A.C. 520 643

Kaine, In re Estate of, [1938] 3 W.W.R. 224 455
Kalling, Deceased, 32 Ir. L.T.R. 131 (1897) 447
Kahan v. Pakistan Federation, [1951] 2 K.B. 1003 ....173, 175
Kahler v. Midland Bank, [1950] A.C. 24 ....545, 548

Kaufman, In the goods of, [1952] P. 325 455
Kaufman v. Gerson, [1904] 1 K.B. 591 550
Kaur v. Ginder, 13 D.L.R. (2d) 465 (1958) 213
Kaye v. Sutherland, 20 Q.B.D. 147 (1887) 137
K.C. v. M.C., Sup. Ct., 13 December 1985, affirming High Ct., Carroll, J., 26 September 1984 ....79, 235
Keegan v. De Burca, [1973] I.R. 223 196
Keith v. Protection Marine Insurance Co. of Paris, 10 L.R. Ir. 51 (1882) 519
Kennedy v. London Express Newspapers Ltd., [1931] I.R. 532 ....520, 524
Keochlin et Cie v. Kestenbaum, [1927] 1 K.B. 889 ....489, 490
Khalifa v. Khalifa, 19 D.L.R. (3d) 460 (1971) 82
Khan's Settlement, In re, [1966] Ch. 567 451
Keane v. Crozier, 27 I.L.T.R. 81 (1893) 159
Keane v. Hanley, [1938] Ir. Jur. Rep. 16 ....107, 634
Keatinge, Ex parte, I.R. 2 Eq. 26 (1867) 542
Keegan v. Keegan, 7 L.R. Ir. 101 (1881) 661
Keith v. Protection Marine Insurance Co. of Paris, 10 L.R. Ir. 51 (1882) 551
Kelly v. Bank of Ireland, Batty 593 (1826) 453
Kelly, deceased, In bonis, 31 I.L.T.R. 169 (1897) 455
Kelly v. Dixon, I.R. 6 C.L. 25 (1870) 132, 144, 148
Kelly v. Jameson, unreported, Sup. Ct., 1 March 1972 582
Kelly v. O'Brian, 31 D.L.R. 770 (1916) 328
Kelly v. Selwyn, [1905] 2 Ch. 117 503
Kennedy v. Keane, [1901] 2 I.R. 640 665
Kennedy v. Kelly, 7 Ir. Jur. (n.s.) 326 (1862) 67, 68
Kennedy v. London Express Newspapers, [1931] I.R. 532 163
Kennedy v. Trites, 10 W.W.R. 412 (1816) 592
Kent Co. Co. v. C.S., [1984] I.L.R.M. 14, 25, 337, 633
Kenward v. Kenward, [1950] P. 71 240
Kenwood v. Kenwood, [1951] P. 124 245
Keresz v. Keresz, [1954] V.L.R. 195 107
Keresztessy v. Keresztessy, 73 D.L.R. (3d) 347 (1976) 280
Kern v. Kern, [1972] 3 All E.R. 207 131
Kernot, Re, [1965] Ch. 217 330
Kervorkian v. Burney (No. 2), [1937] 4 All E.R. 468 ....658, 660
Keserue v. Keserue, [1962] 1 W.L.R. 1406 295
Kett v. Robinson, 4 I.C.L.R. 186 (1854) 140, 142
Kevens v. Joyce, [1896] 1 I.R. 442 474
Keys v. Keys, [1919] 2 I.R. 160 ....114, 305, 306, 308, 601
Khan v. Khan, 21 D.L.R. (2d) 171 (1959) 251, 252
Kianta Osakeyhtio v. Britain and Overseas Trading Co. Ltd., [1954] 1 Lloyd's Rep. 247 618
Kildare (Lord of) v. Eustace, 1 Vern. 419; 22 E.R. 905 (1686) 406
Killiney U.D.C. v. Kirkwood & Moorhead, [1917] 2 I.R. 614 ....137, 142. 184
Kilpatrick v. Kilpatrick, [1929] 3 W.W.R. 463; [1930] 1 D.L.R. 288 83
Kindersley, In re, [1944] I.R. 111 ....86, 321, 331, 332
King v. Attorney-General, I.R. 4 Eq. 464 (1870) 356
King, The v. International Trustee for the Protection of Bondholders A/C, [1937] A.C. 500 521
King, In re Estate of; King v. Long, 53 I.L.T.R. 60 (1918) 512
King v. King, [1941] Ir. Jur. Rep. 29 626
King v. Ridle, 1 I.C.L.R. 85 (1851) 132
Kingston's (Duchess of) Case, 2 Sm. L.C. (13th ed.) 644 (1776) 606
Kingston (Earl of) v. Sheehy, Hayes & Jones, 358 (1833) 659
Kionta Osakeyhtio v. Britain and Overseas Trading Co. Ltd., 1 Lloyd's Rep. 247 617
Kirwan v. Lindsay, 2 Ir. Ch. Rep. 23 (1852) 633
Kisbey v. Chester & Holyhead Ry. Co., 6 I.C.L.R. 393 (1857) 146, 148

Kitson v. Kitson, 1945 S.C. 434 326
Kleinwort Sons & Co. v. Ungarische Baumwolle Industrie A/G, [1939] 2 K.B. 678 548
Klingemann, In the Goods of, 3 Sw. & Tr. 18; 164 E.R. 1178 (1862) 108
Kloebe, Re; Kannreuther v. Geiselbrecht, 28 Ch. D. 175 (1884) 458, 459, 648
Knock, Re, 25 O.R. (2d) 312 (1979) 456
Knox deceased, In re; Snodgrass v. Gamble, [1910] 1 I.R. 508
Kochanski v. Kochanska, [1958] P. 147 229
Kohnke v. Karger, [1951] 2 K.B. 670 642
Koitaki Para Rubber Estates Ltd. v. Federal Commissioners of Taxation 484
Kondor Plas Ltd. v. Honeywell Leasing Ltd., 104 I.L.T.R. 220 (1969) 136, 144
Koop v. Bebb, 84 C.L.R. 626 (1951) 149
Kooperman, Re, [1928] W.N. 101 478
Korner v. Witkowitzer, [1950] 2 K.B. 128 627
Korvine's Trusts, In re, [1921] 1 Ch. 343 500
Kroch v. Rossell et Compagnie Société de Personnes à Responsabilité Limitée,
   [1937] 1 All E.R. 725 148
Kruppstahl A.G. v. Quitman Products Ltd., [1982] I.L.R.M. 551 ....498, 520
Krzus v. Crow's Nest Pass Coal Co. Ltd., [1912] A.C. 590 436
Kuklycz v. Kuklycz, [1972] V.R. 50 228
Kuwait Oil Co. v. Indemitsu Tankers K.K.; The Hida Maru, [1981] 2 Lloyd's Rep.
   510 136
Laane v. Estonian State Cargo & Passenger S.S. Line, [1949] S.C.R. 530 206, 207
La Carte v. La Carte, 60 D.L.R. (3d) 507 (1975) 280
Lacon v. Higgins, 3 Stark. 178, 171 E.R. 813 (1822) 219
Ladbroke v. Biggs, Batty, 619 (1826) 542
Lahiff, A person of unsound mind, In re, [1904] 1 I.R. 147 381
Lambe v. Manuel, [1903] A.C. 68 397
Landsdowne v. Landsdowne, 1 Ir. L.R. 204 (1839) 542
Langley's Settlement Trusts, Re, [1962] Ch. 541 381
Langston v. Massey, 4 Ir. L.R. 412 (1842) 132
Larkin v. National Union of Mineworkers, High Ct., Barrington, J., 18 June 1985 99,
                                                           106, 193, 197, 330
Lashley v. Hog, 2 Coop. t. Cott. 449, 47 E.R. 1243 (1804) 420
La Société Anonyme la Chemo-Sérothér-apiè Belge v. Dolan (Dominick A.) & Co.
   Ltd., [1961] I.R. 281 ....586, 587, 602, 604
Latimer v. Dumican, 44 I.L.T.R. 150 (1910) 523
Lauriè v. Carroll, 98 C.L.R. 310 (1958) 125, 127
Lavelle, In re; Cassidy v. A.G., [1940] Ir. Jur. Rep. 8 629
Lavender's Policy, In re, [1898] 1 I.R. 175 541
Law v. Gustin, [1976] Fam. 155 ....261, 263
Lawrence v. Lawrence, [1985] 2 All E.R. 733 233
Lawson v. Commissioners of Inland Revenue, [1896] 2 I.R. 418 113,
                                                           392, 396, 397
Lazard Bros. & Co. v. Midland Bank Ltd., [1933] A.C. 289 ....105, 111
Lazarewicz v. Lazarewicz, [1962] P. 171 229
Lazarus-Barlow v. Regent Estates Co. Ltd., [1949] 2 All E.R. 118 ....598, 599
L.B. v. H.B., [1980] I.L.R.M. 257 ....66, 106, 276, 277,
                                          282, 284, 285, 286, 587, 608
Leake v. Douglas, 88 I.L.T.R. 4 (1952) 106, 273, 308
Lear v. Lear, 51 D.L.R. (3d) 56 (1974) 104
Lebel v. Tucker, L.R. 3 Q.B. 77 (1867) 489
Leckham v. Gresham, 2 Ir. C.L.R. 139 (1852) 668
Lecky, a Bankrupt in England, In re, 95 I.L.T.R. 38 (1961) 478
Lee, In bonis, [1898] 2 I.R. 81 455
Lee v. Abdy, 17 Q.B.D. 309 (1886) 502
Lee Hing, In the will of, 1 S.R. N.S.W. (Eq.) 199 (1901) 431
Lee v. Lau, [1967] P. 14 213
Leeson v. Leeson, 4 Ir. Ch. Rep. 28 (1853) 653, 668

Le Feuvre v. Sullivan, 10 Moo. P.C. 1, 14 E.R. 389 (1885) 503
Leguia, In the Estate of, [1934] P. 80 456
Le Mesurier v. Le Mesurier, [1895] A.C. 517 33
Lemons Infants, In re, 19 L.R. Ir. 575 (1887) 322
Leonard v. Scofield (No. 2), [1938] Ir. Jur. Rep. 31 ....539, 631, 632
Lepre v. Lepre, [1965] P. 52 ....259, 262
Leroux v. Brown, 12 C.B. 801, 138 E.R. 119 (1852) 554, 631, 632
Lesage v. De Frith, 12 I.L.T. 161 (1878) 133
Leslie v. Baillie, 2 Y. & C. Ch. Cas. 91, 63 E.R. 40 (1843) 431
Lessee Nagle v. Power, 1 Jones 420 (1835) 659
Lessee Stewart v. Bartholomew, 1 Ir. L.R. 377 (1839) 652
Lett v. Lett, [1906] 1 I.R. 618 ....51, 109, 170, 404, 519, 638
Lett's Trusts and Trustee Relief Act, In re; Ex parte Lett, 7 L.R. (Ir.) 132 (1881) 106,
                                                                          417, 418, 420
Levene v. I.R.C. [1928] A.C. 217 ....101, 138
Levison v. Hodges, 8 Ir. L.R. 112 (1846) 669
Levy's Trusts, In re, 30 Ch. D. 119 (1885) 478
Lewal's Settlement, Re, [1918] 2 Ch. 391 450
Lewis v. Belshaw, 54 C.L.R. 188 (1935) 456
Lewis v. Nixon, 7 Ir. L.R. 359 (1843) 144
Lightbody v. West, 18 T.L.R. 526 (1902) 228
Lim v. Lim, [1973] V.R. 370 54
Limerick Corporation v. Crompton, [1909] 2 I.R. 120, aff'd [1910] 2 I.R. 416 134, 595
Lim Poh Choo v. Camden & Islington Area Health Authority, [1980] A.C. 174 644
Lindgram v. Lindgram, [1956] V.L.R. 215 130
Lindsay v. Crawford & Lindsays, 45 I.L.T.R. 52 (1911) 127, 128
Lindsay v. Miller, [1949] V.L.R. 13 509
Linke (otherwise Van Aerde) v. Van Aerde, 10 T.L.R. 426 (1894) 253
Lisburn Council v. Shortt, 46 I.L.T.R. 132 (1912) 139
Lister & Co. v. Stubbs, 45 Ch. D. 1 (1890) 646
Liston v. Munster & Leinster Bank Ltd., [1940] I.R. 77 490
Littauer Glove Corporation v. Millington (F.W.) (1920) Ltd., 44 T.L.R. 746 (1928) 590
Littles, In re, 10 Ir. Eq. Rep. 275 (1847) 598, 599
Liverpool Marine Credit Co. v. Hunter, L.R. 4 Eq. 62 (1867) 499
Livesley v. Clements Horst Co., [1924] S.C.R. 605 ....15, 586, 625, 643
Livingston v. Commissioner of Stamp Duties, 107 C.L.R. 411 (1960) 397
Llangennech Coal Co. v. Old Park Printing Co., 13 I.L.T.R. 74 (1879) 486
Lloneux, Limon & Co. v. Hong Kong & Shanghai Banking Corporation, 33 Ch.
    Div. 446 (1886) 131
Lloyd & Guibert, L.R. 1 Q.B. 115 (1865) 113, 143, 520, 530
Loader v. Millar, [1942] Ir. Jur. Rep. 38 ....653, 659
Lockhart, In the goods of, 69 L.T. 21 (1893) 455
Lockhart's Trust, Ex parte Lady Lockhart, 11 Ir. Jur. (n.s.) 245 (1866) 66
London Finance and Discount Co. v. Butler, [1929] I.R. 90 ....519, 549
Long v. Long, 1 Ir. Chy. Rep. 618 (1851) 668
Long v. Tottenham, 1 Ir. Chy. Rep. 127 (1850) 658, 668
Lorillard, In re, [1922] 2 Ch. 638 459
Loucks v. Standard Oil Co., 224 N.Y. 99, 120 N.E. 198 (1918) 568
Louis-Dreyfus v. Patterson Steamships Ltd., 43 F. 2d 824 (1930) 543
Lowden v. Accident Insurance Co., 43 I.L.T.R. 277 (1904) 141, 519
                                                                          523, 649
Lowenstein v. Allen, [1958] C.L.Y. 491 502
Lucan (Lord) v. Latouche, 1 Hogan 448 659
Luck, Re, [1940] Ch. 864 ....359, 362
Lurgan U.D.C., Ex parte; In re Kearns, [1902] 1 I.R. 154 454
Luther v. Sagor, [1921] 3 K.B. 532 ....177, 178, 206
Lynch v. Clarkin, 33 I.L.T.R. 157 (1899) 668
Lyons (an Infant), Re, 72 I.L.T.R. 37 (1937) 270

M., In re., [1937] N.I. 151 ....49, 361
M.C. v. K.E.D. (otherwise K.C.), Sup. Ct., 13 December 1985 ....80, 262, 276
                                                          279, 280, 282
M.K. (otherwise McC.) v. F.McC., [1892] I.L.R.M. 277 287
M.P.D. v. M.D., [1981] I.L.R.M. 179 639
Maatschappij Voor Fondsenbezit v. Shell Transport & Trading Co., [1923] 2 K.B. 166 655
Macartney, Re; Macfarlane v. Macartney, [1921] 1 Ch. 522 638
M'Caffrey v. Brennan, 10 Ir. C.L.R. 159 (1860) 666
M'Cann v. Allen, 27 I.L.T.R. 64 (1893) 161
M'Cann v. Thomson, 11 Ir. L. Rep. 201 (1847) 127
McCarthy v. Walsh, [1965] I.R. 246 644
Macaura v. Smith, [1939] Ir. Jur. Rep. 46 660
M'Clelland v. Tyrell, 31 I.L.T.R. 84 (1897) 132, 160
McClement, a Bankrupt, In re, [1960] I.R. 141 463
McComiskey, deceased, In re; Gibson v. Patterson, [1939] I.R. 573 271
M'Cormick v. Garnett, 5 D.M. & G. 278, 43 E.R. 877 (1854) 105
McCowan v. Menasco Manufacturing Co., [1941] O.W.N. 133 139
M'Crea v. Knight, [1896] 2 I.R. 619 ....133, 134, 140, 141
M'Cullagh, In bonis, 13 L.R. (Ir.) 242 (1884) 454
McCulloch, Ex parte, 14 Ch. D. 716 (1880) 465
MacDonald, Re, 44 D.L.R. (2d) 208 (1964) 349
M'Donaugh v. McCartney, 3 Ir. C.L.R. 239 (1854) 132
M'Donnell v. Alcorn, [1894] 1 I.R. 274 118
M'Donnell v. M'Donnell, [1921] 2 I.R. 148 ....114, 306, 308
                                                     309, 586, 587, 601, 602
M'Dougal v. O'Shaughnessy, I.R. 1 C.L. 86 (1867) 132, 138
MacDougall v. Chitnavis, 1937 S.C. 390 213
M'Elroy v. M'Allister, 1949 S.C. 110 ....569, 640
M'Evers v. O'Neill, 4 L.R. (Ir.) 517 (1879) 134, 144
McFadden v. Colville Ranching Co., 8 W.W. 163 (1915) 591
McFee Engineering Pty. Ltd. (in Liquidation) v. C.B.S. Constructions Pty. Ltd., 44
   Fed. L. Rep. 340 (1979) 142
McGee v. A.G., [1974] I.R. 284 ....81, 224, 335
Magees Infants, In re, 31 L.R. (Ir.) 513 (1892) 326, 328
M'Gettigan v. North-Eastern Ry Co. of England, [1899] 2 I.R. 375 ....139, 141
Maghee v. M'Allister, 3 Ir. Chy. Rep. 604 (1853) 79, 270, 278, 288, 358
McGill v. L.S., [1979] I.R. 283 629
M'Ginn v. Delbeke, 61 I.L.T.R. 117 (1926) 392, 432
MacGregory v. Application des Gaz, [1976] Qd. R. 175 150
Machado v. Fontes, [1897] 2 Q.B. 231 ....575, 576
McHenry v. Lewis, 22 Ch. Div. 397 (1882) 167
Mackay v. Douglas, L.R. 14 Eq. 106 (1872) 463
McKee v. McKee, [1951] A.C. 352 330
Macken & Son v. Ellis, I.R. 8 C.L. 151 (1874) 146, 147
Mackender v. Feldia A.G., [1967] 2 Q.B. 590 536
M'Kendrick v. Buchanan, 20 L.R. (Ir.) 206 (1886) 54
Mackenzie, Re, [1911] 1 Ch. 578 423
MacKenzie, Re, [1941] Ch. 69 94
Mackenzie v. Corballis, 40 I.L.T.R. 28 (1905) 643
Mackie v. Darling, L.R. 12 Eq. 319 (1871) 328
McKie v. McKie, [1933] I.R. 464 ....54, 107
McKinney v. McKinney, 17 R.F.L. (2d) 308 (1980) 419
MacKinnon v. Iberia Shipping Co. Ltd., 1955 S.C. 20 580
McLaffey v. McLaffey, [1905] 2 I.R. 292 606
M'Laughlin, Re, Roulston v. M'Laughlin, 25 L.R. (Ir.) 513 (1890) 132
McLean v. Pettigrew, [1945] 2 D.L.R. 65 575
M'Loughlin, In re Estate of, 1 L.R. (Ir.) 421 (1878) 219, 227, 629
McLoughlin v. Life Association of Scotland, 49 I.L.T.R. 166 (1915) 140

McM. v. McM. and McK. v. McK., [1936] I.R. 196 ....242, 243
M'Mahon v. M'Elroy, Ir. R. 5 Eq. 1 (1869) 629
M'Mahon v. Northwestern Ry. Co., Ir. R. 5 C.L. 200 (1870) 147, 483
McMillin v. McMillin, 114 Colo. 247, 158 P. 2d 444 (1945) 86
McMullen v. Wadsworth, 14 App. Cas. 631 (1889) 68
MacNamara v. Ejector, 6 Ir. L.R. 421 (1844) 160
MacNamara v. Owners of *S.S. Hatteras*, [1933] I.R. 675 ..105, 108, 109, 111, 542
McNeary v. Maguire, [1923] 2 I.R. 43 ....655, 662
MacNeill v. MacNeill, 53 D.L.R. (3d) 486 (1974) 280
Maconchy v. Trower, 30 L.R. (Ir.) 480 (1892) 134, 140
Macrae v. Macrae, [1949] P. 272 302
Macreight, Re, 30 Ch. Div. 165 (1885) 65
M'Sweeney, deceased, In the Estate of; M'Sweeney v. Murphy, [1919] 1 I.R.
  16 ....454, 457, 460
McWhinney v. McWhinney, 248 Minn. 303, 79 N.W. 2d 683 86
M'Williams v. Gilbert & Millard Bros., Ltd., 47 I.L.T.R. 297 (1913) 158
Maddison v. Alderson, 8 App. Cas. 467 (1883) 632
Madzinbanuto v. Lardner-Burke, [1968] 3 All E.R. 561 178
Maharanee of Baroda v. Wildenstein, [1972] 2 Q.B. 283 125
Mahon v. Harrison, [1934] L.J. Ir. 79 139
Mahon v. Hodgens, I.R. 6 Eq. 344 (1872) 457
Mahood, a Ward of Court, In re, [1946] Ir. Jur. Rep. 17 386
Majot's Estate, In re, 199 N.Y. 29, 92 N.E. 402 (1910) 422
Malaysia-Singapore Airlines Ltd. v. Parker, [1972] 3 S.A.S.R. 300 597
Maldonado, deceased, In the Estate of, [1954] P. 228 429
Malley v. Malley, 6 Ir. L. Rep. 154 (1843) 633
Malo v. Clement, [1943] 4 D.L.R. 773 626
Manderville v. Eyre, 13 Ir. L. Rep. 225 (1849) 138
Manifold, Re, [1962] Ch. 1 ....456, 459
Manning v. Manning, L.R. 2 P. & D. 223 (1871) 73
Manning v. Manning, I.R.M. Eq. 520 (1873) 297, 299
Mansfield, deceased, In re; Hibernian Bank Ltd. v. Mansfield, [1962] I.R. 454 106, 109
Mareva Companie Naviera S.A. v. International Bulkcarriers S.A., [1975] 2
  Lloyd's Rep. 509 646
Marie Constance, The, 3 Asp. M.L.C. 505 (1877) 162
Marine Steel Ltd. v. Government of Marshall Islands, [1981] N.Z.L.R. 1 175
Marlborough, Duke of, v. A.G., [1945] Ch. 78 ....424, 510
Marseilles Extension Railway & Lank Co., Re, 30 Ch. D. 598 (1885) 105
Marshall v. Houghton, [1923] 2 W.W.R. 553 596
Marshall v. Marshall, [1952] Q.W.N. 308 82
Marshall v. Murgatroyd, L.R. 6 Q.B. 31(1870) 317
Martin, Re, Loustalan v. Loustalan, [1900] P. 211 ....27, 416, 449
Martin v. Nadel, [1906] 2 K.B. 26 505
Martin v. Russell, 21 L.R. (Ir.) 196 (1888) 656
Martyn v. Kelly, 5 Ir. R.C.L. 404 (1871) 132
Mason v. Mason (otherwise Pennington), [1944] N.I. 134 ....251, 252, 294
Massey v. Allen, 12 Ch. D. 807 (1879) 665
Massey v. Heynes, 21 Q.B.D. 330 (1880) 157
Matalon v. Matalon, [1952] P. 233 295
Matheson Brothers Ltd., Re, 27 Ch. D. 25 (1884) 485
Mattar and Saba v. Public Trustee, [1952] 3 D.L.R. 399 595
Matthews v. Alexander, 7 Ir. R.C.L. 575 (1873) 144
Maubourquet v. Wyse, Ir. R. 1 C.L. 471 (1867) 596, 598, 603, 608
Maudslay Sons & Field, Re; Maudslay v. Maudslay Sons & Field, [1900] 1 Ch.
  602 505
Maule v. Murray, 7 T.R. 470, 101 E.R. 1081 (1978) 587
Mauroux v. Sociedade Comercial Abel Pereira de Fouseca S.A.R.L., [1972] 2 All
  E.R. 1085 ....134, 548

Maxwell v. Martin, Fox & Smith 275 (1824) 659
May (A.S.) & Co. v. Robert Redford Co. Ltd., [1969] 2 O.R. 611, 6 D.L.R. (3d)
    288 164
Mayo-Perrott v. Mayo-Perrott, [1958] I.R. 337 ....213, 214, 238, 273, 290, 585
Mayor, etc., of Limerick v. Crompton & Co., [1910] 2 I.R. 416 ....133, 140
Medley, a Minor, In re, Ir. R. 6 Eq. 339 (1871) 330
Megaw v. Di Lizardi, 5 I.L.T.R. 62 (1871) 146
Mégret, In re, [1901] 1 Ch. 547 451
Mehta v. Mehta, [1945] 2 All E.R. 690 ....214, 242
Meinertzhagen v. Davies, 1 Coll N.C. 335 (1844) 511
Melbourn, Ex parte, L.R. 6 Ch. App. 64 (1870) 480
Merker v. Merker, [1963] P. 283 ....229, 260, 261, 262, 605
Messiniaki Tolmi, The, [1983] 1 Lloyd's L. Rep. 666 167
Metal Industries (Salvage) Ltd. v. Owners of S.T. *Harle*, 1962 S.L.T. 114 198,
                                                                                    199
Metamorphosis, The [1953] 1 All E.R. 723 142
Mette v. Mette, 1 Sw. & Tr. 416, 164 E.R. 792 (1859) 233
Metzenburgh v. Chadwick, 13 Ir. L.R. 59 (1848) 655
Meyer, Re, [1971] P. 298 287
Middleton v. Cottesloe, [1949] A.C. 418 395
Middleton v. Middleton, [1967] P. 62 608
Middleton's Settlement, Re, [1947] Ch. 583 395
Midland Bank Ltd. v. Crossley-Cooke, [1969] I.R. 56 ....653, 658
Mighell v. Sultan of Johore, [1894] 1 Q.B. 149 173
Miliangos v. George Frank (Textiles) Ltd., [1976] A.C. 443 ....491, 649, 650
Miller, Re; Baillie v. Miller, [1914] 1 Ch. 511 ....445, 513
Miller v. Allison, 33 D.L.R. 144 (1917) 234
Miller v. Teale, 92 C.L.R. 406 (1954) 236
Miller v. Wheatley, 28 L.R. (Ir.) 144 (1891) 629
Milligan v. Milligan, [1942] P. 78 300
Milward Jones & Cameron v. Fitzhenry (M. & C.M.) Ltd., 36 I.L.T.R. 211 (1902) 128
Minchin, In re; Minchin v. Stevens, 38 I.L.T.R. 189 (1904) 459
Missouri Steamship Co., In re, 42 Ch. D. 321 (1889) 520, 545, 549
Mitchell, In re, [1937] I.R. 767 78
Mitford v. Mitford, [1923] P. 130 ....260, 262
Mizachi v. Nobel's Explosives Co. Ltd. (1978) (11) 32 P.D. 115 149
Moffett v. Moffett, [1920] 1 I.R. 57 ....46, 50, 52, 56, 58, 65, 69, 107, 359
Mogowan v. Mogowan, [1921] 2 I.R. 314 306
Molony v. Gibbons, 2 Camp. 502, 170 E.R. 1232 (1810) 591
Monaghan v. Swan & Co., unreported, High Ct., McLoughin, J., December 1961 148
Monro (George) Ltd. v. American Cyanamid & Chemical Corporation, [1944]
    K.B. 432 149
Monsarrat v. Barron, 4 N.I.J.R. 21 (1906) 134, 144
Mooney, In bonis, [1938] I.R. 354 656
Moore, an Infant, In re, 11 Ir. C.L.R. 1 321
Moore, deceased, In re; Moore v. His Holiness Pope Benedict XV, [1919] 1 I.R.
    316 507
Moore v. Belfast & Ballymena Ry. Co., 6 Ir. C.L.R. 441 (1857) 128
Moore v. Darell, 4 Hag. Ecc. 346, 162 E.R. 1472 (1832) 432
Moore v. Johnston, 26 I.L.T.R. 92 (1892) 127, 132
Moore v. Moore, I.R. 5 Eq. 371 (1871) 55, 129
Moorhouse v. Lord, 10 H.L. Cas. 272, 11 E.R. 1030 (1863) 56, 61, 62, 64
Moran v. Pyle National (Canada) Ltd., 43 D.L.R. (3d) 239 (1972) 148, 149, 150
Morgan v. Larivière, L.R. 7 H.L. 423 (1875) 177
Morgardshammar A.B. v. H.R. Radomski & Co. Ltd., 5 D.L.R. (4th) 576 (1984) 104, 113
Morocco Bound Syndicate, Ltd. v. Harris, [1895] 1 Ch. 534 153
Morris v. Baron & Co., [1918] A.C. 1 632
Morson v. Second National Bank of Boston, 306 Mass. 588, 29 N.E. 2d 19 (1940) 500

Moulis v. Owen, [1907] 1 K.B. 746 ....105, 112, 552
Mouncer v. Mouncer, [1972] 1 All E.R. 287 88
Mount Albert Borough Council v. Australian Temperance & General Mutual Life
  Assurance Society, [1938] A.C. 224 543
Moxham, The M., 1 P.D. 107 (1876) 580, 647
Muldoon v. Doyle, 79 I.L.T.R. 134 (1944) 474, 641
Mulhern v. Clery, [1930] I.R. 649 629
Mullaly v. Walsh, I.R. 6 C.L. 314 (1872) 629
Multinational Gas Co. v. Multinational Gas Services, [1983] Ch. 238 158
Municipal Council of Sydney v. Bull, [1909] 1 K.B. 7 ....:............................198
Munro v. Munro, 7 Cl. & Fin. 842, 7 E.R. 1288 (1840) 358
Munster & Leinster Bank v. O'Connor, [1937] I.R. 462 ....58, 72, 75
Murphy (Joseph) Structural Engineers Ltd. v. Manitowoc (U.K.) Ltd., Sup. Ct., 30
  July 1985 ....165, 167, 169
Murray v. Champernowne, [1901] 2 I.R. 232 ....391, 397, 408, 411
                                         430, 432, 451, 455, 513
Murray v. Comerford, 33 I.L.T.R. 12 (1898) 129
Murray v. Finkle, 48 I.L.T.R. 178 (1914) 134, 139
Murray v. Laverty & Sons, 40 I.L.T.R. 131 (1905) 669
My v. Toyota Motor Co. Ltd., [1972] 2 N.Z.L.R. 113 150
Myerson v. Martin, [1979] 1 W.L.R. 1390 127

N.F. v. M.T. (otherwise known as F.), [1982] I.L.R.M. 545........................242
N.M. v. E.F.M., unreported, High Ct., Hamilton, J., July 1978 ....276, 290, 313
Naamlooze Vennootschaap Beleggings Compagnie "Uranus" v. Bank of England,
  [1948] 1 All E.R. 465 653
Naamlooze Vennootschap de Faam v. Dorset Manufacturing Co., [1949] I.R. 203 208,
                                         546, 550, 552
Nachimson v. Nachimson, [1930] P. 217 ....212, 372
National Bank Ltd. v. Hunter, [1948] Ir. Jur. Rep. 33 ....178, 181
National Mortgage & Agency Co. of New Zealand v. Gosselin, 38 T.L.R. 832 (1922) 142
National Trust Co. v. Ebro Irrigation & Power Co., [1954] 3 D.L.R. 326 484
Naville v. Naville, 1957 (1) S.A. 280 66
Naylor v. Naylor, [1962] P. 253 88
Neale v. Cottingham, Wallis by Lyne 54 (1770) 404, 467, 478, 480
Neil v. Silcock, 38 I.L.T.R. 5 (1903) 634
Nelson, In re; Ex parte Dare & Dolphin, [1918] 1 K.B. 459 481
Nelson v. Bridport, 8 Beav. 547, 50 E.R. 215 (1846) 407, 408, 445, 513
Nesbitt, Re, 14 L.J.M.C. 30 (1844) 105
Neville v. Pononsby, 1 Ir. L.R. 204 (1839) 542
Newcomb, Re, 192 N.Y. 238, 84 N.E. 950 (1908) 53, 68
Newmarch v. Newmarch, [1978] Fam. 79 303
New York Breweries Co. v. A.G., [1899] A.C. 62 460
New Imperial & Windsor Hotel Co. v. Johnson, [1912] 1 I.R. 327 568
New York Life Insurance Co. v. Public Trustee, [1924] 2 Ch. 101 ....399, 501
New York Security and Trust Co. v. Keyser, [1901] 1 Ch. 666 ....386, 387
Niboyet v. Niboyet, 4 P.D. 1 (1878) 81
Nielsen v. Nielsen, [1971] 1 O.R. 541, 16 D.L.R. (3d) 33 (1970) 324
Ninemia Maritime Corporation v. Trave Schiffahrtsgesellschaft m.b.H. und Co.
  K.G., [1983] 1 W.L.R. 1412 647
Nixon v. Loundes, [1909] 2 I.R. 1 ....602, 606
Njegos, The, [1936] P. 90 542
Nolan v. Fitzgerald, 2 Ir. C.L.R. 79 (1851) 127, 132
Nouvion v. Freeman, 15 App. Cas. 1 (1889) 587, 601
Norris, Re, 4 T.L.R. 452 (1882) 101
Norris v. A.G., [1984] I.R. 36 81
Norris v. Chambres, 29 Beav. 246, 54 E.R. 621 (1861) 406
Norris v. Duckworth, 6 Ir. Ch. Rep. 57 (1856) 658

Norske Atlas Insurance Co. Ltd. v. London General Insurance Co. Ltd., 43 T.L.R. 541 (1927) 616
Northampton Co. Co. v. A.B.F. and M.B.F., [1982] I.L.R.M. 164 ....14, 25, 335, 337, 338, 341
Northern Bank Ltd. v. Edwards, [1986] I.L.R.M. 167 ....412, 542, 651
Northern Ontario Power Co. Ltd., Re, [1954] 1 D.L.R. 627 504
Northern Trust Co. v. McLean, [1926] 3 D.L.R. 93 ....625, 648, 649
Norton v. Florence Land & Public Works Co., 7 Ch. D. 332 (1877) 648
Norton v. General Accident, Fire & Life Assurance Co., 74 I.L.T.R. 123 (1940) 180
Nouvelle Banque de l'Union v. Ayton, 7 T.L.R. 377 (1891) 113
Nova (Jersey) Knit Ltd. v. Kammgran Spinneri G.m.b.H., [1977] 1 Lloyd's L.R. 463 489
Nugent v. Vetzera, L.R. 2 Eq. 704 (1866) 328
Nunn v. Nunn, 8 L.R. (Ir.) 298 (1880) 305, 306, 601

O'B. v.. S., [1984] I.R. 316 420
O'Brien, Infants, In re, [1938] I.R. 323 324
O'Brien, In re, [1940] Ir. Jur. Rep. 60 629
O'Brien v. Carr, 5 Ir. C.L.R. 316 (1856) 633
O'Callaghan v. O'Sullivan, [1925] 1 I.R. 90 ....105, 106, 107, 110, 111, 118, 520, 521
Ocean Steamship Co. v. Queensland State Wheat Board, [1941] 1 K.B. 402 523
O'Connell v. Holland, [1900] 2 I.R. 448 ....53, 64
O'Connor v. Bernard, 4 Ir. Eq. Rep. 689 (1842) 626
O'Connor & Lemieux, Re, [1927] 3 D.L.R. 77 139
O'Connor v. Star Newspaper Co., 30 L.R. (Ir.) 1 (1891) 126, 133
O'D., Infants, In re; O'D. v. O'D., unreported, High Ct., Hamilton, J., 14 June 1979 ....333, 334
O'Daly v. Gulf Oil (Ireland) Ltd., [1983] I.L.R.M. 163 ....398, 580, 581
O'Domhnaill v. Merrick, [1984] I.R. 151 641
Ogden v. Folliott, 3 Term Rep. 726, 100 E.R. 825 (1790) 194
Ogden v. Ogden, [1908] P. 46 ....28, 218, 219, 227
Ogilvie, In re, [1918] 1 Ch. 492 439
O'Hagan v. Sun Life Ins. Co. of Canada, [1932] I.R. 741 629
O'Hara, An Infant, In re, [1900] 2 I.R. 232 321
O'Haran v. Divine, 100 I.L.T.R. 53 (1974) 88
O'Kane v. Campbell, [1985] I.R. 115 568
O'Keefe, deceased, Re; Poingdestre v. Sherman, [1940] Ch. 124 ....42, 43, 47
Ó Laighléis, In re, [1960] I.R. 93 207
Oldenberg, In the goods of, 9 P.D. 234 (1884) 108
Oldham v. Shaw, 4 Ir. L. Rep. 1 (1841) 127
O'Leary v. Law Integrity Insurance Co., [1912] 1 I.R. 479 141
O'Loghlen, Ex parte; In re O'Loghlen, L.R. 6 Ch. App. 406 (1871) 464
Olpherts v. Brinkley, I.R. 4 Eq. 208 (1869) 132
O'Mara Ltd. v. Dodd, [1912] 2 I.R. 55 144
Omychurd v. Barker, 1 Atk. 22, 26 E.R. 15 (1744) 218
O'Neill, deceased, In re; Humphries v. O'Neill, [1922] N.Z.L.R. 468 .....392, 397
O'Neill v. O'Neill, 6 L. Rec. (N.S.) 159 (1838) 656
O'Neill v. Doran, I.R. 10 Eq. 187 (1876) 626
O'Neill v. M'Erlean, 30 I.L.T.R. 162 (1896) 126
O'Neill v. St. Brigid's Well Co., [1895] 2 I.R. 442 128
Onobrauche v. Onobrauche, 8 Fam. Law 107 (1978) 214
Oppenheim & Co. v. Mahomed Haneef, [1922] 1 A.C. 482 617
Oppenheimer v. Cattermole, [1976] A.C. 249 144
Oppenheimer v. Losenthal (Louis) & Co. A/G, [1937] 1 All E.R. 23 144
Original Blouse Co. Ltd. v. Bruck Mills Ltd., 42 D.L.R. (2d) 174 (1963) 148
Orlando v. Fingal (Earl of), [1940] Ir. Jur. Rep. 281 ....106, 329
Orr, deceased, In re Estate of; M'Dermott v. Anderson, [1915] 1 I.R. 191 508
Orr-Lewis v. Orr-Lewis, [1919] 1 K.B. 410 169

Osborn, In re, [1931] B. & C.R. 189 ....473, 478
O'Sullivan v. Dwyer, [1971] I.R. 275 582
O'Toole (Jack) Ltd. v. MacEoin Kelly Associates, Sup. Ct., 24 July 1986 667
Ottoman Bank of Nicosia v. Chakarian, [1938] A.C. 260 111
Otway v. Ramsey, 3 Stra. 1090 (1736) 603

P., In re, [1945] Ir. Jur. Rep. 17 ....49, 88, 361
P. (G.E.) (an Infant), Re, [1965] Ch. 568 ....101, 324, 325, 327
P. v. C., unreported, High Ct., McWilliam, J., 22 February 1980 629
Pacat Finance Corporation, In re, 295 Fed. 394 (1923) 468
Pacific Star (S.S.) v. Bank of America National Trust and Savings Association,
   [1965] W.A.R. 159. 159 601
Padolecchia v. Padolecchia, [1968] P. 314 ....233, 237, 253
Paget v. Paget, 11 L.R. (Ir.) 26 (1882) 425
Pain v. Holt, 19 S.R. (N.S.W.) 105 (1919) 436
Paine, Re, [1940] Ch. 46 ....233, 348, 351, 353
Paley Olga (Princess) v. Weisz, [1929] 1 K.B. 718 206
Palsgraf v. Long Island Railroad Co., 162 N.E. 99 (1928) 18, 574
Papadopoulos v. Papadopoulos, [1930] P. 55 ....240, 605
Paramount Ltd. v. Republic of Zaire, [1980] Lloyd's L. Rep. 393 175
Parana Plantations Ltd., Re, [1946] 2 All E.R. 214 113
Parchim, The, [1918] A.C. 157 113
Pardo v. Bingham, L.R. 6 Eq. 485 (1884) 648
Parke v. Parke, 1 I.C.L.R. 632 (1851) 668
Parker v. Dickie, 4 L.R. (Ir.) 244 (1879) 643
Parnell v. Parnell, 7 Ir. Ch. Rep. 322 (1858) 170
Parojcic v. Parojcic (otherwise Ivetic) [1958] 1 W.L.R. 1280 ....242, 287
Part v. Scannell, Ir. R. 9 C.L. 426 (1875) 610
Partenreederei MS Tilly Russ and Ernest Russ v. NV Haven & Vervoerbedriff
   Nova, [1984] E.C.R. 2417 191
Patterson v. D'Agostino, 8 O.R. (2d) 367 (1975) 107, 596
Paul v. Chandler & Fisher Ltd., [1924] 2 D.L.R. 479 149
Paulin, In re, [1950] V.L.R. 462 ....436, 437, 438, 439
Pavitt, An Infant, In re, [1924] 1 I.R. 234 ....108, 323, 324
Payne v. The King, [1902] A.C. 552 397
Pearse's Settlement, Re, [1909] 1 Ch. 304 513
Pearson, Re, [1946] V.L.R. 356 375
Pedlar v. Johnstone, [1920] 2 I.R. 450 ....171, 172
Pêlêgrin v. Coutts & Co., [1915] 1 Ch. 696 386
Pemberton, Re; Fisher v. Barclays Bank Ltd., 59 D.L.R. (2d) 44 (1966) 431
Pemberton v. Hughes, [1899] 1 Ch. 781 ....605, 608
Penhas v. Tan Soo Eng, [1953] A.C. 304 ....228, 230
Peninsular & Oriental Steam Navigation Co. v. Shand, 3 Moo. P.C. (N.S.) 272, 16
   E.R. 103 (1865) 520, 545
Penn v. Lord Baltimore, 1 Ves. Sen. 444, 27 E.R. 1132 (1750) 403, 404, 406
People (A.G.) v. Byrne, [1974] I.R. 1 627
People (A.G.) v. Edge, [1943] I.R. 115 346
People v. Ruttledge, [1978] I.R. 376 23
Peppard & Co. Ltd. v. Bogoff, [1962] I.R. 180 ....656, 665, 667
Perkins, deceased, Re, [1950] S.R. (N.S.W.) 1 436
Perlak Petroleum Maatschappij v. Deen, [1924] 1 K.B. 111 107
Permanent Trustee Co. (Canberra) Ltd. v. Finlayson, 122 C.L.R. 338 (1968) 459
Perpetual Executors & Trustees Association of Australia Ltd. v. Roberts, [1970]
   V.R. 732 509
Perpetual Trustee Co. Ltd. v. Bolger, 67 I.L.T.R. 259 (1933) 663, 666
Perrin v. Perrin, [1914] P. 135 ....298, 299, 300
Perrini v. Perrini, [1979] Fam. 84 ....237, 261, 264
Perry v. Stratham, [1928] I.R. 580 661

Personal Service Laundry Ltd. v. National Bank Ltd., [1964] I.R. 49 656
Pezet v. Pezet, 47 S.R. (N.S.W.) 45 (1946) 236
Phelan v. Johnson, 7 Ir. L.R. 527 (1844) 132
Philippine Admiral, The, [1977] A.C. 373 174
Philipson-Stow v. Inland Revenue Commissioners, [1961] A.C. 727 ..443, 445, 513
Phillips v. Batho, [1913] 3 K.B. 25 ....595, 597
Phillips v. Eyre, L.R. 6 Q.B. 1 (1870) 152, 153, 572, 573, 574, 575, 576,
                                                577, 578, 580, 581, 582, 643
Phillips v. Hunter, 2 H. Bl. 402 (1795) 467
Phrantzes v. Argenti, [1960] 2 Q.B. 19 638
Picker v. London & County Banking Co., 18 Q.B.D. 515 (1887) 487
Pim, a bankrupt, In re, 7 L.R. Ir. 458 (1881) 468
Pim Bros. v. Wylie, 27 I.L.T.R. 27 (1892) 126, 132
Pindling v. National Broadcasting Corp., 49 O.R. (2d) 58 (1984) 148
Pink v. Perlin & Co., 40 N.S.R. 260 (1898) 419
Pipon v. Pipon, Amb. 25, 27 E.R. 14 (1744) 429
Planche v. Fletcher, 1 Doug. 251, 99 E.R. 164 (1779) 198
Plyler v. Doe, 457 U.S. 202 (1983) 54
Pollack's Estate, In re, [1937] T.P.D. 91 510
Ponticelli v. Ponticelli (otherwise Giglio), [1958] P. 204 245
Poole v. Stewart, 37 I.L.T.R. 74 (1903) 126
Parkasho v. Singh, [1968] P. 233 ....105, 214
Portarlington Light & Power Co. Ltd., In re, [1922] 1 I.R. 100 486
Porter v. Freudenberg, [1915] 1 K.B. 857 ....127, 171, 172
Porto Alexandre, The, [1920] P. 30 174
Potinger v. Wightman, 3 Mer. 67, 36 E.R. 26 (1817) 83
Potts v. Batty, 6 I.R. 10 Eq. 188 (1876) 633
Pouey v. Hordern, [1900] 1 Ch. 492 451
Powell v. Atlantic Steam Navigation Co., 10 Ir. C.L.R. App. xl (1860) 146
Powell v. Cockburn, 68 D.L.R. (3d) 700 (1976) 280
Powell v. Powell, 31 D.L.R. (3d) 419 (1972) 82
Power, In bonis, 25 L.R. (Ir.) 509 (1890) 454
Power v. Irish Civil Service (Permanent) Building Society, [1968] I.R. 158 663,
                                                                                        664
Power v. Webber, I.R. 10 Eq. 188 (1876) 633
Powerscourt Estates v. Gallagher, [1984] I.L.R.M. 123 646
Preston v. Melville, 8 Cl. & Fin. 1, 8 E.R. 1 (1841) 458
Preston v. Preston, [1963] P. 411 ....229, 230
Price, In re; Tomlin v. Latter, [1900] 1 Ch. 442 444
Price v. Dewhurst, 3 Sim. 279, 59 E.R. 111 (1837) 607
Prins Bernhard, The, [1964] P. 117 162
Prior-Wandesforde v. Revenue Commissioners, 1 Repts. of Irish Tax Cases 148
    (1928) 68, 70
Pritchett v. Jordan, I.R. 3 Eq. 273 (1869) 132
Prowse v. European & American Steam Shipping Co., 13 Moo. P.C. 484, 15 E.R.
    182 (1860) 105
Pryce, Re, [1911] 2 Ch. 286 451
Pugh v. Pugh, [1951] P. 482 233
Purdy v. Purdy, [1919] 2 W.W.R. 551 252
Purser v. Purser, [1913] 1 I.R. 422 549
Puttick v. A.G., [91980] Fam. 1 54

Quarrier v. Colston, 1 Ph. 147, 41 E.R. 587 (1842) 552
Queensland Mercantile & Agency Co. Ltd., Re; Ex parte Union Bank of Australia,
    [1892] 1 Ch. 219 505
Quinn v. Kelly, [1951] Ir. Jur. Rep. 45 ....401, 402
Qureshi v. Qureshi, [1972] Fam. 173 ....274, 303

R. v. R., [1984] I.R. 296 321
R. (Armstrong) v. Co. Ct. Judge of Wicklow, [1924] 2 I.R. 139 129
R. (Stewart) v. Baldrick, 71 I.L.T.R. 57 (1937) 96
R. v. Blane, 13 Q.B. 769 (1849) 318
R. v. Brentwood Marriage Registrar, [1968] 2 Q.B. 956 ....237, 264
R. v. Burke, 5 Ir. L.R. 549 (1843) 118, 219, 231
R. v. Griffin, 4 L.R. (Ir.) 497 (1879) 105, 115, 218, 219, 228, 626, 630
R. v. Gyngall, [1983] 2 Q.B. 232 321
R. v. Hammersmith Superintendent Registrar, [1917] 1 K.B. 634 213
R. v. Humphreys, ex p. Ward, [1914] 3 K.B. 1237 318
R. v. International Trustee, [1937] A.C. 500 543
R. v. Millis, 10 Cl. & Fin. 534, 8 E.R. 844 (1844) 115
R. v. Williams, [1942] A.C. 541 504
R. v. Wilson, ex p. Pereira, [1953] 1 Q.B. 59 318
Radcliffe, In re, [1916] 2 I.R. 534 463
Radio Corporation of America v. Rauland Corporation, [1956] 1 Q.B. 618 635, 636, 637
Radwan v. Radwan, [1973] Fam. 35 213
Raeburn v. Raeburn, 44 T.L.R. 384 (1928) 295
Rahimtoola v. Nizam of Hyderabad, [1958] A.C. 379 177
Rahman v. Abu-Taha, [1980] 1 W.L.R. 1268 646
Rail v. Rail, 12 R.F.L. (2d) 265 (1979) 422
Rainford v. Newell-Roberts, [1962] I.R. 95 ....125, 129, 131, 586, 588, 589,
                                                                        591, 594, 595, 596, 597
Ralli Bros. v. Compania Naviera de Sota y Aznar, [1920] 2 K.B. 287 198, 546, 548
Ralston, In re; Perpetual Executors and Trustees Association, [1906] V.L.R.
   689 397
Ramsay v. Liverpool Royal Infirmary, [1930] A.C. 588 ....57, 58, 75
Ramsey-Fairfax v. Ramsey-Fairfax, [1956] P. 115 ....246, 254
Rand v. Flynn, [1948] Ir. Jur. Rep. 30 550
Rashid Hasan v. Union of India, [1967] A.I.R. 154 86
Raulin v. Fisher, [1911] 2 K.B. 93 ....193, 195
Razelos v. Razelos, [1969] 3 All E.R. 929 406
Razelos v. Razelos (No. 2), [1970] 1 W.L.R. 392 428
Rea Deceased, In the matter of; Rea v. Rea [1902] 1 I.R. 451 .107, 391, 392, 393,
                                                                        408, 409, 430, 437, 440, 441
Reddy v. Bates, [1984] I.L.R.M. 197 644
Redmond v. Mooney, 14 Ir. C.L.R. xvii (1862) 46, 653
Redondo v. Chaytor, 4 Q.B.D. 453 (1879) 653, 658
Reg. v. Barnet L.B.C., Ex p. Shah, [1983] 1 A.C. 309 102
Regal Ltd. v. Plotkins, [1961] S.C.R. 566, 29 D.L.R. (2d) 282 ....502, 504
Regazzoni v. Sethia, [1956] 2 Q.B. 490 551
Reilly, A Bankrupt, In re, [1942] I.R. 416 ....408, 469, 471, 475
Reilly v. White, 11 Ir. C.L.R. 138 (1860) 144, 148, 152
Reiman, In re, Fed. Cas. No. 11, 673, 20 Fed. Cas. 490 (1874) 462
Renak, The, [1979] 1 All E.R. 398 162
Republic of Spain v. National Bank of Scotland, Ltd., 1939 S.C. 413 205
Republica de Guatemala v. Nunez, [1927] 1 K.B. 669 ....501, 502, 503, 504
Revenue Commissioners v. Matthews, 92 I.L.T.R. 44 (1953) 67, 71, 76
Revenue Commissioners v. Pelly, [1940] I.R. 122 ....424, 509
Revenue Commissioners v. Shaw, [1982] I.L.R.M. 433 ....46, 70, 72, 76
Revenue Commissioners v. "Z", 101 Ir. L.T. & Sol. J. 492 (1967) 58
Richardson v. Allen, 28 D.L.R. 134 (1916) 591, 593
Richardson v. Army, Navy & General Assurance Association, [1924] 2 I.R. 96 142, 163
Richardson v. Gregory, 4 Ir. C.L.R. 248 (1854) 633
Richardson v. Richardson, [1927] P. 228 505
Ridge v. Newton, 4 Ir. Eq. Rep. 389 (1842) 164
Riera v. Riera, 112 L.T. 223 (1914) 295

Rio Tinto Zinc Corporation v. Westinghouse Corporation, [1978] A.C. 547 ....636, 637
Risk v. Risk, [1951] P. 50 213
Robert (otherwise de la Mare) v. Robert, [1947] P. 164 ....243, 244. 245. 246
Roberta, The, 58 Ll. L. Rep. 159 (1937) 627
Robertson v. Brandes, Schönwald & Co., 8 F. 815 (1906) 543
Robinson, a Bankrupt, Re, 11 Ir. Ch. Rep. 385 (1860) 117, 465
Robinson v. Bland, 1 W. Bl. 234, 96 E.R. 129, 2 Burr. 1077, 97 E.R. 717
    (1760) 9, 208, 518
Robinson v. Fenner, [1913] 3 K.B. 835 ....608, 609
Robinson v. M'Entee, 73 I.L.T.R. 53 (1939) 661
Robinson v. Palmer, [1901] 2 I.R. 489 454
Rockware Glass Ltd. v. MacShannon, [1978] A.C. 795 166
Rogers, a Bankrupt, In re, 9 Ir. Ch. Rep. 150 (1859) 464
Roper, deceased, In re, [1927] N.Z.L.R. 731 ....436, 437
Rosenbaum v. Hicks, 58 I.L.T.R. 93 (1923) 661
Rosencrantz v. Union Contractors Ltd., 23 D.L.R. (2d) 473 (1960) 544
Rosler v. Rottwinkel, [1986] Q.B. 33 190
Ross, Re, Ross v. Ross, [1930] 1 Ch. 377 ....42, 43, 67, 513
Ross v. Burke, L.R. 6 Eq. 328 (1872) 633
Ross v. Eason & Son Ltd., [1911] 2 I.R. 459 157
Ross Bros. Ltd. v. Shaw (Edward) & Co., [1917] 2 I.R. 367 ....546, 551
Rossano v. Manufacturers' Life Insurance Co., [1963] 2 Q.B. 352 107, 395, 505, 596
Ross Smith v. Ross Smith, [1963] A.C. 280 ....244, 245, 253, 263, 295
Rouquette v. Overmann, L.R. 10 Q.B. 525 (1875) 492
Rousou's Trustee v. Rousou, [1955] 2 All E.R. 169 141
Rousillon v. Rousillon, 14 Ch. D. 351 (1880) 549, 550, 595
Rouyer Guillet & Compagnie v. Rouyer Guillet & Co., [1949] 1 All E.R. 244 111, 112
Rowett, Leakey & Co. v. Scottish Provident Institution, [1927] 1 Ch. 55 ..542, 543
Rowland v. Rowland, 42 D.L.R. (3d) 205 (1973) 65
Royal v. Cudahy Packing Co., 195 Iowa 759, 190 N.W. 427 (1922) 216
Royal Bank of Canada and Corriveau, Re, 30 O.R. (2d) 653 (1981) 175
Royal Bank of Canada (London) Ltd. v. Krogh, [1986] 1 All E.R. 611 440
Royal Trust Co. v. Kritzwiser, [1924] 3 D.L.R. 596 ....648, 649
Royal Trust Co. v. Provincial Secretary Treasurer of New Brunswick, [1925] 2
    D.L.R. 49 397
Rudd v. Rudd, [1924] P. 72 608
Ruding v. Smith, 2 Hag. Con. 371, 161 E.R. 744 (1821) 228, 231
Russ v. Russ (No. 2), 106 Sol. J. 632 (1962) 252. 274
Russell (John) & Co. Ltd. v. Cayzer, Irwine & Co. Ltd., [1916] 2 A.C. 298 ...159
Russell v. Kitchen, 3 Ir. C.L.R. 613 (1854) 117, 503, 637
Russell v. Murphy, 16 Ir. Chy. Rep. 54 (1865) 471
Russell v. Russell, [1924] A.C. 687 630
Russell v. Smyth, 9 M. & W. 810 (1842) 602
Russell v. United Provident Assurance Co. Ltd., 41 I.L.T.R. 200 (1907) 129
Russian Commercial & Industrial Bank v. Comptoir d'Escompte de Mulhouse,
    [1923] 2 K.B. 630 A 112
Russian and English Bank v. Baring Brothers & Co., [1936] A.C. 405 485
Ryan v. A.G., [1965] I.R. 294 224

S., Estate of, [1928] N.I. 46 ....93, 94
S. v. S., unreported, Sup. Ct., 1 July 1976 ....242, 243, 248
S. v. S., [1983] I.R. 68 630
S.A. Consortium General Textiles v. Sun & Sand Agencies, Ltd., [1978] Q.B. 279 593
Sachs v. Standard Bank (Ireland) Ltd., Sup. Ct., 18 July 1986, affirming High
    Ct., Barrington, J., 30 July 1985 ....277, 291, 568, 585
Sadler v. Robins, 1 Camp. 253, 170 E.R. 948 (1808) 602, 603
Said Ajami v. Comptroller of Customs, [1954] 1 W.L.R. 1405 108

St. Pierre v. South American Stores Ltd., [1936] 1 K.B. 382 ....165, 166, 167, 402, 542, 627
Salmon v. Belfast Alhambra Ltd., 37 I.L.T.R. 72 (1903) 655
Salter's Trusts, In re, 17 Ir. Ch. Rep. 176 (1866) 330
Salvesen v. Administrator of Austrian Property, [1927] A.C. 641 ....227, 599
Samuelson v. Andrews, Ir. R. 3 C.L. 575 (1868) 668
Sanders v. Van der Putte, [1977] E.G.R. 2383 184
Sanderson, In re, Ir. Chy. Rep. 421 (1861) 464
Sanderson v. Cunningham, [1919] 2 I.R. 234 ....139, 140, 141
Santos v. Santos, [1972] Fam. 247 88
Saorstát & Continental Steamship Co. v. De Las Morenas, [1945] I.R. 291 .....173, 175
Sara v. Sara, 36 D.L.R. (2d) 499 (1962) 213
Saul v. His Creditors, 5 Mar. (n.s.) 569, 16 Am. Dec. 212 (1827) 422
Savage v. General Life Insurance Co., 47 I.L.T.R. 158 139
Saxby v. Fulton, [1909] 2 K.B. 208 ....105, 552
Sayers v. International Drilling Co.,[1971] 1 W.L.R. 1176 545
Sayer v. Sheehan, 26 L.R. Ir. 417 (1890) 661
Scanlon v. Abbey Service Garage, 98 I.L.T. & Sol. J. 464 (1964) 668
Scanlon v. Hartlepool Seatonia Steamship Co. Ltd., 63 I.L.T.R. 21 (1927) 542
Scarpetta v. Lowenfield, 27 T.L.R. 509 (1911) 609
Schibsby v. Westenholz, L.R. 6 Q.B. 155 (1870) 585, 591, 597, 608
Schnapper, Re, [1928] Ch. 420 431
Schopperles Trusts, In re, [1932] I.R. 457 13
Schorsch Meier GmbH v. Hennin, [1975] Q.B. 416 649
Schulhof, In the Goods of, [1948] P. 66 457
Schwebel v. Ungar (or Schwebel), 42 D.L.R. (2d) 622 (1963) 33, 34, 234, 237, 265
Scott, an alleged lunatic, In re, 22 W.R. 748 (1874) 382
Scott v. De Barros, 11 P.D. 128 (1886) 240
Scott v. Nesbit, 14 Ves. 438, 33 E.R. 589 (1808) 406
Scott v. Pilkington, 2 B. & S. 11 (1862) 601, 604
Scott v. Scott, 1937 S.L.T. 632 263
Scrimshire v. Scrimshire, 2 Hag. Con. 395, 161 E.R. 782 (1752) 218, 227, 231
Seaton v. Clarke, 26 L.R. (Ir.) 297 (1890) 126
Sebba, Re, [1957] Ch. 166 105
Sedgewick v. Sedgewick, 9 W.W.R. (N.S.) 704 (1953) 219
S.E.E. Co. Ltd. v. Public Lighting Services Ltd. and Petit Jean (U.K.) Ltd., Sup. Ct., 12 May 1986 ....667, 668
Segoura v. Bonakarian, [1976] E.C.R. 1851 191
Seifert v. Seifert, 32 O.L.R. 433, 23 D.L.R. 440 (1914) 449
Seren v. Douglas, 489 P. 2d 601 (1972) 54
Services Europe Atlantique Sud (S.E.A.S.) v. Stockholms Rederiaktiebolag Svea, [1979] A.C. 685 650
Settlement Corporation v. Hochschild, [1966] Ch. 10 170
Sexton v. Looney, High Ct., Murphy, J., 8 July 1985 (83/40m) 235, 276
Sexton v. O'Halloran, [1904] 1 I.R. 123 ....131, 136
Sexton v. O'Keefe, [1966] I.R. 204 645
Sfeir & Co. v. National Insurance Co. of New Zealand, Ltd., [1964] 1 Lloyd's Rep. 330 595
Shahnaz v. Rizwan, [1965] 1 Q.B. 390 551
Shanks v. Shanks, 1965 S.L.T. 330 85
Shannon, deceased, 76 I.L.T.R. 53 (1942) 50, 51, 74
Sharpe v. Crispin, L.R. 1 P. & D. 611 (1869) 93
Sharples v. Eason & Son, Ltd., [1911] 2 I.R. 436 157
Sharps Commercials v. Gas Turbines, Ltd., [1956] N.Z.L.R. 819 597
Shaw v. A.G., L.R. 2 P. & D. 156 (1870) 608
Sheehan v. Gamplovitch, 46 I.L.T.R. 80 (1912) 135

Shipsey v. British & American Steam Navigation Co., [1936] I.R. 65 133,
                                                                142, 184
Sigurdson v. Farrow, 121 D.L.R. (3d) 183 (1981) 625
Sill v. Worswick, 1 Hy. Bl. 665, 126 E.R. 379 (1791) 467, 494
Sillar, deceased, In re; Hurley v. Wimbush, [1956] I.R. 344 ....45, 57, 58,
                                                        68, 69, 70, 72, 75, 443
Sim v Sim, [1944] P. 87 295
Simonds v. Simonds, 154 F. 2d 326 (1946) 86
Simonin v. Mallac, 2 Sw. & Te. 67, 164 E.R. 917 (1860) 227, 252
Simons v. Simons, [1939] 1 K.B. 490 253
Sims v. Thomas, 3 Ir. L.R. 415 (1841) 609
Sinclair v. Sinclair, [1896] 1 I.R. 603 ....270, 276, 278, 295, 300
Sinclair v. Sinclair, [1968] P. 189 ....53, 65
Sinnott v. Quinnsworth Ltd., [1984] I.L.R.M. 523 644
Sirdar Gurdyal Singh v. Faridkote, [1894] A.C. 670 ....129, 595, 597, 598
Siskina, The; Siskina v. Distos Compania Naviera S.A., [1979] A.C. 210 154, 156, 646
Sisson v. Cooper, 4 Ir. L.R. 401 (1842) 656, 659
Skottowe v. Young, L.R. 11 Eq. 474 (1871) 365
Skyrotors Ltd. v. Carsere Technical Industries, Ltd., 26 O.R. (2d) 207 (1979) ...150
Slater v. Mexican National Railway, 194 U.S. 120 (1904) 15, 568
Slattery, In re; Slattery v. Slattery, [1941] Ir. Jur. Rep. 13 129
Slingsby v. A.G., 33 Times L.R. 120 (1916) 357
Smith (E.R.), Re, 12 T.L.R. 223 (1896) 65
Smith, Re; Lawrence v. Kitson, [1916] 2 Ch. 206 413
Smith v. Buchanan, 1 East 6, 102 E.R. 3 (1800) 481
Smith v. Cork & Bandon Ry. Co., [1903] 1 I.R. 512 504
Smith v. Cotton, 27 S.R. (N.S.W.) 41 (1926) 649
Smith Kline & French Laboratories, Ltd. v. Bloch, [1983] 1 W.L.R. 730 171
Smith v. Nicolls, 5 Bing. N.C. 208, 132 E.R. 1084 (1839) 587, 603
Smith v. Smith, 1970 (1) S.A. 146 ....49, 54, 112, 132
Smullen v. Benoit & Co., 68 I.L.T.R. 260 (1933) 133
Smyth v. Dolan, 47 I.L.T.R. 287 (1913) 127
Société Anonyme Metallurgique de Prayen, Prooz, Belgium v. Koppel, 77 S.J. 800
  (1933) 640
Société Générale de Paris v. Dreyfus Bros., 29 Ch. D. 239 (1885) 134
Solomon v. Solomon, 29 W.N. (N.S.W.) 68 (1912) 54
Soltykoff, Re, [1898] W.N. 77 382
Somafer S.A. v. Saar-Ferngas A.G., [1978] E.C.R. 312 ....186, 187
Somers v. Connolly, 1 Ir. Eq. Rep. 416 (1839) 132
Somjee v. Minister for Justice & A.G., [1981] I.L.R.M. 96
Sottomaior (a lunatic), In re, L.R. 9 Ch. App. 677 (1874) 382, 387
Sottomayor v. De Barros, 5 P.D. 94 (1879) 219, 235, 236, 240, 241, 253, 425
Soutar v. Peters, 1912 1 S.L.T. 111 150
South African Republic v. Compagnie Franco-Belge-du Chemin de Fer du Nord,
  [1898] 1 Ch. 190 174
Spaight v. Dundon, [1961] I.R. 201 88
Spaine v. Spaine, 10 Ir. Ch. Rep. 49 (1858) 132
Spartan Steel & Alloys, Ltd. v. Martin, [1973] Q.B. 27 643
Spence v. Parkes, [1900] 2 I.R. 619 159
Spencely, In the Goods of, [1892] P. 255 457
Spivack v. Spivack, 46 T.L.R. 243 (1930) 215
Sproule v. Hopkins, [1903] 2. I.R. 133 ....50, 59, 66, 73, 252, 295, 296
Spurrier v. La Cloche, [1902] A.C. 446 545
Spurway v. Spurway, [1894] 1 I.R. 385 ....53, 66, 67, 83, 91, 138, 144
Stafford Allen & Sons, Ltd. v. Pacific Steam Navigation Co., [1956] 2 All E.R. 716 523
Stanhope v. Hospitals Trust Ltd. (No. 2), [1936] Ir. Jur. Rep. 25 ...109, 112, 197,
                                                        546, 547, 643, 645
Stanley v. Barnes, 3 Hag. Ecc. 447, 162 E.R. 1190 (1830) 432

Starkowski v. A.G., [1954] A.C. 155 ....221, 222, 223, 227
State (Dowling) v. Brennan, [1937] I.R. 483 203
State (Dowling) v. Kingston (No. 2), [1937] I.R. 699 ....172, 203, 610
State (Gilsenan) v. McMorrow, [1978] I.R. 360 ....23, 475, 487
State (Goertz) v. Minister for Justice, [1948] I.R. 45 ....54, 101, 102
State (Griffin) v. Bell, [1962] I.R. 355 113
State (Hully) v. Hynes, 100 I.L.T.R. 145 (1961) 203
State (Kennedy) v. Little, [1931] I.R. 39 ....23, 310, 383
State (Kinvarra Shipping Ltd.) v. Neylon, [1974] I.R. 11 161
State (K.M. and R.D.) v. Minister for Foreign Affairs, [1979] I.R. 73 .....330, 345
State (Lavelle) v. Carroll, unreported, High Ct., 25 October 1963 113
State (Nicolaou) v. A.G., [1966] 567 ....321, 334, 336
State of Victoria v. Hansen, [1960] V.R. 582 142
State (Sumers Jennings) v. Furlong, [1966] I.R. 183 207
State (Trimbole) v. Governor of Mountjoy Prison, [1985] I.R. 550 334
Statathos v. Statathos, [1913] P. 46 81
Steele v. Braddell, 6 Milw. 1 (1838) 219
Stein v. Valkenhuysen, E.B. & E. 65, 120 E.R. 431 (1858) 125, 590
Stephen v. M'Farland, 8 Ir. Eq. Rep. 444 (1845) 92
Stevenson v. London North-Western Railway, I.R. 1 C.L. 672 (1867) 142
Stevenson v. Masson, L.R. 17 Eq. 78 (1873) 630
Stewart v. Ballance, 10 I.C.L.R. App. 1 (1860) 668
Stewart v. Conyngham (Marquis of), 1 Ir. Ch. Rep. 534 (1849) 97
Stewart v. Stewart, 16 Ark. App. 164, 698 S.W. 2d 516 (1985) 76
Stockholms Enskilda Bank Artiebolag v. Schering Ltd., [1941] 1 K.B. 424 551
Stoughton, deceased, In re, [1941] I.R. 166 ....30, 391, 393-396, 408, 411, 430
Strabane Canal Co. Ltd. v. London & N.W. Ry., [1912] 2 I.R. 147 161
Stransky v. Stransky, [1954] P. 428 101
Strauss & Co. v. Goldschmid, 1 T.L.R. 512 (1892) 158
Street v. Mason, 26 L.R. (Ir.) 298n (1890) 126
Stubbs, In re; Russell v. Le Bert, [1896] 1 I.R. 334 ....133, 136, 137, 139
Studd v. Cook, 8 App. Cas. 577 (1883) 513
Sullivan v. National Bank, 73 I.L.T.R. 95 (1939) 490
Sussex Peerage Case, 11 Cl. & F. 85, 8 E.R. 1034 (1844) 228
Svinskis v. Gibson, [1977] 2 N.Z.L.R. 4 607
Swan, Re, 2 V.R. (I.E. & M.) 47 (1871) 105, 234, 236
Swan v. Miller, Son & Torrance Ltd., [1919] 1 I.R. 151 632
Swedish Central Rail Co. Ltd. v. Thompson, [1925] A.C. 495 483
Swift & Co. v. Bankers Trust Co., 280 N.Y. 135, 19 N.E. 2d 992 577
Swift v. Swift, 1 Ball & B. 326 (1810) 458, 460
Swifte v. A.G. for Ireland, [1912] A.C. 176 219
Swiss Bank Corporation v. Boehmische Industrial Bank, [1923] 1 K.B. 673 505
Synge's Estate, In re, [1900] 1 I.R. 92 633
Szechter (otherwise Karsov) v. Szechter, [1971] P. 286 ....233, 241, 254, 287

T. v. T., [1983] I.R. 29 ....74, 75, 80, 277, 278, 585
Taczanowska v. Taczanowski, [1957] P. 301 229
Tallmadge, In re; Re Chadwick's Will, 181 N.Y. Supp. 336 (1919) 41
Tamburrini, In re, [1944] I.R. 508 ....29, 369
Tassell v. Hallen, [1892] 1 Q.B. 321 137
Taylor v. Begg, [1932] N.Z.L.R. 286 603
Taylor v. Low, 3 Ir. C.L.R. 223 (1854) 668
Tedcastle M'Cormick v. Robertson, [1929] I.R. 597 ....134, 139, 140, 145, 519
Teh Hu, The, [1970] P. 106 649
Tellett v. Lalor, 10 L.R. (Ir.) 357 (1882) 668
Temilkovski v. Australian Iron & Steel Pty. Ltd., 67 S.R. (N.S.W.) 211 (1966) .110
Thalle v. Soares, [1957] I.R. 182 ....664, 667
Thelwall v. Yelverton, 14 Ir. C.L.R. 188 (1862) 219

Theodores, The, [1977] 2 Lloyd's Rep. 428 129
Theophile v. Solicitor-General, [1950] A.C. 186 463
Third Chandis Corp. v. Unimarine S.A., [1979] 3 W.L.R. 122 646
Tipperary Election Petitions, In re, I.R. 9 C.L. 217 (1875) 97
Tisdall v. Humphrey, 1 I.R.C.L. 1 (1897) 126
Thompson v. Haughton, 11 Ir. L. Rep. 201 (1847) 127
Thomson v. Kindell, 1910 2 S.L.T. 442 148
Thorne v. Watkins, 2 Ves. Sen. 35, 28 E.R. 24 (1750) 429
Thornton v. Thornton, 11 P.D. 176 (1886) 298
Thornton v. Thornton, 65 W.N. (N.S.W.) 87 (1947) 637
Thornton's Estate, In re, 1 Cal. (2d) 1, 33 P. (2d) 1 (1934) 420
Tinneny v. O'Keefe, 85 Ir. L.T. & Sol. J. 307 (1951) 662
Tobin v. London & North-Western Ry. Co., [1895] 2 I.R. 22 532
Tolten, The, [1946] P. 135 407
Tomkinson v. First Pennsylvania Banking & Trust Co., [1961] A.C. 1007 ....543, 544
Torni, The, [1932] P. 27 112
Toronto General Trusts Co. v. The King, 39 D.L.R. 380 (1917) 397
Tozier v. Hawkins, 15 Q.B.D. 650 (1885) 153
Traill v. Porter, 1 L.R. (Ir.) 60 (1878) 138
Travers v. Holley, [1953] P. 246 ....259, 261, 373, 586, 597
Traynor v. Fegan, [1985] I.R. 585 135
Trendtex Trading Corporation v. Central Bank of Nigeria, [1977] Q.B. 529 175
Trendtex Trading Corporation v. Credit Suisse, [1980] 3 All E.R. 721 167
Trepca Mines, Re, [1960] 1 W.L.R. 1273 600
Trevethick v. Leary, 28 I.L.T.R. 8 (1893) 153
Trottier v. Rajotte, [1940] S.C.R. 203 47
Trumbal v. Ejector, 5 Ir. L.R. 358 (1843) 132
Trustees Executors & Agency Co. Ltd. v. I.R.C., [1973] Ch. 254 398
Trustees Executors & Agency Co. Ltd. v. Margottini, [1960] V.R. 417 426
Tucker, In bonis, 3 Sw. & Tr. 585, 164 E.R. 1402 (1864) 454
Tudor Furnishers Ltd. v. Montague & Son, [1950] Ch. 113 655
Tudor v. Lawson, 15 Ir. C.L.R. 144 (1864) 53
Tunstall v. Tunstall, [1953] 1 W.L.R. 770 428
Tuohy v. Great Southern Ry. Co., 32 I.L.T.R. 139 (1898) 146
Turnbull v. Walker, 67 L.T. 767 (1892) 596, 597
Tursi v. Tursi, [1958] P. 54 296
Twomey, Deceased, In the goods of; O'Leary v. Stack, [1900] 2 I.R. 560 652, 654, 655
Tyler v. Judges of Court of Registration, 175 Mass. 71, 55 N.E. 812 (1900) 124
Tzortzis v. Monark Line A/B, [1968] 1 W.L.R. 406 ....522, 524, 616

Ua Clothasaigh v. McCartan, 83 I.L.T.R. 6 (1947) 88
Udny v. Udny, L.R. 1 H.L. (Sc.) 441 (1869) 51, 55, 56, 60, 62, 66, 71, 76, 83, 359
Ulster Bank, Ltd. v. Walsh, 62 I.L.T.R. 68 (1928) 384
Underwood v. Darracott, I.R. 8 Eq. 348 (1873) 633
Ungar v. Ungar, [1967] 2 N.S.W.R. 618 236
Union National des Co-opératives Agricoles et Céréales v. Catterall (R.) & Co.
 Ltd., [1959] 2 Q.B. 44 ....617, 618
Union Trustee Company of Australia Ltd. v. Commissioner of Stamp Duties,
 [1926] St. R. (Queensland) 304 82
Unit Construction Co. Ltd. v. Bullock, [1960] A.C. 351 484
United General Life Assurance Co. v. Beale, 8 Ir. C.L.R. xxx (1858) 668
United Railways of the Havana and Regla Warehouses, Re, [1960] Ch. 52 543, 544, 649
Urquhart v. Butterfield, 37 Ch. D. 357 (1887) 90, 94
U.S.A. v. Dollfus Meig etc. Compagnie S.A., [1952] A.C. 582 ....176, 177
Ussher v. Ussher, [1912] 2 I.R. 445 ....219, 228, 230, 235
Vadala v. Lawes, 25 Q.B.D. 310 (1890) 603, 607
Vagliano, In re; Vagliano v. Vagliano, 75 L.J. Ch. 119 (1905) 512
Valentine's Settlement, Re, [1965] Ch. 831 ....373, 375

Valier v. Valier (otherwise David), 133 L.T. 830 (1925) 242, 253
Vamvakidis v. Kirkoff, [1929] 4 D.L.R. 1060 252
Vander Donckt v. Thellusson, 8 C.B. 812; 137 E.R. 727 (1849) 108
Van Grutten v. Digby, 31 Beav. 561; 54 E.R. 1256 (1863) 427, 510
Vanquelin v. Bouard, 15 C.B.N.S. 341; 143 E.R. 817 (1863) 605
Vervaeke v. Smith, [1981] Fam. 77 ....241, 261, 262, 263
Viditz v. O'Hagan, [1900[2 Ch. 87 ....426, 510
Vile v. Von Wendt, 20 O.R. (2d) 513 (1979) 149
Viner v. Bond, 4 Ir. L.R. 433 (1841) 132
Vita Food Products, Inc. v. Unus Shipping Co. Ltd., [1939] A.C. 277 412, 521, 522, 549
Vitkovice Horni A Hutni Tezirstvo v. Korner, [1951] A.C. 869 ....139, 627
Vogel v. Kohnstamm Ltd., [1973] Q.B. 133 ....591, 595, 596
Voghell v. Voghell, 33 W.W.R. 673 (1960) 82
Voinet v. Barrett, 55 L.J.Q.B. 39 (1885) 593
Volkl v. Rotunda Hospital, [1915] 1 K.B. 857 171
Von Lorang v. Administrator of Austrian Property, [1927] A.C. 641 ......254, 256,
                                                                    258, 263, 264
W. v. W., unreported, High Ct., Doyle, J., 5 July 1978 74
Waddell v. Norton, [1966] N.I. 85 ....136, 158
Wadsworth v. McCord, 12 S.C.R. 466 (1886) 50
Waite's Settlement Trusts, [1958] Ch. 100 451
Wakely v. Triumph Cycle Co., [1924] 1 K.B. 214 ....610, 661
Wallace, In Bonis, 29 L.R. (Ir.) 118 (1891) 457
Wallach, deceased, Re, [1950] 1 All E.R. 199 78
Walker and Walker, Re, 14 D.L.R. (3d) 155 (1970) 324
Walker v. Bennett, I.R. 5 C.L. 366 (1871) 633
Walker v. Lorton (Lord), 6 Ir. Ch. Rep. 329 (1857) 392, 412
Walker v. Witter, 1 Doug. 1 (1778) 603
Wallis v. Austin, 3 Ir. L.R. 258 (1841) 126
Walsh v. Great Western Ry. Co., 6 Ir. R.C.L. 532 (1872) 150
Walsh v. Kennedy, 68 I.L.T.R. 238 (1934) 127
Walsh v. Moffat, 7 L.R. (Ir.) 446 (1881) 133
Walshe, In bonis, [1897] 1 I.R. 167 457
Walter, Ex parte, [1960] Ir. Jur. Rep. 60 24
Walter v. Atkinson, [1895] 1 I.R. 246 663
Wansborough Paper Co. Ltd. v. Laughland, [1920] W.N. 344 140
Ward v. Coffin, 27 D.L.R. (3d) 58 (1972) 404
Ward v. Harris, 8 L.R. (Ir.) 365 (1880) 145
Ward v. McMaster and Louth Co. Co., [1986] I.L.R.M. 43 643
Ward v. Skeehan, [1907] 2 I.R. 1 654
Ward v. Ward, [1960] N.I. 122 294
Warner Bros. Pictures Incorporated v. Nelson, [1937] 1 K.B. 209 638
Warrender v. Warrender, 2 Cl. & Fin. 688, 6 E.R. 1239 (1835) 81, 276
War, Secretary for, v. Booth, [1901] 2 I.R. 692 629
Waterhouse v. Stansfield, 9 Hare 234, 68 E.R. 487 (1851) 406
Watkins v. North American Land & Timber Co. Ltd., 20 T.L.R. 534 (1904) 125, 126, 590
Watson v. Armstrong, 4 Ir. L.R. 219 (1841) 132
Watson v. Atlantic Royal Mail Steam Navigation Co., 10 Ir. C.L.R. 163 (1860) 145
Watson v. Chadwick, 8 Ir. L.R. 291 (1845) 668
Watson v. Pim, 2 Ir. Eq. Rep. 26 (1839) 668
Watson v. Porter, [1907] 2 I.R. 341 ....656, 665
Way v. Way, [1950] P. 71 240
Wayland, In the Estate of, [1951] 2 All E.R. 1041 ....454, 455
Waziristan, The, [1953] 1 W.L.R. 1446 580
Webb's Estate, In re, I.R. 5 Eq. 235 (1871) 629
Weir v. Lohr, 65 D.L.R. (2d) 717 (1967) 198, 199
Weiss, In the Estate of, [1962] P. 136 459
Welch v. Tennent, [1891] A.C. 636 422

Wellington, Duke of, Re, [1948] Ch. 118 ....107, 407, 513

Wells v. Wells, [1960] N.I. 122 296

Welsh, deceased, In re; O'Brien v. Phelan, [1931] I.R. 161 ....454, 460, 461

West (Richard) & Partners (Inverness) Ltd. v. Dick, [1969] 2 Ch. 424 404

West (H.) & Son Ltd. v. Shephard, [1964] A.C. 326 644

Westby, In re, [1932] I.R. 444 105

Westby Minors (No. 2), In re, [1934] I.R. 310 ....330, 331

West of England Steamship Owners Protection & Indemnity Association Ltd.,
    [1957] 3 All E.R. 421n 127

Wheeler & Co. Ltd. v. Jeffrey (John) & Co., [1921] 1 I.R. 395 140

Whicker v. Hume, 7 H.L. Cas. 124, 11 E.R. 50 (1858) 44, 45, 430

Whitaker v. Berry, 28 I.L.T.R. 8 (1893) 138

White, deceased, In re; Ingram v. White, [1918] 1 I.R. 19 ....106, 328

White v. Carroll, I.R. 8 C.L. 296 (1874) 652, 661

White Cliffs Opal Mines, Ltd. v. Miller, 4 S.R. (N.S.W.) 150 542

White v. Hardwick, 23 S.R. (N.S.W.) 6 (1922) 131

White v. Tennant, 31 W. Va. 790, 8 S.E. 596 (1888) 54

White v. White, [1937] P. 111 ....251, 637

White v. White, 59 Man. R. 181 (1950) 82

Whitehead's Will Trusts, In re, [1971] 1 W.L.R. 833 511

Whitelegg, In the goods of, [1899] P. 267 107

Whyte v. Rose, 3 Q.B. 493, 114 E.R. 596 (1842) 457

Wilby, Re, [1956] P. 174 ....29, 372, 373, 375

Wilcox v. Wilcox, 6 W.W.R. 213, 24 Man. R. 93, 16 D.L.R. 491 (1914) 256

Wilkie v. McCalla (No. 3), [1905] V.L.R. 276 107

Wilkin, Ex parte, 5 Ir. Ch. Rep. 397 (1856) 633

Willans v. Patterson, 8 Ir. C.L.R. xxix (1858) 663

Williams, In re, [1945] V.L.R. 213 397

Williams & Humbert Ltd. v. W. & H. Trade Marks (Jersey) Ltd., [1986] 1 All
    E.R. 129 ....195, 199, 205

Williams v. Jones, 13 M. & W. 628, 153 E.R. 262 (1845) 308, 586, 602, 640

Williams v. Lloyd, 50 C.L.R. 341 (1934) 463

Williams v. Usher, 94 C.L.R. 450 (1955) 105

Williams v. Wheeler, 8 C.B. (N.S.) 299, 141 E.R. 1181 (1860) 632

Willis v. London & North-Western Ry. Co., I.R. 10 C.L. 95 (1876) ..133, 146, 147

Willoughby, An Infant, In re, 30 Ch. D. 324 (1885) 323, 324

Wilson, Re, [1954] Ch. 733 ....29, 372, 373

Wilson v. National Livestock Insurance Co. Ltd., 48 I.L.T.R. 77 (1914) 163

Wilson v. Wilson, [1903] P. 157 107

Winans v. A.G., [1904] A.C. 287 ....55, 57, 74, 75

Winans v. Winans, 205 Mass. 388 (1910) 54

Winson v. Winson, [1948] 3 D.L.R. 319 47

Winter v. Winter, [1894] 1 Ch. 421 138

Wisconsin v. Pelican Insurance Co., 127 U.S. (20 Davis) 265 (1888) 193

Witted v. Galbraith, [1893] 1 Q.B. 577 157

Wolf, In the goods of, [1948] P. 66 457

Wolfenden v. Wolfenden, [1946] P. 61 ....228, 230

Wolff v. Oxholm, 6 M. & S. 92, 105 E.R. 1177 (1817) 551

Wood v. Wood, 37 Ont. L.R. 428 (1916) 195

Wood v. Wood, [1957] P. 254 303

Woodley v. Woodley, 3 Ir. L.R. 86 (1840) 656

Woods v. Byron, [1947] Ir. Jur. Rep. 42 654

Woodward v. Woodward, [1981] 6 W.W.R. 385 419

Worms v. De Valdor, 49 L.J. Ch. 261 (1880) 369

Wrench v. Rothwell, 4 N.I.J.R. 21 (1903) 134

Wright's Trust, In re, 2 K. & J. 595, 69 E.R. 920 (1856) 83, 361, 362

Wycherly's Trusts, In re, 1 L.R. (Ir.) 60 (1878) 138

Wykenham, a Lunatic, Re, T. & R. 537, 37 E.R. 1207 (1823) 382

Wyndham v. Ennismore, 1 Keen 467, 48 E.R. 386 (1837) 330
Wynne v. Knox, 14 Ch. Rep. 149 (1863) 658

Yarborough v. Yarborough, 290 U.S. 202 (1933) 16
Yates v. Thompson, 3 Cl. & F. 544, 6 E.R. 1541 (1835) 624, 625, 626
Yelverton v. Yelverton, 1 Sw. & Tr. 524, 164 E.R. 866 (1859) 300
Yool v. Ewing, [1904] 1 I.R. 434 ....355, 357
Yorke v. M'Loughlin, Ir. R. 8 C.L. 547 (1847) 661
Yorkshire Tannery & Boot Manufacturing Co. Ltd. v. Eglinton Chemical Co. Ltd., 54
L.J. Ch. 81 (1884) 159
Young, In re; Trustees Executors and Agency Co. Ltd. v. Young, [1942] V.L.R. 4 397

Z Ltd. v. A-Z, [1982] Q.B. 558 646
Zarine v. *S.S. Ramava* (owners of), [1942] I.R. 149 ....174, 175, 177, 205, 207
Zelger v. Salinitri, Case 56/79, [1980] E.C.R. 89, [1980] 2 C.M.L.R. 635 184
Zivnostenska Banka v. Frankman, [1950] A.C. 57 545
Zodiac International Products Inc. v. Polish People's Republic, 81 D.L.R. (3d)
656 (1977) 175

BIBLIOGRAPHY

ABRAHAM	G. Abraham, *The Law and Practice of Lunacy in Ireland* (1886)
ANTON	A.E. Anton, *Private International Law: A Treatise from the Standpoint of Scots Law* (1967)
von BAR	L. von Bar, *The Theory and Practice of Private International Law* (Gillespie trans., 2nd ed., 1892)
BATE	J. Bate, *Notes on the Doctrine of Renvoi in Private International Law* (1904)
BATY	T. Baty, *Polarized Law* (1914)
BEALE	J. Beale, *The Conflict of Laws* (1935)
BENTWICH	N. Bentwich, *The Law of Domicile in its relation to Succession* (1911)
BINCHY	W. Binchy, *A Casebook on Irish Family Law* (1984)
BLOM-COOPER	*Bankruptcy in Private International Law* (1954)
BOGERT & BOGERT	G.C. & G.T. Bogert, *The Law of Trusts and Trustees* (revised 2nd ed., 1977)
BOULANGER	F. Boulanger, *Les successions internationales: problemes contemporains* (1981)
BRADY	J. Brady, *Religion and the Law of Charities in Ireland* (1976)
BRADY & KERR	J. Brady & T. Kerr, *The Limitation of Actions in the Republic of Ireland* (1984)
BRESLAUER	W. Breslauer, *The PIL of Succession in England, America and Germany* (1937)
BROMLEY	P. Bromley, *Family Law* (6th ed., 1981)
BROWNE	A. Browne, *Ecclesiastical Law of Ireland* (1803)
BURN	R. Burn, *Ecclesiastical Law* (9th ed., 1842)
CASTEL	J.G. Castel, *Canadian Conflict of Laws* (1975)
CAVERS	*The Choice of Law Process* (1965)
CHESHIRE & NORTH	Cheshire & North, *Private International Law* (10th ed., by P.M. North, 1979)
CLARK	R. Clark, *Contract* (1982)
COHN	E. Cohn ed., *Manual of German Law*, vol. 2 (1968), vol. 2 (1971)
COLLINS	L. Collins, *The Civil Jurisdiction and Judgments Act 1982* (1983)
COOK	*Logical and Legal Bases of the Conflict of Laws* (1942)
CRETNEY	S. Cretney, *Principles of Family Law* (3rd ed., 1979)
CROSS	R. Cross *Evidence* (5th ed., 1979)
DELANY	V.T.H. Delany, *Law Relating to Charities in Ireland* (1962)
DELANY & LYSAGHT	V.T.H. Delany, *The Administration of Justice in Ireland* (4th revised ed., by C. Lysaght, 1975)
DICEY & MORRIS	*Dicey & Morris on the Conflict of Laws* (10th ed., J.H.C. Morris, Gen. Ed., 1980)

FALCONBRIDGE	J. Falconbridge, *Essays on the Conflict of Laws* (2nd ed., 1954)
FARNSWORTH	A. Farnsworth, *The Residence and Domicile of Corporations* (1939)
FLEMING	J. Fleming, *The Law of Torts* (6th ed., 1983)
FLETCHER	I. Fletcher, *Conflict of Laws and European Community Law* (1982)
FORDE	M. Forde, *Company Law in Ireland* (1985)
FORSYTH	C.F. Forsyth (assisted by T.W. Bennett) *Private International Law* (1981)
FREEMAN & LYON	M.D.A. Freeman & C.M. Lyon, *Cohabitation without Marriage: An Essay in Law and Social Policy* (1983)
GEARY	N. Geary, *The Law of Marriage and Family Relations* (1892)
GOODRICH	H. Goodrich, *Handbook of the Conflict of Laws* (3rd ed., 1949)
GRAVESON	R.H. Graveson, *Conflict of Laws: Private International Law* (7th ed., 1974)
GRIMES & HORGAN	*Introduction to Law in the Republic of Ireland* (1980)
HANCOCK	M. Hancock, *Torts in the Conflict of Laws* (1942)
HARTLEY	T.C. Hartley, *Civil Jurisdiction and Judgments: The Application in England of the Convention on Jurisdiction and the Enforcement of Judgments in Civil and Commercial Matters under the Civil Jurisdiction and Judgments Act 1982* (1984)
HARTLEY, S.F.	S.F. Hartley, *Illegitimacy* (1975)
HEYWOOD & MASSEY	Heywood & Massey, *Court of Protection Practice* (11th ed., by N.A. Whitehorn, 1985)
HOGAN & MORGAN	G. Hogan & D. Morgan, *Administrative Law* (1986)
HOGGETT & PEARL	B.M. Hoggett & D.S. Pearl, *The Family, Law and Society: Cases and Materials* (1983)
HONORÉ	A.M. Honoré, *The South African Law of Trusts* (3rd ed., 1985)
HUNTER	John M. Hunter, *Northern Ireland Bankruptcy Law and Practice* (1984)
JACKSON	J. Jackson, *The Formation and Annulment of Marriage* (2nd ed., 1969)
JUDGE	N.E. Judge, *Irish Income Tax*
KEANE	Mr Justice R. Keane, *Company Law in the Republic of Ireland* (1985)
KEETON & SHERIDAN	*G.W. Keeton & L.A. Sheridan, The Law of Trusts (11th ed., 1983)*
KELLY	John Maurice Kelly, *The Irish Constitution* (2nd ed., 1984)
KELLY & CARMICHAEL	F.N. Kelly & K.S. Carmichael, *Ireland Income Tax and Corporation Tax* (9th ed., 1976) (looseleaf)
KISBEY	W. Kisbey, *The Law of the Court for Matrimonial Causes and Matters* (1871)
KRAUSE	H.D. Krause, *Illegitimacy: Law and Social Policy* (1971)
KUHN	A. Kuhn, *Comparative Commentaries on Private International Law of Conflict of Laws* (1937)
LALIVE	P. Lalive, *The Transfer of Chattels in the Conflict of Laws* (1955)
LEFLAR	R. Leflar, *American Conflicts Law* (1968) ed.)
LIPSTEIN	K. Lipstein, *Principles of the Conflict of Laws, National and International* (1981)
LORENZEN	E. Lorenzen, *Selected Articles on the Conflict of Laws* (1947)
McCLEAN	J.D. McClean, *Recognition of Family Judgments in the Commonwealth* (1983)
McGUIRE	W. McGuire, *the Succession Act 1965: A Commentary* (2nd ed., by R.A. Pearce, 1986)

McLEOD	J. McLeod, *The Conflict of Laws* (1983)
McMAHON & BINCHY	B. McMahon & W. Binchy, *Irish Law of Torts* (1981)
McQUEEN	J. McQueen, *Husband and Wife* (4th ed., by W. Paine, 1905)
MARSH	H. Marsh, *Marital Property in the Conflict of Laws* (1952)
MEILI	F. Meili, *International Civil and Commercial Law* (A. Kuhn trans., 1905)
MENDELSSOHN-BARTHOLDY	A. Mendelssohn-Bartholdy, *Renvoi in Modern England Law* (1937)
MORRIS	J.H.C. Morris & P. North, *The Conflict of Laws* (3rd ed., 1984)
MORRIS & NORTH	J.H.C. Morris & P. North, *Cases and Materials on Private International Law* (1984)
MORSE	C. Morse, *Torts in Private International Law* (1978)
NADELMANN	K. Nadelmann, *Conflict of Laws: International and Interstate* (1972)
NORTH	P.M. North, *The Private International Law of Matrimonial Causes in the British Isles and the Republic of Ireland* (1977)
NORTH ED.	P.M. North, ed., *Contract Conflicts: The E.C.C. Convention on the Law Applicable to Contractual Obligations:* A Comparative Study (1982)
NUSSBAUM	A. Nussbaum, *Principles of Private International Law* (1943)
NYGH	P. Nygh, *Conflict of Laws in Australia*, (4th ed., 1984)
O'DONNELL & JONES	W.J. O'Donnell & D.A. Jones, *The Law of Marriage and Marital Alternatives* (1982)
PAGET	*Paget's Law of Banking* (9th ed., by M. Megrah & F. Ryder, 1982)
PALSSON	L. Palsson, *Marriage and Divorce in Comparative Conflict of Laws* (1974)
PEARCE	R. Pearce, *Land Law* (1985)
PIGGOTT	F. Piggott, *Foreign Judgments and Jurisdiction* (3rd ed., 1908)
PHILLIPSON	C. Phillipson, *The International Law and Custom of Ancient Greece and Rome* (1902)
POPE	H.M. Pope, *A Treatise on the Law and Practice of Lunacy* (2nd ed. by J.H. Boome & V. de S. Fowke, 1890)
POWER	W.K. Power, *Family Law in Canada* (4th ed. of *Power on Divorce*, by C. Davies, 1984)
POWLES	D.G. Powles, *The Mareva Injunction and Associated Orders* (1985)
POYNTER	T. Poynter, *Marriage and Divorce* (2nd ed., 1824)
PROSSER & KEETON	*Prosser & Keeton on the Law of Torts* (5th ed., W.P. Keeton, gen. ed., 1984)
RABEL	E. Rabel, *The Conflict of Laws: A Comparative Study* (2nd ed., 1958)
ROGERS	F. Rogers, *Ecclesiastical Law* (2nd ed., 1849)
READ	H. Read, *Recognition and Enforcement of Foreign Judgments in the Common Law Units of the British Commonwealth* (1938)
REESE & ROSENBERG	W.L.M. Reese & M. Rosenberg, *Conflict of Laws: Cases and Materials* (8th ed., 1984)
ROBERTSON	A.H. Robertson, *Characterization in the Conflict of Laws* (1940)
SAVIGNY	*Conflict of Laws* (Guthrie's Translation) (2nd ed., 1880)
SCHMITTHOFF	C. Schmitthoff, *The English Conflict of Laws* (3rd ed., 1954)
SCHWARTZ	V.E. Schwartz, *Comparative Negligence* (2nd ed., 1986)
SCOLES & HAY	E. Scoles & P. Hay, *Conflict of Laws* (1982)

SCOLES & WEINTRAUB	E. Scoles & R. Weintraub, *Cases and Materials on Conflict of Laws* (2nd ed., 1972)
SHANNON & ARMSTRONG	G.W. Shannon & W.R. Armstrong, *The Law of Income Tax in the Irish Free State* (1934)
SHARPE	R. Sharpe, *Interprovincial Product Liability Litigation* (1982)
SHATTER	A. Shatter, *Family Law in the Republic of Ireland* (3rd ed., 1986)
SHELFORD	L. Shelford, *The Law of Marriage and Divorce* (1841)
SHERIDAN & DELANY	L. Sheridan & V.T. Delany, *The Cy-Près Doctrine* (1959)
SPEISER	S. Speiser, *Recovery for Wrongful Death* 2nd ed., 1975)
SPRATT & McKENZIE	Spratt & McKenzie's *Law of Insolvency* (1972)
STIMSON	E. Stimson, *Conflict of Laws* (1963)
STORY	J. Story, *Commentaries on the Conflict of Laws* (2nd ed., 1841)
STRÖMHOLM	S. Strömholm, *Torts in the Conflict of Laws* (1961)
SYKES	E.I. Sykes, *A Textbook on the Australian Conflict of Laws* (1972)
THEOBALD	Sir H. Theobald, *The Law Relating to Lunacy* (1924)
THOMAS	J. Thomas, *Private International Law* (1955)
TRINDADE & CANE	F.A. Trindade & P. Cane, *The Law of Torts in Australia* (1985)
USSHER	P. Ussher, *Company Law in Ireland* (1986)
VERWILGHEN	M. Verwilghen, dir., *Régimes Matrimoniaux, Succession et Libéralités: Droit international privè et Droit comparé* (Union Internationale du Notariat Latin Commission des Affaires Europeénes, 1979)
WEINTRAUB	R. Weintraub, *Commentary on the Conflict of Laws* (1971)
WEBB, CALDWELL & DAVIS	P.R.H. Webb, R.A. Caldwell & J.L.R. Davis, *Source Book of Family Law* (1967)
WESTLAKE	*Private International Law* (7th ed., 1925)
WEYRAUCH & KATZ	W. Weyrauch & S.N. Katz, *American Family Law in Transition* (1983)
WILLIAMS	G. Williams, *Joint Torts and Contributory Negligence* (1951)
WOLFF	*Private International Law* (2nd ed., 1950)
WYLIE	J. Wylie, *Irish Land Law* (2nd ed., 1986)
ZAPHIROU	G. Zaphirou, *The Transfer of Chattels in Private International Law: A Comparative Study* (1956)

PART I

PRELIMINARY TOPICS

CHAPTER 1

THE HISTORICAL BACKGROUND

INTRODUCTION

The conflict of laws is a necessary part of our law because human transactions may often have connections with more than one legal system.[1] A few examples will bring the problem into focus. A man born in Dublin, of English parents, spends most of his early years with an aunt in Belfast, before going to live in Toronto at the age of 16. Four years later he marries a Californian girl aged 17, whose parents are Italian. The wedding is in New Jersey. By what law or laws should the validity of the marriage be determined? A couple from France are touring the Ring of Kerry in their Italian-designed car; the axle breaks and the car crashes, injuring both of them. If the couple claim that the car was defectively manufactured, by what law or laws is the question of the tortious liability of the manufacturer to be determined? And where should the proceedings be taken?

There may be no obvious answers to questions such as these. It would be plainly unjust and arbitrary if an Irish court were unthinkingly to assert jurisdiction and apply the rules of Irish internal[2] law to situations such as these. The conflict of laws is thus a body of principles that goes at least some way towards providing the courts with answers as to what law is the most appropriate to apply and which forum is appropriate to determine the issue. These answers should be reached after a consideration of questions of justice, practicality and common sense. It must be frankly admitted at the outset of our discussion on the subject that many of the answers are tentative, in the absence of relevant judicial decisions; the conflict of laws is a subject, more than most, in which the writings of jurists have had a marked influence on the development of the law.

CONFLICT OF LAWS IS PART OF IRISH LAW

A point which should also be stressed is that the conflict of laws is *part of Irish law*. Although it deals with problems with an international dimension, it is not "international" in the sense of being a supra-national legal system binding several countries or the world as a whole. At first it may seem odd that there should be as many systems of conflict of laws as there are countries. As the subject unfolds the position becomes easier to understand. Of course, it would be possible for there to be a supra-national, genuinely international, system of conflict of laws and indeed there have been moves in this direction, especially at EEC level and at the Hague Conference on Private International Law. But for historical reasons each country

---

[1] Cf. Beckett, *The Question of Classification ("Qualification") in Private International Law*, 15 Br. Yrbk. of International L. 46, at 46 (1934), who observes that the conflict of laws "is in a sense the antithesis of universal unification of law. Its *raison d'être* is the existence in different countries, and sometimes within the same country, of different systems of law".

[2] Sometimes referred to as "domestic" or "municipal" law.

has developed its own system of conflict of laws, just as each country has developed its own system of internal law. There are some trends towards unification and harmonisation of national domestic laws[3] but we are still very far from being governed by one "World law".

OBJECTIVES OF CONFLICT OF LAWS

Conflict of laws has several objectives, not all of which are easy to reconcile either in general or in specific instances. The desire to do justice is, of course, an important consideration. It may be quite unjust in some cases to apply to an individual the rules of a legal system with which he or she has only a passing, fortuitous connection; thus justice may require that the application of the law of a particular country should be based on a more sustained connection. Equally, the forum's conception of justice may be so outraged by a particular rule in the legal system of a foreign jurisdiction that it may consider itself obliged to refuse to give effect to the foreign rule.

As well as justice, other objectives of the conflict of laws include the protection of the legitimate expectations of parties, predictability and uniformity of results, the discouragement of forum shopping and ease of practical administration.[4]

HISTORICAL DEVELOPMENTS

We must look briefly at the historical development of conflict of laws. We will consider a wide variety of theories that have commanded support at various times. As we shall see, the story is not one of the gradual dawning of judicial enlightenment; instead there are continual ebbs and flows, with "black letter" rules being preferred at one time and broad discretion at another. Similarly, the forum may assert a dominant claim at some times, and recede into relative insignificance at others.

Greece and Rome[5]

It is the nature of empires that conflict of laws problems will arise. Inevitably there will be a divergence of legal traditions falling under a central system of power; moreover questions of status will also be bound to occur. Of course, the very strength of dominant imperial values has sometimes served to weaken the development of a coherent, articulated body of conflict rules, since those operating the dominant legal system may be so filled with contempt for the law of the subjugated people that, while tolerating the continued existence of their law, they treat it as an inferior phenomenon worthy of no respect in its own right.[6]

The influence of the Greek and Roman legal systems on the development of modern conflicts of law was not great.[7] It appears that "certain rudiments"[8] of private international law were recognised in Greece. Fuller development was impossible, "on account of the very conditions of private and public life in antiquity, the concept of exclusive citizenship, the imperfect notion of comity and of balance of power, the comparatively small international intercourse, coupled with national instability, and, subsequently, absorption of the conquered races by the 'barbarous' conquerors,

---

[3] See *Symposium: The International Unification of Law*, 16 Amer. J. of Compar. L. 1 (1968).

[4] Cf. *Castel*, vol. 1, pp. 9-11.

[5] See *Meili*, 51-58, Yntema, *The Historic Bases of Private International Law*, 2 Am. J. of Comp. L. 297, at 300-303 (1953), *Cheshire & North*, 15-17, Lewald, *Conflits de lois dans le monde Grec et Romain*, 57 Rev. Crit. de Dr. Internat. Privé 420, 615 (1968) *Forsyth*, 20-22.

[6] See *Wolff*, 20. See also *Phillipson*, vol. 1, 39-42, 301. Cf. Graveson, 'The Origins of the Conflict of Laws', in *Festschrift für Konrad Zweigert* 93, at 97-98 (1981).

[7] Lipstein, *The General Principles of Private International Law*, 1972-I Recueil des cours 99, at 1106, *Meili*, 51.

[8] *Phillipson*, vol. 1, 192. See also Yntema, *The Historic Bases of Private International Law*, 2 Amer. J. of Compar. L. 297, at 300 (1953).

and the consequent severance of the continuity of organic development."[9]

The *ius sanguinis* was "the veritable basis of citizenship".[10] Thus aliens, even those permanently resident within the territory, were not normally amenable to the ordinary judicial structures. A special jurisdiction had to be introduced to cater for them. Accordingly special magistrates, the *xenodikai*, were appointed for trying questions in which foreigners were involved.[11]

Roman law's *Corpus Juris Civilis* was "innocent of any texts useful for the development of private international law".[12] Several reasons for this have been suggested. The fact that the *praetor peregrinus* was charged with the task of applying the *ius gentium* to *peregrini* (who included the inhabitants of most of the Roman provinces and the subjects of friendly foreign states[13]) reduced the scope of potential conflicts.[14] Later, when the *Constitutio Antoniana* of 212 AD established common Roman citizenship throughout the Empire, the effect was to apply the *ius civile* to so large a group that again the potential for conflicts was minimised.[15]

There were, however, rudimentary elements of conflicts principles throughout the whole period of the Roman Empire. Phillipson has traced these elements in several parts of the law, including marriage,[16] family property,[17] adoption,[18] emancipation,[19] contracts[20] and succession.[21]

After the Fall

When the Roman Empire eventually fell, the barbarian tribes gained control over areas hitherto within the province of Roman Law. Each of the tribes — Franks, Visigoths, Saxons, Alemanni, Frisians, Burgundians, Lombards and others — retained its own tribal law,[23] just as today Hindus and Muslims within India have their own separate family and religious laws.[24]

Since the tribes did not live as isolated communities but often interacted with each

---

[9] *Phillipson*, vol. 1, 192.

[10] *Id.*

[11] *Id.*, 193.

[12] *Forsyth*, 20. See, to similar effect, *Wolff*, 19.

[13] *Phillipson*, vol. 1, 233.

[14] *Forsyth*, 20-21.

[15] *Forsyth*, 21, *von Bar* (Guthrie trans.), para. 11, *Phillipson*, vol. 1, 30-31, Mancini, *De l'utilité de rendre obligatoires pour tous les Etats, sous la forme d'un ou de plusieurs traités internationaux, un certain nombre de règles générales du Droit international privé*, 1 J. du dr. internat. priv. 221, at 221 (1874).

[16] Cf. *Phillipson*, vol. 1, 285.

[17] *Id.*, 286-288.

[18] *Id.*, 288.

[19] *Id.*, 288-289.

[20] *Id.*, 290-291.

[21] *Id.*, 292-295.

[22] See *Cheshire & North*, 17, *Forsyth*, 22-23, Lipstein, *The General Principles of Private International Law*, 1972-I Recueil des cours 99, at 107-109, *Meili, op. cit.*, 58-61. For a comprehensive, scholarly analysis of this period of the conflicts of laws, see Guterman, *The First Age of European Law: The Origin and Character of the Conflict of Laws in the Early Middle Ages*, 7 N.Y.L. Forum 131 (1961) and Guterman, *The Principle of the Personality of Law in the Early Middle Ages: A Chapter in the Evolution of Western Legal Institutions and Ideas*, 21 U Miami L. Rev. 259 (1966).

[23] Meijers, *l'histoire des principes fondamentaux du droit international privé à partir du moyen âge spécialement dans l'Europe Occidentale*, [1934] - III Recueil des cours 543, at 549.

[24] Lipstein, *supra*, at 107, *Cheshire & North*, 17, *Meili*, 60. As *Forsyth*, 23, points out:
"the idea of a personal law — which applies to a person wherever he may be by virtue of his being a member of a certain group (a nation or other community) — lives on, albeit in attenuated form, for all systems of private international law use either the *lex domicillii* or the *lex patriae*, as the governing law in matters of status and the family, wherever the *propositus* may happen to be at the time."

other,[25] this sometimes resulted in difficulties,[26] as the "famous complaint"[27] by Bishop Agobard, Archbishop of Lyons, illustrates: commenting on the law of the Burgundians, he said:

> *"Tanta diversitas legum quanta non solum in singulis regionibus aut civitatibus, sed etiam in multis domibus habetur. Nam plerumque contingit ut simul eant aut sedeant quinque homines et nullus eorum communem legem cum altero habeat."[28]*

A clear-cut solution was necessary:[29] this took the form of a *professio juris* whereby a person could freely elect as to the system of law which would govern his transactions.[30] This profession would be made publicly on a solemn occasion, such as coming of age, and it would be registered.[31] A husband's profession generally bound a wife.[32]

Feudalism[33]

The growth of feudalism in the eleventh and twelfth century led to the eclipse of the personal law by an "essentially territorial"[34] approach. All persons and things within the boundary of a particular territory were subject to its law exclusively.[35] One's racial origins were no longer relevant. A person who left his own fief often lost the power to transmit his property on his death,[36] and his rights depended largely on the goodwill of his new lord.

The Statutists[37]

During the eleventh, twelfth and thirteenth centuries, there was a revival of Roman law studies in Italy. The glossators of the eleventh century whose annotations, or glosses, on the *Corpus Juris* had given an impetus to this revival,[38] were succeeded by the post-glossators who carried the process well beyond explanation and analysis of the text into entirely new areas of legal thought. There were practical pressures on these jurists to come up with new solutions: the number of almost autonomous city States in Italy and the commercial connections between them had given rise

---

[25] *Forsyth*, 22.
[26] Yntema, *The Comity Doctrine*, Vom deutschen zum europäischen recht, Bd. II, 65, at 66 (Festschrift für Hans Dolle, 1963).
[27] Lipstein, *supra*, at 107.
[28] Quoted by Meijers, *supra*, at 108, *Meili*, 59, and Lipstein, *supra*, at 108.
[29] Lipstein, *supra*, at 108.
[30] *Id.* See further Guterman, *The Principle of the Personality of Law in the Early Middle Ages: A Chapter in the Evolution of Western Legal Institutions and Ideas*, 21 U. Miami L. Rev. 259, at 292-294 (1966).
[31] *Meili*, 60.
[32] *Id.*, Guterman, *supra*, 21 U. Miami L. Rev., at 302-302.
[33] See Lipstein, *supra*, at 109-110, *Meili*, at 61-62.
[34] *Cheshire & North*, 18. See also *Meili*, 61, Mancini, *De l'utilité de rendre obligatoires pour tous les Etats, sous la forme d'un ou de plusieurs traités internationaux, un certain nombre de règles générales du Droit international privé*, 1 J. du dr. internat. priv. 221, at 222 (1874). Cf. Guterman, *The First Age of European Law: The Origin and Character of the Conflict of Laws in the Early Middle Ages*, 7 N.Y.L. Forum 131, at 153ff (1961).
[35] *Meili*, 61.
[36] *Cheshire & North*, 18.
[37] See Lipstein, *supra*, at 110-121, Yntema, *The Comity Doctrine*, vom deutschen zum europäischen recht (Festschrift für Hans Dolle), Bd. II, 65, at 66-71 (1963), Yntema, *The Historic Bases of Private International Law*, 2 Amer. J. of Comp. L. 297, at 301-306 (1953), Meijers, *L'histoire des principes fondamentaux du droit international privé a partir du moyen âge*, [1934] - II Recueil des cours 543, ch. 2, de Nova, *Historical and Comparative Introduction to Conflict of Laws*, [1966] - II Recueil des cours 435, at 441-448, *Kuhn*, 4-9, Gutzwiller, *Développement historique du droit international privé*, [1929] - IV Recueil des cours 291, at 310ff.
[38] *Cheshire & North*, 19.

to the need "to allocate to each territorial law its proper space".[39]

Seizing on the opening sentence of the Digest,[40] the post-glossators developed an elaborate system of conflicts rules. The technique generally adopted was to examine the local laws of every city to determine their "rightful sphere of application".[41] These laws were called "statutes" but this term should not be understood in its modern sense. It was "applied to all positive laws of the cities, whether derived from usages and custom or from direct executive or legislative enactment".[42]

Laws could be either *personal, real* or *mixed.*[43] Personal statutes were those which had for their principal object the person and his status. Real statutes were directed primarily at immovable property. There was disagreement as to the proper scope of mixed statutes. Some post-glossators considered that they should be limited to the form of acts and obligations of individuals; others extended their scope to the substance of these acts and obligations.[44] According to some jurists mixed statutes embraced what we might today call civil procedure; others argued that they extended to both persons and things.[45]

It is, of course, easy to find fault with this approach[46] but, in its historical context it was a great achievement.[47] In prescribing choice of law rules of general application, modified by the entitlement to refuse to apply foreign *statuta odiosa*[48] (repugnant laws), the statutists laid the foundation for the development of the conflict of laws as we know it today.

The most famous of the Italian post-glossators were Bartolus[49] (1314-1357), Professor of Italian law at Bologna, and later Pisa and Perugia, his successor, Baldus (1327-1400), and Saliceto (1363-1412). Bartolus articulated a wide range of conflicts rules which played an important role in the development of the subject and which continue to do so even today.[50] Thus, we find such principles as that contracts should be governed by the *lex loci contractus,* that the *lex loci* should generally govern formalities, that the *lex situs* should govern the law of property and that the *lex fori* should determine matters of procedure.

The French School of the Sixteenth Century[51]

The French school of the sixteenth century developed further the thinking of the statutists. The most notable representatives of this school were Dumoulin (1500-1566) and D'Argentré (1519-1590). Dumoulin stressed the power of the parties to select the applicable law; he was thus "largely responsible for the introduction of the free

---

[39] *Schmitthoff*, 20. See also *Kuhn*, 4, de Nova, *Historical and Comparative Introduction to Conflict of Laws*, [1966] - II Recueil des cours, at 443-445.

[40] The law in question, *De summa Trinitate et fide Catholica*, began as follows:
   "Cunctos populos quos clementiae nostrae regit imperium in tali volumus religione versari quam divinum Petrum apostolum tradidisse Romanis religio usque adhuc ab ipso insinuata declarat."

[41] *Cheshire & North*, 20. See further *Meili*, 62-63.

[42] *Kuhn*, 5.

[43] *Phillimore*, vol. IV, 247, 250-252.

[44] *Id.*, 251.

[45] *Id.*, *Cheshire & North*, 20, fn. 5

[46] Cf. Lorenzen, *The Jurisdiction of Sovereign States and the Conflict of Laws*, 31 Colum. L. Rev. 368, at 381 (1931), Lipstein, *supra*, at 118, *Story*, paras. 14-16

[47] Cf. Lipstein, *supra*, at 119-120.

[48] *Id.*, at 116.

[49] See *Bartolo on the Conflict of Laws* (trans. by Clarence Smith), 14 Amer. J. of Legal History 157, 247 (1970). See also Ehrenzweig's criticism of Beale's translation of Bartolus, 12 Amer. J. of Comp. L. 384 (1963).

[50] Cf. *Meili*, 64, Harrison, *Le droit international privé ou le conflit des lois au point du vue historique, particulièrement en Angleterre*, 5 J. du dr. internat. privé et de la jurispr. comp. 417, at 423 (1880).

[51] See *Meili*, 70-75, *Kuhn*, 9-11.

choice of law into private international law".[52] To him may be attributed the notion of *tacit* choice of law in respect of contracts, most notably marriage contracts.[53] In contrast, D'Argentré was a strong proponent of the autonomy of the provinces. A Breton historian, jurist and legislator, his horizons "did not extend beyond Brittany; to its cause he consecrated his life".[54] In stressing the claim of the provinces D'Argentré "resembles the modern states' rights man who excitedly attacks the broader development of federal power".[55] Although D'Argentré reasserted the scope of *statuta reala,* he conceded that *statuta personalia* governed in some exceptional instances. He treated *statuta mixta* in the same way as *statuta reala.*[56] Thus D'Argentré represented a re-emphasis on the territorial principle,[57] echoing the feudal approach,[58] but capable of gaining a new vitality once the focus shifted to international rather than interprovincial rivalries.[59]

The Dutch School[60]

We must now consider the important influence of Dutch jurists in the development of the conflict of laws in the seventeenth century. It is interesting to ask why the Netherlands should have been at the centre of conflicts thinking at this time, and why Huber (and other Dutch jurists) could have had such influence in common law jurisdictions.

So far as the first question is concerned the answer appears to be that the existence of seven provinces in the Netherlands after the attainment of independence from Spain led inevitably to the development of conflicts problems which required practical resolution.[61] But broader cultural forces also played their part:

> "The protracted conflict with Spain released unsuspected energies and evoked a remarkable expansion of commerce, culture and industry ... The Netherlands became the chief mart of world commerce, not only in goods but also in ideas ..."[62]

So far as the second question is concerned, it must be remembered that there were at the time very close mercantile and cultural relations between England and the Netherlands.[63] Indeed, John Voet's *Commentaries* were dedicated to William III.[64]

---

[52] Lipstein, *supra,* at 120.

[53] This notion exerts a continuing influence: see, pp.416-418 *infra.*

[54] *Meili,* 71.

[55] *Id.*

[56] Cf. *von Bar* (Gillespie trans., 2nd ed., 1892), 35-36.

[57] Cf. *Schmitthoff,* 22, *Kuhn,* 10.

[58] Cf. p.6, *supra.*

[59] Cf. *Westlake,* 7th ed., by N. Bentwich, 1925, p. 18.

[60] See *Lorenzen,* ch. 66, *Kuhn,* 11-12, Llewelyn Davies, *The Influence of Huber's De Conflictu Legum on English Private International Law,* 18 Br. Yrbk. of Internat. L. 49 (1937), Nadelmann, *Some Historical Notes on the Doctrinal Sources of American Conflicts Law,* Ius et lex; Festgabe für Gutzwiller 263, at 265-276 (1959), Lipstein, *The General Principles of Private International Law,* [1972] - I Recueil des cours 97, at 122-130, Yntema, *The Comity Doctrine,* vom deutschen zum europäischen recht (Festschrift für Hans Dolle), Bd. II, 65, at 79ff. (1963), Yntema, *The Historic Bases of Private International Law,* 2 Am. J. of Compar. L. 297, at 1306-1307 (1953), de Nova, *Historical and Comparative Introduction to Conflict of Laws,* [1966] - II Recueil des cours 435, at 448-451.

[61] See Llewelyn Davies, *supra,* at 52, *Lorenzen, supra,* at p. 138, de Nova, *Historical and Comparative Introduction to Conflict of Laws,* [1966] - Recueil des cours 435, at 448-449.

[62] Yntema, *The Comity Doctrine,* vom deutschen zum europaischen recht (Festschrift für Hans Dolle), Bd II, 65, at 72-73 (1963). See also de Nova, *supra,* at 448.

[63] Llewelyn Davies, *supra,* at 52-53, *Kuhn,* 29, *Meili,* 83.

[64] Llewelyn Davies, *supra,* at 53, fn. 1.

Moreover, there was a still greater connection between Scottish and Dutch lawyers.[65]

This probably explains how the great Judge, Lord Mansfield, was largely responsible for introducing the work of the Dutch jurists to the English courts[66] in the famous decision of *Robinson* v. *Bland.*[67] In its turn, since, "[n]o decision of Lord Mansfield was, to be sure, overlooked by the Bar in England or on th[e other] side of the Atlantic",[68] the works of the Dutch jurists gained a wide audience. In the United States, Huber gained further influence by being included, in translation as an appendix to a law report of a United States Supreme Court case.[69] In turn, Huber influenced the thinking of Story,[70] who played such an important role in the development of conflicts theory in common law jurisdictions.

It is worth examining Huber's theory, in view of the fact that his work exercised "by far the greatest influence in the development of private international law in the common law countries".[71] Huber's approach was well summarised in three maxims which govern his whole thinking on the subject:

" (1) The laws of every sovereign authority have force within the boundaries of its state, and bind all subject to it, but not beyond.
(2) Those are held to be subject to a sovereign authority who are found within its boundaries, whether they be there permanently or temporarily.
(3) Those who exercise sovereign authority so act from comity that the laws of each nation having been applied within its own boundaries should retain their effect everywhere so far as they do not prejudice the power or rights of another state or its subjects."[72]

As may be seen from these maxims, laws are regarded as being strictly territorial,[73] rather than as attaching to the person wherever he might happen to be at any particular time. But, as a modification of this principle of territoriality, the third maxim allows states to "so act from comity" as to permit laws of foreign countries to "retain their effect everywhere" (so far as they do not prejudice the rights of another state or its subject). These three notions, of territoriality, comity, and the extraterritorial recognition of vested rights, continue to provoke controversy even today. We will examine them below,[74] but first it is necessary to consider briefly the influence of two leading theorists of the nineteenth century: von Savigny and Mancini.

---

[65] Cf. *Id.*, at 53:
"The frequent practice, adopted by Scottish advocates during the seventeenth and eighteenth centuries, of completing their legal studies in Holland had made them directly acquainted with the works of Huber and the Voets, and there is evidence that the subject had received greater study in Scotland than in England ..."
See further Anton, *The Introduction into English Practice of Continental Theories on the Conflict of Laws*, 5 Int. & Comp. L.Q. 534, at 535-536 (1956).
[66] Llewelyn Davies, *supra*, at 53, Nadelmann, *supra*, at 265-266. Anton, *supra*, at 539, warns against over-emphasising Lord Mansfield's rôle.
[67] 1 W. Bl. 234, 256, 96 E.R. 129, 141, 2 Burr. 1077, 97 E.R. 717 (K.B., 1760). See also *Holman* v. *Johnson*, 1 Cowp. 341, 98 E.R. 1120 (1775).
[68] Nadelmann, *supra*, at 266.
[69] *Emory* v. *Grenough*, 3 Dall. 369, at 370-377 (1797). See Nadelmann, *supra*, at 267, Llewelyn Davies, *supra*, at 56.
[70] Story, para. 31; cf. Llewelyn Davies, *supra*, at 60, Lainé, *De l'application des lois étrangères en France et en Belgique - 2*, 23 J. de dr. internat. 481, at 486 (1896).
[71] Llewelyn Davies, *supra*, at 53. See also Harrison, *Le droit international privé ou le conflit des lois au point de vue historique, particulièrement en Angleterre*, 7 J. de dr. internat. 417, at 428 (1880).
[72] *De Conflictu Legum*, para. 2 (trans. by Llewelyn Davies, *supra*, at 65). See further Yntema, *The Comity Doctrine*, vom deutschen zum europäischen recht (Festschrift für Hans Dolle) Bd. II, 65, at 81-82 (1963).
[73] Llewelyn Davies, *supra*, at 57.
[74] Cf. *infra*, pp. 12-15.

von Savigny[75]

We now must turn to consider the influence of Friedrich Carl von Savigny, whose eighth volume of the *System des heutigen römischen Rechts,*[76] published in 1849, "did more for the development of the law — not only in Germany — than any other work devoted to law as it stands".[77]

Savigny, influenced by Wächter,[78] sought to develop conflicts rules on a universal basis.[79] In his view, it was in the interests both of different individuals and different states that in cases of conflict of laws, the same rules should apply, "whether the judgment be pronounced in this state or in that".[80] Savigny looked to the interdependence of sovereign states[81] as the source of the universal approach which he favoured:

> "The standpoint to which this consideration leads us, is that of an international common law of nations having intercourse with one another; and this view has in the course of time always obtained recognition, under the influence of a common Christian morality, and of the real advantage which results from it to all concerned."[82]

Where there was a "collision"[83] between the laws of different states, the task was to "*discover for every legal relation (case) that legal territory to which, in its proper nature, it belongs or is subject (in which it has its seat).*"[84]

This notion of a "seat" for every legal relation is clearly metaphorical but that is scarcely a criticism since metaphors are the tools of the legal trade.[85] It is true that in some cases it may be very difficult to identify the "seat" of a particular legal relation,[86] but that is perhaps more a reflection on the complexity of human life than on the lack of clarity of Savigny's basic criterion.

Savigny's approach led inevitably away from an exaggerated emphasis on the *lex situs*.[87] In Savigny's theory, the "seat", so far as matters of status and succession were concerned, lay at the domicile. This approach contributed to making Savigny's theory particularly attractive to common law commentators.[88] Savigny also

---

[75] See *Wolff*, 34-38, *Lorenzen*, 195-196, *Forsyth*, 36-38, *Lipstein*, 21-23, *Meili*, 91-92, 97, de Nova, *supra*, at 456-464, Audit, *A Continental Lawyer Looks at Contemporary American Choice-of-Law Principles*, 27 Am. J. of Compar. L. 589, at 590-593 (1979), Yntema, *supra*, at 309-311.

[76] The volume was translated into English by William Guthrie, a Scottish advocate, under the title *A Treatise on the Conflict of Laws, and the Limits of Their Operation in Respect of Time and Place*, (1869, 2nd ed., 1880).

[77] *Wolff*, 34.

[78] Cf. *Lipstein*, 21, Nadelmann, *Wächter's Essay on the Collision of Private Laws of Different States*, 13 Amer. J. of Comp. L. 414, at 416 (1964).

[79] *Lorenzen*, 195.

[80] *Savigny* (Guthrie trans, 2nd ed.), p. 70.

[81] *Lorenzen*, 195.

[82] *Savigny*, (Guthrie trans, 2nd ed.), p. 70.

[83] *Id.*

[84] *Id.*, p. 135. *id.*, p. 71.

[85] Cf. *Wolff*, 37-38. Later writers have replaced "seat" by "the centre of gravity" or the "most closely connected" law: *id., 37, Anton*, 25.

[86] von Bar's criticism, to the effect thata legal relation "never belongs exclusively" to any one territorial law (*von Bar*, 2nd ed., 1892, Gillespie, trans., p.56), is surely misconceived. The task is to identify as the "seat" one of several competing laws, each of which has a definite, possibly substantial, connection with the legal relation in question. Wengler (*The General Principles of Private International Law*, [1961] - III Recueil des cours 273, at 356) argues that, though it may often be possible to *exclude* certain laws as being unsuitable, "the intrinsic nature of a legal or a social relation cannot always indicate with certainty one allocation factor leading to *one* local law, which would furnish the most appropriate solution". He contends (*id.*) that it "can never be proved" that in principle the law of the domicile is better suited to family relations than the *lex patriae.*

[87] *Westlake*, 21, *Forsyth*, 36.

[88] Notably Westlake, who considered that Savigny had made "the most remarkable contribution" to conflicts theory since the eighteenth century: *Westlake*, 21.

considered that the *situs* of immovables was the "seat", and that the place of performance constituted the "seat" for contracts.

The "Achilles heel"[89] in Savigny's theory is his assumption that legal relations are uniform throughout every legal system. As Yntema points out, legal relations "are legal and not natural conceptions".[90] As we have seen,[91] different countries may characterise a single set of facts in several different ways. The task of identifying a single "seat" in these cases presents formidable conceptual difficulties.[92]

Mancini[93]

We must mention briefly the effect of Mancini's thought on the development of conflicts theory. Pasquale Stanislas Mancini (1817-1888) was an Italian nationalist, a Neapolitan exile who was appointed Professor of International Law at the University of Turin in 1851.

In his inaugural lecture Mancini argued that nationality is the basis of both public and private international law. In his Report to the Institut de Droit International in 1874,[87] Mancini set out his views on the conflict of laws. The principle of *nationality* required that, as a general rule, matters relating to the person, the family and succession should be governed by the *lex patriae*.[95] The principle of *liberty* meant that people should be free to change their nationality, as well as to choose the law to govern their contractual relationships.[96] The principle of *sovereignty* played a role in the conflict of laws in sanctioning resort to a state's *ordre public* when necessary.[97]

Mancini's ideas were very influential in shaping the conflicts rules adopted by the Italian Civil Code and several other European Codes.[98] The principle of nationality endorsed by Mancini was "altogether consonant with the political trend of the epoch, characterised by popular insurrectional outbursts against the oppression of foreign monarchies".[99] His stress on individual autonomy in contract was "an unquestionable concession to the prevailing liberalistic doctrines of the time, favouring free enterprise."[100] It would be quite wrong to view Mancini's support for nationality as being inward looking and parochial. On the contrary, Mancini was

---

[89] Yntema, *supra,* at 312.

[90] *Id.*

[91] *Infra,* Ch. 3.

[92] *Cheshire & North,* 24.

[93] See *Wolff,* 38-40, *Anton,* 26-27, *Meili,* 94-96, *Forsyth,* 39-41, de Nova, *supra,* at 464-468, Catellani, *Les maîtres de l'école italienne du droit international au XIXe siècle,* [1933] - Recueil des cours 709, Diena, *La conception du droit international privé d'après la doctrine et la pratique en Italie,* [1927] - II Recueil des cours 347, Farrelly, *The New Italian School of Private International Law,* 5 Jurid. Rev. 105, 197 (1893), Nadelmann, *Mancini's Nationality Rule and Non-Unified Legal Systems,* 17 Amer. J. of Comp. L. 418 (1969), Vitta, *International Conventions and National Conflict Systems,* [1969] - I Recueil des cours III, at 126-137.

[94] Mancini, *De l'utilité de rendre obligatoires pour tous les Etats, sous la forme d'un ou de plusieurs traités internationaux, un certain nombre de règles générales du Droit international privé,* 2 J. du dr. internat. priv. 221, 285 (1874). This report was first published in Italian in 1876; more recently it reappeared in 13 Diritto Internat. 367 (1959). Important extracts, translated into English, appear in A. Von Mehren & D. Trautman, *The Law of Multistate Problems* 46-51 (1965). See further Nadelmann, *supra,* at 423 ff., Kahn-Freund, *General Problems of Private International Law,* [1974] - III Recueil des cours 139, at 275-276.

[95] *Id.,* at 298.

[96] *Id.,* at 298-299.

[97] *Id.,* at 299. Cf. de Nova, *New Trends in Italian Private International Law,* 28 L. & Contemp. Prob. 808, at 808-809 (1963).

[98] Cf. Vitta, *supra,* at 126-127, de Nova, *supra,* at 809. See also McCusker, *The Italian Rules of Conflict of Laws,* 25 Tul. L. Rev. 70, at 72 (1950).

[99] Vitta, *supra,* at 126.

[100] *Id.,* at 127.

of the view that, only through the adoption by all states of the same appropriate connecting factor (which he considered nationality to be), could there be any hope of universal concord in the conflict of laws. As early as 1867 he began a campaign for an international conference aimed at concluding conventions for unifying the conflict systems of the contracting States on the basis of the principle of nationality.[101] As Minister of Foreign Affairs of the Kingdom of Italy, in 1881, he began diplomatic negotiations with other states to bring about this goal.[102] The Hague Conferences on Private International Law, at the beginning of this century were in large part inspired by him.[103]

We shall later[104] examine in some detail the merits and disadvantages of nationality as a predominant connecting factor in the conflict of laws. Suffice it at present to comment that much of Mancini's argument reads unconvincingly to the modern reader, since it involves some rather crude sociological assertions and doubtful explanations of differences among national laws.[105]

The Territorialist Approach

As we have seen[106] the territorialist approach reflects the emphasis on sovereignty which affected the thinking of the Dutch jurists at the time of Huber, and, more broadly, of nationalist thought throughout much of Europe. According to this view, each state should be regarded as supreme within its own territory, and inevitably would have to concede a similar supremacy to other states within their territories. Thus Story could assert that:

"... every nation possesses an exclusive sovereignty and jurisdiction within its own territory. The direct consequence of this rule is that the laws of every state affect and bind directly all property, whether real or personal, within its territory, and all persons who are resident within it, whether natural-born subjects, or aliens, and also all contracts made and acts done within it. A state may, therefore, regulate the manner and circumstances under which property, whether real or personal, or in action within it shall be held, transmitted, bequeathed, transferred, or enforced; the condition, capacity, and state of all persons within it; the validity of contracts and other acts done within it; the resulting rights and duties growing out of these contracts and acts; and the remedies and modes of administering justice in all cases calling for the interposition of its tribunals to protect and vindicate and secure the wholesome agency of its own laws within its own domains."[107]

And Story went on to support the proposition that:

"no state or nation can, by its laws, directly affect or bind property out of its own territory, or bind persons not resident therein, whether they are natural-born subjects or others. This is a natural consequence of the first proposition; for it would be wholly incompatible with the equality and exclusiveness of the sovereignty of all nations, that any one nation should be at liberty to regulate either persons or things not within its own territory. It would be equivalent to a declaration that the sovereignty over a territory was never exclusive in any nation, but only concurrent with that of all nations; that each could legislate for all, and none for itself; and that all might establish rules which

---

[101] *Id.*, at 127-128.
[102] *Id.*, at 128.
[103] *Anton*, 27. The use of nationality in these Conferences meant that they had no appeal for countries that favoured domicile as a connecting factor.
[104] *Infra.*, pp.97-98.
[105] See *Sereni*, 170-171.
[106] *Supra*, pp.8-9.
[107] *Story*, para. 18.

none were bound to obey. The absurd result of such a state of things need not be dwelt upon."[108]

Of course, it is impossible to reconcile a strictly territorialist approach with the realities of the conflict of laws over the centuries. As a matter of fact, courts everywhere, to a greater or a lesser extent, have had regard to foreign laws when determining cases with a foreign dimension.[109] The real conceptual problem lies in explaining how and why the courts do this, and in prescribing rules by which this process should be achieved. The territorialist approach is useful, even today, in reminding us that private legal entitlements do not arise in some supra-national vacuum, unaffected by the frequently inevitable clash of competing claims, interests and values of different states. But, so far as the territorialist approach stresses the notion of sovereignty, it has today a dated air, which contrasts with a sentiment favouring international conventions and agreements in conflicts of law.[110]

The Comity Doctrine[111]

The notion of comity fits in easily with the territorialist approach. As Story observed:

"The true foundation on which the administration of international law must rest is, that the rules which are to govern are those which arise from mutual interest and utility, from a sense of the inconveniences which would result from a contrary doctrine, and from a spirit of moral necessity to do justice, in order that justice may be done to us in return."[112]

In saying this Story reflected Huber's statement to the effect that the subject of the conflict of laws was:

"to be derived not simply from the civil law, but from the convenience and tacit consent of nations, for although the laws of one country cannot have any direct force in another, yet nothing could be more inconvenient to the commerce and general intercourse of nations than that which is valid by the law of one place should be rendered invalid elsewhere owing to a difference in the law."[113]

Since the comity doctrine did not require courts to embrace foreign law uncritically, but rather let them apply it cautiously when the need arose, it proved attractive to both English[114] and Irish courts, especially during the formative years of conflict of laws in these jurisdictions. For well over a century comity has been invoked in

---

[108] *Id.*, para. 20.

[109] "Every civilised country recognises the laws of other countries, whether they are foreign to or associated with each other, and is willing to apply those laws within its borders whenever it is necessary to do so": *In re Schopperle's Trusts,* [1932] I.R. 457, at 464 (High Ct., Johnston, J.).

[110] Graveson, *Comparative Aspects of the General Principles of Private International Law,* [1963] - II Recueil des cours l, at 29ff., Nadelmann, *Méthodes d'unification du droit international privé,* 47 Rev. crit. de dr. internat. priv. 37 (1958), Valladâo, "Private International Law, Uniform Law, and Comparative Law" in *XXth Century Comparative and Conflicts Law: Legal Essays in Honor of Hessel E. Yntema* 98 (1961). Vitta, *International Conventions and National Conflict Systems,* [1969] - I Recueil des cours lll.

[111] See *Lorenzen,* 158-162, *Kuhn,* 28-33, Yntema, *The Comity Doctrine,* vom deutschen zum europäischen recht (Festschrift für Hans Dolle) Bd. II, p. 65 (1963), reprinted (with Introduction by Nadelmann), 65 Mich. L. Rev. 1 (1966), Lipstein, *The General Principles of Private International Law,* [1972] - I Recueil des cours 97, at 121-125, Cheatham, *American Theories of Conflict of Laws: Their Role and Utility,* 58 Harv. L. Rev. 361, esp. at 367ff (1945).

[112] *Story,* para. 35.

[113] Huber, *De Conflictu Legum,* para. 2 (trans by Llewelyn Davies, *supra,* at 65-66).

[114] Cf. Kegel, *The Crisis of Conflict of Laws,* [1961] - II Recueil des cours 95, at 105.

Irish cases.[115] In the recent decision of *Larkins* v. *National Union of Mineworkers*,[116] however, Barrington, J. attacked the notion, describing the phrase, "comity of courts" as "a misnomer".[117] He added:

> "No doubt the courts of one country have respect for the courts of another arising from the fact that both are engaged in the administration of justice in accordance with the laws of their respective jurisdictions. But that is not what private international law is about. It is about attempting to do justice between private citizens when their rights arise under the law of one country but fall to be enforced, if enforced at all, under the law of a different country."[118]

The Theory of Vested Rights[119]

If comity did not adequately explain how sovereignty was not infringed by the reference to foreign law, then some other explanation was called for. Inherent in Huber's third axiom[120] was what came to be known as the theory of "vested rights". On this view, the courts of one state enforced, "not foreign laws, but rights acquired under foreign laws".[121] In doing so, they were not in any way compromising the sovereignty of their own state. A right, even a foreign right, was "a fact".[122] A right could of course be changed "by the law that created it, or by any other law having power over it,"[123] but proponents of the theory of vested rights considered that "[i]f no law having power to do so has changed a right, the existing right should everywhere be recognised; since to do so is merely to recognise the existence of a fact."[124]

For a time, the vested rights theory had a great deal of influence. Dicey[125] and Beale[126] were strong supporters. Beale's approach greatly influenced the *First Restatement*,[127] of which Beale was the Reporter. There was also some judicial

---

[115] Cf., e.g. *Re Corcoran, an Infant*, 86 I.L.T.R. 6, at 8 (Sup. Ct., *per* Murnaghan, J., 1950) and at 22 (*per* Black, J., dissenting), *Gaffney* v. *Gaffney*, [1975] I.R. 133, at 155 (Sup. Ct., *per* Henchy, J.), *Northampton Co. Co.* v. *A.B.F.*, [1982] I.L.R.M. 164, at 165 (High Ct., Hamilton, J., 1981), *Kent Co. Co.* v. *C.S.*, [1984] I.L.R.M. 292, at 297 (High Ct., Finlay, P., 1983).

[116] High Ct., Barrington, J., 18 June 1985 (1984-8465P).

[117] At p. 15 of the judgment.

[118] At pp. 15-16 of the judgment. In accord, *Cheshire & North*, 4-5. *Graveson*, 11, puts the point well: "The responsibilities of comity are broadly comprehended in the primary duty of a court to do justice according to law. It is in pursuance of that duty that reference is made to systems of foreign law. No lesser justification is sufficient. No greater justification exists."

[119] See Cook, *passim*, Pillet, *La théorie génerale des droits acquis*, [1925] - III Recueil des cours 489, Carswell, *The Doctrine of Vested Rights in Private International Law*, 8 Int. & Comp. L.Q. 268 (1959), Arminjon, *La notion des droits acquis en droit international privé*, [1933] - I Recueil des cours 1, Lipstein, *The General Principles of Private International Law*, [1972] - I Recueil des cours 97, at 135-140, Nadelmann, *Some Historical Notes on the Doctrinal Sources of American Conflicts Law, Ius et Lex: Festgabe für Gutzwiller* 263, at 276-280 (1959), Cheatham, *American Theories of Conflict of Laws: Their Role and Utility*, 58 Harv. L. Rev. 361, at 379-385 (1945).

[120] The doctrine may be traced to still earlier origins: cf. Lipstein, *supra*, at 136, Arminjon, *supra*, at 8-9, Carswell, *supra*, at 271.

[121] *Dicey*, 3rd ed., 1922, p. 11. See further Arminjon, *supra*, ch. III, Kaeckenbeeck, *The Protection of Vested Rights in International Law*, 17 Br. Yrbk. of Internat. L. 1, at 5-7 (1936).

[122] Beale, *A Selection of Cases on the Conflict of Laws*, 501 (1902). See further Arminjon, *supra*, ch. IV.

[123] *Id.*

[124] *Id.*

[125] Probably influenced by Holland: cf. Nadelmann, *supra*, at 276-279, Lipstein, *supra*, at 136, Yntema, *The Historic Bases of Private International Law*, 2 Amer. J. of Compar. L. 297, at 308 (1953).

[126] Cf. Juenger, *American and European Conflicts Law*, 30 Amer. J. of L. Compar. 117, at 119 (1982): "Beale cribbed the vested rights theory from Dicey". (Citing *Cavers* 5-6).

[127] American Law Institute, *Restatement of the Law of Conflict of Laws*, sections 33, 378 (1934).

support.[128] Today, the theory has virtually no adherents. Commentators have ridiculed the view that a court "can give no help to a party unless he can pull out of his pocket a legal right which he, quite fictitiously, of course, is carrying about with him".[129] Critics have also stressed the fact that the vested rights theory ignores the concrete world in which difficult policy choices may have to be made.[130] The whole thrust of conflicts thinking internationally over the past fifty years has been away from "black letter" rules of universal or general application in favour of a more contextual examination of the policy goals which the rules are designed to serve.[131] Moreover, as Savigny pointed out as long ago as 1849, the vested rights theory "leads into a complete circle; for we can only know what are vested rights, if we know beforehand by what local law we are to decide as to their complete acquisition."[132] Finally, the vested rights theory is difficult to reconcile with the fact that the choice of law rules of many countries often involve the enforcement of rights that are not recognised by the chosen law.[133]

It would be wrong, however, to conclude that the vested rights theory had nothing to be said in its favour: the stature of its proponents is testimony to its attraction. It did, after all, seek to do justice in cases involving international dimensions[134] and to protect the reasonable expectations of the parties concerned. Moreover, it encouraged a process for seeking solutions outside the narrow confines of a state's internal law.

The Local Law Theory[135]

Sixty years ago, when the weaknesses of the vested rights theory were being widely attacked in the United States, many of these critics put forward, as an alternative, what became known as the "local law" theory. At that time, legal realism was in the ascendancy. There was a widespread feeling of excitement that the old sterile "black letter" rules, not only of conflicts law but of law generally, had been exposed as no more than cloaks for the true position, which was that what the judges *did*, not what they *said*, was the law.[136] A "rule of law" was thus seen as the expression

---

[128] Cf. *Livesley* v. *Horst*, [1924] S.C.R. 605, at 607, [1925] 1 D.L.R. 159, at 161 (per Duff, J.), *Slater* v. *Mexican National Ry.*, 194 U.S. 120 at 126 (per Holmes, J.), criticised by Cook, *The Logical and Legal Bases of the Conflict of Law*, 33 Yale L.J. 457, at 480-481 (1924), *Dalrymple* v. *Dalrymple*, 2 Hag. Con. 54, at 58, 161 E.R. 665, at 667 (*per* Sir William Scott, 1811), *Re Askew*, [1930] 2 Ch. 259, at 267 (*per* Maugham, J.).

[129] Willis, *Two Approaches to the Conflict of Laws: A Comparative Study of the English Law and the Restatement of the American Law Institute*, 14 Can. Bar Rev. 1, at 3 (1936).

[130] Cf. Yntema, *The Hornbook Method and the Conflict of Laws*, 37 Yale L.J. 468, at 476-483 (1928).

[131] Cf. Cook, *An Unpublished Chapter of The Logical and Legal Bases of the Conflict of Laws*, 37 Ill. L. Rev. 418, at 418-423 (1943). See also Lorenzen, *Territoriality, Public Policy and the Conflict of Laws*, 33 Yale L.J. 736 (1924), Heilman, *Judicial Method and Economic Objectives in Conflict of Laws*, 43 Yale L.J. 1082, at 1097 (1934).

[132] *Savigny* 147 (Guthrie trans., 2nd ed., 1880). See also Stumberg, *Conflict of Laws. Foreign Created Rights*, 8 Tex. L.Rev. 173, at 191-193 (1930).

[133] *Cheshire & North*, 26.

[134] Cf. *Graveson*, 38-39.

[135] See Cook, *The Logical and Legal Bases of the Conflict of Laws*, 33 Yale L.J. 457 (1924), de Sloovere, *The Local Law Theory and Its Implications in the Conflict of Laws*, 41 Harv. L. Rev. 421 (1928), Cavers, *The Two "Local Law" Theories*, 63 Harv. L. Rev. 822 (1950), Yntema, *The Historic Bases of Private International Law*, 2 Amer. J. of Compar. L. 297, at 314-317 (1953), Lipstein, *The General Principles of Private International Law*, [1972] - I Recueil des cours 97, at 140-143, Ehrenzweig, 60-62, Cheatham, *American Theories of Conflict of Laws: Their Role and Utility*, 58 Harv. L. Rev. 361, at 385-391 (1945).

[136] Cf. Oliphant, *A Return to Stare Decisis*, 14 Amer. Bar Assoc. J. 71, 107, 159, at 161 (1928):
"…. we have focused our attention too largely on the *vocal behaviour* of judges in deciding cases. A study with more stress on their *non-vocal behaviour*, i.e., what the judges actually do when stimulated by the facts of the case before them, is the approach indispensable to exploiting scientifically the wealth of material in the cases."

of a conclusion rather than as a governing principle. We are not here concerned with testing the adequacy of United States legal realism, though, as we shall see, some of the general criticisms of this school of jurisprudence have particular force in respect of the "local law" theory in the conflict of laws.

The leading proponent of the "local law" theory was Walter Wheeler Cook.[137] The notion of a "vested" foreign right was abhorrent to him. The forum was no doubt always free to create such a right by way of analogy with the position in the foreign legal system but, if it did so, the right was one of the forum's and in no way a foreign import.[138]

When first formulated, the "local law" theory held much attraction for many in its war against legal metaphysics[139] but, as time went by, it became clear that apart from its central insight into the workings of the law, the theory contributed nothing to the solution of legal problems in the real world. Having dispatched "vested rights" as the basis for referring to a foreign law, the "local law" theory was left with the barren assertion that, whatever solution was to be favoured, and however, international its perspective, it would inevitably be one involving the law of the forum.[140]

Currie[141]

Professor Brainerd Currie proposed the replacement of conventional choice-of-law rules[142] by an analysis of competing "governmental interests".[143] His theory

---

[137] Cook taught at Chicago, Yale and Columbia in the decade before he published his seminal article, *The Logical and Legal Bases of the Conflict of Laws*, 33 Yale L.J. 457 (1924). He had there taught and influenced many of the leading members of the realist school: Cavers, *Book Review*, 56 Harv. L. Rev. 1170, at 1171 (1943).

[138] Cf. *Cook*, 20-21:

"The forum, when confronted by a case involving foreign elements, always applies its own law to the case, but in doing so adopts or enforces as its own law a rule of decision identical, or at least highly similar though not identical in scope with a rule of decision found in the system of law in force in another state or country with which some of all of the foreign elements are connected ... The forum thus enforces not a foreign right but a right created by its own law."

[139] Cf. Williams, *Language and the Law-V*, 62 L.Q. Rev. 387 (1946), Cheatham, *supra*, at 381-382.

[140] It is worth recording Yntema's strong criticism of Cook's conclusion that in conflicts law there can be no law but the *lex fori*:

"This is a truism, which contains neither truth nor virtue. On the one hand, it does not explain why, as Savigny noted, every modern legal system in some substantial measure provides for reference to foreign law in the determination of foreign cases. On the other hand, it cannot be useful, and may even be misleading, to instruct courts confronted with cases presenting foreign aspects, in which it may be desirable to refer to foreign law and not to apply the ordinary rules of the local law, that, technically speaking, they must enforce their local law."

The Historic Bases of Private International Law, 2 Amer. J. of Comp. L. 297, at 316 (1953). Cheatham, *supra*, at 386 warns that in "[l]aying the emphasis on the freedom of the forum state to do what it wishes, [the theory] may engender the unfortunate attitude that the freedom should be widely used."

[141] Currie's major articles were collected in *Selected Essays on the Conflict of Laws* (1963). Later articles include *The Disinterested Third State*, 28 L. & Contemp. Problems 754 (1963) and *Full Faith and Credit, Chiefly to Judgments: A Role for Congress*, [1964] Sup. Ct. Rev. 89. Brainerd Currie died in 1965. For analysis of Currie's theory, see Traynor, *Conflict of Laws: Professor Currie's Restrained and Englightened Forum*, 49 Calif. L. Rev. 845 (1961), Hill, *Governmental Interest and the Conflict of Laws - A Reply to Professor Currie*, 27 U. Chic. L. Rev. 463 (1960), Sedler, *The Governmental Interest Approach to Choice of Law: An Analysis and a Reformulation*, 25 U.C.L.A. L. Rev. 181 (1977), Westbrook, *A Survey and Evaluation of Competing Choice-of-Law Methodologies: The Case for Eclecticism*, 40 Missouri L. Rev. 407, at 417-418, 421-423 (1975), Lipstein, *The General Principles of Private International Law*, [1972] - I Recueil des cours 97, at 154-157, Kegel, *The Crisis of Conflict of Laws*, [1964] - I Recueil des cours 91 (Part 1), and the *Symposium on Interest Analysis in Conflict of Laws: An Inquiry into Fundamentals with a Side Glance at Products Liability*, 46 Ohio St. L.J. 457 (1985), which contains a stinging critique of Currie's theory, by Professor Lea Brilmayer (*Governmental Interest Analysis: A House without Foundations, id.*, 459).

[142] Including characterisation, *renvoi* and public policy.

[143] The concept is not new: see, e.g. *Yarborough* v. *Yarborough*, 290 U.S. 202, at 227 (*per* Stone, J., dissenting, 1933), *Alaska Packers Association* v. *Industrial Accident Commission*, 294 U.S. 532, at 547 (*per* Stone, J., 1935). Cf. Hill, *Governmental Interest and the Conflict of Laws - A Reply to Professor Currie*, 27 U. Chic. L. Rev. 463, at 483, fn.97 (1960).

contains many useful insights into the deficiencies of the conventional approach. Whether his own proposal is workable may, however, be doubted.

First let us consider briefly the main features of Currie's theory. He himself provided a helpful, though skeletal, summary:

> "(1) Normally, even in cases involving foreign factors, a court should as a matter of course look to the law of the forum as the source of the rule of decision.
>
> (2) When it is suggested that the law of a foreign state, rather than the law of the forum, should furnish the rule of decision, the court should first of all determine the governmental policy — perhaps it is helpful to say the social, economic, or administrative policy — which is expressed by the law of the forum. The court should then inquire whether the relationship of the forum state to the case at bar — that is, to the parties, to the transaction, to the subject matter, to the litigation — is such as to bring the case within the scope of the state's governmental concern, and to provide a legitimate basis for the assertion that the state has an interest in the application of its policy in this instance.
>
> (3) If necessary, the court should similarly determine the policy expressed in the proffered foreign law, and whether the foreign state has a legitimate interest in the application of that policy to the case at bar.
>
> (4) If the court finds that the forum state has no interest in the application of its law and policy, but that the foreign state has such an interest, it should apply the foreign law.
>
> (5) If the court finds that the forum state has an interest in the application of its law and policy, it should apply the law of the forum even though the foreign state also has such an interest, and *a fortiori* it should apply the law of the forum if the foreign state has no such interest."[144]

There is of course much to be said for taking account of state interests: no good purpose is served by applying the law of a country which simply has nothing to do with the case or the parties involved in the litigation. But the concentration on *state* interests may be regarded by some as "too political in a field which is mostly concerned with private relations".[145]

Moreover, Currie's insistence[146] that the *lex fori* should prevail where several states, including the *forum* state, have an interest in applying their own law denies the court the opportunity to weigh these competing interests.[147] Currie's reluctance to counsel a balancing of interests in this context was based on a number of arguments: that the courts lack the necessary resources for weighing competing state interests, that this process is a political function which should not be committed to courts in a democracy and on the notion that application of a foreign law by a court would be tantamount to the Court declaring its own law inferior.

To the first of these arguments it has been replied that state courts "weigh

---

[144] Currie, *The Constitution and the Choice of Law: Governmental Interests and the Judicial Function*, 26 U. Chi. L. Rev. 9, at 9-10 (1958).

[145] *Castel*, vol. 2. Cf. Hill, *Governmental Interest in the Conflict of Laws — A Reply to Professor Currie*, 27 U. Chic. L. Rev. 463, at 485 (1960):

> "When Professor Currie says that a court should effectuate the Governmental interests of the forum he means no more than that it should effectuate such policies to the extent that substantial local contacts of a contemporaneous nature afford a reasonable basis for doing so. Up to this point, at least, his approach is one which would have provoked no serious demurrer on the part of Ulrich Huber."

See also Sedler, *The Governmental Interest Approach to Choice of Law: An Analysis and a Reformulation*, 25 U.C.L.A. L. Rev. 181, at 191-192 (1977).

[146] Modified in later writings.

[147] *Castel*, vol. 2. See also Ehrenzweig, *A Counter-Revolution in Conflicts Law? From Beale to Cavers*, 80 Harv. L. Rev. 377, at 389 (1966). See, however, *Forsyth*, 49, fn. 219 describing the preference for the *lex fori* as "understandable if chauvinistic". And see Sedlar, *The Governmental Interest Approach to Choice of Law: An Analysis and a Reformulation*, 25 U.C.L.A. L. Rev. 181, at 219 (1977).

competing interests in common-law[148] and statutory interpretation[149] cases every day''.[150] There is nothing essentially different about the task facing a court where an international element is involved. To the second argument it may be responded that much of what sails under the flag of legal principle is in fact a matter of "practical politics".[151] There is nothing unique about conflicts problems in this regard. If the courts were to retreat from all issues with a political dimension, many of our judges would surely become redundant. Neither has the third argument a great deal of attraction. Where the court applies a foreign law, all it is saying is that in the particular circumstances the interests of another state are more concerned with the facts of the problem with which the court has to deal. This is not a statement of weakness, merely one of fact.

Having said this, it must be admitted that Currie's elevation of forum interests may well harmonise with what courts tend to do rather than say, and who can argue that their approach is self-evidently misconceived?[152]

Currie's failure[153] to resolve the problem where the *forum* has no interest in applying its own law but two foreign states have conflicting interests should also be noted. The selection of the *lex fori*, as he proposed, is scarcely satisfactory in view of its admitted irrelevance.

Critics of Currie's approach have argued that it is not so revolutionary as it may first appear. Under Currie's system a court would still have to choose between local and foreign law or, less frequently, between the laws of two or more foreign jurisdictions. Thus, "he is not so much proposing the abolition of choice-of-law rules as proposing that the traditional rules be abandoned in favour of a different approach to the problem".[154]

Some commentators[155] have argued that, while Currie's theory may be workable within the United States where the interests of the various states may be discerned with relative ease, matters become far less manageable when truly international conflicts arise. It is often hard enough to establish what is the foreign law on a particular subject; to ask our courts to investigate the differing governmental interests in the laws of several foreign countries is in many cases to expect the impossible.

It has also been suggested that there is a risk that the forum state may exaggerate its own interest and downplay foreign interests.[156] Moreover, the inevitable

---

[148] Cf. *McMahon & Binchy*, 154 ff.

[149] Cf., *id.*, ch. 15.

[150] Traynor, *Conflict of Laws: Professor Currie's Restrained and Enlightened Forum*, 49 Calif. L. Rev. 845, at 854 (1961).

[151] *Palsgraf* v. *Long Island Railroad Co.*, 162 N.E. 99, at 103 (N.Y. Ct. Apps., *per* Andrews, J. (dissenting), 1928).

[152] Cf. Sedlar, *The Governmental Interest Approach to Choice of Law: An Analysis and a Reformulation*, 25 U.C.L.A. L. Rev. 181, at 227 (1977):

"Whenever the forum has decided that it has a real interest in the application of its law, it has necessarily concluded that the policy behind the law would be significantly impaired if it were not applied to this particular situation containing a foreign element. It is clearly legitimate for a court to decide that the implementation of that policy is more important than implementation of 'multistate policies'; courts simply do not view their function in a conflicts case to be that of 'policing the interstate and international legal order'. In practice, courts tend to see a conflicts case as essentially a domestic case with a foreign element added; when the same reasons that call for the application of their law in a domestic case are equally present in a conflict case, they naturally enough want to apply their own law."

[153] Cf. *Morris*, 518.

[154] Hill, *Governmental Interest and the Conflicts of Laws — A Reply to Professor Currie*, 27 U. Chic. L. Rev. 463, at 474 (1960).

[155] See, e.g. *Castel*, vol. 2, 19.

[156] *Cavers*, 74.

consequence of giving prominence to the *lex fori* is that the outcome will depend on which state first determines the case.[157]

Reese's criticism of Currie's approach is worth recording:

> "One thing is apparent. Professor Currie is a simplicist. In his view, a single approach will satisfactorily handle the myriad of problems that may arise in choice of law. In his view also, there is one choice of law policy of such paramount importance that it will always outweigh other countervailing policies. This may be all to the good. Simplicity is indeed a virtue if it can be attained. The fact remains that Professor Currie in his own way is as dogmatic and doctrinaire as was the much maligned Professor Beale."[158]

Furthermore, Currie's insistence that a specific determination of state interests should be made in each *individual* case, rather than in each *type* of case[159] makes the task of planning one's personal or business life a dangerously uncertain one. A person who wishes to marry abroad or enter into a contract with a French company does not want a disquisition on the comparative weights of the interests of several states, ending in a "maybe"; he or she wants no more than reasonably clear guidance on the legal implications of the proposed course of conduct.

Finally, it has been argued that Currie's critique of conventional choice of law rules is less incisive than might at first appear. He never provides empirical proof for his contention that these rules yield unsatisfactory results; on the contrary he concedes that the conventional approach does not work as much hardship as one might expect because "[a] sensitive and ingenious court can detect an absurd result and avoid it ..."[160]

Cavers[161]

David Cavers made an important contribution[162] to the development of conflicts theory in the United States, at a time when the controversy between the vested rights and local law theories was raging. Cavers stressed that in cases with a foreign element, just as much as in cases without this element, the court was called on to embark on "a penetrating analysis of the controversy and the transaction out of which it arose, an exacting inquiry into and appraisal of the competing rules, a deliberate weighing of the equities."[163] In conflicts cases, the stress on jurisdiction-selecting

---

[157] Traynor, *Conflict of Laws: Professor Currie's Restrained and Enlightened Forum*, 49 Cal. L. Rev. 845, at 847 (1961).

[158] Reese, *Book Review*, 16 U. of Toronto L.J. 228, at 229 (1965).

[159] See Forsyth, *Interest Analysis and the Myth of Legislative Intent*, 78 Mich. L. Rev. 392, at 402-407 (1980), Reese, *Choice of Law: Rules or Approach?*, 57 Corn. L. Rev. 315 (1972).

[160] Currie, *Notes on Methods and Objectives in the Conflict of Laws*, [1959] Duke L.J. 171, at 179. Cf. Hill, *Governmental Interest and the Conflict of Laws — A Reply to Professor Currie*, 27 U. Chic. L. Rev. 463, at 469 (1960).

[161] See D. Cavers, *The Choice of Law Process* (1965); leading articles by Cavers include *Contemporary Conflicts Law in American Perspective*, [1970] - III Recueil des cours 131, *The Value of Principled Preferences*, 49 Tex. L. Rev. 211 (1971), *A Critique of the Choice-of-Law Problem*, 47 Harv. L. Rev. 173 (1933). For analysis see Morris, 512-516, Anton, 36-37, Westbrook, *A Survey and Evaluation of Competing Choice-of-Law Methodologies: The Case for Eclecticism*, 40 Missouri L. Rev. 407, at 423-427 (1975), Ehrenzweig, *A Counter-Revolution in Conflicts Law? From Beale to Cavers*, 80 Harv. L. Rev. 377 (1966). For a useful recent analysis of the theories of Cavers and Currie, see Maslechko, *Revolution and Counter-revolution: An Examination of the Continuing Debate over "Interest Analysis" in the United States and its Relevance to Canadian Conflict of Laws*, 44 U. Toronto Fac. of L. Rev. 57 (1986).

[162] The article that occasioned most attention was published over fifty years ago: *A Critique of the Choice-of-Law Problem*, 47 Harv. L. Rev. 173 (1933). It is useful to read this in conjunction with a *Comment* by Cavers nearly forty years later: *A Critique of the Choice-of-Law Process: Addendum 1972*, 17 Harv. Internat. L.J. 651 (1976).

[163] Cavers, *A Critique of the Choice-of-Law Problem*, 47 Harv. L. Rev. 173 (1933).

rules was in his view unduly mechanical and likely to yield quite inappropriate decisions:

> "The court is not idly choosing a law; it is determining a controversy. How can it choose wisely without considering how that choice will affect that controversy?"[164]

Rather than automatically applying a mechanical formula, such as the *lex loci contractus* rule in respect of contracts, Cavers proposed that the courts should examine the *content* of the respective laws of interested states; in some instances this examination would reveal that an apparent conflict between different laws was not a real one. Thus, for example, limitations on a person's contractual capacity according to the law of a particular state based on minority[165] or insanity might well be considered not to affect those who are domiciled or resident in some other state.[166]

Cavers argued that the courts should release themselves from "the blindfold of a theory which has compelled them to grope for solutions to problems for which perspicacity is peculiarly essential ..."[167] Instead the following approach should be adopted:

> "When a court is faced with a question whether to reject, as inapplicable, the law of the forum and to admit in evidence, as determinative of an issue in a case before it, a rule of law of a foreign jurisdiction, it should
> (1) scrutinise the event or transaction giving rise to the issue before it;
> (2) compare carefully the proffered rule of law and the result which its application might work in the case at bar with the rule of the forum (or other competing jurisdiction) and its effect therein;
> (3) appraise those results in the light of those facts in the event or transaction which, from the standpoint of justice between the litigating individuals or of those broader considerations of social policy which conflicting laws may evoke, link that event or transaction to one law or the other ..."[168]

The end-product of this process of evaluation and analysis would be the application to the case of a rule of law derived either from the municipal law of the forum or some foreign state:

> "The choice of that law would not be the result of the automatic operation of a rule or principle of selection but of a search for a just decision in the ... case."[169]

But, as Cavers admitted, "lawyers are a rulemaking sect";[170] and from this simple decision the seed of a rule or principle for the choice of law might spring. Gradually, with sufficient decisions using this approach, a body of law could well develop which would lend itself to analytic analysis expressed in terms of "rule", but Cavers stressed that these "rules" should reflect rather than dictate the outcome of cases.

Cavers conceded that his proposed approach would sacrifice some of the certainty and predictability involved in the black-letter jurisdiction-selecting rules, but he argued

---

[164] *Id.*, at 189. See also *Cavers*, 72. It may be argued that, in their practical application and interpretation of professedly mechanical conflicts rules, our courts are far from blind to the implications for the parties, as well as for broader social policies. Cf. Fawcett, *Result Selection in Domicile Cases*, 5 Oxford J. of Leg. Stud. 378 (1985).

[165] Cf. The Law Reform Commission's *Report on Minor's Contracts* (LRC 15-1985).

[166] A general reference to the *lex domicilii* in commercial matters may, however work just as unsatisfactorily as a general reference to the *lex loci contractus:* cf: *infra*, pp. 494, 501.

[167] Cavers, *supra*, at 192.

[168] *Id.*, at 192-193.

[169] *Id.*, at 193.

[170] *Id.*

that certainty under these rules had been bought at too high a price. He made the interesting observation that the application of mechanical rules of law in cases with an international (rather than interprovincial or inter-state) dimension might be regarded as:

> "necessary to safeguard the alien litigant from xenophobia. Discretion is a safe tool only in the hands of the disinterested. Such disinterestedness may more readily be credited to courts within the bounds of a federal union."[171]

Cavers and Currie are in accord in regarding the choice of law problem as involving a choice between two specific rules of law rather than between the legal systems of two jurisdictions.[172] There are echoes of this approach in the recent Supreme Court decision of *Grehan* v. *Medical Incorporated & Valley Pines Associates.*[173] Whether this development is an indication of a more general adherence by the Court to this approach remains to be seen.

[171] *Id.*, at 203.
[172] *Castel*, vol. 2, 24.
[173] [1986] I.L.R.M. 627 (Sup. Ct) *cf. infra*, 151-154, 578-580.

CHAPTER 2

IRELAND AND THE CONFLICT OF LAWS

Having regard to its history and to its geographical position it is scarcely surprising that this island should have had a good deal of practical experience of "conflict of laws situations". Patterns of emigration and trade inevitably throw up these questions. Moreover, the fact that Ireland has been the object of Britain's attention over the centuries has left its mark. Several cases have come before the courts involving questions of title to land or other property in Ireland owned by English, Welsh or Scottish domiciliaries or residents. More importantly, especially after the Act of Union, questions as to the effect of British legislation on Ireland frequently arose. Of course, the more important effect of the Act of Union was to introduce such a degree of uniformity between the laws of Britain and Ireland as greatly to minimise the scope of potential conflicts. The law of contract was essentially the same, and most (though not all) of the principles of property law were identical. Thus in the nineteenth century most of the conflicts questions related to the connecting factors of the conflict of laws — jurisdiction, domicile, identifying the *lex situs* or the *lex loci celebrationis*, for example.[1] Support for the Union was scarcely consistent with an emphasis on every possible legal distinction between Ireland and the other countries comprising the Union. Thus we find cases in which relevant substantive conflicts issues were not raised by the court.

After Independence, it is fair to say that this tendency to ignore conflicts issues was slow to die away. The relative lack of attention in the conflict of laws until recently by the legal educational institutions must have contributed to this process. In recent years, however, the position has greatly improved.

Ireland's membership of the European Economic Community, greater investment by foreign and multinational companies, as well as important differences between our marriage law and the law of many other countries have all contributed to an increasing consciousness of the conflicts dimensions to legal issues.

Two conflicts issues merit particular attention: (a) the effect of Independence on British legislation relating to Ireland, and (b) the effect of the Constitution on our conflict of laws. Let us consider each of these issues in turn.

The effect of independence on British legislation relating to Ireland

With Independence in 1922 the Irish Free State came into being. Article 73 of the Constitution of Saorstát Éireann provided that, subject to the Constitution and to the extent to which they were not consistent with it, the laws in force in the Irish Free State at the date the Constitution came into force should continue to be of full force and effect until they might be repealed or amended by enactment of the Oireachtas.

[1] The question whether a particular British statute applied to Ireland during this period is an issue that may, even today, come before the courts; see e.g. *Flynn* v. *Buckley* [1980] I.R. 423 (Sup. Ct.).

The Adaptation of Enactments Act 1922 was designed to smooth this process of transition. Of particular interest in section 3, which provides that:

"for the purpose of the construction of any British statute the name 'Ireland', whether used alone or in conjunction with the expression 'Great Britain', or by implication as being included in the expression 'United Kingdom', shall mean Saorstát Éireann."

In the Supreme Court case of *State (Gilsenan)* v. *McMorrow*,[2] Henchy, J. said:

"The range of adaptation effected by the section was this:-
1. Whenever one finds the name 'Ireland' alone in a British statute, one reads it as meaning Saorstát Éireann.
2. Whenever one finds the expression 'Great Britain and Ireland' in a British statute, one reads it as meaning Great Britain and Saorstát Éireann.
3. Whenever one finds the expression 'United Kingdom' (*i.e.* of Great Britain and Ireland) in a British statute, one reads it as meaning Great Britain and Saorstát Éireann."

In *The State (Kennedy) v Little*,[3] in 1930, a person resident in the Free State and arrested under a Canadian warrant on a charge of obtaining money by false pretences, contended that the Fugitive Offenders Act 1881, under which the warrant had been executed in the Free State, had no longer continued in force by virtue of its inconsistency with Article 73 of the Constitution. The High Court unanimously rejected this argument.

Johnston, J.'s analysis was particularly clear. He considered that the court should be "very slow to do anything that would have the effect of depriving the Saorstát of the benefit of the vast body of useful statutory law which regulated hundreds and thousands of necessary matters in the body politic at the date of the coming into operation of the Constitution." He considered that this view was:

"confirmed and strengthened by the fact that ... Article [73] itself expressly indicates that the Oireachtas may repeal or amend any law that ought to be repealed or amended; and, further, it is reasonably plain from the Adaptation Act that a statute of the United Kingdom, which was in force in Ireland in 1922, is not to be rejected merely because of some difficulty of terminology, of procedure, or of change of circumstance. There must be something in the Act which renders it unworkable in principle by reason of its inconsistency with the Constitution before it can be regarded as not coming within the scope of the Article."[4]

The Court rejected the argument that only "municipal" or "domestic" legislation came within the operation of Article 73. Three types of British legislation were identified. The first embraced Acts operative only in the "dominions", "colonies" or "possessions" of the Crown and had no primary operative force at all in any part of the United Kingdom. The second embraced Acts having a primary operative force in both the United Kingdom and all British possessions. The Fugitive Offenders Act 1881 was an example. The third and final type embraced legislation having a primary force in the United Kingdom only. It was "obvious", said Johnston, J. "that different considerations apply to each of these classes of legislation, and even to the various Acts which are included in each class, and no useful result can be achieved by bulking them together as 'imperial', or 'colonial', or 'reciprocal', or 'non−municipal'. When they come to be considered in the Irish Courts, each must be viewed in the light of its own object and provisions."[5]

[2] [1978] I.R. 360, at 372 (Sup. Ct.). See also *People (A.G.)* v. *Ruttledge,* [1978] I.R. 376 (Sup. Ct., 1947). The anomalies that may result in regard to Northern Ireland are considered in *Gilsenan.*
[3] [1931] I.R. 39 (High Ct., 1930).
[4] *Id.,* at 45.
[5] *Id.,* at 46.

In *Irish Transport & General Workers Union v Green and Transport & General Workers Union*,[6] Meredith, J. had to decide whether a tort action against the defendant union should be dismissed under section 4(1) of the Trade Disputes Act 1906, which precludes the taking of an action against a trade union in respect of a tortious act. This defence would not be available if section 6 of the Trade Union Act Amendment Act 1876 applied. Section 6 provided as follows:

> "Trade Unions carrying or intending to carry on business in more than one country should be registered in the country in which their registered office is situate; but copies of the rules of such unions, and of all amendments of the same, shall, when registered, be sent to the registrar of each of the other countries, to be recorded by him, and until such rules be so recorded the union shall not be entitled to any of the privileges of this Act or the principal Act, in the country in which rules have not been recorded, and until such amendments of rules be recorded the same shall not take effect in such country. In this section 'country' means England, Scotland, or Ireland."

The effect of section 3 of the Adaptation of Enactments Act 1922 was that this provision would provide for the registry of unions doing business in more than one of the countries, England, Scotland and Saorstát Éireann. Northern Ireland would be excluded even though the effect of the British adaptation provisions was that section 6 of the 1876 Act applied to England, Scotland and Northern Ireland, but not to Saorstát Éireann. Meredith, J. was so troubled by these implications that he held that section 6 no longer had effect. He said:

> "If ... the section were to continue to be applicable it would purport to make provision as much for things to be done and effects to follow in England and Scotland as for things to be done and effects to follow in Saorstát Éireann. That, of course, is impossible. The section could only apply to Saorstát Éireann, and it could not have any application in Saorstát Éireann alone unless England and Scotland were countries in Saorstát Éireann which they are not. The whole basis of the section is a legislative union, and it provides for recognitions and reciprocal obligations for which a section applicable only to, and in, Saorstát Éireann could not possibly provide. That being so, it is unnecessary to point out the inconsistencies with our Constitution, by reason of the vesting of important jurisdictions in external authorities, that would result from a partial or one-sided application — entire application being quite impossible — of the section in Saorstát Éireann."[7]

The holding and analysis cannot be faulted; but the case does raise some interesting constitutional and other legal questions. First, where the whole basis of a statutory provision is *not* a legislative union, does the fact alone that the section purports to confer or recognise a jurisdiction in a law district outside the Republic constitute a reason for rejecting the application of the section? The answer must surely be no. As we shall see,[8] there are several of these statutory provisions which appear to have continuing vitality.

Secondly, does the fact that a statutory provision has lost its reciprocal effect by reason of Independence necessarily mean that it thereby became inapplicable and inconsistent with the Constitution? Again the answer appears to be so. This is clear from Walsh, J.'s resolution of the issue arising in *re Gibbons, a Bankrupt in England. Ex parte Walter*.[9]

Thirdly, and arising from the question just considered, does the fact alone that

---

[6] [1936] I.R. 471 (High Ct., Meredith, J., 1935). Cf. Hickling, *Legal Personality and Trade Unions in the British Isles,* 4 Western L. Rev. 7, at 19 (1965).

[7] *Id.,* at 481. See also *Ulster Bank Ltd* v. *Walsh* 62 I.L.T.R. 68, at 68 (Meredith, J., 1928), quoted *infra*, p. 384, fn. 29.

[8] For example, in relation to bankruptcy.

[9] [1960] Ir. Jur. Rep. 60 (High Ct., Walsh, J.). cf. *infra*, pp. 473-474.

a statutory provision has ceased to apply in England and Scotland by virtue of British adaptation provisions after our Independence mean that the provision can no longer apply under our law? Yet again the answer appears clearly to be no. The whole purpose of the British adaptation process after 1922 was to restrict the scope of a former range of statutory operation and in some cases to kill it completely. For the Saorstát, the policy was in some respects the opposite: to continue and protect the operation of formerly applicable legislation, albeit often narrowed in scope to the Saorstát rather than (as formerly) to Britain.

The Role of the Constitution[10]

The relationship between the Constitution and the conflict of laws raises fascinating questions, most of which have yet to be addressed by the courts.

The Constitution is, of course, the basic law of the State and all statutory and non-statutory Irish law is subject to its provisions. But, of their nature, conflicts rules embrace reference to the laws of other countries, and it might be considered that they should be permitted to operate freely, without constitutional restraint.[11] This approach seems inconsistent with the view[12] of conflicts rules as part of the domestic law rather than as constituting some supra-national system of law.[13]

The Irish Constitution is based on a philosophical vision of human capacity, rights and responsibilities. That vision is consistent with a natural law analysis, and is universalist in its scope. It sees *all* people, not just Irish citizens, as having the right to life, as well as to marry and own property, for example. In many instances, the Constitution recognises, rather than confers, these rights. This approach has particular implications in relation to the conflict of laws. If, for example, a person with little or no connection with Ireland comes here and seeks protection under Article 41 (in respect of the Family), our courts may be presented with a difficulty. The vision of family rights and responsibilities may well be universal and transcend all national boundaries, but the practical implications of extending Constitutional protection to persons without substantial connections with this country are significant.[14] We will be examining this question in greater detail in the chapter on minority.[15]

If we accept that there must be *some* limits to the range of protection afforded by the Constitution, the question arises as to how those limits are to be determined. One approach would seek to make distinctions on the basis of how fundamental the right in question might be.[16] Another approach would seek to distinguish between

[10] See Muller—Freienfels, *Conflicts of Law and Constitutional Law*, 45 U. Chi. L. Rev. 598 (1978).

[11] Cf. *id.*, *supra*, at 602-603 (footnote references omitted):

"Even in nations that grant primacy to constitutional law, it is not indisputable that courts with constitutional review jurisdiction should invalidate 'unconstitutional' conflicts rules. Some scholars have argued that the rules of private international law should not be viewed as positive, national law but rather as transnational prescriptions that are not subject to any national constitution. The conflict rules are simply neutral, formal provisions − rules of expediency, devoid of substantive justice. Furthermore, it might be argued, the participants in the establishment of the constitution probably never intended that constitutional provisions such as those providing equal rights to spouses or between legitimate and illegitimate children should be applied to conflicts rules. Rather, the existence of these rules was presupposed in drafting the individual country's constitution. Since the constitutional provisions were adopted within the framework of existing conflicts law, the argument runs, constitutional law should be considered subject to private international law in the hierarchy of norms."

[12] Cf. *supra*, pp. 3-4, 15-16.

[13] Cf. Muller—Freienfels, *supra*, at 603.

[14] The problem of forum shopping is an obvious example: Cf. *id.*, at 610.

[15] *Infra*, ch.15. See *Northampton Co. Co.* v. *A.B.F. and M.B.F.*, [1982] I.L.R.M. 164 (High Ct., Hamilton, J., 1981), *Kent Co. Co.* v. *C.S.*, [1984] I.L.R.M. 292 (High Ct., Finlay, P., 1983).

[16] Cf. Muller—Freienfels, *supra*, at 609.

"general" human rights and citizenship rights.[17] As against this, it has been suggested that "analysis wedded to abstract concepts should be eschewed in favour of careful consideration of the interests involved in each case."[18]

In some instances, the Constitution has expressly provided for the continued application of conflicts rules. Thus, for example Article 41.3.3° gives to the legislature the power to alter the rules as to the recognition of foreign divorces. It is surely correct that the Constitution had not the effect of freezing the common rules of recognition in perpetuity. But that does not mean that the legislature necessarily has a totally free hand when it comes to framing statutory rules of recognition.[19]

A broader issue yet to be considered by the courts is the extent to which questions historically regarded as essentially part of conflicts of law may be reinterpreted, entirely or in part, as being questions of constitutional law. Thus, for example, the rules relating to jurisdiction,[20] the recognition of foreign judgments[21] and limitation of actions,[22] may on reflection be considered to give effect to important constitutional principles, including those relating to the right to fair judicial procedures, due process and equal treatment as well as the somewhat complicated protection of the right to property afforded by the Constitution.

If within our domestic law a person is deprived of his home or livelihood by fraudulent abuse of the legal procedure he may have a remedy, if needs be, under the Constitution. Why should it be any different where the deprivation is effected by the abuse of a foreign legal procedure? If constitutional justice, like natural justice, affords protection under our domestic law, why should it not do so under our conflicts rules, which are, after all, part of our domestic law in the wider sense?

In many instances, the conflicts rules, as they have been developed, will afford such significant protection that recourse to constitutional principles would be otiose; but there is no reason to suppose that the two approaches will always necessarily coincide. Where conflicts rules have been based on obsolete notions, such as sex inequality, which was at the heart of the wife's domicile of dependency, the Constitution can, of course, override the conflict rules. The specific question of the domicile of dependency of married women is far from moot. Although the Domicile and Recognition of Foreign Divorces Act 1986 has abolished the concept, it has done so only propectively. Thus, our courts may well have to address the issue of the constitutionality of the rules relating to the domicile of dependency of married women before 2 October 1986.

---

[17] Cf. *id.,* at 609-610, discussing Swiss case on the right to marry, judgment of 16 December 1897, BG Switz., 23 Part 2 entschiedungen des schweizerischien Bundesegerichtes, autliche Sammlung [B G E] 1 1390.

[18] Muller — Freienfels, *supra,* at 609.

[19] Cf. *infra*, pp. 275, 279.

[20] Cf. *infra*, ch.9; and see Hertz, *The Constitution and the Conflict of Laws: Approaches in Canadian*

[21] Cf. *infra*, ch. 33.

[22] Cf. *infra*, pp. 639-641.

CHAPTER 3

CHARACTERISATION

Every day, in legal proceedings, the courts are constantly characterising the raw facts of human interrelationships. Sometimes the process is so obvious and simple that it is easy to overlook. Yet facts *of themselves* have no particular legal significance.[2] That legal significance can come only from a hierarchy or hierarchies of intermeshing legal norms. If we think of any human occurrence, we can properly examine its possible legal significance for the purposes of Irish law only if we are familiar with the entire corpus of Irish law. If, for example, a man puts up a large building which blocks light to his neighbour's house, the problem may perhaps be legally characterised as private nuisance, interference with an easement, breach of covenant, breach of the planning legislation, or all or none of these.

Problems of characterisation such as this may sometimes be complex in our internal law. But when we turn to consider conflicts of law the difficulties may be multiplied. Frequently, of course, no problem arises. There may be widespread agreement internationally as to how to characterise certain modes of conduct or of interrelationship. Much of our tort law is similarly characterised in the laws of other countries, but even here there are some differences. Our law may characterise as tortious conduct what some other countries characterise as a breach of contract and *vice versa*.[3]

A much quoted example of the possible conflict of classification that can arise concerns the question whether a will is revoked by marriage: is this an issue of *matrimonial law*[4] or of *succession*[5]? The reasonable reply might seem to be that it

---

[1] See generally Robertson, *Characterization in the Conflict of Laws* (1940), *Falconbridge*, 50-123, *Wolff*, ch. 13, *Jackson*, chs 5 – 6, Beckett, *The Question of Classification ("Qualification") in Private International Law*, 15 Br. Yrbk of Internat. L. 46 (1934) Lorenzen, *The Theory of Qualifications and the Conflict of Laws*, 20 Colum. L. Rev. 247 (1920), Pascal, *Characterization as an Approach to the Conflict of Laws*, 2 La. L. Rev. 715 (1940), Meriggi, *Les qualifications en droit international privé*, 28 Rev. de Dr. Internat. Priv. 201(1933), Overton, *Analysis in Conflict of Laws: The Problem of Classification*, 21 Tenn. L. Rev. 600 (1951), Cormack, *Renvoi, Characterization, Localization and Preliminary Question in the Conflict of Laws*, 14 So. Calif. L. Rev. 221, at 223 – 240 (1941), Mendelssohn – Barehaldy, *Delimitation of Right and Remedy in the Cases of Conflict of Laws*, 16 Br. Yrbk of Internat. L. 20 (1935), Morse, *Characterization: Shadow or Substance*, 49 Colum. L. Rev. 1027 (1949), Cheatham, *Internal Law Distinctions in the Conflict of Laws*, 21 Corn. L.Q. 570 (1936), Ehrenzweig, *Characterization in the Conflict of Laws: An Unwelcome Addition to American Doctrine*, in *XXth Century Comparative and Conflicts Law*, 395 (1961), Turpin, *Characterization and Policy in the Conflict of Laws*, [1959] Acta Jurid. 222, Bland, *Classification Re-Classified*, 6 Int. & Comp. L.Q. 10 (1957).

[2] Cf. Lederman, *Classification in Private International Law*, 29 Can. Bar Rev. 3, at 10 (1951), Falconbridge, *Renvoi, Characterization and Acquired Rights*, 17 Can. Bar Rev. 369, at 374 (1939).

[3] For example, actions for breach of promise of marriage which, until their abolition by statute in 1981 (cf. infra) were characterised as involving breaches of *contract* under our law but which constitute torts (delicts) in some civil law jurisdictions.

[4] As decided in the English case of *Re Martin, Loustalan* v. *Loustalan*, [1900] P. 211, discussed *infra*, p.449.

[5] As is the view under most civil law systems: see *Wolff*, 146.

is truly an issue of *both*; but that will not satisfy conflicts lawyers, since choice of law rules in the conflict of laws "require mutually exclusive classes of rules."[6] What the conflict of laws has historically tried to do is to confront the totality of human experience and break it down into discrete categories and subcategories. To each of these categories and subcategories particular choice of law rules apply. Thus, for example, under conflicts rules, the formal requirements for marriage are to be governed by the law of the place where the marriage is celebrated (the *lex loci celebrationis*).[7]

This approach guarantees that questions of classification *must* arise. Is a polygamous marriage a marriage, for the purpose of this rule?[8] In a proxy marriage, where is the place of celebration?[9] Is the requirement of parental consent for marriage one of form or of substance?[10] To complicate matters, other countries, in their conflict of laws, have also attempted to break down the totality of human experience into specific categories and subcategories. It is too much to expect that there would be a total uniformity of approach between all countries. In fact, there is a good deal more uniformity of approach than might have been expected, but nonetheless important differences remain.

It is perhaps worth reflecting briefly at this point on the philosophical implications of attempting to categorise or sub-categorise in legal terms the totality of human experience. All such categorisation must involve some loose ends. But ordinary life, let alone the legal process, would become unmanageable if we were to avoid the categorisation process until all categories had been thoroughly refined. The truth of day-to-day life is that we have to live with rough edges for our categories, verbal and legal, because, on balance, the categorisation process contributes to our understanding of the world, to social harmony and to communication.

The very process of legal categorisation takes place, not in a social vacuum but with very definite social goals in mind. In many respects, legal categorisation is *purposive*.

As Pound observed:

"Classification is not an end. Legal precepts are classified in order to make the materials of the legal system effective for the ends of law."[11]

Let us now consider briefly the problem of characterisation in the context of the conflict of laws. One approach[12] would be for the court of the forum to characterise legal rules in accordance with the concepts of its internal law. This approach makes it easy for the court to apply its own choice of law rules.[13] But it also can involve difficulties where a rule or institution of foreign law finds no counterpart in the

---

[6] Lederman, *Classification in Private International Law — 1*, 29 Can. Bar Rev. 3, at 13 (1951).

[7] See *infra*, pp. 218-219.

[8] Cf. *infra*, pp. 212-213.

[9] Cf. *infra*, p. 221.

[10] Cf. the notorious decision of the English Court of Appeal in *Ogden* v. *Ogden*, [1908] P. 46, where requirements under French law (the man's *lex domicilii*) which required parental consent as a condition of the validity of the marriage were characterised as formal, following the classification of the *lex fori*, which was the *lex loci celebrationis*, rather than substantive, as they clearly were under French law. See further Wolff, 329, *Cheshire & North*, 50–52.

[11] Pound, *Classification of Law*, 37 Harv. L. Rev. 9033, at 944 (1924). Cf. Morse, *Characterization: Shadow or Substance*, 49 Colum. L. Rev. 1027 (1949), Bland, *Classification Re-Classified*, 6 Int. & Comp. L.Q. 10 (1957), Turpin, *Characterization and Policy in the Conflict of Laws*, [1959] Acta Jurid. 222.

[12] Put forward by Bartin, *De l'impossibilité d'arriver à la suppression définitive des conflits de lois*, 24 Clunet 225, at 466, 720 (1897). In accord were Kahn, Noboyet, Arminjon and Pillet.

[13] Cf. Beckett, *supra*, at 51.

forum's internal law.[14] Moreover, the forum-based approach can result in the application of the law of a foreign country in cases where, according to the notions of the foreign law, it is not applicable at all: "in other words, applying a law which is not ... the law of any country whatsoever."[15]

Another approach[16] would characterise in accordance with the *lex causae*, that is, "the appropriate foreign law."[17] In favour of this approach it has been argued that the forum "avoids the danger of distorting a foreign rule by reflecting it in the mirror of its own legal concepts."[18] Moreover, unlike the forum-based approach, foreign rules unknown to the forum will simply be characterised in accordance with the *lex causae*.

But the *lex causae* approach "bristles with difficulties."[19] Most obviously, it is impossible to know which is the *lex causae* until a process of characterisation has resulted in its identification.[20] Perhaps, the notion of a putative *lex causae*, akin to that of the putative proper law of the contract[21] or proleptic domicile,[22] would mitigate the force of this objection.

Under the third approach, proposed by Beckett, characterisation should be performed in accordance with analytical jurisprudence, "that general science of law, based on the results of the study of comparative law, which extracts from this study essential general principles of professedly universal application − not principles based on, or applicable to, the legal system of one country only."[23] Beckett did not deny that even analytical jurisprudence "may have something of a national character"[24] and that consequently a national judge will follow the ideas of his own country regarding analytical jurisprudence. Moreover, the *lex fori's* characterisation would prevail where general jurisprudence could give no answer because the laws of different countries were more or less equally divided and there was no logical reason for adopting one view rather than another.[25]

This third approach has been criticised for being easier to state than to apply in practice. The principles of "analytical jurisprudence" are of quite uncertain scope.[26] Moreover, the fact that different countries adopt different rules as to characterisation does not greatly help us in deciding which law is to be preferred.

These competing theories as to the proper approach to characterisation have not greatly troubled the judges, who tend to get on with the process of characterisation with little discussion of the difficulties involved. As we will see, Irish courts have taken the view that domicile should be determined in accordance with the *lex fori*,[27]

---

[14] Cf. Nussbaum, *Book Review*, 40 Colum. L. Rev. 1461, at 1470 (1940). Bartin suggested that this absence of a counterpart meant that the foreign rule or institution must be so alien to the forum as to be excluded on the grounds of public policy. This seems too extreme a solution: cf. Beckett, *supra*, at 57. In *In re Tamburrini*, [1944] I.R. 508, discussed, *infra*, pp. 367-368, the High Court gave short shift to the claim of an adoptive father to assert parental rights in regard to his adopted child. At that time adoption was lawful under Scots, but not Irish, law. See also *Re Wilson*, [1954] Ch. 733 (Vaisey, J.); cf. *Re Wilby*, [1956] P. 174 (Barnard. J.).

[15] Beckett, *supra*, at 55.

[16] Favoured by *Wolff*, 154, and Despagnet, *Des conflits des lois relatifs a la qualification des rapports juridiques*, 25 J. du droit internat. privé 253 (1898).

[17] Dicey & Morris, 36.

[18] *Nygh*, 158-159; see also Beckett, *supra*, at 580, but cf. Ehrenzweig, Characterization in the Conflict of Laws: An Unwelcome Addition to American Doctrine, in *XXth Century Comparative and Conflicts Law: Legal Essays in Honour of Hessel Yntema* 395, at 402(1961).

[19] Dicey & Morris, 36.

[20] Beckett, *supra*, at 51.

[21] Cf. *infra*, p. 528.

[22] Cf. *infra*, pp. 91, 433.

[23] Beckett, *supra*, at 59.

[24] *Id*.

[25] *Id*.

[26] Cf. *Dicey & Morris*, 37.

[27] Cf. *infra*, p. 50.

that the *lex situs* should determine whether property is moveable or immoveable,[28] that the *lex fori* should characterise matters as substantive or procedural.[29]

In determining whether a foreign law is penal, the courts of the forum characterise the issue for themselves and are not bound by how the courts of the foreign country characterise their law; but, as we shall see,[30] in the recent case of *Larkins v National Union of Mineworkers*[31] Barrington, J. appeared to place some weight on how the foreign courts characterised the law in issue.

The question of how marriage should be characterised is discussed later.[32] Irish courts have yet to confront the issue of whether a marriage subject to virtually immediate dissolution at the uniliteral demand of either spouse should necessarily be treated as a marriage for all purposes. Deference to international realities suggests that it would, though conceptually this approach may be difficult to defend in certain cases. Perhaps this is an example of the approach advocated by Beckett; more probably it is merely evidence of the pragmatic dimension to the conflict of laws.

---

[28] Cf. *infra*, p. 392. The problem of circularity in determining what is the *lex causae*, mentioned *supra*, p. 29, applies in this context: see *infra*, p. 395. In *In re Staughton*, [1941] I.R. 166 (High Ct., 1940), English securities, the proceeds of the sale of Irish land, were treated as though they were Irish land; cf. infra, pp. 393-396.

[29] Cf. *infra*, pp. 625-626.

[30] *Infra*, pp. 195-197.

[31] High Ct., Barrington, J. 18 June 1985 (1984—8465P).

[32] *Infra*, pp. 211-212.

CHAPTER 4

THE "INCIDENTAL QUESTION"

We must now consider a problem[1] which has excited much academic analysis but which has yet to enter the mainstream of judicial thought.[2] This is the "incidental question", referred to generally in the continental literature as the "preliminary question" (*question préalable, vorfrage*).

For the classic case involving an incidental question, three elements must exist:

> "The law applying to the principal question must be a foreign law; a subsidiary issue must arise which is capable of arising in its own right and for which choice-of-law rules are available; the forum's choice-of-law rules must select a different system to settle the subsidiary issue than would the choice-of-law rules of the country chosen to apply to the main question."[3]

An example may make the problem clear. Under our law, the *lex domicilii* generally controls questions of succession to movables. Let us assume that the *lex domicilii* specifies that the testator's wife is to inherit a specified portion of his moveable estate. A woman who is regarded as his wife by the conflict rules of the *lex domicilii* relating to marital status but is not so regarded by the conflict rules of our marriage law claims this portion. The principal question is one of succession; the incidental question concerns the marital status of the claimant. Should the *lex domicilii's* conflict rules also answer that question (in which case, on the facts of the chosen example, the claimant would succeed)? Or should our own conflict rules determine the question of her status, as they unquestionably would if her status were raised as a principal question (in which case the claim would fail)? Or should no hard and fast rule be adopted?

---

[1] See Gotlieb, *The Incidental Question in Anglo-American Conflict of Laws*, 33 Can. Bar Rev. 523 (1955), Gotlieb, *The Incidental Question Revisited — Theory and Practice in the Conflict of Laws*, 26 Int. & Comp. L.Q. 734 (1977), *Robinson*, Ch. 6, Robertson, *The 'Preliminary Question' in the Conflict of Laws*, 55 L.Q. Rev. 565 (1939), Cormack, *Renvoi, Characterization, Localization and Preliminary Question in the Conflict of Laws*, 14 So. Calif. L. Rev. 221, at 243-249 (1941), Raape, *Les rapports juridiques entre parents et enfants*, [1934] - IV Recueil des cours 401, at 485-495, Maury, *Règles génerales des conflits de lois*, [1936] - III Recueil des cours 325, at 554-563, van Hoogstraten, *Le droit international privé néerlandais et la question préalable*, [1962] Nederlands Tijdschrift voor Internat. Recht 209, Lalive, *Tendances et Méthodes en droit international privé*, [1977] - II Recueil des cours l, at 280-299, Francescakis, *Les questions préalables de status personnel dans le droit de la nationalité*, 23 Rabels Zeitschrift 466 (1958), Lagarde, *La règle de conflit applicable aux questions préalables*, 49 Rev. Crit. de Droit Internat. Priv. 459 (1960), Bouckaert, *La question préalable en droit international privé*, 40 Rev. Jur. du Congo 245 (1964), Schmidt, *The Preliminary Question and the Question of Substitution in Conflict of Laws*, 12 Scandinavian Studies in Law 92 (1968).

[2] *Nygh*, 180, goes only slightly too far where he says that "judges have remained blissfully unaware of its existence."

[3] Gotlieb, *The Incidental Question Revisited — Theory and Practice in the Conflict of Laws*, 26 Int. & Comp. L.Q. 734, at 737 (1977); see also *Dicey & Morris*, 46. For consideration of other cases in which the incidental question can arise, see Gotlieb, *The Incidental Question in Anglo-American Conflict of Laws*, 33 Can. Bar Rev. 523, at 524-529 (1955).

Support for each of these possible approaches may be found among the legal scholars.[4]

The lex causae approach

In favour of the view that the law[5] governing the principal question (the *lex causae*) should also determine the incidental question, it is argued that this approach promotes international harmony in the conflict of laws.[6] One does not generally come across a problem of a person's legitimacy in the abstract; what tends to happen is that the legitimacy issue arises in a concrete context — the question of a person's entitlement to succeed to property, for example.[7] It has been argued that it makes more sense for the rules of the foreign law governing the question of succession to determine the legitimacy question than for the forum to apply its conflict rules concerning this question.[8] When the foreign law provides the concepts, "it is only reasonable to allow [it] to specify what is their content."[9] To take this course does not involve the difficulty of the *circulus inextricabilis* associated with *renvoi*[10] since that arises where a single question is being "bounced" between two countries, whereas here the court refers the succession question to the *lex causae* and then applies the rules of the *lex causae* on the entirely separate question of legitimacy.[11]

The approach favouring the conflict rules of the forum

Proponents of the view that the conflicts rules of the forum should determine both the principal and the incidental question argue that considerations of consistency,[12] simplicity and even public policy dictate that the forum should not concede to the *lex causae* the control over important matters such as marital status and legitimacy. The fact that these matters may present themselves to the court of the forum as "incidental" questions should not disguise their importance in relation to the social and legal policies of the forum.[13] As against this, our conflict rules can always make a distinction between status and its incidents.[14] This may moderate the impact of the *lex causae* so far as the forum's basic policies are concerned.

The Eclectic Approach

The third approach argues that "there are no overall general rules that are applicable to the incidental question".[15] The attraction of this approach is that it harmonises with actual judicial practice. Moreover, it seems plain that neither the *lex causae* nor the *lex fori* works successfully when applied inflexibly to all cases where an incidental question arises. In some cases, the forum's interests may be sufficiently strong to outweigh those of the *lex causae,* but not in all.

---

[4] Cf. Gotlieb, *The Incidental Question Revisited — Theory and Practice in the Conflict of Laws,* 26 Int. & Comp. L.Q. 734, at 757 (1977).

[5] Including its conflict rules.

[6] Robertson, *The 'Preliminary Question' in the Conflict of Laws,* 55 L.Q. Rev. 565, at 570 (1939).

[7] *Infra,* pp. 354-355.

[8] Cf. Lagarde, *supra,* at 470-471, *Anton,* 70-71. See also Gotlieb, 26 Int. & Comp. L.Q. at 758.

[9] Robertson, *supra,* at 570.

[10] Cf. pp. 35-38, *infra.*

[11] *Robertson, supra,* at 571-572, *Anton,* 68-69.

[12] Cf. *Wolff,* 209, Raape, *supra,* at 493-494, Maury, *supra,* at 560, Robertson, *supra,* at 570, Kegel, *The Crisis of Conflict of Laws,* [1964] - II Recueil des cours 93, at 231.

[13] Cf. van Hoogstraten, *Le droit international privé néerlandais et la question préalable,* [1962] Nederlands Tijdschrift voor Internat. Recht. 209, at 214-215. Falconbridge, *Renvoi, Characterization and Acquired Rights,* 17 Can. Bar Rev. 369, at 377 (1939).

[14] Cf. pp. 303-304, *infra.*

[15] Gotlieb, 26 Int. & Comp. L.Q., at 758.

JUDICIAL ANALYSIS OF THE ISSUE

The courts internationally have adopted differing strategies to the incidental question, often in apparent ignorance of the exact nature of the problem.

One of the more impressive discussions of the issue was provided by the Supreme Court of Canada in *Schwebel* v. *Ungar*[16] in 1963. A married couple, domiciled in Hungary and members of the Jewish religion, were divorced in Italy by Ghett. This divorce was invalid by both Hungarian and Italian Law. They later acquired a domicile in Israel, which recognised the divorce. The wife, while still domiciled in Israel, married again in Ontario. Her second husband subsequently sought an annulment on the basis that the wife's first marriage was still subsisting when she celebrated the second.

The principal question concerned the wife's capacity to marry the second time; the incidental question concerned the validity of the divorce. The Supreme Court of Canada, affirming the Ontario Court of Appeal, applied Israeli law in holding that the defendant had the capacity to remarry in Ontario. The divorce recognition rules of the country whose law governed the principal question were thus applied to the incidental question.

It is worth quoting from the judgment of McKay, J. in the Ontario Court of Appeal — which met with the enthusiastic endorsement of Ritchie, J.[17] on appeal to the Supreme Court of Canada:

"The decision in the present case turns on the marital status of the defendant at the time of her marriage to the plaintiff. To determine that status, I think our enquiry must be directed not to the effect to be given under Ontario law to the divorce proceedings in Italy as at the time of the divorce, but to the effect to be given to those proceedings by the law of the country in which she was domiciled at the time of her marriage to the plaintiff in 1957, namely, Israel, a domicile that she retained until her marriage to the plaintiff was actually performed, or, to put it another way, the enquiry is as to her status under the law of her domicile and not to the means by which she acquired that status. To hold otherwise would be to determine the personal status of a person not domiciled in Ontario by the law of Ontario instead of by the law of that person's country of domicile. This would be contrary to a basic principle of international law and would result in the social evil referred to by Lord Watson, in the *Le Mesurier*[18] case of a person being regarded as married in one jurisdiction and unmarried in another. If [the first husband] or the defendant, after arriving in Israel, had attempted to obtain a divorce, any such application would have been rejected on the ground that the marriage had already been dissolved. If, in any proceedings in the courts of Israel the defendant's status had been called into question, it would undoubtedly have been held that her status was that of a single person; if the defendant had married while in Israel, the marriage being valid according to the law of Israel should not be different because the marriage took place in Ontario."[19]

Schwebel v. *Ungar* has provoked much discussion, not all of it in favour on the approach it adopted. One commentator has observed that some lawyers "may well think that the Ontario court has ceased to be master in its own house if it is willing to throw to the winds its own private international law rules as to the recognition of foreign divorces and allow itself to be forced into making new rules owing to the exigencies of the domestic and conflict of law rules of Israel."[20] Certainly the

[16] [1965] S.C.R., 148, 48 D.L.R. (2d) 644, approved in *Padolecchia* v. *Padolecchia*, [1968] P. 314. *Schwebel* v. *Ungar* is noted by Lysk, 43 Can. Bar Rev. 363 (1965), Hartley, 4 Western L. Rev. 99 (1965) and Webb, 14 Int. & Comp. L.Q. 659 (1965).

[17] [1965] S.C.R., at 155, 48 D.L.R. (2d), at 649.

[18] [1895] A.C. 517.

[19] [1964] 1 O.R. 430, at 441 (C.A., 1963).

[20] Webb, *Note: Bigamy and Capacity to Marry*, 14 Int. & Comp. L.Q. 659, at 622 (1965).

decision created a problem of internal dissonance,[21] since the Ontario courts might in other contexts have to pronounce the first marriage still effective, as, for example, where the first husband acquired an Ontario domicile and married a woman domiciled there. In such a case where both the principal and incidental questions were a matter for Ontario law alone, it is difficult to see how the second marriage by the husband should not be annulled.[22]

Later[23] we will examine the effect of Article 41 of the Constitution in general and of Article 41.3.3° in particular on the right to remarry. It is at least arguable that the solution favoured in *Schwebel* v. *Ungar* would be excluded in some cases.

A problem which should be noted is that there may in some instances be uncertainty as to which is the principal, and which the incidental, question. For example, it can be argued that in *In re Interview Ltd*[24] in 1975 Kenny J. might more appropriately have considered assignment rather than contract as the principal question raised by the facts of the case.

---

[21] Cf. *Wolff*, 209.

[22] Cf. Lysk, *Comment*, 43 Can. Bar Rev. 363, at 378 (1965). If the husband's second marriage took place after the decision in *Schwebel* v. *Ungar* upholding the validity of his former wife's second marriage, strong policy considerations would be in favour of upholding the validity of his second marriage.

[23] *Infra*, pp. 236-240, 271-280.

[24] [1975] I.R. 382 (High Ct., Kenny, J.). See further *infra*, pp. 496-498.

CHAPTER 5

RENVOI

We must now consider the topic of *renvoi*,[1] "the *bête noire* of conflict of laws".[2] It has been described by *Rabel* as "the most famous dispute in conflicts law, a classical example of violently prejudicial literature confronting naïvely consistent practice".[3] Having suitably alarmed the reader, let us proceed to examine the doctrine.

Conflict of law rules select the law that is to apply to a problem before the court. But what is meant by the Irish court saying that "the law of France", for example, applies? One view is that the Irish court should apply the rules of French domestic law without regard to French conflicts of law.

To apply French domestic law has the advantage of being simple and clear — "a merit that becomes increasingly attractive as the other theories are considered".[4] It avoids deciding the same question twice over, and "can never involve more than one crossing of the frontier in search of the correct municipal law".[5] There is, moreover, much to be said for the view that when Irish law refers to a person's *lex domicilii* (in marriage, divorce or succession cases, for example), it intends that the internal law of the country of domicile should be applied on the basis that, by becoming domiciled in the country, the person has become integrated

---

[1] See generally I. Bate, *Notes on the Doctrine of Renvoi in Private International Law* (1904), T. Baty, *Polarized Law*, 115-120 (1914), Griswold, *Renvoi Revisited*, 51 Harv. L. Rev. 1165 (1938), Munro, *The Magic Roundabout of Conflict of Laws*, [1978] Jurid. Rev. 65, Forsyth, *Renvoi — Is There an Answer?*, 1 Natal U.L. Rev. 321 (1976), Welling & Hoffman, *"The Law of" in Choice of Law Rules: "Renvoi" Comme Nostalgie de la Boue*, 23 U.W. Ontario L. Rev. 79 (1985), Raeburn, *The "Open Offer" Formula and the Renvoi in Private International Law*, 24 Br. Yearbook of International L. 211 (1948), Bentwich, *The Development of the Doctrine of Renvoi in England in Cases of Succession*, 4 Zeitschrift für Auslandisches und Int. Privatrecht 433 (1930), Morris, *The Law of the Domicil*, 18 Br. Yearbook of International L. 32 (1937), Falconbridge, *Renvoi, Characterization and Acquired Rights*, 17 Can. Bar Rev. 369 (1939), Falconbridge, *Renvoi and the Law of the Domicile*, 19 Can. Bar Rev. 311 (1941), Falconbridge, *Renvoi in New York and Elsewhere*, 6 Vanderbilt L. Rev. 708 (1953), Bentwich, *Recent Application of the Renvoi in Matters of Personal Status*, 14 Can. Bar Rev. 379 (1936), Falconbridge, *Renvoi and Succession to Movables*, 46 L. Q. Rev. 465 (1930), 47 L.Q. Rev. 271 (1931), Cowan, *Renvoi Does Not Involve a Logical Fallacy*, 87 U. Pa. L. Rev. 34 (1938), Cormack, *Renvoi, Characterization, Localization and Preliminary Question in the Conflict of Laws*, 14 So. Calif. L. Rev. 221 (1941), Lorenzen, *The Renvoi Theory and the Application of Foreign Law*, 10 Colum. L. Rev. 190, 327 (1910), Schreiber, *The Doctrine of the Renvoi in Anglo-American Law*, 31 Harv. L. Rev. 523 (1918), Allemès, *The Problem of Renvoi in Private International Law*, 12 Grotius Society Transactions 63 (1927), Abbot, *Is the Renvoi a Part of the Common Law?*, 24 L. Q. Rev. 133 (1908), Pollock, *The 'Renvoi' in New York*, 36 L. Q. Rev. 91 (1920), Sewell, *Observations on Renvoi in the Case of the Movable Succession of British Subjects Dying Intestate in France*, 27 Int. Law Assn. 334 (1912), Brown, *In re Johnson*, 25 L.Q. Rev. 145 (1909), Morris, *Renvoi*, 64 L.Q. Rev. 264 (1948), Mann, *Note: Succession to Immovables Abroad*, 11 Modern L. Rev. 232 (1948), Pagenstecher, *Renvoi in the United States: A Proposal*, 29 Tulane L. Rev. 379 (1955), Weintraub, *Conflicting Choice-of-Law Rules*, 43 Iowa L. Rev. 519 (1958).

[2] Munro, *The Magic Roundabout of Conflict of Laws*, [1978] Jurid. Rev. 65, at 65.

[3] Rabel, vol. 1, 75-76.

[4] Forsyth, *Renvoi — Is There an Answer?*, 1 Natal U. L. Rev. 321, at 323 (1976).

[5] Morris, *The Law of the Domicil*, 18 Br. Yrbk. of Internat. L. 32, at 33 (1937). See also *Baty*, 116.

into its internal social and legal framework. To apply the private international law rules of the country would defeat the purpose and lead to arbitrary and certainly unintended results in some cases.

A drawback to this approach, however, is that it does not lead to uniform decisions, since the outcome of a case depends on which country hears the proceedings. Moreover, if the foreign internal law is applied, the result may be that the Irish court will have regard to a law which the foreign court would reject as completely inapplicable.

The second approach, sometimes known as the doctrine of "partial *renvoi*", requires the Irish court, when interpreting the law of France, to be guided by the choice of law rule of French private international law where the choice of law rule refers such a case either to Irish law (*remission*) or to the law of a third country (*transmission*).[6] On this approach, the Irish court would apply the internal law of Ireland, or of the third country, as the case may be. This approach "can never involve more than two crossings of the frontier. Logically the reference back to the law of the nationality from the *lex domicilii* must be to its municipal laws, and not to its private international law with a consequent further reference back, for the excellent reason that part of its law has spent itself in the first reference."[7]

The second approach has a number of disadvantages. There is something arbitrary[8] about recognising *two* references to other legal systems, although "the cynic might point out ... that it means that in all remission cases the *lex fori* will be applied."[9] Moreover, the second approach shares with the first the problem of lack of uniformity of decisions between different countries.[10]

This approach finds little support among Irish decisions and decisions in common law jurisdictions elsewhere.[11] It did, however, commend itself to Kenny, J., in *In re Interview Ltd.*,[12] a decision analysed later in the chapter.[13]

The third approach also requires the Irish court to refer to the relevant foreign law, but if that foreign law proceeds on a different basis than Irish law, as, for example, by referring to the *lex patriae* rather than the *lex domicilii,* the Irish court should apply Irish internal law in default.[14] This theory, sometimes referred to as the *desistement* theory, was supported by Westlake.[15]

Under the fourth approach,[16] if an Irish court is referred by our conflict of law rules to the law of (let us say) France, the Irish court should find out, and apply, the law that a French court would apply to the case in question. If a French court would apply French internal law, then the Irish court should also apply French internal law. If a French court would apply Irish internal law, then so should the Irish. If the French court were to apply the internal law of a third country, then again the Irish should follow suit. This "will involve as many as three crossings of the frontier..."[17]

---

[6] Cf. Griswold, *Renvoi Revisited,* 51 Harv. L. Rev. 1165, at 1169-1170 (1938).

[7] Morris, *The Law of the Domicil,* 18 Br. Yrbk. of Internat. L. 32, at 34 (1937).

[8] Pace Cowan, *Renvoi Does Not Involve a Logical Fallacy,* 87 U. Pa. L. Rev. 34 (1938), who argues that this approach is necessary to avoid a vicious circle. Cf. Cheatham, *Problems and Methods in Conflict of Laws,* [1960] - I Recueil des cours 233, at 338, Griswold, *Renvoi Revisited,* 51 Harv. L. Rev. 1165, at 1177 (1938).

[9] Forsyth, *supra,* at 324.

[10] *Id.*

[11] Cf. *id.*

[12] [1975] I.R. 382 (High Ct., Kenny, J.).

[13] *Infra,* p. 44.

[14] Cf. Griswold, *Renvoi Revisited,* 51 Harv. L. Rev. 1165, at 1168 (1938).

[15] *Westlake,* 29-33.

[16] See Griswold, *Renvoi Revisited,* 51 Harv. L. Rev. 1165, at 1168 (1938).

[17] Morris, *The Law of the Domicil,* 18 Br. Yrbk. of Internat. L. 32, at 34 (1937).

The advantage frequently attributed to this approach is that it encourages "a high degree of uniformity of decision, which the other solutions lack."[18]

The disadvantages are, first, that if the foreign court also adopts the same approach the vicious circle will be restored. As Lorenzen observes, it is difficult to "approve a doctrine which is workable only if the other country rejects it".[19] Secondly, it has been pointed out that, since *renvoi* is an area of uncertainty in many legal systems, "it is thus often difficult to determine what the attitude of a foreign legal system to *renvoi* is".[20] Whatever problems this may cause a court,[21] "how much more difficult is it for a solicitor or counsel to advise a client in ignorance of the expert evidence that may have been collected on the other side?"[22] Thirdly this approach may damage national pride in that it involves a high degree of deference to the conflicts rules of the foreign country.[23]

Where the doctrine is recognised in both there is the prospect of an infinite regress, an international game of lawn tennis,[24] or "hall of mirrors",[25] which can be broken only arbitrarily. As against this the fact that the critics who make this point admit of its operation in exceptional cases "suggests that the objection is of a practical rather than a logical kind".[26] If practical convenience is to be the ruling criterion, the court need have no fear of an infinite regress, since the court, rather than the rule, will be the master.[27]

A particular difficulty with the "foreign court" approach, as we shall see, is that it forces Irish law to interpret the *lex patriae* where the foreign court would apply the *lex patriae* of a national of a country with several law districts, such as Britain, for example. There is no "British" law, only English law, Scottish law, and so on. A wide variety of solutions has been suggested, many of them rather crude and none without distinctive problems. Westlake[28] suggested that the *lex domicilii* should be applied on the basis that there simply is no other possible alternative; but, as Morris points out, if this is so, Westlake "stultifies his own theory of *renvoi*, since in the majority of cases the only remission would be from the foreign law to itself".[29]

Another solution would be to look to the dominant country within the group of

---

[18] Forsyth, *Renvoi — Is There an Answer?*, 1 Natal U.L. Rev. 321, at 326 (1976). It would be wrong to place too much emphasis on this factor, which may not exist in some cases: cf. Lorenzen, *The Renvoi Theory and the Application of Foreign Law — I*, 10 Colum L. Rev. 190, at 205-206 (1910), Morris, *The Law of the Domicil*, 18 Br. Yrbk. of Internat. L. 32, at 38-39 (1937).

[19] Lorenzen, *The Qualification, Classification, or Characterization Problem in the Conflict of Laws*, 50 Yale L.J. 743, at 753 (1941). See also Schreiber, *The Doctrine of the Renvoi in Anglo-American Law*, 31 Harv. L. Rev. 523, at 534 (1918), Weintraub, *Conflicting Choice-of-Law Rules*, 43 Iowa L. Rev. 519, at 524 (1958).

[20] Forsyth, *Renvoi — Is there an Answer?* 1 Natal U.L. Rev. 321, at 325 (1976). Cf. *Re Duke of Wellington*, [1947] Ch. 506, at 515 (Wynn-Parry, J.):

"It would be difficult to imagine a harder task than that which now faces me, namely, of expounding for the first time either in this country or in Spain the relevant law of Spain, as it would be expounded by the Supreme Court of Spain, which up to the present has made no pronouncement on the subject, and having to base this exposition on evidence that satisfied me that on this subject there exists a profound cleavage of legal opinion in Spain and two conflicting decisions of two courts of inferior jurisdiction."

[21] Cf. Falconbridge, *Renvoi and the Law of the Domicile*, 19 Can. Bar Rev. 311, at 316-317 (1941).

[22] Morris, *The Law of the Domicil*, 18 Br. Yrbk. of Internat. L. 32, at 35 (1937).

[23] Cf. Pagenstecher, *Renvoi in the United States: A Proposal*, 29 Tulane L. Rev. 379, at 387 (1955), Morris, *The Law of the Domicil*, 18 Br. Yrbk. of Internat. L. 32, at 36 (1937).

[24] Cf. Lorenzen, *The Renvoi Theory and the Application of Foreign Law — I*, 10 Colum. L. Rev. 190, at 198, fn. 33 (1910), quoting Buzzati.

[25] *Anton*, 60.

[26] *Id.*

[27] *Id.*, 61.

[28] *Westlake*, 27. *Baty*, 119, is in substantial accord.

[29] Morris, *The Law of the Domicil*, 18 Br. Yrbk. of Internat. L. 32, at 36, fn. 2 (1937).

law districts. But apart from its questionably imperialist assumptions, it would involve quite inappropriate attributions in many instances.[30] A third solution, which has some support in English cases but not among the commentators, is to have resort to the domicile of origin of the person in question. But in cases where that domicile has long since ceased to apply,[31] the result is difficult to defend. There is, moreover, a special problem where the person's domicile of origin is outside any of the law districts of which he or she is a national.[32]

It is interesting, though perhaps dangerous, to speculate as to why *renvoi* has not presented itself more frequently to the Irish courts. The *renvoi* problem normally has arisen where a person is domiciled in a country whose choice of law rules provide that nationality should govern the personal law, and the person's national law provides that the law of the domicile should govern the personal law. This situation could, of course, happen where an Irish person becomes domiciled in any of the countries in Europe where nationality is the test of the personal law. But for the past couple of centuries the trend has been for Irish people to emigrate and become domiciled in countries which also are governed by domicile — Britain, the United States, the Canadian provinces, the Australian states, New Zealand, South Africa[33] and Argentina, for example. This has minimised the potential effect of *renvoi* on our law. With the increasing movement by Irish people to Europe, sometimes on a long-term basis, we may expect the issue to gain greater practical relevance in the future.

RENVOI AS PART OF THE COMMON LAW

We must now consider the extent to which the *renvoi* doctrine has become part of the common law.[34] In England, *De Bonneval* v. *De Bonneval*[35] in 1838, has been tentatively identified[36] as the first case in which the doctrine was implicitly recognised. The case concerned the question of the formal validity of a will made in France, the country of the testator's domicile at the time of his death. Sir Herbert Jenner suspended proceedings in England on the will until its validity or invalidity had been pronounced by the French Courts, which were "the competent authority" to decide the issue. He did not make it clear whether he meant French internal law or conflict of law rules: "[o]nly on the assumption that [he] meant to say the latter can the case be made to support the *renvoi*".[37]

In *Collier* v. *Rivaz*,[38] three years later, a British subject of Irish domicile of origin, but of English domicile of choice, died domiciled in the English, but not the Belgian sense, in Belgium. He left a will and six codicils, four of which were not executed according to the forms required by Belgian law, though they complied with English requirements. The English court — again Sir Herbert Jenner — upheld the validity of all instruments. The will and two codicils executed in accordance with Belgian law were admitted to probate without dispute. The four other codicils were also upheld. Sir Herbert Jenner was of the view that:

> "[e]very nation has a right to say how far the general law shall apply to its own born
> subjects and the subject of another country; and the Court, sitting here to determine

---

[30] *Id.*, at 36.
[31] As in *Re O'Keefe (Deceased); Poingdestre* v. *Sherman*, [1940] Ch. 124, considered *infra*, p. 42.
[32] Cf. Morris, *The Law of the Domicil*, 18 Br. Yrbk. of Internat. L. 32, at 36-37 (1937).
[33] Cf. Forsyth, *supra*, at 327.
[34] See *Morris*, 471-474, *Bate*, ch. 2, Schreiber, *The Doctrine of the Renvoi in Anglo-American Law*, 31 Harv. L. Rev. 523, at 537-571 (1918), Lorenzen, *The Renvoi Theory and the Application of Foreign Law-II*, 10 Colum. L. Rev. 327, at 332-344 (1910).
[35] 1 Curt. Ecc. 856, 163 E.R. 296 (1838).
[36] Schreiber, *supra*, at 537-539.
[37] *Id.*, at 538. In fact the French Court did apply the French conflict-of-law rule to sustain the will: Cf. *id.*
[38] 2 Curt. Ecc. 855, 163 E.R. 608 (1841).

it, must consider itself sitting in Belgium under the particular circumstances of the case."[39]

The judgment has been widely criticised for its failure to address the possibility that the Belgian court might have accepted the *renvoi* from English law and applied Belgian internal law.[40]

In spite of the absence of "an iota of evidence"[41] on the question whether *renvoi* was part of Belgian law, *Collier* v. *Rivaz* can best be understood as a decision, however deficient, supporting the total *renvoi* theory.[42]

In *Frere* v. *Frere*,[43] in 1847, a will formally invalid according to the internal law of Malta, the country of the testator's nationality and domicile, but valid under English internal law, was upheld by Sir Herbert Jenner Fust (as he had become) on the basis that a Maltese court would uphold the validity of a will made "according to the law of the country where it was executed". There was no argument as to the application of the foreign law theory, which was accepted as correct and duly applied. The question of Maltese law's attitude to the *renvoi* doctrine was not investigated.

In *Bremer* v. *Freeman*[44] in 1857, the Privy Council first addressed the issue. It disapproved of *Collier* v. *Rivaz,* and declined to admit to probate in England a will of a British testatrix who had died domiciled in France, according to the English notion of domicile, but in England according to the French notion, since she had not obtained from the French government authorisation to establish such domicile as would carry with it the full enjoyment of all civil rights.[45]

Although the rejection of *Collier* v. *Rivaz* was expressed quite clearly, the reasoning in *Bremer* v. *Freeman* is so intricate[46] and so ambiguous[47] that "it has been claimed as an authority both for and against the [*renvoi*] doctrine, and few modern lawyers have the patience to unravel its intricacies"[48] The result of the decision in *Bremer* v. *Freeman* was so unsatisfactory that it led to the passing of Lord Kingdown's Act in 1861.[49] That Act enabled British[50] testators disposing of

---

[39] 2 Curt. Ecc., at 858-859, 163 E.R., at 609. See also 2 Curt. Ecc., at 863, 163 E.R., at 611: "The Court sitting here decides from the evidence of persons skilled in [Belgian] law, and decides as it would if sitting in Belgium".

[40] *Morris,* 471, Falconbridge, *Renvoi and Succession to Movables — I,* 46 L.Q. Rev. 464, at 479 (1930). Schreiber, *supra,* at 541, criticises the decision for its inconsistency in holding that the will and two codicils complying with Belgian law should be upheld as well as the four codicils complying with English, but not Belgian internal law. The *favor testamenti* principle may, however, be invoked to justify a rule of alternative reference to test the formal, as opposed to essential, validity of wills. As *Morris,* 471-472, states:

> "In ... cases [of essential validity] the court must choose between the domestic rules and the conflict rules of the foreign law. It cannot apply both, for it must decide whether or not the testator had disposing power, whether or not he died intestate, and if so who are his next-of-kin. It is one thing to uphold a will if it complies with the formalities prescribed by either the domestic rules or the conflict rules of the foreign law. It is quite another thing to allow the next-of-kin entitled under the domestic rules of the foreign law to share the property with the next-of-kin entitled under its conflict rules."

[41] Schreiber, *supra,* at 541.

[42] Lorenzen, *The Renvoi Theory and the Application of Foreign Law — II,* 10 Colum. L. Rev. 327, at 333 (1910). Cf. Schreiber, *supra,* at 541.

[43] 5 Notes of Cases 593 (1847).

[44] 10 Moo. P.C. 306, 14 E.R. 508 (1857).

[45] Article 13 of the *Civil Code* provided that "[t]he foreigner who shall have been admitted by the government to establish his domicile in France shall enjoy there all civil rights as long as he continues to reside there".

[46] Falconbridge, *Renvoi and Succession to Movables — I,* 46 L.Q. Rev. 465, at 480 (1930).

[47] *Dicey & Morris,* 68.

[48] *Id.*

[49] *Falconbridge, supra,* at 481. For consideration of the provisions of the Act, see *infra,* p. 432.

[50] And Irish testators: the Act applied to Ireland which was then part of a political unit with Britain.

personal estate to choose between the forms prescribed by four different systems of law.[51]

In re Johnson; Roberts v. *A.G.*,[52] in 1903, was the first case in which the term *renvoi* was used by an English court.[53] In this case, the testatrix, a British national with a Maltese domicile of origin, died in Baden, where she had acquired a domicile of choice. A question arose as to whether certain movables not disposed of by her will should be distributed according to Baden law or some other law.

Farwell, J. came to the conclusion that Maltese law should be applied as the testatrix's national law. He held that, in view of Baden law's reference to nationality rather than domicile as the criterion for succession to property, there had been no *de facto* change of domicile from Malta to Baden and that the case was accordingly remitted to him as one where the *propositus* had intended, but had failed, to obtain an effectual domicile of choice:

> "No change is effectual unless the *factum* is proved, and the *factum* cannot exist in a country where the law refuses to recognize it. The result is that this Court must conclude that a domicile of choice, ineffectual to create any rights and liabilities governing the distribution of movables in the country supposed to have been chosen, is for this purpose no domicile at all, and that the *propositus,* therefore, is left with his domicile of origin unaffected. The Baden Courts would in effect have disavowed him and disclaimed jurisdiction."[54]

This approach has been widely criticised. The Baden courts would not in fact have declined to exercise jurisdiction over the moveable property of the testatrix in Baden, though it may be doubted whether they would have applied the *lex domicilii*.[55] Moreover the notion that the acquisition of a domicile of choice could be indefinitely postponed until some foreign law recognised it "does violence to language ... "[56]

Farwell, J.'s alternative line of reasoning for holding in favour of Maltese law also proved controversial. Since the Baden courts referred to the *lex patriae* of the *propositus*, this presented difficulty in relation to Britain, which comprised several different systems of law. Farwell, J. considered that the rules of English law as to domicile should be applied:

> "Foreign States are in diplomatic relation with this country as representing the whole Empire. They know nothing officially of Scotland or Canada, or the Colonies, still less, perhaps, of the Channel Islands or the Isle of Man ... The only possible solution appears to me to be that foreign courts must necessarily refer such questions as these to, and decide them according to, the law of the country with which alone they are in diplomatic relation; and inasmuch as the law of England distributes such movables in accordance with domicile of origin substantial justice is done to all His Majesty's subjects ... I conclude, therefore, that distribution according to the law of the nationality means according to English law, but according to that law as applicable to the particular *propositus,* and not to Englishmen generally without regard to their domicile of origin."[57]

Critics of this approach have pointed out[58] that it is not the case that "the law of England distributes such movables in accordance with domicile of origin".

[51] *Morris,* 472.
[52] [1903] 1 Ch. 821, analysed by Brown, *In re Johnson,* 25 L.Q. Rev. 145 (1909).
[53] Bentwich, *The Development of the Doctrine of Renvoi in England in Cases of Succession,* 4 Zeitschrift für Ausändisches und Int. Privatrecht 433, at 437 (1930).
[54] [1903] 1 Ch., at 828.
[55] Morris, *The Law of the Domicil,* 18 Br. Yrbk of International L. 32, at 46, fn. 4 (1937).
[56] Schreiber, *The Doctrine of the Renvoi in Anglo-American Law,* 31 Harv. L. Rev. 523, at 555 (1918).
[57] [1903] 1 Ch., at 832-835.
[58] Schreiber, *supra,* at 556.

Moreover, although on the facts of *Re Johnson* the first and alternative approaches yielded the same answer, this would not always be the case.[59] *Re Johnson* therefore does not represent a satisfactory model of how the *renvoi* issue should be resolved.[60]

In *Re Annesley, Davidson* v. *Annesley,*[61] in 1926, the issue concerned the validity of testamentary dispositions made by an Englishwoman long resident in France. She was domiciled in France, according to English law, but not according to French law, since she had not taken the steps prescribed by Article 13 of the French Civil Code to apply for Governmental authorisation to acquire a French domicile.

Having decided that the domicile of the testatrix at the time of her death was French, Russell, J. said:

> "French law accordingly applies, but the question remains: what French law? According to French municipal law, the law applicable in the case of a foreigner not legally domiciled in France is the law of that person's nationality, in this case British. But the law of that nationality refers the question back to French law, the law of the domicile; and the question arises, will the French law accept this reference back, or *renvoi*, and apply French municipal law?"[63]

After considering the evidence of experts in French law, Russell, J. came to the conclusion that he:

> "ought to accept the view that according to French law the French courts, in administering the movable property of a deceased foreigner who, according to the law of his country, is domiciled in France, and whose property must, according to that law, be applied in accordance with the law of the country in which he was domiciled, will apply French municipal law, and that even though the deceased had not complied with art. 13 of the Code."[64]

Critics of *Re Annesley* have pointed out that French private international law referred the material validity of the will to English law, not because English law was the law of the testatrix's *nationality* (as Russell, J. said) but because it was the law of her domicile, according to principles of French law.[65] Russell, J. was thus guilty of having "fallen into the logical error of setting up for reconsideration that French view of the testatrix's domicile which he had already decided was irrelevant".[66] Having found that the testatrix was domiciled in France according to English rules of private international law, Russell, J. should simply have applied the internal rules of French succession law without launching out on a further international journey.[67]

---

[59] Morris, *The Law of the Domicil*, 18 Br. Yrbk of Internat. L. 32, at 47 (1937). A minority view is perhaps worth recording. Dr J.T.B. Sewell, in a review of *Re Johnson (Observations on Renvoi in the Case of the Movable Succession of British Subjects Dying Intestate in France)*, 27 Int'l Law Assn. 334, at 342 (1912)) said:
> "For my part, ... I fully believe if a vote could be taken of English persons domiciled abroad they would prefer the English law of the domicile of origin to be applied."

[60] *Re Johnson* was followed in *In re Bowes; Bates* v. *Wengel*, 22 Times L.R. 711 (Chy. Div., Swinfen Eady, J., 1906). *In re Bowes* was seriously criticised by Russell, J. in *In re Annesley, Davidson* v. *Annesley*, [1926] Ch. 692. Having read the shorthand notes of *In re Bowes*, Russell, J. had "no hesitation in saying that the case should never have been reported. The point was neither discussed nor argued; nothing was cited of *In re Johnson* except the headnote": [1926] Ch., at 706.

[61] [1926] Ch. 692.

[63] *Id.*, at 706-707.

[64] *Id.*, at 708.

[65] Morris, *The Law of the Domicil*, 18 Br. Yrbk of Internat. L. 32, at 40 (1937).

[66] *Id.* Cf. Falconbridge, *Renvoi and Succession to Movables — I*, 46 L.Q. Rev. 465, at 478-479 (1930).

[67] Cf. *Cheshire & North*, 70. In fairness to Russell, J. it should be pointed out that he was aware of this "much more direct route" to the same conclusion as that which he had reached, and he noted that "this simple solution" had been adopted seven years earlier by the Surrogate Court of New York in *In re Tallmadge, Re Chadwick's Will*, 181 N.Y. Supp. 336 (1919): [1926] Ch., at 709.

In *Re Ross*,[68] another succession case, the testatrix had been domiciled in Italy (in both the English and the Italian sense) for many years before her death. A question arose as to whether her son, whom she had excluded from her will, was entitled to his *legitim portio*[69] under Italian law, the *lex domicilii,* so far as movables were concerned and the *lex situs,* so far as the immovables were concerned. Luxmoore, J., applying the "foreign court" approach, found that the Italian court would have referred to the *lex patriae* and would have rejected the remission to it from English law; accordingly English internal law was applied. The result of the case was that the testatrix "was allowed to evade one of the cardinal rules of the legal system, the protection of which she had enjoyed for the last fifty-one years of her life".[70]

In *Re O'Keefe (Deceased); Poingdestre v. Sherman,*[71] a question arose as to which law should determine the distribution of the estate of one Mary Alice O'Keefe, an unmarried woman, who died intestate in 1937, domiciled in Italy. Her father had been born in Ennis, Co. Clare, in 1835. Around 1857 he went to India and there in 1858 he married a woman of Irish parentage. Mary Alice was born in 1860.

In 1867, Mary Alice and her sister were brought to Europe. Mary Alice settled in Naples, where she remained until her death forty-seven years later. In 1878, she had visited Ireland with her father for a period of about three weeks. Her nationality was at all times British.

Crossman, J. noted that, under Italian law, intestate succession was regulated by the national law of the deceased. Italian lawyers, he found,[72] could not say what was the meaning of the law of the nationality where there was more than one system of law of the nationality, but he had undisputed evidence from experts in Italian law that the Italian law would hold that the succession was "regulated by the law of the country to which the intestate belonged, and belonged I think at the time of her death".[73]

The judge noted that Mary Alice O'Keefe "could not in the circumstances have been a citizen of Éire, at her death".[74] Nevertheless, he said,

"looking at the whole of the facts and considering the evidence of the Italian lawyers ..., as to which I think there is no real doubt, I have come to the conclusion that the only part of the British Empire to which the intestate can be said to have belonged in the circumstances is the part from which she originated; and finding, as I have found, that her domicil of origin was Southern Ireland, I hold that the law now applicable to the distribution of her estate is the law of Eire applicable to a person dying intestate domiciled in Éire."[75]

It is very easy to criticise the *O'Keefe* decision. The inappropriateness of the result has occasioned much comment.[76] It is a fiction, rarely consistent with a person's true intent, to equate nationality with the domicile of origin.[77]

---

[68] [1930] 1 Ch. 377 (Luxmoore, J., 1929).

[69] A somewhat more potent equivalent of a child's entitlement under section 117 of our Succession Act 1965.

[70] *Cheshire & North*, 70-71.

[71] [1940] Ch. 124 (Crossman, J., 1939), analysed by Falconbridge, *Renvoi and the Law of the Domicile,* 19 Can. Bar Rev. 311 (1941).

[72] [1940] Ch., at 129.

[73] *Id.*

[74] *Id.* Cf. Art. 3 of the First Schedule to the Irish Free State Constitution Act 1922.

[75] [1940] Ch., at 130.

[76] See, e.g. *Cheshire & North,* 67:

"In the result ... the succession to [Ms O'Keefe's] property was governed by the law of a country which she had never entered except during one short visit some sixty years before her death; which was not even a separate political unit until sixty-two years after her birth; of whose succession laws she was no doubt profoundly and happily ignorant; and under the law of which it was impossible in the circumstances for her to claim citizenship."

[77] Cf. *Castel,* vol. 1, 46.

In *Re Adams Deceased; Bank of Ireland Trustee Co.* v. *Adams,*[78] in 1967, a testator died domiciled (according to Irish law) in France. It was contended by the second defendant that, in accordance with modern decisions, the estate ought to be administered in accordance with the law of the testator's nationality, which was Irish. As Budd, J. noted:

> "She stated in layman's language that this was because the doctrine of *renvoi* applied, and she cited and quoted from the following cases in particular as supporting her proposition:- *In re Johnson, Roberts* v. *Attorney General;*[79] *In re Ross, Ross* v. *Waterfield;*[80] *Re O'Keefe, Poingdestre* v. *Sherman.*[81] "[82]

Budd, J.'s analysis of the issue of *renvoi* makes it clear that he was of the view that the doctrine had utility. He discussed without criticism the English decisions just cited, and he sought to distinguish them rather than to challenge their adequacy. Thus, *In re Johnson, Roberts* v. *Attorney General*[83] was "clearly distinguishable"[84] on the "fundamental point"[85] that French law (in contrast to the law of Baden) "recognise[d] the law of the domicil"[83] of a deceased person as governing the succession to movables. To this it may be replied that, although it is unquestionably true that French law — unlike the law of Baden — had no regard for nationality, its recognition of "the law of the domicil" of a deceased person was of a *different* law of domicil than that of Irish law. In other words, French and Irish law were not the same on the connecting factor, though they used the same name ("domicile") to describe their respective connecting factors and the result, so far as the application of their differing connecting factors was concerned, would (probably) be identical.

Budd, J. went on to distinguish *In re Ross, Ross* v. *Waterfield,*[87] again on the basis that no question of reference to the nationality of the *propositus* arose, the French Courts "not tak[ing] the same view as the Italian courts and accept[ing] the law of domicil".[88] Similarly, *In re O'Keefe, Poingdestre* v. *Sherman,*[89] was "clearly distinguishable"[90] from the case before him "by reason of the laws of France accepting the law of domicil as governing the succession to movables".[91] Again, this statement may be challenged. True, French law rejected any reference in this context to the *lex patriae,* but *Re Adams Deceased* was not a case of the law of France "*accepting* the law of domicil"[92] as governing the question of succession to movables. On the contrary, French law, far from "accepting" the law of the domicile, in the sense of receiving any aspect of the content of another country's conflicts rules, instead *prescribed its own conflicts rules.* These included a concept — *domicile* — which happened to share the same word but did not share the same substantive content as the word "domicile" in Irish conflicts of law. There was no question therefore, of French law "accepting" anything from another system of law, but rather there was merely a coincidence of words and of outcome in the application of two different principles.

[78] [1967] I.R. 424 (High Ct., Budd, J.).
[79] [1903] 1 Ch. 821.
[80] [1930] 1 Ch. 377.
[81] [1940] Ch. 124.
[82] [1967] I.R. at 455.
[83] [1903] 1 Ch. 821.
[84] [1967] I.R., at 455.
[85] *Id.*
[86] *Id.,* at 455-456.
[87] [1930] 1 Ch. 377.
[88] [1967] I.R., at 456.
[89] [1940] Ch. 184.
[90] [1967] I.R., at 456.
[91] *Id.*
[92] Emphasis added.

Budd, J. went on to discuss *In re Annesley, Davidson* v. *Annesley.*[93] He noted the change in French law since that decision, whereby a foreigner could become domiciled in France, according to French law, without the legal formalities which prevailed at the time *Annesley* was decided. Budd, J. stated:

"This decision [in *Annesley*] that French municipal law is to be applied in the administration of the estate of a foreigner dying domiciled in France according to English law, even though that person is not so legally domiciled in France according to French law, applies *a fortiori* since the position is now that legal formalities are not required for the acquisition of domicil in France. Since there is now no law in France requiring formalities of a strictly legal nature to be complied with before a person can become legally domiciled in France, the difficulty that arose in the *Annesley Case* does not arise in this case at all. The position in this case is that, according to English and Irish law, on which there is no difference on this point, the law of the place of a deceased person's domicil governs the succession to his movables and therefore the material validity of his will. According to the expert opinions on French law before me the position under French law is the same. Therefore no conflict of laws would appear to arise. Following the decisions in *Whicker* v. *Hume*[94] and in *In re Annesley, Davidson* v. *Annesley,*[95] my view is that the material validity of the will is to be determined in accordance with the law of his domicil, and that is the law of France. Accordingly, as the testator died domiciled in France, his property must be administered according to the laws of that country."[96]

It appears that Budd, J., mistakenly concluded from the fact that French law no longer requires compliance with formalities to have a *domicile,* that this meant that "no conflict of laws would appear to arise". In fact there was a conflicts problem, which, in "[f]ollowing" *Annesley*, Budd, J. himself recognised and resolved. In summary, Budd, J. himself first established the relevant Irish conflicts rule, namely that succession to movables should be determined by the law of the domicile. The "law of the domicile" here was to be determined by *Irish*, not French, legal criteria. According to Irish legal criteria, France was found to be the law of the domicile. Budd, J. then went on to consider what French law had to say on the issue. He found that French law — that is, French *conflicts of law* — would also apply French law as the law of the testator's *domicile,* in the French sense. Budd, J.'s holding that French law should apply can thus be interpreted as an application of the partial *renvoi* principle. Alternatively, it may be argued that Budd, J.'s resolution of the case amounted to an enlightened, though largely intuitive, application of the "false conflicts" approach advocated by Currie and Cavers in the United States.[97]

In *In re Interview Ltd.,*[98] Kenny, J. was faced with a complicated conflicts issue regarding title to goods sold to an Irish company by a German company subject to a reservation of title clause. Kenny, J. appears to have regarded the question as one initially to be determined by German law as the proper law of the contract. His reliance on German conflict rules as to the transfer of chattels appears to follow from this reference to German law. Guided by the German conflict rules, Kenny, J. applied Irish law, as the *lex situs*. While this application may be defended on conventional *Irish* conflict rules as to the transfer of chattels, it appears to have been selected on the basis of a "total law" approach, in which German law, as the *lex causae* in contract, was given an unusually potent role in respect of the separate issue concerning the transfer of chattels.

[93] [1926] Ch. 692.
[94] 7 H.L. Cas. 124, 11 E.R. 50 (1858).
[95] [1926] Ch. 629.
[96] [1967] I.R., at 457.
[97] Cf. *supra*, pp. 16-21.
[98] [1975] I.R. 382 (High Ct., Kenny, J.). The case is discussed in detail *infra*, pp. 496-498. See also *Kruppstahl AG* v. *Quitmann Products Ltd.*, [1982] I.L.R.M. 551 (High Ct., Gannon, J.).

CHAPTER 6

DOMICILE AND OTHER CONNECTING FACTORS

In this chapter we will examine some of the principal "connecting factors" in the conflict of laws. Domicile has had a pre-eminent position in our legal system, but in several other jurisdictions nationality has for long been dominant. More recently, habitual residence has gained support internationally. It has much to recommend it, in some, though not all, contexts, as a satisfactory compromise between domicile and nationality.

DOMICILE[1]

The concept of domicile is of central significance in the conflict of laws. It affects questions relating to civil status (such as marriage, matrimonial causes and legitimacy) and property, including succession and taxation. It is a "connecting factor" or link between a person and the legal system or rules which will apply to him in specific contexts.

The central notion embraced by domicile is that of a long-term relationship between person and place: thus one may be said to be domiciled in the country where one intends to live permanently or indefinitely.[2] The idea at the base of this approach

---

[1] See generally *Dicey & Morris*, ch. 7, *Cheshire & North*, ch. 7, *Wolff*, ch. 9, Nygh, *The Reception of Domicil into English Private International Law*, 1 Tasmanian U.L. Rev. 555 (1961), Hickey, *Irish Private International Law*, 42 Rabels Zeitschrift 268, at 275-279 (1978), Tarnopolsky, *The Draft Domicile Act — Reform or Confusion?*, 29 Sask. Bar Rev. 161 (1964), de Winter, *Nationality or Domicile? The Present State of Affairs*, [1969] III Recueil des cours 247, esp. at 400-423, Baty, *The Interconnection of Nationality and Domicile*, 13 Ill. L. Rev. 363 (1919), Cowan & da Costa, *The Unity of Domicile*, 78 L.Q. Rev. 62 (1962), Castel, *Domicile*, 5 McGill L.J. 179 (1958), Reese, *Does Domicile Bear a Single Meaning?* 55 Colum. L. Rev. 589 (1955), Mann, *The Seventh Report of the Private International Law Committee on Domicile*, 12 Int. & Comp. L.Q. 1326 (1963), Weintraub, *An Inquiry into the Utility of "Domicile" as a Concept in Conflicts Analysis*, 63 Mich. L. Rev. 961 (1965), Wade, *Domicile: A Re-Examination of Certain Rules*, 32 Int. & Comp. L.Q. 1 (1983), Corson, *Reform of Domicile Law for Application to Transients, Temporary Residents and Multi-Based Persons*, 16 Colum. J. of L. & Soc. Prob. 327 (1981), Borgen, *Comment: The Determination of Domicile*, 65 Mil. L. Rev. 133 (1974), Lopez, *The Law of the Domicile with Greater Compensation Rule: Toward Policy — Oriented Rules for Choice of Law* 17 Calif. W.L. Rev. 26 (1980), Wurfel, *Jet Age Domicil: The Semi-Demise of Durational Residence Requirements*, 11 Wake Forest L. Rev. 349 (1975), Coudert, *Some Considerations in the Law of Domicil*, 36 Yale L.J. 949 (1927), Hogan, *Joseph Story's Essay on "Domicil"*, 35 Boston U.L. Rev. 215 (1955), Graveson, *Reform of the Law of Domicile*, 70 L.Q. Rev. 492 (1954), Pollak, *Domicile*, 50 S. Afr. L.J. 449 (1933), 51 S. Afr. L.J. 11 (1934), Bohan, *The Domicile and Recognition of Foreign Divorces Act 1986*, 80 Incorp. L. Soc. of Ir. Gazette 269 (1986).

[2] In *Whicker* v. *Hume*, 7 H.L. Cas. 124, at 160, 11 E.R. 50, at 64 (1858), Lord Cranworth observed:
"By domicile, we mean home, the permanent home; and if you do not understand your permanent home, I am afraid that no illustration drawn from foreign writers or foreign languages will very much help you to it."
This passage was quoted with approval by Budd, J., in *In re Sillar; Hurley* v. *Wimbush*, [1956] I.R. 344, at 348-349 (High Ct., 1955). Budd, J. added (at 349):
"While many factors have to be considered in most cases relating to domicil, I cannot help feeling

is that normally it would be appropriate[3] and in harmony with reasonable expectations for important matters affecting a person's civil status and property to be determined by the law of the country of his permanent home rather than by the law of a country with which that person has only tenuous or short-term connections. Whether this is a sensible assumption we shall examine a little later in the chapter.

The rules relating to domicile are fairly simple in theory but in their application to specific cases can be a source of much uncertainty and debate.[4] Recent legislative changes[5] affect only limited[6] (though important) aspects of the subject.

Let us summarise briefly the main features of the law, before going on to examining them in detail. Every person must have a domicile, and it is not possible at any time to have more than one domicile. There are three types of domicile: of origin, of choice and of dependency.

The domicile of origin is the domicile which every person receives at birth. A legitimate child born during the lifetime of his father has his domicile of origin in the country in which the father is domiciled at the time of birth.[7] An illegitimate child or a legitimate child born after his father's death has his domicile of origin in the country where his mother is domiciled at the time of birth.

A domicile of choice[8] is acquired by an independent[9] person by residing in a country with the intention of continuing to do so permanently or indefinitely.[10] All the circumstances throwing light on the question must be considered in determining whether a domicile of choice has been acquired.[11] A person may change his or her domicile as many times as he or she pleases.[12]

A domicile of dependency is ascribed to minors and mentally ill persons, regardless of their own intentions or wishes. A person subject to such a domicile is unable to change it; instead the domicile depends[13] on that of the domicile of his father or mother. Recently, legislation[14] has abolished the domicile of dependency of married women, "that last barbarous relic of a wife's servitude."[15]

---

that at times, in the welter of argument and citation of case law, that simple elementary proposition is in danger of being forgotten.''

See also *Re Adams Deceased; Bank of Ireland Trustee Co. Ltd.* v. *Adams,* [1967] I.R. 424 at 433 (High Ct., Budd, J.).

[3] Cf. Graveson, *The Comparative Evolution of Principles of the Conflict of Laws in England and the U.S.A.,* [1960] I Recueil des cours 25, at 43.

[4] Cf. *Redmond* v. Mooney, 14 Ir. C.L.R. *xvii,* at *xix* (Q.B., *per* Fitzgerald, J., 1862): 'The question of domicile is always of extreme difficulty ....''

[5] Domicile and Recognition of Foreign Divorces Act 1986, sections 1-4.

[6] Cf. 113 Seanad Debs. Col. 212 (Mrs Nuala Fennell, Minister for State at the Dept. of Justice, 4 June 1986).

[7] Cf. *Revenue Commissioners* v. *Shaw,* [1982] I.L.R.M. 433, at 434, (High Ct., McWilliam, J., 1977).

[8] See *Anon., Comment: Domicil of Choice — Fixed Rules* 36 Yale L.J. 408 (1926).

[9] That is, a person who has not a domicile of dependency.

[10] See *infra,* pp. 55-58. In *Moffett* v. *Moffett,* [1922] 1 I.R. 57, at 73 (1919), Powell, J. spoke of residence in a country ''for a period not limited as to time''.

[11] Cf. *Davis* v. *Adair,* [1895] 1 I.R. 379, at 445 (C.A., *per* Palles, C.B.). See also *Hutchinson's Executor* v. *The Master,* 1919 A.D. 71, at 77 (*per* De Villiers, J.): ''No circumstance is too small to be taken into consideration in deciding the question of domicile''. To similar effect is *Drevon* v. *Drevon,* 45 L.J. Ch. 129, at 133 (1864).

[12] *Bell* v. *Bell,* [1922] 2 I.R. 152, at 155 (K.B. Div., Dodd, J.).

[13] Subject to certain exceptional cases: cf. *infra,* pp. 82-92.

[14] Domicile and Recognition of Foreign Divorces Act 1986, section 1.

[15] *Gray* v. *Formosa,* [1963] P. 259, at 267 (C.A., *per* Lord Denning M.R., 1962).

PRELIMINARY CONCEPTS

(1) The area of domicile

Domicile "is used to identify a country possessing a distinct legal system".[16] Thus, one is not domiciled in a town or county, for example, but in a *country*. What constitutes a "country" may not always be easy to determine, however. These difficulties are particularly apparent where federal structures of government exist

It is clear that France, for example, is a "country" for the purposes of domicile. So also are the constituent elements of a State or Union which contains several countries[17] or a federation.[18] Thus a person may be domiciled in England or Scotland,[19] for example, or in one of the Canadian provinces, or in one of the States of the United States or of Australia. It may seem odd to refer to some of these areas as "countries"; other expressions, such as "territory", "law district" and "place" have been suggested but each of them has its own drawbacks.

(2) Change in territorial boundaries[20]

We must now consider the problem that may arise where land originally within the territorial boundaries of one country becomes part of another country. This may happen where, for example, people gain independence from a foreign power, or alternatively where a foreign power incorporates land within its territory, or where a part of a State secedes. Since a person is regarded as being domiciled in a territory governed by a distinct legal system, there may be difficulties when, after a change in the boundaries, a question arises as to what that person's domicile was *before* the change.

There is no easy answer to this question. One approach may be to attribute a retrospective domicile to the person, so that he or she, if living both before and after the change in what is now designated France, but was formerly designated Germany, should be regarded as having been domiciled in France at all material times. Alternatively, the person may be regarded as having changed his or her domicile with the change from German to French control. This change, of course, could not be characterised as involving the acquisition of a domicile of choice, since the person had no necessary intention to change his or her domicile. Indeed the person may well have deeply resented the change but, on account of sickness, family commitments or economic necessity, may have been obliged to remain in the territory after the political and legal controls have altered.

The problem increases in complexity where a single legal unit becomes divided into two or more legal units. A question may arise after the change as to where a person was domiciled before the change, and that question may be posed in such a manner as to make it impossible or inappropriate to answer it by referring to the original unit. In such circumstances, there may be merit in treating the new legal units as if they had existed separately before the change. The effect of doing so would be to treat a person born in Dublin in 1910, for example, to parents domiciled in Ireland as having a domicile of origin in the Republic of Ireland.[21]

---

[16] *McClean*, p. 4, para. 1.05.

[17] Cf. *Dicey & Morris*, 101.

[18] Cf. *A.G. for Alberta* v. *Cook*, [1926] A.C. 444, *Trottier* v. *Rajotte*, [1940] S.C.R. 203, *Winson* v. *Winson*, [1948] 3 D.L.R. 319 (N.S.C.A.).

[19] On occasion, this fact is overlooked; thus, for example, the statement of the facts in *In bonis Wallace*, 29 L.R. Ir. 118, at 118 (Probate, Warren, P., 1891), refers to a person "domiciled in England and Scotland". The judgment in the case makes it clear that no such concept was envisaged by the court.

[20] See *Anton*, 180, *McLeod*, 141.

[21] Cf. *Re O'Keefe*, [1940] Ch. 124, *Re M.*, [1937] N.I. 151 (Chy. Div., Megaw, J., 1936), *In re P.*, [1945] Ir. Jur. Rep. 17 (High Ct., Maguire, J., 1944).

In truth, the question does not easily lend itself to *a priori* resolution. Our courts should not be blind to the social and political contexts in which independent nations emerge or fall under the control of a foreign power. Rather than adopt "black letter" rules of general application, it may be desirable to fashion more subtle solutions, sensitive to the political and social realities.

The first case which we must consider in this context displays just this sensitivity. In *In re Egan*,[22] in 1928, a case involving divorce proceedings, Moore, L.C.J. of the Northern Ireland King's Bench Division held that, after Independence, the petitioner could *elect* to be domiciled in either Northern Ireland or the Irish Free State. He observed that, previous to "the separation of Ireland into two parts,"[23] the petitioner's domicile had been "Ireland, and not a particular part of it".[24]

It should be noted that the petitioner, a civil servant working much of his life in Ceylon, had connections with both parts of the island. His father had lived successively in Co. Dublin (where he was residing when the petitioner was born) and various parts of Antrim as the petitioner was growing up. The petitioner had been educated partly in Belfast and partly in Dublin.

After Independence the petitioner had successfully encouraged his father to live in Northern Ireland and had resided with him in a house that he had bought for him in Belfast. The petitioner stated that he had fully determined never to reside in the Irish Free State, but to make his permanent home in Northern Ireland, and to live there save as far as he was obliged to reside in Ceylon.

In re M.,[25] in 1936, another Northern Ireland decision, the question arose concerning a person's domicile before 1922. The Northern legislation of 1928 introducing legitimation *per subsequens matrimonium* applied to a marriage if the child's father was at the date of the marriage "domiciled in Northern Ireland".[26] The marriage in question took place in 1907. Megaw, J. held that this expression should be interpreted as "domiciled in that portion of Ireland which is now Northern Ireland".[27] He stressed the fact that the child's father had never resided anywhere but in Antrim, and that the continuous residence of a party was "a vital factor"[28] in determining domicile:

"No doubt during his lifetime [the child's father] had an Irish domicile, but it was derived from a residence which would today have given him a domicile in Northern Ireland."[29]

Megaw, J. referred to *Egan* v. *Egan*,[30] and stated that he considered his decision to be consistent with and supported by the judgment of Moore, L.C.J. in that case. He noted that in *Egan* the petitioner had been born in the part of Ireland that afterwards became the Irish Free State and then had come to Northern Ireland. Referring to the right of election recognised in *Egan,* Megaw, J. said:

"It follows, I think, that when a person has lived all his lifetime in an area which is now part of Northern Ireland the ordinary presumption of law arising from continuous residence should be applicable, and that when a division of domicile was effected by the legislature he must be held to be domiciled in the part of the divided territory in which he had so resided."[31]

[22] [1928] N.I. 159 (K.B. Div., Moore, C.J.).
[23] *Id.*, at 161.
[24] *Id.*
[25] [1937] N.I. 151 (Chy. Div., Megaw, J., 1936).
[26] Legitimacy Act (Northern Ireland) 1928, section 1(1).
[27] [1937] N.I., at 154.
[28] *Id.*
[29] *Id.*
[30] *Supra.*
[31] [1937] N.I., at 155.

In *In re P.,*[32] in 1944, a man died intestate leaving a widow and six children, the two eldest of whom had been born before the marriage. The applicant for a grant of letters of administration intestate was the eldest child, born in 1894. His parents had married in 1898, his father at that time being domiciled in that part of Ireland which subsequently became the Irish Free State.

Maguire P. held that the applicant had been legitimated by the Legitimacy Act 1931 and was thus entitled to apply for a grant. He said:

> "On the whole, though I have some doubt in my mind, I must hold that 'Saorstát Éireann' is s. 1(1) of the Legitimacy Act 1931 refers to that part of Ireland which subsequently came under the jurisdiction of the Government of the Irish Free State in 1922. It seems unlikely that the Legislature did not intend to include within the scope of the Act children born to a couple who married subsequently to their birth, but before the establishment of the Irish Free State, and as pointed out in *In re. M.,*[33] to hold that such was the position would amount to holding that this type of case is a *casus omissus.* I am prepared to follow the line of reasoning adopted in *In re. M.,* and to hold that the applicant here became legitimated on the date of the passing of the Act, having been born to parents who were in a position to be married at the time of the birth, and his father having been domiciled, at the time of his subsequent marriage, in that part of Ireland which subsequently became the Irish Free State."[34]

(3) Federations[35]

Some problems with federations may be mentioned briefly. In federal and composite jurisdictions, the Constitution or legislation may provide that for some specific principles of the law — divorce, for example — a person may have a domicile[36] in the federal or composite unit as a whole rather than in an individual law district.[37] Of course, the *lex fori* is free to ignore this characterisation[38] but practical convenience may suggest that it should modify the principle that no person may have more than one domicile at a time.[39]

Another problem which can arise with federations is that a person may be resident in a federal state, intending to live there permanently, but without having formed the intention to live permanently in any one of the constituent components of the state. For example, a man born in Ireland to parents domiciled in Ireland, may have emigrated to the United States of America intending to spend the rest of his days there, never to return to Ireland, but he may have formed no lasting attachment to any particular state within the United States. Under present law, he would not have lost his Irish domicile of origin; yet he clearly intended to reside permanently in the United States. Some other countries have dealt with this problem, either by referring the man's domicile to the state, within the federal structure, with which

---

[32] [1945] Ir. Jur. Rep. 17 (High Ct., Maguire, J., 1944).

[33] [1937] N.I. 151 (Chy. Div., Megaw, J., 1936).

[34] [1945] Ir. Jur. Rep., at 46.

[35] See generally Graveson, *Problems of Private International Law in Non-Unified Systems,* [1974] I Recueil des cours 190, esp. at 235-241.

[36] The English and Scottish Law Commissions call this type of domicile a "super-domicile": *Private International Law: The Law of Domicile,* para. 3.2 (Working Paper No. 88 and Consultative Memorandum No. 63, 1985).

[37] E.g. Australia and Canada: cf. *McClean,* p. 5, para. 1.06.

[38] Cf. *Smith* v. *Smith,* 1970 (1) S.A. 146 (Rhodesia High Ct.), criticised by Carter, in [1970] Annual Survey of Commonwealth Law, at p. 612.

[39] Cf. *McClean,* p. 5, para. 1.06. It is interesting to note that, in *T.* v. *T.,* [1983] I.R. 29 (Sup. Ct., 1982), Henchy, J. (at 33, 34) and Griffin, J. (at 35) referred to "British" domicile. It is also worth noting that Britain's Domicile and Matrimonial Proceedings Act 1973, in Parts I to V, requires proof of domicile for matrimonial proceedings to be in England and Wales, Scotland and Northern Ireland, respectively. Cf. the Domicile and Recognition of Foreign Divorces Act 1986, section 5(2) and (3).

he has for the time being the closest connection[40] or to the state in which he is ordinarily resident.[41] The Law Reform Commission addressed the question in their Working Paper on Domicile and Habitual Residence. They included a provision[42] in the General Scheme of a Bill to Reform the Law of Domicile to the effect that, where a person who has his habitual residence and intends to live indefinitely in a State that has two or more territorial units in which different systems of law apply regarding domicile, but that person has not formed an intention to live indefinitely in any territorial unit forming part of that State, he is to be deemed to live indefinitely —

(a) in that territorial unit in which he has his habitual residence;

(b) if he does not have habitual residence in any such unit, in the territorial unit in which he ordinarily resides; or

(c) if he has neither his habitual residence or his ordinary residence in any such unit, in whichever unit in which he was last ordinarily resident.

(4) Domicile is determined according to Irish law

It seems clear that the law which the court dealing with the question is to apply in determining the matter of a person's domicile is Irish law.[43] In *Re Adams Deceased*,[44] Budd J. referred to the English decision of *In re Annesley: Davidson* v. *Annesley*,[45] where Russell, J. had stated his view very clearly, that the question whether a person is or is not domiciled in a foreign country is to be determined in accordance with requirements of English law as to domicile irrespective of whether the person in question has or has not acquired a domicile of choice in the foreign country in the eyes of the law of that country. Budd, J. noted that, in the case before him, it had been submitted to him that the matter of domicile was to be determined according to the *lex fori,* namely of Ireland. He said that he was "not aware of any distinction between English and Irish law on the point"[46] and determined the question according to Irish law.[47]

(5) The single conception theory of domicile

It is clear that every person, at all times, has a domicile.[48] But does this mean that the notion of domicile is a constant one throughout the law? The conventional position in English and Irish conflicts of law is that the test which determines the

[40] Cf. *McClean,* p. 27, para. 1.B6, *Nygh,* (3rd ed.) 130-131.

[41] Cf. New Zealand's Domicile Act 1976, section 10.

[42] Law Reform Commission's Working Paper No. 10-1981, *Domicile and Habitual Residence as Connecting Factors in the Conflict of Laws,* p. 94, section 8 of the General Scheme of a Bill to Reform the Law of Domicile.

[43] An exception arises under the Succession Act 1965 section 102(4), in relation to the formal validity of wills: see further p. 433 *infra.*

[44] [1967] I.R. 424, at 434-435 (High Ct.). See further *supra,* pp. 43-44.

[45] [1926] Ch. 692.

[46] [1967] I.R., at 435.

[47] The question is of some considerable practical importance in view of the enactment of the Age of Majority Act 1985, section 2 of which confers full age on married persons under the age of 18. The implications for the domicile of dependency of minors are considered *infra,* pp. 90-91.

[48] See e.g., *Shannon Deceased,* 76 I.L.T.R. 53, and 54 (N.I.K.B. Div., Andrews L.C.J., 1942). *Sproule* v. *Hopkins,* [1903] 2 I.R. 133, at 138 (K.B. Div., Andrews, J., 1902). See also *Hood* v. *Hood,* [1959] I.R. 225, at 231 (High Ct., Murnaghan, J., 1958): "It is conceded on behalf of the respondent that a person can only have one domicil at a time ...." And see *Moffett* v. *Moffett,* [1920] 1 I.R. 57, at 73 (Powell, J., 1919) (affirmed by C.A., 1920) (quoting from *Story,* p. 52, para. 45), *Wadsworth* v. *McCord,* 12 S.C.R. 466 (1886), *Tennant* v. *City of St. John,* 5 M.P.R. 107, at 110 (N.S.C.A., 1932).

place of a person's domicile must remain constant no matter what the nature of the issue may be before the court.[49] In *Shannon Deceased,*[50] Andrews, L.C.J. said:

> "No person can be without a domicil; but, although he may have two or more residences, he cannot have two different and concurrent domicils; for domicil, as Lord Westbury put it in *Udny* v. *Udny*[51] is 'the criterion established by law for the purpose of determining civil status'; and the co-existence of different domicils would result in the simultaneous application of conflicting systems of law to the same individual."

This approach is what Cook described as the "single conception theory". Cook took issue with this approach, arguing that "domicile" is a relative term, varying in meaning according to the different contexts in which it is applied.[52] There is much support for Cook's view in the United States of America.[53] It is interesting to note that as long ago as 1874 this issue arose in the Irish decision of *Gillis* v. *Gillis.*[54] The case concerned proceedings for divorce *a mensa et thoro* taken by a husband; the wife would have suceeded in her challenge against the jurisdiction of the court if she could show that the domicile of her husband (and thus of herself)[55] was French rather than Irish, and her argument was based primarily on the long residence of her husband outside Ireland. Her counsel contended that domicile had two meanings, one in connection with the law of succession, and the other in connection with personal jurisdiction; and that in the latter case there had to be territorial residence.

Warren, J. did not reject this argument out of hand. He said that he would

> "merely wish to observe that, if there be a difference as to the nature of domicil as connected with successions and jurisdictions, I should suppose it would be more easy for one to change his status, so as to effect the devolution of his property than so as to oust the municipal jurisdiction founded upon the domicil of origin as regards his matrimonial rights and duties..."[56]

(6) Legality of transaction contingent on domicile in one of two countries

Where a person does an act which will be legal and binding according to the law of one country but not so under the law of another, the courts will give this factor considerable weight in determining his domicile. This is especially so where the

---

[49] See the *Seventh Report of the Private International Law Committee,* para. 12 (Cmnd. 1955, 1963). Cf. *Cheshire & North,* 162.

[50] 76 I.L.T.R. 53, at 54 (N.I.K.B. Div., 1942).

[51] L.R.1 H.L. (Sc.) 441, at 457 (1869).

[52] *Cook,* 194ff.

[53] Cf. Reese, 55 Colum. L. Rev. 589 (1955), *Restatement 2d,* para 11(2). See also the stimulating analysis, from a British standpoint, by Fawcett, *Result Selection in Domicile Cases,* 5 Oxford J. of Leg. Stud., 378 (1985).

[54] I.R. 8 Eq. 597 (Ct. for Mat. Causes, Warren, J., 1874).

[55] A point conceded by her counsel: cf. *id.,* at 604. As has been mentioned *supra,* p. 46, the domicile of dependency of married women was abolished by the Domicile and Recogniton of Foreign Divorces Act 1986, section 1.

[56] *Id.,* at 608-609, citing *Deck* v. *Deck,* 2 Sw. & Tr. 90 (1860). Cf. *Lett* v. *Lett,* [1906] 1 I.R. 618 (Porter, M.R., aff'd by C.A.), where Porter, M.R. said (at 625):
> "It is not impossible that a man may actually have two domicils, one according to the law of one country, and another according to the law of another country. I do not know how that may be; but so far as the decree of the Probate and Matrimonial Division and anything done in that matter, it is absolutely concluded that the domicil of both parties was Irish throughout."

It is submitted that this statement amounts of no more than the correct, but rather obvious, assertion that there is no way of preventing two different tribunals from arriving at two differing findings as to a person's domicile, whether by reason of differences in relevant legal principles as to what constitutes domicile, differences in evidence or differences in inferences arising from the evidence.

act is one of particular moral and social significance, such as marriage[57] or legitimation,[58] but less significant acts such as the adoption of the distinctive testimony formalities of one country[59] may also suffice.

In *Davis* v. *Adair*,[60] a man married his deceased wife's sister in New York. According to New York law, the marriage was valid; according to English law it was void.[61] The couple asserted that they both were domiciled in England at the time of the marriage and that accordingly their marriage was void. Their probable reason for doing so was that, if the marriage were valid, the wife would stand to lose a certain interest in property. The Court of Appeal, affirming Porter, M.R., held that the spouses had been domiciled in New York at the time of the marriage.

Palles, C.B. interpreted the very fact that the couple had married as evidence of a declaration on their part that they were domiciled in New York. He said:

"Take the case of two persons in Paris, who go to the English [sic] Embassy, arrange to be married there, and are in fact married there. Is that, or is it not, a declaration that they are at the time people domiciled in England? There are two formal modes of celebrating marriage there; one between persons who are then domiciled French people, the other between persons whose domicil is English, and the moment that a person appeals to the English law, to be married in Paris according to that law, it appears to me to be an eloquent declaration that he considers himself bound by that English law, and as having an English domicil. But the present case is stronger, because according to the English law there can be no such thing as a marriage between persons in this position, domiciled in England, and their marriage is valid if they are domiciled Americans. In my opinion the very fact of going through a ceremony of marriage as Americans is a declaration of the utmost solemnity that in their opinion they are subject to American law."[62]

Palles, C.B. was strongly influenced by the fact that the spouses had been advised as to the legal position relating to the marriage, so that they must have known that their marriage would not have been legal unless they were domiciled in America, and he imputed to them a clear intention to reside permanently in America, "if for no other purpose to effectuate their primary object of a legal marriage".[63]

Similarly in *Doucet* v. *Geoghegan*[64] where a Frenchman, resident in England, married twice in England, without complying with the requirements of French law, James L.J. said that both the marriages "were acts of unmitigated scoundrelism if he was not a domiciled Englishman".

In *Moffett* v. *Moffett*,[65] a man of Irish domicile of origin left Ireland in 1858 and from the following year until his death in 1893 lived in South Africa. There he married twice, one of these marriages legitimating a son previously born out of wedlock. Powell, J. commented that "if it were unmitigated scoundrelism for Doucet to have contracted in England a marriage which would have been void in France, if he actually intended to return to France, it would, I think, have been a useless performance to have gone through this ceremony, so far as his son was concerned, if he had no intention of continuing to reside in the country in which the ceremony would have the effect of making his son legitimate."[66]

[57] Cf. *Davis* v. *Adair*, [1895] 1 I.R. 379 (C.A.), *Moffett* v. *Moffett*, [1920] 1 I.R. 57 (Powell, J., 1919), *Doucet* v. *Geoghegan*, 9 Ch. Div. 441 (C.A., 1878).
[58] Cf. *Moffett* v. *Moffett*, *supra*.
[59] *Id.*, at 70.
[60] *Supra*.
[61] Lord Lyndhurst's Act 1835.
[62] [1895] 1 I.R., at 452. See, however, Barry, L.J.'s note of caution, *id.*, at 458.
[63] *Id.*, at 453.
[64] 9 Ch. Div. 441, at 457 (C.A., 1878).
[65] [1920] 1 I.R. 57.
[66] *Id.*, at 70.

Where, however, nothing hinges on the legality of the marriage, the place or form of its celebration may well not give rise to any inference regarding domicile. In *Spurway* v. *Spurway*,[67] a couple were married at the British consulate at Nice. The husband was of Irish domicile of origin but had lived some years in France; the wife was born in Jersey, but had lived many years in France, being the widow of a Frenchman. The Master of the Rolls noted that "the marriage must have been performed between two persons who were British subjects," but added: "I do not think the fact of the marriage would be at all conclusive as to domicile".

DOMICILE OF CHOICE

Let us now examine the law relating to domicile of choice. This is the domicile that adults will have in most cases — unless they are subject to a domicile of dependency on account of mental illness or have abandoned the domicile of choice without acquiring another (in which case, as we shall see,[68] their domicile of origin revives).

(1) Acquisition of domicile of choice

Two elements must be established in order to acquire a domicile of choice. These are *residence* and *intention*.[69] It must be proved that the person in question resided in a certain country with the intention of remaining there permanently or indefinitely. Residence must be accompanied by intention although it does not matter which came first. Thus, to use an example from *Cheshire & North*:

"The emigrant forms his intention before he leaves England for Australia; the *émigré* who flees from persecution may not form it until years later."[70]

(a) Residence[71]

The concept of residence, though an essential ingredient in the notion of domicile, has received relatively little judicial analysis. This is perhaps because the term "residence" appears reasonably self-explanatory — though, on reflection, it turns out to be less so.

At all events, it appears that "residence" does not extend to a casual presence in a country, on a shopping expedition, for example — or presence there as a traveller.[72] An American judge captured the essence of the concept when he described residence as "bodily presence as an inhabitant".[73]

There is no minimum period for establishing residence: a residence can be

---

[67] [1894] 1 I.R. 385.

[68] *Infra*, pp. 76-77.

[69] Cf. *Revenue Commissioners* v. "Z", 101 Ir. L.T. & Sol. J. 492, at 492 (Sp. Comms. 1967).

[70] *Cheshire & North*, 165.

[71] For some helpful insights, see McClean, *The Meaning of Residence*, 11 Int. & Comp. L. Q. 1153 (1962), Reese & Green, *That Elusive Word "Residence"*, 6 Vand. L. Rev. 561 (1953), Beale, *Residence and Domicile*, 4 Iowa L. Bull. 3 (1918).

[72] Cf. *Manning* v. *Manning*, L.R. 2 P.& D. 223, at 226 (1871), *Sinclair* v. *Sinclair*, [1968] P. 189 (C.A.).

[73] *Re Newcomb*, 192 N.Y. 238, 84 N.E. 950 (1908). The definition of "residence" has arisen in a wide variety of contexts: see e.g. *Donnelly* v. *Graham*, 24 L.R. Ir. 127 (C.A., 1888), *Charlton* v. *Morris*, [1895] 2 I.R. 541 (C.A., 1894), *O'Connell* v. *Holland*, [1900] 2 I.R. 448 (C.A., 1899), *Snow* v. *Irwin*, 2 I.C.L.R. 378 (C.P., Monahan, C.J., 1852), *Forrest* v. *Maher*, 2 I.C.L.R. 546 (C.P., Monahan, C.J., 1852), *Butler* v. *Corcoran*, 7 I.C.L.R. 276 (Exch., Greene, B., 1857), *Tudor* v. *Lawson*, 15 I.C.L.R. 144 (Exch., Fitzgerald, B., 1864), *Tom* v. *Nagle*, 13 I.C.L.R. App. *xxxviii* (Exch., Fitzgerald, B., 1862). See further McClean, *The Meaning of Residence*, 11 Int. & Comp. L. Q. 1153, at 1155 (1962). As to the residence of a company, see *Hood & Co.* v. *Magee*, [1918] 2 I.R. 34 (K.B. Div., 1917), and *infra*, pp. 482-484.

established immediately on arrival in a country in which one intends to settle.[74]

It should not be thought, however, that an intention to reside is an essential ingredient in the concept of residence: even in the absence of intention on his or her part a mentally disabled person may be held to reside in a particular country.[75] The same applies to children incapable of forming an intention on this matter.[76]

Conversely, an intention or desire to reside in a particular place will not be sufficient if one lacks a sufficient quantum of physical presence there.[77]

Illegal residence

We must now consider the position where a person's residence in a country is illegal.[78] Courts in England,[79] Australia,[80] South Africa,[81] and (what was then) Rhodesia and Nyasaland[82] have held that a domicile of choice may not be acquired on this basis. Courts in the United States[83] and Canada[84] have generally taken the opposite view.[85]

The balance of the argument would appear to favour the view that, while the illegality of a person's residence may often throw light on his or her intention,[86] it should not, of itself, be a reason for denying that he or she is in fact resident in the country in question.[87] It may, of course, be a sound policy for the *lex fori* to

---

[74] *Bell* v. *Kennedy*, L.R. 1 Sc. & Div. 307, at 319 (1868). Cf. *Winans* v. *Winans*, 205 Mass. 388 (per Morton, J. 1910): "The length of the residence is immaterial ... [A] day or an hour ... will suffice for the acquisition of a domicile." In accord is *Mason* v. *Mason*, 4 E.D.C.330, at 349 (*per* Shippard, J., 1985): "Domicile can be fixed even in one moment if there be clear proof of intention." See also the famous decision of *White* v. *Tennant*, 31 W.Va. 790, 8 S.E. 596 (1888), critically analysed by Weintraub, *An Inquiry into the Utility of "Domicile" as a Concept in Conflicts Analysis*, 63 Mich. L. Rev. 961, at 969-971 (1965).

[75] Cf. *Donnelly* v. *Graham, supra, Charlton* v. *Morris, supra;* see also *Re X.Y.*, [1937] Ch. 337 (C.A.), *Berkshire Co. Co.* v. *Reading Borough Council*, [1921] 1 K.B. 787 (K.B. Div.), *Edinburgh Parish Council* v. *Local Govt. Bd. for Scotland*, [1915] A.C. 717, at 723 (H.L.(Sc.), *per* Lord Kinnear, 1915), and cf. *In re Birch (A Lunatic)*, 29 L.R. Ir. 274 (Lord Ashbourne, C., 1892), *In re B--, a Lunatic*, 1 I.R. Eq. 181 (Lord Plunket, L.C., 1839, *The State (Goertz)* v. *Minister for Justice*, [1948] I.R. 45 (Sup. Ct., 1947, aff'g High Ct., Maguire, J., 1947), discussed *infra*.

[76] McClean, *supra*, at 1160.

[77] Cf. *M'Kendrick* v. *Buchanan*, 20 L.R.(Ir.) 206 (C.A. 1886), *Martin* v. *Hanrahan*, 22 L.R.(Ir.) 452 (C.A., 1887), *Hassan* v. *Chambers*, 24 L.R.(Ir.) 139 (C.A., 1888), *Duffy* v. *Chambers*, 26 L.R.(Ir.) 100 (C.A. 1889) (franchise cases).

[78] See Pilkington, *Illegal Residence and the Acquisition of a Domicile of Choice*, 33 Int. & Comp. L. Q. 885 (1984) (a comprehensive analysis); see also Spiro, *Note: Domicile of an Illegal Immigrant*, 12 Int. & Comp. L.Q. 680 (1963).

[79] *Puttick* v. *A.G.*, [1980] Fam. 1 (Sir George Baker, P.) where, however, in spite of Baker, P.'s broad statement that ".... a person cannot achieve status by fraud", it may be argued that the decision stands for no more than the proposition that the forum will not recognise an illegal residence in the forum (as opposed to other countries).

[80] *Solomon* v. *Solomon*, 29 W.N. (N.S.W.) 68 (1912), *Ah Yin* v. *Christie*, 4 Comm. L. R. 1428, at 1431 (*per* Griffith, C.J., 1907), *Lim* v. *Lim*, [1973] V.R. 370. See *Nygh*, 134.

[81] *Ex p. Parker*, [1926] C.P.D. 255, *Ex p. MacLeod*, [1946] C.P.D. 312.

[82] *Smith* v. *Smith*, 1962 (2) S.A. 930.

[83] Cf. *Scoles & Weintraub*, 20, *Reese & Rosenberg*, 16, *Seren* v. *Douglas*, 489 P. 2d 601 (Colo., 1972), *Rzeszotarski* v. *Rzeszotarski*, 296 A. 2d 431 (D.C., 1972), *Plyler* v. *Doe*, 457 U.S. 202, at 227, fn. 22 (1983).

[84] *Jablonowski* v. *Jablonowski*, [1972] 3 O.R. 410, 28 D.L.R. (3d) 440 (High Ct., Lerner, J., 1972).

[85] Cf. *McKie* v. *McKie*, [1933] I.R. 464 (High Ct., Meredith, J.), where Meredith, J. appeared (at 479) to favour the view that a man who had illegally entered the United States and lived for a period in California, where he married, had not a Californian domicile. Nothing hinged in this issue, however, and the judgment gives no indication of the effect, if any, which the illegality of the man's entry into the country played in the determination of his domicile. Nor is it clear whether Meredith, J. considered that the man had never acquired a Californian domicile or that, having done so, he had abandoned it.

[86] Cf. Pilkington, *supra*, at 893ff.

[87] Cf. *Dicey & Morris*, 122. All the judgments in *The State (Goertz)* v. *Minister for Justice*, [1948] I.R. 45 (Sup. Ct., 1947, aff'g High Ct., Maguire, J., 1947), save that of Black, J., appeared to favour the view that the illegality of purpose in staying within the jurisdiction was a reason for depriving the stay of the character of "ordinary residence". Cf. *infra*, pp. 101-103.

deny benefits to persons illegally residing in the forum, but that is a separate question.[88]

Where a person's "days are numbered", so far as residence in a particular country is concerned, he or she may none the less obtain a domicile of choice there.[89] In *Cruh* v. *Cruh*,[90] in 1945, Denning, J. held that an alien whose deportation had been recommended following conviction for an offence had not lost his English domicile of choice: "until the deportation recommendation is actually effected, his domicil of choice remains".[91]

(b) Intention[92]

Questions of domicile "turn very much upon intention".[93] The precise nature of the requisite intention has been a matter of some uncertainty. Several questions need to be resolved. Must a person actually have an intention to remain in the country until he dies, or will an intention to remain indefinitely suffice? And what weight should be given to contingent conditions — where, for example, a person will move from the country in which he resides if he wins a lottery? The courts have experienced some difficulty in articulating clear guidelines. In many decisions the words "permanent" and "indefinite" are used interchangeably. In *Davis* v. *Adair*,[94] Walker, C. observed that it was "obvious that as the word 'indefinite' has no fixed legal meaning, every case must depend on its own special facts". The somewhat unspecific test he applied was whether a person had adopted the country in which he or she was living "as a permanent residence, without any such intention of returning [to the country of his or her domicile of origin] as was not too indefinite to outweigh acts".[95]

In *Udny* v. *Udny*[96] Lord Westbury said:

> "Domicil of choice is a conclusion or inference which the law derives from the fact of a man fixing voluntarily his sole or chief residence in a particular place, with an intention of continuing to reside there for an unlimited time. This is a description of the circumstances which create or constitute a domicil, and not a definition of the term. There must be a residence, freely chosen, and not prescribed or dictated by any external necessity, such as the duties of office, the demands of creditors, or the relief from illness; and it might be a residence fixed, not for a particular purpose, but general and indefinite in its future contemplation. It is true that residence, originally temporary, or intended for a limited period, may afterwards become general and unlimited; and in such a case, so soon as the change of purpose, or *animus manendi*, can be inferred, the fact of domicil is established."

In *Davis* v. *Adair*,[97] Sir P. O'Brien, L.C. commented:

> "This is the language of Lord Westbury in what appears to me to be the greatest, the most luminous, and, though not long, the most comprehensive judgment that is to be found in our English law books upon the law of domicil. It has been adopted as laying down the true test by which domicil has been determined in all subsequent cases, and

---

[88] Cf. Pilkington, *supra*, at 910.

[89] *Puttick* v. *Puttick*, [1980] Fam. 1, at 18 (Sir George Baker, P., 1979), *Boldrini* v. *Boldrini and Martin*, [1932] P. 9.

[90] [1945] 2 All E.R. 545 (P.D.A. Div., Denning, J.).

[91] *Id.*, at 546.

[92] See Heilman, *Domicil and Specific Intent*, 35 W. Va. L.Q. 262 (1929), *Anon., Note: Evidentiary Factors in the Determination of Domicil*, 61 Harv. L. Rev. 1232 (1948).

[93] *Moore* v. *Moore*, I.R. 5 Eq. 371, at 372 (Ct. for Mat. Causes, Warren, J., 1871).

[94] [1895] 1 I.R. 379, at 425 (C.A.).

[95] *Id.*

[96] L.R. 1 H.L. Sc. & Div., 441, at 457 (1869).

[97] [1895] 1 I.R. 379, at 437 (C.A.).

it corrected in the most lucid language the mistake of Mr Justice Story, when he confounded civil with political *status,* a mistake founded on the language of Lord Kingsdown in *Moorhouse* v. *Lord*"[98]

In *Davis* v. *Adair,*[99] the plaintiff's husband, Mr M'Andrew, an Englishman, had gone to the United States at the age of 28. Initially he had worked as agent for his father's business, a London firm; but as the years passed he went into business on his own, eventually returning at the age of 61, a very rich man. A question arose as to his domicile at the time of his marriage, in 1891, when he was 33 years old.

Sir P. O'Brien, C.J., having quoted with approval the passage from Lord Westbury's judgment in *Udny* v. *Udny,*[100] continued:

"Applying this test to ... Mr M'Andrew's life ... before June, 1891, is it not plain that he voluntarily fixed his chief residence in America, with an intention of continuing to reside there for an unlimited time? His residence there was, in my opinion, absolutely indefinite, the word which Lord Westbury uses, and which Lord Bramwell says, in *Re Steer,*[101] he prefers to the word 'permanent'. To say that he went to America to make a fortune, and that therefore he went for a particular purpose, is in my opinion, wholly unsustainable. Lord Westbury illustrates what he means by a particular purpose in the self-same sentence; and to say that being engaged in the multifarious transactions of a great business career is being in America for a particular purpose, as was contended at the bar, is negatived by the illustrations given by Lord Westbury, and indeed by the suggestions of common sense. Nothing, in my opinion, could be more 'general and indefinite in its future contemplation' than Mr M'Andrew's residence in America up to the time of the ... marriage in 1891."[102]

The courts have vacillated on the extent to which residence should give rise to an inference of an intention to reside permanently in a particular country.[103] As Black, J. observed in *In re Joyce; Corbet* v. *Fagan,*[104] it is "possible to cite weighty pronouncements seeming to favour the view that mere length of residence alone will raise a presumption of such an intention, casting the onus of rebuttal upon those who contest it". Yet when these *dicta* are closely examined the more important of them appear to fall short of this proposition; indeed the better view today seems to be that what one must examine is the "quality", rather than mere duration, of the residence.

Discussion of this subject in Britain has been overshadowed by two decisions, where the House of Lords held that the domicile of origin had persisted in spite of an extended sojourn abroad. In part these holdings may be attributed to the tenacity of the domicile of origin,[105] but they have been generally considered to have a wider import for the doctrine of domicile as a whole. To a large degree the decisions were the product of their times and have lost much of their influence in post-colonial Britain. They cannot be ignored, however, as they have been of much influence in a number of Irish cases over the years.

In *Winans* v. *Attorney General,*[106] a person born in the United States resided principally in England for the last thirty-seven of his sixty-four years; indeed for

---

[98]   10 H.L. Cas. 272, 11 E.R. 1030 (1863).

[99]   *Supra.*

[100] L.R. 1 H.L. Sc. & Div. 441, at 457 (1869).

[101] 3 H. & N. 594, 157 E.R. 606 (1858).

[102] [1895] 1 I.R., at 437-438. See also *Moffett* v. *Moffett,* [1920] 1 I.R. 57, at 69-70 (Powell, J., 1919).

[103] A *dictum* going much too far is Blackbourne, C.J.'s in *Conway* v. *Wilson,* 2 Ir. C.L.R. 47, at 48 (Q.B., 1851): "In the plaintiff's affidavit it is stated he has a residence at Kingstown; that implies a domicile".

[104] [1946] I.R. 277, at 302 (Sup. Ct., 1945).

[105] *Infra,* pp. 74-76.

[106] [1904] A.C. 287.

the final years of his life he resided exclusively there. Nonetheless, the House of Lords held that he had not been shown to have abandoned his domicile of origin in the United States. The initial decision to live in England had been dictated by health considerations; moreover, an examination of Mr Winans's outlook, his hopes and his projects revealed (to the satisfaction of the majority)[107] a continuing desire on his part to carry out large schemes relating to maritime development in the United States, to some extent directed against British strategic interests. "[U]p to the very last he had an expectation or hope of returning to America and seeing his grand schemes inaugurated".[108] Moreover, his son testified that he had been "entirely American in all his ideas and sympathies".[109] *Winans*, as Black, J. observed in *In re Joyce; Corbet* v. *Fagan*,[110] "may, therefore, fairly be regarded as a border-line case".

In *Ramsay* v. *Liverpool Royal Infirmary*,[111] a Scotsman, one George Bowie, who had lived for thirty-seven years in England, was held to have retained his Scottish domicile. The House of Lords considered that his residence in England was attributable initially to attachment to his relations who had gone to live there, and to the convenience of being supported by them; at a later stage in his life the "inertness of age", and poor health, supervened.

In *In re Joyce; Corbet* v. *Fagan*,[112] in 1945, the Supreme Court was faced with the question of how to determine domicile in the case of long residence in a particular country, but in the absence of very useful direct evidence as to the person's intention.[113] Mr George Joyce had been born in Galway in 1873. Shortly after he came of age, he became insane and was an inmate of a mental hospital for eighteen months. After having been discharged from the hospital he spent four years in Canada. He then returned to Ireland until 1907, when he went to England, where he resided for the remaining thirty-seven years of his life. For a period of about six years, from 1927 to 1933, he was again in a mental institution. From 1933 until his death he lived in a number of hotels in London.

Overend, J. held that Mr Joyce had acquired an English domicile. The Supreme Court (Geoghegan, J. dissenting) affirmed. Black, J. delivered the leading judgment. He discussed *Winans* and *Ramsay* at length. He distinguished *Winans* on the ground that Mr Joyce's residence in England lasted for thirty-seven years against Mr Winans's thirty-three years, and his exclusive residence there had extended over the whole thirty-seven years as compared with four years for Mr Winans. More convincing was the fact that there was "no evidence that Mr Joyce had any scheme in his mind to inaugurate in the land of his birth, or 'any hope or expectation of returning' there, or that he was entirely, or in any degree, Irish in 'his ideas and sympathies' ".[114] Black, J. observed:

> "If, then, *Winans* v. *Attorney-General* was a border-line case, the present case by comparison would appear to be distinctly over the border on the side of the English domicile."[115]

[107] By two-to-one; the courts below had reached the opposite conclusion. Indeed Lord Halsbury's concurrence with Lord Macnaghten was about as tepid as it could be: cf. *In re Joyce: Corbet* v. *Joyce,* [1946] I.R. 277, at 304 (Sup. Ct., *per* Black, J., 1945).

[108] [1904] A.C., at 298 (H.L.(Eng.), *per* Lord Macnaghten).

[109] *Id.*, (*per* Lord Macnaghten, adopting the words of Mr Winans's son).

[110] [1946] I.R. 344, at 349. See also *In re Sillar; Hurley* v. *Wimbush,* [1956] I.R. 344 (High Ct., Budd, J., 1955).

[111] [1930] A.C. 588.

[112] [1946] I.R. 277 (Sup. Ct., 1945).

[113] Cf. *id.*, at 293 (*per* Geoghegan, J., dissenting), referring to "the want of colour" in Mr Joyce's life.

[114] *Id.*, at 304 (internal citation to *Winans* v. *Attorney-General,* [1904] A.C. 287, at 298 (H.L. (Eng.), *per* Lord Macnaghten)).

[115] [1946] I.R., at 304.

Distinguishing *Ramsay* v. *Liverpool Royal Infirmary* presented no difficulty. Mr Joyce had no family or financial motive for going to England. There was no evidence to show that, apart from mental illness, which had ceased eleven years before his death, he had suffered from poor health; moreover, in his dealings with his bank manager, he had shown none of the "inertness of age" or inanition which had affected Mr Bowie.

Again in contrast to Mr Bowie, Mr Joyce had been financially well off and "had nobody's convenience but his own to consider".[116] He had, moreover, during the two years before his death, remained at his hotel, in London, thereby gravely risking his life,[117] since the whole area around him had been wrecked or burned down by air bombardment. Indeed Black, J. considered[118] that Mr Joyce's twenty years' residence in London *before* his period of time in a mental institution there, constituted a sufficient indication of a probable intention to make England his permanent home.

Geoghegan, J. dissenting, stressed the "stringent presumption"[119] in favour of the continuance of the domicile of origin. He viewed the facts of the case as giving rise to a different series of inferences. Mr Joyce's failure to leave London during the bombardment *could* be seen as evidence of inanition and passivity since he had no tie or link with London and could always have moved to a safer area within England. Mr Joyce's practice of keeping his securities in an Irish bank in London was, in Geoghegan J.'s view, scarcely evidence of an intention to abandon his Irish domicile; equally, the fact that the major portion of his correspondence was addressed to the bank, where he used to call, was "not characteristic of a permanent English resident".[120]

In *In re Sillar; Hurley* v. *Wimbush,*[121] in 1955, Budd, J. emphasised that *Ramsay* v. *Liverpool Royal Infirmary,* though "naturally of great weight",[122] was concerned with a man who was "a somewhat unusual individual and apparently peculiarly inert. It would seem unlikely that a decision on the peculiar facts of his case should fit any other".[123] Budd, J. stressed that:

> "There is no general rule to be applied, old age has many varying effects on individuals ..."[124]

The relevance of a place of business

Does the fact that a person residing in a particular country maintains a business there add to the likelihood that he or she is domiciled there? The answer must be the rather unhelpful one that it all depends. In *Munster & Leinster Bank Ltd.* v. *O'Connor,*[125] in 1935, Meredith, J. attributed a French domicile to a woman born in Ireland who had died in Paris, forty-five years after she had established a business there as a beauty specialist. She had come back to Cork, the place of her birth, every year for two to four weeks and on one occasion had remained there for a year but during that year she had maintained her business in France. She had given instructions

---

[116] *Id.,* at 305.

[117] *Id.,* at 305-306.

[118] *Id.,* at 306.

[119] *Id.,* at 298.

[120] *Id.,* at 296. See also *Revenue Commissioners* v. *"Z",* 101 Ir. L. T. & Sol J. 492 (Sp. Comms., 1967), where a man of South African domicile of origin who came to "try .... out" Ireland as a farmer in 1952 was held, after fourteen years' residence here, not to have acquired a domicile of choice since he had postponed making a final decision as to whether to stay here until his children finished their education.

[121] [1956] I.R. 344 (High Ct., Budd, J., 1955).

[122] *Id.,* at 357.

[123] *Id.,* at 358.

[124] *Id.,* at 359. See also *Moffett* v. *Moffett,* [1920] 1 I.R. 57 (Powell, J., 1919, aff'd by C.A., 1920).

[125] [1937] I.R. 462 (High Ct., Meredith, J., 1935).

as to her burial which "showed clearly"[126] that she contemplated the probability of her continuing to reside in Paris at the date of her death.

In contrast, in *In re De Hosson, Erwin* v. *De Hosson,*[127] two years later, the same judge held that thirty years' residence working as a hairdresser in Ireland by a man with a Dutch domicile of origin did not result in the acquisition of an Irish domicile. In 1931, less than five years before his death, the man married a woman who was, it appears, Irish. At that time he made it plain to her that she must be prepared to go and live with him in the Netherlands within two years. That statement was confirmed by the fact that he made attempts, albeit unsuccessful, to sell his business.

In *Sproule* v. *Hopkins,*[128] the respondent in nullity proceedings had had an Irish domicile of origin but, after some years of employment as a journalist in Dublin, went to London where he had "a variety of journalistic engagements".[129] He lived in London for over seventeen years. Andrews, J. was of the opinion that he had acquired an English domicile. Although the respondent had not acquired a permanent, fixed residence in London, Andrews J. considered that:

> "the proper inference from the facts of his having selected London as the place to earn his livelihood in, of his lengthened residence there, and the character of the employment he obtained, and might naturally expect to continue to obtain there, and the circumstances of his Irish relatives, is that he voluntarily abandoned his Irish domicil of origin and settled in London *animo manendi,* if not absolutely permanently, at least for an indefinite and unlimited time, and without any then existing intention of returning to reside in Ireland."[130]

In re Joyce; Corbet v. *Fagan,*[131] contains some important observations on the subject. Having noted the fact that Mr Joyce had not established any business in London, Black, J. stated that if he had done so:

> "... that, along with the long residence, might well have been sufficient to show an intention to change his domicil ... Yet, many emigrants have established business in foreign countries and long resided in them without ever having had any definitive intention of changing their domicile of origin, and sometimes they have all the time had a contrary intention, and have ended by giving effect to it, disposing of their business and returning to end their days in their native country. This may be the exception and not the rule. Yet from what we know to happen, I do not think it inherently improbable that a man should emigrate and even set up a business in a foreign land, while entertaining all the time the hope or purpose of returning one day to his homeland when he has acquired a certain gain. But if one remains for a great length of time in a foreign country without any tie of family, of health, or of business, but from sheer personal taste and predilection, I should more readily infer a probable intention to remain there permanently than from the mere establishment of a business, strong as the inference of an intended permanent residence from this latter fact might be. One can, and often does, dispose of an established business; but personal taste and predilection, when formed or confirmed by a longer period of years and persisting well into advanced middle age generally tend to become rooted and endure to the end...."[132]

Along with this we have noted, in *Davis* v. *Adair,*[133] Sir O'Brien C.J.'s scornful rejection of the argument that "being engaged in the multifarious transactions of

---

[126] *Id.,* at 466.
[127] [1937] I.R. 467 (High Ct., Meredith, J.).
[128] [1903] 2 I.R. 133 (K.B. Div., Andrews, J., 1902).
[129] *Id.,* at 138.
[130] *Id.,* at 137-138.
[131] [1946] I.R. 277 (Sup. Ct.).
[132] *Id.,* at 306-307.
[133] [1895] 1 I.R. 379, at 438 (C.A.) cf. *supra,* p. 56.

a great business career''[134] was being in a country for a "particular purpose", as understood by Lord Westbury in *Udny* v. *Udny*.[135] Such a suggestion was "negatived by the illustrations given by Lord Westbury, and indeed by the suggestions of common sense".[136]

The Chief Justice was clearly correct in rejecting the argument in relation to the case before him but it would be wrong to conclude that a business abroad — even a very successful one — might not in certain other cases be a "particular purpose". Thus, in *T.* v. *T.*[137] in 1982, the Supreme Court held that a British citizen with a "British"[138] domicile of origin had not acquired an Irish domicile of choice where, in April 1974, eight years after having married an Irish woman in England, he came to Ireland with her and their children and took up permanent and pensionable employment here. He also purchased a dwelling house in Ireland. Two and a half years later, the husband moved from the family home and took up temporary residence in a flat; but he returned in February 1978, as his wife and children had left the home. In August 1978, he was granted a decree of divorce in England. He had filed the petition in February 1977. During the currency of the marriage, the wife had obtained a maintenance order in the District Court against her husband. In July 1979 he applied for a variation of the maintenance order, claiming that the English divorce absolved him from continuing liability to make maintenance payments to his wife, so the question of his domicile at the time of the divorce required consideration.

The Supreme Court held that both the District Justice and the High Court judge had misdirected themselves in law in holding that the husband had acquired an Irish domicile of choice. Henchy, J. considered that they had:

> "wrongly allowed the elements of employment and residence to be the decisive factors. Undoubtedly, the husband left England with his wife and children, set up a family home in Cork and took up permanent employment there. In doing so he did no more than what tens of thousands of people are doing throughout the European Economic Community, where freedom of movement and mobility of employment are the order of the day under the Treaty of Rome. He spent but two years[139] in Cork with his family before he brought in London his petition for divorce. He had gone to Cork, presumably, because there was permanent employment available there and because it was his wife's native place. From these meagre facts or inferences, and they are all we have, it would be an unwarranted deduction to say that, of his own volition, he had stripped himself of his British domicile and had chosen to acquire an Irish domicile in its place. From the facts, as found by the District Justice, I am satisfied that the husband put the position correctly in the divorce petition when he averred that, while he was then residing in Cork, his domicile was British. A man's sojourn abroad with his wife and children for two years, even in a position of permanent employment, is not, without more, capable of displacing the presumption that the domicile of origin has been retained. The period lived abroad may be no more than the external manifestation of the temporary compulsion of circumstances. Such bare facts as we have in this case as to the husband's foreign residence do not show the volitional and factual transition which is a *sine qua non* for shedding a domicile of origin and acquiring a domicile of choice."[140]

---

[134] *Id.*

[135] L.R. 1 H.L. Sc. & Div. 441, at 457 (1869).

[136] [1895] 1 I.R., at 438.

[137] [1983] I.R. 29 (Sup. Ct., 1982).

[138] This term is unfortunate: cf. *supra*, p. 47.

[139] While it is true that the husband had spent only two years *with his family*, he had continued to live for a further fourteen months, at an absolute minimum, in Cork. The report is not clear on when (if at all) the husband ceased to reside there. At all events he was still residing in Cork for over a year after he had filed the petition for divorce.

[140] [1983] I.R., at 34. Contrast *L.B.* v. *H.B.*, [1980] I.L.R.M. 247 (High Ct., Barrington, J.) where

DOMICILE AS AFFECTED BY COMPULSION[141]

Matters become somewhat more complicated when an element of compulsion is involved. If a person is sentenced to a long prison term in a foreign country, does he become domiciled there, when his residence is involuntary? If a person flees from his homeland to escape political persecution, does he become domiciled in the new country or will his (possibly futile) hope that political events will improve at home serve to make him retain his original domicile? If a person leaves the country where he is domiciled because he has been advised to do so on account of medical necessity, does he acquire a new domicile in the country in which he goes to live, or can he be regarded as equivalent to a prisoner in exile, without the requisite intention to reside permanently there? Most of the reported cases have dealt with medical necessity so let us consider them first.

(A) Medical necessity[142]

In Britain in the last century some judges took the view that it was extremely difficult for a British person to change his domicile by residing abroad for health reasons. In *Moorhouse* v. *Lord*[143] in 1863, in a case concerning a Scotsman who had lived in France, Lord Cranworth said:

> "it is not enough that you merely mean to take another house in some other place, and that on acount of your health, or for some other reason, you think it tolerably certain that you had better remain there all the days of your life. That does not signify; you do not lose your domicile of origin, or your resumed domicile, merely because you go to some other place that suits your health better, unless, indeed, you mean either on account of your health, or for some other motive, to cease to be a Scotchman and become an Englishman, or a Frenchman, or a German. In that case, if you give up everything you left behind you, and establish yourself elsewhere, you may change your domicile. But it would be a most dangerous thing in this age, when persons are so much in the habit of going to a better climate on account of health, or to another country for a variety of reasons, for the education of their children, or from caprice, or for enjoyment, to say that by going and living elsewhere, still retaining all your possessions here, and keeping up your house in the country, as this gentleman kept up his house [in Scotland], you make yourself a foreigner instead of a native. It is quite clear that that is quite inconsistent with all the modern improved views of domicile."

In the same case, Lord Kingsdown said:[144]

> "A man must intend to become a Frenchman instead of an Englishman; I can well imagine a case in which a man leaves England with no intention whatever of returning, and not only with no intention of returning, but with a determination and certainty that he will not return. Take the case of a man labouring under a mortal disease. He is informed by his physicians that his life may be prolonged for a few months by a change to a warmer climate — that at all events his sufferings will be mitigated by such change. Is it to be said that if he goes out to Madeira he cannot do that without losing his character of an English subject, without losing the right to the intervention of the English laws as to the transmission of his property after his death, and the construction of his

---

an international businessman from the United States was held to have acquired a French domicile (later abandoned), although there was "no evidence of a firm intention to sever his final links with the United States".

[141] See Erving, *Note: Domicile as Affected by Compulsion*, 13 U. Pittsburgh L. Rev. 697 (1952), *Anon.*, *Note: Domicil of Refugees*, 42 Colum. L. Rev. 646 (1942).

[142] See Erving, *supra*, at 703-707.

[143] 10 H.L.C. 272, at 283, 11 E.R. 1030, at 1035 (1863).

[144] *Id.*, at 292 and 1038, respectively.

testamentary instruments. My Lords, I apprehend that such a proposition is revolting to common sense, and the common feelings of humanity."[145]

Clearly these passages display a lofty contempt for foreigners and their legal systems. They go very far down the road of making the concept of domicile almost identical to that of nationality. They are also noteworthy in their lack of adequately reasoned analysis of the conceptual questions raised by the invalid emigrant. It would be wrong to stigmatise all British decisions on this question, however. Even at that time a different, and more realistic, approach was favoured by some judges.[146]

There are several Irish cases on the subject. In the first of these, *Gillis* v. *Gillis*,[147] in 1874, an Irishman was seeking to obtain a decree of divorce *a mensa et thoro* from his wife. In order to do this it was necessary for him to establish that, although he had spent the previous thirteen years in France, his domicile remained Irish. He testified that his foreign residence in France originated in his ill health, and the advice of medical men to spend his winters out of Ireland; that in the course of thirteen years he spent portions of six summers in Ireland; and that it had been his practice to return to Ireland whenever his health and that of his wife and child permitted. He denied that he had ever formed the intention of permanently residing abroad, and said that it always had been his intention to reside permanently in Ireland, if his health should permit. He relied on declarations of intention contained in his will, and on the fact that he held the bulk of his property in Ireland.

Warren, J. stated:

> "These allegations, if true, are sufficient to rebut the inference or presumption in favour
> of a change of domicile, which would flow from the evidence of the respondent; for
> they would establish that the foreign residence of the petitioner was caused by illness,
> and continued on account of health for a particular purpose; he had hoped or expected
> that a change in his health would enable him to reside in Ireland; and that it was always
> his intention to retain his Irish domicile."[148]

Warren, J. confessed that, if the case rested on them, he would hesitate to decide on these statements of the petitioner as to his health and intentions; "it would have been satisfactory testimony on the former subject, and statements of intentions made by a party on a case are entitled to little weight"; moreover, the judge attached little importance to the occasional visits to Ireland. The declarations in his will resolved the issue, since they were in documents prepared "without any anticipation of the unhappy matters which .... caused this litigation".[149] All the references, save one, in these documents to his foreign residence seemed to the judge to point to "residence for the particular purpose" of health, to a residence " 'prescribed or dictated by the external necessity of relief from illness':[150] to which he had deposed, and certainly consistent with hope of a change which would enable him to return and reside in Ireland." Warren, J. continued:

> "... Was the petitioner 'settled' in France? Was he residing at Pau for the personal
> and particular purpose of health; or had he settled himself and his family there? ...

---

[145] The speeches of Lords Cranworth and Kingsdown in *Moorhouse* v. *Lord* "have since, in *Udny* v. *Udny*, L.R. 1 H.L. Sc. 441, been authoritatively decided not to be law, to depend upon a confusion in thought between the political and civil *status* of the individual, and to destroy the differences between *patria* and *domicilium*": *Davis* v. *Adair*, [1895] 1 I.R. 379, at 442-443 (*per* Palles, C.B.).

[146] Cf. e.g. *Hoskins* v. *Matthews*, 8 De G. M. & G. 13, 44 E.R. 294 (1856).

[147] I.R. 8 Eq. 597 (1874).

[148] *Id.*, at 607.

[149] *Id.*

[150] Quoting from *Udny* v. *Udny*, L.R. 1 Sc. & Div. 441, at 458 (1869).

In my opinion the contents of the draft wills, coupled with the petitioner's statement on the subject of his health, rebut the presumption flowing from his long residence in France and the purchase of the villa at Pau, and the respondent has failed to prove that the petitioner had settled in France, or so resided there *animo et facto* as to have acquired a French domicil in substitution for and in derogation of his domicil of origin.''[151]

In *Bradfield* v. *Swanton*,[152] an Irishman who had emigrated at an early age to America returned to Ireland after his wife's death, when he was aged 68. He made other brief visits to the United States, but remained in Ireland until his death six years later. O'Byrne, J. held that he had reacquired an Irish domicile. Those parties in the case who sought a finding of an American domicile, argued that the man had intended merely to live in Ireland for the good of his health during the winter months, but the judge considered that the evidence pointed to his having been advised by his doctor in Boston that "in the interest of his health it would be necessary for him to live for the remainder of his life out of New England". The judge was of opinion that this was why the man had returned to Ireland: "in the circumstances, and having regard to the fact that he was at the time a childless widower, there seems nothing inherently improbable in his having determined to return to Ireland for the purpose of spending the remainder of his life there".

In *In re Sillar Deceased*,[51] the High Court was required to determine the domicile of an Englishman who had lived in Ireland for nearly fifty years up to his death at the age of ninety-seven. He had retained certain interests in England, and on one occasion, about five years before his death, he had intended to visit a relation in England but had been prevented from going there on account of poor health. Budd, J. held that the man's domicile was Irish. It had been argued that he should find an English domicile because the effect of the man's inability to travel to England in 1948 must have been that he was "coerced by the circumstances of his health" to remain in Ireland for all his life thereafter, and that a decision to remain here in such circumstances was not voluntary. Budd, J. rejected this argument on the basis that the other evidence in the case showed that the man had been a very active person who was perfectly capable of going to live in England up to three months before his death. "Though of great age and handicapped by arthritis", said the Judge, he "was quite mentally competent and alert enough to make a decision as to where he would live in the future. He was sufficiently active physically to carry that decision into effect."

An interesting discussion of the question was made by the same judge in *Re Adams Deceased*.[154] There an Irishman, Mr Adams, had acquired an English domicile but, when in his sixties, went with his wife to live in the south of France, where he remained until his death at the age of 78. It was contended by one of the litigants concerned with the question of inheritance to his property that Mr Adams had not lost his English domicile because he had been forced to go to France for health reasons. Budd, J. rejected this argument. He noted that, when in France, Mr Adams swam three times a day, that he travelled to England and Ireland most summers, that he went on cruises, and that no doctor had advised his departure to France. Budd, J. concluded that "certainly no urgent necessity of health compelled him to choose life abroad ... His choice was a perfectly free one influenced by a preference for the climate there as being better suited to his health and no more". It was not the case, in the judge's view, that Mr. Adams had gone unwillingly to France with the intention of returning when his health permitted.

---

[151] I.R. 8 Eq., at 608.
[152] [1931] I.R. 446 (High Ct., O'Byrne, J.).
[153] [1956] I.R. 344 (High Ct., Budd, J., 1955).
[154] [1967] I.R. 424 (High Ct., Budd, J.).

Reading these decisions, it is relatively easy in most instances to agree with their holdings on the evidence before the court. Nevertheless, by and large, the decisions fall well short of providing an impressive intellectual analysis of the difficult questions raised by invalids living abroad. Of course, some aspects of the problem are relatively easy to resolve, and, indeed, have been adequately dealt with by the courts. At one end of the scale, it is clear that where people go abroad for what is intended to be a short visit, to receive medical attention or simply for the benefit of their health, there is no reason to hold that they thus acquire a foreign domicile. At the other end of the scale, where people, for example, emigrate from Ireland to California because they think that the climate will be conducive to their health, there is every reason to hold that they acquire a foreign domicile. The fact that they would not have gone had the Irish climate been better is no reason for denying the obvious fact that they intend to reside permanently or indefinitely in California. As Budd, J. said in *Re Adams Deceased*,[155] ''a special motive does not negative the necessary intention, indeed it may help to establish it.''

The troublesome issue of principle, which the courts have been reluctant to confront, concerns cases where medical necessity absolutely dictates that a person leave his own country to go abroad. It seems that such a decision, made with the very greatest of reluctance, can involve the severance of connection with his own country which a change of domicile implies. We have seen how, in *Moorhouse* v. *Lord*,[156] Lord Kingsdown could not bring himself to accept that a change of domicile would thus take place. Nevertheless, if the law of domicile is to be applied on a principled rather than an emotional basis, the courts should be willing, even in cases of strict medical necessity, to hold that a change of domicile can take place.

Having made this point, however, it is necessary to mention three qualifications. First, where the departure to another country is accompanied by an intention to return, then there will not be the degree of finality necessary to show an intention to change one's domicile. Secondly, in cases of very serious injury, where the patient is unconscious or unable to form any intention on the question, then, of course, his or her domicile will not change.

Finally, in cases where a fatal illness is diagnosed, and the person goes abroad to ease his or her suffering during the final days, it is possible that a court could legitimately hold that, in some instances, where the person dies very shortly afterwards, his or her residence did not change. This seems to be the effect of Budd, J.'s judgment in *Re Adams Deceased*.[157]

(B) Prisoners

A prisoner normally will be considered to retain during the period of his imprisonment the domicile which he had at its commencement. In *Burton* v. *Fisher*,[158] one Joshua Meredyth, who had an Irish domicile of origin, died as a prisoner in England in 1828. Dr Radcliff stated:

''It could not be supposed that he acquired a domicile in England by residence within the walls of the King's Bench prison. All such residence goes for nothing ... *Bempde* v. *Johnstone*,[159] decides that a residence in any place by contrast, operates nothing in a question of change of domicile, agreeably to the rule of the Roman law, in the passage referred to by Domat (Droit public, livre 1, tit, XVI, sec. iv. No. xiv), to show that

---

[155] *Id.*, at 444.
[156] 10 H.L.C. 272, at 292, 11 E.R. 1030, at 1038 (1863).
[157] [1967] I.R. 424, at 452.
[158] Milw. 183, at 191-192 (1828). Cf. *Donnelly* v. *Graham*, 24 L.R. Ir. 127 (C.A., 1888), *Charlton* v. *Morris*, [1895] 2 I.R. 541 (C.A., 1894), *O'Connell* v. *Holland*, [1900] 2 I.R. 448 (C.A., 1899).
[159] 3 Ves. 198, 30 E.R. 967 (1796). Cf. *infra*, pp. 93-94.

a person banished to any certain place, by order of the Prince, did not thereby lose his original domicile. This case, therefore, can derive no aid from Mr Meredyth's involuntary residence and domicile in England; if acquired at all, it must have been acquired before the first arrest of the prisoner.''

(C) Members of the armed forces[160]

Courts formerly held[161] that, as a matter of law, a member of the armed forces could not acquire a domicile of choice during the period of his service. This was because his residence there was regarded as enforced and because his residence in any place was necessarily precarious.[162] Thus, in *Du Moulin* v. *Druitt*,[163] where a marriage was contracted on board a British troopship heading from Cork to Australia in 1817, Lefroy, C.J. said:

"In point of fact, th[e] parties were not in any degree in the position of colonists who had quitted the mother country with a view to form, and who did form, a domicile in another place, and made there a new home for themselves. The parties in the present case not only did not go abroad with a view to remain abroad, but they went abroad under circumstances which made it an imperative duty for them to return. They were members of a military force which had not will or choice of its own, but must certainly come back to England, the mother country.''[164]

Over the years, the courts have set aside the view that a domicile of choice cannot be obtained by a member of the armed forces. They have come to accept that a soldier may indeed wish to stay on in a foreign country when his or her days of service there have been completed. It is now a question of fact in every case,[165] although, of course, the great majority of those serving abroad will not acquire a domicile of choice there.

In *Gaffney* v. *Gaffney*,[166] the question of the domicile of the defendant arose in proceedings under the Succession Act 1965. The defendant had been born in Ireland. It was contended that the defendant nonetheless had an English domicile. His father had been a member of the British army and it was argued that the court could infer that the defendant's father had been domiciled in England. Kenny, J. rejected this argument. He said:

"Before 1921 there were a number of regiments of the British Army which were recruited almost entirely from men living in Ireland, and I am not prepared to infer from the description of the husband's father as an ex-soldier that he had a domicile of origin in England or that the husband was ever domiciled in England.''[167]

---

[160] See Erving, *Note: Domicile as Affected by Compulsion*, 13 U. Pittsburgh L. Rev. 697, at 699-701 (1952), Hendry, *Note; Conflict of Laws: Limitations on the "Domicile of Choice" of Military Servicemen*, 31 Okla. L. Rev. 167 (1978), Sanftner, *The Serviceman's Legal Residence: Some Practical Suggestions*, 26 JAG J. 87 (1971), Siffert, *Residence and Domicile of Servicemen*, 11 JAG J, 5 (1957).

[161] *Re E.R. Smith*, 12 T.L.R. 223 (1896), *Re Macreight*, 30 Ch. Div. 165, at 168 (1885).

[162] *Dicey & Morris*, 124. In the United States, the *First Restatement* S.21, comment *c* (1934) distinguished between soldiers to whom living quarters were compulsorily assigned and soldiers permitted to live with their families near enough to their posts to enable them to perform their duties. In the latter, but not the former, case a domicile of choice could be acquired. This distinction was criticised for being "basically fallacious because the intention of the soldier may well be the same whether or not he lives on the post": Erving, *Note: Domicile as Affected by Compulsion*, 13 U. Pittsburgh L. Rev. 697, at 700 (1952).

[163] 13 I.C.L.R. 212 (Q.B., 1860).

[164] *Id.*, at 222. Cf. *Sinclair* v. *Sinclair*, [1896] 1 I.R. 603 (Warren, P., aff'd by C.A.), *Johnson (falsely called Cooke)* v. *Cooke*, [1898] 1 I.R. 130 (Q.B. Div., Mat., Madden, J., 1897). See also *In the goods of Butson, Deceased*, 9 L.R. Ir. 21 (Prob., Warren, J., 1882) where the domicile of an army captain serving in India was accepted without argument to the contrary as being Irish. Except when serving with his regiment, the captain resided with his father in Ireland, and had no other permanent residence. All his property, consisting of personal chattels and money, was located in India.

[165] Cf. e.g. *Moffett* v. *Moffett*, [1920] 1 I.R. 57 (C.A., 1920, aff'g Powell, J., 1919). See also *Rowland* v. *Rowland*, 42 D.L.R. (3d) 205, at 208-209 (Ont. High Ct., Larner, J., 1973).

[166] [1975] I.R. 133 (Sup. Ct., 1975, aff'g High Ct., Kenny, J., 1973).

[167] *Id.*, at 138-139.

(D) Diplomats

A diplomat is regarded merely as a particular category of public servant,[168] and his or her domicile is governed by the same principles as apply to public servants in general. The fact that there is immunity from jurisdiction of the local courts is not relevant.[169] Although it is possible for a diplomat to acquire a domicile of choice in the country to which he or she is posted, this, of the nature of things, happens only rarely.[170] Moreover, where a person who has already acquired a domicile of choice in a foreign country is appointed to a diplomatic post in that country by the country of his nationality, he will not automatically be considered to have lost the domicile of choice on this account alone.[171]

DIRECT EVIDENCE AS TO INTENTION

How can the Court establish the intention of a particular person? The simplest way might seem to be to ask him, and indeed it is perfectly permissible[172] for a witness to give evidence in court proceedings as to his present or previous intention in relation to domicile. But such evidence tends to be regarded with suspicion.[173] In the Irish decision of *Gillis* v. *Gillis*[174] which has already been discussed, the petitioner, long resident in France, testified that he had gone there on medical advice and that he had at all times intended to reside permanently in Ireland if his health should permit.

Warren, J. stated:

"I confess that, if the case rested with them, I should hesitate to decide upon these statements of the petitioner as to his health and intentions; it would have been satisfactory to have submitted to the Court some medical testimony on the former subject, and statements of intention made by a party in a cause are entitled to little weight ..."[175]

So also in *Davis* v. *Adair*,[176] Palles, C.B. pointed out that

"... when witnesses are deeply interested in the views that are taken of a particular fact, especially when the fact is their own intention at an antecedent period, the experience of all of us is that the mind is able to believe that it remembers, as having existed at an antecedent period, intentions that really had their origin at a subsequent time."

[168] Cf. *Dicey & Morris*, 126.

[169] Cf. *Casdagli* v. *Casdagli*, [1919] A.C. 145. Nor will the fiction of extra-territoriality of embassies apply in relation to domicile: *A.G.* v. *Kent*, 1 H. & C. 12, at 28, 29, 158 E.R. 782, at 788 (1862).

[170] Cf. *Naville* v. *Naville*, 1957 (1) S.A. 280.

[171] *A.G.* v. *Kent, supra, Sharpe* v. *Crispin*, L.R. 1 P. & D. 611 (1869).

[172] Cf. *D'Etchegoyen* v. *D'Etchegoyen*, 13 P.D. 132 (1882), *Udny* v. *Udny*, L.R. 1 Sc. & Div. 441, at 444 (*per* Lord Hatherley, L.C., 1869). See also *Spurway* v. *Spurway*, [1894] 1 I.R. 385 (C.A., 1894, affirming Porter, M.R. 1893). Relevant Canadian decisions are discussed by J.-G. Castel, *Conflict of Laws: Cases, Notes and Materials*, 3-39ff. (4th ed., 1978).

[173] See *Bell* v. *Kennedy*, L.R. 1 Sc. & Div. 307, at 313 (*per* Lord Cairns, 1868). Cf. *id.*, at 322-323 (*per* Lord Colonsay). See also *Re Craignish* [1892] 3 Ch. 180, at 190-191 (*per* Chitty, J.), *Lockhart's Trust; ex parte Lady Lockhart*, 11 Ir. Jur. (n.s.) 245, at 249 (Berry Cusack Smith, M.R., 1866), *Iveagh* v. *Revenue Commissioners*, [1930] I.R. 386, at 413 (High Ct., *per* Sullivan, P., 1929) (High Court order discharged by Sup. Ct. on grounds not of present relevance). Cf. *Sproule* v. *Hopkins*, [1903] 2 I.R. 133 (K.B. Div., Andrews, J., 1902) (evidence given by respondent as to his intention of returning to London "not ... consistent with his acts and conduct ...."), *L.B.* v. *H.B.*, [1980] I.L.R.M. 257 (High Ct., Barrington, J.). Of course, in many cases such evidence will be perfectly acceptable and fully credible: see, e.g. *Re Adams Deceased* [1967] I.R. 424, at 446 (High Ct., Budd, J.).

[174] I.R. 8 Eq. 597 (Ct. for Mat. Causes, Warren, J., 1874).

[175] *Id.*, at 607.

[176] [1895] 1 I.R. 379, at 454 (C.A., affirming Porter, M.R.). See also *Holden* v. *Holden*, [1968] N.I. 7, at 15 (Q. B. Div. (Mat.), Lord MacDermott, L.C.J. 1967), *Bell* v. *Kennedy*, L.R. 1 Sc. & Div. 307, at 322 (*per* Lord Colonsay, 1868).

Evidence of earlier declarations

As well as direct testimony by the person concerned, his or her intention at an earlier time may be gleaned[177] through evidence as to what he or she *said* on the question, whether formally or informally, publicly or privately. This evidence "as to declarations" has not a very high status with the courts today,[178] although to say that it is "the lowest species of evidence"[179] is probably an overstatement.

The cautious approach of the courts was well expressed in *Ross* v. *Ross:*[180]

"Declarations as to intention are rightly regarded in determining the question of a change of domicile, but they must be examined by considering the person to whom, the purposes for which, and the circumstances in which they are made, and they must further be fortified and carried into effect by conduct and action consistent with the declared expression."

Context in which declaration is made

That the probative force of a declaration depends on its particular context was apparent in the case of *Gillis* v. *Gillis*[181] (already mentioned) where a man, long resident in France, petitioned for divorce *a mensa et thoro,* asserting an Irish domicile. Warren, J. regarded as "evidence of a superior quality"[182] four draft wills prepared by the man "without any anticipation of the unhappy matters which ... caused this litigation, and presenting to my mind every appearance of truthfulness."[183]

Similarly, in *Kennedy* v. *Kelly,*[184] in 1862, there was no reason to doubt the veracity of a declaration. In this case, an Irish parish priest working in the West Indies made a will in which he described himself as "of Liscoleman in the County of Wicklow in Ireland, at present in the parish of St Davids, Grenada". On this declaration was based a finding that the testator's domicile was Irish. Keatinge, J., having quoted this declaration noted that the testator:

"gives Ireland as his domicil,[185] but adds, that at present he is at St. Davids. We all know that a domicil of origin continues until a new one is acquired, and his will, not only affirms that his domicil is in Ireland, but the words added, 'at present', etc. mean that Ireland is his domicil, though he is now residing in Grenada."[186]

On the other hand, human nature being what it is, it is possible that in some cases a statement as to intention may be made which is designed to flatter or deceive the

---

[177] In *Davis* v. *Adair,* [1895] 1 I.R., at 396, Porter, M.R. "entertained some doubts" as to whether evidence as to earlier declarations should be received to prove the intentions of a living person, capable of being examined and actually examined, in order to confirm his evidence in his own favour and interest.

[178] Cf. the former approach expressed in *Burton* v. *Fisher,* Milw. 183, at 188 (Dr Radcliff, 1828): "[A] man ... does not establish his domicile in any place, unless he makes sufficiently known his intention of fixing there, either tacitly or by express declaration."

[179] *Crookenden* v. *Fuller,* 1 Sw. & Tr. 441, at 450, 164 E.R. 804, at 808 (*per* Sir C. Cresswell, 1859). See also *Davis* v. *Adair,* [1895] 1 I.R. 379, at 439 (C.A., *per* Sir P. O'Brien, B.): "Evidence of conversations is said .... to be the lowest class of evidence".

[180] [1930] A.C. 1, at 6-7 (*per* Lord Buckmaster, H.L., 1929). *Dicey & Morris,* 119, fn. 76 consider that "expression" seems to be a misprint for "intention". See also *Revenue Commissioners* v. *Matthews,* 92 I.L.T.R. 44, at 50 (High Ct., *per* Maguire, J. 1953 (reversed by Sup. Ct., 1954)).

[181] I.R. 8 Eq. 597 (Ct. of Mt. Causes, Warren, J. 1874). Cf. *Spurway* v. *Spurway,* [1894] 1 I.R. 385 (C.A., 1894, affirming Porter, M.R. 1893), as explained by Hanna, J., in *Iveagh* v. *Revenue Commissioners,* [1930] I.R. 386, at 419 (High Ct., 1929) (High Court order discharged by Sup. Ct. on grounds not of present relevance).

[182] I.R. 8 Eq., at 607.

[183] *Id.*

[184] 7 Ir. Jur. (n.s.) 326 (1862).

[185] In fact, as has been mentioned, the testator merely described himself as being "of" Liscoleman and made no specific mention of "domicil" cf. *id.,* at 326.

[186] 7 Ir. Jur. (n.s.) at 328.

hearer.[187] In *Re Adams Deceased*,[188] discussed earlier, the Court had to determine the domicile of a man, born in Ireland, who had acquired a domicile of choice in England, where he married, but who had, in his sixties, gone to live in France where he remained until his death there. A friend of the deceased, Miss Hutchings, gave evidence that he had acquired a flat in London and that he had expressed to her the intention of returning to England on his wife's death. Budd, J. appeared to give only small weight to this evidence as to intention, which, as counsel for another party pointed out, was "not a little affected by the consideration that the [deceased] appeared from time to time to have made statements to Miss Hutchings of a kind which she would like to hear."[189]

Conduct must be consistent with declaration

The courts have in several cases laid stress on the requirement that declarations as to intention be backed up by conduct consistent with them: "It is not by naked assertion, but by deeds and acts that a domicile is established".[190] Thus where a person's actual behaviour contradicts the declaration, the court will not give any substantial weight to the declaration.

In *In re Sillar; Hurley* v. *Wimbush*,[191] Budd, J. said:

"Where a person is in fact physically resident in a place and the proper inference from all the known circumstances is that he had formed the intention of remaining indefinitely at that place, he cannot alter the fact that he has acquired a domicil of choice by stating something to the contrary."

This rule has often been applied where the declaration involves a statement of an intention that is contingent on the happening of uncertain events. In *Doucet* v. *Geoghegan*,[192] a Frenchman long resident in England said that when he made his fortune he would go back to France. This declaration did not impress the Court. James, L.J. said:

"A man who says that is like a man who expects to reach the horizon[;] he finds it at last no nearer than it was at the beginning of his journey."[193]

---

[187] Cf. *Cheshire & North*, 169.
[188] [1967] I.R. 424 (High Ct., Budd, J.).
[189] *Id.*, at 450.
[190] *McMullen* v. *Wadsworth*, 14 App. Cas. 631, at 636 (P.C., *per* Sir Barnes Peacock, 1889) (quoting "the doctrine of the Roman law"). See also *Prior-Wandesforde* v. *Revenue Commissioners*, 1 Repts of Irish Tax Cases 148, at 255 (High Ct., *per* Sullivan, P., 1928):
    "Change of domicile cannot be effected by a mere declaration, as domicile is established by conduct and not by assertion."
    Cf., however, *Kennedy* v. *Kelly*, 7 Ir. Jur. (n.s.) 326 (Keatinge, J., 1862). An Australian *dictum* in accord with *McMullen* v. *Wadsworth* is contained in the judgment of Isaacs, J., in *Fremlin* v. *Fremlin*, 16 C.L.R. 212, at 234 (1913). A relevant Canadian authority is *Brewster* v. *Brewster*, [1945] 3 D.L.R. 541 (B.C.C.A.). For consideration of the position in the United States, see *Leflar*, para. 10, *Weintraub*, 12, Heald, *Note: Self-Serving Declarations and Acts in Determination of Domicile*, 34 Georgetown L. J. 220 (1946). See also *Texas* v. *Florida*, 306 U.S. 398 (1939), *In re Dorrance's Estate*, 309 Pa. 151, 163 A. 303 (1932), *In re Dorrance's Estate*, 115 N.J.Eq. 268, 170 A. 601 (1934). In *In Matter of Newcomb*, 192 N.Y. 238, 84 N.E. 950 (1908), it was noted that:
    "While acts speak louder than words, the words are to be heard for what they are worth."
[191] [1956] I.R. 344, at 355 (1955). See also *id.*, at 350, and cf. *In re Annesley, Davidson* v. *Annesley*, [1926] 1 Ch. 692, at 701 (*per* Russell, J.), approved by Budd, J. in *In re Sillar; Hurley* v. *Wimbush*, *supra*, at 356. Of course a false assertion of foreign domicile designed to secure a decree in that foreign jurisdiction will not be effective in conferring a foreign domicile: cf. *Gaffney* v. *Gaffney*, [1975] I.R. 133 (Sup. Ct., aff'g Kenny, J.), discussed *infra*, pp. 286-287, 605, 607-608.
[192] 9 Ch. D. 441 (1878).
[193] *Id.*, at 457.

Similarly, in *Davis* v. *Adair,*[194] where an Englishman long resident in the United States had made statements indicating that he would eventually return to England, the Irish Court of Appeal gave these statements no weight. Palles, C.B. said that:

"declarations such as we have here, indicating an intention to return upon an event which is contingent in fact, which is not contemplated by the individual as reasonably certain, and which cannot happen until after a period of time unlimited and undefined, are consistent with, instead of being destructive of, the necessary intention [to acquire a new domicile in one of the United States]."[195]

In *Re Adams Deceased,*[196] which has already been mentioned, Budd, J. quoted this extract from Palles C.B.'s judgment, when rejecting the argument that the deceased had abandoned his French domicile on account of his statement to Miss Hutchings that he would return to England on his wife's death. Budd, J. noted that:

"The portion of the foregoing observation as to an event reasonably certain does not apply in that death is certain,[197] but that does not detract from the relevance of the rest of what the Chief Baron said."[198]

In the earlier case of *Moffett* v. *Moffett*[199] in 1919, Powell, J. had invoked Palles, C.B.'s statement when holding that an Irishman long resident in South Africa had abandoned his Irish domicile and had not subsequently resumed it, in spite of statements by him at various times that he desired to return to Ireland. Powell, J. gave these statements "no weight".[200] He considered that:

"All these declarations of intention might possibly be evidence of an intention to resume his domicil of origin if in fact he returned to this country; but, in my opinion, they are not sufficient to outweigh the natural result of his acts, and I think that, looking at his acts as a jury ought to do, I can come to no other conclusion than that his domicil was [in] South Africa."[201]

In *Bradfield* v. *Swanton,*[202] the Court was faced with the somewhat different problem of mutually inconsistent declarations as to intention. O'Byrne, J.'s solution was straightforward:

"In these circumstances, I scrutinise the undoubted facts of the case for the purpose of seeing with which alleged expression of intention they are more consistent ."[203]

Declarations by persons ignorant of exact meaning of domicile.

In some cases the evidence will disclose that a person actually declared himself to be "domiciled" in a particular country. This usually occurs in an official or legal context, such as in dealings with tax or immigration authorities or in the making of a will or settlement of property. In *Sillar's*[204] case, Mr Sillar, an Englishman, came to live in Ireland at the age of 50 and remained there until his death 47 years

---

[194] [1895] 1 I.R. 379 (C.A. aff'g Porter, M.R.).

[195] *Id.,* at 441.

[196] *Supra.*

[197] Of course, although death is certain, the time of its occurrence is normally not at all certain. This factor might have been mentioned by Budd, J.

[198] [1967] I.R., at 451.

[199] [1920] 1 I.R. 57 (Powell, J.).

[200] *Id.,* at 71.

[201] *Id.,* at 72.

[202] [1930] I.R. 446 (High Ct., O'Byrne, J.).

[203] *Id.,* at 455. See also *Fleming* v. *Horniman,* 44 Times L.R. 315 (P.D.A. Div., Hill, J., 1928).

[204] [1956] I.R. 344 (High Ct., Budd, J., 1955).

later. In his will made four years before his death, Mr Sillar described himself as a British subject, domiciled in England and resident in Ireland. Budd, J. was not troubled by this description, saying:

> "It is, I feel significant that in his will he couples his statement as to domicil with the assertion that he is a British subject. [His daughter] says of him that he was very insistent that he was not Irish. Laymen do not appreciate as clearly as lawyers the distinction between domicil and nationality. People feel strongly on the political issue of nationality but are little interested in the rather complex and arid subject of domicil. Mr Sillar had no place of residence in England. He had not even visited England for many years before he made his will. He had a settled home here. Just why he should say he was domiciled in England it is difficult to say, but having regard to all the surrounding circumstances I feel that the clue is to be found: the fact that he desired to stress his nationality as is indicated by his description of himself in his will as a British subject and his insistence on the fact that he was not Irish."[205]

The same judge was faced with the same issue twelve years later in *Re Adams Deceased*.[206] The facts of this case have already been stated. When living in France Mr Adams appointed the Bank of Ireland Trustee Department as his executor. During correspondence with the Bank, the issue of his domicile arose. In answer to an inquiry from the Bank as to whether his domicile of origin had been "British", and as to whether he had ever acquired a domicile of choice, Mr Adams replied "I am an Irishman born in Cork .... I hold an Irish passport and I have never acquired a domicile of choice."

Budd, J. accepted the principle that:

> "a declaration as to domicile may carry great weight, particularly if there was reason for supposing that the person concerned had some reasonably clear idea of what is involved in acquiring a domicile of choice, a matter that, I may remark, presents no little difficulty to skilled lawyers."[207]

Returning to the theme of *Sillar's* case, he said:

> "Laymen are apt to confuse the matter of nationality with domicil. From the wording of the testator's letter to the Bank of Ireland in answer to the query as to his domicil, I am left with the impression that he was no exception to this ...."[208]

Declarations made on legal advice

Clearly a declaration made on legal advice may differ in its probative force from one made spontaneously; the declaration is likely to reflect in some part the guiding hand of the lawyer rather than necessarily reflecting the undistilled views of the declarant. In *Revenue Commissioners* v. *Shaw*[209] the testator made a testamentary declaration that: "despite my residence in the Republic of Eire [*sic*] I have looked upon myself as a Scotsman and have retained and desired to retain my Scottish domicile acquired by my choice and .... now retained by me ...." The declaration was made at the instigation of his Scottish solicitor who thought that it would simplify the administration of the estate. McWilliam, J. considered that it was clear from the

---

[205] *Id.*, at 356.
[206] [1967] I.R. 424 (High Ct., Budd, J.).
[207] *Id.*, at 448.
[208] *Id.* See also *Prior-Wandesforde* v. *Revenue Commissioners,* 1 Repts of Irish Tax Cases 248 (High Ct., 1928), where the appellant believed that he could change his domicile by mental act expressed by declaration, with no regard to the question of residence.
[209] [1982] I.L.R.M. 433 (High Ct., McWilliam, J., 1977).

evidence that "the deceased did not really mind which domicile was alleged. Accordingly, the declaration cannot influence my consideration of the domicile of the deceased...."[210]

Declarations referring to "home"

It is not unusual for a person living away from the country of his or her birth to refer to that country as "home". The courts will not normally attach very great significance to this expression as far as gleaning the person's intentions is concerned. In *Bell* v. *Kennedy,*[211] in 1868, a man born of Scottish parents in Jamaica used the expression "coming home" when corresponding with relatives and friends in Scotland about long-term plans to buy a Scottish estate, with the possibility of living there. The House of Lords attached little weight to this expression. It appeared to Lord Cairns, L.C. to be "obviously a form of language that would naturally be used by a colonist in Jamaica speaking of the mother country in contradistinction to the colony".[212]

But as Sir P. O'Brien, C.J. noted in *Davis* v. *Adair:*[213]

"Very different is the expression 'my home', which does import residence, and permanent residence...."

In this case, one of the parties deposed:

"When I left Kenilworth-square in 1882 I went to my father's house in Staten Island. That was my home then. From that time to my marriage I made that my head-quarters except when I was travelling."

Sir P. O'Brien, C.J. considered that the expressions "my home" and "my head-quarters" were

"used not casually, but deliberately in direct reference to residence. 'Head-quarters' means in its ordinary acceptation principal place of residence; and 'Domicile of choice', says Lord Westbury in *Udny* v. *Udny,*[214] 'is a conclusion or inference which the law derives from the fact of a man fixing voluntarily his sole or chief residence in a particular place, with the[215] intention of continuing to reside there for an unlimited time'."[216]

Again, it is necessary to look at the wider picture in every case. It is quite possible that a person living abroad may refer to the home in which his or her family

---

[210] *Id.*, at 437. See also *Revenue Commissioners* v. *Matthews*, 92 I.L.T.R. 43 (Sup. Ct., 1954, reversing High Ct., Maguire, J., 1953). The approach in these cases may be contrasted with *Bell* v. *Bell*, [1922] 1 I.R. 152 (K.B. Div., Dodd, J.) where a marriage settlement drawn up by a lawyer expressly provided that it was to be "construed .... as if the said Isaac Bell were now domiciled in Ireland, and as if the said Isaac Bell and Evadne Cane were to remain henceforth during their respective lives domiciled in Ireland". In holding that the husband had an Irish domicile, Dodd, J. (at 155) considered that " [t]he marriage settlement is cogent evidence. Mr Cane [the wife's father] says it was deliberate. The lawyer who drafted it had the law clearly in mind" (citation omitted). Cf. *Gulbenkian* v. *Gulbenkian*, [1937] 4 All E.R. 618, at 627 (P.D.A. Div., Langton, J.).

[211] L.R. 1 Sc. & Div. 307 (H.L., 1868).

[212] *Id.*, at 310. See also *Davis* v. *Adair*, [1895] 1 I.R. 379, at 458 (C.A., *per* Barry, L.J.):
"We all know that the expression 'home', as applied to the mother country, is used by Australian colonists almost invariably, or at all events extensively; and I have heard travellers remark the difference between Australians and Americans in that respect, that Australians, even those who were born in Australia, when coming on a visit to England, say they are going 'home'."

[213] [1895] 1 I.R. 379, at 433 (C.A.).

[214] L.R. 1 H.L.Sc. 441, at 458 (1869).

[215] In fact Lord Westbury spoke of "an" intention.

[216] [1895] 1 I.R., at 433-434. Cf. *id.*, at 445 (*per* Palles, C.B.).

remain[217] as "home", not to suggest that he or she intends to return to the country of his or her birth but instead to describe the centre of his or her family's life (and a place of fond memories) in warm terms.

Declarations as to apprehended place of death

If a person makes a statement consistent only with his belief that he will die in a certain country, this may be of strong probative value in determining his domicile. In *Munster & Leinster Bank Ltd.* v. *O'Connor*,[218] a woman of Irish domicile of origin worked in Paris for many years. She gave instructions as to her burial which showed clearly that she contemplated the probability of her continuing to reside in Paris at the date of her death. She promised her Irish solicitor that she would leave a note, with instructions as to her burial, in the desk in her apartment in Paris, marked: "To be opened after my death". This, combined with other facts in the case, made it "unarguable,"[219] in the view of Meredith, J., that her domicile was French.

Failure to make declaration

It is worth noting that the *failure* to make a declaration as to intention may in some cases be the basis for inferring that the person did not have a particular intention. In *In re Sillar; Hurley* v. *Wimbush*,[220] an Englishman lived for many years in Ireland, and after his retirement remained here until his death. Budd, J. rejected the argument that he had retained his English domicile:

> "He had ample means to go to England in a comfortable and leisurely fashion. From the time the business was sold and the war was over there was no restraint on his going. He had only himself to please, yet there is not a whisper of any such intention having been envisaged to those to whom it is morally certain he would have communicated it."[221]

ABANDONMENT OF DOMICILE OF CHOICE

A domicile of choice may be abandoned by a person ceasing to reside[222] in the country in which he or she has been domiciled, with the intention of no longer being domiciled there. The onus of proving this is on the person alleging it.[223] It appears that "the evidence to establish the abandonment of an acquired domicil and the

---

[217] Cf. *id.*, at 446-447 (*per* Palles, C.B.).

[218] [1937] I.R. 462 (High Ct., Meredith, J., 1935). See also *In re Sillar; Hurley* v. *Wimbush*, [1956] I.R. 344, at 351-352, 360-361 (High Ct., Budd, J.). Contrast *In re Joyce; Corbet* v. *Fagan*, [1946] I.R. 277 (Sup. Ct., affirming Overend, J., 1945), where the deceased, an Irishman, died in England after a long period of residence there. He was held to have acquired an English domicile. *Per* Black, J., at 307:

> "I regard the fact that [the deceased] left an Irish will made forty-two years before his death, which contained a provision that *if* he died in Ireland he should be buried in the family vault in County Galway, as a negligible circumstance, and the more so having regard to his subsequent history."

Cf. Geoghegan, J. (dissenting) at 297-298. See also the facts of *Shannon deceased*, 76 I.L.T.R. 53 (N.I.K.B. Div., Andrews, L.C.J., 1942).

[219] [1937] I.R., at 467. Contrast *In re De Hosson; Erwin* v. *De Hosson*, [1937] I.R. 467 (High Ct., Meredith, J.) where it was held that, in spite of thirty years' residence in Ireland, the deceased had not abandoned his Dutch domicile, since the evidence showed that he intended to return to the Netherlands shortly.

[220] [1956] I.R. 344 (High Ct., Budd, J., 1955).

[221] *Id.*, at 355. See also *id.*, at 360:

> "While evidence of a negative nature is not enough I start with the fact that there is not a scintilla of evidence of his ever having even talked of moving after the war."

Cf. *Re Adams Deceased*, [1967] I.R. 424, at 439 (High Ct., Budd, J.).

[222] *Bank of Ireland Trustee Co. Ltd.* v. *Adams, supra*, at 452 (High Ct., Budd, J.).

[223] *Revenue Commissioners* v. *Shaw*, [1982] I.L.R.M. 433, at 436 (High Ct., McWilliam, J., 1977). See also *Gillis* v. *Gillis*, I.R. 8 Eq. 597, at 605 (Ct. for Mat. Causes, Warren, J., 1874).

resumption of a domicil of origin need not be so strong as the evidence which is requisite to establish the abandonment of a domicile of origin, and the acquisition of a new one''.[224]

The easiest way an intention to abandon may be shown will normally be through the establishment of an intention to acquire another domicile of choice.

But it is clear that a person may abandon his or her domicile of choice without actually seeking to acquire any other domicile.[225] In this case the domicile of origin revives and continues to apply until the person acquires a new domicile of choice or one of dependency.[226]

This was brought out clearly in *Re Adams Deceased. Bank of Ireland Trustee Co. v. Adams,*[227] where Budd, J., relying on *Dicey,*[228] summarised the legal position as follows:

> "A person abandons a domicil of choice in a country by ceasing to reside there and by ceasing to intend to reside there permanently or indefinitely and not otherwise. On abandoning a domicil of choice, a person either acquires a new domicil of choice or resumes his domicil of origin."

Bell v. *Bell*[229] is a difficult decision. The respondent in proceedings for restitution of conjugal rights had a domicile of origin in one[230] of the United States of America but had acquired an Irish domicile of choice several years previous to the taking of the proceedings. He subsequently had left his wife, informing her that he intended to live with another woman. In correspondence with his wife he stated that his "permanent address" was at a house in London. Shortly after having left his wife he transferred to her his interest in the family home.

Dodd, J. held that the respondent had not changed his Irish domicile:

> "As a man may change his domicile, has the respondent by purporting to do so and going to England, effectively changed it? He cannot do so according to our law and, I think, also, clearly not according to English law."[231]

Unfortunately the report throws little light on the sincerity of the respondent's assertion that his London residence was his "permanent address". Nor is there any discussion of his circumstances at the time of the petition. If the holding amounts to no more than one that the respondent had *in fact* retained his Irish domicile, no particular problem arises. But the passage quoted from Dodd, J.'s judgment appears to suggest that a man who leaves his wife cannot gain a foreign domicile where to do so may result in preventing the court from exercising jurisdiction in certain matrimonial proceedings against him. The perceived wrongfulness of the respondent's conduct, rather than the insincerity of his attempt to change his domicile, seems to have weighed heavily with the judge.[232] If this was the judge's holding, it was in error. When a person's motive for acquiring a new domicile is investigated, it may sometimes show that an apparent acquisition of a new domicile was not in fact

---

[224] *Sproule* v. *Hopkins,* [1903] 2 I.R. 133, at 138 (K.B. Div., Andrews, J., 1902).

[225] *Id.*

[226] See *infra,* p. 76. Since the abolition of the domicile of dependency of married women, the only domicile of dependency that may occur in the present context is that of mentally disabled persons; *ex hypothesi,* the abandonment of a domicile of choice must be made by an adult.

[227] [1967] I.R. 424, at 434 (High Ct., Budd, J.).

[228] 7th ed., 1958, p. 112-113.

[229] [1922] 2 I.R. 152 (K.B. Div., Dodd, J.).

[230] The report does not indicate which.

[231] [1922] 2 I.R., at 155, citing *Manning* v. *Manning,* L.R. 2 P. & D. 223 (1871), a decision which does not appear to be of particular assistance in the present context.

[232] Cf. [1922] 2 I.R., at 155.

a real one, since the person may have been attempting to deceive others (such as a potential petitioner) or may have intended secretly to return when the "heat has died down". But if the motive shows that the person did in fact intend to acquire a new domicile, then he should be held to have done so, regardless of the moral quality of his motive. If this presents a problem, then the rules for jurisdiction should be changed, rather than interfering with the concept of domicile.

One final difficulty with *Bell* v. *Bell*[233] is that Dodd, J. did not discuss, and may well have overlooked, the possibility that the respondent, though not necessarily acquiring an English domicile, had none the less abandoned his Irish domicile of choice, whereupon his domicile of origin would have revived.

THE DOMICILE OF ORIGIN

The domicile of origin differs in several respects from a domicile of choice. First, and self-evidently, the domicile of origin is acquired without any choice on the part of the person to whom it attaches. Secondly, it appears that the domicile of origin is more tenacious than a domicile of choice: it "adheres more closely"[234] and is less easily shaken off than a domicile of choice. The courts have not been entirely consistent in their formulation of the approach to be applied. In the Supreme Court decision of *T.* v. *T.*,[235] in 1982 Henchy, J. noted that "[t]he rebuttable presumption" is in favour of continuance of the domicile of origin.[236] Over a hundred years ago,[237] Warren, J. had asserted that ".... unless the acquisition of a new domicil be shown with perfect clearness and satisfaction, the domicil of origin continues."

In the English decision of *Winans* v. *A.G.*[238] in 1904 Lord Macnaghten thought that an intention to abandon a domicile of origin was:

> "not to be inferred from an attitude of indifference or a disinclination to move increasing with increasing years, least of all from the absence of any manifestation of intention one way or the other. It must be, to quote Lord Westbury[239] ...., a 'fixed and settled purpose'. 'And', says his Lordship, 'unless you are able to show that with perfect clearness and satisfaction to yourselves, it follows that a domicil of origin continues.' So heavy is the burden cast upon those who seek to show that the domicil of origin has been superseded by a domicil of choice! And rightly I think."

In the High Court decision of *Hood* v. *Hood*,[240] in 1958, however, Murnaghan, J. made it plain that he did

---

[233] *Supra.*

[234] *Davis* v. *Adair,* [1895] 1 I.R. 379, at 432 (C.A., *per* P. O'Brien, C.J.).

[235] [1983] I.R. 29, at 34 (Sup. Ct., 1982).

[236] See also *In re Joyce; Corbet* v. *Fagan,* [1946] I.R. 277, at 298 (Sup. Ct., *per* Geoghegan, J., dissenting, 1945); cf. *W.* v. *W.*, unreported, High Ct., Doyle, J., 5 July 1978 (1978-336Sp.), at p. 1: "It is settled law that cogent evidence is required to displace a domicile of origin and to demonstrate that it has been superseded by a domicile of choice".

[237] In *Gillis* v. *Gillis,* I.R. 8 Eq. 597, at 605 (Ct. for Mat. Causes, 1874). See also *Shannon Deceased,* 76 I.L.T.R. 53, at 54 (N.I. K.B.Div., Andrews, L.C.J., 1942) ("The importance ... of domicil of origin must never be overlooked, especially as the tendency of modern authority makes it increasingly more difficult to displace it by an alleged domicil of choice"); *Moffett* v. *Moffett,* [1920] 1 I.R. 57, at 62 (*per* Powell, J., 1919) (affirmed by C.A., 1920) ("The domicil of origin continues, unless a fixed and settled intention of abandoning the first domicil and acquiring another as the sole domicil is clearly shown"). In accord is *L.B.* v. *H.B.* [1980] I.L.R.M. 257 (High Ct., Barrington, J.). In the Canadian decision of *Haut* v. *Haut,* 86 D.L.R. (3d) 757, at 759 (Ont. High Ct., 1979), Carruthers, J. required "[s]trict and conclusive proof" to displace the domicile of origin by a domicile of choice "because of the grave consequences flowing from a change in domicile".

[238] [1904] A.C. 287, at 290 (H.L. (Eng.)).

[239] In *Bell* v. *Kennedy,* L.R. 1 H.L.Sc. 307, at 321 (1868).

[240] [1959] I.R. 225, at 232 (High Ct., Murnaghan, J., 1958).

"not interpret what Lord Macnaghten said as meaning anything more than that a Court should be slow legally to draw an inference that a person had the intention to acquire a new domicil, particularly as a change of domicil may involve far-reaching consequences."

It is possible that the greater difficulty in shaking off a domicile of origin derived from the view of English courts over a century ago, during the formative period of the principles of domicile, that persons with an English domicile of origin would be very slow to abandon it. This was perhaps a correct inference when, at the height of British imperialism, Britain exercised control over countries spread throughout the world. The pattern of colonists frequently sending their children back to Britain for their education and of retiring there supported the view that the domicile of origin would be difficult to dislodge.[241] There was also perhaps a degree of racism in this approach: certainly the decisions which formerly held that a person of European origin could never acquire a domicile in an oriental country would give credence to this view.

The Law Reform Commission in their Working Paper No. 10-1981 have observed that:

" [w]hilst national sentiments towards one's own country make it reasonable that the Courts should not too hastily find that a domicile of origin has been abandoned, it would appear that 'English courts have given an exaggerated emphasis to this aspect of the domicile of origin'."[242]

In the Working Paper, the Commission recommended[243] that, if domicile was to continue as a connecting factor, the rule that a domicile of origin is more difficult to abandon than a domicile of choice should be abandoned. The Commission accepted that the decisions in this country[244] do not manifest such an exaggerated emphasis as in England.

In contrast to a domicile of choice, which may be extinguished by departure from a country with the intention of not returning, but without necessarily acquiring a new domicile, the domicile of origin cannot be lost by abandonment of residence alone. It continues until a domicile of choice (or new domicile of choice as the case may be) or of dependency is acquired. In the Supreme Court decision of *In re Joyce; Corbet* v. *Fagan*,[245] Black, J. observed that:

---

[241] Cf. the English and Scottish Law Commissions' *Private International Law: The Law of Domicile*, para. 509 (Working Paper No. 88 and Consultative Memorandum No. 63, 1985):
"It could be argued that the pre-Second World War attitudes displayed in cases such as *Winans* v. *Attorney General*, [1904] A.C. 287 and *Ramsay* [v. *Liverpool Royal Infirmary*], [1930] A.C. 588 are anachronistic today, being a direct response to the demands of a now vanished Empire and the desire of imperial and colonial servants and the businessmen who accompanied them to retain their domiciles in the United Kingdom. However, the void left by the imperial administrator and soldier has been filled by ever-expanding population in the international business community, and, in our view, whatever may be the other objections to the tenacity of the domicile received at birth, anachronism is not one."

[242] Law Reform Commission, Working Paper No. 10, *Domicile and Habitual Residence as Connecting Factors in the Conflict of Laws*, p. 79 citing Graveson, 199.

[243] *Id.*

[244] See, e.g. *In re Joyce; Corbet* v. *Fagan, supra, Munster & Leinster Bank Ltd* v. *O'Connor*, [1937] I.R. 462 (High Ct., Meredith, J.).

[245] [1946] I.R. 277, at 301 (Sup. Ct., 1945). See also, to similar effect, *In re Sillar; Hurley* v. *Wimbush*, [1956] I.R. 344, at 349 (High Ct., Budd, J., 1955), *Re Adams Deceased, Bank of Ireland Trustee Co. Ltd.* v. *Adams*, [1967] I.R. 424, at 433 (High Ct., Budd, J.), *T.* v. *T.*, [1983] I.R. 29, at 35 (Sup. Ct., *per* Griffin, J., 1982), *Bell* v. *Kennedy*, L.R. 1 H.L. (Sc.) 307, at 310 (*per* Lord Cairns, L.C., 1868).

"... one principle at least is beyond doubt, namely that the domicil of origin persists until it is proved to have been intentionally and voluntarily abandoned and supplanted by another [domicil]."

And in *Revenue Commissioners* v. *Shaw,*[246] McWilliam, J. observed, in relation to the domicile of origin:

"In order to acquire another domicile a person must have the intention of doing so together with actual residence in the country of his choice. The intention must be an intention to reside in that country for an unlimited time. A domicile of origin persists until it has been shown to have been abandoned and another acquired and the onus of proving a change of domicile is on the person alleging it. No question arises of ascertaining whether there is evidence of an intention to retain the domicile of origin; the person alleging a change must establish an intention to acquire another domicile."

The next difference concerns the notion of revival of the domicile of origin. Where a person abandons a domicile of choice, then, in the hiatus until he or she acquires a new domicile, of choice or one of dependency, his or her domicile of origin revives.[247] Thus, where a person with an Irish domicile of origin acquires an English domicile of choice, which he later abandons — for example by leaving England and becoming a wanderer on the European mainland — his Irish domicile of origin will revive and continue to apply until he acquires a new domicile of choice or one of dependency. Similarly, if the same person left England by boat for America, having abandoned his English domicile of choice, intending to live for the rest of his days in New York, the domicile of origin would revive, for the duration of the voyage at least, until the New York domicile of choice was acquired.

In *Revenue Commissioners* v. *Matthews,*[248] the Supreme Court had to decide whether the case was one involving revival of the domicile of origin. A man of Irish domicile of origin acquired a domicile of choice in the Sark domiciliary area in 1935, residing on an island which he himself had bought, and on which he had built a mansion. In 1940 he bought a house in Guernsey, a separate domiciliary area. He supervised alterations to this house and visited it frequently but never took up residence there. He decided to live in this house, but before he could move there the Germans occupied the Channel Islands and he was forced to flee to England. He died four years later in Scotland.

The Supreme Court, reversing Maguire, J. rejected the argument of the Revenue Commissioners that the man had abandoned his Sark domicile, whereupon, in the absence of the acquisition of a domicile in Guernsey, the Irish domicile of origin would revive. The Supreme Court was impressed by the fact that his staff, as well as his furniture and other movable property, remained in Guernsey, so that "until his 'lares et penates' were installed, [the Guernsey property] could not be regarded as his home nor did [the Sark property] cease to be such even though he did not physically occupy it again."

As may be appreciated this doctrine of revival is a mixed blessing, especially when it is recalled that the person may have only the most tenuous connection with the country of his or her domicile of origin. The problem is not easy to resolve. In the United States[249] and Australasia[250] the law of the domicile just abandoned continues

---

[246] [1982] I.L.R.M. 433, at 435-436 (High Ct., McWilliam, J., 1977).

[247] *Udny* v. *Udny,* L.R. 1 Sc. & Div. 441 (1869). See also *Davis* v. *Adair,* [1895] 1 I.R. 379, at 416-417 (C.A., *per* Walker, C.).

[248] 92 I.L.T.R. 44 (Sup. Ct., 1954, rev'g High Ct., Maguire, J., 1953).

[249] See *Leflar*, 18, *Stewart* v. *Stewart*, 16 Ark. App. 164, 698 S.W. 2d 516 (Ct. Apps., 1985). A clear analysis of the policy issues is presented in *In re Estate of Jones*, 192 Iowa 78, 182 N.W. 227, 16 A.L.R. 1286 (1921). For criticism of the outcome of that decision, see Weintraub, *An Enquiry into the Utility of "Domicile" as a Concept in Conflicts Analysis*, 63 Mich. L. Rev. 961, at 965-968 (1965).

[250] Cf. Australia's Domicile Act 1982, section 7; see also New South Wales's Domicile Act 1979, section 6, and New Zealand's Domicile Act 1976, section 11.

until a new domicile is acquired. But, though this rule may work less arbitrarily than the revival principle, it is scarcely a totally satisfactory answer since, as the Law Reform Commission point out, *ex hypothesi* the person affected by the rule "has abandoned the domicile [of choice], possibly for strong personal reasons of antipathy towards the country or State in question, and he might resent his incapacity to 'shake off' that connection until a new domicile is acquired".[251]

Once the doctrine of revival is set aside, and the other distinguishing feature of the domicile of origin — its relative tenacity — is removed (as the Law Reform Commission have proposed),[252] the domicile of origin serves little useful function. It seems that in such circumstances the concept may safely be abandoned,[253] leaving the other rules as to domicile of choice or dependency to fill the void.

THE DOMICILE OF MARRIED WOMEN

Prior to its abolition in 1986 the domicile of dependency of married women had provoked a great deal of critical analysis.[254] The essence of the concept was that, on marriage, a woman's domicile became that of her husband, and was thereafter determined by reference to his domicile at any particular time. Precisely why this doctrine developed is a matter of some discussion. It appears to have been part of the wider notion of the "unity of husband and wife"[255] brought about by marriage. Unquestionably the wife's legal identity became subservient to that of her husband, and in some respects was entirely obliterated. But it would be wrong to approach this question with the view that the only explanation for the doctrine was that it was "the last barbarous relic of a wife's servitude".[256]

Undoubtedly a single matrimonial domicile (albeit one which was based on sex discrimination) was practically convenient and conducive to some degree of certainty in determining the status, and consequently the rights and obligations, of the spouses.[257] There was, moreover, a basis for assuming that spouses would wish to share a common domicile, since normally they would be living together and,

---

[251] Law Reform Commission, Working Paper No. 10-1981, *Domicile and Habitual Residence as Connecting Factors in the Conflict of Laws*, p. 80. See also Atkin, *The Domicile Act 1976*, 7 N.Z.U.L.Rev. 286, at 289 (1977), Forsyth, *Reform of the Law of Domicile in Australia with Particular Reference to the New Zealand Domicile Act 1976*, 4 Otago L. Rev. 95, at 99 (1977). The Commission, on the basis that domicile is to continue as a connecting factor, proposed (*op. cit.*, pp. 80-81) that the rule favoured in the United States, New Zealand, and Australia should be adopted; the Commission considered this preferable to a more complex alternative rule which would determine a person's domicile in the period between abandonment and acquisition by reference to "the country with which he is most closely connected." The English and Scottish Law Commissions have provisionally come to a similar conclusion, in *Private International Law: The Law of Domicile*, para. 5.21 (Working Paper No. 88 and Consultative Memorandum No. 63, 1985).

[252] W.P. No. 10 — 1981, p. 80.

[253] Cf. *McClean*, pp. 23-24, para. 1.30. This step has been taken in New Zealand: Domicile Act 1976, section 12.

[254] See generally the Law Reform Commission's Working Paper No. 10-1981, *Domicile and Habitual Residence as Connecting Factors in the Conflict of Laws*, chs. 4-7, *Shatter*,117-118, 119, Shatter, *The Mixed Blessing of an Independent Domicile*, 193-194 Irish Times, 30 November 1976, Matthews, *Dependent Domicile of Irish Wives*, 111 Ir. L. T. & Sol. J. 17 (1977), Duncan, *The Domicile of a Married Submission to the Law Reform Commission*, (1977) 1 Dublin U.L.J. 38, Beale, *The Domicile of a Married Woman*, 11 So.L.Q. 93 (1917), Goodrich, *Matrimonial Domicile*, 27 Yale L.J. 49 (1917), Crozier, *Domicile in Marriage Law*,17 Boston U. L. Rev. 293 (1937), Hogg, *Domicile of a Married Woman in Relation to Divorce*, 6 Can. Bar Rev. 655 (1928).

[255] See generally Williams, *The Legal Unity of Husband and Wife*, 10 Modern L. Rev. 16 (1947); Bracton, *De Legibus*, Lib. V. c. 25, s. 10, Blackstone, *Commentaries on the Laws of England*, vol. 1, 442.

[256] *Gray* v. *Formosa*, [1963] P. 259, at 267 (C.A. *per* Lord Denning, M.R., 1962). See also Lord Denning's observations during the Second Reading of the (abortive) Domicile Bill 1959 in the House of Lords: H.L. Debs., vol. 214, cols. 250-251 (12 February 1959). And see Crozier, *supra*, at 321-327.

[257] Cf. the *Royal Commission on Marriage and Divorce*, 1951-55, para. 820 (Cmd. 9678, 1956).

formerly, the husband, who was likely to be the breadwinner,[258] would have the final say, legally, as to where they should live.[259]

The Domicile and Recognition of Foreign Divorces Act, 1986 has abolished the domicile of dependency of married women. Section 1 provides as follows:

"(1)   From the commencement[260] of this Act the domicile of a married woman shall be an independent domicile and shall be determined by reference to the same factors as in the case of any other person capable of having an independent domicile and, accordingly, the rule of law whereby upon marriage a woman acquires the domicile of her husband and is during the subsistence of the marriage incapable of having any other domicile is hereby abolished.

(2)   This section applies to the parties to every marriage, irrespective of where and under what law the marriage takes place and irrespective of the domicile of the parties at the time of the marriage."

Two other provisions should also be mentioned in this context. Section 2 provides that "[t]he domicile that a person had at any time before the commencement of this Act shall be determined as if this Act had not been passed"; and section 3 provides that "[t]he domicile that a person has at any time after the commencement of this Act shall be determined as if this Act had always been in force".

A number of points about these provisions may be noted. First, section 1 seeks to prescribe an independent domicile for all married women, regardless of the domicile of the parties at the time of the marriage, and regardless of where the marriage took place.[261] Secondly it is worth noting that section 1(1) speaks of "*the* rule of law whereby upon marriage a woman acquires the domicile of her husband and is during the subsistence of her marriage incapable of having any other domicile".[262] Clearly the assumption here is that such a rule of law represented the situation existing at the time of the legislation.[263] As we shall see,[264] there is at least some doubt as to whether this was in fact so.

Thirdly, the abolition of a married woman's domicile of dependency is not retrospective. Thus, for example, if the question as to what was the domicile of a married woman in 1975 arises in proceedings in 1987, the answer must be determined "as if this Act had not been passed".[265] The court in 1987 would be required to treat the issue as one to which common law rules (subject to the provisions of the Constitution) would apply.[266]

---

[258] Cf. *In re Bushbey*, 112 N.Y.S. 262, at 263 (*per* Crosby, Surrogate, 1908):
"Either the husband or the wife must have the final say in the matter of where their home is to be; and, so long as the husband is burdened with the responsibility of feeding and clothing the family, the wife, and children, that very responsibility ought to carry with it the authority to determine the location where his toil will earn its best reward for their benefit."
See also *Re Wallach Deceased*, [1950] 1 All E.R. 199, at 200 (P.D.A.Div., Hodson, J., 1949).

[259] Cf. *In re Mitchell*, [1937] I.R. 767 (Sup. Ct., 1937, aff'g High Ct., 1936). See further *Binchy*, 185.

[260] 2 October 1986: cf. section 7.

[261] Cf. section 1(2).

[262] Emphasis added. Section 1(1) closely follows section 5(1) of New Zealand's Domicile Act 1976.

[263] Contrast section 1(1) of the General Scheme of a Bill to Reform the Law of Domicile, included in the Law Reform Commission's Working Paper No. 10-1981, *Domicile and Habitual Residence as Connecting Factors in the Conflict of Laws*, p. 86, which refers to "any rule of law".

[264] *Infra*, pp. 80-82.

[265] Section 2.

[266] It would seem that, in interpreting the effect of the Constitution, a court in 1987 would be entitled to have regard to the standards and attitudes of 1987 rather than of 1937 or 1975. It may perhaps be argued that the court would also be permitted to apply common law rules as of 1987 rather than 1975, though there may be some conceptual difficulty in attempting to discern a common law rule in circumstances where a statute has intervened, so far as concerns events after the commencement of the statute. In the narrow, technical, sense the court, when dealing with pre-statute cases, must determine the question of a married woman's domicile "as if th[e] Act had not been passed". But from a broader standpoint, the court would surely be entitled to have regard to changing social attitudes towards sex equality, of which the 1986 Act is evidence, when determining the present content of

A fourth point worth noting about the legislation is that section 3 (following New Zealand and Australian models) ensures that there is no "hangover" from the domicile of dependency rules so far as the determination of a married woman's domicile *after* the commencement of the Act is concerned. Her domicile is to be determined as if the Act "had always been in force", just as the domicile of any other person capable of having an independent domicile is determined. This approach is far preferable to that adopted in Britain in 1973,[267] whereby a wife is treated as retaining her domicile of dependence (as a domicile of choice if it is not also her domicile of origin) unless and until it is changed by acquisition or revival of another domicile either on or after the commencement date. The effect of this approach is "to treat women who were married before [the commencement date] somewhat less favourably than those who marry on or after that date".[268]

Since the Irish legislation of 1986 expressly provides[269] that the domicile a person had at any time before the commencement of the Act is to be determined as if the Act had not been passed, the question as to what exactly the law was before the commencement of the Act is far from academic. The domicile of every woman married before that date for the duration of her married life until 2 October 1986 must be determined as though the Act had not been passed. It is useful, therefore, to examine what the position may be in relation to this period.

In cases dealing with the domicile of married women, the judges were mainly[270] content to proceed on the basis that the rule applied and admitted of no exception. Thus, in *Sinclair* v. *Sinclair,*[271] in 1896, the court appeared to accept without question that if the husband's domicile was Irish the wife's domicile was also Irish. Similarly, in *Lett* v. *Lett,*[272] in 1906, where the defendant wife had obtained a decree of divorce *a mensa et thoro* from the plaintiff husband eighteen years previously, Porter, M.R., having noted that the plaintiff's Irish domicile at all times had not been denied, observed that:

> "[i]f this is so, it follows, as a necessary consequence that the defendant also was and is domiciled in Ireland, for, according to our law, the domicil of the wife is that of her husband."[273]

---

common law rules relating to the domicile of dependency of married women.

[267] Domicile and Matrimonial Proceedings Act, 1973, section 1(2).

[268] *Inland Revenue Commissioners* v. *Duchess of Portland* [1982] Ch. 314, at 318 (Chy. Div., Nourse, J.). See also *id.,* at 320: "It seems clear that a woman living in England who was married before [the commencement date] can only free herself from the shackles of dependency by choosing to leave her husband for permanent residence in another country. This is a very limited freedom ...." See further Wade, *Domicile: A Re-Examination of Certain Rules,* 32 Int. & Comp. L. Q. 1 (1983), Thompson, *Domicile of Dependence: The Last Remnant of a Relic?,* 32 Int. & Comp. L. Q. 237 (1983).

[269] Domicile and Recognition of Foreign Divorces Act, 1986, section 2.

[270] But cf. *Gaffney* v. *Gaffney,* [1975] I.R. 133, at 152 (*per* Walsh, J.), and *K.C.* v. *M.C.,* Sup. Ct., 13 December 1985 (292/84) (*per* McCarthy, J.), considered *infra.*

[271] [1896] 1 I.R. 603 (Mat., Warren, P., aff'd by C.A.). The evidence disclosed that at the time of a divorce obtained earlier in England, the wife, who had deserted her husband, was living there with another man. The question of the wife's long-term intentions was not investigated. The argument of counsel for the petitioner in the proceedings (for divorce *a mensa et thoro*) brought by the husband before the Irish court, was to the effect that "[t]he domicil of the wife followed that of the husband ....": *id.,* at 606.

[272] [1906] 1 I.R. 618 (C.A., aff'g Porter, M.R.).

[273] *Id.,* at 623. *Maghee* v. *M'Allister,* 3 Ir. Ch. Rep. 604 (Brady, L.C., 1853) is of interest since it contains a possible suggestion that the wife's assumption of a domicile of dependency might not be automatic. There a Scotsman, domiciled in Scotland, married an Irish wife in London. Three months later, the couple having apparently lived together in London in the meantime, the husband "returned to Scotland with his wife, *and she became a domiciled Scotchwoman ....*"(*Id.,* at 609, *per* Brady, L.C.) (emphasis added). It could perhaps be argued that this means that only where the wife actually went to the country of her husband's domicile should it be considered to apply to her. However, the case appears also to support the view that, once the Scottish domicile applied to the wife, she was not capable of shaking it off of her own accord by residing elsewhere.

Most recently in *T.* v. *T.*,[274] in 1983, the Supreme Court appeared to accept without question that the domicile of a wife, living apart from her husband, was dependent on his; otherwise it is difficult to see on which basis recognition would have been afforded to the divorce obtained by the husband in England,[275] where he was domiciled.[276]

In the earlier Supreme Court decision of *Gaffney* v. *Gaffney*,[277] however, in 1975, Walsh, J. had stated:

> "The law has been that during the subsistence of a marriage the wife's domicile remains the same as, and changes with, that of her husband. For the purpose of this case it is proper to adopt this view, although it is possible that some day it may be challenged on constitutional grounds in a case where the wife had never physically left her domicile of origin while her deserting husband may have established a domicile in another jurisdiction."

This proviso merits close examination. It fell well short of an assertion that the rule of law attributing a domicile of dependency of married women was completely inconsistent with the Constitution. Walsh, J. referred only to a case where the wife had "never physically left her domicile of origin". Taken literally these words would not apply to a woman with an Irish domicile of origin, who had at any time in her life, possibly even before the marriage, gone on a week's visit to London, for example. A more reasonable interpretation would be that what was envisaged here was a departure of more substantial dimensions. A strict application of the requirement relating to domicile of origin could also lead to some arbitrary results. The best way of responding to this proviso would therefore seem to be that it constituted a sound warning that the rules relating to the domicile of dependency of married women raised constitutional doubts, at all events in cases where injustice or hardship to the wife would, as a general rule or in a specific case, be likely to follow. It is worth noting also that in the Supreme Court case of *M.C.* v. *K.C.*,[278] McCarthy, J. referred to Walsh, J.'s comments in *Gaffney* regarding the question of the wife's domicile of dependency, and observed that he was "not to be taken as accepting that any such legal principle survived the enactment of the Constitution".

What are the constitutional dimensions to the question? First, we must consider the guarantee of equality under Article 40.1.[279] Clearly there was no equality of treatment with the domicile of dependency of married women. But that does not necessarily mean that the rule was inconsistent with the Constitution. It might be argued that the discrimination was not invidious, because it served beneficial policies such as the encouragement of family unity and the simplification of the determination of domicile.[280] Whether this argument would succeed today is most doubtful. Alternatively, it might be argued that being a wife is a different "social function" from being a husband or a single woman. Again, this defence of the discriminatory rule appears unconvincing.

---

[274] [1983] I.R. 29 (Sup. Ct., 1982).

[275] As has been noted, *supra*, p. 60, the court spoke of a "British" domicile.

[276] *Cf. infra*, pp. 277-280.

[277] [1975] I.R. 133,at 152. For analysis of the decision, see *North*, 379ff., Duncan, 9 Ir. Jur. (n.s.) 59 (1975). This passage from Walsh, J.'s judgment was not quoted or discussed in *T.* v. *T.*, which cited *Gaffney* v. *Gaffney* merely for the proposition that, if the husband's domicile in *T.* v. *T.* had been Irish rather than British, the divorce would have been given without jurisdiction and could not have been acted on in Ireland. It should be noted that, in *Gaffney*, the orthodox view was set forth without qualification by Griffin, J. ([1975] I.R., at 157).

[278] Sup. Ct., 13 December 1985 (292/84), at p. 5 of judgment.

[279] *Cf.* Forde, *Equality and the Constitution*, 17 Ir. Jur. (n.s.) 295 (1983).

[280] *Cf.* Graveson, *The Special Character of English Private International Law*, ch. 1 of R. Graveson, *Comparative Conflict of Laws,* vol. 1, at p. 11 (1977), *Royal Commission on Marriage and Divorce, 1951-1955*, para. 820 (Cmd. 9678, 1956).

The next constitutional attack would concentrate on the personal rights of the citizen under Article 40.3, coupled with the right to property under Article 43. The rules relating to the domicile of dependency of married women prejudiced the property interests of women in some instances. If, for example, an Irish husband domiciled in Ireland with an Irish wife deserted her in 1975 and established — perhaps without even her knowledge — a domicile in Argentina, it may be argued that the wife's constitutional rights in relation to property would be interfered with by rules which would result in her having her share in the property altered to her detriment by Argentinian law. Questions of access to justice could also arise.

Article 41 could also be invoked in the constitutional attack on the wife's domicile of dependency. A rule permitting a man to desert his wife and obtain a divorce recognised here in a country with which the wife has absolutely no connection may be considered to defy the guarantee to "protect the family in its constitution and authority".[281] This is especially so since the wife so divorced would thereupon lose her rights under the Succession Act 1965 and, it would appear, under the Family Law (Maintenance of Spouses and Children) Act 1976 and the Family Home Protection Act 1976. It is difficult to estimate the relevance in this context of the constitutional right to marital privacy[282] or the right to privacy generally.[283] It could perhaps be argued (speculatively) that marital privacy (or, indeed, the general right to privacy) protects a wife against the unwarranted intrusion of a foreign legal system into the privacy of her life on intimate matters such as divorce, for example.

Whatever the outcome of a constitutional challenge to the domicile of dependency of married women may be, it is worth considering whether, even at common law, the position was as stark as is widely believed. During the last century, when the main principles of the law of domicile were being developed, there was considerable disagreement among the judges as to what principles should apply. There was, however, respectable authority (generally *obiter*) favouring the view that in at least some cases the rule regarding dependency of married women should be qualified or even ignored. Thus, in *Dolphin* v. *Robins,*[284] a House of Lords decision in 1859, Lord Cranworth expressed the view that

"... there may be exceptional cases to which, even without judicial separation, the general rule would not apply, as for instance, where the husband has abjured the realm, has deserted his wife, and established himself permanently in a foreign country, or has committed felony and been transported."[285]

The question was finally resolved, in favour of an inflexible application of the dependency rule, in two decisions in the nineteen twenties,[286] but the solution

---

[281] Article 41.1.2°.

[282] Cf. *McGee* v. *A.G.,* [1974] I.R. 284 (Sup. Ct., 1973).

[283] Cf. *Norris* v. *A.G.,* [1984] I.R. 36 (Sup. Ct., 1983).

[284] 7 H.L.C. 390, 11 E.R. 156 (1859).

[285] *Id.,* at 418-419 and 167-168, respectively. See also Lord Cranworth's remarks, *id.,* at 416-417 and 166-167, respectively. Cf. the more conservative positions adopted by Lords Kingsdown and Campbell L.C., *id.,* at 420 and 168, respectively, and at 423 and 169, respectively. Lord Cranworth's approach was supported by *Le Sueur* v. *Le Sueur,* 2 P.D. 139 (Sir R. J. Phillimore, 1876), *Niboyet* v. *Niboyet,* 4 P.D. 1 (C.A. 1878), *Firebrace* v. *Firebrace,* 4 P.D. 63 (Sir James Hannen, P., 1878), *Armytage* v. *Armytage,* [1898] P. 178 (Gorell Barnes, J.), *Ogden* v. *Ogden,* [1908] P. 46, at 78 (C.A., *per* Sir Gorell Barnes, P., 1907), *Stathatos* v. *Stathatos,* [1913] P. 46 (Bargreave Deane, J., 1912), *De Montaigu* v. *De Montaigu,* [1913] P. 154 (Sir Samuel Evans, P.). An approach favouring the application of the dependency principle without exception was adopted in *Warrender* v. *Warrender,* 2 Cl. & Fin. 688, 6 E.R. 1239 (H.L.(Sc.) 1835), *Re Daly's Settlement,* 25 Beav. 456, 53 E.R. 711 (Sir John Romilly, M.R., 1858).

[286] *Lord Advocate* v. *Jaffrey,* [1921] A.C. 146 (H.L. (Sc.), 1920), *Attorney-General for Alberta* v. *Cook,* [1926] A.C. 444 (P.C.). For an analysis of the tendency of courts after the First World War to elevate the principle of certainty in conflicts of law above that of equity, see Neuhaus, *Legal Certainty Versus Equity in the Conflict of Laws,* 28 L. & Contemp. Problems 795, at 797 (1963).

adopted was criticised[287] by many commentators for its harshness and inappropriateness in many cases.[288]

Conclusion

In view of the frailty of the legal arguments in favour of the domicile of dependency of married women, so far as both the Constitution and the common law are concerned, it may be argued that in a case where section 2 of the Domicile and Recognition of Foreign Divorces Act 1986 is relevant, our courts would be justified in taking the bold step of holding that the domicile of dependency of married women had ceased to be part of our law long before the 1986 legislation. A more timid approach, which might commend itself to the courts, would be that the domicile of dependency of married women did indeed apply but operated only so long as the spouses continued to reside together. As against this, our courts may well take the view that there are strong policy reasons for not overturning retrospectively a rule of such practical importance as that of the domicile of dependency of married women. The implications of such retrospective overturning in relation to such matters as matrimonial status, property and tax would be alarming and the potential source of considerable injustice unless the courts were also disposed to work out detailed supplementary rules to mitigate the potential hardship and injustice. Faced with the choice between abolition by legislation on a specific date and a retrospective abolition by judicial decree, the courts may well prefer the more cautious solution.

DOMICILE OF MINORS[289]

The law relating to the domicile of minors is in several respects uncertain. The shadow of history still occludes our understanding of some of the central principles. Legislation[290] has recently changed the position where the parents of a legitimate child, whether by birth or adoption, are living apart, and the child has his home

---

[287] Cf. *Read*, 242, Cowen, *The Conflict of Laws: The Experience of the Australian Federation*, 6 Vand. L. Rev. 638, at 663 (1953), *Anon., Casenote*, 35 Yale L.J. 1015 (1926).

[288] Nevertheless Canadian courts continued to apply the *Cook* principle even after Canada had rid itself of the right of ultimate appeal to the Privy Council: see, e.g. *Capon* v. *Capon*, 42 D.L.R. (2d) 675 (1965). *Christenson* v. *Christenson*, 45 W.W.R. (N.S.) 47 (1963), *Voghell* v. *Voghell*, 33 W.W.R. 673 (N.W.T. C.A., 1960), *Marshall* v. *Marshall*, [1952] Q.W.N. 308, *D.* v. *D.*, [1973] 3 O.R. 82 (H. Ct.), *Solomon* v. *Walters*, 18 W.W.R. 257 (B.C. Sup. Ct., 1956), *White* v. *White (No. 2)*, 59 Man. R. 181 (1950), aff'd. 59 Man. R. 210 (1950), *Harris* v. *Harris*, [1930] 1 W.W.R. 173 (Sask, C.A.), aff'g [1929] 2 D.L.R. 546, *Jablonowski* v. *Jablonowski*, 28 D.L.R. (3d) 446 (Ont. H. Ct., Lerner, J., 1972), *Khalifa* v. *Khalifa*, 19 D.L.R. (3d) 460 (N.S. Sup. Ct., Tr. Div., Gillis, J., 1971), *Armstrong* v. *Armstrong*, 21 D.L.R. (3d) 140 (Ont. H. Ct., Grant, J., 1971), *Powell* v. *Powell*, 31 D.L.R. (3d) 419 (H. Ct., Cromarty, J., 1972). Australian decisions following *Cook* include *Boardman* v. *Boardman*, 36 S.R. (N.S.W.) 447 (Jordan, C.J., 1939). Cf. *Union Trustee Company of Australia Ltd.* v. *Commissioner of Stamp Duties*, [1926] St. R. (Queensland) 304, at 308-309 (Full Ct., *per* Blair, C.J.).

[289] See Duncan, *The Domicile of Infants*, 4 Ir. Jur. (n.s.) 36 (1969), Binchy, *Reform of the Law Relating to the Domicile of Children: A Proposed Statute*, 11 Ottawa L. Rev. 279 (1979), Blaikie, *The Domicile of Dependent Children: A Necessary Unity?*, [1984] Jurid. Rev. 1, Palmer, *The Domicile of an Infant — Some Comments upon the 1973 Act*, 4 Family L. 35 (1974), Clive, *The Domicile of Minors*, [1966] Jurid. Rev. 1, Spiro, *Domicile of Minors Without Parents*, 5 Int. & Comp. L.Q. 196 (1956), Tarnopolsky, *The Draft Domicile Act — Reform or Confusion?*, 29 Sask. Bar Rev. 161, at 166, 173-174 (1964), *Anon., Note: The Power to Change the Domicile of Infants and of Persons Non Compos Mentis*, 30 Colum. L. Rev. 703 (1930). Rafferty, *Domicile — The Need for Reform*, 7 Man. L.J. 203, at 204-205, 201, 211, 214 (1977), Crozier, *Domicile in Marriage Law*, 17 Boston U.L. Rev. 293 (1937), *Wolff*, 108-110, 117-120, *Leflar*, 23-26, Stumberg, *The Status of Children in the Conflict of Laws*, 8 U. Chic. L. Rev. 42, at 45-46, 59-62 (1940), the Law Reform Commission's Working Paper No. 10-1981, *Domicile and Habitual Residence as Connecting Factors in the Conflict of Laws*, ch. 8, the English and Scottish Law Commissions' Working Paper No. 88 and Consultative Memorandum No. 63, *Private International Law: The Law of Domicile*, Part IV (1985), *Shatter*, 118-119.

[290] Domicile and Recognition of Foreign Divorces Act 1986, section 4.

(at least for some time) with his or her mother; but beyond this narrow change, the common law remains unaffected.[291]

The domicile of a child under the age of majority[292] is a domicile of dependency: that is to say, it is, in general, determined by the domicile of the person upon whom the child is regarded by the law as being dependent. At common law it was well established that the domicile of a legitimate child, during the lifetime of his or her father, would be determined by that of the father.[293] Thus, in *Spurway* v. *Spurway*,[294] in 1893, Porter, M.R. said of a person born in Ireland of a father whose domicile was English, that

> "his domicil followed that of his father. The circumstances of his having been born in Ireland would not give him an Irish domicile, for that would remain English until his father had changed his English domicil for an Irish one. His domicil, while he was under age, would follow that of his father."[295]

Whether this is the best approach may be seriously doubted.[296] As well as the recent limited legislative change,[297] it may well be that in the light of constitutional[298] and other legal changes, the law on this subject in general, as articulated in the older decisions, requires substantial modification.

There is no direct authority on the domicile of a legitimated child. *Dicey & Morris* consider that, upon legitimation, "at any rate if the legitimation is due to the marriage of the minor's parents,"[299] the child's domicile, having been dependent on his mother's, becomes dependent on the father's. It would appear, however, that unless the legitimation has retroactive effect — and legitimation under our Legitimacy Act 1931[300] has not — the child's domicile of origin remains what it was at the time of birth.[301]

The domicile of a legitimate child after the death of his father is generally determined by the domicile of his mother,[302] although as we shall see, this rule will not always apply, either under common law rules or under the recent legislative provisions. The domicile of an illegitimate child is determined by that of his mother.[303] There is no authority on the domicile of origin of a foundling. The

---

[291] Cf. *id.*, section 4(3).

[292] See the Age of Majority Act 1985, section 2 and *infra*.

[293] *Udny* v. *Udny*, L.R. 1 Sc. & Div. App. 441, at 457 (H.L., *per* Lord Westbury 1869), *Forbes* v. *Forbes*, Kay 341, at 353, 69 E.R. 145, at 150 (1854), *Re Duleep Singh; Ex parte Cross*, 6 T.L.R. 385 (C.A., 1890), *Gulbenkian* v. *Gulbenkian*, [1937] 4 All E.R. 618 (P.D.A.), *Kilpatrick* v. *Kilpatrick*, [1929] 3 W.W.R. 463, [1930] 1 D.L.R. 288, *Baker* v. *Baker*, 49 Man. R. 163, [1941] 2 W.W.R. 389, [1941] 3 D.L.R. 581 (C.A.).

[294] [1894] 1 I.R. 385 (Porter, M.R., 1893).

[295] *Id.*, at 392.

[296] Cf. *Infra*, p. 91.

[297] Domicile and Recognition of Foreign Divorces Act 1986, section 4.

[298] Cf. the Law Reform Commission's Working Paper No. 10-1981, *Domicile and Habitual Residence as Connecting Factors in the Conflict of Laws*, para. 87.

[299] *Dicey & Morris*, 135. The Law Reform Commission have stated that "[t]he question of the domicile of a child legitimated other than by the marriage of his or her parents (as, for instance, by recognition) appears to be entirely open": Working Paper No. 10-1981, *Domicile and Habitual Residence as Connecting Factors in the Conflict of Laws*, para. 90.

[300] Cf. section 1(1) of the 1931 Act.

[301] *Wolff*, 118-119, *Cheshire & North*, 179.

[302] See *Potinger* v. *Wightman*, 3 Mer. 67, at 79, 36 E.R. 26, at 30 (Ch., 1817), *Johnstone* v. *Beattie*, 10 Cl. & Fin. 42, at 138, 8 E.R. 657, at 694 (H.L., *per* Lord Campbell, 1843), *In re Wright's Trust*, 2 K. & J. 595, 69 E.R. 920 (1856), *Udny* v. *Udny*, L.R. 1 Sc. & Div. App. 441, at 457 (H.L., *per* Lord Westbury, 1869), *Children's Aid Society of Eastern Manitoba* v. *Rural Municipality of St Clements*, 6 W.W.R. (n.s.) 39 (Man. C.A., 1952).

[303] Cf. the Law Reform Commission's Working Paper No. 10-1981, *Domicile and Habitual Residence as Connecting Factors in the Conflict of Laws*, paras. 10, 88.

commentators generally take the view[304] that it should be the place where he or she is found. Perhaps the better rule would be that there should be a presumption to this effect, but one capable of being rebutted where the evidence indicated otherwise.[305]

Adopted children

In the absence of legislative provisions clarifying the position, the domicile of an adopted child is a matter of some uncertainty.[306] The Adoption Act 1952, expressly resolves[307] the question of the *nationality* of an adopted child, but the issue of the child's *domicile* is not specifically addressed. Section 24 of the Act provides that, on an adoption order being made —

"(a) the child shall be considered with regard to the rights and duties of parents and children in relation to each other as the child of the adopter or adopters born to him, her or them in lawful wedlock
(b) the mother shall lose all parental rights and be freed from all parental duties with respect to the child."

This provision does not resolve the issue of domicile expressly, and it would be somewhat difficult to contend that it does so by implication.[308] To regard domicile as either a "right" or a "duty" is odd; yet the purpose, if not the express words of the section, would seem consistent with letting the domicile of the adopted child be determined by that of his adoptive father or mother.

It is "generally assumed, but without judicial or legislative authority",[309] that a child once adopted becomes dependent for his domicile on his adoptive father (or mother if she is not married). The Domicile and Recognition of Foreign Divorces Act 1986[310] deals with only one aspect of the question, namely, the position where parents of a legitimate child are living apart. In such circumstances the child's domicile follows that of the mother. Section 4(4) of the Act provides that " [i]n the application of this section to a minor who has been adopted, references to the father or mother of such minor shall be construed as references to the adoptive father or adoptive mother of such minor". Clearly, therefore, an adopted child is to be treated exactly as a natural child in these limited circumstances. It is reasonable to assume that the legislation was drafted on the assumption that, so far as the other aspects of domicile are concerned, adoptive children are also in the same position as natural children; but the Act does not expressly so provide.

---

[304] *Dicey & Morris*, 109, *Graveson*, 195, *Cheshire & North*, 179, *Westlake*, s. 248. See also the Law Reform Commission's Working Paper No. 10-1981, *Domicile and Habitual Residence as Connecting Factors in the Conflict of Laws*, para. 90.

[305] As, for example, "where a small baby babbling in Swedish is discovered as a stowaway on a ship that has put in to a South African port from Stockholm": Kahn, *The South African Law of Domicile of Natural Persons*, [1971] Acta Jurid. 1, at 19. See also Forsyth, *Reform of the Law of Domicile in Australia with Particular Reference to the New Zealand Domicile Act 1976*, 4 Otago L. Rev. 95, at 98 (1977).

[306] Cf. the Law Reform Commission's Working Paper No. 10-1981, *Domicile and Habitual Residence as Connecting Factors in the Conflict of Laws*, para. 90, Report of the Review Committee on Adoption Services, *Adoption*, para. 13.13 (Pl. 2467, 1984), *Wolff*, 119-120. *Shatter*, 118, states the position without any reservation.

[307] By section 25.

[308] See *Wolff*, 119.

[309] Report of the Review Committee on Adoption Services, *Adoption*, para. 13.13 (Pl. 2467, 1984). *Dicey & Morris*, (9th ed., 1973) rule 15(5), tentatively propose this principle. They concede (at 121) that there is no English authority which supports it, but they point to statutory developments on these lines in Australia and New Zealand, as well as to the fact that the United States *Restatement of the Law, Second, Conflict of Laws*, 22, comment *q* follows the same approach, which they observe, "seems reasonable in principle".

[310] Section 4.

The position of an adopted child before adoption may affect his or her domicile afterwards, since the child's domicile of origin may revive at any later time in his life if he abandons one domicile of choice and fails to acquire another. It would appear that the child's domicile of origin remains that of the natural mother, if the child is illegitimate, or of the natural father, if the child is legitimate.[311] The Law Reform Commission in its Working Paper No. 10-1981, proposed that:

> "the domicile of an adopted child should be the same as if he were the child of the adopter or adopters born in wedlock to him, her or them; but his domicile of origin should be determined by the domicile of his adopter or adopters at the time of the adoption; and, if they have no common domicile, the domicile of origin of the child should be determined by their habitual residence."[312]

This proposal was endorsed by the Review Committee on Adoption Services in its Report[313] in 1984.

Changing a minor's domicile

Let us now consider the position where a parent changes his or her domicile. At common law, it seemed that the domicile of a legitimate child would change automatically with a change in the domicile of his father. The position of a legitimate child of a widowed mother or of a child born out of wedlock was less certain. In *In re Beaumont*,[314] which involved the child of a widowed mother, Mr Justice Stirling considered the better view to be that:

> "the change in the domicil of an infant which .... may follow from a change of domicil on the part of the mother, is not to be regarded as the necessary consequence of a change of the mother's domicil, but as the result of the exercise by her of a power vested in her for the welfare of the infant, which in their interest she may abstain from exercising, even when she changes her own domicil."[315]

The commentators were of the view that the same rule applied to the mother of an out-of-wedlock child.[316]

Where parents live apart

At common law, there was considerable uncertainty regarding the domicile of the children of parents who were divorced, legally separated, or otherwise living apart.[317] In the Scottish decision of *Shanks* v. *Shanks*,[318] in 1965, Lord Fraser stated that the general rule that the father's domicile controls "does not suffer exception"

---

[311] Cf. the Law Reform Commission's Working Paper No. 10-1981, *Domicile and Habitual Residence as Connecting Factors in the Conflict of Laws*, para. 90. In England, the effect of attempted legislative clarification (Children Act 1975, schedule I, para. 3(1), (4) (prospectively repealed and re-enacted in the Adoption Act 1976, section 39)) is uncertain: cf. *Cheshire & North*, 178, fn. 7, *Dicey & Morris*, 109, fn. 5, the English and Scottish Law Commission's Working Paper No. 88 and Consultative Memorandum No. 63, *Private International Law: The Law of Domicile*, para. 3.4, fn. 47.

[312] *Domicile and Habitual Residence as Connecting Factors in the Conflict of Laws*, p. 84.

[313] *Adoption*, Pl. 2467 (1984), para. 13.15.

[314] [1898] 3 Ch. 490. See also *Re G.*, [1966] N.Z.L.R. 1028.

[315] *Id.*, at 496-97.

[316] *Dicey & Morris*, (9th ed., 1973) 120; *Cheshire & North*, 181; *Wolff*, 118.

[317] See *Anon.*, *Note: The Power to Change the Domicile of Infants and of Persons Non Compos Mentis*, 30 Colum. L. Rev. 703, at 706ff. (1930), Wertz, *Note: Domicile of Child After Death of Divorced Parent Having Custody of Child*, 21 Neb. L. Rev. 325 (1942), M.I.S., *Note*, 16 Tulane L. Rev. 285 (1942).

[318] [1965] Sc. L.T. 330 (Outer House). For criticism of *Shanks*, see *Anton*, 171.

where there has been a divorce and the child is in his mother's custody.[319] In the Northern Ireland decision of *Hope* v. *Hope*,[320] two years later, Lord McDermott, L.C.J., came to a different view, stating:

"On principle, it would seem that this rule [that the father's domicile controls] must be based on the authority and responsibility that a father has to act for his child; and it is, I think, clear that on the death of the father his capacity to change the child's domicil will ordinarily pass to the surviving parent. This recognised the rule as a manifestation of parental authority and responsibility. But why should it apply to tie the domicil of the child to the will of a father who has abjured his responsibility by walking out of his child's life and by so conducting himself that his marriage is dissolved by a competent court which grants custody of the child to the mother? In such a case the status and position of the father to which the rule is related have gone, and the mother has become the parent in charge and responsible for the welfare of the child."[321]

This qualification of the general rule that the father's domicile controls was welcomed by many commentators.[322] In times of "no fault" divorce based on marriage breakdown and on unilateral repudiation by the petitioner, however, the *ratio* of *Hope* v. *Hope* would appear difficult to harmonise with the divorce philosophy of many countries today. Perhaps *Hope* v *Hope* would sustain a reference to the mother's domicile in cases where the spouses remain married but the father has deserted the home and she has custody of the children, whether by court order, agreement or otherwise.

It is worth nothing in this context the Irish decision of *In re Kindersley, an Infant*.[323] That case was concerned with the custody of a boy who had been born in England at a time when both his parents were domiciled there. After the parents divorced, the mother, a member of "a well known Irish family"[324] remained and lived in Ireland. The boy came to stay with his mother in Ireland. Initially this was with his father's approval but later his father disagreed and obtained an order in the English Court of Appeal that he should be sent back to England to stay at the home of his paternal grandfather.

In the Supreme Court, O'Byrne, J. observed:

"The boy was born in England at a time when both his parents were domiciled there, and he has never lost his domicile of origin."[325]

And, in subsequent proceedings in the High Court, Gavan Duffy, J. noted that

---

[319] [1965] Sc. L.T., at 332.

[320] [1968] N.I. 1 (Q.B. (Mat.), 1967). This case was analysed by Carter, *Domicil, Infancy and Hope v. Hope*, 20 N.I.L.Q. 304 (1969). Carter refers (at 306) to an Indian decision of similar effect, *Rashid Hasan* v. *Union of India*, [1967] A.I.R. (Allahabad), 154 (H.C.). In the United States, the *Restatement (Second) of Conflicts of Law*, s.22, comment *d*, takes broadly the same position as that adopted in *Hope*. The decisions of most courts are in accord: see, e.g., *McMillin* v. *McMillin*, 114 Colo. 247, 158 P. 2d 444 (Sup. Ct., 1945); *Evans* v. *Evans*, 136 Colo. 6, 314 P. 2d 291 (Sup. Ct., 1957); *MacWhinney* v. *MacWhinney*, 248 Minn. 303, 79 N.W. 2d 683 (Sup. Ct., 1956); *State ex rel. Larson* v. *Larson*, 252 N.W. 329 (Sup. Ct. Minn., 1934) (criticised in 18 Minn. L. Rev. 591 (1934)); *Simonds* v. *Simonds*, 154 F. 2d 326 (D. Cir. 1946). See further Beale, *The Progress of the Laws, 1919-20: The Conflict of Laws*, 34 Harv. L. Rev. at 50, 58-59 (1920).

[321] *Hope* v. *Hope*, [1968] N.I., at 4-5.

[322] See, e.g., Dicey & Morris (9th ed., 1973) 119; *Graveson*, 214 (6th ed., 1969). See also *Hannon* v. *Eisler*, 13 W.W.R. 565, at 572, [1955] D.L.R. 183, at 189 (Man. C.A., 1954), where Coyne, J.A. stated that "a child's domicile is that of the father, at least until he permanently loses custody".

[323] [1944] I.R. 111 (Sup. Ct., 1944, aff'g High Court., 1943).

[324] *Id.*, at 112 (*per* Gavan Duffy). The family in question were the Guinnesses.

[325] *Id.*, at 132.

the boy's "domicile of origin was English and a domiciled Englishman he remains".[326]

This treatment of the domicile issue is a summary one. Its tone suggests that the divorce was considered to have had no effect on the rule that a child's domicile is determined by that of his father. It would, of course, be possible to interpret the decision as resting on the fact that the mother, at the time of the proceedings, was acting in defiance of an English order regarding her son's custody, but O'Byrne, J.'s comments expressly and Gavan Duffy J.'s comments (on any reasonable interpretation) are to the effect that the continuity of the application of the father's domicile had never been broken. Yet the boy had spent the period from 1939 to 1940 in his mother's home with his father's "assent to this course as a temporary measure".[327] Whether this amounted to full custody on her part, however, may be doubted. There was already an order of the English High Court, made with the consent of both parents, making the boy a ward of court, giving his father the right to select his school (subject to the mother's reasonable approval) and providing that the boy was to spend the greater part of his school holidays with his mother but a portion of them with his father, or father's nominee, or his paternal grandparents.

None of these specific elements in the history of the boy's life after his parents' divorce was mentioned by either O'Byrne, J. or Gavan Duffy, J. in the context of domicile and it seems more reasonable to regard their comments as supporting the view that the father's domicile continues to control even after a divorce.

Legislative changes

The recent legislation has modified the common rules in an important, though limited, manner. Section 4(1) of the Domicile and Recognition of Foreign Divorces Act 1986 provides as follows:

> "The domicile of a minor at any time when his father and mother are living apart shall be that of his mother if —
> (a) the minor then has his home with her and has no home with his father, or
> (b) the minor has at any time had her domicile by virtue of paragraph (a) of this subsection and has not since had a home with his father."

And section 4(3) provides that the section is not to affect any existing rule of law as to the cases in which a minor's domicile is regarded as being, by dependence, that of his mother.

Some points about these provisions may be noted. First, section 4(1) deals only with legitimate minors, since at common law, as we have seen,[328] the domicile of illegitimate minors is one dependent on that of their mother, and section 4(3) expressly provides that section 4 is not to affect any existing rule of law as to cases in which a minor's domicile "is regarded as being, by dependence, that of his mother".[329] Secondly, section 4(1) is relevant *only where the minor's parents are living apart*. The expression "living apart" is not defined. Presumably, at the very least, it refers to cases where the parents have ceased to cohabit, by desertion, court decree,[330] separation agreement or informal mutual agreement. Whether the expression also

---

[326] *Id.*, at 135.

[327] *Id.*, at 113 (*per* Gavan Duffy, J.).

[328] *Supra*, p. 83.

[329] Cf. the *Explanatory Memorandum to the Bill as Initiated*, para. 9. The Memorandum also refers to the case where a child is born posthumously; but that case will not arise under section 4(1) since, *ex hypothesi*, the child's parents are not "living apart".

[330] Including a decree for divorce *a mensa et thoro* and (as would seem reasonable) a barring order.

includes cases of imprisonment[331] or hospitalisation[332] or cases where the spouses are amicably living mainly in two separate locations, perhaps on account of work requirements, but are still conducting an interpersonal, sexual relationship, is not clear.[333]

The converse case must also be considered. A couple may cease to cohabit, and establish separate households under the same roof.[334] It seems that in such circumstances, if a child had his home with his mother in one part of the premises and had no home with his father, the child's domicile would depend on his mother's. If the child also had fairly frequent contact with his father, difficult questions of interpretation would arise. The court would first have to decide whether, during the periods the child stayed with his mother, he had "his house" with her and had "no home" with his father. It would also have to decide the duration of each such period. In this context it should be noted that section 4(1) ceases to apply, not when the child has "his home" with his father and "no home" with his mother but rather when the child has "a home" with his father. Thus where a child started seeing more of his father and spending more periods of time in his father's part of the premises, while still having a home with his mother, the father's domicile would reassert itself, once the connection between child and father was sufficiently strong for it to be said that the child had "a home" with the father.

It is perhaps worth looking a little closer at the notions of having "one's home" and "a home" with a parent. The mover of the British legislation[335] on which our section 4 is based explained that "the purpose of using the word 'home' is in a demonstration of warmth and closeness".[336] One commentator has responded that "[t]his may be so but it is not very helpful".[337] The British commentators generally cite the observations of Lord Denning M.R. in *Re P (G.E.) (An Infant)*,[338] as throwing light on the meaning of "home", but in fact the Master of the Rolls in these remarks appeared more anxious to provide a meaning of the concept of "ordinary residence" than that of "home". There is also some uncertainty as to the extent to which the intention of the child is to be taken into account in determining

---

[331] Cf. *Santos* v. *Santos* [1972] Fam. 247 (C.A.), *Cretney*, 154-158. One should not rely too heavily on the analysis of this question presented in cases concerned with divorce and other matrimonial causes, since the domicile of children raises somewhat broader issues.

[332] Cases dealing with hospitalisation in the context of actions for loss of *consortium* may throw some light on the question, but can scarcely determine the resolution of the issue. Cf. *Spaight* v. *Dundon*, [1961] I.R. 201 (Sup. Ct., 1960), *O'Haran* v. *Divine*, 100 I.L.T.R. 53 (Sup. Ct., 1974), *McMahon & Binchy*, 412-414.

[333] *Dicey & Morris*, 138, consider that "[i]f, for example, one spouse travels abroad on business, the spouses will only 'live apart' if the period of employment abroad is such that the absent spouse can be regarded as having a separate household". Cf. section 5(1)(b)(iii) of the Family Law (Maintenance of Spouses and Children) Act, 1976, and section 4(3) of the Family Home Protection Act, 1976, which use the expression "living separately and apart": this expression would clearly appear to exclude the kind of case envisaged above. See also *Ua Clothasaigh* v. *McCartan*, 83 I.L.T.R. 6 (High Ct., Maguire, J., 1947).

[334] Cf. *Hopes* v. *Hopes*, [1949] P. 227, at 235 (C.A., *per* Denning, L.J., 1948): "The husband who shuts himself up in one or two rooms of his house and ceases to have anything to do with his wife is living separately and apart from her as effectively as if they were separated by the outer door of a flat. They may meet on the stairs or in the passageways, but so they might if they each had separate flats in one building." See further *Naylor* v. *Naylor*, [1962] P. 253 (P.D.A. Div., Lord Merriman, P. and Scarman, J., 1961). Cf. *Mouncer* v. *Mouncer*, [1972] 1 All E.R. 289 (Fam. Div., Wrangham, J., 1971). See also *Shatter*, 440, *Cretney*, 152-154, *Alexander* v. *Burke (The French College and St Joseph College Cases)*, 22 L.R. (Ir.) 443 (C.A., 1887), *Alexander* v. *Burke (Mount Argus Case)*, 22 L.R.(Ir.) 458 (C.A., 1887).

[335] Cf. the Domicile and Matrimonial Proceedings Act, 1973, section 4 (c. 45).

[336] Mr Ian MacArthur, M.R., H.C. Standing Committee C, col. 62, quoted by Freeman, *Annotation*, Current Law Statutes Annotated 1973, note to section 4 of the Domicile and Matrimonial Proceedings Act 1973 (c. 45).

[337] Freeman, *supra*.

[338] [1965] Ch. 568, at 585-586 (C.A., 1964).

where (if anywhere) his home is.[339] At all events section 4 of the 1986 Act is drafted in such a way as to imply strongly[340] that a child may have a home in more than one place.

Thus, it would seem that a joint custody arrangement[341] involving a child in spending different parts of the week in either parent's home would not activate the subsection, since it would be hard to say that the child, though perhaps spending most of the week with his mother, had "no home" with his father. Where the gap is larger, as, for example, where a child by prior agreement, spends six months with one parent and six months with the other, a court might be willing to hold that the child has "no" home with the father for the period that the child is with the mother. Wherever the line may be drawn, the effect is that, once beyond it, the child will find that his domicile swings from one parent to the other, depending (a) on which parent he has his home with at any particular time, and (b) on whether, though having "his" home with his mother at any particular time, he also has "a" home with his father.

The next point to note is that, once a minor's domicile is that of his mother's by virtue of section 4(1), it continues automatically to follow her domicile even in cases where the minor ceases to have his home with his mother, until either (i) the minor establishes (or re-establishes, as the case may be) a home with his father,[342] or (ii) the parents cease to live apart.[343] In case (i), as has been mentioned, the child's domicile would appear to revert to one of dependency on the father's domicile. In case (ii) it would also appear that the father's domicile prevails, since section 4(1) will no longer apply and the common law position will thus reassert itself.

Thus, even in cases where the child has had his home with his mother for only a short period when his parents are living apart, the minor's domicile will continue to be that of his mother's for the duration of the period *after* the minor ceases to have his home with her, until either he has a home with his father or his parents cease to live apart. So, if the mother, after her husband has left her, keeps her children with her for (say) two months, and then leaves them in the charge of her aunt, for the following decade, the children's domicile depends on that of their mother. It should also be noted it is not possible for a mother to refrain from changing the domicile of her children where this would be for their benefit, as it appears[344] she can do where the children are illegitimate or where the mother is widowed. This distinction is one that seems difficult to defend.

At common law, there were no authorities on the question of the domicile of a legitimate child after the death of both his parents[345] or of the domicile

---

[339] Cf. Forsyth, *Reform of the Law of Domicile in Australia with Particular Reference to the New Zealand Domicile Act 1976*, 4 Otago L. Rev. 95, at 97 (1977).

[340] Section 4(1)(a), in referring to the case of a child having "his home" with his mother and "no home" with his father, appears to allow for the factual possibility that in another case (outside the scope of section 4(1)(a)) a child, while still having "his home" with his mother, could nonetheless have "a home" with his father. This interpretation is supported by section 4(1)(b), which, in referring to the possibility of a child having "a home" with his father, does not go on to provide that in such a case the child would no longer have "his home" with his mother.

[341] Cf. Furstenberg & Nord, *Parenting Apart: Patterns of Childrearing after Marital Disruption*, 47 J. of Marriage & Family 983, at 902 (1985).

[342] Cf. section 4(1)(b) (".... and has not since had a home with his father"). Both section 4(1)(b) and 4(2) use the expression "a home", in contrast to "his home" in section 4(1)(a). It may be argued that having "a home" involves less strong connections than having "one's" home with a particular person.

[343] Cf. section 4(1) ("the domicile of a minor at *any time when his father and mother are living apart....*") (emphasis added).

[344] Cf. *supra*, p. 85.

[345] Cf. *Anon, Note,* 30 Colum. L. Rev. 703, at 707 ff (1930).

of an illegitimate child after the death of his mother.[346] The recent legislation has changed the position in a narrow area. Section 4(2) of the Act provides that the domicile of a minor whose mother is dead "shall be that which she last had before she died if at her death the minor had her domicile by virtue of subsection (1) of this section and has not since had a home with his father". In simple terms, this provision affects *only* a minor whose domicile follows that of his mother because his parents are living apart and he has his home with her. If the mother dies during the child's minority, then the child's domicile remains frozen as it is at the time of her death unless and until the minor has a home with his father. Thereafter, it seems the minor's domicile is determined by that of his father.[347] Outside the narrow range of circumstances covered by section 4(2), the common law rules, uncertain as they are, continue to apply.

The Age of Majority Act 1985, which came into effect on 1 March 1985, reduces[348] the age of majority from 21 to 18 or to the time of marriage if the marriage takes place under the age of 18. What is the position, therefore, where an Irish court has to determine the domicile of a married 15-year-old in England (where marriage does not confer full age)? As far as English law is concerned, the child has a domicile of dependency; as far as Irish internal law is concerned, the child is of full age.

The Act makes no reference to the termination of domicile of dependency of minors. It would appear most probable, however, that an Irish court would hold that persons who are no longer minors by reason of the Act no longer are subject to a domicile of dependency.[349] On this view, regardless of what domicile English, or other foreign, law attributes to a married 15-year-old, the Irish court should treat this person as having an independent domicile. It will be recalled[350] that, in *Re Adams Deceased*,[351] in 1967, Budd, J. had held that Irish law, the *lex fori*, should determine the matter of a person's domicile.

Consistent with this approach, English decisions[352] have generally treated minors domiciled in Scotland as having a domicile of dependency, even though under Scots law they had a capacity to acquire an independent domicile. On the other hand, in *In re Ferguson's Trusts*,[353] in 1874, two minors, aged 19 and 13, respectively, were held to have a Scottish domicile where their deceased father's domicile had been Scottish, but their widowed mother's domicile was English. Both the minors had been born and spent all their lives in Scotland. No discussion of the domicile issue is included in the report, which merely refers to the statement by the Master of the Rolls that ".... it was clearly shown that the minors were Scotch, and that their

---

[346] *Id.*

[347] The indirect effect of section 4 as a whole on the common law rules as to a child's domicile of dependency on his father is unclear. Section 4(3) preserves existing common law rules regarding the child's domicile of dependence on his *mother* only. On ordinary principles of statutory construction, it would appear that section 4(2) should be interpreted as covering only the period between the mother's death and the time the child has a home with his father. Thereafter, since they are unaffected by the subsection, common law rules, under which the child's domicile is, by dependence, that of his father, should continue to apply.

[348] In section 2.

[349] An amendment clarifying the issue was proposed by Deputy Alan Shatter during the Committee Stage of the Bill but was withdrawn on the basis of a Ministerial assurance that, in the light of section 2 of the Age of Majority Act 1985, a minor, on attaining majority by marrying, "[t]herefore .... acquires the capacity to have an independent domicile": 365 Dáil Debates, col. 2259 (30 April 1986).

[350] Cf. *supra*, p. 50.

[351] [1967] I.R. 424, at 434-435 (High Ct., Budd, J.). See also *In re Annesley: Davidson* v. *Annesley*, [1926] Ch. 692.

[352] Cf., e.g. *Re Beaumont*, [1893] 3 Ch. 490, *Henderson* v. *Henderson*, [1967] P. 77 (Sir Jocelyn Simon, P., 1964). But see *Urquhart* v. *Butterfield*, 37 Ch. D. 357 (C.A., 1887).

[353] I.R. 8 Eq. 563 (Sullivan, M.R., 1874).

domicile was in Scotland ...."[354] We may speculate as to why the minors were not held to have had an English domicile, in view of the fact that this was the domicile of their widowed mother.[355] Perhaps the court overlooked the normal rule. It is possible, however, that Sullivan, M.R. had regard to the fact that, under Scots law, a minor male child, at the age of 14, had the legal capacity to choose a domicile of his own, at all events where he was forisfamiliated (as where both his parents were dead).[356] An affidavit of a Scottish advocate was presented in evidence in the *Ferguson's Trusts* case, to the effect that a male minor, aged 14 or over, was "not in a state of total incapacity like a pupil ... but in a state of limited capacity. He is capable of consenting and acting for himself, but his acts require in general, in order to [give them] complete validity, the concurrence of his curator .... A man domiciled in Scotland is entitled to obtain possession of .... a legacy [where there is no restriction as to time or mode of payment under the terms of the gift] even if it should be lodged with the officers of the Court out of Scotland".[357]

Domicile on attaining majority

Where a minor attains majority, he or she may acquire a domicile of choice different from the domicile of origin. The change may be immediate where the minor has already acquired what would be a domicile of choice in the new country if this had not been neutralised by the operation of the rule of domicile of dependency.[358] Moreover, it appears that the evidence of a change of domicile, from that of origin to choice, need not be very strong, where the minor has already, prior to reaching majority, acted in a manner inconsistent with the desire to retain the domicile of origin. In *Spurway* v. *Spurway*,[359] in 1893, Walker, C. stated strongly that "[o]nce a man's domicil — be it domicil of origin or domicil of choice — is established ..., a new domicil will not be imputed to him except on the clearest evidence of an intention to change his own domicil". He went on to note, however, that the evidence required to prove a change of domicile might "vary enormously in different cases".[360] Thus, although a person could do nothing to disturb the domicile of origin while a minor, nevertheless:

> "if during a man's minority we find in his conduct evidence conflicting with the supposition that he intends to retain his domicil of origin — acts and declarations not in harmony with such an intention — then I think, upon his attaining age, the Court would require less evidence in order to be convinced that his intention was not to stereotype his domicil of origin, but have one in accordance with his declared conduct."[361]

Of course, as one commentator has pointed out,[362] this *dictum*, suggesting that proleptic effect may be given to a minor's intentions, is consistent with the view that a minor's intentions may sometimes be of a sufficient clarity to lend them some weight. This consideration raises broader policy issues, to which we now turn.

---

[354] *Id.*, at 564.

[355] Cf. *supra*, p. 83.

[356] Cf. *Anton*, 171-172.

[357] I.R. 8 Eq., at 564. The fact that, under the law of the place where a minor is domiciled according to Irish law, the minor has adult status may be a reason for paying funds out of Court in Ireland in recognition of that status and its corresponding entitlements: cf. *Donohue* v. *Donohue*, 19 L.R.(Ir.) 349 (Chatterton, V.C., 1887).

[358] Cf. *Davis* v. *Adair*, [1895] 1 I.R. 379, at 428 (C.A., *per* Walker, C.).

[359] [1894] 1 I.R. 385, at 403 (C.A., 1893).

[360] *Id.*

[361] *Id.*

[362] Duncan, *The Domicile of Infants*, 4 Ir. Jur. (n.s.) 36, at 47-48 (1969).

Policy considerations[363]

Perhaps the most basic question of policy concerns the need for a domicile of dependency for minors at all. Why should not some or all minors have an independent capacity to acquire and change a domicile, as adults do? Perhaps the most obvious reason for having a domicile of dependency for minors is that the domicile is premised on a capacity to form an intention as to long term goals.[364] It can also be argued that, for domicile to be an effective connecting factor, this intention must be a mature and balanced one. But does that commit the law to an inflexible rule that under the age of 18 (or of marriage if younger than 18) no person should legally be entitled to have a domiciliary capacity, however mature he may be? This question opens up for our consideration the broader issue of when a child becomes mature enough to make decisions as to where he will live, with whom he will make his home, and what he will do with his life in the short or long term. The law of guardianship, and especially custody of children, has to confront these questions regularly. Over the past century there have been several decisions[365] in which courts have spelt out a principle, of somewhat uncertain and variable scope, to the effect that, somewhere between 12 and 14 or perhaps a little older, a child's wishes as to where he or she should reside must be given great weight, if not, indeed, be determinative, especially as the child reaches the later teens. Statutory policy[366] points in a similar direction. There is something anomalous about our guardianship law recognising the fact of a teenager's capacity to form a mature decision as to where he or she wishes to live while our law of domicile contains no similar recognition.

There is some slender Irish authority in favour of the view that at least some mature minors are capable of acquiring an independent domicile. In *Stephen* v. *M'Farland*[367] in 1845, the court had to determine the question of the domicile of a minor insolvent debtor living in South Australia. The minor's father had died fourteen years previously in Ireland, and it appears that the minor's mother remained in Ireland. Blackburne, M.R. held that the minor was domiciled in South Australia. He said:

> "The objection that the [minor] was not domiciled [there] is, I think, not maintainable: as has been observed, [he] might have been born in the colony; and at all events, having been engaged in trade, and received credit in that country, there is enough *prima facie* to subject his personal property to its law."[368]

Although the Master of the Rolls did not expressly hold that the minor's domicile was in South Australia, it has been observed that "[s]ince the rule was accepted that questions of personal property are to be referred to the *lex domicilii*, the case emerges as an instance where a judge has been prepared to accept that where a son carries on a trade in a domicile separate from that of his parent he may be permitted to acquire a domicile there".[369]

---

[363] Cf. *id.*, at 39ff for an excellent analysis.
[364] See *id.*, at 46.
[365] Cf. *Binchy*, 460-463.
[366] Cf. Guardianship of Infants Act 1964, section 17(2).
[367] 8 Ir. Eq. R. 444 (Blackburne, M.R., 1845).
[368] *Id.*, at 455.
[369] Duncan, *supra*, at 42. The author continues (at 42-43):

"It must be admitted that strictly this was a case where the infant's domicile depended on that of his mother.... It might, therefore, be suggested that the Master of the Rolls, by a remarkable piece of foresight, was simply anticipating the *Re Beaumont* exception. Yet in all discussions on the point it was assumed that the rule was the same whether it was the domicile of the mother or the father which governed that of the son...."

THE DOMICILE OF MENTALLY ILL PERSONS[370]

The domicile of mentally ill persons is difficult to state with any degree of certainty. There are relatively few reported decisions, and the analysis in them is somewhat confused. This is perhaps not surprising. Since intention is an important aspect of the concept of domicile, it is difficult to apply the concept to persons whose intentions may be unclear or otherwise affected by mental illness.

An early decision is *Bempde* v. *Johnstone*[371] in 1796. In this case Loughborough L.C. stated of a man who had become insane during adulthood:

"I am not clear, that the period of his lunacy is totally to be discarded. But I will take him to have died then."[372]

The effect of this statement would appear to be that, on the onset of insanity, the domicile of the affected person is frozen for all time at what it then is.

In *Sharpe* v. *Crispin*,[373] in 1869, the evidence was not clear as to whether the person whose domicile was in question had become insane before or after reaching full age. The evidence disclosed that he was "always of somewhat weak mind, [and] was certainly as early as 1829 or 1830 [when he was fifteen or sixteen] — probably even earlier — unfit, from mental incapacity, to manage his own affairs or be employed in any business or occupation, and that from that time to his death he was more or less constantly under medical supervision and control as a person of unsound mind, having in the year 1858 been actually found lunatic under a commission."[374] Sir J. P. Wilde made an important legal distinction, which continues to apply in the law today. Where insanity occurs *after* a child has reached full age, the child's father should not be able to change his son's domicile, but where the child is or becomes insane *during minority* and continues in the same condition after reaching full age, the father should be able to change the child's domicile even after the child has become an adult.

Sir J. P. Wilde defended the first part of his proposition as follows:

"If a man had grown up, married and established himself in business in the country of his original domicil, and had afterwards become a lunatic, and in that state had been taken charge of by his father, the emigration of his father to a foreign country with the view of becoming domiciled there, taking his son with him, might fail to work a change in the domicil of that son. It is not difficult to conceive cases in which injustice might be done to the interests of others, if the general proposition were admitted that the custody of a lunatic necessarily carried with it the power of changing his domicil at will."[375]

Thus, fear that "great injustice might be done to others" is the only reason given by Sir J. P. Wilde for depriving the father of an adult insane person of the capacity to change his domicile. Why a similar fear would not arise in relation to the general

---

[370] See *Harris*, 77, *Abraham*, 341, Binchy, *The Domicile of Mentally Ill Persons*, 3 Ir. L. Times, (n.s.) 22 (1985), the Law Reform Commission's Working Paper No. 10-1981, *Domicile and Habitual Residence as Connecting Factors in the Conflict of Laws*, paras. 123-124, and their *Report on Domicile and Habitual Residence as Connecting Factors in the Conflict of Laws*, paras. 16-17, 21 (LRC 7-1983), Anon, Note: *The Power to Change the Domicile of Infants and of Persons Non Compos Mentis*, 30 Colum. L. Rev. 703, at 712-714 (1930).

[371] 3 Ves. Jun. 198, 30 E.R. 967 (1796).

[372] *Id.*, at 201 and 968, respectively. See also *Estate of S.*, [1928] N.I. 46, at 50 (*per* Moore, L.C.J.) and 53 (*per* Best, L.J.).

[373] L.R. 1 P. & D. 611 (1869).

[374] *Id.*, at 616.

[375] *Id.*

capacity of any father to change the domicile of his *minor* son is not explained by the judge.

Sir J. P. Wilde defended the second part of his proposition as follows:

> "It would seem to me that the same reasoning which attaches the domicil of the son to that of his father while a minor would continue to bring about the same result, after the son had attained his majority, if he was continuously of unsound mind. The son in this case continued under the control of his father, [and] was presumably supported by him .... At no period could he, according to the hypothesis, have acted for himself in choosing a domicil, and if his next of kin and those who had the control of his movements and life were not capable of changing his domicil, that domicil would, from the moment of his majority, have become indelible. The better opinion, in my judgment, is that the incapacity of minority never having in this case been followed by adult capacity, continued to confer upon the father the right of choice in the matter of domicil for his son...."[376]

Again, the logic and consistency of the approach favoured by Sir J. P. Wilde may be questioned. If it is bad for a domicile to become "indelible" where a person becomes insane *before* he reaches majority, is it not equally bad where the person becomes insane *after* he reaches majority? Moreover, the fears of "great injustice .... to others" which affected the judge in relation to the exercise of paternal discretion in respect of a child becoming insane *after* majority must be equally applicable where the child becomes insane *before* majority.

Later decisions[377] are generally in accord with those decisions already discussed. In the Northern Ireland Court of Appeal case of *Estate of S.*,[378] where a man who had been domiciled in Northern Ireland spent ten months in a mental hospital in the Free State, Moore, L.J. said "We cannot look to what has happened since, as that is the crucial date by which his rights are to be determined".[379] In *Re Joyce; Corbet* v. *Fagan*,[380] where an Irishman long resident in England spent a period of six years in a mental hospital in England, neither Overend, J. in the High Court nor the Supreme Court judges resolved the question of how this should affect the determination of his domicile. This was because, even if these years were ignored, Overend, J.[381] and the majority in the Supreme Court[382] were satisfied that the man had still acquired an English domicile.

The New Zealand decision of *Re G.*[383] is worthy of note. There the Court followed the principle favoured in *Sharpe* v. *Crispin*[384] that, where insanity occurs before majority, the domicile of the father will control after majority. In *Re G.*, however, the domicile of the mother was in question and the Court followed English authority[385] to the effect that the mother, in changing her own domicile, need not change that of her child if it is in the child's interests that it not be changed.

Uncertainty surrounds the domicile of children (or insane adults) whose domicile depends on that of an insane parent, and the effect of any change in an insane parent's

---

[376] *Id.* The distinction based on the time of the onset of insanity is described as "somewhat irrational" by *Cheshire & North*, 181.

[377] E.g. *Urquhart* v. *Butterfield*, 37 Ch. D. 357 (1887), *Crumpton's Judicial Factor* v. *Finch-Noyes*, 1918 S.C. 378, *Re Mackensie*, [1941] Ch. 69, at 71 (referring to previous unreported decision), *Re G.*, [1966] N.Z.L.R. 1028 (Sup. Ct., Wilson, J.).

[378] [1928] N.I. 46 (C.A., 1927).

[379] *Id.*, at 50. See also Best, L.J., at 53.

[380] [1946] I.R. 277 (Sup. Ct., 1945).

[381] Cf. *id.*, at 284.

[382] Cf. *id.*, at 306 (*per* Black, J.).

[383] *Supra.*

[384] *Supra.*

[385] *In re Beaumont*, [1893] 3 Ch. 490. See Binchy, *Reform of the Law Relating to the Domicile of Children: A Proposed Statute*,11 Ottawa L. Rev. 279, at 280-282 (1979).

domicile on the domicile of those whose domicile depends on him. These are murky waters on which almost no light has been shed. It seems impossible to envisage that a court today, if confronted by the arbitrariness of the law of domicile in this context, would not go some way at least towards restoring rationality to rules which have lost their connection with commonsense.

There does not appear to be any authority in Ireland, or the other common law jurisdictions[386] outside the United States on the precise nature and extent of the mental incapacity that renders a person incapable of acquiring a domicile of choice. As *Dicey & Morris*[387] point out, all the English cases, save one, involved "lunatics so found" by inquisition and in the solitary exceptional case[388] the person in question was "admitted to be a declared lunatic". In the United States, where there has been some discussion of this issue in the cases, the courts have made it clear that the test of domiciliary capacity is different from, and less demanding than, that of capacity to execute a deed or will.[389]

In Ireland, the Law Reform Commission, in their Working Paper on *Domicile and Habitual Residence as Connecting Factors in the Conflict of Laws,*[390] addressed the issue.[391] They considered that the present law affords "a rather blunt and uncompromising solution"[392] in freezing the domicile at what it was before the onset of the illness. They took the view that "a degree of flexibility"[393] should be introduced by enabling the Court, on application to it by an interested party, to change the domicile of a mentally ill person "where it appears to the Court to be in the interest of the person, and, having regard to the interests of other persons, proper to do so."[394]

The Commission did not consider it wise to retain the rule that the domicile of a mentally ill child after majority still depends on that of his parents for the rest of his life or until he gets well. In their view, the present rule involved "too great an assumption of a continuing close association of interests between parent and child".[395] The Commission, therefore, tentatively suggested[396] that it would be better to let the child retain the domicile which he had before reaching majority, permitting it, in an appropriate case, to be changed by the Court. They recommended also that there should be power to apply to the courts for a change of domicile on behalf of a child whose domicile is dependent on that of a mentally ill person.[397]

---

[386] Cf. *Dicey & Morris*, 139-140, *McLeod*, 151.

[387] *Dicey & Morris*, 139.

[388] *Re Bariatenski*, 13 L.J. Ch. 69 (Lord Lyndhurst, L.C., 1843).

[389] Cf. *Scoles & Hay*, 207, *Anon.*, *Note: The Power to Change the Domicile of Infants and of Persons Non Compos Mentis*, 30 Colum. L. Rev. 703, at 713 (1930), H.S.J., *Note: Degree of Mental Capacity Required to Change Domicil*, 3 Calif. L. Rev. 491 (1915), *Restatement on Conflict of Laws*, 2d, 23 Comment *a*.

[390] W.P. No. 10-1981.

[391] *Id.*, paras. 123-124.

[392] *Id.*, para. 123.

[393] *Id.*

[394] *Id.* In cases where there is a Committee of the mentally ill person's estate, the Commission considered that it would be the appropriate applicant.

[395] *Id.*, para. 124.

[396] *Id.*

[397] *Id.* See also the broadly similar recommendations made by the Manitoba Law Reform Commission in its Report on Domicile, para. 2.23 (1982). The English and Scottish Law Commissions, in their Working Paper No. 88 and Consultative Memorandum No. 63, *Private International Law: The Law of Domicile*, published in April 1985, provisionally recommended that an adult who lacks mental capacity to acquire an independent domicile of choice should be domiciled in the country with which he or she is for the time being most closely connected. They considered that it would be inappropriate to introduce a rule that the domicile of a mentally incompetent person should be changed only with the consent of a competent authority:

"Domicile is a conclusion of law drawn from the facts of each case irrespective of what the party concerned may directly wish in the matter and whether or not it is to his advantage or disadvantage.

(These tentative proposals have, of course, been overtaken by the Commission's recommendations in their Report that domicile should be replaced by habitual residence.)

OTHER CONNECTING FACTORS

Nationality[398]

We must now consider nationality as a connecting factor in conflicts of law. Nationality represents a person's "political status, by virtue of which he owes allegiance to some particular country".[399] Nationality depends on such matters as place of birth,[400] parentage,[401] marriage,[402] adoption[403] and naturalisation.[404] Irish rules for the acquisition of nationality are liberal,[405] in contrast to the approach in some other countries.

Prior to the French revolution domicile was the dominant connecting factor, not only in common law jurisdictions but also in civil law systems. The French *Code Civil* of 1804 is generally mentioned[406] as the first which endorsed the principle of nationality. Article 13, paragraph 3 of the *Code* provided that: "The laws concerning the status and capacity of persons govern French persons, even though residing abroad". Austria adopted a similar approach in 1811,[407] the Netherlands in 1829.[408] Belgium and Luxembourg, which adopted the French *Code*, also made this change.[409]

It was not until the time of Mancini that the theoretical arguments in favour of nationality were presented with intellectual force.[410] The Italian Civil Code[411] gave effect to Mancini's view. Many apostles of Mancini, including Esperson and Fiore

---

Hence, if a person has his home permanently or indefinitely in a country he becomes domiciled there irrespective of whether he wishes to be, and irrespective of any advantage or disadvantage to him. In our view, giving a court an express power to refuse to recognise a change in domicile in circumstances where a person would otherwise be treated as having received a new domicile would significantly add to the potential for artificiality in the law." *Id.*, para. 6.7.

[398] See *Rabel*, vol. 1, 120ff., Schmidt, *Nationality and Domicile in Swedish Private International Law*, 4 Int. L.Q. 39 (1951), Reed, *Note: Domicile and Nationality in Comparative Conflict of Laws*, 23 U. Pittsburgh L. Rev. 979 (1962), Nadelmann, *Mancini's Nationality Rule and Non-Unified Legal Systems*, 17 Am. J. Comp. L. 418 (1969), Graveson, *Comparative Aspects of the General Principles of Private International Law*, [1963] — II Recueil des Cours, ch. 5, at 63-66, de Winter, *Nationality or Domicile? The Present State of Affairs*, [1969] — III Recueil des cours 347 (a comprehensive analysis), Baty, *The Interconnection of Nationality and Domicile*, 13 Ill. L. Rev. 363 (1919), *Anton*, 157-161, *Cheshire & North*, 183-185, L. Palsson, *Marriage and Divorce in Comparative Conflict of Laws*, 81-105 (1974).

[399] *Cheshire & North*, 183. See generally C. Parry, *Nationality and Citizenship Laws of the Commonwealth and of the Republic of Ireland*, ch. 17 (1957), Reed, *Note: Domicile and Nationality in Comparative Conflict of Laws*, 23 U. Pittsburgh L. Rev. 979, at 987-988 (1962).

[400] Cf., e.g. the Irish Nationality and Citizenship Act 1956, section 6(1).

[401] Cf., e.g. *id.*, sections 6(2)-(4), 7(2).

[402] Irish Nationality and Citizenship Act 1986, section 3; cf. *Somjee* v. *Minister for Justice & A.G.*, [1981] I.L.R.M. (High Ct., Keane, J., 1979), considered by *Kelly*, 41, *Binchy*, 181, Forde, *Equality and the Constitution*, 17 Ir. Jur. (n.s.) 295, at 325-326, 336-337 (1982).

[403] Cf., e.g. the Irish Nationality and Citizenship Act 1956, section 11.

[404] Cf., e.g. *id.*, Part III as amended by the Irish Nationality and Citizenship Act 1986, sections 4-6.

[405] See *Kelly*, 39-42. Cf. *Rex (Stewart)* v. *Baldrick*, 71 I.L.T.R. 57 (N.I. Co. Ct., Derry, Judge Osborne, 1937).

[406] Cf. *Anton*, 157-158, *Rabel*, vol. 1, 121, de Winter, *supra*, at 367-370.

[407] Cf. Schmidt, *Nationality and Domicile in Swedish Private International Law*, 4 Int. L. Q. 39, at 40 (1951).

[408] Cf. *Anton*, 158.

[409] *Id.*

[410] See de Winter, *supra*, at 371-375.

[411] In Article 6: see *Anton*, 158-159.

in Italy, Laurent in Belgium, Weiss in France and Von Bar and Zitelmann in Germany,[412] also successfully pressed for the adoption of nationality as a connecting factor.

Nationality had become the dominant criterion in most of the continental European countries by the early part of this century. It also spread to China, Egypt, Iran, Japan, and most Central and South American countries, but not Argentina, Brazil and Paraguay, which prefer domicile.[413]

The principal attraction of nationality, in contrast to domicile, is its practicability: it is after all "a relatively clear and simple concept compared with the uncertainties and multiformity of domicil, especially in its British varieties".[414] Moreover it prevents easy evasion of a state's policy which habitual residence can involve. But, of course, this very strength of nationality is also its weakness. Nationality as a sole connecting factor can deprive individuals of the entitlement to escape from the laws of a country which they find oppressive or unjust.[415]

Statelessness presents particular difficulties for legal systems favouring nationality as a connecting factor.[416] When nationality was gaining widespread support as a connecting factor, statelessness was not such a major problem, but "[u]ntold numbers"[417] of individuals have been rendered stateless by the political events of the present century.

The approach generally favoured has been to refer to the law of a stateless person's domicile or habitual residence, or in default to the law of his or her temporary residence[418]; another solution, formerly adopted by the German Civil Code,[419] was to refer to the person's previous national law.[420]

Another problem with nationality is that a person may have dual (or even multiple) nationality. This may result in clashing rules, with formidable complexities for private international law.[421] Finally, nationality presents difficulties in states with multiple legal systems.[422]

Emigration is a social phenomenon which has been of considerable importance in shaping attitudes towards nationality and domicile. Countries with a tradition of immigration, such as the United States, Canada, Australia, New Zealand and Argentina, have tended to prefer domicile to nationality as domicile more easily supports "the desire of immigration countries to incorporate new immigrants into the legal life of their country as soon as possible, and thereby to avoid the difficulties

---

[412] *Anton*, 159, fn. 20.

[413] *Anton*, 159; see further *Rabel*, vol. 1, ch. 4.

[414] *Rabel*, vol. 1, 166.

[415] Cf. *Anton*, 160, de Winter, *supra*, at 382-384. In Ireland, prior to Independence, Irish men and women were British nationals. In *Stewart* v. *Marquis of Conyngham*, 1 Ir. Ch. Rep. 534, at 546 (1849), Cusack Smith, M.R. expressed the opinion that "since the Act of Union, every subject of the Crown, in every part of the United Kingdom, is a person of British race, blood or name, within the meaning of that covenant". See also *Davies* v. *Lynch*, I.R. 4 C.L. 570 (Q.B., 1868) and *In re Tipperary Election Petitions*, I.R. 9 C.L. 217 (Com. Pleas, 1875), where John Mitchel was disqualified from taking his seat in the House of Commons because he had become a naturalised citizen of the United States.

[416] See de Winter, *supra*, at 381-382.

[417] *Rabel*, vol. 1, 132.

[418] Cf. *id.*, 132-133.

[419] E.g. art. 29. See *Rabel*, vol. 1, 133.

[420] As *Rabel*, vol. 1, 133, points out:
"This provision compelled the German courts to decide the private status and the incidents of family relations of Russian *emigrés* in accordance with the legislation of the Soviet Union, i.e., the country which was their very enemy and which had refused to accept the role of successor to the former Russian Empire."

[421] See de Winter, *supra*, at 384-386, Baty, *supra*, at 365. Cf. *Davies* v. *Lynch*, I.R. 4 C.L. 570 (Q.B.D., 1868).

[422] See *Anton*, 161, de Winter, *supra*, at 386-387 and the English Law Commission's Working Paper No. 88 and Scottish Law Commission's Consultative Memorandum No. 63, *Private International Law: The Law of Domicile*, para. 2.7 (1985).

that would arise if each new immigrant prior to naturalization were to be judged in accordance with the laws of his home country".[423]

Countries with a tradition of heavy emigration, on the other hand, have been attracted by a principle which "tends to preserve the ties between the emigrant and his home country".[424] It would be wrong to stress this consideration too strongly. As *Rabel* points out:

> "Until very recent times, neither Germany nor Italy pursued any consistent policy in preserving relations with their emigrants. Until 1913, a German citizen living abroad even lost his citizenship after ten years, unless he had himself expressed his desire to retain allegiance by formally registering with the German consulate."[425]

The fact that some common law countries with a tradition of emigration have retained domicile as a connecting factor may at first sight appear to conflict with the suggestion that nationality is preferred by countries with a pattern of emigration. However, we should not overlook the potency of the doctrine of the domicile of origin,[426] "which has often been compared with the bonds effected by the principle of nationality, a doctrine maintained and developed to satisfy the natural desire of a home country from which innumerable colonizers have gone out into the world".[427]

Habitual residence[428]

We must now consider the concept of habitual residence. This concept has played a role of growing importance in recent years throughout Europe including Ireland[429] and Britain.[430] It has been widely used in the Hague Convention on Private International Law. This is no surprise since the concept of habitual residence is close to the notion of domicile as understood in civil law systems.[431] Moreover, it offers a possible compromise resolution to the impasse between the common law's adherence to domicile and the civil law's regard for the nationality principle.

What does "habitual residence" mean, and how is a person's habitual residence determined? There has been relatively little judicial analysis of the concept, but it is at least clear that habitual residence is a less conceptually cluttered notion than domicile. There is, for example, no such doctrine as an "habitual residence of origin". Moreover, intention, though still relevant, is a less controlling factor in the determination of habitual residence than it is for domicile. The courts need not in every case venture into the inner recesses of the subject's mind before coming

---

[423] *Rabel*, vol. 1, 163. See also *Castel*, vol. 1, 106, de Winter, *supra*, at 401, 407, Baty, *supra*, at 367.

[424] *Rabel*, vol. 1, 165.

[425] *Id.*, 165-166.

[426] Cf. *supra*, pp. 74-75.

[427] *Rabel*, vol. 1, 165. Cf. the English Law Commission's Working Paper No. 88 and the Scottish Law Commission's Consultative Memorandum No. 63, *Private International Law: The Law of Domicile*, para. 5.18 (1985).

[428] See generally *Castel*, vol. 1, 144-146, de Winter, *Nationality or Domicile? The Present State of Affairs*, [1969] — III Recueil des cours 347, esp. chs. 4-6, Hall, *Cruse v. Chittum: Habitual Residence Judicially Explored*, 24 Int. & Comp. L.Q. 1 (1975), Cavers, *"Habitual Residence": A Useful Concept?*, 21 Am. U.L. Rev. 475 (1972), Nadelmann, *Habitual Residence and Nationality as Tests at the Hague: The 1968 Convention on Recognition of Divorces*, 47 Tex. L. Rev. 766 (1969).

[429] See the Succession Act 1965, Part VIII (formal validity of wills). See also the Air Navigation and Transport Act 1973, section 11(4) and (5). Simple "residence" has also been used as a connecting factor: see, e.g. the Copyright Act 1963, section 7(5)(a).

[430] See e.g. the Wills Act 1963, section 1 (formal validity of wills), the Recognition of Divorces and Legal Separations Act 1971, section 3, and the Domicile and Matrimonial Proceedings Act 1973, section 5.

[431] Cf. the Irish Law Reform Commission's Working Paper No. 10-1981, *Domicile and Habitual Residence as Connecting Factors in the Conflict of Laws*, pp. 13-14.

to a conclusion as to where he or she has his or her habitual residence. This may ease the task of lawyers, administrative officials and the public generally.[432] The drawback is that it is not clear how long a residence must last before it should be denominated habitual. For all its faults, domicile does at least allow for the possibility of the acquisition of a domicile of choice immediately on arrival in the country where one intends to reside permanently or indefinitely.

While a person may have only one domicile, it is less clear that a person may have only one habitual residence.[433] Another problem with habitual residence is that it may be difficult to determine where a person has his habitual residence if he is constantly on the move, having little or no continuing connection with any of the countries through which he passes. However, no connecting factor provides a totally convincing answer to this problem. Nationality clearly does not even attempt to resolve the issue and domicile's response — revival of the domicile of origin (under the law in this country and in England) or the artificial continuation of a domicile that the person in question does not wish to continue (in the United States, Australia and New Zealand) — scarcely seems adequate.

The Law Reform Commission, in their *Report on Domicile and Habitual Residence as Connecting Factors in the Conflict of Laws*, published in 1983, came to the conclusion that, on balance, the better course would be to replace domicile by habitual residence.[434] The Commission took the view that it would be better for the legislation to define "habitual residence", rather than leave the question entirely to the courts to determine. In taking this approach, of course, the Commission have necessarily run the calculated risk that "a statutory formulation, even in the form of commonsense presumptions, could lead to the development of technical rules".[435]

The central recommendations of the Commission are incorporated in sections 3 to 6 of a General Scheme of a Bill contained in the Appendix to the Report. Section 3 is as follows:

"(1) Provide that the habitual residence of a person shall be determined having regard to the centre of his personal, social and economic interests.
(2) Provide that, in making a determination under subsection (1), account shall be taken of the duration of the interests therein specified and of the intentions of the person relative thereto.
(3) Provide that the habitual residence of any person shall not be determined by that of a spouse, a parent of any other person."

Section 4 provides as follows:

"(1) Provide that although the habitual residence of one spouse does not depend upon that of the other spouse, the habitual residence of one spouse may be taken into account in determining the habitual residence of the other spouse.
(2) Provide that, where the spouses are residing together, they shall each be presumed to have the same habitual residence, unless the contrary is shown."

Section 5 provides that an unmarried child under the age of sixteen is to be presumed to have the habitual residence of his or her parent or of the parent with whom he or she has his/her home unless the contrary is shown or the circumstances indicate otherwise. And section 6 is to the effect that:

[432] Cf. *McClean*, 31. See also the English and Scottish Law Commissions, *Private International Law: The Law of Domicile*, para. 2.2 (Working Paper No. 88 and Consultative Memorandum No. 63, 1985).
[433] Cf. *Private International Law: The Law of Domicile, supra*, para. 2.4
[434] This recommendation echoed their provisional view, explained in their Working Paper No. 10-1981, *Domicile and Habitual Residence as Connecting Factors in the Conflict of Laws*, p. 13.
[435] *McClean*, 30.

"a person may have his habitual residence only in one State or territorial unit of a state and ... he shall be deemed to have his habitual residence in that State until such time as he acquires an habitual residence in another State."

In view of the reference in section 3(1) to "the *centre* of [one's] personal, social and economic interests"[436] it is perhaps not surprising[437] that section 6 should provide that one's habitual residence may be "only in one State ...." The Commission also explain the inclusion of section 6 on the basis that providing for a single habitual residence "removes the possibility of a person's status or legal rights being determined by conflicting systems of law".[438]

Turning to section 4, the Commission go on to say that the rebuttable presumption which it contains:

"would not appear likely to work injustice, whilst at the same time it would greatly facilitate the determination of the question of the spouses' habitual residence outside the context of formal legal proceedings."[439]

Two difficulties present themselves about the section. First it appears to involve a vicious circle, for how may the court take into account "the habitual residence of one spouse" in determining the habitual residence of the other, when, in order to determine the habitual residence of the first, that of the second would be a relevant factor? Only an arbitrary choice will break the circle. Perhaps the answer to this difficulty is that section 4(1) does not require the court in *every* case to keep looking from one spouse to the other, thereby being unable to come to any determination as to the habitual residence of either. In some cases the habitual residence of one spouse may, for particular reasons, be clear, without regard to the habitual residence of the other. In these instances, this definite habitual residence of the first spouse *may* be taken into account in attempting to determine the habitual residence of the other spouse.

This leads us to the second difficulty, which relates in particular to section 4(2). It is not clear which of two quite different notions the subsection envisages. One is that, *without any regard to the factual question of what the habitual residence of either of the spouses may be,* there is a presumption that the spouses *will not have separate habitual residences.* The second notion is that the spouses are presumed *to share an actual habitual residence.* The better view would appear to be that the subsection endorses the first of these two notions; but if this is so it is difficult to see how exactly a court would be expected to give effect to it. That spouses are residing together, of itself, throws no light on what in fact is the habitual residence of either of them. No further light on this question results from the establishment of the presumption that the spouses share a single habitual residence.

An important aspect of section 3(2) should be noted. The subsection requires that, in determining a person's habitual residence, account is to be taken of the duration of his or her personal, social and economic interests "and of the intentions of the person relative thereto". This specific reference to intentions might raise the spectre of domicile, where intention plays such a significant role. The Commission were satisfied that the draft gave the Court "an appropriate discretion",[440] which would not result in perverse findings in cases where a person through unsoundness of mind or lack of age is incapable of forming any intention on these matters.

---

[436] Emphasis added.
[437] Cf. LRC 7-1983, para. 27.
[438] *Id.*
[439] *Id.*, para. 22.
[440] *Id.*, para. 21. Cf. *id.*, paras. 16-17.

Ordinary residence

The notion of "ordinary residence" is of some importance especially in relation to taxation.[441] It is accepted that, in contrast to the concept of domicile,[442] "ordinary residence", is not a term of art with only one inflexible meaning.[443] The proper approach is that "the words 'ordinarily resident' should be construed according to their ordinary meaning and with the aid of such light as is thrown upon them by the general intention of the legislation in which they occur and, of course, with reference to the facts of the particular case."[444]

The extent, if any, to which "ordinary residence" differs from mere "residence" is unclear.[445] In *Levene* v. *I.R.C.*,[446] Viscount Cave, L.C. observed that ordinary residence "connotes residence in a place with some degree of continuity and apart from accidental or temporary absences". Each case must be dealt with on its particular facts.[447] "The expression, 'ordinarily resident' ", said Maguire, J. in *The State (Goertz)* v. *Minister for Justice*[448], "appears to point to the way in which a person's life is usually ordered". As Lord Sumner commented in *I.R.C.* v. *Lysaght,*[449] "the converse to 'ordinarily' is 'extraordinarily' ". Thus, the term "must imply that [the residence] is not casual or uncertain, but that the person held to reside does so in the ordinary course of his life".[450]

It seems that a person may be ordinarily resident in more than one country;[451] and that he may be ordinarily resident in one country while being resident in another.[452] Our courts have yet to consider the question of the ordinary residence of children. Where a child is too young to decide the question of his own residence it may well be that he should be considered to be ordinarily resident in his parents' home.[453] Where the parents live apart, and the child is living with one of them, his home would normally be likely to constitute the place of his ordinary residence. The matter is not one for arbitrary rules such as those at common law which affected the domicile of children whose parents live apart.[454]

---

[441] Cf. the Income Tax Act 1967, sections 76, 199, *Capital Gains Tax Act 1975*, section 4(1). See *Kelly & Carmichael*, 332-333, *Judge*, 1, 602, *Grogan*, 102.
[442] Cf. *supra*, pp. 45-51.
[443] Cf. *The State (Goertz)* v. *Minister for Justice*, [1948] I.R. 45, at 55 (Sup. Ct., *per* Maguire, C.J., 1947, aff'g High Ct., Maguire, J., 1947). Maguire, C.J. considered that the House of Lords cases, *Levene* v. *I.R.C.* [1928] A.C. 217 and *I.R.C.* v. *Lysaght,* [1928] A.C. 234, afforded "no sure guidance as to the meaning of the term" in a different statutory context. In *Goertz*, at 57-58, Black, J. observed that " [i]n *Ex parte Breull. In re Bowie*, 16 Ch. D. 484, Cotton, L.J. declared that the word, 'residence', is an ambiguous term, and I agree with him. Further in *Levene* v. *I.R.C.* [1928] A.C., at 225, Viscount Cave L.C. said, in effect, that the addition of the word, 'ordinarily', made little difference. I agree with that also, unless there is something in the context which throws light on the meaning; and if Viscount Cave L.C. is right, the word, 'resided', loses little of its ambiguity by being modified by the adverb, 'ordinarily'."
[444] *The State (Goertz)* v. *Minister for Justice*, [1948] I.R., at 55 (*per* Maguire, C.J.).
[445] Cf. *Dicey & Morris*, 143.
[446] [1928] A.C., at 225, quoted in part by Black, J., in *Goertz*, at 58, and echoed in the language of Maguire, J., *id.*, at 50.
[447] *The State (Goertz)* v. *Minister for Justice, supra*, at 50 (*per* Maguire, J.).
[448] *Id.*
[449] [1928] A.C., at 217, at 243 (H.L. (Eng.), 1928).
[450] *The State (Goertz)* v. *Minister for Justice, supra*, at 50 (*per* Maguire, J.).
[451] *Re Norris*, 4 Times L.R. 452 (C.A., 1888), *Cooper* v. *Cadwalader*, 5 Tax. Cas. 201 (1904), *Dicey & Morris*, 144.
[452] Cf. *Stransky* v. *Stransky*, [1954] P. 428, *Dicey & Morris*, 143.
[453] Cf. *Re. P. (G.E.) (An Infant)*, [1965] Ch. 568 (C.A.) considered *infra*, pp. 324-325.
[454] Cf. *supra*, pp. 85-87.
[455] *Supra*.

The question of the relevance of voluntariness to ordinary residence arose in *The State (Goertz)* v. *Minister for Justice.*[455] The prosecutor in *certiorari* and *habeas corpus* proceedings was a member of the German Air Force who had landed here by parachute, without permission, in May 1940. He spent the next eighteen months in the country under a veil of secrecy. He was then arrested and interned until September 1946. A deportation order was served on him in August 1946 but was not enforced. Having been released initially on daily parole, he was then released without detention. He took up employment in Dublin, which continued until April 1948, when he was again served with a deportation order, this time with the clear intention on the part of the authorities that it should be enforced immediately. The prosecutor sought that the order should be quashed since, he said, he had been "ordinarily resident" within the jurisdiction for a period of not less than five yers and was thus entitled to 3 months' advice of deportation.[456]

The prosecutor's application was unsuccessful. Maguire, J. and four members of the Supreme Court took the view that his residence was either involuntary or what might be called furtively illegal. Maguire, C.J. said:

> "In this case the applicant came here unlawfully. Although not explicitly stated on affidavit, it is reasonably clear that his object as a member of the armed forces of Germany was to assist his country in her war effort ... There is no evidence that, during the period when I assume he was in hiding or interned, he intended to reside here, save in the sense that he intended to remain here physically in order to carry out the object he had in view ... The argument for the appellant seems to me to come down to this, that the mere physical presence of an alien here for the requisite period constitutes ordinary residence. In my view, so to construe the words, 'ordinarily resident' would produce an absurd result, of which the present case, if it were to be successful, would afford an illustration.'"[457]

Murnaghan, J., concurring, also rejected the argument that mere physical presence within the jurisdiction was embraced by the term "ordinarily resident", as it appeared in the subsection. He added:

> "A person who came here and who remained here under various disguises, could not reasonably be held to be ordinarily resident, although physically in this country. The phrase should, I think, refer to the character, as well as to the duration, of the residence.'"[458]

Although both Maguire C.J. and Murnaghan, J. made observations of apparently general import as to the scope of the expression "ordinarily resident", a close reading of both judgments makes it plain that they were made very much in the specific context of the Aliens Act 1935 and in the light of its particular policies.[459]

Black, J. pursued a radically different analysis, though he reached the same conclusion. He left "out of account altogether"[460] the *motive* of the appellant's sojourn in this country. He did:

> "not see how the man's motive could affect the nature of his stay in Ireland during a period when his motive could have had no effect on that stay and when he had no choice in the matter. Apart from that, and even if his whole stay here had been voluntary, his motive for that stay would, in my view, be immaterial to the question we have to determine. The motive might greatly affect the desirability of the stay, but not, I think, its actuality or its comprehension in the phrase, 'ordinarily resident'. Criminals

---

[456] Cf. the Aliens Act 1935, section 5(5)(c).
[457] [1948] I.R., at 56.
[458] *Id.*, at 57. In accord, *Reg.* v. *Barnet L.B.C., Ex p. Shah*, [1983] 1 A.C. 309.
[459] Cf. [1948] I.R., at 55, 56 (*per* Maguire, C.J.) and 57 (*per* Murnaghan, J.).
[460] *Id.*, at 58.

often come to spend their lives in a given locality for the express purpose of making it the area of their activities; yet if they made their permanent home in that area, nobody would say that they did not ordinarily reside there."[461]

The "serious question"[462] in the case was the issue of *voluntariness* as affecting ordinary residence. In Black, J.'s view, the word "ordinarily" merely connoted continuity rather than voluntariness. The word "residence" equally was not premised on proof of free will.[463] In an important passage, Black, J. said:

"I look upon 'ordinarily' doing anything as doing it often enough or long enough to justify its being regarded as usual or habitual. Whether it is done freely or compulsorily appears to me to have nothing to say to its being 'ordinarily'. If one said that a person ordinarily walked a mile every day, I should think the statement equally correct, whether the person in question covered a mile, daily, solely from inclination or whether he did it by way of compulsory exercise in a prison yard. Similarly, if I were to take the words 'ordinarily resident' alone and without regard to their context, I should think that a person had ordinarily resided in this country if he had spent all his days and nights here continuously for five years or even for a much shorter period. If the fact that such residence was compulsory prevented such a resident from being ordinarily resident here, it would seem to follow that lunatics in an asylum, prisoners in gaol, and, it may be, boys in boarding schools, would not be ordinarily resident in these respective places, which would appear a *reductio ad absurdum* of the contention that one cannot be ordinarily resident in a place unless one is voluntarily resident there."[464]

Thus, Black, J. would have been of opinion that the appellant *had* ordinarily resided here for not less than five years, were it not for the distinctive manner in which the subsection was drafted.

Up to this point, Black, J.'s analysis is of formidable intellectual force, presenting a strong and attractive argument against reading into the term "ordinarily resided" qualifications that it may not necessarily embrace. On the specific question of interpreting the subsection, however, Black, J.'s approach is far less convincing. He took the view that, had the phrase "ordinarily resident" stood alone, the word "ordinarily" would merely have connoted some degree of continuity of residence. But the words "for ... not less than five years" themselves connoted this degree of continuity. Therefore, said Black, J., to avoid redundancy the word "ordinarily" had to connote something not already in the phrase "for ... not less than five years", and hence something more than, and different from, mere continuity. It therefore had to be presumed to have been intended to exclude some kind of residence which the phase "for not less than five years" would not exclude. Black, J. was unable to conceive of any sort of continuous residence for five years which it would exclude, if it did not exclude residence in internment as distinct from the residence of a free citizen.[465]

This conclusion is quite unwarranted. If we accept Black, J.'s interpretation of ordinary residence as connoting some degree of continuity, there was nothing to prevent the subsection, consistent with the interpretation, from requiring that the ordinary residence, thus defined, continue for five years. To introduce such a specific requirement supplements rather than replaces the meaning of ordinary residence.[466]

---

[461] *Id.*
[462] *Id.*
[463] *Id.*
[464] *Id.*, at 59.
[465] *Id.*, at 60.
[466] A recent Northern Ireland decision dealing with the question of ordinary residence is *Deighan v Sunday Newspapers Ltd.*, [1985] N.I.L.R. Bulletin of Judgments, No. 3, p. 18 (Q.B.D., Carswell, J.).

CHAPTER 7

PROOF OF FOREIGN LAW

In this chapter we examine the question of proof of foreign law. As a general rule, when foreign law applies in a case, that law must be pleaded and proved as a fact to the satisfaction of the court.[1] In the Supreme Court decision of *MacNamara* v. *Owners of The S.S. "Hatteras"*,[2] in 1933, FitzGibbon, J. said:

> "Foreign law, *i.e.*, the law of a foreign country, must be proved as a matter of fact in our Courts, if a question depending upon that law is in dispute. This principle applies not only to the laws of foreign countries[3] but to those of the colonies,[4] the Channel Islands[5] [and] Scotland[6] and is now not open to question."

---

[1] Cf.*Dicey & Morris*, Rule 210(1), *Falconbridge*, 833ff., *Rabel*, vol. 4, ch. 76, Hirschfield, *Proof of Foreign Law*, 11 L.Q.Rev. 241 (1895), Chase–Casgrain, *Proof of Foreign Extraprovincial Laws*, 3 Can. Bar Rev. 240 (1925), Lafleur, *Foreign Law and its Proof*, 3 Rev. Lég (n.s.) 393 (1897), McInerney, *Some Notes on Proof of Foreign Law*, 11 Proc. of the Canadian Bar Assoc. 200 (1926), Castel, *Proof of Foreign Law*, 22 U. Toronto L.J. 33 (1927), Nussbaum, *Proof of Foreign Law in New York. A Proposed Amendment*, 57 Colum. L. Rev. 348 (1957), Nussbaum, *The Problem of Proving Foreign Law*, 50 Yale L.J. 1018 (1941), Sommerich & Busch, *The Expert Witness and the Proof of Foreign Law*, 38 Cornell L. Q. 125 (1953), Sass, *Foreign Law in Civil Litigation: A Comparative Survey*, 16 Amer. J. of Comp. L. 332 (1968), Yasseen, *Problèmes relatifs à l'application du droit étranger*, [1962] – II Recueil des cours 498, Kahn, *Note: What Happens In a Conflicts Case when the Governing Foreign Law Is Not Proved?* 87 S.A.L.J. 145 (1970), Kahn, *Note: Proving the Law of Our Friends and Neighbours*, 82 S.A.L.J. 133 (1965), Zajtay, *The Application of Foreign Law*, ch. 14 of International Encyclopedia of Comparative Law, vol. 3, *Private International Law* (1974), Furmston, *Note: Proof of Foreign Law*, 22 Modern L. Rev. 317 (1959), Alexander, *The Application and Avoidance of Foreign Law in the Law of Conflicts*, 70 Nw. U.L.Rev. 602 (1976), Stern, *Foreign Law in the Courts: Judicial Notice and Proof*, 45 Calif. L. Rev. 23 (1957), Schlesinger, *A Recurrent Problem in Transnational Litigation: The Effect of Failure to Invoke or Prove the Applicable Foreign Law*, 59 Cornell L. Rev. 1 (1973), Shava, *Proof of Foreign Law in Israel: A Comparative Study*, 16 N.Y.U.J. of Internat. L. & Pol. 211 (1984). Two relatively recent symposia on proof of foreign law (and related matters) should also be noted: 18 Va. J. of Internat. L. 609–751 (1978) and 19 Stan. J. of Internat. L. 1–206 (1983). Of particular relevance are Hunter, *Proving Foreign and International Law in the Courts of England and Wales*, 18 Va. J. of Internat. L. 665, at 665–677 (1978) and Merryman, *Foreign Law as a Problem*, 19 Stan. J. of Internat. L. 151 (1983).

[2] [1933] I.R. 675, at 698 (Sup. Ct., 1933, reversing Meredith J., 1932). See further, *Canadian National Steamships Co.* v. *Watson*, [1939] S.C.R. 11, [1939] 1 D.L.R. 273, *Furlong* v. *Burns & Co. Ltd.*, [1964] 2 O.R. 3, 43 D.L.R. (2d) 689 (High Ct., Hughes, J.), *Lear* v. *Lear*, 51 D.L.R. (3d) 56 (Ont. C.A., 1974), *Archie Colpitts Ltd.* v. *Graimmer*, 83 D.L.R. (3d) 281 (N.S. Sup. Ct., App. Div., 1978), *Morgardshammar A.B.* v. *H.R. Radomski & Co. Ltd.*, 5 D.L.R. (4th) 576 (Ont. C.A., 1984), aff'g. 145 D.L.R. (3d) 111 (Ont. High Ct., Craig, J., 1983).

[3] Cf. *Bowden Bros & Co.* v. *Imperial Marine & Transport Insurance Co.*, 5 S.R.(N.S.W.)614 (1905).

[4] Citing *The Peerless*, Lush. 103, 167 E.R. 53, 13 Moo. P.C. 484, 15 E.R. 182 (1860). It appears that legislation enacted by the British parliament facilitating proof of laws of British colonies and dominions (British Law Ascertainment Act 1859, Foreign Law Ascertainment Act 1861, Colonial Laws Validity Act 1865, section 6, Evidence (Colonial Statutes) Act 1907; cf. *Dicey & Morris*, 1214–1215, *Anton*, 570–571) has had no continuing application here after Independence.

[5] Citing *Brenan & Galen's Case*, 10 Q. B. 492, at 498, 116 E.R. 188, at 190 (*per* Patteson, J., 1847).

[6] Citing *Dalrymple* v. *Dalrymple*, 2 Hag. Con. 54, at 80–83, 161 E.R. 665, at 675 (Lord Stowell, 1811).

Although foreign law must be proved as a matter of fact, it is "a question of fact of a peculiar kind".[7] The courts accept that in the last analysis the application and interpretation of a foreign law is very much a legal process. Thus we do not find in this context the same degree of appellate deference to the trial court as would apply to other findings of fact by the trial judge. *MacNamara* v. *Owners of the S.S. Hatteras*[8] is itself a good example: the Supreme Court gave scant regard to Meredith, J.'s findings as to foreign law.

FOREIGN LAW MUST BE PROVED

Foreign law must be proved in every case where it is asserted:[9] it cannot be deduced from previous Irish decisions in which the same rule of foreign law has been before the court.[10] In *The Queen* v. *Griffin*,[11] in 1879, Fitzgerald, B. said:

"The Courts of Justice in this country can take no judicial notice of what the law of a foreign State as to any matter in question is, or indeed that there is any law of such State relating to such matter."

Similarly in *O'Callaghan* v. *Sullivan*,[12] Kennedy, C.J. said of the Canon Law:

"It is, of course, true to say that it is a subject matter of which these courts cannot take judicial notice without proof."

On rare occasions, however, the courts have taken judicial notice of foreign law as a notorious fact: thus in one English case[13] judicial notice was taken of the fact that roulette is not unlawful in Monte Carlo and in another[14] that the common law of England prevailed in Ireland.[15] But the court will not be lightly deflected from the general rule.

Modes of Proof

Foreign law must generally be proved by expert evidence.[17] In *O'Callaghan* v.

---

[7] *Parkasho* v. *Singh*, [1968] P. 233, at 250 (*per* Cairns, J., 1966).

[8] [1933] I.R. 675 (Sup. Ct., 1933, reversing Meredith, J., 1932).

[9] The parties may agree as to what the foreign law is on the subject: cf. *Du Fogassieras* v. *Duport*, 11 L.R. Ir. 123 (prob., 1881). See also *Moulis* v. *Owen*, [1907]1 K.B. 746 (C.A.), *Prowse* v. *European & American Steam Shipping Co.,* 13 Moo. P.C. 484, at 506, 15 E.R. 182, at 190 (1860), *Williams* v. *Usher*, 94 C.L.R., 450 (1955). Alternatively the parties may request the judge to determine the foreign law – a course the courts are reluctant to take except in cases concerning the interpretation of foreign statutes: *Beatty* v. *Beatty*, [1924] 1 K.B. 807 (C.A.). See further *infra*, p. 112-113.

[10] *Dicey & Morris*, 1207, *Lazard Brothers & Co.* v. *Midland Bank Ltd.*, [1933] A.C. 289 (H.L. (Eng.), 1932), *M'Cormick* v. *Garnett*, 5 D.M. & G. 278, 43 E.R. 877 (1854), *Re Marseilles Extension Ry. & Land Co.*, 30 Ch. D. 598 (Pearson, J., 1885). See, however, *Re Sebba*, [1959] Ch. 166 (Danckwerts, J., 1958). Moreover, a decision as to the effect of the law of a foreign country handed down by a court in some other foreign country will have no weight in an Irish court: *Callwood* v. *Callwood*, [1960] A.C. 659 (P.C.). See Webb, 23 Modern L.Rev. 556 (1960), Carter, 36 Br.Yrbk. of Int.L. 408 (1960).

[11] 4 L.R. (Ir.) 497, at 506 (Cr. Cas. Res., 1879).

[12] [1925] 1 I.R. 90, at 107 (Sup. Ct.). See also *Re Swan*, 2 V.R. (I.E. & M.) 47 (Molesworth, J., 1871), *R.* v. *Ford*, 32 N.Z.L.R. 1219, at 1225 (C.A., *per* Chapman, J., 1913).

[13] *Saxby* v. *Fulton* [1909] 2 K.B. 208, at 211 (Bray, J., 1908). See also *Harold Meyers Travel Service Ltd* v. *Magid*, 60 D.L.R. (3d) 42, at 44 (Ont. High Ct., Fraser, J., 1975). More generally, see Stern, *Foreign Law in the Courts: Judical Notice and Proof*, 45 Calif. L. Rev. 23, at 39–44 (1957), F.R., *Comment: Conflict of Laws – Judicial Notice of Foreign Law*, 30 Mich. L. Rev. 747 (1932).

[14] *Re Nesbitt*, 14 L.J.M.C. 30, at 33 (Bail Ct., Patterson, J., 1844).

[15] See also *In re Schopperle's Trusts*, [1932] I.R. 457 (High Ct.), where Johnston, J. interpreted provisions of the *British Finance (No.2) Act 1931* without the assistance of foreign legal experts. Cf. *In re Dyas*, [1932] I.R. 427 (Kennedy, C.J.) and *In re Westby*, [1932] I.R. 444 (Kennedy, C.J.).

[17] Cf. *O'Callaghan* v. *O'Sullivan*, [1925] 1 I.R. 90, at 109–110, 119–120 (Sup. Ct., *per* Kennedy,

O'Sullivan,[18] Kennedy, C.J. quoted with approval extracts from the works of two leading authorities on evidence, Stephen and Taylor. Stephen's *Digest of the Law of Evidence*, stated:

"When there is a question as to a foreign law, the opinions of experts who in their profession are acquainted with such law are the only admissible evidence thereof."[19]

Taylor on Evidence stated:

"In conformity with the general rule which admits in evidence the opinions of skilled witnesses on all subjects of science, the existence and meaning of the laws, as well written as unwritten, and of usages and systems of foreign states, may, and indeed *must*, be proved by calling professional or official persons to give their opinions on the subject."[20]

As to the question of who is a competent expert, " [n]o precise or comprehensive answer can be given".[21] A judge or legal practitioner from the foreign country is always competent.[22] Thus, in *MacNamara* v. *Owners of the S.S. "Hatteras"*,[23] the

---

C.J.). See also *McNamara* v. *Owners of the S.S. "Hatteras"*, [1933] I.R. 675, at 691 (Sup. Ct., *per* Kennedy, C.J.), *Baron de Bode's Case*, 8 Q.B. 208, 115 E.R. 854 (1845), *The Earldom of Perth*, 2 H.L.C. 865, 9 E.R. 1322 (1846). *Castrique* v. *Imrie*, L.R. 4 H.L. 414, at 430 (1870).

[18] [1925] 1 I.R. 90, at 109−110.

[19] Article 49.

[20] Vol. 2, section 1423, p. 973 (11th ed.).

[21] *Dicey & Morris*, 1209.

[22] *Baron de Bode's Case, supra.* See, e.g., *In re Lett's Trusts and Trustee Relief Act; Ex Parte Lett*, 7 L.R. (Ir.) 132 (Chatterton, V.C., 1881) (evidence on affidavit fom counsellor-at-law practising in State of New York accepted), *In re Bolton*, [1920] 2 I.R. 324 (K.B. Div., Dodd, J.) (evidence of practising barrister of the Supreme Court of the Union of South Africa accepted), *In re White Deceased: Ingram* v. *White*, [1918] 1 I.R. 19 (Chy. Div., Barton, J., 1917) (evidence on affidavit from "practising attorney of experience at the Philadelphia Bar" accepted), *Donohue* v. *Donohue*, 19 L.R. Ir., 349 (Chatterton, V.C., 1887) (evidence on affidavit from a "Missouri lawyer" accepted), *Dennis* v. *Leinster Paper Co.*, [1901] 2 I.R. 337 (C.A., aff'g K.B. Div., Kenny, J.) (evidence as to law of New York and of United States Supreme Court received from attorney and counsellor-at-law, practising in the Courts of the State of New York and in the United States Supreme Court), *In re Mansfield Deceased; Hibernian Bank Ltd.* v. *Mansfield*, [1962] I.R. 454 (High Ct., 1961) (evidence as to English law, given on affadavit, accepted from member of the English bar and evidence as to Canon Law, also given on affadavit, received from Rev'd Gerard Sheehy, who had "the unusual qualifications of being a Roman Catholic Priest, a holder of the degree of Doctor of Canon Law and a member of the Irish Bar" (*id.*, at 460)), *In re Lett's Trusts*, 7 L.R. Ir. 132 (Chatterton, V.C., 1881) (evidence on affidavit from counsellor-at-law practising in the State of New York accepted), *Dharamal* v. *Lord HolmPatrick*, [1935] I.R. 760 (High Ct., Johnston, J.) (Court accepted the affidavit sworn by an Indore barrister as to the constitutional position of the Indore State, and as to the personal law of the minor concerned, which was Hindu law), *Orlando* v. *Earl of Fingal*, [1940] I.R. 281 (High Ct., Gavan Duffy, J.) (affidavit as to New York law accepted from attorney and counsellor-at-law, duly qualified as a practitioner and licensed to practise before all the Courts of the State of New York and the Federal Courts), *In re Ferguson's Trusts*, I.R. 8 Eq. 563 (Sullivan, M.R.,1874) (evidence on affidavit from Scottish advocate accepted), *Leake* v. *Douglas*, 88 I.L.T.R. 4 (Circuit Ct., Judge Conroy, 1952), (evidence from Professor E. F. Ryan, Barrister-at-Law, Middle Temple and of King's Inns, Professor of Common Law at University College, Cork, accepted in a case involving the question as to the enforceability of an order for alimony made in English divorce proceedings), *L.B.* v. *H.B.*, [1980] I.L.R.M. 257 (High Ct., Barrington, J.) (evidence of person in practice "as a professional lawyer" in France and also qualified as a solicitor in England accepted by the Court), *In re Interview Ltd.*, [1975] I.R. 382 (High Ct., Kenny, J.) (evidence as to law of Federal Republic of Germany given by one Dr Joachim Michael, Kenny, J. stating (at 392) that he accepted "all his evidence" but giving no further details as to his qualifications or experience), *Cripps Warburg Ltd.* v. *Cologne Investment Co. Ltd.*, [1980] I.R. 321 (High Ct., D'Arcy, J., 1979) (evidence as to English law given by practising barrister in the Chancery Courts of the English High Court), *In the Goods of Dyas, Deceased*, [1937] I.R. 479 (High Ct., Hanna, J.) (at 481: "In the consideration of this case I have been greatly assisted by the affidavit of Mr Robert L. Sandes, a Member of the Bar, of the English Bar, and also of the South African bar, known to us as an authority on the Roman Dutch law as applied in the Courts of the Union of South Africa"), *Larkins* v. *National Union of Mineworkers Ltd.*, High Ct., Barrington,

Supreme Court regarded as competent to give evidence as to the Federal law in the United States a solicitor practising in England but who was also a member of the New York Bar and had practised as such for some years, specialising in advising on American statute and Federal law. In the same case the Court also recognised as competent a member of the Bar of the Supreme Court of the United States who was also a member of the New York and English Bars, and who specialised in American law. In *McKie* v. *McKie*,[24] the High Court accepted evidence as to *Californian* law given by a member of the Bar of the State of *Illinois* and of the Bar of the United States, but who was not apparently a member of the Bar of the State of California.

A former practitioner in the foreign country[25] whose law is in question may also be competent; similarly a person entitled to practise in the foreign country but who has not done so.[26] At a further remove, the courts have accepted evidence from a person who has practised in *another* foreign country whose law is the same as that of the foreign country whose law is under consideration.[27] The courts have been reluctant to accept evidence from persons who merely studied the foreign law, without having practised or resided in the foreign jurisdiction,[28] but in rare cases[29] such evidence has been accepted.

In *O'Callaghan* v. *Sullivan*,[30] where Canon Law was the foreign law under consideration, the Supreme Court held that evidence had rightly been received from two witnesses: the first was a Doctor of Canon Law, Professor of Canon Law at Maynooth, and qualified by a special course of study of Canon Law in Rome; the second was a Doctor of Canon Law and Professor of Canon Law and Moral Theology. In the same case no weight was attached to the evidence of a classical scholar of Trinity College who was well able to translate the texts of Canon Law submitted to him but of whom ''[n]either the plaintiff nor this witness [himself] stated that he had ever studied, or even read a line of Canon Law, or of any book on the subject, or had any acquaintance whatever with it.''[31]

In *G. v G.*[32] in 1984, Finlay, P. (as he then was), in determining the law of

---

J., 18 June 1985 (1984−8465P) (evidence received from three English barristers, one of whom was a legal author), *Moffett* v. *Moffett*, [1920] 1 I.R. 57 (C.A., 1920, aff'g Powell, J., 1917) (affidavit as to Cape Colony Law accepted from one William R. Bisschop, L.L.D., Barrister; report silent as to whether he was then practising there). Some problems associated with the use of affidavits rather than oral testimony are considered by Spankling & Lanyi, *Pleading and Proof of Foreign Law in American Courts*, 19 Stan. J. of Internat. L. 3, at 49−51 (1983). Evidence as to foreign law may be taken on commission in certain cases of difficulty: cf. *Keane* v. *Hanley*, [1938] Ir. Jur. Rep. 16 (Sup. Ct., varying High Ct., O'Byrne, J.).

[23] [1933] I.R. 675 (Sup. Ct. 1933, reversing Meredith, J., 1932).

[24] [1933] I.R. 464 (High Ct., Meredith, J.).

[25] Cf. *In the Matter of Rea Deceased: Rea* v. *Rea*, [1902] 1 I.R. 451 (Porter, M.R.), *Re Duke of Wellington*, [1947] Ch. 506, at 514-515 (Wynn-Parry, J.); *Keresz* v. *Keresz*, [1954] V.L.R. 195; *Elter* v. *Keresz*, 26 D.L.R. (2d) 209 (1960), *Patterson* v. *D'Agostino*, 8 O.R. (2d) 367 (Griffiths, Co. Ct. J., 1975). A long absence from the country in which the lawyer practised may disqualify a witness: cf. *Wilkie* v. *McCalla (No. 3)*, [1905] V.L.R. 278, at 283 (Madden, C.J., 1904 (aff'd by Full Ct., 1904)).

[26] *Barford* v. *Barford*, [1918] P. 140 (Horridge, J.); *Perlack Petroleum Maatschappij* v. *Deen*, [1924] 1 K.B. 111 (C.A.).

[27] *Reinblatt* v. *Gold*, 45 Que. K.B. 136 (Greenshields, J., 1928); affirmed [1929] S.C.R. 74.

[28] Cf. *Bristow* v. *Sequeville*, 5 Ex. 275, 155 E.R. 118 (1850), *In the Goods of Bonelli*, L.R. 1 P.D. 69 (Sir J. Hannen, P., 1875).

[29] Cf. *Brailey* v. *Rhodesia Consolidated Ltd.*, [1910] 2 Ch. 95 (Warrington, J.), *Barford* v. *Barford*, *supra*, *Wilson* v. *Wilson*, [1903], P. 157 (Jeune, P.), *In the Goods of Whitelegg*, [1899] P. 267 (Jeune, P.), *Rossano* v. *Manufacturers' Life Insurance Co.*, [1963] 2 Q.B. 352 (McNair, J., 1962).

[30] [1925] 1 I.R. 90 (Sup. Ct.).

[31] *Id.*, at 106 (*per* Kennedy, C.J.).

[32] [1984] I.R. 368 (High Ct., Finlay, P.).

Massachusetts in family litigation, acted on the affidavit of a counseller-at-law in Massachusetts entitled to practise before the courts of that State. This affidavit dealt with questions of the law of Massachusetts as well as dealing with the facts of the case in which he was counsel acting on behalf of the plaintiff. There is, perhaps, some reason to doubt the general advisability of obtaining evidence as to foreign law from a lawyer who has actually been involved in the proceedings.

The courts have frequently accepted the evidence of non-lawyers when their practical experience is considered to give them sufficient authority.[33] Thus an ex-Governor-General of Hong Kong,[34] an ambassador, [35] an embassy official,[36] a merchant[37] and a bank official[38] have all been held competent. But the court will not lightly permit non-lawyers to give evidence as to foreign law. The "best evidence" rule ensures that this will be allowed only where it is not practicable for legal experts to testify.[39]

Mere familiarity with foreign law does not, itself, suffice. In *The Goods of Gentili*[40] the court rejected evidence consisting of a letter written by "a person professing to be acquainted with Roman or Italian law".[41] This person supplied no affidavit to verify his opinion, nor even an affidavit that he was a professional lawyer. Warren, J. said:

> "I think such a letter is not evidence, and ought not to be received, and that it would
> be highly dangerous to rights of property, if such evidence of foreign law were to be
> received and acted upon; *in judicio non creditur nisi juratis* is the general rule ..."[42]

Where evidence as to foreign law given by an expert witness is not met by conflicting evidence it appears that it will not be strengthened by reference to the case law of the foreign legal system. In *MacNamara* v. *Owners of the S.S. "Hatteras"*,[43] Kennedy, C.J. said:

> "In the absence of any evidence conflicting with it, I think we are bound to accept
> th[e] evidence of [one of] th[e] expert witness[es] as stating the [foreign] rule
> ... and, that being so, nothing is added to its value as expert evidence by the fact that
> it appears to be supported clearly by the [foreign] case ... cited by [this] expert."

On occasions the courts appear to have adopted an unduly relaxed approach towards the question of proof of foreign law. In *In re Pavitt, an Infant*,[44] for example, Meredith, M.R. acted on the affidavit from the next friend of the petitioner, an infant, which stated that she had been "informed by her legal advisors" and believed "that

---

[33] See Sommerich & Busch, *The Expert Witness and the Proof of Foreign Law*, 38 Cornell L.Q. 125, at 150−152 (1953).

[34] *Cooper-King* v. *Cooper-King*, [1900] P.65 (Gorrell Barnes, J.).

[35] *In the Goods of Oldenburg*, 9 P.D. 234 (Butt, J., 1884), *In the Goods of Klingemann*, 3 Sw. & Tr. 18, 164 E.R. 1178 (1862).

[36] *In the Goods of Dost Aly Khan*, 6 P.D. 6 (Sir James Hannen, P., 1880) (second secretary to Persian Embassy permitted to give evidence as to the law of Persia, there being no professional Persian lawyers at that time).

[37] *Vander Donkt* v. *Thellusson*, 8 C.B. 812, 137 E.R. 727 (1849).

[38] *De Beeche* v. *South American Stores Ltd.*, [1935] A.C. 148 (H.L. (Eng.), 1934) (bank director); *Said Ajami* v. *Comptroller of Customs*, [1954] 1 W.L.R. 1405 (P.C.) (bank manager).

[39] Cf. Wood, *Proof of Foreign Law in the Manitoba Courts*, 15 Manit. L.J. 53, at 73 (1985), *Direct Winters Transport Ltd* v. *Duplate Canada Ltd*, [1962] O.R. 360 (High Ct., Gale, J.).

[40] I.R. 9 Eq. 541 (Prob., 1875).

[41] *Id.*, at 542.

[42] *Id.* Subsequently the person filed an affidavit "verifying the legal opinion contained in his letter, and stating his professional capacity as an Italian advocate": *id.*, at 551. On this basis the court granted a general administration.

[43] [1933] I.R. 675, at 694 (Sup. Ct., 1933 reversing Meredith, J., 1932).

[44] [1907] 1 I.R. 234 (Meridith, M.R.).

under the circumstances of the case the French Courts would not appoint a guardian of the infant (who was resident in Ireland) but that they would recognise the authority of a guardian appointed by the Irish Court to receive interest payable under a legacy. It is not clear from the report whether these legal advisers were Irish or French: it appears that they gave no evidence, in person or by affidavit, to the Court. So also, in *Lett* v. *Lett*[45] the Court of Appeal did not disturb the trial judge's acceptance of the (non-lawyer) plaintiff's evidence[46] as to the law of matrimonial property in Argentina, no expert in the law of Argentina having been heard.

In *Stanhope* v. *Hospitals Trust Ltd. (No. 2)*,[47] Hanna, J. at trial and the majority of the Supreme Court on appeal favoured a novel mode of proof of foreign law. The case involved an action for breach of contract and negligence brought by a professional seller of sweepstake tickets in Durban. The gravamen of the claim was that certain counterfoils sent by the plaintiff to the Hospitals Trust, with the appropriate payment, had not been included in the draw, with the result that the public lost confidence in him and his occupation was destroyed.

When giving evidence, the plaintiff, who was an engineer by profession,[48] frankly admitted that his occupation was illegal. This was not an issue that the defendants wished to raise but it was clearly one that greatly interested Hanna, J., who directed a verdict in favour of the defendants on this account.

The Supreme Court held that, since the contract was to be performed in Ireland,[49] where it was legal, Hanna, J. should not have withdrawn the case from the jury, and accordingly a new trial was ordered. The Court also held that so far as the plaintiff's case sought damages for loss of an illegal business it was not sustainable. But the members of the Court could not agree on the propriety of acting on the plaintiff's evidence as to the law of Durban. FitzGibbon and Murnaghan, JJ. were happy to do so. FitzGibbon, J. was:

"unable to follow the contention that because no South African lawyer was called to prove that the trade carried on by the plaintiff in the town of Durban was illegal there, the Court was entitled to disregard the express evidence of the plaintiff himself on the point. I agree that if foreign law is in dispute the proper evidence to establish what the foreign law is that of a person who is an expert on that law, but if no issue is raised as to what the foreign law is, then I confess that it seems to me that the admissions of the parties themselves are as good legal evidence of foreign law as they are of any other question of fact on which the Court has to come to a conclusion, and that where the plaintiff himself admits three times over that the trade he is carrying on is illegal there is no need to call any further evidence of its illegality. I do not know who should call evidence to contradict it, but at any rate the onus was on the defendants. That being so, it seems to me that the Court had specific evidence that the plaintiff was claiming damages for the loss of an illegal trade, and that the Court was not only justified in taking, but was bound to take, notice of that specific evidence, and was bound to see that the Courts in this country were not made the means of enforcing that illegality."[50]

So far as FitzGibbon, J. sought to justify reliance on the evidence on "the admissions of the parties themselves", the *principle* is unexceptionable;[51] but it seems difficult to reconcile this approach with the fact that, at trial, plaintiff's counsel

---

[45] [1906] 1 I.R. 618 (C.A., aff'g. Porter, M.R.). Holmes, L.J.'s dissenting judgment should be noted.

[46] Cf. *id.*, at 623.

[47] [1936] Ir. Jur. Rep. 25 (Sup. Ct.), rev'g in part [1936] Ir. Jur. Rep. 21 (High Ct., Hanna, J. with jury, 1935). See further *infra*, pp. 547-548.

[48] Cf. [1936] Ir. Jur. Rep., at 27.

[49] The fact that the proper law seems also to have been Irish appears to have been a factor in Fitzgibbon, J.'s judgment: cf. *infra*, p. 548.

[50] [1936] Ir. Jur. Rep., at 28.

[51] Cf. *infra*, pp. 112-113.

"could not give [the trial judge] an assurance"[52] as to the illegality of the plaintiff's business, and counsel for the defendants, far from admitting its illegality, sought not to raise the question of illegality at all.[53] Neither Hanna, J. nor Murnaghan, J. attempted to justify inclusion of the evidence on the basis of the admission of the parties. Murnaghan, J. appeared to conceive of a principle akin to estoppel applying: he failed to see how anyone could think it "necessary to call an expert lawyer to prove [the illegality] when the plaintiff himself said that the business for the loss of which he was asking damages was illegal."[54]

It is easy to agree with Kennedy, C.J.'s dissenting remarks on the issue. He was of opinion that evidence as to illegality under the law in Natal could:

> "not to be said to have been established by the casual remarks of the plaintiff, who is an engineer by profession, that it is so prohibited and illegal, and that the trial Judge could not properly act upon evidence of the sale of or other dealings in these tickets, being illegal in any country, other than evidence tendered in the recognised manner in Natal. The casual haphazard remarks of the plaintiff in his evidence to the effect that he suffered inconvenience through his business being illegal is a general statement which does not convey to me sufficient evidence of definite prohibition, or of what the limits of legality or illegality may be in Natal regarding the sale of these sweepstake tickets."[55]

Perhaps the approach favoured by the majority in *Stanhope's* case was inspired more by considerations of the forum's public policy than by a desire to introduce a general expansion of the ways in which foreign evidence may be admitted.

Statutory and Other Documentary Material

The expert witness may incorporate in his or her evidence[56] extracts from relevant statutes, decisions or other legal texts. But he or she is not required to do this. In *O'Callaghan* v. *O'Sullivan*,[57] Kennedy, C.J. said:

> "The rule is that the foreign law applicable to a case must be taken from the statement of the expert witness as to what the law is and not from textbooks or codes referred to by him."

The Chief Justice quoted[58] with apparent approval a passage from *Baron de Bode's Case*,[59] where Lord Denman, C.J., explained:

---

[52] [1936] Ir. Jur. Rep., at 23 (*per* Hanna, J.).

[53] *Id.*

[54] *Id.*, at 29.

[55] *Id.*, at 27.

[56] And he or she may consult these texts when giving evidence: *Sussex Peerage Case*, 11 Cl. & F. 85, 8 E.R. 1034 (1844), *Baron de Bode's Case*, 8 Q.B. 208, 115 E.R. 854 (1845). Cf. *Callwood* v. *Callwood*, [1906] A.C. 659 (P.C.). And see *Temilkovski* v. *Australian Iron & Steel Pty Ltd.*, 67 S.R. (N.S.W.) 211, at 216 (*per* Sugarman, J.A. 1966).

[57] [1925] 1 I.R. 90, at 119 (Sup. Ct.).

[58] *Id.*, at 120.

[59] 8 Q.B. 208, at 251, 115 E.R. 854, at 870 (1845).

[60] [1933] A.C. 289, at 289 (H.L.(Eng.), 1932). See, however, *In re Bolton*, [1920] 2 I.R. 324 (K.B. Div.), where Dodd, J. said (at 327):
> "I am asked to aid the Court in South Africa, and I am supplied with all the materials that any Judge could be supplied with. I have the opinion of the eminent counsel who has presented the law to me from South Africa. But I have also before me a printed copy of the Act, and, though the interpretation of that Act is in one sense entirely a matter of adjudication upon a delivered opinion by an expert in the Colonies, I cannot overlook the fact that in so far as it is necessary for me to decide what insolvency in South Africa means, it is within my right to refer to this statute of South Africa, being guided, of course, in my interpretation of that statute by the expert opinion of the legal gentleman who has furnished me with his opinion. I would do the same interpreting a Scottish statute. Having the statute, and having the opinion of the barrister, I am then in a position to know what the word 'insolvency' means in South Africa."

"Properly speaking, the nature of such evidence is, not to set forth the contents of the written law, but its effect and the state of law resulting from it. The mere contents, indeed, might often mislead persons not familiar with the particular system of law: the witness is called upon to state what law does result from the instrument."

Normally the court may not place its own interpretation on a code or statute. As Lord Wright stated in *Lazard Bros & Co.* v. *Midland Bank*:

"The text of the foreign law if put in evidence by the experts may be considered, if at all, only as part of the evidence and as a help to decide between conflicting expert testimony."

Where a *document* is involved, however, the court has a far more active role. As Lord Greene, M.R. said in *Rouyer Guillet & Cie* v. *Rowyer Guillet & Co. Ltd.*,[61]

"evidence on the construction of a private document ... is admissible so far as it deals with [foreign] rules of construction or [foreign] rules of law or the explanation of [foreign] technical terms, but evidence as to its meaning after those aids have been taken into account is not admissible. It is for the court to construe the document, having fortified itself with the permissible evidence."

Uncontradicted Evidence by Expert

Where uncontradicted evidence as to foreign law is given by an expert, the courts will usually abide by it. In *MacNamara* v. *Owners of the S.S. "Hatteras"*,[62] FitzGibbon, J. expressed the opinion that:

"if an expert in the law of a foreign county whose qualifications and credibility are unimpeached, gives evidence upon oath that the law of that country is so, or that a particular contract, or clause of a contract, is, or is not, valid according to the law as administered in the Courts of that country, and his testimony is not contradicted by the evidence of another expert, or broken down by cross-examination, the Court which has to decide the question is just as much bound to accept and act upon that evidence as it would be to accept and act upon the evidence of any credible and uncontradicted witness upon any other question of fact or opinion. In the words of Lord Stowell,[63] *oportet discentem credere*. The Court cannot reject the evidence of the expert because it would itself have come to a different conclusion on perusal of the text of the foreign law or on consideration of the terms of the document which is to be interpreted or whose validity is to be decided in accordance with that law."

But if the evidence of the expert or experts, although uncontradicted, is "obviously false"[64] the court should not accept it.

Where the Experts Disagree

What is the court to do where the experts disagree between themselves? It appears

[61] [1949] 1 All E.R. 244, at 244 (C.A., 1948).
[62] [1933] I.R. 675, at 699 (Sup. Ct. 1933, reversing Meredith, J., 1932). See also *Re Adams Dec'd: Bank of Ireland Trustee Co. Ltd.* v. *Adams*, [1967] I.R. 424, at 455, 457, 458 (High Ct., Budd, J.), *Ottoman Bank of Nicosia* v. *Chakarian*, [1938] A.C. 260, at 270 (P.C., 1937).
[63] In *Dalrymple* v. *Dalrymple*, 2 Hag. Con. 54, at 83, 161 E.R. 665, at 675 (1811).
[64] *O'Callaghan* v. *O'Sullivan*, [1925] I.R. 90, at 119 (Sup. Ct., *per* Kennedy, C.J.). See also *Buerger* v. *New York Life Assurance Co.*, 43 Times L.R. 601, at 607 (C.A., *per* Atkin, L.J., 1927), *A/S Tallinina Laevauhisus* v. *Estonian State SS. Line*, 80 Lloyd's L. Rep. 99, at 108 (C.A., *per* Scott, L.J., 1946) ("The witness, however expert in the foreign law, cannot prevent the court using its common sense; and the court can reject his evidence if he says something patently absurd, or something inconsistent with the rest of his evidence ...").

that "the Court must decide the matter for itself".[65] In the Supreme Court decision of *MacNamara* v. *Owners of the S.S. "Hatteras"*,[66] FitzGibbon, J. said that:

> "if the evidence of the experts is conflicting, either as to the text of the law, or as to its interpretation, or as to the way in which the question at issue would be decided by the foreign court which might have to administer the law, then the Court must make up its own mind as best it can, using the material at its disposal, and deciding between the experts as it would have to do if they were giving their opinion upon any specific question."

In the same case, Murnaghan, J. interpreted the powers of the court even more liberally. In his view, where the experts disagree, the court is "entitled to do more than balance the authority of the experts"[67] and it "may form [its] own opinion"[68] of Foreign legislation. Murnaghan, J. "entirely agree[d]"[69] with the view of Bankes, L.J. in *Russian Commercial and Industrial Bank* v. *Comptoir d'Escompte de Mulhouse*[70] that:

> "[to] a large extent, and in the main, the question is ... one of construction of the decrees themselves, of which there are agreed translations, and which as translated are to a large extent free from technical terms. Under such circumstances this Court is, I think, free to put its own interpretation upon the language and is not bound to accept the view of either set of witnesses[71]... The Court must, I think, be guided by the views of these witnesses as to which of the documents called respectively orders, decrees, resolutions, or instructions have the force of law and as to the meaning of any technical terms."

So far as FitzGibbon, J. was concerned, he had to decide for himself, as a matter of fact, whether he should adopt the opinion of one expert or the doubt of the other,[72] this contrasts with Murnaghan, J.'s view[73] that the disagreement between the experts left the Court free, not merely to choose between them, but to form its own independent view of the foreign law, guided no doubt by their evidence but in no sense limited conclusively by it, at all events so far as interpretation of that law was concerned.

WHERE FOREIGN LAW IS NOT PROVED

Foreign law need not be proved if it is admitted. The court may decide a question of foreign law without proof if requested to do so by both parties;[74] it will be slow

---

[65] *MacNamara* v. *Owners of the S.S. "Hatteras"*, [1933] I.R. 675, at 706 (Sup. Ct., 1933, *per* Murnaghan, J., reversing Meredith, J., 1932).

[66] *Id.*, at 699–700. See also, to similar effect, *Rouyer Guillet & Cie* v. *Rouyer Guillet & Co. Ltd.*, [1949] 1 All E.R. 244, at 244 (C.A., *per* Lord Greene, M.R., 1948), *Buerger* v. *New York Life Assurance Co.*, 43 Times L.R. 601, at 607 (C.A., *per* Atkin, L.J., 1927).

[67] *Id.* at 706.

[68] *Id.*

[69] *Id.*

[70] [1923] 2 K.B. 630, at 643 (C.A.). The House of Lords ([1925] A.C. 112) reversed the Court of Appeal on grounds not of present relevance.

[71] Citing *Di Sora* v. *Phillips*, 10 H.L.C. 624, at 636, 11 E.R. 1168, at 1173 (*per* Lord Chelmsford, 1863). (In fact Lord Chelmsford's remarks on this issue were reported at 637 and at 1173–1174, respectively.)

[72] [1933] I.R., at 701.

[73] *Id.*, at 706.

[74] Cf. e.g. *Moulis* v. *Owen*, [1907] 1 K.B. 746 (C.A.), *The Torni*, [1932] P. 27, at 78 (C.A.), *Smith* v. *Smith*, 13 W.W.R. (n.s.) 207, [1954] 1 D.L.R. 229 (B.C., Clyne, J.). See also *MacNamara* v. *Owners of the S.S. "Hatteras"*, [1931] I.R. 337 (Sup. Ct.) where the Supreme Court held that the contracts in the case should be construed by United States law, "which said law should be proved or admitted ..." in the High Court proceedings relating to those contracts. Cf. *Stanhope* v. *Hospitals Trust Ltd. (No.2)*, [1936] Ir. Jur. Rep. 25, at 28 (Sup. Ct., *per* FitzGibbon, J.), and *supra*, p. 109.

to take this course except in cases concerning the interpretation of foreign statutes.[75]

Frequently in cases with a foreign legal dimension the parties will ignore this element. They may do so out of sheer inadvertence to the legal implications, or because it would be too expensive and troublesome to go into this question with foreign legal experts. However uncertain domestic litigation may be, the introduction of foreign law may be regarded by both parties as simply too intimidating a prospect.[76] Where foreign law is not proved, the court will normally apply Irish law.[77] This approach is sometimes described in terms of *presuming* foreign law to be the same as Irish law until the contrary is proved.

This principle was strongly endorsed in the High Court case of *The State (Lavelle) v. Carroll*,[79] where Davitt, P., speaking for a Divisional Court, took the view that "the principle of the identity of laws was sufficiently well established in 1922 to become part of our laws by virtue of the combined operation of Article 73 of the Construction of Saorstát Éireann and Article 50 of our present Constitution."[80] Applying this principle, Davitt, P. took judicial notice of the fact that a Justice of the Peace in Ireland before 1922 had power to issue a warrant for the arrest of a person against whom an information had been made, and he considered that he "must presume that a Justice of the Peace in England had the same power."[81] Thus the failure to prove the powers of the English Justice of the Peace did not vitiate extradition proceedings of foot of an English warrant.

In contrast to this approach, the general view among commentators,[82] surely correct, is that the rule should be expressed in more realistic terms, namely, that where foreign law is not pleaded or is not proved, the law of the forum will be applied.

---

[75] *Dicey & Morris*, 1208, citing, *inter alia, Beatty* v. *Beatty*, [1924] 1 K.B. 807 (C.A.).

[76] See Sprankling & Lanyi, *Pleading and Proof of Foreign Law in American Courts*, 19 Stan. J. of Internat. L. 3, at 9-13 (1983), Merryman, *Foreign Law as a Problem*, *Id.*, 151, at 151–155, Schlesinger, *A Recurrent Problem in Transnational Litigation: The Effect of Failure to Invoke or Prove the Applicable Foreign Law*, 59 Cornell L. Rev. 1, at 2–3(1973).

[77] See, e.g. *Lloyd* v. *Guibert*, 1 Q.B. 115, at 129 (1865), *Nouvelle Banque de l'Union* v. *Ayton*, 7 Times L.R. 377 (C.A., 1891), *Hartman* v. *Konig*, 50 Times L.R. 114, at 117 (H.L. (Eng.), *per* Viscount Buckmaster (for the Court), 1933), *Re A/S Tank of Oslo & Agence Maritime L. Strauss of Paris*, [1940] 1 All E.R. 40, at 42 (C.A., *per* Scott, L.J. (for the Court)), *Re Parana Plantations Ltd.*, [1946] 2 All E.R. 214, at 217–218 (C.A., *per* Lord Greene, M.R.); cf. *Lawson* v. *Commissioners of Inland Revenue*, [1896] 2 I.R. 418, at 435 (Ex. Div., *per* Palles, C.B., 1895).

[78] Cf., e.g. *Bieber & Co.* v. *Rio Tinto Co.*, [1918] A.C. 260, at 295 (H.L. (Eng.), *per* Lord Dunedin), *The Parchim*, [1918] A.C. 157, at 161 (P.C., 1917), *The Colorado*, [1923] P. 102, at 111 (C.A., *per* Atkin, L.J.). *Casey* v. *Casey*, [1949] P. 420, at 430 (C.A., *per* Bucknill, L.J.), *Canadian National Steamships Co. Ltd.* v. *Watson*, [1939] S.C.R. 11, at 13–14, *Morgardshammar AB* v. *H.R. Radomski & Co.*, 5 D.L.R. (4th) 576 (Ont. C.A., 1984), aff'g 145 D.L.R. (3d) 111 (Ont. High Ct., Craig, J., 1983). See also Kales, *Presumption of the Foreign Law*, 19 Harv. L. Rev. 401 (1906), F.R., *Comment: Conflict of Laws – Judicial Notice of Foreign Law*, 30 Mich. L. Rev. 747, at 755ff (1932). Where the *lex fori* requires the application of a statutory provision of the forum, the "presumption" that foreign law is identical would be particularly tenuous: cf. Von Moschzisher, *Presumptions as to Foreign Law*, 11 Minn. L. Rev. 1 (1926), *Anon., Note.*, 33 Harv. L. Rev. 315 (1919). An alternative strategy of applying pre-statutory common law rules has been stigmatised by Nussbaum as "particularly objectionable in that it represents the foreign common law system in point as thoroughly petrified and antiquated": *The Problem of Proving Foreign Law*, 50 Yale L.J. 1018, at 1038 (1941). The judicial authorities are not settled on this issue: see Wood, *Proof of Foreign Law in the Manitoba Courts*, 15 Manit. L.J. 53, at 57–58 (1985).

[79] Unreported, High Ct., 25 October 1963 (1963–108SS). I am grateful to Mr Gerard Hogan for bringing this case to my attention. See also *The State (Griffin* v. *Bell)*, [1962] I.R. 355.

[80] P. 10 of Davitt, P.'s judgment.

[81] *Id.*

[82] E.g. *Dicey & Morris*, 1216, Castel, *Cases*, 2–113. Cf. Hunter, *Proving Foreign and International Law in the Courts of England and Wales*, 18 Va. J. of Internat. L. 665, at 666 (1978), Alexander, *The Application and Avoidance of Foreign Law in the Law of Conflicts*, 70 Nw. U.L. Rev. 602, at 608–614 (1975), Hay, *International versus Interstate Conflicts of Law in the United States*. 35 Rabels Zeitschrift 429, at 446–447 (1971).

Some Irish Cases Where Foreign Law Was Not Proved

The decision of *M'Donnell* v. *M'Donnell*,[83] in 1920, presents some interesting contrasts in the judicial approach to problems resulting from failure to prove the foreign law. The plaintiff was seeking in the Irish Court £840 arrears due under an order for support and maintenance against her late husband which she had obtained in the District Court of the Third Judicial District of the State of Montana. The order required the husband "to pay into the office of the Clerk of the Court the sum of forty dollars per month for the support and maintenance of the plaintiff, such payments to be made until further order of the court". The defence was that the order was not such a final and conclusive judgment as to be enforceable by the Irish court. No evidence was given as to the law in Montana or as to the effect of an order of the type on which the plaintiff based her case.

By a majority,[84] the King's Bench Division, reversing the trial judge, rejected the plaintiff's case. Gordon, J., one of the majority, noted this evidential *lacuna*. He observed:

> "It was not a proceeding for divorce or judicial separation, such as we have in this country, and in which an order might be made for alimony; such an order, if made, could not be enforced by an action founded on non—compliance with its terms[85] ... But in the absence of any evidence as to the foreign law, one should think that this order, judgment, or decree (whatever it may be called) must be analogous to our orders for alimony. It could hardly be supposed that the wife was to continue to get the monthly payment no matter how she might have misconducted herself. Part of the plaintiff's case in her complaint was that she was unable to earn a living for herself and her child. Might not questions in reference to the child arise which could cause the Court to exercise control over the payment of these monthly sums? These or other considerations must have been present to the Court when it made the order in the form in which it was made. The order is not that the forty dollars a month should be paid to the plaintiff, but that the defendant should pay it into the office of the Clerk of the Court for the support and maintenance of the plaintiff, and that such payments be made until the further order of the court."[86]

Gordon, J.'s approach was thus not to analyse the situation simply in terms of Irish law but instead to stress the analogy with Irish law, pressing such similarities between the two laws as seemed sensible and fair. In doing this, of course, Gordon, J. indulged in dangerously uncontrolled speculation: who would wish to order his or her personal affairs in the United States on the basis of legal advice of this quality? Molony, C.J. disposed of the problem more summarily:

> "No evidence was given to the law in Montana, and in the absence of such evidence I think it is clear that the object of requiring the money to be paid to the Clerk of the Court, and not directly to the Plaintiff, was that the Court might retain control over the money, or be in a position to vary the order, or substitute another order, or abrogate it altogether in case facts were brought to their notice which would justify their intervention."[87]

This statement does not clearly reveal Molony, C.J.'s approach to the problem of unproven foreign law. It suggests that, in default of such proof, an Irish court should be free (if not, indeed, required) to examine the text of the foreign order

[83] [1921] 2 I.R. 148 (K. B. Div., 1920).
[84] Molony, C.J. & Gordon, J.; Pim, J. dissenting.
[85] Referring to *Keys* v. *Keys*, [1919] 2 I.R. 160 and the cases there cited.
[86] [1921] 2 I.R., at 154.
[87] *Id.*, at 162.

and attempt to construe it itself, rather than apply Irish law automatically.

Pim, J. who dissented, felt sufficiently confident to interpret the legal meaning of the foreign order himself with the aid of some sociological speculation:

"In the western States of America life is a shifting thing. Men and women move about in a way which is not at all understood here, and it is probable that the only way in which the money directed to be paid would be sure of reaching the hands of the person entitled to it would be to order it to be paid into the office of the Clerk of the Court to be held at the disposal of the person entitled thereto ..."[88]

A troublesome problem resulting from the failure of expert evidence as to foreign law arose in the bigamy case of *The Queen* v. *Griffin*[89] in 1879. The defendant, an Irishman, had been married according to Catholic rites in Kerry in 1871. Shortly afterwards he went to the United States and about a year or two later, went through a ceremony of marriage in a Catholic Church in Illinois with another woman, his wife still being alive. In 1878 the defendant, who had returned to Ireland, was prosecuted in Kerry and convicted of bigamy.

The defendant challenged the conviction on the basis that no evidence had been adduced during the trial as to the marriage law of the state of Illinois. At his counsel's request, the trial judge reserved the case for the consideration of the Court of Crown Cases Reserved. That Court was clearly unsympathetic to this line of argument, since the accused's case was clearly without substantive merits. The Court, with two dissentients,[90] held that the evidence was sufficient to sustain a conviction.

The members of the majority of Court took somewhat differing positions on the question. Lawson, J. said:

"In my opinion, supposing it to have been necessary to show that this marriage was a valid one according to the law of Illinois, it must be presumed to be so, in the absence of evidence to the contrary. The ceremony was publicly performed by the clergyman of the Church of which the contradicting parties were members, after publication of banns, and in the most solemn manner; it was a contract *per verba de praesenti*, to which the *benedictio sacerdotis,* which was held to be requisite in *Reg.* v. *Millis,*[91] was added, and was a good marriage at common law. We are not to be supposed to be ignorant of the fact that the Catholic religion prevails over the world, that its priests and places of worship are recognised; and if we found that a ceremony was publicly performed according to the rites of that Church, are we to require the presence of an expert to depose that such a marriage is a legal one in the State of Illinois? We should presume, in the absence of evidence to the contrary, that the clergy were acting according to law, and that they solemnized a valid marriage.[92] I am, therefore, of opinion that, assuming it to be necessary that this marriage should be shown as valid according to the laws of Illinois, there was evidence that it was valid, and the instruction of the learned Judge to the jury[93] was correct."[94]

Fitzgerald, B. favoured a separate approach, although his conclusion was the same as that of Lawson, J:

---

[88] *Id.,* at 157.

[89] 4 L.R. (Ir.) 497 (Cr. Cas. Res., 1879).

[90] May, C.J. (with whom O'Brien, J. concurred).

[91] 10 Cl. & Fin. 534, 8 E.R. 844 (H.L.(Ir.), 1844).

[92] It is worth testing the merits of this approach in respect of Catholic weddings in France, for example where such marriages are (and even when *The Queen* v. *Griffin* was decided were) void, constituting a criminal offence under French law. Cf. *infra,* p. 223.

[93] The trial judge had refused to accede to the argument of counsel for the defence as to failure of proof of the marriage law of Illinois; he recommended the jury, if they believed the evidence of a witness (the woman whom the prisoner had "married" in Illinois) as to the fact of the second marriage ceremony, to find the prisoner guilty.

[94] 4 L.R. (Ir.), at 502–503.

"There is no authority for the proposition that a party relying on a contract, be it matrimony or any other contact — if he shows that the *factum* has what I may call the natural essence[95] of a contract of the kind in question — is bound to show, in the first instance, when that contract is made in a foreign country, that the foreign country has a law relating to contracts of the kind, and that it is conformable to such law. It may be, and it often is, necessary or convenient that he should show in the first instance what the foreign law is. It may be necessary if the construction of the language used would be different by the foreign law from what it is in England, or where any other effect which he seeks to give to the contract is different from the effect which would be given to it in England. It may be convenient because proof of its conformity to the foreign law may be the easiest way of proving that it has what is of essence of the contract. But if proper evidence be given that it has what is of the essence of the contract, it will be presumed to be according to the foreign law (if any such there be), without any evidence of such foreign law, until the contrary is shown.

In every case of marriage, the presence of a clerk in holy orders is evidence that the contract has what is of its natural essence − and, therefore, though the marriage be in a foreign country, if such presence be proved, a foreign law invalidating the marriage must be shown by him who impeaches it."[96]

Whether the concept of the "natural essence" of a contract is helpful in interpreting the validity of a foreign marriage so far as formal requirements are concerned may be debated. It could be argued that it is not proper for the prosecuting authorities to fail to do their homework as to the legality of the defendant's conduct, so far as the foreign jurisdiction is concerned, yet expect that the defendant − who frequently will be entirely ignorant of legal matters − should do this work for them. In some cases it might well be reasonable to assume that the defendant knew about these legal requirements, but in other cases, especially where the defendant's contacts with the foreign state were tenuous, no such assumption could properly be made.

May, C.J. and O'Brien, J. differed from their colleagues. May, C.J. considered that, save as to marriages specifically declared valid by the Marriages Confirmation Act 1823:

"the validity of a marriage celebrated between British subjects in a foreign country must be determined by the law of that country, not by the law of England. And I think it is also clear beyond doubt, if the validity of a marriage celebrated in a foreign country comes in question in a British Court of Justice, the foreign law governing the marriage must be proved as a fact by proper testimony on oath before the adjudicating tribunal. I also think it clear that, in a case of bigamy at least, the second marriage, which constitutes the offence, must be proved as a fact, and cannot be inferred or presumed from cohabitation of the parties or otherwise. And from these propositions it would appear to me to follow as a legitimate consequence that, in the present case, in order to establish that the ceremony deposed to by the witness ... was sufficient to constitute a marriage between herself and the prisoner, some evidence should have been given as to the law of Illinois on the subject of marriage, by a witness competent to depose on that subject."[97]

May, C.J. continued:

"It is said[98] in this case, the marriage was celebrated in a Roman Catholic church, and by a Roman Catholic priest, and it is also presumed that such marriage was valid. But I apprehend the question is not one of presumption or inference, but of actual proof of oral evidence taken on oath. Such a marriage may or may not be valid, according to the canon law, or according to the canon law of this country. The court is, in my

---

[95] Anson would scarcely have relished the term: see *Anson's Law of Contract*, 262 (26th ed., by A. G. Guest, 1984). Cf. Husserl, *The Foreign Fact Element in the Conflict of Laws*, Part II, 26 Va. L. Rev. 453, at 470−471 (1940).

[96] 4 L.R. (Ir.), at 510−511.

[97] *Id.*, at 514.

[98] Cf. the extract from Lawson, J.'s judgment quoted *supra*.

opinion, entirely without information as to the requirements of the law of Illinois on the subject of marriage, and is not in a position to decide that this marriage was valid according to that law.

Whether an explicit admission by the defendant of the validity of his second marriage would supply the place of regular proof, it is not, I think, necessary to consider, as I find no evidence of any such admission.''[99]

In *Re Robinson, A Bankrupt*,[100] in 1860, the question arose as to the extent to which New York law would recognise the rights of assignees in bankruptcy of a person adjudicated bankrupt in Ireland, so far as goods of the bankrupt situated in New York were concerned. Neither side in the proceedings furnished any legal evidence other than by way of citation of American authorities. Lynch, J. was not impressed by this approach. He said:

"Had I considered that this was the principal point of the case, or that I was required to expound the American law on the subject, I would require legal evidence to be laid before me respecting it, and I would not rely on my own research into the American authorities, as a proper foundation for a judgment in so serious a case.''[101]

Lynch, J. explained that he had examined the authorities and he proceeded[102] to express a tentative view as to the law on the question before him in the United States.

Russell v. *Kitchen*[103] in 1854 involves a curious, and doubtful, amalgam of two rules of law. The case involved an assumpsit action in Ireland brought by the indorsee of a promissory note made and indorsed in Capetown. Only the plaintiff gave evidence as to the law of the Cape of Good Hope, and the report contains no suggestion that he was a lawyer or had any particular competence to give evidence on this question.

The Queen's Bench held that the law of the Cape, as the *lex loci contractus*, determined the validity of the indorsement and of other aspects of the plaintiff's entitlement to sue. Against the defendant's argument that the indorsement had not been shown to be legal under the law of the Cape, the Court held that the onus lay on the defendant to establish its unlawfulness, and that the defendant had failed to discharge this onus.

Crampton, J. said:

"The question then is, whether this instrument was legal, according to the law of the Cape? We have no evidence of that — the only thing having the appearance of such evidence is, that it is payable to order on the face of it; how far that is evidence, it is unnecessary to say. Are we to assume that the indorsement was void, or should we not presume the contrary, in the absence of any evidence on the subject? The question then comes to this — whether the *onus probandi* lies on the plaintiff or defendant? It is plain that a party relying on the law of a foreign country is bound to prove what that law is. *Brown* v. *Gracey*[104] is an express decision on that point. The effect of that decision is this, that, in the absence of all evidence as to the law, we are to presume that the law of the foreign country is conformable to the law of England, and not the contrary. That decision, therefore, rules the ... point.''[105]

But there is, of course, an obvious difference between a case where a plaintiff fails to prove the foreign law and the case proceeds on the basis that the foreign

[99] 4 L.R. (Ir.), at 515−516.
[100] 11 Ir. Ch. Rep. 385 (Lynch, J., 1860).
[101] *Id.*, at 391
[102] *Id.*, at 391−392.
[103] 3 Ir. C.L.R. 613 (Q.B., 1854).
[104] 1 D. & R., N.P. Cas. 41n., 171 E.R. 911 (1821).
[105] 3 Ir. C.L.R., at 615−616.

law is the same as Irish law, on the one hand, and a case where the plaintiff asserts a legal right on the basis of a foreign law but fails to establish that law through satisfactory expert evidence, on the other hand. Having found that the law of the Cape applied, as the *lex loci contractus*, the court should not have made any assumption as to its content, the plaintiff having failed to put forward the necessary evidence.

To add insult to injury, so far as the defendant was concerned, the court acted on evidence from the plaintiff that the law of the Cape, in contrast to Irish law, allowed for no days of grace. Thus, the defendant had the worst of both worlds, with Irish legal principles being applied to sustain one aspect of the plaintiff's claim and an asserted but unproven legal principle of the Cape denying him a defence.

IS CANON LAW A "FOREIGN LAW"?

A question that is of particular interest in the Irish context is whether Canon law should be considered a "foreign law". It has been strongly asserted that Canon law is no part of Irish law. In *Reg* v. *Burke*,[106] the Court of Queen's Bench repudiated the argument that a marriage invalid under Canon law was on that account invalid under Irish law.[107] Crampton, J. said:

"Now, this argument supposes the rules and discipline of the Church of Rome to be a part of the law of the land − than which there cannot be a more monstrous assumption; even the Canonical law has no dominion in this country, save so far as it has been received and accepted and made part of the Queen's Ecclesiastical law, which is itself part and parcel of the law of the realm."[108]

In *O'Callaghan* v. *O'Sullivan*,[109] in 1924, the Supreme Court held that canon law should be treated as a foreign law. The case involved a dispute between a parish priest and his superiors as to the legality of his removal from his parish. The parish priest contended that his contractual relationship with his superiors was governed by the Canon Law, which, he said, was not foreign law requiring proof by experts; in his submission, the *Codex Juris Canonici* contained a contract between the parties in a foreign language.

The trial judge and the Supreme Court rejected these arguments. Kennedy, C.J. said:

"It has never before, so far as I know, been contended that the Canon law is not a scientific legal system and body of law, both substantive and adjective, a body of rules emanating from a legislating authority for the ordering of the conduct, regulating the social and domestic relations, and punishing the disobedience of those who recognise that authority, which speaks and gives judgments through its own tribunals, but now, in these countries, always without coercive power because of the machinery of coercion is, at least in this State, kept in the exclusive control of the civil government and parliament for compelling obedience to such laws only as its parliament enacts. Every student of jurisprudence knows to what extent the Roman Canon Law was assimilated

---

[106] 5 I.L.R. 549 (Q.B., 1843).

[107] Cf. *infra*, pp. 231-232.

[108] 5 I.L.R., at 556. It is perhaps significant that the House of Lords had just decided R. v. *Millis*, 10 Cl. & Fin. 534, 8 E.R. 844 (H.L., 1843).

[109] [1925] 1 I.R. 90 (Sup. Ct.). Thirty three years earlier, in *M'Donnell* v. *Alcorn*, [1894] 1 I.R. 274 (C.A., 1894), aff'g. Porter, M.R., 1892), Porter, M.R., in considering whether a valid marriage had been celebrated, had said (at 288):

"I have not to go into any question of the canon law as administered in the Roman Catholic Church in relation to discipline. To me, sitting here, it is to a great extent a foreign law as to any purely canonical question. I should require it to be fully discussed if it arose."

by, or influenced national legal systems in Europe. Every student of English Common Law knows that the Canon Law is one of the sources of that Common law, and, indeed, was citable as law in some English Courts down to comparatively recent times."[110]

Kennedy, C.J. noted that the evidence given in the case had been to the effect that Canon Law "has had life and growth, so that it came to be codified anew in our own time", [111] in a Code promulgated in 1917. He added:

"For aught we know the Code may, in the years since 1917, have been added to or altered by the same legislating authority as reduced the then body of Canon Law to the systematic form of a code."[112]

The Chief Justice went on to say that:

" [N]o jurist — certainly none whose study is English Common Law — would deny to what is called 'the Canon Law' of the Roman Catholic Church the character and description of a body or system of law, and on the facts before us in the present case it is shown to be a living system of law, administered by certain tribunals constituted for that purpose under the same authority from which the laws are derived."

The plaintiff had urged that the Canon Law could not be described as "foreign", on the grounds that it is not the law of any particular state or country and that it purports to be universal and therefore of purported validity in this State. Kennedy, C.J. disposed of these arguments robustly:

"In my opinion all law is foreign to these Courts other than the laws which these Courts have been set up under the Constitution of Saorstát Éireann to administer and enforce, that is to say, other than the laws given force and validity by Article 73 of the Constitution and the enactments of the Oireachtas made after the coming into operation of the Constitution. No other laws are known to us judicially; nor can we take judicial notice of any other laws, unless they are proved to us as facts. All other laws are extrinsic to these Courts of Justice of the Saorstát and in that sense 'foreign' to the Courts. So it is that Scots law is 'foreign' in the part of Great Britain which is England."[114]

This approach is of doubtful attraction. The mere fact that a law is not Irish does not make it foreign. It might be part of a system of law that no longer is in operation anywhere throughout the world, or one that has been proposed and widely discussed, but not yet accepted anywhere in the world.

Kennedy, C.J. also noted that the plaintiff's argument:

"prescinds from our consideration facts of which we must properly take notice, namely, the facts of the existence and international position of the Holy See which retains diplomatic relations with upwards of a score of States and, amongst others, Great Britain, the Crown having an accredited Minister at the Vatican, and the fact of the existence within a certain guaranteed area in Rome of the Curia and Tribunals of the Holy See administering this very Canon Law as their proper law."[115]

This would suggest a vision of Canon Law as localised rather than universal. On this view, Canon Law would truly be a foreign law, located in the Vatican.

In *Re Mansfield Deceased; Hibernian Bank Ltd* v. *Mansfield*,[116] Kenny, J.

[110] [1925] 1 I.R., at 107–108.
[111] *Id.*, at 108.
[112] *Id.*
[113] *Id.*, at 108–109.
[114] *Id.*, at 109.
[115] *Id.* See also *In re Howley dec'd, Noughton* v. *Hegarty*, [1940] I.R. 109 (High Ct., Gavan Duffy, P., 1939), considered *infra* p. 511.
[116] [1962] I.R. 454 (High Ct., Kenny, J., 1961).

appeared satisfied that Canon Law was a foreign law which, if relied on, had to be proved by the evidence of expert witnesses.[117] In this case, a testator, troubled by the fact that a nephew had married outside the Catholic Church, made a bequest in his favour subject to the condition that, within a year of the testator's death, the nephew should have married his wife "in a manner recognised by the Roman Catholic Church". The testator also required that the nephew should within the year have delived to the executors "a certificate of his marriage ... issued with the authority of the Roman Catholic Church ..."

The original marriage had taken place in England and under English law it was not possible for a couple already married to each other to marry each other again. Accordingly the nephew applied for and obtained from the appropriate Catholic Bishop in England a matrimonial *sanatio in radice,* a canonical remedy for the nullity or invalidity of a judicial act. This had the effect of validating the marriage under Canon Law.

Kenny, J. received in evidence as to Canon Law an affidavit from a member of the Irish Bar who was also a Catholic priest and the holder of a Doctorate in Canon Law. One of the arguments made by those seeking to establish that the nephew had not complied with the testator's conditions was that he had not delivered to the executor a certificate of his marriage. Kenny, J. said:

> "The certificate delivered was not a certificate of marriage but was a certificate of conformation of his marriage and I think that this was a compliance with [the clause in the will]. Even if it were not a certificate of marriage in accordance with the civil law, the evidence is that it was a certificate of marriage under Canon Law and this matter has to be decided on that law for it is the law which the testator has selected."[118]

This passage seems consistent with the view that Canon Law was the applicable law, rather than merely a cluster of non-legal norms.

The implications of treating Canon Law as a foreign law have yet to be fully examined by our courts. Of most practical importance is the position in relation to Catholic marriages. Many Catholics who marry in a Catholic ceremony are of the view that the Catholic marriage is recognised by Irish law; they are surprised to learn that the legal effects of the Catholic dimension of the marriage extend only to formal requirements. The argument has been heard that, if a couple marry in accordance with Canon Law, that law determines questions of essential, as well as formal, validity.

As against this it may be noted that there is a range of judicial precedent to the contrary, and that our conflicts rules as to the essential validity of marriage have up to now been based on domicile rather than being so pluralist as to permit a free choice of a governing law.

---

[117] *Id.,* at 462.
[118] *Id.,* at 464. Cf. *Blake* v. *Blake,* 4 Ir. Ch. Rep. 349 (Chy., Brady, L.C., 1853), esp. at 354—355, 356, 358.

PART II

JURISDICTION AND RELATED MATTERS

CHAPTER 8

JURISDICTION

INTRODUCTION[1]

The first question which a court faced with a case involving a foreign element may have to address is whether it has jurisdiction[2] in that particular case at all. The world is divided up into a number of different territorial units for legal purposes and it would be absurd if each of these units were to claim jurisdiction over every dispute regardless of where the facts giving rise to it occurred, of the domicile or habitual residence of the parties or their presence or otherwise with the jurisdiction in question. There are clearly some cases in which a particular country will have a strong interest in having a case heard by its courts because some element in the case is so strongly connected with that jurisdiction. Equally clearly there are other cases in which there is no such connection and no interest in exercising jurisdiction. In between, there are many cases where the question whether it would be appropriate to exercise jurisdiction is not so clear: there may be connections between the particular legal system and the case in question but it may be debatable whether they are of such a nature as to warrant the assertion of jurisdiction.

Every legal system lays down rules as to when its courts will exercise jurisdiction in cases involving a foreign element.[3] One might be excused for expecting such rules to relate to the residence, domicile and nationality of the parties or the nature of the cause of action and its connections with the legal system in question. However, in common with their English counterparts from which they derive historically, the Irish rules relating to jurisdiction are primarily procedural in their emphasis. Irish

[1] See generally Gill, *Jurisdiction and the Enforcement of Foreign Judgments in Ireland*, 4 J. of Irish Soc. for European L. 3 (1980), Beale, *The Jurisdiction of a Sovereign State*, 36 Harv. L. Rev. 241 (1923), Graveson, *Choice of Law and Choice of Jurisdiction in the English Conflict of Laws*, 28 Br. Yrbk. of Internat. L. 273 (1951), Pryles, *The Basis of Adjudicatory Competence in Private International Law*, 21 Int. & Comp. L. Q. 61 (1972), Smit, *Common and Civil Law Rules of In Personam Adjudicatory Authority: An Analysis of Underlying Policies*, 21 Int. & Comp. L. Q. 335 (1972), Mann, *The Doctrine of Jurisdiction in International Law* [1964] - 1 Recueil des cours 1, Clarence Smith, *Personal Jurisdiction*, 2 Int. & Comp. L. Q. 510 (1953).

[2] In *Garthwaite* v. *Garthwaite* [1964] 2 All E.R. 233 at 241, Diplock L.J. defined the term "jurisdiction" as follows:

"In its narrow and strict sense, the 'jurisdiction' of a validly constituted court connotes the limits which are imposed on its power to hear and determine issues between persons seeking to avail themselves of its Process by reference (i) to the subject of the issue, or (ii) to the persons between whom the issue is joined or (iii) to the kind of relief sought, or any combination of these factors. In its wider sense it embraces also the settled practice of the court as to the way in which it will exercise its power of hear and determine issues which fall within its 'jurisdiction' (in the strict sense), or as to the circumstances in which it will grant a particular kind of relief which it has 'jurisdiction' (in the strict sense) to grant, including its settled practice to refuse to exercise such powers or to grant such relief in particular circumstances."

[3] For a good consideration of the competing interests of the plaintiff, the defendant and the State, see Smit, *Common and Civil Law Rules of In Personam Adjudicatory Authority: An Analysis of Underlying Policies*, 21 Int. & Comp. L.Q. 335, at 350-354 (1972).

courts have jurisdiction in a case involving a foreign element if the defendant has been duly served with an originating summons in accordance with the rules governing issue and service of summonses. If the rules allow for service of a summons in a case of the kind concerned and if service has been duly affected, jurisdiction exists. But the rules are not entirely procedural in character, divorced from any consideration of the facts and substance of the case. As we will see,[4] a number of procedural rules themselves involve consideration of such factors as the domicile of the defendant and the nature of the cause of action.

WHEN JURISDICTION IS NOT EXERCISED

The statement that jurisdiction exists if an originating summons has been duly served in accordance with the procedural rules needs some qualification. The subject matter of the case may be such that, on the grounds of policy, the court will refuse jurisdiction even if the procedural requirements have been compiled with: it may concern foreign immovables[5] or foreign revenue laws[6], for example. Similarly, some persons (alien enemies) may not invoke the jurisdiction[7] and others (sovereign states and diplomatic and consular agents) may claim immunity from the jurisdiction.[8] Also, in some cases in the family law area[9], the service of the originating document is not sufficient: jurisdiction will exist only if the relevant party is domiciled (or resident) within the jurisdiction. Finally, even where it has jurisdiction, the court may in its discretion decide to decline jurisdiction and stay proceedings either because there is a *lis alibi pendens*[10] or the proceedings are frivolous or vexatious or, in some cases, the balance of commonsense favours a trial somewhere else.

THE *IN PERSONAM* — *IN REM* DISTINCTION

In discussing the question of jurisdiction a distinction must be drawn between actions *in personam* and actions *in rem*. Mr Justice Holmes explained this distinction clearly in *Tyler* v. *Judges of Court of Registration*[11]:

"If the technical object of the suit is to establish a claim against some particular person, with a judgment which generally in theory, at least, binds his body, or to bar some individual claim or objection, so that only certain persons are entitled to be heard in defence, the action is *in personam,* although it may concern the right to, or possession of, a tangible thing. ... If, on the other hand, the object is to bar indifferently all who might be minded to make an objection of any sort against the right sought to be established, and if any one in the world has a right to be heard on the strength of alleging facts which, if true, show an inconsistent interest, the proceeding is *in rem.* ... All proceedings, like all rights, are really against persons.... Personification and naming the *res* as defendant are mere symbols, not the essential matter. They are fictions, conveniently expressing the nature of the process and the result; nothing more."

ACTIONS *IN PERSONAM*[12]

Jurisdiction based on personal presence

At common law any person may be made subject to the jurisdiction of the Irish courts provided that personal service of an originating summons has been duly effected

[4] *Infra*, pp. 132-160.
[5] *Infra*, pp. 402-403.
[6] *Infra*, pp. 198-204.
[7] *Infra*, pp. 171-172.
[8] *Infra*, pp. 173-181.
[9] *Infra*, pp. 294-300.
[10] *Infra*, pp. 168-171.
[11] 175 Mass. 71, at 76, 55 N.E. 812, at 814 (1900).
[12] See Gill, *Jurisdiction and the Enforcement of Foreign Judgments in Ireland,* 4 J. of Irish Soc. for European L. 3, at 4-17 (1980), Clarence Smith, *Personal Jurisdiction,* 2 Int. & Comp. L.Q. 510 (1953).

upon him. Irish courts in the case of actions *in personam* rest their jurisdiction "upon the presence of the defendant within the territorial jurisdiction so as to be available for service of the writ of summons"[13]. Provided he is present and has been duly summonsed within the jurisdiction, it does not matter that he is a foreigner on a mere fleeting visit to Ireland or that the facts of the case are in no way connected with Ireland or that Irish law has no application to the case.

Thus, a Canadian stopping over for a few hours at Shannon Airport on his way to the Far East may be made subject to the jurisdiction of the Irish courts provided he is properly served with a summons during his stopover. This rule as to the existence of jurisdiction even where the defendant's presence is merely fleeting has never been specifically asserted by an Irish court.[14] It is, however, well established in English law and was reaffirmed in *Maharanee of Baroda* v. *Wildenstein*.[15] In that case a writ was served on the defendant, a French art dealer of international renown, when he was on a short visit to England to attend Ascot races. Edmund Davies, C.J. observed that the plaintiff "was doing no more than our law permits, even though it may have ruined his day at the races."[16]

The rules are not, of course, a model of justice or even of practicality. To take the example of the Canadian served while on a stopover at Shannon Airport, the resulting decision of an Irish court would have to be enforced in Canada in order to be effective, and enforcement by a foreign court of a judgment based upon such a dubious ground of jurisdiction would not be a likely prospect.[17] Jurisdiction on the basis of temporary presence is one of the exorbitant grounds of jurisdiction listed in Article 3(2) of the EEC Convention on Jurisdiction in Civil and Commercial Matters[18] and, as such, will cease to be exercisable vis-a-vis EEC domiciliaries when the Convention is implemented in Irish law.

Jurisdiction on the basis of service within the State is not entirely unqualified. The presence of the defendant within the jurisdiction must not have been induced by fraud for the sole purpose of serving him with a summons.[19] If the defendant has been tricked into coming into Ireland for that sole purpose he will be able to

---

[13] *Rainford* v. *Newell-Roberts* [1962] I.R. 95, at 102 (High Ct., Davitt, P., 1961), referring to the position in English law. See also *Laurie* v. *Carroll*, 98 C.L.R. 310, at 323 (High Ct. of Austr., 1958): "The defendant must be amenable or answerable to the command of the writ. His amenability depended and still primarily depends upon nothing but presence within the jurisdiction." Cf. *Carrick* v. *Hancock*, 12 T.L.R. 59 (Q.B. Div., 1895), *Colt Industries Inc.* v. *Sarlie*, [1966] 1 All E.R. 673, *Maharanee of Boroda* v. *Wildenstein* [1972] 2 Q.B. 283 (C.A.), *Australian Assets Co. Ltd* v. *Higginson*, 18 L.R. (N.S.W.) Eq. 189 (Simpson, J.), *Forbes* v. *Simmons*, 20 D.L.R. 100 (Alta. Sup. Ct., Simmons, J., 1914).

[14] See Gill, *supra*, at 6, fn. 16. See, however, *Traynor* v. *Fegan*, [1985] I.R. 586, at 593 (High Ct., Barrington, J.) considered *infra*, fn. 92.

[15] [1972] 2 Q.B. 283 (C.A.).

[16] *Id.*, at 294.

[17] Cf. *Infra*, pp. 589-591.

[18] *Infra*, p. 615, and L. Collins, *The Civil Jurisdiction and Judgments Act 1982*, 47-49 (1983).

[19] *Stein* v. *Valkenhuysen*, E.B. & E. 65, 120 E.R. 431 (1858), *Watkins* v. *North American Land and Timber Co. (Ltd.)*, 20 T.L.R. 534 at 535-536 (H.L. (Eng), *per* Lord Davey, 1904), *Colt Industries Inc.* v. *Sarlie* [1966] 1 All E.R. 673, at 676. Fraud must be distinguished from other cases where the defendant's volition has been affected. In *Doyle* v. *Doyle*, 52 D.L.R. (3d) 143 (Newfoundland Sup. Ct., 1974), the defendant a resident of Montreal, had been arrested in Montreal and brought to Newfoundland where he was imprisoned and released on bail on a criminal charge there. The terms of the bail included a condition that he remain within Newfoundland until the trial was completed. In upholding service of a summons on the defendant, Furlong, C.J. said (at 145):

"I can find no precedent for saying that an involuntary or accidental entry into the jurisdiction renders a person safe from service of process; nor can counsel. Were I to so hold it would virtually be saying that the present defendant, whose stay in Newfoundland may be protracted, would be safe from service of civil process of any sort whilst he was so within the jurisdiction of the Court. It requires little imagination to envisage the complications which such state of affairs could create. It is inconceivable that anybody should be given such extensive right of sanctuary as this might entail."

move successfully to have the summons set aside. If, however, the defendant was induced to come within the jurisdiction for some other genuine purpose, such as the transaction of some other business, as well as for the purpose of serving him with the summons, the proceeding will not be set aside.[20] This exception is, therefore, an extremely narrow one.

Modes of Service

The mode of service of an originating summons is prescribed by the Rules of the Superior Courts 1986. No service is required when the defendant by his solicitor accepts service and undertakes in writing to enter an appearance.[21] Otherwise service must normally be effected by personal service if this is reasonably practicable[22]. Personal service is effected by delivering a copy of the summons to the defendant in person and showing him the original or duplicate original.[23] Where it appears by affidavit that the defendant is personally within the jurisdiction and that due and reasonable diligence has been exercised in endeavouring to effect personal service, service may be effected instead by delivering a copy of it at the defendant's house or place of residence or at his office or other place of business.[24] The copy may be delivered to the spouse, child, parent or brother or sister of the defendant[25] and that person must be shown the original or duplicate original of the summons.[26]

Substituted Service

If it is made to appear to the Court that the plaintiff is from any cause unable to effect prompt personal service or other service of the kind referred to above, the Court may make an order for substituted service, or for the substitution for service of notice by advertisement or otherwise.[27] If there is no difficulty about effecting service in the ordinary way apart from the fact that the defendant is from the beginning out of the jurisdiction and the case does not fall within the rules for allowing service out of the jurisdiction[28], substituted service will not be allowed.[29] In *Smyth* v.

[20] *Watkins* v. *North American Land and Timber Co. Ltd.*, 20 Times L.R. 534 at 536 (H.L. (Eng), *per* Lord Davey, 1904).

[21] Order 9, Rule 1.

[22] *Id.*, Rule 2.

[23] *Id.*, Rule 3.

[24] *Id.*, Rule 2.

[25] The person to whom the copy is delivered must be aged 16 or over; *id.*

[26] *Id.*, Rule 2.

[27] Order 10, Rule 1. See, e.g., *Pim Bros.* v. *Wylie*, 27 I.L.T.R. 27; (O'Brien, J., 1892) (order for substituted service on defendant's solicitor in London, it appearing that defendant was keeping out of the way to avoid his creditors), *Carson* v. *Crozier*, 51 I.L.T.R. 38 (K.B. Div., Pim, J., 1917) (similar facts). Cf. *Wallis* v. *Austin*, 3 Ir. L.R. 258 (Exch. of Pleas, 1841), *O'Neill* v. *M'Erlean*, 30 I.L.T.R. 162 (Chy. Div., Chatterton V.C., 1896). *Fitzgerald* v. *Lowe*, 3 Ir. L.R. 259 (Exch. of Pleas, 1841), *Guinness* v. *Armic*, 3 Ir. L.R. 165 (Comm. Pleas, 1841), *Burke* v. *Quinlan*, 3 Ir. L.R. 310 (Q.B., 1841).

[28] See infra, pp. 132-160.

[29] Cf. Palles, C.B.'s clear statement of this principle in *Clonkey* v. *London and North Western Railway Co.*, [1905] 2 L.R. 251 (K.B. Div., 1904). See also *O'Connor* v. *Star Newspapers Co.*, 30 L.R. Ir. 1 (Q.B. Div., 1891). In *Fry* v. *Moore*, 23 Q.B.D. 395, at 398 (C.A., 1889), Lindley, L.J. said:

"You cannot affect a principal through an agent when you could not affect the principal himself. If in such a case an order for substituted service could be made, the process might very easily be abused. Nothing could be easier than to issue an ordinary writ against a foreigner who was residing out of the jurisdiction, and then to obtain an order for substituted service, and thus the very mischief at which the rules relating to service out of the jurisdiction are directed would be brought back. Both principle and authority are against such a practice."

Cf. *Smith* v. *Hibernian Mine Co.*, 1 Sch. & Lef. 238 (Baron Redesdale, L.C. 1803). See also *Seaton* v. *Clarke*, 26 L.R. (Ir.) 297 (Q.B. Div., 1890) (where leave to serve outside the jurisdiction had been granted and plaintiff had exhausted all means to serve writ of summons personally, Court permitted substituted service by registered letter). Cf. *Street* v. *Mason*, 26 L.R. (Ir.) 298n (Q.B., 1890), *Tisdall* v. *Humphrey*, 1 I.R.C.L. 1 (Com. Pleas, 1867), *Poole* v. *Stewart*, 37 I.L.T.R. 74 (K.B. Div., Madden, J., 1903).

Dolan,[30] however, it was held that, if the defendant was within the jurisdiction at the time of issue of the writ but left before it could be served on him, an order for substituted service might be made: no qualification is to be imported into the terms of the rule that, if the impossibility of effecting personal service arises by reason of the defendant's leaving the country directly after he learns of the litigation, the rule cannot be applied.[31]

Evasion of Service

What is the position where it can be shown that the defendant left the jurisdiction, *before* issue of the writ, in order to evade service? In the English case of *Porter* v. *Freudenberg*[32] it was said that substituted service would be allowed in such circumstances, and Sullivan, P. appeared to favour the same approach in *Walsh* v. *Kennedy,*[33] However, the High Court of Australia in *Laurie* v. *Carroll*[34] rejected this strategy on the basis that a person's motive for leaving the jurisdiction could not confer jurisdiction otherwise lacking. To permit substituted service would conflict with the doctrine that, where a writ might not be served personally, an order for substituted service might not be made. The approach taken in *Laurie* v. *Carroll* received support from Lord Denning, M.R. in *Myerson* v. *Martin.*[35]

Service on Partners

Under Order 14 of the Rules of the Superior Courts 1986 any two or more persons being liable as co-partners and carrying on business within the jurisdiction may be sued as partners in the name of their firm.[36] In such a case the summons is to be served:

(i) upon any one or more of the partners,[37] or
(ii) at the principal place of business of the partnership within the jurisdiction, upon any person having control or management of the partnership business there.

This is deemed good service upon the firm even if any of the members of the firm are out of the jurisdiction. No leave to issue a summons against these members is necessary.[38]

---

[30] 47 I.L.T.R. 287 (K.B. Div., 1913).

[31] *Smyth* v. *Dolan,* 47 I.L.T.R. 287, at 289 (1913), quoting Lord Halsbury's observations in *Jay* v. *Budd,* [1898] 1 Q.B., at 16. See also *Michigan Trust Co.* v. *Ferry,* v. *Dunlevy,* 241 U.S. 518 (1916).

[32] [1915] 1 K.B. 857.

[33] 68 I.L.T.R. 238 (High Ct., Sullivan, P., 1934).

[34] 98 C.L.R. 310, at 332 (1958).

[35] [1979] 1 W.L.R. 1390.

[36] Order 14, Rule 1. See *Anon., Service on Partners and Firms,* 13 I.L.T. & Sol. J. 131 (1879).

[37] See *Heydon* v. *Hammond and Murray,* 10 Ir. L. Rep. 268 (C.P., 1848). Cf. *M'Cann* v. *Thomson,* 11 I.L. Rep. 201 (Q.B., 1847), *Thompson* v. *Haughton,* 11 I.L. Rep. 201, 2 (1847), *Oldham* v. *Shaw,* 4 I.L. Rep. 1 (Com. Pleas, 1841), *M'Kenny* v. *Mark,* 2 I.L.R. 161 (1839), *Moore* v. *Johnston,* 26 I.L.T.R. 92 (Q.B., 1892), *Nolan* v. *Fitzgerald,* 2 I.R. C.L.R. 79 (Com. Pleas, 1851).

[38] *Id.* But where a co-partnership has been dissolved to the knowledge of the plaintiff before the commencement of the action, the summons must be served on every person within the jurisdiction sought to be made liable: *id.* Where a firm has been properly served with a summons in England under Order 14, the Court may, under Order 11, Rule 1(h), give leave to serve a partner who is out of the jurisdiction. Cf. *West of England Steamship Owners Protection and Indemnity Association Ltd.,* [1957] 3 All E.R. 42ln (Chy. Div.), where Roxburgh, J. criticised (somewhat incoherently), the Irish case of *Lindsay* v. *Crawford & Lindsays* 45 I.L.T.R. 52 (K.B. Div., 1911). While accepting that the practice was "convenient, though perhaps illogical", Roxburgh, J. proposed, as an alternative, that the plaintiff could make all the partners parties individually, with the addition of the words: "trading as X & Sons." Where a judgment or order is made against a firm, execution may issue against (a) any property of the partnership within the jurisdiction; (b) any person who has appeared in his own name under Rules 5 or 6 of Order 14, or who has admitted on the pleadings that he is, or who

Service on Companies

Service of the documents on companies is provided for by the Companies Act 1963.[39] An originating summons may be served on a company which is incorporated in the State by leaving it at or sending it by post to the registered office of the company or, if the company has not given notice to the registrar of companies of the situation of its registered office, by registering it at the office for the registration of companies.[40]

Different provisions apply in relation to service of an originating summons on a company incorporated outside the State which has established a place of business[41] within the State.[42] In the first place such a company is obliged to deliver to the registrar of companies the names and addresses of some one or more persons authorised to accept service of process on its behalf, as well as the address of the company's principal place of business in the State.[43] Any process secured on the company is sufficiently served if it is addressed to any of these persons and is left at or sent by post to the address specified.[44] If the foreign company fails to deliver to the registrar the relevant information or if all these persons are dead or have ceased to reside in the State or refuse to accept service or for any other reason cannot be served the originating summons may be served by leaving it at or sending it by post to any place of business established by the company in the State.[45]

A foreign company does not necessarily have a place of business within the State at which it can be served just because some business is transacted within the State on its behalf. Thus, in *Donovan* v. *North German Lloyd Steamship Co.*,[46] O'Byrne J. held that the Irish High Court had no jurisdiction to hear negligence proceedings taken by a passenger against the defendant company arising out of a fall when the ship was on the high seas. The company was a foreign corporation, whose vessels from time to time made calls to Irish ports, particularly Cobh. At Cobh there had for some time been an office bearing the name of the defendant company in large letters. Moreover, the defendant company's name was listed in the telephone directory and they were the rated occupiers of the premises of which the office was a part.

As against this, the premises were in fact leased by an Irish company which carried on business there and acted as passenger agents, not only for the defendant company but also for various other foreign companies.

Beyond the ordinary duties of passenger-brokers and ship-brokers, the Irish company had no authority to transact business for, or to enter into contracts on behalf of, the defendant company.

---

has adjudged to be, a partner; (c) any person who has been individually served, as a partner, with the summons and has failed to appear: Order 14, Rule 8 (1). Except as against the partnership property, a judgment against a firm does not affect any member of the firm who was out of the jurisdiction when the summons was issued, and who has not appeared to the summons unless he has been made a party to the action under Order 11 or has been served within the jurisdiction after the summons in the action was issued: Order 14(2). See further *Lindsay* v. *Crawford & Lindsays, supra.*

[39] As to the former law, cf. *Moore* v. *Belfast & Ballymena Ry. Co.*, 6 Ir. C.L.R. 441 (Q.B., 1857), *O'Neill* v. *St. Brigid's Well Co.*, [1895] 2 I.R. 442 (Q.B. Div.), *Cooper* v. *General Accident Corporation*, 36 I.L.T.R. 24 (Co. Ct., 1901).

[41] As what constitutes a place of business, see *Deverall* v. *Grant Advertising, Inc.*, [1955] Ch. 111 (C.A., 1954). Cf. *Donovan* v. *North German Lloyd Steamship Co.*, [1933] I.R. 33 (High Ct., O'Byrne, J., 1932). See also *Crawford* v. *Wright & Butler*, 27 I.L.T.R. 75 (Ex Div., 1892); cf. *Milward Jones & Cameron* v. *FitzHenry (M. & C.M.) Ltd.*, 36 I.L.T.R. 211 (K.B. Div., Wright, J., 1902).

[42] Cf. *Devine* v. *Cementation Co. Ltd.*, [1963] N.I. 65 (C.A., 1962). As to the position of foreign companies in Ireland see generally *Forde*, 521-524.

[43] Companies Act 1963, section 352 (1) (c).

[44] *Id.*, section 356 (1).

[45] *Id.*, section 356 (2).

[46] [1933] I.R. 33 (High Ct., O'Byrne J., 1932).

O'Byrne, J. considered that, on these facts, the employee of the Irish company on whom the originating summons was served was "in no sense an officer or clerk of the defendant company,"[47] which accordingly had not been properly served.

If a person or place of business is available within the jurisdiction upon whom or at which service may be effected but is not one that is provided for by the Companies Act, it is not possible to seek to circumvent the provisions of that Act by seeking an order for substituted service on that person at that place. The substituted service procedure is meant to be available where the plaintiff is for any reason unable to effect prompt service, whereas in such a case there is not any difficulty in effecting service in the ordinary way; the difficulty is that such service will not subject the defendants to the obligation of appearing in this country because it does not comply with the provisions of the Companies Act. The rule as to substituted service "was not intended to to authorise service within the jurisdiction in a case in which the proper service should have been made out of the jurisdiction, and in which the Court had not power to give liberty to effect such service."[48]

If a foreign company incorporated outside the State has established a place of business within the State, the only procedure available for service of process on it within the jurisdiction is that provided for in the Companies Act 1963.[49] It is not sufficient to effect personal service of the summons on, say, the chairman of the company while he is on a visit to Ireland.

Submission to the jurisdiction

Even if a defendant is not personally present in Ireland so as to enable personal service of process on him, he may submit to the jurisdiction of the Irish courts.[50] Submission may come about in a number of different ways.

(i) By instructing a solicitor to accept service

Under Order 9, Rule 1 of the Rules of the Superior Courts 1986 no service of a summons is required when the defendant, by his solicitor, accepts service and undertakes in writing to enter an appearance. A defendant abroad who takes this course will be held to have submitted to the jurisdiction of the Irish courts.[51] Substituted service on solicitors may be allowed even where they have no instructions to accept but have taken some steps previously on behalf of the defendant in relation to the matter in issue.[52]

(ii) By entering an unconditional appearance

A person served with a summons outside the jurisdiction is not obliged to appear to it unless leave to serve out the jurisdiction has been obtained. Where leave has not been obtained and the person not within the jurisdiction has been improperly served, submission to the jurisdiction is implied if he nevertheless appears voluntarily

---

[47] *Id.* at 35.

[48] *Clokey* v. *London and North Western Railway Co.*, [1905] 2 I.R. 251, at 257 (K.B. Div., *per* Palles, C.B., 1904). See also *Russell* v. *United Provident Assurance Co., Ltd.*, 41 I.L.T.R. 200 (K.B. Div., 1907).

[49] Cf. *The Theodores* [1977] 2 Lloyd's Rep. 428 (Q.B. Div. (Admiralty Ct.), Brandon, J.).

[50] *Rainford* v. *Newell-Roberts*, [1962] I.R. 95, at 100-101, citing *Cheshire*, 3rd ed., 1947, 787. Cf. *Cheshire & North*, 10th ed., 83-84. See also *R. (Armstrong)* v. *Co. Ct. Judge of Wicklow*, [1924] 2 I.R. 139, at 152 (C.A. (I.F.S.), *per* Pim, J.) quoting from Lord Selborne's speech in *Sirdar Gurdyal Singh* v. *Rajah of Faridkote*, [1894] A.C. 670, at 684 (P.C.).

[51] *Heffernan* v. *Atkin*, 47 I.L.T.R. 245 (C.A., 1913).

[52] *Murray* v. *Comerford*, 33 I.L.T.R. 12 (Q.B. Div., Prob., 1898), *Fitzpatrick* v. *Irwin*, 35 I.L.T.R. 250 (K.B. Div., Prob., 1901), *In re Slattery; Slattery* v. *Slattery*, [1941] Ir. Jur. Rep. 13 (High Ct., Maguire, J., 1940).

as a defendant and contests the action on its merits[53]. Unconditional appearance is a submission to the jurisdiction[54]. However, an appearance merely to protest against the jurisdiction of the court, without addressing the merits of the case, does not constitute submission[55].

Lord Denning put the distinction well in *Re Dulles' Settlement (No. 2):*[56]

> "I cannot see how anyone can fairly say that a man has voluntarily submitted to the jurisdiction of a court when he has all the time been vigorously protesting that it has no jurisdiction. If he does nothing and lets judgment go against him in default of appearance, he clearly does not submit to the jurisdiction. What difference in principle does it make, if he does not merely do nothing but actually goes to the court and protests that it has not jurisdiction? I can see no distinction at all. I quite agree, of course, that if he fights the case, not only on the jurisdiction, but also on the merits, he must then be taken to have submitted to the jurisdiction, because he is then inviting the court to decide in his favour on the merits; and he cannot be allowed, at one and the same time, to say that he will accept the decision on the merits if it is favourable to him and will not submit to it if it is unfavourable. But when he only appears with the sole object of protesting against the jurisdiction, I do not think he can be said to submit to the jurisdiction."

It has to be said, however that entry even of a conditional appearance to contest the jurisdiction of the court is a risky business for a foreign defendant if he has assets in other common law jurisdictions because, as we will see[57] in the chapter on recognition of foreign judgments, the defendant may find that, if he loses the jurisdictional point and judgment is given against him, the judgment will be enforceable in other common law jurisdictions on the basis that he submitted to the jurisdiction of the Irish courts.

(iii) By commencing an action as a plaintiff

A person not present within the State who commences an action as a plaintiff before the Irish courts will make himself amenable to the jurisdiction of these courts over a counterclaim by the defendant in the action but not over an entirely independent claim.[58]

(iv) By seeking interlocutory relief that is consistent only with an intention to contest on the merits

A defendant may be deemed to have submitted to the jurisdiction by seeking interlocutory relief, in the proceedings against him, in a manner that is consistent only with an intention to contest them on the merits.[59] Thus, for example, courts

---

[53] *Boyle* v. *Sacker*, 39 Ch. D. 249 (C.A., 1888), *Re Dulles' Settlement* v. *Trusts* [1951] Ch. 265, at *Heffernan* v. *Atkin, supra.*

[54] Cf. *Moore* v. *Moore*, I.R. 5 Eq. 371 (Ct. for Mat. Causes, Warren, J., 1871).

[55] *Gallen* v. *Lee*, [1936] I.R. 142, at 149 (High Ct., *per* Hanna, J., 1935), *Heffernan* v. *Atkin, supra,* at 246 (*per* Holmes, L.J.). *Re Dulles' Settlement (No. 2)* [1951] Ch. 842 (C.A.). Cf. *Nelson* v. *Payne,* 64 W.W.R. 175 (B.C. Sup. Ct., Kirke Smith, J., 1968). As to the entitlement of a defendant to raise an objection to jurisdiction on appeal where he has done so unsuccessfully in the court of first instance and has gone on to fight the case on the merits, there is divided authority in Australia: see *Lindgran* v. *Lindgran*, [1956] V.L.R. 215 (Smith, J., 1955) and cf. *Colbert* v. *Tocumwal Trading Co. Pty Ltd.,* [1964] V.R. 820, at 826 (Full Ct., *per* Sholl, J., 1963).

[56] [1951] Ch. 842, at 850 (C.A.).

[57] *Infra,* pp. 591-594.

[58] See *In Re Belfast Shipowners Co. (Ltd.),* [1894] 1 I.R. 321 (C.A., 1894, aff'g Chatterton, V.C., 1893), *South African Republic* v. *Compagnie Franco-Belge du Chemin de Fer du Nord,* [1898] 1 Ch. 190; *High Commissioner for India* v. *Ghosh,* [1960] 1 Q.B. 134 (C.A., 1959).

[59] Cf. *Fry* v. *Moore,* 23 Q.B.D. 395 (C.A., 1889), *Donald Export Trading Ltd.* v. *Vandevelde PVBA,* [1981] Recent L. 353 (N.Z.C.A., 1981) (noted by P.R.H.W[ebb]).

in several jurisdictions[60] have held that applying for security of costs may[61] amount to submission.

(v) By agreement to submit to the jurisdiction

Even though the defendant is not present within the jurisdiction, he may have agreed by contract to submit to the jurisdiction of the Irish courts. It is quite standard practice in international contracts of a commercial nature for the parties to agree in their contract to submit any dispute that might arise between them to the jurisdiction of the courts of a particular country (or to arbitration in a particular country). Such clauses in contracts are usually referred to as choice-of-forum or choice-of-jurisdiction clauses. Contracts containing such clauses will also normally provide for a method of service of process on parties who are not present within the jurisdiction chosen. In the absence of such a provision, the court has discretionary power to allow service of the summons out of the jurisdiction.[62]

Order 11, Rule 3(1) of the Rules of the Superior Courts 1986 provides that the parties to any contract may agree —

(a) that the Irish Court is to have jurisdiction to entertain any proceeding in respect of that contract, and also, or in the alternative,

(b) that service of any summons in any such proceeding may be effected at any place within or out of the jurisdiction on any party (or on any person on behalf of any party) or in any manner specified or indicated in the contract.

In such a case, notwithstanding anything contained in the Rules, service of a summons at the place or on the party (or person) or in the manner specified or indicated in the contract is deemed good and effective service wherever the parties are resident. If no place or mode or person is so specified or indicated, then service of the summons out of the jurisdiction may be ordered.[63]

Finally, it must be mentioned that submission to the jurisdiction of the Irish courts cannot operate so as to confer jurisdiction on those courts over matters which would otherwise be outside their jurisdiction altogether. In family law cases, where domicile is the normal ground of jurisdiction, submission of the parties to the Irish jurisdiction will not avail to found jurisdiction if the requirements as to domicile are not satisfied.[64] Nor will submission of itself give an Irish court jurisdiction over questions of title to foreign land.[65]

Nationality of the defendant not a basis of jurisdiction

If the defendant is an Irish national does this *per se* make him amenable to the jurisdiction of the Irish courts? In *Rainford* v. *Newell-Roberts*,[66] a case concerned with the recognition of a foreign judgment rather than the exercise of jurisdiction

---

[60] *Lloneux, Limon & Co.* v. *Hong Kong and Shanghai Banking Corporation*, 33 Ch. Div. 446 (Bacon, V.C., 1886), *White* v. *Hardwick*, 23 S.R.(N.S.W.) 6 (Street, C.J. in Eq., 1922), *Catalyst Research Corp.* v. *Medtronic, Inc.*, 131 D.L.R. (3d) 767 (Fed.C.A.), aff'g 120.D.L.R. (3d) 159 (Fed. Ct., Tr.Div., Mahoney, J., 1981).

[61] *Catalyst Research Corp.* v. *Medtronic, Inc.*, 131 D.L.R. 767, at 768 (Fed. C.A., *per* Thurlow, C.J. (for the Court), 1982).

[62] Rules of the Superior Courts 1986, Order 11, rule 3(2). This provision represents the only major divergence between the Irish and English rules for service out of the jurisdiction.

[63] *Id.*

[64] *Armitage* v. *A.G.*, [1906] P. 135, at 140; *De Reneville* v. *De Reneville*, [1948] 1 All E.R. 56, at 61; *Kern* v. *Kern*, [1972] 3 All E.R. 207, at 210.

[65] *British South Africa Co.* v. *Companhia de Mocambique*, [1893] A.C. 602; *infra* pp. 401-403.

[66] [1962] I.R. 95. Cf. Fitzgibbon L.J.'s brief reference to the question in *Sexton* v. *O'Halloran*, [1904] 1 I.R. 123, at 128 (C.A., 1902).

by the Irish Court, Davitt P. cited with approval the following passage from Cheshire:[67]

> "Personal jurisdiction in this country depends upon the right of a Court to summon the defendant. Apart from special powers conferred by statute it is obvious that, since the right to summon depends upon the power to summon, jurisdiction is in general exercisable only against those persons who are present in England. If the defendant is absent from a country and has no place of business there, then, whether he be a citizen or an alien, he would appear to be immune from the jurisdiction, unless he has voluntarily submitted to the jurisdiction of the court."[68]

Not all commentators agree with this approach. Clarence Smith for example, finds "nothing unreal in an absent subject, always ready to run to his national consul for protection",[69] being within the jurisdiction of his national courts.

Assumed jurisdiction — Service out of the jurisdiction under Order 11[70]

There may be many situations in which the defendant is not present within the jurisdiction but the case is so closely connected with Ireland or with Irish law that there is ample justification for its being tried here. Indeed the nature of the claim may be such that not only is Ireland a very suitable forum but it is the most appropriate forum. Strict adherence to the common law position whereby our courts have jurisdiction only where the defendant is served with process here would scarcely work justice to the plaintiff in such cases. For instance, the claim might concern a tort or breach of contract committed here or the defendant might be an Irish domiciliary evading service by absenting himself abroad. Substituted service was formerly permitted in wide-ranging circumstances,[71] but in the latter part of the last century,[72] Rules of the Superior Courts provided that the Irish Courts might permit service of an originating summons or notice of an originating summons[73] out of the

---

[67] [1962] I.R. 95, at 100.

[68] *Cheshire*, 3rd ed., 1947, p. 779.

[69] Clarence Smith, *Personal Jurisdiction*, 2 Int. & Comp. L.Q. 510, at 531 (1953).

[70] See F. Piggott, *Service Out of the Jurisidiction* (1892), *Anon., Service of Writ Out of the Jurisdiction*, 56 Ir. L.T. & Sol. J. 197 (1922), *Anon., Service Out of the Jurisdiction*, 55 Ir. L.T. & Sol.J. 167 (1921), *Anon., The New Rules of Practice: Service*, Part 1, 25 Ir. L. T. & Sol. J. 255, Part 3, *Id.*, 269, Part 4, 283 (1891), *Anon, Service Out of the Jurisdiction*, [1933] L.J. Ir. 133.

[71] Cases dealing with the question include *Phelan* v. *Johnson*, 7 Ir. L. R. 527 (Exch. of Pleas. 1844), *Executors of Bruce* v. *Poe*, 4 Ir. L.R. 4 (Comm. Pleas, 1841), *Watson* v. *Armstrong*, 4 Ir. L.R. 219 (Comm. Pleas, 1841), *Langston* v. *Massey*, 4 Ir. L.R. 412 (Comm. Pleas, 1842), *Viner* v. *Bond*, 4 Ir. L.R. 433 (Exch. of Pleas, 1841), *Atteridge* v. *Executors of Lord Audley*, 5 Ir. L.R. 90 (Comm. Pleas, 1842), *Trumbal* v. *Ejector*, 5 Ir. L.R. 358 (Q.B., 1843), *Eiffe* v. *Caledonian Insurance Co.*, 5 Ir. L.R. 138 (Exch. of Pleas, 1842), *Martyn* v. *Kelly*, 5 I.R.C.L. 404 (Exch. 1871), *Gillespie* v. *Cummins* 2 I.L.R. 200 (1840), *Seaton* v. *Clarke*, 24 I.L.T.R. 82 (Q.B., 1890), *Moore* v. *Johnston*, 26 I.L.T.R. 92 (Q.B., 1892), *Smith* v. *Lipton*, 26 I.L.T.R. 91 (C.A., 1892), *Grove* v. *Boyle*, 26 I.L.T.R. 22 (Ex., 1892), *Pim Bros.* v. *Wylie*, 27 I.L.T.R. 27 (Q.B. Div., O'Brien, J., 1892), *Lewis* v. *Herbert*, 16 L.R. Ir. 340 (C.A., 1885), *Crawford* v. *Wright & Butler*, 27 I.L.T.R. 75 (Ex., 1892), *M'Clelland* v. *Tyrell*, 31 I.L.T.R. 84 (Ex., Chatterton, V.C., 1897), *Olpherts* v. *Brinkley*, I.R. 4 Eq. 208 (Chy., Lord O'Hagan, L.C., 1869), *Pritchett* v. *Jordan*, I.R. 3 Eq. 273 (V.C. Ct., Chatterton, V.C., 1869), *Smith* v. *Smith*, I.R. 6 Eq. 180 (V.C. Ct., Chatterton, V.C., 1871), *Somers* v. *Connolly*, 1 Ir. Eq. Rep. 416 (O'Loghlen, M.R., 1839), *Splaine* v. *Splaine*, 10 Ir. Ch. Rep. 49 (Cusack Smith, M.R., 1858), *King* v. *Ridle*, 1 I.C.L.R. 85 (Perrin. J., 1851), *Nolan* v. *Fitzgerald*, 2 I.C.L.R. 79 (Com. Pleas, 1851), *Byrne* v. *Sherlock*, 8 I.C.L.R. App. *xxxii* (Consol. Cham., Ball, J., 1858), *Cartwright* v. *Ball*, 3 I.C.L.R. 31 (Q.B., 1853), *M'Donaugh* v. *McCartney*, 3 I.C.L.R. 239 (Q.B., Perrin, J., 1854), *Kelly* v. *Dixon*, I.R. 6 C.L. 25 (Q.B., 1870), *M'Dougal* v. *O'Shaughnessy*, I.R. 1 C.L. 86 (Consol. Cham., Deasy, B., 1867).

[73] In *In re M'Laughlin. Roulston* v. *M'Laughlin*, 25 L.R. (Ir.) 513 (1890), Porter, M.R. held that to permit service of the writ itself, rather than notice of it, where the defendant was a foreigner residing out of the British Dominions in Philadelphia "would be to assume a jurisdiction over the subjects of a foreign State, and within its limits, which would be inconsistent with the principles of international

jurisdiction on an absent defendant in certain specified instances. Order 11 of the Rules of the Superior Courts 1986 now enumerates the circumstances in which service out of the jurisdiction of an originating summons or notice of an originating summons may be allowed by the High Court.[74]

The first point to be noted is that Order 11 says that service out of the jurisdiction *may*, not must, be allowed. The fact that one or more of the conditions specified in the Order for service out have been fulfilled does not entitle the plaintiff as of right to succeed in his application for leave to serve out.[75] The matter is one entirely at the discretion of the Court. This is a point which we will return to later when discussing the question of *forum conveniens* and Order 11.

Secondly, Order 11 is "obviously exhaustive — *expressio unius est exclusio alterius;* it plainly deals with the only subjects of suit in which leave can be given to serve personally out of the jurisdiction".[76] Thus, however disposed a court may be towards giving leave to serve *ex juris,* it simply cannot do so unless the case falls within the scope of one or more of the specific categories mentioned in Order 11.

Thirdly, it should be noted that the Court must exercise its discretion strictly in accordance with the Rules. There is no scope for a general unfocused approach. As Kennedy, C.J. observed in *Shipsey v. British & American Steam Navigation Co.*[77]:

> "I think that it is very important that, in a matter of the international comity of Courts, the High Court, when making an order giving leave for service out of the jurisdiction, should specifically mention in the order the particular class of action within which the Court decides the intended action to fall, so as to confine jurisdiction to allow service out of the jurisdiction within the express terms ... of the Rules ...."

Rule 2 of Order 11 provides that the Court is to have regard to the amount or value of the claim or property affected and to the comparative cost and

---

law and contrary to public policy. Serious complications might arise if the Court were to assume compulsory jurisdiction over foreign subjects residing in a foreign State, although I do not apprehend that an order such as sought, would necessarily involve our country in a war with the United States"; *id.*, at 514. See also *Craik* v. *Korth*, 17 I.L.T.R. 45 (Andrews, J., 1883), *James* v. *Despott*, 14 L.R. Ir. 71 (Q.B. Div., O'Brien, J., 1884); cf. *Walsh* v. *Moffatt*, 7 L.R. Ir. 446 (Chatterton, V.C., 1881), *Lesage* v. *De Frith*, 12 I.L.T. 161 (Chatterton, V.C., 1878), *Smullen* v. *Benoit & Co.*, 68 I.L.T.R. 260 (High Ct., Johnston, J., 1933). See further Collins, *Some Aspects of Service Out of the Jurisdiction in English Law*, 21 Int. & Comp. L.Q. 656, at 657−658 (1972).

[74] As to the Circuit Court's jurisdiction cf. *Jeffrey* v. *Jeffrey*, 81 I.L.T.R. 22 (Circuit Ct., Judge McCarthy, (1946).

[75] See Order 11, rules 1 and 5. Cf. *Joynt* v. *M'Crum*, [1899] 1 I.R. 217, at 224 (Chatterton V.C.), *Grehan* v. *Medical Incorporated and Valley Pines Associates*, [1986] I.L.R.M. 627 (Sup. Ct.), *M'Crea* v. *Knight*, [1896] 2 I.R. 619 (C.A.). In the latter case, Barry, L.J. said, at 628: "...I think that where, as here, the jurisdiction is one of a somewhat discretionary character, this Court ought to be very slow to disturb the exercise of its discretion by the Court below". See also *Willis* v. *London and North-Western Ry. Co.*, I.R. 10 C.L. 95, at 100−101 (Q.B., *per* O'Brien, J. 1876) and at 98 (*per* Fitzgerald, J., dissenting), *Bennett* v. *Cook*, 35 I.L.T.R. 153, at 153 (C.A., *per* Fitzgibbon, L.J. 1901) and cf. *Mayor etc. of Limerick* v. *Crompton & Co.*, [1910] 2 I.R. 416 (C.A., 1909). See further Gill, *Jurisdiction and the Enforcement of Foreign Judgments in Ireland*, 4 J. of Irish Soc. for European L. 3 at 1ff (1980), Inglis, *Jurisdiction, The Doctrine of Forum Conveniens, and Choice of Law in Conflict of Laws*, 81 L.Q. Rev. 380, at 384−385 (1965).

[76] *O'Connor* v. *The Star Newspaper Co. (Ltd.)*, 30 L.R. (Ir.) 1, at 4 (Q.B. Div., *per* Sir P. O'Brien, C.J., 1891). Cf. *Dickson* v. *Capes*, 11 I.C.L.R. 345 (Exch., 1860).

[77] [1936] I.R. 65, at 83 (Sup. Ct., 1935). See also *id.*, at 83−84, 88 (*per* Fitzgibbon, J.). Cf. *Bevan* v. *Gillows & Co.*, 40 I.L.T.R. 251, at (K.B. Div., *per* Palles, C.B.), and see *Brennan* v. *Lockyer*, [1932] I.R. 100, at 107 (Sup. Ct., *per* Kennedy, C.J., 1931).

See, however, *Russell* v. *Le Bert*, [1896] 1 I.R. 334, at 339 (Porter, M.R., 1895):
> "It is desirable that the rules in reference to service out of the jurisdiction should be construed widely, and so as to make them applicable to a case...., clearly within the spirit of the rules where there is a question of substance to be determined, which really ought to be, on analogy at least to the rest of the rules, submitted to the Irish Courts, and where no reason to the contrary, founded on convenience, [is] alleged."

convenience[78] of proceeding in Ireland, or in the place of the defendant's residence. Particularly in cases of small demands where the defendant is resident in England, Scotland or Northern Ireland it must have regard to the powers and jurisdiction of the courts of limited or local jurisdiction in these jurisdictions. Rule 5 of Order 11 goes on to specify that the affidavit grounding an application for leave to serve out of the jurisdiction must state the particulars necessary for enabling the court to exercise a due discretion under Rule 2 and that no leave shall be granted unless it is made sufficiently to appear to the Court that the case is a proper one for service out of the jurisdiction.

The mere fact of the existence of proceedings elsewhere related to the same subject matter is not of itself sufficient reason for refusing to allow an action to be commenced or to proceed but it is an element which will enter into the exercise of such discretion.[79] The intending plaintiff must show that Ireland is the *forum conveniens* for the hearing of the action.[80] It is a very serious question, even in a case that falls clearly with one of the sub-heads of Order 11, Rule 1, whether or not it is necessary for the jurisdiction of the Court to be invoked and a foreigner be put to the inconvenience and annoyance of being brought to contest his rights in this country.[81]

The granting of liberty to serve a summons out of the country is a jurisdiction that must be exercised with great care.[82] If on the construction of any of the sub-heads of Order 11, Rule 1 there is any doubt, it ought to be resolved in favour of the foreign defendant.[83] The case should fall within the spirit as well as the letter of one of the various classes of case provided for.[84]

In *Limerick Corporation* v. *Crompton & Co.*[85] an interesting issue arose. A contract was made between Limerick Corporation and an engineering company, under which the company undertook to supply electrical plant to the Corporation. The contract was accepted by the Corporation by a letter posted in Limerick.[86] Thus the contract was made in Ireland. The contract contained an arbitration clause and a provision that the contract should ''in all respects be construed and operate as an English contract, and in conformity with English law; and all payments thereunder shall be made in England and in sterling money.'' The Corporation took proceedings in the Irish King's Bench Division for damages for breach of contract and obtained leave to issue the writ out of the jurisdiction. The defendant company successfully instituted a motion requesting the Court to set aside the order giving leave to issue the writ out.[87] Andrews, J. referred to the provision in the contract which has been quoted above and said:

[78] This means "fitness, propriety, and suitableness — each and all three in the most general sense" — *per* Fitzgibbon L.J. in *M'Crea* v. *Knight* [1896] 2 I.R. 619, at 626.

[79] *Tedcastle M'Cormick & Co.* v. *Robertson* [1929] I.R. 597 at 602 (Sup. Ct., per Kennedy C.J. 1927).

[80] *Mouraux* v. *Pereira* [1972] 1 W.L.R. 962 at 965. For cases where service out was refused because the *forum conveniens* was elsewhere, see e.g. *Bennett* v. *Cook* (1901) 35 I.L.T.R. 153; *Murray* v. *Finkle*, 48 I.L.T.R. 178 (1914); *Wrench* v. *Rothwell*, 4 N.I.T.R. 21 (1903); *Brennan* v. *Lockyer* [1932] I.R. 100; *Freedman* v. *Opdehyde* [1945] Ir. Jur. Rep. 22. For cases where the *forum conveniens* issue was considered and service out allowed, sede e.g. *M'Evers* v. *O'Neill* 4 L.R. Ir. 517; (Ex. Div., 1879); *Maconchy* v. *Trower*, 30 L.R. Ir. 480 (Q.B. Div., 1892); *M'Crae* v. *Knight*, [1896] 2 I.R. 619; *Black* v. *Baird* 31 I.L.T. & Sol. J. 8 (C.A., 1876); *Monsarrat* v. *Barron*, 4 N.I.J.R. 4, (1904), *Dunlop* v. *Dunlop Rubber Co.*, [1920] 1 I.R. 280; [1921] 2 I.R. 173; [1921] A.C. 367, *Tedcastle, M'Cormick & Co.* v. *Robertson*, [1929] I.R. 597.

[81] *Société Générale de Paris* v. *Dreyfus Brothers* 29 Ch. D. 239 at 242–3 (1885).

[82] *Freedman* v. *Opdehyde*, [1945] Ir. Jur. Rep., at 23 (*per* Haugh, J.)

[83] *The Hagen* [1908] P. 189.

[84] *Johnson* v. *Taylor Bros.* [1920] A.C. 144.

[85] [1910] 2 I.R. 416 (C.A., 1909), aff'g [1909] 2 I.R. 120 (K.B. Div.).

[86] As to this rule, cf. *infra*, pp. 533-535.

[87] The defendant company also requested the Court to stay all future proceedings under section 14 of the Common Law Procedure Amendment Act (Ireland) 1856. In view of the Court's holding in the request to set aside the order, it was not necessary to give any decision on the request to stay proceedings.

"To 'operate as an English contract' means to take effect as an English contract; and if the contract is in all respects to take effect as an English contract, it must have all the incidents of such a contract, and must therefore, in our opinion, be treated as a contract made in England.

Under this contract the English jurisdiction is, in our opinion, exclusive, and an English Court is, in effect, the *forum* agreed on for the judicial determination of all questions arising in relation to it. The contract is not framed to oust the jurisdiction of the Courts of this country. It is a contract by which the parties (as we construe it) have, in effect, agreed to have recourse to an English tribunal only."[88]

This approach appears to leave no scope for going against the will of the parties where the contract having "all the incidents" of a foreign contract (surely the proper law of the contract) prescribes, expressly or implicitly, a foreign forum.

The Court of Appeal affirmed.[89] Some differences of emphasis among the judgments may be noted. Walker, L.C. did not think that the court was necessarily deprived of jurisdiction but he considered that, when exercising that jurisdiction, the Court was bound to give effect to the words in the contract, unless "some paramount reason to the contrary"[90] was shown. Fitzgibbon, L.J. considered that the Court could not, consistently with its rules, disregard the agreement between the parties. But Holmes, L.J. was not prepared to say that the parties' agreement deprived the Court of jurisdiction. He observed:

"I doubt that by such a stipulation the parties can free themselves from the authority of a Rule having the force of a statute. An order for service out of the jurisdiction might be made, if necessary for the proper trial of the action; or if, without such an order, there could not be a trial at all. But I hold, without hesitation, that a Court in the exercise of its judicial discretion ought, in the absence of convincing reasons to the contrary, to support the agreement of the parties to treat this contract as if entered into in England."[91]

The procedure under Order 11

The procedure for applying for leave to serve out of the jurisdiction under Order 11 is by way of an *ex parte* motion supported by affidavit or other evidence.[92] The grounding affidavit must state that in the belief of the deponent the plaintiff has a good cause of action and show in what place or country the defendant is or probably may be found.[93] It must state whether the defendant is a citizen of Ireland or not[94] and state the particulars necessary to enable the Court to exercise a due discretion in the matter.[95]

Since, as we have seen,[96] the enumeration of cases in Order 11, Rule 1 in which an order for service out of the jurisdiction may be made is exhaustive, it is, therefore,

[88] [1909] 2 I.R., at 124.

[89] [1910] 2 I.R. 416.

[90] *Id.*, at 418

[91] *Id.*, at 419–420.

[92] Order 11, Rule 5. The application for leave to serve a summons out of the jurisdiction must be made before the issue of the summons. In *Traynor* v. *Fegan,* [1985] I.R. 586 (High Ct.), Barrington, J. criticised the administrative practice that had grown up in the previous decade of refusing to issue a plenary summons when the proposed defendant was resident out of the jurisdiction unless the plaintiff had a court order authorising such service or could produce a letter from the proposed defendant's solicitor agreeing to accept service. He pointed out (at 593) that the plaintiff's solicitor "might discover that a proposed defendant resident abroad was passing through Ireland on a fleeting visit and might wish to serve proceedings on him during his stay."

[93] *Id.*

[94] If he is not, notice of the summons, and not the summons itself, is served on him: Order 11, Rule 8. Cf. *Sheehan* v. *Gamplovitch*, 46 I.L.T.R. 80 (K.B. Div., Kenny, J., 1912).

[95] Order 11, Rule 5.

[96] *Supra*, p. 133.

necessary in an application for an order under the Rule that the applicant should bring himself within one or other of the enumerated cases and the affidavit grounding the *ex parte* application for the order must show the facts which bring the alleged cause of action within the Rule.[97] On an *ex parte* application of this kind there is a long established rule requiring *uberrima fides* on the part of the applicant.[98]

The established canon governing these applications is:

> "... that an affidavit which sets out ... to bring the alleged cause of action within Rule 1 of Order 11, and which does not recite fully the relevant facts but avers as a fact what is really a conclusion of fact (whether rightly or wrongly drawn from the facts not stated) is not such an honest disclosure of facts as the court should act upon, and an order ought not to be made upon such an affidavit."[99]

Cases in which service out may be ordered

We turn now to the cases specified in Order 11, Rule 1 in which service out of the jurisdiction[100] may be allowed by the Court.

(a) *Whenever the whole subject-matter of the action is land situate within the jurisdiction (with or without rents or profits) or the perpetuation of testimony relating to land within the jurisdiction*[101]

The jurisdiction here is limited to cases in which the *whole* subject-matter is land within the jurisdiction. So, if a person becomes entitled, under the same title, to two estates, one in England and the other in Ireland, "it is right that the title to each should be litigated in the Courts of the country where it is situated. The *lex loci rei sitae* applies; and, further, the process of the Court must, that the ligitation be effective, affect the land itself ..."[102]

(b) *Whenever any act, deed, will, contract, obligation or liability affecting land or hereditaments situate within the jurisdiction, is sought to be construed, rectified,*[103] *set aside, or enforced in the action*[104]

No limitation similar to that contained in (a) above (viz. that the *whole* subject-matter of the action must be land within the jurisdiction) can be imported by implication into this clause:[105]

> "To be within the clause, the only condition is that the 'obligation or liability' shall affect land or hereditaments within the jurisdiction, but it will not the less affect them because it also affects other property. But further, suits to construe, set aside, or rectify deeds relating to lands within the jurisdiction are also within the clause. The [contrary] argument ... would therefore involve this, that in such a suit a deed which included

---

[97] *Brennan* v. *Lockyer*, [1932] I.R. 100, at 107 (Sup. Ct., *per* Kennedy, C.J., 1931). See also *Kondor Plas Ltd.* v. *Honeywell Leasing Ltd.*, 104 I.L.T.R. 220 (High Ct., Murnaghan, J., 1969), *Waddell* v. *Norton*, [1966] N.I. 85 (Q.B. Div., Lord MacDermott, L.C.J., 1965).

[98] *Brennan* v. *Locker, supra*.

[99] *Id.*, at 107–108 (Sup. Ct., *per* Kennedy, C.J. 1931). See also e.g., *The Hagen* [1908] P. 189; *Bloomfield* v. *Serenyi*, [1945] 2 All E.R. 646; *Kuwait Oil Co.* v. *Indemitsu Tankers K.K.; The Hida Maru*, [1981] 2 Lloyd's Rep. 510.

[100] As to permissible modes of service, cf. *Mahon* v. *Skeehan*, 88 I.L.T.R. 36 (High Ct., Davitt, P., 1953).

[101] Order 11, Rule 1(a).

[102] *Attorney-General* v. *Drapers' Co.*, [1894] 1 I.R. 185, at 201 (*per* Palles, C.B.). See also *In re Stubbs. Russell* v. *Le Bert*, [1896] 1 I.R. 334, at 338 (Porter, M.R. 1895). Cf. *A.G. (ex rel. Johnston)* v. *The Irish Society*, 26 I.L.T.R. 56 (Chy., Porter, M.R., 1892), *Fitzpatrick* v. *Stewart*, 51 I.L.T.R. 14 (K.B. Div., Gordon, J., (1916), *Sexton* v. *O'Halloran*, [1904] 1 I.R. 123, at 128 (C.A., 1902).

[103] Cf. *Sexton* v. *O'Halloran, supra*.

[104] Order 11, Rule 1(b).

[105] *Attorney-General* v. *Drapers' Co.*, [1894] 1 I.R. 185, at 196 (*per* Palles, C.B.).

property other than land could not be set aside or rectified as a whole, and that the construction adopted by the Court would be binding only as regards the realty in Ireland. There can be no implication which would involve such consequences.''[106]

Therefore, a suit relating to a charge on two properties, one within and the other outside the jurisdiction, is covered by clause (b).[107] However, there must be some relief sought in relation to land within the jurisdiction: Order 11, Rule 1(b) does not cover a case concerning a settlement consisting of lands within the jurisdiction and personalty outside the jurisdiction if the only question is about the property outside the jurisdiction.[108]

In *Clare Co. Council* v. *Wilson*[109] the plaintiff took proceedings under section 1 of the Public Roads (Ireland) Act 1911, which enabled a county council incurring extraordinary expenses in repairing a road, by reason of damage caused by excessive weight or extra-ordinary traffic, to recover the amount of the expenses from any person who had caused the weight or traffic to be conducted. It was held that the action was not one to enforce an obligation or liability affecting land or hereditaments within the jurisdiction. Holmes, L.J. said:

"There is here no obligation or liability *affecting* land. These words must mean something that attaches to and affects the land itself, such as carrying out the trusts relating thereto under a will or deed, suits for redemption or foreclosure, the renewal of leases and similar actions in which orders for service out of the jurisdiction are frequently made. In this case the road is no doubt land; but the action does not affect it in any way. The defendants are under no obligation to repair it; and to attempt to do so by them would be a trespass. The repairs can only be done by the plaintiffs; and their right is confined to recovering by a personal action portion of their expenses from the defendants.''[110]

The English authorities on the subject were considered. Lavery, L.J. noted that:

"in England it has been held that the sub-clause does not apply to an action for slander of title: *Casey* v. *Arnott*,[111] or to an action for rent against the assignee of a lease: *Agnew* v. *Usher*,[112] but that it does apply to an action for damages for breach of covenant to repair: *Tassell* v. *Hallen*,[113] and to an action for compensation for tenant-right according to the custom of the country: *Kaye* v. *Sutherland*.[114] 'The land is affected,' says Stephen, J.,[115] in that case, 'in the sense that it is held subject to the custom which forms part of the contract under which land is usually taken in that part of the country.' I find it difficult to reconcile this last case with the decision of the same Court in *Agnew* v. *Usher;* but even if it is to be considered as rightly decided, it cannot help the plaintiffs here very much.''[116]

In *In re Killiney U.D.C.* v. *Kirkwood & Moorhead*,[117] it was held that a claim for town rates was not one in respect of an obligation affecting land within the jurisdiction. Such a rate was not a charge on land, nor did it directly affect land: it was a personal obligation payable in respect of the occupation of lands.[118]

[106] *Id.*, at 197 (*per* Palles, C.B.)
[107] *Id.*
[108] *In re Stubbs. Russell* v. *Le Bert*, [1896] 1 I.R. 334 (Porter, M.R., 1895).
[109] [1913] 2 I.R. 89 (C.A., 1912, aff'g K.B. Div., 1912).
[110] *Id.*, at 107.
[111] 2 C.P.D. 24 (1876).
[112] 14 Q.B.D. 78 (1884).
[113] [1892] 1 Q.B. 321.
[114] 20 Q.B.D. 147 (1887).
[115] *Id.*, at 150.
[116] [1913] 2 I.R. 89, at 111.
[117] [1917] 2 I.R. 614.
[118] *Id.*, at 616 (*per* Pim J.).

(c)   *Whenever any relief is sought against any person domiciled or ordinarily resident within the jurisdiction*[119]

Normal principles for the determination of a person's domicile[120] will, of course, apply for the purpose of determining whether the defendant is domiciled in Ireland.[121] In view of the flimsiness of the connection that may exist between a person and the country of his domicile under existing rules for the determination of domicile, this is scarcely an appropriate connecting factor to apply to all in the present context. The Law Reform Commission have recommended the replacement of domicile by habitual residence as a connecting factor in the conflict of laws[122] but some less rigorous connection than habitual residence might be appropriate in Order 11, Rule 1(c).[123] "Ordinary residence" generally denotes a lesser degree of permanency of residence than "habitual residence". In the taxation context it has been interpreted as connoting a residence in a place with some degree of continuity and apart from accidental or temporary absences.[124]

(d)   *Whenever the action is for the administration*[125] *of the personal estate of any deceased person who, at the time of his death, was domiciled within the jurisdiction, or for the execution (as to property situate within the jurisdiction) of the trusts of any written instrument, of which the person to be served is a trustee, which ought to be executed according to the law of Ireland*[126]

This paragraph covers only personal estate.[127] Jurisdiction over foreign land is properly a matter for the *lex situs*.[128] Administration of real estate situated within the jurisdiction would be covered by paragraph (a) above. It is important to note that the part of the paragraph referring to execution of trusts is not confined to personal property.[129] In an English case, leave to serve out was refused where the defendant trustee had sold the entire trust property and had gone abroad with the proceeds,[130] but in the Irish case of *Attorney-General* v. *Drapers' Co.*[131] Fitzgibbon L.J. said *obiter:*

"I guard myself against saying that a trustee of property situate within the jurisdiction can escape being sued here because he has conveyed the property away ..."

[119]   Order 11, Rule 1 (c).

[120]   See ch. 6 *supra*.

[121]   For an instance where the defendant was held not to be domiciled in Ireland for the purpose of Order 11, rule 1 (c), see *Spurway* v. *Spurway*, [1894] 1 I.R. 385, (C.A., 1893). In *Whitaker* v. *Berry*, 28 I.L.T.R. 8 (Q.B., Johnson, J., 1893), the defendant was domiciled and ordinarily resident in Ireland. (The report erroneously states that he was "ordinarily domiciled ... and resident" in Ireland).

[122]   In its Working Paper No. 10-1982, *Domicile and Habitual Residence as Connecting Factors in the Conflict of Laws*.

[123]   See *supra*, pp. 98-100.

[124]   *Levene* v. *Inland Revenue Commissioners*. [1928] A.C. 217, at 235. Cf. *supra*, pp. 101-103.

[125]   As to administration generally, see *infra*, Ch. 24.

[126]   Order 11, Rule 1 (d). For cases on the former law, see *Ex parte Crawford*, 2 Ir. Ch. Rep. 573 (Berry Cusack Smith, M.R., 1853), *Ex parte Bernard*, 6 Ir. Ch. Rep. 133 (Berry Cusack Smith, M.R., 1856), *Newland* v. *Arthur*, I.R. 2 Eq. 277 (Walsh, M.R., 1868); see also *Drapers' Co.* v. *M'Cann*, 1 L.R. Ir.) 13 (Chatterton, V.C., 1878), *In re Wycherley's Trusts*, 1 L.R. (Ir.) 60 (Chatterton, V.C., 1878), *Traill* v. *Porter*, 1 L.R. (Ir.) 60 (Chatterton, V.C., 1878), *Manderville* v. *Eyre*, 13 Ir. L. Rep. 225 (Exch. of Pleas, 1849), *Freeman* v. *Freeman*, 4 Ir. Ch. Rep. 39 (M.R., 1853), *M'Dougal* v. *O'Shaughnessy*, I.R. 1 C.L. 86 (Consol. Cham., Deasy, B., 1867), *Freeman* v. *Freeman*, 4 Ir. Ch. Rep. 39 (Cusack Smith, M.R., 1853), disapproved of in *Attorney General* v. *Drapers' Co.*, [1894] 1 I.R. 185 (C.A., 1893).

[127]   From the standpoint of the conflict of laws the notion of movables rather than personal estate might have been preferable, Cf. *infra*, p. 392.

[128]   See *infra*, 401.

[129]   *Attorney-General* v. *Drapers' Co.*, [1894] I.R. 185, at 202.

[130]   *Winter* v. *Winter*, [1894] 1 Ch. 421.

[131]   [1894] 1 I.R. 185, at 207.

(e) When the action is one brought to enforce[132] *rescind, dissolve, annul or otherwise affect*[133] *a contract, or to recover damages or other relief for or in respect of the breach of a contract,*[134] *where any one*[135] *of the following three conditions is fulfilled:*

(i) The contract was made within the jurisdiction[136]

It is not sufficient merely to aver in the affidavit grounding the application that the contract upon which the intending plaintiff relied was made in this country. It is necessary that it should set out the facts which will enable the Court to determine for itself where the contract was made and not to accept what is no more than the deponent's opinion or conclusion upon undisclosed facts, without regard to the material upon which the interested party's conclusion is based.[137] The cases in which difficulties have arisen as to whether a contract was made within the jurisdiction for the purpose of Order 11, Rule 1 (e) have generally been those where one of the parties was within the jurisdiction and the other not at the time of conclusion of the agreement. The question of how the fact of agreement and the place of contracting should be determined in such cases is discussed below in the chapter on the law applicable to contracts.[138]

---

[132] In *Russell* v. *Le Bert*, [1896] 1 I.R. 334 (1895), Porter, M.R. interpreted the concept of enforcement of a contract broadly, holding that it included the construction of a power of appointment under a marriage settlement. The instrument executing the power was made outside the jurisdiction; the marriage settlement within. The Master of the Rolls said (at 338-339): "It is a well-known rule of law that, generally speaking, a power is to be read into the instrument creating it. But the difficulty is whether the contract is one which is 'sought to be enforced or rescinded, dissolved, annulled or otherwise affected in the action or for the breach thereof... relief is demanded.' I rather think that it is a contract in reference to which relief is asked, and it was made within the jurisdiction. The originating summons is brought for the purpose of having the settlement construed by an authoritative decision of the Court, for the guidance of the parties. That, I think, may fairly be deemed to be either the enforcement of the contract, if not relief in respect of its breach, or it may be (though I have more doubt about this) that it is sought to be 'affected' by the proceeding."

[133] "The words 'or otherwise affect' are very wide and cover a claim for a declaration that a contract has become discharged, whether as the result of frustration, repudiation or otherwise": *per* Kerr J., in *B P Exploration Co. (Libya) Ltd.* v. *Hunt,* [1976] 3 All E.R. 879, at 885.

[134] "Contract" here does not necessarily envisage one whose legal validity has been established beyond reasonable doubt: it is enough for the plaintiff to make a good arguable case as to its validity: *Vitkovice Horni A Hutni Tezirstyo* v. *Korner,* [1951] A.C. 869, at 880 (H.L. (Eng), *per* Lord Simonds). See also *Hemelryck* v. *William Lylall Shipbuilding Co. Ltd.,* [1921] 1 A.C. 698 (P.C.), *Re O'Connor* v. *Lemieux,* [1927] 3 D.L.R. 77 (Ont. Sup. Ct., Lennox J.), *McCowan* v. *Menasco Manufacturing Co.,* [1941] O.W.N. 133 (High Ct., Urquhart, J.), cf. *Murray* v. *Finkle,* 48 I.L.T.R. 178, at 180 (C.A., *per* Holmes, L.J., 1914). See also *Mahon* v. *Harrison,* [1934] L.J. Ir. 79 (High Ct., O'Byrne, J.), where an order for service out was permitted although a claim for breach of contract appeared to be statute-barred; since this defence had to be specifically pleaded, O'Byrne J. thought it better to make the order and "let the defendant take his own course" as to whether or not he would plead the statute.

[135] Cf. *Wansborough Paper Co. Ltd.* v. *Laughland,* [1920] W.N. 344 (C.A.). And see *Betham* v. *Fernie,* 4 I.C.L.R. 92 (Com. Pleas, 1854), *Frew* v. *Stone,* 6 Ir. Jur. 267 (Com. Pleas, 1854), *Kisbey* v. *Chester & Holyhead Ry. Co.,* 6 I.C.L.R. 393 (Com. Pleas, 1857), *Reilly* v. *White,* 11 I.C.L.R. 138 (Exch., 1860), *Kelly* v. *Dixon,* I.R. 6 C.L. 25 (Q.B., 1870), *Adams* v. *Geralopolo,* 5 Ir. Jur. N.S. 217 Exch., 1860).

[136] Order 11, Rule 1 (e) (i).

[137] *Brennan* v. *Lockyer* [1932] I.R. 100, at 107, (Sup. Ct., *per* Kennedy C.J., 1931).

[138] For cases where the place of contracting has been determined for the purpose of O. 11, R. 1(e), see *O'Leary* v. *Law Integrity Insurance Co.,* [1912] 1 I.R. 479 (Barton, J.,); *Savage* v. *General Life Insurance Co.,* 47 I.L.T.R. 158 (1913); *Sanderson* v. *Cunningham,* [1919] 2 I.R. 234; *Dooley* v. *Egan* 72 I.L.T.R. 155 (1938); *Tedcastle M'Cormick & Co.* v. *Robertson,* [1927] I.R. 597; see also *Atkins* v. *Thompson,* [1922] 2 I.R. 102 (K.B. Div., S.I. Molony, C.J.) (too briefly reported), *M'Gettigan* v. *North-Eastern Ry. Co. of England,* [1899] 2 I.R. 375 (Q.B. Div., Johnson, J.), *Deane* v. *Sandford,* I.R. 9 C.L. 228 (Q.B., 1875), *Connellan* v. *Fallon,* [1953–1954] Ir. Jur. Rep. 43 (High Ct., Murnaghan, J., 1954); and cf. *Lisburn Council* v. *Shortt,* 46 I.L.T.R. 132 (K.B. Div., 1912) (of interest, although not an Order 11 case). See also *Black* v. *Baird,* 31 L.T. & Sol. J. 8 (C.A., 1896) (where

As an example, in *Wheeler & Co. Ltd* v. *Jeffrey (John) & Co,*[139] an Irish firm agreed to act as agents for a Scottish firm, but no reference was made to any date on which the agency was to begin. The Irish firm wrote a letter stating that they would agree to carry on the agency as from the following 1 July; to this the Scottish firm replied, noting that the Irish firm were agreeable to start on that date. The Court of Appeal, reversing the King's Bench Division, held that the Irish company's letter had introduced a new and material term, which had been accepted by the reply from the Scottish company. Had the Irish company left out any reference to a specific date, the date of commencement would have been what was a reasonable one in the circumstances, but since the Irish company had volunteered to name a specific date, it was open to the Scottish company to accept or reject it. Their letter of acceptance established the contract, which thus was made in Scotland rather than Ireland.

In *Brennan* v. *Lockyer,*[140] the plaintiff, an Irish resident, had applied for membership of a trade union in England. This involved a proposal being sent by the Dublin Secretary of the union to England, where a certificate of membership was issued. The plaintiff contended that the contract was made within the jurisdiction as, he said, it was complete only on notification to him that application had been approved. The Supreme Court rejected this argument. FitzGibbon, J. considered that the plaintiff had waived any entitlement to notification, in view of his conduct, whereby, even before his application had been sent to England, he had purported to exercise a privilege confined to members of the union, in proposing his wife as a member of the union. The plaintiff's conduct was "wholly inconsistent with an intention or belief on his part that he was not to become a member or possess any of the rights or privileges of membership unless and until the fact of his election had been communicated to him."[140]

There have been several of Irish cases[142] under Order 11 involving application of the "postal" rule whereby a contract comes into existence at the place and time of posting rather than at the place and time of the arrival of the letter at its destination.

But if a contract is made within the jurisdiction by reason only of the operation of such a technical rule, the court may be very reluctant to order service out where "[a]ll considerations of propriety and convenience"[143] indicate otherwise.

---

a contract was made in Ireland, the fact that the amount sued for was small was held not to be a sufficient reason for refusing the order for service *ex juris*). Cf. *Bennett* v. *Cook*, 35 I.L.T.R. 153 (C.A. 1901), where the plaintiff purchased from the defendant's agent in Cork a ticket for a tour to Egypt and up the Nile. The contract was thus made in Ireland, but the Court of Appeal held that an order for service out should not be granted. Fitzgibbon, L.J. observed (at 153) that the fact that the contract was "only technically" an Irish one meant that making such an order would be "a strong conclusion".

139 [1921] 2 I.R. 395 (C.A., 1920, rev'g K.B. Div., 1920). See also *Tedcastle M'Cormick & Co. Ltd.* v. *Robertson* [1929] I.R. 597 (Sup. Ct., 1927) ("Sale Note" for the sale of coal containing new terms sent from England to Dublin, where it was accepted by signing "Purchase Note" and posting it back to England; Supreme Court unanimous that contract made in Irish Free State; contention that there had been oral contract in England subsequently reduced to writing rejected by the Court). Contrast *Sanderson* v. *Cunningham*, [1919] 2 I.R. 234 (C.A.). See also *Deane* v. *Sandford*, I.R. 9 C.L. 228 (Q.B., 1875).

140 [1932] I.R. 100 (Sup.Ct., 1931).

141 *Id.*, at 113 (*per* Fitzgibbon, J.).

142 *Wheeler & Co. Ltd.* v. *Jeffrey (John) & Co.*, [1921] 1 I.R. 395 (C.A., 1920, rev'g K.B. Div., 1920), *Sanderson* v. *Cunningham*, [1919] 2 I.R. 234 (C.A.), *M'Crea & Knight*, [1896] 2 I.R. 619 (C.A.), *Tedcastle, M'Cormick & Co.* v. *Robertson*, [1929] I.R. 597 (Sup. Ct., 1927) (especially at 599, *per* Kennedy, C.J.), *Bevan* v. *Gillows & Co.*, 40 I.L.T.R. 251 (K.B. Div., 1906), *Mayor etc. of Limerick* v. *Crompton & Co.*, [1910] 2 I.R. 416 (C.A., 1909), aff'g [1909] 2 I.R. 120 (K.B. Div.), *Maconchy* v. *Trower*, 30 L.R. Ir. 480 (Q.B. Div., 1892). See also *Wansborough Paper Co. Ltd.* v. *Laughland*, [1920] W.N. 344 (C.A.). Cf. *Clarke* v. *Harper and Robinson*, [1938] N.I. 162 (K.B. Div., Andrews, L.C.J.), *Deane* v. *Sandford*, I.R. 9 C.L. 228 (Q.B., 1875), *Kett* v. *Robinson*, 4 I.C.L.R. 186 (Q.B., 1854); cf. *McLoughlin* v. *Life Association of Scotland*, 49 I.L.T.R. 166 (C.A., 1915).

143 *M'Crea* v. *Knight*, [1896] 2 I.R. 619, at 626 (C.A., *per* Fitzgibbon, L.J.). In this case, the Court

The postal rule will not easily be extended to other types of case. In *O'Leary* v. *Law Integrity Insurance Co.*,[144] an insurance proposal was sent to the defendant insurance company's registered office in Liverpool from Dublin. The policy had been signed by the plaintiff in Dublin and transmitted by the company's agent. The policy was signed and sealed in Liverpool. It contained a number of important conditions. It was then returned to the agent, who delivered it to the plaintiff.

Barton, J. was satisfied that the contract was in the circumstances made in Dublin:

> "The proposal was signed in Dublin, and contemplated delivery, in Dublin, of the policy to the proposer, and that he was then to read the conditions printed on the policy and to become bound by them as the basis of the contract. The parties contemplated that the policy would not be completely binding on either party until delivery in Dublin. I do not see that this is affected by the fact that the company sealed the policy in Liverpool. Whatever consequences the sealing of the policy might have, it would not make the policy binding on both parties until delivered to the proposer in Dublin. This case is distinguishable from the common cases of contract by correspondence when the post office is treated as the agent of the proposer. Here we have a contract made by an agent in Dublin in which the parties have stipulated for delivery to the proposer in Dublin of the policy, and communication to the proposer of conditions which were to be the basis of the contract. The contract was then binding on both parties, but not before."[145]

Another type of problem relates to a complex of contractual relationships where it is not clear that, if this complex is unravelled, the particular contract was made within the State. Thus, for example, in *M'Gettigan* v. *North-Eastern Railway Co.*,[146] the plaintiff entered into a contract with a steamship company in Ireland for the through carriage of livestock from Derry to him in York. The carriage was in three stages: the steamship company brought the livestock to Liverpool; a second company brought the livestock from Liverpool to Leeds; and the third company, the defendants, brought the animals from Leeds to York. The plaintiff claimed that loss had been occasioned by delay caused by the defendants on this final stage.

Johnson, J. came to the conclusion on the evidence that there "was not one but a succession of independent contracts."[147] The last was an implied contract by the defendants with the plaintiff, having received his cattle, to convey and deliver them to the plaintiff at York on payment of the through freight and charges. If there was a breach of contract, it was one that took place in York, and thus was not within the Rules as to service out of the jurisdiction.

In England[148] and Australia[149] it has been held that obligations under a quasi-contract arising within the jurisdiction are within the local equivalent of Rule

---

of Appeal judges reluctantly affirmed the Queen's Bench Division's order for service out of the jurisdiction, not so much because they thought in their discretion that they should do so, but rather because they considered that they should be "very slow" to disturb the exercise of its discretion by the Court below.

[144] [1912] 1 I.R. 479 (Barton, J.). Cf. *Sanderson & Co.* v. *Cunningham*, [1919] 2 I.R. 234 (C.A.), *Atkins & Co. Ltd.* v. *Thompson*, 56 I.L.T.R. 107 (K.B. Div., Molony, L.C.J., 1922).

[145] *Id.* [1912] 1 I.R., at 483−484. Cf. *Cannon* v. *Fallon*, 52 I.L.T.R. 34 (K.B. Div., Pim, J., 1918), *Deane* v. *Sandford*, I.R. 9 C.L. 228 (Q.B., 1875). *Lowden* v. *Accident Insurance Co.*, 43 I.L.T.R. 277 (K.B. Div., 1904). Cf. *Hamilton* v. *Foreign & Mercantile Co.*, 3 Ir. L.T. & Sol. J. 389 (Exch., 1869).

[146] [1899] 2 I.R. 375 (Q.B. Div., Johnson, J.).

[147] *Id.*, at 379. Contrast *Cumming* v. *Great Northern Ry., Co.*, 27 I.L.T.R. 74 (Ex., 1893). It is clear that a contract may be made within the jurisdiction, having been preceded by a less formal agreement made abroad: *Gibbon* v. *Commerz und Creditbank A/G*, [1958] 2 Ll. Rep.113, *M'Crea* v. *Knight*, [1896] 2 I.R. 619 (C.A.).

[148] *Bowling* v. *Cox* [1926] A.C. 751; *Trustee of Rousou* v. *Rousou* [1955] 2 All E.R. 169; and see *B.P. Exploration Co. (Libya) Ltd.* v. *Hunt* [1976] 3 All E.R. 879, at p. 887.

[149] *Adcock* v. *Aarons*, 5 W.A.R. 140 (Full Ct., 1903), *Belyando Shire Council* v. *Rivers*, 2 Q.J.P.R.

1(e)(i). However, the Irish courts have displayed a reluctance to extend the rule to obligations akin to those of a contractual nature arising by way of statute. In *Clare County Council* v. *Wilson*[150] it was held that a statutory obligation on the part of the defendants to pay for the repair of roads damaged by them was not covered by what is now Order 11, Rule 1(e)(i).

> "The legal as well as the popular conception of a contract is an agreement expressed or implied between two persons; and an action *ex contractu* is an action brought by one of them against the other in relation to what has been so agreed. I am unable to see how an obligation imposed by a public statute upon persons against their will or at least, without their consent, can be described as the result of a contract."[151]

In *Killiney U.D.C.* v. *Kirkwood*,[152] an action for town rates, the Court rejected the suggestion that the relation between an urban council and its ratepayers might be regarded as that of "statutory contractor and contractee", so as to bring the case within what is now Order 11, Rule (e)(i). Finally, in *Shipsey* v. *British and South American Steam Navigation Co*,[153] the Supreme Court held that a statutory obligation imposed by a local and personal Act was not a contractual obligation and therefore not within the terms of what is now Order 11, Rule 1(e)(i). Fitzgibbon, J. observed that "while every contract creates an obligation, it is not true that every obligation arises out of a contract, and to give jurisdiction under [the Rule] there must have been a contract made or entered into within the jurisdiction.[154]

Some support for the Irish approach may be gleaned from McLeod's observation that "[i]t is questionable whether contract should ... include 'quasi-contract' today, in light of the developments in the law of restitution.[155] Restitution/unjust enrichment has become a distinct aspect of law, separate from contract."[156]

(ii)   *the contract was made by or through an agent trading or residing within the jurisdiction on behalf of a principal trading or residing out of the jurisdiction*[157]

Where the terms of a contract have been arranged through the mediation of an agent trading or residing within the jurisdiction on behalf of a principal trading or residing outside the jurisdiction, the contract has been made "through an agent", even though the agent had no authority to enter into contracts and the contract was actually made by the principal abroad.[158]

(iii)   *the contract is, by its terms or by implication, to be governed by Irish Law ....*[159]

---

47 (Full Ct., 1908), *Durra* v. *Bank of New South Wales*, [1940] V.L.R. 170 (O'Bryan, J.), *Chenoweth* v. *Summers* [1941] A.L.R. 364 (Judge Magennis), *State of Victoria* v. *Hansen*, [1960] V.R. 582 (Sup. Ct., Adam, J.), *Earthworks and Quarries Ltd.* v. *Eastment (F.T.) & Sons Pty. Ltd.*, [1966] V.R. 24 (Sup. Ct., Dean J., 1965), *McFee Engineering Pty. Ltd (in Liquidation)* v. *C.B.S. Constructions Pty. Ltd.*, 44 Fed. L. Rep. 340 (N.S.W. Sup. Ct., Yeldham, J., 1979). See further *Nygh*, 31, 54.

150 [1913] 2 I.R. 89.

151 *Id.*, at 105 (*per* Holmes, L.J.).

152 [1917] 2 I.R. 614. But cf. *Fitzpatrick* v. *Stewart*, 51 I.L.T.R. 14 (K.B. Div., Gordon, J., 1916).

153 [1936] I.R. 65 (Sup. Ct., 1935).

154 *Id.*, at 88.

155 Citing Goff and Jones, *The Law of Restitution*, pp. 5–11 (2nd ed., 1978).

156 *Mcleod*, 97.

157 Order 11, Rule 1 (e) (ii). See *Richardson* v. *Army, Navy, and General Assurance Association*, [1924] 2 I.R. 96 (K.B. Div., (I.F.S), *O'Brien* v. — *Insurance Co.*, 10 Ir. L. Rep. 183 (Q.B., 1846). See also *Duffy* v. *Cowgill*, 13 Ir. L. Rep. 84 (Exch. of Pleas, 1849) (substituted service), *Eiffe* v. *Caledonian Insurance Co.*, 5 Ir. L. Rep. 138 (Exch. of Pleas, 1842), *Stevenson* v. *London North-Western Ry. Co.*, I.R. I.C.L. 672 (Comm. Pleas, 1867), *Kett* v. *Robinson*, 4 I.C.L.R. 186 (Q.B., 1854), *Bennett* v. *Cook*, 35 I.L.T.R. 153 (C.A., 1901). Cf. *Cumming* v. *Great Northern, etc., Rys.*, [1894] 2 I.R. 208 (C.A., 1893, aff'g Ex. Div., 1893), *Frew* v. *Stone*, 6 Ir. Jur. 267 (Com. Pleas, 1854).

158 *National Mortgage & Agency Co. of New Zealand* v. *Gosselin* 38 T.L.R. 832 (1922); see also *The Metamorphosis* [1953] 1 All E.R. 723 (P.D.A. Div., Karminski, J.).

159 Order 11, Rule 1 (e)(iii).

Under this heading the law applicable to the contract (or what is referred to as the "proper" law of the contract) must be Irish. The question of the ascertainment of the proper law of the contract is considered[160] in the chapter on contracts.

Brief reference may be made here to the Northern Ireland decision of *Clarke* v. *Harper and Robinson*.[161] A contract was made in London for the sale of turkeys by the plaintiff, a poultry merchant residing in Keady, Co. Armagh, to the defendants in London. A dispute arose as to some consignments which the defendants refused to pay for, and the plaintiff sought liberty to serve a writ outside the jurisdiction. His claim was based on Order II, rule 1(e)(ii) of the Rules of the Supreme Court (Northern Ireland) 1936, which was drafted in the same way as Order 11, rule 1(e)(iii) of the Rules of the Superior Courts 1986.

Andrews, L.C.J., setting aside the order of Brown, J., held that the plaintiff should not have had liberty to serve *ex juris*. He rejected the argument of counsel for the defendant that clause (iii) of rule 1(e) was intended to apply only to cases in which different systems of law prevail in Northern Ireland and in the other country for which jurisdiction is contended. In the instant case, this argument, if accepted, would have been fatal to the plaintiff, since the Sale of Goods Act 1893 applied both to Northern Ireland and England. The Lord Chief Justice said:

"Let us suppose that in the present case the parties, perhaps in ignorance or forgetfulness that the law in both countries was identical, had expressly provided that the contract should be governed by the law of Northern Ireland. Could it be reasonably contended in such circumstances that the case did not come within the rule merely because the two systems of law were in fact identical? In my opinion the answer must be in the negative — that the existence of two different systems of law is not absolutely essential for the application of the rule, though I recognize that in most cases in practice such different systems probably would so exist."[162]

In the present case the parties had made no express selection of the governing law. Andrews. L.C.J. noted that "[p]rima facie the law governing a contract is presumed to be the *lex loci contractus*";[163] however, it was agreed that the contract was wholly to be performed in Northern Ireland, and "several cases could be cited"[164] in which it had been held that a contract, made in one country but wholly to be performed in another, might in the absence of other circumstances be regarded as intended by the parties to be governed by the *lex loci solutionis*. As against this, Andrews, L.C.J. was of the opinion that:

"there is a circumstance in the present case which is absolutely fatal to a presumption of any such intention by the parties, namely, that the law of both countries .... in regard to the contract is identical. I can well understand that where the law of the two countries is different the parties may intend that their rights and obligations should be determined by the law of the country where the contract is to be performed.[165] It may be, as I have already pointed out, that the parties through ignorance or forgetfulness may expressly provide for the application of the *lex loci solutionis* even though it is identical with the *lex loci contractus*, but I find it impossible to *presume* any such intention where the *lex loci contractus* and the *lex loci solutionis* are the same."[166]

---

[160] *Infra*, pp. 521-531.
[161] [1938] N.I. 162 (K.B.Div., Andrews, L.C.J.).
[162] *Id.*, at 170.
[163] *Id.*, at 171.
[164] *Id.*, at 172, citing *Chatenay* v. *Brazilian Submarine Telegraph Co.*, [1891] 1 Q.B. 79.
[165] Citing the judgment of the Exchequer Chamber in *Lloyd* v. *Guibert*, L.R. 1 Q.B. 115, at 122 (1865).
[166] [1938] N.1., at 172.

... or is one brought in respect of a breach committed within the jurisdiction of a contract wherever made, even though such breach was preceded or accompanied by a breach out of the jurisdiction which rendered impossible the performance of the part of the contract which ought to have been performed within the jurisdiction[167]

A contract may be broken by repudiation[168] (express or implied) or by failure to perform. So far as express repudiation is concerned, it appears that a repudiation by letter will constitute a breach within the jurisdiction only when the letter is posted within the jurisdiction;[169] but where a party abroad seeking to repudiate a contract uses an agent within the jurisdiction to inform the other party, the contract will be broken within the jurisdiction. Thus, in *Oppenheimer* v. *Losenthal (Louis) & Co., A.G.*,[170] the plaintiff, a German national of the Jewish faith, was manager of the London branch of a German company; he alleged that he had been wrongfully dismissed by his German employers, who, not having his address to hand, sent notice of his dismissal through their agents in London. The English Court of Appeal held that the breach had been "clearly committed"[171] in London.

Breach by implied repudiation consists of an act inconsistent with the actor's performance of the contract, such as burning, or selling to another person, an item which the actor had contractually undertaken to sell to the other party to the contract. Although there is no authority on the question, *Dicey & Morris* consider that the breach in such a case "presumably occurs where the inconsistent act is done."[172]

Where the breach consists of the failure by a party to perform some or all of his obligations under the contract, it appears necessary to show that the part of the contract that was breached ought to have been performed within the jurisdiction.[173] Of course, most contracts do not specify in express terms where the contract (or particular parts of the contract) must be performed. It will be sufficient if this intention may be gleaned from the circumstances of the particular case.

Thus, in *O'Mara Ltd* v. *Dodd*,[174] the Irish King's Bench Division held that a

---

[167] Order 11, Rule 1(e) (iii).

[168] See *M'Evers* v. *O'Neill*, 4 L.R. (Ir.) 517 (Ex. Div., 1879). Cf. *Matthews* v. *Alexander*, 7 I.R.C.L. 575 (Q.B., 1873).

[169] *Dicey & Morris*, 208, citing several common law authorities. Cf. *Kelly* v. *Dixon*, I.R. 6 C.L. 25 (Q.B., 1870). See also *Deane* v. *Sandford*, I.R. 9 C.L. 228 (Q.B., 1875), *Matthews* v. *Alexander*, 7 I.R. C.L. 575 (Q.B. 1873).

[170] [1937] 1 All E.R. 23 (C.A., 1936).

[171] *Id.*, at 25 (*per* Greer, L.J.). As to the question of *forum conveniens*, Greer, L.J. observed (*id.*) that "[t] his need occasion no difficulty as there is in London at present a large number of German Lawyers. ..." Had the case proceeded in Germany there was said to be grave reason to suppose that the plaintiff would not be allowed to be represented by an advocate. He would, said Greer, L.J., "be under a real risk of being arrested and put in a concentration camp". See also *Oppenheimer* v. *Cattermole*, [1976] A.C. 249 (H.L. 1975).

[172] *Dicey & Morris*, 208.

[173] *Id.*, 209. In *M'Evers* v. *O'Neill*, 4 L.R. Ir. 517 (Ex. Div., 1879), in an action for breach of promise, service *ex juris* was permitted against a British subject, resident in London, who, having become engaged to the plaintiff in Cork, had subsequently broken off the engagement from London. Fitzgerald, B. observed (at 520): "The cause of action is in Ireland. The ... promise was made here, where the plaintiff resides. The breach is not the marrying a woman resident in Ireland". The latter sentence may suggest that, even if the contract had not been made in Ireland, it would still have been considered to have been *broken* there. Whether the plaintiff's residence was the most appropriate reference point may, however, be debated. See also, *Adams* v. *Mavro*, 17 I.C.L.R. 686 (Comm. Pleas, 1866), *Kondor Plas Ltd.* v. *Honeywell Leasing Ltd.*, 104 I.L.T.R. 220 (High Ct., Murnaghan, J., 1969), *Reilly* v. *White*, 11 I.C.L.R. 138 (Exch., 1860), *Deane* v. *Sandford*, I.R. 9 C.L. 228 (Q.B., 1875), *Gilliland & Son* v. *Latta*, 41 I.L.T.R. 91 (C.A., 1907), *Monsarrat* v. *Barron*, 4 N.I.J.R. 4 (C.A., 1903), *Jeffrey* v. *Jeffrey*, 81 I.L.T.R. 22 (Circuit Ct., Judge McCarthy, 1946), *Kelly* v. *Dixon*, I.R. 6 C.L. 25 (Q.B., 1870), *Spurway* v. *Spurway*, [1894] 1 I.R. 385 (C.A., 1893, aff'g Porter, M.R.).

[174] [1912] 2 I.R. 55 (K.B. Div., Kenny, J., 1911). Cf. *Lewis and Pringle* v. *Nixon*, 7 Ir. L.R. 359 (Exch. of Pleas, 1843), *Connellan* v. *Fallon*, [1953-1954] Ir. Jur. Rep. 43 (High Ct., Murnaghan, J., 1954).

breach had taken place within the jurisdiction in the following circumstances. A course of dealing existed between the parties whereby goods were ordered in the Isle of Man by the defendant trader from the plaintiff company in Ireland; the goods were supplied by the company directly to the trader; and payment was made by the trader by cash order sent directly to the company. When, after several successful sales in accordance with this practice, the trader failed to make payment though he had received the goods, the company successfully sought liberty to serve out of the jurisdiction. The course of trading showed that the trader's breach in failing to pay took place in Ireland, where it might, by then, have been expected, rather than in the Isle of Man.

In *Ward* v. *Harris*,[175] May, C.J. observed:

> "If a trader in England promises to deliver goods, or to pay money to a person resident in Ireland at the time of the contract, it seems to me that contract can be fulfilled only by a delivery or payment to the promisee in Ireland, and that there is a breach in Ireland if the contract be not so fulfilled."

In *Ward* v. *Harris*, the plaintiff, an owner of a vessel belonging to the port of Belfast, obtained a policy of insurance from the defendants in London. The process was somewhat complicated: the plaintiff received the policy from an insurance agent in Belfast who in turn had acted through a London agent. The owner paid the premium to the Belfast insurance agent from whom he received the policy. The policy was underwritten at Lloyds in consequence of a proposal made by the London agent.

The vessel and cargo were destroyed, and the plaintiff claimed payment on the policy. The defendants contended that any money under the policy, according to the usage of Lloyds, could be paid in London only. The plaintiff denied that he had been aware of this usage. The Irish Court of Appeal held that the plaintiff had no reason to be aware of the usage, and that the breach through non-payment was in Ireland rather than England.[176]

In the nineteenth century, before the tort of negligence had gained an independent status,[177] several cases involved plaintiffs suing for the negligent breach of contracts of carriage. Often the goods would have been damaged or destroyed in an accident outside the jurisdiction while they were on their way to or from Ireland. In such cases, the courts generally held that the contract had been breached within the jurisdiction, through non-performance.

The courts arrived at this position after some debate. In *Watson* v. *Atlantic Royal Mail Steam Navigation Co.*,[178] in 1860, the defendant, an English shipping company, contracted in New York to convey the plaintiff and his luggage to Galway on their ship. The ship was wrecked on the journey, and the plaintiff's luggage was lost. In proceedings for breach of contract brought in Irish Court of Exchequer, the plaintiff unsuccessfully sought an order for substituted service. Greene, B. considered that no "necessary ingredient"[179] of the cause of action had occurred within the

---

[175] 8 L.R. Ir. 365, at 371 (C.A., 1880).

[176] Cf. *Tedcastle, M'Cormack & Co. Ltd* v. *Robertson* [1929] I.R. 597 (Sup. Ct., 1927). The defendant had contracted to sell coal to the plaintiffs at a specified price per ton c.i.f. Dublin. The coal was shipped at Antwerp, and was allegedly of the wrong quality. The Supreme Court ordered service out of the jurisdiction, since the contract had been made in the Irish Free State; but FitzGibbon, J. observed (at 604) that:

> "[t]he breach, if there was one, of the contract took place on the shipment of the coal. It took place apparently neither in England nor in the Free State, but at Antwerp, where the coal was shipped ...."

[177] See *McMahon & Binchy*, 149, 160-161 (1981), Winfield, *The History of Negligence in the Law of Torts*, 42 L.Q. Rev. 184 (1926).

[178] 10 I.C.L.R. 163 (Exch., Greene, B., 1860).

[179] *Id.*, at 166.

jurisdiction of the Irish courts. The mere non-delivery in Galway of the plaintiff's luggage was not sufficient to satisfy him that any part of the cause of action had arisen within the jurisdiction.[180]

What is of particular interest in Greene, B.'s judgment is his acceptance of the view that the plaintiff's case was "substantially founded upon a tort."[181] Save for the claim based on non-delivery, the plaintiff had rested his case on "breaches of duty on the part of the defendant, negligence and carelessness".[182] There is here an anticipation of the complete severance from contract of the tort of negligence, which has occurred during this century.

In *Powell* v. *Atlantic Steam Navigation Co.*,[183] the case again involved the loss of luggage on its way from New York to Galway. The defendant shipping company contended that the luggage had probably been taken in Newfoundland by a passenger of the same name, who landed there. The issues were fully canvassed in argument, *Watson's* case being cited by both sides. The Court of Exchequer, which included Greene, B., ordered substituted service, without giving a written judgment. Greene, B. "practically acknowledged the error of his decision in [*Watson's* case] by joining in the judgment of the other members of the Court in complete opposition to his previous order in *Watson's* case".[184]

The approach favoured in *Powell's* case triumphed. It found support in *Aston* v. *London and North-Western Ry. Co.*,[185] and again in *Macken & Son* v. *Ellis*,[186] *Adams* v. *Davison*,[187] *Megaw* v. *Di Lizardi*[188] and *Chambers* v. *London and North-Western Ry. Co.*[189]

In *Willis* v. *London and North-Western Ry. Co.*,[190] The Queen's Bench confronted the issue squarely. The plaintiffs, husband and wife, claimed that the wife had been injured and their luggage lost in a collision outside Holyhead Harbour, when they were being carried on the defendant company's boat from Holyhead to Greenore. The majority of the Court held that enough of the cause of action had arisen within the jurisdiction to warrant an order to substitute service.

The majority considered[191] that the defendant had breached its contractual undertaking to carry the plaintiffs and their luggage safely to Greenore. They were clearly impressed by the volume, if not the analytic power of the earlier decisions in favour of assuming jurisdiction. Moreover, the fact that in *Watson's* case Green, B. had overlooked the Plaintiffs' plea based on the defendant's role as common carrier, as well as his later participation in *Powell's* case, made it easy for them to differ from the more impressive analysis in *Watson's* case.

Nevertheless, there is much more force in Fitzgerald, J.'s dissenting judgment:

---

[180] *Id.*, at 167. Greene, B. went on to say (at 167-168): "If the action were brought against the defendants as common carriers, bound to deliver the goods in Galway, the case might be different. It is not for me to say what the effect of that might have been; it might be held that the non-delivery was the foundation of the action ..." But, as O'Brien, J. noted in *Willis* v. *London and North-Western Ry. Co.*, I.R. 10 C.L. 95, at 100 (Q.B., 1876), in fact the plaintiff *had* pleaded a case against the defendants as common carriers (cf. 10 I.C.L.R., at 163).

[181] 10 I.C.L.R., at 167. Cf. *Tuohy* v. *Great Southern Railway Ry. Co.*, 32 I.L.T.R. 139, at 140 (Q.B. Div., *per* O'Brien, J., 1898).

[182] 10 I.C.L.R., at 167.

[183] 10 I.C.L.R. App. xlvii (Exch., 1860).

[184] *Willis* v. *London and North-Western Ry. Co.*, I.R. 10 C.L. 95, at 103 (Q.B., *per* Whiteside, C.J., 1876). See also *Kisbey* v. *Chester & Holyhead Ry. Co.*, 6 I.C.L.R. 393 (Com. Pleas, 1857).

[185] I.R. 1 C.L. 604 (Com. Pleas, 1867).

[186] I.R. 8 C.L. 151 (Q.B., 1874).

[187] 6 Ir. Jur. (N.S.) 390 (1861).

[188] 5 I.L.T.R. 62 (Consol. Chamb., Hughes, B., 1871).

[189] 9 I.L.T. p. 175 (Consol. Chamb., Fitzgerald, B., 1875). See also *Finnigan* v. *London & N.W. Ry. Co.* 9 I.L.T.R. 230 (Consol. Chamb., Dowse, B., 1875).

[190] I.R. 10 C.L. 95 (Q.B., 1876).

[191] Cf. *id.*, at 98-99 (*per* O'Brien, J.) and at 101-102 (*per* Whiteside, C.J.).

"The breach of contract or of duty of which the Plaintiffs complain took place at Holyhead, and nothing whatever took place in this country which it would be necessary for the plaintiffs to prove or rely on. The contract, the breach, and all the facts to be proved on either side, took place in England. The personal injury of which the Plaintiffs complain took place at Holyhead; the luggage was there lost in the sunken vessel, and the contract was there not only broken but became incapable of being performed, and was so far at an end.

It seems to me, therefore, that the cause of action did not, nor did any part of it, arise within the jurisdiction."[192]

Fitzgerald, J. went on to draw out the implications of holding that, because the terminus of the journey was in Ireland, the breach was committed there:

"Suppose the contract to have been made in Philadelphia with an American company to carry from thence to Dublin, and broken by a railway collision between Philadelphia and New York, we could not refuse to assert jurisdiction and make an order to serve the American company in Philadelphia."[193]

(f) The action is founded on a tort committed within the jurisdiction[194]

To found jurisdiction under this heading, the tort must have been committed within the jurisdiction. In some cases, determining this question presents no difficulty. If for example, a driver carelessly runs over a child in Cavan town, the jurisdictional requirement normally is clearly fulfilled. But what about a case where an accident takes place south of the border, but the car involved in the accident has been negligently repaired in a garage in Co. Fermanagh, or the driver has been rendered intoxicated by an over-generous host north of the border?

Several approaches have been adopted at various times in different jurisdictions towards the question of determining the *locus delicti*.[195] The holding of the Supreme Court in *Grehan* v. *Medical Incorporated and Valley Pines Association*,[196] inspired to a degree by developments within the European Economic Community, goes very far in removing the artificiality which has plagued this area of law.

It is desirable to set out briefly each of the approaches adopted before *Grehan* and then to describe the Court's response.

The requirement that all elements of tort be committed within jurisdiction

The first approach requires that all elements of the tort should have been committed within the jurisdiction before an order for service outside the jurisdiction may be made. It has certain robust linguistic common sense, since it is difficult to see how a tort which, to use a neutral word, "unfolded" in more than one state may be said to have been committed in one state only.[197] But in the world of reality this

---

[192] *Id.*, at 97.

[193] *Id.*

[194] Order 11, Rule 1(f) of the Rules of the Superior Courts 1986.

[195] See generally Webb & North, *Some Thoughts on the Place of Commission of a Non-Statutory Tort*, 14 Int. & Comp. L.Q. 1314 (1965), Morse, ch. 6, Fridman, *Where Is a Tort Committed?* 24 U.T.L.J. 247 (1974); Cowen, *The Locus Delicti in English Private International Law* 25 B.Y. B.I.L. 394 (1948), Hebenton, *Jurisdiction: The Place Where a Tort is Committed*, 2 U. Br. Col. L. Rev. 361 (1964), Ehrenzweig, *The Place of Acting in International Multistate Torts: Law and Reason versus the Restatement*, 36 Minn. L. Rev. 1 (1951), McClean, *Note: Locus Delicti*, 14 I.C.L.Q. 997 (1965), Bissett-Johnson, *Comment*, 48 Can. Bar Rev. 548 (1970), Goldstein, *Note: Jurisdiction Over Foreign Manufacturers Concerning Damage That Occurs in Israel*, 14 Israel L. Rev. 504 (1979).

[196] [1986] I.L.R.M. 627 (Sup. Ct.).

[197] See *Macken* v. *Ellis*, I.R. 8 C.L. 151, at 156 (Q.B., *per* Fitzgerald, J., dissenting 1874). Cf. *Willis* v. *London and North-Western Ry. Co.* I.R. 10 C.L. 95, at 98 (Q.B. *per* O'Brien, J., 1876) and at 97 (*per* Fitzgerald, J., dissenting), *M'Mahon* v. *North-Western Ry. Co.*, I.R. 5 C.L. 200 (Com. Pleas, 1870), *Kelly* v. *Dixon*, I.R. 6 C.L. 25 (Q.B., 1870).

"somewhat draconian"[198] solution would be quite impractical. As Walsh, J.
observed in the *Grehan* decision, "in the nature of things it is highly unlikely that
in conflict of law situations everything would be connected with one jurisdiction.
If that were to be the rule underlying the Court's discretion in an application [for
service *ex juris*], it would indeed be a very rare case in which the plaintiff would
be able to obtain service out of the jurisdiction."[199]

The "last event" approach

There is some support among the cases[200] for the view that a tort is
"committed", for jurisdictional purposes at least, in the state where the last event
necessary to make the defendant liable for the alleged tort takes place. It has been
argued[201] that in a negligence action the plaintiff does not sue the defendant for the

[198] [1986] I.L.R.M., at 636 (Sup. Ct., *per* Walsh, J.), adopting this description from Dickson, J.'s judgment
in *Moran* v. *Pyle National (Canada)* Ltd., [1974] 2 W.W.R. 586, at 596, 43 D.L.R. (3d) 239, at
249 (Sup. Ct. Can., 1973). This approach had received support in *Abbot-Smith* v. *Governors of University
of Toronto*, 45 D.L.R. (2d) 672, at 696, (Nova Scotia Sup. Ct., *per* MacDonald, J. 1964), but in
the Privy Council decision of *Distillers Co. (Biochemicals) Ltd* v. *Thompson*, [1971] A.C. 458, at
467, Lord Pearson had criticised it as being too restrictive for the needs of modern times. One
commentator put the point more directly: "One is tempted to say that if this indeed is the law, the
law is an ass ...." Gerber, *Tort Liability in the Conflict of Laws* — I, 40 A.L.J. 44, at 45 (1966).
See also Webb & North, *supra*, at 1331, Fridman, *supra*, at 257. The decisions on contract are worth
comparing on this question: see, e.g., *Betham* v. *Fernie*, 4 I.C.L.R. 92 (Com. Pleas, 1854), *Kisbey*
v. *Chester & Holyhead Ry. Co.*, 6 I.C.L.R. 393 (Com. Pleas, 1857), *Reilly* v. *White*, 11 I.C.L.R.
138 (Exch., 1860), *Kelly* v. *Dixon*, I.R. 6 C.L. 25 (Q.B., 1870), *Deane* v. *Sandford*, I.R. 9 C.L.
228 (Q.B., 1875).

[199] [1986] I.L.R.M., at 636.

[200] Cf. *Monaghan* v. *Swan & Co.*, unreported, Circuit Appeal, McLoughlin, J., December 1961 discussed
in *Locus of Tort*, 96 Ir. L.T. & Sol. J. 93 (1962), Webb & North, *supra*, at 1328, fn. 58a, McClean,
supra, at 1000, Hebertson, *supra*, at 375, fn. 61. A number of decisions on malicious injury should
also be noted, though these tend to rely on analogies with criminal law and are to a large degree insensitive
to policy considerations: see *Fermanagh Co. Co.* v. *Farrendon*, [1923] 2 I.R. 180 (N.I.C.A.),
Fermanagh Co. Co. v. *Board of Education of Donegal Presbytery*, [1923] 2 I.R. 184 (C.A., N.I.),
Canning v. *Donegal Co. Co.*, [1961] Ir. Jur. Rep. 7 (High Ct., Budd, J., 1960). More recent decisions
are discussed by D. Greer & V. Mitchell, *Compensation for Criminal Damage to Property*, 44-46 (1982).
The "last event" approach in torts litigation was favoured in the American Law Institute's first
Restatement of the Conflict of Laws, section 377 (1934), and in several (though far from all) decisions
on negligence in the United States courts: see *Morse*, 120-121, Webb and North, *Thoughts on the
Place of Commission of a Non-Statutory Tort*, 14 I.C.L.Q. 1314, 1317-1320 (1965); cf. the New Zealand
decisions of *Adastra Aviation* v. *Airparts (N.Z.).*, [1964] N.Z.L.R. 393, at 395, (Sup. Ct., Hardie
Boys, J., 1963).
In many decisions on defamation and misrepresentation also, in a number of countries, the courts
have favoured the "last event" test (though some of these decisions are not inconsistent with the view
that jurisdiction could also have rested, as an alternative, on the place where the defendant's conduct
took place): Cf. Webb and North, *supra*, at 1334, 1337, *Evans (Joseph) & Sons* v. *Stein (John G)
& Co.*, 7 F. 65, 12 S.L.T. 143, (1904), *Thomson* v. *Kindell*, 1910 2 S.L.T. 442, *Kroch* v. *Rossell
et Compagnie Société de Personnes à Responsabilité Limitée*, [1937] 1 All E.R. 725 (C.A.), *Bata*
v. *Bata*, [1948] W.N. 366 (C.A., 1948), *Eyre* v. *Nationwide News Proprietary Ltd.*, [1967] N.Z.L.R.
851 (Sup. Ct., Wellington, McGregor, J.), *Jenner* v. *Sun Oil Co.*, [1952] O.R. 240, [1952] 2 D.L.R.
526 (Ont. H. Ct., McRuer, C.J.), *Pindling* v. *National Broadcasting Corp.*, 49 O.R. (2d) 58 (High
Ct., Montgomery, J., 1984), *Original Blouse Co. Ltd.* v. *Bruck Mills Ltd.*, 42 D.L.R. (2d) 174 (B.C.
Sup. Ct., Aikins J., in Chambers, 1963), *Diamond* v. *Bank of London and Montreal Ltd.*, [1979]
2 W.L.R. 228 (C.A., 1978). In the latter decision, Lord Denning M.R. said (at 234):
"The truth is that each tort has to be considered on its own to see where it is committed. In many
torts the place may be where the damage is done ... Every tort must be considered separately.
In the case of fraudulent misrepresentation it seems to me that the tort is committed at the place
where the representation is received and acted upon; and not the place from which it was sent.
Logically, it seems to me, the same applies to a negligent misrepresentation by telephone or by
telex. It is committed where it is received and acted upon."

[201] Goodrich, *Conflict of Laws* (2nd ed., 1938), p. 236. See also *Cheshire*, 3rd ed., 1947, p. 386, Cowen,
The Locus Delicti in English Private International Law, 25 Br. Yrbk of Internat. L. 394, at 396, 398
(1948).

act of negligence but because the negligence has caused him damage. But, as Walsh, J. observed, the counterweight to this argument is that "it can equally be said that the plaintiff does not sue the defendant because he has suffered damage but because that damage was caused by the defendant's negligence."[202]

Rather than entertain these somewhat sterile modes of argument, Walsh, J. adopted an approach harmonising with the "interest analysis" favoured in much of modern conflicts thinking:

> "It can be argued that the State in which the injury occurs has a legitimate interest in the application of its laws to the victim of the tort[203] and it should facilitate compensation of a victim by permitting him to sue, within the jurisdiction, a foreign manufacturer of defective goods.[204] For all practical purposes it would not be a real option if he was obliged to sue the foreign manufacturer in that manufacturer's foreign place of business. On the other hand if the manufacturer has no assets within the jurisdiction there is no guarantee that judgment can be enforced abroad. But that also raises the question of whether in a case where the injury occurs in a country in which the defendant could not reasonably have anticipated or which has only a passing connection with the injured plaintiff the application of the 'last event' approach is not inappropriate."[205]

The "place of acting" approach

The third approach identifies as the *locus delicti* the place where the defendant's conduct[206] occurred.[207] It has the support of a number of cases in England,[208] Canada,[209] Australia[210] and Israel.[211] The argument most frequently put forward in favour of this approach is that the defendant is entitled to be judged in accordance with the standard under which he acted.[212] But, as Walsh, J. observed, " [t]hat appears to overlook the fact that the plaintiff also has a right to be judged according to the law under which he is living when injured."[213]

The "substance of the cause of action" approach

Another approach that has received much support over the past twenty years or so is what may be called the "substance of the cause of action" approach. It first surfaced in England in *Cordova Land Co. Ltd.* v. *Victor Brothers Inc.*,[214] and

---

[202] [1986] I.L.R.M., at 635.

[203] Cf. *Moran* v. *Pyle National (Canada) Ltd.*, [1974] 2 W.W.R. at p. 596, 43 D.L.R. (3d), at 251 (*per* Dickson, J), *Morse*, at 119.

[204] Cf. Bissett-Johnson, *supra*, at 554. See also *Vile* v. *von Wendt*, 20 O.R. (2d) 513, at 518 (High Ct., Linden, J., 1979).

[205] [1986] I.L.R.M., at 635.

[206] Or omission, though, as Walsh, J. observed (at 632), "in the case of omissions there may be certain conceptual difficulties as it can be said that a person's failure to act frequently has no physical location."

[207] Cf. *Butler* v. *Bianconi*, 11 Ir. L.R. 286 (Q.B., Blackburne, C.J., 1847). Cf. Fitzgerald, J.'s observations in *Deane* v. *Sandford*, I.R. 9 C.L. 228, at 232 (Q.B., 1875), a wrongful dismissal case. *Bevan* v. *Gillows & Co.*, 40 I.L.T.R. 251 (K.B. Div., 1906) may perhaps be interpreted as being premised on acceptance of the "place of acting" approach. See also *Quinn* v. *Kelly*, [1951] Ir. Jur. Rep. 45 (Circuit Ct., Judge Fawsitt, 1943).

[208] *Monro (George) Ltd.* v. *American Cyanamid and Chemical Corporation*, [1944] K.B. 432, at 439 (*per* Goddard, L.J.) and 441 (*per* du Parcq, L.J.).

[209] *Anderson* v. *Nobels Explosive Co.*, 12 O.L.R. 644 (Div. Ct., 1906), *Paul* v. *Chandler & Fisher Ltd.*, [1924] 2 D.L.R. 479 (Ont. Sup. Ct., Orde, J., 1923), *Beck* v. *Willard Chocolate Co. Ltd.*, [1924] 2 D.L.R. 1140 (N.S., Sup. Ct.).

[210] Cf. *Koop* v. *Bebb*, 84 C.L.R. 626 (1951).

[211] *Mizachi* v. *Nobel's Explosives Co. Ltd.*, (1978) (11) 32 P.D. 115, cited and criticised by Goldstein, 14 Israel L. Rev. 504 (1979).

[212] See, e.g. Fridman, *supra*, at 262.

[213] [1986] I.L.R.M., at 632. See also S. Stromholm, *Torts in the Conflict of Laws: A Comparative Survey* (1961), 133, Ehrenzweig, *The Place of Acting in International Multistate Torts: Law and Reason versus the Restatement*, 36 Minn. L. Rev. 1, at 2 (1951).

[214] [1966] 1 W.L.R. 793 (Q.B. Div., Winn, J., 1964).

received the *imprimatur* of the Privy Council in the *Distillers*[215] case, where Lord Pearson said:

> "The right approach is, when the tort is complete to look back over the series of events constituting it and ask the question, where in substance did this course of action arise?"

In *Distillers*, however, Lord Pearson declined[216] to express any opinion as to what rule should apply where the defendant acted negligently in one country and the plaintiff was injured in another.

In turn, *Distillers* has received support in English,[217] New Zealand[218] and Australian[219] cases.

A case of some interest in this context is *Walsh* v. *Great Western Ry. Co.*,[220] in 1872. The action, under Lord Campbell's Act, concerned the death of a sailor in the course of his employment on board the defendant's ship, during the passage from Milford to Waterford, when a boiler exploded on account of corrosion. The accident occurred at sea, outside the jurisdiction of the Irish courts. But the deceased sailor's widow argued that the process of corrosion must have extended over a period of at least three months beforehand during which time the ship, on several occasions, had been in Ireland. Deasy, B., of the Court of Exchequer, was not receptive to this line of argument and declined to make an order for substituted service on the defendant company's agents in Ireland. He said:

> "The negligence consisted in dispatching the steamer from Milford while the boiler was in an improper state."[221]

The "real and substantial" connection approach

In 1973, in *Moran* v. *Pyle National (Canada) Ltd.*,[222] the Supreme Court of Canada developed further the approach that had been favoured in the *Distillers* case. Dickson, J. discerned in *Distillers* a move "toward a form of real and substantial test ..." He considered that:

> "[g]enerally speaking, in determining where a tort has been committed, it is unnecessary, and unwise, to have resort to any arbitrary set of rules. The place of acting and the place of harm theories are too arbitrary and inflexible to be recognised in contemporary jurisprudence. In the *Distillers* case and again in the *Cordova*[223] case a real and substantial connection text was hinted at. Cheshire[224] has suggested a test very similar to this; the author says that it would not be inappropriate to regard a tort as having occurred in any country substantially affected by the defendant's activities or its consequences and the law of which is likely to have been in the reasonable contemplation of the parties."

[215] [1971] A.C., at 468.
[216] *Id.*, at 469,
[217] *Castree* v. *Squibb (E.R. & Sons) Ltd.*, [1980] 1 W.L.R. 1248, *Multinational Gas Services Ltd.*, [1983] Ch. 258.
[218] *My* v. *Toyota Motor Co. Ltd.*, [1972] 2 N.Z.L.R. 113 (Sup. Ct., Wellington, Wild, C.J.).
[219] *Buttigeig* v. *Universal Terminal & Stevedoring Corporation*, [1972] V.R. 626 (Sup. Ct., Crockett, J., 1971), *Hall* v. *Australian Capital Territory Electricity Authority*, 31 A.L.R. 557 (Sup. Ct., of N.S.W. in exercise of Fed. Jur., Master Sharpe, 1980), *Jacobs* v. *Australian Abrasives Pty. Ltd.*, [1971] V.R. 92 (Sup. Ct. (in Chambers), Burbury, C.J.), *MacGregory* v. *Application des Gaz*, [1976] Qd. R. 175 (Sup. Ct., Brisbane, Mathews, J., 1975). But cf. *Nygh*, 36.
[220] 6 Ir. R. C. L. 532 (Exch., 1872).
[221] *Id.*, at 533. Cf. *Soutar* v. *Peters*, 1912 1 S.L.T. 111 (Ct. of Session, Outer House, Lord Ormsdale).
[222] [1974] 2 W.W.R. at pp. 597-598, 43 D.L.R. (3d), at p. 250. *Moran* has been applied in a number of decisions, including *Skyrotors Ltd.* v. *Carsere Technical Industries Ltd.*, 26 O.R. (2d) 207 (High Ct., Osler, J., 1979) and *Drost* v. *Freightliners of Canada Ltd.*, 2 C.C.L.T. 49 (Sask, Q.B., Johnson J., 1976).
[223] *Cordova Land Co. Ltd.* v. *Victor Bros Ltd.*, [1986] 1 W.L.R. 793.
[224] 8th ed., 1970, p. 281.

The elective approach

The elective approach permits the plaintiff to select from the relevant legal systems the one that is most favourable to him. Clearly, this gives generous protection to the interests of the injured party. The elective approach received some support in German law.[225] More recently the European Court of Justice in *Handelskwekerij G.J. Bier B.V.* v. *Mines De Potasse d'Alsace S.A.*[226] has endorsed this procedure when applying Article 5 (3) of the Convention on Jurisdiction and Enforcement of Judgments in Civil and Commercial Matters. Article 5 (3) refers to 'the place where the harmful event occurred'. In *Bier,* it was alleged that a French company had polluted the river Rhine in France, causing damage to the plaintiff's commercial nursery in the Netherlands. The question was whether the Netherland courts had jurisdiction under Article 5(3).

In favouring the elective approach the European Court of Justice stated:

"The form of words 'the place where the harmful event occurred', used in all the language versions of the Convention, leaves open the question of whether, in the situation described, it is necessary, in determining jurisdiction, to choose as the connecting factor the place of the event giving rise to the damage, or the place where the damage occurred, or to accept the plaintiff has an option between the one and the other of those two connecting factors. As regards this, it is well to point out that the place of the event giving rise to the damage no less than the place where the damage occurred can, depending on the case, constitute a significant connecting factor from the point of view of jurisdiction. Liability in tort, delict or quasi-delict can only arise provided that a causal connexion can be established between the damage and the event in which that damage originates. Taking into account the close connexion between the component parts of every sort of liability, it does not appear appropriate to opt for one of the two connecting factors mentioned to the exclusion of the other, since each of them can, depending on the circumstances, be particularly helpful from the point of view of the evidence and of the conduct of the proceedings. To exclude one option appears all the more undesirable in that, by its comprehensive form of words, Art. 5(3) of the Convention covers a wide diversity of kinds of liability. Thus the meaning of the expression 'place where the harmful event occurred' in Art. 5(3) must be established in such a way as to acknowledge that the plaintiff has an option to commence proceedings either at the place where the damage occurred or at the place of the event giving rise to it."[227]

In *Grehan* v. *Medical Incorporated and Valley Pines Association,*[228] the Supreme Court favoured an approach which in essence is an elective one. Walsh, J. (for the Court) noted that, in determining whether or not a tort was committed within the State within the meaning of Order 11, rule 1(*f*), it was "clear that the issue is not merely a mechanical one because that would inevitably lead to arbitrary results."[229] He continued:

"The Court must have regard to the implications for the plaintiff or the defendant if the trial is to take place within the State. The task of the Court is to interpret and to apply the rule in a way designed to ensure that justice and practical common sense prevail. The Court therefore should interpret the rule in the light of a broad policy and in the light of its choice of law implications.[230] If more than one possible

---

[225] Cf. *Morse,* 125-126, *Collins,* 59-60, Kuratowski, *Torts in Private International Law,* 1 I.L.Q. 172, at 182-183 (1947).

[226] [1976] E.C.R. 1735.

[227] *Id.,* at 1746.

[228] [1986] I.L.R.M. 627 (Sup. Ct.).

[229] *Id.,* at 637.

[230] For consideration of this aspect of the case, see *infra.,* pp. 578-580.

interpretation of the rule is available the one which serves to encourage the operation of sensible choice of rules should be followed rather than one which would tend to frustrate them.''[231]

Walsh, J., considered that the Irish courts should be sufficiently flexible to be capable of responding to the individual issues presented in each case and to the social and economic dimensions of applying any particular choice of law rule in the proceedings in question.[232] He went on:

> "As to jurisdiction, if it appears that any significant element in the commission of the tort occurs within this jurisdiction then the plaintiff will have at least fulfilled the threshold requirements set out in O.11, r.1(f). But that is not sufficient to raise a presumption or an inference that the Court should exercise discretion in favour of making an order for service out of the jurisdiction. Any approach which insists on any one constituent element of the commission of the tort occurring within the jurisdiction can only give rise to difficulty. [In a]ny case before the Court which clearly calls for the hearing of the proceedings in Ireland and for the application of Irish law to the case [an] order for service outside the jurisdiction should not be denied merely because of the fact that some significant element or elements in its commission occurred outside the jurisdiction. For example, in many cases it would be quite inappropriate that the invocation either of 'the place of injury' or 'the last event rule' should deny to a plaintiff the right of service out of the jurisdiction. It seems to me sufficient if *any* significant element has occurred within the jurisdiction. To require that the element should be *the most* significant one could render a plaintiff's task more uncertain and the outcome more arbitrary.''[233]

Walsh, J. noted that:

> "There is, of course, a heavy burden on the Court to examine the circumstances of each case before exercising its discretion to make an order for service out of the jurisdiction. It would be clearly wrong to refuse it on the application of any technical rule which insists on one element occurring in the jurisdiction as it would be equally inappropriate if the Court were to permit service out of the jurisdiction where the case only had a tenuous connection with the country on its facts and in terms of the law likely to govern questions of liability and related matters.''[234]

In *Grehan*, the plaintiff had claimed that a heart valve which was inserted in his heart by open heart surgery in a hospital in Dublin was defective, causing him injury. The second-named defendants had manufactured the heart valve[235] in California and had supplied it to the first-named defendants in the United States. The second-named defendants attempted unsuccessfully to resist an order for service out of the jurisdiction, made by the High Court. Their appeal to the Supreme Court was unsuccessful.

Applying the view that an order for service *ex juris* might be justified if any significant element occurred within the jurisdiction, Walsh, J. said:

> "Admittedly other significant elements occurred outside this jurisdiction but for the reasons already given that should not preclude the Court from making the order. The case cannot be said to have only a tenuous connection with this jurisdiction. The appliance was fitted to the plaintiff's heart in this jurisdiction and the injury alleged occurred here. The plaintiff might well have instituted his proceedings in the United States where the law on products liability would be much more favourable to him. However he has

---

[231] [1986] I.L.R.M., at 637. In *Grehan* Walsh, J. reviewed the choice of law rules, roundly criticising the rule in *Phillips* v. *Eyre* as having ''nothing to recommend it because it is capable of producing quite arbitrary decisions and it is a mixture of parochialism and a vehicle for being, in some cases, unduly generous to the plaintiff and, in others, unduly harsh.'' *Id.* See further *infra*, pp. 578-580.
[232] *Id.*, at 638.
[233] *Id.* Cf. the contract case of *Reilly* v. *White*, 11 I.C.L.R. 138, at 141 (Exch., *per* Pigot, C.B., 1860).
[234] [1986] I.L.R.M., at 638.
[235] Or at least a component part of the heart valve: *Id.*, at 629.

chosen to have Irish law applied in proceedings in Ireland where he resides and in which the appliance was fitted. In my view, the elements which occurred in this jurisdiction are sufficiently significant to warrant the order made.''[236]

Implications of Grehan

Grehan appears to be a strongly "pro-plaintiff" decision. In removing technical jurisdictional obstacles, it is in harmony with the approach adopted by the European Court of Justice in *Bier*. It would, however, be unwise to overlook Walsh J.'s statement that the Court "must have regard to the implications for the plaintiff *or the defendant* if the trial is to take place within the State.''[237] Clearly, the interests of the defendant cannot be ignored. It remains to be seen whether the courts in applications under Rule 1 (f) of Order 11 will make any serious investigation of the choice of law dimensions of the case. If, as *Grehan* indicates, the rule in *Phillips* v. *Eyre* should be replaced by a less specific, more contextual, approach,[238] it would seem that the courts in some applications under Rule 1(f) could have a great deal of work to do. This is scarcely a criticism of *Grehan,* however; an inflexible rule may be easier to apply but its results would be less fair to the parties.

(g) *any injunction is sought as to anything to be done within the jurisdiction, or any nuisance within the jurisdiction is sought to be prevented or removed whether damages are or are not also sought in respect thereof*[239]

The purpose of this paragraph is to allow relief to be given as regards something that is to be done within the jurisdiction.[240] The claim for an injunction must be *bona fide*[241]. The court should be satisfied not only that the plaintiff has a good cause of action for an injunction but also that there is a reasonable probability that he will obtain an injunction.

In *Caudron* v. *Air Zaire,*[242] the Supreme Court discussed in detail the scope of this ground for service out of the jurisdiction. The plaintiffs were ex-employees of the defendant, the national airline of Zaire. The plaintiffs were owed a substantial sum of money for arrears of salary and loss of pension rights and, in some instances, sought damages for breach of contract, including wrongful dismissal. There was no question of successfully sustaining proceedings in this country for breach of contract, as the contracts had been neither made nor broken here, nor had any connection with Irish law.

What attracted the plaintiffs to Ireland was the fact that a valuable Boeing 737 plane was within the Irish jurisdiction. It had been delivered to Dublin Airport for repairs, under a contract with Aer Lingus and Aer Rianta. The amount owing on this contract was about £1.8 million, and Aer Lingus and Aer Rianta claimed a lien on the plane until that amount was satisfied.

The plaintiffs had run into difficulties in pursuing their claim abroad. Proceedings brought by them in Belgium had proved unrewarding as the Belgian courts lacked

---

[236] *Id.,* at 638-639.

[237] *Id.,* at 637 (emphasis added).

[238] Cf. *infra,* pp. 578-580.

[239] Order 11, Rule 1(g); *Tozier* v. *Hawkins,* 15 Q.B.D. 650 (1885); *British Marine Assoc.* v. *Macinnes* 31 Sol. Jo. 95 (1886), *"Morocco Bound" Ltd. Syndicate* v. *Harris* [1895] 1 Ch. 534; *Joynt* v. *M'Crum* [1899] I.R. 217 (Chatterton, V.C.): *Dunlop* v. *Dunlop Rubber Co. Ltd.* [1921] A.C. 367, (H.L.Ir.) aff'g. [1921] 1 I.R. 173 (C.A., 1920) and [1920] 1 I.R. 280 (Powell, J.), *Trevethick* v. *Leary* 28 I.L.T.R. 8 (Q.B. Div., Johnson, J., 1893).

[240] Cf. *Spurway* v. *Spurway,* [1894] 1 I.R. 385, at 402 (C.A., *per* Walker, C., 1893).

[241] *De Bernales* v. *New York Herald* [1893] 2 Q.B. 97.

[242] [1986] I.L.R.M. 10 (Sup. Ct., 1985, rev'g High Ct., Barr, J., 1985). For a preceptive analysis of the decision, see Gill, *Order XI, "Mareva Injunctions' and the Jurisdiction of the Irish Courts in Private International Law,* 4 Ir. L. Times (N.S.) 70 (1986).

jurisdiction. The plaintiffs hoped to be able to obtain an order from the Irish courts preserving the plane as an asset within the jurisdiction, ready to satisfy a judgment against the defendant company which would have had to be obtained in a foreign court. It seemed clear that, even with the amount of £1.8 million subtracted, the plane was worth more than enough to satisfy the plaintiffs' claims.

The plaintiffs therefore, in the endorsement of their plenary summons, sought an injunction, restraining the defendant company from removing out of the jurisdiction, parting with possession of, or selling or mortgaging or otherwise disposing of the plane, so as to reduce its unencumbered value to less than the amount of their claims. They also sought damages for breach of contract.

The plaintiffs successfully applied to court seeking leave to serve the plenary summons outside the jurisdiction. The plaintiffs then sought a *Mareva* injunction, pending the determination of the action. The defendant company resisted this application and sought an order[244] setting aside the original order giving leave to serve the plenary summons outside the jurisdiction.

Barr, J. considered that the issue resolved itself into "one basic question", namely, whether the right to a *Mareva* injunction, and nothing more, brings a claimant within the ambit of rule 1(g) of Order 11, thus entitling the court to permit service outside the jurisdiction. Barr, J. drew much inspiration from the statutory origin of granting relief by way of injunction—section 28(8) of the Supreme Court of Judicature (Ireland) Act 1877. That section permitted an injunction by an interlocutory order to be granted "in all cases in which it shall appear to the court to be just or convenient that such an order shall be made ..."

Rule 1(g) of Order 11 had not been changed since its articulation in the Rules of the Supreme Court (Ireland) 1905, made pursuant to the 1877 Act. In contrast to other parts of the rule, Rule 1(g) did not refer to "the action" or the "proceeding", and specified "any injunction" without qualification.

Barr, J. considered that:

> "[i]t follows therefore, having regard to the guiding principle laid down in s. 28(8) of the 1877 Act, that where the court is satisfied that in justice or convenience an injunction should be granted as to property of the proposed defendant within its jurisdiction, then, whether the injunction amounts to substantive relief in the proposed action or not, service out should be granted."[245]

In view of the implicit acceptance by the defendant airline that substantial monies were owing to the employees and that the only free asset outside Zaire which might be availed of by the plaintiffs was the plane in Ireland, and in view of the facts that the plaintiffs' prospects of executing in Zaire on foot of a judgment were remote, Barr, J. was satisfied that the plaintiffs were entitled to the order permitting service out of the jurisdiction.

Barr, J. distinguished the English case of *The Siskina*[246] on the basis that the relevant English rule which had originally been drafted on the same lines as the Irish rule, had been altered in 1965,[247] so as to incorporate the phrase "the action" and substitute the phrase "an injunction" for "any injunction". These "material

---

[243] Under Order 12, rule 26 of the Rules of the Superior Courts 1962. Rule 26 is unchanged in the 1986 Rules.

[244] [1986] I.L.R.M., at 13.

[245] *Id.*

[246] [1979] A.C. 210 (H.L. (Eng.), 1977).

[247] R.S.C. 1965, Order 11, r. (1)(1)(i), which permits service out of the jurisdiction:

"if in the action begun by the writ an injunction is sought ordering the defendant to do or refrain from doing anything within the jurisdiction (whether or not damages are also claimed in respect of a failure to do or the doing of that thing)."

alterations''[248], Barr, J. noted, had been relied on by Lord Diplock in his rejection of the majority judgments in the Court of Appeal.

The Supreme Court reversed. Finlay, C.J., for the court, succinctly summarised the principal issue between the parties:

> "The plaintiffs contend that, once the injunction by way of *Mareva* injunction is *bona fide* sought by them, then, irrespective of whether it is temporary or ancillary in nature as distinct from being a substantive part of their claim, it brings their originating summons within O. 11 r.1(g) and that that, being so, they are automatically entitled to add as a further claim to be determined on that summons, their claim for damages for breach of contract.
>
> The defendants, on the other hand, contend, firstly, that in order for the court to have jurisdiction to issue and serve notice of an originating summons out of the jurisdiction, the injunction sought therein would have to be the substantive or part of the substantive relief claimed and not a relief of an interlocutory or ancillary nature and, secondly, and in the alternative, that, even if it was within the jurisdiction of the court to give liberty to issue and serve out of the jurisdiction in cases where a summons sought an interlocutory or ancillary jurisdiction, it could not do so in any case where there was added to that claim in the originating summons any other claim which was not of itself within one of the sub-rules of Order 11 rule 1 capable of being the subject matter of an order giving liberty to serve out of the jurisdiction.''[249]

Finlay, P. accepted[250] that many forms of interim and interlocutory relief might properly be obtained between the issue of the originating summons and the final determination of the claim endorsed on it. But these were not the relief sought in the action before the Court, nor "on the true interpretation of the Rules, matters which should be claimed by way of endorsement on the summons itself.''[251]

The Chief Justice considered that when the phrase "any injunction was sought" is used in Order 11, rule 1(g), it had to be interpreted in the light of the provisions of Order 11, rule 1 itself, which provide for service out of the jurisdiction of an originating summons or notice of an originating summons:

> "The injunction sought, referred to in sub-rule (g), must therefore, on the interpretation of the order and rule, freed from any authority, be an injunction necessarily and properly sought in the originating summons, which is the document with the issue and service of which outside the jurisdiction the entire order is concerned. It cannot, in my opinion, be an injunction which is properly sought not as part of the endorsement of claim on the summons but rather by means of a motion *ex parte* or on notice.''[252]

Finlay C.J. noted that the "real relief"[253] sought by the plaintiffs by way of injunction was a temporary injunction pending the determination of the action only:

> "The distinction between that type of relief by way of injunction, which I would describe as ancillary or interlocutory, and an injunction of a permanent nature to be obtained at the final determination of the action is indicated by the fact that the plaintiffs, in order to gain the relief which they sought by way of injunction from the High Court, were obliged to seek and obtain [originally], not only liberty to issue and serve notice of their summons out of the jurisdiction upon the defendants but also specifically an order purporting to grant them liberty to serve a notice of motion for the relief by way of injunction out of the jurisdiction.''[254]

---

[248] [1986] I.L.R.M., at 16.
[249] *Id.*, at 20.
[250] *Id.*, at 21.
[251] *Id.*
[252] *Id.*
[253] *Id.*
[254] *Id.*

In the absence of any relevant Irish decisions on rule 1(g) being cited to the Court, Finlay, C.J. was "reinforced"[255] in the view he had taken on its interpretation by the House of Lords decision in *The Siskina*.[256] He rejected the argument by counsel for the plaintiffs that that case should be distinguished in view of the different wording of the English rule. He could "not see that this distinction should alter the principle of the decision nor that it makes any difference to the true interpretation of the rule."[257] He added:

> "As I have already indicated, the injunction must be sought in something and, in my view, under the rule in Ireland the injunction must be properly and necessarily sought in the endorsement of claim contained on the originating summons which is what the plaintiffs claim in the action."[258]

Furthermore, a consideration of the opinions in *The Siskina* did not indicate to the Chief Justice that any reliance was placed on the use of the words changed in 1965, "particularly, as the judgments refer to and appear to interpret in identical terms the rule in England previously in force which is, for practical purposes, identical to our sub-rule (g)".[259]

As far as matters of policy were concerned, the plaintiffs pressed the Court to favour Lord Denning M.R.'s approach in the Court of Appeal in *The Siskina*.[260] Finlay, C.J. noted that it was:

> "clear from the decision of Lord Denning M.R. that he was largely influenced by what he described as two policy considerations by reason of which the judges should themselves extend the jurisdiction of the High Court to authorise service of its process out of the jurisdiction, they being: 1. to enable it to adjudicate upon the merits of actions of any kind which a plaintiff wished to bring against a foreign defendant so long as the defendant had some assets belonging to him in England, or 2. so as to enable the High Court to attack those assets so that they might be kept available to satisfy some future judgment of a foreign court which has got jurisdiction to adjudicate on the dispute between the plaintiffs and the foreign defendant."[261]

The Chief Justice considered that there could be "little doubt"[262] that such a policy of law would be attractive. The plaintiffs, on the affidavits, faced considerable hardship. There might, indeed, be "much to be said"[263] for extending the concept of the Admiralty action *in rem* "to what has now become an even more mobile and frequently used method of transportation than was shipping at the time of the development of the Admiralty Case."[264] But it seemed to the Chief Justice to be "wholly inappropriate for this Court to seek to implement such a policy, which would appear to be a matter for international convention or agreement and for the introduction of substantive domestic legislation, by an interpretation of a statutory rule which is not open on the rule itself."[265]

---

[255] *Id.*
[256] *Supra.*
[257] [1986] I.L.R.M., at 22.
[258] *Id.*
[259] *Id.*
[260] [1979] A.C. 210 T(H.L. (Eng.), 1977).
[261] [1986] I.L.R.M., at 23.
[262] *Id.*
[263] *Id.*
[264] *Id.*
[265] *Id.*

(*h*) *any person out of the jurisdiction is a necessary or proper party to an action properly*[266] *brought against some other person duly served within the jurisdiction.*[267]

In *Ross* v. *Eason & Son Ltd.*[268] and *Sharples* v. *Eason & Son Ltd.*[269] the Dublin newsagents, Eason & Son, were joined as defendants with the publishers of a London newspaper in an action for libel contained in papers sold by Easons who were unaware of the libel and were not agents of the publishers. In the former case the summons against Easons was issued only after the London publishers had refused to nominate a solicitor to accept service in Dublin, while in the latter the action against Easons was discontinued as soon as leave to serve a concurrent summons on the London publishers was received and notice of trial served on them. It was held that the actions against Eason & Son were not *bona fide* actions but an abuse of the rule, which should not be sanctioned. Eason & Son were introduced merely for the purpose of bringing the other defendants within the jurisdiction and the actions were not ones properly brought against them within the jurisdiction. The Irish Court of Appeal applied the test adumbrated by the English Court of Appeal in *Witted* v. *Galbraith:*[270]

"Supposing that both the defendant firms were resident within the jurisdiction, would they both have been joined in the action?"

These two cases were distinguished in *Cooney* v. *Wilson and Henderson,*[271] an action for libel contained in certain posters written and printed by the defendant, Wilson, who lived in England. The posters were widely circulated in Ireland in the vicinity of the plaintiff's residence by Henderson, a bill-poster resident in Ireland, who was employed by Wilson for that purpose. Henderson was "no mark for damages or costs".[272] It was held[273] that, since both defendants were proper parties if they were within the jurisdiction, and since the action clearly lay against the party actually resident within the jurisdiction, the other party might be served just as if he also were resident within the jurisdiction.

Holmes, L.J. said:

"Here an English principal acted through an Irish agent. Both are responsible for the publication. It is said that the Irish defendant is too poor to pay damages; but that is no reason for holding that the plaintiff was not justified in suing him for what is *prima facie* a most serious libel, and for joining with him another person equally responsible. The action is properly brought against the Irishman; and the Englishman is a proper defendant to it. Hence the case comes within the rule ..."[274]

The Court distinguished *Ross* v. *Eason & Sons Ltd.* and *Sharples* v. *Eason & Sons Ltd.* on the basis that, in the *Ross* case, there had been "no real cause of action against Eason & Son".[275] Similarly in the *Sharples* case, the basis of the Court's order had been that the conduct of the plaintiff had "amounted to an admission that he had no cause of action against Eason & Son, and that the foundation for the order

---

[266] See *Boyd* v. *Lee Guinness, Ltd.,* [1963] N.I. 49 (C.A., 1962).

[267] See *Joynt* v. *M'Crum,* [1899] 1 I.R. 217 (Chatterton, V.C.).

[268] [1911] 2 I.R. 459.

[269] [1911] 2 I.R. 436.

[270] [1893] 1 Q.B. 577, at 579.

[271] [1913] 2 I.R. 402.

[272] *Id.,* at 403.

[273] Adopting a test laid down in *Massey* v. *Heynes,* 21 Q.B.D. 330 (1888).

[274] [1913] 2 I.R., at 409.

[275] *Id.,* at 407 (*per* O'Brien L.C.). See also *id.,* at 409 (*per* Cherry, L.J.).

for substitution of service had disappeared."[276] Moreover, in *Cooney,* there was the relationship of principal and agent between the two defendants, and, Cherry, L.J. observed; " [p]rincipal and agent usually and properly are sued together in such cases as this."[277]

The three Irish cases were discussed recently by the English Court of Appeal in *Multinational Gas Co.* v. *Multinational Gas Services Ltd.*[278] The *Eason* cases met with unqualified support. *Cooney,* however, provoked some disagreement. May, L.J. (dissenting) referred to the case with apparent approval, but Dillon, L.J. observed:

> "It was not clear whether it was a factor in the minds of the court [in *Cooney's* case] that the plaintiff might reasonably have wanted to sue the [billposter] in Ireland despite [his] poverty, as the most obvious way of clearing the plaintiff's name in Ireland from a very grave libel. Unless, however, the court did have some such factor in mind, I find it difficult to support *Cooney's* case. Whether an action is properly brought against a particular defendant within the meaning of sub-head must surely depend on the substance of the matter in the light of all the circumstances, and not on the mere form of the pleading and whether there is technically a cause of action."[279]

The *Cooney* and the *Eason* cases were decided at a time when there was no provision in the rules of court comparable to the present Order 11, Rule 1(f). All three cases concerned torts alleged to have been committed within the jurisdiction, so a similar case would now probably fall to be decided under sub-head (f). However, they are still leading authorities on the application of sub-head (h).

An example of a case where the latter sub-head would be more likely to be invoked nowadays is provided by the Northern Ireland case of *Waddell* v. *Norton,*[280] which concerned a tort committed outside the jurisdiction. Two cars, one driven by a resident of Northern Ireland and the other by a resident of the Republic, were involved in a collision in the Republic. Both drivers were killed, as were all the passengers but one, who was injured. The surviving passenger and the personal representative of one of the deceased passengers brought an action in Northern Ireland against the personal representatives of the two drivers. Lord McDermott, applying the *Witted* v. *Galbraith* test already referred to, found that the action was "properly brought" within the meaning of Order 11, Rule 1(h). He did so despite a submission based on police evidence which tended to suggest that the Northern Ireland driver had not been to blame for the collision. In *The Brabo*[281] the House of Lords had held that an action which, on the accepted facts, was bound in point of law to fail against the parties served within the jurisdiction was not "properly brought" within the meaning of the rule. Lord McDermott distinguished the instant case:

> "Though Lord Porter said,[282] 'The plaintiff must show to the satisfaction of the court that he has a probable cause of action,' the opinions delivered do not attempt to define the words 'properly brought' and do not seem to me to suggest that in cases, such as present, which raise issues of fact rather than law, the court should proceed to a finding of fact in order to determine whether the action is 'properly brought'. That is not to say that the evidence available against those served within the jurisdiction is never to be examined or assessed. It may be so flimsy or suspect as to indicate that those served

---

[276] *Id.,* at 408 (*per* Holmes, L.J.).

[277] *Id.,* at 409. See also *McCartan* v. *Hutton & Co. Ltd.,* 56 I.L.T.R. 152 (C.A., 1922), aff'g *id.,* 131 (K.B. Div., 1922).

[278] [1983] Ch. 258 (C.A.).

[279] *Id.* at 285-286.

[280] [1966] N.I. 86.

[281] [1949] A.C. 326. See also *Ellinger* v. *Guinness, Mahon & Co.,* [1939] 4 All E.R. 16, *Strauss & Co.* v. *Goldschmid,* 1 T.L.R. 512 (1892). Cf. *M'Williams* v. *Gilbert and Millard Bros., Ltd.,* 47 I.L.T.R. 297 (K.B. Div., 1913).

[282] [1949] A.C., 326, at 339-40.

have been joined in order to bring the application within the paragraph (*h*), or the evidence to the contrary may be so cogent and overwhelming as to carry conviction even in the course of interlocutory proceedings. But I do not think such considerations apply in the case of a road accident like that with which I am now dealing. It was an occurrence that should never have happened, and it is a fair assumption from the circumstances that one or other or both drivers were at fault and that the plaintiffs accordingly have a right to relief against either or both defendants. [Counsel for defendant outside the jurisdiction] has contended, in his able argument, that the facts as now revealed show that the fault was not that of the [Northern Ireland] driver ... and, in consequence, that the claim against his personal representative is bound to fail. It may be that, ultimately, that view will prove to be right. But I cannot decide that as matters stand."[283]

The other defendant must have been "duly served within the jurisdiction". The court has no power to grant leave to serve a summons on a defendant resident out of the jurisdiction until the defendant within the jurisdiction has been actually served.[284] Nor is it sufficient that the other defendant has been served out of the jurisdiction under some other sub-head of Order 11 or has voluntarily submitted to the court's jurisdiction.[285] However, if the other defendant has become a defendant because he commenced an action as a plaintiff within the jurisdiction and was served with a counterclaim at his address for service, it has been held in England that the counterclaim is "properly brought against a person duly served within the jurisdiction" for the purpose of the rule.[286]

(*i*) *The proceeding relates to an infant or person of unsound mind domiciled in, or a citizen of, Ireland*[287]

(*j*) *The proceeding relates to an interpleader proceeding relating to property within the jurisdiction*[288]

The EEC Judgments Convention[289] does not allow the assumption of jurisdiction based on the *situs* of moveable property, so when it is implemented the presence of moveable property within the jurisdiction will not be available as a ground of jurisdiction in interpleader proceedings relating to the property, as against domiciliaries of EEC Member States.

(*k*) *The proceeding relates to an arbitration held or to be held within the jurisdiction*[290]

(*l*) *The proceeding relates to the enforcement of an award under Part III of the Arbitration Act 1980 or of the pecuniary obligations imposed by an award under Part IV of the Arbitration Act 1980*[291]

---

[283] [1966] N.I. 86, at 90-91.
[284] *Yorkshire Tannery and Boot Manufacturing Co. Ltd.* v. *Eglinton Chemical Co. Ltd.*, 54 L.J.Ch. 81 (1884). See also *Collins* v. *North British & Mercantile Insce. Co.*, [1894] 3 Ch. 228; *The Duc D'Aumale* [1903] P. 18; and *Tassell* v. *Hallen*, [1892] 1 Q.B. 321 where it is queried whether previous service on the other defendant is a condition precedent to an order being made under Order 11, notwithstanding the decision in the *Yorkshire Tannery* Case. Cf. *Dicey & Morris*, 217.
[285] *John Russell & Co. Ltd.* v. *Cayzer Irvine & Co. Ltd.* [1916] 2 A.C. 298.
[286] *Derby & Co. Ltd.* v. *Larsson*, [1976] 1 All E.R. 401. However, this decision turned to a large extent on the working of Order 15, rule 3 of the English Rules of the Supreme Court relating to counterclaims, which differs materially from the corresponding Irish Order (Order 21).
[287] Order 11, Rule 1 (i). Cf. *infra*, pp. 381-386.
[288] Order 11, Rule 1 (j). See *City of Dublin Steam Packet Co.* . *Cooper*, [1899] 2 I.R. 381 (Q.B. Div.), *Galabrun* v. *Bruce, Symes and Williams*, [1903] 2 I.R. 488 (K.B. Div., 1902), *Keane* v. *Crozier*, 27 I.L.T.R. 81 (Q.B. Div., 1893), *Spence* v. *Parkes*, [1900] 2 I.R. 619 (Q.B. Div.).
[289] See *infra*, pp. 181-191.
[290] Order 11, Rule 1(k).
[291] Order 11, Rule 1(l).

(m) *The proceeding is by a mortgage or mortgagor in relation to a mortgage*[292] *of personal property situate within the jurisdiction and seeks relief of the nature or kind following, that is to say sale, delivery of possession by the mortgagor, redemption, reconveyance, delivery of possession by the mortgagee; but does not seek (unless and so far as permissible under the sub-head(e) of this rule) any personal judgment or order for payment of any moneys due under the mortgage*[293]

This essentially *in rem* jurisdiction[294] fills the gap created by the English decision of *Deutsche National Bank* v. *Paul*,[295] which held that an action for foreclosure or redemption of a mortgage of personal property could not be treated as an action for breach of contract, in relation to which service *ex juris* might be permitted. Rule 1(m) is limited to property within the jurisdiction,[296] regardless of where the parties are domiciled or resident. So far as personal jurisdiction over persons outside Ireland is concerned, Rule 1(m), in express terms, makes it plain that it extends only to proceedings seeking personal judgment in respect of breach of contract or otherwise under Rule 1(e).[297]

(n) *The proceeding is brought under the provisions relating to carriage by air of the Air Navigation and Transport Act, 1936*[298]

(o) *The proceeding relates to a ship registed or required to be registered under the Mercantile Marine Act 1955, or any share or interest therein*[299]

(p) *The proceeding relates to the ownership of a trade mark registered or sought to be registered in the Industrial and Commercial Property Registration Office*[300]

JURISDICTION OVER ACTIONS *IN REM*

Actions *in personam* are actions "against a person". Actions *in rem* are proceedings against a *res* whereby the thing in question may be arrested and appropriated to satisfy the plaintiff's claim.

> "The action *in rem* is in essence a proceeding against property which, once instituted, may be made effective by the arrest and detention of the property proceeded against, and followed, if necessary, by the judical sale of the property and with the claim satisfied out of the proceeds of sale."[301]

---

[292] "Mortgage" here means a mortgage, charge or lien of any description; "mortgagee" means a party for the time being entitled to or interested in a mortgage; and "mortgagor" a party for the time being entitled to or interested in property subject to a mortgage: Order 11, Rule 1(l).

[293] Order 11, Rule 1(m). Cf. *MacNamara* v. *Ejector*, 6 Ir. L.R. 421 (Q.B., 1844), *M'Clelland* v. *Tyrrell*, 31 I.L.T.R. 84 (Ex., Chatterton, V.C. 1897).

[294] *Dicey & Morris*, 220, *McLeod*, 95.

[295] [1898] 1 Ch. 283 (Stirling, J.).

[296] Cf. *Cantieri Riuniti Dell'Adriatico di Monfalcone* v. *Gdynia Ameryka Linje Zeglugowe Spolka Akcyjna*, [1939] 4 D.L.R. 491 (N.S.S.C., Chisholm, C.J.) (ship in port held to be "personal property within the jurisdiction").

[297] This may be contrasted with the Scottish approach of arrestment of movables *ad jurisdictionem fundatam*, where the dispute may have no connection with the property within the jurisdiction: cf. *In re Littles*, 10 Ir. Eq. Rep. 275 (Chy., Brady, L.C., 1847), *Dicey & Morris*, 220. See further Collins, *The Jurisdiction and Judgments Convention — Some Practical Aspects of United Kingdom Accession, with Particular Reference to Jurisdiction*, in K. Lipstein ed., *Harmonization of Private International Law by the E.E.C.* 91, at 94 (1978).

[298] Order 11, Rule 1 (n).

[299] Order 11, Rule 1 (o).

[300] Order 11, Rule 1 (p). Cf. *Bayer* v. *Connell Bros. & Co.*, [1897] 1 I.R. 544 (Porter, M.R.).

[301] D.R. Thomas, *Maritime Liens*, p. 38 (1980).

Such a proceeding is not available against all forms of property of course. In fact, the only action *in rem* that exists in Irish law is an admiralty action[302] brought in the High Court against a ship or some other *res* connected with the ship such as its cargo. The reason why an action *in rem* is available against ships is because they "are elusive. The power to arrest in any port and found thereon an action *in rem* is increasingly required with the custom of ships being owned singly and sailing under flags of convenience."[303]

When proceeding against the ship,

> "[t]he writ may be issued against the owner .... and the owner may never appear, and you get your judgment against a ship without a single person being named from beginning to end. That is an action *in rem*, and it is perfectly well understood that the judgment is against the ship."[304]

If the owners do not decide to make themselves parties to the suit in order to defend their property, no personal liability can be established against them in that action. This remains so despite the fact that the form of summons now prescribed for use in admiralty actions *in rem* names and is directed to, specified defendants.[305]

Actions *in rem* must be distinguished from judgments *in rem*. The judgment in an admiralty action *in rem* is itself a judgment *in rem*, that is, a judgment effective against the whole world, not simply as between the parties to the action. There are other judgments which, though they do not arise from actions *in rem*, are similarly effective − for example a judgment affecting the marital status of the parties, granting probate of a will or dissolving a company.

The High Court's admiralty jurisdiction[306] may be either *in rem* or *in personam*. This jurisdiction extends to such matters as claims for the sale of a ship,[307] or in respect of a mortage of or charges on a ship,[308] claims arising out of bottomry[309] or pilotage.[310]

Jurisdiction on the part of the Irish courts in an action *in rem* exists if the originating summons is served on the *res* within the jurisdiction or if the solicitor of the defendant agrees to accept service and undertakes in writing to enter an appearance and to put in bail.[311] In this context presence "within the juridiction" means, of course, presence in internal waters or within the territorial waters of the State.[312] An originating summons in an action *in rem* cannot be served out of the jurisdiction.

---

[302] See Order 64 of the Rules of the Superior Courts 1986.

[303] *The Atlantic Star*, [1974] A.C. 436, at 472 (H.L. (Eng.), *per* Lord Simon, 1973).

[304] *The City of Mecca*, 5 P.D. 106 (1881).

[305] Cf. Appendix J., Forms Nos. 1-3 of the Rules of the Superior Courts 1986.

[306] See Yale, *A Historical Note on the Jurisdiction of the Admiralty in Ireland*, 3 Ir. Jur. (N.S.) 146 (1968), *Strabane Canal Co. Ltd.* v. *London & North Western and Lancashire & Yorkshire Ry. Cos.*, [1912] 2 I.R. 147 (K.B. Div.), *Hayes* v. *Reid*, 12 Ir. L.R. 119 (Q.B., 1848). *The State (Kinvarra Shipping Ltd.)* v. *Neylon*, [1974] I.R. 11 (High Ct., O'Keeffe, P., 1971), *M'Cann* v. *Allen*, 27 I.L.T.R. 64 (Recorder of Belfast, 1893), *Bull* v. *Pile ("The Erminia")*, 27 I.L.T.R. 136 (Admiralty, Johnson, J., 1893), *Cummins & Sons, Carrigaloe Gridiron and Works Co.*, v. *E.C. Corry*, 29 I.L.T.R. 144 (Recorder of Cork, 1895), *Flash* v. *Thorsen*, 30 I.L.T.R. 116 (Recorder of Belfast, 1896), *Officers of the S.S. "Vicia"* v. *Master & Owners (No. 2)*, 76 I.L.T.R. 110 (High Ct., Admiralty, Hanna J., 1942). See also *Officers of the S.S. "Vicia"* v. *Master & Owners*, 76 I.L.T.R. 59 (High Ct., Hanna, J., 1941), *Higgins* v. *Irish Shipping Ltd.*, [1944] I.R. 178 (Sup. Ct., 1944, aff'g High Ct., Haugh, J., 1943). The judgments of Walsh and Henchy, J.J., in *Cox Ltd.* v. *Owners of M.V. Fritz Raube*, Sup. Ct., 1 August 1974 (104/106-1974) comprehensively analyse the origins and scope of Irish Admiralty jurisdiction.

[307] Order 64, Rule 1(b) of the *Rules of the Superior Courts 1986*.

[308] *Id.*, Rule 1(d).

[309] *Id.*, Rule 1(e).

[310] *Id.*, Rule 1(g).

[311] Order 64, Rule 8 of the Rules of the Superior Courts 1986.

[312] It is not settled whether a ship must be anchored within territorial waters or whether a ship in course of navigation may be arrested. See Art. 20 of the *Geneva Convention on the Territorial Sea and the Contiguous Zone*.

In admiralty actions *in rem* service of a summons or warrant of arrest must be effected by the Admiralty Marshal or his substitutes[313] by nailing or affixing the original for a short time on the main mast or on the single mast or some other conspicuous part of the vessel and by leaving a true copy nailed or affixed in its place when the original is taken off.[314] If the *res* is cargo and it has been landed or transhipped, service of the summons or warrant is to be effected by placing it for a short time on the cargo and leaving a true copy of it on the cargo.[315] Failure to follow the prescribed method of serving a writ against a ship vitiates the service. Therefore, service on the captain or master, even on board the ship, is not sufficient.[316] If on the other hand cargo is in the custody of a person who will not permit access to it, service of the summons or warrant may be made upon that person.[317] No warrant for the arrest of property in admiralty actions *in rem* is to be issued until an affidavit by the party seeking it or his agent has been filed containing certain specified particulars,[318] including, the name and description of the party at whose instance the warrant is to be issued, the nature of the claim or counterclaim, the name and nature of the property to be arrested, and a statement that the claim or counterclaim has not been satisfied.

A party may obtain an order for the release of any property by paying into Court the sum in respect of which the action was commenced and a sum for costs[319] but there is a procedure whereby a party desiring to prevent this release can file a *caveat* against release.[320] If an action *in rem* is stayed, either under the Court's general discretionary power to stay proceedings[321] or under the mandatory provisions of the Arbitration Act 1980,[322] the arrested property or other security cannot be retained by the court as security for the other proceedings (such as arbitration proceedings) in whose favour the stay is granted.[323] However, in the case of a discretionary stay the court can get round this lack of power to retain security by making the stay conditional on the provision of alternative security by the defendant.[324] It has been held in England[325] that, even in a case where a mandatory stay under the Arbitration Act is being applied, the court need not necessarily release the security unconditionally, but this decision is at least partially based on an English rule of court that has no direct equivalent here.

STAYING PROCEEDINGS[326]

The Irish Superior Courts have an inherent discretionary jurisdiction to stay

---

[313] Order 64, rule 9 of the Rules of the Superior Courts 1986.
[314] *Id.*, r.10.
[315] *Id.*, r.11.
[316] *The Prins Bernhard* [1964] P. 117, at 130-132, following *The Marie Constance*, 3 Asp. M.L.C. 505 (1877).
[317] Order 64, Rule 12 of the Rules of the Superior Courts 1986.
[318] *Id.*, Rule 6.
[319] *Id.*, Order 11, Rule 20.
[320] *Id.*, Rules 23 and 26.
[321] Section 27(5) of the Supreme Court of Judicature (Ireland) Act 1877.
[322] *Infra* pp. 621-622.
[323] *The Attenee*, 11 Ll.L. Rep. 6 (1922), *Foresta Romana S.A.* v. *Georges Mabro*, 66 Ll.L. Rep. 139 (1940); *The Fehmarn*, [1957] 1 W.L.R. 815, *The Cap Bon*, [1967] 1 Lloyd's Rep. 543, *The Golden Trader*, [1974] 2 All E.R. 686.
[324] *The Eleftheria*, [1970] P. 94, *The Atlantic Star*, [1974] A.C. 436, *The Golden Trader*, [1974] 2 All E.R. 686.
[325] *The Renak*, [1979] 1 All E.R. 397.
[326] See generally Granger, *The Conflict of Laws and Forum Shopping: Some Recent Decisions on Jurisdiction and Free Enterprise in Litigation*, 6 Ottawa L. Rev. 416 (1974), Schuz, *Controlling Forum-Shopping: The Impact of MacShannon* v. *Rockware Glass Ltd.*, 35 Int. & Comp. L.Q. 374 (1986), Verheul, *The Forum (Non) Conveniens in English and Dutch Law and Under Some International Conventions*, 35 Int. & Comp. L.Q. 413 (1986).

proceedings in the interests of justice. This jurisdiction is recognised by section 27(5) of the Supreme Court of Judicature (Ireland) Act 1877.[327] Though we are concerned here only with its application to proceedings involving a foreign element, the jurisdiction exists in purely domestic proceedings as well.

In cases involving a foreign element the court may be invited to exercise its discretion to stay proceedings in Ireland for one or more of several reasons. It may be alleged that the parties have chosen a foreign forum;[328] proceedings may already be pending in some foreign jurisdiction; the nature of the case may be such that it ought more properly to be tried somewhere else. Alternatively, the Irish court may be asked to restrain by injunction proceedings that are pending or about to be instituted abroad. Though a number of the principles guiding the courts in these various contexts overlap to some degree, it is useful to examine first the case where the parties have chosen a foreign forum, and then go on to consider the other types of case separately.

Choice of a foreign forum[329]

The case we must here consider will usually arise in a contractual context. The parties to a contract may have agreed that any dispute arising between them is to be referred to arbitration in a foreign country or to be heard before the courts of a foreign country. It is quite common for international contracts, particularly of a commercial nature, to contain such a choice of forum clause. When a dispute does arise one party may, in contravention of the agreement to litigate in a foreign forum, seek to sue before the Irish courts, either by serving a summons on the defendant within the jurisdiction or by invoking Order 11.

So far as the latter strategy is concerned,[330] where the parties have agreed to litigate in a foreign forum, the Court will exercise its discretion, unless some paramount reason to the contrary is shown, by giving effect to the choice of forum clause. This is the position at least where under the contract the foreign jurisdiction chosen is exclusive, in that the parties have agreed to have recourse only to the tribunals of a particular country.[331] Whether the choice of forum is exclusive or not is a matter of interpretation of the contract and would seem, therefore, to fall to be determined by the proper law of the contract.[332]

Even in non-Order 11 cases where the defendant has been served within the jurisdiction and the Court's jurisdiction is clear cut, the Court still has a discretion to stay Irish proceedings if the parties have agreed to the exclusive jurisdiction of a foreign forum. Indeed, once the fact of the agreement has been established, the principle, *pacta sunt servanda,* places a heavy burden on the plaintiff (though not as heavy as in Order 11 cases) to show that the choice of forum clause ought to be disregarded and that the Irish proceedings ought to be allowed to continue.[333]

---

[327] Cf. *Anon., Stay of Actions Pending Administration or Liquidation Proceedings,* 13 Ir. L.T. & Sol. J. 379 (1879), *Anon., Stay of Proceedings,* 22 Ir. L.T. & Sol. J. 127, 137, esp. at 138 (1888), Murray, *Staying Proceedings,* 18 N. Ir. L.Q. 65, esp. at 69-70 (1967).

[328] Cf. *Wilson* v. *National Live Stock Insurance Co. Ltd.,* 48 I.L.T.R. 77 (C.A., 1914), *Richardson* v. *Army, Navy, and General Assurance Association,* [1924] 2 I.R. 96 (K.B. Div., (I.F.S.)).

[329] See Spiro, *Jurisdiction by Consent,* 84 S.A.L.J. 295 (1967), Bissett-Johnson, *The Efficacy of Choice of Jurisdiction Clauses in International Contracts in English and Australian Law,* 19 Int. & Comp. L.Q. 541 (1970), Cowen & Mendes da Costa, *The Contractual Forum: A Comparative Study,* 53 Can. Bar Rev. 453 (1965), Kahn-Freund, *Jurisdiction Agreements: Some Reflections,* 26 Int. & Comp. L.Q. 825 (1977).

[330] Cf. *supra* p. 131.

[331] *Evans Marshall & Co. Ltd.* v. *Bertola SA.,* [1973] 1 W.L.R. 349, at 360, 364 *Limerick Corporation* v. *Crompton,* [1909] 2 I.R. 120 (K.B. Div.).

[332] *Evans Marshall & Co. Ltd.* v. *Bertola SA.,* [1973] 1 W.L.R. 349 at 361-362. See also *Kennedy* v. *London Express Newspapers,* [1931] I.R. 532, at 543.

[333] Cf. *The Fenmarn,* [1958] 1 W.L.R. 159 (C.A.)

The principles governing the exercise of the Court's discretion whether or not to grant a stay[334] have been summarised in an English case as follows:[335]

> "(1) Where plaintiffs sue in England in breach of an agreement to refer disputes to a foreign court, and the defendants apply for a stay, the English court, assuming the claim to be otherwise within its jurisdiction, is not bound to grant a stay but has a discretion whether to do so or not.
> (2) The discretion should be exercised by granting a stay unless strong cause for not doing so is shown.
> (3) The burden of proving such strong cause is on the plaintiffs.
> (4) In exercising its discretion the court should take into account all the circumstances of the particular case.
> (5) In particular, but without prejudice to (4), the following matters, where they arise, may properly be regarded:-
> (*a*) In what country the evidence on the issues of fact is situated, or none readily available, and the effect of that on the relative convenience and expense of trial as between the English and foreign courts.
> (*b*) Whether the law of the foreign court applies and, if so, whether it differs from English law in any material respects.
> (*c*) With what country either party is connected, and how closely.
> (*d*) Whether the defendants genuinely desire trial in the foreign country, or are only seeking procedural advantage.
> (*e*) Whether the plaintiffs would be prejudiced by having to sue in the foreign court because they would:
> (i) be deprived of security for their claim;
> (ii) be unable to enforce any judgment obtained;
> (iii) be faced with a time bar not applicable in England; or
> (iv) for political, racial, religious or other reasons be unlikely to get a fair trial."

Staying proceedings in other cases[336]

The courts also have jurisdiction to stay actions in this country or abroad in cases where the parties have not contractually agreed upon a forum. Again there is a broad judicial discretion:[337] the important question concerns the limits of this discretion. The development of the law on this subject is of particular interest in view of a fairly significant divergence historically between English, Australian and Canadian law,

---

[334] See *Brand* v. *National Life Assurance Co.*, [1918] 3 W.W.R. 858, 44 D.L.R. 412 (Man. K.B., Mathers, C.J.K.B., 1918), *May (A.S.) & Co.* v. *Robert Reford Co.*, [1969] 2 O.R. 611, 6 D.L.R. (3d) 288 (High Ct., Keith, J.), *G. & E. Auto Brokers Ltd.* v. *Toyota Canada Inc.*, 25 B.C.L.R. 145, 117 D.L.R. (3d) 707 (B.C. Sup. Ct. Macfarlane, J., 1980).

[335] *The Eleftheria*, [1970] P. 94, at 100.

[336] See Morgan, *Discretion to Stay Jurisdiction*, 31 Int. & Comp. L.Q. 582 (1982), Jefferson, *The Jurisdiction to Stay Actions: The Abidin Daver*, 14 Kingston L. Rev. 154 (1984), Barma & Elvin, *Forum Non Conveniens, Where To From Here?* 101 L.Q. Rev. 48 (1985), Edinger, *The MacShannon Test for Discretion: Defence and Delimitation*, 64 Can. Bar Rev. 283 (1986), Briggs, *Forum non conveniens–now we are ten?* 3 Legal Studies 74 (1983), Briggs, *No Interference with Foreign Court*, 31 Int. & Comp L.Q. 189 (1982), Schuz, *Controlling Forum-Shopping: The Impact of MacShannon* v. *Rockware Glass Ltd.*, 35 Int. & Comp. L.Q. 374 (1986), Barrett, *The Doctrine of Forum Non Conveniens*, 35 Calif. L. Rev. 380 (1947), Blair, *The Doctrine of Forum Non Conveniens in Anglo-American Law*, 29 Colum. L. Rev. 1 (1929), Dainow, *The Inappropriate Forum*, 29 Ill. L. Rev. 867 (1935), Inglis, *Jurisdiction, The Doctrine of Forum Conveniens, and Choice of Law in Conflict of Laws*, 81 L.Q. Rev. 380 (1965), J.-G. C[astel], *Comment: Jurisdiction and the Exercise of Discretion by the Court Forum Conveniens*, 49 Can. Bar Rev. 466 (1971), Gill, *Jurisdiction and the Enforcement of Foreign Judgments in Ireland*, 4 J. of Irish Soc. for European L. 2, at 15-17 (1980), Verheul, *The Forum (Non) Conveniens in English and Dutch Law and Under Some International Conventions*, 35 Int. & Comp. L. Q. 413 (1986).

[337] Cf. *Ridge* v. *Newton*, 4 Ir. Eq. Rep. 389 (Chy., Sugden, L.C., 1842), *Heenan* v. *Clements*, 1 Ir. C.L.R. 44 (Com. Pleas, Monaghan, C.J., 1850).

on the one hand, and the approach in Scotland[338] and the United States,[339] on the other.

The first group of countries tended towards a relatively narrower definition of the circumstances in which the Court might exercise its discretion, but in the past decade has gradually relaxed its approach so that the difference between the two groups has now effectively disappeared. In a recent case[340] the Supreme Court has expressed approval for the approach adopted in some of the English cases. The extent to which the case has endorsed recent English developments is, as we shall see,[341] a matter of some uncertainty.

It is useful at this point to examine the question *why* the Court should stay an action. Three possible answers suggest themselves.[342] First that the court should be anxious to protect a party from malicious or devious conduct by an opposing party to the litigation; secondly that the Court should seek to determine which is the more appropriate forum in the light of the administration of justice;[343] third, that the court should, in broad terms, seek to balance the respective interests of the parties themselves. These competing policies are often intertwined in the cases. With this confusion of purpose, one finds a wide variety of judicial formulae, which cannot be satisfactory reconciled.

Up to 1973 the *locus classicus* in English law on the exercise of the Court's discretion to stay was the following passage from the judgment of Scott L.J. in *St. Pierre* v. *South American Stores Ltd.*:[344]

> "(1) A mere balance of convenience is not a sufficient ground for depriving a plaintiff of the advantages of prosecuting his action in an English court if it is otherwise properly brought. The right of access to the King's court must not be lightly refused.
> (2) In order to justify a stay two conditions must be satisfied, one positive and the other negative: (*a*) the defendant must satisfy the court that the continuance of the action would work an injustice because it would be oppressive or vexatious to him or would be an abuse of the process of the court in some other way; and (*b*) the stay must not cause an injustice to the plaintiff. In both, the burden of proof is on the defendant."

This approach clearly gave effect to the first of the three policies mentioned above. The judicial concentration was on the subjective bad faith of the party against whom a stay was sought. Thus, the *bona fide,* but erroneous, belief by the plaintiff that he would have a real advantage in suing in England was sufficient to prevent a stay.[345]

Several decisions since the 1970s have considerably altered the position regarding

---

[338] See *Anton*, 148ff.

[339] See *Gulf Oil Corporation* v. *Gilbert*, 330 U.S. 501, (1947).

[340] *Murphy (Joseph) Structural Engineers Ltd.* v. *Manitowoc (U.K.) Ltd.*, Sup. Ct., 30 July 1985 (328–84).

[341] *Infra*, pp. 167-168.

[342] See Briggs, 3 Legal Stud., at 78 ff.

[343] This approach is at the core of the *forum non conveniens* doctrine in Scotland and the United States: see Edinger, *supra*, at 286–287, *Scoles & Hay*, 363 ff.

[344] [1936] 1 K.B. 382, at 398, quoted by Griffin, J., in *Murray (Joseph) Structural Engineers Ltd.* v. *Manitowoc (U.K.) Ltd., supra*, at pages 9–10 of Griffin, J.'s judgment and by Lord MacDermott, L.C.J. and Black, L.J., in *Devine* v. *Cementation Co. Ltd.*, [1963] N.I. 65, at 68 and 71 respectively (C.A., 1962). Lord McDermott, L.C.J. (at 69) considered it "clear .... that the test does not depend on the balance of convenience, but on whether the inconvenience and expense involved work an injustice ...." Cf. *Parnell* v.*Parnell*, 8 Ir. Ch. Rep. 556 (Cusack Smith, M.R., 1858); although the Master of the Rolls described the English proceedings as "wanton and unnecessary" and "unjust and oppressive", it is submitted that the decision did not depend on such findings and that it proceeded on the basis of a broader exercise of discretion as to the respective merits and disadvantages of the English and Irish proceedings.

[345] Schuz, *supra*, at 379.

the grounds for a stay in respect of proceedings both within the jurisdiction and abroad.

In *The Atlantic Star; Atlantic Star (Owners)* v. *Bona Spes (Owners)*,[346] a stay was granted on the basis that the words "vexatiously, oppressively or in abuse of the process of the court" were flexible words and should be interpreted more liberally than they had been previously.[347] In considering whether a stay should be granted, the Court would have to take into account "(i) any advantage to the plaintiff (ii) any disadvantage to the defendant."[348] This was "the critical equation",[349] said Lord Wilberforce. This advantage to the plaintiff need not be "fanciful";[350] a "substantial"[351] advantage would suffice. A *bona fide* advantage to the plaintiff "is a solid weight in the scale, often a decisive weight, but not always so."[352] To prevail against the plaintiff's advantage, the disadvantage to the defendant would have to be still more substantial.[353] The House of Lords refused, however, to adopt a doctrine of *forum non conveniens* similar to the Scottish, preferring to seek any change within the existing framework of English law.

In *Rockware Glass Ltd.* v. *MacShannon*[354] the House of Lords took matters much further and decided that in order to obtain a stay of proceedings the defendant was no longer under a duty to show that the institution of proceedings in England was vexatious or oppressive, even in an extended or liberal sense.[355] Lord Diplock endorsed the first part of Scott L.J.'s statement in *St. Pierre* v. *South American Stores Ltd.*[356]; but he reformulated the second part in radically different terms:

> "In order to justify a stay two conditions must be satisfied, one positive and the other negative: (*a*) the defendant must satisfy the court that there is another forum to whose jurisdiction he is amenable in which justice can be done between the parties at substantially less inconvenience or expense, and (*b*) the stay must not deprive the plaintiff of a legitimate personal or juridical advantage which would be available to him if he invoked the jurisdiction of the English Court".[357]

Lord Keith adopted an approach that involved a balancing process between the parties. He considered that it was "necessary to weigh against each other the advantages to the plaintiff and the disadvantages to the defendant, and a stay will not be granted unless the court concludes that to refuse it would involve injustice to the defendant and [the grant would involve] no injustice to the plaintiff"[358] Lord Salmon adopted a substantially similar approach.[359]

The notion of a "natural forum" for an action attracted much support in

---

[346] [1974] A.C. 436.
[347] *Id.*, at 454 (*per* Lord Reid).
[348] *Id.*, at 468 (per Lord Wilberforce).
[349] *Id.*
[350] *Id.*
[351] *Id.*
[352] *Id.*, at 469.
[353] *Id.*
[354] [1978] A.C. 795, analysed by Carter, 49 Br. Yrbk of Internat. L., at 291–295 (1978).
[355] *Id.*
[356] [1936] 1 K.B. 382, at 398. See p. 165, *supra*.
[357] [1978] A.C., at 812 (H.L.(Eng)).
[358] *Id.*, at 829. The words in square brackets were inserted by Lord Keith in *The Abidin Daver*, [1984] A.C. 398, at 416 (H.L.(Eng.)).
[359] *Id.*, at 819. Schuz, *supra*, at 397, considers that Lord Salmon's test, in contrast to that of Lord Keith, "seems to be entirely relative and thus the balance will tilt in favour of the result which causes the least injustice." It is true that Lord Salmon said (at 819) that "the real test of stay or no stay depends upon what the court in its discretion considers that justice demands." But in a carefully drafted reformulation of Scott, L.J.'s test in *St. Pierre* case, Lord Salmon (*id.*) committed himself to a rule which would deny a stay where to grant one would cause "an injustice to the plaintiff", even where the defendant showed that the continuance of the action would work an injustice.

MacShannon.[360] Lord Keith understood the term as meaning the forum "with which the action has the most real and substantial connection."[361]

The House of Lords in *MacShannon* still maintained that it was not applying a doctrine of *forum non conveniens* in the Scottish sense, though it was acknowledged that the distinction might be a fine one.[362]

Decisions in England since *MacShannon* have tended to *cite* Lord Diplock's formulation, but to apply a far less rigid test.[363] As to the first limb of this formulation, courts have not concerned themselves with the narrow questions of comparative convenience and expense. Instead they have sought to find the natural forum or, in cases of competing fora, the more natural forum.[364] This approach is consistent with the second, rather than the first, of the three policy approaches mentioned earlier in this discussion.[365] It is in general harmony with the Scottish approach. It therefore comes as no surprise that in *The Abidin Daver*[366] should observe that "judicial chauvinism has been replaced by judicial comity to an extent which I think the time is now ripe to acknowledge frankly is, in the field of law with which this appeal is concerned, indistinguishable from the Scottish legal doctrine of *forum non conveniens*".

Lord Diplock's requirement in *MacShannon* that the stay must not deprive the plaintiff of a *legitimate* personal or juridical advantage has not constituted a distinctive hurdle: in *Castanho,*[367] Lord Scarman said that "[n]o time should be spent in speculating what is meant by 'legitimate'." The word appears to have been equated[368] with "real" as opposed to "speculative".

We must now consider the recent case of *Murphy (Joseph) Structural Engineers* v. *Manitowoc (U.K.) Ltd.*[369] The Supreme Court there accepted that the same principles applied in the case of an application to stay proceedings brought within the jurisdiction as would apply to enjoin proceedings brought in a foreign country. Griffin, J. (for the Court) noted that it had "long been established that the Courts have an inherent jurisdiction to stay or strike out an action or to restrain by injunction the institution or continuance of proceedings in a foreign court whenever it is necessary to prevent injustice."[370]

After a review of *St. Pierre, The Atlantic Star* and *McShannon*, Griffin, J. said:

> "The effect of these decisions is that (1) a mere balance of convenience is not a sufficient ground for depriving a plaintiff of the advantages of prosecuting his action in an English Court if it is otherwise properly brought, but (2) ... a stay will be granted if (a) the continuance of the proceedings will cause injustice to the defendant and (b) a stay will not cause injustice to the plaintiff. That fundamental question can generally be answered by an application of Lord Diplock's restatement of the rule stated by Scott, L.J. in the *St. Pierre* case. I would accept that these are the principles which should properly be applied in this case."[371]

---

[360] Cf. [1978] A.C., at 812 (*per* Lord Diplock), 818 (*per* Lord Salmon), and 829–83 (*per* Lord Keith).

[361] *Id.*, at 829.

[362] [1978] A.C., at 812 (*per* Lord Diplock). See also *id.*, at 822 (*per* Lord Fraser).

[363] See Schuz, *supra*, at 381.

[364] *Id.*, at 382. See also *Dimskal Shipping Co. S.A.* v. *International Transport Workers Federation,* [1986] 2 Lloyd's L. Rep. 165 (Hirst, J.).

[365] *Supra*, p. 165.

[366] [1984] A.C. 398, at 411 (H.L. (Eng.)). See, however, the cautious observations of Jefferson, *supra*, at 162–167.

[366] [1981] A.C. 557, at 575. See Edinger, *supra*, at 295, Jefferson, *supra*, at 167–169.

[367] *Castanho* v. *Brown* and *Root (U.K.) Ltd.,* [1981] A.C. 557.

[368] Cf. *Trendtex Trading Corporation* v. *Credit Suisse* [1980] 3 All E.R. 721, at 734 (Goff, J. (aff'd by C.A.) The *"Messiniaki Tolmi"*, [1983] 1 Lloyds L. Rep. 666 (Mustill, J.), *European Asian Bank A.G.* v. *Punjab & Sind Bank,* [1982] 2 Lloyd's L. Rep. 356 (C.A.) Jefferson, *supra*, at 167.

[369] Sup. Ct., 30 July 1985 (328–84).

[370] Page 8 of Griffin, J.'s judgment, citing, as an example, *McHenry* v. *Lewis.* 22 Ch. Div. 397 (1882).

[371] Pages 11–12 of Griffin, J.'s judgment.

A number of observations on this important statement are in order. First, it seems that the first limb of Scott, L.J.'s test in the *St. Pierre* case has been endorsed verbatim. As to the second limb, Griffin J. places central emphasis on *justice*.[372] True, he refers to Lord Diplock's restatement in *MacShannon,* but he does not appear to regard this as gospel, since he considers that it provides the answer "generally" rather than universally.

The notion of justice is essentially one giving effect to the third of the three policies mentioned earlier in our discussion.[373] Griffin, J.'s formula is extremely close to that adopted by Lord Keith in *MacShannon,*[374] but there is an important difference: unlike Lord Keith, who considered it "necessary to weigh against each other the advantages to the plaintiff and the disadvantages to the defendant," Griffin, J.'s formula contains no such express balancing process. To be entitled to a stay, what must be proved are two facts,[375] one positive, and the other negative: injustice to the defendant resulting from the continuance of the proceedings and the absence of injustice to the plaintiff resulting from a stay.

It is doubtful, however, if the court can easily avoid a covert balancing process. Certainly, as we have seen, this has been the experience in recent English cases. The express terms of Griffin, J.'s formula appear to have a number of implications which will surely encourage the courts to resort to this process. First, it appears that once the two facts are established, a stay is to be ordered even where it will cause greater inconvenience to the plaintiff than the defendant. This conclusion could be avoided if the courts were invariably to hold that in these circumstances greater inconvenience *must* constitute "injustice" to the plaintiff; but this surely involves an unwarranted restriction on the scope of the concept of injustice. Next it appears that a stay must[376] be denied even though it causes the defendant injustice if the granting of a stay would cause the plaintiff injustice: in other words, where one or other party must suffer injustice, depending on whether or not a stay is ordered, the court must refuse a stay. Moreover, a stay will be refused when no question of "causing injustice" to the defendant arises but where the balance of convenience lies in favour of granting a stay.

It is useful at this point to consider separately the two specific contexts of (*a*) staying proceedings within the jurisdiction and (*b*) staying foreign proceedings.

Staying proceedings within the jurisdiction

Requests for a stay of proceedings within the jurisdiction can easily occur in view of the considerable room for overlap that exists between the different grounds for jurisdiction exercised by various countries. In cases where proceedings are launched in Ireland and a foreign country, a plea of *lis alibi pendens* may be raised in the proceedings before the Irish courts. The plea stems from the principle: *Nemo debet bis vexari pro eadem causa.* The plea can arise in a purely domestic context as well as in an international one.

---

[372] In *The Abidin Daver* [1984] A.C. 398, at 412 (H.L. (Eng.)), Lord Diplock spoke in terms of "injustice" to the plaintiff rather than "legitimate personal or juridical advantage. Jefferson, *supra,* at 157 observes that it "is not clear whether Lord Diplock fully comprehended the differences in the formulation".

[373] *Supra,* p. 165.

[374] [1978] A.C., at 829, quoted *supra,* p. 166.

[375] Strictly, these facts involve estimates as to the future repercussions of granting, or refusing, a stay. It is not clear whether Griffin, J.'s use of the word "will" requires the Court to be certain as to these repercussions, or whether it suffices for the Court to be of opinion, on the balance of probabilities, that these repercussions are likely to follow.

[376] Perhaps "may" is the more appropriate word. Griffin, J.'s formula states the circumstances in which a stay "will" be granted. It can be argued that the formula merely specifies the circumstances in which a stay *has to be granted,* while leaving open the question of the circumstances in which it *may, but need not necessarily, be granted.*

Two types of case must be distinguished. The first is where the plaintiff in Ireland is also plaintiff abroad; the second is where the plaintiff in Ireland is defendant abroad or vice versa. The court is less reluctant to intervene by way of a stay in the first type of case than in the second. If the same person is plaintiff in both jurisdictions the Court may stay the Irish proceedings, restrain the foreign proceedings by injunction[377] or require the plaintiff to elect which of the two sets of proceedings to pursue.

The court will be very reluctant to intervene and stay proceedings where the plaintiff here is defendant abroad or *vice versa*. In *Orr-Lewis* v. *Orr-Lewis*,[378] Scrutton, L.J. said:

> "Where the plaintiff in the foreign action is not plaintiff, but defendant, in the English action, the case against interference is even stronger, for the person to be stayed has not himself initiated two proceedings. He has initiated one, and has been compelled to appear in another over which he has, as defendant, no control."

In *Murphy (Joseph) Structural Engineers Ltd.* v. *Manitowoc (U.K.) Ltd.*,[379] the Supreme Court stayed proceedings in the Irish High Court where proceedings involving the same parties and the same issue were already well established in the English High Court. The litigation involved claims for negligence and breach of contract (and a counterclaim), arising from an accident at Moneypoint in which a crane was blown over during heavy winds. All the parties save the plaintiff in the Irish proceedings were English companies, and the plaintiff was an associate of an English parent company.

The Supreme Court was strongly affected by the delay on the part of the Irish plaintiff in advancing the proceedings here, coupled with its failure to have applied in England for a stay of the proceedings there. Griffin, J. (for the Court) considered that, had an application been made to stay the English proceedings shortly after they had been issued, it seemed "quite likely"[380] that a stay would have been granted. Although the accident had occurred in Ireland and, so far as the witnesses were concerned, the balance of convenience would lie with continuing the Irish proceedings, the Supreme Court considered that these proceedings should be stayed "in particular in the absence of any explanation for failure on behalf of [the plaintiff in the Irish proceedings] to apply to have the English proceedings stayed."[381] In Griffin, J.'s opinion, it would have been unjust to the defendant not to grant a stay, and he was satisfied that there would be no injustice to the plaintiff, who had a forum, the jurisdiction of which it had accepted, which was competent to determine all the matters at issue between the parties. Griffin, J. noted that a stay "would not deprive the plaintiff of a legitimate personal or juridical advantage."[382]

Restraining foreign proceedings

Reference has already been made[383] to the fact that, in addition to staying Irish proceedings where there are proceedings pending elsewhere, the Irish courts will also, in an appropriate case, restrain by injunction foreign proceedings where there

[377] Cf. *infra*, pp. 169-170.
[378] [1919] 1 K.B. 410, at 414, Cf. *French* v. *Royal Exchange Assurance Co.*, 6 Ir. Ch. Rep. 523 (Brady, L.C., 1857), where proceedings brought in England by respondents in an Irish case were stayed, on their application.
[379] Supreme Court, 30 July 1985 (328−84).
[380] Page 13 of Griffin, J.'s judgment.
[381] Page 14 of Griffin, J.'s judgment.
[382] Page 13 of Griffin, J.'s judgment.
[383] *Supra*, p. 163.

are proceedings pending here. The case of *Lett* v. *Lett*[384] is an example of this.[385] The plaintiff, an Irish domiciliary, had been married to the defendant, who in 1888 obtained a decree for divorce *a mensa et thoro*. In 1889 a deed was executed containing the terms of an agreement between the parties which released the plaintiff from all present or future claims against him in respect of the relief sought by the defendant in the 1888 proceedings. The plaintiff then went to Argentina where he acquired considerable wealth and in 1903 the defendant instituted proceedings against him in Argentina claiming divorce and maintenance. In 1906 the plaintiff, having come to Ireland, instituted proceedings here for a declaration that the 1888 decree was a definite and binding sentence of divorce *a mensa et thoro* between the parties and sought an injunction to restrain the defendant from continuing proceedings in the Argentine courts. It was held that the case was a proper one for the exercise of the jurisdiction to restrain the foreign proceedings because it was inequitable that the defendant who was a party to the deed of 1889 and the agreement that preceded should seek to throw these agreements aside and proceed to assert rights contrary to them.

Porter, M.R. explained:

> "The old and established jurisdiction of this country in reference to cases in foreign tribunals was founded not on any arrogant assumption of powers in our Courts over foreign tribunals, but upon an undoubted control over the subjects of the realm, as a personal right to restrain them from committing injustice by prosecuting inequitable claims in respect of property, wherever asserted."[386]

As the order of the court in such cases is directed solely at the individual, and does not extend to the tribunal where the suit or proceeding is pending, it is immaterial that the party to whom it is addressed is prosecuting his action in the Courts of a foreign country.[387] Nevertheless, the injunction, although it binds only the defendant, has the effect of preventing a foreign Court from entering on or proceeding with litigation within its jurisdiction and thus is a step which at least until recently Irish courts considered they should be slow to take.[388] As we have seen,[389] however, in *Murphy's* case, Griffin, J. (for the Court) accepted that the same principles apply in the case of applications to enjoin foreign

---

[384] [1906] 1 I.R. 618.

[385] See also *In Re Belfast Shipowners' Co.* [1894] 1 I.R. 321 where the stay was granted in pursuance of an express statutory power to restrain further proceedings against a company after presentation of a petition but before the making of an order for winding up. In *Parnell* v. *Parnell*, 7 Ir. Ch. Rep. 322 (Cusack Smith, M.R. 1858), where administration proceedings were in progress in both the Irish and English Courts, Cusack Smith, M.R. had "no doubt" that the Court of Chancery in Ireland, had jurisdiction to restrain the executor from going on with the case in England without the permission of the English Master of the Rolls. In his turn, the English Master of the Rolls referred the question to the Irish court, for a determination as to which court should hear the case. Cusack Smith, M.R. held that the Irish suit should proceed. The procedure in the Irish court involved less expense; moreover, the only object to be attained by the English proceedings was "to put costs in [the] English solicitor, and to diminish the surplus coming to [the] relatives, the petitioners in the Irish suit": 8 Ir. Ch. Rep. 556, at 562 (1858). Cusack Smith, M.R. was not impressed by the fact that, in the English proceedings, twenty-seven parties had been made defendants, all of whom (save the petitioners in the Irish suit) were clients of the English solicitor. He asked: "Can any impartial person ... come to any other conclusion, but that it was an unjust and oppressive proceeding to file a bill in the Court of Chancery in England, after the plaintiff had appeared, by his Irish solicitor, in the Irish suit?" *id.*, at 566.

[386] [1906] 1 I.R. 618, at 629.

[387] Id., citing *Kerr on Injunctions*. See also *Parnell* v. *Parnell*, 7 Ir. Ch. Rep. 322, at 330–331 (Cusack Smith M.R., 1858), *Elderman Lines* v. *Read* [1928] 2 K.B. 144, at 151–152, 155; *Settlement Corporation* v. *Hochschild* [1966] Ch. 10, at 15.

[388] [1906] 1 I.R., at 645. (per Holmes L.J. *dissenting*). See also *Cohen* v. *Rothfield*, [1919] 1 K.B. 410 at 413; *Settlement Corporation* v. *Hochschild*, [1966] Ch. 10 at 15.

[389] *Supra*, p. 167.

proceedings as apply in respect of applications to stay proceedings brought within the jurisdiction. This is in line with recent English developments.[390] Whether it is a desirable change has given rise to some debate. It has been argued[391] that respect for foreign proceedings should entail a more restrained approach than prevails in applications for a stay of proceedings within the jurisdiction, and that only where there is "oppression and vexation" should an injunction be ordered.[392]

INELIGIBLE AND EXEMPT PARTIES

Persons Who May not Sue

As a general rule, any person, of whatever nationality, domicile or place or residence, may sue in the Irish courts, provided the necessary procedural and jurisdictional requirements are met. There is, however, one exceptional category of person who is ineligible to sue: an alien enemy.

An alien enemy is one whose Sovereign or State is at war with Ireland.[393] An alien friend, on the other hand, is one whose Sovereign or State is not at war with Ireland.[394] The question whether an alien is an alien enemy or an alien friend thus "does not depend upon the personal feelings of the person whose status is inquired into. It depends on whether the State of which he is a subject is friendly or hostile."[395] So, during the First World War, "a German who loved England and hated his own country was nevertheless an enemy alien; *e converso* a Frenchman who hated France and loved Germany was a friendly alien".[396]

By way of exception to this general principle, an alien enemy residing in the State by lawful permission may bring an action before the Courts here.[397] Thus, in *Volkl v. Rotunda Hospital*[398] the plaintiff, a subject of the Austro-Hungarian Empire after the declaration of war between the United Kingdom and Austro-Hungary, who had become duly registered as an alien here with a residence permit, was held to be entitled to sue the Rotunda Hospital in Dublin for alleged negligence on their part when she was in the hospital.

In *Pedlar v. Johnstone*,[399] in 1920, the plaintiff, William Pedlar, who had been born in Ireland but had become a naturalised citizen of the United States in January 1916, returned to Ireland in that year and took part in the Easter Rising. Having been imprisoned in Frongach and later released he came back to Ireland, was deported, returned again and was imprisoned on a charge of illegal drilling. At the time of his arrest, the police seized a sum of money and a cheque found in his possession. The plaintiff sued for the return of the money and cheque, claiming damages for detinue or conversion.

The Court of Appeal,[400] reversing the King's Bench Division, held that the

---

[390] Cf. *Castanho* v. *Brown & Rook (U.K.) Ltd.*, [1981] A.C. 557, *Smith Kline & French Laboratories Ltd.* v. *Bloch*, [1983] 1 W.L.R. 730, *Bryant* v. *Bryant*, [1981] Fam. L. 85, Schuz, *supra*, at 380, 403–404.

[391] Cf. *M. & R.* v. *A.C.L.I.*, [1984] 2 Lloyd's L. Rep. 598 (C.A.).

[392] Schuz, *supra*, at 404.

[393] *Pedlar* v. *Johnstone*, [1920] 2 I.R. 450, at 467 (C.A., per Ronan, L.J.). See also *Banco Nacional de Cuba* v. *Sabbatino*, 376 U.S. 398 (1964), and cf. *Scoles & Hay*, 374.

[394] *Pedlar* v. *Johnstone*, *supra*, at 467.

[395] *Id.*

[396] *Id.*

[397] *Volkl* v. *Rotunda Hospital*, [1914] 2 I.R. 543 at 546; *Pedlar* v. *Johnstone* [1920] 2 I.R. 450, at 465–466, 479–480; *Porter* v. *Freudenberg*, [1915] 1 K.B. 857 at 869.

[398] [1915] 1 K.B. 857, at 880 (*per* Lord Reading C.J.). See also *Robinson & Co.* v. *Continental Insurance Co. of Mannheim*, [1915] 1 K.B. 155, at 159–161.

[399] [1920] 2 I.R. 450 (C.A., 1920, rev'g K.B. Div., 1919).

[400] By a majority: Ronan and O'Connor, L. J.; O'Connor, M.R. dissenting.

plaintiff should succeed. O'Connor, L.J. noted that although the plaintiff's history showed him to be, "personally, most unfriendly to the Government of this country",[401] he was nonetheless, "in spite of his open and notorious hostility to the King",[402] an alien friend. He said:

> "Now, if an alien friend, not being thereto forbidden, comes and lives within the realm, certain consequences follow; he acquires certain rights; he is subject to certain duties. He comes within the King's protection ... and because of that he owes allegiance to the King. ... The alien friend also becomes subject to the ordinary laws of the realm ... and acquires a right to resort to the King's Court in personal actions. This limited right to sue is stated in some authorities as based upon the reason that otherwise he would be incapacitated to trade; but I think it is more logical to put it on the ground that it is a necessary consequence of his being in the King's protection. ..."[403]

The House of Lords affirmed[404] the Irish Court of Appeal. Lord Atkinson said:

> "It is true that the respondent flagrantly violated his allegiance. It is true that he abused the rights which the protection of the King secured for him. It is true that he might presumably have been tried for high treason. It is certain that he might have been expelled from the country. But none of those things has been done. The protection to a resident alien is given by the Crown. The Crown alone can withdraw it. The [respondent] is still the subject of a State at amity with Great Britian. He does not come within the definition of an alien enemy, and the Crown has given no indication whatever that it had withdrawn his implied licence to reside within this realm. The fact that he has shown himself unworthy of the Sovereign's protection, has abused his privileges and violated his allegiance, cannot, in my view, *ipso facto* terminate the protection with all the rights which flowed from it which the Sovereign extended to him, or *ipso facto* withdraw the implied licence which the Sovereign gave him to reside in this country."[405]

Lord Phillimore reserved[406] his opinion on two possible exceptional cases. The first was where an alien who would have been refused admission to the country if his entrance had been known landed surreptitiously and remained in the country surreptitiously.[407] The second was where an alien of a friendly State came to the country with private hostile intent and retained that intent "so that his whole stay was one transaction, and a continuous act of high treason".[408]

A person may be treated as the subject of an enemy State, whatever his nationality, if he carries on business in the hostile territory (because by doing so he is assisting the alien enemy)[409] or is voluntarily resident there (because he has elected to live under the protection of the enemy State).[410]

---

[401] [1920] 2 I.R., at 478.

[402] *Id.*, at 480.

[403] [1920] 2 I.R., at 479–480 (citations omitted). O'Connor, J., dissenting, considered that the mere fact of being the subject of a friendly State was not the sole test of who should be regarded as an alien friend. Carrying on trade in an enemy country was ground for treating a person as an alien enemy. "How much more strongly does this reason apply to an alien who, when war is raging with an enemy country, comes into the Kingdom to upset the King's Government?" *Id.*, at 464.'

[404] [1921] 2 A.C. 262 (H.L. (Ir.)). For approval of the decision, *obiter*, see *The State (Dowling)* v. *Kingston (No.2)*, [1937] I.R. 699, at 715 (High Ct., *per* Gavan Duffy, J.)

[405] *Id.*, at 284–285.

[406] *Id.*, at 297–298.

[407] *Id.*, at 297.

[408] *Id.*

[409] *Porter* v. *Freudenberg*, [1915] 1 K.B. 857, at 868–869, *Pedlar* v. *Johnstone*, [1920] 2 I.R., at 463–464 (*per* O'Connor, M.R., dissenting, dissent not affecting this issue).

[410] *Id.*

Persons Who May Not Be Sued

Certain persons may claim to be exempt from the jurisdiction of the Irish courts. We may consider this aspect of the subject under the two headings: *foreign sovereign states* and *diplomatic immunity.*

Foreign sovereign states[411]

The immunity of sovereign states and their rulers from the jurisdiction of the courts of other states has long been recognised as a principle of international law and must now be accepted as a part of our municipal law by reason of Article 29, section 3 of our Constitution, which provides that Ireland accepts the generally recognised principles of international law as its rule of conduct in its relations with other states.[412] The principle is a consequence of the absolute independence of every sovereign authority and of the international comity which induces every sovereign state to respect the independence and dignity of every other sovereign state.[413]

The general principle has been refined by Lord Atkin into two well-established principles:

"The first is that the courts of a country will not implead a foreign sovereign. That is, they will not by their process make him against his will a party to legal proceedings, whether the proceedings involve process against his person or seek to recover from him specific property or damages.

The second is that they will not by their process, whether the sovereign is a party to the proceedings or not, seize or detain property which is his, or of which he is in possession or control".[414]

A sovereign may, of course, voluntarily submit to the jurisdiction, either by instituting proceedings himself, or by entering an unconditional appearance in proceedings brought against him personally or in respect of property which he claims.[415] Even if an independent foreign sovereign comes into the country *incognito* and enters into contracts here under an assumed name, as if a private individual, he is not liable to proceedings against him personally unless he consents to the jurisdiction.[416] Waiver of immunity by submitting to the jurisdiction can take place only at the time when the jurisdiction of the Court over the foreign sovereign is invoked and not earlier.[417] If therefore a sovereign, having agreed to submit to jurisdiction, refuses to do so when the question arises, he may be guilty of a breach

---

[411] See Fitzmaurice, *State Immunity from Proceedings in Foreign Courts,* 14 Br. Yrbk of Internat. L. 101 (1933), Hanbury, *The Position of the Foreign Sovereign Before English Courts,* 8 Current Legal Prob. 1 (1955), Lauterpacht, *The Problem of Jurisdictional Immunities of Foreign States,* 28 Br. Yrbk of Internat. L. 220 (1951), Brookfield, *The Immunities of Foreign States Engaged in Private Transactions,* 20 J. Comp. Legislation, 3rd Series, 1 (1938), Johnson, *The Puzzle of Sovereign Immunity,* 6 Austr. Yr. Bk. of Internat. L.1 (1974), Sinclair, *The Law of Sovereign Immunity: Recent Developments,* [1980] − 1 Recueil des cours 113, Hill, *A Policy Analysis of the American Law of Foreign State Immunity* − 50 Fordham L. Rev. 155 (1981), and the detailed analysis of the subject presented in the Australian Law Reform Commission Report No. 24 *Foreign State Immunity* (1984).

[412] *Saorstát and Continental Steamship Company* v. *De Las Morenas* [1945] I.R. 291, at 298 (Sup. Ct., *per* O'Byrne, J., 1944).

[413] *Id.,* citing *Mighell* v. *Sultan of Johore* [1894] 1 Q.B. 149, at 159 (*per* Brett, L.J.). For a critical analysis of the several rationales for the principle which have been put forward at various times, see Hanbury, *The Position of the Foreign Sovereign Before English Courts,* 8 Current Legal Prob. 1, at 19−23 (1955).

[414] *The Cristina,* [1938] A.C. 485 at 490, cited by O'Byrne J. in *Saorstát & Continental Steamship Company* v. *De las Morenas,* [1945] I.R., at 299.

[415] *Saorstat & Continental Steamship Co. Ltd.* v. *De Las Morenas,* [1945] I.R., at 300 (*per* O'Byrne, J.).

[416] *Mighell* v. *Sultan of Johore,* [1894] 1 Q.B. 149, at 154−156.

[417] *Mighell* v. *Sultan of Johore, supra, Duff Development Co.* v. *Kelantan Government,* [1924] A.C. 797, *Kahan* v. *Pakistan Federation,* [1951] 2 K.B. 1003.

of his agreement but he does not thereby give actual jurisdiction to the court.[418] There can be no submission unless it is made by a person with knowledge of the right to be waived, with knowledge of the effect of our law of procedure and with the authority of the foreign sovereign.[419]

The effect of a submission to the jurisdiction by a foreign sovereign is strictly limited. Where he brings an action here himself he submits only to a counterclaim which is sufficiently connected with or allied to the subject matter of the claim as to make it necessary in the interests of justice that it should be dealt with along with the claim.[420] He does not lay himself open generally to counterclaims or cross-actions.[421]

Many of the cases relating to the immunity of the property of foreign sovereign and states have been concerned with actions *in rem* against ships. One of the most controversial questions arising in such cases has been whether the immunity extends to ships used for commercial purposes or whether it is confined to vessels destined for public use. Up to 1976, the English courts adopted the view that the immunity did extend to ships employed for ordinary commercial purposes.[422] This doctrine was out of keeping with the general trend in international law[423] and was strongly criticised;[424] in 1976 the Privy Council held that sovereign immunity could not be claimed in cases where an action *in rem* was brought against a vessel owned by a foreign government if that vessel was being used, either by the government itself or by a third party, for trading purposes and not for the public service.[425]

In Ireland, the modern position on this general question has yet to be resolved definitively. Seventy years ago, in The *"Eolo"*,[426] O'Connor, M.R. spoke of the immunity of arrest of ships which are State property "and employed for State purpose". It would seem wrong, however, to conclude from this reference to use for State purposes that the Master of the Rolls was finally committed to excluding from immunity ships belonging to the State which were used for commercial purposes. The *"Eolo"* was concerned, not with that question, but with the converse question as to whether a privately owned vessel requisitioned by a foreign Government and used for State purposes fell within the scope of the immunity.

In Zarine v. Owners of S.S. Ramava,[427] in 1941, Hanna J., having given consideration to the English cases[428] and to the opinions of authorities upon public international law, concluded that there is no rule or usage of public international law granting immunity from process to State owned trading vessels[429] and that the immunity for State vessels does not apply to these vessels which are used for private trading purposes but only to such vessels as are *publicis usibus destinata*.[430] The

---

[418] Cf. *Duff Development Co.* v. *Kelantan Government* [1924] A.C. 797, at 821 (*per* Lord Dunedin).

[419] *Baccus S.R.L.* v. *Servicio Nacional Del Trigo*, [1957] 1 Q.B., at 473.

[420] *High Commissioner for India* v. *Ghosh*, [1959] 3 All E.R. 659 at 662, *South African Republic* v. *Compagnie Franco-Belge du Chemin de Fer du Nord*, [1898] I Ch. 190.

[421] *High Commissioner for India* v. *Ghosh*, [1959] 3 All E.R. 659, at 662.

[422] *The Porto Alexandre*, [1920] P. 30, *The Cristina*, [1938] A.C. 485.

[423] *The Philippine Admiral* [1977] A.C. 373.

[424] See the Australian Law Reform Commission Report No. 24, p. 9 (1984).

[425] *Philippine Admiral* v. *Wallen Shipping*, [1977] A.C. 373. The State Immunity Act 1978 now governs the matter in England: section 10 provides that there is no immunity where a ship was in use or intended for use for commercial purposes. For commentary on the Act, see Bowett, 37 Camb. L.J. 193 (1978), Mann, 50 Br. Yrbk of Internat. L. 43 (1979).

[426] [1918] 2 I.R. 78, at 87 (K.B. Div., O'Connor, M.R. 1917).

[427] [1942] I.R. 149.

[428] Hanna, J. attached particular weight to *The Charkieh*, L.R. 4 Adm. & Ecc. 59 (1873), which held that, if "a sovereign assumes the character of a trader, and sends a vessel belonging to him to this country to trade here, he must be considered to have waived any privilege which might otherwise attach to the vessel as the property of a sovereign".

[429] [1942] I.R. 148, at 170.

[430] *Id.*, at 171.

case was appealed to the Supreme Court which upheld Hanna J., without having to pronounce on this particular question, though one of the judges, Meredith J., did take the opportunity to cast doubt[431] upon the suggestion that a sovereign State forfeits its right to object to being indirectly impleaded in an action *in rem* if it engages in trading operations as not being supported by authority. To modern readers, Hanna, J. appears to have had the better of the argument.

When does a foreign sovereign have a sufficient proprietary interest in property to warrant the application of the doctrine of immunity to that property? In *Zarine v. Owners of S.S. Ramava*[432] Hanna J. took the view that in public international law either ownership or possession must be established. The same distinction as was applied in the *S.S. Ramava* case between *ships* engaged in trade and those used for the public service should also be applied in relation to *transactions generally* that are entered into by a foreign State. A foreign State should not be immune as regards purely commercial transactions entered into by it. In a number of English cases prior to 1977 it was held that immunity did exist in such cases,[433] but in that year the Court of Appeal[434] held that the rule of international law that the doctrine of sovereign immunity was not applicable to the ordinary commercial transactions, as distinct from the governmental acts, of a sovereign state was part of English law. It is submitted that this rule of international law, embodying the internationally well-recognised distinction between *acta jure imperii* and *acta jure gestionis*,[435] is certainly part of Irish law in view of the provisions of Article 29.3 of the Constitution.

It has already been mentioned[436] that a state immunity arises where a foreign State has been either directly or indirectly impleaded in proceedings. There is only one way in which a sovereign or state may be directly impleaded: by being named as defendant in the preceedings.[437] But indirect impleading may arise in a number of ways.

The most obvious example arises in Admiralty proceedings *in rem* against a ship. Here no person is named as defendant; but if the owners are not to see their property go by default they must as a matter of practical necessity defend the proceedings. Where a foreign Sovereign claims to be the owner of the ship in such circumstances, ''it is clear that he is being impleaded.''[438] A Sovereign is also impleaded, though not named as a party, in ''any proceedings in which the Court seizes or detains, or attempts or is required to enforce its process against, any property which the Sovereign claims to be his, or of which he claims to be in possession or control''.[439]

Is a foreign sovereign state indirectly impleaded because the defendant is sued

[431] *Id.*, at 175.

[432] [1942] I.R., at 165.

[433] See, e.g. *Compania Mercantil Argentina* v. *United States Shipping Board*, 131 L.T. 388 (1924); *Kahan* v. *Pakistan Federation*, [1951] 2 K.B. 1003, at 1011; *Baccus S.R.L.* v. *Servicio Nacional del Trigo*, [1957] 1 Q.B. 438.

[434] *Trendtex Trading Corpn.* v. *Central Bank*, [1977] Q.B. 529. For later decisions to similar effect see *Hispano Americana Mercantil S.A.* v. *Central Bank of Nigeria*, [1979] 2 Lloyd's L. Rep. 277, *Paramount Ltd.* v. *Republic of Zaire*, [1980], Lloyd's L. Rep. 393; and cf. The House of Lords decision in *I Congreso del Partido*, [1983] 1 A.C. 244. Other common law guidelines echo this trend: See, e.g. *Zodiac International Products Inc.* v. *Polish People's Republic*, 81 D.L.R. (3d) 656 (1977), *Ferranti-Packard Ltd.* v. *Cushman Rentals Ltd.*, 26 O.R. (2d) 344 (Sup. Ct., Master (Davidson) 1979), *Re Royal Bank of Canada* v. *Corriveau*, 30 O.R. (2d) 653 (High Ct., Cromarty, J., 1981), *Amanat-Khan* v. *Fredian Travel Inc. (No. 2)*, 36 O.R. (2d) 17 (High Ct., Steele, J., 1982), *Marine Steel Ltd.* v. *Government of the Marshall Islands*, [1981] N.Z.L.R.I. (Barker, J). See further the Australian Law Reform Commission Report No. 24, pp. 9-10 (1984).

[435] See, for example, Article (7) of the *European Convention on State Immunity* (1972).

[436] *Supra*, p. 173.

[437] *Saorstát and Continental Steamship Co.* v. *De Las Morenas* [1945] I.R. 291, at 300-301 (Sup. Ct., *per* O'Byrne, J., 1944).

[438] *Id.*, at 303 (*per* O'Byrne, J.).

[439] *Id.*

in respect of some transaction in to which he entered as agent for that state? In *Saorstát and Continental Steamship Company* v. *De Las Morenas*[440] the defendant was a colonel in the Spanish Army who came to Ireland as head of a commission appointed by the Spanish Government to purchase horses for the use of the Spanish Army. He entered into a contract with the plaintiffs whereby it was agreed that they should reserve space for a number of horses on board one of their vessels. The contract provided that, if the defendant failed to tender the horses for shipment when the vessel was ready to load, he should become liable for dead freight. The contract was in the form of a booking note addressed to the "Spanish Commission for the purchase of horses, *per* Col. de las Morenas". The defendant applied to have the proceedings set aside on the ground that, as he had entered into the contract as a representative of and on behalf of the Spanish Government, the proceedings impleaded a sovereign State. He pointed out that he would be entitled to be indemnified out of State funds for any expenses incurred by him in carrying out his mission, including any damages awarded against him in the proceedings, as well as costs he might incur. The Supreme Court, affirming Haugh, J., rejected the application.

It was quite clear, said O'Byrne J., for the Court, that no property belonging to Spain or its Government could be made available to satisfy any judgment which might be obtained against the defendant.[441] The defendant was sued in his personal capacity and any judgment would bind merely him personally and could not be enforced against any property save his.[442] O'Byrne J. was not aware of any rule of international law under which mere agents of a foreign State could claim immunity from the jurisdiction of the Courts of the State in which they were carrying out their duties.[443] Where the sovereign was not named as a party and where there was no claim against him for damages or otherwise, and where no relief was sought against his person or his property, Byrne J. failed to see how he could be said to be impleaded, either directly or indirectly.[444]

It is clear[445] that a ship requisitioned by a State but remaining in the ownership of the private owner and under the charge of the master and crew falls within the scope of immunity, since it is under the orders of a sovereign State for the service of the State.[446] In *The "Eolo"*[447] a ship had been requisitioned by the Italian Government who were paying her owners for her services. It carried a gun served by gunners of the Italian Navy and material for munitions of war, but was under the private owners' master and crew. The ship was held to be not liable to arrest.

"Possession", for the purpose of the doctrine of immunity, has been held to include a right to immediate possession. Actual physical possession by the foreign sovereign or his servants is not essential to immunity — possession by a bailee on foot of a bailment made by or on behalf of the foreign sovereign is enough.[448] In the *Zarine*[449] case, matters were not quite so simple. The captains of certain Estonian and Latvian vessels that were in port in Cork had signed "certificates of delivery" of their vessels to agents of the government of the U.S.S.R. following the invasion of Estonia and Latvia by the U.S.S.R. and the nationalisation of private property,

---

[440] [1945] I.R. 291.
[441] *Id.*, at 301.
[442] *Id.*, at 300.
[443] *Id.*, at 301. O'Byrne, J. distinguished the cases of *Fenton Textile Association Ltd* v. *Kraggin*, 38 T.L.R. 259 (C.A., 1921) and *Compania Mercantil Argentina* v. *U.S. Shipping Board*, 93 L.J.K.B. 816 (1924).
[444] [1945] I.R. 291, at 303.
[445] *Cheshire & North*, 7th ed., 93.
[446] *The "Eolo"*, [1918] 2 I.R. 78 at 88. See also *The Broadmayne*, [1916] P. 64; *The Arantzarn Mandi* [1939] 1 All E.R. 719; *The Messicano* 32 T.L.R. 519 (1916).
[447] [1918] 2 I.R. 78.
[448] *U.S.A.* v. *Dollfus Meig etc. Compagnie S.A.*, [1952] A.C. 582 (H.L. (Eng.).
[449] [1942] I.R. 148.

including the marine fleet. The captains had done so after having been apprised of a law which stated that captains disobeying the orders of the Government would be regarded as traitors "whereby members of their families and near relations are made responsible". The captains retained actual physical possession of the ships.

In actions *in rem* brought by the captains against the ships, the U.S.S.R. government claimed sovereign immunity on the basis that the ships were their nationalised property. Hanna J. held[450] *inter alia* that the certificates of delivery were not effective legal substitutes for the actual physical control or possession which still remained in the masters and crews who held the ships on behalf of the private owners. The Supreme Court affirmed Hanna, J.'s judgment, but on a narrow ground[451] which did not address the question of title to the vessels.

The kind of property in respect of which immunity may be claimed is not confined to chattels but extends to choses in action.[452] However, a claim to sovereign immunity will not lie in a case where there is a claim in respect of a trust fund or other item of trust property within the jurisdiction.[453] It would seem also that sovereign immunity does not apply in the case of immovables situated within the jurisdiction.[454]

If there is any doubt as to whether a particular person or government is an independent sovereign authority, the recognised practice is to submit through the Master of the High Court the decision for the Irish Government and to accept the answer of the Minister for Foreign Affairs as to whether the Government recognises the particular sovereign authority or not.[455] In *Zarine* v. *Owners of S.S. Romana*,[456] already mentioned, U.S.S.R., the U.S.S.R. moved to set aside the proceedings on the ground that they, a sovereign State, where impleaded. It was held by Hanna, J. in the High Court and, on appeal by the Supreme Court, in view of the answer given by the Minister to the effect that the Government did not recognise the U.S.S.R. as a sovereign independent State either *de jure* or *de facto* in Latvia or Estonia, the claim by the U.S.S.R. to ownership of the ships in question could not be recognised by the Courts, and the U.S.S.R. was not in any way affected by the proceedings.[457]

It is clear from the *Zarine* case that a government recognised as the government

---

[450] *Id.*, at 158. See further p. 205, *infra*.

[451] That the Irish Government did not recognise the U.S.S.R. as the sovereign Government of Latvia or Estonia, either *de facto* or *de jure*.

[452] *Rahimtoola* v. *Nizam of Hyderabad*, [1958] A.C. 379 (H.L. (Eng.)).

[453] *U.S.A.* v. *Dollfuss Mieg et Compagnie SA*, [1952] A.C. 582, at 617 (H.L. (Eng.) *per* Lord Radcliffe) citing *Morgan* v. *Lariviere*, L.R. 7 H.L. 423 (1875).

[454] See *obiter dictum* of Sir Robert Phillimore in *The Charkiel*, L.R. 4 A. & E. 59 at 97 (1873).

[455] *Zarine* v. *Owners of S.S. Ramava* [1942] I.R. 148, at 161.

[456] [1942] I.R. 148.

[457] Different views have been expressed on the question whether the failure of their Government to recognise a particular foreign Government either *de jure* or *de facto* deprives the courts of the power to afford recognition to that foreign Government in civil proceedings. Favouring the view that the executive and the courts must speak with one voice were *Luther* v. *Sagor*, [1921] 1 K.B. 456, at 476 (Roche, J.), *Carl Zeiss Stifftung* v. *Rayner & Keeler Ltd.* (*No. 2*). [1965] Ch. 596, at 656 (*per* Diplock, L.J.) and *Government of the Republic of Spain* v. *S.S. Arantzazu Menti (The Arantzazu Mendi)*, [1939] A.C. 256, at 264 (*per* Lord Atkin); favouring the opposite view were Lord Wilberforce in the *Carl Zeiss Stifftung* case, on appeal, [1967] 1 A.C. 853, at 954 and Lord Denning M.R. and Scarman, L.J. in *In re James (In Insolvent) (Attorney General Intervening)*, [1977] Ch. 41, at 62 and 70, respectively. In *Hesperides Hotels Ltd.* v. *Aegean Turkish Holidays Ltd.*, Lord Denning M.R. said that if it were necessary to make a choice between these conflicting doctrines he would "unhesitatingly" hold that the courts could recognise the laws or acts of a body in effective control of a territory, even though it had not been recognised by the British Government, at any rate in regard to the laws which regulate the day to day affairs of the people, such as their marriages, their divorces, their leases, their occupations and so forth. The question of recognition *de facto* or *de jure* did not determine the outcome of the case in the Supreme Court decision of *Re Carl Zeiss Stiftung* unreported 29th February 1972 (178-1968).

de facto of a particular State may be entitled to claim sovereign immunity even if it is not recognised as the government *de jure.* "A *de jure* government is one which, in the opinion of the person using the phrase, ought to possess the powers of sovereignty, though at the time it may be deprived of them. A *de facto* government is one which is really in possession of them, although the possession may be wrongful or precarious."[458] For the purpose of sovereign immunity no distinction is drawn between the effect of the recognition of the one form of government or the other — if the government of this country has recognised a particular government as the government really in possession of the powers of government in a particular State, then the acts of that government must be treated by the courts of this country with all the respect due to the act of a duly recognised foreign sovereign State.[459]

The law relating to sovereign immunity is complex and technical. Implementation of the European Convention on State Immunity drawn up the Council of Europe in 1972, which Ireland has signed but not ratified, would provide a very suitable vehicle for simplification and clarification of the law and narrower delimitation of the scope of the immunity.

Diplomatic immunity[460]

It has long been established internationally that ambassadors and other political or diplomatic representatives are accorded immunity similar to that accorded to the sovereign state which they represent. In the past such immunity was afforded at common law in this country.[461] The matter is now governed by the Diplomatic Relations and Immunities Act 1967, which gives effect to a number of international conventions concerned with the privilege and immunities of diplomats and international organisations.

The most important effect of the Act is that it gives the force of law in the State to the 1961 Vienna Convention on Diplomatic Relations.[462] The Convention provides[463] for the immunity that is to be enjoyed by a diplomatic agent from the civil and administrative jurisdiction of the receiving State. A "diplomatic agent" is the head of the mission or a member of the diplomatic staff of the mission.[464] The premises of the mission[465] and the private residence of the diplomatic agent[466] are inviolable. The person of a diplomatic agent is also inviolable.[467] He enjoys immunity from the criminal jurisdiction of the receiving State.[468] He also enjoys immunity from its civil and administrative jurisdiction except in the case of three specified kinds of action:

(a) a real action relating to private immovable property situated in the territory of the receiving State, unless the diplomatic agent holds it on behalf of the sending State for the purposes of the mission;

(b) an action relating to succession in which the diplomatic agent is involved

---

[458] *Luther* v. *Sagor* [1921] 3 K.B. 532, at 543, (citation omitted).
[459] *Id.*, See also *Banco de Bilbao* v. *Sando* [1938] 2 All E.R. 253 *Carl Zeiss Stiftung* v. *Rayner and Keeler Ltd. (No. 2)*, [1966] 2 All E.R. 536. *Madzinbanuto* v. *Lardner-Burke,* [1968] 3 All E.R. 561.
[460] See Beckett, *Consular Immunities,* 21 Br. Yrbk of Internat. L. 34 (1944), Dugard, *Consular Immunity,* 83 S.A.L.J. 126 (1966).
[461] See, for example, *Norton* v. *General Accident, Fire and Life Assurance,* 74 I.L.T.R. 123 (1940), *National Bank Ltd.* v. *Hunter,* [1948] Ir. Jur. Rep. 33.
[462] Section 5(1) and 1st Schedule.
[463] Article 31(1).
[464] Article 1(e).
[465] Article 22.1.
[466] Article 30.1.
[467] Article 29.
[468] Article 31(1).

as executor, administrator, heir or legatee as a private person and not on behalf of the sending State;

(c) an action relating to any professional or commercial activity exercised by the diplomatic agent in the receiving State outside his official functions.[469]

A diplomatic agent is not obliged to give evidence as a witness[470] and no measures of execution may be taken in respect of him except in the three cases mentioned above and even then the measures concerned must be taken without infringing the inviolability of his person or of his residence.[471]

Apart from the specific exceptions mentioned above, the immunity enjoyed by a diplomatic agent extends to acts performed outside the course of his official duties as well as to those performed within. However, if the diplomatic agent is a national of or permanently resident in the receiving State, he enjoys immunity from jurisdiction, and inviolability, only in respect of official acts performed in the exercise of his functions, except insofar as additional privileges and immunities may be granted by the receiving State.[472] The members of the family of a diplomatic agent forming part of his household enjoy the same privileges and immunities as the diplomatic agent himself if they are not nationals of the receiving State.[473]

Privileges and immunities are not confined to members of the diplomatic staff of the mission. Members of the administrative and technical staff, together with members of their families forming part of their respective households, if they are not nationals of or permanently resident in the receiving State, enjoy the same privileges and immunities as diplomatic agents, except that the immunity from civil and administrative jurisdiction does not extend to acts performed outside the course of their duties.[474] Members of the service staff of the mission (i.e. members of the staff of the mission in the domestic service of the mission[475]) who are not nationals of or permanently resident in the receiving State enjoy immunity in respect of acts performed in the course of their duties.[476] Members of the staff of the mission other than diplomatic agents, who are nationals of or permanently resident in the receiving State, enjoy privileges and immunities only to the extent admitted by the receiving State but the receiving State must exercise its jurisdiction over these persons in such a manner as not to interfere unduly with the performance of the functions of the mission.[477] The same position obtains in respect of private servants of members of the mission,[478] whether they are nationals of or permanently resident in the receiving State[479] or not.[480]

The immunity from jurisdiction of all the persons referred to above may be waived by the sending State.[481] Waiver must always be express[482] but the initiation of proceedings by a person enjoying immunity from jurisdiction precludes him from invoking immunity in respect of any counter-claim directly connected with the principal claim.[483] Waiver of immunity from jurisdiction is not to be held to imply

---

[469] Article 31(1).
[470] Article 31(2).
[471] Article 31(3).
[472] Article 38(1).
[473] Article 37(1).
[474] Article 37(2).
[475] Article 1(g).
[476] Article 37(3).
[477] Article 38(2).
[478] "Members of the mission" are the head of the mission and the members of the diplomatic staff, of the administrative and technical staff and of the service staff of the mission: Art. 1(b) & (c).
[479] Article 38(2).
[480] Article 37(4).
[481] Article 32(1).
[482] Article 32(2).
[483] Article 32(3).

waiver of immunity in respect of the execution of the judgment, for which a separate waiver is necessary.[484]

Every person entitled to privileges and immunities enjoys them from the moment he enters the territory of the receiving State on proceeding to take up his post, or, if he is already in its territory, from the moment when his appointment is notified to the Ministry for Foreign Affairs.[485] When such a person's functions come to an end, his privileges and immunities normally cease at the moment when he leaves the country, or on expiry of a reasonable period in which to do so but, with respect to acts performed in the exercise of his functions as a member of the mission, immunity continues to subsist.[486]

The 1967 Act also gives the force of law in the State to the 1963 Vienna Convention on Consular Relations.[487] Under that Convention consular officers[488] and consular employers[489] are not to be amenable to the jurisdiction of the judicial or administrative authorities of the receiving State in respect of acts performed in the exercise of consular functions.[490] This immunity does not, however, apply in respect of a civil action either:

(a) arising out of a contract concluded by a consular officer or employee in which he did not contract expressly or impliedly as an agent of the sending State; or

(b) by a third party for damage arising from an accident in the receiving State caused by a vehicle, vessel or aircraft.[491]

The Convention also contains provisions[492] for waiver of privileges and immunities by the sending State similar to those contained in the Convention on Diplomatic Relations.[493]

Provision is also made in the 1967 Act for the privileges and immunities of numerous international organisations, including the United Nations[494] and its specialised agencies,[495] the Council of Europe,[496] the Organisation for Economic

---

[484] Article 32(4).

[485] Article 39(1).

[486] Article 39(2). At common law it had been held in *Norton* v. *General Accident, Fire and Life Assurance Co.*, 74 I.L.T.R. 123 (1940), that immunity lapsed when a diplomatic agent ceased to be accredited. That case had also held (following *Dickinson* v. *Del Solar: In re Mobile and General Insurance Company Ltd.*, [1930] 1 K.B. 376) that diplomatic privilege does not confer immunity from legal responsibility, but merely immunity from legal jurisdiction. The action was one against an insurance company for damages as a result of a road accident involving one of their insured, a foreign diplomat who, following issue of the summons against him, had entered a conditional appearance without prejudice to his right to raise his diplomatic privilege and who had in the meantime left the country. Under section 78(1) (*d*) the Road Traffic Act 1933 the court had power to allow an injured person to proceed directly against an owner or driver's insurers or guarantors if it was satisfied that he was not in the State, or could not be found, or could not be served with process, or that it was for any other reason just and equitable. Maguire J. held that it was just and equitable to allow the insurance company to be proceeded against because the plaintiff would be greatly impeded and delayed in obtaining relief if the application was not granted, the reason for the delay being that the "proper defendant" had raised his diplomatic privilege.

[487] Section 6(1) and 2nd Schedule.

[488] "Consular officer" means any person, including the head of a consular post, entrusted in that capacity with the exercise of consular functions (Article 1(d)). "Consular post" means any consulate general, consulate, vice-consulate or consular agency.

[489] "Consular employee" means any person employed in the administrative or technical service of a consular post.

[490] Article 43(1).

[491] Article 43(2).

[492] Article 45.

[493] *Supra*, pp. 178-180.

[494] Sections 7-15 and 3rd Schedule.

[495] Sections 16-20 and 4th Schedule. Among the agencies covered are the WHO, the ICAO, the ILO, UNESCO, the IMF.

[496] Sections 21-25 and 5th Schedule.

Cooperation and Development[497] and the Customs Cooperation Council.[498]

The Act also provides for the general immunities of any other international organisation designated by order[499] and of any international judicial body established under an agreement to which the State is a party.[500] Finally, it enables general immunities to be extended to persons attending international conferences in the State on behalf of a government or State.[501] The privileges and immunities of the European Communities are provided for by Article 28 of, and the Protocol to, the 1965 Brussels Treaty establishing a Single Council and a Single Commission of the European Communities (the "Merger Treaty") which was made part of the law of the State by section 2 of the European Communities Act 1972.

One last point should be mentioned. In *National Bank Ltd.* v. *Hunter*[502] the court gave judgment in default of appearance in an action for a liquidated sum against the consul-general for a foreign state at Dublin, the defendant having taken no step to indicate an intention of relying upon such diplomatic privilege (if any) as he might have been entitled to. The grounds of the judgment are not specified in the report but one of the submissions made by counsel for the plaintiff[503] was that the defendant had neither appeared nor pleaded nor had he claimed privilege and there was nothing to oust the jurisdiction of the court; no question of diplomatic immunity should be considered unless raised by the defendant and his right to raise it established in evidence by a statement from the Minister for External (now Foreign) Affairs. These propositions would seem to remain unaffected by the 1967 Act as they concern procedural matters that are not provided for as such in the Vienna Conventions.

THE EEC JUDGMENTS CONVENTION[504]

The EEC Convention of 1968 on Jurisdiction and the Enforcement of Judgments

[497] Sections 26-31.
[498] Sections 32-36. See also the Air Navigation (Eurocontrol) Act 1983, section 2.
[499] Sections 39-42 of the 1967 Act.
[500] Section 43.
[501] Sections 44-45.
[502] [1948] Ir. Jur. Rep. 33.
[503] Citing *Engelke* v. *Musmann*, [1928] A.C. 433.
[504] See G. Droz, *La Compétence judiciare et l'effet des jugements dans la CEE* (1972), M. Weser, *Convention communautaire sur la compétence judiciare et l'execution des décisions* (1975), L. Collins, *The Civil Jurisdiction and Judgments Act 1982*, chs. 1, 4 (1983), Moloney & Kremlis, *The Brussels Convention on Jurisdiction and the Enforcement of Judgments*, 79 Incorp. L. Soc. of Ireland Gazette 329 (1985), 80 Incorp. L. Soc. of Ireland Gazette 5 (1986), (Part 1 deals with jurisdiction), Pointon, *The EEC Convention on the Recognition and Enforcement of Civil and Commercial Judgments, and Its Implications for English Law*, 1975/2 Leg. Issues of Eur. Integration 1, McClellan, *The Convention of Brussels of September 27, 1968 on Jurisdiction and the Recognition and Enforcement of Judgments in Civil and Commercial Matters*, 15 C.M.L.R. 228 (1978), Collins, *The Jurisdiction and Judgments Convention — Some Practical Aspects of United Kingdom Accession, with Particular Reference to Jurisdiction*, in K. Lipstein ed., *Harmonization of Private International Law by the EEC*, 91 (1978), Gill, 1 *Jurisdiction and Enforcement of Foreign Judgments in Ireland*, 4 J. of Irish Soc. for European L. 3 (1980), Terry, *Convention of Accession of Denmark, Ireland and the United Kingdom to the Convention on Jurisdiction and Enforcement of Judgments in Civil and Commercial Matters*, 4 J. of Irish Soc. for European L. 26 (1980), Hartley, *The Case Law on the Application of the 1968 Convention in the Six Original Member States*, 4 J. of Irish Soc. for European L. 56 (1980), Kohler, *The Case Law of the European Court on the Judgment Convention*, 7 Eur. L. Rev. 3, 103 (1982), Gothot & Holleaux, *La Convention entre les Etats membres de la Communauté économique européenne sur la compétence judiciare et l'exécution des décisions en matière civile et commerciale*, 98 J. du Ir. Internat. 747 (1971), Zaphiriou, *The EEC Convention on Jurisdiction and Enforcement of Judgments*, [1969] J. of Bus. L. 74, Goldman, *Un traité fédérateur: La Convention entre les Etats membres de la CEE sur la reconnaissance et l'exécution des décisions en matière civile et commerciale*, 7 Rev. trim. de dr. Eur. 1 (1971), Herzog, *The Common Market Convention on Jurisdiction and the Enforcement of Judgments: An Interim Update* 10 Virg. J. of Internat. L. 417 (1977), Giardina, *The European Court and the Brussels Convention on Jurisdiction and Judgments*, 27 Int. & Comp. L. Q. 263 (1978),

in Civil and Commercial Matters[505] came into force between the original six Member States of the European Communities in 1973. On becoming members of the Community, Denmark, Ireland and the United Kingdom undertook to accede to the Convention and to this end to enter into negotiations with the original Six in order to make the necessary adjustments to it.[506] A Convention of Accession of the three to the Convention was signed in 1978[507] which made a number of amendments to the 1968 text.[508] Ratification of the Convention, as amended, is an obligation of membership of the European Communities and requires legislation to make the Convention part of Irish law. In December 1986, the Judgments (European Communities) Bill 1986 was published. Its progress in the Seanad was halted by the general election in February 1987 but, in view of its uncontroversial content, the Bill, or a close equivalent, is very likely to reappear shortly on the agenda of the Oireachtas.

The implementation of the Convention will bring about substantial changes in Irish law relating to jurisdiction and the enforcement of judgments in relation to civil and commercial matters.[509] It should, of course, be remembered that the Convention applies only in relation to E.E.C. States. It does not disturb the continued application of the common law rules as to jurisdiction where other States are concerned.

The Convention specifically prohibits the application of certain types of exorbitant jurisdiction[510] against persons domiciled in another Contracting State, including, in the case of Ireland, jurisdiction founded on the document instituting the proceedings having been served on the defendant during his temporary presence in Ireland.[511]

This limitation does not apply in relation to persons domiciled outside the European Economic Community.[512] Thus, service on a Canadian domiciliary temporarily present here will continue to be effective.[513] However, Article 59 permits a Contracting State to agree, by Convention, not to recognise judgments given in other Contracting States against defendants domiciled or habitually resident in a country

---

Hanschild, *The Convention of 27 September 1968 on Jurisdiction and the Enforcement of Judgments in Civil and Commercial Matters,* in R. M. Goode & K. R. Simmonds eds., *Commercial Operations in Europe,* 51 (1978).

[505] See *Bulletin of the European Communities,* Supplement to 2/1969 for English text of the original convention; see also Jenard Report on the Convention and Protocol in Official Journal of the European Communities, Vol. 22, No. C.59, 5 March 1979.

[506] Article 3(2) of the Act of Accession *(Official Journal of the European Communities,* No. L 73, Special Edition, 27 March 1973). See further Terry, *Convention of Accession of Denmark, Ireland and the United Kingdom to the Convention on Jurisdiction and Enforcement of Judgments in Civil and Commercial Matters,* 4 J. of Irish Soc. for European L. 26, at 26-27 (1980), T. C. Hartley, *Civil Jurisdiction and Judgments,* chs. 1-4 (1984), Herzog, *The Common Market Convention on Jurisdiction and the Enforcement of Judgments: An Interim Update,* 10 Virg. J. of Internat. L. 417, at 433-439 (1977).

[507] For text see OJ, vol. 21, No. L. 304, 30 October 1978: for *Schlosser Report,* see OJ, vol. 22, No. C. 59/7, 5 March 1979.

[508] For the consolidated text, as amended by the Convention of Accession, see OJ, Vol. 21, No. L. 304, 30 October 1978. The 1978 Accession has been in force as between the original six and Denmark since 1 November 1986, and as between the original six, Denmark and the United Kingdom since 1 January 1987. The Accession Convention for Greece, signed in 1982, is not yet in force.

[509] Article 1(1). The Convention does not extend to revenue, customs or administrative matters, nor does it apply to certain specified family law matters, wills and succession, bankruptcy and winding-up proceedings, social security and arbitration. Article 1(2) See further *infra* p. 605. For consideration of the jurisdictional rules of the original six Member States before the Convention came into force for those countries, see Weser, *Bases of Judicial Jurisdiction in the Common Market Countries,* 10 Amer. J. of Comp. L. 323 (1961). For a more wide-ranging study, see de Vries & Lowenfield, *Jurisdiction in Personal Actions — A Comparison of Civil Law Views,* 44 Iowa L. Rev. 306 (1959).

[510] Cf. De Winter, *Excessive Jurisdiction in Private International Law,* 17 Int. & Comp. L.Q. 706 (1968). Article 16 of the 1968 Convention by way of exception to this general principle is considered *infra,* pp. 189-190.

[511] Article 3(2). See *Schlosser Report,* para. 85.

[512] Article 4.

[513] Subject to Article 16, which deals with exclusive jurisdiction: cf. Article 4.

outside the European Economic Community where the judgments are based on one of the exorbitant jurisdictions specified in Article 3(2).

It should be noted that the concept of 'domicile' as used in the Convention has greater affinities with that concept as used in Civil Law countries as a factor connecting an individual to a particular place for jurisdictional and administrative purposes than it has to the concept as used in common law countries mainly as a factor connecting a person to a particular legal system for such purposes as status and succession.[514] It was envisaged when the Convention of Accession was being drawn up that Ireland and Britain would provide in their implementing legislation for a concept of domicile, for the purposes of the Convention, which would tend to reflect more the concept of domicile as understood in the original EEC Member States.[515] Habitual residence[516] or ordinary residence or residence are possible alternatives for use as a definition of 'domicile' for the purpose of the Convention.[517]

The Convention is a double one based on direct rules of jurisdiction. It does not merely lay down rules as to the bases on which jurisdiction must have been exercised in order for a foreign judgment to be enforced in a Contracting State. Many international Conventions contain such indirect rules of jurisdiction — rules which operate in the country recognising or enforcing a judgment rather than in the country where the case is heard. Instead the rules of jurisdiction laid down in the EEC Convention are to be applied in each Contracting State independently of any question of proceedings for recognition and enforcement. The Convention therefore lays down common rules for the Contracting States as to the bases on which jurisdiction is to be exercised *vis-a-vis* domiciliaries of other Contracting States and if jurisdiction is exercised in a case being heard in a State where the Convention is in force otherwise than in accordance with its rules, then the defendant can (and indeed, in view of Article 28, para. 3, *should*) object to the jurisdiction at that point rather than wait until enforcement of the judgment given in that State is being sought in some other Contracting State.

The general jurisdictional principle is that persons domiciled in a Contracting State must be sued in the courts of that State.[518] A number of instances of special jurisdiction are also provided for. In these instances a person who is domiciled in a Contracting State, in addition to being sued in the courts of that State, may also be sued in the courts of certain other Contracting States.[519] Under the principle of these special jurisdictional rules a defendant may be sued:

[514] See *Schlosser Report*, paras. 71-72, Terry, *Convention of Accession of Denmark, Ireland and the United Kingdom to the Convention on Jurisdiction and Enforcement of Judgments in Civil and Commercial Matters*, 4 J. of Irish Soc. for European L. 26, at 28 (1980), Collins, *The Jurisdiction and Judgments Convention — Some Practical Aspects of United Kingdom Accession, with Particular Reference to Jurisdiction*, in K. Lipstein ed., *Harmonization of Private International Law by the E.E.C.*, 91, at 92-93 (1978).

[515] *Schlosser Report*, para. 73. See also *Collins*, ch. 3, and Britain's Civil Jurisdiction and Judgments Act 1982, section 41.

[516] See *supra*, pp. 98-100.

[517] See Terry, *supra*, at 28-29. The Judgments (European Communities) Bill 1986 addressed this question: see section 13 and Part I of the Fifth Schedule. Under the Bill, an individual would be domiciled in the State, or in a state other than a Contracting State "if, but only if, he is ordinarily resident in the State or in that other State". An individual would be domiciled *in a place* in the State, "if, but only if, he is domiciled in the State and is ordinarily resident or carries on any profession, business or occupation in that place." This latter concept is required for certain purposes of the 1968 Convention, which allow proceedings to be brought in courts for the particular place where one of the parties is domiciled (cf., e.g., Article 5.2). The draft adopted in the Bill reflected venue provisions of our domestic law: Courts of Justice Act 1924, section 79 and Courts (Supplemental Provisions) Act 1961, Third Schedule: see the *Explanatory and Financial Memorandum to the Jurisdiction of Courts and Enforcement of Judgments (European Communities) Bill 1986*, para. 49.

[518] Article 2(1) of the Convention.

[519] Article 3(1).

(a) in matters relating to a contract, in the courts for the place of performance[520] *of the obligation in question*[521]

This means that certain grounds of jurisdiction provided for in Order 11, Rule 1(e) of the Rules of the Superior Courts 1986[522], namely, that a contract was made[523] within the jurisdiction or is governed by Irish law, will no longer be available against EEC domiciliaries.[524]

A transitional provision[525] was included in the 1978 Convention on Accession which permits the Irish courts to exercise jurisdiction where the parties have agreed in writing before the entry into force of the Convention that the contract is to be governed by Irish law.[526]

The scope of the concept of "contract" for the purposes of Article 5(1) requires some consideration. Questions of characterisation may give rise to difficulty. The concept should be given a Community interpretation.[527] Thus, it may be that quasi-contractual claims arising under statute, which do not fall within the scope of rule 1(e)(i) of Order 11,[528] could be regarded as coming under Article 5(1).

One commentator has expressed the view that ".... there can be little doubt that claims arising out of an ineffective contract or claims to necessary goods supplied to a person under incapacity are covered by Art. 5(1); other claims may be closer to tort claims, and included, if at all, under Art. 5(3)".[529]

Jurisdiction under Article 5(1) may be invoked even in cases where the defendant denies the existence of a contract. Practical considerations require that a defendant should be prevented from escaping from the application of Article 5(1) by mere assertion that there was no legally binding agreement. The European Court accepted this in *Effer SpA* v. *Kantner*,[530] where it was stated that, if the national court had no jurisdiction to determine this question,

> "Article 5(1) of the Convention would be in danger of being deprived of its legal effect, since it would be accepted that, in order to defeat the rule contained in that provision, it is sufficient for one of the parties to claim that the contract does not exist. On the contrary, respect for the aims and spirit of the Convention demands that provision should be construed as meaning that the courts called upon to decide a dispute arising out of a contract may examine, of its own motion even, the essential preconditions for its jurisdiction, having regard to conclusive and relevant evidence adduced by the party concerned, establishing the existence or the inexistence of the contract."[531]

---

[520] Where the law applicable to the contract permits the parties to specify the place of performance of an obligation without complying with any special condition of form, an agreement on the place of the performance of the obligation will be sufficient to found jurisdiction in that place: *Zelger* v. *Salinitri*, Case 56/79, [1980] E.C.R. 89, [1980] 2 C.M.L.R. 635; see further *Collins*, 55-56.

[521] Article 5(1).

[522] See *supra*, pp. 139-143.

[523] Whether through an agent or otherwise.

[524] *Terry, supra*, at 33. It should also be noted that Article 5(1) does not exactly coincide with our jurisdictional ground based on the breach of a contract within the State. It is quite possible that a contract to be performed outside Ireland may be breached within the State, by repudiation, for example. See *supra*, p. 144, and *Collins*, 52.

[525] Article 35. See Terry, *supra*, at 33-34, *Collins*, 52.

[526] The provision applies similarly to Britain, but does not affect Scotland, since courts there do not exercise jurisdiction on the basis of the law governing the contract: *Collins*, 52.

[527] *Id.*, 53.

[528] *Clare Co. Co.* v. *Wilson*, [1913] 2 I.R. 89, *Killiney U.D.C.* v. *Kirkwood*, [1917] 2 I.R. 614, *Shipsey* v. *British and South American Steam Navigation Co.*, [1936] I.R. 65 (Sup. Ct.). See further *supra*, pp. 141-142.

[529] *Collins*, 53 (footnote reference omitted).

[530] Case 38/81, [1982] E.C.R. 825.

[531] [1982] E.C.R., at 834. The Court derived support from Case 73/77, *Sanders* v. *Van der Putte*, [1977] E.C.R. 2383, which had held that the jurisdiction in relation to tenancies of immovable property applies even where there is a dispute as to the existence of a lease.

So far as determining the place of performance is concerned, the national courts must each apply their own rules of conflict of laws.[532] This means, of course, that two (or more) courts could each hold that the place of performance was within their own country.[533] The problems that may result from this will largely be resolved when the Contractual Obligations Convention comes into force.[534]

In *Ets. A. de Bloos SPRL* v. *Bouyer*,[535] the European Court held that the word "obligation" in Article 5(1) "refers to the contractual obligation forming the basis of the legal proceedings".[536] In *Ivenel* v. *Schwab*,[537] however, the Court, influenced by the Contractual Obligations Convention, modified its approach so as to give prominence to the "characteristic obligation" of the contract. *Ivenel* v. *Schwab* was concerned with an employment contract, which, like insurance and consumer contracts, commands special rules under the Contractual Obligations Convention. The Judgments Convention, however, contains special jurisdictional rules for only insurance and consumer contracts. It may well be that the Court, in view of how the Contractual Obligations Convention had unfolded, decided that the time was opportune to harmonise the approaches as far as possible.[538]

It is not clear whether the concept of "characteristic obligation" extends to all contracts or is limited to employment contracts. The strong emphasis on social policy in the decision might suggest that the Court favoured the latter solution.[539] Moreover the Court in *Ivenel* v. *Schwab* sought to distinguish its holding in *De Bloos* v. *Bouyer*[540] on the basis that the problem raised in the case before the Court in *Ivenel* v. *Schwab* was "whether the same criterion must be applied to cases of the kind described by the national court".[541]

One advantage of the approach favoured in *Ivenel* v. *Schwab* is that it offers a simple, workable solution where the plaintiff claims for several breaches of contract, occurring in a number of different countries.[542]

(*b*) *in matters relating to maintenance, in the courts for the place where the maintenance creditor is domiciled or habitually resident or, if the matter is ancillary to proceedings concerning the status of a person, in the court which, according to its own law, has jurisdiction to entertain these proceedings, unless that jurisdiction is based solely on the nationality of one of the parties*[543]

A distinction should be drawn between status proceedings (such as proceedings for divorce), which are excluded by Article 1 of the Convention, and proceedings for maintenance ancillary to a divorce, which fall within the scope of Article 5(2).[544] Maintenance agreements appear to fall under Article 5(1) rather than

---

[532] *Industria Tessili Italiana Como* v. *Dunlop AG*, Case 12/76, [1976] E.C.R. 1473, where it was stated at 1485:

> "It is for the court before which the matter is brought to establish under the Convention whether the place of performance is situate within its territorial jurisdiction. For this purpose it must determine in accordance with its own rules of conflict of laws what is the law applicable to the legal relationship in question and define in accordance with that law the place of performance of the contractual obligation in question."

[533] *Hartley*, 43.

[534] *Id.*, 43-44. Cf. Giardina, *The European Court and the Brussels Convention on Jurisdiction and Judgments*, 27 Int. & Comp. L.Q. 263, at 269-270 (1978). See further *infra*, p. 565.

[535] Case 14/76, [1976] E.C.R. 1497.

[536] [1976] E.C.R., at 1508.

[537] Case 133/81, [1982] E.C.R. 1891, noted by Hartley, 7 Eur. L. Rev. 328 (1982).

[538] See *Hartley*, 46-47.

[539] *Id.*, 47.

[540] *Supra*.

[541] [1982] E.C.R., at 1899.

[542] Cf. *Hartley*, 45-46.

[543] Article 5(2) (as amended by the 1978 Accession Convention).

[544] See *De Cavel* v. *De Cavel (No. 1)*, Case 143/78, [1979] E.C.R. 1055, [1979] 2 C.M.L.R. 547, and contrast *De Cavel* v. *De Cavel (No. 2)*, Case 120/79, [1980] E.C.R. 731 [1980] 3 C.M.L.R. 1.

Article 5(2),[545] unless the maintenance agreement "merely crystallizes an existing
maintenance obligation which originated from a family relationship".[546] To fall
within the scope of Article 5(2), it is not necessary that the maintenance order be
for a periodical payment: orders for lump sums and even the creation of charges
on property and the transfer of property come within its purview.[547]

*(c) in matters relating to tort, delict or quasi-delict, in the courts for the place where
the harmful event occurred* [548]

*(d) as regards a civil claim for damages or restitution which is based on an act
giving rise to criminal proceedings, in the court seized of those proceedings, to the
extent that that court has jurisdiction under its own law to entertain civil
proceedings*[549]

Courts in civil law jurisdictions, and to a lesser extent common law
jurisdictions,[550] have power to award damages in criminal proceedings. The
jurisdictional rule contained in Article 5(4) is very straightforward, enabling the
criminal court to make these awards without any worries as to problems of jurisdiction
and enforcement.[551]

*(e) as regards a dispute arising out of the operations of a branch, agency or other
establishment, in the courts for the place in which the branch, agency or other
establishment is situated* [552]

The meaning of the concepts contained in this heading must be interpreted by the
criteria of the Convention itself rather than by purely national standards.[553] The
European Court[554] has prescribed the characteristics of a branch, agency or other
establishment. Rather than consider each of these three types of business
establishments separately, ascribing distinctive characteristics to each, the Court has
adopted a unified approach.[555]

It is essential that there be "a place of business which has the appearance of
permanency ...",[556] that the establishment be "subject to the direction and control

---

[545] *Schlosser Report*, para. 92.
[546] *Id.* Cf. the Illegitimate Children (Affiliation Orders) Act 1930, sections 8, 18.
[547] *Schlosser Report*, para. 93.
[548] Article 5(3). See *Handelskwekerij C.J. Bier B.V. and De Stickting "Rainwater"* v. *Mines de Potasse
d'Alsace*, Case 21/76, [1976] E.C.R. 1735; [1977] 1 C.M.L.R. 284. See further pp. 151-153 *supra*.
[549] Article 5(4). See further *Collins*, 61. For orders for the delivery of property see the Police Property
Act 1897, section 1.
[550] Cf. the Probation of Offenders Act 1907, sections 1(3) and 1(4), Summary Jurisdiction over Children
(Ireland) Act 1884, section 7, Children Act 1908, s.99, E. Ryan & P. Magee, *The Irish Criminal
Process*, 411 (1983), and the Consumer Information Act 1978 section 17(3).
[551] *Hartley*, 53. Art. II of the Protocol to the Convention contains special rules for cases where the accused
is tried *in absentia*. See Case 157/80 *Rinkan*, [1981] E.C.R. 1391, holding that the reference in Art.
II to "an offence which was not intentionally committed" should be understood as meaning "any
offence the legal definition of which does not require, either expressly or as appears from the nature
of the offence defined, the existence of intent on the part of the accused to commit the punishable
act or omission". For analysis of *Rinkan*, see Hartley, 6 Eur. L. Rev. 483 (1981).
[552] Article 5(5). See Fawcett, *Methods of Carrying on Business and Article 5(5) of the Brussels Convention*,
9 Eur. L. Rev. 326 (1984), Moloney & Kremlis, *supra*, at 333.
[553] Case 33/78, *Somafer SA* v. *Saar-Ferngas AG*, [1978] E.C.R. 2183, at 2190-2191. See Hartley, 4
Eur. L. Rev. 127, at 128-129 (1979).
[554] Case 14/76, *Ets. A. de Bloos SPRL* v. *Bouyer*, [1976] E.C.R. 1497, noted 2 Eur. L. Rev. 61 (1977).
Case 33/78, *Somafer SA* v. *Saar-Ferngas AG*, [1978] E.C.R. 213, noted by Giardina, 27 Int. & Comp.
L.Q. 263, at 267-268 (1978), Kohler, 7 Eur. L. Rev. 3, at 7-13 (1982), Hartley, 4 Eur. L. Rev.
127 (1979), Case 139/80, *Blanckaert and Willems PV PA* v. *Luise Trost*, [1981] E.C.R. 819, noted
by Hartley, 6 Eur. L. Rev. 481 (1981).
[555] Fawcett, *supra*, at 328-329.
[556] *Somafer*, [1978] E.C.R., at 2192. See Fawcett, *supra*, at 330. Cf. *Donovan* v. *North German Lloyd
Steamship Co.*, [1933] I.R. 33 (High Ct., O'Byrne, J., 1932) discussed *supra*, pp. 128-129.

of the parent body,"[557] although itself having "a certain autonomy";[558] and that it should have a management and be "materially equipped to negotiate business with third parties so that the latter, although knowing that there will if necessary be a legal link with the parent body, the head office of which is abroad, do not have to deal directly with such parent body but may transact business at the place of business constituting the extension."[559]

On the question whether it is essential that the establishment should be without legal personality the position is unclear. So far as branches are concerned, it is accepted[560] that they lack legal personality. The Court's disposition to apply identical rules to all types of establishment in prescribing their essential characteristics suggests that agencies and other establishments should also lack legal personality. Whether this is a desirable approach has been doubted.[561] Translating the general characteristics required of establishments into practical reality, it seems clear that a branch office (however described) comes within the scope of Article 5(5).[562]

In contrast a sales representative normally will not come within its scope, since he will not work from an office, will usually be only temporarily in a country where he is soliciting sales and will lack sufficient autonomy to conclude contracts on behalf of his company.[563] Moreover, the Court has held that Article 5(5) embraces neither an exclusive sales distributor[564] nor an independent commercial agent who merely negotiates and transmits orders to the parent body, and who is not required to devote any fixed minimum amount of time to the work.[565] It should be noted that Article 5(5) relates only to defendant companies or firms with the parent body in one Contracting State and an establishment in another Contracting State; where the parent body is outside the Contracting States, the position is covered by Article 4, which provides that the jurisdiction of the courts of each Contracting State[566] is to be determined by the law of that State.

(f) in his capacity as settlor, trustee or beneficiary of a trust created by the operation of a statute, or by a written instrument, or created orally and evidenced in writing, in the courts of the Contracting State in which the trust is domiciled[567]

The 1968 Convention contained no reference to trusts since the concept of trusts is not a part of the law of the original six Member States. The solution adopted by the Convention of Accession is to confer jurisdiction on the courts of the State where the trust is domiciled. As Mr. Patrick Terry has observed:

"The application to trusts of the general jurisdictional provisions of the Convention could result in a foreign court, to the exclusion of an Irish or U.K. court, being called

---

[557] *De Bloos*, [1976] E.C.R., at 1510.
[558] *Id.*, at 1519 (Advocate-General Reischl). See further Fawcett, *supra*, at 330-331.
[559] *Somafer*, [1978] E.C.R., at 2192. See *Collins*, 62-63.
[560] *De Bloos*, [1976] E.C.R., at 1519 (Advocate-General Reischl).
[561] Fawcett, *supra*, at 333.
[562] *Id.*
[563] Cf. Case 33/78, *Somafer SA* v. *Saar-Ferngas AG*, [1978] E.C.R. 213. See Fawcett, *supra*, at 334-335.
[564] Case 14/76, *De Bloos Sprl* v. *Buyer SA*, [1976] E.C.R. 1497, [1977] 1 C.M.L.R. 60. See Fawcett, *supra*, at 336-337.
[565] Case 139/80, *Blanckaert and Willems PVBA* v. *Trost*, [1981] E.C.R. 819, [1982] 2 C.M.L.R. 1. See Fawcett, *supra*, at 1335-336.
[566] Subject to the instances of exclusive jurisdiction provided for by Article 16: cf. *infra*, pp. 189-191. Note also that insurers (Article 8(2)) and suppliers of goods and services to consumers (Article 13(2)) whose parent body is outside the Contracting States but with a branch, agency or other establishment in one of the Contracting States are deemed to be domiciled in that State so far as disputes arising out of the operations of the branch, agency or establishment are concerned.
[567] Article 5(6). See also Article 17.

upon to decide questions in a highly complex and technical area of law with which the foreign court could be presumed to be unfamiliar. It was clearly in the interests of trustees and beneficiaries that questions relating to the internal affairs of the trust should be capable of being determined by a court familiar with the law relating to trusts.[568]

Constructive or implied trusts are not included;[569] nor are testamentary trusts or trustees in bankruptcy, since they are excluded by Article 1.[570] Where a trust relates only to land situated in Ireland, the Irish courts have exclusive jurisdiction.[571]

It appears that Article 5(6) is meant to deal with the internal, rather than external, relations of a trust:[572] thus, proceedings for breach of trust brought by a beneficiary against a trustee would be within Article 5(6), but not an action against the trustee by third parties.[573]

In determining whether a trust is domiciled in a Contracting State, the court of that State should apply its own rules of private international law.[574]

(g) *as regards a dispute concerning the payment of remuneration claimed in respect of the salvage of a cargo or freight, in the court under the authority of which the cargo or freight in question*

　　(i) *has been arrested to secure such payment, or*

　　(ii) *could have been so arrested, but bail or other security has been given provided that this provision applies only if it is claimed that the defendant has an interest in the cargo or freight or had such an interest at the time of salvage*[575]

This provision can best be understood by considering the broader question of admiralty jurisdiction.[576] Had the Convention of Accession not addressed the issue, Irish *in rem* jurisdiction in maritime claims would have been seriously eroded,[577] in view of the application of the general rule basing jurisdiction on domicile. The solution adopted was that all Member States should ratify the 1952 Brussels Convention on the Arrest of Seagoing Ships, which permits the assumption of jurisdiction when a ship (or sister ship) is arrested. By reason of Article 57 of the 1968 Convention, the jurisdictional provisions of the Brussels Convention would then prevail.[578] Neither Ireland nor Denmark has ratified the Brussels Convention. Article 36 of the Convention on Accession contains transitory provisions dealing with this difficulty.

The Brussels Convention does not extend to permitting a maritime lien for salvage in relation to cargo. This lien can be important, especially in cases where only the cargo is salvaged or the salvaged ship is so badly damaged that its value is less than the cost of the salvage operation.[579] Moreover, prior rights can also arise in relation

---

[568] Terry, *Convention of Accession of Denmark, Ireland and the United Kingdom to the Convention on Jurisdiction and Enforcement of Judgments in Civil and Commercial Matters,* 4 J. of Irish Soc. for European L. 26, at 31 (1980).

[569] Cf. the *Schlosser Report,* para. 117.

[570] Cf. *Collins,* 64.

[571] Article 16(1).

[572] Cf. the *Schlosser Report,* para. 117, *Collins,* 64.

[573] *Collins,* 64.

[574] Article 53(2). The British solution, in the Civil Jurisdiction and Judgments Act 1982, section 45(3), is that a trust "is domiciled in a part of the United Kingdom if and only if the system of law of that part is the system of law with which the trust has its closest and most real connection." The Jurisdiction of Courts and Enforcement of Judgments (European Communities) Bill 1986, Fifth Schedule, Part V, adopted the same definition.

[575] Article 5(7).

[576] See *supra,* pp. 161-162, and cf. the *Schlosser Report,* paras. 121-130, Terry, *supra,* at 31-32.

[577] Terry, *supra,* at 31.

[578] *Id.*

[579] *Schlosser Report,* para. 122.

to freight. "If freight is payable solely in the event of the safe arrival of the cargo at the place of destination, it is appropriate that the salvage firm should have a prior right to be satisfied out of the claim to freight which was preserved due to the salvage of the cargo."[580]

Article 5(7) ensures that jurisdiction will lie after the arrest of salvaged cargo or freight claims. Furthermore Article 6A ensures that, where there is jurisdiction in actions relating to ships, that jurisdiction will extend to claims for limitation of liability.[581]

Insurance and Consumer Cases

Special exclusive jurisdiction rules are also laid down which are designed to protect the interests of weaker parties to contracts in which there is unequal bargaining power. In matters relating to insurance, the policy holder is provided with a choice of jurisdictions, among them the courts of his own domicile, in which he may sue the insurer.[582] In the case of contracts of insurance relating to certain types of risks of such a nature that they would be made between large concerns, freedom of the parties to agree on jurisdiction is provided for.[583]

Where consumer contracts[584] are concerned, the consumer is allowed to sue in the courts of his own domicile and may only be sued himself in those courts.[585]

Exclusive Jurisdiction

The Convention also provides that in certain types of action the courts of a specified contracting State are to have exclusive jurisdiction, regardless of domicile.[586] This exclusive jurisdiction overrides any attempt by the parties by agreement to grant, or submit to, the jurisdiction of another court.[587] Failure to comply with the Convention's requirements as to exclusive jurisdiction is a ground for non-recognition of a judgment given on foot of this improper jurisdiction.[588] The most important of these exclusive jurisdictions should be noted:

---

[580] *Id.*

[581] Cf. *id.*, paras. 124-127.

[582] Articles 8 and 9. For detailed analysis of the jurisdictional provisions in relation to insurance contracts, see *Collins,* 68-74.

[583] Articles 12(5) and 12A.

[584] That is, a contract concluded by a person "for a purpose which can be regarded as being outside his trade or profession," where the contract is (1) for the sale of goods in instalment credit terms, (2) for a loan repayable by instalments, or for any other form of credit, made to finance the sale of goods, or (3) any other contract for the supply of goods or a contract for the supply of services, and (a) in the State of the consumer's domicile, was preceded by a specific invitation addressed to him or by advertising, and (b) the consumer took, in that State, the steps necessary for the conclusion of the contract: Article 13. Contracts of transport are, however, excluded: *id.*

[585] Articles 13 and 14. The requirements of Articles 13 and 14 may be departed from only by agreement either (1) entered into after the dispute has arisen, or (2) which allows the consumer to bring proceedings in courts other than those indicated in Articles 13 and 14, or (3) entered into by the consumer and the other party, when at the time of conclusion of the contract both are domiciled or habitually resident in the same Contracting State, which confers jurisdiction on the courts of that State, provided the agreement is not contrary to the law of that State: Article 15. For a detailed analysis of the jurisdictional rules as to consumer contracts, see *Hartley,* 58-61, *Collins,* 74-77. *Collins,* 77, comments that:

"[a]lthough the conferment of jurisdiction on the courts of the plaintiff-consumer's domicile may appear at first sight very far-reaching, the practical effect of these provisions in the United Kingdom is not likely to be very marked; except perhaps in relation to the Republic of Ireland, sales of goods to consumers in other contracting States for purchases by United Kingdom consumers from other Contracting States must rarely be on the credit terms which Article 13 contemplates."

[586] Article 16.

[587] Cf *Collins,* 77.

[588] Cf. Articles 28 and 34.

(i) *in proceedings which have as their object rights in rem in, or tenancies of, immoveable property, the courts of the Contracting State in which the property is situated have exclusive jurisdiction*[589]

This provision gives a predominant role to the court of the *situs*. The concept of proceedings having "as their rights *in rem*" in immoveable property is one well established in civil law jurisprudence but less familiar to common law thinking on property. It seems that an action to establish title to immoveable property falls within the scope of the provision, but that actions for damages for injury to an immovable or for breach of contract to purchase it, do not.[590]

Thus, it has been suggested that "if two Englishmen agree on the sale of a house in France from one to the other, one could sue the other in England for failure to complete or for an order requiring completion, but they would have to go to the French courts if an order for possession was required."[591]

As to leases, the decision of *Rosler* v. *Rottwinkel*[592] throws light on the limits of exclusive jurisdiction. The Court held that:

> "any dispute concerning the existence of tenancies or the interpretation of the terms thereof, their duration, the giving up of possession to the landlord, the repairing of damage caused by the tenant or the recovery of rent and of incidental charges payable by the tenant, such as charges for the consumption of water, gas or electricity, falls within the exclusive jurisdiction conferred by article 16 (1) ... on the courts of the state in which the property is situated. Disputes concerning the obligations of the landlord or of the tenant under the terms of the tenancy fall within that exclusive jurisdiction. On the other hand, disputes which are only indirectly related to the use of property let, such as those concerning the loss of holiday enjoyment and travel expenses, do not fall within the exclusive jurisdiction conferred by that article."

(ii) *in proceedings relating to certain company matters such as dissolution, the Courts of the Contracting State in which the company has its seat*[593] *have exclusive jurisdiction*[594]

(iii) *if the parties have made a choice of jurisdiction agreement,*[595] *then the courts of the Contracting State which have been so chosen have exclusive jurisdiction*[596]

Even in a case where the courts of a Contracting State do not have jurisdiction in accordance with the rules outlined above, they will have jurisdiction if the defendant enters an appearance, but not where appearance was entered solely to contest the jurisdiction or where another court has exclusive jurisdiction under (i) or (ii) above.[597]

We must now consider the position where there is jurisdiction by consent. The first paragraph of Article 17 provides that, if the parties, one or more of whom is domiciled in a Contracting State, have agreed that a court or the courts of a

---

[589] Article 16(1).
[590] *Collins*, 79.
[591] *Id.*
[592] [1986] Q.B. 33, at 60 (E.C.J., 1985).
[593] See Article 53. This concept is new to Irish law and requires definition in the implementing legislation. See Terry, *supra*, at 29. Cf. the Jurisdiction of Courts and Enforcement of Judgments (European Communities) Bill 1986, Fifth Schedule, Art III, and the Explanatory and Financial Memorandum to the Bill, paras. 50-54.
[594] Article 16(2).
[595] The agreement must be either in writing or evidenced in writing or, in international trade or commerce, in a form which accords with practices in that trade or commerce of which the parties are or ought to have been aware.
[596] Article 17. Agreements purporting to exclude the jurisdiction of the courts under Article 16 have no legal force: Article 17.
[597] Article 18.

Contracting State is or are to have jurisdiction to settle "any disputes which have arisen or which may arise in connection with a particular legal relationship", that court or those courts shall have exclusive jurisdiction. The scope of this provision is worth noting. The clause need not be restricted to disputes arising out of the contract in question: it may extend to a disagreement in respect of a continuing relationship between the parties, such as may arise between employer and employee or principal and agent.[598]

To be effective the agreement must be:

(a) in writing or
(b) evidenced in writing, or
(c) in international trade or commerce, in a form which accords with practices in that trade or commerce of which the parties are or ought to have been aware.[599]

The Convention contains rather rigid rules regarding *lis pendens* and related actions. Where proceedings involving the same cause of action and between the same parties are brought in the courts of different Contracting States, any court other than the court first seised is required of its own motion to decline jurisdiction in favour of that court.[600] Where related actions are brought in the courts of different Contracting States, any court other than the court first seised may, while the actions are pending at first instance, stay its proceedings.[61] Where actions come within the exclusive jurisdiction of several courts, any court other than the court first seised must decline jurisdiction in favour of that court.[602] There is no provision in the Convention for a doctrine of *forum conveniens* or *forum non conveniens*:[603] in none of the types of case just mentioned does the court first seised itself have power to decline jurisdiction on the ground that there is another more convenient forum in which the case might better, in the interests of justice, be heard.

---

[598] *Hartley*, 68.

[599] Article 17, first paragraph. See *Hartley*, 69, Terry, *supra*, at 37-38. The 1968 Convention had contained only the first two of these conditions. Decisions of the European Court prior to the Convention of Accession (Case 24/76, *Colzani* v. *Ruwa*, [1976] E.C.R. 1831 and Case 25/76, *Segoura* v. *Bonakarian*, [1976] E.C.R. 1851) had applied to them so restrictive an interpretation that, in the interests of international trade, the third condition was incorporated: see the *Schlosser Report*, para. 179, *Hartley*, 69-70. The Court has since considered the scope of all three conditions, in Case 71/83, *Partenreederei MS Tilly Russ and Ernest Russ* v. *NV Haven & Vervoerbedrijf Nova*, [1984] E.C.R. 2417.

[600] Article 21(1).

[601] *Id.*

[601] Article 23.

[603] *Supra*, pp. 162-171.

CHAPTER 9

EXCLUSION OF A FOREIGN LAW[1]

In some circumstances our law excludes the application of a particular foreign law which would otherwise apply according to the ordinary principles of the conflict of laws. These circumstances may be considered under five headings: (1) foreign penal laws; (2) foreign revenue laws; (3) foreign expropriatory legislation; (4) other public laws of a foreign state; and (5) foreign laws repugnant to Irish public policy.

FOREIGN PENAL LAWS[2]

In *Buchanan Ltd.* v. *McVey*,[3] in 1950, Kingsmill Moore, J. said:

"The principle that 'the courts of no country execute the penal laws of another'[4] has long standing authority both in England and in the United States."

In *Buchanan Ltd.* v. *McVey* this approach was favoured by Kingsmill Moore, J. and by the Supreme Court on appeal.

What is the basis of the principle? In the Privy Council decision of *Huntington* v. *Attrill*,[5] Lord Watson sought to answer this question:

"The rule has its foundation in the well-recognised principle that crimes, including in that term all breaches of public law punishable by pecuniary mulct or otherwise, at the instance of the State Government, or of some one representing the public, are local in this sense, that they are only cognizable and punishable in the country where

---

[1] See generally, *Dicey & Morris*, chs. 6, 21, *Cheshire & North*, ch. 6, *Castel*, vol. 1, ch. 4, *Morris*, chs. 4, 22.

[2] See generally Mann, *Foreign Penal Laws and the English Conflict of Laws*, 42 Gr. Soc. Transactions 133 (1956), Mann, *Prerogative Rights of Foreign States and the Conflict of Laws*, 40 Gr. Soc. Transactions 25 (1954), Leflar, *Extrastate Enforcement of Penal and Governmental Claims*, 46 Harv. L. Rev. 193 (1932), Stoel, *The Enforcement of Foreign Non-Criminal Penal and Revenue Judgments in England and the United States*, 16 Int. & Comp. L.Q. 663 (1967), Kutner, *Judicial Identification of "Penal Laws" in the Conflict of Laws*, 31 Okla. L. Rev. 590 (1978).

[3] [1954] I.R. 89, at 100 (High Ct., Kingsmill Moore, J., 1950, affirmed by Sup. Ct., 1951). Both Kingsmill Moore, J. (at 100) and Maguire, C.J. (Murnaghan and O'Byrne, JJ. concurring) (at 115-116) quoted two passages from *Dicey* (6th ed., 1940): General Principle Number 2 stated:

"English Courts will not enforce a right otherwise acquired under the law of a foreign country which is ordinarily applicable in virtue of the English rules of the conflict of laws, where the enforcement of such right involves the enforcement of foreign penal or confiscatory legislation or a foreign revenue law."

and Rule 22 stated:

"The Court has no jurisdiction at common law to entertain an action for the enforcement, either directly or indirectly, of a penal, revenue or political law of a foreign State."

[4] *The Antelope*, 23 U.S. (10 Wheat.) 66, at 123 (*per* Marshall, C.J. 1825). For a re-assessment of what Marshall, C.J. actually intended by these words, see Janis, *The Recognition and Enforcement of Foreign Law: The Antelope's Penal Law Exception*, 20 Internat. L. 303 (1986).

[5] [1893] A.C. 150, at 156 (1892).

they were committed. Accordingly no proceeding, even in the shape of civil suit, which has for its object the enforcement by the State, whether directly or indirectly, of punishment imposed for such breaches by the *lex fori,* ought to be admitted in the Courts of any other country.''

This attempted justification may not satisfy everyone. For even if we concede the obvious fact that most offences are ''local'' in the sense mentioned by Lord Watson, it is far from clear that conflicts of law rules should on that account adopt a ''hands off'' approach to foreign penal law. Penal laws, after all, frequently deal with antisocial and wrongful conduct. Human nature does not respect national boundaries. True, there is some degree of divergence between countries as to the content of the penal code. But neither this divergence nor the fact that a State's exercise of its *imperium* is ''inherently limited to [its own] territory''[6] affords a compelling reason why our conflicts of law should adopt such a timid approach towards the penal laws of other countries.

What constitutes a "Penal Law"?

The Irish court must decide whether or not the foreign law is penal. In coming to this conclusion it is not bound by the classification adopted by the foreign country in question. In *Huntington* v. *Attrill,*[7] Lord Watson said:

''Judicial decisions in the State where the cause of action arose are not precedents which must be followed, although the reasoning upon which they are founded must always receive careful consideration, and may be conclusive. The Court appealed to must determine for itself, in the first place, the substance of the right sought to be enforced; and, in the second place, whether its enforcement would either directly or indirectly involve the execution of the penal law of another State. Were any other principle to guide its decision, a court might find itself in the position of giving effect in one case and denying effect in another to suits of the same character, in consequence of the causes of action having arisen in different countries; or in the predicament of being constrained to give effect to laws which were, in its own judgment, strictly penal.''

What constitutes a ''penal'' law may be relatively easy to establish in some cases but the precise scope of this notion may at times be difficult to draw.[8] Clearly, from the passage of Lord Watson's speech already quoted, crimes are penal; but equally clearly ''the expressions 'penal' and 'penalty', when employed without any qualification, express or implied, are calculated to mislead, because they are capable of being construed so as to extend the rule to all proceedings for the recovery of penalties, whether exigible by the State in the interest of the community, or by private persons in their own interest''.[9]

In the United States Supreme Court decision of *Wisconsin* v. *Pelican Insurance Company,*[10] in 1888, Gray, J. explained that the rule that courts will not execute the law of a foreign country applies, not only to criminal prosecutions and sentences

---

[6] Mann, *Prerogative Rights of Foreign States and the Conflict of Laws,* 40 Gr. Soc. Transactions 25, at 29 (1954).

[7] [1893] A.C. 150, at 155 (P.C., 1892). In accord, *Raulin* v. *Fisher,* [1911] 2 K.B. 93 (Hamilton, J.), *Burchell* v. *Burchell,* 58 Ont. L.R. 515 (Grant, J., 1926), *Brown, Gow, Wilson* v. *Beleggings-Societeit N.V.,* [1961] O.R. 815, at 849 (High Ct., McRuer, C.J.H.C.). See however, *Larkins* v. *National Union of Mineworkers,* as yet unreported, High Ct., Barrington, J., 18 June 1985 (1984-8465P.), at p. 25, considered *infra,* pp. 195-197.

[8] This may be attributable to the English courts' adherence to an *ad hoc* approach in preference to one starting from a broad principle. Cf. Mann, *Prerogative Rights of Foreign States and the Conflict of Laws,* 40 Gr. Soc. Transactions 25, at 45-46 (1954).

[9] *Huntington* v. *Attrill,* [1893] A.C. 150, at 157 (P.C., *per* Lord Watson, 1892).

[10] 127 U.S. (20 Davis) 265, 32, L.Ed. 239, at 243 (1888).

but "to all suits in favor of the State for the recovery of pecuniary penalties for any violation of statutes for the protection of its revenue, or other municipal laws, and to all judgments for such penalties". In *Huntington* v. *Attrill*,[11] the Judicial Committee of the Privy Council enthusiastically endorsed this exposition of the law. Lord Watson explained that, in their opinion, it disclosed:

> "the proper test for ascertaining whether an action is penal within the meaning of the rule. A proceeding, in order to come within the scope of the rule, must be in the nature of a suit in favour of the State whose law has been infringed. All the provisions of Municipal Statutes for the regulation of trade and trading companies are presumably enacted in the interest and for the benefit of the community at large; and persons who violate these provisions are, in a certain sense, offenders against the State law, as well as against individuals who may be injured by their misconduct. But foreign tribunals do not regard these violations of statute law as offences against the State, unless their vindication rests with the State itself, or with the community which it represents. Penalties may be attached to them, but that circumstance will not bring them within the rule, except in cases where these penalties are recoverable at the instance of the State, or of an official duly authorized to prosecute on its behalf, or of a member of the public in the character of a common informer. An action by the latter is regarded as an *actio popularis* pursued, not in his individual interest, but in the interest of the whole community."[12]

In *Huntington* v. *Attrill,* a New York statute for the protection of members of the public dealing with corporations imposed stringent obligations on directors and officers regarding publication of the true condition of the finances of the corporation. One section of the statute made all the directors and officers who vouched the accuracy of financial reports or certificates which proved to be false in any material representations, personally liable for all the debts of the corporation contracted during their period of office.

The Privy Council held that the section was remedial rather than penal and was thus enforceable in Ontario. Lord Watson explained:

> "In one aspect of them, the provisions of [the section] are penal in the wider sense in which the term is used. They impose heavy liabilities upon directors in respect of failure to observe statutory regulations for the protection of persons who have become or may become creditors of the corporation. But, in so far as they concern creditors, these provisions are in their nature protective and remedial. To use the language of Mr Justice Osler,[13] they give 'a civil remedy only, to creditors whose rights the conduct of the company's officers may have been calculated to injure, and which is not enforceable by the State or the public'. In the opinion of their Lordships, these enactments are simply conditions upon which the Legislature permits associations to trade with corporate privileges, and constitute an implied term of every contract between the corporation and its creditors."[14]

---

[11] [1893] A.C. 150 (P.C., 1892).

[12] *Id.*, at 157-158.

[13] 18 Ont. App. Rep. 136, at 155 (1890).

[14] [1893] A.C., at 159. In proceedings in the United States, the United States Supreme Court came to the same conclusion. Mr Justice Gray said:
> "The test whether a law is penal, in the strict and primary sense, is whether the wrong sought to be redressed is a wrong to the public, or a wrong to the individual ... The question whether a statute of one State, which in some aspects may be called penal, is a penal law, in the international sense, so that it cannot be enforced in the courts of another State, depends upon the question whether its purpose is to punish an offence against the public justice of the State, or to afford a private remedy to a person injured by the wrongful act."

146 U.S. 657, at 668 (1892). See also *Ogden* v. *Folliott*, 3 Term Rep. 726, 100 E.R. 825 (1790) (action to recover money due on bond met by defence that plaintiff had been deprived of his property rights by State of New York during War of Independence; plea rejected as to have admitted it would

The distinction between an "offence against the public justice of the State" and a "private remedy" to an injured person can be difficult to draw in cases where a person's "private remedy" reflects a significant policy of the state. This is particularly so where a civil claim based on breach of statutory duty is in question.[15] The mere fact that compensation is awarded in favour of a claimant in proceedings involving the prosecution of a defendant for a crime does not necessarily mean that the award is of a "penal" nature. In *Raulin* v. *Fisher*,[16] a French alien was injured by a woman who recklessly galloped her horse into him. Under French law he was permitted to intervene in the prosecution with a civil claim. Hamilton, J. had "no doubt" that the public prosecution and private suit were "two quite separate and distinct proceedings although ... for purposes of procedure combined in one".[17]

Similar problems can arise in relation to punitive damages,[18] as well as the right of a private individual to seek damages for public nuisance.[19] The courts should be reluctant to resort to a penal characterisation in these instances since the effect will be to deny all or part of a remedy to an individual in cases where he has unquestionably been the victim of the defendant's misconduct. It would be wrong to regard the concept of "a private remedy" as existing in a social vacuum. To a large extent every "private" remedy reflects, albeit in varying measures, societal concern at the behaviour which occasions the remedy. The fact that this concern may, in overt terms, appear to place little stress on the compensatory element should not prevent the court from recognising that element where to fail to do so will leave the victim without appropriate compensation.

The subject was considered in some detail by Barrington, J., in the recent case of *Larkins* v. *National Union of Mineworkers*.[20] The proceedings arose from the British miners' strike, and related to money, the property of the union, which had been placed on deposit with an Irish financial institution. English sequestrators and an English receiver sought to recover the money, pursuant to orders from the English High Court. The sequestrators had been appointed as a result of the refusal of the union to obey injunctions restraining the union and its executive committee from urging members of the union in the Yorkshire area to strike or not to cross picket-lines.

A fine of £200,000 had been imposed for contempt of court and, when the union failed to pay the fine, a writ of sequestration had been issued, directed to the sequestrators, which provided that it should remain in force until the union should

---

have resulted in enforcement of penalty imposed by foreign state); *Wood* v. *Wood*, 37 Ont. L.R. 428 (App. Div., 1916) (action for arrears of alimony held not penal); *Banco de Vizcaya* v. *Don Alfonso de Borbon y Austria*, [1935] 1 K.B. 140 (forfeiture of former King of Spain's property by Republican Government held penal), and *Williams & Humbert Ltd.* v. *W. & H. Trade Marks (Jersey) Ltd.*, [1986] 1 All E.R. 129 (H.L.(Eng.)), discussed *infra*, pp. 205-206.

[15] See Fricke, *The Juridical Nature of the Action Upon the Statute*, 76 L.Q. Rev. 240 (1960), McMahon & Binchy, ch. 15, Thayer, *Public Wrong and Private Action*, 27 Harv. L. Rev. 317 (1914), Lowndes, *Civil Liability Created by Criminal Legislation*, 16 Minn. L. Rev. 361 (1932), Leflar, *Extrastate Enforcement of Penal and Governmental Claims*, 46 Harv. L. Rev. 193, at 210-211 (1932), Kutner, *Judicial Identification of "Penal Laws" in the Conflict of Laws*, 31 Okla. L. Rev. 590, at 622 (1978).

[16] [1911] 2 K.B. 93 (Hamilton, J.).

[17] *Id.*, at 99. Cf. *Alaska Trainship Corp.* v. *Canadian Merchant Service Guild*, 41 D.L.R. (3d) 116 (B.C. Sup. Ct., Hutcheon, Co. Ct. J. (L.J.S.C.), 1973) (injunction against picketing of Liberian-registered ship refused as no evidence that breach of criminal law gave rise to any private right on part of plaintiff shipowner). On the question of severability, see further *Burchell* v. *Burchell*, 58 Ont. L.R. 515 (Grant, J., 1926).

[18] Cf. Leflar, *supra*, at 210, Kutner, *Judicial Identification of "Penal Laws" in the Conflict of Laws*, 31 Okla. L. Rev. 590, at 608ff. (1978), McMahon & Binchy, 559-563.

[19] Cf. *McMahon & Binchy*, 475-477.

[20] As yet unreported, High Ct., 18 June 1985 (1984-8465P).

have purged its contempt or until further order. The union submitted that this writ for sequestration was a criminal process in that, first, it had been issued to collect a fine imposed for criminal contempt and, secondly, that it was, by its very nature, punitive.[21]

The sequestrators replied that the sequestration proceedings had resulted from the failure by the union to obey injunctions in civil proceedings, and that thus the claims for the money in the Irish financial institution were "private proceedings, civil and coercive in nature",[22] to which the principles discussed in *Buchanan* v. *McVey* had no application. The sequestrators further contended that they were not seeking, in the proceedings before the Irish court, the specific recovery of the fine, but rather possession of the union's funds in Ireland with a view to coercing the union to comply with the order of the English High Court. Responding to these competing arguments, Barrington, J. noted that, in *Buchanan* v. *McVey*,[23] Kingsmill Moore, J. appeared to have accepted that the reason behind the rule was that courts were "not competent to arbitrate on, and should not in fact enquire into, the justice of the penal laws of a foreign state".[24]

The nub of the issue concerned the nature of contempt of court, which had been the "trigger" for the £200,000 fine. In both Ireland and England a distinction is drawn between criminal and civil contempt. Criminal contempt involves some wrongful interference with the administration of justice, and is a crime punishable by fine or imprisonment.[25] Civil contempt, however, "consists merely in a refusal by one party to litigation to obey an Order of the Court. The contemnor may be committed to prison for his civil contempt but the object of the imprisonment is coercive and not punitive."[26] Nevertheless, as Barrington, J. noted, "where the object of civil contempt is undoubtedly coercive, and not punitive, the execution of the warrant of committal is an exercise of State power and the warrant has no force outside the State's territory".[27]

The English courts divide civil contempts into two sub-categories: mere civil contempts and contumacious civil contempts. The latter, said Barrington, J. "involve not merely disobedience to the Court's Order but some form of defiance of the Court's authority with the result that the matter ceases to be a mere matter between private litigants but calls in question the authority of the Court".[28]

After a detailed review of the judgments of the English High Court in which sequestration and the fine had been ordered, Barrington, J. came to the conclusion that the contempt was contumacious civil contempt and that "it touched not only issues between the parties but on the whole question of the maintenance of the rule of law in the United Kingdom".[29]

Barrington, J. said:

---

[21] Invoking *Buchanan* v. *McVey* [1954] I.R. 89 as authority for the proposition that one state will not enforce penal or punitive provisions of the laws of a foreign state, and that the refusal to enforce the revenue claims of a foreign state is merely one application of this wider principle.

[22] Page 6 of Barrington, J.'s judgment.

[23] [1954] I.R. 89.

[24] Page 16 of Barrington, J.'s judgment.

[25] *Id.*, p.17.

[26] *Id.* See also *Keegan* v. *De Burca,* [1973] I.R. 223, at 227 (Sup. Ct., *per* Ó Dálaigh, C.J., 1972), quoted by Barrington, J., at pp. 17-18 of his judgment.

[27] Page 18 of Barrington, J.'s judgment.

[28] *Id.*

[29] *Id.*, p. 24. Barrington, J. noted that the wording of the Court Order giving the plaintiffs in the sequestration action "liberty to issue" a writ of sequestration seemed more consistent with a civil than criminal procedure. But the writ had been issued in the name of Queen Elizabeth II, and in these circumstances Barrington, J. considered that it might "not be wise to attach too much significance to a procedure which probably dates from a time when the distinction between civil and criminal process was not very clear".

"The sequestration .... clearly raises issues as between private litigants, as well as issues touching the authority of the English High Court. But it appears to me that the latter is the predominant issue and was seen as such. Moreover, I accept [the] opinion [of a witness as to English law] that the process, whether civil or criminal and whether coercive or punitive in purpose, is essentially penal in effect.[30] Accordingly, I do not think that this Court has any function in relation to the sequestration and I would dismiss the sequestrators' claim."[31]

Barrington, J. then turned to the receiver's claim and considered whether this should also be unenforceable as involving, or springing from, a penal process. He did not accept as decisive in favour of the receiver's claim the fact that he had been appointed by the English Court on the basis of evidence which was sufficient for the English Judge to consider it proper to remove the trustees. Nor did the fact that the Receiver, once appointed, was an officer of the Court independent of the plaintiff who had him appointed, resolve the question. Barrington, J. observed:

"The plaintiff in *Buchanan* v. *McVey* was also an officer of the Court properly appointed by a High Court Judge on the basis of the evidence correctly presented to him. I think it is possible, without casting doubt on the integrity of the process, to enquire what the litigant hoped to achieve by invoking it."[32]

It appeared that the idea of appointing a Receiver came from Continental lawyers engaged in attempting to trace the Union's assets and not because of any difficulties peculiar to the Irish litigation. The English Judge had taken the view that *prima facie* the plaintiffs in the receivership action had grounds to be concerned about what was happening to the assets of their union and that they had made out a case for the temporary removal of the trustees and the appointment of a Receiver. Barrington, J. therefore considered that there were "independent grounds"[33] for the appointment of the Receiver, so the receivership was not therefore simply an indirect method of enforcing the sequestration.

"Penal" discriminatory rules

It should be noted that it is sometimes said that our law will not give effect to "penal" rules imposing incapacities or distinctions based on such matters as slavery,[34] race or colour,[35] as, for example, where the property of one particular religious or ethnic group is confiscated. It is indeed true that our law will not give effect to these rules, but its refusal to do so is better regarded as one specific aspect of the operation of public policy[36] than as bearing any direct relationship with the questions raised in such cases as *Huntington* v. *Atrill*,[37] *Buchanan* v. *McVey*,[38] and *Larkins* v. *National Union of Mineworkers*.[39]

---

[30] Strictly, of course, the opinion of this witness as to the penal effect of the process under English law should not directly control the determination of its effect according to Irish law: cf. p. 30, *supra*.

[31] Page 25 of Barrington, J.'s judgment.

[32] *Id.* p. 28.

[33] *Id.*

[34] Cf. *Stanhope* v. *Irish Hospitals Trust*, [1936] Ir. Jur. Rep. 21, at (High Ct., *per* Hanna, J, 1935), revd in part, [1936] Ir. Jur. Rep. 25 (Sup. Ct.).

[35] Cf. *Conlon* v. *Mohamed*, High Ct., Barron, J., 25 July 1986 (1984-8937P.), discussed *infra*, pp. 230-231.

[36] See Mann, *Foreign Penal Laws and the English Conflict of Laws*, 42 Grotius Soc. Transactions 133, at 136ff (1956).

[37] [1893] A.C. 150.

[38] [1954] I.R. 89.

[39] *Supra*.

FOREIGN REVENUE LAWS[40]

In *Holman* v. *Johnson*[41] in 1775 Mansfield, C.J. observed that "no country ever takes notice of the revenue laws of another". That statement clearly goes so far[42] but it contains an important degree of truth. There is indeed a significant restriction on the enforceability of foreign revenue laws in this country.

It might be considered that there is no reason to create a particular rule for foreign revenue laws; a revenue law and a penal law are, after all, "similar in the sense that they are both governmental regulations of a civic duty. The right under each accrues in favour of the state without the consent of the citizen involved and it is a well-established principle of law universally admitted that the courts of one state will not enforce the penal laws of another."[43] But there are also important differences between a revenue and a penal law: a tax "is not a penalty but a duty; it is imposed not as an punishment but as a civil obligation".[44]

What constitutes a revenue debt?

The scope of what constitutes a revenue debt may be a matter for debate. It has been held to encompass municipal rates on property owners for street improvements,[45] and employers' company contributions to a state health insurance and family benefits scheme,[46] but not a claim for hospital expenses where the claimant was obliged to account to the foreign State's Hospital Commission for the sum awarded[47] or a claim for costs in divorce proceedings where the sum, if recovered, would be payable to the foreign State's Legal Aid Committee.[48]

Policy basis of the non-enforceability rule

What is the reason for the rule of non-enforceability of foreign revenue law? The English decisions have given few insights, being content to state the principle "as

[40] See Castel, *Foreign Tax Claims and Judgments in Canadian Courts*, 42 Can. Bar Rev. 277 (1964), Freeze, *Extra-territorial Enforcement of Revenue Laws*, 23 Wash. U.L.Q. 321 (1938), Sack, *(Non)-Enforcement of Foreign Revenue Laws in International Law and Practice*, 81 U. Pa. L. Rev. 559 (1933), Mann, *Note: The House of Lords and Foreign Revenue Laws*, 4 Int. & Comp. L.Q. 564 (1955), E.K[ahn], *Comment: Enforcement of Foreign Revenue Laws*, 71 S. Af. L.J. 275 (1954), Stoel, *The Enforcement of Foreign Non-Criminal Penal and Revenue Judgments in England and the United States*, 16 Int. & Comp. L.Q. 663, at 671-679 (1967), Kutner, *Judicial Identification of Penal Laws in the Conflict of Laws*, 31 Okla. L. Rev. 590, at 597-599 (1978), Albrecht, *The Enforcement of Taxation Under International Law*, 30 Br. Yrbk of Internat. L. 454 (1954).
[41] 2 Cowp. 341, at 343, 98 E.R. 1120, at 1121 (1775). See also the same judge's *obiter* statement in *Planche* v. *Fletcher*, 1 Doug. 251, at 253, 99 E.R. 164, at 165 (1779).
[42] Cf. Albrecht, *supra*, at 461, *Foster* v. *Driscoll*, [1929] 1 K.B. 470, at 518 (C.A., *per* Sankey, L.J., 1928), *Ralli Bros* v. *Compania Naviera Sota y Aznar*, [1920] 2 K.B. 287, at 300 (C.A., *per* Scrutton, L.J.). In *Buchanan Ltd* v. *McVey*, [1954] I.R. 89, at 100 (Sup. Ct., 1951, aff'g. High Ct., Kingsmill Moore, J., 1950); Kingsmill Moore, J. said:
"I doubt whether Lord Mansfield intended his remarks to preclude a court from informing itself as to the provisions of a foreign revenue law in order to determine the question whether a foreign transaction was or was not fraudulent and void according to the law of that country. But, if he so intended, having regard to this case and opinions I have cited, I must refuse to follow his view."
[43] *Castel*, vol. 1, 80.
[44] Albrecht, *supra*, at 463.
[45] *Municipal Council of Sydney* v. *Bull*, [1909] 1 K.B. 7 (Grantham, J., 1908).
[46] *Metal Industries (Salvage) Ltd.* v. *Owners of the S.T. "Harle"*, 1962 S.L.T. Repts 114 (Outer House, Lord Cameron, 1961).
[47] *Weir* v. *Lohr*, 65 D.L.R. (2d) 717 (Man. Q.B., Tritschler, C.J.Q.B., 1967).
[48] *Connor* v. *Connor*, [1974] 1 N.Z.L.R. 632 (Sup. Ct., Roper, J., 1973) ("I do not think the authorities support the proposition that merely because enforcement of a judgment may result in reimbursement of a fund which has the blessing, or even the financial support, of a foreign State, enforcement of that judgment by another State would be contrary to public policy": *id.*, at 636-637).

if it were of long standing and so well established, so self evident, as to require no justification".[49] In the United States, Judge Learned Hand attempted to analyse the underlying considerations:

> "While the origin of the exception in the case of penal liabilities does not appear in the books, a sound basis for it exists, in my judgment, which includes liabilities for taxes as well. Even in the case of ordinary municipal liabilities, a Court will not recognise those arising in a foreign State, if they run counter to the 'settled public policy' of its own. Thus a scrutiny of the liability is necessarily always in reserve, and the possibility that it will be found not to accord with the policy of the domestic State. This is not a troublesome or delicate inquiry when the question arises between private persons, but it takes on quite another face when it concerns the relations between the foreign State and its own citizens or even those who may be temporarily within its borders. To pass upon the provisions for the public order of another State is, or at any rate should be, beyond the powers of a Court; it involves the relations between the States themselves, with which Courts are incompetent to deal, and which are entrusted to other authorities. It may commit the domestic State to a position which would seriously embarrass its neighbour. Revenue laws fall within the same reasoning; they affect a State in matters as vital to its existence as its criminal laws. No court ought to undertake an inquiry which it cannot prosecute without determining whether those laws are consonant with its own notions of what is proper."[50]

In the leading Irish decision of *Buchanan Ltd* v. *McVey*,[51] Kingsmill Moore, J. described Learned Hand's reasons as "convincing and illuminating", and as "suggest[ing] the importance of guarding against any attempt to evade the rule or to whittle away the scope of its application". Kingsmill Moore, J. noted that, in deciding cases between private persons, courts have always exercised the right to reject foreign law on the ground that it conflicts with public policy or affronts the accepted morality of the domestic forum. He went on:

> "If then, in disputes beween private citizens, it has been considered necessary to reserve an option to reject foreign law as incompatible with the views of the community, it must have been equally, if not more, necessary, to reserve a similar option where an attempt was made to enforce the governmental claims (including revenue claims) of a foreign State. But if the Courts had contended themselves with an option to refuse such claims, instead of imposing a general rule of exclusion, the task of formulating and applying the principles of selection would have been one, not only of difficulty, but danger, involving inevitably an incursion into political fields with grave risks of embarrassing the executive in its foreign relations and even of provoking international complications. Neither common morality nor 'settled public policy' would have sufficed to cover the area of necessary rejection; for the nature and incidence of governmental and revenue claims are not dictated by any moral principles, but are the offspring of political considerations and political necessity. Taxation originally expressed only the will of the despot enforceable by torture, slavery and death. Though it may be conceded

[49] *Buchanan Ltd.* v. *McVey*, [1954] I.R., at 105 (*per* Kingsmill Moore, J.).
[50] *Moore* v. *Mitchell*, 30 F. 2d 600, at 604 (1929).
[51] [1954] I.R., at 106. *McVey's* case is noted by Donaldson, 3 Int. & Comp. L.Q. 161 (1954) and by Mann, 40 Gr. Soc. Transactions 25, at 36 (1954) ("[a] remarkable and .... well founded decision"). The decision is of international significance, having been discussed with approval by the House of Lords in *Government of India, Ministry of Finance* v. *Taylor*, [1955] A.C. 491 (tempered somewhat by Lord Mackay's lack of enthusiasm, apparent in his speech in *Williams & Humbert Ltd* v. *W. & H. Trade Marks (Jersey) Ltd*, [1986] 1 All E.R. 129, at 142-143 (H.L. Eng. 1985)), by Lord Cameron in the Scots decision of *Metal Industries (Salvage) Ltd* v. *Owners of the S.T. Harle*, 1962 S.L.T. Repts 144 (Outer House, 1961), by the Supreme Court of Canada in *U.S.A.* v. *Harden*, [1963] S.C.R. 366, 41 D.L.R. (2d) 721, in Australia (*Bath* v. *British & Malayan Trustees Ltd.*, 90 W.N. (Part I) (N.S.W.) 44 (Helsham, J., 1969)) and New Zealand (*Connor* v. *Connor*, [1974] 1 N.Z.L.R. 632 (Sup. Ct., Roper, J., 1973)). *McVey* was distinguished in *Weir* v. *Lohr*, 65 D.L.R. (2d) 717 (Man. Q.B., Tritschler, C.J.Q.B. 1967).

that in modern times it is more often designed to further a benevolent social policy, and that the civil servant has usurped the position of the executioner as the agent enforcing it, yet in essence taxation is still arbitrary and depends for its effectiveness only on the executive power of the State. Nor is modern history without examples of revenue laws used for purposes which would not only affront the strongest feelings of neighbouring communities, but would run counter to their political aims and vital interests. Such laws have been used for religious and racial discrimination; for the furtherance of social policies and ideals dangerous to the security of adjacent countries; and for the direct furtherance of economic warfare. So long as these possibilities exist, it would be equally unwise for Courts to permit the enforcement of the revenue claims of foreign States or to attempt to discriminate between those claims which they would and those which they would not enforce. Safety lies only in universal rejection. Such a principle appears to me to be fundamental and of supreme importance."[52]

Kingsmill Moore, J. considered that:

"[i]f the strict application of the principle were in any way relaxed evasion would be easy and the Court would be faced with all the difficulties which the adoption of the rule was designed to avoid."[53]

To demonstrate this line of argument he gave the example of a foreign national, made bankrupt abroad, being pursued by the foreign revenue authorities in litigation in Ireland, where the national has bought some movable property:

"In the course of the hearing it appears that the tax was incurred as the result of discriminatory legislation of a type repugnant to the political views of the enormous majority of the citizens of this country and that the bankrupt has sought asylum here as a political refugee, bringing with him the remnants of his fortune. The Court may admit the claim, may refuse it because of the nature of the legislation, or may reject it on the broad principle that it is an attempt to collect the tax of a foreign revenue. To do the first would be to bring the courts into contempt in the eyes of the people and to offend against their own highest principles; to do the second would be publicly to censure the behaviour of a foreign State, a procedure dangerous and possibly arrogant; in the third course alone safety, propriety, and a recognition of the feeling of the community are combined."[54]

There is perhaps something less than fully convincing about the argument put forward by Judge Learned Hand and developed by Kingsmill Moore, J. All statutes reflect to some degree the public policy of the State where they were enacted.[55] If embarrassment about making distinctions beween just and unjust foreign tax laws is sufficient reason to refuse to enforce any of them, then logic would suggest that the same principle should apply to a host of other types of foreign laws which may be unjust in the eyes of the forum. Yet our courts are content in these other areas to invoke public policy where necessary rather than as an all-embracing blanket.

Indeed, Kingsmill Moore, J. may be regarded as reflecting the view of judges of an earlier era when taxation was viewed with some degree of suspicion. For Kingsmill Moore, J., as we have seen, the nature and incidence of governmental and revenue claims are "not dictated by any moral principles, but are the offspring of political considerations and political necessity".[56] He concedes, somewhat grudgingly, that in modern times taxation "is more often designed to serve a

---

[52] [1954] I.R., at 106-107.
[53] *Id.*, at 107.
[54] *Id.*, at 108.
[55] *Castel*, vol. 1, pp. 83-84.
[56] [1954] I.R., at 107.

benevolent social policy'';[57] but immediately afterwards asserts that ''in essence taxation is still arbitrary''[58] and depends for its effectiveness ''only on the executive power of the State''.[59] He goes on to mention revenue laws which have been used for religious and racial discrimination, for the furtherance of social policies and ideals dangerous to the security of adjacent countries, and for the direct furtherance of economic warfare. This suggests a vision of taxation as an amoral weapon, often admittedly designed to further a benevolent social policy but in essence arbitrary and capable of injustice on a massive scale. While this vision conforms with the more conservative economic and political views of some of the Irish judiciary of thirty years ago, it is doubtful whether it would accord with contemporary judicial attitudes.[60] The result of non-enforcement of a foreign revenue claim is, of course, that revenue debtors, however socially irresponsible, are let go unhindered; as one commentator has asked: ''What 'justice' is there in facilitating fiscal evasion by itinerant taxpayers?''[61]

The case which Kingsmill Moore, J. had to decide involved the following facts. The plaintiff company registered in Scotland, had been put in liquidation by the revenue authorities there under a compulsory winding up order in relation to a large claim for income tax and excess profits tax. The claim resulted from the defendant's disposition of the company assets. The defendant held 99 shares of the capital of the company, the remaining share being held by an employee as trustee for him. The two shareholders were also the directors of the company. The defendant and the other directors, in an elaborate sequence of transactions, succeeded in removing the assets of the company out of Scotland to Ireland, paying off all creditors save the revenue authorities. The liquidator sued the defendant, who was by now in Ireland, for breach of trust and money had and received for the use of the company.

Kingsmill Moore, J. dismissed the liquidator's action. The ''sole object''[62] of the liquidation proceedings in Scotland and the proceedings in Ireland was to collect a revenue debt. Had the liquidator been successful, the ordinary creditors would not have been paid out of the assets, since the revenue authorities had priority. Thus the ''substance of the suit''[63] was to collect the revenue claim of a foreign State. The Supreme Court affirmed. Maguire, C.J. (for the Court) accepted that, if the payment of a revenue claim were ''only incidental''[64] and had there been other claims to be met, it would be difficult for our Courts to refuse to lend assistance to bring assets of the Company under the control of the liquidator; but there was ''no question of that here''.[65]

Non-enforcement does not imply non-recognition

It should be noted that the refusal to *enforce* a foreign revenue law does not commit our courts to refuse also to have regard to the reality of its existence. So, where a foreign contract is illegal in that it defies a foreign revenue law, then, although that revenue law could not be enforced in an Irish court, the Irish court would still have regard to it so that an attempt made to enforce the contract here would fail. In *Buchanan Ltd* v. *McVey*,[66] Kingsmill Moore, J. held that ''the whole

---

[57] *Id.*
[58] *Id.*
[59] *Id.*
[60] The judicial analysis of Article 43 of the Constitution is worth noting in this context: see *Kelly*, 644ff.
[61] Albrecht, *The Enforcement of Taxation Under International Law*, 30 Br. Yrbk of Internat. L. 454, at 462 (1953).
[62] [1954] I.R., at 108.
[63] *Id.*
[64] *Id.*, at 117.
[65] *Id.*
[66] *Id.*, at 98.

object" of the defendant's transactions had been to defeat the tax claims of the Scottish Revenue and that these would thus be categorised by Scots law as "highly fraudulent".[67] Counsel for the defendant argued that the Irish court could not recognise or even inform itself of the Scottish revenue provisions, and that therefore it had to "blind its eyes" to the existence of excess profits tax and to find that the distribution had been made only out of net profits. Kingsmill Moore, J. entirely rejected this contention. The Supreme Court affirmed. Maguire, C.J., for the Court expressed:

"agreement with the trial Judge that to take notice of the revenue law of a foreign country in order to [determine whether the defendant's conduct was honest] is not to conflict with the proposition of law ... that no country will enforce the revenue law of a foreign country".[68]

In *In re Gibbons, A Bankrupt in England. Ex Parte Walter,*[69] in 1960, the facts were as follows. One Gibbons was adjudicated bankrupt by the High Court in England, in respect of sums of money due by him to the English Commissioner of Inland Revenue. The applicant, who was the official receiver and trustee in the matter, sought an order from the High Court of Justice in Ireland under Section 71 of the Bankruptcy (Ireland) Amendment Act, 1872, directing its officers to aid the English High Court in Bankruptcy in realising property in Ireland belonging to the bankrupt.

Counsel for the bankrupt argued that section 71 should be treated as unconstitutional insofar as it was intended to enable the Irish courts to act in aid of the Bankruptcy Court in England in proceedings which had been initiated for the purpose of collection of revenue debts due in that country. Walsh, J. did not accept this contention. He had "no doubt"[70] that the Oireachtas had power under the Constitution to enact legislation which would make provision for the making of orders by the Irish courts enabling the English revenue authorities to collect monies in Ireland on foot of revenue debts due to the English revenue authorities. Walsh, J. construed section 71 as enabling rather than mandatory: the Court might exercise the powers created under the section if it considered "fit to do so in the exercise of its discretion".[71]

Walsh, J. referred to the circumstances of the case before him in which he had been requested to exercise his discretion. He said:

"It is a well established principle that it is contrary to the policy of our courts to permit jurisdiction to be invoked for the purpose of enforcing the collection of foreign revenue debts or claims. This policy was not in force at the date of the passing of the 1872 Act when this country and England were both of one fiscal system. The position is now completely different and two distinct and separate fiscal systems exist.

The policy of the Irish courts has been clearly stated in the decision in *McVey's* case,[72] and it appears to me that it would be quite wrong for me to exercise a discretion in some way which would be contrary to the established policy of the courts. If the statute enabled the aid sought to be provided by executive action only this could be done by the proper authority without involving the Court, but when it is the Court which is involved the Court must have regard to the established policy of the courts in considering the question of the exercise of its discretion and, as the section is not mandatory, I am bound to exercise my discretion in accordance with the policy of the courts as settled in *McVey's* case. Accordingly, I refuse the order sought ...."[73]

[67] *Id.*
[68] *Id.*, at 118.
[69] [1960] Ir. Jur. Rep. 60 (High Ct., Walsh, J.).
[70] *Id.*, at 61.
[71] *Id.*
[72] *Buchanan Ltd.* v. *McVey,* [1954] I.R. 89 (Sup. Ct., 1951, aff'g High Ct., Kingsmill Moore, J., 1950).
[73] [1960] Ir. Jur. Rep., at 62.

The case is of interest in showing that Walsh, J. saw nothing inconsistent with the Constitution in enforcing of foreign revenue claims by legislative decree or through executive action. Nor, it would appear (though he did not expressly so state), did Walsh, J. consider that the discretionary decision by a court to *enforce* a foreign revenue decree under section 71 would necessarily be inconsistent with the Constitution. Thus, if the courts were to change their approach to the question of enforcement, section 71 would not on this account necessarily be held to be inconsistent with the Constitution.

Some further light was thrown on these questions in the Supreme Court decision of *The State (Hully)* v. *Hynes,*[74] in 1961. *Hully* was concerned with the procedure for "backing" warrants issued in Britain, later struck down in *The State (Quinn)* v. *Ryan.*[75] Of present interest is not the general question of extradition[76] but merely the judicial attitude to foreign revenue-based offences discernable in *Hully.* There a prosecutor for *habeas corpus* challenged the constitutionality of his arrest by warrant endorsed for execution under the provisions of the Petty Sessions (Ireland) Act, 1851. The charge was for forgery in England under section 4(1) of the Forgery Act 1913. The prosecutor contended that the warrant had not in fact been issued for the purpose of prosecuting the offence alleged in it, and that the real purpose was to bring him within the English jurisdiction in order to pursue proceedings against him in respect of an offence against the fiscal laws of England. He contended that the warrant thus should not be enforced here.

The Supreme Court made absolute a conditional order of *habeas corpus,* on grounds not of present relevance. On the issue relating to revenue offences, Kingsmill Moore, J. regarded it as "undoubted law"[77] that the courts would not lend their aid to the enforcement of the fiscal laws of another country, either directly or indirectly. But, whatever might be the practice of the *courts,* he could find no authority for the view that the executive could not, if it so desired, deport a non-citizen (and possibly also a citizen) to stand trial abroad for a fiscal offence.

That there might be grave reasons of policy, or even a recognised practice among civilised states, not to extradite for political or fiscal offences did not prevent the executive from doing so if authorised by law.

Kingsmill Moore, J. felt constrained by precedent[78] to hold that, if the Assistant Commissioner exercised his discretion to endorse a warrant issued in England for a revenue offence, the courts could not interfere. In fact, it appeared that the practice was not to endorse warrants for fiscal offences. In the present case, however, the warrant had taken the form it did in order to conceal the real object and so evade this established practice. Since the endorsement was procured by non-disclosure of the true facts, so preventing the Assistant Commissioner from exercising his discretion along established lines, it had to be treated as a nullity.

The other judgments of the Supreme Court were in accord. It is worth recording, also, Lavery, J.'s statement that:

"It is a recognised principle of international law that a state does not enforce or aid in the enforcement of political or fiscal offences against the laws of another state."[79]

The Extradition Act 1965[80], enacted in the wake of the *Quinn* decision, provides,

---

[74] 100 I.L.T.R. 145 (Sup. Ct., 1961). See J. Kelly, *The Irish Constitution,* 184, 535 (2nd ed., 1984).
[75] [1965] I.R. 70 (Sup. Ct., 1964, rev'g High Ct., 1963).
[76] Cf. *Kelly,* 533-542.
[77] 100 I.L.T.R., at 166.
[78] *State (Dowling)* v. *Brennan,* [1937] I.R., 483 (High Ct.), *State (Dowling)* v. *Kingston (No. 2),* [1937] I.R. 699 (Sup. Ct.), *State (Duggan)* v. *Tapley,* [1952] I.R. 62 (Sup. Ct., 1950, aff'g High Ct., 1950). These decisions must now be read in the light of *Quinn's* case: cf. *Kelly,* 535.
[79] 100 I.L.T.R., at 61.
[80] See *Kelly,* 536.

in section 13, that extradition is not to be granted for revenue offences.[81] Moreover the reconstituted procedure for endorsement and execution of warrants, contained in Part III of the Act, enables the Minister for Justice or the High Court to direct that a warrant is not to be endorsed if of opinion that the offence to which it relates is a revenue offence.[82] The expression "revenue offence" means an offence in connection with taxes, duties or exchange control; it does not include an offence involving the use or threat of force or perjury or the forging of a document issued under statutory authority; nor does it extend to an offence alleged to have been committed by an officer of the revenue of the country or place from which the warrant emanates, in his capacity as such officer.

EXPROPRIATORY LEGISLATION[83]

We must now consider the extent to which foreign expropriatory legislation will be recognised in Ireland. Expropriatory legislation may consist of: (a) requisition of property for a limited period, in the public interest, as for example, where ships are requisitioned during times of war or other emergency; (b) nationalisation of property in return for compensation; or (c) confiscation of property without any compensation.[84]

It is a general rule of the conflict of laws that, if the property is situated within the jurisdiction of the foreign sovereign at the time of the foreign decree of expropriation, the Irish courts should recognise its effect, even though the property may have subsequently been brought to Ireland before or during the proceedings in Ireland.[85]

It appears that this rule will apply whether or not the affected property belongs to persons who are nationals of the foreign state, provided that the decree of expropriation is not discriminatory; in *Re Helbert Wagg & Co. Ltd.*,[86] Upjohn, J. said:

"If the principle be true in respect of a State in relation to its own nationals, it must surely be conceded in relation to those persons who, though not subjects of the State, nevertheless bring their movables within its jurisdiction for business or private reasons or for the like reasons enter into contracts governed by the law of the State, and in general enjoy the same benefits and protection and are subject to the same disadvantages and disabilities as subjects of the State."

Where the property is situated outside the territory of the foreign state, however, it seems that Irish courts would not recognise a foreign decree purporting to affect the property. In *Bank voor Handel en Scheepvaart N.V.* v. *Slatford*,[87] Devlin, J. noted that grounds for refusing recognition in these circumstances had been variously stated:

[81] See *Rey* v. *Fleming*, unreported, High Ct., Hamilton, J., 29 January 1980. (1979- No. 792).

[82] Section 44 (2).

[83] See Wortley, *Observations on the Public and Private International Law Relating to Expropriation*, 5 Am. J. of Comp. L. 577 (1957), *Wolff*, 525-529, Seidl-Hohenveldern, *Extra-Territorial Effects of Confiscations and Expropriations*, 13 Modern L. Rev. 69 (1950), Mann, *Outlines of a History of Expropriation*, 75 L.Q. Rev. 188 (1959), Mann, *The Confiscation of Corporations, Corporate Rights and Corporate Assets and the Conflict of Laws*, 11 Int. & Comp. L.Q. 471 (1962), Katzarov, *The Validity of the Act of Nationalisation in International Law*, 22 Modern L. Rev. 639 (1959), Domke, *On the Nationalization of Foreign Shareholders' Interests*, 4 N.Y.L. Forum 46 (1948), McNair, *Problems Connected with the Position of the Merchant Vessel in Private International Law, with Particular Reference to the Power of Requisition*, 31 Grotius Soc. Trans. 30 (1946), Fawcett, *Some Foreign Effects of Nationalisation of Property*, 27 Br. Yrbk. of Internat. L. 355 (1950).

[84] *Cheshire & Morris*, 137.

[85] Cf. *id.*, 138ff., *Castel*, vol. 1, 94, *Morris*, 374, *Dicey & Morris*, Rule 85.

[86] [1956] Ch. 323, at 348.

[87] [1953] 1 Q.B. 248 (C.A., 1952, rev'g Devlin, J., 1951).

"Sometimes it is said that the decree is confiscatory. In the textbooks it is said sometimes that as a matter of public international law no State ought to seek to exercise sovereignty over property outside its own territory, and therefore the principle of comity is against enforcement; and sometimes it is said that the principle of effectiveness is against enforcement, since no State can expect to make its laws effective in the territory of another State."[88]

Devlin, J. noted that several considerations of principle could be advanced against giving extra-territorial effect to foreign confiscatory legislation: the presumption was that a statute was not intended to have extra-territorial effect unless the contrary was made clear; the refusal to recognise the extra-territorial effect of legislation was "in harmony with the principle which favours the *lex situs* generally";[89] moreover, the law of the forum would be constricted if extra-territorial effect were given to foreign property legislation.[90]

A similar approach is apparent in the Irish case of *Zarine* v. *Owners of S.S. "Ramava"*,[91] where decrees in Estonia and Latvia, after the U.S.S.R. invasion, nationalising private property were (it seems) considered not to have affected ships from Estonia and Latvia, registered in these countries, which remained outside them. The issue was, however, essentially one relating to an (unsuccessful) assertion of sovereign immunity by the U.S.S.R. and the analysis did not concentrate on the extra-territorial effectiveness of the Estonian and Latvian decrees.

In the recent case of *Williams & Humbert Ltd.* v. *W. & H. Trade Marks (Jersey) Ltd.*,[92] Lord Templeman accepted the principle that

"an English court will recognise the compulsory requisition law of a foreign state and will recognise the change of title to property which has come under the control of the foreign state and will recognise the consequences of that change of title. The English court will decline to consider the merits of compulsory acquisition."

In this case legislation in Spain had expropriated (with compensation) the shares of a family in a Spanish company. The Spanish government caused the company to take proceedings in England alleging that the family had improperly diverted the company's trade marks to a Jersey company for their own benefit, as well as 46 million dollars from Spanish banks. The House of Lords[93] held that the defence that these proceedings constituted an attempt to enforce a foreign penal law should be struck out.

Lord Templeman pointed out that compulsory acquisition is "universally recognised and practised",[94] with such important historical support as the Declaration of the Rights of Man in 1789 and the Fifth Amendment to the United States Constitution in 1791. There was "undoubtedly"[95] a domestic and international rule which prevented one sovereign state from changing title to property so long as that property was situated in another state; but this territorial limitation on compulsory acquisition was not relevant to the acquisition of shares in a company incorporated in the acquiring state. The internal rule with regard to the non-enforcement of penal laws was

---

[88] *Id.*, at 258.

[89] *Id.*, at 259.

[90] *Id.*

[91] [1942] I.R. 148 (Sup. Ct., 1941, aff'g. High Ct., Hanna, J., 1941). Cf. *Republic of Spain* v. *National Bank of Scotland Ltd.*, 1939 S.C. 413, considered by Kutner, *Judicial Identification of "Penal Laws" in the Conflict of Laws*, 31 Okla. L. Rev. 590, at 595-596 (1978).

[92] [1986] 1 All E.R. 129, at 135 (H.L. (Eng.), 1985).

[93] Affirming the Court of Appeal ([1985] 2 All E.R. 619) and Nourse, J. ([1985] 2 All E.R. 208).

[94] [1986] 1 All E.R., at 133. For a detailed analysis, see Mann, *Outlines of a History of Expropriation*, 75 L.Q. Rev. 188 (1959).

[95] [1986] 1 All E.R., at 133.

"absolute,"[96] but it was doubtful whether the Spanish expropriation law could be described as penal. If the family who resisted the proceedings were correct then the practical effect of the Spanish law was to release from liability, outside Spain, every tortfeasor guilty of inflicting a wrong against any one of the group of expropriated companies as well as every contracting party who defaulted on his obligations with any of these companies. A submission producing such "anarchic results"[97] simply had to be fallacious, in Lord Templeman's view.

Counsel for the family had relied heavily[98] on *Buchanan* v. *McVey*[99] which, he said, applied in the instant case because the object of the proceedings was to collect assets which would indirectly inure for the benefit of a foreign government. Lord Templeman rejected this argument on the basis that *Buchanan* v. *McVey* "only concerned a revenue claim"[100]. The principle that a country cannot collect its taxes outside its territories could "not be used to frustrate or contradict the principle that the courts of this country will recognise the law of compulsory acquisition of a foreign country of assets within the foreign country and will accept the consequences of that compulsory acquisition."[101]

It is worthwhile, at this point recalling Lord Templeman's statement, quoted above,[102] that the English court "will decline to consider the merits of compulsory acquisition."[103] This appears to confirm the view[104] that it is not the function of the courts to investigate the adequacy of the amount of compensation provided or proposed. There are clear practical advantages in this course, but they are bought at the price of a concern for justice, where, for example, recognition is conferred on a foreign government for reasons of political expediency.[105]

An important caveat should here be noted. The Constitution contains positive protection of private property rights, as well as introducing specific limitations on the State's power to abolish the right of private ownership or to regulate rights relating to private property.[106] At the same time, Article 29.3 of the Constitution provides that Ireland "accepts the generally recognised principles of international law as its rule of conduct in its relations with other States".[107] Whether this provision operates as part of our conflicts rules[108] or merely as a signpost to the State in

---

[96] *Id.*, at 134.

[97] *Id.*

[98] *Buchanan's* case, in the words of Lord Mackay (*id.*, at 140), was the "sheet anchor" of counsel's submission.

[99] [1954] I.R. 89.

[100] [1986] 1 All E.R., at 137.

[101] *Id.* Cf. Mann, *The Confiscation of Corporation, Corporate Rights and Corporate Assets in the Conflict of Laws*, 11 Int. & Comp. L.Q. 471, at 481 ff. (1962). Lord Mackay rejected the relevance of *Buchanan's* case on a somewhat different ground. An "essential feature" of the principle enunciated in that case for refusing to allow the action to succeed was the existence of an as yet unsatisfied claim by the foreign revenue authorities. In the instant case, however, there was no allegation of any unsatisfied claim under Spanish law and, in Lord Mackay's view, *Buchanan* gave "no basis for the substitution in place of such an unsatisfied claim, of a general desire on the part of the foreign state to secure a particular result, object or purpose from the enactment of the law." [1986] 1 All E.R., at 143.

[102] *Supra*, p. 205.

[103] [1986] 1 All E.R., at 135.

[104] See *Luther* v. *Sagor*, [1921] 3 K.B. 532, *Princess Paley Olga* v. *Weisz*, [1929] 1 K.B. 718, *Bank voor Handel en Scheepvart N.V.* v. *Slatford*, [1953] 1 Q.B. 248, *Re Helbert Wagg & Co. Ltd's Claim*, [1956] Ch. 323, at 349. Cf. *Laane & Baltsen* v. *Estonian State Cargo & Passenger Steamship Line*, [1949] S.C.R. 530.

[105] Cf. *Morris*, 380-381, Mann, *Outlines of a History of Expropriation*, 75 L.Q. Rev. 188, at 218-219 (1959).

[106] Cf. *Kelly*, 644-661.

[107] See also Article 29.1, under which Ireland affirms "its devotion to peace and friendly cooperation amongst nations founded on international justice and morality".

[108] Cf. *Saorstát & Continental Steamship Co.* v. *De Las Morenas*, [1945] I.R. 291, at 298 (Sup. Ct., 1944) (discussed *supra*, p. 176), where O'Byrne, J. observed that State immunity from jurisdiction "has long been recognised as a principle of international law, and must now be accepted as a part of our municipal law by reason of Article 29, para. 3, of our Constitution ...".

international relations,[109] it may be argued that the expropriation by a foreign State of the property of a person with close connections with Ireland — nationality, domicile and residence, for example — may not now be recognised under our conflicts rules as easily as formerly. The extent (if any) to which our courts would be willing to modify these formerly accepted rules is a matter of considerable uncertainty.

This leads us to a further consideration. A foreign law or act will be recognised where the Irish court is satisfied that it is one emanating from a foreign government recognised, whether *de jure* or *de facto,* by our government,[110] or from a subordinate body set up by that government to act on its behalf.[111] The certificate from the Minister for Foreign Affairs is conclusive evidence on this question.[112] It is not necessary that recognition should have been extended to the foreign government before it made the expropriation decree: it is sufficient that the government should have this recognition at the time of determination of the proceedings.[113]

Zarine v. *Owners of S.S. "Ramava"*[114] should be mentioned in this general context. The facts of this case have already been mentioned. The holding in the case was that, since the Irish Government did not recognise the U.S.S.R. as the sovereign Government of Estonia and Latvia, either *de jure* or *de facto,* the claim by the U.S.S.R. to ownership of the vessels in question could not be recognised. It is worth noting, however, that at trial Hanna, J. found "as a fact"[115] that the vessels were "never at any time in the physical possession of the Latvian and Estonian Governments or of the U.S.S.R. or their agents, and remained at all relevant times in the possession of the masters on behalf of the [ir] respective private owners. ..."[116] Hanna, J. drew no explicit legal conclusion from this finding; we may only speculate as to whether he sought to imply that this afforded a basis for holding that the title to the vessels remained in the private owners.

OTHER PUBLIC LAWS

Apart from penal, revenue and expropriatory laws, there is a residual category of foreign public laws which may not be enforced by our courts. These public laws are those "enforced as an assertion of the authority of central or local government".[117] They include such matters as import and export regulations, price control regulations and anti-trust legislation.[118]

FOREIGN LAWS REPUGNANT TO IRISH PUBLIC POLICY[119]

Our law reserves the right not to apply a foreign law where the conflicts rules would otherwise call for its application if to do so would be contrary to our public

---

[109] Cf. *In re Ó Laighléis,* [1960] I.R. 93, at 103 (High Ct., *per* Davitt, P., 1957) and 124 (Sup. Ct., *per* Maguire, C.J. (for the Court), 1957), *The State (Sumers Jennings)* v. *Furlong,* [1966] I.R. 183 (High Ct., 1966), *Kelly,* 184.

[110] *Zarine* v. *Owners of S.S. Ramava,* [1942] I.R. 148 (Sup. Ct., 1941, aff'g High Ct., Hanna, J., 1941), *Luther* v. *Sagor,* [1921] 1 K.B. 456.

[111] *Carl Zeiss Stiftung* v. *Rayner & Keeler Ltd (No. 2),* [1967] 1 A.C. 853.

[112] *Zarine* v. *Owners of S.S. "Ramava",* supra.

[113] *Luther* v. *Sagor, supra, Gdynia Ameryka Linie Zeglugowe* v. *Boguslawski,* [1953] A.C. 11 (H.L. (Eng.), 1952), *Civil Air Transport Inc.* v. *Central Air Transport Corporation,* [1953] A.C. 70 (P.C., 1952).

[114] [1942] I.R. 148 (Sup. Ct., 1941, aff'g High Ct., Hanna, J., 1941).

[115] *Id.,* at 170.

[116] *Id.*

[117] *Dicey & Morris,* 93.

[118] *Id.,* 94.

[119] See de Belleville Katzenback, *Conflicts on an Unruly Horse: Reciprocal Claims and Tolerance in Interstate and International Law,* 65 Yale L.J. 1087 (1956), Paulsen & Sovern, *Public Policy in the Conflicts of Laws,* 56 Colum. L. Rev. 969 (1956), Kahn-Freund, *Reflections on Public Policy in the English Conflict of Laws,* 39 Gr. Soc. Transactions 39 (1953).

policy. In *Buchanan Ltd.* v. *McVey*,[120] Kingsmill Moore, J. said:

> "In deciding cases between private persons in which there is present such a foreign element as would ordinarily induce the application of the principles of a foreign law, Courts have always exercised the right to reject such law on the ground that it conflicted with public policy or affronted the accepted morality of the domestic forum."

This right will not be exercised lightly: otherwise private international law would lose much of its effectiveness.

The notion of public policy was well established at common law, but it has been modified and developed in the light of the Constitution. In later chapters we shall be examining different aspects of public policy in relation to several specific questions.

It seems clear that a foreign judgment may not be recognised here if it offends against our fundamental conceptions of justice.[121] Thus, the denial of an opportunity to a party to present his case to the foreign court would offend against our principles of natural justice. This denial could arise through the defendant's not being present in the foreign jurisdiction or through an interference with his right to put his case to the court.

Questions of public policy may also arise in the economic context. Decisions of both the High Court and the Supreme Court have held that where an Exchange Control Order is in force preventing the payment of funds outside the scheduled territories it is not possible for the Court to enforce payment through a judgment. In *Namlooze Venootschap de Faam* v. *Dorset Manufacturing Co.*,[122] Dixon, J. said:

> "Whatever the terms of the Court's order, the legal effect of it would be to put the plaintiffs in a position to secure payment of the amount in question and it would thus, even if indirectly, compel the defendants to do an act prohibited by the law for the time being in force. Put thus, I feel that on general principles it would be improper and contrary to public policy for the Court to give judgment for the plaintiffs on their claim as now framed."

In *Fibretex Lté* v. *Beleir Ltd*,[123] he reiterated the public dimension. The Supreme Court affirmed his judgment, Maguire, C.J. stating[124] that he thought Dixon, J. was right in the view he had taken for the reasons given in his judgment in *Namlooze*.

In the area of sexual morality[125] and family life, public policy plays a role. Our courts have addressed the issue of public policy in a number of cases relating to the recognition and enforcement of foreign divorces. These are considered below.[126]

---

[120] [1954] I.R. 89, at 106 (High Ct., 1950, aff'd by Sup. Ct., 1951).
[121] The question is dealt with *infra*, pp. 608-609.
[122] [1949] I.R. 203, at 207 (High Ct., Dixon, J., 1948).
[123] 89 I.L.T.R. 141, at 143 (Sup. Ct., aff'g High Ct., Dixon, J., 1949).
[124] *Id.*
[125] See *Robinson* v. *Bland*, 2 Burr. 1007, at 1084, 97 E.R. 717, at 721 (1760).
[126] *Infra*, ch. 12.

PART III

FAMILY LAW AND RELATED MATTERS

CHAPTER 10

MONOGAMY AND POLYGAMY

In Irish law, we generally use the concepts of "marriage", "husband" and "wife" almost without thinking, and they are most important parts of the scaffolding of the family law; these concepts generally have had similar meaning throughout the domestic laws of foreign countries; but in cases where differences arise, some important and troubling problems are presented. The difficulties cannot be removed by definitional *fiat*: it is necessary to confront the basic policy issues involved.

First we must ask: What does "marriage" mean in our domestic law? The answer is that marriage involves a legally binding irrevocable commitment of exclusivity for life made by both spouses. Two elements, permanence and exclusivity, are inherent in this concept; without one or the other, an interpersonal union, whatever social merits it may possible have, is not marriage under our domestic law.

If we look around the world, however, we see that in most countries marriage no longer involves these two elements. Modern divorce law is inconsistent with permanence (and thus exclusivity), while polygamy is inconsistent with exclusivity between one man and one woman. Our conflicts rules could, of course, take the view that, on this account, neither marriages that are subject to divorce nor polygamous marriages should be treated as marriages for the purpose of the conflict of laws. But to do so would exclude from the definition of "marriage" virtually every union so described under the laws of most countries in the world.

Without at this point attempting to resolve finally the best approach to the issue, let us examine briefly how conflicts rules have developed in respect of the questions of (a) permanence of marriage, and (b) polygamy.

PERMANENCE OF MARRIAGE

As has been mentioned, marriage in our family law involves an *irrevocable* commitment for the joint lives of the spouses. It has been said that, in marrying, what the spouses are undertaking is *not to divorce*. How, therefore, can a marriage that is subject to divorce nonetheless be called, and treated as, a marriage? The answer, so far as conflicts of law rules are concerned, can best be understood from an historical rather than a logical standpoint. When divorce was introduced in a number of countries after the Reformation, it was generally regarded as a limited and exceptional remedy in cases of extreme hardship or injustice. The concept of marriage as a lifelong, irrevocable commitment, though dented, was still part of the culture of these countries. More recently, however, and especially in the past twenty years, divorce based on breakdown of marriage has become the international norm. This generally means that either spouse may obtain a divorce, with or without the consent of the other spouse. In truth, marriage under this system of divorce is not a legal commitment for life: indeed, if spouses sought by contract to enter into such a legal commitment, their attempt to do so would quite possibly be held contrary to public policy. Yet even in countries with this system of divorce, the courts and other institutions are slow to abandon the verbal adherence to marriage as being for life.[1]

In *Nachinson* v. *Nachinson*,[2] the English Court of Appeal held that a post-Revolutionary marriage in the USSR[3] which was subject to easy unilateral divorce by *ex parte* registration, should nonetheless be characterised as a marriage for the purposes of the conflict of laws.

Lord Hanworth, M.R. said:

"It may be that our minds, trained to regard marriage as in most cases sanctified by religious rites - in others by a civil procedure not less binding - recoil from the recognition of a union capable of being dissolved so easily as the marriage of these spouses when contracted in Russia appears to have been.

Nevertheless that marriage has the essential legal ingredients. It is the union of one man and one woman to the exclusion of all others; it is to last for life unless it is dissolved in a manner that is made definite and final by registration. It was duly entered into in accordance with the forms required by the *lex loci* of the domicil of the parties to it. I find myself unable consistently with the authorities, to criticise or to weigh the strength that ought to be attached to the tie which forms the nexus and union of the spouses or to qualify the essence of the marriage by consideration of the means whereby it may be dissolved if and when that question falls to be determined by the law of the domicil of the parties...."[4]

It is difficult to see how this approach is consistent with the concept of marriage as retaining the ingredients of permanence and exclusivity.[5]

POLYGAMOUS MARRIAGES[6]

A polygamous marriage is one "under a system of law which permits one of the

---

[1] See Symes, *Indissolubility and the Clean Break*, 48 Modern L. Rev. 44, at 53-54 (1985).

[2] [1930] P. 217 (C.A.) analysed by Vesey-FitzGerald, *Nachimson's and Hyde's Cases*, 47 L.Q. Rev. 253 (1931).

[3] For consideration of the history of divorce law in the U.S.S.R. see Gsovski, *Marriage and Divorce in Soviet Law*, 35 Geo. L. J. 209 (1947), Stone, *The New Fundamental Principles of Soviet Family Law and Their Social Background*, 18 Int. & Comp. L.Q. 392 (1969), Bolas, *No-Fault Divorce: Born in the Soviet Union?*, 14 J. of Fam. L. 31 (1975), Mendelstham, *Divorce in the USSR*, 1 Fam. L. Rev. 133 (1978), Berman, *Soviet Family Law in the Light of Russian History and Marxian Theory*, 56 Yale L. J. 26 (1946).

[4] [1930] P., at 227.

[5] Cf. the judgment of Hill, J., [1930] P., 85 at 98 (1929), reversed by the Court of Appeal:

"I hold that 'marriage' in English law means a voluntary union of one man and one woman to the exclusion of all others, which is by them indissoluble except by death. If this be the true meaning of marriage in English law, it is the antithesis of a union which the parties or a party can dissolve at will by complying with the forms prescribed by law."

[6] See Lorenzen, *Polygamy and the Conflict of Laws*, 32 Yale L. J. 471 (1923), Beckett, *The Recognition of Polygamous Marriages under English Law* 48 L.Q. Rev. 341 (1932), Morris, *The Recognition of Polygamous Marriages in English Law*, 66 Harv. L. Rev. 961 (1953), Sinclair, *Polygamous Marriages in English Law*, 31 Br. Yrbk. of Internat. L. 248 (1954), Furmston, *Note: Polygamy and the Wind of Change*, 10 Int. & Comp. L.Q. 180 (1961), Mendes da Costa, *Polygamous Marriages in the Conflict of Laws*, 44 Can. Bar Rev. 293 (1966), James, *Polygamy and Capacity to Marry*, 42 Modern L. Rev. 533 (1979), Hartley, *Bigamy in the Conflict of Laws*, 16 Int. & Comp. L.Q. 680 (1967), Karsten, *Capacity to Contract a Polygamous Marriage*, 36 Modern L. Rev. 291 (1973), Davis, *Comment: Capacity to Contract a Polygamous Marriage*, 5 Fed. L. Rev. 294 (1973), Schuz, *Note: When is a Polygamous Marriage Not a Polygamous Marriage?*, 46 Modern L. Rev. 653 (1983), Stone, *Capacity for Polygamy — Judicial Rectification of Legislative Error*, 13 Family L. 76 (1983), Schuz, *Note: When Is a Polygamous Marriage Not a Polygamous Marriage?* 46 Modern L. Rev. 653 (1983).

parties to the marriage to take another spouse at a later date even though the marriage still subsists".[7] Polygamy has a long cultural heritage.[8] The law on the subject is complex and uncertain, with little Irish authority on some of the major questions.

The term "polygamous marriage" embraces two types of marriages, according to the terminology widely used in the reported cases:

"(a) a potentially polygamous marriage, in which neither party has, at the relevant time, any other spouse, but in which one party is capable of taking another spouse; and
(b) an actually polygamous marriage, in which one party has, at the relevant time, another spouse or other spouses in addition to the other party."[9]

The *lex loci celebrationis* prescribes the nature and incidents of the marriage;[10] in view of these, the Irish court must determine whether the marriage is monogamous or polygamous.[11] Thus, for example, if a man or woman domiciled in Ireland goes through a ceremony of marriage in polygamous form in Pakistan, the marriage is polygamous;[12] whereas if a man or woman domiciled in Pakistan goes through a ceremony of marriage in an Irish registry office, he or she contracts a monogamous marriage.[13]

The fact that a polygamous marriage is valid under the *lex loci celebrationis* does not mean that it must be treated as valid under Irish law; if either of the parties to the marriage lacks capacity under his or her *lex domicilii*[14] to contract a polygamous marriage it seems that it will not be valid under our law. Thus it appears that a person domiciled in this country is incapable of contracting a *valid* polygamous marriage.

It was formerly accepted that a marriage potentially polygamous when contracted remained a polygamous marriage even though the husband did not in fact take a second wife.[15] More recently, decisions in some common law jurisdictions have

---

[7] English Law Commission, *Report on Polygamous Marriages*, para. 2 (Law Com. No. 42, 1971).
[8] Cf. Marasinghe, *Polygamous Marriages and the Principle of Mutation in the Conflict of Laws*, 24 McGill L.J. 395, at 395 (1978):
   "Religious creeds traceable to Islam limit the plurality of wives to four. Orthodox Hinduism has no such limitation and Buddhism, both of the Mahayana and the Theravada schools, sets out no rules at all to govern the institution of marriage; the Mahayanists practice polygamy mainly as a cultural tradition which is not prohibited by religion. African native law and custom espouse polygamy, both as a religious fact and as a cultural facet of African tribal life."
   See further Vesey-FitzGerald, *Nachimson's and Hyde's Cases*, 47 L.Q. Rev. 253, at 262-266 (1931).
[9] English Law Commission's *Report on Polygamous Marriages*, para. 2 (Law Com. No. 42, 1971).
[10] See *Lee* v. *Lau* [1967] P. 14, at 20 (Cairns, J., 1964); cf. *Conlon* v. *Mohamed*, High Ct., Barron, J., 25 July 1986 (1984-8937P). See further *Dicey & Morris*, 309-310.
[11] *Lee* v. *Lau*, supra, at 20.
[12] See *Re Bethell* 38 Ch. D. 220 (C.A., 1888), *Risk* v. *Risk*, [1951] P. 50 (Barnard, J., 1950). Cf. *Conlon* v. *Mohamed*, supra, where the potentially polygamous marriage was invalid under the *lex loci celebrationis*.
[13] See *R.* v. *Hammersmith Superintendent Registrar*, [1917] 1 K.B. 634 (C.A.) cited with approval by Kingsmill Moore, J., in *Mayo-Perrott* v. *Mayo-Perrott*, [1958] I.R. 337, (Sup. Ct.). See also *MacDougall* v. *Chitnavis*, 1937 S.C. 390.
[14] Cf. *Risk* v. *Risk*, supra, *Crowe* v. *Kader*, [1968] W.A.R. 122. See, however, Davis, *Comment: Capacity to Contract a Polygamous Marriage* 5 Fed. L. Rev. 294, at 295-296 (1973) and cf. James, *Polygamy and Capacity to Marry*, 42 Modern L. Rev. 533, at 535-536. In *Radwan* v. *Radwan (No. 2)*, [1973] Fam. 35, Cumming-Bruce, J. held that the law of the parties' intended matrimonial home should govern capacity to contract a polygamous marriage. See further James, *supra*, at 537-539, and *infra*, pp. 232-235 The Canadian decisions of *Kaur* v. *Ginder*, 13 D.L.R. (2d) 465 (B.C. Sup. Ct., Brown, J., 1958) and *Sara* v. *Sara*, 36 D.L.R. (2d) 499 (B.C. C.A., 1962), held that reference should be made only to the *lex loci celebrationis* on this question. This approach has received some support from academic commentators: cf. Hartley, 32 Modern L. Rev. 155, at 159 (1969), James, 42 Modern L. Rev. 533, at 535-536 (1979), but was rejected by Cumming-Bruce, J., in *Ali* v. *Ali*, [1968] P. 564. See further the English Law Commission W.P. No. 83 and the Scottish Law Commission Consultative Memorandum No. 56, *Polygamous Marriages: Capacity to Contract a Polygamous Marriage and the Concept of the Potentially Polygamous Marriage*, paras. 3.2-3.4 (1982).
[15] *Hyde* v. *Hyde*, L.R. 1 P. & D. 130 (1866), *Sowa* v. *Sowa*, [1961] P. 70.

recognised that such a marriage[16] may subsequently be transformed into a monogamous marriage in certain circumstances,[17] the most important arising where the parties originally domiciled in a country where polygamy is permitted later acquire a domicile of choice in a country where it is not.[18] Pragmatically this approach has some attractions,[19] but it can result in serious anomalies[20] and injustice.[21] Whether an Irish court would favour the same approach is not clear. In *Conlon* v. *Mohamed*,[22] the question did not arise as the plaintiff was at all stages domiciled in Ireland.

Even more uncertain is the converse question whether a marriage, initially monogamous, may subsequently become polygamous. Statements by the courts[23] and commentators[24] support the view that it may not, but is difficult to be dogmatic as to the effect on a monogamous marriage of a subsequent valid polygamous marriage contracted by the husband abroad.[25]

The most important effect of polygamy, so far as the conflict of laws is concerned, is that neither party to a polygamous marriage is entitled to matrimonial relief in our courts. In the leading case of *Hyde* v. *Hyde*,[26] in 1866, Lord Penzance declined to adjudicate on a petition for divorce in respect of a polygamous marriage contracted by Mormons in Utah. English matrimonial law, adopted to the view of marriage as monogamous,[27] was "wholly inapplicable to polygamy".[28] The notions of

[16] As long as it remains *potentially* polygamous: *Onobrauche* v. *Onobrauche*, 8 Fam. Law 107 (Comyn, J., 1978), *Re Schota*, [1978] 1 W.L.R. 1506.

[17] E.g. where the *lex loci celebrationis* subsequently forbids polygamy *(Parkasho* v. *Singh*, [1968] P. 233), or where the parties, domiciled in a country where the personal law is a religious law, change their religion from one permitting polygamy to one that does not *(The Sinha Peerage Claim*, 171 Lords Journals 350, [1946] 1 All E.R. 348n), as explained in *Cheni* v. *Cheni*, [1965] P. 85, at 90-91 and *Parkasho* v. *Singh*, *supra*, at 253). See English Law Com. No. 42, para. 10 (c).

[18] *Ali* v. *Ali*, [1968] P. 564, *Sara* v. *Sara*, 31 D.L.R. (2d) 566 (B.C. Sup. Ct., Lord, J., 1962), aff'd on other grounds, 36 D.L.R. (2d) 499 (B.C.C.A., 1962), *Re Hassan and Hassan*, 12 O.R. (2d) 432 (High Ct., Cory, J., 1976). For critical analysis, see Tolstoy, *The Conversion of a Polygamous Union into a Monogamous Marriage*, 17 Int. & Comp. L.Q. 721 (1968), Marasinghe, *Polygamous Marriages and the Principle of Mutation in the Conflict of Laws*, 24 McGill L.J. 395 (1978).

[19] Notably that it entitles the spouses to avail themselves of matrimonial remedies.

[20] Especially in relation to divorce and legal separation, where the grounds on which a decree is sought embrace conduct that may have extended over periods before and after the change of domicile. Cf. Davis & Webb, *The Dissolution of Initially Polygamous Marriages, Part II, Grounds for Divorce*, 15 Int. & Comp. L.Q. 1185 (1966).

[21] A unilateral change of domicile by the wife was held in an English decision *(Onobrauche* v. *Onobrauche, supra,)* to be insufficient to render the marriage monogamous: the effect of a similar change by the husband "is not clear": English Law Com. No. 83 and Scottish Law Com. Consultative Memorandum No. 56, p. 30, fn. 63. Plainly, injustice may result from one spouse being capable of transforming the character of the marriage against the wishes of the other: cf. Tolstoy, *supra*, at 723. (It is hard not to be reminded here of the unhappy consequences of section 5(1) of the Domicile and Recognition of Foreign Divorces Act 1986: cf. *infra*, pp. 281-282).

[22] *Supra*.

[23] In *Mayo-Perrott* v. *Mayo-Perrott*, [1958] I.R. 336, at 349 (Sup. Ct.), Kingsmill Moore, J. stated that *R.* v. *Hammersmith Superintendent Registrar of Marriages* [1917] 1 K.B. 634 (C.A., 1916) "suggests that our law would not ... recognise as effective the dissolution of a marriage essentially monogamous by a form suitable only to the dissolution of a polygamous marriage". This *dictum* scarcely addresses the issue of capacity to transform the character of a marriage from monogamous to polygamous, but it may perhaps be regarded as being premised on the assumption that such transformation is not possible. For more direct consideration of the question, to the effect that transformation *is* possible, see *Mehta* v. *Mehta*, [1945] 2 All E.R. 690, at 693 (Barnard J.), *Cheni* v. *Cheni*, [1965] P. 85, at 90 (Sir Jocelyn Simon, P., 1962), *Parkagho* v. *Singh*, [1968] P. 233, at 243-244. But see *A.G. of Ceylon* v. *Reid*, [1965] A.C. 720 (P.C.).

[24] E.g., *Dicey & Morris*, 313.

[25] English Law Commission W.P. No. 83 & Scottish Law Commission Consultative Memorandum No. 56, paras. 3.13, 4.43, 5.15-5.25.

[26] L.R. 1 P. & D. 130 (1866).

[27] Though Lord Penzance spoke of "Christian" marriage, it is plain that what is important is whether

adultery and bigamy would be difficult to apply in relation to polygamous marriages.

Lord Penzance made it clear that his judgment did not address the questions of succession or the legitimacy of the children born of polygamous unions; all that was decided in the case was that the parties to a polygamous marriage were not "entitled to the remedies, the adjudication, or the relief of the matrimonial law of England".[29]

This approach was favoured in later decisions[30] in England before the law was changed there in 1972.[31] Whether an Irish court would take the same view today is not clear. Undoubtedly there are difficulties in modifying matrimonial remedies to cater for polygamous marriages, but these are scarcely so formidable as to justify the refusal to attempt this process in *any* case.

The real issue is one of social policy. If we accept that our *ordre public* does not prevent us from affording recognition to a polygamous marriage valid under the *lex domicilii* of each of the parties, it then becomes a matter of deciding how entitlements in our law premised on monogamous marriages may most appropriately be applied, or not applied, as the case may be, in relation to polygamous marriages, with whatever modifications that may seem desirable. We should not treat the word "spouse" as though it were capable only of a single meaning in the conflict of laws, with identical implications, however unjust or inappropriate. Thus, for example, our courts would scarcely grant a decree for divorce *a mensa et thoro* to the first wife of a polygamous marriage where the "adultery" alleged against her husband consisted of sexual relations with his second wife;[32] but there is no reason why such a decree should not be granted[33] in a case where the husband had sexual relations with a woman who is not his wife.

An interesting issue arises in respect of interspousal maintenance obligations. We can answer the question whether these should extend to polygamous marriages only if we are clear on why the law requires spouses to maintain one another. A credible explanation is that monogamous marriage is perceived as a mode of family organisation that should be strongly encouraged by the law, in view of the benefits generally resulting for the spouses, their children and society.[34] Non-marital cohabitation is not perceived as having similar benefits, and maintenance obligations do not attach to it.[35] It may be argued that a polygamous marriage, valid under the *lex domicilii* of each of the spouses, is closer to the former category, so far as social policy is concerned.[36]

---

the marriage is monogamous: cf. *Isaac Renhas* v. *Tan Soo Eng,* [1953] A.C. 304 (P.C.), *Spivack* v. *Spivack,* 46 Times L.R. 243 (Div., Ct., 1930), *Conlon* v. *Mahomed, supra.*

[28] L.R. 1 P. & D., at 135.

[29] *Id.,* at 138.

[30] *Nachimson* v. *Nachimson,* [1930] P. 217 (C.A.), *Baindail* v. *Baindail,* [1946] P. 122 (C.A.), *Sowa* v. *Sowa,* [1961] P. 70 (C.A.).

[31] Matrimonial Proceedings (Polygamous Marriages) Act 1972.

[32] Cf. *Hyde* v. *Hyde, supra,* at 137. See also English Law Com. No. 42, paras. 50, 80.

[33] At the suit of either (or perhaps both) of the wives.

[34] This is not the only consideration, of course. In England (prior to statutory changes in 1973), the English Law Commission commented that "[t]he man in the street does not readily understand why a polygamously married wife (unlike every other wife resident in this country) should be without a remedy when she is left destitute and should become a charge on our welfare services": English Law Com. No. 42, para. 91 (1971).

[35] Though of course the parents have maintenance responsibilities to their children.

[36] Cf. Pearl, *Cross-Cultural Interaction Between Islamic Law and Other Legal Systems: Islamic Family Law and Anglo-American Public Policy,* 34 Clev. St. L. Rev. 113 (1985). And see Poulter, *Polygamy–New Law Commission Proposals,* 13 Family L. 72, at 73 (1983):

"…. [I]t has to be recognized that monogamy in the traditional sense of 'the union for life of one man and one woman to the exclusion of all others' has been deeply undermined by the massive increase in divorce and remarriage which has occurred in recent years. The widespread practice of 'serial monogamy' in which the marriages are consecutive rather than concurrent is not, of

The international trend in recent years has been towards extending maintenance entitlements to polygamously married spouses. Whether this may be explained in terms of a vision of polygamous marriage as serving social functions closely similar to monogamous marriage in debatable, however, in view of a parallel trend in the domestic law of many countries towards imposing maintenance obligations on those who are cohabiting outside marriage.

Succession entitlements[37] raise an issue not dissimilar to that in relation to maintenance entitlements. The trend of judicial authority[38] in other jurisdictions is to hold that polygamously married spouses are entitled to statutory succession rights. Perhaps the Irish courts would take the same view. Of course this would result in some necessary modifications: the shares under the Succession Act 1965 would have to be divided in cases where there was more than one spouse.[39].

The Family Home Protection Act 1976 might at first sight appear to present difficulties so far as its application to polygamous marriages is concerned. But is there any insurmountable objection? The Act is concerned with the prevention of unilateral dispositions of the family home; it does not seek to give a spouse an exclusive right of occupation.[40] The definition of "family home"[41] ensures that only a spouse who has lived (or is living) in the home with the spouse who wishes to dispose of it can raise an objection. Of course the Court, in deciding whether a polygamously married spouse's refusal to consent to the disposition of the home was reasonable[42] would necessarily take into account circumstances that do not arise in respect of monogamous marriage; but that should present no difficulty in principle.

It also seems that polygamously married spouses should not be excluded from taking proceedings under section 12 of the Married Woman's Status Act 1957.[43] Where the dispute was solely between the wives, however, it seems clear that section 12 would not be available, in view of the express words of the section. Again on principle there seems no reason to restrict the statutory provisions relating to barring orders and protection orders to monogamously-married couples.[44] Similarly, social policy would surely dictate that a polygamously-married spouse should be able to take fatal accidents proceedings under Part IV of the Civil Liability Act 1961.[45]

---

course, the same as polygamy but it is hardly totally dissimilar. It is far from clear which system promotes the greater happiness among its adherents and if both really are social maladies which we should be better off without, polygamy is probably actually practised by a far smaller percentage of those to whom it is available than is divorce and remarriage in our own country at the present time. Yet no steps are apparently being taken to tighten up our divorce laws. For all its imperfections, polygamy does at least allow a husband to take a second wife without the necessity of discarding the first, with all the misery which that may involve."

[37] Succession entitlements do not constitute "matrimonial relief" and thus fall outside the scope of the exclusion specified by Lord Penzance in *Hyde* v. *Hyde*. For a considerable time after *Hyde* v. *Hyde*, the English courts treated polygamous marriages as incapable of recognition even where no question of matrimonial relief arose. Since The *Sinha Peerage claim*, 171 Lord's Journals 350, [1946] 1 All E.R. 348n, this tendency has been halted: cf. English Law Com. No. 42, para. 111.

[38] Cf. *Coleman* v. *Shang*, [1961] A.C. 481 (P.C.), *Cheang Thye Phin* v. *Tan Ah Loy*, [1920] A.C. 369 (P.C., 1919), *The Six Widows' Case*, 12 Straits Settlements L.R. 120 (C.A., 1909). *Re Dalip Singh Bir's Estate*, 83 Cal. App. 2d 256, 188 P. 2d 499 (1948). See further *Scoles & Hay*, 445-446.

[39] The right of appropriation of the matrimonial home under section 56 of the Succession Act 1965 might present some (scarcely insurmountable) difficulty where there is more than one surviving spouse.

[40] Cf. English Law Com. No. 42, para. 122. And see the Matrimonial Homes and Property Act 1981, section 3(Eng.).

[41] Family Home Protection Act 1976, section 1(1). See further *Binchy*, 323, 325-328.

[42] Section 4 of the Act. See *Binchy*, 343-345.

[43] Cf. English Law Com. No. 42, para. 123.

[44] Cf. *id.*, para. 124. See *Binchy*, 272.

[45] Cf. *Scoles & Hay*, 445, citing *Royal* v. *Cudahy Packing Co.*, 195 Iowa 759, 190 N.W. 427 (1922) (a Workmen's Compensation case).
In the United States and Canada, there is some judicial and academic support for entitling unmarried

So far as legitimacy is concerned, it is well established that the children of a polygamous marriage may succeed to their deceased parents' property as their legitimate issue.[46]

---

persons living together to sue for loss of consortium and for the survivor to sue under fatal accidents provisions: cf. *Binchy*, 196-197, Meade, *Consortium Rights of the Unmarried: Time for a Reappraisal,* 15 Family L.Q. 223, at 236-251 (1981). This development would make it all the more incongruous to deny similar rights to polygamously married spouses.

[46] *The Sinha Peerage Claim, supra, Bamgbose* v. *Daniel,* [1955] A.C. 107 (P.C., 1954).

CHAPTER 11

MARRIAGE VALIDITY AND ANNULMENT

In this chapter we shall examine conflicts of law aspects of the validity of marriages. Formerly, the courts subjected all questions of validity to the same conflict rules, but for some time a distinction has been made between the *formalities* and the *essentials* of marriage. Formalities relate to such matters as the time and place at which a marriage may be celebrated, the number of witnesses, the minimum period of prior notice and so on; the essentials concern such elements as mental capacity and duress. This distinction is easy to draw in some cases but in others it may be less clear: for example, is the requirement that a minor over the age of sixteen should have the consent of his guardians to marry, a matter of form or of essentials? The courts that have addressed this general question have not provided conceptually convincing criteria as to how the distinction should be drawn.[1]

The judicial authorities generally have held that the question whether a particular requirement is one relating to form or the essentials should be determined by the *lex fori*. If the courts discharged this function sensitively, by having regard to broader social context in which a particular requirement operated, this approach could be justified.[2] In fact, some courts[3] have been guilty of adopting a crude approach which ignores the function and operation of particular rules in certain foreign legal systems.

FORMAL VALIDITY[4]

It has for long been accepted[5] that, as a general rule, the *lex loci celebrationis*

---

[1] *Reg* v. *Griffin* 4 L.R. Ir. 497, at 508 (Cr. Case Res., 1879).

[2] Cf. *Falconbridge*, 89.

[3] See, e.g. *Ogden* v. *Ogden*, [1908] P. 46, and cf. *supra*, p. 28.

[4] See generally L. Pålsson, *Marriage and Divorce in Comparative Conflict of Laws*, ch. 6 (1974) 209-250, *Falconbridge*, 715-724, *North*, 118-119, *Rabel*, vol. 1, 223-262, Sykes, *The Formal Validity of Marriage*, 2 Int. & Comp. L.Q. 78 (1953), Mendes da Costa, *The Formalities of Marriage in the Conflict of Laws*, 7 Int. & Comp. L.Q. 217 (1958), Keyes, *The Validity of the Law Common Marriage in Ontario*, 1 Osgoode Hall L. J. 58 (1958), the Law Reform Commission's *Report on Private International Law Aspects of Capacity to Marry and Choice of Law in Proceedings for Nullity of Marriage*, pp. 9-46 (L.R.C. 19-1985) and its *Report on Jurisdiction in Nullity Proceedings and Recognition of Foreign Annulments* (L.R.C. 20-1985), the English Law Commission Working Paper No. 89 and Scottish Law Commission Consultative Memorandum No. 64, *Private International Law: Choice of Law Rules in Marriage*, paras 2.1-2.3 (1985). The present chapter, based largely on the Law Reform Commission's two reports, also traces much of its information as to English laws to W.P. No. 89 and C.M. No. 64, and to Law Com. No 137, Scot. Law Com. No. 88 (1984), which contain a comprehensive treatment of the subject. Moreover, several ideas of Dr Peter North, found in *The Private International Law of Matrimonial Causes in the British Isles and the Republic of Ireland* (1977), are reflected throughout the chapter.

[5] The first clear recognition of the principle was by Lord Hardwicke, *obiter*, in *Omychund* v. *Barker*, 1 Atk. 22, at 50, 26 E.R. 15, at 33 (1744). Thereafter the authorities followed in quick succession: see *Scrimshire* v. *Scrimshire*, 2 Hag. Con. 395, 161 E.R. 7782 (1752), *Butler* v. *Freeman*, Amb. 301, at 303, 27 E.R. 204, at 205 (*per* Lord Hardwicke, 1756), *Compton* v. *Bearcroft*, 2 Hag. Con. 444n, 161 E.R. 799 (Court of Delegates, 1769), *Dalrymple* v. *Dalrymple*, 2 Hag. Con. 54, 161 E.R.

is the appropriate law for determining the formal validity of a marriage. As Lord Cranworth stated in *Brook* v. *Brook*,[6] in 1861:

"...in the case of marriage celebrated abroad the *lex loci contractus* must *quoad solemnitates* determine the validity of the contract..."

This means, as a general principle, that if a marriage is valid according to the *lex loci celebrationis* then it "is good all the world over",[7] even though it would not constitute a valid marriage in the country of the domicile of either of the spouses; conversely, if a so-called marriage is not a valid marriage according to the *lex loci celebrationis,* then "there is no marriage anywhere",[8] even in a case where the same marriage, if celebrated in the place of the parties' domicile, would have been a perfectly valid marriage.

In the Irish case of *In re Estate of M'Loughlin*[9] it was clearly accepted that the *lex loci celebrationis* should apply to formal requirements. There the parties, both domiciled in Ireland, went through a ceremony of marriage in Wales, celebrated by a Catholic clergyman. By the law of England and Wales at the time, the marriage was void as the parties had wilfully consented to its performance when it neither complied with *Lord Hardwicke's Act* nor was performed in a Protestant church. Flanagan, J. accepted without serious question that the marriage was void for the purposes of Irish law. He relied strongly[10] on the evidence that the parties themselves had admitted that the ceremony was null and void and had subsequently contracted another marriage with each other. He did not discuss the argument[11] of counsel seeking to uphold the validity of the marriage, to the effect that *Lord Hardwicke's Act* was merely territorial, and that it did not bind parties domiciled in Ireland; on this argument the common law of England and Wales would continue to apply and the marriage would accordingly be valid.

Similarly, in *Du Moulin* v. *Druitt*,[12] the court accepted the general rule that the *lex loci celebrationis* should apply.

In *Swifte* v. *Attorney General for Ireland*,[13] the House of Lords, affirming the

---

665 (1811), *Lady Herbert* v. *Lord Herbert*, 3 Phill. Ecc. 58, 161 E.R. 1257 (1819), *Lacon* v. *Higgins,* 3 Stark 178, 171 E.R. 813 (Abbott, L.C.J., 1822) (especially at 183 and 815, respectively). See generally Mendes da Costa, *The Formalities of Marriage in the Conflict of Laws,* 7 Int. & Comp. L.Q. 217, at 218-220 (1958).

[6] 9 H.L.C. 193, at 224, 11 E.R. 703, at 715 (1861). See also, to similar effect, *Ussher* v. *Ussher,* [1912] 2 I.R. 445, at 523 (K.B.Div., *per* Gibson, J.), *Re Alison's Trusts,* 31 L.T. 638, at 639 (*per* Malins, V.C., 1874), *Sottomayer* v. *De Barros,* 3 P.D. 1, at 5 (C.A., *per* Cotton, L.J., 1877), *Berthiaume* v. *Dastous,* [1930] A.C. 79, at 83 (*per* Viscount Dunedin, 1929). In accord are *Hyde* v. *Hyde,* L.R. 1 P. & D. 130 (1866) and *Ogden* v. *Ogden,* [1908] P. 46. Canadian decisions are in accord: see *Forbes* v. *Forbes,* 30 W.N. 557, 20 O.W.R. 924, 3 D.L.R. 243 (High Ct., Latchford, J., *Johnson* v. *Hazen*, 43 N.B.R. 154 (Chy. Div., McLeod, 1912), (1914), *Re Howe Lewis,* 14 D.L.R. (3d) 49 (B.C.C.A., J., 1970), *Hunt* v. *Hunt,* [1958] O.W.N. 332, 14 D.L.R. (2d) 243 (High Ct., Ferguson, J., 1958), *Sedgewick* v. *Sedgewick,* 9 W.W.R. (N.S.) 704 (Sask. Q. B. Taylor, J., 1953), *Frew (otherwise Reed)* v. *Reed,* 69 W.W.R. 327, 6 D.L.R. (3d) 617 (B.C. Sup. Ct., Harvey, C. Ct. J., 1969).

[7] *Berthiaume* v. *Dastous,* [1930] A.C. 79, at 83 (*per* Viscount Dunedin, 1929).

[8] *Id.*

[9] 1 L. R. Ir. 421 (1878). Cf. *Steele* v. *Braddell,* 6 Milw. 1 (1838), *Thelwall* v. *Yelverton,* 14 I.C.L.R. 188 (Com. Pleas, 1862), *Butler* v. *Butler,* 6 I.C.L.R. 77 (Exch., 1856). See also the broad statement by Crampton J. in *Reg.* v. *Burke,* 5 I.L.R. 549, at 557 (1843), which draws no distinction between matters of formal and of essential validity, and cf. *id.,* at 552 (*per* Burton, J.) and 558 (*per* Perrin, J.). The case of *Reg.* v. *Griffin,* 4 L.R. Ir. 497 (Cr. Cas. Res., 1879) involves some confused analysis of the issue.

[10] Cf. *id.,* at 427.

[11] Cf. *id.,* at 424-425.

[12] 3 I.C.L.R. 212 (Q.B., 1860).

[13] [1912] A.C. 176 (H.L. (Ir.)).

order of the Irish Court of Appeal,[14] held that section 1 of the statute 19 Geo. 2, c. 13 (Ir.) was not extra-territorial in its operation. That section provided that any future marriage

"between a Papist and any person who hath been or hath professed him or herself to be a Protestant at any time within twelve months before such celebration of marriage, or between two Protestants, if celebrated by a Papish priest, shall be and is hereby declared absolutely null and void to all intents and purposes, without any process, judgment or sentence of law whatever."

In *Swifte,* a marriage between a domiciled Irish Protestant and an Austrian Catholic, celebrated according to the rites of the Catholic Church in Austria, was held to be unaffected by the Irish provision. Earl Loreburn, L.C. said:

"It is obviously and admittedly a valid marriage unless it is made invalid by the operation of the Act of 19 Geo. 2 c. 13 (Ir.). Now, if that Act was only an intra-territorial Act in its operation, it is clear that the marriage was good. Was it an intra-territorial Act in its operation and no more? It was a statute not only not forbidding marriages between Protestants and Roman Catholics, but recognising that such marriages might be lawful, in accordance with the law of Ireland. All that it did was to say that they should be invalid if celebrated by a Roman Catholic priest. In other words the Act related not to the capacity of the parties to the marriage contract to enter upon a matrimonial contract, but it related to the form and ceremony, however solemn and important, of its celebration.

Now, my Lords, I cannot suppose that the Irish Parliament intended to prescribe what was to be done by an Austrian priest[15] in Austria, or that it intended to affect the rule that a marriage which might be validly made in one country is good when made in compliance with the *lex loci* of its celebration."[16]

Where is the Lex Loci Celebrationis?

Determining *where* the marriage is contracted may in some instances raise difficulties. Discussion has centred around three particular types of case. The first concerns *marriages by correspondence.*[17] Should it suffice for such a marriage to comply with the law of the place where the contract is concluded (however that place is determined) or should it be necessary to comply with the requirement of the laws of both places? Some commentators[18] have argued in favour of the second option. *Dicey & Morris* are somewhat less certain. They consider that the English courts:

"[p]robably . . . would require to be satisfied that a marriage could be concluded in this manner by the laws of each of the two countries; but it is just possible that they

[14] [1910] 2 I.R. 140 (C.A., 1909).

[15] *Quaere* if the priest had been Irish, and the parties (both Irish nationals, domiciliaries and residents) had deliberately sought to overcome the statutory obstacle by going abroad for a few days? Cf. [1910] 2 I.R., at 160 (*per* Cherry, L.J.). Holmes, L.J. was "prepared to construe the Act as applying only to a marriage celebrated by a priest in Ireland, or celebrated elsewhere, by a priest who was an Irish subject": *id.,* at 157. This was, he considered, because "[t]he statutes on this subject were especially directed against the priest who celebrated the marriage. For him, as declared in the Act of 1745, it was a hanging matter; and that Act seems to have been levelled more against him than against the parties . . .."

[16] [1912] A.C. at 179. See also *id.,* at 280 (*per* Earl Loreburn), and [1910] 2 I.R., at 145-146 (Porter, M.R.), 154-155 (*per* Walker, L.C.) and 160-161 (*per* Cherry, L.J.).

[17] See L. Palsson, *Marriage and Divorce in Comparative Conflict of Laws,* 208ff. (1974), *Rabel,* vol. 1, 242-243, *Leflar,* 534, Lorenzen, *Marriage by Proxy and the Conflict of Laws,* 32 Harv. L. Rev. 473 (1919), and the Law Reform Commission's *Report on Private International Law Aspects of Capacity to Marry and Choice of Law in Proceedings for Nullity of Marriage,* pp. 14-15 (L.R.C. 19-1985).

[18] E.g. *Wolff,* 344.

might apply the rules as to contracts made by correspondence or over the telephone."[19]

On the latter hypothesis, only one law would apply: in the case of an acceptance by letter, this would be the law of the place where the letter is posted. There is some support for this approach in the United States[20] and in some Continental European countries.[21]

Proxy marriages are permitted by several countries.[22] Their characteristic feature is that one of the spouses is not personally present at the marriage ceremony but gives consent through an authorised agent. It is generally accepted that the law of the country where the proxy participates in the ceremony governs the formal validity of the marriage.[23]

Marriages by *habit and repute* present particularly intractable problems so far as the place of contracting is concerned. These spring from the fact that, of their nature, these marriages cannot be created instantaneously, and require the passage of some unspecified period of time before they are established. Usually, a country that allows for marriages by habit and repute requires them to be fulfilled within the boundaries of that country.[24] This reduces the scope of the potential difficulties.

The Lex Loci Celebrationis and the Problem of Time

In referring the question of formal validity to the *lex loci celebrationis,* it is not sufficient merely to state that the *lex loci celebrationis* determines the issue: this *"lex"* is "not a static conception, but is a changing body of rules".[25] The choice of law rule must therefore not merely point to a particular legal system: it should tell us at what particular moment (or moments) in its development such reference is to be made.[26]

At first sight, the answer may appear simple: the date the marriage is contracted would appear to be the obvious reference point. In the ordinary case, of course, this moment will be the one that counts; but what is the position where a country enacts retrospective legislation purporting to validate an invalid marriage, or to invalidate a valid marriage, already celebrated in that country? It is useful to examine each of these possibilities separately.[27]

(a) Retrospective validating legislation

First we must consider the position where legislation in the place of celebration purports retrospectively to validate a marriage that was formally invalid at the time of celebration. In England, in *Starkowski* v. *A.G.*,[28] in 1953, the House of Lords held that a marriage formally invalid by Austrian law (the *lex loci celebrationis),*

---

[19] *Dicey & Morris,* 265. See also the English Law Commission Working Paper No. 89 and the Scottish Law Commission Consultative Memorandum No. 64, para. 2.38 (1985).

[20] *Great Northern Ry. Co.* v. *Johnson,* 254 F. 683 (8th Cir. 1918), noted 32 Harv. L. Rev. 848 (1919). See also *Scoles & Hay,* 425, Beale, *Progress of the Law, 1918-1919,* 33 Harv. L. Rev. 1, at 13 (1919), Palsson, *supra,* 209, *Anon.,* Comment, *The Validity of Absentee Marriage of Servicemen,* 55 Yale L. J. 735, at 743-744 (1946).

[21] Cf. Palsson, *supra,* 209-210, who is critical of this approach.

[22] See *Id.,* 218-230, *Scoles & Hay,* 425-426, *Wolff,* 334, *Dicey & Morris,* 264, 265, 305, Lorenzen, *Marriage by Proxy and the Conflict of Laws,* 32 Harv. L. Rev. 473 (1918), *Anon.,* Comment, *The Validity of Absentee Marriage of Servicemen,* 55 Yale L. J. 735 (1946), Carter, *Proxy Marriages,* 35 Can. Bar Rev. 1195 (1957), *Anon.,* Comment, *Recognition of Marriages by Proxy Abroad,* 33 Yale L.J. 777 (1924).

[23] Palsson, *supra,* 218.

[24] *Id.,* 212.

[25] Mendes da Costa, *supra,* at 251.

[26] *Id.*

[27] The question of retrospective legislation purporting to *invalidate* a validly contracted marriage is considered *infra,* p. 227.

[28] [1954] A.C. 155 (H.C. (Eng.), 1953).

but subsequently validated by retrospective legislation in Austria, should be recognised as valid by English law. The House of Lords preferred to leave to another day the troublesome question as to the effect of such retrospective legislation on a second marriage contracted before the legislation, on the basis (then correct) that the first marriage was invalid. The balance of academic opinion is to the effect that "it would be unjust to deprive a person of a status acquired by him or her on the basis of the then existing state of the law."[29] As we shall see[30] the problem is somewhat more complicated than may at first appear.

In the British Columbia decision of *Re Howe Lewis,*[31] in 1970, retrospective legislation in Saskatchewan validating a marriage celebrated there according to Chinese custom was held effective in British Columbia. The Court was influenced by *Starkowski* but also by the federal status of Canada. The earlier case of *Ambrose* v. *Ambrose (otherwise Harnish or Hornish),*[32] in 1969, also from British Columbia, raised some fascinating issues. Briefly, the facts were as follows. In 1935, the petitioner, a man domiciled in British Columbia, married the respondent in Washington. At the time the respondent was still married to a Californian-domiciled man: a divorce was in the process of being obtained but had not been finalised. In the events that transpired, the full divorce was not obtained until 1939. In 1958, benefiting from Californian legislation which came into effect around 1955, the respondent obtained in California a new divorce decree which was retrospective in its effect, extending to a time *before* the respondent went through the ceremony of marriage with the petitioner.

The petitioner successfully sought an annulment of his marriage with the respondent. Sheppard, J.A. (Sidney Smith, J.A. concurring) noted that *Starkowski* related to formal invalidity, where the law in question was the *lex loci celebrationis,* rather than in the instant case, where the court was dealing with the personal law of domicile. As long as the respondent had remained married to her first husband, she retained a Californian domicile, but once she had been divorced in 1939, her Californian domicile had ended. Moreover, *Starkowski* had not involved a situation where a second marriage had taken place in the interim period between the initially invalid marriage and its subsequent retrospective validation. This was an element on which Lords Morton, Cohen and Tucker had reserved their position. Sheppard, J.A. said:[33]

> "The alleged marriage of the respondent with this petitioner did occur before the enactment of the statute of California and the making of the order pursuant thereto. The respondent in the meantime had gone through the alleged marriage with the petitioner and as a result of that ceremony having been entered into, and the lack of capacity of the respondent, the petitioner had the right to treat that marriage as a nullity. The subsequent legislation and order of the State of California, if here recognized, would divest that right from the petitioner, notwithstanding that the petitioner had not been subject to the legislative jurisdiction of California by reason of his having been resident and domiciled throughout in the province of British Columbia.
>
> Also that legislation and order purport to confer retroactively on the respondent, then resident and domiciled in British Columbia, the capacity to have married, and in consequence to make valid the alleged marriage which was initially void and performed, not in California, but in the State of Washington. In effect, the statute and order purport

---

[29] English Law Commission Working Paper No. 89 and Scottish Law Commission Consultative Memorandum No. 64, *Private International Law: Choice of Law Rules in Marriage,* para. 2-10 (1985), referring to *Dicey & Morris,* 263-264, *Cheshire & North,* 315, Mann, 31 B.Y.B.I.L. 217, at 243 (1954), Mendes da Costa, 7 I.L.C.Q. 127, at 257 (1958), Thomas, 3 I.C.L.Q. 353 (1954).
[30] *Infra,* pp. 223-227.
[31] 14 D.L.R. (3d) 49 (B.C.C.A., 1970).
[32] 32 W.W.R. 433, 25 D.L.R. (2d) 1 (B.C.C.A., 1960).
[33] 32 W.W.R., at 450, 25 D.L.R. (2d), at 16-17.

to define the marital status of two parties neither of whom were domiciled or subject to the State of California at the time of such statute or order. Under the circumstances, the *Starkowski* case can have no application to the case at bar.''

The Lourdes marriages[34]

At this point it is useful to refer briefly to the ''Lourdes marriages''. For a period in the 1950s, the practice developed of Irish couples marrying each other in Lourdes by a Catholic ceremony. This was in breach of French law, which recognised only civil marriages as valid.[35] The practice was eventually halted in 1960 when the legal problems had become known to the religious authorities. By then, thirty-three of these marriages had been celebrated.[36]

According to Irish law, the validity of these marriages was in serious doubt. The general rule is that the *lex loci celebrationis* should determine the formal validity of a marriage, and here the law of France held such marriages void.[37] Possibly, a liberal application of the ''common law'' exception could have upheld the validity of the marriages, but there was a considerable doubt as to whether this would be so.

To remedy the position section 2 of the Marriages Act 1972 was enacted. It provides as follows:

''(1) This section applies to a marriage —
(a) which was solemnised before the passing of this Act solely by religious ceremony in the dèpartment of Hautes Pyrênêes, France, and
(b) was between persons both or either of whom were or was citizens or a citizen of Ireland on the day of the marriage.
(2) A marriage to which this section applies shall be and shall be deemed always to have been valid as to form if it would have been so valid had it been solemnised in the State.
(3) An Ard-Chláraitheoir may, on production of such evidence as appears to him to be satisfactory, cause a marriage to which this section applies to be registered in a register to be maintained in Oifig an Ard-Chláraitheora.
(4) The register in which a marriage is entered under subsection (3) of this section shall be deemed to be a register maintained under the Registration of Marriages (Ireland) Act, 1863, and that Act shall apply and have effect accordingly.''

Some points may be noted about this section. First, it purports to validate the marriages retrospectively. There is nothing particularly unusual about this type of legislation. There are examples in the State's domestic law,[38] and in the domestic and conflicts law of other countries.[39] An important feature of the legislation, however, is that it involves the *lex patriae,* rather than the *lex loci celebrationis,* validating marriages that were (or may have been) formally invalid according to the *lex loci celebrationis.* This differs from the position in *Starkowski,* where the retrospective legislation was that of the *lex loci celebrationis* itself.

---

[34] See *Shatter,* 94-95, *Binchy,* 21-22.
[35] It is worth noting that although, according to French law these marriages were invalid, they would have been valid by French conflict of law rules had they been celebrated by Irish nationals in another country which required a civil ceremony. This is because according to French conflicts of law, a marriage may be normally valid if celebrated *either* according to the *lex loci celebrationis* or to the national law of the parties. Cf. *Rabel,* vol. 1, 254. A broadly similar position prevails in the German Democratic Republic: see *Cohn,* vol. 2, 300. Cf. *I.E.* v. *W.E.,* [1985] I.L.R.M. 691 (High Ct., Murphy, J., 1984), where the issue was not investigated.
[36] 263 Dáil Debates, col. 834 (speech of the Minister for Health, Mr Erskine Childers, 7 November 1972). Cf. *id.,* col. 840 (speech of Mr James Tully, T.D.).
[37] Cf. *Rabel,* vol. 1, 235, fn. 68.
[38] Cf. the Marriages Act 1936, section 4, and the Marriages Act 1972, section 3.
[39] Cf. *Starkowski* v. *A.G.,* [1954] A.C. 155.

Section 2 of the Marriages Act 1972 is an interesting example of the constitutionally complex issues that retrospective legislation may raise. The effect of the legislation is to render valid marriages that were (let us assume) void. Many of the parties in all probability had become aware of the problem before the legislation was enacted. Apart altogether from the particular difficulty concerning cases where a party had contracted a second marriage in (justified) reliance on the invalidity of the first,[40] it is necessary to consider whether the Constitution permits legislation to "foist" the status of marriage on a person who does not then wish to accept the status. In favour of the view that the legislation is unconstitutional it may be argued that the essence of marriage is the full consent of the parties *at the time of the marriage*, subject only to modification by the doctrines of approbation and ratification, both of which are under the substantial control of one or both of the parties concerned. In other words, a person who marries under duress has the option whether or not to approbate or ratify[41] the marriage, and normally approbation or ratification cannot easily be foisted from outside upon the parties. But where legislation changes the status of a person who is not validly married, without his or her consent or acquiescence, then it may be argued that this wrongfully interferes with his or her right to marry[42] as well as (one may presume) the right *not* to marry both in general and in respect of the particular partner concerned. Other constitutional rights, including those in relation to property and the rights of association and of privacy, might also be regarded as having been improperly disturbed.

It would have been possible for the validating legislation to have limited the retrospective validation to cases where both[43] spouses concurred, possibly manifesting their concurrence by an external act, such as registration, whether as a pre-condition, or as evidence, of their concurrence.

The argument in favour of the constitutionality of section 2 is that it gives retrospective effect to what must have been the presumed intention of the parties when marrying. It cannot credibly be suggested that any of them went through the ceremony of marriage with the intention of creating a void marriage. The legislation merely removes the invalidating effect of a technicality in an abstruse area of law which clearly was not in their minds at the time they married.

It seems fair to say that if, *per impossibile*, the legislation could have been enacted before any party had become aware of the problem of the invalidity of his or her marriage, then the legislation would have raised scarcely a constitutional ripple.[44] But since this did not in fact happen, it is necessary to consider the question of constitutionality complicated by the factors of detrimental reliance and of interference with justified expectations. Once a party became aware of the invalidity of his or her marriage then inevitably he or she must have had to make a decision based on this information. In many cases, of course, the decision will have been to treat the marriage as valid, but in other cases there may have been conduct based on the premise of the invalidity of the marriage.

It is possible that a court would take the view that, in the large majority of cases, a party who availed himself or herself of the invalidity of the marriage and ceased

---

[40] As to which, see *infra*, p. 225.

[41] There is some uncertainty as to whether marriages invalid for consent are subject to approbation or ratification. Cf. the Law Reform Commission's *Report on Nullity of Marriage*, p. 73 (LRC 9-1984), Shatter, 104-105.

[42] Cf. *Ryan* v. *A.G.*, [1965] I.R. 294, at 313 (High Ct., Kenny, J., 1962; affirmed by Sup. Ct., 1964), *McGee* v. *A.G.*, [1974] I.R. 284, at 301 (Sup. Ct., *per* FitzGerald, C.J., dissenting, 1973). See further *Kelly*, 486.

[43] Where only one of the spouses was willing to accept the retrospective validation, particular difficulties would inevitably ensue.

[44] If, however, a party subsequently learned of the initial invalidity but, remaining in ignorance of the validating legislation, were thereafter to marry, a new constitutional difficulty would arise. Cf. L. Palsson, *Marriage and Divorce in Comparative Conflict of Laws*, 310-311 (1974).

to live with the other spouse was behaving in an inequitable manner, or at all events was a person whose "sharp practice" estopped him or her from making a serious constitutional case. But it is possible to consider cases where a spouse's conduct would not be inequitable, as, for example, where an Irish woman, deserted by her husband, subsequently learnt of the invalidity of their marriage contracted in Lourdes. If on finding out this fact (prior to the 1972 legislation) she were to treat herself, in matters relating to property, for example, as a single woman, it would be difficult to treat her conduct as being other than sensible and fair.

The question becomes still more difficult where a spouse, having learnt of the invalidity of the marriage, has married another person before the retrospective legislation is enacted.[45] In the English decision of *Starkowski* v. *A.G.*,[46] as we have seen, this issue was specifically left unresolved. But a passage from Lord Reid's speech is of particular interest in relation to the problem of the Lourdes marriages. He considered that there was:

> "... at first sight compelling force in the ... argument that a person ought at any time to be able to find out with certainty whether he or she is married or not, and that the law of England ought not to recognize a principle which may result in a person being for the moment unmarried in law but knowing that he is liable to become married retrospectively. If there were any substantial likelihood of this happening I would be inclined to agree, but one must look at realities. I find it difficult to suppose that in any country there would be substantial delay in deciding whether to legislate retrospectively once the reason for the invalidity had come to light, and I cannot think that any one who had discovered that his marriage was formally invalid would for long be in any real doubt whether there was to be remedial legislation."[47]

In Ireland there *was* some considerable delay. It could perhaps be said that the parties could always have sought a decree of nullity of their marriage, but it is doubtful whether this is a sensible suggestion, in view of the high cost of such proceedings at the time.

Some other features of the section should be noted. It is only retrospective: thus parties marrying in Lourdes after the passage of the Marriages Act 1972[48] must take their chances without this statutory assistance. So far as the legitimacy of children is concerned the statutory provision is silent. But this does not necessarily mean that children born before then are illegitimate. It could be that, even before the legislation, the children were already legitimate, on the basis that the invalidity of their parents' marriage did not necessarily consign them to the status of illegitimacy.[49] On the other hand, if the children were illegitimate before the legislation, it may well be that the legislation would be interpreted as conferring legitimate status on them. Although it may be argued that merely changing the marital status of the parents does not itself necessarily change the status of the children, the courts might well be disposed to interpret the legislation as impliedly conferring legitimate status on them; the latter result could also be reached by the alternative route of applying ordinary conflicts principles regarding legitimacy[50] to the marriage so retrospectively validated.

---

[45] See Mendes da Costa, *The Formalities of Marriage in the Conflict of Laws,* 7 Int. & Comp. L.Q. 217, at 257 (1958), Thomas, *Note,* 3 Int. & Com. L.Q. 353, at 355 (1954), Morris, *The Time Factor in the Conflict of Laws,* 15 Int. & Comp. L.Q. 424, at 434 (1966).

[46] [1954] A.C. 155, at 172. See further Mendes da Costa, *supra,* at 257-258 (1958).

[47] [1954] A.C. 155, at 172. See further Mendes da Costa, *supra,* at 157-158 (1958).

[48] On 20 December 1972.

[49] Cf. *Dicey & Morris,* Rule 62. Cf. *infra,* ch. 16.

[50] Or legitimation, though *quaere* whether this is a case of legitimation *per subsequens matrimonium.*

A more difficult question concerns the issue of legitimacy of children of a Lourdes marriage where, before the Marriages Act 1972, the parents have married again (with other partners). If, as the body of academic opinion considers,[51] the validity of the second marriage should not be disturbed, that might suggest that the children of the Lourdes marriage, if illegitimate before the Act, would have to remain so afterwards. The inherent unfairness of this outcome suggests that no court would be likely to endorse it. The reason why, exceptionally, the validating legislation does not affect the validity of the second marriage is that it is considered just and sensible to protect the parties to that marriage (and, we may presume, their children). Certainly, there is no suggestion that keeping the children of the first union illegitimate, when they would otherwise not be, serves the interests of justice. One possible solution[52] would be to interpret the legislation as validating the Lourdes marriage up to the time the second was contracted, and as having no retrospectively "illegitimating" effect on the children of the first union. In view of the broad implications[53] for the parents which this solution would involve, the courts may well reject it.

It should be noted that section 2 of the Marriages Act 1972, being a provision of *Irish* conflict of laws, cannot, of itself, confer validity on these marriages under the conflict rules of *other* countries. Thus, for example, if the validity of one of these marriages were to be determined by an English court, the fact that the Irish legislation has been enacted would not *override* the normal rule (in English, as in Irish, conflict of laws) that the *lex loci celebrationis* should be applied. But in applying the *lex loci celebrationis,* the English court would probably include a reference to the conflict rules of France, and according to those rules it is possible, though far from certain, that the retrospective validation by the Irish legislation would be recognised. The case against such recognition, of course, is that these marriages offended against the French public policy of requiring a civil ceremony there, and, however much the Irish legislature may wish that these marriages should be recognised, French law does not owe the parties concerned an obligation to set aside this important public policy. If such foreign retrospective legislation were to be recognised, it may be argued, why should not prospective legislation also be recognised? To do so would obviously damage French public policy on this issue.

It may, however, be argued that the human realities of the situation are so strong and unusual that French public policy could well bear the strain of recognising as valid thirty-three marriages celebrated on French soil by foreign nationals acting entirely in good faith, especially where their national legislature has gone to the trouble of enacting retrospective validating legislation on their behalf.

It should also be noted that, according to the conflict rules of some other countries, the Lourdes marriages either were always valid or were retrospectively validated by the legislation. Article 7 of the Hague Convention on the Celebration of Marriages, 1902 provides that a marriage void as regards form in the country where it was celebrated shall be considered valid in the other countries adhering to the Convention if the form prescribed by the national law of each of the parties has been observed. This approach had already been adopted in Switzerland since 1891 and in Germany since 1900. It is interesting to note that in the German Democratic Republic the same approach prevails.[54]

On account of the fairly widespread support among many European countries for the option of the national law of the spouses as an alternative to the *lex loci celebrationis,* it was probably, on balance, preferable that Section 2 should refer

[51] See the several authorities cited by Palsson, *op. cit.,* 311, fn. 513.
[52] *Id.,* 311.
[53] On such matters as maintenance and succession for example.
[54] Cf. *Cohn,* 300 (section by J. Tomass).

to nationality rather than domicile. To have used domicile would have gained little so far as the conflict rules of other countries are concerned, as well, perhaps, as alienating such support as may exist among the countries favouring the *lex patriae*. Moreover, in view of the background to, and the purpose of, the legislation, the test of domicile could well have proved a more arbitrary and less satisfactory one than nationality.

(b) Retrospective invalidating legislation

We must now consider the converse case of legislation in the country of celebration purporting retrospectively to invalidate a marriage for lack of due formality when the marriage was formally valid when contracted. There are no judicial authorities on this question in Ireland, England or Scotland. However, the ''preponderance of academic opinion''[55] is against recognising the foreign invalidating legislation on the grounds of public policy.

Certainly the stress on the policy of *favor matrimonii*[56] would run against recognition. Thus no principle of legal symmetry would require our law to recognise invalidating legislation merely because it (quite rightly) recognises validating legislation.

Lex Loci Prevails Over Personal Law

It should be noted that the *lex loci celebrationis* prevails even in cases where the sole object of the parties in celebrating the marriage abroad was to avoid some irksome requirement of their personal law: this is the effect of *Ogden* v. *Ogden*,[57] *Scrimshire* v. *Scrimshire*[58] and *Simonin* v. *Mallac*.[59] But in such circumstances, it appears that a decree of nullity obtained in respect of the marriage in the country of their common domicile will be recognised[60] subject to certain exceptional limitations.[61]

Renvoi

When we speak of the *lex loci celebrationis,* do we mean the *internal* law of the country of celebration or do we mean the *whole* of that law, including its choice of law rules? There is no clear answer to this question in the Irish decisions. *In re Estate of M'Loughlin*[62] would appear to favour the internal law, since as we have seen, Flanagan, J. did not even address himself to counsel's argument that the formal requirements under the law of England and Wales were merely territorial and did not bind parties marrying in Wales but domiciled in Ireland. In a number of English decisions, however, reference was made to the *whole* law.[63]

Whether the *renvoi* doctrine may be used only to sustain a marriage is ''not entirely clear''.[64] There is no clear authority on this question in this country or in England;[65]

---

[55] English Law Commission Working Paper No. 89 and Scottish Law Commission Consultative Memorandum No. 64, *Private International Law: Choice of Law Rules in Marriage,* para. 2.11 (1985).
[56] See, e.g., *Starkowski* v. *A.G.,* [1954] A.C. 155, at 180 (H.L. (Eng.), *per* Lord Cohen, 1953).
[57] [1908] P. 46.
[58] 2 Hag. Con. 395, 161 E.R. 782 (1752).
[59] 2 Sw. & Tr. 67, 164 E.R. 917 (1860).
[60] *Salveson* v. *Administrator of Austrian Property,* [1927] A.C. 641.
[61] Cf. *infra*, pp. 262-263.
[62] 1 L. R. Ir. 421 (1878).
[63] *Taczanowska* v. *Taczanowski,* [1957] P. 301, *Hooper* v. *Hooper* [1959] 1 W.L.R. 1021. The English and Scottish Law Commissions note, however, that there is no English case in which a marriage has actually been upheld as formally valid by applying the *renvoi* doctrine: *op. cit.,* at p. 13, fn. 34.
[64] *Id.,* para. 213.
[65] Cf. *Hooper* v. *Hooper,* [1959] 1 W.L.R. 1021, as interpreted by the English and Scottish Law Commissions, *op. cit.,* at p. 13, fn. 34.

the academic commentators[66] consider that a marriage should be valid if it complies with the formal requirements of either the internal law of the *lex loci* or the law of the country denominated by the application of the *renvoi* doctrine, as required by the law of the country of the celebration. The effect of this approach, of course, is that a limping marriage may be created.

Exceptions to Application of Lex Loci Celebrationis

A common law marriage is not valid if contracted in England or Ireland. *R.* v. *Millis*,[67] a highly controversial and historically dubious decision, held that in England or Ireland a marriage must be performed by an episcopally ordained priest or deacon; under canon law prior to the Council of Trent parties could marry each other without the necessity of a priest or deacon witnessing the marriage.[68]

In the conflict of laws, a common law marriage may be recognised where the common law is in force in the foreign *locus celebrationis*. The common law was considered to apply to settlers in British colonial territories, but only to the extent that it was suitable to the local conditions. Thus, it seemed only reasonable that the presence of an episcopally ordained clergyman should not be required as a condition of the validity of marriages contracted[69] in the early period of British colonisation before the Church had been established in outlaying areas — for example, in Australia many years ago.[70] The same rule applied "where the Crown by capitulatory agreement exercised extra-territorial jurisdiction over British subjects",[71] as, for example, arose in China[72] and Singapore[73] earlier this century. In other cases, where compliance with the local formalities was prevented by some insuperable difficulty, the parties could also resort to the common law — i.e. marry, whether with or without an episcopally ordained priest, simply by pledging their troth to each other.

What amounts to "insuperable difficulty"? In the early part of the 19th century, Lord Eldon held that a marriage between Protestants in Rome solemnised by a Protestant clergyman was valid on the basis that no Catholic priest would be allowed to perform the ceremony.[74] Australian courts have upheld[75] as valid marriages

---

[66] *Dicey & Morris*, 76, *Cheshire & North*, 76.

[67] 10 C. & Fin. 534 (1844). Cf. *Beamish* v. *Beamish*, 11 I.C.L.R. 511 (H.L.(Ir.), 1861), *Reg.* v. *Griffin*, 4 L.R. Ir. 497 (Cr. Cas. Res., 1879) (especially Fitzgerald, B.'s judgment).

[68] The Tametsi Decree of the Counsel of Trent regarding clandestinity was issued in 1563 but promulgated in different dioceses at different times. In Ireland the dates of promulgation in the various dioceses ranged from the middle of the Seventeenth Century until 1827, when it came into force in Dublin, Kildare, Ferns and Ossory, Meath and Galway: see *Murphy dec'd; Byrne* v. *A.G.*, High Ct., Dixon, J., 20 December 1955 (evidence of Professor Patrick Francis Cremin, D.D.). See generally *Jackson*, 16-17, *Ussher* v. *Ussher*, [1912] 2 I.R. 445.

[69] Cf. *Beamish* v. *Beamish*, 9 H.L. Cas. 274, at 348, 352, 11 E.R. 735 at 764, 766 (1861), *Lightbody* v. *West*, 18 Times L. Rev. 526, at 529 (P.D.A. Div., Jeune, P., 1902).

[70] *Catteral* v. *Catteral*, 1 Rob. Ecc. 580, 163 E.R. 142 (1847).

[71] English and Scottish Law Commission Working Paper No. 89 and Consultative Memorandum No. 64, p. 18, fn. 60.

[72] *Wolfenden* v. *Wolfenden*, [1946] P. 61, *Phillips* v. *Phillips*, 38 Times L.R. 150 (P.D.A. Div., Sir Henry Duke, P., 1921) ("a remote part of China").

[73] *Isaac Penhas* v. *Tan Soo Eng*, [1953] A.C. 304 (P.C.), where the Privy Council held (at 319) that, "in a country such as Singapore, where priests are few and there is no true parochial system, where the vast majority are not Christians, it is neither convenient, nor necessary" that a marriage between a member of the Jewish faith and a non-Christian Chinese should be contracted in the presence of an episcopally ordained clergyman. The English and Scottish Law Commissions consider that this "would appear to afford some support for th[e] view [that the requirement of the presence of an episcopally ordained clergyman would not apply] perhaps, where it would be unreasonable to expect compliance, e.g., where the parties are non-Christian": *op. cit.*, para. 2.21, p. 20, fn. 67.

[74] *Lord Cloncurry's Case* (1811), cited by *Cruise on Dignities and Titles of Honour*, 276. In fact the Roman law was incorrectly stated (cf. *Sussex Peerage Case*, 11 Cl. & F. 85, 8 E.R. 1034 (1844)). See also *Ruding* v. *Smith*, 2 Hag. Cons. 371, 161 E.R. 744 (1821).

[75] *Kuklycz* v. *Kuklycz*, [1972] Q.R. 50.

contracted in Germany in 1945 at a time when no registry offices were open and the registrars had left their posts, and in Russia in 1942 as the German army advanced. In England for some years from 1957 the courts went very much further, taking a far more lax view of when the test of insuperable difficulty had been fulfilled. In *Taczanowska* v. *Taczanowski*,[76] the English Court of Appeal held that the doctrine *locus regit actum* rests on the presumption that parties who marry in a foreign country intend to submit themselves to the local law so far as formalities are concerned; if this is not their intention, the presumption is rebutted and they are free to fall back on the common law. The court considered that there is often no submission by a member of the military forces in occupation of a country and such was the case in *Taczanowska*. The parties were Polish nationals and domiciliaries. The husband was serving in the Polish army and he married in Italy in 1946, the ceremony being performed by a Polish priest but not in compliance with Italian law because the relevant articles of the Italian civil code were not read to the parties and the marriage was not recorded in the register of marriages. The marriage would have been valid under Italian private international law if it had complied with the law of Poland, the national law of the parties; but under Polish law the marriage was invalid. The marriage was upheld by the Court of Appeal.[77]

English courts went still further in *Kochanski* v. *Kochanska*.[78] There Sachs, J. upheld the validity of a marriage celebrated by Polish nationals, occupants of a displaced persons' camp in Germany, which did not comply with the formal requirements of German law. Neither party to the marriage was a member of the armed forces of occupation, nor was it impossible to comply with the local law. Nevertheless the marriage was held valid because:

> "[a]ny presumption that the recently liberated members of this community had, at the material time, subjected themselves to the laws of a country which they then hated fervently and at whose violent hands they had suffered severely is, to my mind, clearly rebutted."[79]

The central principle endorsed by *Kochanski* v. *Kochanska* was that parties might or might not at their option submit to the *lex loci celebrationis;* if they did not so submit, then the common law was applied. The same principle was applied in *Lazarewicz* v. *Lazarewicz*[80] in 1962.

In the decisions of *Merker* v. *Merker*,[81] and *Preston* v. *Preston*,[82] the English courts have adopted what *Cheshire & North* describe as "a less dangerous"[83] approach. In *Merker* v. *Merker*, Simon, P. held that the *lex loci celebrationis* should be subject to exception only in respect of marriages within the lines of a foreign army of occupation or of persons in a strictly analogous situation to the members of that army, "such as members of an organised body of escaped prisoners of

---

[76] [1957] P. 301.
[77] Cf. *Cheshire & North*, 324:
> "The result was that the Court of Appeal, animated perhaps by a desire to save other similar marriages, said to number between three and four thousand, recognised as valid at common law a marriage void both by the *lex loci celebrationis* and by the personal law of the parties."
[78] [1958] P. 147.
[79] *Id.*, at 153.
[80] [1962] P. 171. See *Cheshire & North*, 325.
[81] [1963] P. 283.
[82] [1963] P. 411.
[83] *Cheshire & North*, 327.

war".[84] In *Preston* v. *Preston* a similar interpretation was suggested, somewhat more ambiguously.[85]

In the recent case of *Conlon* v. *Mohamed*[86] Barron, J. discussed the conflicts aspects of common law marriage in some detail. The case has already been mentioned in relation to polygamous marriages.[87] Briefly, the issue in the case concerned the validity or otherwise of a marriage celebrated by Islamic religious ceremony in South Africa between a man domiciled in South Africa, who was a Moslem, and an Irish woman, domiciled in Ireland. The parties intended to have a civil ceremony later before a registrar in Dublin. By reason of the ban on marriage between persons of different colour then applying in South Africa, it was not possible for them to comply with the law there as regards formal validity.[88] Moreover, the marriage was not valid under South African law because it was potentially polygamous. The parties did not in fact have a civil ceremony in Dublin, because the woman, under influence from her father and aunt, declined to do so. When the validity of the marriage was considered in court in Ireland, it was accepted by both parties that the sole issue was whether the marriage was a valid common law marriage.

After a review of two cases[89] concerned with conflicts aspects of common law marriages, as well as the Irish case of *Ussher* v. *Ussher*,[90] which dealt with the common law position under Irish law, it seemed clear to Barron, J. from the principles established in these cases that "the existence of a valid common law marriage must be determined by the nature of the ceremony and not as to [the parties'] belief as to its effect".[91] Accordingly, he said, the validity of their marriage was not affected by their belief that they could not be legally married in South Africa. Nor did their decision to have a registrar's marriage in Dublin mean that the religious ceremony was in any way conditional. It was immaterial whether or not that decision had been prompted by their belief as to the validity of the religious ceremony: "They intended to be bound by that ceremony and any mistake as to its effect would not alter its legal validity".[92]

Barron, J. concluded that, since it was accepted that an Islamic religious marriage was potentially polygamous, it followed that the essential ingredients of a common law marriage were not present, and that accordingly the parties were not husband and wife according to Irish law. It would thus appear that, if the parties had entered a *monogamous* marriage, the fact that the marriage was contrary to South African race laws would not have rendered the marriage invalid *as a common law marriage*. What Barron, J. did not address was the question whether, apart altogether from the possibility of upholding the marriage as a common law marriage, the invalidity of the marriage, so far as it related to marriages between persons of mixed race, ought to have been ignored because our public policy is opposed to

---

[84] [1963] P. at 295.

[85] For consideration of the Australian decisions on the subject, see the Law Reform Commission's *Report on Private International Law Aspects of Capacity to Marry and Choice of Law in Proceedings for Nullity of Marriage*, pp. 38-40 (L.R.C. 19 - 1985). Of particular interest is *Maksymec* v. *Maksymek*, 72 W.N. (N.S.W.) 552 (1954) where Myers, J. considered that the *lex domicilii* rather than English common law should apply where there is no available *lex loci celebrationis*. See further Donovan, *Formal Validity of Foreign Marriages*, 25 Austr. L.J. 165 (1951); cf. Fleming, *Correspondence, id.*, 406, *Sykes*, 83.

[86] High Ct., Barron, J., 25 July 1986 (1984-8937P.).

[87] *Supra*, p. 214.

[88] See also *Hahlo*, 39-40, *Forsyth*, 241.

[89] *Wolfenden* v. *Wolfenden*, [1945] 2 All E.R. 539 (Merriman, P.), *Penhas* v. *Tan Soo Eng*, [1953] A.C. 304.

[90] [1912] 2 I.R. 445.

[91] P. 12 of judgment.

[92] *Id.*

such racial discrimination.[93] Nor did Barron, J. consider specifically the separate question whether, again apart from common law marriage, the validity of a potentially polygamous marriage might be capable of recognition here.[94]

Marriages celebrated on the high seas present more difficulties. In the Irish decision of *Du Moulin* v. *Druitt*,[95] a marriage celebrated between a woman stowaway and a soldier on board a troop ship headed for Australia was held void (in the absence of a clergyman), the court holding that the marriage was not one of necessity since the vessel would be putting in at places where a clergyman would be available.

The Foreign Marriages Act 1892

The Foreign Marriages Act 1892 confers formal validity on marriages celebrated abroad by British citizens before specified "marriage officers" — British ambassadors and consuls and other members of the diplomatic missions.[96] It also contains a specific provision[97] dealing with soldiers' marriages. This Act applied to Ireland. After the establishment of the State, it could be argued that the Act should continue to apply, by virtue of section 3 of the Adaptation of Enactments Acts 1922, which provides that, for the purpose of the construction of any British statute, the name Ireland "whether used alone or in conjunction with the expression 'Great Britain' or by implication as being included in the expression 'United Kingdom' shall mean Saorstát Éireann". As against this, it could be argued that the Act, of its nature, was not susceptible to modification through interpretation and that it does not apply to Ireland. This view is the one that has commanded support in official circles, since there are no procedures for foreign marriages to be performed by "marriage officers" or army chaplains or officers.[98]

Capacity to Marry[99]

Assuming that the parties comply with the formal requirements of the *lex loci celebrationis*, we must now consider what law or laws should determine the essential requirements for marriage. Until about the middle of the nineteenth century, courts[100] applied the *lex loci celebrationis* to all aspects of the validity of marriage — formal and essential. Thus, in *Reg.* v. *Burke*,[101] for example, in 1843, the Court of Queen's Bench referred to the *lex loci* as determining the essential validity of a marriage. The case involved a prosecution for bigamy. The defendant alleged that the first marriage was void. That marriage, celebrated according to Catholic rites, was within the prohibited degrees of relationship prescribed by Canon Law, but not within the prohibited degrees prescribed by legislation[102] of Henry VIII. It was necessary for the defendant, therefore, to convince the court that the legislation did not extend to Catholic marriages.

---

[93] It may be argued strongly that the constitutional right to marry (cf. *Kelly*, 486, *Binchy*, 17) cannot be consistent with a conflicts rule of non-recognition of the validity of a marriage based on racial grounds, whether under the *lex loci celebrationis* or the *lex domicilii* of either party.

[94] Cf. *supra*, pp. 213-214.

[95] 13 I.C.L.R. 212 (1860).

[96] Sections 11, 21(6).

[97] Section 22.

[98] Cf. the Law Reform Commission's Nineteenth Report, p. 41.

[99] See generally *Dicey & Morris*, 285ff.

[100] *Scrimshire* v. *Scrimshire*, 2 Hag. Con. 295, 161 E.R. 782 (1752), *Dalrymple* v. *Dalrymple*, 2 Hag. Con. 54, 161 E.R. 665, *Ruding* v. *Smith*, 2 Hag. Con. 371, at 389-392, 161 E.R. 774, at 780-781 (1821).

[101] 5 I.L.R. 549 (Q.B., 1843).

[102] 33 Hen. 8, c. 6.

Perhaps not surprisingly the court was unreceptive to this principle.[103] Crampton, J. noted that, at the time of the legislation, there was no recognition of Catholics as forming "a distinct sect of religionists";[104] instead "all the King's subjects were looked upon as members of the Church of England, some obedient members of it, and some recusants, who as such were subjected to penalties for not attending and conforming to its rules and ceremonies as established by law".[105]

It was, however, argued on behalf of the defendant that the first marriage would be void in Italy or Spain, and that "the principle of the law of England is to recognise the law of marriage to which the parties owe their obedience".[106] Crampton, J.'s response is of particular interest:

> "I admit this principle, but deny its applicability to this case. The law of England does recognise foreign marriages, and tries their validity not by the law of England, but by the *lex loci*; and if their marriage had been celebrated at Rome, we should try its validity by the law of Rome. But the marriage in question was celebrated in Ireland, where the laws of Rome have no authority, and therefore we must try its validity not by the law of Rome, but by the law of Ireland, the *lex loci*."[107]

In 1861, a new approach was adopted, somewhat unclearly, by the House of Lords in *Brook* v. *Brook*.[108] In that decision Lord Campbell L.C. said:

> "There can be no doubt of the general rule that 'a foreign marriage, valid according to the law of a country where it is celebrated, is good everywhere'. But while the forms of entering into the contract of marriage are to be regulated by the *lex loci celebrationis*, the law of the country in which it is celebrated, the essentials of the contract depend upon the *lex domicilii*, the law of the country in which the parties are domiciled at the time of marriage, and in which the matrimonial residence is contemplated ... [I]f the contract of marriage is such, in essentials, as to be contrary to the law of the country of the domicile and it is declared void by that law, it is to be regarded as void in the country of domicile, though not contrary to the law of the country in which it was celebrated."

As may be seen, this statement of the new approach adopted by the House of Lords was ambiguously expressed. It could mean that the essentials of marriage must comply with the law of the country or countries in which the parties are domiciled at the time of the marriage, or it could mean that the essentials of marriage should be determined by reference to the parties' contemplated matrimonial domicile.

In Ireland, the reported decisions favour the former approach, which is generally referred to as the "dual domicile" test. We will examine these decisions below,[109] but first we will consider briefly the position in other common law jurisdictions.

---

[103] Cf. 5 I.L.R., at 556 (*per* Crampton, J.):
"Now, this argument supposes the rules and discipline of the Church of Rome to be a part of the law of the land — than which there cannot be a more monstrous assumption; even the Canonical law has no dominion in this country, save so far as it has been received and accepted and made part of the Queen's Ecclesiastical law, which is itself part and parcel of the law of the realm."
[104] *Id.*
[105] *Id.*
[106] *Id.*, at 557 (*per* Crampton, J., describing counsel's argument).
[107] *Id.*, at 557. Cf. *id.*, at 558 (*per* Perrin, J.).
[108] 9 H.L. Cas. 193 (H.L. (Eng.), 1861).
[109] *Infra*, pp. 234-235.

In England "the balance of authority"[110] also supports the "dual domicile" test. This test is not a cumulative one. It is sufficient that each spouse should have capacity to marry according *to the law of his or her domicile* at the time of the marriage; it is not necessary that he or she should also pass the test of the law of the other party's domicile.[111] There is, however, some degree of judicial support[112] for the "intended matrimonial home" test.

In the recent case of *Lawrence* v. *Lawrence*,[113] none of the members of the Court of Appeal expressed a final preference as between the general tests of ante-nuptial domicile and intended family home, since they were prepared to decide the case on narrower grounds.[114] Ackner, L.J. acknowledged that "[t]he traditional and still prevalent view is that the capacity to marry is governed by what may conveniently be called the dual domicile doctrine".[115] And Sir David Cairns said that his "own inclination would be to hold that either basis of recognition would suffice".[116]

Purchas, L.J. discussed the strengths and weaknesses of the two approaches. The test of the ante-nuptial domicile had "the advantage of certainty and the further advantage of applying a standard law of domicile both to capacity to marry, the recognition of the marriage for other purposes and other personal issues (such as status, legitimacy, succession, etc.) where these are governed by the *lex domicilii*".[117] But "[o]n the other hand, the rigid adherence to the concept of domicile in alone giving jurisdiction in the case of foreign divorces produces obvious anomalies ..."[118]

The test based on the law of the intended domicile had "the advantage of applying a 'meaningful' law which is accepted in the area in which the parties are to live",[119] but had the disadvantage of uncertainty:

"Parties may genuinely intend to live in a certain jurisdiction at the time they are entering the marriage but this may be overtaken by events, or perhaps, more naturally, the parties may change their minds."[120]

Purchas, L.J. noted that:

---

[110] English Law Commission Working Paper No. 89 and Scottish Law Commission Consultative Memorandum No. 64, *Private International Law: Choice of Law Rules in Marriage*, para. 3.4 (1985). See *Mette* v. *Mette*, 1 Sw. & Tr. 416, 164 E.R. 792 (Sir Creswell Cresswell, 1859), *Re Paine*, [1940] Ch. 46 (Bennett, J.), *Pugh* v. *Pugh*, [1951] P. 482 (Pearce, J.), *R.* v. *Brentwood Superintendent Registrar of Marriages ex parte Arias*, [1968] P. 314 (C.A.), *Padolecchia* v. *Padolecchia*, [1968] P. 314, at 336 (Sir Jocelyn Simon, P.), *Szechter* v. *Szechter*, [1971] P. 286 (Sir Jocelyn Simon, P.). See further L.R.C. 19-1985, pp. 48-52.

[111] See English Law Commission Working Paper No. 89 and Scottish Law Commission Consultative Memorandum No. 64, *Private International Law: Choice of Law Rules in Marriage*, para. 3.3 (1985), at p. 58, fn. 172 explaining *Pugh* v. *Pugh*, [1951] P. 482.

[112] See *Cheshire & North*, 334ff. The decisions include *De Reneville* v. *De Reneville*, [1948] P. 101, at 114 (C.A., *per* Lord Greene, M.R.) and at 121-122 (*per* Bucknill, L.J.), *Kenward* v. *Kenward*, [1951] P. 124, at 144-146 C.A., *per* Denning, L.J.), *Radwan* v. *Radwan* (No. 2), [1973] Fam. 35 (Cumming Bruce, J., 1972) (which, in being expressly limited to the question of capacity to contract a polygamous marriage, "does not detract from and might even be construed as affording indirect support for the view that as a general rule capacity is determined by the dual domicile test": English and Scottish Law Coms., *op. cit.*, p. 60, fn. 178).

[113] [1985] 2 All E.R. 733 (C.A.).

[114] Based on the interpretation of section 3 of the *Recognition of Divorces and Legal Separations Act 1971*.

[115] [1985] 2 All E.R., at 737.

[116] *Id.*, at 746.

[117] *Id.*, at 740.

[118] *Id.*

[119] *Id.*

[120] *Id.*, at 740-741.

"[o]ne view common to all protagonists in this field is that the validity of a marriage must be determined at the moment of celebration. It would be hopelessly inadequate if, before deciding on which system of law to apply, it was necessary to wait to see in which jurisdiction the parties in fact settled down. The question immediately arises: how long would they have to establish their home before qualifying?"[121]

Purchas, L.J. noted that the trial judge had applied the law of the intended domicile. For the reasons just mentioned, Purchas, L.J. considered that he had to express "considerable doubt whether this would be justified as a general proposition".[122] But it was "happily"[123] not necessary to resolve this "extremely difficult but interesting academic controversy"[124] into which the trial judge had seen fit to enter. In his view, as in the view of the other members of the Court, the case could be disposed by on narrower grounds.

In other common law jurisdictions (apart from the United States, where a different approach has been taken) the balance of support appears to be in favour of the ante-nuptial domicile test rather than that of the intended matrimonial home. This appears most clearly in Canada[125] and New Zealand.[126] Decisions in Australia are scanty. In the Victoria decision of *In the Will of Swan*,[127] in 1871, Molesworth, J. considered that capacity to marry should depend "upon the laws of the country of the parties in which they are afterwards probably to live". It would seem wrong to place much weight on this statement as affording support for the intended matrimonial home,[128] however, in view of the fact that immediately afterwards in his judgment Molesworth, J. referred with apparent approval to other decisions in which the ante-nuptial domicile test had been favoured.

Irish decisions, as has been mentioned, also support the dual domicile test. In *Davis v. Adair*[129] 1895 the Court of Appeal, affirming Porter, M.R., applied this test to determine the validity of a marriage celebrated in New York between a man and his deceased wife's sister. The marriage complied with the provisions of New York law but was in breach of Lord Lyndhurst's Act[130] of 1835.

The wife (who stood to gain a small inheritance from her late husband's estate if she could successfully impugn the validity of her second marriage) sued the trustees of her late husband's estate, contending that both she and her husband had been

---

[121] *Id.*, at 741.
[122] *Id.*
[123] *Id.*
[124] *Id.*
[125] Cf. *Crickmay* v. *Crickmay*, 60 D.L.R. (2d) 734 (B.C.C.A., 1966), *Schwebel* v. *Ungar (or Schwebel)*, 42 D.L.R. (2d) 622 (C.A., 1963), aff'd [1965] S.C.R. 148, 48 D.L.R. (2d) 644 (1964), *Gray* v. *National Trust Co.*, 8 W.W.R. 1061, 23 D.L.R. 608 (Alta. Sup. Ct., 1915), *Ambrose* v. *Ambrose (otherwise Harnish or Hornish)*, 32 W.W.R. 433, 25 D.L.R. (2d) 1 (B.C.C.A., 1960). In some cases, it is difficult to be certain which test was applied, in view of their facts and the manner in which the court disposed of the issue: cf. *Miller* v. *Allison*, 24 B.C.R. 123, [1917] 2 W.W.R. 231, 33 D.L.R. 144 (Sup. Ct., Murphy, J.), *Reed (otherwise Frew)* v. *Reed*, 69 W.W.R. 327, 6 D.L.R. (3d) 617 (B.C. Sup. Ct., Harvey, Co. Ct. J., 1969). Of particular interest is *Dejardin* v. *Dejardin*, [1932] 2 W.W.R. 237 (Man. K.B., Macdonald, C.J.K.B.), which might seem on first reading to support the ante-nuptial domicile test, but may perhaps better be regarded as affording support for the intended matrimonial home test, in view of the facts (in particular, that the marriage took place before one of the parties could have acquired a domicile in Manitoba, whose law was applied).
[126] *Carter* v. *Carter*, [1932] N.Z.L.R. 1104. See, however, *Hassan* v. *Hassan*, [1978] 1 N.Z.L.R. 385, at 389-390, where the issue was left open by Somers, J.
[127] 2 V.R. (I.E. & M.) 47, at 52 (Ecc., 1871).
[128] See *Sykes*, 86, fn. 60. But cf. *Nygh*, 306.
[129] [1895] 1 I.R. 379.
[130] Marriage Act 1835, section 2. See the Law Reform Commission's *Report on Nullity of Marriage*, pp. 45-48 (LRC 9-1984), *Shatter*, 80-81.

domiciled in England or in Ireland at the time of the marriage. Her husband supported this action.[131] At trial, Porter, M.R., noted that:

> "[i]t would, however, be sufficient for her to show that one or other of them had a British or Irish domicil at that time; for a marriage cannot be valid if it is invalid as to one of the contracting parties, else one would be married and the other not, an obvious impossibility."[132]

The wife, on appeal, relied on *Brook* v. *Brook*[133] (also a case involving a marriage by a man with his deceased wife's sister) as authority for the proposition that "the contracting capacity of the parties is governed by the law of their domicil".[134] Counsel for the defendants conceded that the validity of the marriage depended on whether the wife and the husband, "or either of them",[135] had on the day of the marriage "an English domicil".[136]

The Court of Appeal held that both the wife and her husband had an "American domicile" and that the marriage was accordingly valid;[137] it seems beyond doubt that, if either of them had had an English (or Irish) rather than "American" domicile, the marriage would have been held invalid.

A brief observation by Gibson, J. in *Ussher* v. *Ussher*[138] should also be noted. Speaking of marriage, he said:

> "The form is governed by the *lex loci contractus;*[139] the essentials by the *lex domicilii.*"

In *K.E.D. (otherwise K.C.)* v. *M.C.*,[140] in 1984, Carroll, J. held that a person's capacity to marry "is determined by the law of his ante-nuptial domicile". The case concerned a marriage after a foreign divorce. This aspect of the subject of capacity to marry raises important issues, which will be examined below.[141]

Exceptions to the General Rule

Whatever the general rule may be, whether ante-nuptial domicile or intended family home, it is clear that it is subject to a number of exceptions. Let us consider them in turn. In view of the paucity of Irish decisions, it is difficult to state with confidence whether these exceptions would command full support.

(i) The rule in Sottomayor v. De Barros (No. 2)

Under the rule in *Sottomayor* v. *De Barros (No. 2)*,[142] a marriage celebrated within Britain where one of the spouses is domiciled in one of the constituent jurisdictions will be valid in spite of the fact that the other spouse does not have capacity under his or her domiciliary law.

[131] Cf. [1895] 1 I.R. at 459 (*per* Barry, L.J.):
"The case is a remarkable one. It is certainly a curious circumstance that this wealthy man, for the sake of the few thousand pounds at which the life estate of his wife would be valued, would thus seek to establish the invalidity of their marriage."
[132] *Id.*, at 386.
[133] 9 H.L.Cas. 193, 11 E.R. 703 (H.L. (Eng.), 1861).
[134] [1895] 1 I.R., at 407.
[135] *Id.*, at 416 (*per* Walker, C., referring to counsel's argument).
[136] *Id.*
[137] *Id.* Cf. *Dicey & Morris*, 101-102.
[138] [1912] 2 I.R. 445, at 523 (K.B. Div.).
[139] Citing *Brook* v. *Brook*, 9 H.L.C. 193.
[140] High Ct., Carroll, J., 26 September 1984 (1983-No. 3M), at p. 9 of judgment. (Affirmed by Sup. Ct., 13 December, 1985 (292-85)). In accord is *Sexton* v. *Looney*, High Ct., Murphy, J., 8 July 1985 (83/40m).
[141] *Infra*, pp. 236-239.
[142] 5 P.D. 94 (1879). *Sykes*, 87, describes the decision as a "peculiar and somewhat deplorable" one.

Sottomayor v. *De Barros (No. 2)* has received a generally unfriendly reception in Australia,[143] falling short, however, of outright rejection. A leading authority has submitted that, "if directly confronted with the decision, the High Court would not follow it".[144]

(ii) Incapacity by the lex loci celebrationis where this is also the lex fori

Where a marriage is valid or otherwise effective[145] by the personal law of the spouses but void by the *lex loci celebrationis,* and the *lex loci celebrationis* is *foreign,* then it would appear that Irish law should ignore any disability under the *lex loci celebrationis.*[146] The only case[147] in which the contrary has been suggested is the much-criticised decision of *Breen* v. *Breen,*[148] where Karminski J. looked to Irish law, as the law of the place of celebration.

Where the *lex loci celebrationis* is also the *lex fori,* however, it has been strongly argued[149] that a marriage valid by the parties' personal law (or laws) but void by the *lex loci celebrationis* would be considered void. There is no clear authority of this issue here or in other common law jurisdictions. The policy justification would seem to be that the forum should be entitled to protect its own laws from defiance by outsiders who come to the forum to marry. Indeed public policy would probably be invoked in relation to at least some matters of capacity, such as minimum age or prohibited degrees of relationship.[150]

(iii) Capacity to Marry After a Divorce

There is some considerable uncertainty as to the position regarding capacity to marry after a divorce so the present analysis is necessarily a tentative one. At common law it appears that capacity to enter a second (or subsequent) marriage is determined on the same principles as capacity to enter a first marriage, namely that "... capacity to marry is governed by the law of each party's ante-nuptial domicile".[151] Two separate questions may arise. First, is the dissolution of the first marriage recognised under our law? And secondly, did the parties have capacity to marry under the law of each party's domicile? In some cases, the questions will seem to be interlocked, so that the answer to the first will appear to dictate the answer to the second. Thus, for example, if X, domiciled in Ireland, obtains a divorce in England and immediately afterwards remarries in England, we are tempted to conclude that

---

[143] See *Miller* v. *Teale,* 92 C.L.R. 406, at 414 (H. Ct. of Austr., 1954), referring with some disdain to *Pezet* v. *Pezet,* 47 S.R. (N.S.W.) 45 (1946) (in which Bonney, J.'s dissent is worthy of note). In *Ungar* v. *Ungar,* [1967] 2 N.S.W.R. 618 (Sup. Ct.), Selby, J. distinguished *Sottomayor* v. *De Barros (No. 2).*

[144] *Sykes,* 88. Cf. *Nygh,* 306, who, in view of a *dictum* in *Miller* v. *Teale,* considers that an Australian court: "would in all probability hold invalid a marriage celebrated in Australia in accordance with Australian law in which one of the parties by virtue of a foreign personal law lacked capacity to marry the other, unless the lack of capacity could have been cured by a consent or dispensation under the foreign law concerned."

[145] As, for example, where the marriage is voidable, and one of the parties to it dies. Cf. the facts of *In the Will of Swan, infra.*

[146] Cf. *In the Will of Swan,* 2 V.R. (I. & M.) 47 (Ecc., Molesworth, J., 1871), *Reed (orse. Frew)* v. *Reed,* 69 W.W.R. 327, 6 D.L.R. (3d) 617 (B.C. Sup. Ct., Harvey Co. Ct. J., 1969).

[147] Loose statements in *Berthiaume* v. *Dastous,* [1930] A.C. 79, at 83 (*per* Viscount Dunedin) and *Starkowski* v. *A.G.,* [1954] A.C. 155, at 174 (*per* Lord Tucker) may safely be ignored.

[148] [1964] P. 144, criticised by Unger, 24 Modern L. Rev. 784, *Cheshire & North,* 343.

[149] Cf. *Dicey & Morris,* 299-300, the English Law Commission Working Paper No. 89 and Scottish Law Commission Consultative Memorandum No. 64, *Private International Law: Choice of Law Rules in Marriage,* para. 3.8 (1985).

[150] Cf. *Reg.* v. *Burke,* 5 I.L.R. 549 (Q.B., 1843), where the Court rejected the argument that Catholic marriages should be treated as outside the scope of legislation on prohibited degrees of relationship introduced by Henry VIII. See further pp. 231-232. *supra.*

[151] *Dicey & Morris,* 293.

because the divorce is not recognised in Ireland, the country of his domicile, neither will X's second marriage be recognised here. In this example, since capacity to remarry is determined by a person's ante-nuptial domicile, it is in fact the case that X's second marriage will not be recognised, because X was *at the time of the second marriage* domiciled in Ireland.

If we vary the facts somewhat, however, the issue will emerge more clearly. Let us take the case of Y, who, when domiciled in Ireland, obtains a divorce in England, and who remarries in England, not immediately, but some time later, *by which time Y has acquired an English domicile.* Clearly, the divorce will not be recognised here, but equally clearly the second marriage, let us assume,[152] is a valid marriage according to Y's ante-nuptial domicile. There is an important Canadian case[153] which holds that a marriage should be recognised where valid according to the ante-nuptial domicile, even though preceded by a divorce decree which was not recognised by the law of the (then) domicile of the party concerned. As may readily be appreciated, some difficult consequential questions arise from severing the question of divorce recognition from that of capacity to remarry in this way. It would be necessary to determine whether the recognition of the validity of the second marriage necessarily extinguishes all the rights and obligations[154] relating to the first marriage.

The converse position arises where, following a divorce granted[155] under the law of the (then) domicile, a party marries in circumstances where the law of his new domicile, at the time of the marriage, does not regard the divorce as effective. There is English authority,[156] which is not directly in point but which would suggest that the validity of the second marriage should not be recognised since it conflicts with the ante-nuptial domicile. More recent English decisions,[157] inspired by the principle of *favor divortii*, are not in harmony with this approach.[158]

However uncertain the common law rules relating to capacity to remarry after a divorce may be, the position becomes even more complicated when we have regard to the constitutional dimension. Article 41.3 of the Constitution provides as follows:

"1° The State pledges itself to guard with special care the institution of Marriage, on which the Family is founded, and to protect it against attack.

2° No law shall be enacted providing for the grant of a dissolution of marriage.

3° No person whose marriage has been dissolved under the civil law of any other State but is a subsisting valid marriage under the law for the time being in force within the jurisdiction of the Government and Parliament established by this Constitution shall be capable of contracting a valid marriage within that jurisdiction during the lifetime of the other party to the marriage so dissolved."

In the Irish language, Article 41.3.3° provides:

[152] We need not here concern ourselves with how English law would actually determine this issue, since the example is given merely as a model to illustrate a general question.

[153] *Schwebel* v. *Ungar*, 48 D.L.R. (2d) 644 (Sup. Ct. Can., 1964), aff'g 42 D.L.R. (2d) 622 (Ont. C.A., 1963), approved by Simon, P., in *Padolecchia* v. *Padolecchia,* [1968] P. 314, at 339. See further *supra*, pp. 33-34.

[154] In relation to such matters as maintenance, family property, residence in the family home and succession.

[155] Or recognised by that law. For simplicity of analysis, the case of a divorce granted under the law of the domicile is being considered.

[156] *R.* v. *Brentwood Marriage Registrar,* [1968] 2 Q.B. 956 (C.A.).

[157] *Perrini* v. *Perrini,* [1979] Fam. 84, *Lawrence* v. *Lawrence,* [1985] 2 All E.R. 733 (C.A.).

[158] Cf. Collier, *Casenote,* [1979] Camb. L.J. 289, English Law Commission Working Paper No. 89 and Scottish Law Commission Consultative Memorandum No. 64, *Private International Law: Choice of Law Rules in Marriage,* para. 3.9 (1985) and the Law Reform Commission's *Report on Private International law Aspects of Capacity to Marry and Choice of Law in Proceedings for Nullity of Marriage,* p. 65 (LRC 19-1985).

"I gcás pósadh duine ar bith a scaoileadh faoi dhlí shibhialta aon Stáit eile agus an pósadh sin, agus bail dlí air, a bheith ann fós faoin dlí a bheas i bhfeidhm in alt na huaire taobh istigh de dhlínse an Rialtais agus na Parlaiminte a bhunaítear leis an mBunreacht seo, ní fhéadhfaidh an duine sin pósadh ar a mbeadh bail dlí a dhéanamh taobh istigh den dlínse sin an fad is beo don duine eile a bhí sa chuing phósta a scaoileadh amhlaidh."

Judicial interpretation of these provisions, especially of Article 41.3.3°, has concentrated on the circumstances in which the validity of *a foreign divorce decree* will be *recognised* under our law. This is so in spite of the express language of the subsection which (whatever it may mean precisely) clearly speaks of *capacity to marry*.[159]

This approach is apparent in *In Re Caffin dec'd: Bank of Ireland* v. *Caffin*,[160] in 1971, Kenny, J. held that the second, rather than the first, wife of a divorced man was entitled under the Succession Act 1965 to elect to take a legal right, as surviving spouse, in respect of his estate. The man had divorced his first wife in England in 1956, when both he and his first wife were domiciled there. In the same year he married his second wife. At the time of the marriage he was domiciled and resident in England, and his second wife was domiciled and resident in Ireland.

Kenny, J. stated:

"As the marriage of Mr Caffin and [his second wife] took place in Dublin, it would have been invalid if on [that day] Mr Caffin's marriage to [his first wife] was a subsisting valid marriage under the law for the time being in force in the Republic of Ireland."[161]

Kenny, J. held that, since the divorce was recognised here, the first marriage was not subsisting and accordingly that the second wife was entitled to the legal right. He provided no specific analysis of the issue of capacity to marry.[162] The reference to the fact that the marriage took place in Dublin, however, suggests that it was inspired by Article 41.3.3°. What precise relevance this sub-section had to the outcome of the decision is not clear.

Passages from *Mayo-Perrott* v. *Mayo-Perrott*[163] merit extended quotation, since they raise (although they do not clearly resolve) the question of the exact effect of Article 41.3.3° on the capacity to remarry after a divorce. O'Daly, J. said:

"Article 41.3.3° appears to put in the power of the Oireachtas to define from time to time what marriages dissolved by foreign civil tribunals are to be regarded as valid subsisting marriages under our law, *id est.*, what foreign civil divorces shall not be recognised as valid."[164]

---

[159] Cf. Duncan, *The Future for Divorce Recognition in Ireland*, 2 Dublin U.L. Rev. 2, at 4 (1971): "On the face of it this suggestion appears to be laying down a rule governing the capacity of persons to contract a marriage in the Republic. What it says about the recognition of foreign divorces, it says only in relation to this question of marriage capacity, e.g. questions of succession or mutual property rights as between the divorced parties, or questions relating to the legitimacy of children of a second marriage occurring outside Ireland, would not seem to come within the subsection's ambit. Nor would the subsection appear to prohibit recognition of a subsequent marriage which takes place outside Ireland. However, judges have not accepted that the subsection is thus limited."

[160] [1971] I.R. 123 (High Ct.), analysed by O'Reilly, *Recognition of Foreign Divorce Decrees*, 6 Ir. Jur. (n.s.) 293 (1971), Duncan, *Desertion and Cruelty in Irish Matrimonial Law*, 7 Ir. Jur. (n.s.) 213, at 232-235 (1972).

[161] [1971] I.R., at 127.

[162] Cf. *North*, 378.

[163] [1958] I.R. 336 (Sup. Ct.). Cf. *infra*, pp. 273-275.

[164] *Id.*, at 351. See also *Gaffney* v. *Gaffney*, [1975] I.R. 133, at 150-151 (Sup. Ct., *per* Walsh, J.).

Kingsmill Moore, J. observed in relation to Article 41.3.3°:

"The remaining words of Article 41.3, are not without difficulty. They apply only to persons whose divorce in a foreign country is not recognised as effectual by our Courts (e.g. where the divorced persons were not domiciled in that country), and where, therefore, the original marriage is considered to be still valid and subsisting. They say that a person whose marriage is thus considered by the law to be valid and subsisting 'shall not be capable of contracting a valid marriage within that jurisdiction (i.e. our jurisdiction) during the lifetime of the other party to the marriage so dissolved.' The words do not declare that such a person cannot *anywhere* contract 'a marriage valid within our jurisdiction,' but merely prohibit the contracting *within our jurisdiction* of a valid marriage. It is the contracting of the second marriage within the jurisdiction which is prohibited. There is nothing to make it invalid if contracted elsewhere.

The general policy of the Article seems to me clear. The Constitution does not favour dissolution of marriage. No laws can be enacted to provide for a grant of dissolution of marriage in this country. No person whose divorced status is not recognised by the law of this country for the time being can contract in this country a valid second marriage. But it does not purport to interfere with the present law that dissolutions of marriage by foreign Courts, where the parties are domiciled within the jurisdiction of those Courts, will be recognised as effective here. Nor does it in any way invalidate the remarriage of such persons. It avoids the anomalous, if not scandalous, state of affairs ... whereby legitimacy and criminality could be decided by a flight over St. George's Channel."[165]

This passage provokes the following question. Is Article 41.3.3° designed to *modify* or to *replace* the common law rules as to capacity to remarry? This question mirrors the question on which judicial attention has instead concentrated, namely, whether Article 41 modifies or replaces the common law rules relating to the recognition of foreign divorces.

Although the answer to the question regarding capacity to remarry is not certain, it may be argued that Article 41.3.3° modifies rather than replaces the common law rules. If the sub-section were to be interpreted as replacing the common law rules by a single provision rendering persons who have divorced abroad in circumstances where the divorce would not be recognised here incapable of remarrying here but capable of remarrying anywhere else, regardless of their ante-nuptial domicile at the time of the second marriage, this would have the effect of removing any of the common law requirements for capacity to remarry, provided only that the marriage takes place outside the State. There appears to be no rational policy justification for such an interpretation. It seems more reasonable to interpret the subsection as providing that parties whose divorce would not be recognised under our law are not entitled to marry here but that in all other respects the common law rules as to capacity to remarry should continue to apply.

It is, of course, possible that the Constitution has an impact on the common law rules, not by reason of the specific terms of Article 41.3.3°, but on account of broader policy norms reflected in Article 41. Thus, for example, it may well be that in cases where a person's ante-nuptial domicile would permit a remarriage but the divorce obtained by that person is not recognised under our law, the validity of the second marriage will not be recognised. It may also be the case that, though a divorce is recognised under our law, a subsequent marriage that is invalid by the law of the ante-nuptial domicile by reason of that law's non-recognition of the divorce should result in the marriage also being invalid under our law. In the absence of clear judicial guidance, these and related issues must remain for the moment unresolved.

---

[165] [1958] I.R., at 349-350.

(iv) *Public policy*

It seems clear that our courts should not give effect to a capacity or incapacity under the law of a party's ante-nuptial domicile if to do so would be contrary to Irish public policy.[166] Public policy can thus operate in two ways. Our courts should not recognise a foreign incapacity "of a penal or discriminatory nature",[167] such as one based on race,[168] caste,[169] or religion,[170] for example, or one that "discriminates against or penalises a particular section of the population".[171] Conversely our courts should (in rare cases) refuse to recognise a foreign *capacity* to marry which offends our public policy; a "marriage" between persons of the same sex,[172] for example, or one between a brother and a sister,[173] would clearly appear to fall within this category.

It would be wrong to overstate the scope of the operation of public policy in this context: too frequent an application of the concept would serve to defeat the general goals of choice-of-law in the private international law of marriage.

Consent to Marry

In the absence of Irish authority on the question, it is useful to examine the position in other common law jurisdictions. In England, "the weight of authority"[174] favours the view that the issue of the reality of a party's consent (as opposed to the form in which that consent is expressed)[175] should be determined by the law of the parties' domicile.

Support for this approach is evident, albeit somewhat opaquely, in the Court of Appeal decision of *Apt* v. *Apt,*[176] in 1947. In *Way* v. *Way,*[177] in 1949, Hodson, J. placed some reliance on *Apt* v. *Apt* when stating that ". . . questions of consent are to be dealt with by reference to the personal law of the parties rather than by reference to the law of the place where the contract was made". Hodson, J. considered that, since marriage is "essentially a voluntary union"[178] and since "'consent is an emanation of personality'",[179] it was "therefore . . . justifiable and consistent with authority to apply the matrimonial law of each of the parties".[180] English law, as the law of the petitioner's domicile, was accordingly applied. On appeal to the Court of Appeal (*sub. nom. Kenward* v. *Kenward*[181]), Evershed, M.R. referred to

---

[166] Cf. *Dicey & Morris,* 303-304, *North,* 131, the English Law Commission's Working Paper No. 89 and the Scottish Law Commission's Consultative Memorandum No. 64, *Private International Law: Choice of Law Rules in Marriage,* para. 3.10 (1985), L. Palsson, *Marriage in Comparative Conflict of Laws: Substantive Conditions,* 191-197 (1981), *Rabel,* vol. 1, 265-266, 271-280, 297-307, *Stimson,* 58-69.
[167] English & Scottish Law Commissions, *op. cit.,* para. 3.10.
[168] *Sottomayor* v. *De Barros (No. 2),* 5 P.D. 94, at 104 (*per* Hannen, P., 1879). Cf. *Conlon* v.*Mohamed,* High Ct., Barron, J., 25 July 1986 (1984-8937P), discussed *supra,* pp. 230-231.
[169] *Chetti* v. *Chetti,* [1909] P. 67.
[170] *Sottomayor* v. *De Barros (No. 2),* 5 P.D. 94, at 104 (1879), *Papadopoulos* v. *Papadopoulos,* [1930] P. 55.
[171] English & Scottish Law Commissions, *op. cit.,* para. 3.10, citing *Scott* v. *A.G.,* 11 P.D. 128 (1886), as explained in *Warter* v. *Warter,* 15 P.D. 152 (1890).
[172] See *O'Donnell & Jones,* 46-50, *Anon., The Legality of Homosexual Marriages,* 82 Yale L.J. 573 (1973), and the Law Reform Commission's *Report on Nullity of Marriage,* pp. 4-5, 90 (LRC 9-1984).
[173] Cf *Cheni* v. *Cheni,* [1965] P. 85, at 97, *Brook* v. *Brook,* 9 H.L.C. 193, at 227-228 (1861).
[174] English Law Commission Working Paper No. 89 and Scottish Law Commission Consultative Memorandum No. 64, *Private International Law: Choice of Law Rules in Marriage,* para. 5.9 (1985).
[175] Cf. *Apt* v. *Apt,* [1948] P. 83 (C.A., 1947).
[176] [1948] P. 83, at 88 (C.A., *per* Cohen L.J. 1947).
[177] [1950] P. 71, at 78 (Hodson, J., 1949).
[178] *Id.,* at 79.
[179] *Id.,* quoting Dr V.R. Idelson, K.C., counsel for the petitioner.
[180] *Id.*
[181] [1950] P. 71 (C.A.), noted by Jackson, 14 Modern L. Rev. 77 (1951). The Court of Appeal reversed Hodson, J. on a ground not of present relevance.

Hodson, J.'s statement that the issue of the petitioner's consent should be determined by English law, and added: "I assume that that is correct".[182]

In *Szechter (orse. Karsov)* v. *Szechter*,[183] in 1970, the issue was whether a marriage contracted in Poland by Polish domiciliaries was void for duress. The marriage was a device adopted by the parties to secure the release of one of them from a prison, where she had been confined for "anti-state activities". Sir Jocelyn Simon P. held that Polish law, as the *lex domicilii*, was the proper law to apply. He quoted[184] the passage from Hodson, J.'s judgment (already mentioned) and referred[185] to Evershed, M.R.'s endorsement in the Court of Appeal.

Some discussion[186] has been provoked by the fact that, although he decided that Polish law applied, Sir Jocelyn Simon made an extensive examination of English law on the subject of duress. Sir Jocelyn Simon explained this on the basis that the expert witness on Polish law had (on account of illness) been able to give evidence only by way of affidavit and that "[i]f a party adduces no evidence, or insufficient evidence, of the proper foreign law, the court perforce looks to English law".[187] He did, however, note that counsel for the Queen's Proctor had not questioned the accuracy of the averment by the expert as to Polish law, which was to the effect that the marriage would be held void.[188]

It is worth noting that in *Szechter*,[189] Sir Jocelyn Simon adopted *Dicey & Morris*'s suggestion[190] that no marriage is valid if by the law of either party's domicile one party does not consent to marry the other. This approach does not coincide with that favoured by *Cheshire & North*:[191] in their view,[192] the issue of a party's alleged lack of consent to marry should be determined by reference to that person's ante-nuptial domiciliary law.[193]

Support for the *lex domicilii* as the relevant law to determine the issue of consent may also be gleaned from the English Court of Appeal's holding in *Vervaeke* v. *Smith*[194] that the rule in *Sottomayor* v. *De Barros (No. 2)*[195] applied to determine the validity of a marriage where consent was in issue.[196] The House of Lords, on appeal,[197] made no observation on this issue.[198]

---

[182] [1950] P. 133. Cf. *id.*, at 144 (*per* Denning, L.J.).

[183] [1971] P. 286 (Sir Jocelyn Simon, P., 1970).

[184] *Id.*, at 295.

[185] *Id.*

[186] Cf. *Cheshire & North*, 401, fn. 1, Hartley, *The Policy Basis of the English Conflict of Laws of Marriage*, 35 Modern L. Rev. 571, at 580 (1972).

[187] [1971] P., at 195.

[188] Cf. Hartley, *supra*, at 580. See also *Feiner* v. *Demkowicz (falsely called Feiner)*, 42 D.L.R. (3d) 165, at 171 (Ont. High Ct. 1973), where, in the absence of acceptable evidence as to the law of Poland, the parties having intended at the time of the marriage to emigrate, and thereafter having done so (although to Canada rather than Israel, which the plaintiff had recorded as his intended destination), Van Camp. J. applied "the internal law of Canada". Although other parts of the judgment suggest that this may be in tune with the "intended matrimonial home" approach, it seems more easily reconcilable with the application of the *lex fori*.

[189] [1971] P., at 294-295.

[190] 8th ed., 1967, p. 271.

[191] *Cheshire & North*, 401.

[192] See also *Dicey & Morris*, 304-305, *Morris*, 175.

[193] *Cheshire & North*, 401. Cf. Hartley, *supra*, at 581: "Provided the parties consent by English law, the marriage should be valid unless there is no consent by the law of *both* parties' domiciles".

[194] [1981] Fam. 77, at 122 (C.A., *per* Sir John Arnold, P. 1980).

[195] 5 P.D. 94 (1879).

[196] See the English Law Commission Working Paper No. 89 and the Scottish Law Commission Consultative Memorandum No. 64, *Private International Law: Choice of Law Rules in Marriage*, para. 5.9 (1985).

[197] [1983] 1 A.C. 145.

[198] It could perhaps be argued that the issue of a "sham marriage", which confronted the court in *Vervaeke*, may more easily be regarded as falling within the general scope of capacity to marry (to which *Sottomayor* v. *De Barros (No.2)* is a qualification) in contrast to the "normal" type of consent case, which raises issues of individual, more than social, dimensions.

It should be noted that in several English cases the *lex fori* has been applied, without comment, not only where the *lex fori* coincided with the ante-nuptial domicile of the petitioner[199] or the *lex loci celebrationis,*[200] but also where neither supporting element was present.[201] Moreover the *lex loci celebrationis* has been invoked in isolated English[202] and Australian[203] cases as well as in the only Scottish case[204] dealing (*obiter*) with the question of choice of law for consent.

An attempt has been made by one commentator[205] to spell out the "inarticulated premises"[206] on which the English courts have been working. In his view, the *lex fori* is to be applied where the case concerns a party who never intended to acquire the status, in law or reality, of a spouse. A mistake as to the nature of the ceremony or a case of duress would relate to the status in *law* of a spouse; a "sham marriage" would seek to deny the status, in *reality*, of a spouse. Where, however, the party did intend to acquire married status, but alleged that true consent was nevertheless lacking, whether because of a mistaken belief as to the legal effects of the marriage or of one as to the attributes of the other spouse, then the issue should be referred to the law of that party's ante-nuptial domicile.

The policy justification put forward for this distinction is that, since, in the case where the party did not intend to acquire the status of a spouse, the court is acting more as a fact-finding tribunal, it would necessarily have to apply English law as the *lex fori* in reaching its decision and there would be no need for it to refer to any other law.[207] These considerations would not arise in cases where the party did intend to marry but was mistaken as to the effects of the marriage or the qualities of the other spouse.

Impotence[208]

Impotence is a ground of nullity which renders a marriage voidable in Irish law.[209] It consists of a condition of incapacity to have sexual intercourse with the other spouse.[210] This condition must be permanent[211] and must have existed at the

---

[199] *Hussein, (otherwise Blitz)* v. *Hussein,* [1938] P. 159 (Henn Collins, J.), *Mehta (otherwise Kohn)* v. *Mehta,* [1945] 2 All E.R. 690 (P.D.A. Div., Barnard, J.).

[200] *Cooper (falsely called Crane)* v. *Crane,* [1891] P. 369 (Collins, J.), *Valier* v. *Valier (otherwise Davis),* 133 L. T. 830 (P.D.A. Div., Lord Merrivale, P., 1925), *Hussein (otherwise Blitz)* v. *Hussein,* [1938] P. 159 (Henn Collins, J.).

[201] *H.* v. *H.,* [1954] P. 258 (Karminski, J., 1953), *Kassim (otherwise Widmann)* v. *Kassim (otherwise Hassim),* [1962] P. 224 (Ormrod, J.), *Buckland* v. *Buckland (otherwise Camilleri),* [1968] P. 296 (Scarman, J., 1965).

[202] *Parojcic* v. *Parojcic (otherwise Ivetic),* [1958] 1 W.L.R. 1280, at 1283 (P.D.A. Div., Davies, J.). Here the marriage was celebrated in England by two English domiciliaries. Davies, J., in deciding an issue of duress, considered it "plain that the law by which the validity of this marriage is to be tested is English law, the *lex loci contractus*". Carter, 45 Br. Y. Bk. of Int. L. 406, at 407 (1971) observes that, "[i]f this implies that English law was applicable as the law governing formal validity, it is wrong. If, however, it means that in matters of essential validity, at least so far as marriages celebrated in the *forum* are concerned, not only the *lex domicilii* but also the *lex loci* must be complied with, it is perhaps more readily explicable". See further Webb, *Note,* 22 Modern L. Rev. 198 (1959).

[203] *Di Mento* v. *Visalli,* [1973] 2 N.S.W.L.R. 199.

[204] *Di Rollo* v. *Di Rollo,* 1959 S.C. 75, at 78.

[205] Webb, *Note,* 21 Modern L. Rev. 198, at 202-204 (1959).

[206] *Id.,* at 202.

[207] *Id.*

[208] See generally the Law Reform Commission's *Report on Nullity of Marriage,* 48-63, 144-147 (LRC 9-1984), *Shatter,* 123-130, *Binchy,* 82-96.

[209] *McM.* v. *McM. & McK.* v. *McK.,* [1936] I.R. (High Ct., Hanna, J., 1935), *A. O'H. (otherwise F.)* v. *P.F.* [1986] I.L.R.M. 489 (High Ct., Barron, J. 1985), *L.C.* v. *B.C. (otherwise known as B.L.),* [1986] I.L.R.M. 618 (High Ct., Lynch, J., 1985), *M.M. (otherwise G.)* v. *P.M.,* [1986] I.L.R.M. 515 (High Ct., McMahon, J., 1985).

[210] *McM.* v. *McM. & McK.* v. *McK., supra, S.* v. *S.,* unreported, Sup. Ct., 1 July 1976 (1-1976), *N.F.* v. *M.T. (otherwise known as F.),* [1982] I.L.R.M. 545 (High Ct., O'Hanlon, J.).

[211] Cf. *A.* v. *A. sued as B.,* 19 L.R. Ir. 403 (Mat., Warren, J., 1897).

time of the marriage. A refusal by a party to consummate the marriage will not be a ground for annulment, unless the refusal may be traced to "such a paralysis and distortion of will as to prevent the victim thereof from engaging in the act of consummation".[212] In other countries, impotence is very frequently a ground for annulment.[213] In some countries,[214] however, it is a ground for divorce.

While the notion of impotence as an *incapacity* to consummate the marriage is at the base of the ground of impotence in most countries, in some countries a decree of nullity may also be obtained for a wilful refusal to consummate a marriage, whether that refusal is based on incapacity existing at the time of the marriage, a secret intention not to consummate existing at the time or a decision made after the marriage was celebrated. Where the ground depends exclusively on facts and conditions occurring after the marriage was celebrated, particular difficulties are occasioned for the conflict of laws.

There appears to be no reported decision in the State in which the issue of choice of law for impotence and related matters was considered.[215] The position in other common law jurisdictions is far from clear. Support has at various times been given to the *lex loci celebrationis*, the *lex fori* and the *lex domicilii*. Each will be considered in turn. Before doing so, however, it is worth noting that, in England,[216] impotence and wilful refusal to consummate the marriage are often pleaded as alternative grounds for annulment. Thus, when in these cases choice of law is discussed, "there is a tendency to assume that the same choice of law rule applied to both, even though impotence may be regarded as a defect existing at the time of marriage whilst wilful refusal could be classed as a post nuptial defect".[217]

(i) *The lex loci celebrationis*

The place of celebration of a marriage may have so little connection with the lives of the parties that it seems an odd reference point for choice of law on such an intimate question as impotence or wilful refusal. Nevertheless it has some English support. In *Robert (otherwise de la Mare)* v. *Robert*,[218] a wilful refusal case, Barnard, J.

[212] *G.* v. *G.*, [1924] A.C. 349, at 367 (H.L. (Sc.), *per* Lord Shaw). Cf. *McM.* v. *McM. & McK.* v. *McK.*, *supra*, at 201. In *S.* v. *S.*, *supra*, Kenny, J. recognised as a ground of annulment a secret intention, existing at the time of the marriage, not to consummate the marriage. Griffin, J. evinced little sympathy for this approach but Henchy, J. appears to have accepted that a petition based on this ground would lie if it could be shown that the party refusing to consummate had been aware of his "emotional and sexual capacity" at the time of the marriage. See further Duncan, *Sex and the Fundamentals of Marriage*, [1979-80] Dublin U.L.J. 29, and the Law Reform Commission's *Report on Nullity of Marriage*, pp. 44-45.

[213] See L. Pålsson, *Marriage in Comparative Conflict of Laws: Substantive Conditions*, 304-305, 308ff. (1981).

[214] In France in certain cases and in some United States jurisdictions: cf. the English Law Commission Working No. 89 and the Scottish Law Commission Consultative Memorandum No. 64, *Private International Law: Choice of Law Rules in Marriage*, para. 5.42, fn. 420 (1985).

[215] LRC 19-1985, p. 77. See generally Bishop, *Choice of Law for Impotence and Wilful Refusal*, 41 Modern L. Rev. 512 (1978), Jaffey, *The Essential Validity of Marriage in the English Conflict of Laws*, 41 Modern L. Rev. 38, at 49 (1978), Pålsson, *Marriage in Comparative Conflict of Laws*, paras. 100, 102 (1981), *North*, 125-129, *Jackson*, 326-330, Garner, *Jurisdiction and the Choice of Law in Nullity Suits*, 63 L.Q. Rev. 486 (1947), Fleming, *Note: Choice of Law in Nullity Proceedings*, 11 Modern L. Rev. 98 (1948).

[216] And in other jurisdictions where wilful refusal is a ground for annulment: see, e.g. *Addison* v. *Addison*, [1955] N.I. 1.

[217] *North*, 126. See also Mendes da Costa, *Divorce*, ch. 7 of Mendes da Costa ed., *Studies in Canadian Family Law*, vol. 1, 482 (1972).

[218] [1947] P. 164 (Barnard, J.), analysed, in respect of choice of law, by Garner, *Jurisdiction and the Choice of Law in Nullity Suits*, 63 L.Q. Rev. 486, at 489-490 (1947) and by Fleming, *Note: Choice of Law in Nullity Proceedings*, 11 Modern L. Rev. 98 (1948).

applied the *lex loci celebrationis*, primarily[219] on the basis that wilful refusal "must be considered as a defect in marriage, an error in the quality of the respondent".[220] This approach has been roundly criticised. Error "in the quality of the respondent" is not as a general rule, a ground for annulment at all under English common law.

But even if we assume that wilful refusal raises an issue of error — which impotence will clearly do in most cases — the *lex domicilii*, rather than the *lex loci celebrationis*, would appear to be the appropriate law to determine the issue.[221]

In the Northern Ireland decision of *Addison* v. *Addison*,[222] the *lex loci* was again applied. Lord MacDermott said that he:

"very much doubt[ed] if the question of capacity to marry which is to be determined by the law of the domicile has to do with more than juristic capacity. Whether a contracting party is capable in the physical sense of discharging the obligations of matrimony seems to be so linked with the nature and quality of those obligations as to be, naturally and aptly, a matter for the *lex loci contractus.*"

(ii) *The lex fori*

The *lex fori* has been applied in a number of English cases. In *Easterbrook* v. *Easterbrook (otherwise Jervis)*[223] and *Hutter* v. *Hutter (otherwise Perry)*,[224] both decided before *Robert (otherwise de la Mare)* v. *Robert,* the *lex fori* was applied without discussion, although in each case the husband was domiciled outside England and there was no evidence that wilful refusal was a ground for annulment in the foreign jurisdiction.[225] Foreign law was pleaded in neither case. In both cases the marriage had been celebrated in England; in *Easterbrook*, both parties had been resident in England at all material times, and in *Hutter* the respondent was an English national, domiciliary and resident and the petitioner, though a domiciled national of the United States, was resident in England from the time of the marriage.

In *Magnier* v. *Magnier*[226] in 1968, an undefended case, the facts were as follows. The parties were married in Ireland[227] in 1942. Both were Catholics. The husband was of Irish birth and domicile and was still resident in Ireland when he brought proceedings for nullity of marriage in England, on the ground of the wife's impotence or wilful refusal to consummate the marriage. The short report does not indicate the wife's nationality of domicile.

After the parties had married, the wife "steadfastly"[228] refused her husband's requests for sexual intercourse, saying that she did not wish to have children. After two years the husband ceased to ask her to have intercourse with him. Shortly

---

[219] Barnard, J. considered that, if he was wrong to apply the *lex loci*, which was the law of Guernsey, the same result would be reached in applying the *lex domicilii*, which was also the law of Guernsey.

[220] [1947] P., at 167-168.

[221] Cf. *Dicey & Morris*, 376, fn. 64, *North*, 126.

[222] [1955] N.I 1, at 30. The House of Lords case of *Ross Smith* v. *Ross Smith*, [1963] A.C. 280 overruled *Addison* v. *Addison* on the question of jurisdiction but did not expressly dissent from it in relation to choice of law.

[223] [1944] P. 10 (Hodson, J., 1943).

[224] [1944] P. 95 (Pilcher, J.).

[225] In *Easterbrook*, the report states merely that the husband was domiciled "in Canada", and in *Hutter* the report states that the husband's domicile was "in the United States of America". In Canada, wilful refusal to consummate was not in 1943 (and has not since become) a ground for annulment: cf. Hahlo, *Nullity of Marriage*, ch. 10 of D. Mendes da Costa, *Studies in Canadian Family Law*, vol. 2 at 679 (1972), Mendes da Costa, *Divorce, id.,* vol. 1, ch. 7, at 481-482; but refusal to consummate for a period of a year, was made a ground for divorce by the Divorce Act 1968, section 4(1) (d).

[226] 112 Sol. J. 233 (P.D. & A. Div., Mais, J., sitting as a special commissioner, 1968).

[227] Bishop, *supra*, at 513, fn. 14, notes that, though the report speaks only of Ireland, "it may be inferred that the Republic is meant since a Northern Ireland marriage would have presented the husband with no difficulty owing to the fact that wilful refusal has been a nullity ground there since 1939".

[228] 112 Sol. J., at 233.

afterwards the wife left Ireland and went first to the United States and finally to England, where she was resident at the time of the proceedings, which she did not defend.

Mais J. was satisfied that there was "abundant authority"[229] grounding jurisdiction and unhesitatingly applied the *lex fori*. He did, however, acknowledge that doing so "resulted in a situation where a party to a marriage who was domiciled and resident in a foreign country could obtain a decree of nullity against the other party in the country of that other party's residence, but that decree might only be recognised in the country where it was granted and might not be binding on the courts of the petitioner's residence and domicile. That would bring into effect a 'limping divorce' whereby the respondent could re-marry but the petitioner could do so only at his peril".[230]

Finally, it may be noted that the House of Lords case of *Ross Smith* v. *Ross Smith*[231] contains some leanings towards the *lex fori*. *Dicey & Morris* note[232] that in this decision Lords Reid[233] and Morris[234] both gave as one of their reasons for declining jurisdiction the undesirability of granting relief on grounds unknown to the law of the parties' domicile:

"This could be taken to imply that, had jurisdiction not been declined, the *lex fori* would have been applied."[235]

(iii) *The lex domicilii*

There is much support for the *lex domicilii* as the test for wilful refusal in English cases. In *Robert (otherwise de la Mare)* v. *Robert*,[236] Barnard, J. was willing to fall back on the *lex domicilii* if his preference for the *lex loci* should prove to have been mistaken. In *Way* v. *Way*[237] Hodson, J. considered that "the law of the matrimonial domicil" should determine the question of wilful refusal. *Way* has been stigmatised as constituting "support of the weakest sort"[238] for the application of the law of the husband's domicile: counsel had not argued the point and there is no trace of *Robert (otherwise de la Mare)* v. *Robert*[239] having been cited.[240] Nevertheless Hodson, J.'s judgment, in the opinion of Sachs, J. in *Ponticelli* v. *Ponticelli (otherwise Giglio)*,[241] retains "considerable persuasive force", especially since Hodson, J. extra-judicially[242] rejected the argument, favoured in *Robert (otherwise de la Mare)* v. *Robert,* that the *lex loci* should apply.

In *Ponticelli*,[243] Sachs, J. also favoured the *lex domicilii* although, in view of the coincidence between the *lex domicilii* and *lex fori* on the facts of the case, it was "not . . . essential . . . to come to a final conclusion as between the two".[244] Sachs, J. was certain that wilful refusal could "not be said to fall within the categories

---

[229] *Id.*

[230] *Id.* Cf. Bishop's caustic observations, 41 Modern L. Rev., at 513.

[231] [1963] A.C. 280.

[232] *Dicey & Morris*, 377.

[233] [1963] A.C., at 306.

[234] *Id.*, at 313, 322.

[235] *Dicey & Morris*, 377.

[236] [1947] P. 164.

[237] [1950] P. 71 (Hodson, J., 1949), reversed on other grounds, *sub nom. Kenwood* v. *Kenwood*, [1951] P. 124 (C.A., 1959).

[238] Bishop, *supra*, at 515.

[239] *Supra.*

[240] *Ponticelli* v. *Ponticelli (otherwise Giglio)*, [1958] P. 204, at 212 (Sachs, J.).

[241] *Id.*

[242] In his Introduction to the 1st edition of *Jackson*, in 1951: cf. *Ponticelli, supra*, at 212.

[243] [1958] P. 204, analysed by Webb, 21 Modern L. Rev. 416 (1958).

[244] [1958] P., at 216.

of form and ceremony".[245] The choice, in his view, was between the *lex domicilii* and the *lex fori*. The claim of the *lex fori* was based on the view of the ground of wilful refusal as "something akin to matters for which the true remedy is divorce".[246] But against this could be marshalled the robust repudiation by Denning, L.J. in *Ramsay-Fairfax (otherwise Scott-Gibson)* v. *Ramsay-Fairfax.*[247] Moreover, the authorities were, on balance, in favour of the *lex domicilii.*[248] In view of Sachs, J. the *lex fori* failed to provide a uniform general rule by which the initial validity of a marriage could be determined.[249]

Proposals for Reform

The Law Reform Commission have made detailed recommendations for reform of the choice-of-law rules in nullity proceedings.[250] On formal requirements the Commission recommend[251] that the *lex loci celebrationis* should continue to afford the test as a general rule. The *lex loci celebrationis* in this context should include the whole law, rather than the internal law alone, on the basis that this would promote greater uniformity of status and would encourage the *favor matrimonii* principle.[252]

So far as exceptions to the *lex loci* rule are concerned, the Commission recommend, first, that, rather than subject all affected persons of every nationality and residence to the English common law in circumstances where this would be done at present, the law in such cases should simply provide that a marriage would be formally valid if the parties each undertake thereupon to become man and wife.[253] The Commission consider that reference to the formal requirements of the parties' personal law (such as domicile, nationality or habitual residence) would "place undue and impractical demands on many prospective spouses".[254] The Commission are not enthusiastic about introducing special provisions to deal with consular marriages abroad or for marriages by members of the Defence Forces.[255] The Commission have "no evidence that any hardship or injustice of any significant extent results from the absence of this legislative machinery".[256]

The Commmission go on to consider choice-of-law rules in relation to capacity to marry. The dual domicile test is criticised for leaning too heavily in favour of invalidity,[257] and the intended matrimonial test is criticised for its uncertainty in

---

[245] *Id.* at 214.

[246] *Id.*

[247] [1956] P. 115, at 132 (C.A., 1955). Cf. *infra*, pp. 245-255. Lord Denning, L.J. was speaking in the context of jurisdiction. It is interesting however, to note that, at trial, Willmer, J. had observed that "the proper law, i.e., the law of the domicile" [1956] P., at 125) should be applied. See further *Cheshire & North*, 402, Matheson & Webb, *A Note on the Recognition of Foreign Decrees of Nullity Granted to Scots Domiciliaries* [1962] Jurid. Rev. 21, at 22-23, E. Clive, *The Law of Husband and Wife in Scotland*, 111 (2nd ed., 1982).

[248] Cf. [1958] P., at 215, referring to Barnard, J.'s fall-back position in *Robert (otherwise de la Mare)* v. *Robert*, to *Way* v. *Way*, and to the judgments of Lord Greene, M.R. and Bucknill, L.J., in *De Reneville* v. *De Reneville* [1948] P. 100, which, Sachs, J. considered, "clearly tend against the applicability of the *lex fori*". *Cf.* [1958] P., at 213.

[249] [1958] P., at 215-216.

[250] *Report on Private International Law Aspects of Capacity to Marry and Choice of Law in Proceedings for Nullity of Marriage*, ch. 3 (L.R.C. 19-1985).

[251] P. 85 of the Report.

[252] *Id.*, p. 86.

[253] *Id.*, p. 93.

[254] *Id.*

[255] *Id.*, p. 94.

[256] *Id.*

[257] *Id.*, p. 96.

practical application.[258] The Commission propose[259] that habitual residence should constitute the test for capacity to marry: a marriage should be valid as regards capacity when each of the parties has, according to the law of his or her habitual residence, the capacity to marry the other. As with formal validity, the Commission recommend[260] that *renvoi* should apply in relation to capacity to marry.

The Commission reiterate[261] their earlier[262] recommendation that, so far as minimum age and parental consent requirements are concerned, the substantive requirements should apply to any marriage solemnised in the State, regardless of the parties' habitual residence.

The Commission present a detailed analysis of the question of capacity to remarry after a foreign divorce. They propose[263] that, in cases where the dissolution of a marriage would not be recognised here and that marriage continues to be a subsisting valid marriage under our law, a subsequent marriage should not be recognised under our law whether or not it complies with the law as to capacity to remarry of the parties' habitual residence.

The converse case arises where our law recognises a divorce of a marriage which, accordingly, is no longer a valid subsisting one under our law, but where the parties do not have capacity to remarry under the law of their habitual residence because that law does not recognise the divorce. On the one hand, as the Commission note,[264] it may be argued that, if we recognise the divorce, we should disregard the incapacity under the law of the parties' habitual residence because in the reverse case (where we do not recognise the divorce but the law of the habitual residence does) precedence is given to our recognition rule over the law of the parties' habitual residence. As against this, "it may be said that this stress on apparent consistency ignores the more fundamental point that a remarriage, to be effective, must fulfil the requirements of both our divorce recognition rules and our capacity to marry rules. If it fails either of these sets of requirements its validity should not be recognised."[265] Consistent with this approach, the Commission recommend[266] that, where remarriage fails to satisfy the requirements of the law of the parties' habitual residence, its validity should not be recognised, whether or not a prior dissolution is recognised under our law.

Turning to the choice of law rules to determine issues of consent,[267] the Commission consider[268] that the law of the country of the parties' habitual residence at the time of the marriage should govern. Where the parties have their habitual residences in different countries, a marriage should be invalid for lack of consent only where, according to the law applying to the party in question, that party did not provide the requisite consent.[269] This recommendation is in harmony with international trends,[270] and would prevent a spouse who has given a valid consent under the law of his habitual residence from invoking the law of the other spouse's habitual residence[271] to invalidate the marriage.

---

[258] *Id.* See also pp. 110-112.

[259] *Id.*, p. 114.

[260] *Id.*

[261] *Id.*, p. 115.

[262] In their *Report on the Law Relating to the Age of Majority, the Age for Marriage and Some Connected Subjects,* para. 63, and sections 7(2) (a) and 8(4) (a) of the Draft Scheme of Legislation, *id.* pp. 38, 40 (L.R.C. 5-1983).

[263] L.R.C. 19-1985, p. 117.

[264] *Id.*

[265] *Id.*

[266] *Id.*

[267] Cf. *supra,* pp. 240-242.

[268] *Op. cit.*, p. 119.

[269] Cf. L. Pålsson, *Marriage in Comparative Conflict of Laws: Substantive Conditions,* 114 (1981).

The Commission provide a detailed analysis of the choice-of-law rules for impotence. Again the Commission consider[272] that the law of the parties' habitual residence at the time of the marriage should govern the question of impotence. Where the parties have their habitual residences in separate countries, the position becomes more complicated. The suitability of a choice of law rule must depend largely on whether impotence is regarded as involving *an incapacitated person,* a *ground entitling the other party to a decree of nullity*[273] or a *defective interpersonal relationship.*[274] On the latter view, impotence affects *both* parties, insofar as their relationship is subject to a vitiating element.

The Commission consider that the best approach would be to refer to the laws of both the spouses and to entitle the petitioner to a decree of nullity if the petitioner is, in the circumstances, entitled to petition according to the law of either party.[275]

The Commission leave to the courts rather than the legislature the task of dealing with a situation where a foreign law contains no ground of nullity based on impotence.[276] They consider that it would be ''an almost impossible task for the legislation to cover all possible instances of foreign limitations, against an international background of a rapidly changing nullity law.''[277]

Wilful refusal to consummate a marriage presents particular difficulties when formulating choice-of-law rules. No particular problem arises where the refusal reflects a condition of impotence existing at the time of the marriage[278] or, perhaps, a secret intention, existing at that time, not to consummate the marriage.[279] In the former case, the choice of law rules relating to impotence would apply; in the latter, the choice of law rules relating to consent would determine the issue.[280]

The ''really troublesome''[281] case arises where a foreign law provides as a ground of nullity of marriage the fact that the respondent spouse has wilfully refused to consummate the marriage, in circumstances where the petitioner need not prove that at the time of the marriage the respondent had any particular state of mind. In such a case the ground permits a decree of nullity to be based *exclusively on post-nuptial matters.* Such a ground, if introduced as part of our law, would almost certainly be unconstitutional[282] since it would appear to conflict with the prohibition on the dissolution of marriage.

If the ground is not acceptable as part of our law, could it nonetheless be capable of recognition if it is part of a foreign law? The Commission take no final view on the question, leaving[283] it to be determined by the courts on the same principles as they would apply towards any other ground unknown to the internal law of the

[271] L.R.C. 19–1985, p. 120.

[272] *Id.*, p. 124.

[273] Cf. *id.*, pp. 127-128 and the Law Reform Commission's *Report on Nullity of Marriage,* pp. 52-63, 144-145 (L.R.C. 9-1984).

[274] Cf. the Law Reform Commission's *Report on Private International Law Aspects of Capacity to Marry and Choice of Law in Proceedings for Nullity of Marriage,* p. 128 (L.R.C. 19-1985).

[275] *Id.*

[276] The scope of the Commission's recommendation extends beyond impotence to other cases where the foreign law contains no ground equivalent to one in our law: cf. *id.*, pp. 134-135.

[277] *Id.*, p. 135.

[278] Cf. the judgments of Henchy and Griffin, JJ., in *S.* v. *S.*, unreported, Sup. Ct., 1 July 1976 (1-1976), extracted in *Binchy*, 76, 90.

[279] Cf. Kenny, J.'s judgment in *S.* v. *S.*, *supra.*

[280] Cf. L.R.C. 19-1985, p. 130.

[281] *Id.*

[282] The Law Reform Commission go no further than to admit that such a ground ''might well raise difficulties under Article 41 of the Constitution'': *Report on Nullity of Marriage,* p. 146 (L.R.C. 9-1984).

[283] *Report on Private International Law Aspects of Capacity to Marry and Choice of Law in Proceedings for Nullity of Marriage,* p. 133 (L.R.C. 19-1985).

forum.[284] The fact that the ground has no counterpart in the *lex fori* should not *of itself* be a reason for modifying the general choice of law rules proposed by the Commission, but of course public policy would play an important role in this context.[285]

The distinctions between "void" and "voidable" marriages are hard enough to understand in our internal law[286]; in the conflict of laws the position becomes still more complicated. There are formidable complexities as to characterisation. If, for example, a foreign law calls a marriage void but enables only one or both of the parties to petition, is the marriage "really" voidable? And how should our courts characterise foreign hybrid rules, as, for example, where only a party to an allegedly voidable marriage may petition but he or she may do so even after the death of the other party?

Before the Commission's consideration of this issue, there had been little detailed analysis by the courts[287], commentators[288] or law reform agencies.[289] Arguments in favour of the *lex fori's* characterisation are largely based on jurisdictional considerations. The argument in favour of the parties' personal law is to the effect that what is at stake is the validity or invalidity of the marriage and that the law which determines this question should be allowed to "determine what is meant by invalidity, that is, whether it means voidness or voidability."[290]

The Law Reform Commission take the view that it would be wrong to let characterisation occlude rather than enlighten analysis.[291] Rather than be diverted by the issues of "voidness" and "voidability" of marriage, and of related characterisation problems, the Commission consider[292] that the better approach would be for our choice-of-law rules to refer to the law of the parties' habitual residence questions such as entitlement to petition after one party has died, and the bars to the granting of a nullity decree, including approbation and ratification. This reference would be subject to the application of the public policy proviso.

Turning to the *effects* of a nullity decree, the Commission recommend[293] that the *lex fori* should apply to ancillary orders of a financial nature.[294] The question of the retrospective operation of a nullity decree is rather difficult. There is a wide divergence of approach among the internal laws of different countries.[295] So far as conflicts aspects are concerned, it could be argued that the *lex fori* should determine the question of retrospectivity on the basis that "it must be for the law of the forum as the law governing procedure to determine the effect of its own decree."[296] On the other hand, the Commission prefer[297] the argument that the issue of

---

[284] Cf. *id.*, pp. 139-140.

[285] *Id.*, p. 140.

[286] See *Shatter* pp. 104-105, the Law Reform Commission's *Report on Nullity of Marriage*, pp. 72-73 (L.R.C. 9-1984).

[287] Cf. the decisions cited by *North*, 145, fn. 214.

[288] See *Cheshire & North*, 392, 405-406, *North*, 135-138, *Anton*, 293.

[289] Cf. the English Law Commission Working Paper No. 89 and Scottish Law Commission Consultative Memorandum No. 64, *Private International Law: Choice of Law Rules in Marriage*, paras. 5.50-5.53 (1985).

[290] *Cheshire & North*, 392.

[291] Cf. the *Report on Private International Law Aspects of Capacity to Marry and Choice of Law in Proceedings for Nullity of Marriage*, p. 144 (L.R.C. 19-1985).

[292] *Id.*, p. 149.

[293] *Id.*, p. 150.

[294] The present rules of our internal law are indefensibly restrictive: for the Commission's proposals for reform, see their *Report on Nullity of Marriage*, Ch. 12 (L.R.C. 9-1984).

[295] Cf., e.g. the law in New Zealand: see *Webb, Caldwell & Davis*, ch. 5.

[296] English Law Commission's Working Paper No. 89 and Scottish Law Commission's Consultative Memorandum No. 64, *Private International Law: Choice of Law Rules in Marriage*, para. 5.54 (1985).

[297] L.R.C. 19-1985, p. 151.

retrospection is so closely connected with questions of legitimacy[298] and capacity to marry that it should more appropriately be dealt with by the law of the parties' habitual residence.[299]

JURISDICTION IN PROCEEDINGS FOR NULLITY OF MARRIAGE

Much uncertainty attaches to the question of jurisdiction. The courts "have not adopted a consistent position on the question, and the result is that the battlefield presents a somewhat scarred appearance".[300]

The easiest way of approaching the subject is to consider void and voidable marriages in turn.

The Distinction between Void and Voidable Marriages

As has just been mentioned, marriages that are invalid are divided, in Irish law, into two categories: those that are void and those that are voidable. There are several important differences between these two categories. Perhaps most important is the distinction regarding nullity proceedings. In the case of void marriages, no decree is necessary. Any court and any person may treat such marriages as void without being concerned to obtain a judicial decree to this effect (although in practice some categories of void marriages would raise such uncertainty as to their status that a decree might be essential to resolve the issue).

The next most important distinction is that the validity of a void marriage may be challenged by any person with a sufficient interest,[301] even after the death of the parties, whereas a voidable marriage may be challenged only by one of the parties during the lifetime of both; until it is annulled it is regarded as valid. Other differences may be noted. Children of a void marriage are illegitimate. Children of voidable marriages are regarded as legitimate unless or until the marriage is annulled.

Marriages that are void are those invalid on the grounds of nonage, prior subsisting marriage, prohibited degrees of relationship, formal defect and lack of consent (other than at least certain instances of mental incapacity which render a marriage voidable).[302] Impotence also renders a marriage voidable.

Void Marriages

(1) Domicile

There is reasonably clear Irish authority for the proposition that the domicile of the respondent affords a basis of jurisdiction in nullity proceedings in respect of a void marriage. In *Johnson (falsely called Cooke)* v. *Cooke,*[303] the respondent, a domiciled Irishman, already married to another woman in Ireland, went through a ceremony of marriage with the petitioner in India. The petitioner, ten years later, petitioned for a decree of nullity in Ireland, the respondent having returned to live in this country. In her petition the petitioner made no allegation relating to her own

---

[298] The Commission proposed the abolition of illegitimacy in their *Report on Illegitimacy* (L.R.C. 4-1982). So far as nullity of marriage was concerned they saw no reason for proposing more limited entitlements to legitimacy based on the 'good faith' belief by one or both of the parents on the validity of the marriage: Cf. their *Report on Nullity of Marriage*, p. 167 (L.R.C. 9-1984). The Commission left to a general review of conflicts aspects of legitimacy the specific question of legitimacy of children of an invalid marriage: L.R.C. 19-1985, p. 150.

[299] This recommendation would need to be refined further in relation to cases where the parties have their habitual residences in different countries or to cases where the marriage is formally invalid.

[300] *Dicey & Morris,* 8th ed., 1967, p. 349.

[301] Cf. *Jackson,* 100-102.

[302] Controversy surrounds the question whether marriages invalid for lack of consent are void or voidable: see the Law Reform Commission's *Report on Nullity of Marriage*, p. 73.

[303] [1898] 2 I.R. 130 (Q.B. Div. (Mat.), Madden, J., 1897).

domicile: she was at the time residing in England.[304] Madden, J. held that the court had jurisdiction to grant the relief sought, "the respondent being domiciled in Ireland".[305] The decree of nullity specifically stated that the Judge found that the court had jurisdiction, "notwithstanding that it is not stated that the petitioner has an Irish domicil, the respondent having an Irish domicil".[306] It should be noted that, in *Johnson,* the respondent was resident, as well as domiciled, in Ireland, and one commentator has observed that "it is not clear to what extent this fact played a part in the decision".[307]

Scots authority[308] and Canadian *dicta*[309] are in accord with the approach favoured in *Johnson* v. *Cooke.*[310] In *Johnson* v. *Cooke,* the respondent was the husband. On principle (supported by some authority)[311] the same rule should apply in respect of a respondent wife. Even before the changes brought about by section 2 of the Domicile and Recognition of Foreign Divorces Act 1986, women were not affected by a domicile of dependency in this context. The courts took the view that, since the marriage was alleged to be void, the "wife" would never acquire her husband's domicile by operation of law and thus her domicile would be a matter for determination entirely independently of that of the man with whom she went through the ceremony of marriage. So far as jurisdiction was concerned, where a marriage was alleged to be void, the courts assumed the outcome of the proceedings to the extent that they accepted jurisdiction on the assumption that the allegation that the marriage was void was true; otherwise there would have been an unbroken circularity of thought.

In England[312] and Scotland[313], the courts have gone considerably further in accepting the domicile of the petitioner[314] as a basis of jurisdiction in respect of void marriages. One commentator has suggested[315] that an Irish court could take the same view though there are, of course, policy arguments both ways on this question.[316]

(2) *Residence*[317]

There is no direct modern authority on residence as a basis of jurisdiction in proceedings for a decree of nullity of a void marriage. An important case, however, which would be likely to command much respect, is *Mason* v. *Mason (otherwise Pennington)*[318], decided in 1943 by Andrews, L.J.C., of Northern Ireland's King's

---

[304] Cf. *North,* 362:

"From the facts, it seems most unlikely that [the petitioner] was domiciled in Ireland for 'she was born in India of English parents and resided there' [: [1898] 2 I.R. 130, at 132]."

[305] [1898] 2 I.R., at 133.

[306] *Id.,* at 134.

[307] Rafferty, *Recognition of Foreign Nullity Decrees,* 46 Sask. L. Rev. 73, at 78, fn. 41 (1981).

[308] *Aldridge* v. *Aldridge,* 1954 S.C. 58 (following *Johnson* v. *Cooke*). See also *Martin* v. *Buret,* 1938 S.L.T. 479.

[309] *Bevand* v. *Bevand,* [1955] 1 D.L.R. 854 (N.S. Ct. for Div. & Mat. Causes, Doull, J.), *Khan* v. *Khan,* 29 W.W.R. 181, at 184 (B.C. Sup. Ct., 1959), *Re Capon,* 49 D.L.R. (2d) 675, at 684 (Ont. C.A., *per* Schroeder, J.A., 1965). See *Castel,* vol. 2, 166-167, Rafferty, *Recognition of Foreign Nullity Decrees,* 46 Sask. L. Rev. 73, at 78 (1981).

[310] *Supra.*

[311] Cf. *Balshaw* v. *Balshaw,* 1967 S.C. 63, at 73, 84.

[312] *White* v. *White,* [1937] P. 111, *De Reneville* v. *De Reneville,* [1948] P. 100, at 112-113. See also *Apt* v. *Apt,* [1948] P. 83, *Casey* v. *Casey,* [1949] P. 420 (C.A.), *Ross-Smith* v. *Ross-Smith,* [1963] A.C. 280, at 310 (*per* Lord Cohen) and 347 (*per* Lord Guest).

[313] *Balshaw* v. *Balshaw,* 1967 S.C. 63, at 80 (*per* Lord Guthrie).

[314] Whether husband (e.g. *Balshaw* v. *Balshaw, supra, Martin* v. *Buret, supra*) or wife (e.g. *White* v. *White, supra*).

[315] *North,* 361.

[316] See Goodrich, *Jurisdiction to Annul a Marriage,* 32 Harv. L. Rev. 806 (1919).

[317] See North, *Nullity Jurisdiction Based on Residence,* 106 Sol. J. 949 (1962).

[318] [1944] N.I. 134 (K. B. Div. (Mat.), Andrews, L.C.J., 1943).

Bench Division. There, after a detailed review of the judicial and scholarly authorities, Andrews, L.C.J. held that the residence of both parties afforded a good basis of jurisdiction. Rejecting *Cheshire's* advocacy[319] of domicile as the sole basis, Andrews, L.C.J. said:

> "It may be that the law would be more acceptable to the jurists, and that it would be more certain, though perhaps in some ways less convenient, if domicil were made the sole test of jurisdiction in nullity as in divorce; but in my opinion that day has not yet arrived: and when it does come the change — for change I believe it to be — should be effected by clear and unmistakable legislation."[320]

Andrews, L.C.J. made it clear that, in referring to "residence", he was referring to *bona fide* residence not resulting "from any mere desire on the part of either spouse to attract the jurisdiction"[321] of the court.

Of course, the jurisdiction of the Ecclesiastical Courts was based on the residence of the respondent,[322] and it is difficult on this account to see why it should be necessary for the petitioner to establish that both parties were resident in the jurisdiction. It would seem only reasonable that *Mason* v. *Mason (otherwise Pennington)*[323] should not be regarded as having rejected the residence of the respondent as an adequate basis of jurisdiction. Certainly English authority has made such an extension.[324] (In this context, as has been mentioned, Dr. North points out[325] that, in *Johnson* v. *Cooke*[326] the respondent was resident as well as domiciled in Ireland. Whether this factor weighed heavily in the judge's deliberations is, of course, a separate question; it seems clear[327] that Madden, J. in this case did not base jurisdiction on the element of residence.)

There is no Irish authority that supports basing jurisdiction on the residence of the petitioner alone. Authorities in other common law jurisdictions are clearly opposed[328] and there seems little likelihood of our courts accepting this head of jurisdiction.

(3) *Place of Celebration of Marriage*

There is clear Irish authority in favour of basing jurisdiction on the fact that the marriage took place in Ireland. In *Sproule* v. *Hopkins*,[329] the parties went through a ceremony of marriage in Ireland. The petitioner was domiciled and resident here; the respondent had been originally domiciled in Ireland but (he alleged)[330] had acquired an English domicile by the time of the ceremony of marriage. The petitioner

---

[319] 2nd ed., 337-339.

[320] [1944] N.I., at 158.

[321] *Id.*, at 142.

[322] Cf. *id.*, at 143.

[323] *Supra*.

[324] *Russ* v. *Russ (No. 2)*, 106 Sol. J. 632 (1962), where Scarman, J. considered that the previous practice of the Ecclesiastical Courts supported this basis of jurisdiction. See North, *Nullity Jurisdiction Based on Residence*, 106 Sol. J. 949, at 950 (1962). In Canada it was originally held that the residence of the respondent alone would not be a good basis of jurisdiction: *Purdy* v. *Purdy*, [1919] 2 W.W.R. 551, *Vamvakidis* v. *Kirkoff*, [1929] 4 D.L.R. 1060; but later decisions support the view that such residence will suffice: *Adelman* v. *Adelman*, [1948] 1 W.W.R. 1071 (Alta.), *Khan (Worresck)* v. *Khan*, 21 D.L.R. (2d) 171 (B.C., 1959).

[325] *North*, 362.

[326] *Supra*.

[327] From the text of Madden, J.'s judgment as well as from the terms of the decree.

[328] Cf. *De Reneville* v. *De Reneville*, [1948] P. 100, at 116-118 (C.A., *per* Lord Greene, M.R., 1947), *Adelman* v. *Adelman, supra, Shaw* v. *Shaw*, [1946] 1 D.L.R. 168 (B.C.C.A.), *D.* v. *D.*, 36 D.L.R. (3d) 17 (Ont. High Ct., 1973).

[329] [1903] 2 I.R. 133 (K. B. Div. (Mat.) Andrews, J., 1902).

[330] Unsuccessfully, on the evidence: cf. [1903] 2 I.R., at 137-138.

sought a decree of nullity on the basis that the respondent was already married to another woman at the time of the ceremony.

Andrews, J. held that the court had:

"jurisdiction to hear and determine the question of the validity or invalidity of the marriage contracted between the parties in Ireland irrespective of any question as to the respondent's domicil or place of residence."[331]

Andrews, J. relied on the "very learned and well-considered judgment"[332] of Sir Creswell Creswell in *Simonin* v. *Mallac*[333] as authority for this holding. He noted that in the later decision of *Sottomayor* v. *De Barros*[334] *Simonin* v. *Mallac* had been referred to without question.[335]

In *Simonin* v. *Mallac*,[336] Sir Creswell Creswell had said that:

"There is nothing contrary to natural justice in calling upon [a person residing out of the jurisdiction] to have the validity or invalidity of a supposed contract ascertained and determined by the tribunal of the country where it was entered into by him; for, according to Lord Stowell, in *Dalrymple* v. *Dalrymple*,[337] it is an indispensable rule of law, as exercised in all civilised countries, that a man who contracts in a country engages for a competent knowledge of the law of contracts in that country. If he rashly presumes to contract without knowledge, he must take the inconveniences resulting from such ignorance upon himself, and not attempt to throw them upon the other party."

This view of jurisdiction in respect of contracts generally is no longer tenable[338] and it is scarcely surprising that in England the authority of *Simonin* v. *Mallac*[339] has subsequently come into question. The decision has been rejected in respect of jurisdiction for voidable marriages, but in *Ross Smith* v. *Ross Smith*[340], the House of Lords was divided as to its continuing operation with respect to void marriages. Later decisions[341] have interpreted *Ross Smith* in its result, as affirming *Simonin* v. *Mallac* in respect of void marriages.

Voidable Marriages

(1) *Domicile*

There are no Irish decisions in respect of domicile, but in England and Scotland the common domicile of the spouses has been held to afford a good basis for

---

[331] *Id.*, at 136. See also *id.*, at 137.

[332] *Id.*

[333] 2 Sw. & Tr. 67 (1860).

[334] 5 P.D. 94. (1879)

[335] See also *Cooper* v. *Crane*, [1891] P. 369, *Linke (otherwise Van Aerde)* v. *Van Aerde*, 10 Times L.R. 426 (P.D.A. Div., Gorell Barnes, J., 1894), *Valier* v. *Valier*, 133 L.T. 830 (1925), *Hussein* v. *Hussein*, [1938] P. 159, *Simons* v. *Simons*, [1939] 1 K.B. 490, at 498, *Hutter* v. *Hutter*, [1944] P. 95, at 102, *Dicey & Morris*, 8th ed., 1967, 354, fn. 35.

[336] 2 Sw. & Tr., at 75.

[337] 2 Hag. Con. 54, at 61 (1811).

[338] Cf. *Ross Smith* v. *Ross Smith*, [1963] A.C. 280, at 295 (H.L. (Eng.), *per* Lord Reid, 1962):

"It is almost obvious to us today that the mere fact that an ordinary contract has been made in a particular country does not confer jurisdiction on the courts of that country to entertain an action with regard to that contract against a defendant who is neither present, resident nor domiciled in that country when the action is commenced. But the principles of private international law . . . were developed surprisingly slowly, and that was by no means obvious in 1860."

[339] *Supra.*

[340] [1963] A.C. 280 (H.L. (Eng.), 1962).

[341] *Padolecchia* v. *Padolecchia (otherwise Leis)*, [1968] P. 314 (Sir Jocelyn Simon P., 1967), *Garthwaite* v. *Garthwaite*, [1964] P. 356, at 390-391 (C.A., *per* Diplock, L.J.).

jurisdiction.[342] A voidable marriage is regarded as valid until a decree of nullity is obtained. Before the Domicile and Recognition of Foreign Divorces Act 1986 came into force, the "wife" was regarded as taking the domicile of her "husband", so in practice the domicile of the "husband" at the time of the institution of the proceedings was the sole base of jurisdiction.[343] At all events, this was the accepted approach in the several English decisions which considered the question. In the light of the recent statutory change, as well as the constitutional developments in relation to sex equality, it may well be that our courts will be content to rest jurisdiction on the residence of the respondent, whether the "husband" or the "wife".

(2) *Residence*

There are no Irish decisions on the question of residence as a possible basis for jurisdiction in respect of voidable marriages. The developments in England on this question are instructive. In *Inverclyde (otherwise Tripp)* v. *Inverclyde,*[344] in 1930, Bateson, J. took the view that a decree of nullity in respect of a marriage voidable for impotence was in essence a decree for divorce rather than nullity:

"To call it a suit for nullity does not alter its essential and real character of a suit for dissolution. That is a mere difference in form. . . ."

Having taken this approach, Bateson, J. propounded domicile as the exclusive basis for jurisdiction in respect of nullity proceedings for impotence, as it had already been established[345] in relation to divorce.

In *Ramsay-Fairfax (otherwise Scott-Gibson)* v. *Ramsay-Fairfax,* in 1955, the Court of Appeal rejected Bateson, J.'s approach.[346] In *Ramsay-Fairfax* the petitioner alleged that the marriage was voidable on the ground either of impotence or the respondent's wilful refusal to consummate the marriage.[347] Denning, L.J. (as he then was) said:

"Looking at the ground of wilful refusal from a legalistic standpoint, and treating marriage as a contract, the remedy of nullity does look like a remedy of divorce or dissolution, because it depends on events which occur subsequent to the marriage; but looking at it from a sensible standpoint, and having regard to the true ends of marriage, one of the principal aims of which is the procreation of children, it seems to me that the remedy falls more truly within the category of nullity. No one can call a marriage a real marriage when it has not been consummated; and this is the same, no matter whether the want of consummation is due to incapacity or to wilful refusal. Let the

---

[342] *Von Lorang* v. *Administrator of Austrian Property*, [1927] A.C. 641 (H.L.Sc.), *De Reneville* v. *De Reneville*, [1948] P. 100, at 109 (C.A., *per* Lord Greene, M.R., 1947), *Szechter (otherwise Karsov)* v. *Szechter,* [1971] P. 286 (Sir Jocelyn Simon, P. 1970). See also *Ramsay-Fairfax (otherwise Scott-Gibson)* v. *Ramsay-Fairfax,* [1956] P. 115, at 134 (C.A., *per* Denning, L.J., 1955).

[343] Cf. *North*, 363.

[344] [1931] P. 29, at 42. This approach is contrary to Irish law: cf. the Law Reform Commission's *Report on Nullity of Marriage* (L.R.C. 9-1984), P. 146.

[345] *Le Mesurier* v. *Le Mesurier,* [1895] A.C. 517.

[346] [1956] P. 115.

[347] Wilful refusal to consummate a marriage was introduced in England in 1937 as a statutory ground for nullity, rendering the marriage voidable. It is still part of English law: Matrimonial Causes Act 1973, section 12(b). See *Cretney*, 67-72. There is no directly equivalent ground in Irish law. For consideration of private international law aspects of this ground, see the Law Reform Commission's *Report on Private International Law Aspects of the Capacity to Marry and Choice-of-Law in Proceedings for Nullity of Marriage*, pp. 129-133 (L.R.C. 19-1985), and *supra*, p. 248. In its *Report on Nullity of Marriage* (L.R.C. 9-1984) (p. 146), the Commission rejected the argument that wilful refusal to consummate should, of itself, be a ground for nullity of marriage; it proposed (p. 118) that the fraudulent non-disclosure of an intention at the time of entering the marriage not to consummate the marriage should be a ground for a decree of nullity.

theologians dispute as they will, so far as the lawyers are concerned, parliament has made it quite plain that wilful refusal and incapacity stand together as grounds for nullity and not for dissolution: and being grounds for nullity, they fall within the old ecclesiastical practice, in which the jurisdiction of the courts is founded upon residence and not upon domicile.''[348]

Reform Proposals

The Law Reform Commission in their Twentieth Report,[349] have made wide-ranging proposals for reform of jurisdictional requirements in nullity proceedings. Their central policy is to ensure that Irish courts should have jurisdiction in nullity proceedings ''where, in broad terms, the parties have a reasonable connection with the State. In other words, speaking negatively, our courts have no business exercising such jurisdiction over parties neither of whom has any connection with the State.''[350] The Commission consider that the best approach would be for the legislation to set out a list of specific circumstances which constitute a ''reasonable connection'', supplemented by a more broadly-framed, discretionary entitlement. The approach would be on the following lines: a court should have jurisdiction to hear and determine a petition for nullity of marriage in any of the following cases:

(1) Where, at the time of the marriage, the validity of which is in question, either party had his or her habitual residence in the State;

(2) Where, at the time of the proceedings, either party has his or her habitual residence in the State;

(3) Where the marriage was celebrated in the State and a ground on which the marriage is alleged to be invalid is one to which the *lex loci celebrationis* applies;

(4) Where, in the opinion of the Court, either spouse has, or has had, such substantial ties[351] with the State as to make it appropriate to hear and determine the petition.[352]

RECOGNITION OF FOREIGN NULLITY DECREES

If all countries adhered to the same approach towards private international law aspects of marriage, then the question of recognition would be a relatively easy one to resolve. Every country would apply the same choice of law rule when dealing with a nullity petition and courts everywhere would have little difficulty in recognising foreign nullity decrees since they would be based on the same choice of law rules as the courts themselves would have applied.

Unfortunately life is not that simple. Different countries apply widely differing choice of law rules: some refer questions of capacity and consent to the law of the spouses' nationality, others to their domicile, others to the country of their habitual residence; still others apply the *lex fori*, frequently in seeming ignorance of even the existence of a choice of law dimension to the case. Moreover, where recognition of a foreign nullity decree is concerned, some countries concern

---

[348] [1956] P., at 132-133. See also, to the same effect, *Easterbrook* v. *Easterbrook*, [1944] P. 10 (Hudson, J., 1943), *Hutter* v. *Hutter*, [1944] P. 95 (Pilcher, J.).

[349] Law Reform Commission's *Report on Jurisdiction in Proceedings for Nullity of Marriage, Recognition of Foreign Nullity Decrees, and the Hague Convention on the Celebration and Recognition of the Validity of Marriages (1978)*, pp. 32-34 (L.R.C. 20-1985).

[350] *Id.*, p. 33.

[351] Cf. the Scottish Law Commission's *Report on Jurisdiction in Consistorial Causes Affecting Matrimonial Status*, para. 48, (Scot. Law Com. No. 25, 1972).

[352] L.R.C. 20-1985, p. 33.

themselves with the choice of law rules adopted by the court in the foreign country; others are more interested in ensuring that the parties fulfilled various jurisdictional criteria, such as domicile or residence, in the foreign country.

Another factor which comes into play with the recognition of foreign annulments is that, as a matter of practical reality, parties will frequently have their marriages annulled in countries where they are living (or with which they have other close connections) *at the time of the annulment proceedings.* It will often take some time for a particular defect — impotence, for example — to be established with sufficient certainty. Countries called on later to recognise these foreign nullity proceedings may find that the court in question applied the *lex fori* with no regard for the parties' personal law. To deny recognition to such a decree on account of the fact that it ignored the parties' personal law will often run directly contrary to the legitimate expectations of the parties, their families and others whose personal or business relationships with the parties were also premised on the assumption that the nullity decree would be internationally efficacious.

There appears to be no Irish decision on the subject of the recognition of foreign nullity decrees.[353] Dr. North has commented that "[o]ne can merely suggest that the courts will recognise foreign nullity decrees on bases similar to those on which they have been recognised in England".[354] As English law diverges progressively from Irish law, the relevance of English decisions appears to be gradually weakening. But that is not to say that they should not be studied: the issues confronting the courts in many of these decisions are often precisely the same as those which an Irish court must eventually decide, unless legislation resolves the question first. It is necessary to consider briefly the grounds of recognition that have found favour in the English courts, against a background of developments in other common law jurisdictions.

1. Domicile

(a) *Common domicile*

There is clear authority in Britain for recognising a decree of nullity obtained in a country where both parties are domiciled. In *Von Lorang* v. *Austrian Property Administrator,*[355] in 1927, the House of Lords, on appeal from the Court of Session, recognised a decree of nullity of a marriage celebrated in France granted by a German court, the parties being domiciled in Germany at the time of the decree. The decree was based on lack of compliance with the formal requirements of French law, the German court having taken "proper steps to inform itself of the French law and [given] judgment according to the law proved before it".[356] The House of Lords was clearly influenced by the recognition rules applicable to divorce. The judges appeared willing to endorse the questionable syllogism, that since divorce was concerned with status, and nullity was also concerned with status[357], the recognition rules relating to foreign divorce and nullity decrees should be the same.

Yet the two processes, though similar in some respects, involve important

---

[353] See *Castel,* vol. 2, 179-186, Smith, *The Recognition of Foreign Nullity Decrees,* 96 L. Q. Rev. 380 (1980), Rafferty, *Recognition of Foreign Nullity Decrees,* 46 Sask. L. Rev. 73 (1981), Nott, *Foreign Nullity Decrees: Perrini* v. *Perrini,* 29 Int. & Comp. L.Q. 510 (1980), Young, *id.,* 515, Kennedy, *Recognition of Foreign Divorce and Nullity Decrees,* 35 Can. Bar Rev. 628 (1957), Lysyk, *Jurisdiction and Recognition of Foreign Decrees in Nullity Suits,* 29 Sask. Bar Rev. 143, at 151-159 (1964). See generally L.R.C. 20-1985, ch. 3, on which this section is based.
[354] *North,* 386.
[355] [1927] A.C. 641 (H.L.(Sc.)). See Hughes, *Judicial Method and the Problem in Ogden* v. *Ogden,* 44 L.Q. Rev. 217 (1928). Canadian authorities are in accord with *Von Lorang: Castel,* vol. 2, 179, citing *Wilcox* v. *Wilcox,* 6 W.W.R. 213, 24 Man. R. 93, 16 D.L.R. 491 (C.A., 1914).
[356] [1927] A.C., at 663 (*per* Viscount Dunedin).
[357] *Id.,* at 662 (*per* Viscount Dunedin: "Now it seems to me that celibacy is just as much a status as marriage . . . The judgment in a nullity case decrees either a status of marriage or a status of celibacy".

differences: divorce changes a status, whereas a nullity decree does not — it merely declares that a particular status has not been disturbed by the fact that the parties went through a ceremony of marriage; since divorce changes an existing legal relationship, it may be considered reasonable to look to the country of the spouses' common domicile at the time of the divorce; but, since nullity does not change the legal relationship, and merely declares that a vitiating element invalidated a marriage from the start, there is less reason to refer this adjudication to a country with which the parties happen to have long-term ties at some particular time after they have gone through the ceremony of marriage.

If the social realities are examined, this objection may be modified. In some cases where a decree of nullity is sought, the parties to the allegedly invalid marriage will have had an interpersonal relationship after the ceremony, and have lived together as though they were man and wife. Perhaps it is not inappropriate for the recognition criterion to have regard to this dimension. To this argument, it may be replied that in some other cases where nullity proceedings are sought there may have been no such relationship: in "sham" marriages, for example,[358] where the parties never live together as man and wife. There are also cases when the relationship, although seeming normal to the outsider, was not in fact so. These would include some cases of duress,[359] fraud and mistake,[360] insanity[361] and impotence.[362]

There is, moreover, something curious about looking to the country in which the parties happen to be domiciled, possibly several years after the marriage, as having the say in determining whether a vitiating element existed in their marriage from the start. Of course, if that country has a choice of law rule requiring the courts to answer the question of validity according to the same personal law of the parties[363] as the one to which our law refers, there may be no harm in recognising the decree; but if that country instead determines the question of the validity of the marriage by reference to its own law of nullity or to a different personal law, then there may well be reason to be cautious about recognising that decree.

At all events, it is clear that an English court will recognise a nullity decree obtained in a foreign country where both parties are domiciled; and it seems equally clear that it will do so even if the parties of the court of the foreign country applied some choice of law rules other than an English court would have done, or misapplied the choice of law rules. Thus, a foreign decree of nullity given in the country where both spouses are domiciled may be recognised even where the marriage was celebrated in England and even where the marriage duly celebrated there is annulled on the ground of lack of form.

(b) *Decree obtained in the country where one of the parties is domiciled*

When we turn to the position relating to a foreign decree of nullity obtained in a country where *one* of the parties is domiciled, the position becomes quite uncertain. We must examine in particular three decisions,[364] all involving Maltese annulments based on the failure of a Catholic Maltese husband marrying in England to marry in a Catholic Church, as required by Maltese law of all its citizens wherever the marriage might be celebrated. In each of the cases, the husband was domiciled in

---

[358] Cf. Wade, *Limited Purpose Marriages,* 45 Modern L. Rev. 159 (1982), Horton Rogers, 4 Fam. L. 4 (1974), Bromley, 15 McGill L.J. 319 (1969), *Anon.,* 20 U. Chic. L. Rev. 710 (1953).

[359] Cf. L.R.C. No. 9-1984, pp. 32-42.

[360] Cf. *id.,* pp. 42-45.

[361] Cf. *id.,* pp. 13-31.

[362] Cf. *id.,* pp. 144-147.

[363] Or the *lex loci celebrationis,* if a formal defect is alleged.

[364] *Chapelle* v. *Chapelle,* [1950] P. 134 (Willmer, J., 1949), *Gray* v. *Formosa,* [1963] P.259 (C.A., 1962), *Lepre* v. *Lepre,* [1965] P. 52 (Sir Jocelyn Simon, P., 1962).

Malta at the time of the nullity proceedings, the wife living in England with the intention of remaining there.

In none of the cases did the English court recognise the Maltese decree. Two factors were of particular force: the technical and arbitrary operation of the doctrine of domicile of dependency of married women — "the last barbarous relic of a wife's servitude";[365] and the particular effects of Maltese marriage law, which offended against English sensibilities.[366] These factors, no doubt important in their own right, played so great a role that it is difficult to discern any coherent general policy towards the question of recognition of foreign annulments based on the domicile of one of the parties.

In *Chapelle* v. *Chapelle*,[367] in 1949, Willmer, J. considered that he would be following, rather than departing from, the principle laid in *Von Lorang* v. *Austrian Property Administrator*,[368] by holding that the English court should not:

> "accept as binding a decree of the court in Malta which, by its very terms, destroys the one and only ground on which the claim to exercise jurisdiction over the wife would be based."

He did:

> "not think that a wife can, at one and the same time, claim a common domicile with her husband in Malta, and yet rely on the decree of the Maltese court which destroys the foundation on which that claim is based."[369]

In *Gray* v. *Formosa*,[370] in 1962, the refusal by the English Court of Appeal to recognise the Maltese decree was based on the finding that it offended against English views of substantial justice. The Court thus did not have to determine whether the principle stated in *Chapelle* v. *Chapelle*[371] was sound. Lord Denning, M.R. expressed his neutrality in a way[372] that indicated little enthusiasm for Willmer, J.'s approach. Donovan, L.J. would, if necessary, have followed *Chapelle* v. *Chapelle*. Pearson, L.J. favoured a different approach. He said:

> "The argument is that the jurisdiction of the Maltese court depended on the man and woman having a common domicile in Malta, and that common domicile depended on their marriage, and the annulment of the marriage struck at the root of the supposed jurisdiction. But I am not clear as to that argument, because there is a time factor involved. It is clear that after the decree of nullity took effect the wife did not then have the domicile of her husband, but it does not follow that she had her own separate domicile at the earlier time before the decree was made. The material time for the existence or non-existence of jurisdiction presumably is . . . the time of the commencement of the proceedings in Malta. At that time there was, according to the law of England, and probably according to the law of some other countries, a valid marriage subsisting between the man and the woman and they had, according to English law, a common domicile in Malta."[373]

---

[365] *Gray* v. *Formosa*, [1963] P., at 267 (*per* Lord Denning, M.R.).

[366] Cf. *id.*, at 270 (*per* Donovan, L.J.):
"It ill accords with present-day notions of tolerance and justice that a wife, validly married according to our law, should be told by a foreign court that she is a mere concubine and her children bastards, simply on the ground that her husband did not marry her in the church of a particular religious denomination."

[367] [1950] P. 134, at 144 (Willmer, J., 1949).

[368] [1927] A.C. 641 (H.L.(Sc.)).

[369] [1950] P., at 144.

[370] [1963] P. 259 (C.A., 1962).

[371] *Supra.*

[372] "I know that academic writers have criticised . . . *Chapelle* v. *Chapelle*, with all the sophistry at their command. I will not embark on that controversy today."

[373] [1963] P., at 271-272.

In *Lepre* v. *Lepre*,[374] five months later, Sir Jocelyn Simon, P. applied *Gray* v. *Formosa*[375] in refusing to recognise the Maltese decree on the basis that it offended against the concept of justice that prevailed in English courts. He thought that the crux of the Court of Appeal decision was that "it was an intolerable injustice that a system of law should seek to impose extraterritorially, as a condition of the validity of a marriage, that it should take place according to the tenets of a particular faith".[376]

Sir Jocelyn Simon, P. adopted a clear analysis of the issue. The question of the wife's domicile depended on whether the marriage was void, voidable or valid in the eyes of the legal system which should be invoked; if valid or voidable, the wife remained married to the husband until the pronouncement of the decree of nullity and therefore took his domicile until that event; if void she had her own legal domicile throughout. The marital defect in the instant case was clearly one characterised by English law as relating to formalities. Its legal result, according to Lord Greene, M.R., in *De Reneville* v. *De Reneville*,[377] must in those circumstances be referred to the *lex loci celebrationis* — English law. According to English law, the marriage was valid, and the wife thus had a Maltese domicile at the commencement of the Maltese proceedings. The nullity decree "was a judgment of the court of common domicile and should, therefore, be recognised here as binding and conclusive".[378]

Sir Jocelyn Simon, P. conceded that where the jurisdiction of a foreign court was in question it might reasonably be argued that English law should have regard not only to its own characterisation of the nature of the defect in question, but also to how it was characterised by the foreign court. In the case before him, the same result ensued:

> "In truth, there is no real difficulty in the present case: all the systems of law to which reference could be made — the *lex loci contractus,* the *lex domicilii* of the husband, the *leges domicilii* of the wife, the *lex causae* and the *lex fori* — concur at the time the Maltese proceedings started that the wife was married to the husband and domiciled with him in Malta. If that is so, then, whatever the words of the decree, it is inadmissible to relate it back so as to destroy the basis of the jurisdiction to make it."[379]

What Sir Jocelyn Simon P. did not attempt to resolve, outside the context where the *Travers* v. *Holley* principle applies,[380] was the very formidable question of what approach should be favoured where the characterisation of the law of the country called on to recognise the nullity decree differs from that of one or more of the various foreign systems of law to which reference might legitimately be made.

(c) *Decree recognised as valid in the country of the parties' common domicile*

In *Abate* v. *Abate*,[381] Lloyd-Jones, J. applied to recognition of nullity decrees the rule relating to recognition of foreign divorces established in *Armitage* v. *A.G.*[382] In a short judgment, Lloyd Jones, J. was content to rely, without any analysis, on the view of the textbook writers that recognition was desirable where, although the decree was not obtained in the country of the parties' common domicile, it was recognised there.

---

[374] [1965] P. 52 (Sir Jocelyn Simon, P., 1962).
[375] *Supra.*
[376] [1965] P., at 64.
[377] [1948] P. 100.
[378] [1965] P., at 60.
[379] *Id.,* at 61. Sir Jocelyn Simon, P. held that even if the marriage were void *ipso jure,* so that the husband alone was domiciled in Malta at the start of the proceedings, the decree should be recognised in England, on the basis of the *Travers* v. *Holley* principle.
[380] See *infra,* p. 261.
[381] [1961] P. 29 (Lloyd-Jones, J.).
[382] [1906] P. 135. Cf. *infra,* p. 284.

(d) *Decree recognised as valid in the country of the domicile of one party*

There are as yet no decisions in England which have addressed the question whether a decree recognised as valid in the country of the domicile of one of the parties to the marriage should be recognised in England. Commentators generally take the view[383] that it should. The English and Scottish Law Commissions accept[384] that, if both domiciliary laws of the parties agree as to their status it should in principle make no difference that the legal systems of two countries are involved rather than one. That unquestionably is the easier case. The harder case is where the domiciliary laws disagree: here the English and Scottish Commissions are more cautious. They comment that:

> "[i]f, as seems likely, the courts in England and Scotland will recognise a foreign nullity decree on the basis of one party's domicile . . ., then it may be that, despite the statutory rules for divorce recognition,[385] they will recognise a nullity decree which would be recognised as valid in the domicile of one of the parties but not in the domicile of the other."[386]

In Canada, there are only *dicta* to the effect that a decree recognised in the country of the parties' common domicile will be recognised by the courts in Canada.[387] Where the parties do not have a common domicile, the view has been expressed that "presumably the same result would ensue if the foreign decree would be recognised by each of the party's *(sic)* domiciles".[388]

(2) Residence

(a) *Common residence*

There are three English decisions[389] consistent with recognising a foreign decree obtained in the country which was the parties' common residence at the time the proceedings were commenced. In *Mitford* v. *Mitford,*[390] in 1923, a German decree of nullity with respect to a marriage celebrated there, the parties residing in Germany at the time of the proceedings, was recognised by the English court. It is not clear whether each of the two factors (the *locus celebrationis* and the residence of the parties) was independently a sufficient ground for recognition.[391] In *Corbett* v. *Corbett,*[392] in 1957, Barnard, J. did not resolve conclusively whether the parties' residence would suffice: again the *locus celebrationis* was an alternative basis of recognition, on which he relied primarily.[393]

In *Merker* v. *Merker,*[394] in 1962, there again were the two factors of *locus celebrationis* and the parties' residence in the state granting the annulment. Sir Jocelyn Simon, P. made it clear that common residence constituted a sufficient connecting factor in its own right, insofar as England should recognise, on the ground of comity, a foreign jurisdiction which it itself claimed.

---

[383] Cf. *Anton*, 255, *Dicey & Morris*, 383, *Morris*, 212, *Cheshire & North*, 409.

[384] The English and Scottish Law Commissions' Report, *Private International Law: Recognition of Foreign Nullity Decrees and Related Matters,* para. 2.23, fn. 123 (Law Com. No. 137, Scot. Law Com. No. 88, 1984).

[385] Cf. *id.*, para. 2.23.

[386] *Id.*, para. 2.23, fn. 124.

[387] Rafferty, *Recognition of Foreign Nullity Decrees,* 46 Sask. L. Rev. 73, at 80 (1981), citing *Gwyn* v. *Mellen,* 6 W.W.R. 385, at 390 (B.C.C.A.).

[388] Rafferty, *supra,* at 81.

[389] *Mitford* v. *Mitford,* [1923] P. 130, *Corbett* v. *Corbett,* [1957] 1 All E.R. 621, *Merker* v. *Merker,* [1963] P. 283.

[390] [1923] P. 130.

[391] Cf. the English and Scottish Law Commissions' Report, *supra,* para. 2.20.

[392] [1957] 1 All E.R. 621 (P.D.A. Div., Barnard, J.).

[393] Cf. Lysyk, *Jurisdiction and Recognition of Foreign Decrees in Nullity Suits,* 29 Sask. L. Rev. 143, at 156 (1964).

[394] [1963] P. 283.

To the extent that Sir Jocelyn Simon, P. rested recognition on the ground that the English court would itself claim jurisdiction in such circumstances, a question arises in England today as to whether the common residence of the parties continues to afford a ground for recognition, since this is no longer a ground for jurisdiction. The practical scope of the change is, however, small, since the issue will be of significance only in "the rare case"[395] in which the common residence of both parties falls short of being an habitual residence of either of them.[396]

(b) *Residence of one party*

There appears to be no reported decision in which the residence of one of the parties was held sufficient to justify recognition of a foreign nullity decree. One commentator, noting that, at common law, the English courts took jurisdiction themselves on the basis of the residence of the respondent but not of the petitioner, has argued that "there is at least an inference that decrees of the residence of the petitioner alone will not be recognised for that reason".[397]

(c) *Habitual residence*

The English jurisdictional rules in nullity since 1973 permit proceedings to be based on the habitual residence of either party for the minimum of one year before the institution of the proceedings. The application of the *Travers* v. *Holley* principle would afford recognition to foreign decrees based on a similar jurisdictional entitlement.

Reciprocity

Reference has been made earlier to the *Travers* v. *Holley*[398] principle. That decision established that in England courts must recognise foreign divorces obtained in circumstances in which, *mutatis mutandis,* there was jurisdiction in England to grant a decree.[399] The principle has been extended in England to nullity decrees[400] and it seems likely[401] that the Scottish courts would take a similar view. Canadian decisions[402] are in accord.

The "real and substantial connection" test

The "real and substantial connection" test of *Indyka* v. *Indyka*[403] in relation to divorce recognition has so far fared badly in our law in relation to divorce.[404] In England this test has also been applied in relation to the recognition of foreign nullity decrees. In *Law* v. *Gustin*,[405] in 1975, Bagnall, J. had "no doubt" that he ought to follow the lead of *Indyka* and its divorce progeny, and in *Perrini* v. *Perrini*,[406] three years later, Sir George Baker, P. took the same view. He was "unable to

---

[395] English and Scottish Law Commission's Report, *supra,* para. 2.20.

[396] Cf. Britain's Domicile and Matrimonial Proceedings Act 1973.

[397] *North,* 256.

[398] [1953] P. 246.

[399] Cf. the English and Scottish Law Commissions' Report, *supra,* para. 2.10.

[400] Cf. *Merker* v. *Merker,* [1963] P. 283 (Sir Jocelyn Simon, P., 1962), *Vervaeke* v. *Smith,* [1983] 1 A.C. 145.

[401] Cf. the English and Scottish Law Commissions' Report, *supra,* para. 2.11.

[402] *Re Capon, Capon and O'Brien* v. *McLay,* [1965] 2 O.R. 83 (C.A.), *Gwyn* v. *Mellen,* [1979] 6 W.W.R. 385 (B.C.C.A.).

[403] [1969] 1 A.C. 33.

[404] Cf. *infra,* pp. 279-280.

[405] [1976] Fam. 155 (Bagnall, J., 1975).

[406] [1979] Fam. 84, at 92 (Sir George Baker, P., 1978).

discover any reason why any different principle should apply to a decree of nullity and as the English statutory provisions cover both divorce and nullity there is every reason why the principle should apply".[407]

Of course, the "real and substantial connection" test devours many of the older more specific grounds of recognition, and may well in some cases go further than these grounds.

There is no English authority on whether the *Indyka* principle should be extended, in combination with *Armitage* v. *Attorney-General*,[408] so that the English court would recognise a foreign nullity decree *recognised* in a country with which a party has a real and substantial connection. Divorce decisions to similar effect in England would perhaps encourage recognition of nullity decrees on this basis, but the apparent hostility of the Supreme Court to the "real and substantial connection" test in relation to divorce makes it very difficult to anticipate developments in relation to nullity, where, of course, the policy issues are not the same.[409]

The place of celebration

The place of celebration has been held to be a good ground for recognition in a number of English decisions,[410] where the marriage was void. The principle of reciprocity has played an important role in justifying this ground in the more recent cases, and, as we have seen, since the jurisdiction no longer exists with respect to the place of marriage, this ground is more doubtful, at all events so far as reciprocity is its rationale.

Grounds for Withholding Recognition

Five grounds for withholding recognition of a foreign nullity decree may be considered briefly. In the absence of reported Irish authority, we must look elsewhere for guidance.

(1) *Recognition contrary to "substantial justice" or public policy*

The English and Scottish Law Commissions have observed as follows:

> "That an English court might withhold recognition from a foreign nullity decree which offends against English ideas of 'substantial justice' is the least well defined and most controversial[411] ground for denying recognition."[412]

We have seen how in *Gray* v. *Formosa*[413], the English Court of Appeal denied recognition to a Maltese decree of nullity on the ground that certain principles of Maltese marriage law were offensive to English notions of "substantial justice". In *Lepre* v. *Lepre*[414], Sir Jocelyn Simon, P., "with some misgiving" adopted the same approach; and in the House of Lords decision of *Vervaeke* v. *Smith*[415] Lord Simon observed that an English court would exercise this jurisdiction to refuse to recognise a decree "with extreme reserve".

---

[407] *Id.*, Canadian law is in accord: see *Gwyn* v. *Mellen*, [1979] 6 W.W.R. 385 (B.C.C.A.), considered by Rafferty, *supra*, at 85-86.

[408] [1906] P. 135.

[409] Cf. the English and Scottish Law Commissions' Report, *supra*, paras. 2.22-2.23 and contrast *K.E.D.* (*otherwise K.C.*) v. *M.C.* [1987] I.L.R.M. 189, discussed *infra*, pp. 279-280.

[410] *Mitford* v. *Mitford*, [1973] P. 130, *Corbett* v. *Corbett*, [1957] 1 All E.R. 621, *Merker* v. *Merker*, [1963] P. 283. See also *Gwyn* v. *Mellen*, [1979] 6 W.W.R. 385 (B.C.C.A.), considered by Rafferty, *Recognition of Foreign Nullity Decrees*, 46 Sask. L. Rev. 73, at 84-85 (1981).

[411] Citing Carter, 38 B.Y.B.L.L. 497 (1962), Lewis, 12 I.C.L.Q. 298 (1963), Blom-Cooper, 26 M.L.R. 94 (1963), Smart, 99 L.Q.R. 24 (1983), Jaffey, 32 I.C.L.Q. 500 (1983).

[412] *Op. cit.*, para. 2.24.

[413] [1963] P. 259.

[414] [1965] P. 52, at 63.

[415] [1983] 1 A.C. 145, at 164 (H.L.(Eng.)), 1982).

(2) *Fraud in obtaining the foreign decree*

The decision of *Van Lorang* v. *Administrator of Austrian Property*[416] appears to concede that an English or Scottish court could withhold recognition from a foreign nullity decree obtained by fraud. The English and Scottish Law Commissions have noted that:

> "Lord Phillimore's examples of fraud in that case suggest that both fraud as to the foreign court's jurisdiction and fraud as to the actual merits of the petition may be relevant, but the latter was not at common law a sufficient ground for withholding recognition from a foreign divorce."[417]

(3) *Foreign decree offending against the rules of natural justice*

Some English *dicta*[418] and Scottish authorities[419] indicate that recognition may be withheld where the foreign decree offends in some way against the rules of natural justice, but the scope of this exclusion appears relatively narrow.[420] and the mere fact that the proceedings were undefended is not of itself a reason for refusing to deny recognition to the decree.[421]

(4) *Res judicata*

In *Vervaeke* v. *Smith*,[422] the House of Lords applied the doctrine of *res judicata* to deny recognition to a foreign nullity decree, where in English proceedings, prior to the foreign decree, the validity of the marriage had been upheld.

(5) *Extra-judicial Foreign Annulments*

It is open to question whether the fact that a foreign annulment was extra-judicial should be a ground for non-recognition in English law. Certain types of extra-judicial divorces [such as the talaq and gett] are in some circumstances recognised in English law; it may be that a similar development would take place with respect to nullity decrees.

Effects of a Foreign Nullity Decree

The effects of a foreign nullity decree which is recognised in Ireland are not clear, in the absence of case law on the subject. A major question of principle arises as

---

[416] [1927] A.C. 641. See also *Merker* v. *Merker*, [1963] P. 283, at 296 (*per* Sir Jocelyn Simon, P., 1962), *Chapelle* v. *Chapelle*, [1950] P. 134, at 140.

[417] *Op. cit.*, para. 2.24.

[418] Cf. the English and Scottish Law Commission's Report, para. 2.25, citing *Mitford* v. *Mitford*, [1923] P. 130, at 137, 141-142, *Merker* v. *Merker*, [1963] P. 283, at 296, 299 and *Law* v. *Gustin*, [1976] Fam. 155, at 159.

[419] Cf. *id.*, para. 2.25, citing *Crabtree* v. *Crabtree*, 1929 S.L.T. 675, at 676, *Scott* v. *Scott*, 1937 S.L.T. 632 and *Perrin* v. *Perrin*, 1950 S.L.T. 51, at 53.

[420] Cf. *id.*, para. 2.25, noting (in fn. 130) that "[i]n *Mitford* v. *Mitford* the court was prepared to recognise a German decree, even though it was granted during wartime when the English respondent husband was unable to reach Germany ([1923] P. 130, 141); and in *Law* v. *Gustin* the court ignored the fact that the respondent had received only five days' notice in which to enter a defence [[1976] Fam. 155, 158]."

[421] *Id.*, para. 2.25, citing *Von Lorang* v. *Administrator of Austrian Property*, 1926 S.C. 598, 627 (*per* Lord Sands), cited with approval by Lord Hodson in *Ross-Smith* v. *Ross-Smith*, [1963] A.C. 280, 341.

[422] [1983] 1 A.C. 145.

[423] Citing *Von Lorang's case*, [1927] A.C. 641, at 654-655, and *North*, 267.

to how the Irish courts would deal with a situation where the effects of the foreign decree under the law of the foreign country differ from those under Irish law. This problem would arise where under Irish law the marriage was void but under the law of the foreign court was voidable, or vice versa. The English and Scottish Law Commissions have observed that "[t]he cases give no firm guidance on this problem, although a dictum of Viscount Haldane in the *Von Lorang* case might be taken to indicate that the foreign effect of a foreign decree should be recognised".[424]

Capacity to Marry After a Foreign Nullity Decree

As a general rule, the recognition by Irish law of a foreign nullity decree will mean that the parties are free to marry. But another general rule is that a person's capacity to marry is determined by the law of his or her domicile at the time of the marriage. Thus the situation could arise where a foreign nullity decree was recognised in this country but not in the country of a spouse's domicile.[425] In the divorce context in England it was held[426] that the country of the domicile would prevail. In *Perrini* v. *Perrini*,[427] however, Sir George Baker, P., took a different view. Having recognised a nullity decree obtained against an Italian respondent in New Jersey, he said:

"Once the New Jersey decree is recognised here the fact that the respondent could not marry in Italy, the country of his domicile, on April 8, 1967 is, in my opinion, no bar to his marrying in England where by the New Jersey decree he was free to marry. No incapacity existed in English law."[428]

Sir George Baker, P. did not mention *R.* v. *Brentwood Superintendent Registrar of Marriages, Ex Parte Arias.*[429]

Some uncertainty remains as to the effect of *Perrini* v. *Perrini*. There is a passage in the judgment which suggests an adherence to the intended matrimonial residence as a test for validity of the marriages.[430] If, however, the rule is that once an English court has recognised a foreign nullity decree, then any subsequent English marriage will be valid, the position regarding the validity of marriages in other countries is not clear.

Ancillary Relief

There is no Irish authority on the question of ancillary relief; nor is there any authority in England or Scotland directly in point. The English and Scottish Law Commissions suggest[431] that the divorce analogy would be likely to be followed, so that a foreign order for financial relief would be recognised only if it were final

---

[424] *Op. cit.*, para. 2.33.
[425] Cf. *Id.*, para. 2.35.
[426] In *R.* v. *Brentwood Superintendent Registrar of Marriages, Ex Parte Arias*, [1968] 2 Q.B. 956. The Recognition of Divorces and Legal Separations Act 1971, section 7, effectively reversed this decision.
[427] [1979] Fam. 84.
[428] *Id.*, at 92.
[429] *Supra.*
[430] Cf. Nott, *Foreign Nullity Decrees: Perrini* v. *Perrini — I*, 29 Int. & Comp. L.Q. 510, at 514-515 (1980), and Young, *Foreign Nullity Decrees: Perrini* v. *Perrini — II*, 29 Int. & Comp. L.Q. 515, at 517 (1980) criticising *Perrini* for failing to note that in *Radwan* v. *Radwan*, [1973] Fam. 37, Cumming-Bruce, J. acknowledged that *Brentwood Superintendent* had been correctly decided, and had specifically restricted the scope of the intended matrimonial residence test to capacity to contract a polygamous marriage.
[431] English and Scottish Law Commissions' Report, *supra*, para. 2.36.

and conclusive or fell within the statutory rules for the recognition of maintenance orders. In the converse case, where one of the parties wishes to seek financial relief in England following a foreign decree of nullity, it appears that "the English courts will decline jurisdiction on the ground that there is no subsisting marriage".[432]

Where the Foreign Nullity Decree is not Recognised

There is no direct authority on the position where a foreign nullity decree is not recognised in Ireland. On principle, it would appear that the parties must all be regarded by Irish law as married, unless, of course, the marriage is invalid under Irish law.

Where the question of remarriage arises, the position becomes more unclear. If a spouse with such an unrecognised foreign decree remarries and that remarriage is valid according to the law (or laws) of the country (or countries) of domicile of the spouse and the person he or she marries, then we have a similar problem to that arising in the *Brentwood Superintendent Registrar of Marriages* case. In Canada[433] it has been held that the capacity rule rather than recognition should prevail.

Reform Proposals

The Law Reform Commission in their Twentieth Report[434] have recommended the replacement of the existing rules for recognition of foreign nullity decrees by rules which attempt to harmonise with the reasonable expectations of the parties themselves. The Commission propose that a nullity decree obtained outside the State should be recognised here in any of the following cases:

(1) Where the court granting the decree applied the choice-of-law rules which the Commission propose in their 19th Report.[435]

(2) Where the decree was obtained or recognised in the country of either spouse's habitual residence.

(3) Where the decree was obtained or recognised in a country with which either spouse has a real and substantial connection.

So far as grounds for withholding recognition are concerned, the Commission recommend that the courts should continue to develop the law, on the basis that questions of public policy, natural, substantial and constitutional justice and *res judicata* are more easily considered in the context of the exercise of a general judicial discretion than within the confines of a statutory enactment.

So far as fraud is concerned the Commission recommend that fraud, whether as to the foreign court's jurisdiction or as to the actual merits of the petition, should be a ground for non-recognition of a foreign nullity decree. Moreover, where a party's predominant purpose in seeking to establish an habitual residence in, or real and substantial connection with, a particular country was to obtain a nullity decree there which would not otherwise be recognised, the decree should not in such circumstances be recognised. In other words, forum shopping would be discouraged.

---

[432] *Id.*, citing the divorce case of *Quazi* v. *Quazi*, [1980] A.C. 744.

[433] *Schwebel* v. *Ungar*, 48 D.L.R. (2d) 644 (1964), aff'g 42 D.L.R. (2d) 622 (1963). The case involved remarriage after divorce rather than annulment. Cf. *supra*, pp. 33-34.

[434] L.R.C. 20-1985, pp. 36-37.

[435] *Report on Private International Law Aspects of the Capacity to Marry and Choice of Law in Proceedings for Nullity of Mariage* (L.R.C. 19-1985). Cf. *supra*, pp. 246-250.

THE HAGUE CONVENTION ON MARRIAGE (1978)

We now consider briefly the *Hague Convention on the Celebration and Recognition of the Validity of Marriages* (1978).[436] The Convention deals with the celebration of marriages, in Chapter I.[437] Article 2 provides that the formal requirements for marriages are to be governed by the law of the State of celebration.[438] Article 3 provides as follows:

"A marriage shall be celebrated —

(1) where the future spouses meet the substantive requirements of the internal law of the State of celebration and one of them has the nationality of that State or habitually resides there; or

(2) where each of the future spouses meets the substantive requirements of the internal law designated by the choice of law rules of the State of celebration."

Thus, to take the first sub-paragraph, where both the prospective spouses fulfil the requirements of Irish law and one of them is Irish or habitually resides here, then they will be entitled to be married here, regardless of any question of their capacity to marry under their personal law. However, Article 6 provides that a Contracting State may reserve the right, by way of derogation from Article 3, sub-paragraph 1, not to apply its internal law to the substantive requirements for marriage in respect of a prospective spouse who neither is a national of that State nor habitually resides there. Thus, if Ireland were to make a reservation under Article 6, it would no longer be sufficient for this prospective spouse to comply with the requirements of Irish law. The Convention does not specify what law should be applied to that person. In the normal course it would be the personal law of that person, so far as matters of essential validity are concerned, and the *lex loci celebrationis,* so far as matters of formal validity are concerned.

Article 5 provides that the application of a foreign law declared applicable by Chapter I may be refused only if such application is manifestly incompatible with the public policy *(ordre public)* of the State of celebration. The effect of Article 3, sub-paragraph 1 and Article 5 is that if Ireland were to accept the Convention, Irish law would be required to authorise the celebration of a marriage here of persons who may have no connection with the State where those persons meet the substantive requirements of the law of their own country, even though they *do not meet the substantive requirements of Irish law,* unless to allow them to do so would be manifestly incompatible with Irish public policy *(ordre public),* or unless Ireland reserves the right under Article 6, to derogate from Article 3, sub-paragraph 1.

Chapter I suffers from a number of weaknesses. It fails to provide a complete code of choice-of-law rules for the celebration of marriage. Rather than prescribing any general choice-of-law rule for the essential validity of marriage, "it assumes that the State of celebration has such a rule, but without defining it".[439]

The Law Reform Commission considered[440] that Chapter I would on balance present too many difficulties for its incorporation into Irish law. Its reference to the *lex loci celebrationis* and the *lex patriae* do not harmonise with the Commission's

---

[436] For analysis of the Convention, see Lalive, *La Convention de la Haye du 14 Mars 1978 sur la célébration et la reconnaissance de la validité des mariages,* 34 Schweizerisches Jahrbuch für Internationales Recht 31 (1978), Reese, *The Hague Convention on Celebration and Recognition of the Validity of Marriages,* 20 Virginia J. of Internat. L. 25 (1979), Glenn, *Comment: Conflict of Laws — The 1976 Hague Conventions on Marriage and Matrimonial Property Regimes,* 55 Can. Bar Rev. 586, at 588-595 (1977) and the Law Reform Commission's *Report on Private International Law Aspects of Capacity to Marry and Choice of Law in Proceedings for Nullity of Marriage,* Ch. 6 (L.R.C. 19-1985).

[437] Chapter 1 is optional: cf. Article 16.

[438] The expression "law" here includes the choice-of-law rules of the State of celebration. Thus *renvoi* is not excluded.

[439] English Law Commission Working Paper No. 89 and Scottish Law Commission Consultative Memorandum No. 64, *supra,* at p. 165.

emphasis[441] on the country of the habitual residence of the spouses as providing the test for capacity to marry.

Chapter II "forms the core of the Convention".[442] The Chapter "is 'obligatory' in the sense that it is not possible to accept the Convention while excluding Chapter II.[443] The Chapter applies to the recognition in a Contracting State of the validity of marriages entered into in other States.[444]

Article 9, "which may be called the heart of Chapter II",[445] provides as follows:

"A marriage validly entered into under the law of the State of celebration or which subsequently becomes valid under that law shall be considered as such in all Contracting States, subject to the provisions of this Chapter.

A marriage celebrated by a diplomatic agent or consular official in accordance with his law shall similarly be considered valid in all Contracting States, provided that the celebration is not prohibited by the State of celebration."

Article 11 represents an important counterweight to Article 9. It provides as follows:

"A Contracting State may refuse to recognise the validity of a marriage only where, at the time of the marriage, under the law of that State —

(1) one of the spouses was already married; or

(2) the spouses were related to one another, by blood or by adoption, in the direct line or as brother and sister; or

(3) one of the spouses had not attained the minimum age required for marriage, nor had obtained the necessary dispensation; or

(4) one of the spouses did not have the mental capacity to consent; or

(5) one of the spouses did not freely consent to the marriage.

However, recognition may not be refused where, in the case mentioned in sub-paragraph 1 of the preceding paragraph, the marriage has subsequently become valid by reason of the dissolution or annulment of the prior marriage."

Article 12 provides that the rules of Chapter II are to apply even where the recognition of the validity of a marriage is to be dealt with as an incidental question in the context of another question;[446] however, these rules need not be applied where the other question, under the choice-of-law rules of the forum, is governed by the law of a non-Contracting State.[447]

---

[440] Law Reform Commission's *Report on Jurisdiction in Proceedings for Nullity of Marriage, Recognition of Foreign Nullity Decrees, and the Hague Convention on the Celebration and Recognition of the Validity of Marriages*, p. 41 (L.R.C. 20-1985).

[441] In their *Report on Private International Law Aspects of the Capacity to Marry and Choice of Law in Proceedings for Nullity of Marriage*, p. 114 (L.R.C. 19-1985).

[442] Malström Report, *Actes et Documents de la Treizième Session*, tome III, *Marriage*, at p. 298.

[443] *Id.*

[444] Article 7. Five specific marriages are excluded by Article 8: (1) marriages celebrated by military authorities; (2) marriages celebrated aboard ships or aircraft; (3) proxy marriages; (4) posthumous marriages; (5) informal marriages.

[445] *Malström Report*, p. 300.

[446] See *supra*, ch. 4.

[447] Regarding Article 12, the English and Scottish Law Commissions, *op. cit.*, p. 167, fn. 10, comment: "This exception is a pretty rough and ready one. If one assumes that the main question is one of succession and the subsidiary issue is the validity of the marriage of a potential beneficiary, then whether the Convention applies to the latter issue depends on whether the forum's conflict rules, including possibly *renvoi*, apply to the succession laws of a State which has ratified the Convention."

Article 13 provides that the Convention is not to prevent the application in a Contracting State of rules of law more favourable to the recognition of foreign marriages. Article 14 provides that a Contracting State may refuse to recognise the validity of a marriage where such recognition is manifestly incompatible with its public policy *(order public)*. Finally, Article 15 provides that Chapter II is to apply regardless of the date on which the marriage was celebrated. It also provides, however, that a Contracting State may reserve the right not to apply Chapter II to a marriage celebrated before the date on which, in relation to that State, the Convention enters into force.

Some general observations on Chapter II are in order. The Chapter represents a compromise between those states which refer to the law of domicile of the parties to determine the essential validity of marriage and those states which refer to the *lex patriae*. In settling for the *lex loci celebrationis*, the Convention is favouring a rule abandoned long ago by most countries[448] and under attack in the United States,[449] and some other countries[450] where it has had a longer influence.

Chapter II has further deficiencies. It fails to harmonise the choice of law rules of the individual States, and provides no rules for recognition of the validity of marriages which are invalid under the *lex loci celebrationis*.[451]

It should be noted that the term "law" in the first paragraph of Article 9, when referring to the law of the State of celebration, means not only its internal law but also its choice-of-law rules. Thus Article 9 would require us to recognise a marriage even if it fails to comply with our choice-of-law rules (based on domicile[452]) in a case where it complied with the choice-of-law rules of the *locus celebrationis*. We could avail ourselves of the right to refuse to recognise the validity of the marriage by invoking either Article 11 or 14. There are so many gaps[453] in Article 11 that we would be forced back on to the public policy proviso of Article 14 in quite a wide range of cases. As the Law Reform Commission has observed:

> "It could be considered that it is wrong to overload the public policy proviso. A further criticism is that the only reason why Article 9 would work satisfactorily is because it may be effectively eclipsed by the continued operation of Articles 11 and 14."[454]

On balance the Commission came to the view that the Hague Convention would increase rather than reduce the present complexity of the law on this subject, and recommended[455] that the Convention should not be incorporated into Irish law.

---

[448] Cf. *supra*, pp. 231-235.
[449] Cf. *Scoles & Hay*, 421, *Leflar*, 533.
[450] Cf. *Rabel*, vol. 1, p. 264, *Pålsson*, paras. 33-37.
[451] See Glenn, supra, at 593.
[452] See *supra*, pp. 231 ff.
[453] Article 11 does not cover marriages invalid by reason of affinity, marriages invalid for consanguinity between outside relations in the direct line and between brother and sister or marriages affected by impotence; finally the Article does not extend to marriages invalid for failure to have obtained parental consent. The Law Reform Commission has recommended that these marriages should be invalid, regardless of the habitual residence of the spouses: cf. the *Report on the Age of Majority, the Age of Marriage and Some Connected Subjects*, para. 63 (L.R.C. 5-1983) and the *Report on Private International Law Aspects of the Capacity to Marry and Choice-of-Law in Proceedings for Nullity of Marriage*, p. 115 (L.R.C. 19-1985).
[454] L.R.C. 19-1985, p. 47.
[455] *Id.*, p. 48.

CHAPTER 12

DIVORCE[1]

In this chapter we examine the conflict of laws aspects of divorce. This involves a consideration of complicated constitutional provisions, whose exact scope has yet to be determined. A recent statutory intervention,[2] which has brought a measure of certainty to the law, though with debatable social consequences.

We approach the subject by looking first at the position before 1937. Then we shall consider the effect of the Constitution on the previous law. Finally we examine the circumstances in which recognition of a foreign divorce decree may be granted or withheld in the light of the Domicile and Recognition of Foreign Divorces Act 1986.

THE POSITION BEFORE 1937

Before 1937, the common law rules as to recognition of foreign divorces applied. So far as divorce *within* the jurisdiction was concerned, prior to Independence, divorce by Private Act of Parliament was permitted.[3] The 1922 Constitution contained no explicit prohibition against divorce legislation, but as a result of the alteration of Standing Orders in the Oireachtas in 1925, it became effectively impossible to introduce divorce by Private Act.[4]

So far as foreign divorce decrees were concerned, the common law rules of recognition continued to apply. What *were* these common law rules? In summary it may be said that the major principle of recognition was that divorces would be recognised when granted in the country of the spouses' common domicile. The effect of the operation of the principle that a wife's domicile depended on that of her husband's domicile was that a divorce obtained by either spouse in the country of the *husband's* domicile would be recognised, regardless of the wife's place of residence or where she intended to have her permanent home.

This appears to have been the position even before 1871, when the civil courts acquired jurisdiction over matrimonial matters[5] for the first time.

---

[1] See *Shatter*, ch. 10, *North*, 372-386, J.M. Kelly, *Fundamental Rights in the Irish Law and Consititution*, 199-204 (2nd ed., 1967), J.M. Kelly, *The Irish Constitution*, 617-623 (2nd ed., 1984), *Binchy*, ch. 6, Duncan, *The Future of Divorce Recognition in Ireland*, 2 Dublin U.L. Rev. (No. 1) 2 (1971), Duncan, *Foreign Divorces Obtained on the Basis of Residence and the Doctrine of Estoppel*, 9 Ir. Jur. (n.s.) 59 (1975), Lee, *Irish Matrimonial Laws and the Marital Status*, 16 N.I.L.Q. 387 (1965) (reprinted in 103 I.L.T. & Sol. J. 151 (1969)), Kerr, *The Need for a Recognition of Divorces Act*, [1976] 1 Dublin U.L.J. 11, Davitt, *Some Aspects of the Constitution and the Law in Relation to Marriage*, 57 Studies 6 (1968), Grogan, *Comments on the Foregoing Article — I*, 57 Studies 20 (1968), Clarke, *Comments on the Foregoing Article — II*, 57 Studies 24 (1968), Jones, *The Non-Recognition of Foreign Divorces in Ireland*, 3 Ir. Jur. (n.s.) 299 (1968).

[2] Domicile and Recognition of Foreign Divorces Act 1986.

[3] The subject is analysed in detail by Duncan, *Desertion and Cruelty in Irish Matrimonial Law*, 7 Ir. Jur. (n.s.) 213, at 213-221 (1972).

[4] See Nolan, *The Influence of Catholic Nationalism on the Legislature of the Irish Free State*, 10 Ir. Jur. (n.s.) 128, at 133-137 (1975).

[5] Though not divorce *a vinculo*, which remained a matter for private Act of Parliament.

In *Maghee* v. *M'Allister*,[6] a man domiciled in Scotland married an Irish woman[7] in London, where they lived for four months, before going to Scotland.[8] Some time later they returned to England where the wife "separated herself"[9] from her husband. He went back to live in Scotland, and afterwards divorced his wife. The wife later married for a second time. On her death, both husbands claimed a share in her freehold and personal property in Dublin as their "marital right". The question whether the divorce decree should be recognised under Irish law thus required consideration.

Brady, L.C. held that the divorce should be recognised. The first marriage was "a Scottish marriage"[10] although celebrated in England because domicile determined the question.[11] Thus the Irish court was prepared to recognise as effective a divorce obtained in the country of the spouses'[12] domicile, even though the ecclesiastical courts in Ireland could not grant a divorce.

Newly established civil courts acquired jurisdiction over matrimonial proceedings in 1871.[13] Like the ecclesiastical courts, however, whose jurisdiction they replaced, the civil courts had no power to grant decrees for divorce.

Sinclair v. *Sinclair*[14] is of interest because it reveals the attitude of the civil courts towards the recognition of foreign divorces during this period. In *Sinclair's* case a man domiciled in Ireland who had divorced his wife in England was later advised by trustees of the marriage settlement that the decree was ineffective as having been made without jurisdiction. He therefore sought a decree for divorce *a mensa et thoro* from the Irish court as a preliminary to obtaining a private Act of Parliament dissolving the marriage.

Warren, P. held[15] that it was not necessary to take this first step,[16] and accordingly dismissed the petition. His observations on the question of divorce recognition rules, though *obiter*, are of some interest. His impression was that:

> "under the English Divorce Act of 1857, the English Court has jurisdiction to make a decree for a divorce *a vinculo* between British subjects personally present within the jurisdiction of English Courts, where adultery is carried on in England, notwithstanding a foreign domicil, in cases where the petitioner, by the very act of petition, and the respondent, by appearing without protest, or by not appearing at all, submit to the jurisdiction of the Court.[17] On the other hand, I think that by the law of nations, the validity of such a divorce is limited to the country where the decree is made, unless it is the country of the domicil of the parties, and does not extend to foreign countries, and for this purpose, as regards English decrees, Ireland is a foreign country."[18]

In the Northern Ireland case of *Re E.E.L. (An Infant)*,[19] the Court of Appeal took

[6] 3 Ir. Chy. Rep. 372 (Brady, L.C., 1853).
[7] The report does not state the woman's domicile but seems safe to assume that it was Irish: cf. *North*, 372.
[8] For consideration of the question whether the wife's domicile automatically became that of her husband on marrying him or only when the couple went to Scotland, cf. *supra*. p. 79, fn. 273.
[9] 3 Ir. Ch. Rep., at 605.
[10] *Id.*, at 607.
[11] *Id.*, at 608.
[12] The wife's domicile, once it became Scottish, was apparently considered to remain so in spite of her residence outside Scotland.
[13] Matrimonial Causes and Marriage Law (Ireland) Amendment Act 1870.
[14] [1896] 1 I.R. 603 (Mat., Warren, P.).
[15] *Id.*, at 611.
[16] On the basis, first, that the relevant Standing Order of the House of Lords required merely that proceedings should have been taken, rather than that the Court should necessarily have made an order, and, secondly, that the House of Lords had power to dispense with the Standing Order.
[17] As *North*, 393, fn. 168, points out, this conclusion hardly accords with *Le Mesurier* v. *Le Mesurier* [1895] A.C. 517, which Warren, P. himself cited elsewhere in the judgment.
[18] [1896] 1 I.R., at 608.
[19] [1938] N.I. 56, also reported (*sub nom. Re Lyons (An Infant)*), 72 I.L.T.R. 37 (C.A., 1937).

the same view on the question of divorce recognition. The case is of interest since at that time Northern Ireland courts, like their counterparts in the Free State, had no jurisdiction to grant divorces. The case involved a custody application in relation to a child whose parents had been divorced in Florida three years previously. The father was at all material times domiciled in Northern Ireland. The wife had been domiciled in Florida before the marriage.

The Court of Appeal, in determining the custody issue, addressed the question whether the divorce decree was capable of recognition, and held that it was not. Andrews, L.J., delivering the judgment of the Court, said:

> "Now in our opinion the law is clear that our courts will not recognise a decree of divorce as possessing any extra-territorial validity unless at the commencement of the proceedings the parties were domiciled within the jurisdiction of the Court pronouncing the decree. Nothing short of domicile can give a foreign Court jurisdiction to decree a divorce which will be valid in this country. A decree of divorce made in a foreign country without regard to domicile may according to the law of that country be valid within the limits of that country; but to a divorce so pronounced our Courts deny validity within our jurisdiction."[20]

THE EFFECT OF THE CONSTITUTION

We must now consider the effect of the 1937 Constitution on the previous rules as to the recognition of foreign divorces. Article 41.3.2° deals with the internal law of the State. It provides that "[n]o law shall be enacted providing for the grant of a dissolution of marriage". Article 41.3.3° goes on to provide as follows:

> "No person whose marriage has been dissolved under the civil law of any other State but is a subsisting valid marriage under the law for the time being in force within the jurisdiction of the Government and Parliament established by this Constitution shall be capable of contracting a valid marriage within that jurisdiction during the lifetime of the other party to the marriage so dissolved."

On a reasonable interpretation this sub-section appears to be concerned with the question of the capacity to remarry within the State.[21] But judicial interpretation of the sub-section has concentrated on the circumstances in which the validity of a foreign divorce decree will be recognised under our law, the courts generally evincing little interest in the explicit question of capacity to remarry.[22]

Some Early Cases After 1937

The first reported decision in which the question of divorce recognition arose after the Constitution had come into effect was *In re McComiskey, deceased; Gibson* v. *Patterson.*[23] The Court had to determine whether it could properly be said of a

---

[20] [1938] N.I., at 77.
[21] Cf. Duncan, *The Future for Divorce Recognition in Ireland,* 2 Dublin U.L. Rev. (No. 1) 2, at 4 (1971): "On the face of it this subsection appears to be laying down a rule governing the capacity of persons to contract a marriage in the Republic. What it says about the recognition of foreign divorces, it says only in relation to this question of marriage capacity, e.g. questions of succession or mutual property rights as between the divorced parties, or questions relating to the legitimacy of children of a second marriage occurring outside Ireland, would not seem to come within the subsection's ambit. Nor would the subsection appear to prohibit recognition of a subsequent marriage which takes place outside Ireland. However, judges have not accepted that the sub-section is thus limited."
[22] Cf. the Law Reform Commission's *Report on Private International Law Aspects of Capacity to Marry and Choice of Law in Proceedings for Nullity of Marriage,* pp. 65-67 (L.R.C.) 19-1985). See further *supra,* pp. 236-239.
[23] [1939] I.R. 573 (High Ct., Gavan Duffy, J.).

woman who had divorced her husband in England that she had "died unmarried", or had left a husband "surviving her". The husband would be entitled to an interest in property under the will of the woman's father if he fell within the scope of the latter description.

Gavan Duffy, J. held that he did not. He said:

> "I must take [the husband] to have been domiciled in England at the time when the English Court pronounced dissolution of the marriage, and, in the absence of an Irish law invalidating that decree, the law of his domicile must determine whether he is married or not, when that question arises on a claim of which a marriage is the foundation."[24]

Gavan Duffy, J.'s explanation of why the constitutional and public policy issues did not arise raises an interesting jurisprudential question. The title to the property was "not established by proof of a divorce,"[26] but the persons entitled took in default, as a result of "the evidence that [the testator's daughter] did not die unmarried and of the rejection of the claim by the only possible surviving husband to prove that he was her husband at her death".[27] There was therefore no occasion for him to investigate the "interesting"[28] question of constitutional law and public policy as to whether the Irish Court could recognise and enforce the claim, if otherwise well founded, of a person "compelled to establish his title to property by proving and relying upon a decree of dissolution of marriage, pronounced by the Court having divorce jurisdiction in England".[29]

One may doubt the force of this distinction. In truth, the claim of those entitled to the property on proof of there being no surviving husband depended on recognition being afforded to the English divorce. In the absence of that recognition, their claim would necessarily have perished. Of course none of these claimants had obtained a divorce on which they were seeking to rely; but their reliance on the divorce was no less strong on that account. Perhaps Gavan Duffy, J. was envisaging the limited instances in which a person who himself had obtained a divorce was seeking to have it recognised. It would be difficult, however, to believe that the constitutional dimensions of the subject could be kept within such narrow bounds.

It has been suggested[30] that direct confrontation of the issue of divorce recognition in this case might perhaps be avoided by characterising the problem as one merely of status, in respect of which the *lex domicilii* controls.[31] Although this distinction is "a fine one",[32] it receives clear support from Gavan Duffy, J.'s statement that "....the law of [the husband's] domicile must determine whether he is married or not, when that question arises on a claim of which a marriage is the foundation."[33] Thus, as has been pointed out,[34] Gavan Duffy, J.'s approach would appear to lead to indirect recognition of divorce decrees altering status under the *lex domicilii* although obtained elsewhere.[35] It would, however, be inadvisable for a court to attempt to treat questions of "status" *in vacuo*.[36] When matrimonial status is in question, there is no way that our rules relating to recognition of foreign divorces can be ignored.

[24] *Id.*, at 581.
[25] *Id.*, at 580-581.
[26] *Id.*, at 581.
[27] *Id.*
[28] *Id.*
[29] *Id.*
[30] *North*, 375.
[31] Cf. *Armitage* v. *A.G.*, [1906] P. 135.
[32] *North*, 375.
[33] [1939] I.R., at 581.
[34] *North*, 375.
[35] Cf. *Armitage* v. *A.G.*, [1906] P. 135.
[36] Cf. *MacLeod*, 236.

The Circuit Court decision of *Leake* v. *Douglas*[37] may be interpreted (very tentatively) as affording support to the view that Article 41 does not affect the rule that divorces obtained in the country of the spouse's domicile should be recognised here. In this case a couple obtained a divorce in England at a time when, it seems,[38] they were domiciled there. The husband later came to live in Ireland. The wife sought to enforce the order of the divorce court relating to alimony. Judge Conroy rejected her action on the basis that, under English law, orders for alimony were not final and conclusive. Of particular interest is the Judge's rejection of the argument made on behalf of the husband that the judgment on which the claim was based was not enforceable by action in the Irish courts because it was of a kind which, "in the view of the constitutional ban on divorce",[39] it was the policy of the law within the State not to enforce, although the judgment was "unobjectionable by the *lex loci*".[40] Judge Conroy did not accept this argument since the judgment "was not of a penal nature but was a judgment affecting status only, which the Courts here would recognise".[41]

The Mayo-Perrott Case

The first decision of the Supreme Court involving an interpretation of these provisions was *Mayo-Perrott* v. *Mayo-Perrott*,[42] in 1958. In this case, the plaintiff obtained a decree for divorce against the defendant in the English High Court. At the time of the hearing of the proceedings, both parties were domiciled in England. Later the defendant came to live in Ireland and the plaintiff brought proceedings in the Irish High Court for the enforcement of orders for costs made during and pursuant to the English divorce proceedings.

The Supreme Court, affirming Murnaghan, J., held unanimously that these orders for costs were not enforceable here as being against Irish public policy.[43] But there the agreement ended. It seemed to Maguire, C.J. that Article 41.3.3° was:

"clearly....designed to double-bar the door closed in sub-section 2. Far from recognising the validity of a divorce obtained outside the country it seems to me expressly to deny to such a divorce any recognition for it prohibits the contracting of a valid marriage by a party who has obtained a divorce elsewhere. The sub-section says as plainly as it could be said that a valid marriage which is dissolved under the law of another State remains in the eyes of our law a subsisting valid marriage. It may be that the Constitution recognises that a decree of dissolution of marriage elsewhere may be valid in the country where it has been obtained, but to my mind, as I have said, it denies it any validity here. As already stated, it would seem sufficient to dispose of the appellant's case that sub-section 2 prevents the course of action in respect of which the decree sued upon was obtained from being made the basis of proceedings in this country. I have, however, considered the argument which has been so pressed that the Article as a whole merely intended to state the law as it was before 1922. I am not convinced that even if this were so it would assist the appellant.

In my opinion, however, the contention that sub-section 3 of Article 41 qualifies the very clear earlier provisions of the Article in the way suggested is entirely unsustainable. The interpretation which the appellant seeks to place upon the sub-section is almost the exact opposite of what the Article to my mind plainly means."[44]

---

[37] 88 I.L.T.R. 4 (Circuit Ct., Judge Conroy, 1952).

[38] The report does not mention the question of the parties' domicile. They had been married in England twenty years before the divorce. Both parties had later remarried, the wife and her second husband "continuing to reside in England", the husband and his second wife "coming to live in Ireland".

[39] *Id.*, at 5.

[40] *Id.*

[41] *Id.*

[42] [1958] I.R. 336 (Sup. Ct., aff'g High Ct., Murnaghan, J., 1955).

[43] This aspect of the case is considered *infra*, pp. 290-291.

[44] [1958] I.R., at 344.

Mr Justice Kingsmill Moore took an opposing view. He considered that, apart from the difficulties involved in the correct construction of Article 41.3 of our Constitution the law appeared to be well settled. There was, in his view, "no reason"[45] to suggest that in 1921, when Ireland gained its independence, there was any difference between the law of England and of Ireland as to the rules for divorce recognition. A contrary view would "lead to strange and perplexing results".[46] At that time, changes of domicile between the two countries were frequent. If divorces obtained in the country of the parties' domicile had not been recognised, serious problems in relation to legitimacy and bigamy would have arisen.

The 1921 Constitution had not changed matters, in Kingsmill Moore, J.'s view. Turning to Article 41.3.3° the 1937 Constitution, he said:

"First it must be noted that the prohibition is *not* applicable to all cases of dissolution of marriage, but only to cases where, under the law for the time being in force within our jurisdiction, the original marriage is regarded as valid and subsisting, or in other words where, by that law, the divorce is regarded as not being effectual to put an end to the original valid marriage. No doubt the Oireachtas could pass a law that no dissolution of marriage, wherever effected, even where the parties were domiciled in the country of the court pronouncing the decree, was to be effective to annul the pre-existing valid marriage. If it did so, then, by the law for the time being in force, the first marriage would still be valid and subsisting within our jurisdiction. But the Oireachtas has not done so, and the law as existing when the Constitution was passed was that a divorce effected by a foreign Court of persons domiciled within its jurisdiction was regarded as valid in our jurisdiction. Such law was preserved unless inconsistent with the new Constitution and, in the absence of any statement in the Constitution altering such law, inconsistency cannot be spelled out from the words now being interpreted for they are perfectly consistent with the preservation of the pre-existing law which was the 'law for the time being in force.' "[47]

Kingsmill Moore, J. noted that there had been divorce decrees by foreign courts which were not regarded as effectual to put an end to the marriage, "[t]he most obvious instance"[48] being where the parties were not domiciled in the country whose courts granted the divorce. Nor did it appear that our law would recognise as valid a divorce, even in the country of the spouses' domicile, where, by the law of that country, divorce could be brought about without recourse to the courts.[49] Similarly our courts would not recognise the dissolution of a marriage essentially monogamous by a form suitable only to the dissolution of a polygamous marriage.[50] But it seemed highly unlikely to Kingsmill Moore, J. that the Constitution intended, without clear words, to reverse what was a practically universal rule of conflict of laws, so as to result in spouses being treated as married under the law of one country and divorced under the law of another.[51]

Kingsmill Moore, J. considered that the remaining words of Article 41.3 were "not without difficulty".[52] The words of sub-section 3 did not declare that a

---

[45] *Id.*, at 347.

[46] *Id.*

[47] *Id.*, at 348.

[48] *Id.*, at 349.

[49] In England, prior to legislation in 1971 dealing with the subject, the trend of decisions was in favour of recognising extra-judicial divorces: see *Har-Shefi* v. *Har-Shefi (No. 2)*, [1953] P. 220 (Pearce, J.), *Russ (otherwise Geffers)* v. *Russ*, [1964] P. 315 (C.A., 1962), *Qureshi* v. *Qureshi*, [1972] Fam. 173 (Sir Jocelyn Simon, P., 1970), *North*, ch. 11.

[50] Cf. *supra*, p. 214.

[51] [1958] I.R., at 349. This argument is of debatable force. The problem of limping divorces existed before 1937 and remains today. In view of the strong opposition to divorce evident in the Article as a whole, it would seem unwise to interpret Article 41.3.3° as placing any particular emphasis on mitigating the problem of limping divorces.

[52] [1958] I.R., at 349.

divorced person whose marriage continued to subsist under our law could not *anywhere* contract a marriage valid *within our jurisdiction*, but merely prohibited the contracting within our jurisdiction of a valid marriage: "It is the contracting of the second marriage within the jurisdiction which is prohibited. There is nothing to make it invalid if contracted elsewhere."[53]

Unfortunately, Kingsmill Moore, J. did not elaborate on this line of thought. It suggests that a second marriage, contracted abroad after a divorce not recognised under our conflict rules, should be recognised here. This is surely a most unlikely conclusion. Indeed, it would imply that Article 41, far from narrowing the common law rules as to divorce recognition, would have extended them to the point that all foreign divorces would be efficacious. Where a divorce was recognised under the common law rules, a divorced party might validly contract a second marriage within the State; where, however, it was not capable of recognition, a valid second marriage might still be contracted, provided only that the parties took the precaution of marrying outside the State. One suspects that Kingsmill Moore, J. may not have been entirely clear on the distinction between the question of recognition of foreign divorces, on the one hand, and capacity to marry, on the other.[54]

Kingsmill Moore, J. went on to state his conclusions as to the general policy of Article 41:

> "The Constitution does not favour dissolution of marriage. No laws can be enacted to provide for a grant of dissolution of marriage in this country. No person whose divorced status is not recognised by the law of this country for the time being can contract in this country a valid second marriage. But it does not purport to interfere with the present law that dissolutions of marriage by foreign courts, where the parties are domiciled within the jurisdiction of those courts, will be recognised as effective here. Nor does it in any way invalidate the anomalous, if not scandalous, state of affairs stigmatised in the passages which I have already cited whereby legitimacy and criminality could be decided by a flight over St George's Channel."[55]

Maguire, J. expressed no view on the question of recognition of foreign divorces. O'Daly, J. considered it unnecessary to offer any opinion on this question in view of his holding that the order for costs was unenforceable on the grounds of public policy. But he did venture the opinion that Article 41.3.3° appeared "to put in the power of the Oireachtas to define from time to time what marriages dissolved by civil tribunals are to be regarded as valid subsisting marriages under our law, *id est*, what foreign civil divorces shall not be recognised as valid."[56]

This view, if accepted without qualification, would mean, for example, that the Oireachtas, could enact a law providing for the recognition of a foreign divorce based on 24 hours' presence in the foreign country granting the divorce, or in some other manner requiring neither spouse to have any significant connection with that country. Perhaps Article 41.3.3° is not inconsistent with this interpretation but surely such a law would offend against other constitutional provisions, in relation to the Family, for example, as well, perhaps, as those in relation to personal rights and rights as to property.

The Commentators' View of Mayo-Perrott

Kingsmill Moore, J.'s approach received the clear support of most of the

---

[53] *Id.*
[54] See *supra*, pp. 238-239.
[55] [1958] I.R., 336 (Sup. Ct., aff'g High Ct., Murnaghan, J.).
[56] *Id.*, at 351.

commentators,[57] as well as the Irish[58] and English courts.[59] It also appears to harmonise with the intent of the drafters of the Constitution.[60]

Of particular interest is Mr William Duncan's pertinent observation that Kingsmill Moore, J.'s judgment:

"renders Article 41.3.3° otiose. Article 41.3.3° does for the rules of divorce recognition what Article 50.1 at any rate does for all pre-existing laws which are not inconsistent with the Constitution. The rules regulating divorce recognition were part of these pre-existing laws, so there seems little reason to give them a private subsection to ensure their continuance in force."[61]

Recognition Based on Domicile in Cases Since Mayo-Perrott

Overwhelmingly the decisions between *Mayo-Perrott* and the 1986 legislation favoured Kingsmill Moore, J.'s interpretation of Article 41.3.3°, and recognised foreign divorces based on the common domicile of the spouses.[62]

[57] See, e.g. *North*, 376, Webb, *Case Note*, 18 Int. & Comp. L.Q. 744 (1959), J. Kelly, *Fundamental Rights in the Irish Law and Constitution*, 203 (2nd ed., 1967), Jones, *The Non-Recognition of Foreign Divorces in Ireland*, 3 Ir. Jur. (n.s.) 29 (1968), Clarke, *Comments on the Foregoing Article, II*, 57 Studies 24 (1968), Duncan, *The Future of Divorce Recognition in Ireland*, 2 Dublin U.L. Rev. (No. 1) 2 (1971), Kerr, *The Need for a Recognition of Divorces Act*, [1976] 1 Dublin U.L.J. 11, *Contra*, Lee, *Irish Matrimonial Law and the Marital Status*, 16 N. Ir. L.Q. 387, at 389-90 (1969), Davitt, J., writing in 1968, considered the question to be "wide open": *Some Aspects of the Constitution and the Law in Relation to Marriage*, 57 Studies 6, at 15 (1968): cf. *id.*, at 13 and see Clarke, *Comments on the Foregoing Article*, II, 57 Studies 24, at 24 (1968).

[58] *In re Caffin dec'd; Bank of Ireland* v. *Caffin*, [1971] I.R. 123 (High Ct., Kenny, J.) *C.* v. *C.*, unreported, High Ct., Kenny, J., 27 July 1973 (1973-144Sp.) (extracted in *Binchy*, 237), *Gaffney* v. *Gaffney* [1975] I.R. 133 (Sup. Ct., 1975, aff'g High Ct., Kenny, J., 1973), *L.B.* v. *H.B.*, [1980] I.L.R.M. 257 (High Ct., Barrington, J.), *N.M.* v. *E.F.M.*, unreported, High Ct., Hamilton, J., July 1978 (1977-No. 87 EMO), *Dalton* v. *Dalton*, [1982] I.L.R.M 418 (High Ct., O'Hanlon, J., 1981), *T.* v. *T.*, [1983] I.R. 29 (Sup. Ct., 1982 rev'g High Ct., D'Arcy, J., 1981), *M.C.* v. *K.E.D. (otherwise K.C.)*, Sup. Ct., 13 December, 1985 (292-84), *Sexton* v. *Looney*, High Ct., Murphy, J., 8 July 1985 (83/40m).

[59] Karminski, J., in *Breen* v. *Breen*, [1964] P. 144 (1961), criticised by Unger, *Note: Capacity to Marry and Lex Loci Celebrationis*, 24 Modern L. Rev. 784 (1961). See also Kerr, *supra*, at 14.

[60] *North*, 376, fn. 188, referring to J. M. Kelly, *Fundamental Rights in the Irish Law and Constitution*, 2nd ed., p. 201, fn (1967) 12 and Kahn-Freund, [1974] — II Hague Recueil 139, at 231-232.

[61] Duncan, *The Future of Divorce Recognition in Ireland*, 2 Dublin U.L. Rev. 2, at 2 at 5 (1971). Mr Duncan added in a footnote (*id.*, fn. 14):

"The argument might be advanced that Article 41.3.3° was needed to show that the recognition of foreign divorces is not implicitly prohibited within the Republic. But it is not easy to detect such an implication."

Mr Duncan also considered (*id.*) that the historical basis of Mr Justice Kingsmill's view might be weak:

"There were no cases reported between 1922 and 1937 in which the rule was accepted or laid down that a divorce granted by a court of the common domicile of the parties would be recognised in Ireland. Kingsmill Moore, J. therefore relies on the nineteenth century case of *Sinclair* v. *Sinclair*, [1896] 1 I.R. 603, in which an Irish court certainly did state that the . . . English rule was also the Irish rule. And if this was the Irish rule prior to 1922 it must be admitted the Article 73 of the 1922 Constitution guaranteed its continuance in force until 1937. However, there are two facts which weaken the authority of any ruling made in *Sinclair* v. *Sinclair* concerning divorce recognition. First, it was in no way necessary for the decision to determine whether the English divorce should be recognised. The only point which the case decided directly was that a decree of divorce *a mensa et thoro* was not a necessary preliminary to obtaining a full divorce by private Act of Parliament. Second, the Irish courts had been following a different path from the English courts in matters of divorce since 1857, in which year the English courts had, but the Irish courts had not, been given the power to grant a divorce *a vinculo*. Nor were the Irish courts ever given such a power. So there is some reason to suggest that the rules developed by the English courts concerning divorce, including the recognition rules, were not relevant or applicable in Ireland, as was assumed in *Sinclair* v. *Sinclair*."

Mr Duncan pointed out that it might be argued against this interpretation that the English recognition rule itself first appeared before 1857 (cf. *Warrender* v. *Warrender*, 2 Cl. & F. 488 (1835)), at a time when divorce could be obtained in England (as in Ireland) only by private Bill.

[62] Whether recognition might also be afforded on other grounds is considered *infra*, pp. 280-281.

The approach of the courts is of some considerable significance, because section 5(5) of the Domicile and Recognition of Foreign Divorces Act 1986 provides that the new statutory rules for recognition introduced by that Act apply only to divorces granted after the commencement of the Act on 2nd October 1986. Thus, when the question arises, at any time after that date, as to whether a divorce obtained before that date should be recognised, the court must apply the pre-legislative rules of recognition.

In *In re Caffin Deceased; Bank of Ireland* v. *Caffin*,[63] proceedings were taken to determine which of two women was entitled to elect to take a legal right, as surviving spouse, of half the estate of the deceased testator. The first marriage had taken place in England where both parties to it were then domiciled. They were divorced in England while they were again domiciled there. The second marriage took place in Dublin at a time when the second wife was domiciled and resident in Ireland, her husband then being domiciled and resident in England.

Kenny, J. held that the divorce should be recognised and that the second wife was thus entitled to elect. He did not accept the view of Maguire, C.J. in *Mayo-Perrott*[64] that subsection 3 was designed to "double-bar the door in subsection 2": Kenny, J. said:

> "The two sub-sections are dealing with different branches of the law and I do not agree with him that 'the subsection says as plainly as it could be said that a valid marriage which is dissolved under the law of another State remains in the eyes of our law a subsisting valid marriage' — because the sub-section does not say this. If this was the meaning which it was intended to express, the sub-section would have read: — 'No person whose marriage has been dissolved under the civil law of any other State shall be capable of contracting a valid marriage within the jurisdiction of the Government and Parliament established by this Constitution during the lifetime of the other party to the marriage so dissolved.' What Maguire, C.J. said ignores altogether the significance of the words 'under the law for the time being in force within the jurisdiction of the Government and Parliament established by this Constitution'."[65]

In the Supreme Court case of *Gaffney* v. *Gaffney*,[66] Walsh, J. expressly approved of Kingsmill Moore, J.'s interpretation of Article 41.3.3°. He added:

> "It follows, therefore, that the Courts here do not recognise decrees of dissolution of marriage pronounced by foreign courts unless the parties were domiciled within the foreign court in question."[67]

Griffin, J. was more cautious: he observed that, for the purpose of the case before the Court, it was "not necessary to decide whether and to what extent, if at all, the recognition of a decree of divorce *a vinculo* made by a foreign court is inconsistent with or repugnant to any of the articles of the Constitution"[68] and he expressed no view on this question.

In the later decision of *T.* v. *T.*,[69] the Supreme Court's holding was again consistent with Kingsmill Moore, J. 's approach.

[63] [1971] I.R. 123 (High Ct., Kenny, J.) analysed by O'Reilly *Note: Recognition of Foreign Divorce Decrees,* 6 Ir. Jur. (n.s.) 293 (1971), and by Duncan, *Desertion and Cruelty in Irish Matrimonial Law,* 7 Ir. Jur. (n.s.) 213, at 232-235 (1972).

[64] [1958] I.R., at 344.

[65] [1971] I.R., at 130. See also *C.* v. *C.*, unreported, High Ct., Kenny, J., 27 July 1973 (1973-144Sp.), extracted in *Binchy,* 237.

[66] [1975] I.R., at 133, at 150 (Sup. Ct.).

[67] *Id.*

[68] *Id.*, at 159-160.

[69] [1983] I.R. 29. See also *Sachs* v. *Standard Bank (Ireland) Ltd.*, Sup. Ct., 18 July 1986 (284/85) and *L.B.* v. *H.B.*, [1980] I.L.R.M. 257 (High Ct., Barrington, J.), where it was accepted by both parties and the Court that Kingsmill Moore, J.'s approach in *Mayo-Perrott* was correct.

The Proviso as to the Domicile of Dependency of Married Women

Up to this point we have been proceeding on the basis that the domicile of dependency of married women had the effect of making a wife's domicile dependent on that of her husband in every case. In several of the decisions[70] already considered, the wife's domicile, if determined independently, would very probably have been found to have been different from that of her husband.

It should, however, be mentioned[71] in this context that some doubts were cast on this approach in a couple of cases. In *Gaffney* v. *Gaffney*,[72] Walsh, J. considered that it was:

"possible that some day [the principle of a wife's domicile of dependency] may be challenged on constitutional grounds in a case where the wife has never physically left her domicile of origin while her deserting husband may have established a domicile in another jurisdiction."

In *M.C.* v. *K.E.D. (otherwise K.C.)*,[73] McCarthy, J. referred to Walsh, J.'s doubts and observed, again *obiter*, that he was not to be taken as accepting that this principle had survived the entitlement of the Constitution.

A Doubt About Northern Ireland

It is worth recording briefly a doubt about divorces obtained in Northern Ireland raised but not further addressed by Kenny, J., in *Re Caffin deceased; Bank of Ireland* v. *Caffin*.[74] Kenny, J. observed that his judgment in that case was "not a decision on the difficult question ....whether a divorce granted by the Courts in Northern Ireland to a person domiciled there will be recognised by our law...."[75]

It is unclear precisely what doubt was in Kenny, J.'s mind on this matter. On principle there should be no difficulty in our law recognising a divorce obtained in Northern Ireland by spouses domiciled there, since the two jurisdictions are different areas for the purpose of domicile.[76] Possibly the provisions of Articles 2 and 3 regarding the national territory were troubling Kenny, J., though why they should have done is not plain. There seems no prospect that these Articles would be capable of being invoked to deny recognition to a divorce otherwise capable of commanding recognition.

Recognition Based on Grounds other than Domicile

We must now consider whether, before the enactment of the Domicile and Recognition of Foreign Divorces Act 1986, a divorce might have been recognised on grounds other than those of domicile. The issue was never completely resolved, but there is good reason to be cautious about supporting any suggested non-domiciliary ground, if the issue arises in the future in respect of a divorce obtained before 2 October 1986.

The first point to notice is that, within the ordinary rules relating to precedent, it was always possible for our courts (prior to the 1986 Act) to have developed our recognition rules beyond what had previously been articulated in the decisions. A similar power resided in the Oireachtas. In *Gaffrey* v. *Gaffrey*[77] Walsh, J. said:

[70] E.g. *T.* v. *T., supra, Re E.E.L. (An Infant). supra, Sinclair* v. *Sinclair, supra, Maghee* v. *M'Allister, supra.*
[71] Cf. *supra*, p. 80.
[72] [1975] I.R., at 152 (Sup. Ct.).
[73] Sup. Ct., 13 December 1985 (292-84).
[74] [1971] I.R. 123 (High Ct., Kenny, J.).
[75] *Id.*, at 130.
[76] Cf. *supra*, pp. 47-49.
[77] [1975] I.R., at 151.

"Neither Article 73 of the Constitution of Saorstát Éireann nor Article 50 of the present Constitution (by virtue of which the common law recognition principle based on domicile survives) could be construed as freezing our common law or other non-statutory law in the condition in which it was found at the coming into force of the Constitution of 1922 so that it could never be departed from save by enactment of the Oireachtas."

Of course, as has been mentioned, there must be limits to the scope of divorce recognition legislation which the Oireachtas may enact. If, for example, the Oireachtas were to enact legislation recognising the validity of a divorce based on a week's residence abroad, this would scarcely be valid in view of the constitutional pledge of the State in Article 41.3.1° to "guard with special care the institution of Marriage, on which the Family is founded, and to protect it against attack".

Let us now turn to the judicial decisions in which the issue arose. In *M.C.* v. *K.E.D. (otherwise K.C.)*[78] the petitioner challenged the validity of her marriage with the respondent on the basis that he had no capacity to marry her since he was at the time of the marriage, already married to another person. The respondent had obtained a divorce in England from his first wife but the petitioner argued that this divorce was not recognised under Irish law since the respondent was not domiciled in England at the time of the divorce.

The respondent fought the case unsuccessfully at trial on the basis that he had in fact been domiciled in England at the time of the divorce. On appeal to the Supreme Court the respondent argued that the divorce should be recognised, not on the basis of his domicile in England at the time of the divorce, but on the entirely different ground that the evidence adduced disclosed a connection on his part with England "of so substantial and close a nature at the time of the ... divorce proceedings as ought to have induced the trial Court to accord recognition to the decree...."

This ground was not one simply clutched out of the air. It was a ground for divorce recognition which had been accepted by the House of Lords in the decision of *Indyka* v. *Indyka*.[79] Lord Wilberforce in *Indyka* had expressed the opinion that it would be in accordance with social and legal developments and with the trend of legislation

"to recognise divorces given to wives by the courts of their residence wherever a real and substantial connection is shown between the petitioner and the country, or territory, exercising jurisdiction. I use these expressions so as to enable the courts, who must decide each case, to consider both the length and quality of the residence and to take into account such other factors as nationality which may reinforce the connection. Equally they would enable the courts (as they habitually do without difficulty) to reject residence of passage or residence ... resorted to by persons who properly should seek relief here for the purpose of obtaining relief which our courts would not give."[80]

The "real and substantial connection" test did not last long in England. It was stigmatised by the English and Scottish Law Commissions as being "inherently vague and the source of much uncertainty where certainty is desirable".[81] The Commissions recommended that divorces should not be recognised on this basis. An important reason for making this recommendation was that the grounds for recognition in the Hague Convention were so extensive as to render the "real and substantial connection" test entirely otiose.

This advice was followed in the legislation on divorce recognition in Britain in 1971,[82] which specified an exclusive list of grounds for recognition of foreign

---

[78] Sup. Ct., 13 December 1985 (292-84).
[79] [1969] 1 A.C. 33.
[80] *Id.*, at 106. See also *id.*, at 112 (*per* Lord Pearson).
[81] Report on the Hague Convention on Recognition of Divorces and Legal Separations, para. 25, (1970).
[82] Recognition of Divorces and Legal Separations Act 1971. In Canada there has been a considerable body of support for the "real and substantial connection" test: e.g. *Goldin* v. *Goldin*, 104 D.L.R.

divorces, which did not include the "real and substantial connection" test.

Of course, in Ireland, where domicile has afforded the sole basis of recognition the relevance of an argument in favour of the real and substantial test is quite different.

In *M.C.* v. *K.E.D. (otherwise K.C.)*, the issue never got off the ground. The Supreme Court were unanimous that the respondent should not be permitted to change course so radically on appeal. None of the evidence at trial had been directed to the question of whether either of the parties had a real and substantial connection with England. The Supreme Court, said Finlay, C.J., was being asked to decide a point of law "as a moot.... in advance of the hearing of any evidence significantly relevant to the principle of law involved".[83]

The Chief Justice observed:

> "It may well be, as was urged upon the Court, that anomalies exist in the law of domicile when applied to the recognition of foreign divorces. It may well be that this area of law, the reform of which has been recommended by the Law Reform Commission should receive statutory attention, but that is not a reason in itself for considering a test other than the well-established test of domicile which was the only test put forward in the High Court and the only test which arises on the facts of this case."[84]

Finlay, C.J. went on to make some comments which, though *obiter*, indicate a considerable lack of enthusiasm for the proposed new ground of recognition. It was "of importance" that, so far as *Indyka* v. *Indyka* supported the "real and substantial connection" test, all the judgments were largely based on the existence of statutory provisions in England which created exceptions to the general law of domicile in the context of divorce, none of which was applicable in Ireland. So far as the "real and substantial connection" test was based on the principle of reciprocity arising from the entitlement in England to base a divorce petition on three years' residence without domicile, Finlay, C.J. commented that, "in this country where there is no provision for divorce, such a principle does not apply either".

The Chief Justice was quite satisfied that the Court should not entertain a consideration of the ground of recognition proposed by the respondent; to do so "would be much more likely to lead to substantial injustice in the application of any decision of this Court to other parties than it could possibly contribute to any requirement of justice in the instant case before us."[85]

McCarthy, J.'s concurring judgment made the same point in even stronger terms. The Court was being asked:

> "to declare, upon a theoretical set of facts, that decisions of both this Court and the former Supreme Court were fundamentally wrong, notwithstanding that the law of this country and the actions of citizens of this country based upon that law, have assumed it to be as so stated at least since 1957. In that context, public policy is not confined to the status of a child as here, but extends to the affairs of the community as a whole over the last decade (since *Gaffney*) or over 28 years (since *Mayo-Perrott*). In my judgment, it would be utterly wrong to embark upon such an enquiry."[86]

(3d) 76 (Ont. Sup. Ct., Salhany, Co. Ct., J. (L.J.S.C.), 1979), *Clarkson* v. *Clarkson,* 86 D.L.R. (3d) 694 (Man. Q.B., Wright, J., 1978), *Haut* v. *Haut,* 86 D.L.R. (3d) 757 (Ont. High Ct., Carruthers, J., 1978), *Holub* v. *Holub,* 71 D.L.R. (3d) 698 (Man. C.A., 1976) (O'Sullivan, C.J.'s, dissent (at 705) is worth noting), *Keresztessy* v. *Keresztessy,* 73 D.L.R. (3d) 347 (Ont. High Ct., Donohue, J., 1976), *La Carte* v. *La Carte,* 60 D.L.R. (3d) 507 (B.C. Sup. Ct., Andrews, J., 1975), *MacNeill* v. *MacNeill,* 53 D.L.R. (3d) 486 (Ont. Sup. Ct., Winter, Co. Ct. J. (L.C.S.C.), 1974), *Berinton (otherwise Hewitson)* v. *Hewitson,* 47 D.L.R. (3d) 510 (Ont. High Ct., Lacourciere, J., 1974); cf. *Powell* v. *Cockburn,* 68 D.L.R. (3d) 700 (Sup. Ct. Can., 1976), where the issue was raised but did not, in the event, require resolution.
[83] P. 9 of Finlay, C.J.'s judgment (Henchy, Griffin and McMahon, JJ. concurring).
[84] *Id.,* p.10.
[85] *Id.,* p.11.
[86] Pp.4-5 of McCarthy, J.'s judgment.

STATUTORY CHANGES TO DIVORCE RECOGNITION RULES

The Domicile and Recognition of Foreign Divorces Act 1986 has made radical changes in the rules for recognition of foreign divorces. All of the proposed changes relating to the recognition of foreign divorces are contained within a single section − section 5 of the Act.

The central provisions of this section are subsections (1) and (4). Section 5(1) provides as follows:

"For the rule of law that a divorce is recognised if granted in a country where both spouses are domiciled, there is hereby substituted a rule that a divorce shall be recognised if granted in the country where either spouse is domiciled."

And section 5(4) provides that:

"In a case where neither spouse is domiciled in the State, a divorce shall be recognised if, although not granted in the country where either spouse is domiciled, it is recognised in the country or countries where the spouses are domiciled."

Thus, the general rules for recognition of foreign divorces are quite clear under the Act: *a divorce granted in the country where either spouse is domiciled or (where neither spouse is domiciled in the State) recognised in the country or countries where the spouses are domiciled, will be recognised under Irish law.*

An interesting question arises as to the extent to which section 5(1) extends the recognition rules under common law. The answer depends on how one looks at the common law. Prior to the Act, two rules came together to yield a result for which neither, viewed in isolation, was responsible. These were: (1) that a divorce would be recognised here only if obtained in the country of the spouses' common domicile, and (2) that the wife's domicile was one of dependency, determined by her husband's domicile. The combined effect of these two rules was that a divorce obtained by either spouse in the country of the domicile of *one* spouse − the husband − would be recognised here, in spite of rule (1), which required that the divorce be obtained in the country of the domicile of *both* spouses.

Those supporting the change brought about by section 5(1) of the Act argued that it does no more than remove sex discrimination from our law in this context. The common law already permitted recognition of a foreign divorce based on the domicile of *one* spouse (the husband). The Act merely applied the *same* rule to a divorce based on the domicile of the *other* spouse. This, it may be said, is merely an application of the "sauce for the goose" principle.

However, those opposing section 5 of the Act argued that it went further. They contended that the effect of rule (2), at common law, had been to pervert and thwart the operation of rule (1). With the removal of rule (2) from our law (by section 1 of the Act), rule (1) should be permitted to apply without hindrance. Rule (1) required that the divorce be obtained in the country of the domicile of *both* spouses. To introduce a rule (as section 5 of the Act does) basing recognition on a divorce obtained in the country of the domicile of one of the spouses is to reintroduce, quite needlessly, a harmful side-effect of the former rule as to domicile of dependency of married women, and to multiply the problem by two by applying it to both spouses.

On the other hand, opponents of section 5 of the Act were accused of seeking to tighten up the law of divorce recognition. Proponents of section 5 claimed that, unless this extension were made, circumstances which up to then had justified the recognition of foreign divorces here (by reason of the application of the wife's domicile of dependency) would no longer have that effect. To this, the opponents of section 5 replied as follows. It is now universally agreed, by supporters and opponents of divorce alike, that the domicile of dependency was a bad rule, capable of resulting in injustice and hardship to married women. A significant part of that injustice — indeed, probably the *most* significant part of that injustice in the context of divorce — was the effective preference it gave to divorce over marriage.

The effect of section 5(1) is to extend recognition to a divorce obtained in the country where *either* spouse is domiciled. No less than under the former discredited rule of recognition, the effect of section 5(1) is inappropriate and unjust to the wife in resulting in her losing the status of wife by reason of a divorce obtained in a country with which she may have no connection whatsoever. Moreover, the new rule does little to harmonise with the general spirit of Article 41 of the Constitution. All it does is extend this type of injustice to men as well as women.

As against this, we must have regard to the position of a spouse domiciled in a foreign country who wants a divorce where that country permits it. Unless the change made by the Act (or something like that change) was made, that person would have been prevented from obtaining a divorce capable of recognition under our law in any case where the other spouse remained domiciled (or, indeed, had acquired a domicile) in Ireland. It would be wrong also to ignore the fact that the spouse who remains in Ireland may wish to avail himself or herself of the opportunity to obtain a foreign divorce against a spouse who has gone to live abroad permanently.

From the standpoint of legislative policy, a choice must be made. Our conflicts rules of recognition may either permit one spouse unilaterally to break the marriage tie effectively, or they should require that, before this can be done, both spouses should be domiciled in the country where the divorce is obtained or recognised.[87] The Act favours the first option. The effect is that we must recognise a foreign divorce in cases where a spouse leaves the family, goes abroad, acquires a domicile in a foreign country and divorces the spouse who is left behind with the children. The spouse who remains at home loses all rights to succession and maintenance,[88] other than such maintenance rights, however small, as may have been given under the divorce.[89] It would seem also that the spouse who remained at home would lose all rights under the Family Home Protection Act 1976.[90] Indeed, it may be argued that such wide-ranging implications, damaging and unjust to the spouse who remains in Ireland, would be contrary to the Constitution. The domicile of dependency, prior to its abolition, gave rise to constitutional doubts.[91] Fuelling these doubts must be a consideration of the injustice and hardship to a wife resulting from the recognition of a divorce obtained in a country where she was not domiciled.

The effect of section 5 is to re-introduce and extend much of the practical injustice of the domicile of dependency, since the rule that a divorce based on the domicile of only one of the spouses should be recognised here strips the spouse who remains here of much of the legal protection given to married people in Ireland. In blunt terms, the Court may take the view that the right to marry for life should take priority over the right to avail oneself of an opportunity to divorce on unilateral demand offered by the law of the country of domicile of one of the spouses, and denied by the country where the other spouse is domiciled.

Another option open to the Court would be to invoke the rule that the Act should be interpreted, if possible, in a manner consistent with the Constitution and to hold that, on that approach, the "single spouse's domicile" rule could be tolerated if surrounded by implicit protections to be articulated in the fullness of time by the

---

[87] Cf. section 5 (4) of the Act, discussed *infra*, pp. 283-284.
[88] Unless our courts accept the principle of "divisible divorce": cf. pp. 303-304, *infra*.
[89] Where the spouse obtaining the divorce lives in a distant country, these rights of post-divorce maintenance may be of no practical use to the divorced spouse.
[90] This appears to have been accepted in *L.B.* v. *H.B.*, [1980] I.L.R.M. 257 (High Ct., Barrington, J.).
[91] Cf. *Gaffney* v. *Gaffney*, [1975] I.R. 133, at 152 (*per* Walsh, J.), *M.C.* v. *K.E.D. (otherwise K.C.)*, Sup. Ct., 13 December 1985 (292-85), (*per* McCarthy, J.), at p. 5 of his judgment.

Court itself. It is doubtful whether the Court would be attracted by this approach.

Let us now consider briefly subsections (2) and (3) of section 5. Subsection (2) provides that:

"in relation to a country which has in matters of divorce two or more systems applying in different territorial units, this section shall, without prejudice to subsection (3) of this section, have effect as if each territorial unit were a separate country."

Thus, in the United States of America, where each State has its own divorce law, a divorce obtained in California (or, indeed, New Jersey) by a spouse domiciled in New York will not be recognised here under subsection (1) (although, as we shall see, it may in some instances be capable of recognition under subsection (4)). Where a country has a unitary divorce law applying throughout all its constituent States or Provinces, subsection (2) will not apply. Thus, in Canada (which has such a unitary divorce law) a divorce obtained in British Columbia by a spouse domiciled in Ontario will be recognised here by virtue of subsection (1).

Subsection (3) provides as follows:

'A divorce granted in any of the following jurisdictions —

(a) England and Wales,
(b) Scotland,
(c) Northern Ireland,
(d) the Isle of Man,
(e) the Channel Islands,

shall be recognised if either spouse is domiciled in any of those jurisdictions."

This subsection may be explained by the fact that the five jurisdictions it mentions are different "countries" for the purposes of the conflict of laws, but under present British law a divorce obtained in any of them is automatically recognised in the other four. It was considered by the proponents of the legislation that it would be "artificial" to refuse recognition of a divorce obtained by a spouse in such circumstances. As against this view, it can be argued that there is no necessary connection between the grounds for divorce in the five different jurisdictions, nor must it necessarily be the case that British law will continue to adhere to a rule of automatic recognition. It is perhaps a source of concern that the example used by the Minister of State in support of the subsection during both Dáil and Seanad debates was misleading: there is no need to invoke subsection (3) where both spouses are domiciled in England and a divorce is obtained in Scotland, since subsection (4) will ensure that the divorce is recognised. Subsection (3) contributes a distinctive change in the law only in a case where the country in which the divorce is obtained is one in which neither spouse is domiciled, and the divorce would not be recognised under subsection (4).

Section 5(4) of the Act provides that:

"In a case where neither spouse is domiciled in the State, a divorce shall be recognised if, although not granted in the country where either spouse is domiciled, it is recognised in the country or countries where the spouses are domiciled."

Thus, for example, a divorce obtained in the Netherlands where the spouses are domiciled in Sweden will, if recognised in Sweden, also be recognised here. Similarly where a divorce is obtained in the Netherlands and the spouses have *different* domiciles, in Norway and Sweden, respectively, the divorce will be recognised here if recognised in *both* Norway and Sweden. This subsection has no effect on a divorce where Ireland is the country of domicile[92] of either or both of the spouses. The effect of subsection (4) is to provide for recognition of many divorces were the law of the

---

[92] Of course, it is possible that the spouses, or either of them, may be *resident* here; but section 5(4) requires that neither of them be domiciled here.

country (or countries) of the spouses' domicile recognises divorces obtained elsewhere.[93]

Section 5(6) of the Act provides that nothing in section 5 is to affect a ground on which a court may refuse to recognise a divorce, "other than such a ground related to the question whether a spouse is domiciled in a particular country, or whether the divorce is recognised in a country where a spouse is domiciled". Thus, for example, recognition may be denied to a divorce on the ground that is contrary to natural justice or to public policy. It could be argued that public policy may serve to temper some of the injustice that may result from recognition of a foreign unilaterally-obtained divorce in the country of one only of the spouses. The manner in which subsection (6) is drafted makes this a matter of speculation.

Let us finally turn to consider very briefly what the Act does *not* contain. It says nothing about ancillary orders granted in foreign divorce proceedings, nor does it provide any protection to spouses and children who are the victims of a harsh foreign divorce, possibly obtained at the unilateral demand of a deserting spouse. In view of the wide extension of grounds for recognition this seems to contain a potential for considerable harshness and injustice for some family members.

GROUNDS FOR NON-RECOGNITION OF A FOREIGN DIVORCE DECREE

In some cases a divorce which fulfils the jurisdictional requirements of our conflict rules may nonetheless not be recognised. Let us examine each of them in turn.

Fraud

Fraud is an important ground for refusing to recognise a foreign divorce decree. This issue is considered later in the context of foreign judgments.[94] Very briefly, it may be noted here that the general approach in common law countries is to restrict the scope of non-recognition of foreign divorces to cases of fraud as to the jurisdiction of the foreign court.[95] In the Irish decision of *L.B.* v. *H.B.*,[96] however, Barrington, J. refused to recognise a divorce where the parties' lawyers had effectively invented grounds for divorce, since he considered that there had been "a substantial defeat of justice for which the parties, and not the Court, bear the responsibility".[97] Barrington, J. was of the view that in the circumstances of the case, this ground should not be characterised as one of fraud[98] (which had been abandoned in the course of the proceedings). He cited two English decisions[99] in support of the proposition that " [c]learly matters which have been fully heard and determined before a competent tribunal should not lightly be reopened".[100] These decisions restricted the scope of fraud to fraud as to the jurisdiction. There is nothing in Barrington, J.'s judgment committing him to this limitation, however.

---

[93] This principle was recognised in the English case of *Armitage* v. *A.G.*, [1906] P. 135. The question whether this principle was part of Irish law was not addressed in any case. It is possible that it may yet arise in relation to a divorce obtained before 2 October 1986.

[94] *Infra*, pp 606-608.

[95] Cf. *Bater* v. *Bater*, [1906] P. 135 (C.A.) (esp. at 218 (*per* Sir Gorell Barnes), and 239 (*per* Cozens Hardy, L.J.)), *Crowe* v. *Crowe*, [1937] 2 All E.R. 723 (P.D.A. Div., Bucknill, J.) See also *Gaffney* v. *Gaffney*, [1975] I.R. 133 (Sup. Ct., 1975, aff'g High Ct., Kenny, J., 1975).

[96] [1980] I.L.R.M. 257 (High Ct., Barrington, J.), discussed in detail in the section immediately following. For a perceptive, critical analysis of the decision, see Duncan, *Collusive Foreign Divorces — How to Have Your Cake and Eat It*, 3 D.U.L.J. 17 (1981).

[97] *Id.*, at 270. See further *infra*, pp. 608, 609.

[98] Cf. *infra*, pp. 606, 608.

[99] *Bater* v. *Bater*, *supra*, *Crowe* v. *Crowe*, *supra*.

[100] [1980] I.L.R.M., at 268.

Failure to Comply with Natural or Constitutional Justice

Where a divorce is obtained contrary to natural or constitutional justice, it may not be recognised here. This principle applies to all foreign judgments.[101]

In *L.B.* v. *H.B.*,[102] which has just been mentioned, a married couple domiciled in France obtained a divorce there in 1957. Both parties wished to be divorced. The husband had submitted a petition for divorce and the wife a cross-petition. It transpired that the divorce decree was given on the ground of the wrongful behaviour of the wife, based on evidence manufactured by means of documentary evidence arranged with the assistance of lawyers acting for the spouses. If the divorce court had become aware that either the parties or their lawyers had been in collusion to manufacture evidence, it would certainly have rejected the petition. But, once the decree of divorce was made final and absolute, it could not be upset even though it had been obtained by collusion. The parties had already entered into an agreement providing for the wife's maintenance and her occupation of a house in England and for the husband to have custody of their son.

The divorce did not mark the final break between the parties. They continued to "preserve the semblance of a marriage for the sake of their son".[103] Later the husband bought property in Ireland. The wife,[104] who lived in one of these houses, took proceedings against him in the Irish High Court, claiming a maintenance order under the Family Law (Maintenance of Spouses and Children) Act 1976 and a share in the beneficial interest in the house in which she was living. The husband resisted these claims on the basis that the effect of the French divorce was that the plaintiff was no longer his wife. To this the wife originally responded by pleading that the divorce was one that ought not to be recognised on the grounds that it had been obtained "by fraud, which amounted to a substantial denial of justice" to her.[105] During the hearing, the wife's counsel was permitted to substitute a plea of collusion for a plea of fraud.

In the central passage in his judgment, Barrington, J. said:

> "It is clear that the wife's original plea could not succeed as there was no fraud or no substantial denial of justice *inter partes*. The collusion however, between the parties was such that the entire proceedings became a charade and the French Court was unwittingly led to a conclusion which had been pre-determined by the parties. There was a substantial defeat of justice for which the parties, and not the Court, bear the responsibility.... This Court is fixed with knowledge of matters of which the French Court had no knowledge. It is accordingly no disrespect to the French Court if it refused to recognise a divorce obtained in such circumstances. Indeed, once this Court has been fixed with knowledge of what happened in the French divorce proceedings it is hard to see how it could recognise the validity of the divorce and at the same time observe the constitutional duty of the State to uphold the institution of marriage."[106]

The passage provokes a number of observations. First, Barrington, J. holds that fraud as to the grounds for the divorce decree may constitute the basis for non-recognition by the Irish court of the divorce, not under the heading of "fraud" but that of "a substantial defeat of justice[107] for which the parties, and not the Court bear the responsibility". It is difficult to understand Barrington, J.'s rejection of

---

[101] See further, *infra*, pp. 608-609.
[102] *Supra*.
[103] [1980] I.L.R.M., at 260.
[104] For convenience of narration this term is used though the question of her status was of course, at issue.
[105] The wife also (unsuccessfully) contested her husband's French domicile.
[106] [1980] I.L.R.M., at 270-271.
[107] Cf. *Shatter*, 271 who argues that the denial of recognition on this ground "introduced considerable uncertainty into the law... ."

the argument based on the heading of "fraud". It was "clear" to him that this argument could not succeed "as there was no fraud or no substantial denial of justice *inter partes*". But the essence of fraud as a ground for non-recognition of a foreign divorce, whether the fraud goes to the question of jurisdiction or otherwise, is that the *court* was misled; whether one of the parties was also misled is irrelevant to this ground (though it may be of relevance in certain instances in relation to estoppel).

L.B. v. *H.B.* may have some significant implications in view of the current state of divorce law internationally. In many countries where it is possible to obtain a postal divorce by consent or on unilateral demand, there is a certain reluctance by the legislature and the courts to admit openly what this entails. The strategy adopted has been to grant divorces with no questions asked. Many of these divorce decrees are obtained on the basis of untrue or inaccurate assertions made by the spouses. On the basis of *L.B.* v. *H.B.*, they may not be capable of recognition; yet in the countries where they are obtained it appears that often those involved in the judicial process are content to let matters stand. It may seem incongruous that the Irish court should be required to remain solicitous for the integrity of foreign courts if those courts themselves are willing to tolerate the presentation of false evidence to them. What Barrington, J. is anxious to stress is that the Irish court should not become a party to the cheapening of marriage and the judicial process in this way.

Duress

It may happen that a spouse is forced by threats to initiate divorce proceedings or not to oppose them. In such circumstances, should the decree be recognised here? There is relatively little discussion of this question by either the courts or the commentators in common law jurisdictions. It would be possible to refuse recognition on the basis that recognition would offend the forum's public policy[108] or on account of failure to comply with natural justice.[109] Public policy is, however, a somewhat general ground of unpredictable scope. Failure to comply with natural justice offers a more specific solution, since it would be impossible to argue that participation in legal proceedings under duress complied with the principles of natural justice.[110]

In *Gaffney* v. *Gaffney*,[111] recognition was denied to an English divorce obtained by spouses who were not domiciled there. The evidence disclosed that the wife had been coerced by her husband into taking the proceedings. In view of the separate holding that the divorce should not be recognised as failing to fulfil the requirements as to domicile,[112] the Supreme Court did not have to resolve the issue of duress. However, Walsh, J. observed that:

> "it might well be that . . . it would be incumbent upon the plaintiff to have the decree of dissolution, made by the court having jurisdiction, set aside before she could successfully assert the status of wife."[113]

At trial, Kenny, J. had favoured a more direct approach. He said:

> "It is established law that a marriage may be declared null if it is entered into because of duress and, in my view, a similar principle applies to an application for a decree

---

[108] Cf. *supra*, pp. 207-208.
[109] Cf. *infra*, pp. 608-609.
[110] Cf. *Dicey & Morris*, 358, para. 11.
[111] [1975] I.R. 133 (Sup. Ct., 1975, aff'g High Ct., Kenny, J., 1973).
[112] Cf. *supra*, p. 289.
[113] [1975] I.R., at 153-154.

of divorce. There is no reason in logic or in principle why, if the doctrine of duress applies to contracting a marriage, it should not apply to its termination by divorce."[114]

If Kenny, J.'s approach is followed, the question arises as to the extent to which the analogy with duress in the context of marriage should control the resolution of the issue in relation to divorce. Under Irish law, duress vitiates matrimonial consent not merely in cases of threats to life or bodily integrity but also in a wide range of other circumstances where a party's freedom or capacity to consent has been interfered with.[115] It does not matter whether the duress was exercised by the other party to the marriage.

It would be unwise for our courts in divorce recognition cases to apply without modification the principles relating to duress in nullity cases. The policies served by nullity law are different from those in divorce. Both marriage and divorce involve the question of status, but beyond that it is difficult to see close similarities. Our law of nullity, in fashioning rules as to duress, is seeking to prescribe the parameters of a legally binding irrevocable commitment. Thus duress in nullity law embraces pressures imposed by third parties,[116] as well as by the other party to the marriage. But it is not self-evident that third party pressure on one spouse, unknown to the other, should vitiate a divorce. Divorce is not necessarily a consensual process. A spouse affected by duress may be either petitioner or respondent. If, for example, a respondent fails to oppose divorce proceedings because of pressures brought upon him or her by a third party, unconnected with the petitioner, it may be argued that the policy questions are somewhat different from those arising in relation to duress which results in a party going through a ceremony of marriage against his or her will.[117] The suggestion here is not that the scope of duress should be narrower in relation to divorce than to nullity; merely that it is not necessarily identical.

Let us now briefly consider Walsh, J.'s suggestion that it may be necessary for the party affected by duress to have the decree of divorce set aside before being permitted to assert the status of spouse in the Irish courts. The advantages of this approach include the discouragement of forum shopping and of "limping" divorces. A difficulty is that if the law of the country where the divorce is obtained has only a limited entitlement to have the decree overturned on the ground of duress,[118] a spouse who is divorced as a result of duress may be prejudiced.

Estoppel[119]

We must now consider the difficult question of estoppel in relation to divorce. Estoppel may be by *record* or by *conduct*. The former presents no great problem.

---

[114] *Id.*, at 139. Kenny, J. agreed with the approach favoured by Bagnall, J., in *Re Meyer*, [1971] P. 298 (P.D.A. Div., 1970). See further Canton, *Note: Duress and Estoppel in Matrimonial Causes*, 94 L.Q. Rev. 15, at 16 (1978). In England, section 8(2) of the Recognition of Divorces and Legal Separations Act, 1971 effectively rendered duress a matter for the court's discretion to refuse recognition, whether on the grounds of public policy (cf. *Dicey & Morris,* 355) or denial of an opportunity to a party to take part in the proceedings (cf. *id.*, 358, paragraph 11).

[115] Cf. the Law Reform Commission's *Report on Nullity of Marriage*, pp. 32-33 (L.R.C. 9-1984).

[116] See, e.g. N. *(otherwise K.)* v. *K.,* [1986] I.L.R.M. 75 (Sup. Ct., 1985), *M.K. (otherwise M.cC)* v. *F. McC.,* [1982] I.L.R.M. 277 (High Ct., O'Hanlon, J.), *A.C.L.* v. *R.L.*, High Ct., Barron, J., 8 October 1982, *H.* v. *H.,* [1954] P. 258 (Karminski, J., 1953), noted by Woodhouse, *Lack of Consent as a Ground for Nullity and the Conflict of Laws*, 3 Int. & Comp. L.Q. 454 (1954) and by Stone, *Mariage de Convenance*, 17 Modern L. Rev. 149 (1954), *Parojcic* v. *Parojcic*, [1959] 1 All E.R. 1 (P.D.A. Div., Davies, J., 1958), *Buckland* v. *Buckland (otherwise Camileri)*, [1968] P. 296 (Scarman, J., 1965), *Szechter (otherwise Karsov)* v. *Szechter*, [1971] P. 286 (Sir Jocelyn Simon, P., 1970); cf. *Anon., Note*, 30 Colum. L. Rev. 714 (1930).

[117] It is worth noting here the possible relevance of public policy. In view of the constitutional pledge to "guard with special care the institution of Marriage", the courts may be disposed to interpret the scope of duress broadly in relation to divorce.

[118] Cf. *Power*, 324-325.

[119] See *North*, 384-385, Duncan, *Foreign Divorces Obtained on the Basis of Residence, and the Doctrine of Estoppel*, Ir. Jur. 59, at 60-62 (1975).

In *Gaffney* v. *Gaffney*,[120] the Supreme Court gave short shrift to the argument that an English divorce obtained by a false assertion of English domicile should be recognised here in spite of an allegation that the wife had been acting under duress. Part of that argument was to the effect that the wife, being petitioner for the divorce, was estopped by the record from impugning the correctness of what she had put on record by obtaining the divorce decree. Henchy, J. said:

> "The flaw in this argument is that the divorce decree could be a judgment *in rem*, carrying with it the rule of estoppel by record, only if it had been given within jurisdiction.[121] If it be shown that the English court had no jurisdictional competence to make the order, such order is a nullity and is incapable of supporting an estoppel of record. If the absence of jurisdiction had appeared on the face of the decree, there would have been no doubt about its worthlessness as a foundation for estoppel. I fail to see why, although the decree seems good on its face, evidence should not be received to show that its facade conceals a lack of jurisdiction no less detrimental to its validity than if it had been written into the order. To hold otherwise would be to close one's eyes to the available truth and to give effect instead to a spurious divorce which the English court was deluded by sworn misrepresentations into making.
>
> The position is not affected by the fact that it is a foreign decree. The comity of courts under private international law does not require or permit recognition of decisions given, intentionally or unintentionally, in disregard of jurisdictional competence....I am satisfied that there can be no estoppel by record when the record arose in proceedings, domestic or foreign, upon which the court in question had no jurisdiction to adjudicate."[122]

We must now consider estoppel by *conduct*. If a spouse who has participated actively in foreign divorce proceedings, by petitioning or by consenting to the granting of a decree, later seeks to challenge the validity of the divorce, in what (if any) circumstances will he or she be estopped from doing so? This question was also considered by the Supreme Court in *Gaffney* v. *Gaffney*.[123] Walsh, J. said:

> "The paramount issue in the present case is the status of the plaintiff and her husband at the date of his death. The plaintiff was either his wife or she was not. Apart from other legal incidents in this country, certain constitutional rights may accrue to a woman by virtue of being a wife which would not be available to her if she were not. The matter cannot, therefore, by any rules of evidence, be left in a position of doubt nor could the Courts countenance a doctrine of estoppel, if such existed, which had the effect that a person would be estopped from saying that he or she is the husband or wife, as the case may be, of another party when in law the person making the claim has that status. In law it would have been quite open to the husband to have denied at any time after his marriage to the defendant that he was in law her husband. If during the currency of that marriage the plaintiff had claimed that she was his wife, she might have been met with the answer which is being offered on behalf of the defendant in this case — that the plaintiff was estopped from doing so because she had submitted to a jurisdiction which purported to change that status. Consent cannot confer jurisdiction to dissolve a marriage where that jurisdiction does not already exist. The evidence which the plaintiff sought to offer in the present case was directed towards showing that the court in question did not have jurisdiction. In my view, the learned trial judge was quite correct in admitting that evidence."[124]

[120] [1975] I.R. 133 (Sup. Ct., 1975, aff'g High Ct., Kenny, J., 1973).

[121] Citing Halsbury's Laws of England (3rd ed.), vol. 15, p. 168, para. 336, at p. 178, para.351.

[122] [1975] I.R., at 154-155.

[123] *Supra.* In *Maghee* v. *M'Allister*, 3 Ir. Chy. Rep. 604 (1853) and *C.* v. *C.*, unreported, High Ct., Kenny, J., 27 July 1973 (1973-144Sp.), extracted in *Binchy*, 237, the defence of estoppel by conduct was summarily rejected. In C. v. C., Kenny, J. relied on the reasons he had given in *Gaffney* v. *Gaffney*. These are considered *infra*, p. 289.

[124] [1975] I.R., at 152.

Henchy, J. favoured a somewhat different approach. He referred to the argument made on behalf of the husband that the wife was estopped from attacking the divorce because she had executed a deed some time after the divorce in which she commuted the alimony payable to her under the divorce. Henchy, J. conceded that there might be "some force"[125] in this submission if the deed had been the genuine act of the plaintiff. But the trial judge had held that the deed had been procured by duress and no appeal had been made against this finding. It was therefore "impossible"[126] to hold that the plaintiff had approbated the divorce decree when the act of approbation relied on was not her free voluntary act.[127] It would seem that Henchy, J. would countenance the defence of estoppel by conduct where there was no question of duress or other barrier to the voluntariness of the act.

In the High Court, Kenny, J. had expressed his objection to estoppel in forcible, though not fully convincing, terms. There would be

> "startling consequences if it be held that a spouse domiciled in one State who obtains an invalid divorce in another State is estopped in the State of the domicile from establishing that the divorce was invalid, and that she should not be regarded as the spouse for the purposes of succession. Bigamy is an extra-territorial offence.... If the husband had been prosecuted in the Republic of Ireland for bigamy and the invalidity of the English divorce had been established, the jury would have had to convict him because a belief on reasonable grounds (if he had it) that he had been divorced, when in fact he had not, is not a defence to such a charge.... The result then would be that while the plaintiff would be prevented from proving the invalidity of the divorce, the husband would have been convicted of bigamy. If there had been children of the second marriage and if the husband died intestate (as he did), the plaintiff could not have disputed their legitimacy; but the children of the first marriage could have done so as the estoppel would bind the plaintiff only, and could exclude the children of the second marriage from any benefit by succession.... If the law is to avoid these ridiculous consequences, it seems to me that on principle the doctrine of estoppel does not apply to the question of the existence of a valid marriage or the status of being married though it may apply in relation to property rights between husband and wife."[128]

One can legitimately doubt whether the consequences of giving at least some effect to the estoppel defence would be as "ridiculous" as Kenny, J. states. There is, of course, a strong argument for people retaining a consistent status in public law — for voting, income tax, citizenship and so on; but there is an equally strong argument that, where private rights are concerned, a party should not be allowed to "approbate and reprobate" — to assert the validity of the divorce in one context and its invalidity in another.[129] If a spouse has obtained a foreign divorce, and no question of duress arises, why should it be unjust or socially dangerous for the court to hold that he or she was estopped from later asserting maintenance or succession rights against his or her former spouse?[130]

ANCILLARY ORDERS IN FOREIGN DIVORCE PROCEEDINGS

It is one thing to *recognise* a foreign divorce in the sense that the Irish court will accept that the divorce has changed the status of the parties concerned. It is quite another thing to give effect to all aspects of a divorce decree, as, for example, by enforcing orders for costs incurred in the divorce proceedings or orders for maintenance and financial provision.

[125] *Id.*, at 155.

[126] *Id.*

[127] Griffin, J.'s analysis of this question is along similar lines: cf. *id.*, at 157.

[128] *Id.*, at 141-142.

[129] Cf. *Downton* v. *Royal Trust Co.*, [1973] S.C.R. 437, 34 D.L.R. (3d) 403 (1972), Canton, *supra*, at 18-19, Duncan, *Foreign Divorces Obtained on the Basis of Residence, and the Doctrine of Estoppel*, 9 Ir. Jur. (n.s.) 59, at 60-62 (1975).

[130] Cf. Duncan, *supra*, at 62, *Downton* v. *Royal Trust Co.*, 34 D.L.R. (3d) 403, at 412-413 (Sup. Ct. Can., *per* Laskin, J., for the Court 1972), Clark, *Estoppel Against Jurisdictional Attack on Decrees of Divorce*, 70 Yale L.J. 45 (1960), *Scoles* v. *Hay*, 482-485, *Restatement, Second*, section 74.

In Mayo-Perrott v. *Mayo-Perrott*,[131] as we have seen, the Supreme Court unanimously refused to enforce an order for *costs* of foreign divorce proceedings, the Court taking the view that such an order could not be severed from the divorce decree itself. Maguire, C.J.'s judgment displayed such strong opposition to divorce that it seemed reasonable to assume that, had the issue related to alimony rather than costs, he would have held that the foreign order should not be enforced here. In a number of later decisions, however, it has been held that, in wide-ranging circumstances, a foreign maintenance order ancillary to a divorce is enforceable here.

Thus, in *N.M.* v. *E.F.M.*,[132] Hamilton, J. held that an English maintenance order made six years after a divorce there had become absolute could be enforced under the provisions of the Maintenance Orders Act 1974, and did not fall foul of section 9 which provides that a maintenance order made in a reciprocating jurisdiction should not be recognised or enforceable if recognition or enforcement would be contrary to public policy.

The manner in which Hamilton, J. came to this conclusion is of some interest. He accepted "unreservedly" that, if the recognition or enforcement of a maintenance order would have the effect of giving active assistance to facilitate "in any way" the effecting of a divorce or of giving assistance to the process of divorce, such recognition or enforcement would be contrary to public policy. But in the case before him the maintenance order had come six years after the divorce; so in enforcing and recognising this order, it could:

> "not be said that such enforcement or recognition is giving active or any assistance to facilitate in any way the effecting of dissolution of marriage or is giving assistance to the process of divorce. It is merely providing for the maintenance of spouses and as such can not be regarded as contrary to public policy."

One may wonder what Hamilton, J.'s response would have been, had the maintenance order been made directly on the granting of a divorce decree. The fact that he referred to the time-lag suggests that it might have been in some way significant to the outcome of the case; but Hamilton, J. did not attempt to explain its precise role. So far as he approved of the maintenance order as "merely providing for the maintenance of spouses" − in this case, former spouses − Hamilton, J. appeared to lay down no specific limitation on the enforceability of any maintenance order pursuant to divorce.

In *G.* v. *G.*,[133] Finlay, P. was faced with the question whether he should enforce an agreement made between spouses in Massachusetts under which the husband had undertaken to make specific maintenance for the support of their child. That agreement formed part of the subject-matter of an order made the same date by the Family Court in Massachusetts. The wife's claim was based on both the agreement and the order. At the time of the agreement and order, the wife had already filed for divorce, but a divorce *nisi* was not granted until over a year later. The judgment for divorce *nisi* incorporated the earlier order for the support of the child, as was the normal practice in Massachusetts.

Finlay, P. considered himself "of course....bound" by *Mayo-Perrott* not to enforce the order for maintenance unless satisfied that it was clearly severable from the divorce decree. He held that it was indeed so severable. The central passage from his judgment is worth recording in full:

---

[131] [1958] I.R. 336.
[132] Unreported, High Ct., Hamilton, J., July 1978 (1977-No. 87 EMO), extracted in *Binchy*, 255.
[133] [1984] I.R. 368 (High Ct., Finlay, P.).

"The law of this country does not recognise divorce and will not aid it. However, it does recognise, and in recent years has developed a strict and efficient code, for the imposition of liability on a parent to maintain a child. To revert to the test applied by O'Daly, J. (as he then was) in *Mayo-Perrott* v. *Mayo-Perrott*, a claim by a mother who has custody of a child against the child's father for a payment towards its maintenance is a form of action known to the Courts of this country and is regularly enforced by them.

It may well be that different considerations might apply where an order for custody of a child has been granted to one parent for the first time and as an integral part of a decree for divorce in a foreign jurisdiction and where maintenance commenced only upon the making of that order. It does not seem to me that the principles laid down in the *Mayo-Perrott* case and the true interpretation of the relevant provisions of the Constitution would justify me in relieving the defendant from his obligation to pay maintenance for the support of his infant child merely by reason of what ... was a procedural convenience which altered the forum or particular vehicle whereby that liability was imposed without, apparently, altering the liability or reaching a separate conclusion about it."[134]

Finlay, P. was satisfied on the evidence that the order for maintenance was a final judgment capable of being enforced in Ireland.[135]

In *Sachs* v. *Standard Chartered Bank (Ireland) Ltd*[136], the facts were somewhat complex but, expressed simply, the issue arising in the case was whether an order for financial provision made against a husband in English divorce proceedings, requiring him to pay his former wife £35,000 sterling as a lump sum within seven days, was enforceable in Ireland.

Counsel for the husband argued that *Mayo-Perrott* was authority for the proposition that this order was not enforceable here on account of public policy. Barrington, J. and the Supreme Court on appeal rejected this argument without hesitation. Barrington, J. commented:

"A woman's right to have such a financial provision made for her arises not because she was divorced but because she was married and the marriage has broken down. It would be strange if the public policy of Ireland allowed one to recognise the divorce but debarred one from upholding the vestigial rights of the wife."[137]

The Supreme Court, affirmed.[137] Finlay, C.J. considered that it would be an "extraordinarily anomalous position"[138] if the divorce could be recognised but not "a final judgment for maintenance".[139] The Chief Justice stated:

"The provision of maintenance arising from the obligation of a spouse in a marriage to a dependent spouse is something recoverable within the law of this country and something for which ample provision has been made by relatively modern legislation. In these circumstances it seems to me that not only should public policy not be deemed to prevent the enforcement of this judgment, but ... the requirements of public policy seem clearly to favour it."[140]

There would of course be an irony if public policy opposing divorce resulted in a divorced wife or husband or the children becoming destitute. To this extent the decision is to be welcomed. But it may be doubted whether the best way of ensuring

---

[134] *Id.*, at 374.
[135] Cf. *infra*, pp. 308-309.
[136] Sup. Ct., 18 July 1986, aff'g High Ct., Barrington, J., 30 July 1985.
[137] p. 10 of Barrington, J.'s judgment.
[138] Page 5 of Finlay, C.J.'s judgment.
[139] *Id.*, p. 6.
[140] *Id.*, p. 7.

adequate protection for spouses and children with close Irish connections is merely to "rubber stamp" a foreign decree for post-divorce maintenance, which international trends prove to be a paltry and ineffective amount in many cases. Our courts could be empowered by legislation to act on the principles of our existing statutory provisions (such as the Family Home Protection Act 1976, and the Family Law (Maintenance of Spouses and Children) Act 1976) so as to ensure adequate protection for the rights of a spouse divorced abroad (where the divorce is recognised here) with respect to maintenance, and occupation and beneficial ownership of the family home.

The Law Reform Commission has made recommendations on these lines in its Working Paper No. 11-1984, *Recognition of Foreign Divorces and Legal Separations*,[141] and in its later Report[142] on the same subject. The Commission recommended that, in exercising its discretion, the Irish court should have regard to all the circumstances of the case including:

(a) the extent to which each of the spouses actively participated in the foreign divorce proceedings;

(b) the respective resources of the spouses;

(c) the respective ages and health of the spouses;

(d) the extent (if at all) to which the orders ancillary to the foreign divorce decree adequately protect the interests of each spouses.

The Commission said that:

"In the light of international experience especially with regard to maintenance obligations following a divorce, we consider it essential to include statutory provisions along these lines. The general international trend has been towards reducing the amount and duration of support of divorced women. We consider that, for persons with close connections with Ireland, some discretionary protection is necessary, to deal with cases of hardship or injustice."[143]

The Hague Convention on Recognition of Divorces and Legal Separations (1970)[144]

We must now consider very briefly the implications for Irish law of the Hague Convention on Recognition of Divorces and Legal Separations (1970). The Convention prescribes wide-ranging grounds for recognition of divorces: as well as fairly traditional grounds, such as the nationality of the spouses or the habitual residence of the respondent. Article 2 of the Convention provides for recognition based on the habitual residence or nationality of the *petitioner*, if certain extra requirements are fulfilled.[145]

[141] W.P. No. 11-1984, pp. 67-68.

[142] L.R.C. 10-1985.

[143] W.P. No. 11-1984, p. 68.

[144] See Batiffol, *La Onzieme Session de la Conférence de La Haye de droit international privé*, 58 Rev. Crit. de Dr. Int. Priv. 215, at 216-226 (1969), von Mehren & Nadelmann, *The Hague Conference Convention of June 1, 1970 on Recognition of Foreign Divorce Decrees*, 5 Fam. L.Q. 303 (1971), Duncan, *The Future of Divorce Recognition in Ireland*, 2 Dublin U.L. Rev. (No. 1) 2, at 8ff (1969), Graveson, Newman, Anton & Edwards, *The Eleventh Session of the Hague Conference on Private International Law*, 18 Int. & Comp. L.Q. 619, at 620-643 (1969) (*Commission I: The Recognition of Divorces and Legal Separations*, by Professor Anton), and the Law Reform Commission's Working Paper No. 11-1984, *Recognition of Foreign Divorces and Legal Separations*, pp. 31-66.

[145] Where the petitioner's habitual residence is the basis of recognition, it must have continued for at least the previous year in the country in which the divorce is obtained and the spouses must last have habitually resided there together: Article 2(2); when the petitioner's nationality is the basis of recognition *either* (i) it must be supplemented by one year's continuous habitual residence in that country by the petitioner, falling, at least in part, within the two years preceding the institution of divorce proceedings or (ii) the petitioner must have been present in that State at the date of the institution of the proceedings and the spouses must last have habitually resided together in a State whose law, at the date of the institution of the proceedings, did not provide for divorce: Article 2(4) and (5).

The Convention is in harmony with the contemporary international view of marriage and divorce: in countries where divorce may be obtained by consent or at the unilateral insistence of one spouse, without any serious judicial scrutiny,[146] there may seem little point in solicitude about onerous jurisdictional requirements for divorce.[147]

Nevertheless Ireland continues to support the *favor matrimonii* principle. The question thus arises as to what is the best means of harmonising this approach with the preference of countries elsewhere for the *favor divortii* principle.[148] The Convention is reasonably sensitive to cultural pluralism in this context and does not seek to press too far a single normative structure. Article 19(2) permits a Contracting State to reserve the right to refuse to recognise a divorce when, at the time it was obtained, both parties habitually resided in States which did not provide for divorce; and Article 20 permits Contracting States whose law does not provide for divorce to reserve the right not to recognise a divorce where one of the spouses was a national of a State whose law did not provide for divorce.

The Law Reform Commission have proposed[149] that Ireland should ratify the Convention, availing itself of these reservations. The Commission make detailed recommendations designed to ensure that the constitutional protection of the Family is not subverted by over-extensive divorce recognition rules. Thus, the Commission propose that, where both spouses are habitually resident in the State at the date of the institution of the divorce proceedings, a foreign divorce obtained by them should not be recognised here. A person would be deemed to be habitually resident in the State when, having been habitually resident here, he temporarily ceased to reside here and acquired a temporary residence abroad for the primary purpose of obtaining a foreign divorce. The Commission recommend that, where one of the spouses is an Irish citizen and only one of them is habitually resident here, the spouses having last habitually resided together in the State, a foreign divorce should be recognised here only if the spouse habitually resident here submitted to the jurisdiction of the foreign court and the divorce is obtained in the country where the other spouse is habitually resident at the date of the institution of the proceedings.

Of course any attempt to find a *via media* between fundamentally differing views of marriage is bound to lend itself to the easy criticism that the lines of demarcation should have been drawn differently. As in so many other areas of law reform there is a dilemma between adopting "black letter" rules which can create anomalies, and a more discretionary approach, which may lead to unpredicability and variation in application from judge to judge.

[146] Cf. *A Better Way Out: Suggestions for the Reform of the Law of Divorce and Other Forms of Matrimonial Relief*, pp. 14-15 (A Discussion Paper prepared by the Family Law Sub-Committee of the English Law Society, January 1979).

[147] Cf. The Law Reform Commission's W.P. No. 11-1984, pp. 18-20.

[148] Cf. Siehr, *Domestic Relations in Europe: European Equivalents to American Evolutions*, 30 Am. J. of Comp. L. 37, at 50 (1982).

[149] In their *Report on Recognition of Foreign Divorces and Legal Separations* (L.R.C. 10-1985).

CHAPTER 13

DIVORCE A MENSA ET THORO AND
RESTITUTION OF CONJUGAL RIGHTS

DIVORCE A MENSA ET THORO

The purpose of proceedings for divorce a mensa et thoro[1] is twofold. A decree for divorce a mensa et thoro entitles the petitioner to live apart from the respondent, without prejudicing valuable rights, including the right to maintenance and succession. Moreover, in appropriate cases the Court may order the respondent, if the husband, to pay alimony to his wife.

The three grounds for divorce a mensa et thoro are adultery, cruelty and "unnatural practices". Four absolute defences may be raised: recrimination, condonation, connivance and collusion. It also appears that conduct conducing to adultery constitutes a discretionary bar.

Proceedings for divorce a mensa et thoro have become practically redundant for several reasons. Spouses may prefer not to indulge in the process of making accusations and counter-accusations; the award of alimony is restricted in its scope; finally, and of most practical significance, legislation over the past twenty years or so, on such matters as protection of the family home, maintenance, and the custody of the children, have offered more attractive practical remedies. Proposals for changes in the law have been made by the Law Reform Commission, in its Third Report, in 1983. The Joint Oireachtas Committee on Marriage Breakdown also addressed the subject in its Report, published in 1985.

Let us now consider the conflicts aspects of the subject, beginning with the question of jurisdiction.

Jurisdiction

Residence

It seems clear that the residence of the respondent will constitute a good ground of jurisdiction. This was the position[2] before 1870, when the jurisdiction of the Ecclesiastical Courts was transferred to the newly-constituted Civil Court for Matrimonial Causes and Matters. Section 13 of the Matrimonial Causes and Marriage Law (Ireland) Amendment Act 1870 provided that:

"In all suits and proceedings, the said Court for Matrimonial Causes and Matters shall proceed and act and give relief on principles and rules which, in the opinion of the

---

[1] See *Shatter*, ch. 8, *Binchy* , ch. 8, *Geary*, ch. 8, 11-12, 566-567, *Browne*, 276-280, *Shelford*, ch. 5, *Burn*, vol. 2, 495-500a-503a, 503d-508a, Hayes, *The Matrimonial Jurisdiction of the High Court*, 8 Ir. Jur. (n.s.) 55, at 55-60 (1973), and the Irish Law Reform Commission's *Report on Divorce a Mensa et Thoro and Related Matters,* ch. 2 (L.R.C. 8 – 1983).
[2] Cf. *Carden* v. *Carden*, 1 Curt. 558, 163 E.R. 196 (1837). See also *Mason* v. *Mason*, [1944] N.I. 134, *Addison* v. *Addison,* [1955] N.I. 1, *Ward* v. *Ward*, [1960] N.I. 122, *Shelford*, 486.

said Court, shall be as nearly as may be conformable to the principles and rules on which the ecclesiastical courts of Ireland have heretofor acted and given relief...."

In *Gillis* v. *Gillis*[3] and *Sproule* v. *Hopkins*,[4] it was accepted that the residence of the respondent could be a good basis of jurisdiction. In the later decision of *Hood* v. *Hood*,[5] however, there is a suggestion that the residence of both parties would be necessary.

In England (prior to statutory change in 1973) the courts accepted that residence afforded a good ground of jurisdiction. The courts there were divided as to whether the residence of the respondent alone[6] or the residence of both parties[7] was necessary[8]; but they were clear that the residence of the petitioner alone would not suffice.

Domicile

Domicile was not a basis of jurisdiction under ecclesiastical law. Once the civil courts acquired authority over suits for divorce *a mensa et thoro*, however, the influence of domicile, so potent in relation to divorce *a vinculo*, was difficult to withstand.

In *Gillis* v. *Gillis* in 1874, Warren, J., after a review of the English authorities, was "of opinion that domicil without residence is sufficient to sustain the jurisdiction" in proceedings for divorce *a mensa et thoro*. In *Sproule* v. *Hopkins*,[9] in 1902, Andrews, J. also held that the respondent's domicile would afford a good basis for jurisdiction.

Other possible grounds

There is authority from Northern Ireland[10] for the proposition that the country of the matrimonial home of the spouses affords a good ground for jurisdiction in proceedings for divorce *a mensa et thoro*. In England, however, this ground has been rejected.[11] Dr. North[12] suggests that our courts should also reject it.

[3] I.R. 8 Eq. 597, at 603 (Ct. for Mat. Causes, Warren, J., 1874).
[4] [1903] 2 I.R. 133.
[5] [1959] I.R. 255, at 234-235.
[6] *Raeburn* v. *Raeburn*, 44 Times L.R. 384 (1928), *Sim* v. *Sim*, [1944] P. 87, *Sinclair* v. *Sinclair*, [1968] P. 189, *Keserue* v. *Keserue*, [1962] I W.L.R. 1406, *Garthwaite* v. *Garthwaite*, [1964] P. 356, at 390 (C.A., *per* Diplock, L.J., 1964), *Ross Smith* v. *Ross Smith*, [1963] A.C. 280, at 297 (H.L. (Eng.), *per* Lord Reid, 1962); see also *Hutter* v. *Hutter*, [1944] P. 98, at 99 (*per* Pilcher, J.), *Ramsey-Fairfax* v. *Ramsey-Fairfax*, [1956] P. 115, at 120 (*per* Willmer, J.).
[7] *Armytage* v. *Armytage* [1898] P. 178, *Anghinelli* v. *Anghinelli*, [1918] P. 247, *Matalon* v. *Matalon*, [1952] P. 233.
[8] *Graham* v. *Graham,* [1923] P. 31. Cf. *Riera* v. *Riera*, 112 L.T. 223 (1914).
[9] [1903] 2 I.R. 133, at 137. *Gillis* v. *Gillis* was not cited to the Court. See also *Egan* v. *Egan* [1928] N.I. 159 (K.B. Div. (Mat.)), *Eustace* v. *Eustace,* [1924] P. 45 (C.A., 1923). In *Beamish* v. *Beamish*, I.R. 10 Eq. 413 (Ct. for Mat. Causes, Warren, J.), a decree for divorce *a mensa et thoro* was granted against a wife who had gone to Australia. Although the report does not refer to the petitioner's domicile (or residence), it seems not unreasonable to conclude that his domicile, and thus (on the conventional view) that of his wife also, must have been Irish. In *Moore* v. *Moore*, I.R. 5 Eq. 172 (Ct. for Mat. Causes, Warren, J., 1871), I.R. 5 Eq. 371 (Ct. for Mat. Causes, Warren, J., 1871), the English-born respondent, having lived for seven or eight years in Ireland, left his wife and went to live in France. His attempt to challenge to jurisdiction was rejected on procedural grounds, but Warren, J. adverted to the question of domicile and expressed the view that the respondent was not domiciled in England. The implication would appear to be that the respondent was domiciled in Ireland; otherwise, the case could be explained either in terms of (*a*) the petitioner's residence in Ireland; (*b*) the respondent's *former* residence here; (*c*) the fact that the petitioner's domicile would have been Irish if the principle of the domicile of dependency was ignored; or (*d*) the respondent's former domicile in Ireland.
[10] *Wells* v. *Wells*, [1960] N.I. 112.
[11] *Sinclair* v. *Sinclair*, [1968] P. 189.
[12] *North*, 361.

Choice of law

In England, *Dicey and Morris* note that "[i]t has never been doubted"[13] that English domestic law will be applied in suits for legal separation, once the Court is satisfied that it has jurisdiction, even if the parties are domiciled abroad. The English Law Commission in its Report[14] in 1972 recommended that this policy continue. The same approach appears to apply to Northern Ireland.[15]

In this jurisdiction, there has been virtually no discussion of this problem.[16] In *Sproule* v. *Hopkins*,[17] the Court seems to have been disposed to regard the *lex fori* as applicable.

Recognition of Foreign Decrees

In England, *Dicey and Morris* note that "[i]t has never been doubted"[13] that surprising lack of authorities. In the only reported decision, *Tursi* v. *Tursi*[19] a decree for judicial separation[20] granted in Italy, the country of the spouses' domicile, should be recognised in England. Mr. Justice Sachs noted that:

"[a]s regards principle, the main argument pressed against recognition of decrees of judicial separation outside the country of domicile in which they were granted went thus. So far the courts of the country have only accorded recognition to a foreign domiciliary decree when it affected the status of the parties: decrees of judicial separation do not affect the status: accordingly, no such decrees should be here recognised. Whilst appreciating, of course, the practical distinction between those decrees that cut the bond of marriage and those that leave it subsisting, the above proposition, as stated in the way that appears to attract those who put it forward, savours to my mind somewhat of a blend of dogma and absence of precedent. It is the fact that hitherto the courts here have not accorded recognition to domiciliary decrees for judicial separation: but until now they have not been asked to do so — and, indeed, it is not surprising that before the Act of 1949[21] the occasion for such a request did not arise. So the argument against recognition, as thus stated, seems rather to beg the question of principle."[22]

Sachs, J. continued:

"The argument on principle for extra-territorial recognition springs from the fact that by the almost universal view of all civilised countries a special quality attaches to the decrees of domiciliary High Courts touching any contract of marriage between persons domiciled in the country of those courts, when that contract has validly resulted in married status: and then it runs thus. It is that special quality which is 'recognised' in the sense that the domiciliary decrees are treated as operative in other countries. The most drastic way in which a decree of a domiciliary court can affect a marriage is by dissolving it: and if recognition extends to the most drastic decree *a fortiori* it must cover a decree of lesser effect."[23]

Mr. Justice Sachs approved of the approach adopted by the Australian decision

---

[13] *Dicey & Morris*, 341 (9th ed.). See *Armytage* v. *Armytage*, [1898] P. 178.
[14] Law Com. No. 48, para. 66 (1972).
[15] *Wells* v. *Wells*, [1960] N.I. 122.
[16] Cf. *North*, 369.
[17] [1963] 2 I.R. 133.
[18] Recognition of Divorces and Legal Separations Act 1971, as amended by the Domicile and Matrimonial Proceedings Act 1973, s. 2.
[19] [1958] P. 54 (Sachs, J., 1957).
[20] A *separation legale*, on account of the husband's desertion and cruelty.
[21] Law Reform (Miscellaneous Provisions) Act, 1949.
[22] [1958] P., at 62.
[23] *Id.*, at 62-63.

of *Ainslie* v. *Ainslie*,[24] to the same effect as the passage quoted above.

On the possibility of residence as a basis of recognition, *Dicey & Morris* state that this "is an open question"[25], submitting that, if the decree is granted on the basis of the residence of both parties, or of the respondent, it should be recognised, but that if it is based on the residence of only the petitioner, it should not.[26] There are no decisions on this question in Ireland. Dr. North has suggested[27] that the English rules (prior to 1971) should be followed in this country.

RESTITUTION OF CONJUGAL RIGHTS[28]

Desertion is not a ground for divorce *a mensa et thoro* in our law.[29] Where one spouse deserts another, the spouse who has been deserted may avail himself or herself of the right to take proceedings for the restitution of conjugal rights.

If a spouse fails to comply with a decree for restitution of conjugal rights, a statute enacted in 1813 provides for committal to prison for a period not exceeding six months.[30]

The Law Reform Commission have sounded a warning note:

"One spouse may stop living with the other either by leaving the home or by excluding the other spouse from the home. In the case of a spouse who leaves the home, it could well be that the action for restitution of conjugal rights would be held to be inconsistent with one or more of several Constitutional rights, including the liberty of the person, freedom of association, the right to travel and earn a livelihood and the right to privacy. In the case of a spouse who excludes the other spouse from the home, it seems less likely that an action for restitution of conjugal rights would be held to be inconsistent with the Constitution. Indeed, as well as an action for conjugal rights the excluded spouse would in certain cases be entitled to obtain an injunction ordering the offending spouse to desist from all conduct that prevents the excluded spouse from entering the home."[31]

There are a number of defences to the action for restitution of conjugal rights, including those of uncondoned adultery or cruelty.

It is not, however, a good defence to show that the petitioner deserted the respondent. As Warren, J. stated in *Manning* v. *Manning*,[32] in 1873, "desertion, wilful or not, is no bar to restitution of conjugal rights, according to the law of Ireland". The question was examined again in *Dunne* v. *Dunne*[33] in 1947, where

---

[24] 39 C.L.R. 381 (1957). For criticism of extending the *Ainslie* rationale beyond inter-provincial recognition, see Grodecki, *Note: Effect of a Foreign Decree of Judicial Separation*, 20 Modern L. Rev., 636, at 637, fn. 4 (1957).

[25] *Dicey & Morris*, 337 (8th ed., 1967).

[26] Cf. *Hughes* v. *Hughes*, [1958] C.L.Y. 502 (judicial separation obtained in Denmark by petitioner resident but not domiciled there (on account of operation of domicile of dependency, it would appear) not recognised in England, the respondent's domicile and residence remaining English; reliance apparently on English domestic jurisdictional grounds for judicial separation as determinant of recognition of foreign decrees).

[27] *North*, 386.

[28] See generally, *Shatter*, 159-161, *Binchy*, 184-186, *Kisbey*, ch. 5, *Browne*, 261-262, *Shelford*, 574-582, *Burn*, vol. 2, 500b-500d, *Rogers*, 823-825, *Poynter*, ch. 17, *Geary*, 371-378, 565-566, *MacQueen*, 210-211, the Law Reform Commission's *Report on Restitution of Conjugal Rights, Jactitation of Marriage and Related Matters*, ch. 1 (L.R.C. 6–1983).

[29] Cf. Duncan, *Desertion and Cruelty in Irish Matrimonial Law*, 7 Ir. Jur. (n.s.) 213, at 218 (1972).

[30] Ecclesiastical Courts Act 1813, sections 1, 3 (53 Geo. III c. 127). See also *Shelford*, 582.

[31] *Report on Restitution of Conjugal Rights, Jactitation of Marriage and Related Matters*, p. 3 (L.R.C. 6–1983).

[32] I.R. 7 Eq. 520, at 523 (1873).

[33] [1947] I.R. 227 (High Ct., Dixon, J.).

Dixon, J. held that the law in this country was still the same as that expressed in *Manning* v. *Manning*.[34]

The Law Reform Commission have recommended[35] the abolition of the remedy of restitution of conjugal rights. The doubt about the consistency of the action with the Constitution was an important factor. The Commission considered, moreover, that the proceedings might be self-defeating where imprisonment of the unwilling spouse resulted in deprivation of maintenance to the petitioner.

Let us now turn to consider conflict of law aspects of the subject, beginning with the question of jurisdiction.

Jurisdiction

The residence of the respondent has been accepted by the Irish courts as a basis of jurisdiction. In the High Court decision of *Hood* v. *Hood*,[36] Murnaghan, J. held, after a careful analysis of the authorities, that:

"this Court has jurisdiction in a proceeding for the restitution of conjugal rights where the respondent is residing within the jurisdiction."[37]

To this rule the courts have engrafted an exception: where a respondent has no fixed residence, it seems that jurisdiction may be based on his last place of fixed residence. In *Cooper* v. *Cooper*,[38] the respondent husband who had been residing in Dublin, eloped in 1832 with another woman. Immediately after the elopement he made preparations for "abjuring the realm", and practically lived on his yacht. The petitioner took proceedings for restitution of conjugal rights in Dublin in 1835. The respondent challenged the jurisdiction on the basis that he had not been in Ireland for years except for a day at the Kingstown regatta, and except for a visit to the city of Dublin of three or four days' duration, during which he slept on board his yacht in the Bay, six miles off.

Dr Radcliff held that the court had jurisdiction. He referred to the English Statute of Citations[39] which made a fixed residence in the diocese the basis of the Ecclesiastical Court's jurisdiction. He regarded the Statute as "seeming to be in a great measure, declaratory"[40] of the previous law and added:

"The law or law-makers never intended in providing that a party should be convened before his own proper and convenient Judge, that he should, by going from place to place, evade the law altogether, and leave the plaintiff remediless, and to the beyond of losing his witnesses."[41]

There is, perhaps, some suggestion in Dr Radcliff's judgment that it was the departure by the respondent from the jurisdiction rather than the lack of a fixed residence on his part which entitled the petitioner to base jurisdiction on the respondent's former residence:

---

[34] *Supra*.

[35] In its Report on *Restitution of Conjugal Rights, Jactitation of Marriage and Related Matters*, p. 12 (L.R.C. 6–1983).

[36] [1959] I.R. 225 (High Ct., Murnaghan, J., 1958).

[37] *Id.*, at 242. English decisions (prior to the abolition of restitution of conjugal rights in 1971) were in accord: see, e.g. *Thornton* v. *Thornton*, 11 P.D. 176 (C.A., 1886), *Perrin* v. *Perrin*, [1914] P. 135 (Evans, P.).

[38] Milw. 373 (Dr Radcliff, 1836).

[39] 23 Henry VIII, c. 9.

[40] *Supra*.

[41] *Id.*

"His intent clearly was to live abroad, to avoid *all* the proceedings and penalties consequent on his *aime*; but he is constructively domiciled here."[42]

This dimension was again apparent in *Bell* v. *Bell*,[43] in 1922. There, the respondent, domiciled in Ireland, went to England on a short visit in 1921. On 13 August, he wrote to his wife, the petitioner, asking her to meet him at a Dublin hotel. There he informed her that he intended to leave her and live with another woman. It appears that the respondent returned to England shortly afterwards. He wrote to his wife, saying that his intention to leave her was irrevocable. He described his place of residence in London as his "permanent address". On 1 December 1921, the respondent transferred to the petitioner in the Land Registry his absolute interest in their matrimonial home. The petition for restitution of conjugal rights was issued in Dublin thirteen days later and served on the respondent on 9 December 1921.

Dodd, J. held[44] that the residence of the respondent afforded a good basis of jurisdiction:

"It would be a strange procedure that where the spouses are living in England, if the marriage was an Irish marriage, an aggrieved wife should not be entitled to apply to the Court in England for an order that her husband should receive her to his hearth and home there, the place of his residence: still more anomalous if she had to resort to an American Court."[45]

But, of course, the respondent in the case before him had not been living in Ireland during the four months between August and December of 1921. Was he not, therefore, residing in England rather than in Ireland? It appears that Dodds, J. thought that the respondent was still residing in Ireland, since he had "no doubt"[46] about having jurisdiction. His extensive discussion of *Cooper* v. *Cooper*,[47] which he described as an "illuminating"[48] authority, would suggest strongly that he simply regarded the respondent either as being still resident in Ireland, or as having no fixed residence, in which case the principle endorsed in *Cooper* v. *Cooper* would apply. Moreover, the decision of *Manning* v. *Manning*,[49] also discussed by Dodd, J., was concerned in large part with what constitutes *bona fide* residence. What makes one less certain about Dodd, J.'s precise analysis is that he went to some lengths[50] to establish that the respondent's domicile was Irish rather than English: why this should have been necessary if residence rather than domicile is the basis of jurisdiction is not clear. One possible interpretation, suggested by Dr. North, is that *Bell* v. *Bell* is authority for the proposition that "the court will assume jurisdiction if both spouses are domiciled in Ireland at the institution of the proceedings".[51] In England, it was

---

[42] *Id.*, at 389. It is, however, true that, on the same page, Dr Radcliff referred again to the fact that the respondent had "no certain or fixed domicile, residence, or abode, but is a mere wanderer, or vagabond, and . . . his place of abode in Ireland was in his diocese".

[43] [1922] 2 I.R. 152 (K.B.Div., Dodd, J.).

[44] Relying on *Manning* v. *Manning*, L.R. 2 P.&D. 223 (Lord Penzance, 1871).

[45] [1922] 2 I.R., at 155.

[46] *Id.*, at 158.

[47] Milw. 373.

[48] [1922] 2 I.R., at 157.

[49] *Supra*.

[50] Cf. *id.*, at 155.

[51] *North*, 367. Prior to abolition of restitution of conjugal rights in England in 1970, courts recognised the common domicile as a proper basis of jurisdiction in several cases: see, e.g., *Dicks* v. *Dicks*, [1899] P. 275 (Gorell Barnes, J.), *Perrin* v. *Perrin*, [1914] P. 135 (Evans, P.), *Bateman* v. *Bateman*, [1901] P. 136 (Gorell Barnes, J.). *Bateman* v. *Bateman* is of particular interest since its facts closely resemble *Bell* v. *Bell* in that, although the respondent arguably had abandoned his domicile with the jurisdiction, the court, perhaps out of sympathy for the deserted petitioner, held to the contrary. See also *Cowley* v. *Cowley*, 29 Times L.R. 690 (P.D.A. Div., Evans, P., 1913) and *Buckley* v. *Buckley*, unreported,

at one time suggested[52] in 1914 that jurisdiction should also be based on the fact that the parties had a matrimonial home in the country at the date when their cohabitation ceased, but this view was subsequently discredited.[53] In England, the courts have also rejected the residence of the petitioner alone,[54] or the celebration of the marriage in the jurisdiction[55] as grounds for jurisdiction for proceedings for restitution of conjugal rights.

Choice of law[56]

There are no decisions in which choice of law has been discussed.[57] It has been suggested by Dr. North that having regard to the similarity between this action and proceedings for divorce *a mensa et thoro*, the *lex fori* should be applied.[38]

Recognition of foreign decrees

Since most countries have abolished proceedings for restitution of conjugal rights, the question of recognition of foreign decrees is not of any practical importance. In the absence of judicial authority,[59] the courts would probably be disposed to apply rules similar to those relating to divorce *a mensa et thoro*,[60] or, perhaps, to the domestic jurisdictional rules relating to restitution of conjugal rights.[61]

---

cited by counsel in *Perrin* v. *Perrin, supra*, at 137, where the court's sympathy for the deserted petitioner appears to have induced it to extend the scope of domicile very far.
[52] *Perrin* v. *Perrin, supra*, at 140. See also *Milligan* v. *Milligan*, [1942] P. 78 (Henn Collins, J.).
[53] *Sinclair* v. *Sinclair*, [1963] P. 189 (C.A., 1967).
[54] *Yelverton* v. *Yelverton* , 1 Sw. & Tr. 524, 164 E.R. 866 (1859).
[55] *De Gasquet James* v. *Mechlenburg-Schwerin*, [1914] P. 53.
[56] See *North*, 371.
[57] The position in England prior to the abolition of the action in 1970 was similar.
[58] *North*, 371. So also in England, it was "never . . . doubted that . . . domestic law w[ould] be applied . . .": *Dicey & Morris* (8th ed., 1967), 336.
[59] *North*, 300-301, 388.
[60] *Id.*, 300, 38.
[61] *Id.*, 388.

CHAPTER 14

MAINTENANCE ENTITLEMENTS

Most countries contain laws requiring spouses to maintain each other and requiring parents to support the members of their family, whether born within or outside marriage. But these laws have varied widely. Thus, for example, we find that, at different times, some countries have imposed maintenance obligations on the husband alone, others on both spouses equally;[1] some (including Ireland) enable a maintenance order to be made while the spouses are living together; others make separation a precondition of entitlement to apply for maintenance;[2] in some countries maintenance is in nature of a quasi-criminal or public obligation, in others it is viewed as a private civil obligation. Where maintenance of children born outside marriage is concerned, there is again a very considerable divergence,[3] with the role of the state authorities in pursuing fathers ranging from a fairly passive one in most common law jurisdictions to a very active one in some European, especially Scandinavian, countries.[4]

Moreover, the position is at present in a process of rapid change internationally. With the widespread adoption of no fault divorce, maintenance entitlements have been transformed. Since marriage no longer carries an irrevocable commitment for life, courts and legislatures increasingly have regarded lifelong maintenance as being no longer appropriate. Thus we find that spousal maintenance is awarded to fewer spouses, less frequently, in less amounts, and for shorter periods than formerly.[5]

For Ireland, where marriage still involves a lifelong irrevocable commitment, some interesting and difficult issues of policy arise in relation to conflict of laws aspects of maintenance obligations. To what extent should our courts exercise jurisdiction to make maintenance orders if either of the parties has close connections with a country where marriage is now regarded as involving only a revocable commitment? Where the question of the recognition and enforcement of foreign maintenance orders arises, should our courts treat divorce merely as a "response" to marriage breakdown (just as proceedings for maintenance in this country may in some cases be a response to marriage breakdown), and enforce maintenance orders made in divorce proceedings, however small they may be? If so, should our law give some subsidiary support to an Irish woman living here, deserted by her husband, who divorces her abroad in proceedings where the woman receives only a pittance as maintenance?

---

[1] See Binchy, *Family Law Reform in Ireland—Some Comparative Aspects*, 25 Int. & Comp. L.Q. 901, at 901-905 (1976), *Weyrauch & Katz*, 281-282, Payne, *Maintenance Rights and Obligations: A Search for Uniformity, Part I*, 1 Fam. L. Rev. 1 (1978).

[2] See Binchy, *supra*, at 906-907.

[3] See *Krause*, chs. 4-6.

[4] *Eekelaar*, 210.

[5] Bruch, *Of Work, Family Wealth, and Equality*, 17 Fam. L.Q. 99 (1983), Payne, *Policy Objectives of Private Law Spousal Support Rights and Obligations*, ch. 3, of K. Connell-Thouez & B Knoppers eds., *Contemporary Trends in Family Law: A National Perspective* (1984).

These questions are of real practical significance, and require considered analysis by our courts and by the Oireachtas. When the EEC Judgments Convention is given legislative effect, it will be interesting to examine its effects in this context.

JURISDICTION

The Family Law (Maintenance of Spouses and Children) Act 1976[6] has modernised the law relating to family maintenance obligations. Now a spouse may apply for a maintenance order where the other spouse has failed to provide proper maintenance for the family. It is not necessary to show that the respondent spouse is guilty of any other wrong; nor is it necessary that the spouses have ceased to live together. Desertion by the applicant spouse affords an absolute defence, adultery a discretionary defence.

The jurisdictional provisions of the Act[7] do not address the international dimensions. This omission is probably explained by the historical background to the Act. Before 1971 the only jurisdiction exercised by the High Court in respect of spousal[8] maintenance was through the remedy of divorce *a mensa et thoro*, under which periodical payments of alimony might be awarded to the wife.[9] The District Court exercised exclusive jurisdiction under the Married Women (Maintenance in case of Desertion) Act 1886. It seems that there was no jurisdiction where the respondent spouse resided outside the State, and that jurisdiction could not be conferred by the consent of the parties.[10]

The Courts Act 1971 extended to the High Court the jurisdiction under the 1886 Act. The Family Law (Maintenance of Spouses and Children) Act 1976 is in some respects the natural successor to the 1886 Act. Thus it derives from a tradition based on the residence of the respondent spouse in a particular jurisdiction within the State.

In favour of basing jurisdiction on the residence of the respondent spouse it can be argued that otherwise, in cases where the spouses have no real connection with this country, an applicant spouse could "manufacture" jurisdiction here by coming to reside in the State. Spouses are not permitted to do this in relation to other matrimonial remedies, such as *divorce a mensa et thoro*.[11]

As against this, it can be argued that the needs of the applicant spouse should be given priority, since he (or more usually she) may otherwise be left destitute by a spouse who has left the jurisdiction. On this view, at least in cases where the spouses have shared a common residence within the State, jurisdiction based on the residence of the applicant spouse would be permissible, especially in cases where the respondent spouse has deserted the applicant spouse.[12]

CHOICE OF LAW

It seems clear that, when the court exercises jurisdiction under the 1976 Act, it will apply Irish law, regardless of the domicile of the spouses.[13]

---

[6] See Binchy, *supra*, Horgan, *The Irish Republic's New Maintenance Provisions*, 127 New L.J. 743 (1977).

[7] Family Law (Maintenance of Spouses and Children) Act 1976, section 23, as amended by the Courts Act 1981, section 12.

[8] Orders for the maintenance of children under the Guardianship of Infants Acts 1964 are considered *infra*, ch. 15.

[9] Cf. *supra*, p. 292.

[10] *Forsyth* v. *Forsyth*, [1948] P. 125 (C.A., 1947), *Macrae* v. *Macrae*, [1949] P. 272 (C.A.).

[11] Cf. *supra*, pp. 292-293.

[12] Cf. *E.D.* v. *F.D.*, unreported, High Ct., Costello, J., 23 October 1980 (1979—26 Sp.), extracted by *Binchy*, 201. In *L.B.* v. *H.B.*, [1980] I.L.R.M. 257 (High Ct., Barrington, J.), jurisdiction under the 1976 Act was not challenged on the basis of inadequate residential nexus where the respondent spouse, though spending "a considerable part of the year" in Ireland, also spent "a considerable amount of time" in the United States of America.

[13] *Dicey & Morris*, 392, 404, *Cammell* v. *Cammell*, [1965] P. 465 (P.D.A. Div., (Scarman, J., 1964)).

Divisible Divorce[14]

We now must consider the effect of a foreign divorce decree on maintenance entitlements within this jurisdiction. The question may arise where an Irish maintenance order is already in effect at the time of the divorce decree, or where, after a foreign divorce recognised here, one of the former spouses seeks to invoke the Family Law (Maintenance of Spouses and Children) Act 1976 to obtain a maintenance order against the other former spouse. In England, in *Wood* v. *Wood*,[15] the Court of Appeal held that an *ex parte* Nevada divorce, recognised under English conflict rules, did not of itself put an end to a maintenance order which the wife had obtained in England. The divorce had been granted on a ground of the *de facto* separation of the spouses, then[16] not a basis for divorce in England. The decision was professedly based on an interpretation of the statutory provisions relating to the variation and discharge of maintenance orders but clearly an important issue of principle is involved.

Four issues seem to have been of particular interest to the Courts in the English cases: (i) whether the divorce was obtained on a ground available in English law; (ii) whether the respondent spouse had actively participated in the divorce proceedings; (iii) whether the foreign divorce court awarded adequate maintenance in favour of the respondent spouse; and (iv) whether the English maintenance order had been obtained, or at least sought, before the foreign divorce proceedings took place. The English courts have been anxious to protect wives who are in receipt of maintenance under an English court order from destitution by being divorced abroad, on grounds not available in England, in cases where the husband is not required by the foreign court to provide adequate maintenance for his wife.

In Ireland this question assumes more complex dimensions. Since there is no domestic divorce jurisdiction, the first factor mentioned above does not arise. As to the third factor, we have seen that so far our courts have not sought to examine the question of the adequacy of the maintenance awarded in the foreign divorce proceedings. Up to now, our courts have only addressed the related, but different, question of whether a maintenance award ancillary to a foreign divorce decree should be recognised here.[17] In holding that it should, the courts have not expressly foreclosed the option of holding also that an Irish maintenance order made under the Family Law (Maintenance of Spouses and Children) Act 1976 should not automatically cease to have effect by reason of the fact that the parties are no longer "spouses".

Although there are strong policy arguments in favour of preserving the entitlements of a dependent spouse under an Irish maintenance order, it is necessary to consider whether the 1976 Act is drafted in such a way as to permit this. Section 6 of the Act specifies the circumstances in which a maintenance order may be discharged or varied. It does not provide that a maintenance order is discharged on the granting of a foreign divorce. But subsection 1 (b) permits the Court to discharge or vary a maintenance order "at any time, on the application of either party, if it thinks it proper to do so having regard to any circumstances not existing when the order was made . . ." Thus, it could be argued that the Court has a discretion to discharge or vary a maintenance order after a foreign divorce, and that unless and until it so exercises its discretion the respondent former spouse has continuing obligations under the maintenance order. As against this some of the other provisions in section 6

---

[14] See Morris, *Divisible Divorce*, 64 Harv. L. Rev. 1287 (1951), *Scoles & Hay*, 507 ff.

[15] [1957] P. 254 (C.A.). See also *Qureshi* v. *Qureshi*, [1972] Fam. 173 (Simon, P., 1970), *Newmarch* v. *Newmarch*, [1978] Fam. 79 (Rees, J., 1977).

[16] Until the Divorce Reform Act 1969 came into force, grounds for divorce in England were based on fault rather than on separation.

[17] Cf. *supra*, pp. 289-292

which give rise to the possibility[18] or certainty[19] of discharge are clearly based on the fact of a subsisting marriage. This might suggest that section 6, like the Act in general, is based on the premise of a subsisting marriage. To this it may be replied that the fact that certain provisions in section 6 deal with situations arising in a subsisting marriage does not mean that other parts of the section must do so; nothing in the language of subsection 1 (b), or indeed any other part of the section, is inconsistent with the view that a maintenance order continues to be effective after a foreign divorce unless and until discharged under subsection 1 (b), or any other part,[20] of section 6.

If we accept for the moment that the granting of a foreign divorce does not automatically discharge a maintenance order granted under the 1976 Act, we must consider how the Court might respond to an application for a discharge in such circumstances under section 6 (1)(b). The circumstances may vary widely.[21] Presumably the court would invariably (or almost invariably) discharge the maintenance order where the maintenance creditor had sought the divorce or was domiciled in the country where it was obtained.[22] Where, however, the maintenance creditor had at all times been domiciled and resident in the State, it may well be that the order would not be discharged, unless of course the maintenance creditor had sought the divorce.

A somewhat different issue arises where the divorced spouse in need of maintenance has not yet obtained[23] a maintenance order under the 1976 Act before the divorce is granted. On one view of social policy it may be argued that it is immaterial whether or not the order has been obtained, since "in either case the economic problem is the same and should receive the same solution".[24] There is much to be said for this view but it is very difficult to see how it can be reconciled with the language of section 5 of the 1976 Act which expressly requires that the applicant be "a spouse", not a former spouse.

RECOGNITION AND ENFORCEMENT
OF FOREIGN MAINTENANCE ORDERS

The recognition and enforcement of foreign maintenance orders raise some difficult questions. The general rule is that a foreign maintenance order should be treated in the same way as any other foreign judgment for a sum of money. Questions as to finality and conclusiveness may arise. Moreover, in contrast to most commercial judgments, public policy issues may play a prominent role.

Statute has intervened in this area. This aspect of the subject will be examined later in the chapter.[25]

---

[18] Cf. section 6 (4).

[19] Cf. section 6 (2).

[20] There seems to be no reason why section 6 (1) (a), which enables the Court to discharge a maintenance order at any time after one year from the time it was originally made, could not be invoked after a foreign divorce. Either section 6 (2), which deals with desertion by the maintenance creditor, or section 6(4), which deals with adultery by the maintenance creditor, could no doubt by invoked after a foreign divorce provided, it would seem, the conduct occurred before the divorce.

[21] Cf. Morris, *Divisible Divorce*, 64 Harv. L. Rev. 1287, at 1301-1303 (1951).

[22] Or recognised, in cases where section 5(4) of the Domicile and Recognition of Foreign Divorces Act 1986 applies: cf. *supra*, pp. 283-284.

[23] The cases where a spouse has applied for, but not yet obtained, a maintenance order raise particular difficulties. If substance is to have priority over form, such a spouse should be treated in the same way as one who has actually obtained an order, otherwise there might be an incentive to rush for a divorce abroad. On the other hand, to treat an application in the same way as an order might have the converse effect of encouraging dependent spouses to rush to apply for maintenance orders when they are served with foreign divorce papers.

[24] Morris, *supra*, at 1302. Cf. *Dicey & Morris*, 408-409.

[25] *Infra*, pp. 310-317.

Recognition and Enforcement at Common Law

When considering the recognition and enforcement of maintenance orders at common law it is necessary to consider the general principle of conflicts of law that "[t]hese Courts cannot and should not enforce a judgment which is not final."[26] In *G.* v. *G.*,[27] in 1984, Finlay, P. said:

> "A judgment is not final if it can be varied or altered by application to the court that made it in the country in which it was made, though the existence of a right of appeal from that court which has not been exercised or has been unsuccessfully exercised does not detract from the finality of the judgment. In regard to a periodical payment such as this order for maintenance, I am satisfied on a consideration of the authorities that the crucial test must be whether the court which granted the order for maintenance had power within its jurisdiction to vary, rescind or alter the order retrospectively."

This statement of law resolves a great deal of unnecessary confusion which had plagued the Irish cases dealing with this question over the years. It is useful to look briefly at these cases.

The first, *Nunn* v. *Nunn*,[28] in 1880, stated and applied the relevant principles quite satisfactorily. The Irish Court of Appeal, affirming the Queen's Bench Division, held that an English order for alimony pursuant to a decree for legal separation was enforceable here as a final and conclusive award. Lord O'Hagan, C.[29] did not consider that this was an interlocutory order:

> "An interlocutory order is an order made in the course of, and in aid of the progress of, the cause. But an order such as this, which is the final, the material, the conclusive order, cannot properly be regarded as interlocutory. Here we have first the judicial separation, and then we have, as the last step in the cause, led up to by the decree for separation, this order for alimony — an order in which the Petitioner has the greatest possible interest, which may be the most important thing accomplished for her benefit in the suit, and beyond which there is no further judicial determination. Observe the words of the order itself — it fixes 'permanent' alimony. Is not a thing which is made 'permanent' a thing established and settled by the final adjudication of the Court?"[30]

It had been argued that the order was interlocutory because by a subsequent proceeding the alimony might be reduced. Lord O'Hagan, C. rejected this contention, observing that, although, no doubt, the defendant might get the order reduced under certain circumstances, "that would not make the decree less final in its spirit and operation — less final in establishing a principle and conferring a right."[31] Finally, the Court stressed that two sums of alimony had actually accrued; judgment in respect of these sums could hardly be described as interlocutory by reason of the possible chance of a change in the amount of alimony to be awarded in the future.

In *Keys* v. *Keys*,[32] the King's Bench Division favoured a different approach. The case concerned a claim for eleven years' arrears of permanent alimony payable under a consent order made by Andrews, J. in "a matrimonial matter"[33]. The King's

---

[26] *G.* v. *G.*, [1984] I.R. 368, at 374 (High Ct., Finlay, P.).
[27] *Id.*, at 375-376.
[28] 8 L.R. Ir. 298 (C.A., 1880), aff'g 6 L.R. Ir. 115 (Q.B.Div., 1880).
[29] With whom Morris, C.J. and Deasy, L.J. concurred.
[30] 8 L.R. Ir., at 303.
[31] *Id.*
[32] [1919] 2 I.R. 160 (K.B. Div., 1918).
[33] *Id.*, at 160 (presumably proceedings for divorce *a mensa et thoro*).

Bench Division held that the rule[34] that alimony might be increased or diminished by reason of the enhanced or reduced "faculties"[35] "would seem to deprive the alimony order of the character of a final judgment...."[36] The Court noted that English decisions subsequent to *Nunn* v. *Nunn* had taken a different view than had been adopted in that case on the question of the finality of English orders for alimony. The Court considered that "[a]s to the finality and actionable character of their own orders the English Courts were the supreme and sole judges."[37] In one sense this is, of course, true: the scope and effect of the English orders were matters for English law to prescribe. But in another, more important, sense, this statement is positively misleading. The question whether any foreign order is final is a matter which the *Irish* court must decide, in the light of the evidence as to the nature and effect of the foreign order. The fact that the foreign court might not characterise the order as "final" should not affect the issue.

Keys v. *Keys* had an unfortunate influence on the Court in *M'Donnell* v. *M'Donnell*,[38] in 1920. In *M'Donnell's* case, the plaintiff had emigrated from Ireland with her husband to Montana in 1911. Later that year she took maintenance proceedings against him in Montana and the Court ordered her husband to pay to the office of the Clerk of the Court forty dollars a month until further notice. Her husband died in 1918, without having paid anything to the plaintiff. She sued her husband's executor for the arrears in the Irish courts since her husband had left some property in Ireland. She was successful at trial but the King's Bench Division, by a majority[39], reversed.

A fatal flaw in the plaintiff's case was her failure to prove the law applied by the court in Montana. This meant that the Irish court could only speculate on the meaning and effect of the Montana decree. Molony, C.J. thought it clear that the object of requiring the money to be paid to the Clerk of the Court, and not directly to the plaintiff, was that the Court "might retain control over the money, or be in a position to vary the order, or substitute another order, or abrogate it altogether in case facts were brought to [its] notice which would justify [its] intervention".[40] He was not satisfied that this judgment was final and conclusive.

Gordon, J. clearly regarded the maintenance order as being akin to an award of alimony in Irish proceedings for divorce *a mensa et thoro*, which *Keys* v. *Keys*[41] had held was not a final and conclusive judgment. He considered that it

"could hardly be supposed that the wife was to continue to get the monthly payment no matter how she might have misconducted herself. Part of the plaintiff's case in her complaint was that she was unable to earn a living for herself and her child. Might not questions in reference to the child arise which would cause the Court to exercise control over the payment of these monthly sums? These or other considerations must have been present to the Court when it made the order in the form in which it was made. The order is not that the forty dollars a month should be paid to the plaintiff,

---

[34] Matrimonial rule 58 (*Wylie*, p. 966). See now Rules of the Superior Courts 1986, Order 70, rule 55. See further *Halligan* v. *Halligan*, [1896] 1 I.R. 244 (C.A., 1895), *Mogowan* v. *Mogowan*, [1921] 2 I.R. 314 (K.B. Div. (Mat.), Ross, J.), *M.C.* v. *J.C.*, [1982] I.L.R.M. 562 (High Ct., Costello, J.) and the Law Reform Commission's *Report on Divorce a Mensa et Thoro and Related Matters*, pp. 28-30 (L.R.C. 8–1983).

[35] That is, "the property and income of the husband": *Browne*, 280.

[36] [1919] 2 I.R., at 167 (*per* Gibson, J.).

[37] *Id.*, at 168.

[38] [1921] 2 I.R. 148 (K.B. Div., 1920). The personnel of the Court in *M'Donnell* (Molony, C.J., Gordon & Pim, JJ.) were entirely different from those in *Keys* (Gibson, Madden and Kenny, JJ.).

[39] Molony C.J. and Gordon, J.; Pim, J. dissenting.

[40] [1921] 2 I.R., at 162.

[41] [1919] 2 I.R. 160.

but that the defendant should pay it into the office of the Clerk of the Court for the support and maintenance of the plaintiff and that such payments be made until the further order of the Court.''[42]

So far as it suggests that the order capable of subsequent variation, for the future but not retrospectively, was not a final one, this passage no longer commands support.

But both Gordon, J. and Molony, C.J. appeared to contemplate the possibility of the Court still reserving to itself the right to intervene between the time the money was given to the Clerk of the Court and the time it was to be paid to the plaintiff. If this intervention could have the effect of modifying the defendant's provisional liability, then perhaps the case against the finality of the order would be somewhat strengthened. On this view the defendant should be regarded as being under an obligation to pay a sum of money to the Clerk of the Court, provisionally fixed at forty dollars, but crystallising in that actual amount only to the extent that the Court, having reserved its right to intervene in the meantime, exercised its discretion against intervention.

Pim, J.'s dissenting judgment is worthy of particular attention. He said of the maintenance order obtained by the plaintiff:

> ''If it were possible in a case of this kind to make any other order, I should possibly be compelled to hold that this order was not final, but the very nature of the proceeding is such that *ex necessitate* there must be an opportunity left, possibly to rescind and possibly only to vary it. An order made by any Court for maintenance would not satisfy justice if there were not a power left to the Court to make changes in it, if the maintenance directed to be paid became in part or wholly unnecessary. If this order cannot be treated as a final and conclusive order, because of the possible necessity in the future of varying it, then there never can be a final and conclusive order in a suit for maintenance — a proposition which seems to me quite untenable.''[43]

Pim, J. regarded the requirement of payment into Court, rather than directly to the plaintiff, as ''mere machinery for paying the complainant, and probably the Court machinery that could be employed for such purpose in the circumstances.''[44] He noted that:

> ''[I]n the western States of America, life is a shifting thing. Men and women move about in a way which is not at all understood here, and it is probable that the only way in which the money directed to be paid would be sure of reaching the hands of the person entitled to it would be to order it to be paid into the office of the Clerk of the Court to be held at the disposal of the person entitled thereto. There is nothing in the order from which it might be inferred that the money that was paid in was to be at the disposal or under the control of the Court itself, and it must therefore be assumed that whenever, the complainant made an application to the clerk of the office to have the money paid out, it would have been paid out to her as a matter of course; nor do I think the Court had any power to prevent such payment out at any time. All the Court could do, if application was made to it, was to vary the amount. I do not agree that a mere order to pay into Court without any indication that the Court had or desired to exercise any control over the money prevents the order being a final and conclusive one''[45]

---

[42] [1921] 2 I.R., at 154 (*per* Molony, C.J.).
[43] *Id.*, at 156.
[44] *Id.*, at 157.
[45] *Id.* Cf. *supra*, pp. 115-116.

Pim, J. clearly had the better of the argument. His interpretation of the function of the machinery involving the Clerk of the Court was far more credible than that of the majority; moreover, he presented a potent *reductio ad absurdum* of the argument that susceptibility to subsequent (rather than retrospective) variation rendered a maintenance order incapable of being final or conclusive.

Keys v. *Keys* received support, *obiter*, in the Circuit Court case of *Leake* v. *Douglas*,[46] where Judge Conroy is reported as having said that *Keys* v. *Keys* made it plain that "arrears of permanent alimony could not be recovered by action for the reasons that other means for enforcing such an order were provided, and that such an order was not final and conclusive as it remained within the control of the Court making it."[47]

In *G.* v. *G.*[48] in 1984, Finlay, P. gave a clear analysis of the subject. In this case the plaintiff's wife claimed 3,230 dollars from her husband on foot of an agreement between the spouses made on 2 April 1979, whereby the husband had agreed to pay her 40 dollars a week for the support of their child. She also based her claim on an order made by the Probate and Family Court of Massachusetts, which decreed that the spouses should "comply with the stipulation or agreement of the parties dated 2 April 1979 which is filed with the Court and expressly made a part of this order."

The plaintiff obtained a decree of divorce *nisi* on 15 May 1980, which became absolute 6 months later. That decree contained a clause requiring the plaintiff to pay 40 dollars a week for the maintenance of the child until the child became re-employed, all payments "to be made through the Family Service Office".[49]

One of the grounds of objection to enforcement made by the defendant was that the order was not a final order. Finlay, P. rejected this contention. He stressed that, for an order not to be final and conclusive, it would have to be subject to retrospective, rather than subsequent, variation. Yet the evidence as to Massachusetts law given by the foreign legal expert was to the effect that, on the making of an order for maintenance, "the court may, of course, vary it at any time with the altered circumstances of the parties but has not got jurisdiction to alter it retrospectively."[50] Finlay, P. noted that in *M'Donnell* v. *M'Donnell* Pim, J. had made the distinction between retrospective and subsequent variation but that Gordon, J., for the majority, had not. Finlay, P. quoted a passage from the English decision of *Williams* v. *Jones*[51] which had also been quoted by Molony, C.J. for the majority in *M'Donnell* v. *M'Donnell*. In Finlay, P.'s view this passage supported the holding that capacity for retrospective rather than subsequent variation was necessary for a judgment not to be final and conclusive.

As in *M'Donnell* v. *M'Donnell*, the question arose in *G.* v. *G.* as to whether the indirect mode of payment ordered by the Massachusetts court affected the matter of the finality and conclusiveness of the order. Finlay, P. considered that it had no such effect. In his view, payment through the Family Service Office of the Court

---

[46] 88 I.L.T.R. 4 (Circuit Ct., Judge Conroy, 1952).

[47] *Id.*, at 5.

[48] [1984] I.R. 368 (High Ct., Finlay, P.).

[49] The decree also provided that a judgment of contempt issued in April 1980 for arrears of 750 dollars on the support order of 2 April 1979 was "held in abeyance", and that the issue of arrears and support should be reviewed by the Court on 26 June 1980 or on the further Order of the Court. The foreign legal expert gave evidence that arrears under or on foot of the support order could be sued upon in Massachusetts as a liquidated sum and as a simple debt due and that the Court would not alter the amount due as arrears: [1984] I.R., at 371-372. It would seem therefore, as the thrust of Finlay, P.'s judgment would appear to confirm, that there was no question of the Massachusetts Court's having powers with respect to arrears akin to those of the Court in proceedings for divorce *a mensa et thoro*, relative to arrears in alimony.

[50] *Id.*, at 371.

[51] 11 M. & W. 628 (1845).

was "obviously a procedure similar to the procedure (well known to our law) when the payment of maintenance is made through the District Court clerk[52]".[53] Finlay, P. said that he unreservedly accepted[54] the view expressed by Pim, J. in *M'Donnell* v. *M'Donnell* "as to the nature of this provision[55] and of its irrelevance to the determination as to whether the order for maintenance is a final order or not".[56] Finlay, P. continued:

> "Quite clearly, it is a method whereby the service provided is a mere conduit pipe for the transfer of money from the husband to the wife and is, if it is similar to the provisions contained in our law,[57] largely designed to avoid subsequent disputes about whether payment has been made or not. It is wholly different in character from an order directing the payment of money into court to abide subsequent proceedings in the same or another action; that direction would, of course, destroy the final nature of the order."[58]

The Maintenance Orders (Facilities for Enforcement) Act 1920

We must now consider the present status of the Maintenance Orders (Facilities for Enforcement) Act 1920.[59] This Act was designed to provide facilities for the reciprocal enforcement of maintenance orders between England and Ireland, on the one hand, and countries forming part of what was then the British Empire, on the other. The Act defined a maintenance order broadly, to include every order, other than an affiliation order, for the periodical payment of sums of money towards the maintenance of the wife of the person against whom the order was made, as well as others whom he was liable to maintain under the law in force where the order was made.[60]

Sections 1 and 2 of the Act provided for the registration in England and Ireland of maintenance orders made in a country to which the Act extended, and for an equivalent power of registration of English and Irish maintenance orders in any of these countries. For these sections to operate, the court granting the maintenance had to have jurisdiction, independently of the Act. These sections would be of assistance where there was difficulty in enforcing the order, as, for example, where a husband, having been resident in Ireland when a maintenance order was made against him, later went to a far-off British dominion, leaving the wife with a valid, but in practice unenforceable, order in her favour.[61]

Section 3 of the Act dealt with the position where a person resided in a British dominion and an order for maintenance was sought in England or Ireland. The English or Irish court, of summary jurisdiction, was permitted to make a provisional order which the court in the dominion might confirm or, at its discretion, rescind.[62] Section 4 gave an equivalent power to the English or Irish court of summary jurisdiction in relation to a maintenance order made in a British dominion against a person residing in England or Ireland.

---

[52] Cf. the Family Law (Maintenance of Spouses and Children) Act 1976, section 9. See *Shatter*, 449.

[53] [1984] I.R., at 376.

[54] *Id.*

[55] There is, of course, no reason why a provision in Montana law over 60 years ago should *necessarily* operate in the same way as one in Massachusetts in the past decade.

[56] [1984] I.R., at 376.

[57] The doubt on the matter is curious since the evidence of the foreign legal expert as to the exact operation of the Massachusetts provisions could always have been obtained. Perhaps the point arose at too late a stage in the proceedings.

[58] [1984] I.R., at 376.

[59] See *Dicey & Morris*, 395 ff., *McClean* 197-199.

[60] Section 10.

[61] See *Dicey & Morris*, 8th ed., 1967, p. 341; Cf. *id.*, 10th ed., 1980, pp. 397.

[62] Section 3(4).

At the time of Independence, the Act extended to a large number of jurisdictions.[63] The effect of Independence on the operation of the 1920 Act is not entirely clear. The Act has never been repealed. In the light of the general provisions for adaptation of enactments[64] and the considerations mentioned in *The State (Kennedy)* v. *Little*,[65] a strong case, at least in theory, may be made in favour of the view that the Act has continued in force. The opportunity for expanding the protection of abandoned spouses is one that should not lightly be refused; this humane policy is easy to harmonise with the public policy of the State. Indirect pragmatic encouragement for this interpretation is afforded by the fact that some Commonwealth countries, whether falling within the list of those to which the Act extended at the time of Independence or otherwise, have in their legislation made it clear that it embraces the State.[66]

However impressive the theoretical argument in favour of the continuing vitality of the 1920 Act, the practical reality is that no reciprocal arrangements with these countries are in use.[67] That is why the Maintenance Orders Act 1974 is of such importance; and to that Act we now turn.

The Maintenance Orders Act 1974

The Maintenance Orders Act 1974 provides for the enforcement in the State of maintenance orders made in Northern Ireland, England and Scotland and for the making of maintenance orders in the State against persons residing in Northern Ireland, England and Scotland.[68] A similar legislative machinery exists in these reciprocating jurisdictions.[69] The 1974 Act applies to maintenance orders whether made before or after its commencement but does not affect arrears which accrued before its commencement.[70] Let us first consider what orders fall within the scope of the Act. Section 3 (1) provides that:

" 'maintenance order' means –
(a) an order (including an affiliation order or an order consequent thereon) which provides for the periodical payment of sums of money towards the maintenance of any person, being a person whom the person liable to make payments under the order is, in accordance with the law of the jurisdiction in which the order was made, liable to maintain, or
(b) an affiliation order or an order consequent thereon, being an order which provides for the payment by a person adjudged, found or declared to be a child's father of expenses

---

[63] *McClean*, 198 lists the following (without any attempt to express the jurisdictions in modern terms): Basutoland, Bechuanaland, Bermuda, British Solomon Islands Protectorate, Cyprus, the Falkland Islands, the Gambia, Gibraltar, the Gilbert and Ellice Islands, Gold Coast (including Ashanti and the Northern Territories), Grenada, Hong Kong, the Leeward Islands, Malta, the Isle of Man, Mauritius, New Zealand, Nigeria, Northern Rhodesia, Nyasaland, Queensland, St. Lucia, St. Vincent, Seychelles, Somaliland Protectorate, Southern Rhodesia, the Straits Settlements, Swaziland, Tasmania, Trinidad and Tobago, Western Australia, and Zanzibar.

[64] Adaptation of Enactments Act 1922, section 3, Constitution (Consequential Provisions) Act 1937, section 2.

[65] [1931] I.R. 39 (High Ct., 1930). See further *supra*, p. 23.

[66] *McLean*, 198-199 mentions that Botswana, the Cayman Islands, Cyprus, Figi, Guyana, Kiribati, Lesotho, Malawi, Mauritius, Nigeria, St. Lucia, St. Vincent and the Grenadines, Sierra Leone, the Solomon Islands and Zambia have retained the expression "England and Ireland"; Kenya refers to "Eire"; and the Bahamas, Fiji, Gambia, Swaziland and Uganda refer to "the Republic of Ireland".

[67] *Id.*, 198.

[68] See *Shatter*, 461-466, *Woods*, 245-253.

[69] Cf. the Maintenance Orders (Reciprocal Enforcement) Act 1972, Part I, as applied to the State by The Reciprocal Enforcement of Maintenance Orders (Republic of Ireland) Order 1974 (S.I. 1974, No. 2140). Cf. Latham, *Reciprocal Enforcement of Maintenance Orders in the E.C.C.*, 5 Family L. 145 (1975).

[70] Section 4 of the 1974 Act.

incidental to the birth of the child or, where the child has died, of the funeral expenses and, in the case of a maintenance order which has been varied, means that order as varied."

Throughout the Act, the expression "maintenance proceedings" means proceedings in relation to the making, variation or revocation of a maintenance order.[71]

Section 3 (2) goes on to provide that, for the avoidance of doubt, a maintenance order includes three specific types of order. The *first* is "such an order which is incidental to a decision as to the status of natural persons". Thus, a maintenance order made in proceedings for divorce or nullity of marriage[72] would come within the scope of this description. The *second* is "such an order obtained by or in favour of a public authority in connection with the provision of maintenance or other benefits in respect of a person whom the maintenance debtor is, in accordance with the law of the jurisdiction in which the order was made, liable to maintain".[73]

The *third* is:

"a provision in an agreement in writing between spouses for the making by one spouse of periodical payments towards the maintenance of the other or of any of their children or of any child to whom either is *in loco parentis*, being an agreement which has been embodied in or approved by a court order or made a rule of court."

The type of provision covered by this definition would include one falling within the scope of paragraph (a)(i) of section 8 of the Family Law (Maintenance of Spouses and Children) Act 1976.[74]

Enforcement of Maintenance Order Made in a Reciprocating Jurisdiction

Let us now consider the provisions of the Act relating to the enforcement of maintenance orders made in a reciprocating jurisdiction.[75] A maintenance order made in a reciprocating jurisdiction and enforceable there is recognised and enforceable in the State (subject to the other provisions in the Act) when, having

[71] Section 3(1).

[72] This is possible in England, Northern Ireland and Scotland though not yet in the State. The Law Reform Commission in its *Report on Nullity of Marriage,* pp. 170 ff (L.R.C. 9–1984), recommended the introduction of wide-ranging financial provisions in relation to invalid marriages.

[73] Cf. *Bromley* 495-497. In Ireland, section 2 (1) of the Illegitimate Children (Affiliation Orders) Act 1930 provides that "a local body administrating the relief of the poor then giving relief to the mother of an illegitimate child" may apply for an affiliation order. *Shatter,* 604, fn. 19 states that "Whilst in theory such a body could bring affiliation proceedings there is no reported case of a body doing so since the Act's inception."

[74] See *Shatter,* 211-213, *Binchy,* ch. 10. Section 8 provides as follows:
"Where—
(a) the parties to a marriage enter into an agreement in writing (including a separation agreement) after the commencement of this Act that includes either or both of the following provisions, that is to say—
(i) a provision whereby one spouse undertakes to make periodical payments towards the maintenance of the other spouse or of any dependent children of the family or of both that other spouse and any dependent children of the family,
(ii) a provision governing the rights and liabilities of the spouses towards one another in respect of the making or securing of payments (other than payments specified in paragraph (a) (i) of this section), or the disposition or use of any property, and
(b) an application is made by one or both of the spouses to the High Court or the Circuit Court for an order making the agreement a rule of court,
the Court may make such an order if it is satisfied that the agreement is a fair and reasonable one which in all the circumstances adequately protects the interests of both spouses and the dependent children (if any) of the family, and such order shall, in so far as it relates to a provision specified in paragraph (a) (i) of this section, be deemed, for the purpose of section 9 and Part III of this Act, to be a maintenance order."

[75] That is, Northern Ireland, England and Wales, or Scotland: section 3 (1).

received a request for enforcement from an appropriate authority,[76] the Master of the High Court makes an order under section 6 (4) of the Act.[77]

This request must be accompanied by the following documents:

(a) a certified copy of the maintenance order concerned:

(b) where the maintenance order was made in default of appearance, the original or a certified copy of the document which establishes that notice of the institution of the proceedings was served on the person in default,

(c) documents establishing that the order is enforceable according to the law of the jurisdiction in which it was made and that notice of the order has been served on the maintenance debtor[78] outside the State or sent by registered post to him at an address within the state, and

(d) where appropriate, a document showing that the maintenance creditor[79] is receiving legal aid in that jurisdiction.[80]

The maintenance debtor is not, at this stage, entitled to make any submission on the request.[81] The Master considers the request privately and must make an order (known as an "enforcement order") for the enforcement of the maintenance order to which the request relates, unless it appears to him from the documents before him or from his own knowledge that its recognition and enforcement is prohibited by section 9.[82] (We shall be examining section 9 below.)[83]

The Master's decision on the request, whether to enforce or not to enforce, must be brought to the notice of the maintenance creditor.[84] Only where he has made an enforcement order, however, must the Master cause notice of this fact to be served on the maintenance debtor.[85] This notice served on the maintenance debtor must include a statement of his right to appeal,[86] the restriction[87] on the taking of measures of execution against his property and the provisions of section 9 relating to non-recognition and non-enforcement of certain maintenance orders.[88]

Where an enforcement order is made, the maintenance debtor has one month after service of notice of the order on him within which he may appeal to the High Court against the order.[89] The Court may, on the application of the maintenance debtor, stay the proceedings if either:

(a) enforcement of the maintenance order has been suspended in the reciprocating jurisdiction in which it was made pending the determination of any form of appeal, or

---

[76] "Appropriate authority" means the person who, in a reciprocating jurisdiction, has a function corresponding to that of the Master of the High Court under section 19 (3).

[77] Section 6 (1).

[78] That is, the person liable to make payments under the maintenance order: section 3 (1).

[79] That is, the person entitled to the payments for which the maintenance order provides: section 3 (1).

[80] Section 13 (1). Some supplementary provisions should be noted. If the documents specified in paragraphs (b) or (d) are not produced, the Master may allow time for their production, accept equivalent documents or, if he considers that there is sufficient information available, dispense with their production: section 13 (2). Sections 13 (4) and (5) permit the Master to accept without further proof documents containing a request for enforcement and purporting to have been transmitted by or at the instance of an appropriate authority and documents purporting to be certified copies of maintenance orders or other documents signed by a judge, magistrate or officer of a court in a reciprocating jurisdiction.

[81] Section 6 (3).

[82] Section 6 (4).

[83] *Infra*, p. 313.

[84] Section 6 (5).

[85] *Id.*

[86] Under section 7.

[87] Imposed by section 7 (3).

[88] Section 6(6) (a). As to the modes of service of the notice, see section 6(6) (b).

[89] Section 7.

(b) the time for an appeal has not yet expired and enforcement has been suspended pending the making of an appeal.[90]

In the latter case the Court may lay down the time for which it will stay the proceedings.[91]

During the time allowed for an appeal and until the appeal is determined, no measures of execution may be taken against the property of the maintenance debtor other than measures ordered by a court and designed to protect the interest of the maintenance creditor.[92] The judgment given on appeal may be contested only on a point of law.[93]

The maintenance creditor may appeal to the High Court against a refusal by the Master of a request to enforce a maintenance order made in a reciprocating jurisdiction.[94] Notice of this appeal must be served on the maintenance debtor.[95] As with appeals from enforcement orders, the judgment given on the appeal against refusal to enforce an enforcement order may be contested only on a point of law.[96]

Prohibition on Recognition and Enforcement

We must now consider the provisions in the Act prohibiting recognition or enforcement of maintenance orders in certain circumstances. Section 9 provides as follows:

> "A maintenance order made in a reciprocating jurisdiction shall not be recognised or enforceable if, but only if—
> (a) recognition or enforcement would be contrary to public policy,
> (b) where it was made in default of appearance, the person in default was not served with notice of the institution of the proceedings in sufficient time to enable him to arrange for his defence, or
> (c) it is irreconcilable with a judgment given in a dispute between the same parties in the State."[97]

As to the first of these three cases, we have seen that in *N.M.* v. *E.F.M.*,[98] in 1978, Hamilton, J. rejected the argument that recognition or enforcement of an English maintenance order consequent on the grant of a divorce there would be contrary to public policy. Hamilton, J. considered that:

> "in enforcing and recognising this maintenance order it can not be said that such enforcement or recognition is giving active or any assistance to facilitate in any way the effecting of a dissolution of marriage or is giving assistance to the process of divorce. It is merely providing for the maintenance of spouses and as such can not be regarded as contrary to public policy."[99]

We must consider briefly the effect of section 16, which provides that:

> "Nothing in this Act (other than section 9) shall be taken as preventing the recognition of a maintenance order which is made in a reciprocating jurisdiction and which, apart from this Act, would be recognised in the State."

[90] Section 7 (2).
[91] *Id.*
[92] Section 7 (3).
[93] Section 7 (4).
[94] Section 8 (1).
[95] Section 8 (2).
[96] Section 8 (3).
[97] The jurisdiction of the court that made the order may not, however, be examined, nor may the order by examined as to its substance: section 10.
[98] Unreported, High Ct., Hamilton, J., in July 1978 (1977 No. 87 EMO) by *Binchy* 255.
[99] Cf. *Binchy*, 257.

Clearly the intended effect of the section is to confirm that the Act does not disturb common law grounds for recognition of maintenance orders made in reciprocating jurisdiction. But section 16 also makes it plain that section 9 *will* affect these other grounds for recognition. Indeed section 9 is drafted so as to extend non-recognition and non-enforcement not merely to maintenance orders made in reciprocating jurisdictions under the Act but to *all* maintenance orders made in a reciprocating jurisdiction. Having regard to the nature of the three grounds specified in section 9, however, this scarcely disturbs the position as it seems that, even under common law, all these grounds for non-recognition and non-enforcement would in any event have applied.

Partial Enforcement

The Act provides for the possibility of *partial enforcement*. Where, in a maintenance order made in a reciprocating jurisdiction, there are provisions in respect of which enforcement cannot be ordered, an enforcement order may be made in respect of any other provision of the maintenance order.[100] Thus, for example, it might in some cases be possible to enforce that part of the order relating to maintenance for the children but not relating to a spouse, or *vice versa*. Partial enforcement may be requested by those seeking an enforcement order.[101]

No Security for Costs

In contrast with the general approach towards legal proceedings taken in the State by plaintiffs resident outside the jurisdiction,[102] no security or deposit, however described, may be required from a person seeking enforcement of a maintenance order under the 1974 Act, solely on the ground that he or she is not residing in the State.[103] The policy here is to ensure that spouses who are not receiving adequate maintenance will not be prevented from seeking enforcement of maintenance orders here. The injustice of denying them access to the Irish Court is plain. The principles on which security for costs may be ordered or refused could result in the exercise by the Irish court of a discretion to refuse an order for security for costs in these circumstances.[104] But the straightforward approach adopted by section 12 of the 1974 Act has much to recommend it and will remove a shadow of uncertainty which could have been sufficient to dissuade some spouses from seeking enforcement here.

Enforcement By the District Court

The District Court has jurisdiction to enforce an enforceable maintenance order[105] under the Act. The order is deemed to be an order made by the District Court under section 5 of the Family Law (Maintenance of Spouses and Children) Act 1976[106] or section 3 of the Illegitimate Children (Affiliation Orders) Act 1930, as the case may be.[107]

---

[100] Section 11 (1).

[101] Cf. section 11 (2).

[102] Cf. *infra*, ch. 35. ·

[103] Section 12.

[104] Cf. *infra*, ch. 35. The rule that security may not be ordered when the plaintiff's poverty is attributable to the defendant's allegedly wrongful conduct would have mitigated the difficulties facing a petitioner in this context: *infra*, pp. 666-668.

[105] That is, a maintenance order in respect of which an enforcement order, full or partial, has been made: section 14 (1).

[106] Section 14 (2) (a) refers to an order made by the District Court under section 1 of the Married Women (Maintenance in Case of Desertion) Act 1886. This Act was repealed and effectively replaced by the Family Law (Maintenance of Spouses and Children) Act 1976. Cf. section 20 (1) of the Interpretation Act 1937.

[107] Section 14 (2) (a).

The District Court has jurisdiction to enforce an enforceable maintenance order even where the amount payable under it exceeds the maximum amount which the District Court has jurisdiction to award under these Acts.[108] Whether this is permitted by the Constitution is a point worthy of consideration.

Variation and Revocation

Variation or revocation[109] of enforceable maintenance orders are not matters in which the Irish court is involved.[120] Instead, where an enforceable maintenance order is varied by a court in a reciprocating jurisdiction and a certified copy of the variation order is sent to the District Court, the enforceable maintenance order, from the date on which the variation order takes effect, is enforceable here as so varied.[111] And when an enforceable maintenance order is revoked by a court in a reciprocating jurisdiction and a certified copy of the revocation order is sent to the District Court, the enforceable maintenance order, from the date on which the revocation order takes effect, ceases to be enforceable here except in relation to any arrears accrued at that date.[112] Arrears and costs are regarded as sums payable by virtue of a maintenance order made under the 1976 or 1930 Act, as the case may be.[113]

The District Court jurisdiction in maintenance orders is exercised by the justice of the District Court district where the maintenance debtor resides.[114] The machinery of enforcement is as follows. The maintenance debtor pays the sum due under the order to the local district court clerk for transmission to the maintenance creditor or public authority, as the case may be.[115] The maintenance debtor must inform the district court clerk of any change of address: failure without reasonable cause to do so is an offence.[116] Where the maintenance debtor fails to make due payment, and the maintenance creditor so requests in writing, the district court clerk may proceed under section 8 of the Enforcement of Court Orders Act 1940.[117] The attachment of earnings provisions contained in Part III of the Family Law (Maintenance of Spouses and Children) Act 1976 may also be availed of by the district court clerk[118]. The enforcement machinery involving the district court clerk is intended to afford supplementary protection rather than to replace the rights of the maintenance creditor.[119]

Maintenance Orders Made in the State

Let us now consider the reverse position involving the enforcement in Northern

---

[108] Section 14 (2) (b).

[109] "Revocation" includes the discharge of a maintenance order (cf; e.g. section 6 of the Family Law (Maintenance of Spouses and Children) Act 1976) and the termination of a weekly sum payable under a maintenance order: section 3 (1) of the 1974 Act.

[110] Section 14 (3) of the 1974 Act. It seems arguable that where the concept of "divisible divorce" (cf. *supra*, pp. 303-304) is recognised by a court is a reciprocating jurisdiciton, a maintenance order made before the divorce and enforced under the 1974 Act would have continuing effect after the divorce until discharged by the court of the reciprocating jurisdiction.

[111] Section 14 (4).

[112] Section 14 (5).

[113] Section 14 (6). This is subject to section 4 of the Act, which provides that the Act does not have effect in relation to arrears accrued before the commencement of the Act.

[114] Section 14 (7).

[115] Section 14 (8).

[116] Section 14 (9).

[117] Section 14 (8) (b).

[118] Note the definition of "antecedent order" in section 3 (1) of the 1976 Act, which includes an enforceable maintenance order under the Maintenance Orders Act 1974. See also section 10 (1) (a) (iii) (II) of the 1976 Act.

[119] Section 14 (8) (c).

Ireland, England and Wales or Scotland of a maintenance order made in the State.

Where proceedings are instituted under the Family Law (Maintenance of Spouses and Children) Act 1976[120] or the Illegitimate Children (Affiliation Orders) Act 1930, against a person residing in a reciprocating jurisdiction for the making, variation or revocation of a maintenance order, the court here has the same jurisdiction to hear and determine the proceedings as it would have if that person were residing in the State and a summons to appear before the court had been served on him.[121] This jurisdiction, so far as it rests in the District Court, is exercised by the Justice of the district court district where the person instituting the proceedings resides.[122]

Where proceedings of this nature are instituted, the registrar or clerk of the court sends the following documents to the Master of the High Court:

(i)　notice of the institution of the proceedings, including a statement of the substance of the application;

(ii)　a statement signed by the registrar or clerk giving such information as he possesses as to the whereabouts of the person against whom the proceedings have been instituted.

(iii)　a statement signed by the registrar or clerk giving such information as he possesses for facilitating the identification of the person;

(iv)　where available, a photograph of the person, and

(v)　any other relevant document.[123]

The Master of the High Court transmits these documents to the appropriate authority in the reciprocating jurisdiction concerned if it appears to him that the statement giving information as to the person's whereabouts gives sufficient information to justify doing so.[124]

In any proceedings under the 1976 or 1930 Acts against a person residing in a reciprocating jurisdiction, a maintenance order may not be made, varied or revoked unless:

(a)　notice of the institution of the proceedings has been served on him in accordance with the law of the reciprocating jurisdiction in question, and in sufficient time to enable him to arrange for his defence, and

(b)　the notice includes a statement of the substance of the complaint or allegation, as the case may be.[125]

Where the maintenance debtor under a maintenance order made in the State is residing in a reciprocating jurisdiction, the maintenance creditor may apply to the registrar or clerk of the court which made the order, to have the order transmitted to the reciprocating jurisdiction concerned, for enforcement.[126] If it appears to the registrar or clerk that the maintenance debtor is residing in a reciprocating jurisdiction, he must send the debtor notice of the order by registered post.[127] The registrar or clerk must also send [128] the following documents to the Master of the High Court:

---

[120]　Section 17 (1) of the 1974 Act refers to the Married Women (Maintenance in case of Desertion) Act 1886. Cf. fn. 106 *supra*.

[121]　Section 17 (1).

[122]　Section 17 (2). Where the "person instituting the proceedings" is a local authority (cf. section 2 (1) of the Illegitimate Children (Affiliation Orders) Act 1930), presumably the location of the authority will determine jurisdiction under section 17 (2).

[123]　Section 17 (3) (b).

[124]　Section 17 (3) (a).

[125]　Section 18.

[126]　Section 19 (1) and (2).

[127]　Section 19 (3) (i).

[128]　Section 19 (3) (ii).

(i)   a certified copy of the maintenance order,

(ii)   where a maintenance order has been made in default of appearance, the original or a certified copy of the document which establishes that notice of the institution of the proceedings was served on the person in default,

(iii)   a certificate signed by the registrar or clerk certifying that the maintenance order is enforceable in the State and that notice of the order has been sent to the maintenance debtor by registered post,

(iv)   a certificate signed by the registrar or clerk of any arrears under the order,

(v)   a statement signed by the registrar or clerk giving such information as he possesses as to the whereabouts of the maintenance debtor,

(vi)   a statement signed by the registrar or clerk giving such information as he possesses for facilitating the identification of the maintenance debtor,

(vii)   where available, a photograph of the maintenance debtor, and

(viii)   any other relevant document.[129]

The Master of the High Court transmits these documents to the appropriate authority in the reciprocating jurisdiction concerned if it appears to him that the statement giving information as to maintenance debtor's whereabouts gives sufficient information to justify this being alone.[130]

Taking of Evidence

We must now consider the detailed provisions regarding the taking of evidence contained in the Maintenance Orders Act 1974. A court may, for the purpose of any proceedings under the Act or maintenance proceedings under the 1976 or 1930 Acts where the defendant is residing in a reciprocating jurisdiction, send to the Master of the High Court for transmission to the appropriate authority in a reciprocating jurisdiction a request for the taking in that jurisdiction of the evidence of a person resident there in relation to such matters as may be specified in the request.[131]

Where a similar request comes *from* an appropriate authority in a reciprocating jurisdiction, the Master of the High Court requests a Justice of the District Court to take the evidence.[132] After giving notice of the time and place at which the evidence is to be taken to such persons and in such manner as he thinks fit, the Justice takes the evidence and causes a record of it to be sent to the Master for transmission to the appropriate authority from whom the request was received.[133] The court is given wide-ranging powers[134] in relation to evidence including the power to accept without further proof that documents purporting to be judicial documents emanating from reciprocating jurisdictions are genuine documents, unless the court "sees good reason to the contrary".[135]

AFFILIATION PROCEEDINGS

(1) Jurisdiction

The historical background to the modern law relating to affiliation proceedings is that these proceedings could be brought only where the child was born within Ireland.[136] The local authority where the child was born took the proceedings,

---

[129] Section 19 (3) (b).
[130] Section 19 (3) (a) (ii).
[131] Section 20. See *Woods*, 252-253.
[132] Section 21 (1).
[133] Section 21 (2).
[134] Section 22.
[135] Section 22 (1).
[136] Cf. *Dicey & Morris*, 450. It seems that this jurisdiction would extend to cases involving the birth of a child in a ship registered in Ireland: cf. *Marshal* v. *Murgatroyd*, L.R. 6 Q.B. 31 (1870).

which were of a quasi-criminal nature, against the reputed father.[137] Moreover "since jurisdiction to make affiliation orders was and is entrusted to the...courts [of summary jurisdiction], it was desirable to exclude intricate questions of the conflict of laws from their consideration.[138]

In *R.* v. *Blane*,[139] the first English case in which the conflicts dimensions of the subject were analysed, the Court of Queen's Bench held that there was no jurisdiction to make an affiliation order, the child having been born abroad, the mother (apparently) being domiciled abroad. Later English decisions[140] have held that jurisdiction should be denied only where both of these factors can be established: thus, in cases where the mother was domiciled there,[141] though the child was born elsewhere, jurisdiction was held to lie.

When the courts in these cases accepted jurisdiction based on the mother's domicile, they were clearly concerned that a woman should not lose her entitlement to receive financial support for the child from the father merely because he had gone abroad before the birth. It may therefore be argued that the reference to the mother's domicile should not easily extend to a case where the mother had been at all stages resident abroad, though domiciled within England.

When we look at the present Irish legislation, it is possible to argue that the fact that a local authority may take affiliation proceedings, as an alternative[142] to the mother, suggests that jurisdictional grounds should not extend beyond cases where the child was born here or the mother was domiciled[143] here.

So far as the alleged father is concerned, the legislation contains no explicit jurisdictional requirements. However, section 2(2) of the Illegitimate Children (Affiliation Orders) Act 1930 (as inserted by section 28 (1)(b) of the Family Law (Maintenance of Spouses and Children) Act 1976) may cast some light. This provision deals with the extension of the general limitations period of three years after the birth of the child; it enables an application for the issue of a summons to be made:

"....
(d) where the alleged father of the child was not resident in the State at the date of the birth of the child, at any time not later than three years after the alleged father first takes up residence in the State after that date, or
(e) where the alleged father of the child was resident in the State at the date of the birth of the child but ceased to be so resident within three years after that date, at any time not later than three years after the alleged father first takes up residence in the State after that cesser."

These two clauses appear to be premised on the assumption that the man will normally be within the State and they seek to ensure that a man, by going, or staying, abroad will not be able to defeat the woman's right of action. There is, moreover, probably a recognition that in many cases a woman would simply not have the resources to proceed against a defendant abroad. But does this mean that the man's residence, or presence, within the State is an essential jurisdictional requirement? This would surely be a most unsatisfactory approach, since a woman's action would effectively be defeated if a man lived, or went, abroad and *stayed* out of the

---

[137] Cf. Horgan, The financial support of illegitimate children, II Ir. Jur. (n.s.) 59, at 59 (1976).
[138] *Dicey & Morris*, 450, citing *R.* v. *Blane*, 13 Q.B. 769, 773 (1849), *Hampton* v. *Rickard*, 43 L.J.M.C. 133 (1874).
[139] 13 Q.B. 769 (1849).
[140] *O'Dea* v. *Tetau*, [1951] 1 K.B. 184, (K.B Div., 1950), *R.* v. *Wilson, ex p. Pereira*, [1953] 1 Q.B. 59 (Q.B. Div.)
[141] *R.* v. *Humphreys, ex p. Ward*, [1914] 3 K.B. 1237.
[142] In practice local authorities do not take these proceedings: cf. *Shatter*, 604.
[143] Possibly modified by the requirement that the mother should also have been resident within the State.

jurisdiction. The extensions of the limitation period in clauses (d) and (e) would be entirely ineffective in these circumstances.

Perhaps the absence of any equivalent provisions to cover the position where the woman herself is abroad at the time of the birth indicates that her presence in Ireland at or before[144] the birth is not an essential jurisdictional requirement. In *Tetau* v. *O'Dea*[145] Lord Goddard, C.J. drew from similar English provisions the inference that the legislature must have been proceeding on the basis that *R.* v. *Blane* was correct in holding that there was jurisdiction where a woman domiciled within the jurisdiction gave birth outside the jurisdiction.

We have seen[146] that the Maintenance Orders Act 1974 includes affiliation orders within the definition of a "maintenance order".[147] Thus where a woman takes affiliation proceedings in Ireland against a man residing in England (or other "reciprocating jurisdiction"[148]) the Irish court will have the same jurisdiction to hear the proceedings as if the man were residing here and a summons had been served on him.[149]

(2) Choice of Law

Where the Irish courts have jurisdiction in affiliation proceedings it appears that they will apply Irish law.[150] Foreign law may, of course, be relevant in determining whether the child is legitimate or illegitimate.[151]

(3) Recognition of Foreign Orders

Since affiliation orders generally are a species of maintenance order, foreign affiliation orders are capable of being enforced to the same extent as other maintenance orders. We have seen[152] that the Maintenance Orders (Facilities for Enforcement) Act 1920, had no application to affiliation orders.[153] However, as we have also seen,[154] the Maintenance Orders Act 1974 does include affiliation orders within the scope of the definition[155] of maintenance orders.

Whether affiliation orders are likely to raise distinctive issues of public policy[156] has yet to be decided. It seems most unlikely that our courts would refuse to recognise a foreign affiliation order merely because the foreign proceedings were taken later than is permissible under our domestic law. The policy considerations appear to be too divided[157] to justify the extreme step of invoking public policy in this context. Nor would a standard of proof which does not require corroboration of the woman's evidence, as our law still does,[158] seem of itself to be sufficiently significant to warrant resort to public policy. In view of the fact that the Law Reform Commission recommended just this change[159] in 1982 and that it is contained in legislative propo-

---

[144] Cf. clause (a) of section 2 (2) of the 1930 Act (inserted by section 28 (1) (b) of the 1976 Act).

[145] [1951] 1 K.B. 184, at 188-189 (K.B. Div., 1940).

[146] *Supra*, pp. 308-309.

[147] Section 3 (1) of the Act.

[148] I.e., Northern Ireland, Wales or Scotland: *id.*

[149] Section 17 (1).

[150] *Dicey* v. *Morris*, 452.

[151] *Bucheridge* v. *Hall* [1963] 1 Q.B. 614.

[152] *Supra*, p. 309.

[153] Section 10 of the 1920 Act.

[154] *Supra*, pp. 310-311.

[155] Section 3 (1) of the 1974 Act.

[156] Cf. section 9 of the 1974 Act.

[156] Cf. the Law Reform Commission's *Report on Illegitimacy*, pp. 108-110, 116 (L.R.C. 4-1982). The Status of Children Bill 1986 includes no limitation periods for taking maintenance proceedings against an alleged parent.

[158] Illegitimate Children (Affiliation Orders) Act 1930, section 3(2).

[159] L.R.C. 4-1982, p. 111.

sals now before the Oireachtas, the present approach is scarcely likely to be interpreted as containing a basic policy that requires to be upheld in our conflicts of law rules so as to deny recognition to foreign affiliation orders. This is not to suggest that public policy can have no role in relation to affiliation. For example, the approach formerly favoured by Norway of imposing joint responsibility on sexual partners where paternity could not be established[160] might raise some doubts.[161]

[160] Cf. S.F. Hartley, 185.

[161] Perhaps the analogy with section 11 (3) of the Civil Liability Act 1961 suggests that a provision on former Norwegian lines would be upheld; though there is at least a constitutional issue to be resolved, in respect of section 11 (3), as to the extent to which a person may be deprived of property on the basis of 'fault' where no causal relationship is (or can be) established between that person's conduct and another's injury or detriment.

CHAPTER 15

MINORITY[1]

"The jurisdiction of the Court of Chancery in minor matters," said Molony, L.J., in *In re Cunningham Infants*,[2] "has been exercised from time immemorial." It is "a paternalistic jurisdiction, a judicially administrative jurisdiction, in view of which the Chancery Court was put to act on behalf of the Crown, as being the guardian of all infants, in the place of a parent, and as if it were the parent of the child, thus superseding the natural guardianship of the parent."[3]

The Judicature Act 1877, in section 28 (10), declared that in questions relating to the custody and education of infants, the rules of equity should prevail.[4] Under present law jurisdiction in guardianship matters is vested in the High Court and Circuit Court.[5]

What does "guardianship" mean?[6] The term is not defined in our legislation, but clearly it extends to the functions of parents in rearing children, covering such matters as custody[7], education and decisions as to the child's welfare and development. The limits of the concept of guardianship have yet to be determined by our courts.

THE ROLE OF THE CONSTITUTION

The Constitution has had an important role in the development of law relating to guardianship.[8] In Article 41.1.1°, the State recognises the Family[9] as "the natural primary and fundamental unit group of Society" and as "a moral institution

---

[1] See *Rabel*, vol. 1, ch. 15, pp 635 ff., Paulsen, *Appointment of a Guardian in the Conflict of Laws*, 45 Iowa L. Rev. 212 (1960).

[2] [1915] 1 I.R. 380, at 383 (C.A.). See also *In re O'Hara, an Infant*, [1900] 2 I.R. 232, at 251 (C.A., per Holmes, L.J., 1899), *In re Moore, an Infant*, 11 I.C.L.R. 1, at 24-25, 42 (Q.B., per O'Brien, J., 1859.

[3] *The Queen* v. *Gyngall*, [1983] 2 Q.B. 232, at 239 (C.A., per Lord Esher, M.R.), quoted by Molony, L.J., in *In re Cunningham Infants*, [1915] 1 I.R., at 383. See also *In re O'Hara, an Infant, supra*, at 239-240 (per Fitzgibbon, L.J.), 251 (per Holmes, L.J.).

[4] See *In re O'Hara, an Infant, supra*, at 251 (per Holmes, L.J.), *In re Kindersley, an Infant*, [1944] I.R. 111, at 130 (Sup. Ct., per O'Byrne, J., 1943).

[5] Guardianship of Infants Act 1964, section 5, as amended by the Courts Act 1981, section 15: see *R.* v. *R.* [1984] I.R. 296. (High Ct., Gannon, J.), O'Connor, 2 Ir. L. Times (n.s.) 88 (1984), Practice Direction, extracted by *Binchy*, 12, Note 1 (1984). For a thorough analysis, see Hogan, *Constitutional Aspects of the Distribution and Organisation of Court Business*, 6 D.U.L.J. (n.s.) 40 (1984).

[6] See Eekalaar, *What Are Parental Rights?*, 89 L.Q. Rev. 210 (1973), Hall, *The Waning of Parental Rights*, [1972B] Camb. L.J. 248, Hopkins, *Rights and Duties in Relation to Children*, 7 Family L. 169 (1977), Dickens, *The Modern Functions and Limits of Parental Rights*, 97 L.Q. Rev. 462 (1981).

[7] "Custody essentially means the right to physical care and control": *Shatter*, 343. Cf. Article 5 of the *Hague Convention on the Civil Aspects of International Child Abduction* (1980) which provides that "rights of custody" include "rights relating to the care of the person of the child and, in particular, the right to determine the child's place of residence."

[8] See *Kelly* 608 ff especially at 631-639, *Shatter*, 347ff.

[9] Based on marriage: *State (Nicolaou)* v. *An Bord Uchtála* [1966] I.R. 567 (Sup. Ct., 1966, aff'g High Ct., 1965). See *Shatter*, 594-597, Staines, *The Concept of The Family Under the Irish Constitution*,

possessing inalienable and imprescriptible rights, antecedent and superior to all positive law.'' In Article 41.1.2°, the State guarantees to protect the Family in its constitution and authority as the necessary basis of social order and as indispensable to the welfare of the Nation and the State.

In Article 42.1, the State acknowledges that the primary and natural educator of the child is the family and guarantees to respect the inalienable right and duty of parents to provide, according to their means, for the religious and moral, intellectual, physical and social education of their children. Article 42.5, however, allows that ''[i]n exceptional cases, where the parents for physical or moral reasons fail in their duty towards their children, the State, as guardian of the common good, by appropriate means shall endeavour to supply the place of the parents, but always with due regard for the natural and imprescriptible rights of the child.''

It is against the background of these important constitutional provisions that all common law and statutory rules, including the conflicts of law rules[10] must be judged.

On this basis, let us look briefly at some of the main provisions of the Guardianship of Infants Act 1964.[11] The father[12] and mother of a legitimate infant[13] are guardians of the infant jointly.[14] On the death of one parent, the surviving parent is the guardian of the infant, either alone or jointly with any guardian appointed by the deceased parent or by the court.[15] The mother of an illegitimate infant is its guardian.[16] Where an infant has no guardian, the court may appoint a guardian (or guardians) for the infant.[17] The court may remove from office any guardian appointed by will or deed or order of the court,[18] and appoint another guardian in his or her place.[19]

Every guardian is a guardian of the person and of the estate of the infant unless, in the case of a guardian appointed by deed, will or order of the court, the terms of his or her appointment provide otherwise.[20]

Section 11 of the Guardianship of Infants Act 1964[21] is a key provision. It permits a guardian to apply to the Court for its direction on ''any question affecting the welfare''[22] of an infant.[23] The Court may make ''such order as it thinks proper,''[24] specifically in respect of custody,[25] access[26] and maintenance.[27]

11 Ir. Jur. (n.s.) 223 (1976). More generally, see Dickey, *The Notion of 'Family' in Law*, 14 U.W. Austr. L. Rev. 417 (1981).

[10] Cf. pp. 334-339 *infra*.

[11] See *Shatter*, Ch. 13, *Binchy*, 428ff. Section 11 of the Guardianship of Infants Act 1964 was amended by sections 2, 4(g) and 6 of the Age of Majority Act 1965. See Binchy, *Annotation: The Age of Majority Act 1985*, notes to these sections, [1985] *Irish Current Law Statutes Annotated*.

[12] Cf. the definition of ''father'' in section 2.

[13] Cf. *infra*, fn. 23.

[14] Section 6 (1).

[15] Section 6 (2) and (3). As to the power of the father or mother to appoint testamentary guardians, see section 7.

[16] Section 6 (4).

[17] Section 8 (1).

[18] Section 8 (4).

[19] Section 8 (5), See *In re Lemons Infants*, 19 L.R. Ir. 575 (Lord Ashbourne, L.C., 1887), where the Irish Court removed from guardianship (with her consent) a widowed mother where she was permanently resident in England and the infants resided with a paternal uncle in Ireland. The paternal uncle was substituted as guardian.

[20] Section 10 (1). As to the entitlements of guardians relating to custody and the possession and control of the infant's property, see section 10 (2).

[21] As amended by the Age of Majority Act 1985.

[22] Section 11 (1) of the 1964 Act.

[23] An ''infant'' for the purposes of the Guardianship of Infants Act 1964 in general is a person under the age of 18 years who has not married: Guardianship of Infants Act 1964, section 2, amended by the Age of Majority Act 1985, section 2 (3). But section 11 (5) of the 1964 Act, inserted by section 6 of the Age of Majority Act 1985, provides that any reference to an infant in section 11 (except in

APPLICABLE LAW IN PROCEEDINGS RELATING TO CHILDREN

Where the Irish Court hears guardianship proceedings relating to an infant, it seems clear that it should apply the *lex fori*. This appears to follow from section 3 of the Guardianship of Infants Act 1964, which provides as follows:

"Where in any proceedings before any court the custody, guardianship or upbringing of an infant, or the administration of any property belonging to or held on trust for an infant, or the application of the income thereof, is in question, the court, in deciding that question, shall regard the welfare of the infant as the first and paramount consideration."

The scope of this section is very wide. It applies not only in Irish cases involving no foreign element but also in cases where one or both of the parties is of foreign nationality, domicile[28] or residence. It appears clear that section 3 will apply even where a foreign court has already made a guardianship or custody order.[29]

To complicate matters, section 3 must itself be interpreted subject to the constitutional guarantees to the Family. The extent to which these guarantees affect persons abroad is a question yet to be fully answered by our courts.[30]

JURISDICTION OF THE IRISH COURT

We must now consider the question of the jurisdiction of the Irish Court in guardianship proceedings. The Constitution plays an important, if as yet only partially defined, role in determining jurisdiction. We will examine this aspect of the subject below but first it is necessary to consider the position at common law, as modified by statute.

Nationality

At common law, it is well established that jurisdiction will lie where the infant is Irish and resides in Ireland. In *In re Pavitt*,[31] in 1907, Meredith, M.R. accepted[32] that the Irish court:

"has jurisdiction, when the infant is resident within the jurisdiction, and is a British subject, to appoint a guardian, although the infant has no property in this country."

In that case the Master of the Rolls appointed a guardian for an infant, a British subject resident in Ireland, who was entitled to the income of a legacy under the will of her grand-uncle, a French subject, which was invested in French Government Stock, and the interest on which was not being paid owing to the absence of any person who could give a proper receipt for it.

---

section 11 (2) (a), which relates to orders for custody and access) is to include a reference to a child "who has attained the age of eighteen years and is suffering from mental or physical disability to such extent that it is not reasonably possible for him to maintain himself fully". It is doubtful whether this subsection is accurately drafted. It leaves uncertain the status of those who are permitted to apply under it. It would appear to mean that the Court retains a function to make "such order as it thinks proper" (save orders for custody and access) in respect of "any question affecting the welfare" of an *adult* who cannot maintain himself fully on account of physical or mental disability. The subsection was probably intended to allow only for orders for maintenance for these adults, but this is not what it provides.

24 *Id.*
25 *Id.*, section 11 (2) (a).
26 *Id.*
27 *Id.*, section 11 (2) (b). An order for maintenance may not be made under this provision on the application of a natural father of an illegitimate infant: *id.*, section 11 (4).
28 *Dicey & Morris*, 423.
29 *Id.*, and rule 58.
30 Cf., *infra*, pp. 334-339.
31 [1907] 1 I.R. 234, at 236 (Meredith, M.R.).
32 Following *In re Willoughby, an Infant*, 30 Ch. D. 324 (1885).

In the High Court decision of *In re O'Brien, Infants*[33], in 1937, Johnston, J. followed *In re Pavitt*. He appointed the mother of infants resident in the Irish Free State as their guardian for the purposes of establishing their claim to a share in the estate of their late great-aunt in California. The report does not explicitly state that the children were Irish. It is possible that they were not: their great-aunt had died in California; other relatives lived there; their mother had remarried, which is at least consistent with an earlier residence or marriage in the United States, although at the time of the proceedings the family were living in Dublin.

Johnston, J. stated that the infants had "no assets in this country,"[34] although they had claims to the share in the estate of their deceased great-aunt in California. Since, however, Johnston, J. relied so strongly on *In re Pavitt*, stating that he thought that "the same principles apply in this case".[35] it seems more reasonable to conclude that the children had Irish nationality and residence at the time of the proceedings.

The fact that the child is an Irish national, regardless of where he or she may be living or present at the time of the proceedings appears to be a sufficient ground for exercising jurisdiction[36] although it is reasonable that the Irish courts should do so with circumspection.[37]

Ordinary Residence

In England,[38] and Canada[39] jurisdiction can rest, not merely on nationality but on the fact that a minor owes local allegiance to the Crown by virtue of his ordinary residence there. In *Re P. (G.E.) (an Infant)*,[40] in 1964, the English Court of Appeal invoked the controversial decision of *Joyce* v. *Director of Public Prosecutions*[41] in support of the proposition that "the Court of Chancery has jurisdiction to make an order for the custody, education and maintenance of an alien child who is ordinarily resident in this country, even though the child is for the time being absent from this country or taken out of it."[42] The analogy from the law of treason (which Russell, L.J., with impressive understatement, conceded was "peculiarly susceptible to the temper of the moment"[43]) is unfortunate and unhelpful, and it is to be hoped that it will have no attraction for an Irish court.

The most obvious objection to it is that it concentrates on the parent rather than on the child: the notion of allegiance to the State seems to be largely irrelevant to the question whether the Court should intervene in a matter affecting the rights and welfare of a child. But the rejection of the treason analogy should not be a reason for rejecting the ordinary residence of a child as a ground for

[33] [1938] I.R. 323 (High Ct., Johnston, J., 1937).

[34] *Id.*, at 325.

[35] *Id.*

[36] Cf. *Hope* v. *Hope*, 4 De G.M. & G. 328, 43 E.R. 534 (1854), *Re Willoughby (an Infant)*, 30 Ch. D. 324 (1885) (followed in *In re Pavitt, supra*), *Re P. (G.E.) (an Infant)*, [1965] Ch. 568 (C.A., 1964). Cf. *In re Moore, an Infant*, 11 I.C.L.R. 1, at 14 (Q.B., *per* Hayes, J., 1859).

[37] Cf. *R.* v. *Sandbach Justices, Exp. Smith*, [1951] 1 K.B. 62, at (K.B. Div., *per* Lord Goddard, C.J., 1950), *Re P. (G.E.) (an Infant)*, [1965] Ch. 568, at (C.A., *per* Pearson, L.J., 1964), *Harben* v. *Harben*, [1957] 1 All E.R. 379 (P.D.A. Div., Sachs, J., 1956). See also Order 11, Rule 1(i) of the *Rules of the Superior Courts 1986*.

[38] Cf. *Dicey & Morris*, Rule 56 (1), *Re P. (G.E.) (An Infant)*, [1965] Ch. 568 (C.A., 1964).

[39] *Re Walker and Walker*, 14 D.L.R. (3d) 155 (Ont. High Ct., Pennell, J., 1970), *Nielsen* v. *Nielsen*, [1971] 1 O.R. 541, 16 D.L.R. (3d) 33 (High Ct., Galligan, J., 1970), *Re Firestone and Firestone*, 90 D.L.R. (3d) 742, at 746 (High Ct., Cromarty, J., 1978).

[40] [1965] Ch. 568 (C.A., 1964).

[41] [1946] A.C. 347.

[42] [1965] Ch., at 585 (*per* Lord Denning, M.R.).

[43] *Id.*, at 594.

jurisdiction.[44] It may in some cases be a vital factor, especially where the child is no longer actually present in Ireland, having been "kidnapped" by a parent or other person or having been detained while on a short visit abroad.[45]

A disadvantage to the ordinary residence test is that the relatively uncertain dimensions of the concept of "ordinary residence" would create "an undesirable preliminary issue which could only be resolved by the decision of the Court".[46] This can work particular hardship in the "kidnapping" cases, which will be considered later in the chapter.[47]

Assuming that the court applies the ordinary residence ground, the question then arises as to how to determine the ordinary residence of a child who cannot decide for himself where to live. Taking the age of 16 as a dividing point, Lord Denning, M.R. in *Re P. (G.E.) (an Infant)*[48] addressed the problem as follows:

> "So long as the father and mother are *living together in the matrimonial home*, the child's ordinary residence is the home — and it is still his ordinary residence, even while he is away at boarding school. It is his base, from whence he goes out and to which he returns. When father and mother are at variance and living *separate and apart* and by arrangement the child resides *in the house of one of them* — then that home is his ordinary residence, even though the other parent has access and the child goes to see him from time to time. I do not see that a child's ordinary residence, so found, can be changed by kidnapping him and taking him from his home, even if one of his parents is the kidnapper. Quite generally, I do not think a child's ordinary residence can be changed by one parent without the consent of the other. It will not be changed until the parent who is left at home, childless, acquiesces in the change, or delays so long in bringing proceedings that he or she must be taken to acquiesce. Six months' delay would, I should have thought, go far to show acquiescence. Even three months might in some circumstances. But not less."

Habitual Residence

It is possible that, with the increasing international significance of habitual residence as a connecting factor, an Irish court would be more disposed to rest the ground of jurisdiction on habitual rather than ordinary residence. It is worth noting that habitual residence is conceived by the Law Reform Commission[49] as a replacement of domicile.

Domicile

This brings us to the question whether domicile, under present law, affords a good

[44] Cf. *Re P. (G.C.) (An Infant)*, [1965] Ch., at 584 (*per* Lord Denning, M.R.):
"The Crown protects every child who has his home here and will protect him in respect of his home. It will not permit anyone to kidnap the child and spirit it out of the realm. Not even its father or mother can be allowed to do so without the consent of the other. The kidnapper cannot escape the jurisdiction of the court by such a stratagem. If, as in this case, it is the father who flies away with the child, the mother is not bound to follow him to a foreign clime. She can bring her proceedings against him in England. I know that it will be difficult for her to enforce any order the court may make. But it is not impossible. The father may have assets here. Or he may return here for a visit. And if she has eventually to apply to the courts of the foreign country, they will surely respect an order made by the courts of the ordinary residence — just as we should — for the simple reason that it is his home and, as such, is entitled to special consideration."
[45] English Law Commission Working Paper No. 68 and Scottish Law Commission Memorandum No. 23, *Custody of Children — Jurisdiction and Enforcement within the United Kingdom* para. 3.64 (1976), quoting with approval from Michael Albery's Note of Dissent, para. (5), in the Hodson Committee's *Report on Conflict of Jurisdiction Affecting Children*, Cmnd. 842 (1959).
[46] *Id.*
[47] *Infra*, pp. 337-344.
[48] [1965] Ch., at 585-586. See further the English Law Commission Working Paper No. 68 and the Scottish Law Commission Memorandum No. 23, *Custody of Children — Jurisdiction and Enforcement within the United Kingdom*, para. 3.46 (1976).
[49] Law Reform Commission's *Report on Domicile and Habitual Residence as Connecting Factors in Private International Law*, para. 18 (L.R.C. 7 - 1983).

ground of jurisdiction in proceedings affecting minors. Domicile has played an important role in Scots law on this question.[50] In the United States, the first Restatement took the position that the state of the child's domicile had sole jurisdiction in custody proceedings.[51] This rule, not surprisingly,[52] proved unworkable. The Restatement, Second now provides[53] three possible grounds for jurisdiction, based, respectively, on the domicile of the child in the state, his or her presence there, and the existence of a controversy as to the custody of the child between persons who are personally subject to the jurisdiction of the state. Moreover, the Uniform Child Custody Jurisdiction Act 1968, did not adopt domicile as a test, preferring to base pre-eminent jurisdiction on the state of the child's last established home.[54]

Domicile had some advantages as a ground of jurisdiction, but these are largely a matter of history. At a time when the domicile of dependency of married women and of children operated with full force throughout most of the common law world it seemed to make some sense to treat guardianship as yet another part of a larger unity of "family domicile" (albeit one determined by the father).[55]

Once the domicile of dependency of married women was abolished or modified, and the domicile of children became dependent on that of the parent having custody[56] rather than on the father, the rationale for domicile in guardianship proceedings was severely weakened. Moreover, the extension of jurisdiction in matrimonial causes well beyond domicile, to habitual residence and other connecting factors less permanent than domicile, also made an exclusive reference to domicile in guardianship matters difficult to support.[57]

An important disadvantage of domicile as a test in guardianship proceedings is its arbitrariness, which may on occasion result in a quite inappropriate assertion of jurisdiction.[58]

Presence Within the State

The Courts may also exercise jurisdiction based on the mere presence of the child in the State, even where there is no supplementary connecting factor, such as domicile or nationality. This is clear from the decision of *In re Magees, Infants*,[59] in 1892. The case concerned children in Ireland whose father, an Irish emigrant, had become a naturalised American citizen. Porter, M.R. had no hesitation in rejecting the argument that he had no jurisdiction in guardianship proceedings on account of the fact that the children were aliens.

The Master of the Rolls stigmatised as question-begging the argument that the

---

[50] See e.g., *Kitson* v. *Kitson*, 1945 S.C. 434, *Babington* v. *Babington*, 1955 S.C. 115.
[51] Cf. *Restatement of the Law of Conflict of Laws*, pp. 117, 145-146 (1934). See further *Leflar*, 586, *Weintraub*, 194-196.
[52] Cf. *Leflar*, 586-586.
[53] *Restatement of the Law (Second), Conflict of Laws*, p. 79 (1971).
[54] Cf. English Law Commission Working Paper No. 68 and Scottish Law Commission Memorandum No. 23, *Custody of Children—Jurisdiction and Enforcement within the United Kingdom*, para. 3.44, 3.63 (1976), *Scoles & Hay*, 524-525.
[55] W.P. No. 68 & Memorandum No. 23, para. 3.46.
[56] *Hope* v. *Hope* [1968] N.I. 1, and *supra* p. 86.
[57] English Law Commission Working Paper No. 68 and Scottish Law Commission Memorandum No. 23, *Custody of Children—Jurisdiction and Enforcement within the United Kingdom*, para. 3.48 (1976).
[58] In *Re P. (G.E.) (an Infant)*, [1965] Ch. 568, (C.A., 1964), where the English Court of Appeal rejected domicile as a test, Pearson, L.J. said (at 589-590):
    "A child of foreign nationality but English domicile of origin might have lived abroad for many years and have no intention of returning to England, and yet have his English domicile of origin surviving or reviving if he had not acquired or had lost a domicile of choice. The answer made in argument is that the infant, though technically domiciled in this country, had ceased to have any real connection with this country. That answer, however, does not wholly remove the objection to a theory which asserts the existence of a jurisdiction in a case where its existence would be absurd."
    See also *id.*, at 583-584 (*per* Lord Denning, M.R.) and at 592-593 (*per* Russell, L.J.). It should be noted that Order 11, Rule 1(i) of the *Rules of the Superior Courts 1986* enables the Court to order service out of the jurisdiction where the child is domiciled in Ireland.
[59] 31 L.R. (Ir.) 513 (Porter, M.R., 1892).

exercise of jurisdiction by the Crown as *parens patriae* could not extend to children of aliens, to whom the Crown did not stand in the relation of *parens*. A "host of cases"[60] showed that jurisdiction could be exercised in respect of alien infants, "for their benefit and protection".[61] There was in his view "no question"[62] but that the jurisdiction existed.

In England, in *Re P. (G.E.) (an Infant)*,[63] Pearson, L.J. said that:

"[i]t would be unusual for the English court to exercise wardship jurisdiction in such cases, but there might be some occasion for it, for example, in a case of emergency to prevent some grievous wrong being committed, or in a case where an order of the English court could usefully and in furtherance of justice support or supplement an order of the foreign court having jurisdiction by virtue of the nationality or residence of the infant."

The words "for example" should not be overlooked. The court's obligation to protect the welfare of minors should ensure that their mere physical presence here will suffice in some cases, although in the actual exercise of this jurisdiction the Court may well decide that it is better to stand back from the merits of the care and return the child to the country whence he or she came. In *Re A (Infants)*,[64] Harman, L.J. said:

"In my judgment, the children not being here as the result of some deceit or wrongdoing, it is quite unheard of that this court should decline jurisdiction and say that it will have no more to do with them. Such a thing was never heard of before the so-called kidnapping cases came into being. In my judgment, the jurisdiction of the court — which, incidentally, I think is not disputed — results [from] the fact that the children are plainly now in need of protection."

Foreign Guardians

We must now consider the position of guardians appointed by a foreign court. There appears to be no definitive Irish or English[65] case dealing with this question. On the principle of reciprocity it may be argued that our law should recognise the same grounds for jurisdiction as Irish courts accept.[66] This is scarcely controversial save in relation to the ground based on presence of the child within the State. Our courts might be understandably slow to recognise every foreign appointment made on the basis of such a transient connection.

Where the Irish courts recognise the appointment of a guardian by a foreign court, they still preserve the entitlement to intervene in the child's interests. Section 3 of the Guardianship of Infants Act 1964 gives specific power to the Irish court to do so.

Where a foreign guardian's entitlement to exercise the rights of guardianship has

---

[60] *Id.*, at 519.
[61] *Id.*
[62] *Id.*, at 522.
[63] [1965] Ch. 568, at 588 (C.A., 1964).
[64] [1970] Ch. 665, at 674 (C.A.,).
[65] See *Dicey & Morris*, 438.
[66] *Id.*

not been challenged, he may exercise his functions without hindrance, provided that these functions are within the scope of those possessed by a guardian under Irish law, *mutatis mutandis*.[67]

Thus, in the Supreme Court decision of *Re Corcoran, an Infant*,[68] Murnaghan, J. observed that:

> "....the Courts of the country in which the infant actually is will pay the greatest consideration to the law of that country which is the personal law of the child and will follow that law in the absence of sound and compelling reasons to the contrary."

So far as the minor's moveable property within the State is concerned, it appears that in general the foreign guardian's power to dispose of it "should be regulated by the law of the country to which he owes his appointment as guardian."[69] But where there is a fund in court, the Irish court is not obliged to hand over property to the foreign guardian automatically; instead, the court may decline to approve of payment over to the guardian until satisfied that the fund will be duly applied by the guardian.[70]

Broadly speaking, the decisions fall into two classes. In the first, a minor domiciled abroad is entitled to funds in Court in Ireland and reaches an age when, by the law of his domicile, but not by Irish law, he becomes entitled to receive, and give an absolute discharge for, moneys which are his property. In this class of case, "the law of the domicile has been recognised as the governing law in respect of...'moveable property', and the moneys have been paid out to the minor."[71]

In the second class of case, where again an Irish Court holds a minor's property, the minor domiciled abroad is still under the disability of minority according to both the law of his domicile and Irish law. In this class of case, as Kennedy, C.J. observed in *In re Duddy*[72]:

> "[a] different principle governs.... The infant is not, nor is his guardian or any other person applying on his behalf, entitled as of right to have the infant's funds handed over or his monies paid out merely so as to handle and administer them in the place of domicile outside the jurisdiction of the Court. This Court must in such cases be satisfied by evidence that it is to the advantage of the infants to entertain the application; that any moneys paid out will be applied for the benefit of the infants; and that in all the circumstances it is proper, and perhaps necessary, in the interests of the infants to let the moneys go out of the jurisdiction."

[67] *Id.*, 439 referring to *Johnstone* v. *Beattie*, 10 Cl. & F. 42, 113, 114 (1843), and by way of contrast *Nugent* v. *Vetzera*, L.R. 2 Eq. 704, 714 (1866). See also *Cheshire & North*, 475, *Bell & Armstrong*, 31.

[68] 86 I.L.T.R. 6, at 13 (Sup. Ct., 1950). Murnaghan, J. referred with approval to a passage from Page-Wood V.C.'s judgment in *Nugent* v. *Vetzera*, L.R. 2 Eq. 704, at 714 (1866): "The same authority which we claim here on behalf of the Crown as *parens patriae*, is claimed by every other independent state, and should not be interfered with except on some grounds which I do not think it necessary to specify, guarding myself, however, against anything like an abdication of the jurisdiction of this Court to appoint guardians." See also *id.*, at 10 (High Ct., per Davitt, J.); cf. *id.*, at 12 (High Ct., per Dixon, J.). In *In re Magees, Infants*, 31 L.R.(Ir.) 513, at 521-522 (1892), Porter, M.R. referred with approval to *Nugent* v. *Vetzera*.

[69] *Dicey & Morris*, 439, citing *Re Crichton's Trust*, 24 L.T. (o.s.) 267 (1855), *Mackie* v. *Darling*, L.R. 12 Eq. 319 (1871), *Re Ferguson's Trusts*, 22 W.R. 762 (1874), *Hanrahan* v. *Hanrahan*, 19 O.R. 396 (1890), *Kelly* v. *O'Brian*, 31 D.L.R. 770 (1916).

[70] *Dicey & Morris*, 439, referring to *Re Chatard's Settlement*, [1899] 1 Ch. 712 and *Re White, Deceased; Ingram* v. *White*, [1918] 1 I.R. 19 (Barton, J., 1917). In *White's* case, Barton, J. permitted the Irish trustees of a will to pay all accruing income to a Philadelphia trust corporation, which had been appointed guardian of the estate of a minor beneficiary, an American subject.

[71] *In re Duddy, Minors*, [1925] 1 I.R. 196, at 198 (Kennedy, C.J., 1924), citing *Abernethy* v. *Greer*, 36 I.L.T.R. 63 (Barton, J., 1902) and *Donohoe* v. *Donohue*, 19 L.R. Ir. 349 (Chatterton, V.-C., 1887). See further pp. 90-91, *supra*.

[72] [1925] 1 I.R. 196, at 198-199 (Kennedy, C.J., 1924).

The Chief Justice considered that the Irish Court would be "very slow"[73] to hand over property from this jurisdiction where to do so would be of no advantage to the minors on account of the fact that in the place of their domicile they had property yielding income more than sufficient for their every requirement. But where the other extreme applied, where the minors had no property or income whatever in the place of their domicile, it would be the duty of the Irish Court to make such provisions as would secure, so far as their means would allow, the support and education of the minors in their place of domicile.

In *Dharamal* v. *Lord Holmpatrick*,[74] Johnston, J. described this rule as "well settled". In this case a six-year old Indian girl domiciled in Indore, Central India, won a prize of about £230 in the Irish Sweep. Her father was appointed guardian on her person and property by the Indore court. The order made him competent to give receipts for all money received by him for his daughter. The money was paid into Court by the Irish Sweep, and the father applied for payment out of the fund for her benefit.

Johnston, J. declined to pay out the corpus of the fund but made an order authorising payment of the income to the father for a period of seven years, to be used for his daughter's benefit. He noted that the sum involved was small by European standards but that it probably would be "a very considerable fortune"[75] for the girl if it was carefully preserved and kept intact. It was nearly equivalent to her father's total income for four years, and its continued existence as a capital sum would, in the judge's view, render the girl "a much more important personage in her father's household"[76] than if the whole amount were paid out to him to be spent according to his discretion, "even a discretion exercised wisely".[77]

The girl's father had stated in his affidavit that he would use the fund so as "substantially [to] improve her position, help her advancement in life and ultimately settle her well." This did not impress the judge, who regarded it as "no more than an expression of... benevolent intentions."[78] No information had been given as to the social and political conditions under which the girl was being brought up. The judge did not know how the caste system affected her life; nor was he aware of when, if ever, the child would reach full age (or its equivalent mode of emancipation under Indore law). He was "entirely in the dark"[79] as to how the money, if sent to India, would be safeguarded or what facilities there were for investment of trust money.

In *Orlando* v. *Earl of Fingal*[80] Gavan Duffy, J. ordered the payment out of a Sweep prize of about £460 to the father of a 13-year-old boy. The father had been appointed guardian of his son's property by a New York court. Under New York law, the father as guardian was competent to receive all moneys due to the minor.

Counsel for the father referred to *Dharamal* v. *Lord Holmpatrick*[81] and sought to distinguish it on the basis that the laws and conditions in the United States approximated more closely to those pertaining in this country than did those in India. Gavan Duffy J. made the order sought without discussion.

The fact that a guardian has been quite properly appointed by a foreign court is not of itself a conclusive reason for the Irish court to decline to appoint another guardian. The Irish court may appoint a guardian where it is in the interests of the

[73] *Id.*, at 199.
[74] [1935] I.R. 760 (High Ct., Johnston, J.).
[75] *Id.*, at 763.
[76] *Id.*, at 764.
[77] *Id.*
[78] *Id.*
[79] *Id.*
[80] [1940] I.R. 281 (High Ct., Gavan Duffy, J.).
[81] *Supra.*

child to do so. Again section 3 of the Guardianship of Infants Act 1964[82] would appear to demand that the welfare of the child should not be put into second place to an inflexible conflict rule. The fact that a foreign custody order is not final would also be a factor weighing against automatic enforcement here.[83]

Minors Taken Abroad

Where an Irish court has made an order in relation to the custody or welfare of a minor, it does not lose jurisdiction merely because the minor is taken abroad in breach of the terms of the order.[84] In *In re Brown, a Minor*,[85] Brady, L.C. intervened when a minor, in disobedience of an earlier order of the Court,[86] had been removed from the jurisdiction to France, where she was being educated according to religious tenets contrary to those specified in the earlier order. The circumstances bringing about the Lord Chancellor's intervention were interesting. The minor, aged fifteen, had written to him from Boulogne, expressing the wish to be brought under the direct care and supervision of the Court. The Lord Chancellor had sent his secretary to Boulogne, "to wait on the minor, and to bring her over to Dublin".[87] On her arrival in Dublin, the Lord Chancellor "took the earliest opportunity of seeing her, and ascertaining every fact which might be material to the proper exercise of the jurisdiction of the Court."[88]

Of course, before making an order when a minor is not within the jurisdiction, the Court will have regard to the likely practical effects of doing so. The issue is one that has come before the courts increasingly in recent years with the growth of international child abduction by parents. We will be examining this subject later in the chapter.[89]

Proposed Removal of a Minor Abroad

So far as the exercise of the rights of guardianship, whether by a foreign or Irish guardian, would involve the removal of a minor from Ireland, the welfare of the minor is the dominant consideration.[90] Thus, in *In re Medley, a Minor*,[91] in 1871, the Irish Court permitted an orphan living in impoverished circumstances to go to live with his "rich, prosperous, and respectable"[92] great-uncle in Ontario.[93]

Similarly, in *In re Westby Minors (No. 2)*[94], in 1934, the former Supreme Court,

---

[82] Cf. *Re B's Settlement*, [1940] Ch. 54 (Morton, J., 1939), *McKee v. McKee*, [1951] A.C. 352 (P.C.), *Re Kernot*, [1965] Ch. 217, at 224 (Buckley, J., 1964), *Dicey & Morris*, 440-441.

[83] Cf. *Larkins v. National Union of Mineworkers*, as yet unreported, High Ct., Barrington, J. 18 June, 1985 (1984-8465P), where the lack of finality of a foreign order appointing a receiver weighed against its enforcement here.

[84] Cf. *Fabbri v. Fabbri*, [1962] 1 All E.R. 35 (P.D.A. Div., Scarman, J., 1961).

[85] 8 Ir. Ch. Rep 172 (Brady, L.C., 1858).

[86] *In re Browne, a Minor*, 2 Ir. Ch. Rep. 151 (Berry Cusack Smith, M.R., 1852).

[87] 8 Ir. Ch. Rep., at 173.

[88] *Id.*

[89] *Infra*, pp. 339-346.

[90] Cf. *Cheshire & North*, 475, *Bell & Armstrong*, 42. The child's constitutional right to travel appears to be subject to the predominant consideration of its welfare: (*The State (K.M. and R.D.) v. Minister for Foreign Affairs*, [1979] I.R. 73 (High Ct., Finlay, P., 1978).

[91] I.R. 6 Eq. 339 (Chy. 1 Lord O'Hagan, L.C., 1871).

[92] *Id.*, at 341.

[93] The order required one of the guardians of the orphan to enter into security by recognisance, to ensure that the child would be returned to the jurisdiction of the Court when required by the Court, and to ensure that the great-uncle furnished, to the Lord Chancellor at stated periods, "proper and necessary information relative to the condition, progress, and well being of the minor . . .": I.R. 6 Eq., at 342-343. See also *In re Salter's Trusts*, 17 Ir. Ch. Rep. 176 (Cusack Smith, M.R., 1866).

[94] [1934] I.R. (Sup. Ct., 1934 rev'g Kennedy, C.J., 1933), *Wyndham v. Ennismore* 1 Keen 467, 48 E.R. 386 (1837).

by a majority,[95] permitted a minor ward of the Irish Court, aged 12, to be educated at Eton. The minor's mother, who was the guardian of his person and joint guardian of his fortune, was residing in England. She was Irish and had formerly lived in Ireland but objected to returning to live in Ireland because six men had been shot dead in the house she had been living in in November 1920 and she feared that, if she returned to the country, she would be in a constant state of nervous tension, to the detriment of the minor, possibly resulting in the recurrence of a nervous breakdown which she had suffered after this occurrence.

Murnaghan J. said:

> "There can be no question as to the rule under which the Court will not allow a ward to be taken or detained outside its jurisdiction if thereby the Court is deprived of securing compliance with any order which the Court may think fit to make. But so long as the Court is satisfied that its order will be obeyed, a ward may be permitted to depart out of the jurisdiction of the Court if the step proposed to be taken is for the benefit of the ward."[96]

Murnaghan, J. noted that there was:

> "also involved the question of parental control. In my opinion, in so far as the legislation has given no indication of State policy, the Court will better pursue its function by complying as far as possible with the wishes of the parents and near relatives of the ward. It is well known that some parents in the Irish Free State do send their children to school in England in accordance with their views of what is best for the benefit of their children, and in so doing they are acting within their legal right. I am of the opinion that this Court should not on an assumption of national policy[97] force children to be educated in a way which the parents do not approve."[98]

In *Re Corcoran, an Infant*[99] in 1950, the Supreme Court held that a child should not be returned to his English mother who was domiciled and resided in England, where the child was living with his paternal grandmother in Ireland, his father being at the time in prison in England for having defied a custody order of the English High Court. Murnaghan, J. for the majority,[100] noted that, if the mother were to be permitted to remove the child to England, her undertaking to bring him up as a Catholic could not be enforced. At this time, prior to the *Tilson*[101] decision, a father was still considered to have superior rights in regard to the religious upbringing of his children. In England however, since 1925,[102] the welfare of the child had

---

[95] Fitzgibbon and Murnaghan, J.J., Sullivan P. dissenting.

[96] [1934] I.R., at 327-328.

[97] Contrast Kennedy, C.J.'s approach, *id.,* at 314-315:
> "It would . . . be quite abnormal to seek original general education out of the jurisdiction of the Court and outside the Saorstát in which presumably the future lives of wards of the Court will ordinarily be cast. I cannot, sitting in this Court, assume the contrary, that is to say assume that the wards will not be able to live in this country (which no one has ever suggested to me to be overpopulated) and that, therefore, their education must be such as will fit them rather to live elsewhere. Such an assumption on my part would imply grievous disloyalty to the State and to the people whose commission is my authority."

See further Hogan, *Irish Nationalism as a Legal Ideology,* 75 Studies 528, at 529-530 (1986).

[98] [1934] I.R. at 331. Cf. *Kelly,* 639, who observes that this statement "foreshadowed" Article 42 of the Constitution. This raises the question as to the extent to which parents' constitutional right to educate their children embraces a foreign education, and the extent to which judicial concern for the ability of the court to monitor and enforce its orders may modify this right. Cf. *Re Kindersley* [1944] I.R. 111, where these constitutional dimensions were not discussed.

[99] 86 I.L.T.R. 6, (Sup. Ct., aff'g. High Ct., 1950).

[100] Maguire, C.J. and O'Byrne, J. concurring.

[101] [1951] I.R. 1 (Sup. Ct., 150, aff'g High Ct., Gavan Duffy, P., 1950).

[102] Guardianship of Infants Act 1925, section 1.

been made the first and paramount consideration and the father's superior rights expressly extinguished. Murnaghan J. said:

"If the child is removed to England the law of England will not give to the father that claim which the law of Ireland allows to him, and no practical way has been suggested by which the undertaking of the mother can be enforced."[103]

Developing this line of thought into one with constitutional implications, he continued:

"Corresponding to the duty of parents to provide, according to their means, for the religious and moral, physical and social education of their children, the child has a right that such education should be provided. When the Family, which is the natural educator of the child, has been broken up it is the duty of the State to endeavour to supply the place of the parents. When the child is within the jurisdiction of the Court it can weigh all the factors, the welfare of the child, the rights and feelings of the mother, and secure the best arrangement that can be made in the circumstances. But in this case the only proposition before the Court is that the child should be given to the mother in order to be taken out of the jurisdiction. Considering and weighing all the circumstances in this case, I am of the opinion that the Court should not make such an order...."[104]

There is a clear indication here that constitutional considerations in relation to Article 42 should make the Court reluctant to authorise the removal of a child from the State, especially where the parents are no longer living together.

Black, J. dissented. He said:

"If the law were still the same in both countries, I for my part would at once hand over the child to its mother upon the principle of the comity of the Courts, having no doubt that the English Courts would enforce the father's right as to religious upbringing. But, when a child is once within our jurisdiction and entitled to the protection of our laws, I think we are not bound by any principle of comity to send it into another jurisdiction, if, owing to a difference in the law its upbringing within that jurisdiction could be directed in a way which our law would forbid. On the other hand we are not bound to refuse to give it to the mother. For me the question is simply whether I could properly accept the mother's undertaking as to its upbringing. If she were resident within the jurisdiction, I think we could properly accept it, knowing that if she broke it the father would have a right to get an Order to enforce it....Yet, if we took her undertaking and gave her the custody, she being within our jurisdiction, we should still be taking some risk, for she might at any time leave the jurisdiction. I deduce, then, that we are not obliged to eliminate *all* risk. No doubt the risk would be larger if she were out of the jurisdiction *ab initio*, as this mother is. But, I have come to the conclusion that if I would be justified in taking the one risk, I would be justified in taking the other. Unenforceable undertakings were taken in *In re Kindersley*,[105] one from the Irish mother by the English Court and the other from Lord Kindersley by this Court, though he was out of its jurisdiction."[106]

INTERNATIONAL CHILD ABDUCTION[107]

We must now consider the subject of international child abduction. The growth

[103] 86 I.L.T.R. at, 17-18.
[104] *Id.*, at 18.
[105] [1944] I.R. 11 (Sup. Ct., 1944, aff'g High Ct., 1943).
[106] 86 I.L.T.R., at 22.
[107] See O'Connor, *"Kidnapping" and the Irish Courts*, 2 Ir. L. Times (n.s.) 4 (1984), McCutcheon, *Kidnapping Reconsidered*, 3 Ir. L. Times (n.s.) 146 (1985), Cole, *Judicial Discretion in Child-Snatching Cases*, 129 New L.J. 64 (1979), Khan, *Child Abduction and Custody*, 16 Family L. 114 (1986), and the Law Reform Commission's *Report on the Hague Convention on the Civil Aspects of International Child Abduction and Some Related Matters* (L.R.C. 12–1985).

of marriage breakdown and divorce internationally and the spread of relatively cheap air travel have contributed significantly to this problem. But one of the strongest incentives to flee to another jurisdiction has been caused ironically, by the desire of courts in most countries to decide questions of custody, according to what is in the best interests of the child in question. Where all of the parties remain resident in one jurisdiction, this approach has a number of obvious advantages but, where the child is brought from one jurisdiction to another, difficulties may arise. The courts in the country where the child is brought are often unable to make a decision as to what is in the child's welfare without obtaining reports from psychologists, psychiatrists and social workers, as well, perhaps, as receiving information from schools and doctors abroad. All of this takes time and "time is on the side of the abducting parent".[108]

The accepted wisdom among psychologists and psychiatrists today is that continuity in relationships is of very great importance to the child. Thus, if the abducting parent can spin matters out long enough, eventually the psychological evidence will run in his or her favour. This strategy is scarcely in the interests of the child in question; nor indeed do children as a group benefit from the process.

The courts are conscious of this problem.[109] In *O'D. Infants; O'D.* v. *O'D.*,[110] a man brought his children from Alberta to Ireland, without the consent of their mother. The mother had some time previously obtained an order from the Alberta Supreme Court granting her custody. The father who had been living in New Mexico, had obtained a divorce there, the court granting joint custody of the children to both parents but ordering that the children's principal place of residence should be with their mother.

As regards Irish connections, the children's mother was originally from Derry, and the father's second wife was also Irish. When the children were brought to Ireland, they took up residence with the second wife's mother in Dublin.

In proceedings before Hamilton J., the children's mother argued that the children should be returned in her custody to Alberta, which was "the proper jurisdiction with which they had close and continued connection". Their father replied by arguing that their mother was an unsuitable person to have custody on account of the condition of her home, her alleged alcoholism and other factors.

Hamilton, J. held that the proper forum to decide questions concerning the custody of the children was the Supreme Court of Alberta and that, providing the Irish Court was assured that no direct harm would come to the children thereby, they should be returned to their mother's custody. To ascertain whether any direct harm would come to the children, the Court directed a psychiatric examination of the children and of both their parents.[111]

The approach favoured by Hamilton, J. has echoes in decisions in several countries. The English Court of Appeal decision of *Re C (Minors)*[112] placed greater emphasis on the children's welfare than had been apparent in some earlier decisions, including

[108] Editorial, *International Kidnapping: Why the Law Must Be Reformed*, 3 Ir. L. Times (n.s.) 193, at 193 (1985). The Irish courts are conscious of this danger and go to great lengths to prevent children who have been abducted by a parent from being taken out of the jurisdiction. They permit the solicitor for the applicant "to notify by telephone and telegram the Commissioner of the Gardaí and all points of departure from the State of the content of the order": *Shatter*, 370.

[109] Cf. *Re H. (Infants)*, [1966] 1 W.L.R. 381, at 393 (*per* Cross, J.).

[110] Unreported, High Ct., Hamilton, J., 13/14/22 June 1979, as summarised in 73 Incorp. L. Soc. Gazette No. 6 (July-August 1979).

[111] The outcome was that the parties agreed that the children should remain with their mother during all school terms and with their father in Ireland during vacations. All future applications concerning custody and access were to be made to the Alberta courts. See also *A.* v. *H.*, High Ct., D'Arcy, J., 23 August 1978 (1978-484) discussed by *Shatter*, 370 (no written judgment delivered).

[112] [1978] Fam. 105.

Re H. (Infants)[113], which was cited in argument to Hamilton, J., in *O'D. Infants; O'D.* v. *O'D.* The Law Reform Commission have suggested[114] that if the matter is fully argued in the Irish courts it is possible that they will adopt a similar approach to that favoured in *Re C. (Minors)* when dealing with children who have been abducted into the jurisdiction. In many cases this would not lead to a significantly different outcome from that tentatively endorsed by Hamilton, J. in *O'D Infants; O'D.* v. *O'D.* But, as the Commission observe, "the conceptual framework of considering the welfare of the children untrammelled by any binding guideline necessarily gives more scope for a judge, who is so minded, to assume jurisdiction to examine the merits of the case."[115]

THE CONSTITUTIONAL DIMENSION

We must now consider the effect of the Constitution on our conflicts rules relating to guardianship. Our Constitution is imbued with a philosophical notion of human persons, their moral capacities, and their relationship with the State. Since the Constitution is the basic law, our conflicts rules must be applied subject to its provisions. The question therefore arises as to the extent to which the Constitutional guarantees in relation to persons and the family range outwards to embrace people with foreign connections, such as foreign nationality, domicile or residence.

The philosophical notion underpinning many of the Constitutional guarantees is clearly not local in its scope. In other words, this notion of a person as a moral entity, with rights and responsibilities, applies to all human beings. The norms at the base of the Constitution are clearly not consistent with only *Irish* people as having the right to life, to marry and to rear their children, for example[116]. This is

---

[113] [1966] 1 W.L.R. 381 (Cross, J.).

[114] *Report on the Hague Convention on the Civil Aspects of International Child Abduction and Some Related Matters*, p. 9 (L.R.C. 12 – 1985).

[115] L.R.C. 12 – 1985, p. 9.

[116] A number of the constitutional guarantees are limited to "citizens". Cf. *Kelly*, 433. The extent to which a non-citizen may assert a constitutional right in respect of such guarantees has not been fully settled, but the general trend is towards extending protection to non-citizens: see *Kelly*, 433-434, Binchy, *The Need for a Constitutional Amendment*, in A. Flannery, ed., *Abortion and Law*, 116, at 118-119 (1983). In *The State (Nicolaou)* v. *A.G.*, [1966] I.R. 567 (Sup. Ct., 1966, aff'g High Ct., 1965), the Supreme Court left this question open; cf. *id.*, at 645 (*per* Walsh, J., for the Court). In the High Court neither Murnaghan J. nor Henchy, J. showed any enthusiasm for extending constitutional protection to non-citizens; but Tevan, J.'s observations to the contrary (at 599) are of particular relevance:

"The Constitution enjoins legal recognition of the fundamental rights it defines and acknowledges. Those rights do not owe their existence to the Constitution. While the Constitution, governing the rights and duties of citizen to citizen, citizen to State and State to citizen, can guarantee the preservation, maintenance and enforcement of those rights and duties only to citizens, I do not think it follows that we are obliged to deny the constitutional protection of those natural rights enshrined in the Constitution to every non-citizen merely on the ground of his non-citizenship, even to a person who not only lacks citizenship but is also not resident here (for we have resident non-citizens to whom the point would be of more practical importance).

There must, of course, be many cases wherein the non-citizen must submit to a position of inequality with the citizen, where the law will deny to the non-citizen privileges and legal remedies enjoyed by the citizen. Where, however, there is no conflict between the common good and the right sought to be asserted by a non-citizen, I do not think the Court should feel obliged willy-nilly to refuse to hear the non-citizen's plaint; that is to say where, if his case be well founded otherwise, his own personal rights are involved."

In *State (Trimbole)* v. *Governor of Mountjoy Prison*, [1985] I.R. 550 (Sup. Ct., aff'g High Ct., Egan, J.) the constitutional protections available to citizens against being deported improperly were held to extend to an Australian citizen on a temporary visit to Ireland. See especially *id.*, at 581-582 (*per* McCarthy, J.). See also *Attorney-General, ex rel. The Society for the Protection of Unborn Children Ireland Ltd* v. *Open Counselling Ltd and Dublin Well-Woman Centre Ltd.*, High Ct., Hamilton, J., 19 December 1986 (1985-5652 P.). In *In re Electoral (Amendment) Bill*

important when we consider where the "cut off" point should be, beyond which the Constitution extends no protection, on account of insufficient connection with a person claiming its aid.

Obviously there must be *some* limits to the scope of this protection. The fact that the Constitution has a particular vision of human capacity does not mean that every human being can call it in aid. In the particular context of guardianship, the Constitution characterises as fundamental certain parental rights relative to the State and others. In many foreign countries there is no similar characterisation, and, indeed the philosophical tendency in some countries is in the opposite direction. There may well be a tendency, therefore, for parents with fairly tenuous connections with Ireland to invoke the Constitution in cases where their legal rights in a foreign country imperil their relationship with their children.

In the cases where the Irish courts have faced this question, they have tended towards an *ad hoc* solution, rather than to articulate broad principles of general application. We must therefore await a detailed judicial analysis of this important issue.

In *Northampton County Council* v. *A.B.F. and M.B.F.*,[117] in 1981, an English local authority sought the return of a 14-year-old child, where she had been placed in their care by a court order, but (they claimed) had been illegally removed from the jurisdiction of the English courts by her father, who had placed her in the temporary care of the defendants. It was "quite clear"[118] that if the child were returned, it was proposed that she should be legally adopted, contrary to the wishes or consent of her father. The child's mother, however, appeared willing to have her adopted.

Hamilton, J. refused the local authority's application. He admitted that, "in the ordinary course".[119] he would have granted the application without considering the merits of the case, having regard to the fact that the child had been placed in the care of the local authority by the order of an English court "and the degree of comity which exists between the courts of these relevant jurisdictions;"[120] moreover, both parents were English citizens, who had married in England, and were domiciled there; their only child was born in England, and the child had been unlawfully removed from the jurisdiction of the English courts.

The basis for refusing the application was that the effect of granting the order sought by the plaintiff would have been that the child would have been adopted without the consent and in spite of the opposition of its lawful father, "a development which is not permissible under the Irish law of adoption."[121] Hamilton, J. quoted Article 41.1 of the Constitution, and two passages from Walsh, J.'s judgment in *McGee* v. *Attorney-General*.[122]

In the first passage, Walsh, J. had said:

"Articles 40, 41, 42 and 44 of the Constitution all fall within that section of the Constitution which is called 'Fundamental Rights'. Articles 41, 42 and 43 emphatically reject the theory that there are no rights without law, no rights contrary to law and

---

1983, [1984] I.L.R.M. 539, the Supreme Court appeared content to accept that the protections afforded to citizens by such Articles 40 and 44 might properly be interpreted as having the effect, at least in certain circumstances, of not excluding the existence or the granting of similar or identical rights to persons who are not citizens.

[117] [1982] I.L.R.M. 164 (High Ct., Hamilton, J. 1981).
[118] *Id.*, at 164.
[119] *Id.*, at 165.
[120] *Id.*
[121] *Id.*
[122] [1974] I.R. 284, at 310, 317 (Sup. Ct., 1973).

no rights anterior to law. They indicate that justice is placed above the law and acknowledge that natural rights, or human rights, are not created by law but that the Constitution confirms their existence and gives them protection. The individual has natural and human rights over which the State has no authority: and the Family as the natural primary and fundamental group of society has rights as such which the State cannot control."[123]

In the second passage, Walsh, J. said:

"The natural or human rights to which I have referred earlier in this judgment are part of what is generally called the natural law."[124]

Hamilton, J. stated:

"In the course of his judgment in *G* v. *An Bord Uchtála*[125] [Walsh J.] stated that he still held these views, with which I am in complete agreement.

The Supreme Court in *The State (Nicolaou)* v. *An Bord Uchtála*[126] expressly reserved for another and more appropriate case consideration of the effect of non-citizenship upon the interpretation of the Articles in question.

It seems to me however that non-citizenship can have no effect on the interpretation of Article 41 or the entitlement to the protection afforded by it.

What Article 41 does is to recognise the Family as the natural primary and fundamental unit group of society and as a moral institution possessing inalienable and imprescriptible rights antecedent and superior to all positive law, which rights the State cannot control. In the words of Walsh, J. already quoted, 'these rights are part of what is generally called the natural law' and as such are antecedent and superior to all positive law.

The natural law is of universal application and applies to all human persons, be they citizens of this State or not, and in my opinion it would be inconceivable that the father of the infant child would not be entitled to rely on the recognition of the Family contained in Article 41 for the purpose of enforcing his rights as the lawful father of the infant the subject matter of the proceeding herein or that he should lose such entitlement merely because he removed the child to this jurisdiction for the purpose of enforcing his said rights.

These rights are recognised by Bunreacht na h-Éireann and the courts created under it as antecedent and superior to all positive law: they are not so recognised by the law or the courts of the jurisdiction to which it is sought to have the infant returned.

Consequently it is for these reasons that I have at this stage refused to grant the orders sought by the applicant herein viz. that the child be returned to them or their agent.

The child however also has natural rights, As stated by the Chief Justice in *G* v. *An Bord Uchtála*[127] 'having been born, the child has the right to be fed and to live, to be reared and educated, to have the opportunity of working and of realising his or her full personality and dignity as a human being. These rights of the child (and others which I have not enumerated) must equally be protected and vindicated by the State.'

It will be necessary therefore to have a full plenary hearing of this application for the purpose of ascertaining whether the child's rights are being protected before any final order can be made in this case."[128]

This decision clearly raises a large number of questions,[129] especially in relation

---

[123] *Id.*, at 310.
[124] *Id.*, at 317.
[125] [1980] I.R. 32 (Sup. Ct., 1978).
[126] [1966] I.R. 567.
[127] [1980] I.R., at 56.
[128] [1982] I.L.R.M. at, 165-166.
[129] O'Connor, *"Kidnapping" and the Irish Courts*, 2 Ir. L. Times (n.s.) 4, at 4 (1984), raises the following jurisprudential question:
"Is it possible for the citizens of this jurisdiction to alter the natural law by constitutional amendment? If natural law is antecedent and superior to all positive law it suggests that an amendment purporting to alter the Constitution in violation of the natural law would not be valid."

to the conflict of laws. Hamilton, J. appears to have concluded from the fact that the natural law is "of universal application and applies to all persons, be they citizens of this State or not" that it would therefore be "inconceivable" that the father in the proceedings before him would not be entitled to the rights accorded the Family by Article 41. This seems to involve a step from the universality of *vision* of human capacity and entitlement embraced by natural law philosophy to the conclusion that the *protection* afforded by the Constitution is also universal in its scope.

Some obvious difficulties attach to this approach. At a very straightforward, practical level, the laws of very many countries provide for compulsory adoption of legitimate children in certain circumstances, regardless of the wishes of the parents. The constitutionality of such a process in this country is the subject of debate.[130] One may ask whether *Northampton County Council* v. *A.B.F. and M.B.F.* constitutes a precedent for protecting parents throughout the world from having their children adopted against their wishes. Common-sense suggests strongly that it does not; the problem is to identify precisely *why* it does not.

Hamilton, J.'s judgment can perhaps be interpreted as involving merely the denial of the argument that Article 41.1 of the Constitution may not be availed of by a non-citizen who has brought a child to this jurisdiction in defiance of a court order in a foreign jurisdiction. This falls well short of the positive assertion that foreigners, wherever they reside or are domiciled, and regardless of the absence of any connection with Ireland, may avail themselves of the protection of Article 41.1. What *Northampton County Council* v. *A.B.F. and M.B.F.* leaves entirely unresolved is the nature of the connection which will be sufficient to enable a non-citizen to invoke Article 41.1. The decision, therefore, simply does not address the broad issue that, on a casual reading, it may seem to determine.

In *Kent County Council* v. *C.S.*[131], in 1983, the facts were as follows. The respondent, an Irish citizen aged 47, had lived in England since 1956. His first marriage had ended in divorce in 1971. His second marriage, to a 16-year-old girl, was in 1979. The boy who was the subject of the legal proceedings was born a year later. The couple ceased to reside together in 1981. The boy lived for much of the following 18 months in the household of a woman with whom his father had lived for some years after his divorce in 1971. Both the respondent and his wife, in varying degrees, had access to the child during this period. In 1982, the respondent petitioned for a divorce. During the period before a decree *nisi* was granted, an order was made by the court providing that the Social Services Department of the Kent County Council should be at liberty to apply on 48 hours' notice with regard to the access arrangements. When the decree *nisi* was granted in January 1983, the High Court in England made an order that the child should remain in the care of the Kent County Council with leave to place the child with his mother. Supervised access was to be at the discretion of the local authority. The Court ordered that the child was not to be removed from England and Wales without leave of the court until he reached 18.

The father came to an agreement with Kent County Council officials that the child should be left in the care and custody of the woman who had largely been responsible for his upbringing. Two months later, he took the child from this woman, "asserting or pretending to her that he intended to bring it to visit a brother of his who resided in England".[132] In fact he brought the child to Dublin to the home of his elderly parents. He stated in evidence that he did so "because he believed that under the orders of the English courts he would not be able to retain control and custody and

---

[130] Cf. The Review Committee on Adoption Services's Report, *Adoption*, paras 3.7, 3.10 (Pl. 2467, 1984), G. v. *An Bord Uchtála*, [1980] I.R. 32, at 79 (Sup. Ct., *per* Walsh, J., 1978). The Adoption Bill 1986 provided for the adoption of legitimate children in certain circumstances.

[131] [1984] I.L.R.M. 292 (High Ct., Finlay, P., 1983).

[132] *Id.*, at 275.

a proper link with the infant and that it could be placed away in someone else's care or even given in adoption".[133]

Kent County Council sought the return of the child. The proceedings were treated as an application for an enquiry as to the legality of the detention of the child by the respondent under Article 40 of the Constitution.

The respondent asserted a Constitutional right pursuant to Articles 41 and 42 to be regarded as the family in relation to the child and as such to take the responsibility for the upbringing and education of the child. He claimed that he should not be deprived of that right in favour of a stranger except for the gravest of reasons consisting of a dereliction of duty by him and an immediate danger or hazard to the child.[134]

Counsel for Kent County Council submitted that the case was clearly a "kidnapping" one, and that the ordinary principle should be applied whereby the courts of the country in which the child was born, in which the parties resided during their marriage so long as it lasted and in which, the evidence made clear, it was intended that the child should be brought up were the appropriate courts for the determination of the welfare of the child.

Counsel for Kent County Council relied in particular on the fact that the respondent, on the break-up of the marriage, had sought the exercise by the English courts of their jurisdiction and "did so as a person domiciled in England which would be a necessary pre-requisite to his obtaining a decree of divorce in that country;"[135] only after he had exhausted those remedies in a full hearing in which all relevant matters had been canvassed did he take the child out of the jurisdiction of those courts "in plain contempt of and breach of an order of the court for the specific purpose of obtaining a different decision with regard to the custody and care of the child in these courts."[136]

Finally, counsel for the County Council pointed out that, after the respondent had removed the child out of the jurisdiction of the English courts, the child had been made a ward of court there and a specific order made on the wardship side directing his return and the determination of his custody and welfare in the English courts.

Finlay, P. was satisfied that the English courts were hoping that it might be possible to place the boy in the long-term care of his mother with appropriate access to his father. He stressed the fact that the material witnesses as the long-term question of the child's welfare were not normally amenable to be brought before the Irish courts. He added:

> "The entire legal framework as a result of which this child was born of a lawful marriage in England and as a result of which a decree *nisi* in divorce has been granted in England concerning that marriage is a legal framework which is not known to the law of this country."[137]

The relevance of the factor of divorce and remarriage is difficult to appreciate. Our conflicts rules have for long recognised foreign divorces based on domicile, and the courts have made it abundantly plain that Article 41 of the Constitution has not abolished these rules of recognition.

Finlay, P. was satisfied that Kent County Council had no immediate intention to place the boy for adoption against the wishes of his parents. That was the

---

[133] *Id.*
[134] *Id.* The respondent relied on *Re J.M.* [1966] I.R. 295 and *Northampton County Council* v. *A.B.F. and M.B.F., supra.*
[135] [1984] I.L.R.M., at 296.
[136] *Id.*
[137] *Id.*

"fundamental underlying principle"[138] for Hamilton, J.'s decision in the *Northampton* case. Finlay, P. continued:

> "Having regard to my view of the facts of this case and the fundamental importance of the appropriate forum for the determination of the future welfare of this child being the courts in the country in which it was born and intended to be brought up, I am satisfied that there is no question of a deprivation of any of the constitutional rights relied upon by the respondent which should prevent me from applying the principle which I understand to be appropriate in relation to the comity between courts and in making an order for the return of the child to the care of the Kent County Council who must only deal with it in accordance with the determination of the English courts to which the respondent who has originally invoked their jurisdiction has full access. I therefore make the order for the return of the child."[139]

This passage raises a number of questions as to the relationship between the Constitution and the conflict of laws. Finlay, P. appears initially to accept that, had there been an immediate intention to place the child for adoption in England, the Irish court could properly have exercised jurisdiction, based on the constitutional entitlement of the father. On this view, the respondent's assertions were not so much unsustainable as premature. But other parts of this passage are ambiguous: they could perhaps mean (1) that the respondent's constitutional rights, recognised by the Court, would not be jeopardised by making an order for the return of the child to the English local authority, (2) that the respondent had no relevant constitutional rights to assert, or (3) that the respondent, although having constitutional rights capable of vindication through the Irish courts, had waived or otherwise forfeited his entitlement to do so by having originally invoked the jurisdiction of the English courts.

As to the first of these three possible interpretations, which is consistent with Hamilton, J.'s approach in the *Northampton* case, it is perhaps significant that Finlay, P. expressed not one word of disagreement with that decision, which he sought to distinguish merely on its facts. The second possible interpretation seems unlikely: if Finlay, P. had wished to reject the respondent's argument so comprehensively he would surely have said so simply and directly. The third possible interpretation, perhaps supplemented by the practical considerations against exercising jurisdiction mentioned by the President, may be at the base of the decision. It would seem that the concept of waiver[140] should be applied with sensitivity in this context. It would be harsh on some parents to penalise them for invoking a foreign jurisdiction when in truth this was a decision over which they presumably had little control. It would be asking rather much of an English lawyer advising English domiciliaries on their position under English law that he be conscious of the fundamentally important constitutional implications for them under Irish law of this advice.

THE HAGUE CONVENTION ON INTERNATIONAL CHILD ABDUCTION[141]

In 1980, the Hague Conference on Private International Law adopted a Convention on the Civil Aspects of International Child Abduction. The purpose of the Convention is to ensure that when children under the age of 16 years[142] have been wrongfully removed from the country where they are habitually resident to another country or

---

[138] *Id.*, at 297.
[139] *Id.*
[140] See *Kelly,* 438 ff.
[141] For commentary on the Convention, see Anton, *The Hague Convention on International Child Abduction,* 30 Int. & Comp. L.Q. 537 (1981), Bodenheimer, *The Hague Draft Convention on International Child Abduction Comes to Canada,* 4 Can. J. of Family L. 5 (1983).
[142] Article 4.

wrongfully retained in another country, they should, as a general rule, be returned to the country of their habitual residence. The courts of the "receiving" country would not enter into a detailed consideration of the question of welfare. The idea behind the Convention is to make international child abduction so unattractive and pointless as to discourage would-be abductors from resorting to this process. The Convention also contains some provisions under which the courts may, or must, decline to order the return of the child.

The central provisions are to be found in Articles 3, 12, 13 and 20. Article 3 provides that the removal or retention of a child is to be considered wrongful where:

"(a) it is in breach of rights of custody attributed to a person, an institution or any other body, either jointly or alone, under the law of the State in which the child was habitually resident immediately before the removal or retention; and
(b) at the time of the removal or retention those rights were actually exercised, either jointly or alone, or would have been so exercised but for the removal of retention."

These "rights of custody" may arise "in particular by operation of law or by reason of a judicial or administrative decision, or by reason of an agreement having legal effect under the law of the State."[143] What is important to note here is that a right to custody need not have arisen as a result of judicial decree: general rights given by the law[144] will suffice.

Article 12 represents the core of the Convention. Where a child has been wrongfully removed or retained and *less than a year* has elapsed from between the removal or retention and the date the proceedings are commenced, the judicial or administrative authority *must* order the return of the child forthwith.

Where a year or more has elapsed, again the judicial or administrative authority must order the return of the child, but not if "it is demonstrated that the child is now settled in its new enviroment." This proviso may well be fulfilled in many cases: once a year has elapsed it should normally be a relatively easy task to demonstrate that the child has settled in an environment that is now scarcely "new" to the child.[145]

Article 13 *permits, but does not require*[146] the judicial or administrative authority of the requested State to decline to order the return of the child if the person, institution or other body opposing its return establishes that:

"(a) the person, institution or other body having the care of the person of the child was not actually exercising the custody rights at the time of the removal or retention, or had consented to or subsequently acquiesced in the removal or retention; or
(b) there is a grave risk that his or her return would expose the child to physical or psychological harm or otherwise place the child in an intolerable situation."

The Article also permits the judicial or administrative authority to refuse to order the return of the child if it finds that the child objects to being returned and has attained an age and degree of maturity at which it is appropriate to take account of its views.[147]   It should be noted that the judicial or administrative authority has a broader discretionary power to order the return of the child at any time.[148]

---

[143] *Id.* Rights of custody include rights relating to the care of the person of the child and, in particular, the rights to determine the child's place of residence: Article 5, clause (a).

[144] As, for example, section 6 of the Guardianship of Infants Act 1964.

[145] Article 12 also provides that, where the judicial or administrative authority in the requested State has reason to believe that the child has been taken to another State, it may stay the proceedings or dismiss the application for the return of the child.

[146] See also Article 18, which preserves the power of a judicial authority to order the return of the child at any time.

[147] Cf. *Binchy*, 460-463.

[148] Article 18.

Moreover the Convention would also seem to allow a Contracting State to return a child even when its judicial and administrative authorities have declined to do so pursuant to the Convention. "Thus, for example, the power to deport aliens may not be affected by adherence to the Convention."[149]

A further exception to the obligation to return a child to the country of habitual residence is to be found in Article 20, which provides that:

"The return of the child under the provision of Article 12 may be refused if this would not be permitted by the fundamental principles of the requested State relating to the protection of human rights and fundamental freedoms."

The scope of this potentially important provision is necessarily broad and to a large degree uncertain. In the Irish context it would seem to allow an Irish court to refuse to return a child where its return would conflict with the guarantees relating to the protection of human rights contained in the Constitution. As the Law Reform Commission have observed:

"This might be important, for example, in a case such as *Northampton County Council v. A.B.F. and M.B.F.*[150] where a parent is resisting the return of the child to its habitual residence on the ground that it would be placed in the care of a non-parent in circumstances which would conflict with the inalienable and imprescriptible rights of the Family guaranteed under Article 41 of the Constitution."[151]

This raises again the whole question of the interrelationship between the Constitution and conflicts rules. Of course, if Ireland is to give effect to this Convention, this problem has to be confronted, and Article 20 makes it far easier for us to contemplate making the Convention part of our law.

The Convention requires[152] each Contracting State to designate a "Central Authority" charged with the task of co-operating with the Central Authorities of other Contracting States, so as to secure the prompt return of children and to achieve the other objects of the Convention.[153]

Among the more important functions of these Central Authorities is the obligation to take all appropriate measures to discover the whereabouts of a child who has been wrongfully removed or retained, to prevent further harm to the child, to secure his or her voluntary return, and, if necessary, to initiate or facilitate the institution of judicial or administrative proceedings with a view to obtaining the return of the child.[154] This may involve providing legal aid.[155]

To ease this task still more, the judicial or administrative authorities are given some further powers.[156] In ascertaining whether there has been a wrongful removal or taking, they may take notice directly of the law or judicial or administrative decisions of the State of the child's habitual residence without recourse to the normal requirements for proof of foreign law[157] which would otherwise be applicable.[158] Before making an order for the return of the child, the authorities may request the

---

[149] Law Reform Commission, *Report on the Hague Convention on the Civil Aspects of International Child Abduction and Some Related Matters*, p. 12 (L.R.C.12–1985).
[150] *Supra.*
[151] L.R.C. 12–1985, p. 13.
[152] Article 6.
[153] Article 7.
[154] Article 7.
[155] *Id..*
[156] Cf. Articles 14-16.
[157] See *supra*, ch. 7.
[158] Article 14. See further L.R.C. 12–1985, p. 16.

applicant to obtain from the authorities of the State of the child's habitual residence a decision or other determination that the removal was wrongful.[159] The Central Authorities of Contracting States are under a duty "so far as practicable"[160] to assist applicants to obtain this determination.

Where the authorities of the State to which the child has been removed (or in which he or she is being retained) receive notice of the wrongful removal (or retention), they may not decide on the merits of rights of custody unless (a) it has been determined that the child is not to be returned under the Convention or (b) an application under the Convention is not lodged within a reasonable time following receipt of the notice.[161] The sole fact that a decision relating to custody has been given, or is entitled to recognition, in the requested State is not a ground for requiring to return a child under the Convention; however, the authorities of the requested State may take account of the reasons for that decision in applying the Convention.[162]

Article 19 makes it plain that a decision under the Convention concerning the return of the child is not to be treated as a determination on the merits of any custody issue; thus, "if a court refuses to return a child under Article 12 or 13, a separate decision, though not necessarily another hearing, must be given on the question of custody."[163]

Access rights are heard in a manner broadly similar to custody rights under the Convention. Rights of access are defined by Articles as including "the right to take a child for a limited period of time to a place other than the child's habitual residence." An application to make arrangements for organising and securing the effective exercise of rights of access may be presented to the Central Authorities of the Contracting States in the same way as an application for the return of a child.[164] The Central Authorities are under the obligation of co-operation, set out in Article 7,[165] to promote the peaceful enjoyment of access rights[166] and the fulfilment of any conditions to which the exercise of rights may be subject.[167] They may initiate or assist in the institution of proceedings with a view to organising or protecting these rights and securing respect for the conditions to which their exercise may be subject.[168]

The Convention contains some important practical provisions regarding costs of proceedings, designed to smooth the path of those seeking the return of an abducted child. Article 22 provides that "[n]o security, bond or deposit, however described" is to be required to guarantee the payment of costs and expenses in the judicial or administrative proceedings falling within the scope of the Convention. Thus, our Rules[169] regarding security for costs in relation to plaintiffs without financial resources would have no application in this context. Moreover nationals and habitual residents of the Contracting States, in matters concerned with the application of the Convention are entitled to legal aid in any other Contracting State on the same conditions as if they themselves were nationals or habitual residents of that State.[170] Although the Central Authorities have to bear their own costs in applying the Convention and impose no charges in relation to applications submitted under it,[171]

---

[159] Article 15. See L.R.C. 12–1985, pp. 16-17.
[160] Id.
[161] Article 16.
[162] Article 17.
[163] L.R.C. 12–1985, p 17.
[164] Article 21.
[165] See p. 341, *supra*.
[166] Article 21.
[167] Id.
[168] Id.
[169] *Infra*, ch. 35.
[170] Article 25.
[171] Article 26. A Contracting State may, however, by making a reservation in accordance with Article 42, declare that it is not bound to assume any costs resulting from the participation of legal counsel or advisors or from court proceedings, save insofar as they may be covered by its system of legal aid and advice: Article 26.

they may require the payment of the expenses incurred in implementing the return of the child. On ordering the return of a child or issuing an order regarding access, the judicial or administrative authorities may, where appropriate, direct the person who removed or retained the child, or prevented the rights of access, to pay necessary expenses incurred by or on behalf of the applicant, including travel expenses, any costs incurred or payments made for locating the child, the costs of legal representation of the applicant, and those of returning the child.[172]

The Convention does not preclude any person, institution or body who claims that there has been a breach of custody or access rights within the meaning of Article 3 or 21 from applying directly to the judicial or administrative authorities of a Contracting State, whether or not under the provisions of the Convention.[173]

The Law Reform Commission's Proposals

The Law Reform Commission have recommended that Ireland should adhere to the Convention. In their Report on the Hague Convention on the Civil Aspects of International Child Abduction and Some Related Matters,[174] published in 1985, the Commission express the conclusion that the balance of the argument is in favour of adherence.

As to the question of what should constitute the judicial or administrative authority competent to decide on an application to return a child under the Convention, the Commission recommend[175] that this jurisdiction should be vested solely in the High Court. They recommend[176] that a government agency, such as the Department of Justice or the Attorney General, should, at least initially, be designated as Central Authority.

Referring to Article 18,[177] the Commission recommend[178] that the Irish legislation giving effect to the Convention should state that nothing in it is to prevent a child from being returned to another State merely because that return is not required by the Convention. They recommend[179] that the legislation should also provide that in deciding on an application for the return of children to another jurisdiction in a case where that return is not required by the Convention, the court is to have regard to the welfare of the child as the first and paramount consideration. The Commission consider this provision to be appropriate as they do not believe that our courts should ever decide abduction cases other than on the basis of their view of the welfare of the child except in cases concerned by the Convention where reciprocal advantages are obtained for persons resident in Ireland.[180]

The European Convention on Recognition and Enforcement of Decisions concerning Custody of Children and on Restoration of Custody of Children

The Council of Europe has also adopted a Convention on the subject of international aspects of child custody. This European Convention is at present under consideration by the Department of Justice. Unlike the Hague Convention, which is directed towards

---

[172] *Id.*.
[173] Article 29.
[174] L.R.C. 12−1985.
[175] *Id.*, p. 14.
[176] *Id.*, p. 26.
[177] Cf. *supra*, p. 340.
[178] Page 30 of the Report.
[179] *Id.*
[180] *Id.*, pp. 30-31.

resolving the problem of child abduction through provisions for the immediate return of the child, the European Convention is concerned with the general international recognition and enforcement of decisions concerning custody.

Under the European Convention, recognition and enforcement may be refused only on specific grounds. Broadly speaking these are:

(i)   That the defendant was unrepresented and had not been served with the document instituting the proceedings in sufficient time to enable him to arrange his defence;[181]

(ii)   that the decision was given in the absence of the defendant or his legal representative and the competence of the authority giving the decision was not founded on the habitual residence of the defendant or the child or on the last habitual residence of the child's parents;[182]

(iii)   that the decision is incompatible with a decision relating to custody in the State addressed;[183]

(iv)   that the effects of the decision are manifestly incompatible with the fundamental principles of the law relating to the family and children in the State addressed;[184]

(v)   that by reason of a change in circumstances since the original decision its effects are no longer in accordance with the welfare of the child;[185]

(vi)   that the child is a national of the State addressed or was habitually resident there and no such connection existed with the State where the decision was given;[186]

(vii)   that the child, being a national of the State of origin and of the State addressed, was habitually resident in the State addressed.[187]

In certain cases of improper removal, however, the grounds of refusal may be more limited. Improper removal is defined as meaning the removal of a child across an international frontier in breach of a decision relating to its custody given in a Contracting State or a failure to return a child at the end of a period of access.[188] In such a case if the child and his parents have as their sole nationality the nationality of the State where the custody decision is given and the child has its habitual residence in that State, the State addressed must restore custody of the child, provided the request is made within six months.[189]

In other cases of improper removal, recognition may be refused only on grounds (i), (ii) and (iii) mentioned above. But a Contracting State may make a reservation exempting itself from this limitation on the grounds on which it may refuse to recognise and enforce a decision in another Contracting State.

There is no guarantee that the same outcome will be reached under the two Conventions. As the Law Reform Commission point out, "[i]t is conceivable that one would be bound under the Council of Europe Convention to enforce a custody decision given in the country of the child's nationality where the Hague Convention requires the return of the child in accordance with the law of its habitual residence."[190]

---

[181]   Article 9.1.a.
[182]   Article 9.1.b.
[183]   Articles 9.1.c.; 10.2.d.
[184]   Article 10.1.a.
[185]   Article 10.1.b.
[186]   Article 10.1.c.
[187]   *Id.*
[188]   Article 1.d.i.
[189]   Article 8.
[190]   L.R.C. 12–1985, p. 34.

Article 20 of the European Convention is designed to reduce the extent of potential conflict. It provides that the Convention is not to affect "any obligations which a Contracting State may have towards a non-contracting State under an international instrument dealing with matters governed by this Convention;" but conflict may still arise where the States concerned are party to both the European and the Hague Conventions.

The Law Reform Commission go on to spell further distinctions between the two conventions:

> "While the Council of Europe Convention would have similar effects to the Hague Convention in many cases, it goes further in certain respects. It would secure the enforcement of rights of access as well as rights of custody. In cases of improper removal, as between States which make no reservations, it allows of fewer exceptions to the obligation to act on the decision or law of the State where the abducted child was resident. Under it the Central Authority is obliged to take proceedings or cause proceedings to be taken to secure the recognition and enforcement of the decision of the other Contracting State whereas under the Hague Convention the Central Authority need only facilitate the institution of proceedings with a view to obtaining the return of the child. Under the Council of Europe Convention each Contracting State undertakes not to claim any payment from an applicant in respect of any measures taken by its Central Authority except the cost of repatriation, whereas, under the Hague Convention, States may reserve the right not to assume any costs resulting from the participation of legal counsel or advisers or from court proceedings. Accordingly it seems that under the Council of Europe Convention more expense is likely to fall on the Central Authority and less on the individual applicant than under the Hague Convention, especially if reservations are made under Article 26 of the latter."[191]

The Commission consider that, if a choice had to be made between the Hague Convention and the European Convention, it might be preferable to adhere to the Hague Convention, if only because countries such as the United States and Canada with which Ireland has extensive contracts, may become a party to it. But the Commission do not believe that this choice need be made, in spite of some possible inconsistencies between the two Conventions. They point out that in Britain the solution adopted has been to introduce legislation giving effect to both of the Conventions. They therefore recommend[192] that the Department of Justice should continue its consideration of the European Convention with its ratification by Ireland, but that this process should not be allowed to delay adherence to the Hague Convention.

Other Proposed Amendments

At present the only statutory prohibition against the removal of a child out of the jurisdiction is to be found in section 40 of the Adoption Act 1952, so far as that section has survived constitutional challenge.[193] A person may not take a child under seven years out of the jurisdiction without the permission of a parent, guardian or relative.[194] Since the permission of one of these persons suffices, section 40 does

---

[191] *Id.*, pp. 34-35.

[192] *Id.*, p. 35.

[193] In *The State (M.)* v. *A.G.*, [1979] I.R. 73, Finlay, P. held that an illegitimate child's constitutional right to travel abroad with the consent of his or her mother or guardian where this was in the child's welfare rendered invalid parts of section 40 which prohibited absolutely the removal of an illegitimate child out of the jurisdiction except for the purpose of residing with a mother or relative.

[194] "Relative" is defined by section 3 as meaning grandparent, brother, sister, uncle or aunt, whether of the whole blood, of the half-blood or by affinity, relationship to an illegitimate child being traced through the mother only. Thus the consent of the father of an illegitimate child, even where he has the sole care of the child, would not suffice.

not render unlawful the removal by one parent of a child out of the jurisdiction in defiance of the wishes of the other parent, even when this is in clear breach of a written agreement between the parties.

Other offences relating to abduction of children do not appear to have much impact on the problem of international abduction by a parent. Section 55 of the Offences Against the Person Act 1861, while technically applicable to any abduction, "is, in fact, invoked almost entirely in seduction cases with sexual overtones".[195] And section 56 of the same Act has no application in cases where there is a *bona fide* dispute as to custody. Kidnapping is a felony attracting a maximum sentence of life imprisonment.[196] The scope of the offence at common law is uncertain.[197]

The Law Reform Commission have recommended the creation of an offence of abduction of a child under sixteen out of the jurisdiction. This offence would be committed by anyone "who takes or sends or keeps a child (being a child habitually resident in the State) out of the State in defiance of a court order or without the consent of each person who is a parent or guardian or to whom custody has been granted unless the leave of the court is obtained; it should be a defence that the accused (i) honestly believed the child was over sixteen; (ii) obtained the consent of the requisite persons or of the court;[198] (iii) has been unable to communicate with the requisite persons, having taken all reasonable steps, but believes that they would all consent if they were aware of all the relevant circumstances; or (iv) being a parent, guardian or person having custody of the child had no intention to deprive others having rights of guardianship or custody in relation to the child of those rights."[199]

The Commission recommend that no prosecution should be brought without the consent of the person in breach of whose rights in relation to the child that child was abducted out of the jurisdiction.

---

[195] L.R.C. 12-1985, p 39.
[196] Criminal Law Act 1976, section 11.
[197] Cf. *The People (A.G.)* v. *Edge*, [1943] I.R. 115 (Sup. Ct., 1943, rev'g C.C.A. 1942). See further *Binchy, xi*, 462-463, L.R.C. 12–1985, pp. 38-40.
[198] Cf. McCutcheon, *Child Abduction: A New Offence?* 3 Ir. L.T. (n.s.) 233, at 235 (1985), who points out that, if the removal is made without the required consents, "the *actus reus* of the offence is negated, and the suggested defence is needless".
[199] L.R.C. 12-1985, p. 44.

CHAPTER 16

LEGITIMACY AND LEGITIMATION

In this chapter we will examine conflicts aspects of legitimacy and legitimation. The role of conflicts of law is to specify what system of law determines whether a person is born legitimate or whether he is legitimated.[1] Conflicts of law rules present particular difficulty in view of the wide range of social, legal and cultural attitudes towards legitimacy among the legal systems throughout the world. Moreover the rapid changes in legal and social attitudes towards legitimacy in many countries over the past twenty years[2] make it difficult, at the height of this movement, for conflicts rules to work satisfactorily in every case.

LEGITIMACY[3]

Under Irish law the following children are legitimate:

(a) those conceived and born within marriage;
(b) those born within marriage but conceived before marriage;
(c) those conceived within marriage but born after it has ended;
(d) those conceived as the result of pre-marital intercourse where the parents marry but the father dies before the birth of the child;[4]
(e) those who are legitimated by the subsequent marriage of their parents.

A child who does not fall within any of these categories is illegitimate. A child born of a void marriage is illegitimate whether or not any decree of nullity of marriage is obtained.[5] A child born of a voidable marriage will also be illegitimate if the marriage is annulled.[6] In several other countries, the absence of a valid marriage

---

[1] *Cheshire & North*, 440.

[2] Cf. the Law Reform Commission's *Report on Illegitimacy*, ch. 2 (L.R.C. 4-1982), the English Law Commission's Report, *Family Law — Illegitimacy*, paras. 1.3, 2.1-2.3, 4.5 (Law Com. No. 118, 1982), *Hogett & Pearl*, 289-294, *Cretney*, 616-617. Before the recent General Election, a bill proposing some changes in the law (The Status of Children Bill 1986) passed all stages in the Seanad, and thus remains on the order paper. The Bill does not propose the abolition of the concept of illegitimacy, and preserves significant distinctions in relation to guardianship of children.

[3] See generally Guttman, *Whither Legitimacy: An Investigation of the Choice of Law Rules to Determine the Status of Legitimacy*, 14 Rutgers L. Rev. 764 (1960), Welsh, *Legitimacy in the Conflict of Laws*, 63 L. Q. Rev. 65 (1947), Taintor, *Legitimation, Legitimacy and Recognition in the Conflict of Laws*, 18 Can. Bar Rev. 589, 691 (1940), Ester, *Illegitimate Children and Conflict of Laws*, 36 Ind. L. J. 163 (1961), Mann, *Note: Legitimacy and the Conflict of Laws*, 64 L. Q. Rev. 199 (1948), Falconbridge *Legitimacy or Legitimation and Succession in the Conflict of Laws*, 27 Can. Bar Rev. 1163 (1949), and the Law Reform Commission's W.P. No. 10-1981, *Domicile and Habitual Residence as Connecting Factors in the Conflict of Laws*, paras. 82-84.

[4] There is no judicial authority on this question. Cf. *Bromley*, 256. The Law Reform Commission, in their *Report on Illegitimacy*, para. 3, noted that, "[h]ad the father lived, the child would without question have been legitimate, and the fact that the child is born posthumously does not in itself appear to be a reason to deny him legitimate status".

[5] Cf. the Law Reform Commission's *Report on Nullity of Marriage*, p. 72 (L.R.C. 9-1984).

[6] Cf. *id.*, pp. 72-73. The Status of Children Bill 1986, section 6, proposes to change the law in respect of both void and voidable marriages.

between the parents does not necessarily mean that the child is illegitimate. The notion of the "putative marriage" has existed in some countries over several centuries; legislative provisions also confer legitimate status on certain children born outside marriage.

The courts over the years have been conscious that legitimacy presents some difficult problems for the conflict of laws but there has been no attempt to confront the central policy issues in a comprehensive manner. The result has been to leave the law in a state of some conceptual disarray, with fragmented insights littering the law reports.

The best approach towards giving some conceptual order to the subject is to summarise briefly the main approaches which have received support among the courts or commentators and then consider how the unresolved issues should best be addressed.

The Lex Fori

Clearly the *lex fori* must have *some* say in determining questions of legitimacy of children, but its role should not range too widely. The fact that, under the internal law of the *lex fori*, a child is regarded as legitimate only if born in "lawful wedlock" should not mean that legitimate status in the conflict of laws would have to be restricted similarly. According to the law in many countries, as has been mentioned, a valid marriage by the parents is not always a precondition of legitimacy. If legitimacy were to be restricted by the forum to cases of birth within marriage, then children unquestionably legitimate under the foreign law most closely connected with them (or perhaps with their parents) would have to be treated as illegitimate. In some cases this might lead to unpalatable results.

In *Shaw* v. *Gould*,[8] a decision of the House of Lords in 1868, the question arose as to whether a bequest to the "children" of one Elizabeth Hickson and a devise of land in England to her son, "lawfully begotten", applied to children born of a second marriage, to a Scottish domiciliary, by Elizabeth Hickson. Elizabeth Hickson's first marriage, to an English domiciliary, had been dissolved in Scotland, where her husband had not acquired a Scottish domicile. That divorce was not effective under English law. Under Scots law, however, the divorce and second marriage were valid, and the children, being born of a "putative marriage" (a notion of Scots, but not English Law), were legitimate. The House of Lords held that the bequest and devise did not apply to the children of the second marriage, since the dissolution of the first marriage was not effective under English Law. Thus, the issue of legitimacy was "subsumed within the legal issue of essential validity or formal validity of marriage".[9]

The same approach found favour in the later decisions of *Re Bethell*[10] and *Re Paine*,[11] where the possibility that the children might be legitimate by reference to the law of their domicile of origin, or the domicile of either of their parents at the

---

[7] See Cohn, *The Nullity of Marriage: A Study in Comparative Law and Legal Reform: Part I,* 64 L.Q. Rev. 324, at 331 ff, (1948), Brière, *Le Mariage Putatif,* 6 McGill L.J. 217 (1960). Cf. *Jackson,* 52: "There can be no doubt that for a while, English ecclesiastical law, nourished with the same ideas and thought as its continental counterpart, accepted and applied the doctrine of the putative marriage."

[8] L.R. 3 H.L. 55 (1868). See also *Piers* v. *Piers,* 11 H.L.C. 331, 9 E.R. 11 8 (1849), aff'g 10 Ir. Eq. Rep. 341 (1847), where there was an identification between the issues of the validity of the marriage and the legitimacy of the children born of the marriage. It seems however, on the facts, that it would have been impossible for the children to have asserted a legitimate status on any basis other than that of the validity of their parents' marriage. Cf. *In re Darcys Infants,* 11 I.C.L.R. 298 (Com. Pleas, Manahan, C.J., 1860).

[9] *McLeod,* 299.

[10] 38 Ch. D. 220 (1888).

[11] [1940] Ch. 46.

date of their births, notwithstanding the invalidity of the marriages, was not even considered.[12]

But if it is wrong for the *lex fori* to apply in conflicts cases the rules of its internal law as to who is legitimate, it may be argued that the *lex fori* should nonetheless reserve to itself the function of characterising children as legitimate or illegitimate in accordance with the totality of their entitlements under the particular foreign law, regardless of whether that foreign law uses the word "legitimate" or "illegitimate" to describe these children.[13]

The precise question arose in *Re MacDonald*,[14] in 1964, where the Supreme Court of Canada, affirming the Ontario Court of Appeal, held that a daughter born outside marriage in a Mexican State where her father was domiciled should be regarded as the legitimate "issue" of the grandson of an Ontario testator for the purposes of Ontario succession law, even though her status was described as illegitimate under the law of the Mexican State. Under the Mexican law the girl had "the same capacities, incidents and obligations vested in her in relation to her father . . . as she would have had if she had been born as a legitimate child. She ha[d] the same inheritance rights as a legitimate daughter under the Civil Code and by virtue of a paternity judgment [was] entitled to use her father's name; ha[d] the right of support and obligation of support".[15]

It seemed clear to MacKay, J.A., of the Ontario Court of Appeal, that the purpose of the law was "to equalize the rights of children,"[16] whether legitimate or illegitimate. In his view, the Court had to consider what was meant by the word "status":

> "Is it the name which the foreign law attaches or do we look behind to determine what incidents, capacities and obligations the foreign law imposes? In other words, is status the name which the foreign jurisdiction employs to describe the child in question or do we look behind to examine the rights and obligations imposed by the foreign law to determine whether those rights and obligations are so closely akin to those imposed in this jurisdiction in the case of a child born in lawful wedlock? ... I have reached the conclusion that the sum total of the capacities and obligations vested in the child in question by the *lex domicilii* are the same as those of a child born in lawful wedlock."[17]

Affirming the Ontario Court of Appeal's holding, Ritchie J., of the Supreme Court of Canada, expressed the opinion that:

> "the title of 'legitimacy' or 'illegitimacy' when attached to the status of an individual in any jurisdiction reflects the capacity or lack of capacity which the law of that jurisdiction recognizes in the case of the individual concerned. Just as 'legitimate' when used in relation to a child is only a symbol employed to designate the legal rights and obligations which flow from being born in wedlock, so the word 'illegitimate' is used to denote the limitations of capacity which attach to being born out of wedlock, and the word 'legitimation' is descriptive of the legal effects incident to being relieved of those limitations.
>
> [The daughter], the sum total of whose capacities and obligations under the law of the [Mexican] State ... include all those of a child born in wedlock in Ontario, in my opinion has the status of a legitimate child in [Ontario] for the purpose here in question and the fact that some social limitations may attach to her position in Mexico,

---

[12] *Dicey & Morris*, 459.

[13] Cf. *Cheshire & North*, 449.

[14] 44 D.L.R. (2d) 208 (Sup. Ct. Can., 1964), aff'g 34 D.L.R. (2d) 14 (Ont. C.A., 1962).

[15] 34 D.L.R. (2d), at 18 (*per* MacKay, J.A.).

[16] *Id.*

[17] *Id.*, at 21.

and that her status in that country is therefore described as 'illegitimate', can, in my view, have no effect on the standards required in order to qualify as a legitimate child for the purpose of benefiting as one of 'the issue' of the grandson of an Ontario testator."[18]

The Lex Domicilii

We must now consider an entirely different approach, which looks to the *lex domicilii*, rather than the *lex fori*, to resolve the question of legitimacy. The leading English decision in *Re Bischoffsheim; Cassel* v. *Grant.*[19]

The facts in *Re Bischoffsheim* were as follows. Henri Bischoffsheim, by will made in 1903, devised and bequeathed his residuary real and personal estate to his trustees to hold a share (subject to certain prior interests) in trust for his granddaughter, Nesta Fitzgerald, for life with remainder to such of her child or children as being male should attain the age of 21 years or being female should attain that age or marry. The testator died on 11 March 1908. On 30 April, 1908, Nesta married Lord Richard Wellesley. Two children, the first and second defendants, were born of this marriage. In 1914, Lord Richard Wellesley was killed in action. Less than three years later, his widow married Lord George Wellesley, a brother of Lord Richard, in New York. The third defendant, Richard Wellesley, was the only child of that marriage, and was born on 22 June 1920. Nesta died in 1946.

The domicile of origin of Nesta Wellesley (née Fitzgerald) and Lord George Wellesley was English, and therefore, under English law, a marriage between them would be void. But this was not so under New York law. The evidence disclosed that it was the definite aim of both the parties to acquire an "American"[20] domicile of choice before the marriage was celebrated. At all events, it was conceded that they had unquestionably acquired a New York domicile by the time Richard Wellesley was born in 1920.

The question arose as to whether Richard Wellesley was entitled to a share of the testator's residuary estate settled on his mother for life, with remainder to her children. Romer, J. held that he was.

He considered that:

"where succession to personal property depends on the legitimacy of the claimant, the status of legitimacy conferred on him by his domicile of origin (i.e. the domicile of his parents at birth) will be recognised by our courts; and .... if that legitimacy be established, the validity of his parents' marriage should not be entertained as a relevant subject for investigation."[21]

This holding has given rise to much discussion. On the one hand it has been praised for avoiding the *"non sequitur"*[22] that the invalidity of the parents' marriage under conflicts of law rules relating to marriage must necessarily mean that the children are illegitimate according to conflicts of law rules relating to legitimacy. Romer, J.'s strategy, moreover, in harmonising the approaches to legitimacy and legitimation,[23] respectively, avoids the "startling result,"[24] for which there is said to be "no reason of logic or convenience,"[25] that legitimacy and legitimation should be treated differently in conflicts of law.

[18] 44 D.L.R. (2d) 208, at 215.
[19] [1948] Ch. 79.
[20] This is an unfortunate term: the proper question was whether the parties had intended to acquire, and acquired, a *New York* domicile. Cf. *supra,* pp. 47, 49-50.
[21] [1948] Ch., at 92.
[22] *Cheshire & North,* 443.
[23] See *infra,* pp. 357 ff.
[24] *Cheshire & North,* 446.
[25] *Id.*

On the other hand, *Re Bishchoffsheim* has been heavily criticised, for the conceptual inadequacy of its central holding, as well as for its scant regard for precedent. Romer, J.'s attempt to distinguish *Shaw* v. *Gould* has not impressed the commentators. His belief that the relevance of the Scottish divorce was "a matter rather of assumption by the House than one of direct decision,"[26] in *Dicey & Morris's* words, "certainly does not lack boldness, for it treats as *obiter* a substantial portion of the opinions delivered in *Shaw* v. *Gould*".[27]

So far as conceptual inadequacy is concerned, it has been pointed out[28] that it may not always be the case that the child's domicile of origin will be "the domicile of his parents at birth". The parents may have *different* domiciles, and in such cases a vicious circle is created since a child's domicile of origin depends on whether he is legitimate or illegitimate,[29] and the question of legitimacy, according to Romer, J., must depend on his domicile of origin.

How should the law respond to this "logically insoluble"[30] problem? Several possible solutions have been suggested at various times. They include the following: (a) referring to the *lex domicilii* of the father alone; (b) referring to the *lex domicilii* of the mother alone; (c) referring to the *leges domicilii* of *both* parents; (d) referring to the *lex domicilii* of that parent (if there be such) whose law confers legitimate status on the child; (e) referring the *lex domicilii* of the parents, or the *leges domicilii* of the parents, which is, or are, appropriate to apply in the circumstances of the case. Each of these approaches merits brief consideration.

(a) The lex domicilii of the father alone

In favour of having the *lex domicilii* of the father determine the issue of the child's legitimacy, it has been argued that the essence of the notion of legitimacy concerns the relationship between father and child.[31] Moreover, in matters of children's domicile generally, the law has given,[32] and continues to give,[33] preference to fathers. It has, however, been denied that legitimacy is only concerned with the relationship between father and child. As one commentator noted:

> "The issue in both *Shaw* v. *Gould* and *Re Paine* was whether the claimants were the legitimate children of their mother: their relationship with their father was never in issue, and there would seem to be no good reason why their capacity to take under a will in favour of their mother and her 'children' should be determined by the *lex domicilii* of their father, to whom, if they were illegitimate, they were *ex hypothesi* denied any relation."[34]

The fact that the Continental European legal systems appear to place "most emphasis"[35] on the relationship between father and child has been offered as a reason for referring to the *lex domicilii* of the father. In view of rapid moves towards sex equality in the law relating to legitimacy in those jurisdictions in recent years[36] this argument would seem to have lost much of its force.

---

[26] *Re Bishchoffsheim*, [1948] Ch., at 91.

[27] *Dicey & Morris*, 461.

[28] By *Dicey & Morris*, 461-462, *McLeod*, 300, Welsh, *Legitimacy in the Conflict of Laws*, 63 L. Q. Rev. 65, at 70-71 (1947).

[29] Cf. *supra*, pp. 82-84, *Udny* v. *Udny*, L.R. 1 Sc. & Div. 441, at 457 (H.L., *per* Lord Westbury, 1869).

[30] Webb, *supra*, at 71.

[31] *Wolff*, 382, 389; cf. *Re Luck*, [1940] Ch. 864, at 882 (*per* Greene, M.R. and Luxmoore, L.J.).

[32] See *supra*, pp. 82-83.

[33] Domicile and Recognition of Foreign Divorces Act 1986, section 4.

[34] Welsh, *supra*, at 72.

[35] *Cheshire & North*, 448, citing Guttman, 8 Int. & Comp. L.Q. 678, at 685 (1959) in support.

[36] See A. Chloros ed., *The Reform of Family Law in Europe* (1978), Frame, *The Legal Status of Children of Illegitimate Parents: A Comparative Survey*, 2 Comp. L. Yrbk. 47, (1978), Meulders-Klein, *Cohabitation and Children in Europe*, 20 Am. J. of Comp. L. 359 (1981).

Finally, the fact that legitimation refers to the *lex domicilii* of the father[37] rather than the mother may be considered to be a reason, from the standpoint of consistency, to apply the same rule in relation to legitimacy.

(b)   The lex domicilii of the mother alone

As *Cheshire & North* have observed, there is "much to be said"[39] in favour of referring to the *lex domicilii* of the mother, for "it is with the mother that the young child is likely to make his first home."[40] It is easy to think of cases in which the *lex domicilii* of the mother would, from the standpoint of the social reality of the child's life, have a far more pressing claim that that of the father, who may have only the most transient relationship with the mother. But this approach would not be satisfactory in cases where the father played an active role in the child's upbringing.

(c)   The leges domicilii of both parents

The proposal that a child legitimate according to the *leges domicilii* of *both* parents should be treated as legitimate in English law has been made somewhat tentatively by *Dicey & Morris.*[41] This would reconcile *Re Bischoffsheim* with the previous decisions.[42] From the standpoint of policy, it may be argued that our law has generally no business denying a legitimate status to a child where the child is legitimate according to the *leges domicilii* of both parents. The principal issue would appear to be whether this approach is too restrictive from the standpoint of the interests of the child. If legitimacy is considered to be of legal and social advantage to the child, it may be regarded as overcautious for our law to insist that the *leges domicilii* of *both* parents be complied with. This leads us conveniently to the next possible approach.

(d)   The lex domicilii of that parent whose law confers legitimate status on the child

Under this approach a child would be legitimate under Irish law if the *lex domicilii* of *either* of the parents conferred legitimate status on the child. The advantage, of course, from the child's standpoint, is that he or she would have the social and legal benefits of a legitimate status, and would not lose them on account of the fact that the *lex domicilii* of the other parent did not concur. But the disadvantage is that the *lex domicilii* which confers legitimacy may be one which has far less relevance to the factual circumstances of the child's life than the *lex domicilii* of which denies legitimate status. For example, if an Irishwoman, domiciled in Ireland, has a transient relationship with a foreign domiciliary of a country where illegitimacy has been abolished, when he is on a short visit to Ireland, and the child is reared by the woman

---

[37] Cf. *Re Grove,* 40 Ch. D. 216, at 224 (Stirling, J. 1887); see also the Legitimacy Act 1931, sections 1 (1), 8 (1).

[38] Cf. *Cheshire & North,* 448-449.

[39] *Cheshire & North,* 448. It should be noted that other considerations (notably the desire to encourage harmony with the approach favoured by Continental European legal systems, as well as the wish to unify the rules for legitimacy and legitimation) lead *Cheshire & North,* 448-449 to prefer the *lex domicilii* of the father as "the solution most favourable to the child": *id.,* 448.

[40] *Id.* See further the English Law Commission Working Paper No. 88 and Scottish Law Commission Consultative Memorandum No. 63, *Private International Law: The Law of Domicile,* para. 4.6 (1985), analysed by Fawcett, 49 Modern L. Rev. 225 (1986).

[41] *Dicey & Morris,* 462, and *id.,* 456, Rule 62 (2).

[42] *Dicey* v. *Morris,* 462, point out that their proposed rule would mean that, if the first husband in *Shaw* v. *Gould* had acquired a Scottish domicile after the divorce but before the birth of the children, that case would have been differently decided. They add (*id.*):

"It is of course a matter of conjecture what the decision of the House of Lords would have been in that event, but it may be observed that no member of the House referred to the domicile of [the first husband] as being relevant at any time other than that of the proceedings for divorce in Scotland."

in Ireland, it is at least a matter for discussion whether the child's status should more appropriately be considered legitimate. From the general standpoint of children, legitimacy would appear clearly to be to their advantage, but as a matter of practical convenience, these advantages would have to be weighed in the individual case just mentioned against the possible practical inconveniences involved in the entitlement to joint guardianship, for example, exercisable at a distance of several thousand miles.

(e) That lex domicilii of the parent, or the leges domicilii of the parents which is or are, appropriate to apply in the circumstances of the case

This approach is capable of responding to some of the weaknesses of the previous approach. Rather than have legitimacy follow inexorably from a legitimate status according to the *lex domicilii* of *one* parent, however irrelevant that law may be, the present option has regard to the circumstances of each case before determining this question. Only where the parental *lex domicilii* is "appropriate to apply in the circumstances of the case" will reference be made to it.[43]

This approach would, moreover, seem to have something to recommend it in cases such as *Shaw* v. *Gould* and *Re Paine*, where, as we have seen, the children's relationship with their father "was never in issue".[44] It would also have much to offer to deal with problems arising from the fact that under certain foreign laws a child may be the legitimate child of one parent but not the other.[45]

There are, however, some significant problems associated with this approach. If it involves the invariable *selection* of the *lex domicilii* of *one* parent as the more appropriate law in the circumstances, then there will be a difficulty in cases where the *leges domicilii* of both parents are *equally* appropriate but prescribe differing resolutions to the question of the child's legitimacy. If, on the other hand, "appropriateness" is merely a threshold criterion, which the *leges domicilii* of *both* parents may quite possibly fulfil in some instances, then the problem of differing resolutions to the legitimacy issue will be compounded.

[43] It is interesting in this context to refer briefly to the Scottish case of *Smith* v. *Smith*, 1918 1 S.L.T. 156. There, in proceedings for a declaration of legitimacy, Lord Anderson said (at 160):
   "It may be that, as to cases of this nature, no general rule can be laid down as to the law which falls to be applied. The law which is applicable may depend on the facts of the particular case".
   Lord Anderson considered it his duty to apply Scots law — the law of the *mother's* domicile. If that law had not been applied, then the pursuers would never have succeeded in removing the stigma of illegitimacy, as (it appeared) the law of England would not give them the remedy they sought, since the case involved a putative marriage, a concept recognised under Scots but not English law at that time. Moreover, the decree would have no consequences, and, being based on a putative marriage, the remedy sought, in the words of Frazer (*Husband & Wife* 1.151) flowed from considerations of "equity and humanity". Lord Anderson was:
   "unable to appreciate in what respect the father's domicile affects the present applications. Neither his former *status* nor his succession will be affected by [the] decree being granted.... Sir William was the party who was in bad faith in connection with the putative marriage. Why should the domicile of the first party be regulative of the matter?"
   This is an important decision in showing that policy considerations relating to the circumstances of the particular case may serve a more useful function than mere "black-letter" rules of general application. It is not clear from the case what approach would have been favoured if the facts had been more "neutral", normatively speaking. In other words, it seems plain that the innocence of the children, their "undoubted ... entitle[ment] to have the stigma of illegitimacy removed by legal process if they c[ould] succeed in doing so" (*id.*, at 157), the good faith of the mother and the bad faith of the father all combined to make it easy for the court to apply the rule which would confer legitimate status on the children; the fact that no property consequences were raised directly by this option made the choice a still easier one.
   But the case is still an old-fashioned one so far as it concentrates on the relative guilt and innocence of the parents. It gives us no indication of what rule should be applied where neither parent had the intention of marrying the other and the *lex domicilii* of one parent, but not the other, confers legitimate status on the child.
[44] Welsh, *supra*, at 72.
[45] *Id.* See, however, *Wolff*, 382.

Another problem raised by this approach is its emphasis on a contextual solution. What may be "appropriate" in one context at a particular time may not be "appropriate" in another context or at another time. Our conflicts rules would not be able to answer definitively the question: Is this child legitimate? Instead, the answer would depend on the specific context and on the time when the question is put. Perhaps this is not a weakness but a strength: in conflicts law solutions of automatic general application may sometimes be far less satisfactory than solutions limited to particular contexts, with concentration on specific policy goals in the particular case.[46]

The Constructionist Approach

Under this approach the question whether a child is legitimate is one of "construction of words like 'children'[47] or 'issue' in deed, will and statutes",[48] rather than a question requiring an answer in the abstract.[49] Under this approach, a child's legitimacy is a concept relevant only to the particular purpose for which the answer is required and not an abstract issue to be answered in its own right.[50] The solution *would* depend on the somewhat fictional process of attempting to glean the intention of the donor, testator or legislature, as the case may be.

Succession Rights and Legitimacy

We must consider briefly the Irish internal law relating to succession and legitimacy.[51] Legitimate children have generous succession entitlements with respect to their parents' estates. Where a parent dies intestate leaving a surviving spouse and legitimate children, the children are entitled to a third of the estate.[52] Where there is no surviving spouse, the legitimate children are entitled to the whole of their deceased parent's estate.[53] Where a parent dies testate, the legitimate children are entitled to no specific mathematical proportion of his or her estate. Under section 117(1) of the Succession Act 1965, however, where a parent has "failed in his [or her] moral duty make proper provision" for a legitimate child in accordance with his or her means, the court may order that such provision be made for the child out of the estate as the court thinks just. A significant body of decisions on this statutory entitlement has been built up over the past twenty years.[54]

Where a legitimate child dies intestate, unmarried and without children, legitimate or illegitimate, the parents are entitled to all of the estate.[55] If the child has made a will, the parents have no overriding claim.

In contrast to legitimate children, illegitimate children have far more restricted rights.[56] Where the mother of an illegitimate child who has not been legitimated dies intestate leaving no legitimate issue, then the illegitimate child (or, if the child is dead, his or her issue) is entitled to take any interest in the mother's estate to which the child (or, if he or she is dead, his or her issue) would have been entitled

---

[46] Cf. *supra*, pp. 16-21.
[47] Cf. *Andrews* v. *Andrews*, 15 L.R. Ir. 199 (C.A., 1885, aff'g Porter, M.R., 1884).
[48] *Morris*, 240.
[49] *McLeod*, 300.
[50] *Id.*
[51] See *Shatter*, 623-627, *Wylie*, paras. 14.55-14.64, ch. 15, *Binchy*, ch. 13.
[52] Succession Act 1965, section 67(2).
[53] *Id.*, section 67(3).
[54] See Cooney, *Succession and Judicial Discretion in Ireland: The Section 117 Cases*, 15 Ir. Jur. (n.s.) 62 (1980), Fitzpatrick, *The Succession Act, 1965, Section 117*, 110 Ir. L. Times & Sol. J. 77, 83, 89, 95, 101 (1976), Bacon, *The Right of Children and the Discretion of the Courts under Section 117 of the Succession Act, 1965*, 77 Incorp. L. Soc. of Ireland Gazette 223 (1983).
[55] Succession Act 1965, section 67(3).
[56] See the Law Reform Commission's *Report on Illegitimacy*, paras. 88ff (L.R.C. 4-1982).

if the child had been born legitimate.[57] Where the mother dies testate, it appears that her illegitimate child may apply to the court under section 117(1) of the Succession Act 1965.[58] It would also appear that this entitlement is limited to a case where the mother leaves no legitimate issue.[59]

Although the succession rights of the illegitimate child in his or her mother's estate are not entirely certain, the succession rights of the mother in the child's estate are clear. Where the child who has not been legitimated dies intestate, the mother is entitled to take any interest in the child's estate to which she would have been entitled if the child had been born legitimate and she had been the only surviving parent.[60]

So far as the father's estate is concerned, the position for the illegitimate child is bleak. The child has no succession entitlements, whether the father dies intestate[61] or (it seems) testate.

So far as the conflict of laws is concerned, the position appears to be as follows. A person who is recognised as legitimate under the Irish conflict of laws may succeed to property under deeds, wills and intestacies to the same extent as if he or she were legitimate under Irish internal law.[62] Conversely, a person who is not so recognised has only the same rights of succession as if he or she were illegitimate under Irish internal law.[63]

Of course, the relevant succession law need not necessarily be Irish. It may in some cases be a foreign law, as, for example, where there is a devise of French immovables or a bequest of Irish movables by a testator who died domiciled in France.[64] There appears to be no Irish[65] authority on the question. The commentators are of the view[66] that the legitimacy of the donee should be determined in accordance with the conflicts rules of the foreign legal system.

Declarations of Legitimacy

The question of a person's legitimacy[67] may arise in several different contexts — maintenance[68] or succession, for example, or, perhaps, the interpretation of a deed. If the question is determined in one context, in judicial proceedings, this determination does not conclude the issue of legitimacy for all other contexts thereafter. The judgment operates *inter partes* rather than *in rem.*[69]

Therefore, it is quite possible that a person could be held legitimate in one proceeding and illegitimate in separate proceedings a week later. Accordingly, "[t]he desirability of having a procedure to settle for all circumstances disputes over a person's status, resulted in the enactment of the required legislation in the second half of the last century."[70] The relevant statutory provisions are contained in the Legitimacy Declaration Act (Ireland) 1868.

Under section 1 of the 1868 Act:

[57] Legitimacy Act 1931, section 9(1). Section 9(3) provides that the section "does not apply to or affect the right of any person to take by purchase or descent an estate in tail in real property". Nor does the section affect the succession to "any dignity or title of honour": section 10(1).
[58] Cf. L.R.C. 4-1982, para. 90.
[59] Cf. *id.*, para. 91.
[60] Legitimacy Act 1931, section 9(2).
[61] *O'B.* v. *S.,* [1984] I.R. 316 (Sup. Ct., 1984, aff'g High Ct., D'Arcy, J., 1982).
[62] *Morris,* 244.
[63] *Id.*
[64] Cf. *Cheshire & North,* 447.
[65] Or English: *Morris,* 246.
[66] *Cheshire & North,* 447, appear to have no doubt on this question. More cautious are *Morris,* 246, and *Dicey & Morris,* 468.
[67] Whether or not that person is a party to the proceedings (cf. *Dicey & Morris,* 455) or is alive or dead (cf. *Brook* v. *Brook,* 9 H.L.C. 193, 11 E.R. 703 (1861).
[68] Cf. *Yool* v. *Ewing,* [1904] 1 I.R. 434, at 451 (Porter, M.R., 1903).
[69] *Dicey & Morris,* 455, *Shatter,* 285.
[70] *Shatter,* 284.

"[a]ny natural-born subject of the Queen, or any person whose right to be deemed a natural-born subject depends wholly or in part on his legitimacy, being domiciled in England or Ireland, or claiming any real or personal estate situate in Ireland, may apply by petition to the Court of Probate in Ireland, praying for a decree that the petitioner[74] is the legitimate child of his parents and that the marriage of his father and mother, or of his grandfather and grandmother, was a valid marriage, or for a decree declaring either of the matters aforesaid; and any subject or person being so domiciled or claiming as aforesaid may in like manner apply to such Court for a decree declaring that his marriage was or is a valid marriage; and such Court shall have jurisdiction to hear and determine such application, and to make such decree declaratory of the legitimacy or illegitimacy of such person, or the validity or invalidity of such marriage, as to the Court may seem just; and such decree, except as herein-after mentioned, shall be binding to all intents and purposes on Her Majesty and on all persons whomsoever."

A copy of every petition, and accompanying affidavit, must be delivered to the Attorney General, who is a respondent in the hearing.[72] The Court has power,[73] to require that such other persons as it thinks fit are to be made parties to the proceedings, and to oppose the application.

A decree of the Court is not in any case to prejudice any person, unless he has been made a party to the proceedings "or is the heir-at-law or next of kin, or other real or personal representative of, or derives title under or through, a person who has been made a party; nor is the decree to prejudice any person if it is subsequently proved to have been obtained by fraud or collusion."[74] Finally, the proceedings do not affect any final judgment or decree already pronounced or made by any court of competent jurisdiction.[75]

There appears to be no Irish decision dealing with the jurisdictional aspects of the 1868 Act[76] and, as has been observed, "the difficulties that they now cause are manifest".[77] One leading commentator has stated that:

"[i]t seems wholly reasonable to assume that the phrase 'subject of the Queen' will, at least, be taken to include a natural born subject of the Republic of Ireland.[78] However, it does also appear to include a wider range of petitioners, i.e. subjects of the Queen. Secondly, the Irish court's jurisdiction would appear to extend to petitioners domiciled in England, as well as Ireland. Thirdly, the definition of Ireland would appear to be that contained in the Irish Constitution of 1937.[79] It would appear that the obvious anomalies in the 1868 Act are best cured by legislation."[80]

Some less troublesome jurisdictional aspects may be noted. If the domicile of the petitioner depends on his legitimacy or on the validity of a marriage, and the petitioner is not claiming any property situated in Ireland, then "the court will assume the truth of his allegations for the purpose of assuming jurisdiction".[81] This application

[71] The section does not permit the petitioner to establish the legitimacy of his or her child: cf. *Aldrich* v. *A.G.*, [1968] 2 W.L.R. 413. Since 1971 a petitioner may obtain a declaration of *legitimation* of his or her child: Courts Act 1971, section 20, considered *infra*, pp. 366-367.
[72] Section 6 of the 1868 Act. As to costs, cf. *A.B.* v. *A.G.*, I.R. 4 Eq. 56 (Probate, Warren, J., 1869), *King* v. *A.G.*, I.R. 4 Eq. 464 (Probate, Warren, J., 1870).
[73] Section 7 of the 1868 Act.
[74] *Id.*, section 8.
[75] *Id.*, section 9.
[76] *North*, 368.
[77] *Id.*
[78] Citing *Re Duane*, [1936] Ir. Jur. Rep. 60.
[79] Citing Articles 2 and 3 of the Constitution and the Constitution (Consequential Provisions) Act 1937, section 2.
[80] *North*, 368-369.
[81] *Dicey & Morris*, 454, citing *Armitage* v. *A.G.*, [1906] P. 135, a decision which, they note, was criticised by Morris, 24 Can. Bar Rev. 73, at 77-78 (1946), but defended by Tuck, 25 Can. Bar Rev. 226, at 228-230 (1947).

of the notion of proleptic, or anticipatory domicile[82] is essential to prevent the ''impasse''[83] which would otherwise arise.

The scope of the decree which a court may make under the 1868 Act was considered in *Yool* v. *Ewing*,[84] in 1903. Porter, M.R. Held that proceedings under section 1 ''can only be brought to establish, not to negative legitimacy''.[85] He noted that, ''[i] f a person comes into court to have his legitimacy established, and if he fails to do so, of course the decree establishes his illegitimacy''.[86]

When determining the issue of the petitioner's legitimacy under the 1868 Act, the courts may investigate the question of paternity. In *A.B.* v. *A.-G.*,[87] in 1868, Warren, J. held that this is so, ''as it is impossible to decide that a person is the legitimate child of his reputed parents without deciding who his reputed parents are''.

LEGITIMATION

We must now consider the notion of legitimation.[88] In contrast to legitimacy, which is a condition affecting a child at birth, legitimation is concerned with the process of *becoming* legitimate at some point after the child's birth.

Legitimation may be of many types. These include legitimation by subsequent marriage (*per subsequens matrimonium*), by recognition of the child by the father and by decree of the Sovereign or other competent authority.[89]

Let us consider each of these methods of legitimation in turn.

(i) Legitimation per subsequens matrimonium

Legitimation by subsequent marriage (*per subsequens matrimonium*)[90] has a long history. It was part of Roman law from the time of Constantine,[91] and has been a feature of the law of most European and South American countries for centuries.[92] The relationship between the canon law and common law of England on the question of legitimation by subsequent marriage is not entirely clear:[93] plainly this concept had no effect on succession entitlements, but beyond this the question is not so easily resolved. At all events, legitimation by subsequent marriage was finally introduced into English law by statute in 1926. In Ireland, five years later, the passage of the Legitimacy Act 1931 brought the concept into our law.

---

[82] Cf. the Law Reform Commission's Working Paper No. 10-1981, *Domicile and Habitual Residence as Connecting Factors in the Conflict of Laws*, para. 13.

[83] *Dicey & Morris*, 454.

[84] [1904] 1 I.R. 434 (Porter, M.R., 1903).

[85] *Id.*, at 448.

[86] *Id. Quaere* whether the refusal to grant a decree under the section would in every case establish the illegitimacy of the petitioner. For example, the petitioner's failure to comply with the jurisdictional requirements would be a reason for refusing to grant the decree which would have no necessary implications as to his or her status.

[87] I.R. 4 Eq. 56, at 58 (Probate, Warren, J., 1869). Cf. *Slingsby* v. *A.-G.*, 33 Times L. R. 120 (H.L. (Eng.), 1916).

[88] See generally Taintor, *Legitimation, Legitimacy and Recognition in the Conflict of Laws*, 18 Can. Bar Rev. 589, 691 (1940), Mann, *Legitimation and Adoption in Private International Law*, 57 L.Q. Rev. 112 (1941), *Wolff*, 87-89, 393-397.

[89] See *Wolff*, 393-394. So far as legitimation by the decree of the Sovereign or other competent authority is concerned, *Wolff*, 393, notes that legitimation by the Sovereign (*per rescriptum principis (seu Papae)*) originated in Roman and Canon law, and continues to be found in the law of such countries as Italy, the Netherlands and the Scandinavian states; legitimation by judicial edict is permitted in Switzerland, by the President of the Court in the Federal Republic of Germany, and by the Minister of Justice in Greece: *id.*

[90] See White, *Legitimation by Subsequent Marriage*, 36 L.Q. Rev. 255 (1920).

[91] *Cheshire & North*, 451.

[92] Scottish Law Commission, *Reform of the Law Relating to Legitimation per subsequens matrimonium*, para. 7. (Cmnd. 3223, 1967).

[93] See *Castel*, vol. 2, 270-272.

(a) Legitimation per subsequens matrimonium at Common Law

Before considering the provisions of the 1931 Act, it is advisable to refer to the position at common law. In what circumstances should our courts (at common law) hold that a subsequent marriage confers legitimate status on the child?

The answer appears to be determined by reference to the domicile of one or both of the child's parents. In *Re Goodman's Trusts*,[94] in 1881, the English Court of Appeal held that the law of the domicile of the child's parents at the birth of the child determined the issue. Cotton, L.J. stressed the fact that the question of legitimacy was one of status, which depended on "the law of the domicile". He added:

> "If, as in my opinion is the case, the question whether a person is legitimate depends on the law of the place where his parents were domiciled at his birth, that is, on his domicile of origin, I cannot understand on what principle, if he be by that law legitimate, he is not legitimate everywhere, and I am of the opinion that if a child is legitimate by the law of the country where at the time of its birth its parents were domiciled, the law of England, except in the case of succession to real estate in England, recognises and acts on the *status* thus declared by the law of the domicile... [I]n my opinion, in deciding questions of legitimacy, that is of *status*, the law of England looks to the law of the actual, not the hypothetical, domicile."[95]

Re Goodman's Trusts has received the wholehearted endorsement of an Irish court. In *In re Hagerbaum, Deceased; Bond* v. *Pidding*,[96] a case concerned with legitimation by subsequent marriage, Meredith, J. cited the case as authority for the proposition that "[t]he question as to legitimacy is one of status, and status depends on the law of domicile".[97] He did not elaborate as to *whose* domicile was in issue, nor as to *when* that domicile was relevant. The passage from Cotton, L.J.'s judgment quoted above refers to "the place where [the child's] *parents* were domiciled *at his birth*".[98] But in *In re Grove; Vaucher* v. *Treasury Solicitor*,[99] decided seven years after *In re Goodman's Trusts, Cotton, L.J. sought to explain* his earlier remarks. He noted that what he had said in that case:

> "might seem to bear the construction that the only time to be considered is the time of the birth of the child. That was a question which had not really to be considered, or in any way decided, in *In re Goodman's Trusts*. ... What is really necessary, I think, is that the father should at the time of the birth of the child be domiciled in a country allowing legitimation, so as to give to the child the capacity of being made legitimate by a subsequent marriage. But it is the subsequent marriage which gives the legitimacy to a child who has at its birth in consequence of its father's domicil the capacity of being made legitimate by a subsequent marriage.
>
> Where then must that marriage be? It is singular that there is, as far as I am aware, no express decision on that point. But this is probably because as a rule when the parties have been domiciled at the time of the birth in a country allowing legitimation of a child born before marriage, that same country has been their domicil at the time of their marriage. As I said before, the place of birth and the place of marriage is (*sic*) immaterial to the question of domicil. In the absence of authority the incidents and the effects of a marriage must, in my opinion, depend on the domicil of the parties

[94] 17 Ch. D. 266 (C.A., 1881). See also the earlier decision of *Munro* v. *Munro*, 7 Cl. & Fin. 842, 7 E.R. 1288 (1840), referred to with apparent approval by Brady L.C. in *Maghee* v. *M'Allister*, 3 Ir. Ch. Rep. 604, at 607 (1853).

[95] 17 Ch. D., at 291-292.

[96] [1933] I.R. 198 (High Ct., Meredith, J.).

[97] *Id.*, at 200.

[98] Emphasis added.

[99] 40 Ch. D. 216 (Ct. App., 1888).

at the time of the marriage; and it will be strange if a marriage in England, between persons domiciled in England, could produce an effect which by English law is not attributed in any way to marriage."[100]

It seems clear from *Re Grove,* and subsequent English cases[101] that a child must pass *two* hurdles: only where the law of the father's domicile at the time of the birth *and* at the time of the subsequent marriage permit legitimation by subsequent marriage will the legitimation have effect under English law. But does this mean that the same double hurdle must be crossed under our law? Though *Re Hagerbaum* does not answer this question, the earlier decision of *Moffett* v. *Moffett*[102] affords strong support of the view that the double hurdle is indeed part of our law. There, a man whose domicile of origin was Irish was held to have acquired a domicile of choice in Cape Colony by 1864, when his child was born, and to have had the same domicile of choice at the date of his subsequent marriage in 1867. Legitimation by subsequent marriage was permitted by the law of Cape Colony. The child was accordingly held to have been legitimated. The case includes no discussion of the rules for recognition of legitimation by subsequent marriage. Almost all of Powell, J.'s judgment was concerned with the question of the man's domicile.

Powell, J. at first resolved the question of the man's domicile *at the time of his death,* a question which was not relevant to the issue of legitimation but apparently was the only question he had initially been asked to decide by counsel on both sides of the case.[103] After he had delivered judgment in the case (holding that the man had at his death acquired a South African domicile), Powell, J. was told by counsel for the party seeking to attack the legitimation that there were two other questions to be determined, namely the father's domicile at the date of the child's birth and at the marriage. He had no difficulty in holding that the father's domicile at these dates also was South African.

It is worth noting that the same counsel is reported as having argued that, for the legitimation to be recognised, it was "essential to prove"[104] that at both these dates, of birth and marriage, the father's domicile was South African. He had cited *In re Grove*[105] and *Udny* v. *Udny*[106] in support of this proposition. Moreover, counsel seeking to have the legitimation recognised appears[107] not to have contested this assertion. At all events, the holding in the case by Powell, J. seems consistent only with the view that the law of the father's domicile on the two dates, of birth and marriage, had to be complied with. The Court of Appeal affirmed Powell, J.'s judgment without calling on counsel for the respondent.

In *Moffett* v. *Moffett,* the only foreign law at issue was that of South Africa. There appears to be no reported case in which a father was domiciled in one country at the time of the child's birth and another country at the time of the marriage, the laws of both countries permitting legitimation *per subsequens matrimonium.* In *Re Luck,*[108] Scott, L.J. considered that the decisions on legitimation by subsequent marriage "postulate the possession by the natural father of the same domicile at the date of the birth as at the date of the marriage". *Dicey & Morris*[109] consider, however, that

---

[100] *Id.,* at 231-232.
[101] *Re Grey's Trusts* [1892] 3 Ch. 88, *Re Askew,* [1930] 2 Ch. 259, *Re Luck,* [1940] Ch. 864, *Re Hurll,* [1952] Ch. 722.
[102] [1920] 1 I.R. 57 (C.A., 1920, aff'g. Powell, J., 1919).
[103] Cf. *id.,* at 72.
[104] [1920] 1 I.R., at 60.
[105] *Supra.*
[106] L.R. 1 Sc. App. 441.
[107] Cf. [1920] 1 I.R., at 60-62.
[108] [1940] Ch. 864, at 888.
[109] *Dicey & Morris,* 8th ed., 1967, p. 437.

"on principle" it should not matter whether or not the father was domiciled in the same country on both dates: the child should be legitimated in either case.

Where the father is domiciled in a foreign country at the time of the child's birth and domiciled in Ireland at the time of the marriage, it can be argued that the common law rule does not apply in view of the fact that children legitimated under common law have greater rights of succession than those legitimate under the Legitimacy Act 1931.[110] To hold otherwise "would be to repeal"[111] section 4 of the 1931 Act, which prescribes the succession rights of children legitimated under the Act. As against this, it could perhaps be contended that such children should not be denied the superior succession entitlements since their fathers fulfil the *two* requirements of common law legitimation rather than the single requirement under the 1931 Act: the fact that (a) the marriage takes place in Ireland, and (b) certain restricted succession rights attach to children legitimated *by reason only* of a marriage in Ireland, does not require us to conclude that these restrictions should attach also to cases where the father was domiciled at the time of the birth of the child in a country permitting legitimation by subsequent marriage.

We must now consider the position where the law of the father's domicile, either at the birth of the child or at the time of the subsequent marriage, requires something more or less than Irish internal law does for legitimation by subsequent marriage and the additional requirements of the foreign law or of Irish internal law, as the case may be, are not complied with.[112] In the absence of a clear authority, *Dicey & Morris* submit that "on principle"[113] these additional requirements must be complied with if they form part of the law of the domicile, but that they need not be complied with where they form part of the internal law. Thus, for example, if the foreign law requires parental recognition of the child in addition to the subsequent marriage of the child's parents, this extra requirement would have to be fulfilled. On the other hand, if the foreign law permits legitimation *per subsequens matrimonium* in circumstances which would not be sufficient under our internal law, this divergence should not be a ground, in itself, for our law to decline to recognise the legitimation. So if the foreign law permits legitimation *per subsequens matrimonium* in cases where the child has died before the marriage, the legitimation would be recognised even though under our internal law[114] it is essential that the child be alive at the time of the marriage.[115]

It should, however, be noted that there may be cases in which the divergence between the foreign law and the internal law is of such significance as to raise an issue of public policy. For example, it is doubtful whether in 1931 the foreign legitimation of children born as a result of adultery would have been recognised here. As to the position today, it seems far less likely that such a foreign legitimation would be denied recognition on the ground of public policy.

(b) Legitimation per subsequens matrimonium under the Legitimacy Act 1931

The common law position has been supplemented by statute. The Legitimacy Act 1931 introduced into the law the principle of legitimation *per subsequens matrimonium*. Legitimation by subsequent marriage will be effective if the father of the illegitimate person "was or is at the date of the marriage domiciled in [the

---

[110] See *infra*, pp. 360-362.
[111] *Dicey & Morris*, 8th ed., 1967, p.437 (referring to similar English legislative provisions).
[112] *Id.*, p. 438.
[113] *Id.*
[114] Cf. the Legitimacy Act 1931, section 1(1).
[115] The example is taken from *Dicey & Morris*, 8th ed., 1967, p. 438.

State] ...,"[116] provided the father and mother could have been lawfully married to one another at the time of the birth of such person or at some time during the ten months preceding the birth.[117] The idea behind this proviso is to prevent parents of children resulting from an adulterous relationship subsequently legitimating these children. The proviso gives effect to this policy only crudely;[118] moreover, as we have noted, it appears it is out of touch with contemporary values.

In *In re P.*,[119] in 1944, a man died intestate leaving a widow and six children, the two eldest of whom had been born before the marriage. The applicant for a grant of letters of administration intestate was the eldest child, born in 1894. His parents married in 1898, his father at the time being domiciled in that part of Ireland which subsequently became the Irish Free State.

Maguire, P. held the applicant had been legitimated by the Legitimacy Act 1931 and was thus entitled to apply for a grant. He said:

> "On the whole, though I have some doubt in my mind, I must hold that 'Saorstát Eireann' in s. 1(1) of the Legitimacy Act 1931 refers to that part of Ireland which subsequently came under the jurisdiction of the Government of the Irish Free State in 1922. It seems unlikely that the Legislature did not intend to include within the scope of the Act children born to a couple who married subsequently to their birth, but before the establishment of the Irish Free State, and, as pointed out in *In re M.*,[120] to hold that such was the position would amount to holding that this type of case is a *casus omissus*. I am prepared to follow the line of reasoning adopted in *In re M.*, and to hold that the applicant here became legitimated on the date of the passing of the Act, having been born to parents who were in a position to be married at the time of the birth, and his father having been domiciled, at the time of his subsequent marriage, in that part of Ireland which subsequently became the Irish Free State."[121]

As *In re P.* makes clear, section 1(1) of the 1931 Act requires that the husband be domiciled within the State only at the date of the *marriage;* his country of domicile at the date of *the child's birth* is irrelevant. Indeed, the report of *In re P.* does not even mention what the domicile of the father was at that time.

Section 8(1) of the Act provides that, where the parents marry but the father is at the time of the marriage "domiciled in a country other than the State by the law of which the illegitimate person became legitimated by virtue of such subsequent marriage", the child will be recognised as having been legitimated from the date of the marriage,[122] "notwithstanding that his father was not at the time of the birth of such person domiciled in a country in which legitimation by subsequent marriage was permitted by law". Thus the rule laid down in *Re Wright's Trusts*[123] no longer applies in cases falling within the scope of section 8(1).

By reason of section 8(2), all the provisions of the Act relating to legitimated persons and to the taking of interests in property by or in succession to a legitimate person and the spouse, children and remoter issue of a legitimate person apply in the case of a person "recognised as having been legitimated under .... section [8]".

In *Collins* v. *Attorney General*,[124] in 1931, Bateson, J. held that the effect of a similar English legislative provision was that the proviso regarding "adulterine" children did not qualify section 8. In other words a child resulting from an adulterous relationship might be legitimated under section 8 by virtue of the law of the father's domicile (in Germany) at the time of the subsequent marriage without regard to the

[116] Section 1(1) of the 1931 Act.
[117] *Id.*, section 1(2).
[118] Cf. *Shatter*, 283.
[119] [1945] Ir. Jur. Rep. 17 (High Ct., Maguire, J., 1944).
[120] [1937] N.I. 151.
[121] [1945] Ir. Jur. Rep., at 46. Cf. *supra*, pp. 47-49.
[122] Or the time the Act came into force, if later than the date of the marriage.
[123] 2 K. & J. 595, 595, 69 E.R. 920 (1856).
[124] 47 Times L.R. 484 (P.D.A. Div., Batteson, J., 1931).

law of his domicile (in England) at the time of the child's birth. The same view
has been favoured [in other cases].[125]

(ii) Legitimation by Recognition

Legitimation by paternal recognition is permitted by the law of several European
and South American countries, and some jurisdictions in the United States.[126] It is
the successor of the Roman *legitimatio per rescriptum principis.*[127]

The question arises, first, as to whether this mode of legitimation should be
considered effective and, if so, secondly, as to what domiciliary law or laws should
apply. So far as the first issue is concerned, there is no authority in this country,
but judicial authorities and scholarly opinion elsewhere are clearly of the view that
legitimation by this mode should be considered effective. So far as the second issue
is concerned, again there is no Irish authority. In England, in the one case considering
the issue, *Re Luck's Settlement Trusts,*[128] the majority of the Court of Appeal held
that the father's *lex domicilii* at the time of the birth of the child *and* at the time
of the recognition would both have to support legitimation by this means.

Sir Wilfrid Greene, M.R. and Luxmoore, L.J. thought it appropriate to refer to
the father's *lex domicilii* at the child's birth because (echoing Lord Hatherley in *In
re Wright's Will Trusts*[129]) they considered that the law of the father's domicile
should be regarded as "fastening on" the child at his or her birth and as determining
the nature of their relationship:

> "If by the law of that domicil the relationship is immutably that of a putative father
> and illegitimate child, nothing thereafter can change it. If, on the other hand, by the
> law of that domicil such relationship is not immutable but is capable of becoming that
> of father and legitimate child, that capacity when duly fulfilled is to be recognised by
> the courts of this country."[130]

Sir Wilfrid Greene, M.R. and Luxmoore, L.J. spelt out policy reasons which seemed
to them sound ones for referring to the father's *lex domicilii* at the time of birth.
Legitimacy was "not a unilateral matter affecting the child alone".[131] When an
illegitimate child was legitimated, not only the child's status was affected, but also
the status, rights and obligations of the father and other relations. Moreover, to ignore
the father's *lex domicilii* at the birth of the child would mean that the English courts
would have to "recognize the jurisdiction of a foreign legislature to impose upon
a domiciled Englishman the status of paternity which he did not acquire at the date
of the child's birth and the potentiality of acquiring which he did not at the time
possess".[132]

Finally, the majority considered it a matter of practical advantage that the common
law approach to legitimation by subsequent marriage and legitimation by recognition
should be the same. The short answer to this, of course, is that since 1926 in England
— 1931 in Ireland — the common law rules relating to legitimation by subsequent
marriage have been supplemented by a statutory facility which no longer requires
any reference to the father's *lex domicilii* at the time of the child's birth: in the light

---

[125] *Re Askew,* [1930] 2 Ch. 259; *Re Hurll,* [1952] Ch. 722.
[126] *Cheshire & North,* 456, Mann, *Legitimation and Adoption in Private International Law,* 57 L.Q. Rev.
112, at 112 (1941).
[127] Mann, *supra,* at 112.
[128] [1940] Ch. 864.
[129] 2 K. & J. 595, at 612, 69 E.R. 920, at 927 (1856).
[130] [1940] Ch., at 882.
[131] *Id.,* Cf. Mann, *supra,* at 120-121.
[132] *Id.,* Cf. Mann, *supra,* at 121.

of these developments, it is easy to agree with *Cheshire & North's* description of the approach favoured in *Re Luck* on this issue as being "a little eccentric".[133]

The better view appears to be that there is little reason to refer to the father's *lex domicilii* at the time of the birth. There is no question that fathers or their relations would be prejudiced, so far as their reasonable expectations are concerned, by a rule which referred only to the *lex domicilii* at the time of the recognition. Indeed there could well be cases where reference to the *lex domicilii* at birth would actually *frustrate* the reasonable expectations of the father (and, possibly, the relations).

(iii) Legitimation by Foreign Statute

We must now consider the position arising where a foreign statute legitimates a child in circumstances other than those of subsequent marriage or of recognition. We have seen that our own Legitimacy Act 1931, in section 1(1), legitimated a child, born before that statute came into force, where his parents had married before the time the statute came into force, the father being domiciled in the State *at the time of the marriage*. The section did not require that the father should be domiciled in the State, or even that he should be alive, at the time the statute came into force. Similar statutory provisions have been enacted in several other jurisdictions, including Northern Ireland, England, the Canadian provinces and Australian states.[134]

The question arises as to whether we should recognise the efficacy of these foreign statutory provisions in cases where the father had died or, is no longer domiciled in, the foreign jurisdiction at the time the foreign statutory provision comes into force. From one point of view, the foreign statutory provision "would not be *legitimatio per subsequens matrimonium* but *legitimatio per rescriptum principis,* because the legitimation is effected by, and takes effect from the date of, the statute and not the marriage".[135] On this view, section 8(1) of the 1931 Act could not avail the child, since it could not be said that by the foreign law the illegitimate person "became legitimated by virtue of [the] subsequent marriage...."[136]

The issue was raised in *In re Hagerbaum Deceased; Bond* v. *Pidding.*[137] There the applicant's father, domiciled in England, had married her mother in 1876, two years after her birth. Under England's Legitimacy Act 1926, the applicant had become legitimate. The applicant claimed to be one of the next of kin of her father's sister, who died on 9 August 1930, the Irish Legitimacy Act 1931 coming into force on 1 July 1931.

Counsel for the applicant contended that " [i] f a child be legitimate according to the law of the father's domicile the child will be legitimate in this country".[138] He cited *In re Goodman's Trusts*[139] in support of this proposition. He referred to section 8 of the 1931 Act but conceded that the applicant did not come within its provisions since section 10(2) provided that nothing in the Act was to affect any rights under the intestacy of a person dying before the commencement of the Act.

---

[133] *Cheshire & North*, 455. See also Mann, *supra,* at 120.

[134] See *Dicey & Morris*, 8th ed., 1967, p. 442.

[135] *Id.*

[136] This point is debatable. The contrary appears to have been assumed by counsel in *In re Hagerbaum Deceased: Bond* v. *Pidding, infra.*

[137] [1933] I.R. 198 (High Ct., Meredith, J.).

[138] *Id.,* at 199.

[139] 17 Ch. D. 266 (1881).

Counsel for the defendant did not challenge the argument regarding *In re Goodman's Trusts,* save to the extent of contending that it did not apply in view of sections 3 and 8 of the 1931 Act:

> "Since the Legislature has made express provision by ... section [8] as to how persons legitimated by the laws of other countries are to be recognised in the ... State as having been legitimated, that provision is conclusive, and therefore the applicant's argument that the question of her legitimacy depends upon domicile is unsustainable in view of this express statutory provision."[140]

Meredith, J. held that the applicant should succeed. He said:

> "The question as to legitimacy is one of status, and status depends on the law of domicile: *In re Goodman's Trusts.*[141] As the deceased died in 1930, [the applicant]'s claim ... is independent of the Irish Act. But [counsel for the defendant] argued that her claim is prejudiced by sect. 3. But that is only an enabling section applying to persons legitimated under the Act. The [applicant's] legitimacy ... does not depend upon the Act but on the principles expounded in *In re Goodman's Trusts.*"[142]

This holding, in its result, has much to be said for it since it enables us to recognise foreign statutory legitimations even in cases where the father of the child has died, or is no longer domiciled in the foreign jurisdiction at the time the legislation comes into effect.[143] Unquestionably it reduces the problem of "limping" legitimations. One may, however, express doubt as to whether the full dimensions of the issue were pereceived by the court, which appears to have arrived at its conclusion without regard to the specific difficulty raised by a father's change of domicile, or his death, between the birth of the child and the enactment of the legislation.

Succession and Legitimation

In order to understand the succession entitlements of legitimated persons we must go back to the case-law of the nineteenth century. In the House of Lords decision of *Doe, d., Birtwhistle* v. *Vardill,*[144] in 1940, it was held that a child legitimated *per subsequens matrimonium* under Scots law, the *lex domicilii* of his father at the date of the birth and subsequent marriage, could not succeed as heir of his uncle to real estate in England. This represents the nadir of succession entitlements for legitimated children.

As James, L.J. explained in the later case of *Re Goodman's Trusts*;[145]

> "What the assembled judges said in *Doe d., Birtwhistle* v. *Vardill,* and what the Lords held, was, that the case of heirship to English land was a peculiar exception to the rights incident to that character and status of legitimacy, which was admitted by both judges and Lords to be the true character and status of the claimant. It was only an additional instance of the many anomalies which at that time affected the descent of land .... But in this particular case, the exception is, at all events, plausible. The English heirship, the descent of English land, required not only that the man should be legitimate, but as it were *prophyro-genitus,* born legitimate within the narrowest pale of English legitimacy. Heirship is an incident of land, depending on the local law, the law of the country, the county, the manor, and even of the particular property itself, the *forma doni.* Kinship is an incident of the person, and universal."

---

[140] [1933] I.R., at 200.
[141] *Supra.*
[142] [1933] I.R., at 200-201.
[143] Cf. *Dicey,* 8th ed., 1967, p. 449.
[144] 2 Cl. & Fin. 571, 6 E.R. 1270 (1835).
[145] 17 Ch. D. 266, at 299 (1881).

In *Re Goodman's Trusts,* already mentioned,[146] a child legitimated under the law of the Netherlands, the *lex domicilii* of her father at the time of birth and legitimation, was held entitled to succeed to personal property where her aunt died intestate, domiciled in England.

From this decision onwards, the rule in *Birtwhistle* v. *Vardill* "came to look increasingly anomalous and archaic."[147] In *Re Grey's Trusts*[148] in 1892, the rule was held not to apply to gifts by deed or will to children; and, as we shall see, the rule has been further circumscribed by legislation.[149]

Nevertheless, "[a]lthough since 1881 the right to succeed has automatically followed from the determination of the status [of the legitimated person], it cannot be denied that the two questions are distinct."[150] Of course, Irish law, when the *lex successionis,* is free to adopt a narrow or a broad view, so far as the sucession entitlements of legitimated persons are concerned. Where a foreign *lex successionis* is involved the question as to what law governs is "doubtful".[151] *Dicey & Morris* suggest that, if this issue arose in England, the courts there:

> "would probably permit the foreign *lex successionis* to determine not only what classes of persons were entitled to succeed, but also (if legitimacy was a necessary qualification under the foreign law) whether any individual had or had not been legitimated, and what law determined this question."[152]

At this point it is worth mentioning briefly the rules regarding succession and legitimated children under Irish internal law. Where a child has been legitimated and dies intestate, the same persons are entitled to take the same interests in the child's estate as would have been entitled to take if the legitimated child had been born legitimate.[153] So far as the legitimated child is concerned, section 3 (1) of the Legitimacy Act 1931 provides that (subject to the provisions of the Act) a legitimated person[154] is entitled to take any interest:

(a) in the estate of an intestate dying after the date of legitimation;

(b) under any disposition coming into operation after the date of legitimation; or

(c) by descent under an estate in tail created after the date of legitimation,

in like manner as if the legitimated person had been born legitimate.

Where the right to any property depends on the relative seniority of the children of any person, and these children include a legitimated person, the legitimated person ranks as if he or she had been born on the day when he or she became legitimated by virtue of the Act.[155] Section 3 applies only if and so far as a contrary intention is not expressed in the disposition, and it has effect subject to the terms of the disposition.[156]

The "most important point"[157] about the entitlements conferred by section 3(1) on the legitimated child is that he or she may not take any interest in the estate of a person who had died intestate before the date of legitimation, or under any

---

[146] *Supra,* p. 358.
[147] *Morris,* 252.
[148] [1892] 3 Ch. 88.
[149] Legitimacy Act 1931, section 3.
[150] *Dicey & Morris,* 8th ed., 1967, p. 448.
[151] *Id.*
[152] *Id.,* contrasting *Re Johnson,* [1903] 1 Ch. 821 with *Skottowe* v. *Young,* L.R. 11 Eq. 474 (1871).
[153] Legitimacy Act 1931, section 4.
[154] As well as his or her spouse, children or remoter issue.
[155] Legitimacy Act 1931, section 3(2). The effect of section 3(3) is that nothing in the Act affects the succession to any dignity or title of honour or operates to sever any property or interest therein from such dignity or title of honour.
[156] *Id.,* section 3(4).
[157] *Dicey & Morris,* 8th ed., 1967, p. 453 (referring to equivalent English legislation).

disposition coming into operation before that date.[158] As *Dicey & Morris* have pointed out, for the purposes of this section:

> "a will comes into operation on the death of the testator and not when some benefit under the will becomes vested or payable. Hence, if the testator gives property to A for life and then to the children of A, a child of A who is legitimated after the testator's death cannot take a share of property.... Similarly, an appointment under a special power comes into operation at the date of the instrument by which the power was exercised. Hence, if a settlement or will gives property to A for life and then to such of the children of A as A shall appoint, a child of A who was legitimated after the settlement or will came into operation is not an object of the power...."[159]

These limitations are important in relation to conflicts of law because section 8(2) of the Legitimacy Act 1931 states that all the provisions of the Act relating to legitimated persons and to the taking of interests in property by or in succession to a legitimated person[160] apply in the case of a person recognised as having been legitimated under section 8,[161] or who would, had he survived the marriage of his parents, have been so recognised. Thus a person recognised as having been legitimated under section 8 has the same circumscribed succession rights as apply to persons legitimated (under our internal law) by reason of section 1.[162] In contrast, no similar restrictions apply to persons whose legitimation is recognised under common law rules.[163]

Finally, reference should be made to claims under section 117 of the Succession Act 1965. The effect of section 110 of that Act is not certain. It seems that children whose legitimacy resulting from legitimation is recognised under the provisions of the Legitimacy Act 1931 may take proceedings under section 117. Section 110 does not appear expressly to confer a similar entitlement to those children whose legitimacy is recognised under common law rules. It would be odd if such children should not be entitled to take proceedings under section 117. Apart from the fact that this would run directly contrary to their general succession entitlements, which as we have seen,[164] are more extensive than those of children whose legitimate status is recognised under the provisions of the Legitimacy Act 1931, there would seem to be no apparent rational justification for excluding these children.

Declarations as to Legitimation

Section 2(1) of the Legitimacy Act 1931 provides that:

> "[a] person claiming that he is or that any of his parents or remoter ancestors is or was a legitimated person may, whether he is or is not domiciled in Saorstát Éireann and whether he is or is not a natural-born British subject within the meaning of the Legitimacy Declaration Act (Ireland) 1868, institute proceedings under that Act, and that Act shall apply accordingly."

And section 20 of the Courts Act 1971 has inserted, as subsection (1A) of section 2 of the 1931 Act, the following provision:

---

[158] A will comes into effect on the death of the testator. Thus a legitimated child may acquire an interest under a will even where it was made *before* he or she was legitimated, provided the testator died after he or she was legitimated; see the Law Reform Commission's *Report on Illegitimacy,* para. 27 (L.R.C. 4-1982). Of course section 3(4) of the Legitimacy Act 1931, should not be ignored in this context.
[159] *Dicey & Morris*, 8th ed., 1967, pp. 453-454 (referring to equivalent English legislation).
[160] And his or her spouse, children and remoter issue.
[161] Cf. *supra*, pp. 361-362.
[162] Cf. *Re Hepworth*, [1936] Ch. 759 and *Re Hoff*, [1942] Ch. 298.
[163] Dicey & Morris, 487, citing *Re Askew*, [1930] 2 Ch. 259 and *Re Hurll*, [1952] Ch. 722.
[164] *Supra*, pp. 354-355.

"A person claiming that a child of his is or was a legitimated[165] person may, whether the child is or is not domiciled in the State and whether the child is or is not a natural-born British subject within the meaning of the Legitimacy Declaration Act (Ireland) 1868, institute proceedings under that Act praying for a decree that the child is the legitimate child of his parents, and that Act shall apply accordingly."

It appears that, whereas proceedings under section 2(1) are held in public,[166] proceedings under section 2(1A) are heard in chambers.[167] Whether this distinction can be justified on policy grounds is debatable.

We must now consider the question whether jurisdiction under sections 2(1) and 2(1A) extends merely to one who is "a legitimated person" by reason of section 1 or section 8 of the Legitimacy Act 1931, or whether it extends to one who is "a legitimated person" by reason of the operation of common law rules as to recognition of foreign legitimations.[168] Section 11 of the 1931 Act provides that, for the purposes of that Act, unless the context otherwise requires, the expression "legitimated person" means a person legitimated by the Act. It can be argued, on the other hand, that there is no sound policy reason for restricting jurisdiction for declarations as to legitimation to cases of statutory legitimation: a child is no less fully legitimated if this has been achieved by operation of the common law rules. On the other hand, it may be argued that the 1931 Act offers a clear and straightforward criterion for legitimation which is far easier to establish than the common law criteria. Though a case may be made for the *desirability* of extending jurisdiction to instances of common law legitimation it can scarcely be said that "the context ... *requires*"[169] this interpretation in either section 2(1) or 2(1A).[170]

It should be noted that section 2 of the Legitimacy Act 1931, (as amended), though embracing none of the jurisdictional controls of the Legitimacy Declaration Act (Ireland) 1868, relating to "natural-born British subject[s]", does require that the proceedings for a declaration of legitimation be instituted under the 1868 Act, which Act "shall apply accordingly". Thus, the requirements as to notification of the Attorney-General,[171] and as to joinder of other parties,[172] apply to these proceedings as they do to proceedings for a declaration of legitimacy.

The effect of a declaration of legitimation is, moreover, the same as that of a declaration of legitimacy, so far as concerns (a) persons not made parties to the proceedings,[173] (b) decrees obtained by fraud or collusion,[174] and (c) prior final judgments or decrees.[175]

---

[165] It has been noted *supra*, fn. 71 that a parent may not obtain a declaration as to the *legitimacy* of his or her child where that legitimate status is not based on legitimation.

[166] Cf. *Greenaway* v. *A.G.*, 44 T.L.R. 124 (P.D.A. Div., 1927), where Lord Merrivale, P. emphasised the fact that a question of status is determined in proceedings for a declaration of legitimation.

[167] Courts Act 1971, section 20, inserting subsection (1B) into section 2 of the Legitimacy Act 1931.

[168] Cf. *supra*, pp. 358-360.

[169] Emphasis added.

[170] Cf. *Dicey & Morris*, 70, *Collins* v. *A.-G.*, 47 Times L.R. 484 (P.D.A. Div., Bateson, J., 1931).

[171] *Re Clayton,* 43 Times L.R. 659 (P.D.A. Div., Lord Merrivale, P., 1927).

[172] Legitimacy Declaration Act (Ireland) 1868, section 7.

[173] *Id.*, section 8.

[174] *Id.*

[175] *Id.*, section 9.

CHAPTER 17

ADOPTION

INTRODUCTION

Adoption consists of the establishment of a legal relationship of parent and child where this relationship does not necessarily depend on natural ties.[1] This very general definition simplifies a most complex range of adoption laws which have existed in different cultures at different times.[2] The policy of adoption has sometimes been directed towards benefiting the adoptive parents, as in Greece and Rome, where "[f]amily ties were strengthened in consequence and the name and property of ancient and noble houses were preserved from extinction".[3] This policy is reflected even today in the law of some African[4] and Asian[5] countries.

In Ireland, other European countries and North America, the policy of adoption is to promote the welfare of the child. There are, however, significant differences in a number of these countries as to the legal effects of adoption. In many common law countries, including Ireland, adoption has the effect of completely extinguishing the legal relationship between the natural parents and the child who is adopted. In some other countries, however, the legal relationship is only modified. Thus, the child may in some cases have succession rights in the estate of his or her natural and adoptive parents.[6] In some of the countries which traditionally have favoured a complete severance of the legal relationship, a view has developed in recent years in favour of modification of the present position, on the basis that some form of less final and complete placement of their children might appeal to young mothers.[7]

Other differences may be mentioned briefly.[8] In some countries only children may be adopted; in others there is no age limit. In some countries adoption is by private agreement; in others it must be formally approved by a public authority,

---

[1] See *Shatter*, ch. 12, *Binchy*, ch. 14, *Rabel*, vol. 1, ch. 17.

[2] See *Rabel*, vol. 1, 678-679, Scoles & Hay, 545, 546, Lipstein, *Adoption in Private International Law: Reflections on the Scope and the Limits of a Convention*, 12 Int. & Comp. L.Q. 835, at 835-836 (1963). Huard, *The Law of Adoption: Ancient and Modern*, 9 Vand. L. Rev. 743(1956).

[3] Jones, *Adoption in the Conflict of Laws*, 5 Int. & Comp. L.Q. 207, at 207 (1956).

[4] See O'Collins, *The Influence of Western Adoption Laws on Customary Adoption in the Third World*, ch. 18 of P. Bean, ed., *Adoption : Essays in Social Policy, Law, and Sociology*, at 290-292 (1984).

[5] See Yong-Han Kim, *Legislative Tendency of Adoption in the Developing Country*, ch. 15 of F. Bates ed., *The Child and the Law* (1976).

[6] Cf. Jones, *Adoption in the Conflict of Laws*, 5 Int. & Comp. L.Q. 207, at 207 (1956), Cohn, *Note*, 83 L.Q. Rev. 177, at 177-179 (1967), Lipstein, *Adoption in Private International Law: Reflections on the Scope and Limits of a Convention*, 12 Int. & Comp L.Q. 835, at 835-836(1963).

[7] Cf. Amadio & Deutsch, *Open Adoption: Allowing Adopted Children to 'Stay in Touch' with Blood Relatives*, 22 J. of Family L. 59, at 70-72(1983), Katz, *Rewriting the Adoption Story*, 5 Family Advocate No. 1, p. 9 (1982). For a broader analysis of recent trends, see Johnston, *Is Adoption Outmoded?* 6 Otago L. Rev. 15 (1985).

[8] Cf. Hoggett, *Adoption Law: An Overview*, ch. 8 of P. Bean ed., *Adoption: Essays in Social Policy, Law, and Sociology* (1984).

such as an Bord Uchtála in Ireland, or by a court.[9] Some countries restrict eligibility for adoption to orphans and illegitimate children; others, in varying degrees, provide for the compulsory or voluntary adoption of legitimate children. Some countries provide for the extinction of the rights of one parent after a divorce and for the adoption of the child by the other parent and a later spouse, in other countries divorce does not sever parent-child relationships in this way.

Adoption did not become part of Irish law until 1952.[10] Before then, only one reported decision[11] considered the question whether foreign adoptions would be recognised in Ireland, and if so the extent to which their effects would also be recognised. In England, before adoption was introduced there in 1926, Dicey[12] considered that, since adoption was unknown at common law, the courts should not recognise the status of the adopted child. A Canadian decision[13] took the same view.

As against this, courts have been able to recognise the status of legitimation[14] and of declarations of prodigality;[15] it seems "a complete non-sequitur"[16] to suggest that merely because adoption was not part of our law, our courts should deny recognition to this status, provided, of course no consideration of public policy would prevent them from doing so.

Nevertheless, in *In re Tamburrini*,[17] in 1944, the High Court gave short shrift to the claims of a man to have custody of his adopted son based on a foreign adoption order. An Irish woman had gone to live in Scotland where she gave birth to a boy, outside marriage. She sent the child back to be reared by her parents in Ireland, and over the years contributed regularly towards his maintenance. When the boy was four, she married a divorced man in Scotland, who was not the child's father. The following year she and her husband formally adopted the boy under the provisions of the Adoption of Children (Scotland) Act 1930. They later sought custody of the child from his grandparents, who resisted their request.

The High Court rejected the application of the mother and adoptive father, and the child was permitted to remain with his grandparents. The Court was primarily concerned with the child's religious welfare, which, it felt, would not be served by moving the child to Scotland.

Of interest in the present case is the fact that Maguire P., during argument, enquired of counsel for the applicants whether he relied solely on the natural rights of the mother or on "any alleged right of Antonio Tamburrini, as adoptive father."[18] Counsel replied that he relied on the mother's natural rights, adding: "but under the law of Scotland Antonio Tamburrini has now the legal rights of a father and any order made by this Court should give custody to the two prosecutors."[19]

In the judgments of the Court, Maguire P.[20] alone referred to the question of the adoptive father's claim. He said:

"Although Antonio Tamburrini had adopted the child and is anxious to have him come to live with him, we are of opinion that in a case such as this his rights can not be placed on the same plane as a real parent's."[21]

[9] Cf. Lipstein, *supra*, at 836.
[10] Adoption Act 1952. See *Shatter*, 291-292.
[11] *In re Tamburrini*, [1944] I.R. 508 (High Ct.).
[12] 3rd ed., 502-503 (1922).
[13] *Burnfiel* v. *Burnfiel*, [1926] 2 D.L.R. 129.
[14] Cf. *Re Goodman's Trusts*, 17 Ch. D. 266 (1881), *Re Andros*, 24 Ch. D. 637 (1883).
[15] Cf. *Baindail* v. *Baindail*, [1946] P. 122, *Worms* v. *De Valdor*, 49 L.J. Ch. 261 (1880).
[16] Jones, *Adoption in the Conflict of Laws*, 5 Int. & Comp. L.Q. 207, at 209 (1956).
[17] [1944] I.R. 508 (High Ct.).
[18] *Id.*, at 509.
[19] *Id.*
[20] With whom Maguire, J. concurred.
[21] [1944] I.R., at 513.

The case shows how little weight was attached to the status of a foreign adoption order in 1944, when no institution of adoption existed in Ireland. Not only were the rights of the adoptive father given virtually no attention, but the Court also ignored any rights of the mother as adoptive parent of her own child.[22]

Jurisdiction to make an Adoption Order

An adoption order may be made only where the child resides in the State,[23] and where the applicants are ordinarily resident in the State and have been so resident during the year ending on the date of the order.[24]

Thus, the domicile of neither the child nor the applicants is relevant. So far as the child is concerned, this relieves the authorities of the task, which may be a difficult and complex one in many cases, of attempting to discern the domicile of the child's mother or father, as the case may be. As we have seen[25] the whole subject of the domicile of children is plagued by uncertainties. If the authorities were obliged to work out the domicile of children otherwise eligible for adoption, they would have to resort frequently to the court for guidance on the matter. Moreover, a requirement that the child or the applicants should be domiciled within the State would lead to arbitrary results, to the detriment of the child in many instances.[26] "Residence" is probably a better notion than "living", since it connotes a stronger degree of continuity than the latter term.[27] Clearly, what the legislation is seeking to prevent is an adoption of a child whose presence within the State is fleeting. "Residence" accomplishes this goal.

Some other aspects of the question of eligibility to adopt and to be adopted must also be considered. Section 11(1) of the Adoption Act 1952, as amended by section 5 of the Adoption Act 1964 and section 5 of the Adoption Act 1974, renders a "married couple", a "widow" and a "widower" eligible to adopt in specified circumstances. The question arises as to whether Irish law or some other law determines the status of the persons concerned. The Acts throw no direct light on the issue. A reasonable interpretation of these terms is that the capacity of the persons involved to marry is determined by having regard to the conflicts of law rules on this question. In other words if the parties have such a capacity according to the law of the countries of their domicile,[28] then, but not otherwise, do they fulfil the requirements of eligibility. Section 3 of the Adoption Act 1952 defines "relative" as meaning:

> "grandparent, brother, sister, uncle or aunt, whether of the whole blood, of the half-blood or by affinity, relationship to an illegitimate child being traced through the mother only."

Again the statute gives no guidance on the question of what law is to determine

---

[22] This may be because her counsel apparently placed no reliance on these rights: cf. *id.*, at 509.

[23] Adoption Act 1952, section 10.

[24] Adoption Act 1964, section 5(2), substituting a new subsection (4) for the original subsection (4) of section 11 of the Adoption Act 1952. Under the 1952 Act, it was necessary for the applicants to reside in the State (original section 11(4)). Moreover section 11(5), which was deleted by section 5(3) of the 1964 Act, had provided that an adoption order should not be made unless the applicant or, if the applicants were a married couple, the husband, was an Irish citizen or had been ordinarily resident in the State during the five years preceeding the date of the application.

[25] *Supra,* pp. 82-92.

[26] See Morris, *Some Recent Developments in the English Private International Law of Adoption,* Festschrift for Mann 241, at 243 (1977) (criticising for English law, which made domicile the sole jurisdictional criterion). Cf. de Nova, *Adoption in Comparative Private International Law* [1961] 1 Recueil des cours 68, at 80-81.

[27] Cf. McClean & Patchett, *English Jurisdiction in Adoption,* 19 Int. & Comp. L.Q. 1, at 8 (1970).

[28] Cf. pp. 228 ff., *supra.*

the legitimate or illegitimate status of the child. Again it seems reasonable that our conflicts of law rules on the subject of legitimacy[29] should determine the question.

When we turn to consider the subject of eligibility for adoption, similar questions arise. Those eligible for adoption are children residing in the State[30] who are: (a) orphans[31]; (b) illegitimate children;[32] and (c) legitimated children whose birth has not been re-registered.[33] No major difficulty in relation to conflicts of law arises with respect to orphans.[34] So far as illegitimate children are concerned, it seems that our conflicts rules as to legitimacy should determine the question. The position regarding legitimated children is the subject of a specific statutory provision. Section 2(1) of the Adoption Act 1964 permits the adoption of a child "who has been legitimated or whose legitimation has been recognised in pursuance of the provisions of the Legitimacy Act 1931," provided the child's birth has not been re-registered in pursuance of the provisions of the Schedule to the 1931 Act "or in pursuance of the law of a country other than the State." Clearly, a foreign legitimation recognised under the 1931 Act comes within the scope of section 2(1). But what about a foreign legitimation recognised *other than under the 1931 Act?*[35] There seems no sound policy justification for excluding children thus legitimated from the scope of section 2(1), at all events where the legitimation was *per subsequens matrimonium,*[36] but it is not very easy to fit them within its express words. Perhaps it can be said simply that they have "been legitimated"; but if this expression covers *these* children it should be sufficiently strong to cover children whose legitimation has been recognised under the 1931 Act, yet the latter receive specific mention.

Some uncertainty surrounds the requirement that the birth of the legitimated child should not have been re-registered "in pursuance of the law of a country other than the State". Some countries may have provisions requiring re-registration, others not. For those requiring re-registration, section 2(1) provides that no such registration should actually have occurred. So far as those countries not requiring any re-registration are concerned, it is not clear whether this renders the child ineligible under section 2(1) or (more credibly) that this renders irrelevant the requirement as to non-registration. Section 2(1) does not attempt to identify *which* country's law is relevant. This would appear to depend on the choice of law rules as to recognition of foreign legitimations.

Choice of Law

Apart from the limited scope of operation of choice of law rules in respect of eligiblity to adopt and to be adopted, it appears that our law of adoption does not in general involve choice-of-law principles. Thus an adoption complying with the requirements of Irish law will be valid even though it does not comply with the requirements for adoption under the *lex* (or *leges*) *domicilii* of the child and of the applicants.[37]

---

[29] Cf. pp. 345-355. *supra.*
[30] Adoption Act 1952, section 10.
[31] *Id.*
[32] *Id.*
[33] Adoption Act 1964, section 2(1).
[34] The question whether a country's law as to presumption of death is a matter of substance or procedure could perhaps give rise to difficulties in some cases: cf. *infra*, pp. 434, 628-630.
[35] Cf. pp. 358-360, 362-364, *supra.*
[36] The requirements in section 2(1) concerning re-registration suggest (though far from conclusively) that *legitimation per subsequens matrimonium* was envisaged.
[37] Cf. Morris, *Some Recent Developments in the English Private International Law of Adoption*, Festschrift for Mann 241, at 246-247 (1977). For critical analysis of this approach see de Nova, *Adoption in Comparative Private International Law,* [1961] 1 Recueil des cours 68, ch. 1. Of course, the international implications of a proposed adoption could be a factor to be taken into account in determining

Recognition of Foreign Adoptions[38]

We must now consider the question of recognition of foreign adoptions in Irish law. In the absence of legislative guidance or judicial decisions, the question is an open one. The advantage of this position is that our law can review the various strategies considered or applied elsewhere, and select the best approach. These strategies have ranged widely. Some of these are mentioned below.

Refusal to recognise foreign adoptions because the legal nature of adoption varies so greatly from country to country.

One approach would require the Irish court to refuse to recognise foreign adoptions because the legal nature of adoption varies so greatly from country to country. The objections to this solution are obvious. It would result in hardship and injustice to many families; it would yield quite inappropriate solutions in practice; and there is simply no need for our courts to adopt such an unwilling attitude. The fact that a task may at times prove difficult is scarcely a good reason for declining to undertake it at all.

There is, of course, a problem in some instances as to the extent to which a legal process denominated "adoption" in a particular foreign law is akin to adoption under Irish law, but this is by no means a unique type of problem in the conflicts of law.[40] One solution would be to ask an all-or-nothing question: "Is the legal process, whatever its name, sufficiently similar with adoption in our law to be treated as an adoption?" If the answer is yes, then there is no further question to be asked. Even if the foreign legal process is in some respects different to our notion of adoption, these differences will be ignored. If the answer is no, then whatever similarities there may be with our notion of adoption will be ignored. A more complex, though more sensitive, solution would characterise the foreign process *in the specific context* in which the particular issue arises. On this approach, a child could be treated as adopted for some purposes and not for others.

---

whether the adoption should be made: cf. *Re B.(S) (An Infant)*, [1968] Ch. 204 (Goff, J.), but this does not affect the principle that the *lex fori* controls.

[38] See Scarman, *English Law and Foreign Adoptions*, 11 Int. & Comp. L.Q. 635 (1962), Cowen, *English Law and Foreign Adoptions*, 12 Int. & Comp. L.Q. 168 (1963) (a useful comparative study), Morris, *Some Recent Developments in the English Private International Law of Adoption*, Festschrift for Mann 241, at 248-255 (1977), Lipstein, *Adoption in Private International Law: Reflections on the Scope and Limits of a Convention*, 12 Int. & Comp. L.Q. 835, at 839 ff (1963), O'Connell, *Recognition and Effects of Foreign Adoption Orders*, 33 Can. Bar Rev. 635 (1955), Kennedy, *Adoption in the Conflict of Laws*, 34 Can. Bar. Rev. 507, at 521 ff (1956) (an excellent analysis), Jones, *Adoption in the Conflict of Laws*, 5 Int. & Comp. L.Q. 207, at 210-216 (1956), Taintor, *Adoption in the Conflict of Laws*, 15 U. Pittsburgh L. Rev. 222 (1954), Inglis, *Adoption, The Marshall Case, and The Conflict of Laws*, 35 Can. Bar Rev. 1027(1957), Inglis, *Recognition of Foreign Adoptions*, 32 Austr. L.J. 216 (1958), Gerber, *Some Aspects of Adoptions in the Conflict of Laws*, 38 Austr. L.J. 309 (1965), North, *Note: Adoption, Succession, and the Conflict of Laws*, 28 Modern L. Rev. 470 (1965), Groffier, *L'adoption en droit international privé comparé*, [1976] Rev. Critique de Dr. Int. Privé 603, at 635-651, Inglis, *Adoption and Succession in Private International Law*, 6 Int. & Comp. L.Q. 202 (1957).

[39] See *Re Wilson*, [1954] Ch. 733, at 741 (Vaisey, J.). Cf. *Re Wilby*, [1956] P. 174, at 180 (Barnard, J.).

[40] The definition of marriage may present somewhat similar difficulties in certain instances: cf. Scarman, *English Law and Foreign Adoptions*, 11 Int. & Comp. L.Q. 635, at 638(1962), *Nachimson* v. *Nachimson*, [1930] P. 217, analysed *supra*, p. 212. See also Kennedy, *Adoption in the Conflict of Laws*, 34 Can. Bar Rev. 507, at 545-546 (1956):

"We may look to the foreign adoption law to determine whether the adoption resembles adoption as we know it. In cases of foreign marriage, of which there are many forms, we examine the nature of the foreign institution. If it is in substance marriage as we know it, we accept it and treat the parties to it as married. Even if it is polygamous we accept it for succession purposes. So, too, in adoption it is neither necessary nor proper to go beyond the question of substance. Rituals called 'adoptions' but which are in substance something else — for example, a form of ancestor worship — will not be accepted. On the other hand, where we have what is in substance an adoption,

The reciprocity principle

This approach recognises foreign adoptions if carried out in circumstances which, had they occurred in Ireland, would have entitled the Irish authorities to exercise jurisdiction.[41]

In the English decision of *Re Valentine's Settlement*[42], in 1965, Lord Denning, M.R. said:

"[W]hen is the status of adoption duly constituted? Clearly it is so when it is constituted in another country in similar circumstances as we claim for ourselves. Our courts should recognise a jurisdiction which *mutatis mutandis* they claim for themselves: see *Travers* v. *Holley*.[43] We claim jurisdiction to make an adoption order when the adopting parents are domiciled in this country and the child is resident here. So also, out of the comity of nations, we should recognise an adoption order made by another country when the adopting parents are domiciled there and the child is resident there."

A reciprocity principle could work unsatisfactorily so far as our jurisdictional requirements are liberal but our eligibility requirements are narrowly drawn; where a country with similar jurisdictional requirements but wide-ranging eligibility requirements permitted an adoption it is not certain that recognition would necessarily be desirable. To this it may be said that our courts are always free to resort to public policy[44] where the eligibility requirements are too wide-ranging, and secondly, that, whether the reciprocity principle or one based on domicile is favoured, the problem of over-liberal eligibility requirements may arise.

A domicile-based test

It has been argued widely that recognition of foreign adoptions should be based, exclusively or as one of a number of grounds, on domicile. It is perhaps not unreasonable that domicile should play a significant role since adoption (in the law of many countries) changes status,[45] and such an important result should not lightly be recognised. Domicile, it may be said, has a sufficiently strong and permanent force as a connecting factor to base recognition of foreign adoptions upon it.

If domicile is to be the test, *whose* domicile should enter into construction?

One solution would be to recognise a foreign adoption only where it is valid according to the *leges domicilii* of the child *and* the adoptive parents. This cumulative approach was supported by Barnard, J. in *Re Wilby*[46] and Vaisey, J., in *Re Wilson*.[47]

In favour of this view, it may be argued that, since adoption alters the status of both the child and the parents, it should not be recognised unless it is effective under the domiciliary laws of all parties concerned.[48] In this regard it has been noted that adoption differs from legitimation in that adoption involves no necessary prior connection by blood between the parties:

differences in detail do not matter. In both marriage and adoption differences in the age limits, residence periods, consents necessary, and other details do not prevent our acceptance of the foreign institution."

[41] Cf. *Travers* v. *Holley* [1953] P. 246, at 257 (C.A., per Hodson, L.J.), Kennedy, *Reciprocity in the Recognition of Foreign Judgments*, 32 Can. Bar Rev. 359, at 370-372 (1954), O'Connell, *Recognition and Effects of Foreign Adoption Orders*, 33 Can. Bar Rev. 635, at 642 (1955), Kennedy, *Adoption in the Conflict of Laws*, 34 Can. Bar Rev. 507, at 523-525 (1956).

[42] [1965] Ch. 831, at (C.A.)

[43] [1953] P. 246, at 257.

[44] Cf. Morris, *Some Recent Development in the English Private International Law of Adoption*, Festschrift for Mann, 241, at 249 (1977): "Public policy is probably more important a reservation in the law of adoption than in any other part of the conflict of laws, because the laws of some foreign countries differ so sharply from English law as to the objects and effects of adoption."

[45] Cf. O'Connell, *Recognition and Effects of Foreign Adoption Orders*, 33 Can. Bar Rev. 635, at 638-639 (1955).

[46] [1956] 2 W.L.R. 262.

[47] [1954] Ch. 733.

[48] Jones, *Adoption in the Conflict of Laws*, 5 Int. & Comp. L.Q. 207, at 209 (1956).

"Where [blood] ties exist . . . it is adequate to disregard the [child]'s personal law. But if the relationship of father and child is created independently of any natural ties, regard must be had to the child's personal law which, not only in a legal but also in a natural sense is different from that of the adopter, and on which the adopter's personal law has never had a possibility of 'fastening' itself. Moreover, adoption to a large extent disconnects the ties between the child and its family whose interests will be reasonably protected by taking into account the personal law which it has 'fastened' on the child. The situation is, in some respects, similar to that to be faced in connection with marriage the creation of which depends on both spouses' personal law. Before the marriage a woman is no way subject to her future husband's personal law and, therefore, she cannot become his wife but by the force of their respective personal laws. Exclusive reliance on the adopter's personal law would be equally unjustified."[49]

As against this, the cumulative rule restricts the number of adoptions which will be treated as effective. This may cause hardship and injustice in some instances.[50]

If a choice has to be made between the *lex domicilii* of the child[51] and that of the parents, which should prevail? The argument in favour of the child's *lex domicilii* is "based on the consideration that the law from which the child is withdrawn and which provides the existing framework of his legal relations should have some say in the change."[52] The fact that the child in most cases will not be old enough to protect his own interests is a further reason for giving emphasis to the child's *lex domicilii*. Nor should one ignore the interests of the child's natural parent or parents, since, if the adoption is recognised, their rights in relation to their child will no longer be recognised. The phenomenon of international adoptions of children from poor countries by adoptive parents of richer countries should be kept in mind in this context.

The principal argument in favour of selecting the adoptive parents' *lex domicilii* is that in most cases the child, when adopted, will be living in the country of the adoptive parents' domicile; this will be his centre of gravity during the time he is growing up with them, and "[t]o attribute to him a connection with a system of law with which he has, perhaps, had no point of contact since his earliest months might be considered artificial."[53] The analogy with custody proceedings has been pressed, debatably[54] perhaps, on the basis that one should have regard to the best interests of the child[55] by looking to the future rather than the past.

Effects of Adoption[56]

It is one thing to recognise a child's status as an adopted person; it is "a very different thing"[57] to hold that this status controls succession and other entitlements under Irish law.

Let us consider first the position where succession is governed by Irish law.

[49] Mann, *Legitimation and Adoption in Private International Law*, 57 L.Q. Rev. 112, at 123-124 (1941).

[50] Cf. O'Connell, *Recognition and Effects of Foreign Adoption Orders*, 33 Can. Bar Rev. 635, at 638, 641(1951).

[51] A *via media* would be to develop a concept of "divisible adoption", whereby liberal recognition rules would ensure that the child obtained all the benefits of adoption, but the interests of the child's natural parents would nonetheless be protected: cf. Baade, *Interstate and Foreign Adoptions in North Carolina*, 40 N. Car. L. Rev. 691, at 716(1962). This would no doubt be a complex and challenging development, but, in view of its generosity of spirit to all affected parties, merits some consideration, though the price in terms of enhanced legal uncertainty weighs against it.

[52] O'Connell, *Recognition and Effects of foreign Adoption Orders*, 33 Can. Bar Rev. 635, at 641 (1955).

[53] *Id.*, at 642.

[54] Cf. Baade, *Interstate and Foreign Adoption in North Carolina*, 40 N. Car. L. Rev. 691, at 703-704 (1962).

[55] Cf. *Scoles & Hay*, 543.

[56] See O'Connell, *Recognition and Effects of Foreign Adoption Orders*, 33 Can. Bar Rev. 635 (1955), North, *Note: Adoption, Succession, and the Conflict of Laws*, 28 Modern L. Rev. 470 (1965), Inglis, *Adoption and Succession in Private International Law*, 6 Int. & Comp. L.Q. 202 (1957), Inglis, *Adoption, the Marshall Case, and the Conflict of Laws*, 35 Can. Bar Rev. 1027 (1957), de Nova, *Adoption in Comparative Private International Law*, [1961] — 1 Recueil des cours 68, Part II.

[57] Scarman, *English Law and Foreign Adoptions*, 11 Int. & Comp. L.Q. 635, at 636 (1962).

Children adopted under the Adoption Acts 1952-76 are in the same position, for succession purposes, as their adoptive parents' children born within marriage, provided, in cases of testate succession, that they were adopted before the will was executed. But what is the position where there has been a foreign adoption that is recognised under Irish law? On one view, the adopted child should simply have no succession rights since he falls outside the succession entitlements given by the Irish Adoption Acts.[58] This approach has little to commend it on social policy grounds; nor has it much credibility from a conceptual standpoint.

A second, and contrary, approach would treat the adopted child as though he were the legitimate child of his adoptive parents, born to them in marriage.[59] But to do so would having the unfortunate result of giving the child greater rights in some instances than a child adopted under Irish law.[60]

The third possible approach would let the law governing the adoption determine the question.[61] But again this could result in a child adopted abroad being entitled to more than a child adopted here.[62] Moreover, it would be curious if the law governing the adoption should fix certain succession rights at the time of the adoption rather than at the time of the making of the will or at the time of the death of the deceased adoptive parent.[63]

Under the fourth and final approach the court would treat the child, though the subject of a foreign adoption order, as if he had been adopted under Irish law. This has the support of Lord Denning M.R. in *Re Valentine's Settlement*,[64] as well as that of a number of Canadian courts.[65] It has the virtues of simplicity and practicality but suffers from the vice of lacking a fully principled rationale.

Where the succession is governed by foreign law, the best approach would seem to be to refer the whole question to the *lex successionis*.[66] This straightforward solution has much to recommend it.

Reform of the Law

The Review Committee on Adoption Services, in its Report, entitled *Adoption*,[67] published in 1984, addressed some issues relating to conflicts of law. The Committee referred to section 5(2) of the Adoption Act 1964, which stipulates that prospective adopters must be ordinarily resident in the State and have been so resident during the year preceding the date of the adoption order. From the information available to them, they were satisfied that this provision works well, and they recommended no change in the law. The requirement that the prospective adopters be "ordinarily" resident here removed any doubts as to the eligibility to adopt of Irish persons obliged temporarily to live abroad in the course of this work.

The Committee stated that they "would be opposed to any measures which would

---

[58] Cf. the discredited English decision of *Re Wilby*, [1956] P. 174 (Barnard, J.), in the context of which Gareth Jones observed that "English judges tend to regard English statutes as sacred and sacrosanct, so much so as to ignore and overrule the rules of English private international law": 5 Int. & Comp. L.Q., at 213 (1956).

[59] Cf *Re Valentine's Settlement*, [1965] Ch. 831, at (C.A., *per* Salmon, L.J., dissenting).

[60] Cf. *Dicey & Morris*, 9th ed., 1973, 490. See also North, *Adoption, Succession, and the Conflict of Laws*, 28 Modern L. Rev. 470, at 474 (1965).

[61] Cf. *Re Pearson*, [1946] V.L.R. 356, (Gavan Duffy, J.) *Re Brophy*, [1959] N.Z.L.R. 1006 (Gresson, J.) critically analysed by Inglis, *Adoption, The Marshall Case, and the Conflict of Laws*, 35 Can. Bar. Rev. 1027, at 1040-1045 (1957), O'Connell, *supra*, at 651-653.

[62] Cf. *Dicey & Morris*, 9th ed., 1973, 490.

[63] *Id.*

[64] [1965] Ch. 831, at 844.

[65] Cf. *Dicey & Morris*, 9th ed., 1973, 490, fn. 80.

[66] *Id.*

[67] Pl. 2467 (1984).

encourage or facilitate trafficking in children for adoption purposes".[68] They considered that the fact that there may be many young children orphaned or abandoned as a result of conditions of war or poverty or famine should not be regarded as a justification for removing them from their native environment. Instead, concern for the deprived children of distressed or undeveloped countries could "best be shown by assisting the various national and international agencies working to relieve the problems of such areas by improving conditions within them".[69]

The Committee accepted that there will be particular instances in which people living in Ireland may wish to adopt a foreign child and where the circumstances would justify a favourable view being taken of such an application. They recommended however, that it should be obligatory for all applications in respect of the adoption of a foreign child to be made through a registered adoption society or health board.[70] The agencies would have the responsibility to make enquiries about the background of the child and to ensure that the necessary conditions, particularly those relating to consent, had been fulfilled.[71]

On the question of recognition of adoption orders made abroad, the Review Committee recommended that the Minister for Health should be empowered by statute "to designate countries whose adoption orders would be recognised in Ireland".[72] The effect of this recognition would be "to accord the same rights to children adopted in these countries as children who had been adopted under Irish law".[73] The Minister would also be given powers to draw up rules governing the recognition of adoption orders made in non-designated countries.[74] The Committee considered that the recognition of foreign adoptions should have retrospective effect but they suggested that, in framing the law, consideration should be given to making the recognition of foreign orders retrospective without affecting rights that are vested, such as those in relation to succession.[75]

The notion of Ministerial designation of countries whose adoption orders would be recognised here is a new one: under present law, as we have seen,[76] a foreign adoption order will not be recognised here because it is French or German, for example, but because it was obtained in accordance with the law of the domicile of the adoptive parent (or child). Of course, it would be necessary when designating countries to ensure that we would not be required to recognise "back door" adoptions of Irish children (or children with other close Irish connections).

THE HAGUE CONVENTION ON ADOPTIONS

As a possible model for reform it is helpful to consider briefly the Hague Convention on Jurisdiction, Applicable Law and Recognition of Decrees relating to Adoptions,[77] drafted at the 10th Session of the Hague Conference on Private

---

[68] *Id.*, para. 3.13.

[69] *Id.*

[70] *Id.*, para. 3.14.

[71] *Id.*

[72] *Id.*, para. 13.17. This recommendation was no doubt influenced by the approach favoured in Britain: cf. the Adoption Act 1968 section 4(3) and the Children Act 1975, Schedule 1.

[73] *Id.*

[74] Para. 13.17 of the Report.

[75] *Id.*, para. 13.18.

[76] Cf. *supra*, pp. 372-374.

[77] See *Scoles & Hay*, 546-549, Unger, *Hague Conference on Private International Law: Draft Convention on Adoptions*, 28 Modern L. Rev. 463(1965), Lipstein, *The Tenth Session of the Hague Conference on Private International Law, 1964*, [1965] Camb.L.J. 224, at 224-230, McClean & Patchett, *English Jurisdiction in Adoption*, 19 Int. & Comp. L.Q. 1, at 12ff. (1970), Graveson, *The Tenth Session of the Hague Conference of Private International Law*, 14 Int. & Comp. L.Q. 528, at 532-538 (1965), Blom, *The Adoption Act 1968, and the Conflict of Laws*, 22 Int. & Comp. L.Q. 109, at 110-125 (1973), Loussouarn, *La Xme session de la Conférence de la Haye du droit international privé*, 92 J. du dr. internat. 5, at 6-11(1965), Amram, *Report on the Tenth Session of the Hague Conference on Private*

International Law in 1964. The Convention contains some interesting compromise solutions to the conflict between nationality and domicile as connecting factors in adoption, as well as introducing provisions for a modest degree of co-operation between the authorities of different countries when international adoptions are being made.[78] The limits of the Convention should be noted, as they are "at least as important as its provisions".[79] The Convention covers only adoptions with a foreign element: it does not extend to wholly "internal" adoptions, where the adopter or adopters and the child all possess the same nationality and habitually reside in the State of which they are nationals.[80] Thus the question of the recognition abroad of these adoptions, "which are of course much more numerous and thus more important in practice",[81] was left to another day.[82]

The next and arguably most significant[83] limitation is that the Convention does not extend to the incidents and effects of an adoption recognised by another State. It goes only so far as to say (in Article 8) that every adoption granted by an authority having jurisdiction under the terms of Article 3, para. 1 of the Convention is to "be recognised without further formality in all contracting States".[85] The precise content of this recognition is left to be determined by each individual State,[85] since it would be very hard for over twenty different States to reach consensus on this question.

The final limitation in the scope of the Convention that should be noted is that the Convention deals only with adoptions by a single adopting parent, or by spouses, of children under the age of 18 who have not been married.[86] This approach, so far as children are concerned, would harmonise easily with the Age of Majority Act 1985.[87]

The Adoptive Parent or Parents

The Convention applies to an adoption where the adoptive parent possesses the nationality of one of the contracting States and has his or her habitual residence within one of these States, or, in the case of spouses, where each of them possesses the nationality of one of the contracting States and has his or her habitual residence within one of these States.[88] The spouses need not actually habitually reside in the State of the nationality of either or both of them: it is enough that they habitually reside in any one[89] of the contracting States.

International Law, 59 Amer. J. of Comp. L.87, at 88-89(1965).

[78] Cf. Blom, *The Adoption Act 1968, and the Conflict of Laws,* 22 Int. & Comp. L.Q. 109, at 110-112(1973).

[79] *Id.* at 113.

[80] Article 2(b). It should be noted that Irish jurisdictional requirements do not require that either the adoptive parents or the child have Irish nationality: cf. *supra,* pp. 370-371, and see Lipstein, *The Tenth Session of the Hague Conference on Private International Law, 1964,* [1965] Camb. L.J. 224, at 225.

[81] Lipstein, *supra,* at 224.

[82] Cf. Graveson, *The Tenth Session of the Hague Conference of Private International Law,* 14 Int. & Comp. L.Q. 528, at 534 (1965). Hay, *The United States and International Unification of Law: The Tenth Session of the Hague Conference,* [1965] U. Ill. L. Forum 820, at 840.

[83] Cf. Blom. *The Adoption Act 1968, and the Conflict of Laws,* 22 Int. & Comp. L.Q. 109, at 113 (1973). See also Hay, *supra,* at 840.

[84] Article 8 has a similar provision in relation to the recognition of every decision annulling or revoking an adoption granted by an authority having jurisdiction under Article 7.

[85] Blom, *The Adoption Act 1968, and the Conflict of Laws,* 22 Int. & Comp. L.Q. 109, at 114 (1973).

[86] Article 1. Cf. Graveson, *The Tenth Session of the Hague Conference of Private International Law,* 14 Int. & Comp. L.Q. 528, at 533 (1965).

[87] Cf. section 1 of the 1985 Act.

[88] Article 1. Article 10 provides that, for the purposes of the Convention, an adopter or a child who is stateless, or whose nationality is unknown, is deemed to have the nationality of the State of his habitual residence. The exception contained in Article 2(b), already mentioned, should be borne in mind in the present context.

[89] Articles 2(a) and 3.

Jurisdiction to grant an adoption is vested in:

(a)   the authorities of the State where the adopter habitually resides or, in the case of an adoption by spouses, the authorities of the State in which both habitually reside;

(b)   the authorities of the State of which the adopter is a national or, in the case of an adoption by spouses, the authorities of the State of which both are nationals.[90]

The Adopted Child

As well as being under eighteen and unmarried,[91] the child must possess the nationality of one of the contracting States *and* have his or her habitual residence within one of these States[92] (not necessarily the same as the one of which the child is a national).

Choice of Law

The authorities having jurisdiction based on the habitual residence of the adopter (or adopters) must apply their internal law to the conditions governing an adoption.[93] However, they must apply the national law of the child relating to consents and consultations, other than those in respect of an adopter, his family or his or her spouse.[94] Moreover, they must respect any provision prohibiting adoption contained in the national law of the adopter (or adopters)[95] if the State of nationality of the adopter (or adopters) has made a declaration, when signing, ratifying or acceding to the Convention, specifying the provisions of its internal law prohibiting adoptions founded upon:

(a)   the existence of descendants of the adopter or adopters
(b)   the fact that a single person is applying to adopt
(c)   the existence of a blood relationship between an adopter and the child
(d)   the existence of a previous adoption of the child by other persons
(e)   the requirement of a difference in age between adopter or adopters and the child
(f)   the age of the adopter or adopters and that of the child
(g)   the fact that the child does not reside with the adopter or adopters.[96]

Thus an adoption may be granted only where the conditions of the law of the forum are complied with and no prohibition specified by the *lex patriae* applies. In practice, this double requirement restricts the scope of permissible adoptions more than might at first be appreciated;[97] it has also been mooted that this approach may be considered to give undue prominence to the law of nationality.[98]

---

[90]   Article 3. The problem of double nationality is not dealt with in the Convention, "being regarded as a more general question of which the application to the matter of adoption is only a special case": Graveson, *The Tenth Session of the Hague Convention of Private International Law,* 14 Int. & Comp. L.Q. 528, at 534 (1965).

[91]   Article 1.

[92]   *Id.* Article 10 provides that, for the purposes of the Convention, an adopter or a child who is stateless, or whose nationality is unknown, is deemed to have the nationality of the State of his habitual residence.

[93]   Article 4.

[94]   Article 5.

[95]   Article 4. Where the adopters do not possess a common nationality, the prohibitions contained in their respective *leges patriae* are not to be heeded.

[96]   Article 13.

[97]   Blom, *supra,* at 116-117, Hay, *supra,* at 840.

[98]   Cf. Unger, *Note: Hague Conference on Private International Law: Draft Convention on Adoptions,* 28 Modern L. Rev. 463, at 464 (1965) (raising this issue, though taking no position on it himself).

The Interest of the Child

The authorities having jurisdiction to grant an adoption under Article 3 of the Convention must not do so "unless it will be in the interest of the child".[99] Before granting an adoption they must carry out, through the agency of the appropriate local authorities, a thorough inquiry relating to the adopter or adopters, the child and his or her family.[100] As far as possible, this inquiry must be carried out in co-operation with public or private organisations qualified in the field of intercountry adoptions and the help of social workers having special training or having particular experience concerning the problems of adoption.[101] The authorities of all the contracting States are required promptly to give all the assistance requested for the purposes of an adoption governed by the Convention.[102]

Recognition

Every adoption to which the Convention applies is to be recognised "without further formality in all contracting States".[103] Moreover, if any question arises in a contracting State with respect to the recognition of such an adoption, the authorities of that State, in considering the jurisdiction of the authority which granted the adoption, are "bound by the findings of fact on which that authority based its jurisdiction".

Some discussion has centred around the question whether findings as to habitual residence, or nationality are exclusively findings of "fact". The framers of the Convention appear to have acted on this assumption.[104] But since these findings go to the centre of jurisdictional competence it is possible that our courts would be reluctant to surrender the power to investigate this matter where the authority which granted the adoption appeared to have made an improper inference or conclusion of law.[105]

Possibly a constitutional problem could arise in Ireland in relation to this issue: the constitutional requirement that "truth must out"[106] would appear to be in potential conflict with the Article 8 of the Convention in at least some instances.

The Public Policy Proviso

Article 15 is to the effect that the provisions of the Convention may be disregarded in contracting States "only where this observance would be manifestly contrary to public policy". The circumstances under which this provision would come into operation may only be guessed at.[107]

It is possible that a particular foreign law providing for the compulsory adoption of children could offend against our public policy to such a degree as to warrant the non-recognition of an adoption based on this ground.

Another factor worth mentioning in the context of Ireland is the relationship between the Constitution and the Convention. As we have seen,[108] the precise range of protection afforded by the Constitution to persons living abroad is not clear. But it seems likely that an adoption abroad of an Irish child[109] or even perhaps of a child

---

[99] Article 6.
[100] *Id.*
[101] *Id.*
[102] *Id.*
[103] Article 8.
[104] Cf. Blom, *supra,* at 119-120.
[105] Cf. Graveson, *supra,* at 537.
[106] Cf. *S.* v. *S.,* [1983] I.R. 68 (High Ct., O'Hanlon, J., 1982). See also *L.B.* v. *H.B.* [1980] I.L.R.M. 257 (High Ct., Barrington, J.).
[107] Cf. Morris, *Some Recent Developments in the English Private International Law of Adoption,* Festschrift for Mann 241, at 251(1977), de Nova, *Adoption in Comparative Private International Law,* [1961] — 1 Recueil des cours 68, at 85.
[108] *Cf. supra,* pp. 334-339.
[109] Cf. Article 1 of the Convention.

habitually resident here would raise constitutional questions if the adoption was not consistent with the Constitutional rights of the child or of his or her parents. Perhaps the public policy proviso contained in Article 15 of the Convention is sufficient to deal with these different cases. It is also possible that the State could invoke paragraph (c) of Article 13. Whether this would be fully efficacious or appropriate solution to the problem is a matter of debate.

CHAPTER 18

MENTAL INCOMPETENCY[1]

Mental incompetency[2] is a question of status. Thus it might be thought that the *lex domicilii* would control all aspects of mental incompetency.[3] But matters are not so simple. People often become mentally ill in countries where they are not domiciled: they may be resident there or even on a visit.[4] Their condition may be so urgent as to require immediate attention.[5] History also casts its shadow over the development of conflicts rules in this area. The jurisdiction of the President of the High Court traces its legal origins to a British prerogative based on feudal duties relating to land.[6] The tendency over the centuries has been for the courts to concentrate on the question of jurisdiction to declare a person incompetent rather than to investigate issues of choice of law.[7] The result is an amalgam of statutory law and judicial precedent, from which it is hard to disentangle any clearly considered principles.

The easiest way to approaching the subject is to examine it from two standpoints: control over the property and person of the mentally incompetent person, and the position of foreign curators and committees.

CONTROL OF A MENTALLY DISORDERED PERSON'S PROPERTY AND PERSON

The management of the property and person of a mentally disordered person in the State[8] is under the charge of the President of the High Court or other High Court Judge and the Registrar of Wards of Court. Normally a committee of the mentally

---

[1] See *Theobald*, 32, ch. 67, *Abraham*, 54-57, 82-86, 152-158, 173-175, 185-186, *Harris*, 4-8, *Pope*, 31-32, 192-194, Fridman, *Mental Incompetency and the Conflict of Laws*, 4 Sol. Q. 60 (1965), H. Venables, *A Guide to the Law Affecting Mental Patients*, ch. 12 (1975).

[2] A few words about definitions may be desirable. Formerly statutes and judicial decisions used generally refer to people suffering from mental disorder as "lunatics" or "persons of unsound mind" Section 9(4) of the Courts (Supplemental Provisions) Act 1961 encourages the use of the expression "ward of court" or other similar expression for "lunatic" or "person of unsound mind". A lack of intellectual capacity is now generally referred to as mental handicap or retardation. The expression "mental incompetency" is designed to embrace all persons whose condition falls within the scope of any of these terms. It is also worth noting that certain *physical* conditions may occasion a declaration of "incompetency" in some countries: cf. *Re Langley's Settlement Trusts*, [1962] Ch. 541 (C.A., 1961), Grodecki, 11 Int. & Comp. L.Q. 578 (1962), Fridman, *supra*, at 69-71. These cases involve rules similar to those of mental incompetency.

[3] The question of the domicile of a mentally incompetent person is considered, *supra*, pp. 93-96.

[4] Cf. *In re B-, a Lunatic*, 1 Ir. Eq. Rep. 181 (Lord Plunket, L.C., 1839).

[5] Cf. *McLeod*, 313.

[6] Cf. *Theobald*, 1-4.

[7] Cf. Fridman, *supra*, at 63, *McLeod*, 314.

[8] Lord Ashbourne, C. gave a brief historical account of this jurisdiction, in *In re Lahiff, a Person of Unsound Mind*, [1904] 1 I.R. 147, at 152-153 (Lunacy, 1903). See further the Lunacy Regulation (Ireland) Act 1871, (as amended) and the Courts (Supplemental Provisions) Act 1961, section 9, *Harris*, Introduction and ch. 1, and *Abraham*, Introduction and ch. 1.

disordered person's property will be appointed. The committee has wide-ranging statutory powers relating to the management of the property.

The jurisdiction of the President extends to mentally disordered persons who are actually present within the State, regardless of their domicile or nationality or the location of their property.[9] The fact that the person came into the jurisdiction intending only to stay a short time will not deprive the court of jurisdiction. Conversely, there is Irish authority holding that the absence of the person from Ireland, even for a limited period, may deprive the Irish court of jurisdiction. In *In re B-, a Lunatic*,[10] a man possessed of considerable landed property in Ireland, where he usually resided, became of unsound mind when on a visit to England. He was placed by his friends in an "asylum of great respectability"[11] near Bristol. Later a commission was issued under the Great Seal of Ireland and the man was declared a lunatic. The question of appointing a committee to the man's estate then arose. All his property was in Ireland. Lord Plunket, L.C. held that the Irish Court had no jurisdiction to make the appointment. He said:

"I have had some correspondence with the Lord Chancellor of England on this subject. There is a perfect equality of jurisdiction between the Courts of Chancery in England and in Ireland. When the lunatic is resident in Ireland, this court appoints a committee of his person; but when the lunatic is resident in England, as in the present case, the Court of Chancery in England is the proper tribunal to appoint the committee of his person."[12]

The Lord Chancellor considered that "[t]he circumstance, that the lunatic was only accidentally in England where he became of unsound mind, and was placed in an asylum there, makes no difference in the case."[13]

This case could possibly be understood as holding that the fact that the mentally ill person's property is here cannot be a ground, of itself, for exercising jurisdiction in respect of that property; but that would be difficult to harmonise with a number of English decisions[14] which accept the presence of property within the jurisdiction as sufficient for the court to exercise jurisdiction, at all events in regard to the property.[15] Perhaps the more reasonable interpretation of *In re B-, a Lunatic* is that it was a decision of its time, restricted to the narrow question of the respective roles of the Irish and English courts in the nineteenth century.

There is no clear decision on the question whether the court may exercise jurisdiction on the sole basis of the mentally incompetent person's domicile. The commentators generally[16] regard this as an undesirable ground. The very notion of domicile is premised on free choice, which may not be fully present for many mentally incompetent people. In the absence of the choice, the courts have had to fall back

---

[9] See *In re Burbridge*, [1902] 1 Ch. 426 (C.A.) (where, however, Vaughan Williams, L.J. (at 427) thought it "probable that this alleged lunatic has a few personal chattels in this country"), *In re Sottomaior (A Lunatic)*, L.R. 9 Ch. App. 677 (1874), *In re Princess Bariatinski*, 1 Ph. 375, 41 E.R. 674 (1843), *In re Houston*, 1 Russ. 312, 38 E.R. 121 (1826).

[10] 1 Ir. Eq. Rep. 181 (Lord Plunket, L.C., 1839).

[11] *Id.*, at 181.

[12] *Id.*, at 182.

[13] *Id.*, at 183.

[14] *Re Scott, an alleged Lunatic*, 22 W.R. 748 (1874), (where the petitioners were at liberty to take all proper steps for bringing the alleged mentally ill person to England for the inquiry as to his sanity); See also *Re Knight*, [1898] 1 Ch. 257, at 261 (C.A. *per* Lindley, M.R.), *Re Soltykoff*, [1898] W.N. 77 (C.A.) (where proceedings were approved subject to applicant applying to the foreign committee to join in the proceedings).

[15] *Dicey & Morris*, 512 consider that in such cases the court "probably has no jurisdiction over the person of the mentally disordered person; but it may give leave for steps to be taken to have him brought to England" (citing *Re Wykenham a Lunatic*, T. & R. 537, 37 E.R. 1207 (1823) and *Re Scott, supra*).

[16] *Dicey & Morris*, 513, *McLeod*, 314; but see Fridman, *supra*, at 63.

on the notion of a domicile of dependency which, as we have seen, can involve great artificiality. It is easy to think of cases where the exercise of jurisdiction based on such a domicile of dependency could not be defended from a common sense standpoint. But it may be doubted whether the inadequacies of the present rules of domicile of mentally incompetent people, especially at the "outer edges", can constitute a good reason for denying jurisdiction in more clearcut cases where a person with strong connections here becomes mentally ill while temporarily abroad. The better solution may be to reform the present law as to domicile, rather than to reject a jurisdictional ground that would be useful and defensible in some cases.

As a general rule, the President will not make an order directly affecting property that is situated abroad.[17] In such a case the committee can be directed to take whatever steps may be possible to bring the property within its control, as, for example, by appointing an attorney to act in the name of the mentally ill person in selling property and in accounting for the proceeds.[18]

Some specific statutory provisions should, however, be noted in this context. Section 96 of the Lunacy Regulation (Ireland) Act 1871 provides that the powers and authorities given by the Act to the Lord Chancellor extend to "all land and stock within any of the dominions, plantations, and colonies of Her Majesty (except England, Wales and Scotland.)" The precise status of this provision today is not certain. It may be argued that the President of the High Court can continue to assert this jurisdiction.[19] Whether the courts in the other countries will necessarily recognise and give effect to such assertion of jurisdiction is, of course, a separate question.

A degree of harmonisation between the orders of Irish, England and Scottish courts is contained in the Lunacy Act 1890. Let us first examine some of these provisions before considering their present status in the light of political and constitutional change. Section 131 (1) of that Act provides that the powers of management and administration of the estates of lunatics conferred by the Act are to extend, without an inquisition or other proceedings in Ireland, to the personal property in Ireland of a lunatic so found by inquisition in England where the personal property does not exceed £2,000 in value or the income does not exceed £100 *per annum*. The subsection also provides that "the like powers" conferred by the Lunacy Regulation (Ireland) Act 1871 are to extend, similarly without an inquisition or other proceedings in England, to personal property in England of a lunatic so found by inquisition in Ireland, subject to the same maximum amounts of value.

This subsection is limited to cases of "lunatics so found by inquisition" and to personal property. Section 131(4) of the 1890 Act contains no similar limitations. It provides that the powers of management conferred by the Lunacy Regulation (Ireland) Act 1871[20] and by the 1890 Act,[21] where the property of a person of unsound mind does not exceed £2,000 in value, or the income £100 *per annum,* extend to his property in Ireland or England, as the case may be, where the combined total value in the two countries is within the specified monetary limits. Thus, under this provision an Irish court may make an order affecting English land (subject, of course, to the prescribed limits of value) and *vice versa.*[22]

---

[17] *Cheshire & North*, 478.
[18] *Id.*
[19] Cf. *State (Kennedy)* v. *Little*, [1931] I.R. 39 (High Ct., 1930). See also *Harris*, 4. It has been suggested that section 96 extends to land and stock in Northern Ireland: *id.*, 6.
[20] In section 68.
[21] In section 116(1) (e).
[22] *Theobald*, 474.

In the case of a "lunatic so found by inquisition" in Ireland, if the property in England exceeds the prescribed limit, section 107 of the 1890 Act offers a solution. It provides for the transmission of a transcript of the inquisition from Ireland to England; when recorded there, it may be acted on and is "of the same validity and effect, to all intents and purposes," as if the inquisition had been taken in England. Section 107 works in the converse manner as well, so that English transcripts may be transmitted to Ireland where they have full effect.

Where the lunatic is not "so found by inquisition" and the total combined value of his property in England and Ireland exceeds the prescribed limit, a problem arises.[23] One approach would be for the Irish receiver, with power to receive and give a discharge for personal property in England, to maintain an action in England as next friend of the lunatic to recover the property.[24] Alternatively, it may be necessary to go by the longer route of invoking section 107.[25] Where English land is involved, it seems that this latter approach is imperative.[26]

The position regarding Ireland's relationship with Scotland is dealt with in section 131(2) and (3) of the 1890 Act. Section 131 (2) provides that where a person has been found lunatic by inquisition in Ireland and has personal property in Scotland, the committee of the estate of the lunatic is, without cognition or other proceedings in Scotland, to have all the same powers as to that property, or income from it, as might be exercised by a tutor at law after cognition or a duly appointed *curator bonis* to a person of unsound mind in Scotland. It is worth noting that, though this subsection extends only to personal estate, there is no limit in value, in contrast to section 131 (1) and (4). It merely reproduces in statutory form what was already the position according to the case-law.[27]

Section 131(3) gives a tutor at law after cognition or a *curator bonis* appointed to a lunatic in Scotland having personal property in Ireland the same powers as to that property or income produced by it, without an inquisition or other proceedings in Ireland, as might be exercised by the committee of the estate of a lunatic so found by inquisition in Ireland.

We must now consider the present status of these provisions. The simplest view is that, as part of statute law which continues to apply here (in contrast to in England and Scotland)[28] these provisions should continue to apply, but to the Republic, rather than the whole country.[29] This view is to a large degree of academic interest, however, since the orders of the Irish court made under these provisions will not be considered by the courts in England or Scotland to have been made under any legislative authority binding them.

It is of interest to consider briefly the present status of section 110 of the 1890 Act, which provides that the powers and authorities given by the Act to the Judge in Lunacy are to "extend to property within any British possession". This section refers exclusively to the English Judge. It has been repealed in Britain but not here.

---

[23] *Id.*, 475.

[24] On the authority of *Didisheim* v. *London & Westminister Bank*, [1900] 2 Ch. 15: *Theobald*, 475. *Cf. infra*, p. 387.

[25] Cf. *Theobald*, 475.

[26] *Id.*

[27] *Theobald*, 473. See further *Morison (Todd's Curator Bonis), Petitioner*, (1901) 4 F. 144.

[28] Cf. *Heywood & Massey*, ch. 3, *Anton*, 382, *Dicey & Morris*, 513-514.

[29] Cf. *Theobald*, 475. See also *Harris*, 5-6, attempting to grapple with the uncertain position as to Northern Ireland. In *Ulster Bank, Ltd.* v. *Walsh*, 62 I.L.T.R. 68 (1928), it was not necessary, on the facts of the case, for Meredith, J. to decide whether section 131 continued to apply. However, he saw fit to observe (at 68):

> "This is one of the many statutory provisions which provide for reciprocity between England and Ireland, and it is hard to see how such provisions can now continue in force, unless there is something to ensure the continuance of reciprocity. A continuance of the provision, not as a reciprocal arrangement, but as a one-sided arrangement, does not seem to me a continuance of the provision at all, seeing that it was from the beginning essentially one for reciprocity. All such provisions raise the question of the necessity for reciprocal legislation between Great Britain and the Saorstát."

"British possessions" mean British dominions, exclusive of the United Kingdom[30]. Ireland therefore did not originally come within the scope of section 110. But after Independence, the Irish Free State was a dominion. It thus was concluded that the English Judge in Lunacy might make orders dealing with property in Ireland of a lunatic in England, whether or not so found by inquisition.[31] On this theory, the Bank of Ireland, after the establishment of the Irish Free State, acted on orders of the English Master of Lunacy for lodgment of Government Stocks standing in their books in the names of lunatics in England not so found by inquisition.[32] Since Ireland is no longer a British dominion, section 110 no longer has any application to property in Ireland.

Sending a Mentally Ill Person Abroad

It seems clear that an Irish Court having jurisdiction over a person of unsound mind may authorise his removal to a foreign country. In *In re Birch (a Lunatic)*,[33] Lord Ashbourne, C. had "no doubt" that he had "perfect jurisdiction" to sanction the removal of an Irish person of unsound mind from Ireland to reside in a mental asylum in Scotland, but he thought that permission "should not be lightly granted or without some special circumstances to justify it."[34] The Lord Chancellor refused to grant his approval, as he saw no sufficient reasons in the case before him to justify his doing so.

To a modern reader, the decision to leave the person in Ireland may seem of debatable merit. Though Irish, he had been living in the Scottish asylum for twenty-five years. The only reason he was in Ireland was that this had proved the most efficient means of placing him under the care of the Lord Chancellor of Ireland, since he had recently come into possession of a substantial property in Ireland.[35] The medical officer of the Scottish asylum was of the view that to remove him from the place where he had lived for so many years, and to which he had grown accustomed, would be prejudicial to his mental and physical health. This view was opposed by the two Irish medical visitors who examined him. They were of the opinion that his interests would best be served by being placed into the house of a private family who would be willing to receive him.

The Lord Chancellor, in refusing to permit the man to be moved back to Scotland said:

> "The natural place of residence for an Irish lunatic is Ireland. This is his country and all his property is here. There should be some special circumstances to justify any order that he should reside elsewhere."[36]

The Lord Chancellor pointed to some of the practical difficulties:

> "How could I look so well after the lunatic if he were away in Scotland? How could my medical visitors have such ready access? I feel that, having regard to the position and condition of this gentleman, whom I have taken under my care, no adequate reason exists why I should permit his removal from my own jurisdiction when he is amenable to the frequent visits and constant attendance of my medical visitors."[37]

All these factors would no doubt weigh heavily in most cases where the proposal

---

[30] Interpretation Act 1889, section 18(2).
[31] *Theobald*, 476. See further *Dicey*, 5th ed., 1932, by A. Berriedale Keith, p. 574.
[32] *Id.*
[33] 19 L.R. Ir. 274, at 278 (Lunacy, Lord Ashbourne, C., 1892).
[34] *Id.*
[35] Cf. *id.*, at 276.
[36] *Id.*, at 277.
[37] *Id.*, at 278.

is to remove the mentally disordered person abroad for a considerable length of time. Where, however, a short period abroad is envisaged, different factors should come in play. In *In re Hackett, a Lunatic,*[38] the committees of a mentally disordered person sought permission to take her to travel in England or the Continent. They relied on medical evidence that it was advisable to her to "have the advantage of frequent changes of air and scene, and that it would be to her advantage to travel, and remain for a time in the Continental climate." Brady, L.C. made the order permitting her to be taken out of the jurisdiction, but he refused to permit her to be taken out of the United Kingdom. This limitation (which of course has no direct application today since this jurisdiction is independent from Britain) would seem very hard to justify under modern law in view of the constitutional protection of bodily integrity, health and the right to travel.

Termination

The High Court has power, in special circumstances, to terminate a matter notwithstanding the continued insanity of the ward. In *In re Mahood, a Ward of Court,*[39] a woman of unsound mind, resident and domiciled in Northern Ireland, was a ward of court under the jurisdiction in lunacy of the High Court in the Twenty-six Counties which administered a fund to which she was absolutely entitled. Later she became entitled to property in Northern Ireland and was placed under the equivalent jurisdiction in lunacy of the Lord Chief Justice there. The committee of her estate appointed in Northern Ireland successfully applied to the High Court in Dublin for an order transferring the funds under its care to the jurisdiction of the Court in Northern Ireland and terminating the proceedings in the High Court.

Jurisdiction of a Foreign Court

On the question of the jurisdiction of a foreign court, there is little clear authority. It seems that jurisdiction based on the residence, or even the presence, of the mentally incompetent person in the foreign country will suffice.[40] The principle of reciprocity would require us to recognise also jurisdiction based on the presence of property of the mentally incompetent person within the foreign country,[41] at all events to the extent that that jurisdiction extends to the property (as opposed to the person) of the mentally disordered person. It is not clear whether the fact that the mentally incompetent person was domiciled within the foreign country affords a sufficient basis for recognition. Courts in a number of cases have said that it does.[42] But in many of these cases there were also other connecting factors such as residence or nationality.[43]

FOREIGN CURATORS AND COMMITTEES

The powers of foreign curators and committees have grown over the years. Originally they had no entitlement to sue;[44] then the practice grew of permitting

---

[38] 3 Ir. Ch. Rep. 375 (Brady L.C., 1854).

[39] [1946] Ir. Jur. Rep. 17 (High Ct., Davitt, J., 1946).

[40] Cf. *In re B-, a Lunatic,* 1 Ir. Eq. Rep. 181 (Lord Plunket, L.C., 1839), *New York Security and Trust Co.* v. *Keyser,* [1901] 1 Ch. 666 (Cozens-Hardy, J.) (where the mentally ill person was by birth a national of the country in which she resided at the time of her illness), *Re De Larragoiti (A Person of Unsound Mind),* [1907] 2 Ch. 14 (C.A.), *Dicey & Morris,* 513.

[41] Cf. *Dicey & Morris,* 513.

[42] Cf. e.g. *Re Forrest,* 30 D.L.R. (2d) 397, at 400 (Sask. Q.B., Bence, C.J. Q.B., 1961), *Pélégrin* v. *Coutts & Co.,* [1915] 1 Ch. 696 (Sargant, J.).

[43] Cf. *Fridman, supra,* at 63; see also *McLeod,* 314.

[44] *Dicey & Morris,* 515, citing *Re Houston,* 1 Russ, 312, at 312, 38 E.R. 121, at 121 (*per* Lord Eldon, 1826).

them to do so at the court's discretion; finally, in *Didisheim* v. *London and Westminster Bank*,[45] foreign curators and committees were held entitled to sue as of right for movables[46] situated within the jurisdiction.

Lindley, M.R. observed:

"If the title of the lunatic is clear, and the authority to act for him is equally clear, we fail to see what discretion the Court, acting for the trustees, has in the matter. The trustees may properly say that they cannot safely act without the sanction of the Court, but we fail to see what other discretion there is."[47]

The power of the foreign curator is not unlimited. It gives way to that of the Irish court where the mentally incapable person is domiciled in Ireland[48] or where the property of the mentally incapable person is already being administered by the Irish court.

Foreign curators and committees, however, are not entitled to exercise control over the person of a mentally disordered person within the State:[49] although the court may permit the patient resident here to be placed with a foreign curator or committee.[50]

---

[45] [1900] 2 Ch. 15 (C.A.).

[46] As opposed to immovables: cf. *Grimwood* v. *Bartels*, 46 L.J. Ch. 788 (Hall, V.C., 1877).

[47] [1900] 2 Ch., at 51. See also *Abraham*, 292. Section 91 of the 1871 Act deals with the case where stocks or shares are standing in Ireland in the name of and beneficially vested in a person of unsound mind residing out of Ireland. On proof to the satisfaction of the Irish Court that his personal estate has been vested in a curator "or other person appointed for the management thereof, according to the laws of the place where he is residing", the Irish Court may order some fit person to transfer the stocks and shares to the curator or other person so appointed, and also to receive and pay over the dividends as the Court thinks fit. See further *Abraham*, 84-85. Even when Ireland and Britain were part of a political unit, a committee of the fortune in England was held to come within the scope of section 91:cf. *id.*, 85, citing the unreported decision of *Re Pigot*, 18 February 1879 (Ball, L.C.). The discretionary nature of the Court's power is clear from Chatterton, V.C.'s decision in *In re Hill*, [1900] 1 I.R. 349 (1899).

[48] *Id.*, *New York Security & Trust Co.* v. *Keyser*, [1901] 1 Ch. 666 (Cozens-Hardy, J.).

[49] *Dicey & Morris*, 517.

[50] *Re Sottomaior*, L.R. 9 Ch. App. 677 (1874).

PART IV

LAW OF PROPERTY

CHAPTER 19

MOVABLE AND IMMOVABLE PROPERTY

CHARACTERISATION OF PROPERTY

Property may be of several forms. It may be tangible (a radio or a house, for example) or intangible (a debt, stocks and shares or goodwill in a business, for example). Irish law historically has subdivided property into the categories of realty and personalty.[2] This is a distinction made in common law jurisdictions but it is not the approach adopted in civil law jurisdictions, which "make the far more simple and scientific distinction"[3] between moveable and immoveable property.[4]

Our conflict laws have been more cosmopolitan in this regard than in many other areas of conflicts of law. Irish and other common law courts accept that, for the conflicts of law, the distinction that should control is between movables and immovables.[5] As was said in the English decision in *Re Hoyles*[6]:

> "In order to arrive at a common basis on which to determine questions between the inhabitants of two countries living under different systems of jurisprudence, our courts recognise and act on a division otherwise unknown to our law into movable and immovable."

The distinction between movables and immovables is an important one: succession to movables is generally governed by the *lex domicilii* of the deceased, whilst succession to immovables is generally governed by the *lex situs*[7]; a broadly similar distinction is made with regard to transactions *inter vivos*.[8]

---

[1] See Falconbridge, *Immovables in the Conflict of Laws,* 20 Can. Bar Rev. 1 (1942), reproduced in revised form as *Falconbridge,* ch. 21, Cook, *'Immovables' and the 'Law' of the 'Situs',* 52 Harv. L. Rev. 1246 (1939), reprinted as *Cook,* ch. 10.

[2] See generally J. Wylie, *Irish Land Law* (1975), R. Pearce, *Land Law* (1985). Leasehold interests in land constitute the hybrid class of "chattels real": see *Wylie,* para. 4.008, *Pearce,* p. 6.

[3] *Rea* v. *Rea,* [1902] 1 I.R. 451, at 461 (Porter, M.R.). See also *In the Goods of Gentili, Deceased,* I.R. 9 Eq. 541, at 546-547 (Prob., Warren, J., 1875).

[4] See Yinnopoulos, *Movables and Immovables in Louisiana and Comparative* Law, 22 La. L. Rev. 517 (1946).

[5] There have been some attempts judicially to limit the adoption of the distinction between movables and immovables only to cases where one or more of the countries involved in the conflict does or do not adhere to the distinction between real and personal property. Cf. *Re. Hoyles,* [1911] 1 Ch. 179, at 185 (*per* Farwell L.J.), *Re Hole Estate,* [1948] 2 W.W.R. 754, 56 Man. R. 295, [1948] 4 D.L.R. 419, *Haque* v. *Haque (No. 2),* 114 C.L.R. 98, at 109 (High Ct. of Austr., *per* Barwick, C.J., 1965). This approach has received widespread criticism: cf. *Robertson,* 201, *Falconbridge,* 240-241, *Nygh,* 414, *Dicey & Morris,* 523.

[6] [1911] 1 Ch. 179, at 185. See also *In the Goods of Gentili,* I.R. 9 Eq. 541, at 545 (Warren, J., 1875). Cf. *Falconbridge,* 506-508.

[7] Cf. *Rea* v. *Rea,* [1902] 1 I.R. 451, at 461 (Porter, M.R.), *In the Goods of Gentili,* I.R. 9 Eq. 541 (Warren, J., 1875), *Murray* v. *Champernowne,* [1901] 2 I.R. 232, at 236 (Q.B. Div., Prob., Andrews, J., 1900), *In re Stoughton Deceased,* [1941] I.R. 166, at 178 (High Ct., *per* Hanna, J., 1941).

[8] See *Dicey & Morris,* 522, Ch. 20; cf. *In re Duddy, Minors,* [1925] 1 I.R. 196, at 198 (Kennedy, C.J., 1924).

The distinction between movables and immovables is not co-extensive with the distinction between realty and personalty.[9] Personalty includes certain interests in immovables[10]; thus for example one finds Warren, J. in *De Fogassieras* v. *Dupont*[11]; speaking of testator's "immoveable personal estate", Moreover, it has been said that the distinction between movables and immovables is a distinction between different *kinds of interests in things*.[12]

The Irish courts therefore have the task of selecting the appropriate law based on the distinction between movables and immovables, and the rule they have adopted is that the law of the country where a thing is situate (the *lex situs*) determines whether the thing itself is to be categorised as an immovable or a movable.[13] Moreover the *lex situs* determines whether any right, obligation, or document connected with the thing is to be considered an interest in an immovable or a movable.[14] This deference to the *lex situs* appears to be based on the practical commonsense view that in the last analysis, "[by international comity and] for manifest convenience"[15] the only law which can effectively determine whether things are to be treated as movables or immovables is the law of the country where they are situated.[16]

In applying the rule that the *lex situs* determines whether a thing is to be considered an immovable or a movable, Irish law has had to make its own determination as to immovables and movables *when Irish law is the lex situs*.[17] Thus, for example, where a farm in County Kerry is involved, Irish law, as the *lex situs*, will categorise the property.[18]

INTERESTS IN IMMOVABLES

Let us examine some examples of Irish categorisation of proprietary interests in

---

[9] *Dicey & Morris*, 522. Cf. the criticism of *Lawson* v. *Commissioners for Inland Revenue*, [1896] 2 I.R. 418 (Ex. Div. 1895) (considered in detail *infra*, p. 396), by *Nygh*, 417; see also *Haque* v. *Haque* (No. 2), 114 C.L.R. 98, at 114-115 (High Ct., of Austr. *per* Barwick, C.J., 1965). Courts have on occasion been somewhat lax about acknowledging the distinction between movables and personal property; see, e.g. *In re Duddy, Minors*, [1925] 1 I.R. 196, at 198 (Kennedy, C.J., 1924). *Canny* v. *Fox*, I.R. 4 Eq. 410 (V.C. Court Chatterton, V.C., 1870), *Walker* v. *Lord Lorton*, 6 Ir. Ch. Rep. 329 (Cusack Smith, M.R., 1857), *In re Belfast Shipowners Co. (Ltd.)* [1894] 1 I.R. 321 (C.A., 1894 (aff'g Chatterton, V.C. 1893). Cf. *M'Ginn* v. *Delbeke*, 61 I.L.T.R. 117 (N.I.C.A., 1926).

[10] Cf. *infra*, pp. 397-398.

[11] 11 L.R. Ir. 123, at 125, 126 (Ct. of Probate, 1881).

[12] *Falconbridge*, 507, *Dicey & Morris*, 523. *Falconbridge*, 506-508, points out that the distinction between movables and immovables should properly apply to tangible things, and that intangibles should be classified separately. This is not what has happened, however, and intangibles have generally been treated as movables, which, as we shall see, can create some considerable difficulty when determining their *situs*.

[13] *Dicey & Morris*, rule 75(1), *Rea* v. *Rea*, [1902] 1 1 I.R. 451 (Porter, M.R.). See also *In the Goods of Gentili*, I.R. 9 Eq. 541, at 550 (Warren, J., 1875), quoting from *Freke* v. *Lord Carbery*, L.R. 16 Eq. 461, at 467 (*per* Lord Selborne, 1873). Cf. *Lawson* v. *Commissioners for Inland Revenue*, [1896] 2 I.R. 418, at 435 (Ex. Div., *per* Palles, C.B., 1895), *In re O'Neill (Deceased), Humphries* v. *O'Neill*, [1922] N.Z.L.R. 468, at 474-475 (Sup. Ct. (Full Ct.), *per* Salmond, J. (for the Court), 1921).

[14] *Dicey & Morris*, rule 75 (2).

[15] *Rea* v. *Rea* [1902] 1 I.R. 451, at 461 (Porter, M.R.).

[16] Cf. *Dicey & Morris*, 521. See also *Castel*, vol. 2, 330:
"The reason for this rule is that it would be useless for the court [of the forum] to reach a decision at odds with the *lex situs* which has effective control over the thing."
In accord, *Forsyth*, 289.

[17] Or when no evidence is given as to the *lex situs*: cf. *Lawson* v. *Commissioners of Inland Revenue*, [1896] 2 I.R. 418 (C.A.).

[18] In some cases this distinction has not been articulated clearly: see, e.g. *In the goods of Gentili*, I.R. 9 Eq. 541 (1875). It should be noted that in that case, however, there was no conflict between the *lex fori* and the *lex situs*.

things situated in Ireland. In *Rea* v. *Rea*[19], Porter M.R. stated that the *lex situs* applied to immovable property "of whatever tenure". In that case land in fee was involved. It is well established that leaseholds are interests in immovables[20], and it is quite immaterial that Irish law regards them as personal estate.

CHATTELS REAL

In *The Goods of Gentili*[21], in 1875 Warren, J. held that, on both authority[22] and principle, chattels real — leasehold interests, in the case before him — should be categorised as immovables. Warren J. considered that, "[i]n *rerum natura* [chattels real] are certainly not moveable, but immoveable".[23] He admitted that textbooks and law reports frequently stated that the *lex domicilii* governed "personal estate" and that there were also abundant statements that chattels real, according to Irish law were "personal estate". But this did not mean that the *lex domicilii* should govern chattels real:

> "No doubt the last proposition would be a logical conclusion from the premises, if the word *personal* were used in the same sense in both the former propositions; but no such conclusion would follow if *personal* were synonymous with *moveable* in the first proposition, and in the latter were merely a general designation of the property to which the personal representative of a deceased, as distinguished from the heir, succeeded, according to the law of this country.
>
> The two propositions belong to different codes of law; the former was adopted from the civil law, and is universal; the latter is peculiar to the law of England and Ireland. In the civil law the word is *moveable,* and not *personal,* and in the statements in the books of the former proposition the words *moveable* and *personal* are indifferently used as equivalent."[24]

Six years laters in *De Fogassieras* v. *Duport*[25], the same judge reasserted the same conclusion.

CAPITAL MONEYS ARISING UNDER THE SETTLED LAND ACT 1882

We must now consider the position relating to capital moneys arising under the Settled Land Act 1882. Section 22(5) of that Act provides that capital money arising under the Act, while remaining uninvested or unapplied, and securities on which an investment of any such capital money is made, are, for all purposes of disposition, transmission and devolution to be treated as land.

In *In re Stoughton,*[26] the facts were as follows. A testator died in England in 1885 leaving by his will of 1868 all his land in England and Ireland to trustees in

---

[19] [1902] 1 I.R. 451, at 461 (Porter, M.R.). Cf. *In re Bonnet dec'd: Johnston* v. *Langheld,* [1983] I.L.R.M. 359 (High Ct., O'Hanlon, J., 1982).

[20] *In the goods of Gentili,* I.R. 9 Eq. 541 (Ct. of Probate, Warren, J., 1875), *De Fogassieras* v. *Dupont,* 11 L.R. Ir. 123 (Ct. of Probate, Warren, J., 1881), T. Maxwell, *The Practice of the Queen's Bench Division (Probate) and the County Courts of Ireland,* 180 (1900).

[21] I.R. 9 Eq. 541 (Ct. of Probate, Warren, J., 1875).

[22] *Freke* v. *Lord Carbery,* L.R. 16 Eq. 461 (1873), where Lord Carbery, a domiciled Irishman, died possessed of chattels real in Belgrave Square, London. Lord Selbourne, in categorising them as immovables, said:
> "This leasehold property in Belgrave Square is part of the territory and soil of England, and the fact that the testator had a chattel interest in it, and not a freehold interest, makes it in no way whatever less so."

[23] I.R. 9 Eq., at 545.

[24] *Id.,* at 546.

[25] 11 L.R. Ir. 123 (Ct. of Probate, Warren, J., 1881). See also *Rea* v. *Rea,* [1902] 1 I.R. 451, at 461-462 (Porter, M.R.).

[26] [1941] I.R. 166 (High Ct., 1940).

trust for his widow for life and after her death (in the events that happened) to his nephew for life and ultimately for his niece in tail. The testator's domicile was at all material times English. As tenant for life under the Settled Land Acts, the widow sold the land in Ireland under the Land Acts to the occupying tenants. Portion of the proceeds of sale was invested by the trustees in securities in England; the balance was invested in land in England. The widow died in 1924, and her nephew died in 1936. On the nephew's death, the Irish Revenue Commissioners claimed that estate duty was payable on these securities. Estate duty having been paid already in England in respect of the securities, the trustees brought a petition asking for an order that the estate duty on the property passing on the death of the testator's widow should be re-assessed and that consequential relief should be given.

The High Court dismissed the petition. Hanna, J. (with whom Maguire, P. and Maguire, J. concurred) referred to the settlement in the will of 1868, noting that:

> "Except in so far as it dealt with Irish land it had all the formal *indicia* of an English settlement — that is to say, the domicil of the testator; the residence of the trustees; the preparation of the settlement in England and much of the property being in England. But, in so far as the settlement included Irish immovables as Irish land, it was governed by the *lex situs* of the realty, and to that extent was an Irish settlement governed by Irish law....
>
> This disposition of Irish land, as contained in the will, was subject to the Irish law."[27]

One of the "vital questions of law"[28] to be determined in the case, having regard to the physical change of the property from Irish lands to English securities, was the point of time at which it was to be decided under which law the succession fell. On the authorities, Hanna J. concluded that:

> "as regards the Irish land, this settlement and the successions thereunder were controlled by Irish law, inasmuch as that was the *lex situs* at the date of the disposition creating the successions, and all the restrictions and obligations as well as the rights and privileges attaching to this land were imposed or conferred by Irish law and one of these was the right to sell under the provisions of the Irish Land Acts."[29]

Irish law being the law governing the immoveable property and the series of successions, the ultimate question was whether the transfer of the proceeds of the sale of the lands to England and English securities altered the legal situation so as to free the succession of the nephew from the estate duty in Ireland.

The petitioners argued that by reason of the investment of the proceeds in England securities, a different and new succession had been created, and that the succession which would otherwise have been derived from the original disposition had been destroyed. The Court rejected the argument on the basis that what had happened was "little more than a change of investment".[30] Moreover, judicial authority was to the contrary.

However, Hanna, J. gave what he considered to be "a further and . . . complete answer"[31] to the petitioners, even if the case had involved more than a mere change of investment, either within or outside the original jurisdiction. The change had been made "in pursuance of certain statutory rights and privileges given by the Irish law in relation to land".[32] The sale of the lands was "a joint operation"[33] under the

---

[27] *Id.*, at 177.
[28] *Id.*, at 178.
[29] *Id.*, at 179.
[30] *Id.*, at 180.
[31] *Id.*, at 181.
[32] *Id.*
[33] *Id.*

powers of the Settled Land Act 1882 and the Irish Land Act 1903; section 22(5) of the 1882 Act and sections 16 and 34 of the 1903 Act enabled the proceeds of the sale.

"to be followed whenever they may be and in whatever form, so that there is impressed on such proceeds the notional character of Irish land."[34]

In Hanna, J.'s view, the succession of the nephew was a "devolution" within the meaning of the words in section 22(5) of the 1882 Act, under the will, and also one of a series of successions made by the "disposition" thereunder:

"This brings the securities within one or other, or both, of the words in s.22, sub. s.5, of the Settled Land Act. These words cannot refer to the barest legal meaning to be applied to the terms and would, in my opinion, carry with them the legal interests or obligations such as estate duty attached thereto by statute or otherwise."[35]

In re Staughton raises some interesting questions as to how the classification of property into movables and immovables should be made. As a matter of first impression, there is something curious about treating English securities as though they were Irish land.

Logically, it could be argued that the High Court approached the matter in the proper sequence. As *Dicey & Morris* observe,

"the situs of a thing is ascertained by reference to the rules of the *lex fori* because all concepts signifying connecting factors must be interpreted by reference to that system."[36]

Only where this determination of the *situs* of the property has been made, therefore, may the Court go on to consider whether the *lex situs* categorises the property in question as moveable or immoveable.[37] To this extent, the High Court adopted the correct approach; so wherein lies the basis for criticism?

The answer could be that the Court was sidetracked from a realistic determination of the *situs* of the English securities by an undue emphasis on the language of certain statutory provisions which should not have been regarded as addressing such an esoteric matter as location of property for the purposes of conflicts of law.[38] This emphasis led the Court to hold that the property in question was Irish land, yet the physical land in question, so far as it was actual soil, had for several years gone from the family's control into the hands of tenant purchasers and their successors. That "land" was of only historical relevance: the actual property comprised the English securities which, however to be categorised technically, were clearly located in England.

Perhaps the Court's approach may have resulted in part from its having confused the functions of the *lex fori* and the *lex situs*. As the *lex fori*, it was charged with

---

[34] *Id.*

[35] *Id.*

[36] *Dicey & Morris*, 529, citing *Rossano* v. *Manufacturers' Life Insurance Co.* [1963] 2 Q.B. 352, at 379-380.

[37] The problem of circularity should not be overlooked: cf. Sommerfeld, *Comment*, 27 Can. Bar Rev. 225, at 226 (1949): "The *lex situs* of the property must determine its nature. Where . . . the *situs* depends upon the nature of the property, the problem of what system of law is to determine its nature is not easily resolved."

[38] Cf. *Re Midleton's Settlement*, [1947] Ch. 583, at 592 (C.A.) (affirmed (*sub nom Midleton* v. *Cottesloe*) [1949] A.C. 418 (H.L.)), where Lord Greene, M.R. said that section 22(5) of the Settled Land Act 1882. "appears to me to have nothing to do with location. [Location] was not a matter which was relevant for the purposes of the sub-section."

the initial task of determining the *situs* of the property in question — not of making any characterisation of the property as moveable or immoveable. Only if it concluded that the property was situated in Ireland should it have proceeded to determine the next question, which was whether Irish law, as the *lex situs and not as the lex fori* — characterised the property as moveable or immoveable. It seems clear from Hanna J.'s judgment as a whole, especially from his explicit reference to "Irish immovables"[39] being "governed by the *lex situs*"[40], that the second of these two questions was addressed without any clear appreciation that it differed from, and was dependent on the resolution of, the first.[41] In the last analysis, however, the case may be criticised on the basis of its unconvincing statutory interpretation: it was scarcely sensible to hold that statutory provisions should require so implausible a determination of the *locus* of the property for the purposes of conflicts of law.

MORTGAGEE'S INTEREST IN LAND

In *Lawson* v. *Commissioners of Inland Revenue*,[42] it was held that a mortgagee's interest in land should be classified by Irish law as an interest in a movable. Palles, C.B. said:

> "[T]he net question is, what is the effect of these debts being charged upon land in a foreign country? Do they, by reason of the mere circumstance of being so charged, lose the character they otherwise would have borne of moveable property, and by reason thereof become immovable property . . .?
>
> [T]he only matter of law for our determination is whether, according to our law, a debt secured by a mortgage of land in a foreign country is moveable or immoveable property; and we determine this the moment we determine whether the property is in character a debt with an accessory right to resort to the land for payment, or is in character an estate in land, measured by the amount of the debt. Now this cannot depend upon the locality of the land upon which the debt is charged. The character must be the same, whether the land is situate in a foreign country or here. This brings the matter to a point which is absolutely settled and was determined centuries ago, when it was held that the beneficial interest in a mortgage in fee passed, upon the death of an intestate to his administrator, and not to his heir."[43]

Some points about *Lawson* may be noted. It was a revenue case,[44] which applied the *lex fori's* classification in default of any proof as to the laws of the foreign jurisdictions (Victoria and Switzerland) where the freehold property was situate.[45] Moreover, it sought to justify the classification by reference to the distinction between realty and personality, "a fundamental error in reasoning",[46] in the view of one critic.

---

[39] [1941] I.R., at 177.

[40] *Id.*

[41] Cf. *Forsyth*, 292.

[42] [1896] 2 I.R. 418 (Ex. Div., 1895).

[43] *Id.*, at 435-436.

[44] Under the Finance Act 1894, section 2. Cf. *Nygh*, 417. See also Falconbridge, *Comment*, 19 Can. Bar Rev. 746, at 749 (1941). Cf. *Haque* v. *Haque (No. 2)* 114 C.L.R. 98, at 133-134 (High Ct., of Austr., *per* Menzies, J., 1965).

[45] Cf. [1896] 2 I.R., at 435 (*per* Palles, C.B.). See also *Haque* v. *Haque (No. 2)*, 114 C.L.R. 98, at 145 (High Ct. of Austr., *per* Windeyer, C.J., 1965). Cf. *id.* at 127 (*per* Kitto, J.).

[46] *Nygh*, 417. See also *Haque* v. *Haque (No. 2)*, 114 C.L.R. 98, at 114-115 (High Ct. of Austr. 1965), where Barwick, C.J. criticised *Lawson's* case, stating (at 115):
> "That an asset is personalty for municipal purposes is not, in my opinion, relevant to the question whether, in a conflict of laws between systems, one of which does not employ the dichotomy of realty and personalty, that asset is a movable or an immovable: nor, in my opinion, are the reasons or doctrines for or by which an asset is treated for municipal purposes as personalty or as realty . . ."

Courts in other common law jurisdictions are divided on the question.[47] In *Harding* v. *Commissioners of Stamps for Queensland*,[48] the Privy Council came to the same conclusion as *Lawson*, and a number of decisions in Australia[49] and New Zealand[50] are also to this effect.

Decisions in England[51] and Canada,[52] however, have held that a mortgagee's interest in land should be classified as an immovable. In the English decision, *In re Hoyles; Row* v. *Jagg*,[53] *Lawson* v. *Commissioners of Inland Revenue* was cited by counsel, but given short shrift by Farwell, L.J., who observed that, although a mortgage might be a movable for some purposes, "revenue cases have much less reference to actual facts than to the exigencies of the Treasury".[54] The English Court of Appeal placed much reliance on the views of *Story* and *Dicey*.[55] It did not refer to *Harding's*[56] *case*, which apparently had not been brought to its notice. Perhaps the proper approach would be to accept that classification of property into movables and immovables can be most effective if due regard is given to the context in which that classification becomes necessary to be made:[57] what may be appropriate in a revenue case may be quite inappropriate in a succession case.[58]

INTERESTS IN LAND HELD ON TRUST FOR SALE

In *Murray* v. *Champernowne*[59], it was held that interests in land in Ireland held on trust for sale but not yet sold are interests in an immovable, even though under the equitable doctrine of conversion they are treated as personal estate by Irish law.

---

[47] Cf. *Nygh*, 416-417, Kitto, *Are Mortgage Debts Immovables?*, 2 Austr. L. J. 85 (1928).

[48] [1898] A.C. 769 (P.C.), harshly criticised by Falconbridge, *Comment*, 19 Can. Bar Rev. 746, at 748-749 (1941). See also *Payne* v. *The King*, [1902] A.C. 552 (P.C.), *Lambe* v. *Manuel*, [1903] A.C. 68 (P.C. 1902), *Toronto General Trusts Corporation* [1919] A.C. 679 (P.C.).

[49] *In re Ralston. Perpetual Executors and Trustees Association*, [1906] V.L.R. 689 (Cussen, J.), *McClelland* v. *Trustees Executors and Agency Co. Ltd.*, 55 C.L.R. 483, at 493 (High Ct., of Austr. per Dixon, J. 1936), *In re Young. Trustees Executors and Agency Co. Ltd.* v. *Young*, [1942] V.L.R. 4 (Martin, J., 1941), *In re Williams. National Trustees Executors & Agency Co. of Australasia Ltd.* v. *Brien*, [1945] V.L.R. 213 (Full Ct.) (where Gavan Duffy, J. observed (at 215) that *Lawson* v. *Commissioners of Inland Revenue* derived "some additional persuasive authority from the fact that it was Palles, C.B. who delivered the judgment of the Court); *Livingston* v. *Commissioner of Stamp Duties*, 107 C.L.R. 411, at 421 (High Ct. of Austr., per Dixon, C.J., 1960); in *Haque* v. *Haque (No. 2)*, 114 C.L.R. 98 (1965), the High Court of Australia was divided on this question, Kitto J. (at 129) Menzies, J. (at 133-134) Owen, J. (at 152) and Windeyer, J. (very reluctantly) (at 146), supporting the view that, for succession purposes, a mortgagee's interest should be treated as a movable; Barwick, C.J.'s dissent on this point (at 109-118) is worthy of particular attention. An earlier decision, following *In re Hoyles*, is *Re Donnelly*, 28 S.R. (N.S.W.) 34 (Harvey, C.J. in Eq., 1927), criticised by Kitto, *supra*.

[50] *In re O'Neill (Deceased), Humphries* v. *O'Neill*, [1922] N.Z.L.R. 468 (Sup. Ct., (Full Ct.), 1921).

[51] *In re Hoyles. Row* v. *Jagg*, [1911] 1 Ch. 179 (C.A., 1910), followed in *Re Donnelly, supra*.

[52] *Hogg* v. *Provincial Tax Commission*, [1941] 4 D.L.R. 501 (Sask. C.A.) (noted by Falconbridge, 19 Can. Bar Rev. 746 (1941)), *Re Ritchie*, [1942] 3 D.L.R. 330 (Ont. High Ct., Roach, J.). See also *Toronto General Trusts Co.* v. *The King*, 39 D.L.R. 380, at 389 (Sup. Ct. Can., per Duff, J., 1917), *Royal Trust Co.* v. *Provincial Secretary Treasurer of New Brunswick* [1925] 2 D.L.R. 49, at 53 (Sup. Ct. Can., per Duff, J.).

[53] [1911] 1 Ch. 179 (C.A., 1910).

[54] *Id.*, at 182.

[55] *Dicey & Morris*, 525, fn. 23, are strongly of this view, dismissing *Harding* v. *Commissioner of Stamps*, [1898] A.C. 769 (P.C.) as "a taxation case and of no value as an authority in the conflict of laws . . .".

[56] *Supra*.

[57] Cf. *In re Young. The Trustees Executors and Agency Co. Ltd.* v. *Young*, [1942] V.L.R. 4, at 10-11 (Martin, J., 1941).

[58] Cf. *In re Williams. National Trustees Executors & Agency Co. of Australasia Ltd.* v. *Brien*, [1945] V.L.R. 213, at 216 (Full Ct., per Gavan Duffy). See also Cook, *'Immovables' and the 'Law'* of the *'Situs'*, 52 Harv. L. Rev. 1246, at 1253-1254 (1939). Cf. *In re O'Neill (Deceased), Humphries* v. *O'Neill*, [1922] N.Z.L.R. 468, at 478 (Sup. Ct. (Full Ct.), per Salmond, J. (for the Court), 1921).

[59] [1901] 2 I.R. 232, (Q.B. Div., Prob., Andrews, J., 1900).

The case was concerned with the testamentary disposition of the lands of Rathsheagh in County Westmeath by a domiciled Scotsman. The lands had been vested in trustees since 1853 on trust for sale. The will was invalidly executed according to the law of Scotland but validly executed according to Irish law.

It was argued that the lands of Rathsheagh, having been equitably converted into money in 1853, should be regarded as moveable property, in which case the will (judged by the *lex domicilii*) would not be effective to dispose of them. Andrews, J. rejected this argument. He said:

> "The research of counsel failed to find any decided case which would be an authority for this proposition, and I am not aware of any such case. Mr. Dicey (*Conflict of Laws*, page 520, note 2) seems to be of opinion that the succession to the property would, in such a case, be governed by the *lex situs*, and that is my opinion. The lands of Rathsheagh, notwithstanding the doctrine of equitable conversion, are still lands in fact, and may never be sold under the trusts of 1853. If the will of 1862 was sufficient to pass the beneficial interest in them as land, which, in my opinion, it was, the appointee's title is not, in my opinion, destroyed by the fact that the will is invalid to pass moveable property to the testator, which the lands have never, in fact, been converted into, or more accurately speaking, become represented by."[60]

HOW SITUS IS DETERMINED

The next question that must be considered is how the *situs* of things is determined.

Land and chattels

Land, of course, does not normally present a problem.[61] Chattels are generally[62] regarded as being situated in the country where they were at the relevant time.

Choses in action

The problem arises in regard to choses in action, in relation to which it is difficult to see why they are subject to any particular location.[63]

(i) *Simple contract debts and specialty debts*

It is generally accepted that a simple contract debt should normally be regarded as being situate in the country where the debtor resides.[64] A debt due on a deed or other specialty, however, is situate in the country where the deed itself is situate from time to time rather than in the country where the debtor resides.[65]

---

[60] *Id.*, at 236.

[61] We have, however, seen, *supra*, pp. 393-396, how in *In re Staughton*, [1941] I.R. 166, the High Court, through an inversion of the relevant questions of characterisation, concluded that English securities should be treated as Irish land. The basis of the rule that land is governed by the law of the place where it is situated, namely, practical efficacy, finds no reflection in the holding in this case.

[62] Exceptional cases are merchant ships, which may at times be deemed to be situate at their port of registry (*Dicey & Morris*, rule 76, exception 1) and civil aircraft, which may at some time be deemed to be situate in their country of registration (*Dicey & Morris*, rule 76, exception 2). Cf. the Succession Act 1965, section 103, and *infra*. p. 433. Where a ship or aircraft is situated for the time being in a particular country, rather than being on or over the high seas, it may well be the case that its *situs* should be that country rather than the port of registry or country or registration: *Dicey & Morris*, 536-537, *Trustees Executors and Agency Co. Ltd.* v. *I.R.C.* [1973] Ch. 254 (Chy. Div., Pennycuick, V.C. 1972). Cf. *O'Daly* v. *Gulf Oil (Ireland) Ltd.*, [1983] I.L.R.M. 163 (High Ct., Barrington, J. 1982).

[63] Courts formerly rejected the proposition that a *chose in action* had any particular location, but this approach is no longer favoured: *English, Scottish & Australian Bank* v. *I.R.C.* [1932] A.C. 238 (H.L. (Eng.), 1931). Cf. *Ex parte Ballinrobe and Claremorris Light Railway Co. and Kenny*, [1913] 1 I.R. 519 (Barton, J.), *Hutchinson* v. *Cathcart*, 8 Ir. Eq. Rep. 394, at 397 (Equity Exch., 1845).

[64] *In re Finance Act 1894 and Deane Deceased*, [1936] I.R. 556 (High Ct.).

[65] A different problem may arise in respect of mortgage debts, which are normally specialties: since a mortgage confers an interest in land, it will be situate where the land is situate: Cf. *Dicey & Morris*, 531, *Falconbridge*, 573-580.

In a "revenue" case involving death duties it was held the locality of a specialty debt is the place where the specialty is found at the time of the creditor's death.[66] In *In re Finance Act 1894 and Deane Deceased,*[67] Sullivan, P. quoted with approval from Lord Abinger, C.B.'s judgment in *A.G.* v. *Bouwens:*[68]

"As to the locality of many descriptions of effects, household and moveable goods, for instance, there never could be any dispute; but to prevent conflicting jurisdictions between different ordinaries, with respect to choses in action and titles to property, it was established as law, that judgment debts were assets, for the purpose of jurisdiction, where the judgment is recorded; leases, where the land lies; specialty debts, where the instrument happens to be; and simple contract debts, where the debtor resides at the time of the testator's death . . . ."

In *Deane,* counsel for both parties accepted this statement of the law. In this case a man, domiciled in the Irish Free State, died there, having some time previously taken out a life assurance policy with a Scottish society. At the time of his death the policy was in his possession in the Irish Free State. Under the ordinary common law rules, the specialty debt should therefore have been considered to be situate in the Irish Free State.

(ii) *Bills of exchange*

Bills of exchange and other securities which can be transferred validly and effectively by delivery with or without endorsement are situate in the country where the paper representing the security is from time to time to be found.[69]

(iii) *Shares*[70]

It is well-settled law that "the *situs* of shares in a company is at the place where the register of shareholders is kept in accordance with the law".[71] The Supreme Court decision of *In re Ferguson, Deceased,*[72] fully endorsed this principle. In that case, the court resisted attempts to qualify the full force of this rule. Thus the rule applies whether or not the legal and beneficial ownership of the shares are in the same person. Equally it will apply even where proceedings in the Irish courts may be necessary, whether for the purpose of obtaining possession of the certificate or otherwise.[73]

---

[66] *In re Finance Act 1894 and Deane Deceased,* [1936] I.R. 556 (High Ct.).

[67] *Id.,* at 566.

[68] 4 M. & W. 171, at 191, 150 E.R. 1390, at 1398 (1838), cited with approval by Pollock, M.R., in *New York Life Insurance Co.* v. *Public Trustee,* [1924] 2 Ch. 101, at 107 (C.A.).

[69] *Dicey & Morris,* 532. See also *In re Duddy, Minors,* [1925] 1 I.R. 196 (Kennedy, C.J. 1924).

[70] See further *infra,* pp. 504-505.

[71] *In re Ferguson, Deceased,* [1935] I.R. 21, at 65 (Sup. Ct., *per* Fitzgibbon, J., 1934). The Supreme Court "entirely agree[d]" with Hanna, J.'s judgment in the High Court. Hanna, J. had observed (at 49) that it was "clearly established law that the place where the law requires the register of the shares to be kept determines the locality of the shares". See also *id.,* at 52 (*per* O'Byrne, J.). In accord are *A.G.* v. *Higgins,* 2 H. & N. 339, 157 E.R. 140 (1857), *Brassard* v. *Smith,* [1925] A.C. 371 (P.C., 1924), *Erie Beach Co.* v. *A.G. for Ontario,* [1930] A.C. 161, at 167-168 (P.C., *per* Lord Merrivale).

[72] *Supra.*

[73] Cf. *In re Ferguson, dec'd,* [1935] I.R., at 52 (*per* O'Byrne, J.).

(iv) *Interests in unadministered estate*

An interest in an unadministered estate is situate in the country where the executors or administrators may be compelled to administer the estate — that is, at their place of residence.[74] Where there is no personal representative, then *Dicey & Morris* suggest,[75] sensibly, that the interest is situate at the place where administration would normally take place — that is, at the domicile of the deceased.

[74] *Dicey & Morris*, 534, Cf. *Higgins* v. *Byrne*, 42 I.L.T.R. 252 (Ch., Meredith, M.R., 1908).
[75] *Dicey & Morris*, 534 (citing *Minister of National Revenue* v. *Fitzgerald*, [1949] 3 D.L.R. 497).

CHAPTER 20

IMMOVABLES : JURISDICTION

INTRODUCTION

In this chapter, we examine briefly the main features of the law as to jurisdiction in relation to immovables. As a general rule, the court of the *situs* of immoveable property is the only court which can make an effective decree in relation to it.[2] This rule is based on the practical consideration that it is the only court, in the last analysis, whose order with respect to the immoveable property, will be likely to be enforced effectively.[3]

As a corollary to this rule, an Irish court generally has no jurisdiction to adjudicate upon the right of property in, or the right to possession of, foreign immovables, even in cases where the parties are domiciled and residing here.[4]

Formerly, it was thought that this lack of jurisdiction of the Irish court was based on procedural rather than substantive grounds. In times when juries were selected on the basis of their prior knowledge of the parties and of the merits of the case, litigants were required to specify the venue of the proceedings with exactitude — in other words, the place where the facts giving rise to the dispute had arisen — the jury had to be summoned at that place. Clearly this rule made it impossible to take proceedings in Ireland relating to foreign land.

Later a distinction was drawn between local and transitory actions. "If a cause of action was one that might have arisen anywhere, it was *transitory;* if it was one that could have arisen only in one place, it was *local*".[5] In local matters, including claims to the ownership of lands, the venue had still to be stated with accuracy. Local venues were abolished by the Judicature Act and the Rules made under it, so the technical objection to hearing an action in respect of foreign immovables no longer had force.

Did this mean, therefore, that Irish or British courts had gained jurisdiction in respect of these actions? The answer, emphatically in the negative, was given by the House of Lords in 1893 in *British South Africa Co.* v. *Companhia de Moçambique.*[6] The Lords held that the lack of jurisdiction was "substantial and not technical".[7]

---

[1] See Welling & Heakes, *Torts and Foreign Immovables Jurisdiction in Conflict of Laws*, 18 U.W. Ont. L. Rev. 295 (1980).

[2] See, e.g. *Cartwright* v. *Pettus*, 2 Chan. Cas. 214, 22 E.R. 916 (1675), *Barker* v. *Damer*, 1 Salk. 81, 91 E.R. 76 (1691), *Boyse* v. *Colclough*, 1 K. & J. 123, 69 E.R. 396 (1854).

[3] See Keeton, *Trusts in the Conflict of Laws*, 4 Current L. Prob. Ch. 5, at 107 (1951).

[4] *Cheshire & North*, 489.

[5] *Id.*, 490.

[6] [1893] A.C., at 629. See Welling & Heakes, *supra. Cf. Quinn* v. *Kelly,* [1951] Ir. Jur. Rep. 45 (Circuit Ct., Judge Fawsitt, 1943).

[7] [1893] A.C., at 629.

Jurisdiction Excluded in Two Specific Cases

The effect of the *Moçambique* decision is that the court has no jurisdiction where the action concerns:

(a) the title to, or right of posession of, land abroad; *or*

(b) the recovery of damages for trespass to land abroad.[8]

This lack of jurisdiction in respect of actions concerning disputed claims of title to land abroad is based on the fact that any judgment *in rem* the Court might give would be totally ineffective unless implemented by the authorities of the situs.[9] The court's lack of jurisdiction in respect of the recovery of damage for trespass to foreign land "has little to commend it".[10] In *Hesperides Hotels Ltd* v. *Aegean Turkish Holdings Ltd*,[11] the House of Lords declined to depart from, or even modify, the *Moçambique* rule in a case where no question of title arose. The members of the Court were less then enthusiastic about the rule, Lord Fraser going so far as to express "serious doubt whether the rule . . . is either logical or satisfactory in its result".[12] They signalled that legislative reform was desirable, Viscount Dilhorne stating[13] that "if any change in the law is to be made it should only be made after detailed and full investigation of all the possible implications which we sitting judicially cannot make. In my view it must be left to Parliament to change the law if after full consideration that is thought to be desirable."[14] The British parliament has since taken the hint.[15] No similar change has yet taken place in this jurisdiction. The Bill introduced in December 1986 which was designed to give effect to the EEC Judgments Convention contained no reforming measure outside the scope of the Convention itself.

Up to now our discussion has proceeded on the assumption that the *Moçambique* rule has continued as part of Irish law. A shadow of uncertainty has, however, been case by a passage in D'Arcy, J.'s judgment in the High Court case of *Cripp's Warburg Ltd* v. *Cologne Investment Co. Ltd.*[16] That case concerned a contract for the loan of money to purchase an hotel in Dublin, the loan being secured by a mortgage. The mortgage was executed in Ireland. When the purchasers failed to pay the loan, the lender claimed repayment of the money lent (with interest), and also instituted a mortgage suit claiming a declaration that the mortgage was well charged on the premises, together with an order for sale of the premises. D'Arcy, J. held that the contract of loan was governed by English law as its proper law,[17] but he noted that "[d]ifferent considerations"[18] applied to the mortgage suit.

D'Arcy, J. went on to say:

"It is to be noted that [an expert in English law] gave evidence that the Courts of the United Kingdom would not entertain suits concerning foreign immoveable property.

---

[8] Cf. *St Pierre* v. *South American Stores (Gath and Chaves) Ltd.*, [1936] 1 K.B. 382, at 396 (*per* Scott, L.J.), *Quinn* v. *Kelly, supra.*

[9] *Cheshire & North*, 490.

[10] *Id.*, 491. See also *Ehrenzweig*, s. 39, *Anon., Note: Conflict of Laws — Jurisdiction — Trespass to Land as Transitory Action*, 6 Vand. L. Rev. 786 (1953), Welling & Heakes, *supra*, Kahn-Freund, *Precedent and Policy: the Dilema (sic) of the Mozambique Rule* in *Multum Non Multa: Festschrift für Lipstein*, 101 (1980). See, however, *McLeod*, 321.

[11] [1979] A.C. 508 (H.L.(Eng.), 1978).

[12] *Id.*, at 544.

[13] *Id.*, at 541.

[14] See also *id.*, at 544 (*per* Lord Fraser).

[15] Civil Jurisdiction and Judgments Act 1982, section 30. See L. Collins, The Civil Jurisdiction and Judgments Act 1982, 139-140 (1983).

[16] [1980] I.R. 321 (High Ct., Barrington, J.).

[17] See pp. 527-530, *infra.*

[18] [1980] I.R., at 336.

It is not clear whether the reason for this is that it is a general principle of private international law or that the Courts of the United Kingdom lack the jurisdiction and the machinery to deal with such suits. If it be the latter, this Court suffers from no such infirmity, even if the action relating to immoveable property had its origin in a contract governed by English law. I accept [the witness] as an expert on English law. I find that Irish law applies to the suit to realise the mortgage and charge.''[19]

This passage could mean no more than that Irish law should apply to determine the question of the validity and effectiveness of a mortgage of an immovable situated in Ireland. On this quite unexceptional approach, English rules as to jurisdiction and choice of law in the case of foreign immovables would simply be irrelevant. But is there not a hint in D'Arcy, J.'s statement that Irish courts, in contrast to their British counterparts, have jurisdiction to deal with foreign immovables, that is, immovables foreign according to our law? The statement that the Irish Court ''suffers from no such infirmity'', in isolation, may give some support to this interpretation. The general tenor of D'Arcy, J.'s description of the evidence as to English law indicates a degree of ''distance'' from its principles, as though they had no clear counterparts in Irish law. This is compounded by D'Arcy, J.'s uncertainty, and apparent lack of interest, regarding the precise basis of the English approach towards foreign immoveable property. If D'Arcy, J. was of the view that the same principles also applied here, but were irrelevant because the property, so far as Irish law was concerned, was not foreign, he could have said so quite simply.

Exceptions to the exclusion of jurisdiction[20]

There are three exceptions[21] to the exclusion of jurisdiction — three cases where an Irish court will not decline jurisdiction merely because the action is founded on a disputed claim to title to foreign land or is an action for trespass to foreign land. These are: (*a*) actions founded on a personal obligation to the plaintiff; (*b*) questions affecting foreign land arising incidentally in Irish proceedings; and (*c*) admiralty proceedings in respect of trespass to foreign land. The first of these exceptions is of greatest practical significance and to it we now turn.

(a) *Actions founded on a personal obligation to the plaintiff*

The *first* exception relates to actions founded on a personal obligation to the plaintiff: the court, in the exercise of its jurisdiction *in personam*, may order the defendant to deal with foreign land in a particular fashion. The court in such a case is not attempting the futile task of making a declaration *in rem;* rather is it attempting, so far as it can, to oblige a particular individual to behave in a certain way in respect of the foreign land.

Of course exercising this jurisdiction *in personam* may well have an indirect effect on the foreign land but the direct purpose of the order is to affect the conscience of the defendant.[22] The defendant's conscience may be encouraged by a wide variety of practical incentives. As Wright, J. said in *Companhia de Moçanbique* v. *British South Africa Co.:*[23]

''Courts of Equity have, from the time of Lord Hardwicke's decision in *Penn* v. *Lord Baltimore,*[24] in 1750, exercised jurisdiction *in personam* in relation to foreign land

---

[19] *Id.,* at 337.
[20] See Chesterman, *Note: Foreign Land and English Equity,* 33 Modern L. Rev. 209 (1970).
[21] The structure of these exceptions is based on *Cheshire & North,* 493ff. See *Deschamps* v. *Miller,* [1908] 1 Ch. 856, at 863 (Parker, J.), *Companhia de Moçambique* v. *British South Africa Co.,* [1892] 2 Q.B. 358, at 364 (Wright, J.), judgment restored by H.L., [1893] A.C. 602.
[22] Cf. *Cheshire & North,* 493.
[23] [1892] 2 Q.B. 358, at 364 (C.A.).
[24] 1 Ves. Sen. 444, 27 E.R. 1132 (1750).

against persons locally within the jurisdiction of the English court in cases of contract, fraud and trust, enforcing their jurisdiction by writs of *ne exeat regno* during the hearing, and by sequestration, commitment, or other personal process after decree.''

In *Penn* v. *Baltimore*[25] in 1750, an English court gave a decree of specific performance in respect of a scheme arranged for fixing the boundaries of Pennsylvania and Maryland, although it accepted that it had no jurisdiction to make a decree *in rem*.[26]

Since conscience is the basis of this jurisdiction, the court must be satisfied that this element is relevant before it seeks to make an order against the defendant. Several formulae have been advanced by the courts and commentators, to give effect to this requirement. One judge has referred to "contract, fraud and trust",[27] *Westlake* to "[o]bligations arising from, or as from contract or tort",[28] *Dicey & Morris* to a jurisdiction "substantially confined to cases in which there is either a contract between the parties to the action; or an equity between such parties",[29] and *Cheshire & North* to: "some personal obligation arising from [the defendant's] own act".[30] There are three cases[31] in which this personal equity may arise.

Contracts concerning foreign land

First, it is clear that a party to a contract concerning foreign land is under sufficient personal obligation to come under the Courts' equitable jurisdiction.[32] It may be useful at this point to refer to the decision of *Lett* v. *Lett*,[33] in 1906. There the Irish Court of Appeal upheld an order by Porter, M.R., granting an injunction restraining the defendant's wife from proceeding with an action for divorce, division of property and alimony against the plaintiff, her husband, in the courts of Argentina, in breach of a contractual undertaking on her part. The parties had ceased to live together in 1888. Matrimonial proceedings in the Irish courts at the time they separated had been settled on terms by which the defendant on the receipt of a specified issue of money from the plaintiff had executed a deed releasing him from all future claims. Between 1888 and 1903, the plaintiff amassed a considerable fortune in Argentina. In 1895 the wife came to Argentina seeking greater support from her husband; he agreed formally to increase the amount, and he complied with this agreement. In 1903, the defendant initiated the proceedings for divorce, division of property and alimony in the courts of Argentina, without[34] mentioning the earlier proceedings in Ireland.

In the Court of Appeal, Sir Samuel Walker, C. said:

> "Does it make any difference that the proceeding sought to be restrained is a proceeding in a foreign Court? I think not, because the equity against her is founded not upon the tribunal to which she has resorted, but upon the personal contract binding her

---

[25] *Supra.* See Keeton, *Trusts in the Conflicts of Laws,* 4 Current Legal Prob. 107, at 107-112 (1951), Beale, *Equitable Interests in Foreign Property,* 20 Harv. L. Rev. 382 (1906). *Neale* v. *Cottingham,* Wallis by Lyne 54, at 63, fn. 1 (1770).

[26] It should be noted that the Court's *in personam* jurisdiction extends beyond questions concerning foreign land. It may, for example, make an order restraining the taking or continuance of foreign legal proceedings where these are inequitable: cf. *supra,* pp. 169-171.

[27] *Companhia de Moçambique* v. *British South Africa Co.,* [1892] 2 Q.B. 358, at 364 (*per* Wright, J.), judgment restored by H.L., [1893] A.C. 602.

[28] *Westlake,* s. 172.

[29] *Dicey & Morris,* 542.

[30] *Cheshire & North,* 495.

[31] See *id.,* 495ff.

[32] Cf., *Penn* v. *Baltimore,* 1 Ves. Sen. 444, 27 E.R. 1132 (1750), *Archer* v. *Preston,* 1 Eq. Cas. Abr. 133, 21 E.R. 938, cited in *Arglasse* v. *Muschamp,* 1 Vern. 75, at 77, 23 E.R. 322, at 323 (1682), *West (Richard) & Partners (Inverness) Ltd* v. *Dick,* [1969] 2 Ch. 424 (C.A., 1969, aff'g Megarry, J., 1968), *Ward* v. *Coffin,* 27 D.L.R. (3d) 58 (N.B. Sup. Ct., App. Div., 1972).

[33] [1905] 1 I.R. 618 (C.A., aff'g. Porter, M.R.).

[34] So the plaintiff alleged: [1906] 1 I.R., at 622.

conscience. The jurisdiction asserted is not against the foreign tribunal, but against the person within the jurisdiction, who has made a contract not to resort to proceedings; and whether such proceedings are in a foreign Court or not, is immaterial for the purposes of the equity on which the jurisdiction rests — an equity *in personam.*"[35]

And FitzGibbon, L.J. said:

"If there were no other answer to the wife's demand of liberty to prosecute her pending suit in Argentina, it would seem to me to be enough to say that equity can not permit her to do so, so long as she retains and enjoys the agreed consideration for the contract not to sue which the deed of 1889 imports — except upon the terms of accounting, against her present claim, for what she has received, and is receiving, under the contract which she now seeks to 'reprobate'. An injunction which can be enforced if necessary, by sequestration of the Irish property is the appropriate — if not the only — remedy for such a breach of contract, and it is not argument, but caricature, to describe this suit as one 'brought by the plaintiff to put his wife in gaol'."[36]

Fitzgibbon, L.J. went on to state:

"The validity and binding effect of separation deeds have varied under our law, but it was never contended that their operation *in personam* was in any way affected by the situation of property, or governed by any other law than the *lex loci contractus.*"[37]

In his view:

"The personal covenant of a separated wife not to molest or sue a husband is, from its very nature, an obligation for the breach of which there is no practical remedy except a decree, in the nature of specific performance, for an injunction to restrain a suit threatened or commenced; therefore, if the covenant is lawful and proper, the decree for specific performance by injunction, being the only remedy, is *ex debito justitiae* and not discretionary.

If a suit was not maintainable, it could be defeated on the merits; it is only where there is a legal claim, that the interference of a Court of Equity becomes necessary; therefore, proof that the suit which is sought to restrain will, if it proceeds, result in the establishment of a claim against the defendant therein, only shows the necessity of the suit *in personam*, by which its prosecution is to be restrained."[38]

Fraud or other unconscionable conduct

Secondly, fraud or other unconscionable conduct gives rise to a personal obligation. Thus, in the English case of *Cranstown* v. *Johnston*,[39] Arden, M.R., gave equitable relief where the defendant, a creditor of the plaintiff in Eng-

---

[35] *Id.*, at 635.

[36] *Id.*, at 638.

[37] *Id.*, at 639. FitzGibbon, L.J. quoted from Fry's *Specific Performance* (4th ed.), p. 52, s. 126, 127:
"A contract made abroad may be enforced against a defendant within the jurisdiction of this country, and, as the remedies for breach of a contract are clearly governed by the *lex fori*, it follows that it is no objection to the specific performance in England of a foreign contract that the foreign law might have given no such remedy.
This jurisdiction extends to cases of contracts relative to real or immovable property where the defendant is within the jurisdiction of the Court. The maxim is *Aequitas agit in personam*, and any operation of the judgment on the immovable estate abroad is not direct but indirect, and only through the medium of the person affected by the judgment."

[38] [1906] 1 I.R., at 640. Holmes, L.J.'s dissent is worth noting. He had "no doubt" that the Irish Court had jurisdiction to restrain the defendant from proceeding with a suit before a foreign tribunal, the object of which was to enforce against her husband a right from which she had released him but this, in his view, was a jurisdiction which the court should be "slow to take". He stressed the fact that Argentina had been the plaintiff's home for almost forty years, that all his property was in that State, and that the defendant's suit had been initiated nearly three years before the plaintiff's will was issued.

[39] 3 Ves. 170, 30 E.R. 952 (1796).

land, had availed himself of legal proceedings in the island of St Christopher, with no notice to the plaintiff, which resulted in the seizure of the plaintiff's property in St Christopher and sale to the defendant at a gross undervalue. The Master of the Rolls went so far as to "lay down the rule as broad as this: this Court will not permit [the defendant] to avail himself of the law of any other country to do what would be gross injustice."[40]

Fiduciary relationships

The third case in which the personal equity may arise is that of a fiduciary relationship. This can occur where the trust is attached to foreign land and the trustee is present in Ireland.[41] It is not necessary that the author of the trust be subject to Irish jurisdiction.[42] Similarly a personal equity arising from a mortgage of foreign land may be the basis of proceedings in Ireland.[43]

In deciding whether a personal obligation is such as to affect the defendant's conscience is a matter determined by Irish law rather than the *lex situs.*[44]

It should be noted that the doctrine of *Penn* v. *Baltimore* is subject to two important qualifications. *First,* the Irish court will make an order only where it is possible for the decree to be carried into effect in the country were the land is situated.[45] Thus, if the *lex situs* forbids the performance of some act, the Irish court will not engage in the futile and possibly unjust course of ordering the defendant to do that act.[46] *Secondly,* the personal obligation must "have run from the defendant to the plaintiff".[47] in the sense that there must be privity of obligation between the parties.[48] There may, however, be exceptional cases in which, despite the absence of privity, a personal obligation may be enforced. The question the court must resolve is whether the defendant, "though not a party to the original transaction which gave rise to the dispute, is contractually or otherwise personally bound".[49]

The doctrine in *Penn* v. *Baltimore* has not met with universal favour by the commentators, who have on occasion argued that it is difficult to reconcile with the general principles of conflicts of law:[50] indeed Lord Esher observed in *Companhia de Moçambique* v. *British South Africa Co.*[51] that the decision in *Penn* v. *Baltimore,*

> "which has been acted upon by other great judges in equity, seems to me to be open to the strong objection, that the Court is doing indirectly what it dare not do directly."

A question not yet resolved is whether an Irish court would give extra-territorial effect to a foreign decree of a personal nature made on the same principle as in *Penn* v. *Baltimore,* in respect of Irish land.[52] The comity principle,

---

[40] 3 Ves., at 183, 30 E.R., at 959.
[41] *Kildare (Lord of)* v. *Eustace,* 1 Vern. 419, 22 E.R. 905 (1686), *Razelos* v. *Razelos,* [1969] 3 All E.R. 929 (P.D.A. Div., Baker, J.), criticised by Chesterman, *Note: Foreign Land and English Equity,* 33 Modern L. Rev. 209, at 212-213 (1970).
[42] Cf. *Ewing* v. *Orr-Ewing,* 9 App. Cas. 34 (1883).
[43] Cf. *Beckford* v. *Kemble,* 1 Sim. & St. 7, 57 E.R. 3 (1882), *Inglis* v. *Commonwealth Trading Bank of Australia,* 20 F.L.R. 30 (1972), noted by Pryles, *Jurisdiction over Foreign Immovables,* 22 Int. & Comp. L.Q. 756 (1973).
[44] Cf. *Scott* v. *Nesbitt,* 14 Ves. 438, 33 E.R. 589 (1808). See Beale, *supra,* at 385-386.
[45] *Keeton & Sheridan,* 14.
[46] Cf. *Re Courtney, Ex Parte Pollard,* Mont. & Ch. 239, at 250-251 (*per* Lord Cottenham, 1840); see also *Waterhouse* v. *Stansfield,* 9 Hare 234, 68 E.R. 489 (1851).
[47] Beale, *supra,* at 390.
[48] See *Norris* v. *Chambres,* 29 Beav. 246, 54 E.R. 621 (1861), aff'd 3 De G.F. & J. 583, 45 E.R. 1004 (1861), *Deschamps* v. *Miller,* [1908] 1 Ch. 856 (Parker, J.).
[49] *Cheshire & North,* 500.
[50] Cf. *Story,* 758. See also *Cheshire & North,* 501.
[51] [1892] 2 Q.B. 358, at 404-405 (C.A.), affirmed (*sub nom. British South Africa Co.* v. *Companhia de Moçambique*), [1893] A.C. 602 (H.L.).
[52] See Gordon, *The Converse of Penn* v. *Lord Baltimore,* 49 L.Q. Rev., 547 (1933), Keeton, *Trusts in the Conflict of Laws,* 4 Current Legal Problems, Ch. 5, at 111-112 (1951).

it has been said, would dictate an affirmative answer.[53] However, decisions in Canada[54] and the United States[55] are hostile to this view, and the English commentators appear to accept[56] that the argument is not likely to be successful in their courts. The case against giving extra-territorial effect to these foreign decrees is that they were given by courts *in personam* in circumstances where those courts probably never envisaged that they would be enforced in the country where the lands are situate.[57]

(b) *Questions affecting foreign land arising incidentally in Irish proceedings*

We now turn to the second exception to the exclusion of jurisdiction in respect of foreign immovables. It is of uncertain scope in Ireland, in the absence of case law. In England, however, the practice is now well established[58] whereby jurisdiction has been assumed by the court even in cases where title to foreign land was clearly in dispute.

As *Cheshire & North* observed, this

"comes perilously near to destroying the supposedly universal principle that jurisdiction concerning the title to, or possession of, immovables, resides only in the *forum rei sitae*."[59]

Perhaps it can be defended on the basis that it goes no further than embracing the principle that, if an estate or trust which includes English property and foreign movables is being administered in English proceedings, the court should be prepared to determine a disputed title to the foreign immovables.[60]

This question of jurisdiction in respect of foreign immovables may also arise in the context of statutory provisions relating to matrimonial property.[61] This matter is dealt with in chapter [22].

(c) *Admiralty jurisdiction*

In *The Tolten*,[62] the English Court of Appeal held that the *Moçambique* rule did not restrict the right of a plaintiff to take an admiralty action *in rem* to enforce a maritime lien on a ship for damage done to foreign immovable property. Scott, L.J. provided a learned historical analysis of admiralty jurisdiction and its intimate relationship with "the general law of the sea". The *Moçambique* rule, he said, was "in short, a conception wholly foreign to the essential nature of admiralty jurisdiction".[63] If the rule embraced the admiralty action *in rem*, this would interfere with the effectiveness of the maritime lien.[64]

---

[53] *Cheshire & North*, 501.
[54] *Duke* v. *Andler*, [1932] S.C.R. 734.
[55] Cf. Gordon, *supra*, at 550-552.
[56] Cf. e.g. *Cheshire & North*, 501.
[57] Cf. Gordon, *supra*, at 548-549.
[58] Cf. e.g. *Re Duke of Wellington*, [1948] Ch. 118, *Nelson* v. *Bridport*, 8 Beav. 547, 50 E.R. 215 (1846).
[59] *Cheshire & North*, 502.
[60] Cf. *id.*
[61] Cf. the Married Women's Status Act 1957, section 12; see also *Hamlin* v. *Hamlin*, [1985] 2 All E.R. 1037 (C.A.). Cf. *infra*, pp. 427-428.
[62] [1946] P. 135 (C.A.).
[63] *Id.*, at 154.
[64] As to which, cf. Crosbie, *The Ships of State*, [1984] 1 *Obiter Dicta*, p. 18.

CHAPTER 21

IMMOVABLES: CHOICE OF LAW

INTRODUCTION

It is a general rule, not only of the Irish conflict of laws,[1] but of the conflict of laws of most common law[2] jurisdictions, that the *lex situs* determines all questions arising in relation to immoveable property. In *In bonis Gentili,*[3] in 1875, Warren, J. quoted with approval the following passage from *Story:*

> "The consent of the tribunals acting under the common law both in England and America is, in a practical sense, absolutely uniform on the same subject. All the authorities in both countries, so far as they go, recognize the principle in its fullest import, that real estate, or immovable property, is exclusively subject to the laws of the government within whose territory it is situate."[4]

In *In re Rea deceased; Rea* v. *Rea*[5], in 1902, Porter, M.R. said that:

> "In the case of immovable property of whatever tenure the *lex loci rei sitae* applies, instead of the *lex domicilii,* the reason being that immovable property, that is land or things appurtenant to land, forms part of the actual territory controlled by the law at the place, and by international comity and for manifest convenience is deemed to be, for the purposes of descent and inheritance, regulated by the *lex loci.*"

The wide scope of the rule is apparent from a passage in *Story* which states that the common law applies:

> "a simple and uniform test. It declares that the law of the *situs* shall exclusively govern in regard to all rights, interests, and titles in and to immovable property."[6]

---

[1] In *Cripps Warburg Ltd.* v. *Cologne Investment Co. Ltd.,* [1980] I.R. 321, at 336 (High Ct., 1979), D'Arcy J. said:
> "It is a principle of private international law that all questions concerning the rights over immoveables are governed by the *lex situs.*"

See also Miller's *Irish Probate Practice,* 176 (Maxwell ed., 1900), *Murray* v. *Champernowne,* [1901] 2 I.R. 232 (Q.B. Div., Prob., Andrews, J., 1900), *In re Stoughton Deceased,* [1941] I.R. 166 (High Ct., 1940).

[2] But not most civil law jurisdictions: Morris, *Intestate Succession to Land in the Conflict of Laws,* 85 L.Q. Rev. 339, at 344 (1969), *McLeod,* 415.

[3] I.R. 9 Eq. 541, at 545 (Warren, J., 1875).

[4] *Story,* s. 428. See also *Nelson* v. *Bridport,* 8 Beav. 547, at 570, (*per* Lord Langdale, M.R., 1846).

[5] [1902] 1 I.R. 451, at 461 (Porter M.R.). See also *Freke* v. *Lord Carbery,* L.R. 16 Eq. 461, at 466 (*per* Lord Selbourne, 1873), quoted by Porter M.R., [1902] 1 I.R., at 461-462; *In the Matter of Corballis, dec'd,* [1929] I.R. 266, at 271 (Kennedy, C.J., 1928), *In re Reilly, A Bankrupt,* [1942] I.R. 416, at 447 (Sup. Ct., *per* Sullivan, C.J.) and at 451 (*per* Murnaghan, J., dissenting, but dissent not affecting this issue).

[6] *Story,* s. 463.

In *In bonis Gentili, Deceased*,[7] in 1875, Warren, J., having quoted this passage added: "To this rule I know of no exception".

There are some good practical reasons why the *lex situs* should govern, not least the fact that in the last analysis that law will be effective, whatever other laws may say.[8] Moreover, it is arguable[9] that a person owning immoveable property should expect that the law of the country where it is situated would have a say in relation to how, and on what terms, it is to be transmitted, for no other reason than to protect its system of conveyancing and the interests of purchasers.[10] But these considerations fall well short of justifying the inflexible application on the *lex situs* rule, which can lead to harsh and indefensible results.[11]

This is particularly so in view of two developments over the past century: the reduction or abolition of the differences between real and personal property in the law of many countries, and the extension of generous statutory "forced shares" for members of the family or other dependents of the deceased person.[12] If the *lex situs* rule continues to operate unchecked it can involve unsatisfactory solutions, with surviving spouses obtaining "double shares"[13] (or conceivably no share at all in converse cases), as well as having unpalatable results for legatees. We will be examining this question in some detail in the chapter on Succession.[14]

The Meaning of the "Lex Situs"

What does the *"lex situs"* mean? As we have seen when discussing the doctrine of *renvoi*,[15] this is one of the exceptional cases in which the entire law of the foreign *situs* is taken into account. The reason for this approach is not difficult to appreciate. It would be unfortunate if the country where the immovable is situated were obliged to apply its internal law to everyone without regard to whether they have any real connection with that country.[16] Moreover, application of the *lex situs* rule on any other basis would lead to practical difficulties to the extent that it differed from what the courts of the *situs* held to be the answer to the problem in any particular case. At the end of the day, as we have noted, the courts of the *situs* tend to have the last word.

---

[7] I.R. 9 Eq. 541, at 545 (Prob., Warren, J., 1875).

[8] See *Attorney General* v. *Drapers' Co.*, [1894] 1 I.R. 185, at 201 (C.A., *per* Palles, C.B., 1893), *In re Rea deceased; Rea* v. *Rea, supra*, at 461 (*per* Porter, M.R.). Goodrich, *Two States and Real Estate*, 89 U. Pa L. Rev. 417, at 419, fn. 12 (1941); but cf. Weintraub, *An Inquiry into the Utility of "Situs" as a Concept in Conflicts Analysis*, 52 Cornell L.Q. 1, at 4 (1966).

[9] Though far from self-evident: cf. *McLeod*, 415.

[10] But cf. Weintraub, *supra*, at 3.

[11] Cf. Morris, *Intestate Succession to Land in the Conflict of Laws*, 85 L.Q. Rev. 339, at 339 (1969), who goes so far as to state that the *lex situs* rule "makes no sense whatever and leads to absurd and anomalous results." See further Hancock, *"In the Parish of St. Mary le Bow, in the Ward of Cheap"*: *Choice-of-Law Problems Resolved by Statutory Construction: The Charitable Testamentary Gift Cases*, 16 Stan. L. Rev. 561 (1964), Hancock, *Equitable Conversion and the Land Taboo in Conflict of Laws*, 17 Stan. L. Rev. 1095 (1965), Hancock, *Conceptual Devices for Avoiding the Land Taboo in Conflict of Laws*, 20 Stan. L. Rev. 1 (1967). For example, if a man dies intestate, domiciled in Ireland, leaving immoveable property in Italy, it may be debated whether Italian rather than Irish law should prescribe what share his widow and children in the Italian property: cf. Weintraub, *supra*, at 17ff.

[12] See Sheridan, *Disinheritance of a Spouse: A Comparative Study of the Law in the United Kingdom and the Republic of Ireland*, 31 N.I.L.Q. 21 (1980), Volkmer, *Spousal Property Rights at Death: Re-Evaluation of the Proposed Uniform Marital Property Act*, 17 Creighton L. Rev. 95 (1983), Kulzer, *Property and the Family: Spousal Protection*, 4 Rutgers-Camden L.J. 195 (1973) Prager, *Sharing Principles and the Future of Marital Property Law*, 25 U.C.L.A. L. Rev. 1 (1977).

[13] Cf. *In re Rea deceased; Rea* v. *Rea*, [1902] 1 I.R. 451 (Porter, M.R.), discussed *infra*, pp. 440-441.

[14] *Infra*, pp. 435-441.

[15] *Supra*, ch. 5.

[16] Cf. *Cheshire & North*, 504.

Capacity to Take and Transfer Immovables

It is well established that if a person has not the capacity by the *lex situs* to *take* immovables, he or she will be excluded from ownership.[17] Thus, if the *lex situs* excludes aliens from owning land, the courts of other countries must give effect to this exclusion, subject, of course, to public policy.[18]

Capacity to *transfer* immovables is also determined by the *lex situs*.[19] Thus, if a person attains capacity to convey immoveable property under the law of the country of his domicile when 16, he will nonetheless be incapable of executing a valid conveyance of immovables situated in a country under whose law capacity to convey immovables is limited to persons aged at least 18 years.[20] Similarly capacity, under the *lex situs* of the immovables will prevail over any incapacity under a person's *lex domicilii*.[21]

The English decision of *Bank of Africa Ltd.* v. *Cohen*[22] has provoked much discussion. There the Court of Appeal, affirming Eve, J. held invalid, and thus unenforceable, a contract entered into in England by the defendant, a married woman domiciled in England, by which she agreed to mortgage land in Johannesburg to an English bank as security for advances made by the bank to her husband. When the bank sued for specific performance of this contract, the defendant resisted on the basis that, under the law of the Transvaal, a married woman could not be bound as a surety for her husband save in certain exceptional cases, none of which applied.

Eve, J. observed that:

"The court in dealing with a contract relating to immovables is bound to determine this question of capacity by the *lex situs*, and if the *lex situs* shows that the contracting party had not the capacity to contract, the whole contract is void, and nothing can be done in this country to enforce that contract against the contracting party."[23]

And on appeal, Buckley, L.J. said:

"A judgment for specific performance here would mean that this court should order the defendant, after having had her rights explained to her, to renounce the *Senatus Consultum Velleianum* and *Authentica si qua mulier*, whereas the law to be applied is that the wife, after explanation of her rights, may refuse to renounce them. Specific performance in that sense is, in my judgment, impossible. Mr Dicey's language[24] I think is correct, that a person's capacity to make a contract with regard to an immovable is governed by the *lex situs*."[25]

This decision has been widely criticised, but not for such support it may give to the principle that the *lex situs* should determine a person's capacity to transfer an immovable.

A major objection is that neither court made any attempt to determine the policy of the Transvaal law, or how the Transvaal courts would deal with the case.[26] The

---

[17] *Id.*, 505. See *Duncan* v. *Lawson*, 41 Ch. D. 394 (1889) (restrictions under England's Mortmain and Charitable Uses Act 1888 applied to determining capacity of charity to take English freeholds and leaseholds under a foreign will).

[18] Cf. *Dicey & Morris*, 551, *In bonis Gentili, Deceased*, I.R. 9 Eq. 541, at 544-546 (Prob., Warren, J., 1875).

[19] *Cheshire & North*, 505, *Dicey & Morris*, 550.

[20] *Cheshire & North*, 506; as to the position in the United States, cf. *Restatement, Second, on Conflicts of Law*, s. 223, *Scoles & Hay*, 717-720.

[21] *Cheshire & North* 505.

[22] [1909] 2 Ch. 129.

[23] *Id.*, at 135.

[24] *Dicey* 2nd ed., 1908, p. 501.

[25] [1909] 2 Ch., at 143.

[26] Cf. *Dicey & Morris*, 550-551. *Dicey & Morris* criticise the decision for losing sight of the economic and social considerations involved: the bank was left without security for advances made to the defendant's husband in reliance upon her promise, and she was allowed "to break the promise with impunity, although she made it in solemn form and knew quite well what she was doing" *id.*, 551.

fact that the court was dealing, not with a mortgage but a *contract to make a mortgage*, has also been stressed. As we shall see,[27] contracts for the sale or mortgage of immovables are governed by their proper law, which normally (though not invariably) will be the *lex situs*. In *Cohen's* case, the Court made no effort to determine what was the proper law of the contract.

Formalities

When we came to consider formalities of alienation, the drawbacks of a mechanical "black letter" choice of law rule became apparent. It is easy to see the injustice of invalidating a transaction involving immoveable property which complies fully with the formal requirements of the law of the country with which the parties have most connection, but which fails to fulfil a technical formal requirement of the domestic *les situs* of the immoveable property. There is a clear need to examine the policy of the *lex situs* and to enquire whether the purpose of the formal requirement was to cover only transactions having some close connection with the jurisdiction, or to apply to all transactions involving immoveable property situated within the jurisdiction.

There is not a great deal of judicial authority on this question.[28] The leading Irish case is *Murray* v. *Champernowne*.[29] There a man domiciled in Scotland made a will in execution of a power of appointment with respect to Irish land subject to a trust for sale. The will complied with the formal requirements of Irish, but not Scots, law. Andrews, J. upheld the validity of the will. He considered it "settled law that the formalities required for the disposal by will ... of immoveable property in Ireland, are governed by the testamentary law of Ireland (the *lex situs*) . . ."[30] The only question, therefore, was whether the trust for sale altered the application of this general rule, and Andrews, J. was satisfied that it did not. He said:

> "If, as the law unquestionably is, an owner of land in Ireland, no matter what his domicil may be, can only devise it by a will made in accordance with the law of Ireland, I am unable to hold that he can, if domiciled say in Scotland, enable himself to dispose of it by a Scotch will, not in accordance with the law of Ireland, by previously vesting it in a trustee for sale, the trust being unperformed. It is still immovable property, in fact, and the disposition of it is a disposition of immovable property, and not of something else, namely the money by which, if sold, it would be represented, but which before the sale does not, in fact, exist."[31]

Essential Validity of Transfers

The *lex situs* determines the essential validity of transfers of immoveable property.[32] Thus the *les situs* determines whether an interest given infringes the rule against perpetuities or accumulations, for example,[33] or whether a gift to a charity is valid[34] or whether a testator must leave a fixed portion of his or her estate to members of his or her family or other persons or institutions.[35]

---

[27] *Infra*, pp. 412-413.

[28] Cf. *Adams* v. *Clutterbuck*, 10 Q.B.D. 403 (1883) (conveyance by domiciled Englishman of shooting rights over Scottish land valid where it complied with formal requirements of Scots, but not English, law); *Coppin* v. *Coppin*, 2 P. Wms. 291, 24 E.R. 735 (1725) (converse case).

[29] [1901] 2 I.R. 232 (Q.B. Div., Prob., Andrews, J., 1900).

[30] *Id.*, at 236.

[31] *Id.*, at 237. See also *In bonis Gentili, Deceased*, I.R. 9 Eq. 541, at 544-545 (Prob., Warren, J., 1875).

[32] *Murray* v. *Champernowne*, [1901] 2 I.R. 232, at 236 (Q.B. Div., Prob., Andrews, J., 1900), *In re Stoughton Deceased*, [1941] I.R. 166, at 178 (High Ct., *per* Hanna, J., 1940).

[33] *Freke* v. *Carbery*, L.R. 16 Eq. 461 (1873), *In re Grassi*, [1905] 1 Ch. 584, at 592 (Buckley, J.), Dicey & Morris, 625, Cheshire & North, 507-508.

[34] Dicey & Morris, 625, *Re Hoyles*, [1911] 1 Ch. 179 (C.A., 1910).

[35] Cf. *infra*, pp. 435-441.

Contracts relating to immovables

We must now consider the position concerning *contracts* relating to immovables. Briefly, it may be said that, although the *lex situs* plays an important role in many cases, it does not do so in all;[36] nor, in those cases where it does apply, has it an exclusive operation.

In *Cripps Warburg Ltd* v. *Cologne Investment Co. Ltd.*,[37] D'Arcy, J. expressed the view that:

> "the proper law of a contract concerning immoveables, as distinct from moveables, cannot be determined by any one factor alone, except in the case where the parties expressly provide what law should apply or where all the parties live, and the transactions take place, in one jurisdiction. In the end one must come down to the law which has the closest and the most real connection with the contract and transaction. That is the proper law of the contract."

Let us examine this statement. It seems, that the "closest and most real connection" affords the general test, save in two cases. The first is where the parties "expressly provide what law should apply". As we will see in the chapter on contracts,[38] this statement is subject to no modification, such as that the choice be *"bona fide* and legal.*"*[39] Perhaps this is because D'Arcy, J. saw no need, in a case where *no* choice had in fact been made, to specify the precise scope of the rule where a choice is made. It is worth noting[40] that D'Arcy, J.'s words do not extend to instances where the parties failed to provide expressly for a governing law but did so by necessary implication. It may be argued that these instances should also be determined by a single law.

The second exceptional case mentioned by D'Arcy, J. is where "all the parties live, and the transactions take place, in one jurisdiction." In these circumstances, D'Arcy, J. would appear to require that the proper law be determined by "one factor alone". D'Arcy, J. does not, however, state expressly what that factor is. It would surely be reasonable to infer that the proper law would in these circumstances be that of the country where the parties live and the transactions take place. This indeed was the situation in *Cripps Warburg* but in that case there was another important element: the immovable was also situated in the same jurisdiction.

Let us envisage two cases where the immovable is situated in another jurisdiction. In the first, a house in Spain is owned by an Irishman. He mortgages the property to an Irish bank, the transaction taking place in Ireland. It is reasonable to consider that the proper law would be Irish in these circumstances. In the second case, a house in Spain is owned by a Spanish person who is living in Ireland. The house is sold, in Ireland, to another Spanish person. The proper law *may* again be Irish but it is not obvious that it should be. The point to note here is that D'Arcy, J.'s formula works effectively where the immovable is in the same country as where the transaction takes place and the parties live, but where the immovable is elsewhere it is not clear that the proper law is capable of being determined by any "one factor alone".[41]

So far as formal requirements are concerned, it appears that a contract will be

---

[36] See *Walker* v. *Lord Lorton*, 6 Ir. Ch. Rep. 329, at 345-346 (Cusack Smith, M.R., 1857), *Ferguson* v. *Lomax*, 2 Dr. & War. 120 (1842). Cf. *In re Boate's Estate*, 10 Ir. Ch. Rep. 164 (Ch. App., 1859), considered *infra*, p. 427.

[37] [1980] I.R. 321, at 333 (High Ct., 1979).

[38] *Infra*, p. 522.

[39] *Vita Food Products, Inc.* v. *Unus Shipping Co. Ltd.*, [1939] A.C. 277, at 290 (*per* Lord Wright).

[40] Cf. *infra*, pp. 527-530.

[41] Cf. *Northern Bank Ltd.* v. *Edwards*, [1986] I.L.R.M. 167 (Sup Ct., 1985) (owner of immoveable property in Donegal mortgaged it to a bank in Derry where he had an account; *per* McCarthy, J., for the Court, at 169: "There can be no doubt but that the proper law of the contract was the law prevailing in Northern Ireland").

formally valid if it complies with the formal requirements of either its proper law or (perhaps) of the *lex loci contractus*.[42] In a case where the proper law is not the *lex situs*, it appears that a contract to transfer an interest in land which complies with the formal requirements of its proper law or the *lex loci contractus* will be enforceable even if the formal requirements of the *lex situs* have not been met.[43]

So far as material validity, capacity and interpretation are concerned it seems that the proper law of the contract governs.[44] This usually will be the *lex situs* of the immovable, but not invariably so.[45]

[42] See *Cheshire & North*, 509, *Dicey & Morris*, 551, 553 and Rule 148; *Re Anchor Line (Henderson Brothers) Ltd.*, [1937] Ch. 483 (C.A., 1936). The proper law of the contract "is usually the *lex situs*": *Dicey & Morris*, 551. See also *id.*, 553. For criticism of *Bank of Africa Ltd.* v. *Cohen* [1909] 2 Ch. 129 in this context, see *Cheshire & North*, 510.

[43] *In re Smith, Lawrence* v. *Kitson*, [1916] 2 Ch. 206. See also *Castel*, vol. 2, p. 375.

[44] *Dicey & Morris*, Rule 78, Exception 1.

[45] *Id.* See further *Castel*, vol. 2,375. *British South Africa Co.* v. *De Beers Consolidated Mines Co. Ltd.* [1910] 2 Ch. 502 (C.A.) rev'd on other grounds, [1912] A.C. 52 (H.L., 1911), criticised by *Nygh*, 64. See also *Re Smith* [1916] 2 Ch. 206, *Re Anchor Line (Henderson Bros) Ltd.*, [1937] Ch. 483 (Luxmoore, J.).

CHAPTER 22

FAMILY PROPERTY[1]

Throughout the world several different types of marital property systems are in operation.[2] They range from "separate property" systems which historically have commanded support in most common law jurisdictions, to "community of property" systems, mainly favoured by civil law jurisdictions.

The question of what conflicts rules should govern matrimonial property regimes raises far more difficult issues than has generally been appreciated. We here are at a crossroads where policies affecting marriage, property and contract converge. Each of these three policies has a claim to priority. How should these competing claims be resolved? And according to what values?

These questions were a good deal less intractable some years ago, when marriage was widely regarded as essentially lifelong, where the primary maintenance obligations fell on the husband[3] and where relationships outside marriage generated few, if any, mutual legal entitlements and responsibilities.[4] Recently marriage has come to be regarded by the laws of most countries as involving merely a revocable commitment;[5] wives have far less maintenance entitlements;[6] and non-marital

---

[1] See H. Marsh, *Marital Property in Conflict of Laws* (1952), Droz, *Les régimes matrimoniaux en droit international privé comparé*, [1974]-III Recueil des cours 1, Anton, *The Effect of Marriage Upon Property in Scots Law*, 19 Modern L. Rev. 653 (1956), Goldberg, *The Assignment of Property on Marriage*, 19 Int. & Comp. L.Q. 557 (1970), Rafferty, *Matrimonial Property and the Conflict of Laws*, 20 U.W. Ont. L. Rev. 177 (1982), Juenger, *Marital Property and the Conflict of Laws: A Tale of Two Countries*, 81 Colum. L. Rev. 1061 (1981), Deering, *Separate and Community Property and the Conflict of Laws*, 30 Rocky Mtn. L. Rev. 127 (1958), De Funiak, *Conflict of Laws in the Community Property Field*, 7 Ariz. L. Rev. 50 (1965), Neuner, *Marital Property and the Conflict of Laws*, 5 La. L. Rev. 167 (1943), Leflar, *Community Property and Conflict of Laws*, 21 Calif. L. Rev. 221 (1933), Horowitz, *Conflict of Law Problems in Community Property*, 11 Wash. L. Rev. 121, 212 (1936), Stumberg, *Marital Property and the Conflict of Laws*, 11 Tex. L. Rev. 53 (1932), Harding, *Matrimonial Domicil and Marital Rights in Movables*, 30 Mich. L. Rev. 859 (1932), Leyser, *Community of Property — Interests Acquired by Marriage Abroad*, 33 Austr. L. J. 209 (1959), Lay, *Property Rights Following Migration from a Community Property State*, 19 Ala. L. Rev. 298 (1967), Forsyth, *Section 7 of the Matrimonial Property Act 1976; A Choice of Law Rule?*, 7 N.Z.U.L. Rev. 397 (1977).

[2] See I. Brown, *Marital Property*, ch. 40 (1973), de Funiak & Vaughn, *Principles of Community Property Law*, (2nd ed., 1971), A. Kiralfy ed., *Comparative Law of Matrimonial Property*, (1972), A. Bissett-Johnson & W. Holland, eds., *Matrimonial Property Law in Canada* (1980), Lay, *A Survey of Community Property*, 51 Iowa L. Rev. 625 (1966), Powell, *Community Property — A Critique of Its Regulation of Intra-Family Relations*, 11 Wash. L. Rev. 12 (1936), Glendon, *Matrimonial Property: A Comparative Study of Law and Social Change*, 49 Tul. L. Rev. 21 (1974), McLachlan, *Matrimonial Property and the Conflict of Laws*, 12 N.Z.U.L. Rev. 66 (1986).

[3] Cf. Binchy, *Family Law Reform in Ireland: Some Comparative Aspects*, 25 Int. & Comp. L.Q. 901, at 901-905 (1976).

[4] Cf. *Freeman & Lyon*, 6-11.

[5] See Hoggett, *Ends and Means — The Utility of Marriage as a Legal Institution*, Ch. 10 of J. Eekelaar & S. Katz, eds, *Marriage and Cohabitation in Contemporary Societies* (1980), Goldstein & Gitter, *On Abolition of Grounds for Divorce: A Model Statute and Commentary*, 3 Family L.Q. 75 (1969), Zuckman & Fox, *The Ferment in Divorce Legislation*, 12 J. Family L. 515 (1973).

[6] See O'Donovan, *Should All Maintenance of Spouses Be Abolished?*, 45 Modern L. Rev. 424 (1980),

relationships now have clear legal implications.[7] The situation varies from country to country, and it would be wrong to imagine that the progress of the law must continue inexorably in one direction. Ireland finds itself supporting a concept of marriage as involving a lifelong commitment of partnership between the spouses — a perception at variance with most other countries, where the long-term drift is away from the model of committed partnership.[8] Where marriage no longer involves a mutual commitment for life, of course, the notion of "marital property" as a shared partnership makes less sense. It is not surprising, therefore, that the long-term trend in countries with liberal divorce is towards a separate property regime.[9]

It is against this background that we must examine what our conflicts rules concerning family property should be seeking to achieve. Several possible policy goals may be relevant: these include support for marriage, protection of the economically disadvantaged spouse, promotion of sex equality, respect for the individual autonomy of the spouses, protection of third parties, including creditors, and reducing legal complexities resulting from connections between the spouses and the property laws of different countries. At present, most of these goals provoke questions that are not easy to resolve. *Should* our conflicts rules relating to family property seek, even in part, to provide support for marriage? It is easy to conceive of conflict rules that would be damaging to marriage by removing any effective economic security from one of the spouses.[10] The notion of protecting the economically disadvantaged spouse runs contrary to the contemporary view of marriage as a "risk business". The economically disadvantaged spouse — usually the wife — receives scant sympathy in most countries today.[11]

The answer, so far as Irish conflicts rules are concerned, is far from simple. There would seem little point in applying to other countries values as to marriage supported by Irish law: why should spouses from Oklahoma be subject to Irish policies relating to marriage? Perhaps the best solution would be for our courts or legislature to establish distinctive rules applicable to spouses with significant Irish connections,[12]

Hauserman, *Homemakers and Divorce: Problems of Invisible Occupation,* 17 Family L.Q. 41 (1983), Bruch, *Of Work, Family Wealth, and Equality,* 17 Family L.Q. 99 (1983), Olsen, *The Family and the Market: A Study of Ideology and Legal Reform,* 96 Harv. L. Rev. 1497 (1983).

[7] See Glendon, *Marriage and the State: The Withering Away of Marriage,* 62 Va. L. Rev. 663, at 684-697 (1976), Venturatos Lorio, *Concubinage and Its Alternatives: A Proposal for a More Perfect Union,* 26 Loyola L. Rev. 1 (1980), Girard, *Concubines and Cohabitees: A Comparative Look at 'Living Together',* 28 McGill L. J. 977 (1983).

[8] See Oldham, *Is the Concept of Marital Property Outdated?,* 22 J. Family L. 263, at 266 (1984).

[9] See Glendon, *Is There a Future for Separate Property?* 8 Family L.Q. 315 (1974), Pedersen, *Recent Trends in Danish Family Law and the Historical Background,* 20 Int. & Comp. L.Q. 332, at 337 (1971), Sage, *Dissolution of the Family Under Swedish Law,* 9 Family L. Q. 375, at 402 (1975), Angelo & Atkin, *A Conceptual and Structural Overview of the Matrimonial Property Act 1976,* 7 N.Z.U.L. Rev. 237, at 258 (1977), Schmidt, *The Prospective Law of Marriage,* 15 Scand. Studies in L. 191, at 204-205, 215 (1971), Sargisson, *Matrimonial Property Legislation — Its History and a Critique of the Present New Zealand Law,* 3 Auckland U.L. Rev. No. 1 82, at 105-106 (1976). Cf. Oldham, *Is the Concept of Marital Property Outdated?,* 22 J. Family L. 263, at 308 (1984), and Susan Westbery Prager's thoughtful analysis, in *Sharing Principles and the Future of Marital Property Law,* 22 U.C.L.A. L. Rev. 1, at 14-19 (1977).

[10] The notion of "divisible divorce" could mitigate this difficulty, at least to some extent: cf. Dulick, *Note,* 28 Baylor L. Rev. 425 (1976) and *supra,* pp. 303-304.

[11] The position is considered by Brophy & Smart, *From Disregard to Disrepute: The Position of Women in Family Law,* 9 Feminist Rev. 3, at 15 (1981), Glendon, *Matrimonial Property: A Comparative Study of Law and Social Change,* 49 Tulane L. Rev. 21, at 78-81 (1974), Fineman, *Implementing Equality: Ideology, Contradiction and Social Change. A Study of Rhetoric and Results in the Regulation of the Consequences of Divorce,* [1983] Wis. L. Rev. 789.

[12] As well, perhaps, as spouses with significant connections with some other one of the few countries still regarding marriage as involving a truly lifelong commitment.

while leaving spouses without these connections subject to rules reflecting norms as to marital property predominant in many other countries.[13] Thus it would perhaps make sense for our conflicts rules to preserve vested rights under a partnership model, where spouses with strong Irish connections transfer to a country whose law treats spouses as strangers; consistent with this protection, our conflict rules could adopt a more neutral approach towards a change of regime by spouses whose marriage has close connections with a law or laws under which marriage has no significant partnership dimension. The policy of protecting reasonable expectations would seek to ensure that injustice would not occur in individual cases.

Having mentioned the complex policy issues that have yet to be confronted, let us move on to consider how the law on this subject has in fact developed. The approach generally favoured has been to make a division between cases where there is an ante-nuptial contract between the spouses, and cases where no such contract exists.[14] The problem with this approach is that it is hard to place any clear limits on the concept of an ante-nuptial contract.[15]

Let us examine the law under these two headings.

WHERE THERE IS NO ANTE-NUPTIAL CONTRACT

Where the spouses have not entered into an ante-nuptial contract dealing with their property relationships, the courts historically have applied the law of the domicile of the husband to determine their entitlement.[16] In *Hutchinson* v. *Cathcart*,[17] in 1845, some light was thrown on the judicial attitudes at that time to the subject of matrimonial property. In this case, a woman when single was awarded by an Irish Court a certain sum of money, to be realised by a sale of some lands. Before the sale had been completed she married an Austrian subject in Trieste, which was then within the Austrian Empire, and thereafter the couple lived in the Austrian Empire. Later, when the sum was realised, the couple applied to the Irish Court requesting that the money be paid out to their attorney. They stated that, according to the laws of the Austrian Empire, the sum would be at the total disposal of the wife. The wife deposed that she had made no disposition of her rights with respect to the sum for the benefit of her husband. The Court granted the order.

The report of the case merely recites the Court order and contains no record of a judgment. It does, however, include a detailed summary of the argument of counsel for the applicants, and of some judicial responses to it. In particular it is worth noting that counsel pressed the argument that the *lex domicilii* should govern "personal property";[18] and he quoted *Story's* propositions that:

> "[w]here there is no contract the law of the matrimonial domicile will govern, as to all the rights of the parties to their present property in that place, and as to all personal property everywhere, upon the principle that movables have no *situs*, or, rather, that they accompany the person everywhere",[19]

---

[13] The proposals made by the Law Reform Commission in their *Report on Recognition of Foreign Divorces and Legal Separations*, Ch. 3 (L.R.C. 10-1985) provide a useful model of how to distinguish between spouses with, and without, significant Irish connections. Of course, it would be wrong for any law to attempt to squeeze all marriages into a single partnership model. There is within our society a wide variety of spousal roles. The law should seek to take account of this divergence: cf. Kulzer, *Law and the Housewife: Property, Divorce, and Death*, 28 U. Fla. L. Rev. 1, at 47-48 (1975).

[14] *Cheshire & North*, 572-573.

[15] Cf. Goldberg, *supra, passim*. See also *Re De Nicols, De Nicols* v. *Curlier*, [1900] A.C. 21, discussed *infra*, pp. 420-422.

[16] See *In re Martin, Loustalan* v. *Loustalan*, [1900] P. 211, at 233 (C.A., per Lindley, M.R.).

[17] 8 Ir. Eq. Rep. 394 (Equity Exch., 1846).

[18] *Id.*, at 396. As to the inappropriateness of this term, see *supra*, p. 392.

[19] *Story*, s. 186(3).

and

"where there is no change of domicile, the same rule will apply to future acquisitions as to present property. But where there is a change of domicile, the law of the actual domicile, and not of the matrimonial domicile, will govern as to all future acquisitions of moveable property ..."[20]

One of the judges, Lefroy, B., responded to counsel's argument by referring to the decision of *Anstruther* v. *Adair,*[21] where in ordering that a fund under a former settlement be paid to the husband rather than the wife, "the Court ... decided, not on the law of domicile, but on this, that by [a settlement executed by the wife divesting herself of her right to any after-acquired property] the wife had done an act depriving her of her right to any settlement, and on that ground decreed the fund to be paid to the husband. The judgment of the Court in that case, acting on the contract, may be considered as affording an argument against ruling this case on the law of domicile merely."[22] Counsel for the applicants replied by pointing out that, in the instant case, no such contract between the spouses existed and that by the laws of Austria the wife was entitled to the whole sum. In a further intervention, Lefroy, B. sought to distinguish another case[23] as "not strengthen[ing]"[24] counsel's argument, because in it both spouses had been subjects of the foreign country (Denmark) under whose law the husband was entitled to receive the property of the wife without making a settlement on her.

At all events, in spite of Lefroy, B.'s hesitancy, the Court made the requested order, without recording any objection to counsel's central argument based on the application of the matrimonial domicile.[25]

When *Hutchinson* v. *Cathcart* was decided, the matrimonial domicile was (in most cases at least)[26] determined by that of the husband. This approach was defended on the basis of convenience, in that it offered a single test for determining the property relationships of the spouses, and that, since the husband was in most cases likely to be the breadwinner, his choice of where the spouses should live should carry more weight. With changing sex roles and changing attitudes towards sex discrimination, the reference to the husband's domicile in this context has been regarded with increasing disfavour.[27]

In the English decision of *Re Egerton's Will Trusts,*[28] in 1956, Roxburgh, J. still gave priority to the husband's domicile, but the formula he adopted gave room for some unspecified modification. He considered it:

[20] *Id.,* s. 187(4)-(5). This distinction between "matrimonial" and "actual" domicile might mislead. "Matrimonial" here means the domicile of the spouses at the time of the marriage, and "actual" their domicile at some later time cf. *id.,* s. 171. It would seem mistaken to attempt to derive from this passage in *Story* any clear support for the view that the wife's domicile should be treated separately from that of her husband. The facts of the case rendered that question moot, however. The question of "mutability" is discussed *infra,* pp. 418-420.

[21] 2 M. & K. 513, 39 E.R. 1040 (1834).

[22] 8 Ir. Eq. Rep. at 397.

[23] *Dues* v. *Smith,* Jac. 544, 37 E.R. 955 (1822).

[24] 8 Ir., Eq. Rep., at 398.

[25] See also *In re Lett's Trusts and Trustee Relief Act; Ex parte Lett,* 7 L.R.(Ir.) 132 (Chatterton, V.-C., 1881), discussed *infra,* p. 420. In this case, in view of the factual pattern of the spouses' lives, it is impossible to form any view as to the extent (if any) to which the husband's domicile was given greater weight than that of the wife. Since, under New York law, the *lex domicilii* of the spouses, the wife was treated as a *femme sole* for the purposes of entitlement to a distributive share on intestacy from a third party, there would have been a curious irony in invoking the domicile of dependency rules to connect the wife with this entitlement under New York law.

[26] Cf. *supra,* pp. 77-82.

[27] Cf. *Castel,* vol. 1, 420.

[28] [1956] Ch. 593, at 607. See Stone, *The Matrimonial Domicile and the Property Relations of Married Persons,* 6 Int. & Comp. L.Q. 28 (1957).

"reasonably plain that there is a presumption that the law of the husband's domicile applies to a marriage, and that the presumption can be rebutted. It can certainly be rebutted by express contract, and, in my judgment, it could also be rebutted by what is loosely called a tacit contract, if the circumstances warrant the inference of such a tacit contract."

This formula would allow the court to have regard to the changed legal and social position of married women[29] but would not require it to do so. In view of the constitutional and statutory position in Ireland today on the question of sex equality, and in particular the 1986 legislation on domiciles, Roxburgh, J.'s formula seems too half-hearted a response.

Of course in most cases spouses share the same domicile when they marry. In these cases no particular difficulty should arise. In the cases where they have different domiciles at the time of marriage, the Court could look to other factors,[30] including, in appropriate instances, where they intend to live after the marriage.[31] This factor may not always be helpful, especially where the spouses' plans are only provisional, or where they change their minds, or (rarely) where they intend to live in separate countries for some time after the marriage.

The Question of Mutability

We must now consider the question whether spouses, having subjected themselves to one matrimonial property regime (otherwise than by contract), are free to change to another, by changing their domicile, for example. The case against such a power to change, and in favour of what is generally referred to as the principle of immutability, is essentially based on humanitarian concern for the interests of a wife. In *Westlake's* view, "justice is shocked by allowing the husband to affect the wife's position by a change for which he does not require her assent".[32] *Cheshire & North* comment: "What is shocking is suspect, and it is in fact doubtful whether English law has adopted the doctrine of mutability to its full extent".[33]

This argument has some force, at least to the extent that the operation of the doctrine of domicile of dependency of married women enabled a husband to impose on his wife a domicile that she did not seek. But surely it was this distinctive, and indefensible, doctrine, rather than the principle of mutability itself, which should be stigmatised as "shocking"?[34] At least in cases where the spouses are continuing to live together, there is much to be said for recognising the contemporary realities of their marriage relationship. If, for example, an Irish couple marry in Ireland and live there for some years, and then move to California where they buy a house and live in it for twenty years, there is a strong argument that the law of California, rather than Ireland, should determine their matrimonial property entitlements.[35] To continue to apply to them the rules of a legal system which they have long abandoned

---

[29] Cf. *Cheshire & North*, 576.

[30] Cf. Lintner, *Note: Marital Property Rights of Separate Domiciled Spouses and Conflicts of Laws*, 22 J. of Fam. L. 311 (1984).

[31] See *Re Egerton's Will Trusts*, [1956] Ch., at 602-607; cf. Harding, *Matrimonial Domicil and Marital Rights in Movables*, 30 Mich. L. Rev. 859, at 864-865 (1932). The Hague Convention on the Law Applicable to Matrimonial Regimes, completed in 1976, provides (in Article 4, para. 1) that, in the absence of a designated applicable law, the matrimonial property regime of the spouses is to be governed by the internal law of the state where the spouses establish their first habitual residence after marriage. For consideration of the Convention, see Glenn, *Comment*, 55 Can. Bar Rev. 586, at 595-605 (1977), Lienard-Ligny, *Le régime matrimonial en droit international privé et la Convention de La Haye du 14 mars 1978*, 26 Annales de la Fac. de Dr. de Liège 311 (1981), and, at drafting stage, Phillip, *Hague Draft Convention on Matrimonial Property*, 24 Am. J. of Comp. L. 307 (1976).

[32] *Westlake*, 7th ed., 73.

[33] *Cheshire & North*, 578.

[34] Cf. *Dicey & Morris*, 671.

[35] Cf. *Castel*, vol. 1,421. See also *Hutchinson* v. *Cathcart*, 8 Ir. Eq. Rep. 394 (Equity Exch., 1845), *In re Lett's Trusts and Trustee Relief Act; Ex parte Lett*, 7 L.R.(Ir.) 132 (Chatterton, V.-C., 1881).

would seem to defy the very *rationale* of domicile as a connecting factor in private international law. It would be a particularly inappropriate and unjust solution in cases where the spouses have fled from political persecution.[36] From the standpoint of creditors as well, the doctrine of immutability may easily result in hardship.[37]

It is where the spouses no longer live in harmony that a liberal principle of mutability could work particular hardship and injustice on a wife (or, less frequently, a husband). The danger here is that one spouse, by moving from a state with a community of property regime to one with a separate property regime, could effectively deprive the spouse who does not move of an interest attaching under the community regime. An attractive solution would be for our conflicts rules to protect any rights already vested before the change,[38] but to subject after-acquired property to the new regime.[39] A more restricted operation of the principle of mutability would permit the law originally applicable to operate until *both* spouses have abandoned the original regime.[40]

In truth, concern for protection of the wife's interests in this context is a two-edged sword. Let us consider the case of a couple who marry in a country which involves compulsory sharing of all movables, whenever acquired. The wife is mistreated by her husband, so she leaves him and goes to a country with a separate property regime. Receiving no financial support from her husband, she then buys a small house there. Why is it necessarily a good rule that her husband, who chose to stay in the first country, should be entitled to a half-share in the house? Yet that conclusion would appear to follow from requiring the joint abandonment of the original regime.

Assuming that the principle of mutability is to be permitted to have some role, the question arises as to when spouses should be regarded as having changed their matrimonial property regime. Formerly, when the regime applicable at the start of the marriage was generally determined by reference to the husband's domicile, the courts would merely have to examine whether the husband's domicile had changed. But, as we have seen,[41] the present law is less simple, and it seems clear that the determination of the applicable original regime depends on more considerations than that of the husband's domicile alone. Equally, it would seem that what constitutes a change of regime necessarily must be determined by similar wide-ranging criteria.

It is surely reasonable that, in determining the effects of a change of regime, the Court should seek to protect both spouses from injustice or unnecesary hardship. In extreme cases at least, constitutional considerations may require that a spouse should not be rendered destitute by an attempted unilateral change of regime by an economically stronger partner.[42]

---

[36] Cf. *Dicey & Morris*, 672.

[37] Cf. H. Marsh, *Marital Property in Conflict of Laws*, 105 (1952). Legislation protecting the interests of creditors would, of course, go some way towards mitigating the effects of this problem: cf. Leflar, *Community Property and Conflict of Laws*, 21 Calif. L. Rev. 221, at 235 (1933).

[38] Cf. *Cheshire & North*, 579-581, *Castel*, vol. 1, 421, Shava, *Israeli Conflict of Laws Relating to Matrimonial Property — A Comparative Commentary*, 31 Int. & Comp. L.Q. 307, at 313-314 (1982).

[39] Cf. The Canadian cases of *Pink* v. *Perlin & Co.*, 40 N.S.R. 260 (Meagher,J., 1898) (esp. at 262) and *Re Heung Won Lee*, 36 D.L.R. (2d) 177 (B.C. Sup. Ct., Verchere, J., 1962).

[40] See *Cheshire & North*, 580-581. Cf. *McKinney* v. *McKinney*, 17 R.F.L. (2d) 308 (B.C. Sup. Ct., Spencer, L.J.S.C., 1980), distinguished in *Woodward* v. *Woodward*, [1981] 6 W.W.R. 385 (B.C. Sup. Ct., Andrews, L.J.S.C.).

[41] *Supra*, pp. 417-418.

[42] Cf. H. Marsh, *Marital Property in Conflict of Laws*, 105-106 (1952), Juenger, *Marital Property and the Conflict of Laws: A Tale of Two Countries*, 81 Colum. L. Rev. 1081, at 1074-1075 (1981), Leflar, *Community Property and the Conflict of Laws*, 21 Calif. L. Rev. 221, at 237-238 (1933), Welling, *Comment: The Uniform Disposition of Community Property Rights as Death Act*, 65 Ky. L.J. 541, at 543-546 (1976), Gardner, *Comment: Marital Property and the Conflict of Laws: The Constitutionality of the "Quasi-Community" Property Legislation*, 54 Calif. L. Rev. 252 (1966), Oldham, *Property Division in a Texas Divorce of a Migrant Spouse: Heads He Wins, Tails She Loses?*, 19 Houston L.

Such analysis of the question as has been provided in Irish law was in decisions[43] in the nineteenth century, which have today a very dated air. We have already noted *Hutchinson* v. *Cathcart*.[44] Another significant decision is *In re Lett's Trusts and Trustee Relief Act; Ex parte Lett*,[45] in 1881. A married woman and her husband, domiciled in Ireland at the date of their marriage, emigrated to New York where they became domiciled.[46] No settlement had been executed when they married. The wife became entitled to a share of an intestate's estate in Ireland, which was lodged in court under the Trustee Relief Act. She presented a petition for payment of the fund to herself, adducing evidence that, under New York law, a married woman was entitled to receive such a share as if she were a *feme sole*.

Counsel for the petitioner argued that "[t]he law of the actual domicil regulates the rights of the parties" to the fund; since the spouses had changed their domicile, "their mutual rights to personal property now depend on the law of the State in which they are now domiciled".[47] *Story*[48] was again cited in support. Although the report records merely that the Vice-Chancellor made an order that the fund be paid out to the petitioner, this case affords strong support for the "mutability" approach.

ASSIGNMENT WHERE THERE IS AN ANTE-NUPTIAL CONTRACT

Where the spouses make an ante-nuptial contract regulating their future proprietary relations, it will govern their proprietary relations,[49] not only in the original matrimonial domicile but also in any other domicile that they may later acquire.[50] The contract may, of course, be made expressly between the parties.[51] Moreover, in the leading, but controversial, English decision of *Re De Nicols, De Nicols* v. *Curlier*,[52] the House of Lords held that such a contract might be made tacitly. The spouses, both of French nationality and domicile, were married in Paris. They made no express contract as to their proprietary rights. Their property, both present and future, thus became subjected by French law[53] to a system of

---

Rev. 1, at 37ff (1981), *In re Thornton's Estate*, 1 Cal. (2d) 1, 33 P. (2d) 1 (1934). For criticism, see Neuner, *Marital Property and the Conflict of Laws*, 5 La. L. Rev. 167, at 175, fn. 32 (1943). Cf. R.E.P., *Comment*, 15 Calif. L. Rev. 399 (1927), whose argument in defence of constitutionality bears a striking resemblance to that favoured by the Supreme Court in *O'B.* v. *S.*, [1984] I.R. 316, echoing the approach adopted by Mr. Justice Lee in *Eyre* v. *Jacob*, 14 Gratt, (Va.) 422, at 427, 73 Am. Dec. 367, at 372 (1858); but see Leflar, *supra*, at 237, fn 67.

[43] *Hutchinson* v. *Cathcart*, 8 Ir. Eq. Rep. 394 (Equity Exch., 1846), *In re Lett's Trusts and Trustee Relief Act; Ex parte Lett*,7 L.R. (Ir.) 132 (Chatterton, V.-C., 1881).

[44] *Supra*.

[45] 7 L.R. (Ir.) 132 (Chatterton, V.-C., 1881).

[46] The statement of the facts merely decribes the spouses as being "American citizens and resident in the State of New York", but both the headnote and the report of counsel's submissions refer to the spouses as having a domicile in New York.

[47] 7 L.R. (Ir.), at 133.

[48] *Story*, s. 171. Cf. the English decision of *Lashley* v. *Hog.*, 2 Coop. t. Cott. 449, 47 E.R. 1243 (1804), which includes dicta wide enough to embrace the doctrine of mutability: see Rafferty, *Matrimonial Property and the Conflict of Laws*, 20 U.W. Ont. L. Rev. 177, at 192 (1982); but the case has also been interpreted as one involving merely a rule of succession to movables: cf. *De Nichols* v. *Curlier*, [1900] A.C. 211, at 27 (H.L.(Eng.), *per* Lord Halsbury, L.C.), *Cheshire & North*, 577-578, Goldberg, *The Assignment of Property on Marriage*, 19 Int. & Comp. L.Q. 557, at 580-584 (1970). *Dicey & Morris*, 671, adopt a substantially neutral position on this question. See further Burns, *Nichols* v. *Curlier Revisited*, 14 Osgoode Hall L.J. 797 (1976).

[49] Cf. *Heywood* v. *Heywood*, 29 Bev. 9, 54 E.R. 527 (1860) considered by J. Chipman Gray, *The Rule Against Perpetueties*, para. 261 (4th ed., 1942).

[50] *Cheshire & North*, 581.

[51] Cf. Rafferty, *Matrimonial Property and the Conflict of Laws*, 20 U.W. Ont. L. Rev. 177, at 179 (1982), *Devos* v. *Devos*, 10 D.L.R. (3d) 603 (Ont. C.A., 1970).

[52] [1900] A.C. 21 (H.L.(Eng.), 1899), analysed by Burns, *De Nichols* v. *Curlier Revisited*, 14 Osgoode Hall L.J. 797 (1976).

[53] Cf. especially articles 1393 and 1401 of the French Civil Code.

community of goods. The parties later went to live in England, where they became domiciled. The husband died there, still with an English domicile, leaving a will which disregarded his widow's rights under the French doctrine of community of goods. The widow took proceedings in England seeking her community share of the moveable property.[54]

The House of Lords held that under French law the spouses by marrying had entered into an implied matrimonial property contract, which had not been shaken off by the change of domicile. The widow was therefore entitled to a half share of the community assets.

Lord Halsbury, L.C. noted that it had not been denied that if, instead of the law creating these obligations on the mere celebration of the marriage, the parties had themselves by written instrument recited in terms the very contract the law made for them, the change of domicile could not have affected such written contract. He was:

> "wholly unable to understand why the mere putting into writing the very same contract which the law created between them without any writing at all should bar the husband from altering the contract relations between himself and his wife; when if the law creates that contract relation, then the husband is not barred from getting rid of the obligation which upon his marriage the law affixed to the transaction."[55]

The notion of implied contract endorsed in *De Nichols* had been criticised by several writers[56] on the basis that it is fictional to regard the spouses as "choosing" a system specifically prescribed by the law to cater for cases where spouses exercise *no* express choice, especially where the spouses may not even have been aware of this rule. It would, however, be wrong to regard *De Nichols* as adopting an inflexible approach: it is only where the law of the domicile actually implies a matrimonial contract that this implied choice will be attributed to the parties.[57]

De Nicols leaves unresolved some interesting questions. First, it may be asked whether the notion of implied choice of a matrimonial regime can apply to a system of *deferred* community of property, where the spouses during the marriage are generally not entitled to any specific share in each other's property but, on a "day of reckoning" (on divorce, for example), may be awarded a share whether on a pre-ordained or discretionary basis.[58] One commentator has expressed the view that *De Nicols* should not apply to this type of regime because it lacks "the element of partnership during the marriage",[59] but he considers that a different rule could presumably apply if it were "specifically provided"[60] that the regime constituted a contract between the spouses.

---

[54] Cf. *Re De Nicols (No. 2)* [1900] 2 Ch. 410, which dealt with the immoveable property.

[55] [1900] A.C., at 26. See also *id.*, at 33 (*per* Lord Macnaghten), 37 (*per* Lord Shand) and at 44-46 (*per* Lord Brampton).

[56] Cf. *Beale*, 1015, *Falconbridge*, 108-109, H. Marsh, *Marital Property in Conflict of Laws*, 106 (1952), Burns, *supra*, at 801, Anon., *Note: Marital Property Rights and the Conflict of Laws*, 43 Harv. L. Rev. 1286, at 1289 (1930). Goodrich, *Matrimonial Domicile*, 27 Yale L.J. 49, at 58 (1917) observes: "Any explanation of marital rights on the basis of a tacit consent flies in the face of the facts. Laymen generally know very little about the law until they get involved in a lawsuit, and two young people anxious to wed do not sit up nights reading up on the law of matrimonial property."

[57] Cf. *Dicey & Morris*, 658-659, Rafferty, *supra*, at 187-188.

[58] See Hahlo, *A Note on Deferred Community of Gains: Theory and the Practice*, 21 McGill L.J. 589 (1975).

[59] Rafferty, *supra*, at 190. But see Waters, *Matrimonial Property Entitlements and the Quebec Conflicts of Law*, 22 McGill L.J. 315, at 318 (1976):
> "If the domicile of the parties at the time of their marriage solves the property entitlement of the parties by providing that they shall be 'separate as to property', but have the statutory right to seek the exercise of an extensive judicial discretion to allocate assets when the marriage ends, it is a total misrepresentation of that law for another jurisdiction — normally a civil law jurisdiction — to hold simply that they are separate as to property."

[60] Rafferty, *supra*, at 191. Whether the author envisages an express contract between the spouses or a specific provision in the legislation is not made clear.

The second question is whether *De Nicols* extends to a regime of complete separation of property. By way of analogy with the facts in *De Nicols*, it may be argued that our courts should interpret as an implied choice of such a regime the act of spouses who marry under a law prescribing separation of property for those who do not make an express contract. As against this it has been suggested that "to say that the spouses remain separate as to property is to reject the notion that the marriage has any effect on the spouses' proprietary relations".[61] This view may be doubted. A system of separation of property for spouses does not ignore the marriage; rather, it gives effect to the social policy that spouses should have separate entitlements to property. The values at the base of such a policy are deeply immersed in the important issue of what rights should flow from marriage.[62] If it was right that Monsieur De Nicols should continue to be bound by the values underlying the social policy of articles 1393 and 1401 of the French Civil Code long after he and his wife had moved to England, why should it be wrong for a spouse moving from a system of separation, to one of community of property, to continue to invoke the values of the former?

The final question raised by *De Nicols* is the extent to which an express or implied choice of a matrimonial property system should affect immovables. In *Re De Nicols; De Nicols v. Curlier (No. 2)*,[63] Kekewich, J. held that the French Civil Code extended the spouses' community of property regime to immoveable property situated in England. He adopted *Story's* statement that where there is any "special nuptial contract"[64] between the parties, it "ought to be carried into effect everywhere, under the general limitations and exceptions belonging to all other classes of contracts".[65] He considered that nothing in English law rendered the contract unenforceable so far as the immoveable property was concerned. The Statute of Frauds did not apply since the spouses' implied contract should be viewed as an agreement of partnership of parol, which fell outside the scope of the Statute.[66]

In *Callwood v. Callwood*,[67] the Privy Council distinguished *De Nicols (No. 2)* on the basis that the Danish system of community of property, the law of the matrimonial domicile, did not extend to immovables outside the jurisdiction of the country of the matrimonial domicile.[68] There was thus no need to address the "difficult question" of whether to apply Danish law or the *lex situs*,[69] English law, the latter option being "in accordance with the general rule".[70]

---

[61] Rafferty, *supra*, at 190.

[62] Cf. *supra*, pp. 414-415.

[63] [1900] 2 Ch. 410. Contrast *In re Majot's Estate*, 199 N.Y. 29, 92 N.E. 402 (Ct. Apps., 1910), noted 10 Colum. L. Rev. 147 (1910), *Saul v. His Creditors*, 5 Mar. (n.s.) 569, 16 Am. Dec. 212 (La., 1827); and see Juenger, *Marital Property and the Conflict of Laws: A Tale of Two Countries*, 81 Colum. L. Rev. 1061, at 1072-1073 (1981), Neuner, *Marital Property and the Conflict of Laws*, 5 La. L. Rev. 167, at 183-184 (1943), Horowitz, *Conflict of Law Problems in Community Property — II*, II Wash. L. Rev. 212, at 213-214 (1936), Delaume, *Marital Property and American-French Conflict of Laws*, 4 Am. J. of Comp. L. 35, at 45-46 (1955).

[64] *Story*, section 159.

[65] *Id.*

[66] Cf. *Forster v. Hale*, 3 Ves. 696, 30 E.R. 1226 (1798), 5 Ves. 308, 31 E.R. 603 (1800), *Dale v. Hamilton*, 5 Hare 369, 67 E.R. 955 (1846). Cf. *In re Majot's Estate*, 199 N.Y. 29, 92 N.E. 402 (Ct. App., 1910).

[67] [1960] A.C. 659 (P.C.).

[68] The Island of St. Thomas in the Danish Virgin Islands.

[69] The country in question was Great Thatch Island in the British Virgin Islands.

[70] [1960] A.C., at 683, citing *Welch v. Tennent*, [1891] A.C. 639. Cf. the unsatisfactory Canadian decision of *Rail v. Rail*, 12 R.F.L. (2d) 265 (Ont. High Ct., 1979), where Soubliere, L.J.S.C. professed (at 271) to rely on *De Nicols (No. 2)* but applied the *lex situs* without any express consideration of the "implied contract" theory. See further Rafferty, *supra* at 189-190.

SPECIFIC ISSUES

Let us now consider a number of specific issues relating to marriage settlements. It is well established that the proper law generally governs the essential validity, interpretation and effect of marriage settlements.[71] But what is the proper law? The normal rules for finding the proper law of a contract[72] apply to marriage settlements but the courts have laid a considerable emphasis on the law of the matrimonial domicile. In *In re Cloncurry's Estate*,[73] Sullivan, P. observed that the authorities[74] established the proposition that, "in the absence of an indication of a contrary intention, a marriage settlement is to be construed according to the law of the matrimonial domicile".[75]

In this case the Revenue Commissioners claimed estate duty on the property comprised in the marriage settlement of Lord Cloncurry, as being property passing on his death. At the date of the settlement and at the time of the marriage, Lord Cloncurry was domiciled in what became the Irish Free State. The marriage, to an English woman, resident in England, took place in England. Of the three trustees of the settlement, two lived in England and the third had no fixed residence. The settlement was drawn up in England by English solicitors. It authorised a wide range of investments, including investments in land in England, but not in Ireland. No part of the trust funds at any time consisted of Irish property; the bonds or certificates representing the trust funds were held in an English bank.

The Supreme Court, affirming the High Court, held that the settlement was English and accordingly that estate duty was not payable in the Irish Free State. Sullivan, P. said:

"From the contents of the marriage settlement in the present case and from the circumstances in which it was executed, I felt little difficulty in drawing the inference that the parties intended that the legal control of the settled property should be in England and that the forum for deciding any question arising under the settlement should be an English Court. No inference can be drawn from the form of the settlement, that being a form common to both countries, but I think some weight must be attached to the investment clauses, particularly to the authorisation of investment in lands situated in England and Wales but not in Ireland. The most material considerations, however, are: (1) that none of the three original trustees had a residence in the area now comprising the Irish Free State, two of them had residences in England, while the third had no fixed residence; and (2) that from the date of the settlement the bonds and certificates representing the trust funds were held in Barclay's Bank in London in the names of the trustees, and the control and investment of the trust funds were retained in England.

In these circumstances I think that the legal control of the property was in England and that the natural and proper forum to enforce the rights of persons entitled under the settlement would be an English Court; and I am satisfied that the parties so intended ...''[76]

And Hanna, J. said:

---

[71] *Dicey & Morris*, Rule 114(1).

[72] Cf. *infra*, pp. 521-533.

[73] [1932] I.R. 687, at 704 (High Ct., 1931, aff'd by Sup. Ct., 1932).

[74] *In re Bankers, Reynolds* v. *Ellis*, [1902] 2 Ch. 333 (Buckley, J.), *In re Hewitt's Settlement, Hewitt* v. *Hewitt*, [1915] 1 Ch. 228, at 232 (Eve, J., 1914). *Dicey*, 4th ed., p. 713 was also quoted as an authority. *In re MacKenzie, Mackenzie* v. *Edwards — Moss*, [1911] 1 Ch. 578, at 596 when Swinfen Eady, J. said:
"As a general rule, the law of the matrimonial domicil is applicable to a contract in consideration of marriage, but this is not an absolute rule; it yields to the intention of the parties, either expressed, or to be gathered from all the circumstances of the case."

[75] [1932] I.R., at 704.

[76] *Id.*, at 704-705.

"In my opinion the law to be applied in testing this question is quite clear. The only difficulty is in its application.

The law applicable to a marriage settlement is *prima facie* the law of the matrimonial domicile, unless there is either an expressed intention in the deed that the law of some other country is to apply, or unless such an intention can be legitimately inferred from the special surrounding circumstances, including the domicile or residence of the persons bound by the settlement, in terms, and the locality and nature and legal control of the property settled."[77]

Applying this test to the facts of the case, Hanna, J. also considered that the settlement was English.[78]

The Supreme Court affirmed. Murnaghan, J., for the Court, said:

"From an examination of the various authorities which have been dealt with by the President it will be seen that no universal rule or test can be applied, and that the Court must ascertain from all the circumstances whether the property in question is settled by a settlement which has the character of a Free State settlement or which has the character of an English settlement. Various *indicia* have been relied upon. The Revenue authorities point out that Lord Cloncurry must be considered as having an Irish Free State domicile at the date of the settlement and that he continued so domiciled until his death; they say that the law of the matrimonial domicile is the proper law for interpreting the marriage settlement. They further say that so far as any inference can be drawn from the place of residence of the trustees it supports their contention. On the other hand we think that it is of importance that the settlement was drawn and prepared by English solicitors. This was done in accordance with the usual rule that the settlement is prepared by the lady's solicitors — and we think it is the fact that no difference existed at this time between the English law and the law of Ireland. But the professional gentlemen who drafted the settlement did not profess knowledge of any law save that of England. The control of the investments has always been in London, and the securities have been retained there ...

Having regard to the matters already mentioned and to the several considerations relied upon by the President, we are of opinion that they outweigh any countervailing considerations, and that the succession was created by an English settlement, and that the funds dealt with by the settlement would not have been liable to succesion duty in the Irish Free State before 1894 and, accordingly, that the property is not within the Finance Act, 1894, as applied by our Finance Act, 1923."[79]

Capacity[80]

The question of capacity in relation to marriage settlements is a most controversial one. Oversimplifying matters somewhat, it may be said that the decisions, in the main, support the view that the *lex domicilii* of the party whose capacity is in issue should control, while most of the commentators favour the proper law of the contract as the governing law.

Much discussion has centred around three cases. In the first, *Re Cooke's Trusts*[81] a young woman, domiciled in England, while still a minor married a domiciled Frenchman in France. Before the marriage she made a notarial contract in France.

[77] *Id.*, at 705.
[78] O'Byrne, J. concurred with the conclusion at which Sullivan, P. and Hanna, J. arrived: *id.*, at 707.
[79] *Id.*, at 712-713. See also *Revenue Commissioners* v. *Pelly*, [1940] I.R. 122, at 128-129 (High Ct., *per* Hanna, J., 1939), *Iveagh* v. *I.R.C.*, [1954] Ch. 364 (Upjohn, J.). Cf. *Duke of Marlborough* v. *A.G.*, [1945] Ch. 78 (C.A., 1944), criticised by Morris, *Note*, 61 L.Q. Rev. 223 (1945).
[80] See Morris, *Capacity to Make a Marriage Settlement Contract in English Private International Law*, 54 L.Q.R. 78 (1938), Goldberg, *The Assignment of Property on Marriage*, 19 Int. & Comp. L.Q. 557, at 569-573 (1970), Clarence Smith, *Capacity in the Conflict of Laws: A Comparative Study*, 1 Int. & Comp. L.Q. 446, at 446, 450-452 (1952).
[81] 56 L.T. 737 (1887).

Six years after the marriage she separated from her husband. Some time later, wrongly believing him dead, she went through a ceremony of marriage with an Englishman. She then went with this man to New South Wales where they became domiciled. Her true husband died only twenty-five years later. She died the following year, having disposed of her property as an Englishwoman. Her three children argued that the notarial contract precluded their mother from depriving them of vested shares to her estate.[82] Stirling, J. held that her capacity to make the notarial contract was governed by English law, her *lex domicilii* at that time. Stirling, J. relied[83] on passages from Cotton, L.J.'s judgment in *Sottomayor* v. *De Barros*,[84] which have a decidedly dated air in suggesting that *all* contracts should be governed by the law of domicile.

In *Cooper* v. *Cooper*,[85] a young woman aged "about eighteen",[86] and still a minor, domiciled in Ireland, made an antenuptial settlement in Scots form, with her future husband, a domiciled Scotsman. Under the settlement, made in Dublin, the girl purported to relinquish her rights as widow under Scots law. After the marriage the couple went to live in Scotland. Thirty-six years later, when her husband died, domiciled in Scotland, she sought to repudiate the contract. The House of Lords held that she could do so. Lord Halsbury based his rejection on the girl's incapacity under Irish law, her *lex domicilii*.[87] Neither Lord Watson nor Lord Macnaghten was willing to go quite this far; but the fact that the young woman lacked capacity under a law that was the *lex domicilii and* the *lex loci contractus* removed any of their doubts.[88]

The case is blemished by a degree of uncertainty as to what precisely was the Irish law on the subject. The judges agreed that Irish and English law coincided on this question, but Lord Watson considered that the contract might be ratified after majority,[89] while Lord Macnaghten was of the view that the contract was "[p]rima facie ... voidable"[90] and that the woman had "elected to avoid it"[91] twenty-three years after attaining majority! In fact, under Irish law the contract was voidable within a reasonable time after the attainment of majority.[92]

At all events, Lord Watson briefly addressed the question of the effect of transfer from an Irish to a Scottish domicile. He stated that under Scots law any ratification[93] of the contract by the woman after majority "would ... have been recoverable by her as a donation *inter virum et uxorem*".[94] Thus, it appears that, in Lord Watson's view, by the transfer to a Scots domicile the contract's voidable character was replaced, in effect, by a void one.[95] We can only speculate as to what would be the effect of a transfer from a domicile under the law of which a contract is void to a domicile under whose law it is voidable.[96]

[82] This was in fact most unlikely: cf. Morris, *supra*, at 81.

[83] 56 L.T., at 739.

[84] 3 P.D. 1, at 5 (C.A., 1877).

[85] 13 App. Cas. 88 (1888).

[86] *Id.*, at 89, 102.

[87] *Id.*, at 98-99.

[88] Cf. *id.*, at 106 (*per* Lord Watson) and 108 (*per* Lord Macnaghten).

[89] *Id.*, at 106.

[90] *Id.*, at 108.

[91] *Id.*

[92] Cf. *Clark,* 171, and the Law Reform Commission's *Report on Minors' Contracts,* 20-21 (L.R.C. 15-1985). In *Paget* v. *Paget,* 11 L.R. (Ir.) 26 (C.A., 1882), rev'g 9 L.R. (Ir.) 128 (Chatterton, V.C., 1882), a repudiation ten years after majority was held reasonable, where the minor had entered the contract believing himself to be of full age and where, on discovering much later that he had not been, he acted promptly in repudiating the contract.

[93] As we have seen, this is not the correct concept.

[94] 13 App. Cas., at 106.

[95] Cf. *Dicey & Morris,* 665.

[96] Under the Irish law of contract, the concept of "void" contracts which none the less generate rights

In *Viditz* v. *O'Hagan*,[97] the eighteen-year-old daughter of an Irish peer (Viscount Netterville) married a domiciled Austrian in Switzerland. Marriage articles were executed in English form, before the marriage, in Switzerland. This settlement was voidable under English law[98] provided the repudiation took place during or within a reasonable time after her minority. Under Austrian law, she had a right to revoke the settlement at any time. Twenty-nine years later, the couple purported to exercise their right of revocation under Austrian law. The English Court of Appeal held that they were entitled to a declaration that the settlement had been effectively revoked.

It is difficult to be certain about the precise *ratio* of *Viditz* v. *O'Hagan*, Lindley, M.R. was understandably concerned lest the Court commit itself to the "paradox ... that the contract had become irrevocable although the lady never had, either before or after she was married, the capacity to enter into an irrevocable contract".[99] In the opinion of the Master of the Rolls:

"the effect of the change of domicile was that the English doctrine of reasonable time became inapplicable by reason of the impossibility after that change of the wife's effectually ratifying her contract. An alternative view of the case (perhaps it is only the same view in another shape) is that the effect of the change of domicile was to enlarge the reasonable time for repudiation."[100]

Collins, L.J. considered that the rule in English law that repudiation must be within a reasonable time of reaching majority rested on the implication that the voidable contract, after this time had expired, must be presumed to have been ratified and therefore to be incapable of being avoided. Thus, when the wife was debarred by Austrian law from making an irrevocable election, she could not be presumed to have made it.[101]

Essential Validity

As has been mentioned,[102] the essential validity of a marriage settlement is governed by its proper law. As with commercial contracts, the proper law includes subsequent changes in that law. Thus in *Trustees Executors & Agency Co. Ltd.* v. *Margottini*,[103] a decision of the Victoria Supreme Court, the statutory abolition of restraint upon anticipation in England was held to apply to a marriage settlement, the proper law of which was English law, even though the property, the subject of the trust, was in Australia and the trustee was a Victorian company.

Formal Validity

It is now clear that a marriage settlement will be formally valid if it complies with

---

has given rise to much discussion: cf. the Law Reform Commission's *Report on Minors' Contracts*, 23-25 (L.R.C. 15-1985).

[97] [1900] 2 Ch. 87 (C.A.).

[98] Although the young woman was described as "an Irish lady" (*id.*, at 96 (*per* Lindley, M.R.)), the report does not indicate what her domicile was, nor where she had been reared. Her father's estate when he died eighteen years later consisted chiefly of real estate in Ireland (*id.*, at 89). At all events, the Court proceeded on the basis that English rather than Irish law was in question, perhaps because the Court considered there was no difference between the two.

[99] *Id.*, at 98. In one sense this statement is misleading: under English (and Irish) law, the young woman *had* capacity to enter a contract which might *become* irrevocable, depending on her conduct before and for a reasonable time after attaining full age.

[100] *Id.*

[101] *Id.*, at 100. See also *id.*, at 97-98 (*per* Lindley, M.R.), Clarence Smith, *supra*, at 451, captures the point well: "[S]ilence for an unreasonable time makes [the contract] binding not as a failure to revoke but as an implied affirmation".

[102] *Supra*, p. 423.

[103] [1960] V.R. 417 (Sup. Ct., Deane, J.).

Irish Conflicts of Law

either the *lex loci contractus*[104] *or* its proper law.[105]

Interpretation

As a general rule questions of interpretation of a marriage settlement are determined by its proper law.[106] In *In re Boate's Estate*,[107] the question arose as to whether a reference in a marriage settlement to raising "£5,000 of lawful British money" as portions for the younger children of the marriage should be interpreted as referring to British or Irish money. At the time of the settlement, in 1813, the two currencies were on parity, but a later devaluation of the Irish currency in 1826 made the issue a live one.

There were some Irish factors in the case: the husband was domiciled in Ireland, the lands on which the money was to be raised was Irish, and one of the two trustees was Irish. But the English connections were so strong that the Court considered itself obliged to hold that the settlement referred to British currency. The wife was English, as was her father, and at the time of the settlement the husband, a captain in the Waterford Militia, was in England. In the view of Brady, L.C., the "most important"[108] of the circumstances was "the place where the contract is made".[109]

The Lord Chancellor observed:

"Here is a contract made in England, the parties speaking in England, and plainly designating the money to be raised, 'lawful British money', about which, in England, no possible ambiguity could arise. In Ireland those words might have an ambiguous meaning for, in Ireland they might import that the money was to be paid in the currency of Ireland, which would be lawful British money, inasmuch as the money was counted in England... No doubt, [the husband] may say, 'I am contracting to pay Irish money, and why should I pay more?' But the question is, looking at the entire instrument, what did the contracting parties mean? [The husband] may or may not have known what he was contracting to pay, but there is nothing in this deed to show that the other parties contemplated anything but a contract for a sum in gross, of lawful British money."[110]

Proceedings Under Section 12 of the Married Women's Status Act 1957

We now must consider the conflicts aspects to section 12 of the Married Women's Status Act 1957. This important provision, the successor to section 17 of the Married Women's Property Act 1882, does not address the conflicts issue with any clarity. Subsection (1) provides that the section applies to the determination of "any question arising between husband and wife as to the title to or possession of any property". Thus the subsection provides no specific limits as to the location of the property or the connection between the spouses and the State. However, the reference in subsection (3) to "personal property" and "land" rather than to "movables" and "immovables", suggests that the draftsman did not have conflicts questions in mind. This seems even more likely in view of the fact that this subsection refers to "the rateable valuation of the land", which clearly envisages Irish land.

In England, the courts have considered conflicts aspects of section 17 of the 1882 Act, which originally applied to Ireland as well as England. The section provided that "[i]n any question between husband and wife as to the title to or possession of property", either party might apply in a summary way "to any judge of the High

---

[104] *Guépratte* v. *Young*, 4 De G. & Sm. 217, 64 E.R. 804 (1851).
[105] Cf. *Re Bankes*, [1902] 2 Ch. 333, *Van Grutten* v. *Digby*, 31 Beav. 561, 54 E.R. 1256 (1863).
[106] *Dicey & Morris*, Rule 114(1).
[107] 10 Ir. Chy. Rep. 164 (Ch. App., 1859).
[108] *Id.*, at 171.
[109] *Id.*
[110] *Id.*

Court of Justice in England or in Ireland, according as such property is in England or in Ireland ..." In *Razelos* v. *Razelos (No. 2)*,[111] Baker, J. observed that at first sight this provision might seem to mean that only property in England could be the subject of a succession in England, and property in Ireland was specifically the subject of a summons in Ireland, and that therefore, under the section, no property other than property in England could be within the jurisdiction of the English courts. But, on reflection, he had come to the conclusion that the framers of the Act "were unlikely to have had in their minds nice questions of international law. They were merely defining the machinery for enforcing the claims in Ireland as distinct from England."[112]

In *Razelos (No. 2)* the English court was held not to have lost jurisdiction where shares that had been under the husband's control in London had been sent by him out of his possession to the United States. Moreover, in view of Baker, J.'s interpretation of section 17, the court made an order affecting land in Greece where the husband was present in England at the time the summons was issued and no evidence had been adduced that an order affecting the land in Greece would be ineffective.

It seems that there must be property or an identifiable fund on which an order under section 12 can operate.[113] Where all the property is outside the jurisdiction this may present an insurmountable hurdle. Where, however, this problem does not present itself it seems that ordinary jurisdictional rules will operate. Thus, the presence of the respondent spouse within the jurisdiction, or his or her submission to jurisdiction will suffice. It would, moreover, seem possible for the Court in appropriate cases to make an order for service out of the jurisdiction under Rule 1 of Order 11 of the Rules of the Superior Courts 1986.

So far as choice of law is concerned, it appears that the Court in proceedings under section 12 should apply the rules of the matrimonial property regime governing the spouses.[114] This may present practical difficulties for the court, but clearly a blind application of the *lex fori* could be the source of great injustice.

---

[111] [1970] 1 W.L.R. 392, at 402 (P.D.A. Div., Baker, J., 1969).

[112] *Id.*

[113] See *Tunstall* v. *Tunstall*, [1953] 1 W.L.R. 770 (C.A.), as explained in *In re Bettinson's Question*, [1956] Ch. 67 (Wynn-Parry, J., 1955).

[114] Cf. *In re Bettinson's Question, supra*, which could perhaps be given a narrower interpretation than the proposition for which it is here cited.

CHAPTER 23

SUCCESSION[1]

When the estate of a deceased person has been cleared of debts, the administrator must distribute the property among those to whom it beneficially belongs. The position where the deceased dies intestate differs from that where the deceased dies testate. As a general principle[2] the *lex situs* governs succession to immovables and the *lex domicilii* at the time of death determines succession to movables. These rules are subject to some fairly important qualifications, especially in relation to testate succession and powers of appointment.

Let us first consider intestate succession before going on to examine the position relating to testate succession.

INTESTATE SUCCESSION

(a) Movables

It is a long-established rule that succession to moveable property in the case of intestacy is distributed according to the *lex domicilii* of the testator at the time of death.[3] This rule applies only to succession "in the strict sense of that term."[4] It does not apply to the right of a State to take ownerless property as *bona vacantia* or *jus regale*.

The issue was analysed by the English Court of Appeal in *In the Estate of Maldonado, Deceased, State of Spain v. Treasury Solicitor,*[5] in 1953. There, the Court held that the Spanish State, as *ultimus heres,* should succeed to the estate of a woman domiciled in Spain. Against this view, it had been argued that the distinction between succession by a sovereign state as *ultimus heres*[6] and the appropriation of

---

[1] See generally *Rabel*, vol. 4, part 13, *Wolff*, chs. 38-41, W. Breslauer, *The Private International Law of Succession in England, America and Germany* (1937), F. Boulanger, *Les successions internationales: problèmes contemporains* (1981), N. Bentwich, *The Law of Domicile in its Relation to Succession* (1911), von Overbeck, *Divers aspects de l'unification du droit international privé, spécialement en matière de succession,* [1961] — III Recueil des cours 529, Hickey, *Irish Private International Law,* 42 Rabels Zeitschrift 268, at 286-291 (1978). Lewald, *Questions de droit international des sucessions,* [1925] — IV Recueil des cours 1, Scoles, *Conflict of Laws and Nonbarrable Interests in Administration of Decedents' Estates,* 8 U. Fla. L. Rev. 151 (1955). Plimpton, *Conflict of Laws and the Disposition of Decedants' Movables,* 24 Me. L. Rev. 43 (1972), Carteaux, *Comment, Conflicts of Law and Successions: Comprehensive Interest Analysis As a Viable Alternative to the Traditional Approach,* 59 Tul. L. Rev. 389 (1984).
[2] *In bonis G.M. Deceased; F.M.* v. *T.A.M.*, 106 I.L.T.R. 82, at 86 (High Ct., Kenny, J., 1970).
[3] See *In bonis Gentili, Deceased,* I.R. 9 Eq. 541 (Prob., Warren, J., 1875), Miller's *Irish Probate Practice,* 174 (Maxwell ed., 1900), *Pipon* v. *Pipon,* Amb. 25, 27 E.R. 14 (1744), *Thorne* v. *Watkins,* 2 Ves. Sen. 35, 28 E.R. 24 (1750), *Bruce* v. *Bruce,* 6 Bro. P.C. 566, 2 E.R. 1271 (1790), *Balfour* v. *Scott,* 6 Bro. P.C. 550, 2 E.R. 1259 (1793), *Somerville* v. *Somerville,* 5 Ves. Jun. 750, 31 E.R. 839 (1793).
[4] *Dicey & Morris,* 611.
[5] [1954] P. 223 (C.A., 1953, aff'g Barnard, J.).
[6] Which is also the position under Irish law: Succession Act 1965, section 73 (1).

bona vacantia by a foreign state was "a mere matter of words".[7] Jenkins, L.J. responded:

> "This argument is not without persuasive force, but I do not think that the question can truly be said to be one of distinction without difference. The foreign state can only succeed under its own law of succession where the succession is governed by that law. On the other hand, where the case is not one of succession, but of appropriation of ownerless property, the right applies to any ownerless property which may be reached by the law of the foreign state concerned, irrespective of the law by which its devolution is governed, provided only that by the relevant law it is in fact ownerless."[8]

(b) Immovables

It is well established that where a person with an interest in immovables dies intestate, the *lex situs* determines the question of descent or distribution. This is so, regardless of the domicile of the intestate person.[9]

This rule can present particular difficulties where legislation in more than one country confers on a surviving spouse or a member of the family of the deceased intestate person, a specific entitlement to a portion of the estate. This matter is considered in detail below.[10]

TESTAMENTARY SUCCESSION

The general rule in Ireland[11] and other common law jurisdictions is that the *lex domicilii* of the testator at the time of his death exclusively determines testamentary succession to his moveable property,[12] and that the *lex situs* governs testamentary succession to his immoveable property. The fact that Irish assets must be administered in accordance with Irish law does not detract from this principle, since the duty of the Irish executor will be to distribute the moveable property to the persons entitled under the *lex domicilii*.

Let us consider the various questions that arise in testamentary succession.

Capacity

(a) Movables

The capacity of a testator is detemined by the law of his or her domicile.[13] In the English decision of *In the Estate of Fuld (No. 3); Hartley* v. *Fuld*,[14] Scarman, J.said that he knew of no distinction drawn between "lack of capacity due to immaturity or status and incapacity arising from ill health".

There is no problem where the testator has the same domicile at the time of making the will and at his death; but a difficulty arises where the testator has changed his

---

[7] [1954] P., at 248. Cf. *Anton*, 517, Lipstein, [1954] Camb. L.J. 22, at 25-26, L.C.B. G[ower], 17 Modern L. Rev. 167 (1954); Ehrenzweig, *Characterization in the Conflict of Laws: An Unwelcome Addition to American Doctrine*, in *XXth Century Comparative and Conflict Law: Legal Essays in Honor of Hessel Yntema*, 395, at 403 (1961). See, however, Cohn, 17 Modern L. Rev. 381 (1954).
[8] [1954] P., at 248.
[9] *In bonis Gentili*, I.R. 9 Eq. 541 (Warren, J., 1875), *De Fogassieras* v. *Duport*, 11 L.R. Ir. 123 (Warren, J., 1881), *In re Rea deceased; Rea* v. *Rea*, [1902] 1 I.R. 451 (Porter, M.R.), *Cheshire & North*, 511. See also *Murray* v. *Champernowne*, [1901] 2 I.R. 232, at 236 (Q.B. Div., Prob., Andrews, J., 1900), *In re Stoughton, Deceased*, [1941] I.R. 166, at 178 (High Ct., *per* Hanna, J., 1940).
[10] *Infra*, pp. 435-441.
[11] *Cheshire & North*, 599. See also *Re Adams, Deceased. Bank of Ireland Trustee Co.* v. *Adams*, [1967] I.R. 424 (High Ct., Budd, J., 1966).
[12] *Cheshire & North*, 599; *Re Adams, Deceased. Bank of Ireland Trustee Co.* v. *Adams*, *supra*, at 454, quoting from *Whicker* v. *Hume*, 7 H.L. Cas. 124, at 156, 11 E.R. 50, at 63 (*per* Lord Cranworth, 1858).
[13] *Cheshire & North*, 599.
[14] [1968] P. 675, at 696.
[15] Cf. *Wolff*, 581, who mentions, but does not accept, this argument.

domicile between making the will and the time of his death. The commentators are divided on the question whether capacity should be tested by the testator's *lex domicilii* at the time of the making of the will or at the time of his death. In favour of referring to the time of the testator's death, it may be said that the will confers no rights prior to his death.[15] Moreover, other conflicts aspects of succession, such as the essential validity of wills of movables, and intestate succession to movables, take the time of death as their reference point.[16]

In favour of making the time of the will control the outcome, it has been pointed out that certain types of incapacity, such as unsoundness of mind or minority, may not be validated by subsequent events: "[n]o will can be valid unless it is valid when made. On principle it makes no difference that the subsequent event consists in a change of domicil to a new country where the law has a more favourable rule for capacity."[17] This point is a strong one, but should perhaps be restricted to cases of personal, rather than proprietary,[18] capacity,[19] which should better be regarded as involving the question of essential validity.[20]

Rather than making one of these two times the *sole* controlling factor in determining matters of capacity, it would, of course, be possible for our law to require that the testator have capacity at both[21] or, far more generously, either,[22] of these times.

This latter solution gains some support from a similarly "liberal"[23] approach prevailing in relation to the capacity of a legatee to receive a legacy of movables: it will suffice if the legatee has capacity either by the law of his own domicile or by the law of the testator's domicile, which ever first occurs. Thus, if a testator, domiciled in England gives a legacy to his nephew, domiciled in Ireland, and the boy is aged sixteen, the boy may receive the legacy on reaching full age in Ireland by marrying under the age of eighteen,[24] even though in England eighteen is the age of majority in all cases.[25] The converse case arose in *Donohue* v. *Donohue*[26] in 1887, where funds in Ireland, placed to the separate credit of a minor domiciled in Missouri, were paid out on her reaching the age of eighteen, the age of majority in Missouri though not in Ireland.

(b) Immovables

So far as capacity is concerned there is general agreement[27] that the *lex situs* should govern, though clear judicial authority is hard to come by.[28]

---

[16] *Graveson*, 485.

[17] *Cheshire & North*, 600.

[18] As, for example, the power to disinherit one's spouse.

[19] Cf. *Dicey & Morris*, Rule 99.

[20] Cf. *id.*, 615, and *infra*, pp. 434-441. See also *Re Adams Deceased; Bank of Ireland Trustee Co.* v. *Adams* [1967] I.R. 424 (High Ct., Budd, J.), considered *infra*, pp. 434-435.

[21] As suggested by *Thomas*, 130-131 (surely too severe a solution).

[22] Cf. *Graveson*, 486.

[23] Cf. *Dicey & Morris*, 616, *Graveson*, 520.

[24] Age of Majority Act 1985, section 2(1).

[25] See *Hellman's Will*, L.R. 2 Eq. 363 (Lord Romilly, M.R., 1866), *Re Schnapper*, [1928] Ch. 420 (Clauson, J.); cf., however *Leslie* v. *Baillie*, 2 Y. & C.C.C. 91, 63 E.R. 40 (1843) and *Re Will of John Lee Hing*, 1 S.R.N.S.W. (Eq.) 199 (Simpson, C.J. in Eq., 1901), both of which appear to look exclusively to the *lex domicilii* of the legatee. See also *Re Pemberton; Fisher* v. *Barclays Bank Ltd.*, 59 D.L.R. (2d) 44 (B.C.Sup. Ct., Smith Co. Ct. J., 1966), *Graham* v. *Canandaigna Lodge No. 236 of the Independent Order of Oddfellows of the State of New York*, 24 O.R. 255, esp. at 260-261 (Chy. Div., Meredith, J., 1893).

[26] 19 L.R. Ir. 349 (Chatterton, V.-C., 1887).

[27] Cf. *Cheshire & North*, 512, *Dicey & Morris*, 615, *Morris*, 392, *McLean*, 416, *Castel*, vol. 2, 450.

[28] Cf. *Bank of Africa* v. *Cohen*, [1909] 2 Ch. 129, a case dealing with capacity to mortgage land; see also *Re Hernando; Hernando* v. *Sawtell*, 27 Ch. D. 284 (1884). It may be argued that *dicta* in *In the Goods of Gentili, Deceased*, I.R. 9 Eq. 541 (Prob., Warren, J., 1875), are broad enough to embrace the question of capacity.

Formalities[29]

At common law, after some uncertainty,[30] it was accepted in 1830[31] that the law of the domicile exclusively governed the formal validity of a will of movables.[32] This could lead to hardship where a person resident or domiciled abroad made his will in accordance with the formal requirements of the land of his birth. Such a will, if it failed to comply with his place of domicile was invalid, in spite of the testator's best efforts to ensure that the will would be formally valid.[33] As a result of the decision to this effect in *Bremer* v. *Freeman*[34] in 1857, the Wills Act 1861 was passed.

This Act (Lord Kingsdown's Act) improved the position somewhat. Section 1 of that Act provided that every will made outside the United Kingdom by a British subject (whatever his or her domicile at the time of making the will or at his or her death) should be admissible to probate, as regards personal estate, if made in accordance with the formal[35] requirements of the law of the place where it was made or of the law of the place where the person was domiciled when making the will or of the law of his or her domicile of origin if this was in "part of Her Majesty's Dominions".

The Act was, however, "marred by indefensible distinctions".[36] The limitations to British subjects was "embarrassing and insular".[37] Moreover, the reference to personal, rather than moveable, property was out of harmony with the general conflicts classification.[38] Finally, invoking the testator's domicile of origin in this context could result in a will being formally valid by reason of compliance with the law of a country with which the testator had no social links.[39]

So far as immovables were concerned, the position at common law was that the *lex situs* provided the exclusive test for formal validity.[40] A decision involving the application of the *lex situs* is *De Fogassieras* v. *Duport*,[41] in 1881. A French subject, domiciled and resident in France, made a will executed and attested as required by the Irish legislation but not in conformity with the formal requirements of French law. Warren, J. held that the will was effective in relation to the testator's

---

[29] See Lorenzen, *The Validity of Wills, Deeds and Contracts as Regards Form in the Conflict of Laws*, 20 Yale L.J. 427 (1911), Bale, *The Demise of Lord Kingsdown's Act*, 29 Sask. Bar Rev. 179 (1964), Rabel, *The Form of Wills*, 6 Vand. L. Rev. 535 (1953), Morris, *Note*, 13 Int. & Comp. L.Q. 684 (1964), Cohn, *Note*, 22 Modern L. Rev. 413 (1959).

[30] Cf. Lorenzen, *supra*, at 434.

[31] *Stanley* v. *Barnes*, 3 Hagg. Ecc. 447, 162 E.R. 1190 (1830). See also *Moore* v. *Darell*, 4 Hagg. Ecc. 346, 162 E.R. 1472 (1832), *Craigie* v. *Lewin*, 3 Curt. Ecc. 435, 163 E.R. 782 (1842), *Croker* v. *Hertford*, 4 Moo. P.C. 339, 13 E.R. 334 (1844).

[32] *Cheshire & North*, 601.

[33] Cf. *Bremer* v. *Freeman*, 10 Moo. P.C. 306, 14 E.R. 508 (1857).

[34] *Supra*.

[35] Thus, the 1861 Act did "not affect the material validity of a will. Its effect [was] to render formally valid, and thus admissible to probate, a will which might otherwise be defective in form." *Re Adams Deceased; Bank of Ireland Trustee Co. Ltd.* v. *Adams*, [1967] I.R. 424, at 455 (High Ct., Budd, J.).

[36] Bale, *The Demise of Lord Kingsdown's Act*, 29 Sask. Bar Rev. 179, at 181 (1964). See also Morris, *The Choice of Law Clause in Statutes*, 62 L.Q. Rev. 170, at 173-176 (1946), J. Thomas, *Private International Law*, 131-132 (1955), Breslauer, *The Scope of Section 3 of the Wills Act, 1861*, 3 Int. L.Q. 343 (1950).

[37] *Cheshire & North*, 601. See also Morris, *supra*, at 174. Cf. Breslauer, *supra*, at 344-350.

[38] Morris, *supra*, at 175. Cf. *M'Ginn* v. *Delbeke*, 61 I.L.T.R. 117 (N.I.C.A. 1926).

[39] *Cheshire & North*, 602. See also Bentwich, *Recent Application of the Renvoi in Matters of Personal Status*, 5 Can. Bar Rev. 379, at 387 (1936).

[40] *Murray* v. *Champernowne*, [1901] 2 I.R. 232 (Q.B. Div., Prob., Andrews, J., 1900), *De Fogassieras* v. *Duport*, 11 L.R. Ir. 123 (Prob., Warren, J., 1881) (described by *Dicey* 6th ed., 1949, 539, fn. 64 as "undoubtedly sound in principle"); see also *In the goods of Gentili, Deceased*, I.R. 9 Eq. 541, at 544-545 (Prob., Warren, J., 1875). Cf. *M'Ginn* v. *Delbeke, supra*.

[41] 11 L.R. Ir. 123 (1881).

real estate and leaseholds in Ireland. The will, he said, was ''unquestionably valid as a disposition of the testator's real estate in Ireland, for such testamentary dispositions are governed by the *lex loci rei sitae* ...''[42] He held that the leaseholds should also be characterised as immoveable property, and that thus the will was equally valid in regard to them.[43]

The matter was the subject of a Hague Convention in 1961: The Hague Convention on the Conflicts of Laws Relating to the Form of Testamentary Dispositions.[44]

The philosophy of the Convention is very much in favour of upholding the formal validity of testamentary dispositions whenever it is reasonably possible to do so.

Giving effect to this Convention, Part VIII of the Succession Act 1965[45] provides (in section 102 (1)) that a testamentary disposition is valid as regards form if its form complies with the internal law of any of a number of possible countries, that is, the internal law:

(*a*) of the place where the testator made the testamentary disposition;
(*b*) of a nationality possessed by the testator either at the time when he made the disposition or at the time of his death;
(*c*) of a place in which the testator had his domicile either at the time when he made the disposition or at the time of his death;
(*d*) of the place in which the testator had his habitual residence either at the time when he made the disposition or at the time of his death; *or*
(*e*) so far as immovables are concerned, of the place where they are situated.

As a supplement to ground (*a*), section 103 provides that a testamentary disposition made on board a vessel or aircraft is also valid as regards form if its form complies with the internal law of the place with which, having regard to its registration (if any) and any other relevant circumstances, the vessel or aircraft may be taken to have had the most real connection.[46]

Ground (*b*) brings our law into line with civil law jurisdictions,[47] where the *lex patriae*, even today, plays an important role. In countries whose national law consists of a non-unified system, ground (*b*) would present difficulties of interpretation. Section 102(3) accordingly provides that in such a case the law to be applied is to be interpreted by the rules in force in that system and, failing any such rules, by the most real connection which the testator had with any one of the various laws within that system.

So far as ground (*c*) is concerned, there is an important change to the general rule[48] that the *lex fori* determines the meaning of domicile. Section 102(4) provides that the determination of whether or not the testator had his domicile in a particular place is to be governed by the law of that place.[49] The possibility of a testator's being domiciled in more than one country by virtue of this provision should be noted.

Ground (*d*), which refers to the testator's habitual residence, contains no definition

---

[42] *Id.*, at 125.
[43] *Id.*, at 126.
[44] For analysis of the Convention, see Droz, *Les nouvelles règles de conflits francaises en matière de forme des testaments*, [1968] Rev. crit. de dr. internat. priv. 1, Graveson, *The Ninth Hague Conference of Private International Law*, 10 Int. & Comp. L.Q. 18, at 21-25 (1961).
[45] See *Wylie*, paras. 14.51-14.54.
[46] This provision is modelled on section 2 (1) (*a*) of Britain's Wills Act 1963.
[47] Cf. Cohn, *Note*, 22 Modern L. Rev. 413, at 413 (1959). It is interesting to note that Dr. Morris had considered ''startling'' a proposal by an English Committee to this effect: *Note* 22 Modern L. Rev. 65, at 66 (1959). His doubts were not dispelled by Dr. Cohn's note: see Morris, *Note* 13 Int. & Comp. 684, at 686-687 (1964).
[48] See *supra*, p. 50.
[49] This provision derives from Article 1, final paragraph, of the Convention.

as to what that concept means.[50] The liberal policy of Part VIII of the Act towards upholding the formal validity of testamentary dispositions may well affect the judicial interpretation of the concept.[51]

Ground (e), in referring to the *lex situs,* where immovables are concerned, preserves the common law rule. The important difference, of course, is that, at common law, the *lex situs* constituted the *sole* test for immovables whereas, under section 102(1), ground (e) offers merely one of five options for immoveable property. Perhaps it would have been advisable to make this option available for moveable, as well as immoveable, property.[52]

Some other provisions in the Act regarding formalities should be noted. Section 106(1) provides that, for the purposes of Part VIII, any provision of law which limits the permitted forms of testamentary dispositions by reference to the age, nationality or other personal conditions of the testator is to be deemed to pertain to matters of form.[53] In view of the liberal approach adopted by the Hague Convention and section 102 of the Act towards upholding the validity of wills, the effect of this provision, of course, is greatly to enhance the prospects of the will being upheld in respect of matters which formerly would have been characterised as relating to capacity.

Section 107(2) of the Act provides that, in determining whether or not a testamentary disposition complies with a particular law, regard is to be had to the requirements of that law at the time of making the disposition, but that this is not to prevent account being taken of an alteration of law affecting testamentary dispositions made at that time if the alteration enables the disposition to be treated as valid. Thus, retrospective legislation making formal requirements easier than previously would be recognised, but retrospective legislation invalidating a testamentary disposition for non-compliance with formal requirements would not.

Essential Validity

The grant of probate "is conclusive evidence that the instrument proved was testamentary"[54] according to Irish law, but it is not conclusive as to the validity of the disposition to which the will is designed to give effect. This aspect — the essential validity of the will — is determined by the *lex domicilii* at death, so far as movables are concerned, and the *lex situs,* so far as immovables are concerned.[55] In *In Re Adams Deceased; Bank of Ireland Trustee Co.* v. *Adams,*[56] Budd, J. said:

[50] In contrast to the approach favoured by the Law Reform Commission, in its recommendations on the subject of habitual residence as a general connecting factor in private international law: see pp. 99-100 *supra.*

[51] Cf. *Graveson,* 490:

"If, as is possible, a testator, like a cat, has two or more habitual residences, he should be allowed to resort to the law of either or any one of them."

[52] Cf. *Morris,* 394.

[53] The same rule applies to the qualifications of witnesses necessary for the validity of a testamentary disposition and to the provisions of section 82 concerning gifts to an attesting witness or spouse of an attesting witness: section 106(2).

[54] *Re Adams Deceased; Bank of Ireland Trustee Co.* v. *Adams,* [1967] I.R. 424 at 454 (High Ct., Budd, J.), quoting from *Whicker* v. *Hume,* 7 H.L. Cas 124, at 156, 11 E.R. 50, at 63 (*per* Lord Cranworth, 1858).

[55] In this context, it is necessary to distinguish between rules of substance, which are determined by the *lex domicilii* (for movables) or *lex situs* (for immovables), and rules of procedure, which will be governed by the *lex fori.* Rules of substance include the presumption of simultaneous death in cases of uncertainty: cf. Succession Act 1965, section 5, *Wylie,* paras. 7.06, 14.32-14.33, *Re Cohn,* [1945] Ch. 5 (Uthwatt, J., 1944), analysed by 61 L.Q. Rev. 340 (1945), and see *infra,* p. 628. An example of a rule of procedure in this context is the burden of proof of testamentary capacity: see *In the Estate of Fuld (Deceased) (No. 3) Hartley* v. *Fuld,* [1968] P. 675, at 698-699 (Scarman, J., 1965).

[56] [1967] I.R. 424, at 457 (High Ct., Budd, J.). Budd, J. could find "no case ... where it has been held that the expressions used in a will can override the law of domicil as to material validity": *id.,* at 459. He quoted *Dicey,* 7th ed., Rule 119: "The material or essential validity of a will of movables

"The position in this case is that, according to English and Irish law, on which there is no difference on this point, the law of the place of a deceased person's domicil governs the succession to his movables and therefore the material validity of his will."

Accordingly, he applied French law,[57] as the *lex domicilii*, to determine this question. Since the testator's codicil contravened an imperative requirement of French law in that it did not take into account the *réserve légale* (forced-heirship share) to which the testator's daughter was entitled under French law, Budd, J. held that the will and codicil applied only up to the quota which French law permitted the testator to dispose of, having regard to his daughter's claim.

STATUTORY ENTITLEMENTS[59]

An example of the reverse case arose in the English decision of *Re Groos, Groos v. Groos,*[58] where a will made in the Netherlands by a woman domiciled in England was held to operate under English law, which permitted her to leave all her property to her husband, rather than the law of the Netherlands, which would have required three-quarters of her estate to be given to her children.

This may be a useful point to examine in some detail the important question of compulsory statutory entitlements in the estate of deceased person, since it is generally treated as a matter affecting essential validity.

In most countries, legislative provisions confer specific entitlements on intestacy as well as restricting the freedom of a testator to dispose of the whole of his estate as he wishes. Normally the members of his family will have the right to some specific or discretionary share in his estate. There is a wide divergence in the types of legislation in different countries. In Ireland, where a spouse dies intestate[60] leaving a surviving spouse, the surviving spouse is entitled to the entire estate.[61] Where there are issue the surviving spouse is entitled to two-thirds and the issue to the remaining third of the estate.[62] Where a spouse dies leaving a will, the surviving spouse has a "legal right" to a half of the estate of the deceased spouse if there are no issue,[63] and to a third of the estate if there are issue.[64]

The children have no right to any specific proportion of the estate but they may apply to the court, under section 117 of the Succession Act 1965, claiming that their parent has failed in his or her moral duty to make proper provision for them as a prudent and just parent would have done. The court may make an order for such provision out of the estate as it thinks just.

---

or of any particular gift of movables contained therein is governed by the law of the testator's domicile at the time of his death." This passage appears unaltered in *Dicey & Morris*, 10th ed., as Rule 102.

[57] Budd, J.'s consideration of the *renvoi* issue is dealt with *supra*, pp. 43-44.

[58] [1915] 1 Ch. 572 (Sargant, J.).

[59] See Scoles, *Conflict of Laws and Nonbarrable Interests in Administration of Decedents' Estates*, 8 U. Fla. L. Rev. 151 (1955), Scoles, *Conflict of Laws and Elections in Administration of Decedents' Estates*, 30 Ind. L.J. 293 (1955), Heilman, *Interpretation and Construction of Wills of Immovables in Conflict of Laws Cases Involving "Election"*, 25 U. Ill. L. Rev. 778 (1931), Graue, *The Rights of Surviving Spouses Under Private International Law*, 15 Amer. J. of Comp. L. 164 (1967), Scoles & Rheinstein, *Conflict Avoidance in Succession Planning*, 21 L. & Contemp. Prob. 499, at 506-512 (1956), Breslauer, *Conflict of Laws in Restrictions on Freedom and Testation*, 27 Iowa L. Rev. 425, (1942), Ester & Scoles, *Estate Planning and Conflict of Laws*, 24 Ohio St. L.J. 270, at 279-281 (1963), Carteaux, *Comment, Conflicts of Law and Successions: Comprehensive Interest Analysis As a Viable Alternative to the Traditional Approach*, 59 Tul. L. Rev. 389, at 400ff (1984).

[60] For clarity of discussion, it is easier to include the intestacy provisions in the present discussion, rather than treat them separately earlier in the chapter.

[61] Succession Act 1965, section 67(1).

[62] *Id.*, section 67 (2).

[63] *Id.*, section 111(1).

[64] *Id.*, section 111(2).

In other countries, the general trend is to permit applications at least to the extent that the claimants may obtain *maintenance* out of the estate. Some countries go further and permit either specific proportions or discretionary entitlements extending beyond the entitlement to maintenance.[65]

It is worthwhile to consider the policy goals served by this type of legislation. Where, as is often the case, the legislation limits the entitlements of the surviving members of the deceased's family to a *maintenance* claim, it can be argued that the purpose is to prevent destitute families from becoming a charge on the community.[66] Where, however, the legislation provides for a fixed share, as is the case in Ireland in relation to the surviving share, this factor fades in significance. Similarly, a discretionary entitlement not limited to maintenance enables the Court to make a substantial order in favour of an applicant,[67] which goes well beyond the protection of the State purse.

When we come to examine the legislation in most countries, including Ireland, we find a surprising lack of concern on the part of the legislators for the conflicts dimensions. The result is doubly unfortunate. First, the legislation tends to treat the deceased person's estate as a unit, rather than making any distinction between moveable and immoveable property. Secondly, in the light of a wide divergence between the laws of different countries and in the absence of any significant international agreement harmonising practice between the legislation of different countries, there can often be a significant risk of surviving members of the deceased receiving undue or inadequate shares from two or more countries.

Having mentioned these difficulties, let us now consider how the conflicts principles have developed on this subject.

First, as has already been mentioned,[68] it is agreed that a claim for a statutory share, where there is a will, relates to the essential validity of the will,[69] rather than being a matter to be dealt with by the *lex fori* in the administration of the estate.[70]

Secondly, there is widespread support among common law jurisdictions for the view that the domicile or residence of the *claimants* is irrelevant to a claim that is otherwise sustainable. Thus, a child of a testator will not be excluded from making a claim under section 117 of the Succession Act 1965 merely because he was born in Australia and has lived there all of his life. Where, conversely, a testator has abandoned his family and dies domiciled in a foreign country which permits total, or virtually total, testamentary freedom, the fact that the *lex domicilii* of the abandoned family confers substantial rights on the surviving spouse and children is a matter which should surely be given weight. When we are dealing with legislation designed primarily to perform the goal of protecting family members or other dependants of the deceased spouse, reference to their *lex domicilii* would be far from fanciful.[72]

[65] See Graue, *supra*, at 164-172.

[66] Cf. *Re Perkins, Deceased*, [1958] S.R. (N.S.W.) 1, at 9 (Eq., McLelland, J., 1957) (accepting that this was "part of the purpose" of the New South Wales legislation).

[67] See, *e.g. In bonis G.M. Deceased: F.M.* v. *T.A.M.*, 106 I.L.T.R. 82 (High Ct., Kenny, J., 1970).

[68] *Supra*, p. 435.

[69] See *Re Adams Deceased; Bank of Ireland Trustee Co.* v. *Adams*, [1967] I.R. 424 (High Ct., Budd, J.), W. McGuire, *The Succession Act 1965: A Commentary*, 34 (2nd ed., by R.A. Pearce, 1986), *In re Paulin*, [1950] V.L.R. 462, at 464 (Sholl, J.).

[70] See *Pain* v. *Holt*, 19 S.R. (N.S.W.) 105 (Harvey, J., 1919), *In re Butchart (Deceased): Butchart* v. *Butchart*, [1932] N.Z.L.R. 125 (C.A., 1931), *Krzus* v. *Crow's Nest Pass Coal Co. Ltd.*, [1912] A.C. 590, *In re Paulin*, [1950] V.L.R. 462 (Sholl, J.); cf. *In re Found. Found* v. *Seemens*, [1924] S.A.S.R. 237 (Sup. Ct., Murray, C.J., 1924).

[71] *In re Roper (Deceased)*, [1927] N.Z.L.R. 731 (Sup. Ct., Skerrett, C.J.), *Re Donnelly*, 28 S.R. (N.S.W.) 34 (Harvey, C.J. in Eq., 1927), *In re Butchart (Deceased): Butchart* v. *Butchart*, [1932] N.Z.L.R. 125 (C.A., 1931).

[72] Of course, a rule that simply referred to the respective *leges domicilii* of the family members at the time of death would be quite unsatisfactory, in view of its contingent results and complexity in application.

The approach generally favoured by the courts in this context is that the deceased's *lex domicilii* at the time of death governs movables[73] and the *lex situs* governs immovables.[74]

Some important Irish decisions on this subject have been reported. In *In bonis G.M. Deceased; F.M.* v. *T.A.M.*,[75] a testator, domiciled in Ireland, left, among other property, a farm in England. An adopted child of the testator took proceedings under section 117 of the Succession Act 1965, claiming that the testator had not provided for him as a prudent and just parent should. A question arose as to whether the farm should be included in the testator's estate for the purpose of Part IX of the Succession Act 1965, and in particular section 109 (2), which provides as follows:

"In this Part references to the estate of the testator are to all estate to which he was beneficially entitled for an estate or interest not ceasing on his death and remaining after payment of all expenses, debts, and liabilities (other than estate duty) properly payable thereout."

By the time the issue had to be determined by Kenny, J. it had been conceded that the estate, for the purposes of Part IX of the Act, did not include the farm. Kenny, J. said:

"Section 109(2) of the Act has not changed the judge-made rule that the succession to immoveables is governed by the law of the place where they are situate, and that to moveables is regulated by the law of the domicile of the deceased."

Turning to the adopted child's claim under section 117, Kenny, J. said:

"The duty is not one to make adequate provision but to make proper provision in accordance with the testator's means and in deciding whether this has been done, the court may have regard to immoveable property outside the Republic of Ireland owned by the testator. The court, therefore, when deciding whether the moral duty has been fulfilled, must take all the testator's property (including immoveable property outside the Republic of Ireland) into account, but if it decides that the duty has not been discharged, the provision for the child is to be made out of the estate excluding that immoveable property."[76]

After a review of the evidence, Kenny, J. came to the conclusion that a prudent and just parent would have given one half of the estate, excluding the immoveable property in England, to the adopted son.

But this difficulty, of itself, scarcely justifies an unqualified reference to the *lex domicilii* of the deceased spouse.

[73] *In Bonis G.M. Deceased; F.M.* v. *T.A.M.*, 106 I.L.T.R. 82 (High Ct., Kenny, J., 1970), *Re Adams Deceased; Bank of Ireland Trustee Co.* v. *Adams*, [1967] I.R. 424 (High Ct., Budd, J.), *Higgins* v. *Byrne*, 42 I.L.T.R. 252 (Ch., Meredith, M.R., 1908), W. McGuire, *The Succession Act 1965: A Commentary*, 34 (2nd ed., by R. A. Pearce, 1986), *In re Roper (Deceased)*, [1927] N.Z.L.R. 731 (Sup. Ct., Skerrett, C.J.), *Re Donnelly*, 28 S.R. (N.S.W.) 34 (Harvey, C.J. in Eq., 1927), *In re Paulin*, [1950] V.L.R. 462 (Sholl, J.), In *In re Butchart (Deceased): Butchart* v. *Butchart*, [1932] N.Z.L.R. 125 (C.A., 1931), it was acknowledged that the statute, in its express terms, extended to testators not domiciled in New Zealand but it was held that the statute should be read subject to the rule, already established, that the material validity of a will of movables is to be determined by the *lex domicilii* of the testator at the time of death. In *Pain* v. *Holt*, 19 S.R. (N.S.W.) 105 (1919), Harvey, J. took the view that the "presumption" that the *lex domicilii* should apply might be displaced "if the legislature has clearly indicated such an intention". Since no deliberate intention was indicated one way or the other in the New South Wales Act, the *lex domicilii* was applied.

[74] *In bonis G.M. Deceased; F.M.* v. *T.A.M.*, supra. See also *In re Rea Deceased; Rea* v. *Rea*, [1902] 1 I.R. 451 (Porter, M.R.), *In re Roper (Deceased)*, supra, *Re Donnelly*, supra, *In re Paulin*, supra. See also *Re Collens (Deceased); Royal Bank of Canada (London) Ltd.* v. *Krogh* [1986] 1 All E.R. 611 (Chy. Div., Browne-Wilkinson, V.-C., 1985).

[75] 106 I.L.T.R. 82 (High Ct., Kenny, J., 1970).

[76] *Id.*, at 87.

The implications of this case are interesting. Kenny, J. took into account the immoveable property in determining how much the testator should have given his adopted son. Kenny, J. came to this conclusion without regard to the content of the legislation in England or to the conflict rules of that country. If the Irish court chooses to be blind to those considerations in other cases there is a danger that the claimant may receive undue compensation. If we assume that the immoveable property is in Ruritania, whose laws contain a provision exactly the same as section 117 of our Succession Act 1965, how is a court in Ruritania to determine a claim made there? If it adopts a similar approach to that of Kenny, J., and includes the *moveable* property within the total estate against which the testator's duty is to be measured, and compensates the claimant accordingly, the claimant will finish up with unduly extensive compensation. Of course, if the Court in Ruritania has regard to the earlier order made by the Irish court and to the basis on which that award was made, the problem of undue compensation may be mitigated or removed.

We must also consider the position where the court of the *situs* of the immoveable property has *already* made an order in respect of the claimant under its equivalent legislation, *before* the claimant's application under section 117 is determined here. *In bonis G.M. Deceased: F.M.* v. *T.A.M.*[77] is itself authority for the view that, in determining the question of moral duty in applications under section 117, the Court must consider the facts existing at the time of the testator's death rather than of the hearing. This might at first sight seem to foreclose the possibility of the Court's taking into account the outcome of the foreign proceedings. In fact it does not do so. Having addressed the question of the testator's duty, the Court is perfectly entitled (if not required) to have regard to present realities when making its order under section 117.

Next, it seems that Kenny, J.'s reference in the *G.M.*[78] case to the *lex domicilii*, so far as movables are concerned, suggests that he might not have countenanced a claim brought against a testator not domiciled within the State and having no immoveable property here.[79] If the testator had immoveable property here but was not domiciled within the jurisdiction, it seems clear that the Irish Court could make an order under section 117, so far as the immoveable property is concerned, and, on Kenny, J.'s approach, in doing so, it would have regard to the value of the moveable property elsewhere. What is not so clear is whether the Irish Court could in this case go further and attempt to determine the statutory entitlements, akin to section 117, of claimants under the *lex domicilii* so far as the movables are concerned. The inhibition which affected Kenny, J. against trespassing on the jurisdiction of the *lex situs*, so far as immovables are concerned, would not arise in this case. Moreover, the general rule that the essential validity of a will of movables is determined by the *lex domicilii* would appear to permit our courts to attempt to determine statutory claims arising under that law.

If this approach is favoured, the risk of overcompensation by the laws of two separate countries would obviously be reduced. But it may be considered too much to ask of an Irish court to attempt to exercise discretion in the same manner as required

---

[77] *Supra.* See further Cooney, *Succession and Judicial Discretion in Ireland: The Section 117 Cases,* 15 Ir. Jur. (n.s.) 62, at 66 ff (1980), Fitzpatrick, *The Succession Act 1965, Section 117,* 110 Ir. L.T. & Sol. J. 77, at 90 (1976), *Binchy,* 393.

[78] *Supra.*

[79] It is useful in this regard to contrast *In re Found. Found* v. *Seemens,* [1924] S.A.S.R. 237 (Sup. Ct., Murray, C.J., 1924) with *In re Butchart (Deceased): Butchart* v. *Butchart,* [1932] N.Z.L.R. 125 (C.A., 1931) and *In re Paulin,* [1950] V.L.R. 462 (Sholl, J.).

of courts in the country of the domicile by the *lex domicilii*.[80] It may be argued that questions relating to moral duties to family members raise value judgments best resolved in the context of the culture in which they arise. This last observation brings to the surface yet again the inadequacy of a blind adherence to the *lex situs* in relation to movables; for why should the contingent location of immoveable property in a particular country result in the application of the mores of *that* country on an issue which is not its primary concern? If a German domiciled and resident in the Federal Republic of Germany buys a site in County Cork for a holiday home, Irish law should have little interest in imposing on him the mores of our Succession Act 1965, so far as the compulsory entitlements of his wife and children are concerned. The doctrine of total *renvoi* would go only some way towards mitigating the dangers of a "culture clash" here.[81]

It would be unfortunate if the traditional deference afforded to the *lex situs* were allowed to get in the way of basic justice to surviving family members. In the *F.A.M.* case, no difficulty arose, since the assets within the reach of the Irish court were capable of satisfying the claim of the testator's adopted child. But it is possible to think of cases where all the testator's roots and life experiences were in Ireland but the large part of his property at the time of his death consisted of an immovable, perhaps recently purchased in a foreign country whose domestic law had no equivalent of section 117, and whose conflicts rules did not refer the question back to Irish law. In cases such as this, the risk of injustice would be high.

When we come to consider the "legal right" of the surviving spouse, more difficulties arise. If Ireland is the country of the testator's domicile, and the portion of the estate consisting of immoveable property is situated abroad, it would appear from the *F.A.M.* case that the "legal right" would be measured against the *whole* of the estate, but that only that amount of the estate comprising movables would be available to satisfy this claim. The surviving spouse, regardless of whether the "legal right" claim had been fully satisfied against the moveable property, would appear free to proceed independently under the *lex situs* of the immoveable property for such further claim as that law might support.[82] It is to be hoped that the foreign Court would have regard to the claim already made before the Irish Court, but with the present lack of international harmony on this general question, there is no guarantee that this will be so.

Finally, it is worth noting a further complexity. In some countries, the law relating to matrimonial property may give substantial entitlements to a surviving spouse. It is possible to envisage cases where a surviving spouse may have a *combination* of rights under the rules governing succession and matrimonial property.[83]

The easiest response might seem to be that the testator "must be considered as disposing only of that which was properly his, and ... the disposition did not include

---

[80] Cf. *In re Paulin*, [1950] V.L.R. 462, at 467 (Sholl, J.).

[81] Cf. Scoles & Rheinstein, *Conflict Avoidance in Succession Planning*, 21 L. & Contemp. Prob. 499, at 510-511 (1956).

[82] A further complication may arise where the surviving spouse, having taken the benefits under the will so far as the movables (or immovables) are concerned, seeks to assert his or her legal right *against* the will so far as immovables (or movables) are concerned. The possibility of excessive entitlements is a real one. The best solution may be to put the surviving spouse to his or her election: cf. *Wolff*, 575, Scoles, *Conflict of Laws and Elections in Administration of Decedents' Estates*, 30 Ind. L.J. 293, at 297 (1955); see further *Scoles & Hay*, 793-795. Where the doctrine of election occurs in a situation where the testator leaves some of his own property to A but purports to give some of A's property to B, the courts generally look to the testator's *lex domicilii*: see *Cheshire & North*, 516-519, *Wolff*, 573-574, *In re Ogilvie* [1918] 1 Ch. 492. Cf. *In re Allen*, [1945] 2 All E.R. 264 (Cohen, J.), criticised by Morris, 24 Can. Bar Rev. 528 (1946).

[83] See Graue, *The Rights of Surviving Spouses under Private International Law*, 15 Amer. J. of Comp. L. 164, at 180ff (1967).

what would be the wife's under the ... law of community of goods";[84] but, where the surviving spouse, having thus (let us say) obtained half the deceased spouse's moveable property, proceeds against both immoveable and the remaining moveable property in separate countries, under the "forced share" provisions of each, the possibility of overgenerous entitlements is a real one.

In *In re Rea Deceased; Rea* v. *Rea*,[85] in 1902, the facts were as follows. A domiciled Irishman died in Ireland, intestate without issue, leaving a widow surviving him. He had immovables and movables in Ireland, as well as lands in Victoria, Australia which by the law of Victoria were regarded and devolved as personal estate. Administration was taken out in Ireland by the widow, and in Victoria by an appointed person who sold the lands and sent the proceeds to the widow.

By Victoria's legislation a widow was entitled, in the circumstances of the case, to a charge of £1,000 on the estate, the residue to be divided between the widow and next of kin. The widow claimed £1,000 out of the proceeds of sale of the lands in Victoria, as well as £500 out of the real and personal estate in Ireland, under the Intestates' Estates Act 1890. She also claimed dower out of the Irish freeholds and a moiety of the residue of the proceeds of sale of the lands in Victoria and of the Irish personal estate.

The widow's claim was successful. The Master of the Rolls held that the land in Victoria "must in the present case descend in the mode prescribed by the law of that colony, and ... when in fact sold the net proceeds in our Courts must be treated as pure personalty".[86]

The Master of the Rolls stated:

> "The question then arises, is the plaintiff entitled to both these sums of £1000 and £500, or only to one, and if one, to which? I can find no reason to say that either must be surrendered. The £500 under the Act of 1890 is, of course, absolutely secure if there are assets. Then why should the £1000 under the Colonial Act, charged upon colonial assets, be lost? Or why, if the £1000 is legally provided, should it be held to include the £500 under our Act? The latter is a provision out of net assets; but there are no assets till the £1000 charge is first paid. It would, of course, be a different question if the Australian assets had been movable, and, therefore, subject to the law of the country of the domicil. In that case the colonial statute would be of no avail against our law. But that is not so.

> If £1000 had been secured to the wife by settlement, or in any other manner (the settlement not being in bar of her rights under the Statute of Distributions) she would have had both. It seems to me even clearer that she must have both, when both are secured as charges by independent Acts of different Legislatures, each having full jurisdiction over the respective subject matter".[87]

The widow thus was entitled to two statutory legacies, a result that might perhaps be defended on the principle of generosity to widows,[88] but which could not be so easily supported where the shares were higher and the interests of other competing claimants stronger. Morris has roundly criticised the case for its lack of understanding of how conflicts of law operates and, more fundamentally, for its blind application

---

[84] *In re De Nicols. De Nicols* v. *Curlier*, [1898] 1 Ch. 403, at 418. Cf. Morris, *Note*, 24 Can. Bar Rev. 528 (1946), criticising *In re Allen*, [1945] 2 All E.R. 264, Breslauer, *Conflicts of Laws in Restrictions on Freedom of Testation*, 27 Iowa L. Rev. 425, at 438-439 (1942).

[85] [1902] 1 I.R. 451 (Porter, M.R.).

[86] *Id.*, at 463, following *Beaumont* v. *Oliveira*, L.R. 6 Eq. 534 (Stuart, V.C., 1868).

[87] *Id.*, at 465.

[88] See Morris, *Intestate Succession to Land in the Conflict of Laws*, 85 L.Q. Rev. 339, at 350 (1969). Cf. Binchy 389. See also *Re Collens (deceased); Royal Bank of Canada (London) Ltd.* v. *Krogh*, [1986] 1 All E.R. 611, at 616 (Chy. Div., Browne-Wilkinson, V.-C., 1985).

of traditional conflicts rules, so as to reach a result "which seems absurd, because it could not have been contemplated by either of the legislatures concerned."[89] In defence of Porter, M.R., it could be argued that he was rightly conscious of the fact that conflicts rules in relation to succession can operate effectively only where there is a close degree of international co-operation.

In *Higgins* v. *Byrne*,[90] a married man, with no children, who was apparently domiciled in Ireland,[91] died intestate, possessed of immoveable property in Kansas, having failed to exercise a power to dispose of the reversion of settled property in Ireland, subject to a life estate for his widow. The value of the reversion, after deducting the value of the life estate, was less than £500. Section 1 of the Intestates' Estate Act 1890, provided that, where the value of an estate did not exceed £500, it was to belong to the widow absolutely.

Meredith, M.R. considered himself bound by *Rea* v. *Rea*. He noted that "according to law",[92] the land in Kansas passed to the widow, and that neither the land nor the proceeds of the land were assets for distribution. He went on to hold that the widow was entitled to the Irish estate. He said:

> "It so happens that the life estate to which the property of [the deceased] was subject was the life estate of his wife, but as against a creditor it would make no difference if it were the life estate of somebody else of equal age and bodily health. All that any creditor could get at for the payment of debts would be the reversionary interest that [the deceased] was given power to dispose of by the settlement. The wife is entitled to her life estate as property under the settlement and no person claiming under the husband can get anything as regards the assets, except subject to the life estate of the wife, and after full provision has been made for it. Every line of the Intestates Estates Act demonstrates that the wife having a charge of £500 on the assets[93] is in the position of a statutory creditor, and is a chargeant on the estate by Act of Parliament. In this case the net value of the assets at the date of the death of the intestate does not exceed £500, and every sixpence that is not absorbed in payment of costs and debts goes to the widow".[94]

Clearly, Meredith, M.R. was not disturbed at the prospect of the widow receiving the statutory benefit in addition, not only to her life interest, but also to her entitlement to the land in Kansas.

OTHER LIMITATIONS ON THE DISPOSITION OF PROPERTY

We now enter a somewhat less certain area of the law. If we look at the laws of different countries, we find a wide range of limitations on how property may be disposed of. Thus, we note that in Ireland our rule against perpetuities[95] is more

---

[89] Morris, *supra*, at 349, fns. 44, 45:
"The reader will observe [in the passage from *Re Rea* quoted *supra*] the assumption that there is some mysterious super-law known as conflict of laws which would in the case supposed deprive the Victorian Act of all efficacy, irrespective apparently of its content and policy [as well as] the assumption that under the conflict of laws each legislature has a separate 'jurisdiction' assigned to it within which it can operate and outside which it cannot."

[90] 42 I.L.T.R. 252 (Ch., Meredith, M.R., 1908).

[91] The report does not state so expressly, though the headnote refers, without elaboration, to the *lex domicilii*. It is not even certain from the report that the man and his wife were living in Ireland, although this seems likely.

[92] 42 I.L.T.R., at 252. The law referred to here is the law of Kansas, on which evidence was given, to the effect that the widow became absolutely entitled to the property in Kansas.

[93] In fact, where (as in this case) the net value of the estate did not exceed £500, the estate belonged to the widow "absolutely and exclusively", under section 1. It was only where the net value *exceeded* £500 that the widow was given a charge on the property, under section 2.

[94] 42 I.L.T.R., at 252-253.

[95] Cf. *Wylie*, paras. 5032 ff.

stringent than in many other countries;[96] our rules as to charities[97] more liberal than some[98] but more restrictive than others.[99]

From one standpoint it could be argued that these various limitations are controls on the *testator*, but in at least some respects it is surely more realistic to view them as limitations on the *intended recipients*.[100]

There may well be cases where Irish law as the *lex domicilii* of the testator regards a particular bequest as inconsistent with the rule against perpetuities or our law as to charitable trusts, but where the law of the intended recipient's domicile or the country where the trust is to be administered sees nothing wrong with the bequest. Whose law should prevail? There is now general agreement that in such a case, unless the public policy of our law would regard the limitation as so fundamental as to override the foreign entitlement, the foreign entitlement should prevail. There is, moreover, much support for the view that the rule against perpetuities does not have public policy implications.[101] Equally, charitable trusts are not generally seen as giving raise to public policy difficulties.[102]

CONSTRUCTION

The purpose of construction is "to ascertain the expressed intentions of the testator, i.e. the meaning which the words of the will, when properly interpreted, convey",[103] Sometimes, of course, the words are so abundantly plain in their meaning that no doubts as to construction arise; but often testators use ambiguous expressions which call for interpretation. In these latter cases, a question arises as to which system of law should be applied in interpreting the expressions.

(a) Movables

In *Re Adams deceased; Bank of Ireland Trustee Co. Ltd.* v. *Adams*,[104] Budd J., construing a codicil containing a bequest of moneys and securities, said:

[96] Cf. *Bogert & Bogert*, 186-187.
[97] Cf. V.T.H. Delany, *Law Relating to Charities in Ireland* (1962), J. Brady, *Religion and the Law of Charities in Ireland* (1976).
[98] Cf. *Honoré*, 115-123.
[99] Cf. *Bogert & Bogert*, 215.
[100] For example, the policy of preventing the accumulation of wealth in the hands of charitable institutions within the jurisdiction where they are situated. But factors such as the protection of a testator against undue influence and deathbed "soul-saving" gifts (cf. Joslin, *Conflict of Laws Problems Raised by "Modern Mortmain Acts,"* 60 Dick. L. Rev. 7, at 11 (1955), Scoles & Rheinstein, *Conflict Avoidance in Succession Planning,* 21 L. & Contemp. Prob. 499, at 511 (1956)) and the protection of the interests of members of the testator's family (cf. *Dammert* v. *Osborn* 140 N.Y. 30, at 40, 35 N.E. 407, at 410 (1893)) may more properly be regarded as being concerned with the capacity of the testator than of the intended recipient.
[101] Cf. *Cheshire & North*, 608:
    "The object of the perpetuity rule is to restrict the withdrawal of property from the channels of commerce, a purpose which is clearly local, and which, therefore, cannot justifiably be invoked to destroy a bequest of money that is to be enjoyed and administered in a foreign country ..."
    See also *Hope* v. *Brewer*, 136 N.Y. 126, 32 N.E. 558 (1892); Yiannopoulos, *Wills of Movables in American International Conflicts Law: A Critique of the Domiciliary "Rule"*, 46 Calif. L. Rev. 185, at 215-216 (1958).
[102] See *Cheshire & North*, 609. See, however, fn. 100, *supra*. See generally *Annotation*, 91 A.L.R. 491 (1934), Joslin, *supra*, Yiannopoulos, *Wills of Movables in American International Conflicts Law: A Critique of the Domiciliary "Rule"*, 46 Calif. L. Rev. 185, at 212-215 (1958). It seems that, in the United States, courts are inclined to uphold the validity of gifts to charities if they are valid under the law of *either* the testator's or the recipient's domicile: Yiannopoulos, *supra*, at 213.
[103] *Cheshire & North*, 609-610.
[104] [1967] I.R. 424, at 458 (High Ct., Budd, J.).

"Dealing as it does with moveables,[105] it is accepted as a general proposition (in accordance with the well-established law on the matter) that the codicil is to be interpreted and to receive effect in accordance with the law intended by the testator. This will *prima facie* be presumed to be the law of his domicil at the time when the codicil was made, but this is a mere canon of construction which will not be adhered to when there is any reason, from the nature of the will or otherwise, to suppose that the testator wrote it with reference to the laws of another country."

This passage offers an excellent summary of the relevant legal principles regarding construction in relation to movables. The *lex domicilii*'s claim is based on the fact that in many cases it represents the law with which the testator was most familiar;[106] but clearly there are instances where the testator has some other legal system in mind.

It should be noted that the time at which the Court should refer to the *lex domicilii* (or other law, for that matter) will normally be the time of the making of the testamentary disposition rather than that of the testator's death.[107] Obviously, a testator when making a will or codicil can have no certain knowledge of where he is going to die. Common sense requires us to look to his position at the time of the making of the testamentary disposition, if construction is truly concerned with giving effect to the testator's intention.[108] Statutory support for this approach is afforded by section 107(1) of the Succession Act 1965, which provides that the construction of a testamentary disposition is not to be altered by reason of any change in the testator's domicile after the making of the disposition.

In *Re Adams Deceased: Bank of Ireland Trustee Co. Ltd* v. *Adams,*[109] the testator's domicile at the time he made a codicil was French. Nonetheless, Budd, J. held that the codicil should be construed in accordance with Irish law. Budd, J. pointed to the fact that the codicil was in the English language and "in the form appropriate to an Irish will or codicil, in that executors [were] appointed and it [was] attested in the Irish form."[110] Moreover, the executors were Irish companies, and the codicil was not in holograph form as required by French law. There were thus sufficient indications contained in the will itself for the Judge to come to the conclusion that the terms of the will should be construed in accordance with Irish law.

In *In re Sillar; Hurley* v. *Wimbush,*[111] in 1955, a decision that has been discussed

---

[105] As to immovables, cf. *infra*, pp. 445-447.

[106] *Cheshire & North*, 610. See further *Anon., Note, Choice-of-Law Rules for the Construction and Interpretation of Written Instruments*, 72 Harv. L. Rev. 1154, at 1163 (1959).

[107] Although Budd, J. correctly stated the law on this point in the passage quoted above from *Re Adams deceased*, in the earlier case of *In re Sillar; Hurley* v. *Wimbush*, [1956] I.R. 344, at 361 (High Ct., 1955), he had said: "Since the testator died domiciled here his will should *prima facie* be construed according to Irish law." These words appear to make death rather than the time of making the will the relevant point for referring to the *lex domicilii*. But, immediately before making this statement, Budd, J. made the express finding that, both at the date of making the will and at the time of death, the testator had been domiciled in Ireland. It would seem, therefore, that Budd, J. was guilty of no more than infelicitous expression, rather than of misstatement of the rule of law. See further *In re Bonnet Deceased; Johnston* v. *Langheld*, [1983] I.L.R.M. 359 (High Ct., O'Hanlon, J., 1982), *Philipson-Stow* v. *Inland Revenue Commissioners* [1961] A.C. 727, at 761 (*per* Lord Denning).

[108] Cf., however, the objective approach towards intention favoured in *Hamilton* v. *Carroll*, 1 Ir. Eq. Rep. 175 (Lord Plunket, L.C., 1839) where a will was executed before a change in the value of Irish currency and a codicil was executed afterwards; Lord Plunket, L.C. held that the codicil had the effect of republishing the will and that bequests in the will should be interpreted as referring to the new value of the currency. The Lord Chancellor considered that the question he had to decide was "not whether [the testator] intended to alter the distribution of his property, but whether he has, in fact, done an act, the effect of which is to make the whole will as if published at the date of the codicil. I think the codicil had that effect, and, consequently, that these legacies must be paid in [the new value]": *id.*, at 178-179.

[109] *Supra*.

[110] [1967] I.R., at 459.

[111] [1956] I.R. 344 (High Ct., Budd, J., 1955).

in detail in relation to domicile, Budd, J. was called on to determine whether the will of an English national domiciled and long resident in Ireland should be construed according to Irish or English Law. The testator made the will at the age of 92, and two codicils between then and his death a few years later. Budd, J., having stated the general rule somewhat differently than he had in *Adams*,[112] observed that:

"[i]t is a question of the testator's intentions and the court is bound to give effect to the testator's intentions."[113]

Budd, J. held that the will should be construed in accordance with Irish law:

"The background is that the deceased had lived here for approximately half his life in a settled home and there are indications in the will ... that he intended to end his days here. His will was apparently drawn up by Irish solicitors and he appointed Irish solicitors as his executors. It is, perhaps. a small point but I notice that in both codicils the testator directs his will to be construed in a certain fashion which at least shows that the matter of construction was not absent from his mind, and it would have been simple for him to add a direction that his will should be construed according to English law, but he did not do so despite the fact that he apparently wished to stress his nationality."[114]

The testator had described himself in his will as "a British subject and domiciled in England" who was "at present residing at ... Dublin." Accepting that this description was ineffective in establishing that the testator was in fact domiciled in England rather than Ireland, did it nonetheless have the effect of indicating a sufficient intent to have the will construed in accordance with English law? Budd, J. considered not. He accepted that the testator's description of himself was a feature that "should not be lightly disregarded."[115] But he regarded this statement as not involving "anything similar"[116] to one in the English decision of *In re Price, Tomlin* v. *Latter*,[117] where Stirling, J. had held that an expression in the will of a domiciled French subject that it should "be construed in England the same as in France" referred to English law the question whether the document operated as the execution of a power. Moreover (as Budd, J. pointed out), in *In re Annesley, Davidson* v. *Annesley*,[118] Russell J. had construed the will in accordance with French law although the testatrix had "said in so many words that her domicil was English."[119] Budd, J. referred to two earlier English decisions, where wills had been construed according to the law of the domicile. In one[120] the testator, and Englishman domiciled in France had described himself as a British subject, the will being in English form and containing benefactions mainly to English people; moreover, the property comprising the residue was in England. In the other decision,[121] the

[112] Cf. fn. 107, *supra*.
[113] *Id.*, citing *Bradford* v. *Young*, 29 Ch. D. 617 (1885). Budd, J. also referred to *In re Price, Tomlin* v. *Latter*, [1900] 1 Ch. 442, at 452, where Stirling J., having stated that in general a will is to be construed in accordance with the law of the domicile of the testator, had proceeded to quote from *Dicey*, 1st ed., 1896, p. 695:
　　"But this is a mere canon of interpretation, which should not be adhered to when there is any reason, from the nature of the will, or otherwise, to suppose that the testator wrote it with reference to the law of some other country."
　　See now *Dicey & Morris*, 10th ed., 1980, 628.
[114] [1956] I.R., at 362.
[115] *Id.*
[116] *Id.*, at 361.
[117] [1900] 1 Ch. 442.
[118] [1926] 1 Ch. 692.
[119] [1956] I.R., at 362.
[120] *In re Cunnington, Healing* v. *Webb*, [1924] 1 Ch. 68.
[121] *Anstruther* v. *Chalmer*, 2 Sim. 1 (1826).

testatrix, who died domiciled in England, was a Scottish woman who had made a will in Scottish form in Scotland. It contained many expressions peculiar to Scots law. Budd, J. commented:

"These two cases show that some very strong combination of circumstances is required to exclude the rule in the absence of a direct declaration of intention."[122]

Budd, J. in coming to his conclusion that "the rule" had not been excluded, accepted that a large part of the testator's estate consisted of English assets, and that there were many English legatees. The will was in a form suitable in both Ireland and England. The central question was whether the testator's statement that he was domiciled in England indicated an intention that he wished the will to be construed according to the law of England, and Budd J. confessed[123] to being unable in the circumstances to persuade himself that it did; he added[124] that the remaining facts relied on to establish this intention did not convince him in this either.

(b) Immovables

There is some degree of uncertainty as to the best approach to the question of construction of testamentary disposition of immoveable property. There is much to be said for generally applying the *lex domicilii*,[125] and indeed many courts have supported this approach, though, of course, if the testator's disposition evinces his intention that some other law, such as the *lex situs*,[126] should determine questions of construction, that law will be applied. But one difficulty results from the fact that, so far as such questions as capacity and material validity are concerned, the *lex situs* prevails. If the disposition as construed by the system of law intended by the testator is illegal or impossible under the *lex situs*, the construction favoured by the *lex situs* must prevail.[127] The courts "will endeavour to see that the dispositions will operate in the country where the land is situated to the fullest extent that they can operate under the *lex situs*";[128] but if, in spite of these exertions, the disposition cannot be upheld under the *lex situs*, it will not be effective.

In *In re Bonnet Deceased; Roche Johnston* v. *Langheld*,[129] O'Hanlon, J. addressed the general question of what law should be applied to the construction of provisions of a will relating to immovables. The testatrix, a German national who was at her death and "at all other material times"[130] domiciled in Germany, made a will in the German language in which she purposed to dispose of a farm in Ireland in favour of "der Evangelischen Kirche in Ireland". Problems of interpretation arose as to which Church she meant to benefit, and as to what exact interest in the farm she intended to dispose of.

If the *lex domicilii* were to govern interpretation, German law would be applied; on the other hand, if the *lex situs* were to govern, Irish law would[131] be applied. After a brief review of some of the differing views on the question which had been expressed judicially and in the textbooks, O'Hanlon, J. came to the conclusion that he was not obliged to choose between German and Irish law on this issue since he was:

---

[122] [1956] I.R. at 362.

[123] *Id.*, at 362-363.

[124] *Id.*, at 363.

[125] Cf. Section 107 (1) of the Succession Act 1965, which extends to immoveable as well as moveable property.

[126] Cf. *Bradford* v. *Young*, 29 Ch. D. 617, at 623 (1885).

[127] *Cheshire & North*, 515. See *Re Miller. Bailie* v. *Miller*, [1914] 1 Ch. 511, *Nelson* v. *Bridport*, 8 Beav. 547 (1846), *Philipson-Stow* v. *Island Revenue Commissioners*, [1961] A.C. 727.

[128] *Morris*, 399.

[129] [1983] I.L.R.M. 359 (High Ct., O'Hanlon, J., 1982).

[130] *Id.*, at 360.

[131] Cf. *id.*, where O'Hanlon, J. described the disposition as "at first sight [one] of immovables."

"satisfied from the evidence given by experts in German law that the German legal
code incorporates the primary principle of construction which is applicable in our law
also, namely, that whether or not the case contains a foreign element, a will is to be
construed in accordance with the intention of the testator to be gathered from the will.
In the circumstances of the present case it appears to me that the application of that
primary principle is sufficient to enable me to answer the questions of construction
which have been raised ..."[132]

As to the first question of interpretation, all parties agreed that the testatrix had
intended to benefit the Lutheran Church, of which she was a member, and that the
expression used by her "should not be construed as referring to Protestant Churches
in general".[133] The second question of interpretation was more complicated. The
testatrix had not in fact been the owner, in her personal capacity, of a farm in Ireland,
but she or her nominees held the entire shareholding in a limited company which
owned three parcels of land in Co. Laois, comprising 175 acres, together with
buildings, livestock and farm machinery. The company also had a small holding
of bank stock and a small amount of cash in the bank.

O'Hanlon, J. considered that "[t]here was clearly an intention on the part of the
testatrix to give her lands in Ireland to the beneficiary named in the will,"[134] but
the will had "all the appearance of having been prepared in haste",[135] although the
testatrix survived for some months after making it, during which period she added
a codicil. In the Judge's view, the notary who drafted the will must not have discussed
with the testatrix the nature of her beneficial interest in the lands in Ireland and thus
remained unaware of the fact that the legal owner was a company.

He concluded:

"In all these circumstances, having regard to the fact that the expression 'farm' is used
in the German text of the will, which the experts in German law who gave evidence
in the case agreed was one generally used in German only when referring to lands
held abroad, I consider that the text of the will was loosely drawn and loosely expressed
by the testatrix, and should be construed as referring to her property in Ireland.

The testatrix and her husband formed or acquired a small private company — whose
whole *raison d'être* thereafter appears to have been the acquisition, holding and running
of the farm in question, and whose liquid assets at the date of the testatrix's death
comprised only a very limited amount of bank stock and cash. My impression is that
the testatrix intended to hand over the entire enterprise, lock, stock and barrel, with
its assets and liabilities as they then stood, to the beneficiary named in the will."[136]

On this construction, the gift of the farm in Ireland was regarded as capturing
the entire shareholding of the testatrix in the company, with all its assets and liabilities.

The decision is an interesting one. We must consider the statement that under Irish
law, "whether or not the case contains a foreign element, a will is to be construed
in accordance with the intention of the testator to be gathered from the will".[137] Of
course, finding the testator's intention is the purpose of the exercise, but that
represents the goal rather than the means; and we have seen that, where the means
are involved, the question may arise as to which legal system's rules of construction
are to be applied in determining that intention. Moreover, from the fact that, according
to the German experts, German law also seeks to discern a testator's intention, it

---

[132] *Id.*, at 361.
[133] *Id.*
[134] *Id.*, at 362.
[135] *Id.*
[136] *Id.*
[137] *Id.*, at 361.

would not be proper to conclude that Irish and German law adopt the same principles of construction. Sharing the goal does not necessarily involve sharing the means.

REVOCATION

Just as conflicts questions may arise relating to the *making* of a will, so also conflicts questions may affect *revocation*. Rules relating to revocation vary from country to country. Under Irish internal law, a will may be revoked by the testator's making a new will or codicil,[138] by his[139] destroying it *animo revocandi*,[140] or by his subsequent marriage.[141]

Let us take each of these aspects in turn.

Revocation by later will or codicil

A will may be revoked, expressly or impliedly,[142] by a later will or codicil.[143] Whether the revocation is effective depends on whether the later will or codocil is essentially valid, whether the testator had the requisite capacity and whether the formal requirements were satisfied. In this latter regard we must consider a special provision in the Succession Act 1965. Section 102, having set out in subsection (1) the five grounds for formal validity of testamentary dispositions, provides in subsection (2) as follows:

"Without prejudice to subsection (1), a testamentary disposition revoking an earlier testamentary disposition shall also be valid as regards form if it complies with any one of the laws according to the terms of which, under that subsection, the testamentary disposition that has been revoked was valid."

The effect of this provision is as follows. A new will, revoking a former will, is formally valid in either of two cases. First it will be formally valid if it complies with any of the five grounds for formal validity under subsection (1). Thus, for example, if an Irish woman, domiciled in France, makes her first will complying with the law there, that will is formerly valid under ground (c) of the subsection. If that woman later becomes domiciled in Switzerland where she then makes a second will, revoking the first, and that will complies with the formal requirements of Swiss law, though not French law, then that will is also formally valid.

The second case covered by subsection (2) is where a person makes a new will revoking a former will and the *new* will is not formally valid under subsection (1). All is not necessarily lost: if the new will complies with the requirements of any one of the laws qualified to govern the formal validity of the *former* will, then the *new* will is formally valid.[144]

Thus, to vary the example we have already given, if the woman who becomes domiciled in Switzerland makes a will which does *not* comply with the formal

---

[138] Succession Act 1965, section 85(2). This subsection also permits a will to be revoked by "some writing declaring an intention to revoke it and executed in the manner in which a will is required to be executed."

[139] Or by a person who is authorised by him to do so destroying it in his presence: *Id.*

[140] *Id.*

[141] *Id.*, section 85 (1). A will made in contemplation of marriage is not revoked by the subsequent marriage; *id.*

[142] The question whether a will or codicil revokes an earlier will by implication is one of construction, governed (as with testamentary dispositions generally) "*prima facie* by the law of the testator's domicile at the time of making the later will": *Morris*, 401.

[143] Succession Act 1965, section 85(2). As to earlier law, cf. *In bonis Kalling, Deceased*, 32 Ir. L.T.R. 131 (Prob., Andrews, J., 1897).

[144] Cf. *Cheshire & North*, 612.

requirements of Swiss law but which *does* comply with the formal requirements of French law, the will is formally valid.

Revocation by Destruction of a Will

(a) Movables

A problem may arise when a testator possesses one domicile at the time of the act of destruction of a will and another domicile at the time of death. It is possible that the act of destruction may constitute an effective revocation by the law of the testator's domicile at the time of the act but may be ineffective by the law of his domicile at the time of his death.[145]

The better view is surely that the putative revocation by so final an act should be given effect by the law, and that, in cases where the intended revocation was effective under the testator's *lex domicilii* at the time of the revocation, it should not be rendered ineffective merely because the testator, who believed that the will no longer was effective, changed his domicile to a country under whose laws the revocation would not be effective. From the standpoint of the overwhelming majority of testators, the more sensible solution would be to give effect to their intention and uphold the revocation of the will.[146]

The converse case is more troublesome. Let us imagine a testator who destroyed his will in the mistaken belief that this revoked the will according to his *lex domicilii* at the time of the destruction. If that testator later dies domiciled in a country by whose law the destruction is efficacious as a revocation, should the will be regarded as having been revoked? *Cheshire & North*[147] think not: "A chance change of domicil could scarcely infuse life into an act that was legally abortive at birth." Now admittedly it is a matter of chance that a particular rule of the testator's *lex domicilii* at death agrees with his misconceived view as to the rule of his *lex domicilii* at the time of the destruction of the will. But as against this, our conflicts rules should surely give effect as far as possible, to the reasonable expectations of testators. It is not unreasonable for a testator to believe that setting fire to his will revokes it. If his *lex domicilii* at that time and at the time of his death provides otherwise, that is his misfortune but, if his *lex domicilii* at the time of his death coincides with his reasonable expectations, it seems unwise for the law to stand idly by and witness the frustration of the testator's understandable wishes on such an important matter.

(b) Immovables

There has been little discussion about the question of revocation by destruction of a will, so far as immovables are concerned. It has been suggested that "no doubt" the *lex situs* governs.[148]

Revocation by Marriage

Under Irish law a will is revoked by the subsequent marriage of the testator, except

---

[145] For consideration of the wide variety of rules among jurisdictions in the United States on the question of revocation by physical act, see Reese, *American Wills Statutes — Part II*, 46 Va. L. Rev. 856, at 875-880 (1960).

[146] See *Cheshire & North*, 612-613.

[147] *Id.*, 613.

[148] *Morris*, 401. Morris refers to the Iowa case of *Re Barrie's Estate*, 240 Iowa 431, 35 N.W. 2d 658 (1949), where the majority applied the *lex situs* rule. From the standpoint of policy, there is in this instance, as in so many others relating to the *lex situs* rule, a considerable doubt as to the utility and fairness of referring to that law, since the testator almost certainly paid no attention to it and the community living within that territory presumably had little concern as to what law regarding revocation was applied to persons whose only connection with them was that they owned land there: see further Hancock's criticism of the majority approach, in *Conceptual Devices for Avoiding the Land Taboo in Conflict of Laws: The Disadvantages of Disingenuousness*, 20 Stan. L. Rev. 1 (1967).

where the will is made in contemplation of that marriage.[149] This is not the position in some other jurisdictions. The divergence of approach can give rise to difficulties, as, for example, where, in the case of a will disposing of immoveable property, the testator's *lex domicilii* at the time of the marriage differs from the *lex situs* of the property at the time of his death.[150]

A question of characterisation arises: are we dealing with a rule of testamentary, or of matrimonial, law? The commentators generally[151] favour the latter view, which has the support of some judicial authority.[152] Thus, the *lex domicilii* at the time of marriage would be determinative. But there is much to be said for the opposite view that the rule relates more to testamentary law.[153]

POWERS OF APPOINTMENT EXERCISED BY WILL[154]

Under Irish law, one person (the donor) may by will or *inter vivos* settlement give another (the appointer) the power of appointment — that is, power to select which persons are to be entitled to the donor's property. We are here concerned with cases where the appointer exercises the power of appointment by will. The power may be *special,* where the donor must make his selection from a specified class of persons (objects of the power) or *general,* where he may select without any such limitation. This means, of course, that the appointer of a general power may, if he wishes, select himself as beneficiary.

Conflicts of law problems relating to a power of appointment in regard to movables may arise where the donor, the appointer and the donees of the power are not all domiciled in the same country. Which law should control? One approach would refer to the *lex domicilii* of the appointer on the basis that the validity of all wills by movables should be governed by a consistent rule.[155] But certainly in the case of a special power (where he is not an object of the power) and theoretically even in the case of a general power, the appointer is not bequeathing his *own* property but rather is acting as agent for the donor in disposing of the donor's property.[156] This would suggest that we should look instead to the law governing the instrument creating the power of appointment.

Let us consider the subject of powers of appointment under the same headings as we dealt with wills, namely: (1) capacity; (2) formal requirements; (3) essential validity; (4) construction; and (5) revocation.

---

[149] Succession Act 1965, section 85(1). See *Wylie,* para. 14.20.

[150] See *Cheshire & North,* 613, *Falconbridge,* 112-117.

[151] *Cheshire & North,* 613, *Dicey & Morris,* 639.

[152] *Re Martin, Loustalan* v. *Loustalan,* [1900] P. 211, at 240 (C.A., per Vaughan Williams, J.), *Seifert* v. *Seifert,* 32 O.L.R. 433, 23 D.L.R. 440 (Ont. Sup. Ct., Middleton, J., 1914); cf. *Davies* v. *Davies,* 8 W.W.R. 803, 24 D.L.R. 737 (Alta. Sup. Ct., Stuart, J., 1915).

[153] See *Rabel,* vol. 1, 403, *Falconbridge,* 112-117, *Wolff,* 595. Our courts have yet to address the problem created where the testator has been divorced and, under his *lex domicilii* at the time of the divorce, the divorce operated to revoke his will: cf. *Scoles & Hay,* 787-788, Scoles & Rheinstein, *Conflict Avoidance in Succession Planning,* 21 L. & Contemp. Prob. 499, at 505-506 (1956).

[154] See *Morris,* 402-408, *Scoles & Hay,* 812-821, Fridman, *Choice of Law Governing the Testamentary Exercise of Powers of Appointment Over Movables,* 9 Int. & Comp. L.Q. 1 (1960), Durand & Herterich, *Conflict of Laws and the Exercise of Powers of Appointment,* 42 Cornell L.Q. 185 (1957), Mulford, *The Conflict of Laws and Powers of Appointment,* 87 U. Pa. L. Rev. 403 (1939), Ester & Scoles, *Estate Planning and Conflict of Laws,* 24 Ohio St. L.J. 270 (1963), Casner, *Estate Planning — Powers of Appointment,* 64 Harv. L. Rev. 185, at 208-210 (1950), *Anon, Note: Choice of Law Governing Powers of Appointment Over Personalty,* 50 Colum. L. Rev. 239 (1950), D.M.B. *Note: Trusts of Personalty and the Conflict of Laws,* 89 U. Pa. L. Rev. 360 (1941), Halbach, *The Use of Powers of Appointment in Estate Planning,* 45 Iowa L. Rev. 691, at 715-717 (1960), *Anon., Note,* 38 Harv. L. Rev. 661 (1925).

[155] Cf. *Morris,* 403, *Castel,* vol. 2, 469.

[156] *Id.*

Capacity

There is English authority[157] in favour of recognising the exercise of a power of appointment over movables by will where the appointer has capacity under his *lex domicilii* but not by the law governing the instrument creating the power. There is no judicial authority dealing with the position where matters are reversed. It has been suggested[158] that the exercise of a special, but not a general, power should be valid in such a case. This distinction gives effective recognition to the practical distinction between special and general powers.[159] As against this, it may be debated whether a power of appointment is in fact exercised "by will" when the will is not valid by the law governing testamentary capacity.[160] Where the power of appointment is over immovables, it could appear that the *lex situs* should govern.[161]

Formalities

Where a person, under an Irish settlement or will, is given a power of appointment exercisable by will, and he later dies abroad, having made a will in the foreign country, the question will arise as to whether the power of appointment is formally valid. Whose laws should determine this question? The position has been made far easier by the Succession Act 1965. We have already noted that section 102(1), which upholds the formal validity of a will if it complies with any one of five specific laws, also applies to powers of appointment by will.[162] Thus a power of appointment by will is formally valid if it complies with the formal requirements of the *locus actus* or the nationality, domicile or habitual residence of the testator, or, in the case of immovables, of the *lex situs*.

Furthermore, section 104(1) of the Succession Act 1965 provides as follows:

"Without prejudice to section 102, a testamentary disposition shall also be valid as regards form so far as it exercises a power of appointment, if its form complies with the law governing the essential validity of the power."

The subsection is in harmony with a number of earlier authorities, including *Murphy* v. *Deichler*,[163] where the House of Lords affirmed the Irish Court of Appeal. Section 104 (2) of the Succession Act 1965 provides that:

"A testamentary disposition so far as it exercises a power of appointment shall not be treated as invalid as regards form by reason only that its form is not in accordance with any formal requirement contained in the instrument creating the power."

Formerly, compliance with these formalities was necessary where the testamentary disposition derived its formal validity from foreign law.[164]

Essential Validity

When we consider the question of essential validity of a will exercising a power of appointment over movables, we have to bear in mind the distinction between special

---

[157] *Re Lewal's Settlement*, [1918] 2 Ch. 391. See also *Guarantee Trust Co. of New York* v. *Stevens*, 28 N.J. 243, 146 A. 2d 97 (1958).

[158] *Cheshire & North*, 614-615. See also *Morris*, 404, *Dicey & Morris*, 644, *Scoles & Hay*, 816.

[159] See *Castel*, vol. 2, 469-470.

[160] *Goodrich*, 3rd ed., 530. See also Fridman, *Choice of Law Governing the Testamentary Exercise of Powers of Appointment Over Movables*, 9 Int. & Comp. L.Q. 1, at 4 (1960).

[161] Cf. *Castel*, vol. 2 470, *Restatement* 2d 281, *Dicey & Morris*, 644.

[162] Section 102(1) refers to a "testamentary disposition," which is defined, for the purpose of Part VIII of the Act, as meaning any will or other testamentary instrument or act.

[163] [1909] A.C. 446, 43 I.L.T.R. 235 (H.L.(Ir.)), aff'g 42 I.L.T.R. 113 (C.A., 1908). See further *Bentwich*, 123-124.

[164] *Dicey & Morris*, 645, *Barretto* v. *Young*, [1900] 2 Ch. 339.

and general powers. Where the power is special, the *lex domicilii* of the donor rather than of the appointer controls, since the appointer is acting merely as the agent of the donor.[165] Where the power is general, and the appointer deals with the appointed property and his own property "as one mass",[166] this is regarded as so clearly a matter under the appointer's control and concerned with his interests, rather than those of the donor, that the *lex domicilii* of the appointer should control.[167] But where the power is general and the appointer in making an appointment keeps the property subject to the power separate from his own property, the appointer is again regarded as acting as the agent of the donor, whose *lex domicilii* accordingly controls.[168]

So far as immovables are concerned, judicial authority is sparse but the clear rule appears to be that the *lex situs* governs.[169]

Construction

The construction of wills exercising a power of appointment proceeds on the same basis as the construction of wills generally.[170] The courts seek to interpret the will in accordance with the law intended by the testator; in the absence of contrary indications, this is presumed to be the *lex domicilii* at the time the will was made.[171]

In *Murray* v. *Champernowne*,[172] a testator domiciled in Scotland made a will in execution of a general power of appointment, in which he disposed of land in Ireland subject to a trust for sale as yet unsold. The will was invalid under Scots law but valid under Irish and English law.[173] The original deed creating the power of appointment was either Irish or English.

Andrews, J. upheld the disposition, on the basis that the property should be categorised as immoveable, and thus, the will was governed by Irish law.[174] But the Judge was willing to hold that, even if the property should be categorised as movable, the will was still valid. The question was one of construction, and Warren, J. construed the intention of the original deed as being to give the testator "power to appoint by a will made in accordance with Irish or English law, and to be construed in accordance with such law."[175] The words specifying the power, in conjunction with an earlier provision, suggested to the Judge that this construction was correct.[176] The testator "must be taken to have intended"[177] that it should be construed in accordance with the rules of Irish and English law.

Revocation

A power of appointment over movables exercisable by will may be revoked in any of three circumstances:[178]

[165] *Pouey* v. *Hordern*, [1900] 1 Ch. 492. See *Morris*, 406-407.
[166] *Re Pryce*, [1911] 2 Ch. 286, (C.A., per Cozens-Hardy, M.R.), See also *In re Khan's Settlement*, [1966] Ch. 567, disapproving *In re Waite's Settlement Trusts*, [1958] Ch. 100, criticised by Morris, 73 L.Q. Rev. 459 (1957). See further *Dicey & Morris*, 650-652. As to Irish internal law, cf. *Re De Lusi's Settlement*, 3 L.R. Ir. 232 (Chatterton, V.C., 1879).
[167] *Castel* vol. 2, 472.
[168] *In re Mégret* [1901] 1 Ch. 547.
[169] *Re Hernando*, 27 Ch. D. 284 (1884).
[170] See *Dicey & Morris*, 646, *Cheshire & North*, 618.
[171] *Dicey & Morris*, Rule 110 (1), *Re McMorrah*, [1958] Ch. 624 (Harman, J., 1957).
[172] [1901] 2 I.R. 232 (Q.B. Div., Prob., Andrews, J., 1900).
[173] Wills Act 1837, section 27. See now the Succession Act 1965, section 93.
[174] See further pp. 397-398, *supra*.
[175] [1901] 2 I.R., at 237.
[176] *Id*.
[177] *Id*., at 238.
[178] *Cheshire & North*, 618-619.

(*a*) if the will is properly revoked under the law of the donee's domicile,[179]

(*b*) if it is revoked by a later will properly executed under the Succession Act 1965,[180] or

(*c*) if it is revoked by the subsequent marriage of the testator according to the law of his or her domicile at the time of his or her marriage, rather than of his or her death.[181]

---

[179] *Velasco* v. *Coney,* [1934] P. 143 (Langton, J.). See further Mumford, *The Conflict of Laws and Powers of Appointment,* 87 U. Pa. L. Rev. 403, at 421, fn. 101 (1939).

[180] Succession Act 1965, section 85.

[181] *Cheshire & North,* 619.

CHAPTER 24

ADMINISTRATION OF ESTATES

Where a deceased person leaves property, it devolves to his personal representatives, that is, his executors or administrators.[1] Before the personal representatives may carry out the functions of their office, they must first obtain a grant of representation: a grant of probate or (where there is no executor or none willing or able to take up the position) a grant of letters of administration.[2]

The duties of personal representatives are to collect the estate and administer it according to law.[3] The order in which the assets are to be administered is specified by the Succession Act 1965.[4] The personal representatives are also under a duty to distribute the assets among those entitled to them.[5] As we shall see, these two functions, of administration and distribution, "are governed by different principles of private international law".[6]

In Ireland, therefore, property cannot normally be dealt with by anybody without a grant of representation.[7] In civil law jurisdictions, however, the entire property of a deceased person normally passes directly to his heirs or universal legatee, unless they renounce it.[8] This will not have the effect of giving good title to these persons, so far as property situated in Ireland is concerned, unless they obtain an Irish grant of probate or administration.[9]

JURISDICTION OF IRISH COURT

Since succession to moveable property is determined in accordance with the *lex domicilii* of the deceased, it might be thought that courts of the domicile should have jurisdiction on that account alone. But that would not be an ideal solution because a grant would be ineffective where there were no assets within the country of the deceased person's domicile.

Moreover, historical factors play their part in fashioning the modern law. Before 1858, grants of representation were made exclusively by the ecclesiastical courts of the Church of Ireland.[10] Jurisdiction depended on the presence of moveable

[1] See generally *Wylie*, ch.16.
[2] Cf. *Wylie*, para. 1603.
[3] *Wylie*, para. 16.20, Clarke, *Some Aspects of the Succession Act 1965; Caveant Executores; New Powers and Burdens for Personal Representatives*, 1 Ir. Jur. (N.S.) 222 (1966).
[4] See *Wylie*, paras. 16.30 – 16.40. Note especially sections 45-48, 50, 55, 57-61, and 64-65 of the Succession Act 1965.
[5] *Wylie*, paras. 16.41 – 16.63.
[6] *Cheshire & North*, 589.
[7] *Wylie*, para. 16.03. However Section 23 (3) of the Building Societies Act 1976 permits payment out by a society of a sum forming part of the intestate estate of a deceased member or depositor to the person who appears to the directors to be entitled to receive it, without that person taking out letters of administration.
[8] *Cheshire & North*, 589.
[9] *Id.*, 589-590.
[10] See *Wylie*, para. 15.04, *Dicey & Morris*, 589, *Kelly* v. *Bank of Ireland*, Batty 593 (K.B., 1826).

property (*bona notabilia*) within the court's province or diocese.[11] In 1857 this jurisdiction was transferred to the newly constituted Court of Probate.[12] The jurisdiction of that Court in turn was transferred to the High Court in 1877[13], where it remains today, subject to concurrent jurisdiction with the circuit court on certain matters.[14]

The legislation in 1857 preserved for the Probate Court the jurisdictional rules which had applied to the Ecclesiastical Courts and these in turn affected the High Court after 1877. Thus, if the testator left moveable assets within the jurisdiction, probate might be ordered even though the testator had a foreign domicile[15] or residence.[16] But if the testator left no property to be administered within the jurisdiction of the court, it was not possible to order administration.[17] In 1959,[18] however, this position was remedied and this reform was retained by the Succession Act 1965, section 29 of which provides that the High Court has jurisdiction to make a grant of representation in respect of a deceased person, notwithstanding that he left no estate in the State, and to make a *de bonis non* or other form of grant in respect of unadministered estate of the deceased in the State.

This provision ensures that where a person dies leaving property abroad and the foreign court refuses to make a grant of representation until a grant has been obtained in Ireland, the Irish court will be able to make such a grant, thus "obviat[ing] an injustice . . . "[19] which could otherwise arise.[20] An English *dictum* based on similar legislative provisions supports the view that, in cases where the deceased had a foreign domicile it would be "contrary to principle"[21] to make a grant where the deceased leaves no assets in England, since "[s]uch a grant in a case such as this would be nothing more than a piece of paper".[22] Perhaps this is going too far: it is probably sufficient that the Irish court, conscious of the practical realities, should be very reluctant to make a grant in such circumstances.[23]

Separate Wills

In some cases, a testator may make separate wills disposing of his or her property in Ireland and in foreign countries. Where one will confirms the other, the two wills "together constitute the last will of the testator,"[24] and a grant of representation

---

[11] See *Dicey & Morris*, 589.

[12] Probates and Letters of Administration Act (Ireland) 1857, sections 5-6.

[13] Supreme Court of Judicature (Ireland) Act 1877, section 21.

[14] Succession Act 1965, section 6, as amended by the Courts Act 1981, section 4.

[15] *Robinson* v. *Palmer*, [1901] 2 I.R. 489 (K.B. Div. (Prob.), Andrews, J.), *In bonis Gentili, dec'd*, I.R. 9 Eq. 541 (Warren, J., 1875.)

[16] See *In bonis Elliott, dec'd*, 3 L.R. (Ir.) 147 (Prob, Warren, J., 1879), *Ex parte Lurgan U.D.C.; In re Kearns*, [1902] 1 I.R. 154 (Porter, M.R., 1901), *In bonis Grierson*, 7 L.R. Ir. 589 (Prob., 1881).

[17] *In bonis Butson, dec'd* 9 L.R. Ir. 21 (Prob., Warren, J., 1882), *In bonis M'Cullagh*, 13 L.R. Ir. 242 (C.A., aff'g. Warren, J., 1884), *In bonis Tucker*, 3 Sw. & Tr. 585, 164 E.R. 1402 (1864). See also *In bonis Connor, Deceased*, 19 L.R. Ir. 261 (Prob., Warren, J., 1892), *In re Estate of M'Sweeney, dec'd, M'Sweeney* v. *Murphy*, [1919] 1 I.R. 16, at 22 (C.A., *per* O'Connor, L.J., 1981).

[18] Adminstration of Estates Act 1959, section 16.

[19] *In the Estate of Wayland*, [1951] 2 All E.R. 1041, at 1044, (P.D.A. Div., Pearce, J.).

[20] *Dicey & Morris*, 589-590. See further *Wylie*, para. 16.13. Another advantage to a *de bonis non* grant is that it may facilitate a relative who proposes to sue for damages (under the provisions of Part IV of the Civil Liability Act 1961) on behalf of a person who is killed in an accident but leaves no assets here or elsewhere: *Conférence de la Haye de droit international privé, Actes et documents de la Douzième Session*, tôme II, *Administration des successions*, p. 91.

[21] *Aldrich* v. *A.G.*, [1968] P. 281, at 295 (P.D.A. Div., Ormrod, J., 1957).

[22] *Id.*

[23] Cf. *Morris*, 383. Cf. *In the Goods of Dyas, dec'd*, [1937] I.R. 479 (High Ct., Hanna, J.); and see *In re Welsh dec'd; O'Brien* v. *Phelan*, [1931] I.R. 161 (Sup. C. 1930) (deceased domiciled in Ireland; assets from abroad transferred to within the State).

[24] *Morris*, 383. Cf. *In bonis Power*, 25 L.R. Ir., 509 (Prob., Warren, J., 1890) (codicil confirming will made same day). See also *In bonis Fletcher*, 11 L.R. Ir. 359 (Prob., Warren, J., 1883).

for both must be obtained.[25] Where, however, one will does not confirm the other, the two wills are treated independently so far as grants of representation are concerned. Prior to 1959, it appears that it would have been possible to obtain a grant for the will dealing with the Irish property only, since the other will would have fallen foul of the rule[26] that no grant may be obtained here where there are no assets within the jurisdiction. In such circumstances, the Irish property and Irish will were not taken into consideration.

Since 1959, there is no reason for the courts to adopt this somewhat blinkered approach: the better view would appear to be that if some practical benefit will result from making a grant in respect of the foreign will, the court may exercise its discretion to do so.[27]

Person To Whom The Grant Is Made

The High Court has power to grant administration (with or without will annexed) of the estate of a deceased person, and a grant may be limited in any way the Court thinks fit.[28] As a general principle, the person or persons to whom administration is to be granted will be determined "in accordance with rules of the High Court".[29] This principle is qualified by the rule that, where by reason of any special circumstances it appears to the High Court[30] to be necessary or expedient to do so, the Court may order that administration be granted to such person as it thinks fit.[31]

So far as persons domiciled or resident abroad at the time of their death are concerned, we must look at the terms of the 1965 Act. Apart from section 29, there appears to be only one express provision dealing with the position of these persons.[32] Rule 23 of Order 79 of the Rules of the Superior Courts 1986 provides that, in the case of a person residing out of, or about to leave, the jurisdiction of the Court, administration, or administration with the will annexed, may be granted to his attorney, acting under a power of attorney. Though this rule is clearly capable of extending to cases where the deceased died domiciled abroad, it may more easily be understood as envisaging the simpler case of an administrator of an essentially Irish estate who happens to reside abroad.

It seems therefore that the question of the desirability of making a grant here to the person entitled to administer the estate by the law of the deceased's domicile is one that may be resolved by considerations of practicality. In this regard, there is much to be said in favour of making a grant to such a person in the ordinary case.[33]

---

[25] Cf. *Dicey & Morris*, 590, *In bonis Harris*, L.R. 2 P. & D. 83 (1870), *In the Goods of de la Saussaye*, L.R. 3 P. & D. 42 (Sir J. Hannen, 1873), *In the Goods of Lockhart*, 69 L.T.21 (P.D.A. Div., Barnes, J., 1893).

[26] See *supra*, p. 454.

[27] Cf. *Morris*, 383, *Cheshire & North*, 590-591, *Dicey & Morris*, 590, *In the Estate of Wayland*, [1951] 2 All E.R. 1041 (P.D.A. Div., Pearce, J.).

[28] Succession Act 1965, section 27 (1). Cf. *In the Goods of Gentili dec'd*, I.R. 9 Eq. 541 (Prob., Warren, J., 1875), *De Fogassieras* v. *Duport*, 11 L.R. Ir. 123 (Prob., Warren, J., 1883), *Murray* v. *Champerowne*, [1901] 2 I.R. 232 (Q.B. Div., Prob., Andrews, J., 1900), *In bonis Hearst, dec'd*, 40 I.L.T.R. 198 (K.B., Andrews, J., 1906).

[29] *Succession Act 1965*, section 27 (3). Cf. Order 15, Part III, of the Rules of the Superior Courts 1986.

[30] Or, in a case within the jurisdiction of the Circuit Court, that Court: *id.*, section 27 (4).

[31] *Id.*

[32] Section 31 of the Succession Act 1965 deals with the case where a personal representative to whom a grant *has been made* resides abroad. Cf. *In bonis Lee*, [1898] 2 I.R. 81 (Q.B. Div., Prob., Andrews, J., 1896), *In bonis Colclough*, [1902] 2 I.R. 499 (K.B. Div., Andrews, J., 1901). See also *In bonis Grierson*, 7 L.R. Ir. 589 (Prob., Warren, J., 1881), *In bonis Downing*, 19 L.R. Ir. 233 (Prob., Warren, J., 1887), *In bonis Kelly, dec'd*, 31 I.L.T.R. 169 (Q.B. Div., Prob., Andrews, J., 1897).

[33] Cf. *In the Goods of Earl*, L.R. 1 P. & D. 450 (Sir James Wilde, J., 1867), *In the Goods of Briesemann*, [1894] P. 260 (Sir Francis Jeune, P.), *In the Goods of Kaufman*, [1952] P. 325 (Lord Merriman, P.), *In Re Estate of Kaine*, [1938] 3 W.W.R. 224, [1938] 4 D.L.R. 806 (B.C. Sup. Ct., Fisher,

In *In bonis Gentili, dec'd*,[34] Warren, J. went very far in stating that the right of administration "must follow the right of succession . . . " In this case a married woman, who was domiciled in Italy, died intestate there, possessed of a leasehold interest in houses in Ireland. Her Italian husband was held entitled to an unqualified grant of administration. Warren, J. was:

> "of opinion that succession to chattels real depends on the law of the country wherein those chattels real are situate; and inasmuch as in this country a surviving husband alone is entitled to succeed to the chattels real of his deceased wife, Signor Gentili is entitled to have an unqualified administration as to the houses . . . ; but it would be objectionable to give him a grant limited to the houses, if he be also entitled by the law of the domicil [Italy] to a grant of administration of all [the] other . . . assets of his wife, as he would appear to be. . . . "[35]

It would be wrong to think that the Irish court must always appoint as administrator the person authorised by the *lex domicilii* of the deceased.[36] Where, for example, the domiciliary personal representative takes no steps to obtain probate or letters of administration, the Irish court may make a grant to some other person, such as a creditor.[37] *In bonis Dyas, dec'd*,[38] Hanna, J. stated that " [i]n the normal case, a creditor, where the personal representative or the next-of-kin decline to take a grant, is given a grant on satisying the Court that he is a creditor on the particular estate and that there is estate of the deceased in Ireland liable for the debt. But the Court must be always satisfied that there is a distinct and definite interest in the assets." In this case an English nominee of an English firm claiming to be the assignees of a debt incurred to a South African creditor in South Africa fifty years previously by a South Africa domiciliary, sought a grant of letters of administration with the will annexed to the deceased debtor's estate in Ireland. By the direction of the Court the executrix was cited to take out a grant in Ireland but declined to do so. There were no creditors in Ireland.

Hanna, J. expressed considerable uncertainty as to whether the property in Ireland was liable to debts under Roman Dutch law or whether the deceased's wife would have rights which would override the debts, as the spouses had married in community property. Notwithstanding this, he considered that the assignees were entitled to be put in a position where, whatever their rights, they would be protected, and their debts and the liability of the estate investigated (unless the executrix consented to payment) by the competent Court in South Africa. Hanna, J. was therefore willing to issue a grant *ad colligenda bona* to an Irish nominee of the applicants limited to having the money paid out to him, under the obligation to pay it into the appropriate court of the domicile.

Where a grant here is made to a foreign personal representative, it is described as "ancillary", in contrast to the "principal" administration in the country of the

---

J.), *Re Knoch*, 25 O.R (2d) 312 (High Ct., Craig, J., 1979) aff'd 29 O.R. (2d) 60n (C.A., 1980). The fact that a testamentary disposition may be formally valid under Irish rules of conflicts of law though formally invalid under the *lex domicilii* (cf. Succession Act 1965, Part VIII), weakens the strength of the argument that the administrator of the deceased's domicile should be selected because the *lex domicilii* governs succession to movables: cf. *Dicey & Morris*, 593. See further *Re Manifold*, [1962] Ch. 1 (Buckley, J.).

[34] I.R. 9 Eq. 541, at 543 (Prob., Warren, J., 1875).

[35] *Id.*, at 550-551.

[36] See *In bonis Kaufman, supra, Bath* v. *British and Malayan Trustees Ltd.*, [1969] 2 N.S.W.R. 114 (Sup. Ct., Helsham, J.), *Lewis* v. *Belshaw*, 54 C.L.R. 188, at 197 H. Ct. Austr., *per* Starke, J., 1935). Cf. the Succession Act, 1965, section 27 (4), *Dicey & Morris*, 591.

[37] Cf. *In the Estate of Leguia* [1934] P. 80. (Merriman, P., 1933).

[38] [1937] I.R. 479, at 480-481 (Hanna, J.).

deceased person's domicile.[39] An Irish court making a grant to a foreign personal representative need not investigate the ground on which he was appointed in the foreign jurisdiction.[40] But the foreign personal representative is not exempt from the conditions as to capacity to be an Irish personal representative laid down for all personal representatives by Irish law.[41]

Effect of an Irish Grant

We must now consider the effect of an Irish grant. It should be noted that section 10 (1) of the Succession Act 1965 provides that "[t]he real and personal estate of a deceased person shall on his death, notwithstanding any testamentary disposition, devolve on and become vested in his personal representatives". Where the deceased person leaves an effective will appointing an executor or executors, the transmission is immediate. In respect of other cases, section 13 of the Act provides that the deceased person's "real and personal estate, until administration is granted in respect thereof, shall vest in the President of the High Court...."[42]

Although there is no express limitation in the Succession Act 1965 to property situate within the State, the general tenor of many of its provisions[43] strongly suggests that section 10 (1) does not envisage the immediate vesting in the personal representatives of property – at all events, immovables[44] – situate outside the State. So far as movables brought into the State are concerned, the Act again throws no clear light on the position. Indeed, there is uncertainty on this question in other jurisdictions. In the absence of definitive judicial authority, the commentators favour the view that movables brought within the jurisdiction from abroad, before any person has obtained a good title to them in their *lex situs*, should vest in the personal representative within the jurisdiction.[45] It seems, however, that where a third party

---

[39] *Dicey & Morris*, 592, *Cheshire & North*, 591.

[40] *In the Goods of Spenceley*, [1892] P. 255, *In the Goods of Schulhof*, [1948] P. 66 (P.D.A. Div. Willmer, J., 1947); *In the Goods of Wolf*, [1948] P. 66 (P.D.A. Div., Willmer, J., 1947).

[41] Cf. *In the Goods of H.R.H. the Duchesse d'Orléans*, 1 Sw. & Tr. 253, 164 E.R. 716 (1859) (minority). See further *Wylie*, paras. 16.04, 16.12. It should be noted that some statutes enacted in the nineteenth century to facilitate the administration of estates have been repealed after Independence. The Colonial Probates Act 1892 was repealed by the Administration of Estates Act 1959, section 5 and the Probates and Letters of Administration Act (Ireland) 1857 (which included, in section 94, provision for the resealing in Ireland of probates granted in England) was repealed by the Succession Act 1965, section 8. Whether these provisions survived Independence and the consequential legislation is doubtful. Decisions on section 94 include *Mahon* v. *Hodgens*, I.R. 6 Eq. 344 (Prob., Warren, J., 1872) and *Bannon* v. *Macaire*, 7 L.R. Ir 211 (Prob., Warren, J., 1881). See also *In bonis Butson, dec'd*, 9 L.R. Ir. 21, at 23 (Prob., Warren, J., 1882), *In re Estate of Herbert dec'd. Herbert* v. *Herbert* 25 L.R. Ir 102 (Porter, M.R., 1890), *In re Estate of M'Sweeney, Deceased. M'Sweeney* v. *Murphy*, [1919] 1 I.R. 16 (C.A., 1918), *In bonis Haughton, dec'd*, I.R. 4 Eq. 260 (Prob., Warren, J., 1870), *In bonis Walshe*, [1897] 1 I.R. 167 (Prob., Warren, J., 1896), *In bonis Wallace*, 29 L.R. Ir. 118 (Prob., Warren, J., 1891). See further *Miller*, ch. 22.

[42] See further *Wylie*, paras. 16.02-16.03.

[43] Cf., e.g. sections 4, 10 (2), 12.

[44] Save in Part VIII, the Act refers to personal estate and real estate, rather than adopting the conflicts division of property into movables and immovables. (Cf. *supra*, pp. 391-392). It seems clear, especially in view of the dominance of the *lex situs* rule with respect to immovables (cf. *supra*, pp. 392, 401, 408-409), that the foreign immovables would not vest under section 10 (1). The position regarding movables situate abroad is less clear, and the Act throws no light on the question. Perhaps the best way of resolving the uncertainty is in practical, rather than theoretical, terms. As *Cheshire & North*, 595, observe in respect of the position in England, "[a]lthough the theory may be that an English grant extends to property no matter where situated, it is obviously of no practical importance, for whether the administrator is entitled to the property of the deceased in a foreign country must necessarily depend upon the local law." See further *Dicey & Morris*, 559.

[45] *Dicey & Morris*, Rule 89 (2); Cf. *Cheshire & North*, 595. In the English case of *Whyte* v. *Rose*, 3 Q.B. 493, at 506, 114 E.R. 596, at 601 (1842), Parke, B. asked:
"Suppose, after a man's death, his watch be brought to England by a third party, could such party, in answer to an action of trover by an English administrator, plead that the watch was in Ireland

had obtained title to a movable according to the *lex situs* before it was brought to Ireland, that title would be recognised here.[46]

Recovery of Assets

While an Irish personal representative must collect the assets of the deceased person that are situate within the State, his duties with regard to other assets are "less well defined."[47] A prudent personal representative may be slow to touch foreign assets without a foreign grant of representation since otherwise he could well be deemed an executor *de son tort*, or suffer equivalent penalties, under the foreign law.[48] Where the foreign country recognises the claim of the Irish personal representative the question arises as to whether there is an obligation to apply for a foreign grant. The position is uncertain. It seems that if there are sufficient assets available in Ireland to pay the debts, the personal representative is not obliged to take this step and may instead simply assent to the vesting of the foreign assets in the legatee.[49] In *Re Fitzpatrick*,[50] Harman, J. said:

> "Foreign assets do not vest in executors *virtute officii*. If there are debts and no sufficient assets in England to meet them, it may be the duty of English executors to possess themselves of any foreign assets, but, if that is not the case, they can assent to the foreign assets without bringing them to this country. They need only satisfy themselves that they have sufficient assets to pay the debts here."

Choice of Law

The administration of a deceased person's estate "is governed wholly by the law of the country in which the personal representative obtained his grant."[51] The *lex fori* determines the admissibility and priority or debts. In this respect foreign creditors rank equally with Irish creditors.[52] The only difference between a principal and ancillary administration appears to be that an Irish ancillary administrator need not advertise for foreign claims or take active steps abroad to ascertain the position in regard to debts.[53]

The distribution of the assets remaining in the hands of the personal representative after the debts have been cleared is characterised as a matter of succession (generally to be determined by the *lex domicilii*, so far as movables are concerned)[54] rather than of administration.[55] Where an Irish ancillary personal representative has finally collected the assets and paid off the debts here, normally he "will hand over the

---

at the time of the death?"
Cf. *Swift* v. *Swift*, 1 Ball & B. 326 (Lord Manners, L.C., 1810)
[46] *Dicey & Morris*, 597. The position where the third party is a foreign personal representative is discussed *infra*, pp. 460-461.
[47] *Dicey & Morris*, 598.
[48] *Id.*
[49] *Id.*, at 599.
[50] [1952] Ch. 86, at 88 (Ch. Div., Harman, J., 1951).
[51] *Morris*, 387, citing *Preston* v. *Melville*, 8 Cl. & F.1, 8 E.R. 1 (1841), where Lord Cottenham, L.C. observed (at 12-13 and 5-6, respectively): "The domicile regulates the right of succession, but the administration must be in the country in which possession is taken and held, under lawful authority, of the deceased".
[52] *Id.* In *Re Kloebe; Kannreuther* v. *Geiselbrecht*, 28 Ch. D. 175, at 177-178 (Chy. Div., 1884), Pearson, J. said:
> "I know of no law under which the English creditors are to be preferred to foreigners. On the other hand the rule is they are all to be treated equally, subject to what priorities the law may give them, from whatever part of the world they come. . . ."
[53] *In re Achillopoulos*, [1928] Ch. 433, at 445 (Tomlin, J.); cf. *Re Holden*, [1935] W.N. 52 (Farwell, J.).
[54] See *supra*, pp. 429-430.
[55] *Morris*, 387, *Dicey & Morris*, 601.

residue to the foreign administrator or to the person or persons who, according to the foreign law, will take the place of personal representatives".[56]

But it is clear that the Irish Court has a discretionary power to prevent the ancillary administrator from handing over the balance. In the controversial English decision of *In re Lorillard*,[57] Lord Sterndale, M.R., considered the question to be "entirely a matter of discretion".[58] In this case, the testator who had domiciled in New York, died leaving property and creditors both in the United States and England. Administration proceedings were going on in both countries. In England there were no debts, and in the United States there were debts which were statute-barred according to English, but not New York, law. If claims in respect of these debts had been made in England they would have been rejected.[59]

The English administrator asked for the directions of the Court as to what course he ought to pursue. Eve, J. made an order giving the creditors a period of two months within which to bring their claims in England, after which the surplus assets would be distributed among the beneficiaries. This, of course, was an empty entitlement since these claims, if brought, would be rejected. The creditors therefore did not present their claims. The Court of Appeal declined to alter Eve, J.'s order. Lord Sterndale, M.R. could not:

"see any principle under which it is necessary for the English Court in such circumstances to order the administrator here to hand over the surplus assets to the American administrator. No authority has been cited in favour of such a course...."[60]

The decision has been widely criticised[61] for enriching beneficiaries at the expense of creditors entitled to payment in the country of the principal administration, on account of the chance fact that the beneficiaries happened to reside in England, where the Statute of Limitations was classified as procedural.

In *Re Lorillard* has, however, been followed,[62] and has received the approval of Lord Simonds, *obiter*, in *Government of India* v. *Taylor*,[63] as well as being supported in cases in other common law jurisdictions.[64]

---

[56] Irish Government reply to the questionnaire on private international law concerning succession, Conférence de la Haye de droit international privé, *Actes et documents de la Douzième session*, tome II, *Administration des successions*, p. 91. See also *In the Estate of Weiss*, [1962] P. 136, at (P.D.A. Div., Scarman, J., 1961); *Re Achillopoulos*, [1928] Ch. 433. Cf. *Cook* v. *Gregson*, 2 Drew. 286, 61 E.R. 729 (1854), where executors of a testator's will in both Ireland and England proved in both countries and brought a considerable part of the property from Ireland to England without having fully administered the estate in Ireland. Irish judgment creditors were held to have priority over English creditors in the English administration. Kindersley, V.C. observed (at 288 and 730, respectively) that the executor in Ireland "must take care first to pay the debts owing [there], and then, and not until then, if there is a surplus, he may send it to the other country. The duty of the Irish executor was to pay the Irish debts first, according to their order in priority . . . [T]he assets remitted [to England] ought . . . to be administered in as if they had remained and were being administered in Ireland". See further *In re Kloebe; Kannreuther* v. *Geiselbrecht, supra*, at 178-179. Cf. *In re Minchin; Minchin* v. *Stevens*, 38 I.L.T.R. 189 (C.A., 1904).

[57] [1922] 2 Ch. 638 (C.A.).

[58] *Id.*, at 644.

[59] *Id.*, 645 (*per* Lord Sterndale, M.R.).

[60] *Id.*

[61] Nadelmann, 49 Mich. L. Rev. 1129, at 1148-1149 (1951), *Dicey*, 5th ed., by Keith, 984-987. See, however, *Sykes*, 467.

[62] *Re Manifold*, [1962] Ch. 1.

[63] [1955] A.C. 491, at 509 (H.L. (Eng)).

[64] *Dicey & Morris*, 601, *Re Hagen*, [1942] 1 D.L.R. 752, *Permanent Trustee Co. (Canberra) Ltd.* v. *Finlayson*, 122 C.L.R. 338 (1968).

THE POSITION OF A FOREIGN ADMINISTRATOR ACTING IN IRELAND WITHOUT AN IRISH GRANT

It is a general[65] rule that the status of an administrator appointed by a foreign court is not recognised in Ireland.[66] His title relates only to property lying within the jurisdiction of the country from which he derives his authority, and therefore may not take or recover by action property in Ireland without a grant from the Irish court.[67] If the foreign administrator, without an Irish grant, actually succeeds in obtaining property in Ireland, he is "clearly liable as executor *de son tort* to account for the assets received".[68]

Where, however, a foreign personal representative has in a foreign country acquired a good title to any movables of the deceased, and has reduced them into possession, he will also be regarded in Ireland as having a good title to them.[69] In the Supreme Court decision of *In re Welsh, dec'd;O'Brien* v. *Phelan,*[70] in 1930, Fitzgibbon, J. (speaking for the Court) said:

> "When a foreign administrator, who has under the grant of a foreign Court reduced assets of the deceased into his possession, brings these assets into the jurisdiction of another Court, the goods are, by the comity of Courts, regarded as the property of the foreign administrator, and he has a title to them as owner. Accordingly, the foreign administrator can sue for such goods as if they were his own, and he does not require a grant of administration in the local jurisdiction to establish his title."

In *In re Estate of M'Sweeney, dec'd; M'Sweeney* v. *Murphy,*[71] the Court of Appeal held that no decree in an administration suit in Ireland can be made against a party who has not been made a personal representative here, even though that party is resident here and has been appointed administrator in another country. Malony, C.J. adopted[72] as correct the statement of law found in *Williams on Executors,*[73] based on *Story,*[74] to the effect that:

> "....no suit can be brought against any executor or administrator, in his official capacity, in the Court of any country but that from which he derives his authority to act by virtue of the probate or letters of administration there granted to him."

O'Connor, L.J. ventured to express no opinion on the question whether the administratrix in the case before the Court was in some respects in the position of a trustee or quasi-trustee, so that, as equity acts *in personam*, she could be sued in Ireland. The short answer was that the proceedings had not been framed against her as trustee:

> "This was an ordinary administration summons brought against an individual as personal representative, and in the result we find that there is no personal representative before the Court."[75]

Where the foreign administrator sends or brings to Ireland any moveable assets

---

[65] An exception relates to insurance policies. Cf. the Revenue Act 1884, section 11, as amended by the Revenue Act 1889, section 19.

[66] *Cheshire & North,* 595, *Dicey & Morris,* 602-603, *In re Estate of M'Sweeney, Deceased. M'Sweeney* v. *Murphy,* [1919] 1 I.R. 16 (C.A., 1918), *Swift* v. *Swift,* 1 Ball & B. 326 (Lord Manners, L.C., 1810).

[67] *Cheshire & North,* 595. See also *Finnegan* v. *Cementation Co. Ltd.,* [1953] 1 Q.B. 688 (C.A.).

[68] *Cheshire & North,* 595, citing *New York Breweries Co.* v. *A.G.,* [1899] A.C. 62.

[69] *Dicey & Morris,* Rule 92, item (3).

[70] [1931] I.R. 161, at 164 (Sup. Ct., 1930).

[71] [1919] 1 I.R. 15 (C.A., 1918).

[72] *Id.,* at 18-19. See also *id.,* at 21 (*per* Ronan, L.J.).

[73] 10th ed., vol. 2 p. 1565.

[74] Section 513.

[75] [1919] 1 I.R., at 22.

of the deceased, without having accounted for them in the administration in the jurisdiction from which he derives his title, and where he has not, by any specific appropriation, caused these assets to lose their character as part of the deceased's estate, a creditor or beneficiary may maintain an action in Ireland for their judicial administration.[76] Moreover an injunction and receiver will be granted in cases where it is necesary to prevent these assets from being removed out of the jurisdiction.[77]

[76] *In re Welsh, Deceased; O'Brien* v. *Phelan*, [1931] I.R. 161, at 164 (Sup. Ct., *per* Fitzgibbon, J., 1930), quoting from *Westlake*, para. 99.
[77] *Id.*

CHAPTER 25

BANKRUPTCY[1]

Bankruptcy has been defined as being a legal process "for the benefit and the relief of creditors and their debtors,[2] in cases in which the latter are unable or unwilling to pay their debts".[3] Generally, of course, bankruptcy proceedings will

[1] See *Blom-Cooper, passim, Bankruptcy Law Committee Report on the Law and Practice Concerning Bankruptcy and the Administration of Insolvent Estates of Deceased Persons* (Parl. 2714, 1972), Levi & Moore, *Bankruptcy and Reorganization: A Survey of Changes-I*, 5 U. Chic. L. Rev. 1 (1937), Hickey, *Irish Private International Law*, 42 Rabels Zeitschrift 268, at 297-299 (1978), Raeburn, *Application of the Maxim Mobilia Sequuntur Personam to Bankruptcy in Private International Law*, 26 Br. Yrbk of Internat. L. 177 (1949), Burgin, *Private International Law and Bankruptcy and Liquidation of Companies*, 9 Trans. of Grot. Soc. 71, at 71-84 (1923), Rolin, *Des conflits de lois en matière de faillite*, [1926] – IV Recueil des cours 5, Williston, *The Validity of Attachments Made Abroad by Creditors of an Insolvent Debtor*, 5 Harv. L. Rev. 211 (1891).

The leading and most prolific, international authority is Professor Kurt Nadelmann, whose writings have been of considerable influence: see, e.g., *International Bankruptcy Law: Its Present Status*, 5 U. Toronto L.J. 324 (1944) (a wide-ranging comparative study), *The National Bankruptcy Act and the Conflict of Laws*, 59 Harv. L. Rev. 1025 (1946), *Legal Treatment of Foreign and Domestic Creditors*, 11 L. & Contemp. Problems 696 (1946), *Solomons v. Ross and International Bankruptcy Law*, 9 Modern L. Rev. 154 (1946), *Codification of Conflict Rules for Bankruptcy*, 30 Schweizerisches Jahrbuch für internationales Recht 57 (1974).

[2] The policy of imprisoning for debt in former times led to conditions of great hardship. Handel's *Messiah*, first produced in Dublin in 1742, was performed for the benefit of a society formed for improving the condition of such inmates, compounding with their creditors, and releasing as many as possible from prison: Nadelmann, *Compositions — Reorganisations and Arrangements — In the Conflict of Laws*, 61 Harv. L. Rev. 804, at 816, fn. 61 (1948), citing Lecky's *History of England in the Eighteenth Century*, vol. 1, 581 (1878).

[3] *In re Reiman*, Fed. Cas. No. 11, 673, 20 Fed. Cas. 490, at 494 (1874). In *In re Bolton*, [1920] 2 I.R. 324, at 325-326 (K.B. Div.), Dodd, J. said:

"A bankrupt in British phraseology meant a man who had broken his bench, and had indicated thereby that he had not enough money to pay his creditors, and in our vocabulary up till 1872 was applicable to a trader only. The word 'insolvent' was applied to a person, not a trader, who was unable to pay his debts. And from the time of Henry VIII, when relief was granted to bankrupts — that is, traders — and from the time of Queen Elizabeth, when a certain measure of relief was given to other persons unable to pay their debts who were not traders, the words 'bankruptcy' and 'insolvency' have a definite and legal meaning. A bankrupt was, when he got his discharge, relieved from his debts; an insolvent was only released from gaol."

For consideration of historical and comparative aspects of bankruptcy law, see *Blom-Cooper*, ch. 1, Levinthal, *The Early History of Bankruptcy Law*, 66 U. Pa. L. Rev. 223 (1918), Levinthal, *The Early History of English Bankruptcy*, 67 U. Pa. L. Rev.1 (1919), Lipstein, *Jurisdiction in Bankruptcy*, 12 Modern L. Rev. 454, at 456-460 (1949). In Britain, the law of bankruptcy has been radically changed by the Insolvency Act 1985, consolidated by the Insolvency Act 1986. See Woloniecki, *Co-operation Between National Courts in International Insolvencies: Recent United Kingdom Legislation*, 35 Int. & Comp. L.Q. 644 (1986). In Ireland the progress of reforming legislation through the Oireachtas has been at a funereal pace.

The universalist solution attempted by the draft EEC Convention of Bankruptcy (1980) "has little prospect of being adopted by the Member States": Woloniecki, *supra*, at 644. For commentary on the draft Convention see *Fletcher*, ch. 6, Hunter, 21 Int. & Comp. L.Q. 682 (1972), Hunter, *The Draft EEC Bankruptcy Convention: A Further Examination*, 25 Int. & Comp. L.Q. 310 (1976).

be taken in cases where persons cannot pay their debts, but insolvency is not a condition precedent to adjudication: acts of bankruptcy may consist of conduct performed by a solvent person who simply does not want to pay a debt.

The main objects of bankruptcy legislation have been described as follows:

(1) to secure equality of distribution and to prevent any one creditor obtaining an unfair advantage over the others;

(2) to protect bankrupts from vindictive creditors by freeing them from the balance of their debts where they are unable to pay them in full, and to help rehabilitate them.

(3) to protect creditors not alone from debtors who prior to bankruptcy prefer one or more creditors to others but from the actions of fraudulent bankrupts,

(4) to punish fraudulent debtors.[4]

The principal legislation on the subject is contained in the Irish Bankrupt and Insolvent Act 1857, the Bankruptcy (Ireland) Amendment Act 1872, the Debtors Act (Ireland) 1872, the Deeds of Arrangement Acts 1887 and 1890 and the Preferential Payments in Bankruptcy (Ireland) Act 1889.

JURISDICTION OF THE IRISH COURTS[5]

Bankruptcy jurisdiction is based on the fact that a debtor has committed an act of bankruptcy,[6] wherever the debt may have been committed.[7] "Acts of Bankruptcy" occur when, among other cases:

(a) the debtor has, in Ireland or elsewhere, made a conveyance or assignment of his property to a trustee or trustees for the benefit of his creditors generally[8];

(b) where the debtor has, in Ireland or elsewhere, made a fraudulent conveyance, gift, delivery or transfer of his property or any part of it[9];

(c) where the debtor "has, with intent[10] to defeat or delay his creditors,[11] done any of the following things, namely, departed out of Ireland; or being a trader[12] departed from his dwelling house or otherwise absented himself . . . "

Before the 1872 Act, only certain traders[14] were liable to become bankrupt.

---

[4] *Bankruptcy Law Committee Report*, 45.

[5] See *Hunter*, ch. 2, Lipstein, *Jurisdiction in Bankruptcy*, 12 Modern L. Rev. 454 (1949), *Bankruptcy Law Committee Report*, chs. 2, 53.

[6] 1857 Act section 127. An exceptional case where no act of bankruptcy need have been committed arises under section 353 of the 1857 Act: cf. *Hunter*, paras. 2.03, 17.130. The fact that the debtor is an alien is not a ground for exclusion of jurisdiction: section 409 of the 1857 Act.

[7] *Ex parte Pascal*, 1 Ch. D. 509 (C.A., 1876).

[8] Section 21, para. 1, of the 1872 Bankruptcy Act.

[9] *Id.*, para. 2.

[10] The intent must be proven, and the Court is not bound to presume such intent merely from the fact that, by reason of the departure, the creditors have been defeated or delayed: *In re Radcliffe*, [1916] 2 I.R. 534 (C.A., 1915). But the facts surrounding the departure may be sufficiently strong to warrant the presumption of such an intention "in the absence of explanatory circumstances or reasonable explanation of some sort": *In re McClement, a Bankrupt*, [1960] I.R. 141, at 150 (High Ct., Budd, J.).

[11] An intent to defeat *future* creditors will suffice: *Mackay* v. *Douglas*, L.R. 14 Eq. 106 (1872), *Williams* v. *Lloyd*, 50 C.L.R. 341 (High Ct., of Austr., 1934), *Barton* v. *Deputy Commissioner of Taxation*, 48 A.L.J.R. 407 (High Ct., of Austr. 1974).

[12] Where a person who has been carrying on trade in Ireland leaves the country, it appears that he will nonetheless be deemed to be carrying on trade here until all the debts due in respect of the trading have been paid: cf. *Theophile* v. *Solicitor-General*, [1950] A.C. 186 (H.L. (Eng.), *per* Lord Porter).

[13] Section 21, para. 3, of the 1872 Bankruptcy Act

[14] Section 90 of the 1857 Act specified the categories of trader, ranging from apothecaries to wharfingers.

Further, it was necessary to show that the trader was trading in or to Ireland.[15] Thus the commission of an act of bankruptcy whilst temporarily present, or even resident, here did not suffice to found jurisdiction.[16] Section 31 of the 1857 Act provided that the Irish Court was to have exclusive jurisdiction in bankruptcy over traders[17] residing or carrying on business exclusively in Ireland. The effect of this section was to exclude the jurisdiction of the English courts of bankruptcy,[18] rather than to enlarge the jurisdiction of the Irish courts.[19]

The 1857 Act contained provisions for the relief of insolvent debtors who were not traders.[20] Section 178 enabled persons imprisoned for debt in Ireland to apply to the Court for a discharge from custody. Of its nature, this jurisdiction extended only to "Irish residents",[21] albeit of an unwilling nature.

The Debtors (Ireland) Act 1872 abolished imprisonment for debt. The 1872 Bankruptcy Act in turn repealed[22] the provisions in relation to insolvency contained in the 1857 Act, and applied[23] the provisions of the 1857 Act to *all* debtors, whether traders or not. The result, of course, was that the former jurisdictional reference point of trading in or to Ireland became redundant. Yet the 1872 Act contained no specific provisions relating to jurisdiction. Even section 31 of the 1857 Act was left undisturbed; thereafter it would have to be understood[24] as conferring exclusive jurisdiction in bankruptcy on the Irish court over all *debtors* residing or carrying on business exclusively in Ireland.

There is still some considerable uncertainty about the jurisdictional issue.[25] In *In re Hazelton, a Bankrupt*,[26] the members of the Court of Appeal muddied the waters by referring to the "domicile" and "residence" of the debtor in a way that suggests they regarded these terms as identical.[27] A somewhat similar ambiguity may be discerned in the decision of the same Court the following year in *In re Murray*,[28] though the emphasis in that case on domicile is far more slight, resting on an English decision[29] which in fact did not, as O'Brien L.C. thought,[30] involve domicile.

At all events, it seems that residence in this context embraces the place of work as well as the home of the debtor. Whether our courts would go further and accept jurisdiction where a debtor neither resident nor domiciled here commits an act of bankruptcy within the jurisdiction remains to be seen.[31]

The fact that the Irish Court has jurisdiction does not mean that it is obliged to exercise it. Save in cases falling under section 31 of the 1857 Act which have to be heard here and nowhere else, it is always open to the Court to exercise its discretion against assuming jurisdiction[32] as, for example, where foreign proceedings are

---

[15] *Hunter*, para. 2.06.
[16] *Id.*, citing *Re Day*, 7 Ir. Jur. (n.s.) 162, 164, 165 (1862) and *Re Day*, 7 Ir. Jur. (n.s.) 309 (1862).
[17] Though section 31 spoke of "all traders", its effect was linked to the categories of trader specified in section 90, since only they were liable to become bankrupt under the Act.
[18] Cf. *In re Rogers, a Bankrupt*, 9 Ir. Ch. Rip. 150 (Ch. App., 1859), *In re Sanderson*, 11 Ir. Ch. Rep.421 (Ct. of By. & Insolvency, Lynch, J., 1861), *In re Hazelton, a Bankrupt*, 49 I.L.T.R. 29 (C.A., 1914) (esp. at 31 (*per* O'Brien, L.C. and *per* Palles, L.C.B.)
[19] *Hunter*, para. 2.07, *Re Day*, 7 Ir. Jur. (n.s.) 162, 165 (1862), *Re Day*, 7 Ir. Jur. (n.s.) 309, 310 (1862).
[20] *Hunter*, para. 2.09.
[21] *Id.*
[22] Section 5.
[23] Section 17.
[24] Cf. section 17 of the 1872 Act, which provided that the 1857 Act was to be read and construed as if the word "debtor" were inserted throughout, instead of the word "trader".
[25] For a clear and detailed analysis, see *Hunter*, paras. 2.15–2.25.
[26] 49 I.L.T.R. 29 (C.A., 1914).
[27] Cf. *Hunter*, para. 2.19.
[28] [1916] 2 I.R. 554 (C.A., 1915).
[29] *Ex parte O'Loghlen. In re O'Loghlen*, L.R. 6 Ch. App. 406 (1871).
[30] [1916] 2 I.R., at 564. See also *Malone* v. ———, I.R. 7 C.L. 473 (Q.B., 1873).
[31] Cf. *Hunter*, para. 2.23.
[32] *Id.*, para. 2.25, citing *Re Day*, 7 Ir. Jur. (n.s.) 163, 165 (1862); *Re Behrends*, 12 L.T. 149 (1865);

already in progress and there are no assets in Ireland.[33] The converse of this, of course, is that the Irish court, if it chooses, may exercise jurisdiction where foreign bankruptcy proceedings are in progress against the debtor or he has already been adjudged bankrupt. This may be essential in cases where the debtor has immoveable property here, which would be beyond the reach of the foreign court.

VESTING OF PROPERTY

Let us turn now to consider the question of vesting of property. The question is a straightforward one, but not so easy to answer: what effect will an order by an Irish court adjudicating a person bankrupt and vesting the property in the Assignee have on property outside Ireland, and what effect will a vesting order of a foreign court have within Ireland?

(a) Vesting under order of Irish court[34]

We must first consider the position as to vesting under order of the Irish Court. Section 267 of the 1857 Act provides that, when a person is adjudged a bankrupt, "all the personal estate and effects of such bankrupt....present and future, *wheresoever the same may be* ....shall become absolutely vested in the Assignees for the time being, for the benefit of the creditors of the bankrupt...[35] and section 268 contains a similar provision as to the vesting of "all lands, tenements, and hereditaments... wheresoever the same may be situate...."[36]

The scope of section 267 was considered in *In re Robinson a Bankrupt*,[37] in 1860. The facts were as follows. In February 1858, John Robinson was adjudged a bankrupt by the Irish Court of Bankruptcy and Insolvency. The following month, the Northern Banking Company, an Irish bank, with knowledge of the bankruptcy, initiated proceedings in the New York Supreme Court for the enforcement of a debt owing by Robinson to the bank, contracted in Ireland. The bank attached goods which had been sent by Robinson, "for security to answer the final judgment of the Supreme Court of New York".[38] Complicated legal proceedings in New York ensued, in which the assignees participated for a time but from which they ultimately withdrew with the consent of the New York Court and without prejudice to their rights. The Bank having obtained judgment against Robinson, the Sheriff sold the goods, satisfied the judgment and paid the surplus to the assignees.

The assignees and the Bank, in proceedings in Ireland, sought the adjudication of the court as to their respective rights on the basis of these facts.

Lynch, J. first had to consider the extent of the assignment in bankruptcy under the 1857 Act, so far as the bankrupt's chattels were concerned. Section 267 was expressed in terms that were "without limitation or stint as large and comprehensive as words can announce it".[39] So far as Irish law was concerned, the assignment was "without any limitation whatever"[40], giving to the assignees the absolute ownership and property in the goods, though in a foreign state. The operation of the laws of a foreign state were not regarded as a limitation of this assignment.

[32] *Ex p. McCulloch, Ex Parte McCulloch*, 14 Ch. D. 716, 719, 723 (1880).

[33] Cf. *Re Robinson*, 22 Ch. D. 816 (1883), *Re a Debtor (No. 199 of 1922)*, [1922] 2 Ch. 470.

[34] See Nadelmann, *The National Bankruptcy Act and the Conflict of Laws*, 59 Harv. L. Rev. 1025, at 1032-1033 (1946).

[35] Emphasis added. As to earlier law, cf. *Battersby* v. *Rochfort*, 2 Jones & La Touche 431 (Sugden, L.C., 1845).

[36] Emphasis added.

[37] 11 Ir. Ch. Rep. 385 (Ct. of Bankruptcy & Insolvency, Lynch, J., 1860).

[38] *Id.*, at 386.

[39] *Id.*, at 390.

[40] *Id.*

"Our assignment is general and without limit; our law may be incapable of operation
in a foreign state, unless our rule of property be there recognised; but this does not
prevent the operation of our law, as between the subjects of this realm, working the
entire assignment of rights."[41]

The question, therefore, was whether New York law recognised the effect of the
assignment as passing the property in the chattels situate within the boundaries of
the State.

The parties had produced no lawyer to give evidence on this matter, and relied
on citation of relevant authorities.[42] Lynch, J. was satisfied that, although the
question was "not well settled in the American tribunals,"[43] it was "certainly not
true"[44] that the American courts would ascribe to Irish assignments the same
breadth as they had under Irish law; nor did he consider it just that it should be so:

"The domestic creditor could not be affected by it without manifest injustice, and every
State is authorised to protect its own subjects from the operation of a foreign law made
for the protection of the subjects of such foreign State...."[45]

But it seemed to Lynch, J. that the American Law did not treat our assignment
as a nullity; for some authorities went to the length of stating their actual recognition
of it. Those on the opposite side, whilst denying the validity of the transfer, admitted,
at the same time, the recognition of the adjudication as ascertaining a representative
character in the assignees, perhaps in the sense of an indefeasible power of attorney
from the bankrupt to his assignees.[46] Lynch, J. was satisfied that, under American
Law, the assignee had a recognised claim to obtain the chattels of the bankrupt.

Lynch, J. doubted whether the issue in the case before him could be made a question
of foreign law at all. The foreign law was but a means for the creditor obtaining
possession of the property which belonged to the assignees; and the manner of
obtaining that possession, collaterally to the real title, could not alter the rights of
parties in our Courts. But this was subject to the question principally argued before
him as to the effect of a judgment obtained, as the judgment was, in this case, in
a foreign Court.

Lynch, J. was of opinion that the New York proceedings did not constitute a
judgment *in rem* or *quasi in rem*.[47] Had there been a judgment in a suit in which
the assignees were implicated, it would have been "a totally different question".[48]

In a passage of considerable analytic power and impressive moral force, Lynch,
J. stated:

"Is there then in the facts stated anything to give this payment in full to this particular
creditor, in contravention of the rights of all the other creditors, a binding and conclusive
operation here? This is an important question; the extension of trade with foreign
countries, the growth of our foreign markets, make this a question of deep interest.
Every manufacturer, of any extent of trade, has his market in foreign countries as well
as at home, and his produce is to be found in foreign countries, and this is the legitimate
carrying on of his trade as a trader here. Well, he becomes bankrupt – that is, as

---

[41] *Id.*, at 391.
[42] It is not clear whether the court adverted to the fact that New York law, rather than the law of other
jurisdictions in the United States, was the relevant law – save to the extent that it was modified by
Federal law.
[43] 11 Ir. Ch. Rep., at 391.
[44] *Id.*, at 392.
[45] *Id.*
[46] *Id.*
[47] Cf. *supra*, pp. 124, 160-162.
[48] 11 Ir. Ch. Rep., at 395.

an honest man he confesses his insolvency, and tenders fair justice at all his creditors, in offering to them all his property for equitable distribution. Can it be the law that any creditor has a right to look out for some foreign nation, in whose territory part of the bankrupt's goods may be, and, gaining precedence of suit there, to proceed in contravention of the law made for his benefit, to gain for himself an unfair and inequitable distribution of the assets, in payment in full? The assets will admittedly go in a fair course of administration if he does not intervene. Is it not against equity and justice that the creditor should so intervene? This admits the law of America to be as contended for, and yet, even in that case, when I get back the goods here — in possession of the creditor so conducting himself — I cannot understand that such proceedings, so instituted to defeat the purpose of the Bankrupt Law here, and in violation of the rights created by it, have the effect of giving this creditor a right to hold the goods in violation of our law.

The fact that he obtained them by the intervention of the laws of a foreign state cannot, in my opinion, alter the property as established by our laws; and more especially when the very seeking of such intervention was in violation of the duties of citizenship here. But, though I say this, I by no means admit that the American law is open to any fair objection on this head. I think they recognise the title conferred on our assignees, to the extent that justice requires, protecting their own citizens from its unfair operation as far as they are concerned, but never intending to work it out so as to allow the foreign traders, for whose protection the law was made, to make their country a means of working out the defeat of their own institutions.''[49]

Lynch, J. considered that perhaps the true ground of decision in the case before him was that this was no question of foreign law at all; the goods were still the property of the assignees. No suit in America or in Ireland against the bankrupt could affect the title of the assignees, not as a question of foreign law or domestic law, but by the rule that no man could be bound by the acts of a stranger; therefore the property was undisplaced, and still in the assignees.

In *Robinson*, the creditor was clearly Irish and most other significant aspects of the bankruptcy, so far as the creditor was concerned, were also Irish. It was thus not necessary for Lynch, J. to consider the possible limits of the court's power to deprive creditors who have obtained payment abroad, whether by action or not, of property there belonging to a person adjudicated bankrupt in Ireland. It is however, interesting to note Lynch, J.'s description of the creditor's intervention in New York as constituting a "violation of the duties of citizenship here".[50] Citizenship was mentioned as a factor in an earlier English case:[51] but it would seem far too narrow to regard it as the *sole* criterion in *Robinson*. The Irish residence of the creditor was undoubtedly an important factor as well.

In *Sill* v. *Worswick*,[52] in 1791, a creditor resident in England was held not entitled to retain a debt which he recovered in the British West Indies against a person whom he knew to have been adjudicated bankrupt in England. The "crucial factor"[53] was the English residence of the creditor.

Another English decision[54] also at the end of the eighteenth century, is in

---

[49] *Id.*, at 395-396.
[50] *Id.*, at 396.
[51] *Phillips* v. *Hunter*, 2 Hy. Bl. 402, 126 E.R. 618 (1791).
[52] 1 Hy. Bl. 665, 126 E.R. 379 (1791).
[53] *Cheshire & North*, 565.
[54] *Hunter* v. *Potts*, 4 Term Rep. 182, 100 E.R. 962 (1791). Cf. *Cheshire & North*, 564-566 and see *In re Belfast Ship Owners' Co.*, [1894] 1 I.R. 321 (C.A.) (esp, at 332 (*per* Palles, C.B.), discussed *infra*, p. 486. It is useful in this context to consider *Neale* v. *Cottingham*, Wallis by Lyne, Ir. Chy. Rep. 54 (1770), which met with unqualified praise in *Hunter* v. *Potts*, 4 Term Rep., at 194, 100 E.R., at 968-969 (*per* Lord Kenyon, Ch. J. (for the Court). See also *Phillips* v. *Hunter*, 2 H. Bl., at 417, 126 E.R., at 626 (*per* Eyre, L.C.J.). *Neale* v. *Cottingham* is discussed, *infra*, pp. 478-480.

substantial accord with this approach, but modern authority is lacking.[55] The commentators are divided on where precisely the line should be drawn.[56] The fairest and most workable rule seems to be that a creditor obtaining property of the bankrupt situated abroad should be under an obligation to refund it to the assignee if, at the time when he received payment, he was resident in Ireland.[57]

One rule is, however, clear. If an Irish or foreign creditor receives abroad, by judicial proceedings or otherwise, any part of the property of a person against whom proceedings for bankrupty are taken in Ireland, then the creditor will not be permitted to prove under the Irish bankrupty, unless he brings the part of the property thus acquired into the common fund.[58] In *In re Pim, a bankrupt*,[59] in 1881, Walsh, J. clearly accepted this principle, and pointed out[60] the injustice to Irish creditors which would otherwise follow from permitting a creditor "to approbate and reprobate . . . ."[61]

(b) Vesting under order of English court

We now turn to a more difficult question. The statutory provisions as to vesting of *Irish* property in an *English* trustee of bankruptcy, which made sense when England and Ireland were part of the same political unit, have raised a number of problems after Independence. Of course, the sensible solution would have been for new legislation to address the question of the relationship between the two countries, regarding the vesting of what now had become foreign property. In the wake of legislative inertia, the courts were forced to confront basic issues of a constitutional nature and to attempt to work out practical solutions, but there is a pressing need for statutory reform.

Section 53 (1) of the Bankruptcy Act 1914 provided that, "immediately" on a debtor's being adjudged bankrupt in England, the property of the bankrupt "shall vest in the trustee". "Property" includes "money, goods, things in action, land and every description of property, whether real or personal *and whether situate in England or elsewhere . . .* "[62]

These provisions are clearly very wide, and purport to affect property not just in Ireland, England or Scotland, but everywhere else throughout the world. That does not mean, of course, that other countries would necessarily respect provisions of what is, for them, the legislation of a foreign state.

We must now consider the following questions. First did the "vesting" and "property" provisions under the 1914 Act, as originally enacted, apply to Ireland so as to make Irish property vest in the English Trustee in Bankruptcy? Secondly, if they had this effect, was the position changed by reason of our gaining Independence?

The first of these questions was raised in *In re Corballis Deceased*,[63] a decision

---

[55] *Dicey & Morris*, 707.

[56] Cf. Nadelmann, *The National Bankruptcy Act and the Conflict of Laws*, 59 Harv. L. Rev. 1025, at 1053-1054 (1946).

[57] *Dicey & Morris*, 707. *Cheshire & North*, 566, would apply in this context the same jurisdictional rules as apply to debtors. For criticism, cf. *Dicey & Morris*, 707.

[58] *Dicey & Morris*, 706. See generally Nadelmann, *Concurrent Bankruptcies and Creditor Equality in the Americas*, 96 U. Pa. L.Rev. 170 (1947).

[59] 7 L.R. Ir. 458 (By., Walsh, J., 1881).

[60] *Id.*, at 472.

[61] *Id.*, at 469, quoting from *Banco de Portugal* v. *Waddell*, 5 App. Cas. 161, at 169 (H.L. (Eng), *per* Lord Selborne, 1880). To allow a creditor to keep a preference acquired abroad would, moreover, "cause a mad scramble in every bankruptcy proceeding, where the bankrupt owned property in foreign jurisdictions, and create situations wholly repugnant to that equality which the courts declare is the primary object of [bankruptcy legislation]": *In re Pacat Finance Corporation*, 295 Fed. 394, at 402 (S.D.N.Y, Proskauer, Spec. Master, 1923).

[62] Bankruptcy Act 1914, section 167. Emphasis added.

[63] [1929] I.R. 266 (Kennedy, C.J.).

of Kennedy, C.J. in 1928. In this case, land in the Irish Free State devolved upon a person as heir-at-law who had been adjudicated bankrupt in England in 1898 and in Ireland in 1924. Both the English Official Receiver and the Irish Official Assignee claimed the rents of the land accruing after the death of the person from whom the bankrupt inherited the property.

Kennedy, C.J. rejected the view that the effect of the English enactments vesting a bankrupt's property in the Official Receiver in England was that the property, wherever situate, vested automatically in the English Official Receiver. He considered that its true effect was that the bankrupt, if domiciled or resident within the territorial jurisdiction of the English Court, might be subjected to such coercive processes as were there available to compel him to transfer his lands situate outside such territorial jurisdiction to the English Official Receiver, the land itself remaining subject to the *lex loci rei sitae.* If, however, the English Court was not able to procure a legal vesting by the exercise of its own jurisdiction over the bankrupt person within its own jurisdiction, it might then fall back upon any auxiliary jurisdiction, whereby the Court of the place where the land was situate would come to its aid.

In the view of the Chief Justice, it would be "wholly inconsistent with the constitutional status of the Saorstát"[64] to hold that the order of an English Court could automatically transfer land situate in the Saorstát from a citizen of the Saorstát to an official of the English Court. That would not be in accordance with the equal status of the two countries, but would be "to subordinate one country to the jurisdiction of the Courts of the other as regards immoveable property, which on general principle is governed by the *lex loci rei sitae.*"[65]

Kennedy, C.J. did not therefore consider himself bound to treat the Irish land as having been effectively vested in the English Official Receiver. The "only effective order"[66] before him was the vesting order made by the Court of competent jurisdiction in the Irish bankruptcy matter. What the Official Receiver should do, therefore, was to invoke the assistance of the Irish Court under section 71 of the Bankruptcy (Ireland) Amendment Act 1872,[67] which was an Irish Act, providing that the Court in Ireland should act in aid of, and be auxiliary to, the Courts in England in all matters of bankruptcy.

In *In re Bullen*[68] the following year, Johnston, J. took the same view. He accepted that "vesting is of no force or effect unless and until the intervention of this Court is sought and granted."[69]

The issue came before the (former) Supreme Court for the first time in *In re Reilly, a Bankrupt*[70] in 1942. The facts briefly, were as follows. In September 1940, Hugh Reilly was adjudicated a bankrupt by an English Court. He was then the registered owner of certain lands in Ireland. In December 1940, he deposited the land certificate of these lands with the Ulster Bank Ltd., as security for an overdraft. The Ulster Bank had no notice of the adjudication in bankruptcy. On 5 June 1941, Reilly agreed to sell the lands to John Duke. On 27 June 1941, on the *ex parte* application of the English Trustee in Bankruptcy, the Irish High Court made an order in aid of the English Court, recognising the appointment of the Trustee and declaring that the Irish property was vested in him. In October of that year the Trustee's title was registered in the Land Registry. The Ulster Bank applied to the Irish High Court (in Bankruptcy) for an order declaring the amount of Reilly's overdraft with them to be well charged on his interest in the lands and for an order confirming the sale

---

[64] *Id.*, at 271.
[65] *Id.*
[66] *Id.*
[67] See *infra*, pp. 471-477.
[68] [1930] I.R. 82 (High Ct., Johnston, J., 1929).
[69] *Id.*, at 85.
[70] [1942] I.R. 416 (Sup. Ct., 1942, rev'g High Ct., Black, J. 1941).

to Duke. The English Trustee in Bankruptcy and the Irish Official Assignee applied for an order confirming the sales of the lands to Duke and directing payment of the purchase-money to the Official Assignee and an order declaring Reilly's deposit of the land certificate with the Bank to be fraudulent and void, and directing the bank to hand over the land certificate to the Official Assignee.

Black, J. held that the bank's application should be refused and the application of the Trustee and Official Assignee granted. He considered that sections 18 (1) and 167 of the 1914 Act continued in force, and that the lands in question, on adjudication of bankruptcy in England, had been vested in the Trustee in Bankruptcy, but subject to the provisions of the Local Registration of Title (Ireland) Act 1891. Under that Act, although the Trustee in Bankruptcy was a transferee "otherwise than for valuable consideration", there was no provision entitling the bank, an unregistered chargeant, to priority over the Trustee.

The bank's appeal to the Supreme Court was successful but the members of the Court had widely differing views as to the law on a number of questions. As to the question whether the "vesting" and "property" provisions of the 1914 Act had ever been applied to Ireland, there was sharp disagreement.

All the judges, save Murnaghan J.,[71] were of the view that these provisions had indeed applied to Ireland. This interpretation, said Sullivan, C.J., was consistent with the definition of property in section 167 of that Act, as the word "elsewhere" would *prima facie* include Ireland; it was, moreover, consistent with the recognised policy of the bankruptcy laws of England and of Ireland, which always had been that the bankrupt's property of every kind and wherever situate should become the property of the Assignees for the benefit of the creditors.

The next question concerned the possible effect of Independence on these statutory provisions. The four judges for whom the issue was a live one were of the view that no change had in fact resulted. They thus differed from the views of Kennedy, C.J. in *In re Corballis,*[72] and Johnston, J., in *In re Bullen.*[73]

In Meredith, J.'s view, it was "very convenient"[74] that certain reciprocal rights and powers should exist between specified authorities in different countries; the recognition of such rights and powers had never been regarded as a derogation of status as they only existed by agreement and could be repealed immediately. Reciprocal recognition of adjudications in bankruptcy was an instance. If the Act of 1914 had contained a reciprocal power in the Irish Court of Bankruptcy to affect property in England, there could be no question as to the Act's not being consistent with our Constitution. But the absence of such a reciprocal provision could not affect the question since that was a question of policy for the Oireachtas, which could immediately repeal the law if reciprocal recognition was not accorded. Accordingly, in his opinion, the relevant provisions of the Act of 1914 were not inconsistent with the Constitution. He was therefore of opinion that the provisions of the Act of 1914 did vest Irish property in the English Trustee, though "of course only subject to the law of the land."[75]

It is possible that if the issue were to come before the (new) Supreme Court today, in relation to the 1937 Constitution, the Court might be somewhat more cautious about recognising such a wide scope for the English legislation in Ireland today.

---

[71] Murnaghan, J. considered that there was "room at least for a presumption founded upon the analogy of the *lex loci rei sitae* that the statute was not intended to apply to land in Ireland." *Id.,* at 456. If the other judges' interpretation was correct, there would be nothing left on which a subsequent adjudication in Ireland could operate, thus rendering redundant the question that had agitated the Court in *In re Corballis, supra.*

[72] *Supra.*

[73] *Supra.*

[74] [1942] I.R., at 460.

[75] *Id.*

The sovereign nature of the State and the growing recognition of Constitutional rights in relation to property as well as in respect of fair judicial procedures could militate against the view taken in *In re Reilly, a Bankrupt*.

The final matter which required resolution in *In re Reilly, a Bankrupt* related to priorities. This divided the four judges who addressed the issue. Sullivan, C.J. and O'Byrne, C.J. considered that the effect of a vesting order in England was to confer sufficient title on the Trustee to prevail over the equitable charge of the Bank, while Meredith, J., with whom Geoghegan, J. concurred, held that the unregistered title of the Trustee could not prejudice a *bona fide* equitable chargeant, deriving title from the owner, in the absence of evidence of fraud.

The outcome of the case, in view of Murnaghan, J.'s resolution of the first issue, was thus in favour of the Bank. But broader questions remain unresolved. It would seem essential for practitioners advising purchasers and mortgages not to overlook the possibility that the vendor or mortgagor, or a predecessor in title within the period of limitation, may have been declared bankrupt in England (or Northern Ireland). The need for making searches in the relevant registers may thus arise.[76]

Until the law is reformed,[77] injustice may result, whichever strategy is favoured by the courts. If the English adjudication is ineffective to vest an English bankrupt's Irish land in the English Trustee until a vesting order is made by the Irish court, the result is that in the interval "the bankrupt can make away with his Irish land in fraud of the English creditors, and the English Trustee cannot recover it.[78] If, on the other hand, the adjudication is effective in vesting the Irish land immediately in the Trustee without the need to obtain an Irish vesting order, "a very great hardship"[79] may result to persons who purchase or take mortgages of land, if, unknown to them, the party they deal with had been adjudicated a bankrupt in England. The task of inquiry in England is "a very irksome burden calculated to hamper and delay both purchases and mortgages".[80]

MUTUAL AID BETWEEN BANKRUPTCY COURTS

As well as provisions as to vesting of foreign property, our bankruptcy legislation also contains provisions designed to encourage mutual assistance and support among the courts of Ireland, Britain and the former British colonies. These provisions were, of course, originally framed to deal with an entirely different political situation. Since Independence, therefore, our courts have had to look at them in a new light.

SECTION 71 OF THE BANKRUPTCY ACT OF 1872

Section 71 of the Bankruptcy Amendment (Ireland) Act 1872, which is still in operation,[81] provides as follows:

"The Court and the Courts having jurisdiction in England and Scotland, and every British Court elsewhere having jurisdiction in bankruptcy or insolvency, and the officers

[76] Cf. *Hunter*, para. 34.05. For a detailed analysis of the difficulties, see *Anon., The Effect on Lands in Eire of Bankruptcy Adjudications in England*, 77. Ir. L.T. & Sol. J. 101, at 102-104 (1943).
[77] Perhaps on the (satisfactory) lines of the Bankruptcy (Scotland) Act 1913, section 97 (3): cf. *In re O'Reilly, a Bankrupt*, [1942] I.R., at 431 (*per* Black, J.), *Hunter*, para. 34.05, *Anon., The Effect on Lands in Eire of Bankruptcy Adjudications in England*, 77 Ir. L.T. & Sol. J. 101, at 102 (1943).
[78] [1942] I.R., at 432 (*per* Black, J.).
[79] *Id.*, at 431.
[80] *Id.*, Cf. *Russell* v. *Murphy*, 16 Ir. Chy. Rep. 54, at 61-62 (Cusack Smith, M.R. 1865).
[81] Having withstood the argument in *In re Gibbons, A Bankrupt in England. Ex Parte Walter*, [1960] Ir. Jur. Rep. 60 (High Ct., Walsh, J.) that it had not continued in force after the 1937 Constitution came into force. See further, pp. 473-474, *infra*. Section 71 was repealed in Northern Ireland by the Law (Repeals) Act 1981, sl. (1), Sched. 1, pt. 1. Cf. *Hunter*, para. 34.09.

of such Courts respectively, shall severally act in aid of and be auxiliary to each other in all matters of bankruptcy, and an order for the Court seeking aid, together with a request to another of the said Courts, shall be deemed sufficient to enable the latter Court to exercise, in regard to the matters directed by such order, the like jurisdiction which the Court which made the request, as well as the Court to which the request is made, could exercise in regard to similar matters within the respective jurisdictions.''[82]

Section 2 of the Act provides that the Act, ''except in so far as same is expressly provided, apply to England or Scotland''. Clearly, the effect of section 71 is to apply its provisions to England and Scotland, as well, of course as to ''every British Court elsewhere having jurisdiction in bankruptcy or insolvency . . .''

After Independence, the question of the policy of mutual aid in bankruptcy matters was confronted in both Ireland and England. In the Saorstát section 3 of the Adaptation of Enactments Act 1922 provides as follows:

''For the purpose of the construction of any British Statute the name 'Ireland', whether used alone or in conjunction with the expression 'Great Britain', or by implication as being included in the expression 'United Kingdom' shall mean Saorstát Eireann.''

The effect of this provision would be that courts in England and Wales, Scotland and the Saorstát might come to each other's mutual aid under both section 71 of the 1872 Act and section 122 of the 1914 Act.[83] So far as ''every British court elsewhere having jurisdiction in bankruptcy or insolvency'' is concerned, section 3 of the 1922 Act seems not to have changed the position with respect to either section 71 of the 1872 Act or section 122 of the 1914 Act.

There have been several decisions[84] after 1922 in which the Irish courts have acted on the the basis that section 71 of the 1872 Act continues to allow for mutual aid.[85]

---

[82] Section 122 of the Bankruptcy Act 1914 contains a provision similar to that of section 71 of the 1872 Act. Section 122 provides as follows:
''The High Court, the county courts, the courts having jurisdiction in bankruptcy in Scotland and Ireland, and every British court elsewhere having jurisdiction in bankruptcy or insolvency, and the officers of those courts respectively, shall severally act in aid of and be auxiliary to each other in all matters of bankruptcy, and an order of the court seeking aid, with a request to another of the said courts, shall be deemed sufficient to enable the latter court to exercise, in regard to the matters directed by the order, such jurisdiction as either the court which made the request, or the court to which the request is made, could exercise in regard to similar matters within their respective jurisdictions.''
There are thus, in Irish law today, two separate provisions, one in the predominantly Irish Act of 1872, the other in the predominantly English Act of 1914, providing for mutual aid between courts of Ireland, England and Wales, Scotland and ''every British court elsewhere having jurisdiction in bankruptcy or insolvency...'' In England, section 426 of the Insolvency Act 1986 has replaced section 122 of the 1914 Act: see Woloniecki, *Co-operation Between National Courts in International Insolvencies: Recent United Kingdom Legislation*, 35 Int. & Comp L.Q. 644, at 645-647 (1986).

[83] The position regarding Northern Ireland is considered *infra*, pp. 475-476.

[84] Cf. the *Bankruptcy Law Committee Report*, paras. 53.5.2-53.6.1.

[85] There seems to be no reason, however, why, prior to its abolition in 1986, an application under section 122 of the 1914 Act could not also have been entertained here. In Britain, the Irish Free State (Consequential Adaptation of Enactments) Order 1923 provided that section 122 of the 1914 Act was to be construed as including the Irish Free State.
Of course, this provision was not part of Irish law but, practically speaking, it was of some significance. It offered to English and Scottish courts as well as courts falling within the description of ''British court[s] elsewhere'' having jurisdiction in bankruptcy or insolvency the incentive to apply to the Irish court under section 122 of the 1914 Act, as an alternative route to that of section 71 of the 1872 Act, which may well have been repealed in many of these countries. It may also be the case, however, that some countries formerly under British control may wish to rid themselves of the trappings of imperial legislation: cf. *Dicey & Morris*, 703. One commentator has observed that ''[i]t is indeed doubtful whether, immediately before its repeal, any Commonwealth country regarded itself as bound by section 122'': Woloniecki, *Co-operation between National Courts in International Insolvencies: Recent United Kingdom Legislation*, 35 Int. & Comp. L.Q. 644, at 646 (1986).

It seems that, not only British courts, but also courts of former British colonies[86] may still avail themselves of the provisions of section 71 of the 1872 Act. This would be so even in countries where the 1872 Act, as a British statute, was repealed or is no longer legally efficacious since, so far as Irish law is concerned, section 71 of the 1872 Act is part of Irish, rather than British law. Of course, in cases where the statutory link with the 1872 Act has been broken in these countries, the fact that section 71 is still part of Irish law will not enable the Irish Assignee to invoke that section in these countries and demand that their courts act in aid of the Irish Court and Court Officers. Perhaps a question of reciprocity may arise as to whether it is proper that section 71 should be interpreted as providing for what might be called unilateral aid, in cases where the foreign courts provide no equivalent service. Having accepted that the Irish court may act in aid of the English, Scottish, or "British court[s] elsewhere" in bankruptcy proceedings, we must consider the nature of the Irish court's involvement.

In *In re Bullen, A Bankrupt,*[87] in 1929, Johnston, J. considered that section 71 of the 1872 Bankruptcy Act "must be regarded, not as an enactment which deals merely with procedure, but as one conferring a separate and independent class of jurisdiction upon the Court". Similarly *In the matter of Lecky, a Bankrupt in England*[88] in 1961, Budd, J. said in relation to section 71;

> "I agree that this Court has an independent jurisdiction, a statutory jurisdiction. But this Court is not a rubber stamp or even an agent for the English Court. It may have to make substantive decisions."

In *In re Gibbons, A Bankrupt in England, Ex Parte Walter,*[89] in 1960, the official receiver and trustee in bankruptcy in England sought the aid of the Irish court under section 71, in relation to the adjudication of bankruptcy in England of a person who had property in Ireland. Counsel for the bankrupt argued that section 71 must be treated as unconstitutional insofar as it was intended to enable the Irish courts to act in aid of the Bankruptcy Court in England in proceedings initiated for the purpose of collection of revenue debts due in that country.

Walsh, J. did not accept this contention. He had "no doubt"[90] that the Oireachtas has power under the Constitution to enact legislation which would make provision for the making of orders by the Irish courts enabling the English revenue authorities to collect money in Ireland on foot of revenue debts due to the English revenue authorities. Walsh, J. construed section 71 as enabling rather than mandatory: the court might exercise the powers created under the section if it considered "fit to do so in the exercise of its discretion".[91]

---

[86] On the basis that they fall within the definition of "British court[s] elsewhere". Cf. *Reg.* v. *McGlinchey,* [1985] N.I.L.R. Bulletin of Judgments 62 (C.A.). It could, however, be argued that, in the light of their acquisition of independent status, these countries have ceased to be British courts and are thus outside the scope of the section: cf. *Re James (an Insolvent), A.G. intervening,* [1977] Ch. 41 (C.A., 1976), Woloniecki, *supra*, at 645-646.

[87] [1930] I.R. 82, at 84 (High Ct., Johnston, J., 1929).

[88] 95 I.L.T.R. 38, at 40 (High Ct., 1961).

[89] [1960] Ir. Jur. Rep. 60 (High Ct., Walsh, J.)

[90] *Id.*, at 61.

[91] *Id.* Contrast *In re Osborn,* [1931] B. & C.R. 189, at 194, where Farwell, J. interpreted section 122 of the 1914 Act (the equivalent of section 71 of the 1872 Act) as *obliging* the court whose assistance is sought to comply, subject only to "considerations which would arise if there was also a bankruptcy in [that court's] country, as to the rights of the creditors and other persons in [that] country." In *In re Jackson (A Bankrupt in the Republic of Ireland),* [1973] N.I. 67, at 72 (High Ct. (By.), Lowry, L.C.J. favoured virtually the same approach as Farwell, J. Conceding that there might be other examples which had not occurred to him, he stated that, except in cases of conflicting bankruptcies and foreign revenue claims, "this court is bound to give under the relevant provisions every assistance in its power." Although this approach might "vary somewhat" from that of Walsh, J. *In re Gibbons,* Lowry, L.C.J.

Walsh, J. considered the circumstances of the case before him in which he had been requested to exercise his discretion. He noted that it was a "well established"[92] principle that it was contrary to the policy of our courts to permit jurisdiction to be invoked for the purpose of enforcing the collection of foreign revenue debts or claim. This policy was not in force at the date of the passing of the 1872 Act when Ireland and England were both of one fiscal system. The position since Independence was "completely different"[93] since two distinct and separate fiscal systems existed. Walsh, J. added:

"The policy of the Irish Courts has been clearly stated in the decision in *McVey's* case[94] and it appears to me that it would be quite wrong for me to exercise a discretion in some way which would be contrary to the established policy of the Courts. If the statute enabled the aid sought to be provided by executive action only this could be done by the proper authority without invoking the Court, but when it is the Court which is involved the Court must have regard to the established policy of the Courts in considering the question of the exercise of its discretion and, as the section is not mandatory, I am bound to exercise my discretion in accordance with the policy of the Courts as settled in *McVey's* case. Accordingly, I refuse the order sought . . ."[95]

Before Independence it was held that, although the Irish court had a wide discretion as to whether it should act in aid of the English (or other) Court, it was not the task of the Irish court to examine whether or not the English bankruptcy proceedings had been fraudulent. In *Kevens* v *Joyce*,[96] in 1895, an English trustee in bankruptcy sought, in the Irish courts, to set aside mortgages made by the bankrupt person on the grounds of unconscionability. The mortgagee unsuccessfully resisted on the ground, *inter alia,* that the whole of the bankruptcy proceedings had been fraudulent. He argued that the Irish Court of Appeal was at liberty to go into the title of the trustee in bankruptcy and to inquire whether he had been properly appointed or could sustain the suit.

Walker, C. said:

"I should be prepared to go more at length into the circumstances if I thought we were at liberty to do so; but I am of opinion that we are bound by the proceedings in bankruptcy to admit that [the plaintiff] is trustee, clothed with the powers and duties of such, and that any attempt to impeach his title must be made in the Bankruptcy Court in England."[97]

It is most doubtful whether this passivity would be consistent with the present constitutional and legal position.

An interesting issue was raised in *Muldoon* v. *Doyle*.[98] The plaintiff sued in Ireland on an English judgment in an action for money had and received. During the course of the English proceedings the defendant (Jack Doyle, the boxer) had been made bankrupt. An attempt was made by the defendant in the English court

---

concurred in his decision. In *Re a Debtor (Order in Aid No. 1 of 1979) ex parte Viscount of the Royal Court of Jersey,* [1981] Ch. 384 (1980), Goulding, J. expressed a preference for the approach adopted in *Osborn* and *Jackson.*

New Zealand's Insolvency Act 1967, section 135, provides in express terms for the exercise of flexibility, cf. Honsberger, *The Need for a Rapprochement of the Bankruptcy Systems of Canada and the United States,* 18 McGill L.J. 147, at 165 (1972), *Spratt & McKenzie,* 307.

[92] [1960] Ir. Jur. Rep., at 62.

[93] *Id.*

[94] *Buchanan Ltd.* v. *McVey,* [1954] I.R. 89 (Sup. Ct., 1951), aff'g High Ct., Kingsmill Moore, J., (1950).

[95] *Id.*

[96] [1896] 1 I.R. 442 (C.A., 1895, aff'g Monroe, J., 1894).

[97] *Id.,* at 485-486. See also *id.,* at 489 (*per* Fitzgibbon, L.J.).

[98] 79 I.L.T.R. 134 (Sup. Ct., 1945, aff'g High Ct., Maguire, P., 1944).

to have the plaintiff's proceedings in Ireland stopped by injunction; but the injunction was discharged on the plaintiff's undertaking to pay into the English Bankruptcy Court any money he recovered in Ireland.

In the Irish proceedings on foot of the judgment the defendant contended that the effect of the judgment would be to put the plaintiff in a better position than he would occupy in England, since he could enforce the judgment, by execution or otherwise, here, rather than having to prove his debt in the English bankruptcy proceedings in the same way as any other creditor.

This argument was rejected by Maguire, P., and the Supreme Court unanimously affirmed. It was admitted that the effect of *In re Reilly, a Bankrupt*[99] was that, on the adjudication in England, all the property of the bankrupt in Ireland vested in the English Trustee in Bankruptcy. If that was so, Maguire, P. could not see how the fact of the plaintiff's obtaining a judgment have put him in any better position than he was in England. This would scarcely help him very much as the Irish proceedings had been carried on with the full knowledge and approval of the English Court of Bankruptcy. Maguire, P. speculated that the English Court might be making use of the plaintiff's right to sue here on the judgment to make available in the bankruptcy property of the bankrupt which might otherwise be difficult to capture; but he did not feel that he could allow that element to weigh with him.

Northern Ireland

We must now consider the position in relation to Northern Ireland. That part of Ireland which is now described as Northern Ireland fell, of course, within the scope of section 71 of the 1872 Act and section 122 of the 1914 Act, as part of "Ireland". With Independence for the Saorstát, a difficulty arose: "Ireland" meant the Saorstát,[100] so where did Northern Ireland fit in? Two approaches seem possible. One is to adopt a broad principle of interpretation, acknowledging the constitutional changes and seeking to give continuing practical efficacy to sections 71 and 122 in the light of these changes. Another approach is to hunt through the actual language of these sections to see whether words not originally addressing the issue are capable of carrying the load of referring, by good fortune, to Northern Ireland. The first approach seems preferable. In the Northern Ireland case of *In re Jackson (A Bankrupt in the Republic of Ireland)*,[103] in 1973, Lowry, L.C.J. adopting the second approach, was doubtful as to whether section 71 had continuing efficacy in respect of Northern Ireland and the Republic. He noted that the word "elsewhere" in the section originally must have referred to places outside England, Scotland and Ireland, and that after 1922, it required to be modified in order to apply to Northern Ireland from the point of view of a court sitting in the Republic and to the Republic from the point of view of a court sitting in Northern Ireland. Had section 122 not been available,[102] he "should have [had] to consider whether the expression 'elsewhere' ought to read so as to include the Republic"[103]

Lowry, L.C.J. therefore rested the power of acting in aid on section 122 of the 1914 Act rather than section 71 of the 1872 Act. When we look at matters from south of the border, we have no equivalent in our Adaptation of Enactments Act 1922 to the British continuation[104] of the reference to "Ireland" in section 122 of

---

[99] *Supra.*

[100] Cf. the Adaptation of Enactments Act 1922, section 3. See *State (Gilsenan)* v. *McMorrow* [1978] I.R. (Sup. Ct.) considered *supra* p. 23.

[101] [1973] N.I. 67 (High Ct. (By.), Lowry, L.C.J.).

[102] By reason of article 2 of the Irish Free State (Consequential Adaptation of Enactments) Order 1923, whereby the reference to "Ireland" in section 122 of the 1914 Act continues to apply to "Ireland", rather than excluding the Free State: cf. [1973] N.I., at 70.

[103] [1973] N.I., at 71. the expression "British Court" did not cause the Lord Chief Justice difficulty having regard to sections 2 (1) and 3 (2) of the Ireland Act 1949.

[104] Cf. fn. 102, *supra.*

the 1914 Act. Thus the problem of how Northern Ireland fits into the process of acting in aid is the same, so far as our law is concerned, whether section 71 or section 122 is in question.

It is submitted that, adopting the broad interpretative approach, the creation of Northern Ireland makes it necessary to interpret both of these sections as permitting mutual aid between the two jurisdictions. Whether the Supreme Court would be disposed to favour this approach must be regarded as doubtful, if the *Gilsenen* decision is any indicator. So far as Northern Ireland's law is concerned, section 71 no longer applies, having been replaced in 1981,[105] but so far as the Republic is concerned, it continues to apply. Although recourse by the Republic's courts to section 71 should not, even now, render inefficacious a request to the courts in Northern Ireland to act,[106] the more prudent and less controversial course would appear to be for the Republic's courts to base their jurisdiction, whether solely or in conjunction with section 71, on section 122 of the 1914 Act.

"Other British Courts elsewhere having jurisdiction in bankruptcy or insolvency"

Having considered the specific problems in relation to Northern Ireland, let us now consider more generally the position relating to "other British courts elsewhere having jurisdiction in bankruptcy or insolvency". In *In re Bolton*,[107] in 1920, Dodd, J. made an order under section 71, vesting Irish lands in a South African trustee of an insolvent person's estate, for the benefit of his creditors in South Africa. In Roman-Dutch Law, which applied in South Africa, the concept of bankruptcy, as understood in England and Ireland, played no part. Instead there was the concept of insolvency. Dodd, J. said:

> "Now, insolvency in the Roman-Dutch law — for the Dutch held on more to the Roman law than any other country perhaps, except Scotland — was founded on the *cessio bonorum* and *missio in possessionem* of the Romans, and it is clear that under the Roman law the former was a surrender, and the latter a seizure, of all the debtor's proprietary rights in lieu of execution against his person. In other words, all the debtor's property was substituted for his person in satisfaction of his creditor's claims; and this was the view of the Roman-Dutch law as well, which also prevails, and has been adopted and acted upon, in the Act of the Union of South Africa.
>
> Included in the debtor's property, of which he was deprived on insolvency, were such assets as were situated in a foreign jurisdiction, therefore, in holding that 'bankruptcy matters' in section 71 includes 'insolvency matters' in the South African code....
>
> There lies at the root of the whole matter the old well known principle of comity of nations and comity of independent jurisdictions within the same nation. A judgment pronounced by this Court could not formerly have been levied in Britain, but by the Judgment Extension Act and the comity which exists between England and Ireland a judgment of the Court in England can be made a judgment of our Court for the benefit of the English creditor, and in the same way a judgment of our Court can be realized in England or Scotland. This is merely carrying into effect the comity which binds together all its members of the great British Commonwealth of nations."[108]

In the following passage, Dodd, J. gave us some insight into his perception of the Irish court's role under section 71:

[105] By the Statute Law (Repeals) Act 1981 sl. (1), Sched. 1, pt. 1.
[106] Cf. *In re Jackson (A Bankrupt in the Republic of Ireland)*, [1973] N.I. 67, at 70-71 (High Ct. (By.), Lowry, L.C.J.).
[107] [1920] 2 I.R. 324 (K.B.Div., Dodd J.). See also *Re A Debtor (Order in Aid No. 1 of 1979); ex parte Viscount of the Royal Court of Jersey*, [1981] Ch. 384 (Goulding, J., 1980), where *In re Bolton* was referred to with apparent approval.
[108] [1920] 2 I.R., at 328-329.

"But I think I am required to do more than merely grant the application for a vesting order. The trustee would find that would carry him but a short way to realizing the assets in this country, and therefore I place at his service, as required by the section, the machinery of this Court to be used in aid of, and auxiliary to, the Court of South Africa as fully as it could be used in the case of a bankruptcy in this country. At the same time, I must have regard to the interests of creditors in this country, if any there be, who, by virtue of my order, might have been sent far afield unless some such provision is made. I must have regard also to the interests of other beneficiaries. The trustee may need the help of this Court in matters of controversy. The interest of the insolvent is apparently in some of the property held on some kind of joint tenancy with others who are represented before me. Landlords may be entitled to call on the trustee for rent or to elect. I cannot anticipate all matters that may arise in the course of realization. But obviously such matters can only be decided in this country. It is for the benefit of everyone to make provision for the final determination of any matter in controversy. If such application occurred more frequently, it would be necessary to have rules of Court made; but the procedure being novel, all I can do is to frame as carefully as I can regulations for the guidance of the trustee and the Court, such as would be provided by rules of Court and so discharge the duty case upon this Court of aiding the Court in South Africa. Of course, any of these regulations that may not be in aid can be amended, or altered, or rescinded, on proper application, and on reasonable grounds, by the Judge of this Court. But the Official Assignee will act as the auxiliary officer of the trustee, and the whole matter is subject to the control of the South African Court."[109]

Viewed in isolation, the final sentence may give cause for alarm, since it suggests an undue degree of deference to the foreign court. The larger context modifies this, however. It is interesting to note that in the Order of the Court contains the following regulations (among others):

" . . .

(3) That any matters in controversy between the trustee and any person resident in Ireland in his winding up of the estate be determined in this Court.
(4) That the trustee out of the assets do apply to the Official Assignee of this Court for distribution to the creditors such composition or dividend as may be payable on distribution to the creditors in the Union of South Africa.
(5) That the trustee do submit to the jurisdiction of this Court in all such matters, and abide by any order this Court may make, subject to appeal in accordance with the provisions of the rules and orders of the Supreme Court of Judicature in Ireland, and that the law applicable to the decision of such matters be the law of Ireland.
(6) Before taking the proceeds of the sale of the insolvent's property out of Ireland the trustee shall lodge, if so ordered, such sum as the Court may on the application of the Official Assignee direct.
. . . "[110]

MUTUAL ENFORCEMENT PROVISIONS

We must now examine two statutory provisions, one in the 1872 Act and the other in the 1914 Act, regarding the mutual enforcement of Irish, English and Scottish adjudications.

Section 70 of the Bankruptcy (Ireland) Amendment Act 1872 provides as follows:

"Any order made by the Court under the [Irish Bankrupt and Insolvent] Act [1857] as amended by this Act, or under this Act shall be enforced in Scotland and England in the Courts having jurisdiction in bankruptcy in such countries respectively, in the same manner in all respects as if such order had been made by the Courts which are

[109] *Id.*, at 329.
[110] *Id.*, at 331.

hereby required to enforce the same; and in like manner any order made by the Court in Scotland having jurisdiction in bankruptcy shall be enforced in England and Ireland, and any order made by the Court having jurisdiction in bankruptcy in England shall be enforced in Ireland and Scotland, by the Courts respectively having jurisdiction in bankruptcy, in the division of the United Kingdom where the orders made require to be enforced, and in the same manner in all respects as if such order had been made by the Court required to enforce the same in a case of bankruptcy within its own jurisdiction.''

And section 121 of the Bankruptcy Act 1914 provides that:

''Any order made by a court having jurisdiction in bankruptcy in England under this Act or any enactment repealed by this Act shall be enforced in Scotland and Ireland in the courts having jurisdiction in bankruptcy in those parts of the United Kingdom respectively in the same manner in all respects as if the order had been made by the court hereby required to enforce it; and in like manner any order made by a court having jurisdiction in bankruptcy in Scotland shall be enforced in England and Ireland, and any order made by a court having jurisdiction in bankruptcy in Ireland shall be enforced in England and Scotland by the courts respectively having jurisdiction in bankruptcy in the part of the United Kingdom where the orders may require to be enforced, and in the same manner in all respects as if the order had been made by the court required to enforce it in a case of bankruptcy within its own jurisdiction.''

There are some difficulties involved in determining the present status of these provisions. Neither has been repealed expressly here since Independence. There is much force in the argument that, in view of their peremptory terms, they are inconsistent with our independent status and have thereby been repealed. Alternatively, it is possible that they could be read (as has section 71 of the 1872 Act)[111] as prescribing for discretionary rather than an automatic interjurisdictional enforceability.

So far as Britain is concerned, it would appear that, from 1923 until its repeal in 1985, section 121 of the 1914 Act applied only to enforcement between the Courts of England, Scotland and *Northern Ireland*.[112] This is a factor which would surely encourage our courts to be cautious about conceding a generosity of enforcement to orders of foreign jurisdictions who provide no reciprocal facility.

EFFECT IN IRELAND OF FOREIGN ADJUDICATION

Irish courts have for long adhered to the doctrine of universality, whereby all moveable property, wherever situated at the time of the assignment by foreign law, passes to the trustee.[113] This doctrine does not extend to immovables situated in Ireland,[114] though the Irish court may exercise its discretion to permit a foreign trustee to dispose of Irish immovables for the benefit of the bankrupt's creditors.[115] In the Irish case of *Neale* v. *Cottingham*,[116] in 1770, the facts were as follows.

---

[111] Cf. *In re Gibbons, A Bankrupt in England. Ex Parte Walter*, [1960] Ir. Jur. Rep. 60 (High Ct., Walsh, J.).

[112] Cf. the Irish Free State (Consequential Adaptation of Enactments) Order 1923, section 2 (S.R. & O. No. 405).

[113] *Cheshire & North*, 567-570, *Neale* v. *Cottingham*, Wallis by Lyne, Irish Chancery Reports 54 (1770).

[114] *Neale* v. *Cottingham, supra, (semble), Cheshire & North*, 569, *In re Levy's Trusts*, 30 Ch. D. 119, at 123 (Kay, J., 1885).

[115] *Cheshire & North*, 569, *Re Kooperman*, [1928] W.N. 101; *Re Osborn*, [1931] B. & C.R. 189; cf. *In re Bullen, a Bankrupt*, [1930] I.R. 82 (High Ct., Johnston, J., 1929), *In the Matter of Lecky, a Bankrupt in England*, 95 I.L.T.R. 38 (High Ct., Budd, J., 1961); see also *In re Gibbons, A Bankrupt in England*, [1960] Ir. Jur. Rep. 60 (High Ct., Walsh, J.).

[116] Wallis by Lyne, Ir. Chy. Rep. 54 (1770). See further Nadelmann, *Solomons* v. *Ross and International Bankruptcy Law*, 9 Modern L. Rev. 154, at 155 (1946).

John Grattan, a London trader, was made bankrupt in England on 27 October 1763, his whole property being assigned to the plaintiffs in the following month. Two of the defendants, named Haughton, were at the time of Grattan's failure indebted to him in £581.8s "which debt was by the said laws and assignment vested in the plaintiffs".[117] But the bankrupt was indebted at the same time to another defendant, Cottingham, in about £600, and Cottingham, after notice of the bankruptcy, attached the Haughtons' debt, by virtue of a writ of foreign attachment out of the Tholsel Court of Dublin, although that debt was then vested in the plaintiffs under the English bankruptcy laws.

The timing of Cottingham's action should be noted. It appears that he issued foreign attachment on 31 October 1763, and obtained judgment on 9 July 1764, after which the Haughtons paid the money to Cottingham. The plaintiffs sought recovery of this sum. The defendants argued that the English bankruptcy laws did not affect Ireland, nor bound any property of the bankruptcy situated here. Cottingham pointed out that he had never joined in any assignment of property to the plaintiffs. But all the defendants admitted that, by the laws of Ireland and the custom of Dublin, no property could be seized under the foreign attachment save what, at the time of the seizure, was the actual property of the defendant.

The plaintiffs were successful. Lord Lifford, L.J. said:

"Personal property receives the appellation 'personal', because connected with the person, and in contradistinction to real. Grattan, immediately previous to his failure, might have parted with all this property, although situate in Ireland; and that one consideration will show how effectually that property was attached to the person of the bankrupt, to the instant of his failure. And the person of the bankrupt being subject to the effect of the bankruptcy laws, of consequence, the property adhering to that person must be equally liable to those laws. Its owner was a virtual party to the bankrupt laws, and had subjected both himself and his property to the effect of them, by his implied consent to them . . . The law of England has only transferred to the assignees the property inherent in the person of the bankrupt; and they, when thus become owners, have all the rights which the bankrupt before had. In commerce, people trust upon the security of the merchant's general property. His effects, from the nature of trade, must be dispersed; yet, however separated, all unite in procuring his credit.[118] The allowing the property of the bankrupt here to be kept from his assignees, might admit great frauds. A bankrupt might transmit all his effects here, and then openly brave all his creditors; and this would destroy the mutual credit which commerce requires, by making people cautious whom to trust. In this case, therefore, the right being clearly vested in the plaintiffs, they must have such decree as they desire...."[119]

Robinson, J. said:

"The question is not whether the bankrupt laws in general bind Ireland, but whether goods here belonging to the bankrupt at the time of his failure in England are, under those laws, vested in his assignees. Supposing the proceedings in the Tholsel Court to have been legal, (which is a matter rather doubtful,) yet if the goods seized there were, at the time of such seizure, not actually the property of the bankrupt, the defendant in the cause in that Court, the proceedings there were all nugatory.

The question turns upon the authority and interpretation of the bankrupt laws. The power of Great Britain to bind Ireland by special laws, is a matter not now to be disputed....The discovery of America, and of the present course to the East Indies, has created a more liberal way of thinking in these countries, has brought up a new

---

[117] Wallis by Lyne, Ir. Chy. Rep., at 56, stating plaintiff's bill.

[118] Since bankruptcy legislation now extends to all debtors, whether traders or not, the Lord Chancellor's argument must be seen in the light of this revised situation.

[119] Wallis by Lyne, Irish Chancery Reports, at 75-76.

species of commerce, and introduced a new *jus gentium*, arising from the exigencies of that commerce. This introduced the bankruptcy code of laws, springing out of the universality of trade, and founded in universal equity . . . This system was introduced into England as early as the reign of Henry the Eighth, and stands upon one great principle, to secure the goods of the bankrupt, 'wherever found or known', for the general benefit of all his creditors. These words 'wherever found or known', cannot extend to lands, which are territorial, but affects chattels, as being in their nature transitory; and the intention of the legislature was to act upon the goods and debts of the bankrupt, wherever situate . . . Such is the opinion of Serjeant Goodinge in his Bankrupt Law, and adopted by C. B. Comyns, in his Digest. It is an opinion not contraverted, and therefore seems to be acquiesced under. It regards the property of the bankrupt in Ireland as liable to the effect of these laws; and no law of this kingdom clashes with that opinion. The plaintiffs therefore, are entitled to a decree upon this principle; and also upon the principle of giving credit to acts of a competent foreign jurisdiction, and upon the regard which is paid to commerce.[120]

In *Neale* v. *Cottingham,* so far as may be gleaned from the report, the bankrupt's principal connections were in England, where he was made bankrupt. Although it used to be suggested that a foreign trustee must have been appointed by the *lex domicilii* of the bankrupt, this limitation no longer commands support.[121] Perhaps the possession by the bankrupt of assets in the country where he is made bankrupt will suffice;[122] his participation in the foreign proceedings has been held sufficient.[123]

ADMINISTRATION[124]

The administration of the bankrupt's property is governed by Irish law.[125] This is an example of the rule that the *lex fori* governs matters of procedure.[126] Thus, in an Irish bankruptcy, foreign creditors, like their Irish counterparts, may prove in relation to any debt[127] regardless of where the debt was contracted. The debt must be due under its proper law; to this extent the court must have regard to foreign law.

DISCHARGE

A discharge of a bankruptcy through a certificate of conformity in Ireland generally releases the debtor from all debts provable in bankruptcy[128], whether or not they

---

[120] *Id.*, at 72-73. Cf. *id.*, at 73-74 (*per* Clayton, C.J.) referring to the "universal equitable spirit in which these laws are concerned". See also *Solomons* v. *Ross*, 1 H. Bl. 131n, 126, E.R. 79 (1764), analysed by Nadelmann, *Solomons* v. *Ross and International Bankruptcy Law*, 9 Modern L. Rev. 154 (1946), and cf. *Galbraith* v. *Grimshaw*, [1910] A.C. 508 (H.L. (Eng.)).

[121] Cf. Raeburn, *Application of the Maxim Mobilia Sequuntur Personam to Bankruptcy in Private International Law* 26 Br. Yrbk. of Internat. L. 177, at 189 ff (1949).

[122] *Blom-Cooper*, 92.

[123] *Re Anderson*, [1911] 1 K.B. 869; *Re Davidson's Settlement Trusts*, L.R. 15 Eq. 383 (1873); *Re Craig*, 86 L.J. Ch. 62 (Eve, J., 1916); *Bergerem* v. *Marsh*, 125 L.T. 630 (Bailhache, J., 1921). Cf. *Re C.A. Kennedy Co. Ltd. and Stibbe-Monk Ltd.*,74 D.L.R. (3d) 87 (Ont. High Ct., Div. Ct., 1976).

[124] See *Blom-Cooper*, ch. 10. For a comparative study, see Nadelmann, *Foreign and Domestic Creditors in Bankruptcy Proceedings. Remnants of Discrimination*? 91 U. Pa. L. Rev. 601 (1943), also Nadelmann, *Once Again: Local Priorities in Bankruptcy*, 38 Am. J. of Internat. L. 470 (1944).

[125] *Blom-Cooper*, 141, *Wolff*, 566, *Ex parte Melbourn*, L.R. 6 Ch. App. 64 (1870), *Ex parte Holthausen*, L.R. 9 Ch. App. 722 (1874).

[126] Cf. *infra*, p. 625.

[127] *Ex parte Melbourn*, *supra*.

[128] Cf. section 58 of the 1872 Act, which also specifies some exceptions to the general rule. It seems that this process is very rarely invoked. *The Bankruptcy Law Committee Report* (in para. 38.5.1.) mentions that only two applications for a certificate of conformity were made in the thirty years previous to the publication of the report, neither having been granted.

are governed by Irish law.[129] This rule is founded on the need to avoid "the inconsistency, and indeed injustice, of divesting the debtor of all his property wherever located for division amongst all his creditors wherever resident and at the same time leaving him exposed to the claims of local creditors outside the jurisdiction where the bankruptcy occurs".[130] The position regarding a composition with creditors[131] is different. The whole purpose of this process is to enable an insolvent debtor to effect an arrangement with his creditors without publicity.[132]

It would be unfair if foreign creditors were to lose all their rights once the Court grants a certificate of conformity[133] after a composition has been satisfactorily arrived at. True, that certificate operates "to all intents and purposes as if [it] were a certificate of conformity under a bankruptcy . . . "[134] But in spite of this, it is clear that only creditors who have notice of this process are bound by it.[135] Moreover, in contrast to bankruptcy, a composition with creditors does not involve the complete divesting of the debtor of his whole estate for the benefit of the creditors generally.[136] In *In re Nelson; Ex parte Dare & Dolphin,*[137] the English Court of Appeal held that a certificate of conformity granted after a composition with creditors released the debtor only from such debts as creditors should seek to enforce in the Courts of Ireland.[138] Thus a creditor in England with an English claim was entitled to succeed to the full extent of his claim. The Irish courts may well interpret the Irish statutory provisions similarly.

Where a discharge made under the law of a foreign country, it will be effective if made under the proper law of the debt,[139] but not otherwise.[140] This may lead to some difficult results in practice, since Irish law may recognise certain foreign adjudications, and the vesting of the debtor's property in the foreign trustees, while not recognising the subsequent discharge because it does not comply with the proper law of the debt. In these cases "[t]he debtor has lost his assets but not his liability."[141]

---

[129] Cf. *Cheshire & North*, 570

[130] *In re Nelson; Ex parte Dare and Dolphin*, [1918] 1 K.B. 459, at 477 (C.A., *per* Eve., J.).

[131] The history of compositions is well traced by Treiman, *Majority Control in Compositions: Its Historical Origins and Development*, 24 Va. L. Rev. 507 (1938).

[132] *In re Nelson; Ex parte Dare and Dolphin*, [1918] 1 K.B. 459, at 467 (C.A., *per* Swinfen Eady, L.J.).

[133] Section 64 of the 1872 Act.

[134] *Id.*

[135] Cf. section 347 of the 1857 Act.

[136] *In re Nelson; Ex parte Dare and Dolphin*, [1918] 1 K.B. 459, at 478 (C.A., *per* Eve, J., 1918).

[137] *Supra.* See *Blom-Cooper*, 125-129, Nadelmann, *Compositions — Reorganisations and Arrangements — In the Conflict of Laws*, 61 Harv. L. Rev. 804, at 825-826 (1948).

[138] Cf. [1918] 1 K.B., at 475 (*per* Bankes, L.J.).

[139] *Ellis* v. *M'Henry*, L.R. 6 C.P. 228 (1871), *Gardiner* v. *Haughton*, 2 B. & S. 743, 121 E.R. 1247 (1862). Older decisions, which refer to the law of the country in which the debt was contracted or had "arisen" or where it was to be paid, need not be considered inconsistent with this statement in view of the approach at that time to determining the proper law: see *Wolff*, 458, fn. 1.

[140] *Gibbs & Son* v. *Société Industrielle des Métaux*, 25 Q.B.D. 399 (1890); *Smith* v. *Buchanan*, 1 East, 6, 102 E.R. 3 (1800), explaining *Ballantine* v. *Golding*, W. Cooke, *The Bankrupt Laws*, 8th ed., 1823, p. 487, where Lord Mansfield was reported as having made the broad statement (at p. 487) that it was "a general principle, that where there is a discharge by the law of one country, it will be a discharge in another." In *Ballantine's* case the bill of exchange had been drawn in Ireland, payable by the bankrupt, who resided there. The English court had no difficulty in giving effect to a discharge by the Irish court in these circumstances.

[141] *Cheshire & North*, 572.

CHAPTER 26

COMPANIES[1]

In this chapter we will look briefly at the law relating to (a) the residence; (b) the domicile; (c) the nationality; and (d) the winding up, of companies. To speak of a company "residing" or being "domiciled" in a particular country may seem to strain language which is more appropriate to human endeavours,[2] but this is the approach that the courts have favoured. On occasion they have had to resort to striking metaphors, in order to keep alive the analogy with human persons.

RESIDENCE[3]

The question of the residence of a company may arise in a number of contexts, most usually that of taxation. In *De Beers Consolidated Mines Ltd.* v. *Howe,*[4] Lord Loreburn, L.C. said:

> "In applying the conception of residence to a company, we ought, I think, to proceed as nearly as we can upon the analogy of an individual. A company cannot eat or sleep, but it can keep house and do business. We ought, therefore, to see where it really keeps house and does business."

In the Lord Chancellor's view, the "real business"[5] was carried on "where the central management and control actually abides."[6]

In the *De Beers Case,* the House of Lords held that the control of the company (and thus its residence) abided in the three life-governors and sixteen ordinary directors, most of whom resided in Britain, four actually being obliged to live in England. The fact that the company's head office was in Kimberley and that its general meetings were held there did not alter the fact that the company was controlled from England.

The Irish case of *Hood (John) & Co. Ltd.* v. *Magee*[7] presents an interesting contrast. John Hood, the sole director and manager of a "one-man" company[8] was ordinarily resident in the United States. The substantial part of the company's sales took place in the United States under his direction. Nevertheless, the King's Bench

---

[1] See Drucker, *Companies in Private International Law,* 17 Int. & Comp. L.Q. 28 (1968) Seidl-Hohenveldern, *The Impact of Public International Law on Conflict of Law Rules on Corporations,* [1968] — I Recueil des cours 1.

[2] Cf. *Cheshire & North,* 188.

[3] Cf. *Farnsworth,* chs. 4-5, *Ussher,* 34-35, *Keane,* para. 9.07, *Kelly & Carmichael,* para. 193, *Shannon & Armstrong,* 167, 248-249.

[4] [1906] A.C. 455, at 458 quoted with approval by Madden, J., in *Hood (John) & Co. Ltd.* v. *Magee,* [1918] 2 I.R. 34, at 48-49 (K.B. Div., 1917).

[5] [1906] A.C., at 458.

[6] *Id.*

[7] [1918] 2 I.R. 34 (K.B. Div., 1917). See *Ussher,* 34-35, *Farnsworth,* 103-104.

[8] Gibson, J., (at 42) described the company as "an unusually perfect specimen of the one-man type."

Division held unanimously that the Company resided in the United Kingdom, so that it had to pay income tax on the whole of its profits wherever earned.[9]

Gibson, J. said:

"The company in its visible responsible operations, contracts, staff, ownership, distribution of profits, etc., was an Irish company, though its executive dealing were in the hands of Mr Hood as agent. The residence of the company cannot be determined by Mr. Hood's choice of his own residence ... [H]e was not the company; it owned his brain and capacity as well as the business. The tap-root of the fruit-bearing tree was at Belfast."[10]

Madden, J., applying Lord Loreburn's test, asked:

"[W]here does this company keep house? Assuredly in Belfast, for here the registered office must be, under the provisions of the Memorandum of Association, and here the general meetings of the company are in fact held ... In my opinion the central management and control of this company abides with the general meeting of shareholders in Belfast, where the registered office of the company is situated and where the general meetings of the company are held ... If the shareholders in general meeting were to consider it more in the interests of the company that the managing director should reside where the goods in which they deal are manufactured and bought, they might refuse to re-elect him except on the terms of his residing in Belfast. Adopting the analogy suggested by Lord Loreburn, the movement would proceed from the heart and brain of the organization in Belfast by which the action of its organs is controlled."[11]

Kenny, J. observed:

"The test of residence is afforded by the answer to the questions — Where is the seat of government of the company's affairs? Where is the real control of these affairs exercised? The test of residence is not where the company is registered, but where it keeps house and does its real business; and the real business is carried on where the central management and control actually abides."[12]

In Kenny J.'s view, the real seat of government was in Belfast, and the business and trading were controlled from the United Kingdom. It was "a mere accident"[13] that Mr Hood resided in New York. The company, in general meeting could supersede him at any time and appoint a board, any one or more of whom might reside in the United Kingdom. If Mr Hood died or became bankrupt, a new board would have to be appointed.

In England, in *Swedish Central Rail Co. Ltd.* v. *Thompson,*[14] the majority of the House of Lords held that a company could have more than one place of residence, but this view is difficult to harmonise with the notion that a company's residence is determined by the location of its central control and management.[15] Restricting cases of dual residence to those instances where the central control was truly divided down the middle[16] would preserve some conceptual credibility for a development

---

[9] Income Tax Act 1853, section 2, Schedule D.

[10] [1918] 2 I.R., at 43.

[11] *Id.,* at 49-50.

[12] *Id.,* at 53.

[13] *Id.,* at 55.

[14] [1925] A.C. 495. Cf. *Egyptian Delta Land & Investment Co., Ltd.* v. *Todd* [1929] A.C. 1 (H.L. (Eng, 1928). See also *Anon., Residence of a Company for the Purposes of Income Tax* 61, Ir. L.T. & Sol. J. 61 (1927), *M'Mahon* v. *North-Western Ry. Co.,* I.R. 5 C.L. 200 (Com. Pleas, 1870).

[15] Cf. [1925] A.C., at 508 (*per* Lord Atkinson, dissenting).

[16] Cf. *Farnsworth,* 107-120, A. F[arnsworth], *Note,* 67 L.Q. Rev. 446, at 448 (1951).

that has met with little support by the commentators[17] or, indeed, the more recent decisions of the courts.[18]

DOMICILE[19]

A company is domiciled in the country where it is incorporated.[20] That domicile may not be changed thereafter. In *Gasque* v. *Inland Revenue Commissioners,*[21] MacNaghten, J. observed that "[t]he domicil of origin, or the domicil of birth, using with respect to a company a familiar metaphor, clings to it throughout its existence."

Whether this is a sound policy in every case may be doubted.[22] If the laws of both the country of original incorporation and another country where a company proposes to be incorporated concur in permitting a change of domicile, there seems little justification in taking the opposite view. Resort to "the proper law for the time being"[23] of the company, coupled with the *renvoi* doctrine,[24] may go some way towards mitigating the full force of the rule against any change of domicile, but the easier and more credible approach would surely be to permit a change of domicile, at least in cases where no conflict arises between the laws of the original and subsequent domiciles.

NATIONALITY[25]

The nationality of a company is not a question of great importance in our conflict of laws.[26] Statements in English cases[27] have been interpreted[28] as equating nationality with the country of incorporation. In many Continental European countries, however, the nationality of a company is determined by its "real centre of management".[29]

[17] Cf. *Cheshire & North*, 190-191.

[18] Cf. *Koitaki Para Rubber Estates Ltd.* v. *Federal Commissioner of Taxation*, 64 C.L.R. 15, at 19 (*per* Dixon, J., 1940), aff'd., 64 C.L.R. 241 (1941), *Unit Construction Co. Ltd.* v. *Bullock*, [1960] A.C. 351, at 361 (H.L. (Eng), *per* Viscount Simonds 1959), and at 368 (*per* Lord Radcliffe).

[19] See *Farnsworth*, ch. 6, Schuster, *The Nationality of and Domicil of Trading Corporations*, 2 Trans. of Grot. Soc. 57, at 68ff (1917), Francis, *The Domicil of a Corporation*, 38 Yale L.J. 335 (1928).

[20] *Gasque* v. *Inland Revenue Commissioners*, [1940] 2 K.B. 80 (MacNaghten, J.), *National Trust Co.* v. *Ebro Irrigation & Power Co.*, [1954] 3 D.L.R. 326 (Ont. High Ct., Schroeder, J.), *Kelley & Carmichael*, para. 193.

[21] [1940] 2 K.B., at 84.

[22] See Nygh, *The Refugee Corporation*, 12 U.W. Austr. L. Rev. 467, at 469 ff (1976).

[23] *Carl Zeiss Stiftung* v. *Rayner & Keeler Ltd. (No. 3)*, [1970] Ch. 506, at 544 (Buckley, J., 1969).

[24] Cf. Nygh, *supra*, at 470.

[25] See *Farnsworth*, 298-312, Schuster, *The Nationality and Domicil of Trading Corporations*, 2 Trans. of Grot. Soc. 57, at 59-68 (1917), Vaughan-Williams & Chrussachi, *The Nationality of Corporations*, 49 L.Q. Rev. 334 (1933), Hilton-Young, *The Nationality of a Juristic Person*, 22 Harv. L. Rev. 1 (1908), Weidenbaum, *Corporate Nationality and the Neutrality Law*, 36 Mich. L. Rev. 881 (1938) (whose conclusions are criticised by *Farnsworth*, 312), McNair, *The National Character and Status of Corporations*, 4 Br. Yrbk. of Internat. L. 44 (1923).

[26] Cf. Vaughan-Williams & Chrussachi, *supra*, at 336.

[27] Notably *Janson* v. *Driefontein Consolidated Mines Ltd.*, [1902] A.C. 484, at 497 (H.L. (Eng), *per* Lord MacNaghten), 498 (*per* Lord Davey), 501 (*per* Lord Brampton) and 505 (*per* Lord Lindley); *A.G.* v. *Jewish Colonisation Association*, [1901] 1 K.B. 123, at 135 (C.A., per Collins, L.J., 1900).

[28] Cf. *Cheshire & North*, 92; cf. Schuster, *supra*, at 64.

[29] *Wolff*, 308. See also *Rabel*, vol. 2, 22; cf. Seidl-Hohenveldern, *International Law on Conflict of Law Rules on Corporations*, [1968] — I Recueil des cours 1, at 106-107.

WINDING UP

(a) Jurisdiction of the Irish Courts[30]

The Irish courts have jurisdiction to wind up companies registered here, even where they were formed solely to carry on business abroad.[31] The Irish courts may also wind up unregistered companies,[32] including companies incorporated outside the State,[33] where, among other grounds, the company "is dissolved, or has ceased to carry on business, or is carrying on business only for the purpose of winding up its affairs".[34] This provision, which is modelled on a provision in the English legislation,[35] traces its origins to section 199 of the Companies Act 1862. It does not refer in express terms to foreign corporations, but it is now "well settled"[36] that they come within its scope. The words "is dissolved" have been interpreted as extending to companies that *have been* dissolved several years previous to the court's exercise of jurisdiction.[37] It seems, moreover, that it is not necessary to show that the dissolved corporation had established any branch or place of business in Ireland.[38]

Section 345(7) of the Companies Act 1963 provides that:

> "Where a company incorporated outside the State which has been carrying on business in the State ceases to carry on business in the State, it may be wound up as an unregistered company under this Part, notwithstanding that it has been dissolved or otherwise ceased to exist as a company under or by virtue of the laws of the country under which it was incorporated."

This provision indirectly traces its origin to uncertainty as to the position after the 1917 Revolution in the U.S.S.R., when legislation was enacted dissolving companies and confiscating their assets. The English provision on which our section 345(7) is based "was enacted merely for the removal of doubt. It did not alter the previous law, it did not confer any new power to wind up any companies, and it did not add any new requirement to the existing powers to make a winding up order."[39]

The notion of winding up a company that has already been dissolved presents some formidable conceptual difficulties.[40] The English courts have subscribed to the theory of implicit revivification,[41] whereby the dissolution is ignored and results exclusively referable to it are overturned, so far as is practicable, but results not exclusively referable to the dissolution are let stand.[42] In this conceptual morass, it is easy to understand Lord Macmillan's confession that he did:

> "not think ... it ... either necessary or profitable to discuss problems as to the precise legal status of a dissolved company which has been ordered to be wound up. In this connection metaphors may easily be misleading and serve only to create their own puzzles."[43]

---

[30] See *Morris*, 445-447, *Forde*, ch. 15, *Keane*, Part 8.

[31] *Morris*, 334.

[32] Companies Act 1963, Part X.

[33] *Morris*, 445, fn. 19, citing *Re Matheson Brothers Ltd.*, 27 Ch.D. 25 (1884), *Re Commercial Bank of South Australia*, 33 Ch.D. 174 (1886).

[34] Companies Act 1963, section 345 (4) (a).

[35] Companies Act 1948, section 399 (5) (a).

[36] *Cheshire & North*, 624, citing *Re Mercantile Bank of Australia*, [1892] 2 Ch. 204. See also *Dicey & Morris*, 733.

[37] Cf. *Re Family Endowment Society*, L.R. 5 Ch. 118, at 136 (1870), *Cheshire & North*, 624.

[38] Cf. *Banque des Marchards de Moscou* v. *Kindersley*, [1951] Ch. 112, *Re Azoff-Don Commercial Bank* [1954] Ch. 315, *Re Compania Merabello San Nicholas S.A.*, [1973] Ch. 75, *I.R.C.* v. *Highland Engineering Ltd.*, 1975 S.L.T. 203, *Cheshire & North*, 624, *Dicey & Morris*, 734.

[39] *In re Compania Merabello San Nicholas, S.A.*, [1973] Ch. 75, at 86 (Megarry, J., 1972).

[40] Cf. *Cheshire & North*, 625-626.

[41] See *Mann, A Note on The Revivification of a Dissolved Foreign Corporation*, 15 Modern L. Rev. 479 (1952), *Mann, The Dissolved Foreign Corporation*, 18 Modern L. Rev. 8 (1955).

[42] *Cheshire & North*, 626, *Re Banque des Marchands de Moscou*, [1954] 2 All E.R. 746.

[43] *Russian and English Bank* v. *Baring Brothers & Co.*, [1936] A.C. 405, at 439.

So far as jurisdiction to make a winding up order is concerned,[44] it seems essential that a foreign company should have both assets and creditors within the jurisdiction.[45] Otherwise it would be futile for the court to make a winding up order.[46] But the assets need not be assets distributable to creditors by the liquidation in the winding up: it suffices if by the making of the winding up order they will be of benefit to the creditors in some other ways.[47]

Let us now consider briefly the position where certain creditors in Irish winding up proceedings attempt to steal a march on other creditors. In *Re Belfast Ship Owners' Co.*,[48] some creditors, who had successfully petitioned in Ireland for the compulsory winding-up of an Irish company, took proceedings in Massachusetts to attach certain sums, representing cargo freight, which were in the hands of a third party in Boston, and the property of the company, for the purpose of acquiring under Massachusetts law a lien on the freight, which would give them priority over the other creditors. The Court of Appeal held that they should be restrained from continuing with the Massachusetts proceedings.

Walter, C. noted that, if these creditors were successful, the effect might be to upset the Irish proceedings and "to disturb the equality, and the trust ... created by the winding-up order".[49]

He thought it was:

"against those first principles upon which, acting *in personam*, the Court proceeds, whether in a winding-up, or an administration suit, or any other proceedings."[50]

---

[44] As to the position in respect of the winding up of companies registered in England after Independence, see In re *Portarlington Light & Power Co. Ltd.*, [1922] 1 I.R. 100 (Chy. Div. I.F.S., Samuels, J.).

[45] *In re Compania Merabello San Nicholas S.A.*, [1973] Ch. 75, at 86 (Megarry, J., 1972), *Re Kailis Groote Eylandt Fisheries Pty. Ltd.*, 17 S.A.S.R. 35, at 42 (Bray, C.J., 1977).

[46] *In re Compania Merabello San Nicholas S.A.*, *supra*, at 86.

[47] *Id.*, at 91. See, e.g. *In re Eloc Electro-Optieck and Communicatie B.V.*, [1982] 1 Ch. 43 (Nourse, J., 1981).

[48] [1896] 1 I.R. 321 (C.A., 1894, aff'g Chatterton V.C., 1893). See also *Llangennech Coal Co.* v. *Old Park Printing Co.*, 13 I.L.T.R. 74 (C.P.D., 1879).

[49] [1894] 1 I.R., at 331.

[50] *Id.*

CHAPTER 27

NEGOTIABLE INSTRUMENTS

A negotiable instrument[1] is a document containing several distinct contracts. Each party putting his name to the document incurs a separate liability. The original contract between the drawer and the payee is followed by supervening contracts made by the acceptor and indorser. The conflicts of law rules relating to negotiable instruments are largely contained in section 72 of the Bills of Exchange Act 1882, but some important matters, such as that of capacity, have been left to the courts.[2]

Negotiability

Whether an instrument is negotiable is determined by the law of the country where the "negotiation" takes place.[3] In the normal course of events this will be the country in which the instrument is situated at the time of delivery.[4]

Formal Validity

Section 72(1) of the 1882 Act provides that the formal validity of a bill, drawn in one country and accepted, negotiated or payable in another, is to be determined by the law of the place of issue, and that the formal validity of each supervening contract (such as acceptance, indorsement or acceptance *supra protest*) is to be determined by the law of the place where that contract is made.

Section 2 of the Act provides that the "place of issue" is where the first delivery is made, not necessarily, as might have been thought, the place where the bill is signed. Similarly, the place where each supervening contract is made is the place where the contract is completed by delivery.[5]

A difficult threshold question of interpretation arises in regard to the Bills of Exchange Act 1882 in general and Section 72 in particular. There are several references to "the United Kingdom", which prior to Independence, clearly embraced Great Britain and Ireland. Since Independence, that expression has to be given a different meaning. In *The State (Gilsenan)* v. *McMorrow*,[6] the Supreme Court construed section 3 of the Adaptation of Enactments Act 1922 as adapting the expression "United Kingdom" to mean Great Britain and Saorstát Éireann (now the Republic of Ireland). The Court accepted that this interpretation resulted in anomalies regarding Northern Ireland. Manifest further anomalies result from this

---

[1] See generally *Rabel*, vol. 4, Part XII, See J. Milnes Holden, *The Law and Practice of Banking*, vol. 1, ch. 4 (3rd ed., 1982), *Byles on Bills of Exchange, passim,* esp. ch. 25 (25th ed., by M. Megrah & F. Ryder, 1983).

[2] See *Dicey & Morris*, 882-883.

[3] *Cheshire & North*, 252, *Dicey & Morris*, 879; cf. *Picker* v. *London & County Banking Co.* 18 Q.B.D. 515 (C.A., 1887).

[4] *Dicey & Morris*, 879.

[5] *Chapman* v. *Cottrell*, 3 H. & C. 865, 159 E.R. -74 (1-65).

[6] [1978] I.R. 360 (Sup. Ct.), following *The People (A.G.)* v. *Ruttledge* [1978] I.R. 376 (Sup. Ct., 1947). See further *supra*, p. 23.

interpretation in relation to the Bills of Exchange Act 1882. Section 72 of that Act was quite clearly premised on the law of the United Kingdom being one law, rather than a multiplicity of laws. It would be possible for the Court, without abandoning the position in *Gilsenan,* to hold that "business efficacy" requires that references to "the United Kingdom" should be interpreted as referring only to the Republic of Ireland. Until the Court may be disposed to take this step, we must proceed on the basis that the *Gilsenan* interpretation applies.

Section 72(1) specifies two exceptions to the rule that the *lex loci contractus* should apply:

> (*a*) where a bill is issued outside the State or Great Britain, it is not invalid by reason only that it is not stamped in accordance with the law of the place of issue; and
>
> (*b*) where a bill, issued outside the State or Great Britain conforms, as regards requisites in form, to Irish or British law, it may, for the purpose of enforcing payment of it, be treated as valid as between all persons who negotiate, hold or become parties to it in Ireland or Britain, as the case may be.

As regards the first proviso, it appears to be worded with force sufficient to override the rule[7] that an unstamped contract absolutely void according to the law of the place where it is made is also void under our law. Commercial common sense requires that bills and notes should not be under such a cloud.[8]

The apparent object of the second proviso is to remove impediments from negotiability, "for if the validity of a foreign bill depended upon its flawlessness by the law of the place of issue its negotiation in this country might be seriously affected".[9]

The operation of this exception is restricted in two respects. First, a holder relying on it must show that both he and the person against whom he seeks to enforce payment became parties to the bill within the State or Britain. Secondly, the exception relates only to a suit in which the plaintiff seeks to enforce payment of the bill: thus an action for a declaration, it seems, may not suffice.[10]

Capacity

The 1882 Act does not deal with conflicts aspects of matters of capacity: thus the common law prevails. There is some judicial[11] and academic[12] support for the *lex loci contractus,* though it has also been suggested[13] the proper law, objectively ascertained, should govern.

Interpretation and Validity

Section 72(2) of the 1882 Act provides that the interpretation of the drawing, indorsement, acceptance or acceptance *supra protest* of a bill is determined by the law of the place where such contract is made. Thus, there is not one single law to apply to the interpretation of all contracts embodied in the bill: the interpretation of each contract contained in the bill is governed by its own proper law.[14]

---

[7] Cf. *Bristow* v. *Sequeville,* 5 Exch. 275, at 279, 155 E.R. 118, at 120 (*per* Pollock, C.B. 1850), *James* v. *Catherwood,* 3 Dow. & Ry. (K.B.) 190 (1823).

[8] *Dicey & Morris,* 887.

[9] *Cheshire & North,* 253.

[10] See *Guaranty Trust Co.* v. *Hannay* [1918] 1 K.B. 43; cf. [1918] 2 K.B. 623, at 670 (*per* Scrutton, L.J., on appeal). See also *Cheshire & North,* 254, fn. 1.

[11] *Bondholders Securities Corporation* v. *Manville,* [1933] 4 D.L.R. 699.

[12] *Morris,* 367.

[13] Cf. *Cheshire & North,* 254.

[14] *Dicey & Morris,* 889.

Moreover, the proper law of each of these contracts, for the purpose of its interpretation, is the *lex loci contractus*. Thus, for example, whether a bill drawn payable "to X" without the addition of the words "or order" is (as in Ireland) regarded as payable to order and therefore negotiable or (as in the United States) it is not, is a question to be answered by the law of the country in which the drawer delivered the instrument to the payee, and not by the law of the country in which the bill is payable.[15]

One cannot cavil at the attempt by the legislature to provide a "black letter" rule in this context. As *Falconbridge*[16] observed,

> "[i]n the case of bills and notes it would ... be undesirable from the point of view of subsequent holders that the question of the proper law should be a matter of conjecture, and an arbitrary statutory rule is preferable, unless indeed the proper law is designated on the face of the bill."

So far as the selection of the *lex loci contractus* by section 72(2) is concerned, it appears that the intention of the draftsman, Chalmers, had been to prescribe the application of the *lex loci solutionis*. This interpretation could perhaps be sustained by resort to the doctrine of *renvoi*[17] but to do so would be clearly inappropriate, since it would introduce an unsatisfactory degree of uncertainty in an area where certainty is essential.

The reference to "interpretation" in section 72(2) has given rise to difficulty. Normally "interpretation" in contract law relates to the legal *construction of expressions;* there is, however, support in a number of English decisions[18] for the view that the term extends to resolving questions relating to the *essential validity* of the various contracts contained in a bill.

If section 72(2) does not cover the legal effect of the words, then the section offers no guidance as to essential validity. But, as *Morris* points out, "[t]his perhaps is not of much moment, because in a formal contract like the one contained in a bill of exchange the question of essential validity is apt to merge in that of formal validity, ... [which] is ... covered by section 72(2)".[19]

Section 72(2) is subject to the proviso that, where an inland bill[20] is indorsed in a foreign country the indorsement is to be determined, as regards the payer, "according to the law of the United Kingdom". This proviso reflects the position that obtained under common law.[21] The difficulties of interpretation of the expression "the law of the United Kingdom" in this context are obvious. The Supreme Court decision in *Gilsenan*, as we have seen, requires us to interpret the term as meaning the law of Great Britain and the Republic of Ireland. But what is to be done if "the law" in these jurisdictions is not identical? The answer is far from clear.

Since the proviso is effective only "as regards the payer" it does not extend to a dispute between two indorsees where the liability of the acceptor is not at issue.[22]

---

[15] *Id.*, 890.

[16] *Falconbridge*, 328.

[17] Cf. *Id.*, 336.

[18] *Alcock & Smith*, [1892] 1 Ch. 238, at 256, (*per* Romer, J.), *Embiricos* v. *Anglo-Austrian Bank.* [1905] 1 K.B. 677, at 683-686, *Keochlin et Cie* v. *Kestenbaum*, [1927] 1 K.B. 889, at 899, and *Nova (Jersey) Knit Ltd* v. *Kammgran Spinneri G.M.B.H.*, [1977] 1 Lloyd's L.R. 463, at 466 (H.L.(Eng.), *per* Lord Wilberforce, 1976), *Guaranty Trust Co. of New York* v. *Hannay*, [1918] 2 K.B. 623, at 670 (*per* Scrutton, L.J.); *Cheshire & North*, 254, *Morris*, 368, *Byles on Bills of Exchange*, 336 (25th ed., by M. Megrah & F. Ryder, 1983).

[19] *Morris*, 368.

[20] Cf. section 4(1). Unless the contrary appears on the face of the bill, the holder may treat it as an inland bill: section 4(2).

[21] *Lebel* v. *Tucker*, L.R. 3 Q.B. 77 (1867).

[22] *Cheshire & North*, 255, *Morris*, 369, *Alcock* v. *Smith*, [1892] 1 Ch. 238.

Transfer

Under Irish law negotiable instruments, such as bills of exchanges, promissory notes or bank notes, are transferable like chattels by delivery, and may thus be the subject of an action for detinue or conversion.[23]

So far as the conflict of laws is concerned, there is "no doubt"[24] about the principle that the law determining whether property in a negotiable instrument passes is the *lex loci actus,* which in the case of a negotiable instrument, of the nature of things, will be the *lex situs.*[25] Though this principle is clear, the cases[26] have been somewhat confused on the question whether to rely on general conflict rules as to the transfer of chattels or to seek guidance from section 72(2) of the 1882 Act. The commentators[27] generally favour the former approach.

Presentment, Protest and Notice of Dishonour

Where a bill is dishonoured, whether by non-acceptance or non-payment, a holder may take steps against the drawer and the indorsers. By Irish law he is required to give due notice of dishonour of an inland bill to the drawer and to the indorsers.[28] If he merely gives notice to the last indorser, the latter must give notice to any preceding indorsers whom he may wish to make liable, and they in turn must give notice to their predecessors in title.[29] The notice may be in writing or by personal communication, and may be given in any terms which sufficiently identify the bill, and intimate that the bill has been dishonoured by non-acceptance or non-payment.[30] The return of the dishonoured bill is a sufficient notice of dishonour.

In certain circumstances notice of dishonour may be dispensed with,[31] as, for example, where, after the exercise of reasonable diligence, notice cannot be given to or does not reach the drawer or indorser sought to be charged,[32] where notice of dishonour is waived, whether expressly or by implication,[33] where the drawer and drawee are the same person, or where the drawer has countermanded payment.[34]

Where a foreign bill has been dishonoured by non-acceptance or non-payment, then, in addition to notice of dishonour, the bill must be protested. If it is not protested, the drawer and indorsers are discharged.[35] (Where a bill does not appear on the face of it to be a foreign bill, protest in case of its dishonour is not required.[36]).

A protest "is a document drawn up by a notary, or, if no notary is available at the place of dishonour, by a householder in the presence of two witnesses, certifying that the bill was duly presented for payment and that payment was refused".[37] The

---

[23] See *McMahon & Binchy,* 545, *Liston* v. *Munster & Leinster Bank Ltd.,* [1940] I.R. 77 (High Ct., O'Byrne, J., 1939), *Dillon* v. *O'Brien,* 20 L.R. Ir. 300 (Ex. Div., 1887), *Fitzpatrick* v. *Dunphy,* 1 Ir. C.L.R. 366 (Exch., 1851), *Bradley* v. *Archibald,* [1899] 2 I.R. 108 (Q.B. Div., 1897), *Crinion* v. *Minister for Justice,* [1959] Ir. Jur. Rep. 15 (Circuit Ct., Judge Conroy); but see *Sullivan* v. *National Bank,* 73 I.L.T.R. 95 (High Ct., 1939).

[24] *Dicey & Morris,* 894, *Morris,* 369.

[25] *Morris,* 369.

[26] *Alcock* v. *Smith,* [1892] 1 Ch. 238, *Embiricos* v. *Anglo-Austrian Bank,* [1904] 2 K.B. 870, *Koechlin* v. *Kestenbaum,* [1927] 1 K.B. 889.

[27] Cf. *Dicey & Morris,* 897, *Morris,* 371.

[28] Cf. *Cheshire & North,* 255.

[29] Charlesworth's *Mercantile Law,* 291 (12th ed., 1972).

[30] Bills of Exchange Act, 1882, section 49(5).

[31] *Id.,* section 50(2).

[32] *Id.,* para. (*a*).

[33] *Id.,* para. (*b*).

[34] *Id.,* para. (*c*).

[35] *Id.,* section 51(2).

[36] *Id.*

[37] Charlesworth, *supra,* 292. See further *Byles on Bills of Exchange,* ch. 16 (25th ed., by M. Megrah & F. Ryder, 1983).

protest must also contain a copy of the bill. Protest may be dispensed with by any circumstances which would dispense with notice of dishonour.[38] Most European jurisdictions require the protest of a dishonoured bill.

The question of finding the appropriate law of governing the problems that may arise on the dishonour of a bill which has been circulated in more than one country is dealt with by section 72(3) of the Bills of Exchange Act 1882, which provides that:

> "[t]he duties of the holder with respect to presentment for acceptance or payment and the necessity for or sufficiency of a protest or notice of dishonour, or otherwise, are determined by the law of the place where the act is done or the bill is dishonoured."

This provision has been widely criticised by the commentators.[39] It appears that the expression "act is done" refers to presentment for acceptance or payment, and the expression "bill is dishonoured" refers to the need for, or sufficiency of, a protest or notice of dishonour.[40] A basic difficulty, as *Westlake* pointed out,[41] is that there may have been an omission rather than any "act done"; accordingly he suggested that the words "or not done" should be interpolated. *Dicey & Morris* reject this approach on the basis that "[t]he 'law of the country where the act is not done' is the law of any conceivable country in the universe".[42]

Dicey & Morris argue that the scope of the reference to the law of the country "where the act is done" is not clear. It could mean that that law determines whether the holder has to present the bill at all, or, more narrowly, it could refer merely to how he has to do so.[43] On the first view, the words "act is done" would "have to read 'act is done or to be done'".[44] They note, however, that judicial authority[45] runs against this view.

Rate of Exchange

Section 72(4) of the 1882 Act provides that:

> "[w]here a bill is drawn out of but payable in the United Kingdom, and the sum payable is not expressed in the currency of the United Kingdom, the amount shall, in the absence of some express stipulation, be calculated according to the rate of exchange for sight drafts at the place of payment on the day the bill is payable."

There is some difficulty in interpreting this provision in the light of the Supreme Court decision in *Gilsenen*, which we have already considered. If "the currency of the United Kingdom" means "the respective currencies of Great Britain and the Republic of Ireland", it is not clear whether section 72(4) provides any answer to the case where, for example, a bill is drawn in France, payable in the Republic of Ireland and the sum payable is expressed in sterling.

The *Milliangos*[46] decision has led to the repeal of section 72(4) in Britain,[47] and

---

[38] Bills of Exchange Act 1882, section 51(9).

[39] Cf., *e.g. Cheshire & North*, 256: "This obscure section verges perilously on the unintelligible"; see also *Morris*, 372.

[40] *Morris*, 372.

[41] *Westlake*, p. 322, s. 232.

[42] *Dicey & Morris*, 898, fn. 68.

[43] Cf. Mann, *Note: Bills of Exchange and the Conflict of Laws*, 4 Modern L. Rev. 251, at 253-254 (1942).

[44] *Dicey & Morris*, 898.

[45] *Banku Polskiego* v. *Mulder & Co.*, [1941] 2 K.B. 266; affirmed on other grounds [1942] 1 K.B. 497; *Cornelius* v. *Banque Franco-Serbe*, [1942] 1 K.B. 29, at 32, better reported [1941] 2 All E.R. 728, at 732 (K.B. Div., Stable, J.).

[46] *Milliangos* v. *George Frank (Textiles) Ltd*, [1976] A.C. 443. Cf. *Barclay's Bank International* v. *Levin Bros (Bradford) Ltd.*, [1976] Q.B. 270. See also, *infra*, pp. 649-651.

[47] Administration of Justice Act 1977, section 4. Cf. *Paget's Law of Banking*, 580 (9th ed., by M. Megrah & F. Ryder, 1982).

in view of the endorsement of that case by McMahon, J. in *Damen & Zomen* v. *O'Shea*[48] it would appear that a similar repeal is necessary here.

Date of Payment

Section 72(5) of the Bills of Exchange Act 1882, in a concession to the "single law principle",[49] refers to the question of date of payment to the *lex loci solutionis*. It provides that:

" [w]here a bill is drawn in one country and is payable in another, the due date thereof is determined according to the law of the place where it is payable."

Thus, for example, a bill drawn in Paris and payable in Dublin is allowed three days of grace, since this is permitted by Irish law, whereas a bill drawn in Dublin payable in Paris is not entitled to any days of grace, since none are permitted by French law.[50] Similarly, if the law of the place where the bill is payable postpones the maturity of the bill owing to war or state of emergency, payment may not be enforced in Ireland during the period of postponement.[51]

Measure of Damages

Where a bill[52] is dishonoured, the measure of damages, which are deemed liquidated damages, is as follows:

(1) The holder may recover from the party liable on the bill, and the drawer who has been compelled to pay the bill may recover from the acceptor, and an indorser who has been compelled to pay the bill may recover from the acceptor or from the drawer, or from a prior indorser
    (*a*) the amount of the bill;
    (*b*) interest thereon from the time of presentment for payment if the bill is payable on demand, and from the maturity of the bill in any other case; *and*
    (*c*) the expenses of noting or, when protest is necessary and the protest has been extended, the expenses of protest.
(2) Where a bill has been dishonoured abroad, in lieu of the above damages, the holder may recover from the drawer or an indorser, and the drawer or an indorser who has been compelled to pay the bill may recover from any party liable to him, the amount of the re-exchange with interest thereon until the time of payment.
(3) Where by the Bills of Exchange Act 1882 interest may be recovered as damages, this interest may, if justice requires it, be withheld wholly or in part.[53]

This is a rule of Irish internal law rather than of private international law.[54]

It seems clear that the question of the measure of damages on this context is to be treated as a matter of substantive law, governed by the proper law of the

---

[48] High Ct., 25 May 1977 (1977-414). Cf. pp. 650-651, *infra*.
[49] *Morris*, 372.
[50] Cf. *Rouquette* v. *Overmann*, L.R. 10 Q.B. 525, at 535-538 (18-5).
[51] Cf. *Rouquette* v. *Overmann*, *supra*. *Re Francke and Rasch*, [1818] 1 Ch. 470.
[52] And, *mutatis mutandis*, a promissory note: section 89(1).
[53] Section 57. See also section 72(4).
[54] Cf. *Dicey & Morris*, 901.

contract.[55] The "several laws" principle applies here, so that the court must determine each separate contract involved in the transaction, or sequence of transactions, by its own proper law.[56]

[55] *Id.*, 901-902; cf. *In re Commercial Bank of South Australia*, 36 Ch. Div. 522, at 526 (1887), where North, J. considered that previous decisions "show clearly that the liability to damages is to be measured according to the law of the country where the contract which is broken was entered into". See further *Dicey & Morris*, 902, fn. 85, *In re Gillespie. Ex parte Robarts*, 18 Q.B.D. 286, at 292-294 (C.A., *per* Lindley, L.J., for the Court, 1886). Cf. *infra*, pp. 642-643.

[56] *Dicey & Morris*, 502.

CHAPTER 28

TRANSFER OF CHOSES IN POSSESSION[1]

In this chapter we will examine the question of what law governs particular transfers of tangible movables (or *choses* in possession) and the proprietary effect of these transfers. In contrast to general transfers, on death, marriage or on bankruptcy, particular transfers include such matters as transfer by sale, pawning, hire-purchase or gift. At times — in property transactions relating to marriage, for example — the line between general and particular transfers may be difficult to draw.

Several approaches have been proposed to deal with the subject of particular transfers of choses in possession. Let us consider each in turn.

The Lex Domicilii

The first approach, and one that had much support formerly among writers[2] and judges,[3] would be to apply the *lex domicilii* of the owner, echoing the general maxims *mobila sequuntur personam* and *mobilia ossibus inhaerent*.

The mobility, and thus contingent location, of tangible movables has been regarded by some as a reason for establishing a conflicts rule involving a fairly permanent reference point. The *lex domicilii* usually fulfils this requirement, but at a price of considerable commercial impracticability[4] and interference with the legitimate expectations of the parties.[5]

There is, moreover, a somewhat technical difficulty with the *lex domicilii*. In the not infrequent cases where the ownership of a tangible movable is in dispute, "the difficulty is not met by adopting the law of the domicile of the owner as the rules, for the very question to be decided is, who is the owner?"[6]

---

[1] See Lalive, *The Transfer of Chattels in the Conflict of Laws* (1955) G. Zaphiriou, *The Transfer of Chattels in Private International Law: A Comparative Study* (1956), *Dicey & Morris*, 555-569, *Morris* ch. 10, *Cheshire & North*, 520-536, *Nygh* (3rd ed.), 417ff, *Falconbridge*, ch. 19, Morris, *The Transfer of Chattels in the Conflict of Laws*, 22 Br. Yrbk. of Internat. L. 232 (1945), Hellendall, *The Res in Transitu and Similar Problems in the Conflict of Laws*, 17 Can. Bar Rev. 7, 108 (1939), Beale, *The Situs of Things*, 28 Yale L.J. 525 (1919), Beale, *Jurisdiction over Title of Absent Owner in a Chattel*, 40 Harv. L. Rev. 805 (1927), Carnahan, *Tangible Property and the Conflict of Laws*, 2 U. Chic. L. Rev. 345 (1935).
[2] The historical background is set out by *Zaphiriou*, ch. III, *Lalive*, 34-48, *Falconbridge*, 444-445. Story's influence was decisive (*Lalive*, 40), as is apparent from Irish decisions such as *In bonis Gentilii Deceased*, I.R. 9 Eq. 541 (Prob., Warren, J., 1875).
[3] Cf. *Sill* v. *Worswick*, 1 H. Bl. 665, at 690, 126 E.R. 379, at 392 (1791); *Re Ewin*, 1 Cr. & J. 151, at 155; 148 E.R. 1371, at 1373 (1830).
[4] *Zaphiriou*, 24, *Lalive*, 45.
[5] *Cheshire & North*, 522. These objections do not have the same force in relation to *general* assignments of tangible property, such as succession or bankruptcy: cf. *Lalive*, 41-42, 45, Carnahan, *supra*, at 348.
[6] *Cooper* v. *Philadelphia Worsted Co. (Lees* v. *Harding)*, 68 N.J. Eq. 622, at 629, 60 A. 352, at 355 (1905), cited by *Lalive*, 44.

The Lex Situs[7]

The *lex situs* offers considerable advantages as the law to govern the transfer of chattels, in most cases at least. First, since the chattel can be situated in only one country at a time, the *lex situs* offers a single governing law, in contrast to the *lex domicilii*, as the parties do not always share the same domicile. As against this, the *situs* of the chattel may change from time to time, sometimes over a short period. In these cases, "it is no solution to say that the *lex situs* governs: we require to know which *lex situs* to apply".[8]

The *lex situs* has the general advantage of easing commercial transactions[9] and of giving effect to the expectations of the transferor, transferee and third parties.[10] Where, however, the goods have a temporary, contingent location, such as where they are being stored while in transit, the *lex situs* may be quite inappropriate.[11] Moreover, where the *situs* of a chattel is changed by a wrongful act, and the chattel is then disposed of in the new *situs*, an inflexible application of the *lex* of the new *situs* may be unjust to the original owner.[12]

A further claim of the *lex situs* is based on considerations of harsh practicality. The legal system of the *situs* of the chattel, in the last analysis, has control over its fate.[13] The courts of the *situs* may attach the chattel and order its sale. An order of a foreign court, if ignored by the courts of the *situs*, may be a *brutum fulmen*.[14]

More theoretical justifications of the *lex situs*, based on public policy,[15] the sovereignty of the country of the *situs*[16] and the implied submission of the owner,[17] have received little support in common law jurisdictions.

The Lex Loci Actus[18]

The *lex loci actus* at one time received some support, by way of *dicta*, in court decisions.[19] It has fallen into disrepute in recent times. It seems to have no advantage over the *lex situs*, and more drawbacks.[20] If two Irish people are on a holiday in Spain and while there one sells his car, then in a Dublin garage, to the other, there seems little reason to look to Spanish law to govern the transaction. Such support for the *lex loci actus* as was given in former times may be traced by the early influence of the *lex loci contractus* in relation to contracts.[21]

---

[7] See *Zaphiriou*, ch. 6, *Lalive*, ch. 5, Hellendall, *The Res in transitu and Similar Problems in the Conflict of Laws — I*, 17 Can. Bar Rev. 7, at 7-9 (1939). The *lex situs* has considerable judicial support in common law jurisdictions: see e.g. *Cammell* v. *Sewell*, 5 H. & N. 728, (1860), *Re Anziani*, [1930] 1 Ch. 407, at 420 (Maugham, J.), *Bank voor handel en Scheepvart N.V.* v. *Stafford*, [1953] 1 Q.B., at 257 (Devlin, J.), *Hardwick Game Farm* v. *Suffolk Agricultural Poultry Producers Association*, [1966] 1 W.L.R. 287, at 330 (C.A.), *per* Diplock, L.J.) (affirmed by H.L. [1969] 2 A.C. 31). In *In re Interview Ltd*, [1975] I.R. 382, as we shall see, *infra*, pp. 491-493, Kenny, J. applied the *lex situs* of the goods, but only by way of *renvoi* from German law, the proper law of the contract under which the goods had reached Ireland.
[8] Morris, *The Transfer of Chattels in the Conflict of Laws*, 22 Br. Yrbk. of Internat. L. 232, at 233 (1945).
[9] See *Lalive*, 112, 115.
[10] *Zaphiriou*, 41, *Re Anziani*, [1930] 1 Ch. 407, at 420 (Maugham, J.).
[11] Cf. *Cheshire & North*, 524.
[12] Cf. Morris, *The Transfer of Chattels in the Conflict of Laws*, 22 Br. Yrbk. of Internat. L. 232, at 233 (1945).
[13] *Zaphiriou*, 42, *Lalive*, 105-106.
[14] *Morris*, 351.
[15] See *Lalive*, 103-104, *Zaphiriou*, 40.
[16] *Lalive*, 106-110.
[17] *Id.*, 110-112.
[18] See *Zaphiriou*, ch. 4, *Lalive*, 74-83.
[19] For a devastatingly critical analysis, see *Lalive*, 75-81. Perhaps the clearest support for the *lex loci actus* was expressed by Kay, L.J., in *Alcock* v. *Smith*, [1892] 1 Ch. 238, at 267 (C.A.).
[20] Cf. *Zaphiriou*, 29-30.
[21] See *Lalive*, 77, and *infra*, pp. 519-520.

The Proper Law of the Transfer[22]

The final possible governing law which we must consider is the proper law of the transfer, that is, the law of the country with which the transfer has the greatest connection. This solution was advocated by Cheshire,[23] in the context of a wider conceptual approach which has not received general support.[24]

The proper law solution is perhaps most appealing where a single transfer is made of chattels situated in several different countries or of chattels in transit from one country to another.[25] But difficulties arise where there is *no* transfer, as, for example, where a lost chattel is found in one country and brought to another and the finder acquires a presumptive title to it under the law of the latter, but not the former, country.[26]

Perhaps the most fundamental weakness with this solution is that, in giving heavy prominence to the contractual dimensions of transfers, it places insufficient weight on their proprietary effects. If, according to the *lex situs,* no title passes under a particular transfer, practical considerations suggest that that law, rather than the proper law of the transfer, should be respected.[27]

Conclusion

The balance of the competing arguments appears to be in favour of the *lex situs.* Since practicality is such an important consideration, it seems only sensible that the *lex situs* here should mean, not the internal laws of the *situs,* but whatever law the conflict rules of the *situs* prescribe.[28] In other words, there is a case in this narrow context for applying the total *renvoi* theory.[29]

IRISH DECISIONS

Let us now consider the Irish decision of *In re Interview Ltd,*[30] in 1975.

The facts were as follows. An Irish company, EII, agreed with a German company, AEG, to import the German company's goods under a contract governed by German law. By this contract, AEG reserved to itself the property in the goods until payment had been completed, and the Irish company agreed to assign to AEG any claims that the Irish company might acquire against persons to whom the Irish company sold AEG goods.

Later it was agreed that Interview Ltd, another Irish company, should acquire from EII its stock of AEG goods, and that Interview Ltd should be supplied directly by AEG with goods on the same conditions as had applied to the supply of AEG goods to EII. Possession of the AEG goods was transferred by EII to Interview Ltd. Portion of the price was entered as a debt in Interview Ltd's current account with EII and the balance of the price was to be paid by Interview Ltd by the issue of its promissory notes to AEG for the amount of the balance of the price of goods still payable by EII to AEG. Interview Ltd issued the promissory notes but they were dishonoured.

On 29 January 1972, a bank appointed the applicant to be the receiver of the

---

[22] See *Zaphiriou,* ch. 5, *Lalive,* 81-82.

[23] *Cheshire,* 2nd ed., 415-416.

[24] See *Zaphiriou,* 32, *Lalive,* 81-82, *Schmitthoff,* 198, Morris, *The Transfer of Chattels in the Conflict of Laws,* 22 Br. Yrbk. of Internat. L. 232, (1945).

[25] *Morris,* 351.

[26] *Id.*

[27] Cf. *Falconbridge,* 452, *Dicey & Morris,* 557.

[28] *Dicey & Morris,* 558.

[29] See *supra,* p. 36.

[30] [1975] I.R. 382 (High Ct., Kenny, J.).

undertaking and assets of Interview Ltd, pursuant to the powers conferred by a debenture which Interview Ltd had issued to the Bank. At that date Interview Ltd was in possession of a quantity of AEG goods. The receiver applied to the High Court for directions in relation to the conflicting claims of the debenture holder and of AEG.

It is necessary to quote extensively from Kenny, J.'s analysis of the issue. He said:

"Evidence about German law was given by [an expert] and I accept all his evidence. German law distinguishes between a contractual relationship to sell goods and the property relationship involved in the sale. There is a contract for sale and a contract for the transfer of the title to the merchandise, though these two contracts may be in one document. If a person makes an unconditional agreement for sale he may agree that the passing of title will take place only on payment and that until that date, the ownership of or title to the goods remains in the vendor. He said that clause 18 of the terms for deliveries abroad which is headed 'Reservation of ownership' is a very common clause in contracts in Germany where it is known as a 'current account clause'. The first part of the clause is a reservation of title and the effect of it under German law is that the vendor or supplier remains the owner though possession has passed to the purchaser. His evidence was that when goods are sold outside Germany, the German law about reservation of ownership or title prevails. The purchaser is entitled to retain the goods until the vendor can prove delay in payment, and then the vendor may serve a notice of rescission. The vendor cannot take the goods back until he has served the notice of rescission but until he does this, the goods remain his and the purchaser has possession or custody only. The notice of rescission brings about a change in the legal relationship in that the vendor is entitled to take the goods back. However, when the goods are in the custody of a purchaser but the title to them is in the vendor, the effect of a sale by the purchaser is governed, under German law, by the *lex loci rei sitae* which in this case is Irish law. Therefore, the validity of a sale by the purchaser would be governed by Irish law. Similarly, an assignment of the debt arising out of a sale by the purchaser to another person of the goods would be governed by Irish law and not by German law. [The expert] said that if Irish law required the registration of the terms for delivery abroad as a condition of the validity of assignments of debts owing to the purchaser and arising out of a sale by him of goods sold under those terms, then the terms, insofar as they related to the assignment of the debt, would be invalid if they were not registered. Any assignment of a claim by the purchaser arising in Ireland would under German law be governed by Irish law if any question of its validity arose."[31]

Kenny, J. went on to consider clause 18 of the contract dealing with the reservation of ownership in the terms for deliveries abroad. The terms applied to the sale, "because they were part of the contract for sale which provided that German law was to apply".[32] As between EII and AEG, the effect was that the German company remained owner of the goods and that EII had custody and possession of them for the purposes of the Factors Act 1889 and the Sale of Goods Act 1893. Kenny, J. had no doubt that Interview knew that the goods held by EII in March 1972 had been delivered to EII on the terms for deliveries abroad. The effect of clause 18, in his view, was that ownership and property remained in the German company until the goods had been paid for: "[t]hus EII and Interview could transfer the property and ownership in the goods to any person who bought them in good faith and without notice of the claim and right of the German compan[y]".[33]

Kenny, J. went on to hold that the effect of section 9 of the Factors Act 1889 and section 25(2) of the Sale of Goods Act 1893 was that a purchaser in good faith from EII or Interview Ltd of the goods which they had in their possession acquired the property in them. But, Kenny, J. held, Interview Ltd could not rely in either

[31] *Id.*, at 392.
[32] *Id.*, at 393.
[33] *Id.*

Act to validate the transaction as a sale because they had not received the goods in good faith and they had had notice of the rights of the original seller, the German company, in respect of the goods. This was because the goods had never been the property of EII:

> "They had possession and custody of them but not property or ownership because the goods were sold under the AEG terms for deliveries abroad — and Interview knew this. The transfer by EII of the goods to Interview did not transfer the property in the goods which remained in the German compan[y]. Section 1 of the Act of 1893 provides that a contract of sale of goods is 'a contract whereby the seller transfers or agrees to transfer *the property* in goods to the buyer for a money consideration, called the price'. EII could not agree to transfer the property in the goods delivered by the German compan[y] because EII did not have it."[34]

Kenny, J.'s resolution of the conflicts issues raised by the case is not entirely clear. So far as the transfer of chattels is concerned, it appears that Kenny, J. did not seek to apply any rule of *Irish* conflicts of law to the question, such as the *lex situs* or the proper law of the transaction, for example. Instead he appears to have concluded from the fact that the contract provided[35] that all contractual relations should be governed by German law, that the *German* conflicts of law rule as to the transfer of chattels should be applied. Under German conflicts of law, the *lex situs* applied, the *lex situs* being "Irish law".[36] "Irish law" in this context appears to mean Irish internal law, including its statutory law,[37] which Kenny, J. interpreted without regard to international considerations.

In *Kruppstahl A.G.* v. *Quitman Products Ltd.*,[38] Gannon, J. followed *Re Interview Ltd.*[39] The case involved a "retention of title" clause in a contract for the sale and delivery of goods by a German company to a company in Ireland, whose business affairs later resulted in a receiver being appointed to it. The contract was governed by German law. Like Kenny, J., Gannon, J. looked initially to German law to determine the respective rights of the German company and the debenture holder who had appointed the receiver. So far as German law envisaged that Irish law would operate, Gannon, J. recognised and gave effect to it.

Brookes v. *Harrison*[40] is an interesting decision on the question of formal requirements for the transfer of chattels. A bill of sale was made in England between two persons resident and domiciled there. Some of the chattels assigned were in England; the rest consisted of pictures then temporarily in Ireland, on exhibition at the Royal Hibernian Academy. The assignment was registered as a bill of sale in England, but was not so registered in Ireland. An English creditor of the grantor obtained a judgment against him in England, which he enrolled in Ireland under the Judgments Extension Act 1868.[41] The question then arose as to whether he was entitled to take the pictures in execution.

The Common Pleas Division, affirmed summarily by the Court of Appeal, held that the English bill of sale, though not registered here, effectually protected the pictures against execution. Morris, C.J. said:

---

[34] *Id.*, at 394.

[35] Kenny, J. did not discuss why this provision should be given effect by an Irish court. Presumably he considered that the proper law of the contract was German.

[36] [1975] I.R., at 392.

[37] Factors Act 1889, section 9, Sale of Goods Act 1893, section 25(2), Companies Act 1963, section 99(1), (2).

[38] [1982] I.L.R.M. 551 (High Ct., Gannon, J.).

[39] *Supra.*

[40] 6 L.R. Ir. 332 (C.A., 1880), aff'g 6 L.R. Ir. 85 (C.P. Div., 1880), criticised with some astringency, but with no supporting argument, by *Zaphiriou*, 79.

[41] Cf. *infra*, p. 610.

"The property in the pictures followed the person, and was always in [the grantor];
... and there is no express enactment in the [Irish Bills of Sale Act 1854[42]], nor by
implication as within the policy of it, whereby it would invalidate a contract made
in England between parties domiciled there, and dealing with personal property,
principally situate in England, though some of it was then temporarily situate in Ireland
...''[43]

Harrison, J. pointed to the policy of the 1854 Act, which was to prevent frauds
on creditors by secret bills of sale of chattels. He found it:

"difficult to see how any English creditor could be misled as to the credit of his English
debtor, who was possessed of personal effects in Ireland, Scotland, or elsewhere and
affected by an unregistered bill of sale, of the existence of which effects the creditor
cannot be assumed to be aware, and which he could not have made available by seizure
under an execution on foot of his English judgment save through the machinery of
the Judgments Extension Act 1868.''[44]

Attachment of movables

It appears that, so far as *attachment* of movables by a creditor is concerned, "the
creditor enjoys the rights recognised by the country where the movables are situate
at the time of the attachment. Those rights prevail against all persons claiming under
some other law".[45]

Goods in transitu[46]

Where goods *in transitu* are subject to a commercial transaction, such as a sale
or pledge, the question arises as to what law should apply. In contrast to transfers
of goods that are in one place for some time, where the *lex situs* has a credible claim
from the standpoint of practical convenience, goods *in transitu* present far greater
problems in attempting to devise a satisfactory rule or rules. The *lex situs* has obvious
drawbacks, though it is worth bearing in mind that the principal argument in favour
of the *lex situs* as a general governing law, namely that of protecting reasonable
commercial expectations, still applies when the goods are *in transitu*.[47]

There is a need for a governing law that is ascertainable by objective standards.
The law of the place of dispatch would fulfil this requirement,[48] although it may
be considered inappropriate in view of the fact that this law has ceased to be the
law of the actual situation of the goods.[49] The law of the stipulated place of
destination has also been mooted though it has not received much judicial support.[50]
The law of the flag, in cases of carriage by sea, and the proper law have also been
proposed.

Perhaps the best approach is to treat the various problems that may arise according
to the law that is most appropriate.[51] Thus it may be reasonable to apply the *lex
situs* to determine questions of title where the goods are seized by creditors while
applying the law of the flag in respect of carriage by sea in a single ship.[52]

---

[42] 17 & 18 Vict. c. 55.

[43] 6 L.R. Ir., at 88.

[44] *Id.*, at 90.

[45] *Cheshire & North*, 532 referring to *Liverpool Marine Credit Co.* v. *Hunter*, L.R. 4 Eq. 62 (1867);
on appeal 3 Ch. App. 479 (1868), and *Inglis* v. *Robertson*, [1898] A.C. 616.

[46] See Hellendall, *The Res in Transitu and Similar Problems in the Conflict of Laws*, 17 Can. Bar Rev.
7, 105 (1939).

[47] Cf. Hellendall, *supra*, at 33.

[48] *Id.*, at 35.

[49] Cf. *id.*, (stating, but not supporting, this criticism).

[50] Cf. Lord Watson's rejection in *Inglis* v. *Robertson*, [1898] A.C. 616, at 627 (H.L. (Sc.)).

[51] Cf. *Cheshire & North*, 534.

[52] *Id.*, 534-535.

GIFTS[53]

There is very little authority on the question of transfer of movables by gift *inter vivos*. The only English decision[54] on the subject is unhelpful since the foreign law was neither pleaded nor mentioned by the court.

The weight of academic opinion[55] favours the *lex situs*. A *donatio mortis causa,* which falls between a gift *inter vivos* and a testamentary disposition, gives rise to some difficulty in the present context. In the English decision of *In re Korvine's Trusts,*[56] in 1921 a person domiciled in Russia made a *donatio mortis causa* of movables situated in England. In this case, the *lex rei sitae* and the *lex fori* coincided, "so that it was obvious that the nature of the transaction in question had to be determined by the law of England, and that when it had been decided that the transaction was such as to confer a proprietary interest upon the donee and to prevent the subject matter from forming part of the estate of the donor, it became unnecessary, as regards that transaction, to refer to the *lex domicilii*".[57]

In the later decision of *Re Craven's Estate,*[58] however, Farwell, J. characterised such a gift as a testamentary disposition to which the *lex domicilii* would thus apply. He considered that:

> "... if it be necessary, according to English law, that there should be an effective parting with dominion over the property, the property being situated abroad, that which is said to constitute the parting with dominion must be something which would be effective in the place abroad where the property is situated, so as to constitute a sufficient parting with dominion within the meaning of that phrase as used in this connection."[59]

[53] *Id.,* 535-536, *Falconbridge,* ch. 33.

[54] *Cochrane* v. *Moore,* 25 Q.B.D. 57 (1890).

[55] *Morris,* 352, *Cheshire & North,* 535, *Nygh* (3rd ed.) 421, *Falconbridge,* ch. 33. In the Massachusetts Supreme Court decision of *Morson* v. *Second National Bank of Boston,* 306 Mass. 588, 29 N.E. 2d 19, at 20 (1940), it was stated:

> "Doubtless it is true that whether or not there is a completed gift of an ordinary tangible chattel is to be determined by the law of the *situs* of the chattel ..."

[56] [1921] 1 Ch. 343.

[57] *Falconbridge,* 646.

[58] [1937] Ch. 423; [1937] 3 All E.R. 33; reported most fully, 53 Times L.R. 694.

[59] [1937] 3 All E.R., at 40. For criticism of Farwell, J.'s approach, see *Falconbridge,* 643-644.

CHAPTER 29

ASSIGNMENT OF CHOSES IN ACTION[1]

In this chapter we will consider the question of what law should be applied to the assignment of *choses in action,* such as a contract debt, negotiable instrument or share. Four different solutions have been suggested at various times. These are: (a) the law of the creditor's domicile; (b) the *lex situs* of the debt; (c) the *lex loci actus* and (d) the proper law of the debt. Let us consider each in turn.

THE LAW OF THE CREDITOR'S DOMICILE

The *lex domicilii* of the creditor has received the support of several continental authorities and of Story but has not commended itself, in the main, to the courts[2] or commentators of common law jurisdictions. The principal objection is that a person's domicile is generally of little importance in commercial transactions,[3] and that recourse to it would be arbitrary and impractical and would defeat the legitimate expectations of the parties.[4]

THE LEX SITUS

The second approach which has been propounded by some commentators[5] is to refer to the *lex situs.* Before we can examine the merits of this approach we have to consider the prior question of how a debt can be said to have a *situs,* and how that *situs* should be determined. In common law jurisdictions, it is generally accepted that a debt, though "not a matter of which you can predicate position",[6] *has* a *situs* and, further (echoing ecclesiastical law), that that *situs* is the place where the debtor resides.[7]

Of course, residence is not always a straightforward criterion, since the debtor may reside in more than one country. (This may often be the case in relation to corporations.) In such instances, it has been held that the debt is situated in the country in which:

"it is required to be paid by an express or implied provision of the contract or, if there

[1] See *Wolff,* ch. 36, *Castel,* vol. 2, ch. 12.
[2] But cf. *Republica de Guatemala* v. *Nunez,* [1927] 1 K.B. 669, at 689-690 (C.A., *per* Scrutton, L.J., 1926).
[3] Cf. *Morris,* 358.
[4] Cf. *Cheshire & North* 537.
[5] *Westlake,* s. 152, *Dicey,* 5th ed., Rule 153.
[6] *New York Life Insurance Co.* v. *Public Trustee,* [1924] 2 Ch. 101, at 119 (*per* Atkin, L.J.). See also *Lee* v. *Abdy,* 17 Q.B.D. 309, at 312 (*per* Day, J., 1886), *Hutchinson* v. *Cathcart,* 8 Ir. Eq. Rep. 394, at 397 (Equity Exch., 1845). Cf. *English, Scottish and Australian Bank* v. *I.R.C.,* [1932] A.C. 238; and see pp. 398-399, *supra.*
[7] *Cheshire & North,* 537-538; *Wolff,* 542. See *In re Finance Act 1894 and Deane Deceased,* [1936] I.R. 556, at 566 (High Ct., *per* Sullivan, P.).

is no such provision, where it would be paid according to the ordinary course of business."[8]

But even though a debt possesses a situation, based (largely) on the residence of the defendant, it does not follow that the assignment of a debt should necessarily be governed by the *lex situs*. Since the *lex situs* follows the residence of the debtor, difficulties may arise if there are competing assignments in different countries where the debtor happens to be residing at the time of each assignment.[9]

THE LEX LOCI ACTUS

There is some support in the decisions[10] for the *lex loci actus,* the law of the place where the assignment takes place; but it has inspired little enthusiasm among the commentators. *Wolff*[11] comments that "[t]o test an assignment by the place where it was made is to choose the least important of all points of contact, to substitute fortuity for reason".

THE PROPER LAW OF THE DEBT

The idea here is that the assignment should be governed not by its own proper law but by "the proper law of the original transaction out of which the *chose in action* arose".[12] It is reasonable that the assignee should look to the original transaction which is, after all, the basis of the right of action which he is acquiring.[13] Moreover, this approach offers a single solution to govern the problem of competing assignments, rather than referring to more than one legal system, which, as we have seen, is a drawback to the *lex situs* and *lex loci actus* approaches. There is, however, scant judicial support for this approach.[14]

Specific Issues

Let us now turn to consider some specific aspects of the subject.

Capacity

Such judicial authority as there is on the question of the capacity of the parties in relation to the assignment of debts appears to support the *lex domicilii* or *lex loci actus*. In *Lee* v. *Abdy,*[15] in 1886, Day and Willes JJ. favoured this approach, neither judge drawing a distinction between the *lex domicilii* and the *lex loci actus*. In *Republica de Guatemala* v. *Nunez,*[16] Scrutton and Lawrence, L.J. took the same view.

The commentators[17] generally do not like this approach. They stress the fact that in both cases application of the proper law criterion would have yielded the same result as that at which the Court arrived; and they take the view that the proper law

---

[8] *Jabbour (F. & K.)* v. *Custodian of Israeli Absentee's Property of State of Israel,* [1954] 1 All E.R. 145, at 152 (Q.B. Div., Pearson, J., 1953).

[9] Cf. *Cheshire & North,* 539.

[10] Cf. *Lee* v. *Abdy,* 17 Q.B.D. 309 (1886), *Republica de Guatemala* v. *Nunez,* [1927] 1 K.B. 669 (C.A.), both considered *infra*.

[11] *Wolff,* 540.

[12] *Cheshire & North,* 539. Also supporting this approach are *Wolff,* 538, 544 and *Falconbridge,* 494—498.

[13] *Cheshire & North,* 540.

[14] *Morris,* 359.

[15] 17 Q.B.D. 309 (1886). See, however, *Kelly* v. *Selwyn,* [1905] 2 Ch. 117, at 121 (Chy. Div.), where Warrington, J. observed that *Lee* v. *Abdy* "merely decided this: that if a question arises whether an assignment of a chose in action is valid according to the law where it is executed, that question will be determined by the law of the place where it is executed".

[16] [1927] 1 K.B. 669 (C.A. 1926), at 689 and 700—701 respectively. See also *Re Anziani,* [1930] 1 Ch. 407, at 422 (*per* Maugham, J. 1929); but cf. *Lowenstein* v. *Allen,* [1958] C.L.Y. 491 and see *Regas Ltd* v. *Plotkins,* [1961] S.C.R. 566, 29 D.L.R. (2d) 282, as explained by *McLeod,* 348.

[17] *Morris,* 361—362, *Cheshire & North,* 542—543, *Dicey & Morris,* 573—574, *McLeod,* 349—350.

offers ''a far better''[18] test of capacity than either the *lex domicilii* or the *lex loci actus*.

Formalities

On principle, it seems that of the assignment of a *chose in action*, like a contract,[19] should be formally valid if it complies with the requirements of either the *lex loci contractus* or of the proper law.[20] There is, however, a dearth of modern judicial authority on the question, and the only clear statement of law is far more restrictive. In the English decision of *Republica de Guatemala* v. *Nunez*,[21] Scrutton, L.J. expressed support for the view that:

> ''a contract void in the place where it is made, by reason of the omission of formalities required by the law of that place, is void elsewhere ... The authorities are fairly clear ... that where a transaction is invalid or a nullity by the law of the place where the transaction takes place owing to the omission of formalities or stamp, it will not be recognised in England.''

However, Lawrence L.J., dissenting on this point, considered that the formal validity of the debt was governed by the *lex situs*.[22]

Essentials

The same tale unfolds with regard to essentials as in relation to capacity and formalities. The commentators[23] favour the view that the proper law should govern, as it does in relation to contracts in general; but such judicial authority as there is, in its express terms, favours a ''black letter'' rule. In *Re Anziani*,[24] support was given to the *lex loci actus*. Again it has been pointed out[25] that the *lex loci actus* in this case was the proper law.

Priorities

We must now consider the position where there are two or more competing assignments and questions of priorities arises. This issue first arose in *Le Feuvre* v. *Sullivan*[26] where the Privy Council applied the proper law of the debt to determine priorities. A less clear decision is *Kelly* v. *Selwyn*.[27] In 1891, Mr Selwyn, then domiciled in the state of New York, assigned to his American wife all his interest in some English trust funds. According to New York law, notice to the trustees was not necessary to complete an assignment of a chose of action, and no notice of the assignment was in fact given to them until 1903. In the meantime, in 1894, Mr Selwyn assigned the same interest to the plaintiff by way of mortgage and notice of this assignment was given to the trustees without delay.

Warrington, J. held that the question should be determined by English law, under which the plaintiff ranked in priority to Mrs Selwyn. Warrington, J. said:

> ''The ground on which I decide [the question] is that, the fund here being an English trust fund and this being the court which the testator may have contemplated as the

---

[18] *Morris*, 362.
[19] Cf. *infra*, 538.
[20] See *Cheshire & North*, 543–544, *Morris*, 361 *McLeod*, 350. But cf. *Nygh*, 445, *Anning* v. *Anning*, 4 C.L.R. 1049 (High Ct. of Austr., 1907).
[21] [1927] 1 K.B. 699, at 690–691 (C.A., 1926). See also *Re Anziani*, [1930] 1 Ch. 407.
[22] *Id*., at 695–698.
[23] *Morris*, 362, *Cheshire & North*, 544.
[24] [1930] 1 Ch. 407.
[25] Cf. *Cheshire & North*, 544, *Morris*, 362, fn. 23. In *Russell* v. *Kitchen*, 31, C.L.R. 613, at 615 (Q.B., 1854), Crampton, J. invoked the *lex loci contractus*.
[26] 10 Moo. P.C.1, 14 E.R. 389 (1885).
[27] [1905] 2 Ch. 117 (Warrington, J.).

court which would have administrated that trust fund the order in which the parties are to be held entitled to the trust fund must be regulated by the law of the court which in administering that fund.''[28]

The *ratio* of this decision has been a source of much discussion, in view of this opaque language. In support of the view that the *lex fori* was the basis of the judgment are *Westlake*[29] and Scrutton, L.J. in *Republica de Guatemala* v. *Nunez.*[30] But *Cheshire & North* argue that:

"the decisive factor in the mind of the judge, if his language is considered as a whole, was that the subject matter of the assignment consisted of a trust fund, the proper law of which was English Law.''[31]

The *lex fori* would offer an unfortunate choice as a solution to the question of priorities, since there might be competing *fora* on a matter that "must of necessity be referred to one arbiter and to one only".[32]

In both *Jeffrey* v. *Taggart*[33] and *Barber* v. *Mexican Land Co.,*[34] the disentitlement of the assignee to take proceedings in England was attributable to the view that, by the *lex causae,*[35] the entitlement of the assignee was not intended to have extra-territorial effect.[36]

The merits of the argument are generally considered to lie with the view that the rule is substantive. The rule is in aid of debtors,[37] and if, under the *lex causae,* no such protection is available, it is hard to see why creditors' claims should be thwarted by a rule of the forum.[38]

Shares[39]

It is well settled that the validity and legal effects of an assignment of shares *intended to bind the company* will be governed by the *lex situs*. Shares are deemed to be situated in "the country where they can be effectively dealt with as between the shareholder and the company".[40] Thus where shares may be transferred only by an entry in the register, they are deemed to be situated in the country where the register is kept.[41] Where the company keeps registers in more than one country, the shares are deemed to be situated in "the country in which according to the ordinary course of business the transfer would be registered".[42]

The effect of a transfer of shares *as between the parties themselves* is determined

---

[28] *Id.*, at 122.
[29] *Westlake*, 152.
[30] [1927] 1 K.B. 669, at 693.
[31] *Cheshire & North*, 548.
[32] *Id.*
[33] 6 M. & S. 126, 105 E.R. 1190 (1817).
[34] 16 Times L.R. 127 (Ch. Div., Stirling, J., 1899).
[35] Scottish bankruptcy legislation in the first case and the Californian Code of Civil Procedure in the second.
[36] *Morris*, 464, *Regas Ltd* v. *Plotkins*, [1961] S.C.R. 566, 29 D.L.R. (2d) 282, as explained by *Dicey & Morris*, 1191 and *McLean*, 223.
[37] *Morris*, 464–465. In accord, *Dicey & Morris*, 1191.
[38] *Cheshire & North*, 701.
[39] See *Falconbridge*, 498–505.
[40] *Cheshire & North*, 554.
[41] *In re Ferguson, Deceased*, [1935] I.R. 21 (Sup. Ct., 1934), *Brassard* v. *Smith*, [1925] A.C. 371, *Colonial Bank* v. *Cady*, 15 App. Cas. 267 (1890), *Baelz* v. *A.G. for Ontario*, [1930] A.C. 161, *R.* v. *Williams*, [1942] A.C. 541 (P.C.), *Re Thompson Estate*, [1943] O.W.N. 361 (High Ct., Hope, J.). Cf. *Smith* v. *Cork & Bandon Ry. Co.*, [1903] 1 I.R. 512 (Porter, M.R.), distinguished in *R.* v. *Williams*, *supra* at 555. In *In re Belfast Empire Theatre of Varieties Ltd*, [1963] I.R. 41, at 45 (High Ct., 1963), Kenny, J. agreed with the approach of the Privy Council in the *Williams* case. See further *Re Northern Ontario Power Co. Ltd*, [1954] 1 D.L.R. 627, *McLeod*, 189, *Forde*, 295.
[42] *Cheshire & North*, 555.

by reference to the proper law of the transaction,[43] which almost always will be the law of the place where the share certificate is delivered.[44]

Involuntary Assignments

Garnishment [45]

Garnishment is a process whereby a judgment creditor attaches a debt owed by a third party to his judgment debtor. It appears that garnishment proceedings will be permitted "if the debt is properly recoverable, that is situated,"[46] in the State but not otherwise. So a debt due from an Irish bank to a foreign debtor may be garnished[47] but not a debt due from a foreign branch of an Irish or foreign bank to a foreign debtor.[48]

The making of a garnishment order is discretionary, and can be refused where there is a risk that the garnishee will be compelled to pay again abroad.[49] But this must be "a real risk ... A mere speculative or theoretical hazard will not do."[50]

So far as foreign garnishment orders are concerned, it appears that the *lex situs* of the debt governs the question of their enforceability[51] and effect.[52]

---

[43] *Cheshire & North*, 556, *McLeod*, 353.

[44] *Cheshire & North*, 556, *Re Fry*, [1946] Ch. 312.

[45] See Order of the Rules of the Superior Courts 1986, *Buchanan* v. *Darragh*, 36 I.L.T.R. 9 (C.A., 1901). *Morris*, 363–364, *Cheshire & North*, 548-549, *McLeod*, 352.

[46] *Morris*, 364. See *Re Queensland Mercantile & Agency Co. Ltd, Ex Parte Union Bank of Australia*, [1892] 1 Ch. 219 (C.A.) aff'g [1891] 1 Ch. 536, *Re Maudslay, Sons & Field; Maudslay* v. *Maudslay, Sons & FIeld*, [1900] 1 Ch. 602, *Martin* v. *Nadel*, [1906] 2 K.B. 26 (C.A.), *Swiss Bank Corp.* v. *Boehmische Industrial Bank*, [1923] 1 K.B. 673 (C.A.), *Haydon* v. *Haydon*, [1937] 4 D.L.R. 617 (Man. C.A.), *Rossano* v. *Manufacturers Life Ins. Co.*, [1962] 2 All E.R. 214, *Bank of Montreal* v. *Metro Investigation & Security (Can.) Ltd.*, [1975] S.C.R. 546 (all cited by *McLeod*, 362).

[47] Cf. *Swiss Bank Corporation* v. *Boehmische Industrial Bank*, [1923] 1 K.B. 673.

[48] *Martin* v. *Nadel*, [1906] 2 K.B. 26, *Richardson* v. *Richardson*, [1927] P. 228. Cf. *Brooks Associates Inc.* v. *Basu*, [1983] Q.B. 220 (Q.B., Woolf, J., 1982), where the fact that the head office of the National Savings Bank was located in Glasgow for administrative reasons was held not to affect the power of the English court to make an order attaching funds held in the judgment debtor's account with the Bank. Woolf, J. found "great difficulty" in answering the problem by reference to the approach adopted in relation to other banks, in view of the structure of accounts in the National Savings Bank.

[49] *Morris*, 364.

[50] *Employers' Liability Assurance Corporation* v. *Sedgwick, Collins & Co.*, [1927] A.C. 95, 112 (H.L. (Eng.), *per* Lord Summer, 1926).

[51] *Morris*, 364, *Rossano* v. *Manufacturers' Life Insurance Co. Ltd*, [1963] 2 Q.B. 352 (McNair, J., 1962).

[52] *Morris*, 364 *Re Queensland Mercantile Agency Co.*, [1891] 1 Ch. 536 (North, J.), aff'd on other grounds, [1892] 1 Ch. 219 (C.A., 1891).

CHAPTER 30

TRUSTS

The trust[1] is a concept mainly limited to common law jurisdictions, though it has extended its influence into the legal systems of some civil law jurisdictions.[2] When the law of trust was being developed, "no thought existed of the possible relevance of foreign factors".[3] Today, of course, there is a real need for conflicts rules in this area, as trusts with international dimensions frequently play a most important function in family settlements[4] and as commercial investment devices.[5]

Curiously, there is very little case-law on the conflicts aspects of trusts, not only in Irish law, but also throughout the common-law world,[6] save the United States.[7] What has generally happened is that, in conflicts cases, the trust has been viewed in terms of its instrument of creation and the nature of the property it embraces, rather than in its own terms as involving a continuing legal relationship of a specific nature between the trustees and the beneficiaries.[8]

[1] See *Dicey & Morris*, ch. 25, *Morris*, ch. 26, *Keeton & Sheridan*, ch. 27, Croucher, *Trusts of Moveables in Private International Law*, 4 Modern L. Rev. 111 (1940), Cavers, *Trusts Inter Vivos and the Conflict of Laws*, 44 Harv. L. Rev. 161 (1931), Keeton, *Trusts in the Conflict of Laws*, 4 Current Legal Prob. 107 (1951), Delany, *Charitable Trusts and the Conflict of Laws*, 10 Int. & Comp. L.Q. 385 (1961), Lefer & Siegel, *Trusts of Movables in the Conflict of Laws*, 36 N.Y.U.L. Rev. 713 (1961), Dean, *Conflict Avoidance in Inter Vivos Trusts of Movables*, 21 L. & Contemp. Prob. 483 (1956), Latham, *The Creation and Administration of A Trust in the Conflict of Laws*, 6 Current Legal Prob. 176 (1953), Hoar, *Some Aspects of Trusts in the Conflict of Laws*, 26 Can. Bar Rev. 1415 (1948), Castel, *La Fiducie créée par donation entre vifs de biens meubles et le droit international privé quebécois*, 69 Rev. du Notar. 271 (1967), Swabenland, *The Conflict of Laws in Administration of Express Trusts of Personal Property*, 45 Yale L.J. 438 (1935), Beale, *Living Trusts of Movables in the Conflict of Laws*, 45 Harv. L. Rev. 969 (1932), Beale, *Equitable Interests in Foreign Property*, 20 Harv. L. Rev. 382 (1907), W.W.C[ook], *Note, Trusts of Personal Property and the Conflict of Laws*, 19 Colum. L. Rev. 486 (1919), New Brunswick Commissioners' Report to the Uniform Law Section of the Uniform Law Conference of Canada, *Trusts in the Conflict of Laws* (1986).

[2] Cf. Bolgar, *Why No Trusts in the Civil Law?*, 2 Amer. J. of Comp. L. 204 (1953), Batiffol, *The Trust Problem as Seen by a French Lawyer*, 33 J. of Compar. Leg. & Internat. L. 24 (1951), Lapaulle, *Civil Law Substitutes for Trusts*, 36 Yale L.J. 1135 (1927), Hefti, *Trusts and Their Treatment in the Civil Law*, 5 Amer. J. of Comp. L. 553 (1956).

At its Fifteenth Session in 1984, the Hague Conference completed a *Convention on the Law Applicable to Trusts and on Their Recognition:* Actes et documents de la Quinziéme session, Tome II, p. 361. The Convention serves the useful purpose of facilitating the recognition of trusts by States whose law does not include the concept of a trust; moreover, it offers common law jurisdictions some clear conflicts rules to replace the uncertainty which plagues the law in many of these jurisdictions (including Ireland) at present. For consideration of the main features of the Convention, see Williams, *Trusts and the Hague Convention*, 1 Company L. 95 (1986).

[3] *Graveson*, 528.

[4] Cf. Latham, *supra*, at 176.

[5] *Graveson*, 527.

[6] Cf. *Morris*, 419, Hoar, *supra*, at 1415. See also Croucher, *supra*, at 111, describing the English cases as "scanty and often misleading".

[7] Cf. Keeton, *supra*, at 118-121.

[8] *New Brunswick Commissioners' Report, supra*, p. 1.

When approaching the analysis of these conflicts issues, writers have tended to distinguish between trusts of movables and trusts of immovables.[9] From a practical standpoint this may not be all that helpful, since it may often be more suitable to treat the entire trust as a unit. The settlor may well have intended that it should be so treated, and it may be a matter of indifference to him whether the property, over the years, is to be in movable or immovable form. A distinguishing feature of trusts is that they are often intended to last a long time. Their administration may thus continue for decades.

A distinction has been made[10] between questions of validity and administration of trusts. Questions of validity include those relating to the formal and essential validity of a trust, the capacity to create, or be the object of, a trust, and the question whether a trust may be revoked.[11] Administration includes such questions as those relating to the powers and duties of the trustees, investments, the place of accounting,[12] and the power of the Court to frame a scheme for a charitable trust or to direct an application of funds *cy-près*.[13]

Trusts of Movables

The validity of testamentary trusts

Where a will contains trust provisions, it is first necessary, of course, that all the requirements of the will as a testamentary disposition be complied with.[14] Thus, if the will is formally invalid or if the testator lacked capacity to make a will, for example, the trusts contained in the will cannot be upheld.[15] Generally, the validity of a testamentary trust is determined by the testator's *lex domicilii* at the time of his death;[16] but there seems to be no reason why the testator should not be able to set up a trust to be governed by some other law.[17] In such an exceptional case, the validity of the trust will normally be governed by its proper law, which is usually the law of the place of administration.[18]

Where the question concerns whether the trust infringes the rules against perpetuities or accumulations, it seems that the law of the place of administration may govern.[19] Where charitable trusts are concerned, it is necessary that they be valid in accordance with Irish law, as well as the law of the country where they are to be carried out.[20] An example of the first requirement is *In re Moore deceased, Moore v. His Holiness Pope Benedict XV*.[21] Powell, J. held void a bequest of £10,000 to "His Holiness ... the Pope ... to use and apply at his sole and absolute discretion in the carrying out of the sacred office". Powell, J. considered that on the authorities it was "plain that where, as in this case, the objects of the trusts are stated in indefinite terms not capable of being controlled, and, if necessary, executed by the Court, the gift, not being necessarily applicable to charitable purposes as legally defined, and being applicable to purposes not only not charitable, but possibly illegal according to the laws of this country, is void".[22]

---

[9] Cf. Croucher, *supra*, at 112.
[10] *Id.*
[11] *Morris*, 419.
[12] Lefer & Siegel, *Trusts of Movables in the Conflict of Laws*, 36 N.Y.U.L. Rev. 713, at 720 (1961).
[13] Cf. *infra*, p. 512.
[14] Croucher, *supra*, at 111.
[15] *Morris*, 420.
[16] See *Dicey & Morris*, rule 117.
[17] Cf. e.g. *A.G.* v. *Campbell*, L.R. 5 H.L. 524 (1872).
[18] *Morris*, 420.
[19] *Id.*, 421.
[20] Delany, *supra*, at 391-392.
[21] [1919] 1 I.R. 316 (Powell, J.).
[22] *Id.*, at 357. See also *id.*, at 334.

The question of the scope of invalidity under Irish law arose in respect of section 16 of the Charitable Donations and Bequests Act 1844,[23] repealed in 1961.[24] Section 16 provided that "no donation, devise, or bequest for pious or charitable uses in Ireland shall be valid to create or convey any estate in lands, tenements, or hereditaments for such uses, unless the deed, will, or other instrument, shall be executed three calendar months at the least before the death of the person executing the same...." The policy behind this provision was to protect testators from succumbing to the temptation of excessive philanthropy to the neglect of the claims of their family members.[25]

Much uncertainty affected the territorial scope of the prohibition contained in section 16. Chatterton, V.C. did not help matters by producing two directly conflicting judgments[26] on this issue. The interpretation which eventually triumphed[27] was that the words "in Ireland" should be read in connection with the words "donation, devise, or bequest" rather than the words "pious or charitable uses". As Barton, J. observed in *In re Knox dec'd; Snodgrass* v. *Gamble*:[28]

> "The object of the section was not to prevent dispositions in favour of Irish charities as distinguished from English or foreign charities; but to prevent 'the mischief of improvident alienations or dispositions by languishing or dying persons in Ireland'."

That so transient a connection as mere presence in this country should have sufficed may be debated; there is much to be said in favour of having restricted the rule to persons domiciled or resident here. Whether the express words of section 16 would have permitted this interpretation is doubtful, however.

So far as secret trusts are concerned, it seems that, since they take effect outside rather than under the will, their validity should not necessarily be governed by the testator's *lex domicilii* at the time of his death, but that it "may be governed by the law of the country where the legatee accepts the trust and in which the trust is to be carried out".[29]

The Validity of Trusts Inter Vivos

From a practical standpoint, there is much to be said in favour of resolving the question of the validity of an *inter vivos* trust of movables by reference to that a single law.[30] The *lex situs* is scarcely appropriate, since the movables may be in different countries;[31] moreover, where (as is often the case) the movables are intangible, the question of *situs* raises particular difficulties.[32]

The place where the trust is executed may not always be suitable, since it may be fortuitous[33] or contrived.[34] The fact that the trust is something that is often intended to last for a considerable time suggests that a more stable reference-point should control. The *lex domicilii* of the settlor has a reasonably strong claim,[35] as

[23] *Delany*, 107, described section 16 as "[p]robably the most important statutory provision relating to charities in Ireland".

[24] Charities Act 1961, section 4.

[25] *Delany*, 108.

[26] *Boyle* v. *Boyle*, I.R. 11 Eq. 433 (1877), *Brown dec'd Brown* v. *Harrison*, 35 I.L.T.R. 25 (1900).

[27] *In re Knox Deceased; Snodgrass* v. *Gamble*, [1910] 1 I.R. 20 (Barton, J., 1909), *In re Estate of Orr, dec'd; M'Dermott* v. *Anderson*, [1915] 1 I.R. 191 (O'Connor, M.R., 1914). See *Delany*, 112-113.

[28] [1910] 1 I.R., at 22.

[29] *Dicey & Morris*, 676. Cf. *Latham*, *supra*, at 182.

[30] *Morris*, 421.

[31] Cf. *Croucher*, *supra*, at 113.

[32] Cf. *supra*, pp. 398-400.

[33] *Hoar*, *supra*, at 1425, *Morris*, 421.

[34] *Morris*, 421.

[35] *Id.*

does the place of administration, though perhaps in relation to questions of administration rather than validity.

It appears that the validity of an *inter vivos* trust is governed by its proper law, that is, "the system of law with which it has its closest and most real connection".[36] The Irish cases of *In re Cloncurry's Estate*,[37] and *Revenue Commissioners* v. *Pelly*[38] support this approach. In *Pelly,* Hanna, J. said that, in determining which law controlled the deed of trust, the Court had "to look at the surrounding circumstances. It resolves itself into a question of a legal balance sheet, to determine on which side the preponderance of the evidence lies...."[39]

It seems clear that the settlor of the trust may select the proper law. In *Pelly,* Hanna, J. accepted that, at least in cases where the trust was created in the context of a contract,[40] the settlor of the trust had the right of selection. He observed that:

" [i] n particular classes of contracts certain presumptions naturally arise, e.g. marriage settlements, and charter parties; where, in the former, there is a presumption in favour of the matrimonial domicile, and, in the latter, the use of certain phrases may indicate clearly an intention to apply a particular law."[41]

O'Byrne, J. was satisfied that the determination of whether the deed of trust was an English or an Irish settlement was "a question of, and depend [ed] upon, the intention of the parties".[42] He accepted that, had the settlement been entered into voluntarily by the parties, there would be "great force"[43] in the argument that the parties must be presumed to have intended that the settlement should be governed by Irish law, since the principal beneficiaries were domiciled and resident here. But in the case before the Court the settlement had been entered into by way of compromise of legal proceedings in England challenging the validity of a will under which the testator had left no money to his widow and children. The fact that the settlement was executed at all seemed to O'Byrne, J. to be "merely an accidental circumstance",[44] since the compromise might very well have been carried into effect by means of a consent, made a rule of Court in the probate action. In the circumstances, O'Byrne, J. was of opinion that "the reasonable and proper inference"[45] was that the parties intended that the settlement should be governed by English rather than Irish law.

Pelly appears to afford clear support for the view that the question of the proper law of the trust is one of inferring the intention of the parties. Whether this approach should be qualified by the requirement that the chosen law have some substantial connection with the trust[46]remains to be seen.

---

[36] *Dicey & Morris,* Rule 120; See also W.W. C [ook] , *Note; Trusts of Personal Property and the Conflict of Laws,* 19 Colum. L. Rev. 486, at 488-489 (1919).

[37] [1932] I.R. 687, considered *supra,* pp. 423-424.

[38] [1940] I.R. 122 (High Ct., 1939). See also *In re Cuff Knox,* 98 I.L.T.R. 141 (Sup. Ct., 1961, aff'g High Ct., Teevan, J., 1960), where the Supreme Court appeared to accept that Irish law was the proper law of a trust fund constituted by Irish settlements and by the will of a testator domiciled in Ireland. The Court did not, in the event, have to address the question of the validity of the trusts but the case is interesting in showing that the Court was willing to accept that a trust has its proper law.

[39] [1940] I.R., at 128-129. See also *Iveagh* v. *Inland Revenue Commissioners,* [1954] Ch. 364 (Upjohn, J.), a case of interest on its facts to Irish readers, in which *In re Cloncurry's Estate* was considered, at 374-376. McInerney, J. provided a thorough analysis of the subject in *Perpetual Executors & Trustees Association of Australia Ltd.* v. *Roberts,* [1970] V.R. 732 (Sup. Ct., 1969).

[40] Cf. *Lindsay* v. *Miller,* [1949] V.L.R. 13, at 14 (1948), where Lowe, J. accepted that the proper law of a contract provided an appropriate analogy for discerning the proper law of a trust deed.

[41] [1940] I.R., at 128.

[42] *Id.,* at 129.

[43] *Id.,* at 130.

[44] *Id.*

[45] *Id.* See also *id.,* at 127 (*per* Maguire, P.).

[46] Cf. *Morris,* 422; see also Lefer & Siegel, *Trusts of Movables in the Conflict of Laws,* 36 N.Y.U.L. Rev. 713, at 715-716 (1961), Delany, *supra,* at 388-389.

It seems clear that, once a trust has been created, the proper law continues to control its validity.[47] It may be changed only by an agreement by the beneficiaries to change it ,[48] "and thus in effect make a new settlement",[49] or by judicial sanction for the change.[50]

So far as specific aspects of validity of trusts are concerned, it appears that a trust will be formally valid if it complies with either the proper law[51] or the law of the place of execution;[52] that capacity[53] and essential validity[54] are determined by the proper law; and that revocation is similarly determined by the governing law.[55]

Construction

It appears to be accepted that the law determining the construction of a trust is that intended by the settlor or testator.[56] Where the trust is *inter vivos*, it is presumed that the settlor intended that the proper law of the trust should control;[57] where testamentary, it is presumed that the testator intended that *lex domicilii* at the time of making his will should control.[58]

Restraints on Alienation of Beneficial Interests

It appears that the proper law of an *inter vivos* trust or, where the trust is testamentary, the testator's *lex domicilii* at the time of his death, will govern the question whether the beneficiary of the trust may alienate his interest.[59]

Administration

There are very few Irish authorities on questions relating to the administration of a trust. The general rule is these questions are determined by the law of the place of administration. How to determine that law is not entirely settled. In *In re Pollack's Estate*,[60] the Court appeared to favour a broad, discretionary approach which would have regard to the actual or presumed intention of the parties to the trust.[61] Where, therefore, a testator appoints as trustee a trust company of another state, it is not unreasonable to presume that his intention was that the trust should be administered in the latter state, according to its laws.[62]

[47] *Morris*, 422.
[48] Cf. *Duke of Marlborough* v. *A.G.*, [1945] Ch. 78.
[49] *Morris*, 422.
[50] Cf. e.g. the British Variation of Trusts Act 1958, criticised by Mann, *Note: The Variation of Trusts Act, 1958 and the Conflict of Laws*, 80 L.Q. Rev. 29 (1964).
[51] *Van Grutten* v. *Digby*, 31 Beav. 561, 54 E.R. 1256 (1862), *Viditz* v. *O'Hagan*, [1899] 2 Ch. 569, *Re Bankes*, [1902] 2 Ch. 333.
[52] *Guépratte* v. *Young*, 4 De G. & Sm. 217, 64 E.R. 804 (1851).
[53] *Morris*, 422, points out that the English cases on capacity to create the trust all relate to trusts created by a marriage settlement, and are open to more than one interpretation; but that "it is at least a possible interpretation that capacity is governed by the proper law".
[54] Cf. *Lindsay* v. *Miller*, [1949] V.L.R. 13 (Lowe, J., 1948), *Augustus* v. *Permanent Trustee Co. (Canberra) Ltd.*, 124 C.L.R. 245 (1971). Contrast *Permanent Executors and Trustees Association of Australia Ltd.* v. *Roberts*, [1970] V.R. 732. (McInerney, J., 1969).
[55] *Viditz* v. *O'Hagan*, [1900] 2 Ch. 87, *Fattorini* v. *Johannesburg Board of Executors and Trust Co. Ltd.*, 1948 (4) S.A. 806.
[56] *Morris*, 423.
[57] *Dicey & Morris*, Rule 120.
[58] *Philipson-Stow* v. *I.R.C.*, [1961] A.C. 727, at 761.
[59] Cf. *Morris*, 424, *Re Fitzgerald*, [1904] 1 Ch. 573, *Trustees Executors and Agency Co. Ltd.* v. *Margottini*, [1960] V.R. 417.
[60] [1937] T.P.D. 91 (1936).
[61] *Id.*, at 101. cf. *Harris Investments Ltd.* v. *Smith*, [1934] 1 D.L.R. 748 (B.C.C.A., 1933).
[62] *Id.*, at 102. See also *Perpetual Executors & Trustees Association of Australia Ltd.* v. *Roberts*, [1970] V.R. 732 (Sup. Ct., McInerney, J., 1963).

Where the law of the place of administration does not recognise trusts and has no rules covering questions relating to administration, a difficulty arises. One solution would be to hold that a putative selection of such a law must be set aside in favour of another, efficacious, choice since, on the theory of presumed intention, the settlor or testator must be presumed not to have made such a self-defeating choice. Another approach, which would often have the same result in practice, would be simply to fall back on the law governing the validity of the trust.[63]

As to the appointment of trustees, Bruce Knight, V.C. considered that in general it would be "an imprudent and improper exercise of the power of appointing new trustees to appoint foreigners",[64] or even persons habitually resident out of the jurisdiction. But he recognised that in some cases this general rule should not apply.[65] This approach continues to prevail today.[66]

In *In the Estate of Ardagh*,[67] Wylie, J. held that the Irish court had power to appoint the English Public Trustee to act as trustee of an English settlement comprising Irish lands sold under the Land Purchase Acts, and to receive the residue of the purchase moneys arising from the sale. The English Public Trustee had already been appointed sole trustee of the settlement by the person nominated under the settlement to appoint trustees, and the settlement authorised a sole trustee to receive capital moneys arising under the Settled Land Acts.

Wylie, J. had "considerable doubt"[68] as to whether he had jurisdiction to appoint the English Public Trustee as trustee of a settlement *in his capacity of Public Trustee*, since that might be treating the Public Trustee Act 1906 as extending to Ireland,[69] which was clearly not the case.[70] Here the Public Trustee had already been validly appointed trustee of the settlement, which was an English settlement, so Wylie, J. was able to "deal with him as if he were an ordinary trustee".[71]

An interesting question as to the status of trustees was raised, but not resolved, in *In re Howley, dec'd, Naughton v. Hegarty*.[72] There, a testator bequeathed his property to the Bishop and Chapter of the Diocese of Killala, on certain charitable trusts. Under canon law, the chapter is a corporation with perpetual succession, a common seal and the right to hold and administer property.

Gavan Duffy, J. noted that it could be argued that recognition might be afforded to the Chapter because that species of corporation had been absorbed by the common law as part of the canon law before the "temporary pollutions"[73] of statutory interference. Alternatively, the Chapter might possibly be recognised here as a *foreign* corporation. In the event, Gavan Duffy, J. did not attempt to resolve this question because a simpler solution presented itself in having resort to section 15 of the Charitable Donations and Bequests Act 1844.

Re Boswell, Baron Talbot de Malahide, dec'd[74] is an example of how the Irish court will assist trustees so far as the requirements of foreign law are concerned. There the testator, who died domiciled in Ireland, assigned his property in Scotland to his trustees on several trusts. The trustees were anxious to sell some of the property,

---

[63] *Dicey & Morris*, 684.
[64] *Meinertzhagen v. Davies*, 1 Coll. N.C. 335, at 345 (1844).
[65] As, for example, in *In re Barcroft's Trusts*, 32 I.L.T.R. 35 (High Ct., Chy. Div., Porter, M.R., 1897).
[66] Pennycuick, V.C., in *In re Whitehead's Will Trusts*, [1971] 1 W.L.R. 833 presented a good review of the authorities. See also *Georges-Picot v. Henderson*, [1963] N.Z.L.R. 950 (Sup. Ct., Hutchinson, J.); cf. *In re Jones Trusts*, 20 Ont. L.R. 457 (Div. Ct., 1910).
[67] [1914] 1 I.R. 5 (Wylie, J., 1913).
[68] *Id.*, at 7.
[69] *Id.*, at 8.
[70] See section 17(2).
[71] [1914] 1 I.R., at 8.
[72] [1940] I.R. 109 (High Ct., Gavan Duffy, J., 1939).
[73] *Id.*, at 119.
[74] 86 I.L.T.R. 191 (High Ct., Gavan Duffy, P., 1950).

for the purpose of creating leases and feu-duties (corresponding to our ground rents) and generally improving the estate. The trustees lacked full powers of sale under Scots law, but were advised that the Court of Session would grant them the necessary powers only if they obtained an order from the Irish High Court, as the country of the testator's domicile. Gavan Duffy, P. made the necessary order, in an uncontested application.

As to *cy-près*,[75] in *In re Estate of King; King* v. *Long*[76] in 1918 it was admitted by the plaintiff that that doctrine could "not be called in aid of a foreign charity". In *A.G.* v. *Royal Hibernian School*,[77] the charity, "for the care of soldiers' children", that is, children of soldiers of the British army, had been created by letters patent from the British Crown in 1871. It was an Irish corporation situated in the Phoenix Park; its charitable work and administration were intended to be, and were actually, carried out in Ireland; and the charity had its origin "entirely in the benevolence of persons resident and domiciled in Ireland".[78] When, after Independence, the objects and purposes of the charity had failed, the question of a *cy-près* application arose.

Johnston, J. felt that he had "no alternative"[79] but to apply the corporate property of the charity *cy-près* for the carrying on of some charitable work in this country. He added:

"Whatever assistance the Court might give a testator who has bequeathed or devised property to a charitable organization which is resident abroad, there is the gravest doubt whether the court, in applying the *cy-près* principle for the disposal of property which had been devised or bequeathed to a charity within the jurisdiction whose purpose and object have failed, would have jurisdiction at all to endow a charitable organization resident abroad, especially where neither the trustees nor the committee of that organization were resident within the jurisdiction."[80]

Thus he declined to accede to the application of the British Secretary of State for War that a *cy-près* scheme be devised to embrace the Duke of York's Military School at Dover, which existed for a purpose similar to that for which the Royal Hibernian Military School had existed and included boys of Irish parentage and the children of soldiers of Irish regiments in the British army.

Trusts of Immovables

It is scarcely surprising that the *lex situs* should play an important role in regard to trusts of immovables: this is in harmony with the general approach towards immovables in the conflict of laws.[81] It makes obvious sense that questions of future interests, for example, should be determined by the *lex situs*.[82]

Nevertheless, the *lex situs* may not always be the most appropriate law to apply

---

[75] See *Delany*, ch. 13, L. Sheridan & V.T. Delany, *The Cy-Près Doctrine* (1959).

[76] 53 I.L.T.R. 60, at 60 (Chy., O'Connor, M.R., 1918). Where the settlor has nominated suitable trustees in the foreign country to whom the fund can be paid, the Court may direct that payment be so made: *Sheridan & Delany*, 157. This was done in *Collyer* v. *Burnett*, Taml. 79, 48 E.R. 32 (1829), where the testator had given legacies to charities in Ireland; Leach, M.R. ordered the testator's stock and annuities to be sold and the produce paid to the Irish commissioners for charitable donations. In an English case, *In re Vagliano; Vagliano* v. *Vagliano* 75 L.J. Ch. 119 (1905), Buckley, J. directed a scheme in relation to a foreign charitable trust where two of the trustees were resident within the jurisdiction and, by the terms of the trust, the fund was obliged to remain within the jurisdiction.

[77] 63 I.L.T.R. 86 (High Ct., Johnston, J., 1928). See *Sheridan & Delany*, 157.

[78] *Id.*, at 87.

[79] *Id.*

[80] *Id.*, at 87-88.

[81] Cf. *supra*, ch. 21.

[82] *Morris*, 425.

to immovables. This is especially so where the trust property is situated in several countries, perhaps consisting of both movables and immovables. The prospect of a range of different laws being applied to different parts of the property would scarcely appeal to the settlor.[83]

At all events, it seems that questions of essential validity of trusts of immovables are referred to the *lex situs*.[84] As *Morris* points out:

"That law determines what estates can be created;[85] what are the incidents of those estates;[86] whether gifts to charities are valid;[87] and whether the trusts infringe the rules against perpetuities or accumulations[88]."[89]

Where the *lex situs* does not recognise trusts of immovable property, the trust will fail.[90]

Where the property consists of immovables in Ireland, the *lex situs* means Irish domestic law; if, on the other hand, it consists of foreign immovables, the *lex situs* means whatever domestic law the *lex situs* would apply.[91]

Questions of construction of trusts of immovables are determined in accordance with the law intended by the settlor; this need not be the *lex situs*.[92]

It seems clear that Irish courts have jurisdiction to administer a trust even in cases where part of the trust property consists of foreign land.[93] There is little authority on the issue of whether the *lex situs* should govern questions relating to administration rather than to validity; *Morris* considers that this solution "does not seem reasonable".[94] He notes that the English court has sometimes authorised the trustees of an English trust to apply to the Court of Session for leave to sell land in Scotland which formed part of the trust property.[95]

---

[83] *Id.*

[84] *Dicey & Morris*, Rule 118, Delany, *supra*, at 386, Hoar, *supra*, at 1416, *Murray* v. *Champernowne*, [1901] 2 I.R. 232.

[85] *Nelson* v. *Bridport*, 8 Beav. 547, 50 E.R. 215 (1846).

[86] *Re Miller*, [1914] 2 Ch. 511.

[87] *Duncan* v. *Lawson*, 41 Ch. D. 394 (1889); *Re Hoyles*, [1911] 1 Ch. 179.

[88] *Freke* v. *Carbery*, L.R. 16 Eq. 461 (1873).

[89] *Morris*, 426.

[90] *Id.*, citing *Re Pearse's Settlement*, [1909] 1 Ch. 304.

[91] *Morris*, 426, Keeton, *supra*, at 116-117, *Re Ross* [1930] 1 Ch. 377, discussed *supra*, p. 42, and *Re Duke of Wellington*, [1947] Ch. 506.

[92] *Morris*, 426, citing *Studd* v. *Cook*, 8 App. Cas. 577 (1883), *Philipson-Stow* v. *I.R.C.*, [1961] A.C. 727, at 761. See also *Dicey & Morris*, Rule 119.

[93] *Morris*, 426, citing *Hope* v. *Carnegie*, L.R. 1 Ch. App. 320 (1866) and *Ewing* v. *Orr Ewing*, 9 App. Cas. 34 (1883), Cf, *supra*, pp. 404-405.

[94] *Morris*, 426.

[95] *Id.*, 427, citing *Re Forrest*, 54 Sol. J. 737 (1910), *Re Georges*, 65 Sol. J. 311 (1921); and the Scottish cases of *Carruthers' Trustees*, 24 R. 238 (1896), *Allan's Trustees*, 24 R. 718 (1897); *Harris' Trustees*, 1919 S.C. 432 and *Campbell-Wyndham-Long's Trustees*, 1951 S.C. 685.

PART V

LAW OF OBLIGATIONS

CHAPTER 31

CONTRACTS[1]

The central notion of a contract, as a legally binding promise, is easy to understand. Problems of basic characterisation, therefore, play a less important role in relation to contract than in some other areas of private international law. But, if the core concept is a clear one, the range of conduct embraced by the notion of a contract is formidably wide. There may, for example, be contracts for the sale of a house, of a television or of a fur coat, contracts of employment, contracts for the carriage of people or of goods, contracts between large corporations and contracts between family members. Our conflicts rules must seek to give answers to satisfy all these legally binding promises. The chances of general mechanical rules offering satisfactory solutions, therefore, are small.[2]

Some broader issues in the realm of social policy, also play their role in shaping conflicts rules. It has been argued[3] that the very core of the philosophical notion of contract is the freedom of the parties to construct their own legally enforceable rights and responsibilities: they become, as it were, "mini-legislatures" prescribing their own laws. In the domestic law of contract this presents difficulties, since the law of contract has to seek to reconcile this deference to individual autonomy with such other policy goals as social security and protection of the weak and dependent. Indeed, in recent years, the centrality of individual autonomy has been largely circumscribed by legislative and judicial changes. The difficulties for domestic law are multiplied when conflicts issues are involved. The law often seeks to reconcile the freedom of parties to choose the law to govern their contract, on the one hand, with the protection of the social policies of the state with which the parties have most connection, on the other.

It would be wrong to overstress these problems, however. There is broad international agreement, with differences only of emphasis, that parties should be free, by and large, to specify what legal system should govern their contract. There is, moreover, general agreement that in default of their doing so clearly, the court should select the legal system which appears most closely connected to the contract. There is less general agreement on the circumstances in which rules from another legal system should modify the application of these two major principles. It is, however, interesting to note that the recent Rome Convention on the Law Applicable to Contractual Obligations includes an important qualification on the scope of the generally applicable law, enabling the court to give effect to the mandatory rules of the law of another country with which the situation "has a close connection",[4]

---

[1] See *Dicey & Morris*, ch. 28, *McLeod*, ch. 7, *Scoles & Hay*, ch. 18, *Morris*, ch. 15.

[2] Cf. *Morris*, 265.

[3] The issue is one of considerable controversy. See, e.g. P. Atiyah, *The Rise and Fall of Freedom of Contract* (1979), Reiter, *Control of Contract Power*, 1 Oxford J. of Legal Studies 347 (1981), Mensch, *Book Review: Freedom of Contract as Ideology*, 33 Stanford L. Rev. 753 (1981).

[4] Article 7 (1) of the EEC Convention on the Law Applicable to Contractual Obligations. Cf. *infra,* pp. 561-562.

after having had regard to "their nature and purpose and to the consequences of their application or non-application". It is also interesting to note that this Convention includes specific choice-of-law rules to deal with consumer contracts and contracts of employment.

THE DOCTRINE OF THE PROPER LAW OF THE CONTRACT[5]

We must now consider the doctrine of the proper law of the contract. The proper law is "the law which has the closest and most real connection with the contract and transaction".[6] This definition, simple in its conceptual structure, disguises some rather formidable difficulties of application in concrete cases.

Origins of the Doctrine

The origins of the proper law approach have generally been attributed[7] to Lord Mansfield's statement in *Robinson* v. *Bland*,[8] in 1760:

"[T]he general rule established *ex comitate et jure gentium* is, that the place where the contract is made and not where the action is brought, is to be considered, in expounding and enforcing the contract. But this rule admits to an exception, where the parties (at the time of making the contract) had a view to a different kingdom."

In the earlier case of *Connor* v. *Earl of Bellamount*,[9] decided in 1742, the English Court of Chancery had to decide whether English or Irish law should determine the rate of interest payable on a contract debt made in England but secured by a bond on Irish immovables given in Ireland. The Lord Chancellor allowed the (higher) Irish rate of interest. In doing so, he "went some way towards accepting the idea of the obligations of contract being governed by some other law than the *lex loci contractus*".[10] The Lord Chancellor clearly was affected by a consideration of the unsatisfactory social consequences which would follow from an inflexible application of the *lex loci contractus*.[11]

---

[5] See Mann, *The Proper Law of the Contract*, Int. 3 L.Q. 60 (1950), Morris, *The Proper Law of the Contract: A Reply*, 3 Int. L.Q. 197 (1950), Cheshire, *The Significance of the Assunzione*, 32 Br. Yrbk. of Internat. L. 123 (1955), Graveson, *The Proper Law of Commercial Contracts as Developed in the English Legal System*, in *Lectures on the Conflict of Laws and International Contracts* 1, (U. of Michigan, 1951), Leflar, *Conflict of Laws, Contracts, and the New Restatement*, 15 Ark. L. Rev. 163 (1961), Beale, *What Law Governs the Validity of a Contract*, 23 Harv. L. Rev. 1, 78, 260 (1909), Schmitthoff, *The Doctrine of the Proper Law of the Contract in the English Conflict of Laws*, 28 Geo. L.J. 445 (1940), Morris & Cheshire, *The Proper Law of a Contract in the Conflict of Laws*, 56 L. Q. Rev. 320 (1940), Devos, *Freedom of Choice of Law for Contracts in Private International Law*, [1961] Acta Jurid. 1, Wolff, *The Choice of Law by the Parties in International Contracts*, 40 Jurid. Rev. 110 (1937), Vischer, *The Antagonism Between Legal Security and the Search for Justice in the Field of Contracts*, [1974] – II Recueil des cours 1.

[6] *Cripps Warburg Ltd.* v. *Colgate Investment Co.*, [1980] I.R. 321, at 333 (High Ct., D'Arcy, J., 1979).

[7] Morris, 267, Dicey & Morris, 751, Beale, *What Law Governs the Validity of a Contract – I*, 23 Harv. L. Rev. 1, at 4 (1909).

[8] 1 W. Bl. 257, at 258-259, 96 E.R. 141, at 141 (1760). Burrow's report of this passage is as follows: "The law of the place can never be the rule, where the transaction is entered into with the express view to the law of another country, as the rule by which it is to be governed." 2 Burr. 1977, at 1978, 97 E.R. 717, at 718.

[9] 2 Atk. 382, 26 E.R. 631 (1742).

[10] Graveson, *The Proper Law of Commercial Contracts as Developed in the English Legal System, in Lectures on the Conflict of Laws and International Contracts* 1, at 3 (U. of Michigan, 1951).

[11] Cf. 2 Atk., at 382, 26 E.R., at 631. In the still earlier case of *Foubert* v. *Turst*, 1 Brown Parl. Cas. 129, at 130-131, 1 E.R. 464, at 465 (1703) in 1703, which was concerned with a marriage settlement, counsel for the plaintiff had used language close to that later adopted by Lord Mansfield, when he argued that "all lawful contracts, as well as marriage, as relative to any thing else, ought to be fully performed between the parties and their representatives, according to the apparent intent of such contracts...." Commenting on this, Graveson observes that "it is clear that the idea of an objective proper law, if not its judicial expression, was first formulated at least half a century before *Robinson* v. *Bland*..." (Graveson, *supra*, at 3).

At all events, the proper law approach, as articulated by Lord Mansfield, met with little judicial support in Ireland[12] or England for about a century[13]. This may well have been because the common law judges and practitioners were suspicious of a doctrine which appeared to have "more affinity with equity and Roman law than with their own strict and still largely formal system."[14]

The Lex Loci Contractus Formerly Preferred

The result was that in Ireland and England, and for much longer in the United States,[15] there was a judicial preference for a "black letter" approach, determining matters affecting the contract by reference to the *lex loci contractus*. This rule had some advantages, notably certainty and predictability, valuable features in commercial transactions.[16] But equally there were clear drawbacks. The place of contracting might be chosen by the parties to defeat an important legal policy in their own country, or it might be entirely fortuitous, as, for example, where a person accepted an offer by posting a letter when on a stop-over in India while on his way by plane to Australia.[17] Moreover, there might be considerable uncertainty in some cases as to *where* the contract had been made because the rules as to the conclusion of a contract vary from country to country.[18]

In spite of these difficulties, the place of contracting as the governing law commanded widespread judicial support at one time. Thus, in *Lett* v. *Lett*,[19] FitzGibbon, L.J. observed that it had "never" been contended that the operation of separation deeds were governed "by any other law than the *lex loci contractus*". Similarly, in *Tedcastle, M'Cormick & Co.* v. *Robertson*,[20] in 1927, there are clear statements of approval. The contract in this case was made in Dublin. One party was Irish the other English. Kennedy, C.J. referred to the fact that the contract in question was made in Dublin, "and therefore governed by our law (if there be any difference in the law applicable here and in England)...."[21] And Murnaghan, J. said "[t]he contract having been made here, the interpretation of it will be governed by the law here, if there is in fact any difference between our law and the law of England".[22]

Two years later, in *London Finance and Discount Co.* v. *Butler*,[23] Hanna, J. said of a contract alleged to be unenforceable under the Moneylenders Act 1900:

> "The contract was made and the security given within the Free State, and their validity and legality must be tested by the law of the place where the contract was made...."

This approach expressly supports the *lex loci contractus*, without qualification; but perhaps it would be better to interpret the statement in the narrower, specific,

---

[12] Cf. *Keith* v. *Protection Marine Insurance Co. of Paris*, 10 L.R. Ir. 51 (Ex. Div., 1882), where a potentially interesting issue as to the proper law of the contract had to give way to a question of statutory interpretation.

[13] Cf. *Bannantyne* v. *Barrington*, 9 Ir. Ch. Rep. 406 (Ct. of App. in Chy., 1858).

[14] Graveson, *supra*, at 9. Cf. C. Fifoot, *Lord Mansfield*, ch. 5 (1936).

[15] Cf. *Scoles & Hay*, 551-552.

[16] *Morris*, 266.

[17] The "postal" rule of acceptance itself raises particular difficulties in the conflict of laws: cf. *infra*, pp. 533-535.

[18] *Morris*, 266.

[19] [1906] 1 I.R. 618, at 639 (C.A., aff'g. Porter, M.R.). *In re Boate's Estate*, 10 Ir. Chy. Rep. 164 (Ch. App., 1859) (construction of term in marriage settlement).

[20] [1929] I.R. 597 (Sup. Ct., 1927).

[21] *Id.*, at 603.

[22] *Id.*, at 605. See also *Lowden* v. *Accident Insurance Co.*, 43 I.L.T.R. 277 (K.B. Div., 1904).

[23] [1929] I.R. 90, at 94 (High Ct., Hanna, J.).

context of the illegality issue.[24] In any event, in the more recent decision of *Cripps Warburg Ltd* v. *Cologne Investments Co.*,[25] in 1979, D'Arcy, J., without referring to *London Finance and Discount Co.* v. *Butler*, applied the proper law of the contract when dealing with a somewhat similar issue with respect to the Moneylenders Act 1900.[26]

Lex Loci Contractus No Longer the Test

The move away from a strict adherence to the *lex loci contractus* approach towards the approach favoured by Lord Mansfield was carried out in an uneven and intellectually unimpressive manner. 1865 is generally regarded[27] as the watershed in Britain.

By 1889, in the English Court of Appeal decision of *In re the Missouri Steamship Co.*,[28] Cotton, L.J. could observe that the English decisions had:

> "laid down that *prima facie* the law of the country where the contract is made will
> govern the contract, decide what its incidents are, decide what its true construction
> is and its validity, but that the court must look at the circumstances of the case, and
> from them may come to the conclusion that the contract is to be governed by the law
> of some other country."

In *Apicella* v. *Scala*,[29] Meredith, J. declined to make a declaration as to the bare ownership of an Irish Hospitals Sweepstake ticket on the ground that the declaration had been sought only for the purpose of enforcing a contract for the performance in England of acts of violation of section 41 of the Lotteries Act 1823. Section 41 prohibited the sale of any ticket or scheme in a foreign lottery, and it was upon this alleged sale that the plaintiffs' claim depended. Meredith, J. proceeded on the basis that the contract was an Irish one, since this had been assumed by the parties and there were considerations that could be urged in support of this view. His own view, however, was that in the absence of some strong countervailing reason, the contract should be regarded as an English contract since it had been made there and the precise acts to be performed by the defendant in pursuance of the contract, as well as any payment by the plaintiffs, were all acts to be performed in England. He cited *In re Missouri Steamship Co.*,[30] in support of this view.

In the Supreme Court decision of *Kennedy* v. *London Express Newspapers Ltd.*,[31] it is equally plain that the *lex contractus* was regarded as an important, but not determinative, factor in identifying the applicable law. The contract in question was

---

[24] Cf. *infra*, pp. 545-552.

[25] [1980] I.R. 321 (High Ct.,, D'Arcy, J., 1979).

[26] Another decision supporting in express terms the *lex loci contractus* is *Russell* v. *Kitchen*, 3 Ir. C.L.R. 613 (Q.B., 1854), where a promissory note was the subject of litigation. The reported facts of the case suggest that the *lex loci contractus* was also the proper law. Further support for the *lex loci contractus* may be gleaned from observations of Fitzgerald, B., in *Reg.* v. *Griffin*, 4 L.R. (Ir.) 497, at 507 (Cr. Cas. Res., 1879). This was, however, a bigamy prosecution, somewhat removed from the refinements of the law relating to commercial contracts.

[27] Cf. *Peninsular & Oriental Steam Navigation Co.* v. *Shand*, 3 Moo. P.C. (n.s.) 272, 16 E.R. 103 (1865), *Lloyd* v. *Guibert*, L.R. 1 Q.B. 115 (1865).

[28] 42 Ch. D. 321, at 338 (C.A., 1889). See further Graveson, *The Proper Law of Commercial Contracts as Developed in the English Legal System*, in *Lectures on the Conflict of Laws and International Contracts* 1, at 16 (U. of Michigan, 1951).

[29] 66 I.L.T.R. 33 (High Ct., Meredith, J., 1931). See also *O'Callaghan* v. *O'Sullivan*, [1925] 1 I.R. 90 (Sup. Ct.), *In re Interview Ltd.*, [1975] I.R. 382 (High Ct., Kenny, J.), *British Leyland Exports Ltd.* v. *Brittain Group Sales Ltd.*, [1982] I.L.R.M. 359 (High Ct., O'Hanlon, J., 1981), *Kruppstahl A.G.* v. *Quitmann Products Ltd.*, [1982] I.L.R.M. 551 (High Ct., Gannon, J.).

[30] *Supra*.

[31] [1931] I.R. 532 (Sup. Ct., 1931).

made in the Saorstát and was to be performed there, but it prescribed London as the place where arbitration was to be held. The Court held that the contract was governed by the law of the Saorstát. Kennedy, C.J. considered that "[t]he first — and most important clues to the intention of the parties are generally the *locus contractus* and the *locus solutionis*"; their concurrence in the case before the Court was an "important fact".

The Modern Approach Based on the "Proper Law"

The modern law has thus favoured a less categorical approach than the *lex loci contractus*. This approach involves two central features; first, as a general rule, giving priority to the parties' choice of law, where this is express or otherwise plain; and secondly, in the absence of such choice, identifying the law which should govern the contract, having regard to the circumstances of the case. In what has been identified as "[t]he most important English case"[32] this century, *The King* v. *International Trustee for the Protection of Bondholders A/C*,[33] Lord Atkin in the House of Lords said:

"The legal principles which are to guide an English court on the question of the proper law of a contract are now well settled. It is the law which the parties intended to apply. Their intention will be ascertained by the intention expressed in the contract if any, which will be conclusive. If no intention be expressed the intention will be presumed by the Court from the terms of the contract and the relevant surrounding circumstances."

A great deal of controversy has lingered over the precise scope of each of these rules. Should the parties have complete freedom to choose any law they wish, provided their choice is *bona fide*, or is it necessary for there to be some objective link between them and that law? To what extent should an unexpressed intention be given weight? When the court addresses the second principle, should it proceed on the basis that it is divining the parties' intention, however opaque, or should it abandon any pretence of investigating the parties' intention and instead concentrate on objective factors suggesting a connection between the contract and a particular law or, alternatively, country?

Let us consider each of the two central principles in turn.

Where the parties choose the law to govern their contract[34]

There has been support in conflicts theory stretching back to Huber[35] for the view that the parties to a contract should be free in at least some circumstances to choose for themselves the law to govern it. There are clear advantages to this approach, most obviously those of certainty, predictability and, not least the contractual freedom it gives to the parties. By the mid-nineteenth century, the time was ripe for the development of this approach, with its elevation of an individualistic norm.

In the Privy Council case of *Vita Food Products Inc.* v. *Unus Shipping Co.*,[36] Lord Wright (for the Judicial Committee) said that:

[32] Graveson, *supra*, at 16. ·

[33] [1937] A.C. 500 (H.L. (Eng.)).

[34] See *Anon.*, *Note: Commercial Security and Uniformity Through Express Stipulations in Contract as to Governing Law*, 62 Harv. L.Rev. 647 (1949).

[35] Huber, *De Conflictu Legum, Praelectiones*, vol. II, Book 1, tit. iii, No. 10: cf. Llewelyn Davies, *The Influence of Huber's De Conflictu Legum on English Private International Law*, 18 Br. Yrbk. of Internat. L. 49, at 54-55 (1937). For an excellent historical and comparative study, see Yntema, *"Autonomy" in Choice of Law*, 1 Am.J. of Compar. L. 341 (1952).

[36] [1939] A.C. 277, at 290 (P.C.). Cf. *O'Callaghan* v. *O'Sullivan*, [1925] 1 I.R. 90, at 115 (Sup. Ct.), where Kennedy, C.J. espoused the cause of party autonomy without limitation. He said of two Irish parties, who made a contract in Ireland, that "[t]hey might have agreed to be bound by Scots Law or by the Code Napoléon". The context of his remark indicates strongly that he would have had no objection to such choices.

"where the English rule that intention is the test applies, and where there is an express statement by the parties of their intention to select the law of the contract, it is difficult to see what qualifications are possible, provided the intention expressed is *bona fide* and legal, and provided there is no reason for avoiding the choice on the ground of public policy."

The troublesome expressions in this formula are the words *"bona fide"* and "legal". To what extent may parties to a contract choose a law to govern their contract where that law has little or nothing to do with either of them or the contract? For example, if two Irish people resident here with no connection with California were to include in a contract of sale a provision to the effect that Californian law should govern the contract, would that choice, however eccentric, have to be respected?

Two factors would be likely to play an important role in answering this question: the degree of connection between the contract and the chosen law, and the extent to which the chosen law may frustrate the mandatory provisions of the law which has in fact the closest connection with the contract.

The courts have been reluctant to articulate a specific minimum degree of connection which must exist in every case between the contract and the chosen law. This is because of the very wide range of contracts which may be made. In some of them, a chosen law which has little connection with the contract would have no real claim; in others, commercial necessity and practical convenience may dictate the selection of a single law to cover a rapid sequence of interconnecting contracts where, judged in isolation, so far as at least some of the parties are concerned, the chosen law has little connection with them.[37]

One finds therefore that the courts go only so far as to say that they *"will not necessarily regard"* an express choice of law "as being the governing consideration where a system of law is chosen which has no real or substantial connexion with the contract looked upon as a whole."[38] And in the *Vita Food*[39] case, Lord Wright accepted, by way of *dictum*, that "connection with English law is not as a matter of principle essential".

In the Irish decision of *Cripps Warburg Ltd.* v. *Cologne Investment Co. Ltd.*,[40] D'Arcy, J. expressed the view that the proper law of a contract concerning immovables, as distinct from movables, "can not be determined by any one factor alone, except in the case where the parties expressly provide what law should apply or where all the parties live, and the transactions take place, in one jurisdiction". In this case the parties had *not* selected a governing law, and this should be borne in mind when attempting to interpret D'Arcy, J.'s remarks on the position where a law *has* been selected. D'Arcy, J.'s formula contains no limitations as to the parties' good faith, for example, or as to public policy. But it would surely be mistaken to conclude from this omission that D'Arcy, J. regarded these elements as unnecessary. The more reasonable explanation must be that D'Arcy, J. was attempting to sketch in broad strokes the rules applicable where the parties have chosen a law. The details would be a matter for a case in which the issue arose directly.

It is useful at this point to consider briefly the debate between the subjective and objective approaches to the case of express selection by parties of the proper law. This debate, at times heated, may not seem of great moment when considered in

---

[37] Cf. *Compagnie D'Armement Maritime S A* v. *Compagnie Tunisienne de Navigation S.A.*, [1971] A.C. 572, at 609 (H.L.Eng., *per* Lord Diplock, 1970).

[38] *Re Helbert Wagg & Co. Ltd's Claim*, [1956] Ch. 323, at 341 (Upjohn, J., 1955) (emphasis added). See, however, *Tzortzis* v. *Monark Line A/B*, [1968] 1 W.L.R. 406, at 411 (C.A., *per* Lord Denning, M.R.): "It is clear that, if there is an express clause in a contract providing what the proper law is to be, that is conclusive in the absence of some public policy to the contrary".

[39] [1939] A.C., at 290.

[40] [1980] I.R. 321, at 333 (High Ct., 1979).

isolation. But the outcome of this issue in the context of *express* choice by the parties serves to throw light on the more important debate between the subjective and objective approaches where the parties *have not* expressly selected the proper law.[41]

The subjective approach achieves certainty[42] but at the price of having to recognise a possibly capricious selection of the proper law.[43] The objective approach would bring the court's practice into line with its approach to many of the domestic rules of the law of contract, such as mistake, "where subjective theories have for the most part been discarded".[44]

Incorporation of a foreign law[45]

We should here draw a distinction between a case where the parties expressly select a law as the proper law of the contract, on the one hand, and, on the other, a case where parties to an Irish contract incorporate into it a provision (or a number of provisions) of a foreign law. In the latter case the contract remains an Irish one. So if, for example, an Irish contract incorporates the provisions of the British Carriage of Goods by Sea Act 1971, these provisions operate "not as a statute but as a set of contractual terms agreed upon by the parties."[46] This right of incorporation may be freely exercised.[47]

In *Griffin* v. *Royal Liver Friendly Society*,[48] Murnaghan, J., in the High Court, gave effect to a provision of British legislation dealing with insurance where the terms of that provision, synopsised, had been incorporated into an insurance policy made in Ireland, the proper law of which appears without doubt to have been Irish. Murnaghan, J. said:

> "This synopsis is printed on the back of the policy, and in the body of the contract it is referred to as governing the contract. Although not forming part of our law, it is, I think, made by agreement part of the contract entered into between the parties."[49]

The right of incorporation is, however, subject to any statutory prohibition to the contrary.[50] Thus, for example, section 23 of the Sale of Goods and Supply of Services Act 1980 ensure that sections 12 to 15 and 55 of the Sale of Goods Act 1893 will continue to apply to a contract (subject to section 61 (6)[51]) even in cases

---

[41] See *infra*, pp. 526-530.

[42] Mann, *The Proper Law of the Contract*, 3 Int. L.Q. 60, at 69 (1950).

[43] Morris & Cheshire, *The Proper Law of a Contract in the Conflict of Laws*, 56 L.Q. Rev. 320, at 333-339 (1940). But see Mann's reply, *op. cit.*, *supra*, at 64.

[44] Morris, *The Proper Law of a Contract: A Reply*, 3 Int. L.Q. 197, at 198 (1950).

[45] See Mann, *Proper Law and Illegality in Private International Law*, 18 Br. Yrbk. of Internat. L. 97, at 101-102 (1939), Kelly, *Reference, Choice, Restriction and Prohibition*, 26 Int. & Comp. L.Q. 857 (1977) (an excellent, provocative analysis), Reese, *Power of Parties to Choose Law Governing Their Contract*, [1960] Proc. of Amer. Soc. of Internat. L. 49, at 50-51, Lowe, *Choice of Law Clauses in International Contracts: A Practical Approach*, 12 Harv. Internat. L. J. 1, at 20-22 (1971), McCartney, *The Use of Choice-of-Law Clauses in International Commercial Contracts*, 6 Wayne L. Rev. 340 (1960) (esp. at 359).

[46] *Morris*, 274. See *G.E. Dobell & Co.* v. *Steamship Rossmore Co.*, [1895] 2 Q.B. 408, at 413 (*per* Lord Esher), *Griffin* v. *Royal Liverpool Friendly Society*, [1942] Ir. Jur. Rep. 29, at 32 (High Ct., Murnaghan, 1941), but cf. Kelly, *supra*, at 860-861.

[47] *Griffin* v. *Royal Liverpool Friendly Society*, *supra*, *G.E. Dobell & Co.* v. *Steamship Rossmore Co. Ltd.*, [1895] 2 Q.B. 408 (C.A.); *Ocean Steamship Co.* v. *Queensland State Wheat Board*, [1941] 1 K.B. 402 (C.A., 1940); *Stafford Allen & Sons, Ltd.* v. *Pacific Steam Navigation Co.*, [1956] 2 All E.R. 716 (C.A.); cf. *Ex parte Dever: In re Suse and Sibeth*, 18 Q.B.D. 660 (C.A., 1887) (especially Bowen, L.J.'s judgment). See also *Lowden* v. *Accident Insurance Co.*, 43 I.L.T.R. 277 (K.B. Div., 1904), *Latimer* v. *Dumican*, 44 I.L.T.R. 150 (Chy. Div., Barton, J., 1910).

[48] [1942] Ir. Jur. Rep. 29 (High Ct., Murnaghan, J., 1941).

[49] *Id.*, at 32.

[50] See Kelly, *Reference, Choice, Restriction and Prohibition*, 26 Int. & Comp. L.Q. 857, at 871ff (1977), Mann, *The Amended Sale of Goods Act 1893 and the Conflict of Laws*, 90 L.Q. Rev. 42 (1974).

[51] See *infra*, pp. 532-533.

where the contract contains a term which purports to substitute or has the effect of substituting, provisions of the law of some other country for any of these sections. Similarly section 36 of the 1980 Act preserves the application of sections 26 to 29 and 31 of that Act to hire-purchase agreements containing a similar type of term. Finally section 42 of the Act preserves the application of sections 39 and 40 to contracts for the supply of a service in the course of a business. Of course, what the 1980 Act is seeking to prevent is the resort to a foreign law, whether by attempting to specify it as the proper law[52] or by the process of incorporation, which would defeat the social policy of the Act.

Where there is an inferred choice of the proper law

In some cases where there is no express choice of the proper law, the parties' intention may nonetheless be inferred. It would clearly be wrong for the courts to fail to give effect to the parties' intention to choose the proper law merely because the parties did not use express words to this effect. The circumstances in which this intention may be inferred are understandably very broad; many of the reported cases, however, deal with instances where the parties have included a provision for arbitration[53] in a particular country.

In England some of the decisions went very far in inferring a choice of the proper law from the inclusion of an arbitration clause providing for arbitration in England. In *Tzortis* v. *Monark Line A/B,*[54] the Court of Appeal considered that "this choice raises an irresistible inference which overrides all the other factors".[55] In *Compagnie d'Armement Maritime S A* v. *Compagnie Tunisienne de Navigation S A,*[56] however, the House of Lords favoured a more moderate approach. Lord Diplock said:

> "Strong as the implication may be, it can be rebutted as other implications of intention can be rebutted. It is not a positive rule of law which is independent of the intentions of the parties."

We have seen how, in *Kennedy* v. *London Express Newspapers,*[57] in 1931, the Supreme Court held that an arbitration clause selecting London could not prevail over the "important fact" of the concurrence of the *lex loci contractus* and the *lex loci solutionis,* which were Irish.

In *Hammond Lane Industries Ltd.* v. *Ongree Steel Trading Co. Ltd.,*[58] in 1956, the facts of the case were as follows. Hammond Lane Industries Ltd. entered into a contract by correspondence with Ongree Steel Trading Co. Ltd for the purchase of a quantity of galvanised steel sheets. Hammond Lane was an Irish Company, Ongree English. The goods being sold had their origin in Belgium. The agreement was for delivery f.o.b. at Antwerp. Hammond Lane alleged that some of the sheets were received in Dublin in a rusted state. They contended that the damage had been caused before shipment. Ongree denied this.

Clause 17 of the Conditions of Sale provided that:

---

[52] Cf. *infra,* p. 532.
[53] On the validity and effect of these clauses, see Pryles, *Comparative Aspects of Prorogation and Arbitration Agreements* 25 I.C.L.Q. 543 (1976), Kahn-Freund, *Jurisdiction Agreements: Some Reflections,* 26 I.C.L.Q. 825 (1977).
[54] [1968] 1 W.L.R. 406.
[55] *Id.,* at 413.
[56] [1971] A.C. 572, discussed by Carter, 44 B.Y.B.I.L. 220 (1970).
[57] [1932] I.R. 532 (Sup. Ct., 1931).
[58] 99 I.L.T.R. 5 (Sup. Ct., 1956, aff'g High Ct., Murnaghan, J. 1956).

"Any dispute arising out of this contract shall be settled by arbitration in London in accordance with the Arbitration Act 1889 or any statutory modification or re-enactment thereof".

Ongree sought an order under section 12 (1) of the Arbitration Act 1954[59] staying all proceedings in the action pending reference of the matters in dispute to arbitration in London pursuant to clause 17.

Murnaghan, J. was satisfied that clause 17 "sufficiently indicate[d] that the intention of the parties was that their rights thereunder should be determined according to the law of England".[60] Accordingly he stayed all further proceedings pending the outcome of the arbitration. The Supreme Court affirmed. The Court regarded the question whether the proper law of the contract was English or Irish as being "in itself of no moment".[61] It was agreed that the contract was made in Ireland but the contract documents were silent as to the law which was applicable to it. "In these circumstances", said O'Daly, J. for the Court, "the intention of the parties has to be inferred, and, whatever inference be drawn the result will be the same as if the parties had dealt with the matter by express stipulation".[62] Even if an express stipulation had been included in the contract, this would not be a reason for nullifying the stipulation as to arbitration. There were several reasons why the Court considered that it would have been "otiose"[63] for the Court to express any opinion on the question of the proper law of the contract. Of present relevance, O'Daly, J. noted that it was

"a matter which will fall to be decided in the first instance by the arbitrator; and then if a higher opinion than his should be required the question will come to be determined not here but in the English courts. Moreover the parties themselves are unaware that there are any differences between the law of England and law of Ireland as affecting such a dispute as theirs; and indeed the dispute as disclosed in the correspondence appears to resolve itself into nothing more complex than a question of fact."[64]

Other factors from which a choice of the proper law may be inferred include the form of the contractual documents which the parties adopt,[65] the residence of the parties,[66] and the nature and location of the subject matter of the contract.[67]

[59] Section 12 (1) provided that:
"If any party to an arbitration agreement or any person claiming through or under him commences any proceedings in any court against any other party to the agreement or any other person claiming through or under him in respect of any matter agreed to be referred, any party to such proceedings may at any time after appearance and before delivering any pleadings or taking any other steps in the proceedings, apply to that court to stay the proceedings, and that court, if it is satisfied that there is not sufficient reason why the matter should not be referred in accordance with the agreement and that the applicant was, at the time when the proceedings were commenced, and still remains, ready and willing to do all things necessary to the proper conduct of the arbitration, may make an order staying the proceedings."
This provision was repealed by section 4 of the Arbitration Act 1980.
[60] 99 I.L.T.R., at 6.
[61] *Id.*, at 8 (*per* O'Daly, J. for the Court).
[62] *Id.*
[63] *Id.*
[64] *Id.*
[65] *Chamberlain* v. *Napier*, 15 Ch. D. 614 (1880); *Rossano* v. *Manufacturers, Life Insurance Co.*, [1963] 2 Q.B. 352; *James Miller & Partners Ltd.* v. *Whitworth Street Estates (Manchester) Ltd*, [1970] A.C. 583; *Compagnie d'Armement Maritime SA* v. *Compagnie Tunisienne de Navigation SA*, [1971] A.C. 572, at 583: see *Cheshire & North*, 205. See also *Macnamara* v. *Owners of the Steamship "Hatteras"*, [1931] I.R. 337 (Sup. Ct.).
[66] *Jacobs* v. *Crédit Lyonnais*, 12 Q.B.D. 589 (1884), *Keiner* v. *Keiner*, [1952] 1 All E.R. 643.
[67] *Lloyd* v. *Guibert*, L.R. 1 Q.B. 115, at 122-123 (1865); *British South Africa Co.* v. *De Beers Consolidated Mines Ltd.*, [1910] 1 Ch. 354, at 383; reversed on another point, *sub nom. De Beers Consolidated Mines Ltd* v. *British South Africa Co.*, [1912] A.C. 52; cf. *Kahler* v. *Midland Bank Ltd.*, [1950] A.C. 24.

The currency in which payment is to be made may also point to the selection by the parties of a particular legal system, but each case depends on its facts. In *Ladbrooke* v. *Biggs*[68] in 1826, a bill was drawn by A. in Ireland, on the defendant resident in Ireland, whereby he required him to pay to his order in London £500 sterling. The bill was accepted by the defendant in Ireland, payable at the house of K. The declaration averred that it was drawn for £500 Irish Currency and at trial it was proved that the bill was protested in London and that K. resided there; and the drawer proved that he drew the bill for £500 Irish Currency. The defendant objected to the sufficiency of the stamp. The stamp was enough for £500 Irish pounds but too small for £500 sterling. The defence was unsuccessful.

Jebb, J. said:

> "A bill drawn in Ireland upon a person in England, is generally payable in British currency.[69] There are two parties to the contract; one Irish, the other English; and the English acceptor contracts to pay in the currency of his own country. But this bill is drawn by a person in Ireland upon a person in Ireland, to be paid in London. It is not like the other case, and there is not the same reason for holding it to be payable in British currency. Both parties are Irish and residing in Ireland, and may be supposed to look to the law and custom of that country: and therefore the acceptor does not undertake to pay in the currency of England."[70]

Where there is no choice of the proper law

In many cases parties to a contract with international dimensions will make no express choice as to the proper law. In such circumstances how is the proper law to be determined? Two competing approaches have at various times held sway. The first, the subjective approach, rests on the presumed intention of the parties, akin to an implied term.[71] The problem with this approach is that the court is "required to speculate upon an intention common to two or more parties",[72] a task which, if seriously undertaken, will involve complex psychological comparisons.

According to the second view, the judge attempts to determine, not what the parties presumably intended but rather "what as reasonable men they *should* have intended had they addressed their minds to the question at the time of the contract".[73] On this view, the Court "imposes a solution on the parties irrespective of what law one of them would have preferred".[74] This approach may be justified on the basis that the parties themselves "by their own acts localized the contract in the sense that by establishing a number of connecting factors with this or that country they have placed its centre of gravity in the country where those factors are most enduring and most impressive".[75]

---

[68] Batty 619 (K.B., 1826). See also *Neville* v. *Ponsonby*, 1 Ir. L.R. 204 (Exch. of Pleas, 1839), *Ex parte Keatinge*, I.R. 2 Eq. 26 (Walsh, M.R. 1867), *Fitzgerald* v. *Boate's Estate*, 10 Ir. Chy. Rep. 164 (Chy. App., 1859).

[69] See *Taylor* v. *Booth*, 1 Car. & Payne 287, 171 E.R. 1198 (1824).

[70] Batty, at 626.

[71] See, e.g. *Lloyd* v. *Guibert*, L.R. 1 Q.B. 115, at 120 (*per* Willes, J., 1865), *R.* v. *International Trustee*, [1937] A.C. 500, at 529 (*per* Lord Atkin). Cf. *Kennedy* v. *London Express Newspapers Ltd.,* [1932] I.R. 532, at 544 (Sup. Ct., *per* Kennedy, C.J., 1931).

[72] Cheshire, *The Significance of the Assunzione*, 32 Br. Yrbk of Internat. L. 123, at 124 (1955).

[73] *Id.*, at 125 (1955). See *Bonython* v. *Commonwealth of Australia*, [1951] A.C. 201, at 219 (*per* Lord Simmonds), *The Assunzione*, [1954] P. 150, *Re United Railways of Havana and Regla Warehouses Ltd.*, [1960] Ch.52, at 91-92 (*per* Jenkins, L.J.) and 115 (*per* Willmer, L.J.); affirmed, *sub nom.* *Tomkinson* v. *First Pennsylvania Banking and Trust Co.*, [1961] A.C. 1007, at 1068 (*per* Lord Denning) and 1081-1082 (*per* Lord Morris); cf. *Cripps Warburg Ltd.* v. *Cologne Investment Co. Ltd.*, [1980] I.R. 321, at 333 (High Ct., D'Arcy, J., 1979).

[74] Cheshire, *supra*, at 125.

[75] *Id.*

Although, logically, these two approaches "cannot live together",[76] in practice it does not matter greatly which approach is favoured,[77] since the theory of "presumed intention" concedes to the court considerable freedom in attributing to the parties an intention which, psychologically speaking, they may well not have had.[78]

In *The Assunzione*[79] in 1953, "[a]ll doubts as to the correct approach to the matter were ....virtually dispelled by the decision of the Court of Appeal...."[80] Singleton, L.J. said:

> "'...the court ... has to determine for the parties what is the proper law which, as just and reasonable persons, they ought ... [to] have intended if they had thought about the question when they made the contract'. That, I believe, is the duty upon us, and in seeking to determine the question we must have regard to the terms of the contract, the situation of the parties, and generally all the surrounding facts... [O]ne must look at all the circumstances and seek to find out what just and reasonable persons ought to have intended if they had thought about the matter at the time when they made the contract. If they had thought that they were likely to have a dispute, I hope it may be said that just and reasonable persons would like the dispute determined in the most convenient way and in accordance with business efficacy."[81]

The Assunzione affords a good example of how the courts must resolve the question where the case involves several factors, pointing in different directions. The charterers of the ship, who were also the shippers under the bills of lading, were a French organisation; the contract was entered into by a charterparty made in France, and the bills of lading were issued in France; the charterparty was in the English language (with a French supplement), the bills of lading in French. The ship was Italian, owned by two Italians in partnership, and flew an Italian flag. The master was Italian. The charterparty contract was for carriage from the port of Dunkirk to Venice; the charterparty provided that freight and demurrage should be paid in Italian currency.

Weighing all these facts, and placing "very considerable importance"[82] on the form and place of payment, both in Italy, coupled with the fact that the ship was Italian and that the destination was an Italian port, Singleton, L.J. was satisfied that the scales came down in favour of the application of Italian law; Birkett and Hodson, L.J. were of the same opinion.

The issue was considered by the Irish High Court in 1979, in *Cripps Warburg Ltd.* v. *Cologne Investments Co. Ltd.*[83] The facts, briefly, were as follows. In early

---

[76] *Id.*, at 126. But see the attempted harmonisation by Lord Wright in *Mount Albert Borough Council* v. *Australasian Temperance & General Life Assurance Society Ltd.*, [1938] A.C. 224, at 240.

[77] Cf. Mann, *The Proper Law of the Contract*, 3 Int. L.Q. 60, at 69 (1950), Morris, *The Proper Law of a Contract: A Reply*, 3 Int. L.Q. 197, at 197 (1950).

[78] See *Cook*, 418, Nussbaum, *Principles of Private International Law*, 161 (1943). Cf. Cheshire, *supra*, at 126-128.

[79] [1954] P. 150.

[80] *Cheshire & North*, 207.

[81] [1954] P., at 175, 179 (internal quotation cited from *Mount Albert Borough Council* v. *Australian Temperance and General Mutual Life Assurance Society Ltd.*, [1938] A.C. 224, at 240 (P.C., 1937)). Commenting on Singleton, L.J.'s statement, *Cheshire & North*, 208, state:
  "In other words, where it has not been expressly chosen, the proper law depends upon the localization of the contract. The court imputes to the parties an intention to stand by the legal system [with] which, having regard to the incidence of the connecting factors and of the circumstances generally, the contract appears most properly to belong."
  See also *Revenue Commissioners* v. *Pelly*, [1940] I.R. 122, at 128-129 (Sup. Ct., *per* Hanny, J., 1939) (emphasis added):
  "In determining whether the deed of trust under consideration is an English or an Irish contrct we have to look to the surrounding circumstances. *It resolves itself into a question of a legal balance sheet,* to determine on which side the preponderance of the evidence lies...."

[82] [1954] P., at 178.

[83] [1980] I.R. 321 (High Ct., D'Arcy, J., 1979).

1973, a syndicate was formed consisting, amongst others, of two architects, and a chartered surveyor. The purpose was to purchase an hotel in Stillorgan, acquire planning permission for a change of use to office premises, carry out this change quietly and resell the premises at a profit. Speed was of the essence, and the intention was to borrow money for what was expected to be only a very short period.

The plaintiffs were a merchant bank in the City of London. Although they carried on the business of bankers on a global basis, their only office was in London. An intermediary acting as spokesman for the architects and surveyor gave general information of the syndicate's plan to the executive director of the plaintiff bank, a man with whom the intermediary had previously worked in banking in New York. This led to a meeting between the members of the syndicate and the executive director in London, at which agreement was reached on the basic terms of the loan and the necessary security.

In the events that transpired, the plaintiffs lent money to an investment company (Cologne) which acted as trustee for a friendly society (Aran), which was the vehicle through which the transaction was carried out. The architects and chartered surveyor executed a letter of guarantee whereby they jointly and severally guaranteed to the plaintiffs repayment of the money so advanced. Cologne, as trustee for Aran, mortgaged and charged most of the hotel property as security for the repayment of advances to Aran. Aran executed a deed of participation with Talent Participation Ltd., a wholly owned subsidiary of the plaintiffs, entitling Talent Participation to a share of any profits on resale of the premises. The deed contained provisions for the submission to arbitration of any questions arising under it to an arbitration subject to Britain's Arbitration Act 1950.

Payment of the sums advanced to Aran was made through a London bank which in turn credited its subsidiary bank in Dublin, thereby effectively paying off an interim loan which had been already made by the subsidiary bank to Aran some weeks previously. The principal reason for the adoption of this "circuitous route"[84] for the transfer of the money was the desire for speed: it ensured that the money advanced by the plaintiffs could be applied in Dublin to the directions of Aran within one day.

Payments were made on foot of the agreement. The following year, the loan was extended for a further period. Later, liabilities accrued on the loans, and the plaintiffs sought repayment of the sums due on foot of the guarantees to repay, and sought to realise the mortgage and charge. The defendants contested liability on a number of grounds, one of which was that the guarantees were illegal and void because the plaintiffs, in advancing the money, had acted as moneylenders within the meaning of the Moneylenders Act 1900 (as amended) without a requisite moneylenders' licence.

D'Arcy, J. considered it necessary to determine the proper law of the contract. In his view:

> "the proper law of a contract concerning immoveables, as distinct from moveables, can not be determined by any one factor alone, except in the case where the parties expressly provide what law should apply or all the parties live, and the transactions take place, in one jurisdiction. In the end one must come down to the law which has the closest and most real connection with the contract and transaction. That is the proper law of the contract".[85]

In reaching this conclusion, D'Arcy, J. was influenced by the opinion of the Judicial

---

[84] *Id.*, at 329.
[85] *Id.*, at 333.

Committee of the Privy Council in *Bonython* v. *Commonwealth of Australia*[86], where Lord Simmonds had said that:

> "the substance of the obligation must be determined by the proper law of the contract i.e. the system of law by reference to which the contract was made or that with which the transaction had its closest and most real connection".

D'Arcy, J. went on to quote in detail from a number of English decisions, including *The Assunzione*[87] and *Coast Lines Ltd.* v. *Hudig and Veder Chartering N V*[88], where Lord Denning, M.R. said that:

> "[i]n order to determine the proper law of the contract the courts at one time used to have a number of presumptions to help them. Now we have to ask ourselves: What is the system of law with which the transaction has the closest and most real connection? This is not dependent on the intentions of the parties. They never thought about it. They had no intentions upon it. We have to study every circumstance connected with the contract and come to a conclusion."[80]

D'Arcy, J. then considered the facts, so far as they would affect the determination of the proper law of the contract. He listed seventeen facts, without explicitly identifying which way any of them in isolation affected this determination. He said:

> "(1) The defendants either personally or by their agents went to London to obtain the loan.[90]
>
> (2) The basic heads of agreement to make the loan were agreed in London on the 19th of April, 1973. The money for the loan was raised in London.[91]
>
> (3) The formal contract for the loan was contained in the facility letter.... and the written acceptance of it by Aran. This expressly provided that the offer to make a loan should not be binding upon the plaintiffs until they received the payment of the commitment fee; that payment of £6,500 was received in London. The contract was completed in that city. If this fact stood alone, I would not pay attention to it.[92]
>
> (4) At the time the contract was made, none of the parties had any intentions as to what the proper law should be. They never applied their minds to the question. It is clear from [the] evidence [of the executive director of the plaintiff bank] that the only geographical distinction which he had in mind, was the difference between the 'sterling' and 'non-sterling' area. He never thought of any distinction between municipal and foreign law. [The executive director]'s evidence is the only evidence before me on the point. The defendants neither gave nor called evidence.[93]
>
> (5) Had the question of proper law been considered at the time of the making of the contract, on the balance of probability I hold that the parties would have agreed that English law must govern it. [The executive director] has given evidence, which I accept, that it is the practice 'almost without exception' of bankers in the City of London to insist on the insertion in a foreign contract of a term stipulating that English law shall apply to it. The defendants would have agreed to such insertion, had the matter been raised — otherwise they would not have got the loan.[94]
>
> (6) The Participation agreement ... contained a reference to the Arbitration Act 1950, which is a statute of the United Kingdom.[95]

---

[86] [1951] A.C. 201, at 219.
[87] [1954] P. 150.
[88] [1972] 2 Q.B. 34.
[89] *Id.*, at 45.
[90] A factor presumably weighing in favour of English law.
[91] Also a factor presumably weighing in favour of English law.
[92] This is also presumably a factor weighing in favour of English law.
[93] Largely neutral, it seems; perhaps a slight tilt towards English law.
[94] A fairly strong English indicator.
[95] Clearly an English indicator.

(7) The guarantee... contained a reference to the Companies Act 1948, which is a statute of the United Kingdom.[96]

(8) It was agreed that Williams and Glynn's base lending rate as increased was the rate of interest chargeable on the money lent. This was a United Kingdom lending rate.[97]

(9) All the defendants reside in this jurisdiction.[98]

(10) The facility letter was received by the defendants in this country, although it should be noted that it was expressed not to be binding until the commitment fee had been received in London.[99]

(11) Acceptance of the facility-letter was executed in Dublin.[100]

(12) The guarantees were executed in Dublin.[101]

(13) The mortgages and charges were executed in Dublin.[102]

(14) The property mortgaged is situated in Dublin.[103]

(15) The monies lent were paid to the defendants' credit in Dublin.[104]

(16) The plaintiffs took the mortgage in the name of Mars Securities Ltd., an Irish company.[105]

(17) The mortgage and charge....contains a reference to the Land Act 1965, which is an Irish statute.[106]

None of these factors, alone, can determine what is the proper law of this contract and guarantee.''[107]

D'Arcy, J. continued:

"In order to ascertain what is the proper law applicable, I have to balance these factors, one against the other. I have to ascertain the law 'with which the transaction has its closest and most real connexion'. In my view English law has the closest and most real connection with the contract and guarantees with which we are concerned. I find that English law is the proper law and that it applies to the claim for the repayment of the loans and monies on foot of the guarantees.''[108]

D'Arcy, J. went on to consider the mortgage suit. He considered it a principle of the conflict of laws that "all questions concerning the rights over immoveables are governed by the *lex situs*''.[109] On this basis, Irish law applied to the mortgage suit.

Contracts made in one country to be performed in another

We must now consider the position where the contract is made in one country and to be performed in another country, and the contract is silent on the proper law. The authorities lean towards the law of the country of performance.

In *Lloyd* v. *Guibert*,[110] there was a clearer statement. Willes, J. said:

---

[96] Clearly an English indicator.
[97] Clearly an English indicator.
[98] An Irish indicator, of uncertain weight.
[99] Ambiguous, with perhaps a slight tilt towards Ireland.
[100] An Irish factor.
[101] An Irish factor.
[102] An Irish indicator.
[103] An Irish indicator.
[104] An Irish indicator.
[105] An Irish indicator.
[106] An Irish indicator.
[107] [1980] I.R., at 335-336.
[108] *Id.*, at 336.
[109] *Id.*, (citations omitted). See further ch. 21, *Supra*.
[110] L.R. 1 Q.B. 115, at 122 (Exch. Ch. *per* Willes, J. (for the Court) 1865.)

"It is ... generally agreed that the law of the place where the contract is made, is *prima facie* that which the parties intended, or ought to be presumed to have adopted as the footing upon which they dealt, and that such law ought therefore to prevail in the absence of circumstances indicating a different intention, as for instance, that the contract *is to be entirely performed elsewhere....*"

This passage was cited by Bowen, L.J. in *Jacobs* v. *Crédit Lyonnais*.[111]

In the Northern Ireland case of *Clarke* v. *Harper and Robinson*,[112] in 1938, the position was somewhat complicated. The contract was made in England but was to be performed in Northern Ireland. It was silent as to the proper law. Andrews, L.C.J. began from the starting point that "[p]rima facie" the law governing a contract is presumed to be the *lex loci contractus....*"[113] He acknowledged that this presumption might be rebutted by other circumstances, one of which was that the contract was wholly to be performed in another country. But that exception was itself subject to qualification. In the Lord Chief Justice's opinion there was a circumstance in the case before him which was:

"absolutely fatal to a presumption of any such intention by the parties, namely, that the law of both countries — England and Northern Ireland [—] in regard to the contract is identical. I can well understand that where the law of the two countries is different the parties may intend that their rights and obligations should be determined by the law of the country where the contract is to be performed....It may also be....that the parties through ignorance or forgetfulness may expressly provide for the application of the *lex loci solutionis* even though it is identical with the *lex loci contractus*, but I find it impossible to presume any such intention where the *lex loci contractus* and the *lex loci solutionis* are the same. The truth is....that such a matter would in all probability never enter into the minds of the parties where the same system of law prevails in both countries."[114]

Lest it be thought a matter of no moment whether the *lex loci contractus* or the *lex loci solutionis* be chosen where they are the same, it should be noted that this question can have considerable practical significance. In *Clarke* v. *Harper and Robinson*,[115] Andrews, L.C.J.'s finding that English law was the proper law meant that service *ex juris* was not permissible.

Lex fori sometimes applied

Sometimes,[116] the courts apply the *lex fori* without reference to a conflicts dimension. This may in certain instances be attributed to the strategy (or oversight) of the litigating parties; in others it may simply be because the proper law seems beyond question to be Irish or because the parties are of the view that no difference exists between Irish law and the relevant foreign law. This latter possibility explains many of the cases, especially in the nineteenth century, where the facts shared an Irish and English dimension.[117]

[111] 12 Q.B.D. 589, at 600 (C.A., 1884).
[112] [1938] N.I. 162 (K.B. Div., Andrews, L.C.J.).
[113] *Id.*, at 171.
[114] *Id.*, at 172 (citations omitted). See also *Hamlyn & Co.* v. *Talisker Distillery*, [1894] A.C. 202 (H.L. (Sc.)), distinguished by Andrews, L.C.J., at 172-173.
[115] *Supra.*
[116] See, e.g. *Michel Frères Societé Anonyme* v. *Kilkenny Woollen Mills (1929) Ltd.*, [1961] I.R. 157 (High Ct., Davitt, P., 1959), *Curran* v. *Midland Great Western Co. of Ireland*, [1896] 2 I.R. 183 (Ex. Div., 1895), *Hamilton* v. *Magill*, 12 L.R. (Ir.) 186 (Ex. Div., 1883), *M'Clelland* v. *Stewart*, 12 L.R. (Ir.) 125 (Ex. Div., 1883). Cf. *Russell* v. *Kitchen*, 3 I.C.L.R. 613 (Q.B., 1854).
[117] E.g. *Garrick* v. *Bradshaw*, 10 Ir. L.R. 129 (Q.B., 1846), *Kernahan* v. *Corporation of the National Assurance Co. of Ireland*, 10 Ir. L.R. 319 (Q.B., 1847), *The "Castlegate"*, 29 L.R. (Ir.) 55 (C.A., 1891), *M'Carthy* v. *Great Western Ry. Co.*, 18 L.R. (Ir.) 1 (C.A. 1885), *King* v. *Hinde*, 12 L.R. (Ir.) 113 (Ex. Div., 1883), *Ronan* v. *Midland Ry. Co.*, 14 L.R. (Ir.) 157 (C.P. Div., 1883), *Provincial Bank of Ireland (Ltd.)* v. *Brocklebank*, 26 L.R. (Ir.) 572 (Q.B. Div., 1890), *Rae* v. *Joyce*, 29 L.R. (Ir.) 500 (C.A., 1892), *Haughton* v. *Morton*, 5 I.C.L.R. 329 (Q.B., 1855).

Tobin v. *London & North-Western Ry. Co.*,[118] may be quoted as a case where the *lex fori* was applied in default of reference by either party to the foreign dimension in the case. This was a carrier case. Until the trial "both parties apparently acted under the assumption that the contract had been entered into with the agents for the defendant company at Waterford".[119] Gibson, J. said:

> "The entire cause of action, both contract and breach, took place in England, but no remark was made by counsel in reference to this point, as to which therefore I say nothing."[120]

Statutory Exceptions to Application of the Proper Law[121]

It is always possible for a statute to exclude the application of the proper law. This has happened fairly recently in relation to the action for breach of promise of marriage. Proceedings for breach of promise involving conflict of laws aspects[122] were "rare and notable events"[123] in English and Irish courts.[124] The action was abolished in Ireland by the Family Law Act 1981, section 2 of which provides that:

> "an agreement between two persons to marry one another, whether entered into before or after the passing of this Act, shall not under the law of the State have effect as a contract and no action shall be brought in the State for breach of such an agreement, whatever the law applicable to the agreement."

Thus no action may be brought in the State for breach of promise, whatever the proper law of the agreement.

The Sale of Goods and Supply of Services Act 1980 has been noted earlier. The purpose of some of its provisions is to prevent the more economically powerful party from evading the social policy of the Act by specifying a foreign proper law. The Act includes a number of changes to the Sale of Goods Act 1892, strengthening the buyer's position in relation to conditions and warranties, and restricting the permissible scope of excluding implied terms and conditions. Section 23 of the 1980 Act inserts a new provision, section 55A, into the 1893 Act. It provides that:

> "[w]here the proper law of a contract of sale of goods would, apart from a term that it should be the law of some other country or a term to the like effect, be the law of Ireland....,sections [12 to 15 and 55 of the 1893 Act] shall, notwithstanding that term but subject to section 61 (6) of this Act, apply to the contract."

Section 61 (6) of the 1893 Act is in fact a new provision, inserted by section 24 of the 1980 Act. It is to the following effect:

> "(a) Nothing in section 55 or 55A of this Act shall prevent the parties to a contract for the international sale of goods from negativing or varying any right, duty or liability

---

[118] [1895] 2 I.R. 22 (Q.B. Div., 1894).

[119] *Id.*, at 22, fn. 2.

[120] *Id.*, at 38-39.

[121] See Kelly, *Reference Choice, Restriction and Prohibition*, 26 Int. & Comp. L.Q. 857, at 871 ff (1977), Mann, *The Amended Sale of Goods Act 1893 and the Conflict of Laws*, 90 L.Q. Rev. 42 (1974).

[122] See Webb & Brown, *Engagements to Marry and the Conflict of Laws*, 15 Int. & Comp. L.Q. 947 (1966), Hahlo & Kahn, *Casenote: A Matter of Breach of Promise*, 78 S. Afr. L.J. 355 (1961).

[123] Graveson, *Note: Breach of Promise of Marriage – Questions of Jurisdiction and Choice*, 13 Conv. (N.S.) 299, at 299 (1949).

[124] Cf. *Harvey* v. *Johnston*, 6 C.B. 295, 136 E.R. 1265 (1848), where the plaintiff, a Toronto resident, came to Co. Tyrone to marry the defendant, at the defendant's request. The Court did not address the conflicts dimensions of the case, perhaps because the proper law was Irish, more plausibly because these dimensions were overlooked: see Webb & Brown, *supra*, at 953, fn. 20.

which would otherwise arise by implication of law under sections 12 to 15 of this Act.
(b) In this subsection 'contract for the international sale of goods' means a contract
of sale of goods made by parties whose places of business (or of they have none,
habitual residences) are in the territories of different States and in the case of which
one of the following conditions is satisfied:
    (i) the contract involves the sale of goods which are at the time of the conclusion
    of the contract in the course of carriage or will be carried from the territory
    of one State to the territory of another; or
    (ii) the acts constituting the offer and acceptance have been effected in the
    territories of different States; or
    (iii) delivery of the goods is to be made in the territory of a State other than
    that within whose territory the acts constituting the offer and acceptance have
    been effected.''

Some other sections in the 1980 Act are also of interest. Section 36 preserves
the application of sections 26 to 29 and 31 to hire-purchase agreements whose foreign
proper law would be Irish in the absence of a term selecting that proper law. Similarly
section 42 preserves the application of sections 39 and 40 to contracts for the supply
of a service in the course of business where there is an equivalent term.

SPECIFIC ISSUES

Offer and Acceptance[125]

We must now consider how to determine the applicable law (or laws) to govern
questions of offer and acceptance. Under the Irish internal law of contract, a contract
normally is concluded when the acceptance of the offer is communicated to the
offeror;[126] but this rule is modified where the contemplated mode of acceptance is
by post: in such a case the contract is completed when the letter accepting the offer
is posted.[127] Moreover, an offeror is not permitted to impose on the offeree the task
of declining the offer under pain of being contractually bound.[128] Finally, a
distinction is drawn between an acceptance, a counter-offer and a mere request for
further information; whether or not a contract exists depends on how the offeree's
response is categorised.[129] In several other countries, however, different rules as to
offer and acceptance prevail. Thus, in some countries, an acceptance, though posted,
is inefficacious until it reaches the offeror;[130] or an offeror may require of an
offeree that he either refuse the offer or be contractually bound.[131] Finally, the
principles as to what constitutes a counter-offer[132] differ from country to country.

If, therefore, a contract exists from the standpoint of one country's law and does
not exist according to another's on account of lack of acceptance, by what conflict
rules should the efficacy of the contract be determined?

Four approaches may be considered. The first would refer to the *lex loci*

---

[125] See Jaffey, *Offer and Acceptance and Related Questions in the English Conflict of Laws*, 24 Int. &
Comp. L.Q. 603, at 604-613 (1975), Lewis, *Note: The Formation of a Contract*, 10 Int. & Comp.
L.Q. 908 (1961), Libling, *Formation of International Contracts*, 42 Modern L. Rev. 169 (1979). Gill,
The EEC Convention on the Law Applicable to Contractual Obligations, 6 J. of the Irish Soc. for
Eur. L. 1, at 15-16 (1983).

[126] See R. Clark, *Contract*, 8 (1982).

[127] Cf. *Wheeler & Co. Ltd.* v. *Jeffrey (John) & Co.*, [1921] 1 I.R. 395 (C.A., 1920, rev'g K.B. Div.,
1920), *Sanderson* v. *Cunningham*, [1919] 2 I.R. 234 (C.A.), *M'Crea* v. *Knight*, [1896] 2 I.R. 619
(C.A.), *Tedcastle M'Cormick & Co.* v. *Robertson*, [1929] I.R. 597 (Sup. Ct., 1927).

[128] *Clark*, 8-9, *Russell & Baird Ltd.* v. *Hoban*, [1922] 2 I.R. 159 (C.A., 1921).

[129] *Stevenson, Jacques & Co.* v. *McLean*, 5 Q.B.D. 346 (Lush, J., 1880), *Brown & Gracie Ltd.* v. *F.W.
Green & Co. (Pty.) Ltd.*, [1960] 1 Lloyd's Rep. 289 (H.L. (Sc.).

[130] Cf. *Wolff*, 439.

[131] *Id.*

[132] As to Irish law cf. *Brien* v. *Swainson*, 1 L.R. (Ir.) 135 (Chatterton, V.C., 1877).

contractus. This is satisfactory, so far as the question of communication of the acceptance is concerned, where the communications between the parties are instantaneous or "virtually instantaneous",[133] as, for example, where a person in Louth shouts his acceptance of an offer to the offeror who is standing just across the border in Armagh, or, more usually, where an offer is accepted by telephone[134] or telex.[135]

Where, however, communication of the acceptance is not so immediate, the *lex loci contractus* offers no clear guide, since the "place of contracting" may itself vary according to which law's rules as to formation of a contract are chosen. Thus "solv[ing] the problem by arbitrarily preferring one of the two relevant laws to the other is to beg the question".[136]

The temptation to apply the *lex fori* in such a case is no doubt a strong one,[137] but this offers an unsatisfactory solution where the *forum* has only a fortuitous connection with the contract or the parties.[138]

The third possible approach, advocated by many writers,[139] is to determine the question of offer and acceptance by reference to "the putative proper law," that is, the law which "would be the proper law of the contract if the contract was validly concluded".[140]

Some difficulties with this approach have been identified.[141] There may be disagreements between the parties as to which law should govern, and in that event the selection of one of two (or more) competing laws on the basis that it is the "putative proper law" has a potential for hardship and injustice. It is one thing to apply the proper law test to parties who, at the least, regarded themselves as being involved in a contractual relationship with each other. It is another thing to impose on persons who are only negotiating to enter into a contract the rules of offer and acceptance of the law of a country to which (so far as they are concerned) they have not yet bound themselves. Secondly, there is no reason to adopt a presumption that a valid contract has been concluded, in a case where one person asserts and the other denies that this is the case.[142]

Conversely, application of the "putative proper law" test would defeat the contractual expectations of the parties in some cases, as, for example, where the parties both considered that there was, or would be, contractual efficacy because they were seeking to comply with the law of their country of residence or business, but the rules of the putative proper law specified otherwise. Thus, for example, if an Irish author and an Irish publisher were, in Ireland, to negotiate an agreement

---

[133] *Mendelson-Zeller Co. Inc.* v. *T. & C. Providores Pty. Ltd.*, [1981] 1 N.S.W.L.R. 366, at 369 (Rogers, J.).

[134] *Re Modern Fashions, Ltd.*, 8 D.L.R. (3d) 590 (1969) (acceptance by telephone call made from Quebec to Manitoba; contract held to have been made in Manitoba).

[135] *Entores Ltd.* v. *Miles Far East Corporation*, [1955] 2 Q.B. 327, *Hampstead Meats Pty. Ltd.* v. *Emerson and Yates Pty. Ltd.*, [1967] S.A.S.R. 109 (Bright, J.), *Mendelson-Zeller Co. Inc.* v. *T. & C. Providers Pty. Ltd.*, *supra*.

[136] *Cheshire & North*, 216.

[137] *Id.*

[138] *Nygh*, 232.

[139] *Dicey & Morris*, Rule 146, *Cheshire & North*, 216, *Morris*, 282, *Wolff*, 439 *McLean*, 488, *Nygh*, 232. This approach receives some support from *Albeko Schuhmaschinen* v. *The Kamporian Machine Co. Ltd.*, 111 L.J. 519 (1961), noted by Lewis, 10 Int. & Comp. L.Q. 908 (1961) and much support from the New South Wales case of *White Cliffs Opal Mines Ltd.* v. *Miller*, 4 S.R. (N.S.W.) 150 (Simpson, C.J. Eq., 1904) where reliance was placed on *Dicey* and *Westlake* in referring to the "proper law" and the law of the country with which "the transaction has the most real connection".

[140] *Dicey & Morris*, Rule 146. Cf. *Cheshire & North*, 216, and see Libling's criticism: *Formation of International Contracts*, 42 Modern L. Rev., at 170, fn. 4 (1979).

[141] Cf. Jaffey's penetrating analysis, 24 Int. & Comp. L.Q., at 604-613.

[142] Jaffey, *supra*, at 609. See also Libling, *Formation of International Contracts*, 42 Modern L. Rev. 169, at 170 (1979).

to publish a book in Ireland, but the law of Ruritania was specified as the proper law in the draft contract, and if the author posted a letter of acceptance of the contract in Ireland, and died the next day, it would surely defeat the expectations of the parties to hold that no contract had come into existence because in Ruritania postal acceptance must be communicated before it is efficacious.[143]

This leads us to the fourth possible approach to the question of formation of a contract. This is more elaborate and complex, and less certain, than that of the putative proper law. Though lacking a name, or indeed a great deal of support among the commentators, this approach would attempt to examine the circumstances of each case more closely before prescribing a solution.

Thus, after a detailed analysis, Jaffey concludes that "*(a)* where the laws of both parties' countries produce the same result, they should be applied in deciding whether or not a party is bound; *(b)* where they give a different result then a party who contends that he is not bound should be held bound, if he is so bound by his own law,[144] or, if he is not bound by his own law, if he is bound by the *lex fori*, provided that where the relevant acts of both parties are done in the country of one party, that party should be able to rely on the law of his country for the conclusion that he is not bound or that the other party is bound."[145]

Jaffey's somewhat complex solution is designed to give practical effect in specific terms to common-sense notions of justice and of respect for the reasonable expectations of parties who seek to contract with one another. Perhaps there would be merit in having a broad discretionary rule, based on these notions, which would be applied having regard to the individual circumstances of each case. Such a rule could cope with the difficulty, mentioned by *Wolff*,[146] of contractual negotiations between businessmen in two countries, one of whose laws considers silence as being capable of constituting acceptance, and the other of which does not. *Wolff* considers that "[t]he silence of a person can be deemed to be an act of legal significance only if that is so under the law of the person's residence or place of business."[147] Such a conclusion would no doubt in most cases harmonise with ordinary notions of justice and of the reasonable expectations of the parties; but it would scarcely do so in all.[148] If an Irish businessman has done business in the past with a Danish businessman (under whose law silence may constitute consent) and if the Irish businessman is well aware of the Danish rule and receives an offer from the Danish businessman, whose draft contract (as in the past) contains a clause that the contract is to be governed by Danish law, the equities could well tilt towards applying the Danish rather than the Irish rule as to acceptance. All must surely depend on the nature of the rule and the circumstances of each case.

Lack of Consent[149]

A contract may be void for lack of consent attributable to one or more of many factors, such as mistake, misrepresentation, duress or undue influence. Although lack of consent affects the validity of contracts in every legal system the extent to which it does, and the effect of its doing so, can vary widely from one law to another. By which law should this question be determined?

---

[143] Cf. Jaffey, *supra*, at 609-610.
[144] That is, the law of the country where he resides or, in the case of a business contract, carries on business. If he resides or carries on business in more than one country, the court should look to the law of the country in which he has his principal residence or principal place of business: Jaffey, *supra*, at 609.
[145] Jaffey, *supra*, at 613.
[146] *Wolff*, 439.
[147] *Id.*
[148] See Libling, *Formation of International Contracts, supra*, at 171-172.
[149] Cf. Jaffey, *supra*, at 613-616, Libling, *supra*, at 174-181 (1979).

There is very little judicial authority in Ireland[150] or, indeed, in other common law jurisdictions. In the English case of *Mackender* v. *Feldia A.G.*,[151] the Court of Appeal groped towards a distinction, which has some intuitive attraction, between cases where there simply was no meeting of minds and cases where minds did go some way towards meeting but the consent was what might be designated substandard. In the case of the first category the *lex fori* would apply since what had taken place did not constitute a contract at all according to that law. But in the case of the second category, the proper law should determine whether the contract should stand or fall.

There are two principal difficulties with this approach. First, the distinction is difficult to apply in practice since there is a fairly wide band of cases where the lack of true consent could credibly be attributed to either of the two categories. Secondly, and more importantly from the standpoint of conflicts of law, legal systems contain widely differing rules in relating to consent. In Irish law, for example, the first category, of a complete absence of a meeting of minds, is clearly reflected in the doctrines of common mistake and *non est factum*,[152] and to a lesser extent in other doctrines, such as duress and certain instances of unilateral mistake. But neither common mistake nor *non est factum* is restricted to this precise category. So far as the second category is concerned, several doctrines exist under Irish law: these include fraud, misrepresentation, non-disclosure, certain other instances of unilateral mistake and undue influence. Again, these doctrines, though substantially embracing the notion of substandard consent envisaged by the second category, are not specifically limited to this concept. The same can be said of other legal systems.

What *Mackender* v. *Feldia A.G.* attempted to do was to isolate certain specific doctrines of English *domestic* law of contract and categorise them for the purposes of conflicts of law.[153] Thus Lord Denning M.R.[154] and Diplock, L.J.[155] accepted that *non est factum* was probably a matter for English law to determine since this raised the question whether there was any real consensus *id idem*. In contrast, innocent misrepresentation or non-disclosure in insurance cases did not result in the absence of any consent; in these cases the affected party "did in fact consent but would not have done so if he had known then what he knows now".[156] Accordingly, the Court of Appeal held, the proper law rather than the *lex fori* should determine the outcome of the case, which was concerned with alleged non-disclosure in relation to an insurance contract.

---

[150] Cf. *Lecky* v. *Walter*, [1914] 1 I.R. 378 (O'Connor, M.R., 1913), where bonds of a Dutch Company having oil fields in Wyoming were purchased in Dublin through an agent of the defendant, who carried on business in London. The plaintiff's action for rescission, based on innocent misrepresentation, was decided in accordance with principles in the English cases. This approach may be explained on the basis that Irish law, whether as the *lex fori* or the proper law of the contract, prevailed, the Master of the Rolls looking to English cases to determine the governing principles in Irish law. Alternatively, and quite unconvincingly, it could be argued that English law, as the proper law, was applied. In the absence of any indication that this aspect was in the mind of either the Master of the Rolls or of counsel, this explanation carries no conviction. It should, however, be noted that O'Connor, M.R. was conscious of at least some of the international legal dimensions of the case: cf. *id.*, at 382. See also *Schawel* v. *Reade*, [1913] 2 I.R. 64 (H.L. (Ir), 1912, rev'g C.A., 1911), where principles expounded in English cases were also applied in a case involving an allegation of breach of warranty and misrepresentation in relation to the sale of a horse. The plaintiff, "an Austrian gentleman, of some position", was buying horses for the Austrian Government (*id.*, at 81), and bought the horse in question from the defendant in Ireland. When the horse was shipped to Austria, it was found that he was suffering from an eye inflammation. No reference was made to the question of the proper law of the contract.

[151] [1967] 2 Q.B. 590, noted by Carter, 42 Br. Yrbk of Internat. L. 298 (1967).

[152] Cf. *Bank of Ireland* v. *M'Manamy*, [1916] 2 I.R. 161, at 173. (K.B. Div., *per* Cherry, L.C.J. 1915).

[153] Carter, *supra*, at 299, stigmatises this approach as "insular".

[154] [1967] 2 Q.B., at 598.

[155] *Id.*, at 603-604. Russell, L.J. (at 605) reserved on this question.

[156] *Id.*, at 604 (*per* Diplock, L.J.). Lord Denning, M.R. took the same view: *id.*, at 598.

Some troubling questions remain. Into which category does fraud fall?[157] One commentator has suggested that since the victim of fraud may affirm the contract and be satisfied with damages in tort, "the doctrine of fraud does not affect consensus"[158] and thus should be a matter for the proper law rather than the *lex fori*. The position is less clear in relation to duress, where there is a degree of fluidity of judicial thought[159] on the question whether duress deprives a party of the *animus contrahendi* or merely renders his consent revocable.

Consideration

In Irish law, a contract not under seal requires consideration.[160] In many civil law jurisdictions there is no necessity for consideration, the concept of *cause* playing an important role. What is the position where a contract without consideration comes before an Irish court? It appears that where the contract is connected exclusively with a foreign law which does not require consideration, it should be treated as valid here.[161] Where the connection is less than exclusive, the position is less certain. It has been suggested that "[i]n the nature of things",[162] the putative proper law will be applicable.

Formal Validity

The formal validity of a contract raises some interesting, and as yet unresolved, issues.[163] Three main approaches have been canvassed: first that the *lex loci contractus* should determine formal validity; second that the proper law of the contract should control; and finally that a contract should be upheld if fulfilling the formal requirements of *either* the *lex loci contractus* or the proper law. Let us consider each of these approaches in turn.

The lex loci contractus

There is old judicial authority[164] favouring the *lex loci contractus* as providing the exclusive test of formal validity. Moreover, this general principle has for long been accepted (subject to limited exceptions) in relation to marriage,[165] which is without question[166] a contract, albeit one of unique characteristics.

Reference to the *lex loci contractus* may be supported on the basis of practical

---

[157] *In Mackender v. Feldia*, Diplock, L.J. (at 604) and Russell, L.J. (at 605) left this question open.
[158] Libling, *supra*, at 178.
[159] See *Universe Tankships Inc. of Monrovia v. International Transport Workers Federation*, [1983] 1 A.C. 366 (H.L. (Eng.), 1982), *Anson*, 242, Atiyah, *Note: Economic Duress and the "Overborne Will"*, 98 L.Q. Rev. 197 (1982), Tiplady, *Note: Concepts of Duress*, 99 L.Q. Rev. 188 (1983), Atiyah, *Note: Duress and the Overborne Will Again*, 99 L.Q. Rev. 353 (1983), Libling, *supra*, at 179-180.
[160] See *Clark*, 20-21. Cf. the Ontario Law Reform Commission's *Report on Amendment of the Law of Contract*, ch. 2 (1987).
[161] Cf. *Re Bonacina*, [1912] 2 Ch. 394. See *Dicey & Morris*, 776.
[162] *Cheshire & North*, 218. Cf. *Nygh*, 234.
[163] See *Rabel*, vol 2, ch. 31, Gill, *supra*, at 16-17, Batiffol, *Form and Capacity in International Contracts*, in *Lectures on the Conflict of Laws and International Contracts*, 103, at 103-107 (U. of Michigan, 1951). More generally, see Tötterman, *Functional Bases of the Rule Locus in English Conflict Rules*, 2 Int. & Comp. L.Q. 27 (1953).
[164] *Alves v. Hodgson*, 7 Term Rep. 241, 101 E.R. 953 (1797), *Clegg v. Levy*, 3 Camp. 166, 170 E.R. 1343 (1812), *Trimbey v. Vignier*, 1 Bing. N.C. 151, 131 E.R. 1075 (1834), *Bristow v. Sequeville*, 5 Exch. 275, 155 E.R. 158 (1850), *Anthony v. Popwich*, [1949] 4 D.L.R. 640 (Man. K.B., Montague, J.).
[165] Cf. *Steele v. Braddell*, Milw. 1 (1838), *In re the Estate of M'Loughlin*, 1 L.R. Ir. 421 (1878), *Reg. v. Burke*, 5 I.L.R. 549 (1843), *Du Moulin v. Druitt*, 3 I.C.L.R. 212 (1860), *Swifte v. A.G. for Ireland*, [1912] A.C. 176 (H.L.(Ir), aff'g [1910] 2 I.R. 140 (C.A., 1909), *Berthiaume v. Dastous*, [1930] A.C. 79 (P.C.); see further *supra*, pp. 218-221.
[166] *Pace Wolff*, 447-448.

convenience. When parties are concluding their negotiations and entering into a contract there is much to be said for enabling them to rely on local law and local legal advice as to the formal requirements for drawing up the agreement.

But this consideration scarcely justifies making the *lex loci contractus* the *sole* test of formal validity. To do so would run contrary to the general reference to the proper law in matters contractual. Moreover, the place of contracting may sometimes be of little or no concern to the contracting parties. Finally, there may be some difficulty in determining *where* the place of contracting is, especially in cases where Irish rules of offer and acceptance differ from those of the other country involved.[167]

The Proper Law

The proper law has a strong claim to govern the question of formal validity, as it does other aspects of the validity of the contract. It has some judicial support,[168] Moreover, the cases seemingly opposed to the application of the proper law must be considered in their historical context.[169]

It is worth noting that formal requirements in relation to contract are not always concerned with mere administrative convenience. In some instances they may serve important social goals—protecting the interests of an immature or economically vulnerable person against exploitation, for example.[170] The formal requirements may be designed to discourage those who would seek to put improper pressure on persons who are in a situation of danger. To allow an untrammelled reference to the proper law in relation to formalities might weaken this protection in some instances. Perhaps, following Cheshire, a stress on the objective ascertainment of the proper law would minimise this difficulty.

The lex loci contractus or the proper law

The consensus among the academic commentators is that compliance with the formal requirements of *either* the *lex loci contractus or* the proper law should suffice.[171] Some judicial authority is in accord.[172] As we have seen,[173] this alternative selection has no operation in relation to the contract of marriage.

Exceptional cases of imperative public policy

In some cases, a country's law may require parties to a contract to comply with rigorous formalities, the purpose being to alert an economically weak or dependent party and to discourage others from exploiting him. If the forum has such a law the court may well choose to apply the *lex fori* regardless of the proper law, in order to protect the weaker party. To do so would give effect to a basic policy of that state's law.[174] It has also been suggested[175] that compliance with the *lex loci*

---

[167] Cf. *Dicey & Morris*, 785-786, and *supra,* 533-535.
[168] *Van Grutten* v. *Digby*, 31 Beav. 561, 54 E.R. 1256 (1862), a case concerned with a marriage settlement rather than a mercantile contract, but one which has nonetheless received much attention from the commentators. Cf. *Walker* v. *Lord Lorton*, 6 Ir. Ch. Rep. 329 (Cusack Smith, M.R., 1857), *Bannantyne* v. *Barrington*, 9 Ir. Ch. Rep. 406 (Ct. of App. in Chy., 1859).
[169] Cf. *Dicey & Morris*, 786.
[170] Cf. *id.*, 787-788, *Castel*, vol. 2, 546.
[171] This is the approach favoured in most civil law jurisdictions: cf. *Wolff*, 446, *Rabel*, vol 2, 490.
[172] See *Sharn Importing Ltd.* v. *Babchuk*, 21 D.L.R. (3d) 349 (B.C. Sup. Ct., Wilson, C.J.S.C., 1971), *Ward* v. *Coffin*, 27 D.L.R. (3d) 58, at 71-72 (N.B. Sup.Ct., App. Div., *per* Hughes, J.A. (for the Court) 1972), *Re Dunn: Ex parte Andrew*, 35 A.L.R. 466, at 471 (Fed. Ct. of Austr. Gen. Div., Lockheart, J. 1981). Cf. *O'Donovan* v. *Dussault*, 35 D.L.R. (3d) 280 (Alta. Sup. Ct. App. Div., 1973).
[173] *Supra*, pp. 218-221.
[174] Cf. *English* v. *Donnelly*, 1958 S.C.494, (hire purchase agreement), cited by *Dicey & Morris*, 788, and discussed by *Anton*, 209.
[175] *Castel*, vol. 2, 546.

contractus should not suffice where: (i) the place of contracting is fortuitous, bearing no real relation to the transaction and the parties; (ii) the formal requirements of the system of law with which the transaction has its most real and substantial connection have been disregarded; (iii) these latter requirements are designed for the protection of the parties; and (iv) they involve the implementation of "a strong social policy".

Certain formal requirements treated as procedural

An important qualification to the principles discussed above should be noted. The Statute of Frauds 1695, as we shall see,[176] provides that no action is to be brought to enforce certain specified agreements and undertakings unless they are in writing. This requirement is treated as a matter of procedure, to which the *lex fori* rather than the *lex causae* applies. Thus if a contract of guarantee, for example, is not in writing but fulfils the formal requirements of the proper law it will not be enforceable here because it fails to comply with the Statute of Frauds.[177]

Capacity

There has been much academic discussion[178] but somewhat less judicial analysis[179] regarding the question as to what law should determine a party's contractual capacity. Over the years, some facile "black-letter" rules have been supported, with little regard to the complexity of the question.[180]

It is perhaps worth pointing out at the beginning of our discussion of this problem that laws in relation to capacity embrace a wide range of social policies. A country's law of contract may seek to restrict a party's capacity to enter a *particular* contract, or *contracts generally,* for one of several reasons. These policies include the protection of vulnerable or immature[181] persons and the removal from the commercial scene of fraudulent or uncreditworthy people. Sometimes an incapacity may be imposed so as to give effect to broader political or economic goals.[182]

Let us examine the various approaches to the conflicting dimensions of the subject which have found favour. Three solutions have dominated discussion; the *lex domicilii* the *lex loci contractus* and the proper law. Whether any one of these, without modification, affords the true answer to the wide variety of questions that can arise may be doubted.

The lex domicilii

There was formerly some judicial support for the *lex domicilii*[183] but it has been

[176] *Infra*, pp. 631-632.
[177] Cf. *Leroux* v. *Brown*, 12 C.B. 801, 138 E.R. 1119 (1852), *Rabel*, vol. 2, 501-505.
[178] See Batiffol, *Form and Capacity in International Contracts*, in *Lectures on the Conflict of Laws and International Contracts*, 103, at 107-111 (U. of Michigan, 1951), Clarence Smith, *Capacity in the Conflict of Laws*, 1 Int. & Comp. L.Q. 446 (1952), Fisher, *The Law Governing Capacity with Regard to Bills of Exchange*, 14 Modern L.Rev. 144, at 147-148 (1951).
[179] As to why this should have been so, cf. Graveson, *The Proper Law of Commercial Contracts as Developed in the English Legal System*, In *Lectures on the Conflict of Laws and International Contracts* 1, at 30 (U. of Michigan, 1951). In view of the considerable reduction in the age of contractual capacity brought about by the Age of Majority Act 1985, the issue is likely to be of greater practical importance in the coming years: cf. Binchy, *The Age of Majority Act 1985*, [1985] *Irish Current Law Statutes Annotated*, note to section 2.
[180] Cf. *McLeod*, 491.
[181] Cf. the Law Reform Commission's *Report on Minors' Contracts*, ch. 4 (LRC 15-1985).
[182] Cf. *Bodley Head Ltd.* v. *Flegon*, [1972] 1 W.L.R. 680.
[183] *Sottomayor* v. *De Barros*, L.R. 3 P.D. 1, at 5 (C.A., by Cotton, L.J., for the Court, 1877), stigmatised by Sir James Hannen, in *Sottomayor* v. *De Barros (No.2)*, L.R. 5 P.D. 94, at 100 (1879) as laying down "a novel principle, for which up to the present time there has been no English authority". See also *Cooper* v. *Cooper*, 13 App. Cas. 88 (1888), *Republica de Guatemala* v. *Nunez*, [1927] 1 K.B. 669, at 689-690 (C.A., 1926).

largely eclipsed by more recent *dicta*[184] in favour of the *lex loci contractus*—a solution which has in turn been criticised. The *lex domicilii* has little support among the commentators today. As we have seen, its role in relation to the complex and rapid commercial transactions of today would often be to frustrate rather than to accommodate the parties.[185] It must be admitted that the *lex domicilii* may, in certain cases at least, be of sufficient importance to be given some weight. Where an incapacity serves a protective function—one based on minority, mental illness or prodigality, for example—its efficacy would be greatly reduced if the person under the incapacity had "only to cross a border to be able to do quite regularly what was impossible otherwise".[186] But in these cases the interests of the other contracting party must also be respected. If the *lex domicilii* adopts a particularly wide-ranging policy of protection—fixing the age of majority at 25, for example—it may well be unjust for this policy to have effect outside the country of the domicile. On the other hand, if the *lex domicillii* offers unusually narrow protection, it may be argued that the *favor contracti* principle should ensure that a contract entered into elsewhere by a person with capacity under his *lex domicilii* should be upheld.

Other modifications have been suggested. One is to distinguish (as Irish law does in some respects) between commercial contracts and contracts of a more "personal" nature, such as marriage or adoption. In respect of the latter category of contracts the *lex domicilii* appears to have a stronger claim. Another approach, so far as commercial contracts are concerned, would treat incapacities of a long-term nature differently from those of a short-term, passing, nature, such as temporary insanity or drunkenness. The *lex domicilii* would apply only to incapacities the former category.

The lex loci contractus

The *lex loci contractus* has had some judicial support,[187] though not in recent years. In its favour it has been argued that it offers a readily ascertainable test, which

---

[184] *Baindail* v. *Baindail*, [1946] P. 122, at 128. See also *Bondhouse Securities Corporation* v. *Manville*, [1933] 4 D.L.R. 699 (Sask. C.A.), *M'Feetridge* v. *Stewarts & Lloyds, Ltd.*, 1913 S.C. 773 where a minor domiciled in Ireland but working in Scotland was held bound by a contract made and performed in Scotland, in spite of his incapacity under Irish law. See further *Anton*, 201-202, and *infra*, fn. 186.

[185] Cf. *McLeod*, 491, Batiffol, *Form and Capacity in International Contracts*, in *Lectures on the Conflict of Laws and International Contracts*, 103, at 108 (U. of Michigan, 1951).

[186] Batiffol, *supra*, at 108. *M'Feetridge* v. *Stewarts & Lloyds Ltd.*, *supra*, is perhaps an example of the hardship that may result from overriding an incapacity under the *lex domicilii*. The pursuer, a 16-year-old youth, domiciled in Ireland but working in Scotland, was injured by a machine in the factory where he worked. With no legal advice, he agreed to accept compensation under the Workmen's Compensation Act 1906. He thereby lost his right to proceed against his employers for negligence in having failed to fence the machine. He later sought to have this agreement set aside as it was not binding under Irish law. The court rejected this action, as it considered that it would be unfair on employers to have to investigate the domicile of their employees. Moreover, reference to the *lex domicilii* "would hamper persons coming from other parts of the Kingdom in their efforts to obtain employment, for employers would be slow to engage a worker who if an accident happened to him could compel his master to accept an alien law which might be detrimental to his interest": 1913 S.C., at 784. See also *id.*, at 789. Under Scots law minors who were forisfamiliated (living on their own away from their families) were bound by such contracts (subject to reduction for enorm lesion). As against this distinct rule which displayed a clear legal policy in respect of the capacity of minors in the position of the pursuer, it is perhaps not surprising that the *lex domicilli* should have taken second place.

[187] See *Baindail (otherwise Lawson)* v. *Baindail*, [1946] P. 122, at 128 (C.A., *per* Lord Greene, M.R.). See also *Male* v. *Roberts*, 3 Esp. 163, 170 E.R. 574, (1790), *McFeetridge* v. *Stewarts & Lloyds, Ltd.*, 1913 S.C. 773, *Bondholders Securities Corporation* v. *Manville*, 1933 4 D.L.R. 699 (Sask. C.A.), (criticised by *Cheshire & North*, 222, *Falconbridge*, 384 and *Castel*, vol. 2, 548, but defended by *McLeod*, 492 on the basis that it was concerned with a negotiable instrument, in respect of the transfer of which the *lex loci contractus* plays an important role). See also *In re Lavenders Policy*, [1898] 1 I.R. 175 (C.A., 1897), mentioned *infra*, p. 541, which, if not supporting the proper law, may very tentatively be interpreted as affording support for the *lex loci contractus*.

is in the interests of both parties. Commercial decisions seek to minimise uncertainty wherever possible, and the rules of capacity in the law of the place of contracting may easily be determined by the parties before entering the contract.[188] Moreover, legal systems do not lightly deny contractual capacity, so in many cases a policy regarded as important by the law of the place of contracting will be frustrated if the *lex loci contractus* is ignored.

Of course the principal weaknesses of the *lex loci contractus* in this context (as in others) is that the place of contracting may be entirely fortuitous: it is easy to see the folly of applying the *lex loci contractus* to invalidate a contract made by parties which is perfectly valid under their *lex domicilii* and the proper law.[189]

The proper law

Most of the commentators[190] today consider that capacity, at least as a general rule, should be determined by the proper law objectively ascertained.

There is judicial support for this approach in Canada[191] and England.[192] The Irish case of *In re Lavender's Policy*,[193] offers some possible support for this approach, but it is of little assistance since the conflicts issue in the case was conceded[194] rather than determined by the Court.

The proper law or the law of the defendant's domicile and residence as alternative bases for capacity

It is possible to conceive of cases where, according to the proper law, the defendant lacks capacity but, according to the law of his domicile and residence, he has capacity. The principle of *favor negotii* may be invoked[195] in favour of upholding the contract in such circumstances. It is difficult to see how the parties to the contract can complain: the defendant can hardly be heard to say that he is prejudiced by a rule upholding a contract which he may be presumed to have entered with a view to fulfilling rather than rejecting. Moreover the social policies of his country of domicile and residence are satisfied.

Interpretation

Where a Court is faced with the task of interpreting a word or expression in a contract it must naturally seek to discern what the parties *intended* it to mean. In answering this question it would be quite wrong for the court to ignore the international dimensions and invariably apply the rules of interpretation of the *lex fori*: to do so would in some cases frustrate the intention of the parties. The court must instead resort to the rules of interpretation of the system of law which the parties wished should govern questions of interpretation.

---

[188] Cf. *McLeod*, 494.

[189] The converse also may apply: if the parties lack capacity under their *lex domicilii*, they should not be able to confer capacity on themselves merely by making a trip across the border to a country where the law contains no similar rule rendering persons in their circumstances incapable of contracting: cf. *Charron* v. *Montreal Trust Co.*, [1958] O.R. 597, at 603 (C.A., *per* Morden, J.A.(for the Court)).

[190] See *Falconbridge*, 384-385, *Cheshire & North*, 222, *Castel*, vol. 2, 548, *Dicey & Morris*, 779-781, *Nygh*, 230, *Schmitthoff*, 112-113; cf. *McLeod*, 491-492.

[191] *Charron* v. *Montreal Trust Co.*, [1958] O.R. 597 (C.A.). It should be noted that in this case, the court was dealing with a separation agreement — a contract of a type strongly affected by family law policies. It is interesting that Morden, J.A. referred to the place of marriage (Ontario) apparently as a relevant factor. This indicates that the Court was conscious that it was not dealing with an "ordinary" commercial contract. Cf. *Auten* v. *Auten*, 308 N.Y. 155, 124 N.E. 2d 99, 50 A.L.R. 2d 246 (1954), *Scoles & Hay*, 657-658.

[192] *Bodley Head, Ltd.* v. *Flagon*, [1972] 1 W.L.R. 680.

[193] [1898] 1 I.R. 175 (C.A., 1897).

[194] Cf. *id.*, at 183.

[195] Cf. *McLeod*, 492.

Where the parties expressly specify a system of law to govern questions of interpretation no problem arises. But frequently they will not do this. In such cases the court must strive to infer their intention from the language of the contract as a whole and from the context in which it is made. There is a "strong presumption"[195] in favour of the proper law.

The question has arisen in several Irish decisions relating to the interpretation of terms such as "pounds" or "shillings". In *Neville* v. *Ponsonby,*[196] for example, a long lease was made of lands in Ireland in 1721, reserving a rent of "£100 sterling, current and lawful money of Great Britain". At that time the currency of Great Britain and Ireland was the same; but in 1737 the Irish currency was reduced, making English money current in Ireland at 1/13th more than in England. A question later arose as to whether the rent was payable in Irish or British currency.

The Court held that it was payable in Irish currency. Of particular interest are Wolfe, C.B.'s observations:

> "I think...that when [the parties] contracted in 1721...they had not in view the payment of th[e] rent in any foreign currency, or in any other currency than the current money of Ireland. Generally speaking, when parties enter into a money contract, without specifying the particular currency in which that contract is to be performed, they must be taken to mean the currency of the country wherein the contract is made.[197] There may be circumstances to show that the parties contracted in another currency (which of course it is competent for them to do), for instance, in dollars, moidores, or guineas, or in any other currency different from that of the country in which the contract was made; but, in the absence of such circumstances, and of any proof that they so dealt, it must be taken that they contracted in the currency of their own country, such as it was at the time the contract was made. Now, in this case, all the circumstances (notwithstanding the terms employed), appear to me, to denote that the parties contracted in *Irish* currency. The parties were domiciled in Ireland: the contract was to be performed in Ireland; and the subject matter of the contract (namely, the land out of which the rent was to grow due), was situated in Ireland. All these circumstances are indications that the contract was for Irish currency."[198]

The parties' use of the words "lawful money of Great Britain" did not contradict this interpretation, since it was not disputed that this expression had acquired the same import as the words "lawful money" generally or "lawful money of Ireland". A similar view had been taken in *Lansdowne* v. *Lansdowne,*[199] where the House of

---

[195] *Cheshire & North*, 240, *Chartered Mercantile Bank of India, London and China* v. *Netherlands India Steam Navigation Co. Ltd.*, 10 Q.B.D. 521 (C.A., 1883) especially at 529 (*per* Brett, L.J.); cf. *id.*, at 540 (*per* Lindley, L.J.), *Chatenay v. Brazilian Submarine Telegraph Co. Ltd.*, [1891] 1 Q.B. 79 (C.A., 1890), *White Cliffs Opal Mines, Ltd.* v. *Miller*, 4 S.R. (N.S.W.) 150 (Simpson, C.J. in Eq., 1904), *Rowett, Leakey & Co.* v. *Scottish Provident Institution*, [1927] 1 Ch. 55 (C.A., 1926) (especially at 69 *per* Warrington, L.J.), *St Pierre* v. *South American Stores (Gath & Chanes) Ltd.*, [1937] 3 All E.R. 349 (C.A.) (firmly rejecting the argument that the *lex solutionis* should control), *Goldsbrough Mort & Co. Ltd.* v. *Hall*, 78 C.L.R. 1 (High Ct. of Austr., 1949), aff'g [1948] V.L.R. 145 (Sup. Ct., Fullagar, J., 1947). See also *Scanlon* v. *Hartlepool Seatonia Steamship Co., Ltd.*, 63 I.L.T.R. 21, at 22 (High Ct., *per* O'Bryne, J., 1927), *MacNamara* v. *Owners of the Steamship "Hatteras"*, [1931] I.R. 337, at 338 (Sup. Ct.).
  There is, of course, a risk of some degree of circularity here, since in determining what *is* the proper law, the court may have regard to the terms of the contract: cf. *Goldsbrough Mort & Co.* v. *Hall*, [1948] V.L.R. 145, at 152 (Sup. Ct., Fullagar, J., 1947, (aff'd 78 C.L.R. 1); *The Njegos*, [1936] P. 90 (Merriman, P., 1935).

[196] 1 Ir. L.R. 204 (Exch. of Pleas, 1839). See also *Ex parte Keatinge*, I.R. 2 Eq. 26 (Walsh, M.R., 1867), *Ladbrooke* v. *Biggs*, Batty 619 (K.B., 1826), *Fitzgerald* v. *Carew*, 1 Ir. Eq. Rep. 346 (Lord Plunket, L.C., 1839), *In re Boate's Estate*, 10 Ir. Chy. Rep. 164 (Chy. App., 1859) (considered *supra*, p. 427, *Northern Bank Ltd.* v. *Edwards*, [1986] I.L.R.M. 167 (Sup. Ct., 1985). (Sup. Ct., 1985).

[197] Cf. *In re Boate's Estate, supra*, at 171 (Ch. App., *per* Brady, L.C. 1859).

[198] 1 Ir. L.R., at 216-217

[199] 2 Bligh 60, 4 E.R. 250 (1820).

Lords, on appeal from the Irish courts, held that in order to ascertain the real meaning of the contracting parties, it was necessary to take into account all the circumstances of the contract : the place where the contract was made; the residence of the parties; the place where it was to be performed, and the scope and bearing of other portions of the contract upon those words. Adopting this approach the House of Lords came to the conclusion, that the contracting parties in the case intended that Lord Lansdowne's jointure should be paid in English, rather than Irish currency, even though the words used in the contract to describe the currency, standing by themselves, would, in an Irish contract have meant Irish currency.[200]

But it should be stressed that there can be only a presumption that the proper law will determine questions of interpretation. This presumption will not apply in some cases. If, for example, parties to a contract whose proper law is Irish use a technical legal expression which has no meaning under Irish law but has a distinct meaning under another country's law, it may well be reasonable, indeed imperative, to interpret the expression according to the latter law.[201]

Of course, the interpretation of an expression cannot alter its actual legal effect. The court may be satisfied that, applying the appropriate system of law to the interpretation of a particular expression, the parties *intended* that a particular action should have a certain legal effect.[202] But this legal effect may result only when permitted by the governing law.

Discharge

A contract may be discharged in a number of ways: by performance, novation, frustration, accord and satisfaction and illegality, for example. The general rule is that the proper law of the contract is effective.[203] Discharge under some other law, will not be effective.[204]

Let us examine the position a little more closely in relation to (i) performance and (ii) novation.

Performance[205]

In certain instances the proper law and the law of the country where the contract is to be performed (the *lex loci solutionis*) may differ. There have been *dicta*[206]

---

[200] Cf. 1 Ir. L.R., at 217-218 (*per* Wolfe, C.B.).

[201] In *Rowett, Leakey & Co.* v. *Scottish Provident Institution*, [1927] 1 Ch. 55 (C.A., 1926, aff'g Astbury, J., 1926), Astbury, J. held that the expression *"bona fide* onerous holders" in relation to insurance policies was "more or less meaningless" according to English legal phraseology, English law being the proper law; accordingly he allowed evidence to be given as to its meaning in Scots law, the defendants being a Scottish company. The Court of Appeal held that the words could be given a meaning under English law, and did not resort to Scots law for any guidance. Cf. *The Industrie*, [1894] P. 58, at 73 (C.A., *per* Lord Esher, M.R. 1893).

[202] Cf. *Chatenay* v. *Brazilian Submarine Telegraph Co.*, [1891] 1 Q.B. 79, at 85 (C.A., *per* Lindley, L.J., 1890). See also *Robertson* v. *Brandes, Schönwald, & Co.*, 8 F. 815, at 819 (Ist Div., *per* Lord Kinnear, 1906).

[203] Cf. *Dicey & Morris*, 818-819, *Cheshire & North*, 241, *Castel*, vol. 2, 557, *Rabel*, vol. 2, 541.

[204] See *Cheshire & North*, 241, *Jacobs* v. *Crédit Lyonnais*, 12 Q.B.D. 589 (C.A., 1884), *Mount Albert Borough Council* v. *Australian Temperance & General Mutual Life Assurance Society*, [1938] A.C. 224 (P.C., 1937), *Re United Railways of the Havana and Regla Warehouses*, [1960] Ch. 52, at 88-91, (C.A., *per* Jenkins, L.J., 1958) affirmed, in part, *sub nom. Tomkinson* v. *First Pennsylvania Banking and Trust Co.*, [1961] A.C. 1007(1960). Cf. *Cummings* v. *Stewart (No.2)*, [1913] 1 I.R. 95 (O'Connor, M.R., 1912).

[205] See Morris, *The Eclipse of the Lex Loci Solutionis — A Fallacy Exploded*, 6 Vand. L. Rev. 505 (1953).

[206] Cf. Morris, *supra*, at 508 *Chatenay* v. *Brazilian Submarine Telegraph Co.*, [1891] 1 Q.B. 79, at 82-83 (C.A. *per* Lord Esher, 1890), *Adelaide Electric Supply Co. Ltd.* v. *Prudential Assurance Co.*, [1934] A.C. 122, at 151, (H. L. (Eng.), *per* Lord Wright, 1933), *R.* v. *International Trustee*, [1937] A.C. 500, at 574 (H.L. (Eng.), *per* Lord Roche), *Hardy (M.W.) & Co. Ltd.* v. *Pound & Co.*, [1955] 1 Q.B. 499, at 512, (C.A., *per* Lord Goddard, C.J.). See also *Louis-Dreyfus* v. *Paterson Steamships Ltd.*, 43 F. 2d 824 (1930).

which suggest that the *lex loci solutionis* should in these cases determine whether a party has performed his part of the contract. But the more widely accepted view[207] is that the proper law should govern the question of performance.

As regards relations between the principal, agent and third parties, there is considerable judicial authority supporting the *lex loci solutionis* to determine questions affecting the manner of performance as opposed to the substance of the contract.[208]

Novation

Novation must be distinguished from the assignment of a debt. In the case of novation[209] a debt is extinguished and a new contract substituted, by replacing one of the parties to the original debt, or by a new contract between the same parties, for example.[210] In the case of assignment, whether voluntary[211] or involuntary[212], of a debt, however, the original creditor may be replaced by a new one, but the original contractual obligation remains intact.

Some important implications for the conflict of laws follow from this distinction. For novation to be effective, the original debt must be extinguished, and whether or not this occurs may be determined only by the proper law of the contract under which the debt was created.[213] So far as the assumption by a new debtor of the debt is concerned, it appears probable that this process is governed by "the system of law with which the substitution of the new debtor is most closely connected, *i.e.* in the absence of an agreement to the contrary, normally his personal law or the law of his residence or place of business".[214] Where the novation involves merely a new contract between the same parties, it appears that the proper law of the original contract should govern.[215]

Essential Validity[216]

We must now consider briefly the conflicts aspects of the essential validity of a contract. There may be cases where the parties are perfectly competent to contract and the contract is formally valid but none the less the contract lacks essential validity. The most obvious instances would be where the contract is illegal, void or unenforceable. These are sufficiently important to merit separate discussion.[217] Other instances relate to what has been called the "substance of the obligation".[218]

---

[207] *Mount Albert Borough Council* v. *Australian Temperance and General Mutual Life Assurance Society*, [1938] A.C. 224, at 240-241 (P.C., 1937), *Bonython* v. *Commonwealth of Australia*, [1951] A.C. 201, at 219 (P.C., 1950). Cf. *Byrne* v. *Limerick Steamship Co. Ltd.*, [1946] I.R. 138 (High Ct., Overend, J.), and the Admiralty case of *Officers of the S.S. "Vicia"* v. *Master and Owners (No.2)*, 76 I.L.T.R. 110 (Hanna, J., 1942), where the *lex fori* was applied without comment, counsel for the plaintiffs having contended in the latter case (at 111) that it should govern.

[208] Cf. *Cheshire & North*, 238.

[209] See *Pitner Lighting Co. of Ireland* v. *Geddis*, [1912] 2 I.R. 163 (K.B. Div.).

[210] See *Wolff*, 458 quoted with approval by Jenkins, L.J., in *In re United Railways of the Havana and Regla Warehouses Ltd*, [1960] Ch. 52, at 84-85 (C.A., 1958), affirmed in part by H.L., *sub nom.* *Tomkinson* v. *First Pennsylvania Banking and Trust Co.*, [1961] A.C. 1007 (1960).

[211] Cf. ch. 29, *supra.*

[212] Cf. ch. 25, *supra.*

[213] *In re United Railways of the Havana and Regla Warehouses Ltd.*, [1960] Ch. 52, at 85 (C.A., *per* Jenkins, L.J., 1958) affirmed in part, *sub nom.* *Tomkinson* v. *First Pennsylvania Banking and Trust Co.*, [1961] A.C. 1007.

[214] *Dicey & Morris*, 824, citing *In re United Railways of Havana and Regla Warehouses Ltd.*, *supra.* In accord is *Anton*, 223.

[215] *Dicey & Morris*, 824, citing *Rosencrantz* v. *Union Contractors Ltd.*, 23 D.L.R. (2d) 473 (B.C. Sup. Ct., Wilson, J., 1960).

[216] See *Wolff*, 440 ff, *Rabel*, vol. 2, Ch. 29, Jaffey, *Essential Validity of Contracts in the English Conflict of Laws*, 23 Int. & Comp. L.Q. 1 (1974).

[217] *Infra*, pp. 545-552.

[218] *Cheshire & North*, 231.

These may concern such matters as whether the defendant should be excused for non-performance,[219] or whether an exemption clause is effective.[220]

It is now agreed that the essential validity of a contract or of any contractual term,[221] should generally be determined by the proper law. There used to be support[222] for the view that, regardless of its proper law, a contract's essential validity should be determined by the *lex loci contractus* or the *lex loci solutionis*[223] The former was unsuitable in view of its fortuitous role in many cases.[224] The latter also led to difficulties in that it might not be easy to determine in some instances where the contract was to be performed.[225] The development of the law in regard to these issues is considered in greater detail in the analysis of illegal contracts.[226]

In some circumstances, as we have seen, the proper law will not control. For example, section 2(1) of the Family Law Act 1981 provides that no action for breach of promise of marriage may be brought in the State, whatever the law applicable to the agreement. The Sale of Goods and Supply of Services Act 1980[227] contains a number of provisions which exclude the proper law from determining (*inter alia*) questions relating to essential validity in respect of certain contracts of sale,[228] hire purchase[229] and the supply of a service.[230]

Illegality[231]

A contract may be illegal under its proper law, the law of the place of performance on the *lex loci contractus*. It may, moreover, be void as being against the public policy of the forum or because it is contrary to a statutory provision of the law of the forum. Let us examine the position in regard to each of these cases.

Illegality under the proper law

Where a contract is illegal under its proper law, it may not be enforced by the Irish courts.[232] There is some irony in applying the proper law chosen by the parties themselves where to do so means that the contract will be invalid.[233] But, as Morris observes, "[t]he irrationality (if any) is part of the price we have to pay for allowing the parties such a wide freedom to choose the governing law."[234]

---

[219] *Jacobs* v. *Crédit Lyonnais*, 12 Q.B.D. 589 (1884).

[220] See the relevant cases cited in fn. 221 *infra*.

[221] Cf. *P. & O. Steam Navigation Co.* v. *Shand*, 3 Moo. P.C. (n.s.) 272, 16 E.R. 103 (1865), *Re Missouri Steamship Co.*, 42 Ch. D. 321 (C.A., 1889), *Jones* v. *Oceanic Steam Navigation Co.*, [1924] 2 K.B. 730 (Lord Hewart, C.J., and special jury), *Sayers* v. *International Drilling Co.*, [1971] 1 W.L.R. 1176 (C.A.) (all concerned with exemption clauses); *Hamlyn & Co.* v. *Talisker Distillery*, [1894] A.C. 202, (H.L. (Sc.)), *Spurrier* v. *La Cloche*, [1902] A.C. 446 (P.C.) (both cases concerned with arbitration clauses).

[222] Cf. *Foote*, 379-399.

[223] Cf. *Bannatyne* v. *Barrington*, 9 Ir. Chy. Rep. 406, at 423-424 (Ct. of App. in Chy., *per* Brady, L.C., 1859).

[224] Cf. *Dicey & Morris*, 791.

[225] *Id.*

[226] *Infra*, pp. 545-552.

[227] Cf. *Supra*, pp. 532-533.

[228] Section 23.

[229] Section 36.

[230] Section 42.

[231] See Hogan, *Banks and Other Financial Institutions*, ch. 13 of P. Ussher ed., *Doing Business in Ireland*, para. 13.04 (1987), Dowrick, *The Irish Sweep and Irish Law*, 2 Amer. J. of Comp. L. 505 (1953), Jaffey, *Essential Validity of Contracts in the English Conflict of Laws*, 23 Int. & Comp. L.Q. 1 (1974), Mann, *Proper Law and Illegality in Private International Law*, 18 Br. Yrbk of Internat. L. 97 (1937).

[232] *Cripps Warburg Ltd.* v. *Cologne Investment Co. Ltd.*, [1980] I.R. 321 (High Ct., D'Arcy, J., 1979), *Kahler* v. *Midland Bank*, [1950] A.C. 24, *Zivnostenska Banka* v. *Frankman*, [1950] A.C. 57.

[233] Cf. Jaffey, *supra*, at 3.

[234] *Morris*, 289.

In *Cripps Warburg Ltd.* v. *Cologne Investment Co. Ltd.*,[235] the question of illegality had to be considered where, so far as the contracts of loan and guarantee were concerned, the proper law was English but so far as the action on the supporting mortgage was concerned, the proper law was Irish. D'Arcy, J. held that under neither law was illegality established. So far as English law was concerned, the contracts of loan were not illegal and were enforceable because the plaintiff bank had obtained a certificate of exemption under the Moneylenders Acts as a firm *bona fide* carrying on the business of banking. Although they had no equivalent exemption under the Irish legislation,[236] the loan was held to be valid because it was an isolated transaction, and thus the bank was not "carrying on business" as a moneylender in Ireland.[237]

Illegality under the lex loci solutionis

Where a contract whose proper law is Irish is illegal under the *lex loci solutionis*, it will not be enforced here.[238] Public policy will cover many of the cases where this situation arises,[239] especially where there is a conspiracy to violate the laws of a foreign state. But where Irish law is neither the proper law of the contract nor the *lex loci solutionis*, it is not clear that illegality under the *lex loci solutionis* but not under the proper law will invalidate the contract according to our rules of private international law. The judicial authorities are not definitive and the commentators are divided.[240]

In *Apicella* v. *Scala*,[241] Meredith, J. gave an extended analysis of the issue. Here the parties, Italian nationals resident in England, had agreed to purchase Irish Sweepstake tickets and to share the winnings. This agreement was of an elaborate nature. Of present relevance is the fact that the agreement, though treated (reluctantly)[242] by Meredith, J. as being governed by Irish rather than English law, was one which was to be performed by breaking the English law. A dispute arose between the parties as to ownership of the winning ticket.

Meredith, J. dismissed the plaintiff's action. He said:

---

[235] [1980] I.R. 321 (High Ct., D'Arcy, J., 1979). See further *supra*, pp. 412, 522-523, 527-530.

[236] Moneylenders Act 1900, section 6, Moneylenders Act 1933, section 5 (5)(b).

[237] Cf. Hogan, *supra*, para. 13.04, who observes that:

"the consequence of the *Cripps Warburg* decision is that it makes the lending into Ireland of unlicensed banks a decidedly doubtful business. Certainly a foreign bank may be able to argue successfully, like the plaintiff in *Cripps Warburg*, that it engaged only in isolated loan transactions, but there are obvious risks attached to this strategy. Equally, the unlicensed foreign bank could seek to protect itself by choosing the law of some country other than Ireland as the proper law of the contract, but again there must be a doubt about this course of action where the transaction involves a security taken over immovable property in Ireland. Probably the most prudent move is for such banks to obtain an exemption under Section 6 of the Moneylenders Acts, as bodies corporate from the Department of Industry, Trade, Commerce and Tourism, so that there can be no question of their loans being rendered illegal or unenforceable by reason of the Moneylenders Acts". In accord is Dickson, *Lending into Ireland*, 1 Bus. L. Rev. 81, at 82 (1980).

[238] *Ralli Bros* v. *Compania Naviera de Sota y Aznar*, [1920] 2 K.B. 287, *Stanhope* v. *Hospitals Trust Ltd. (No.2)*, [1936] Ir. Jur. Rep. 25 (Sup. Ct.), rev'g in part [1936] Ir. Jur. Rep. 21 (High Ct., Hanna, J., with jury, 1935), *Apicella* v. *Scala*, 66 I.L.T.R. 33 (High Ct., Meredith, J., 1931). See also *Ross Bros. Ltd.* v. *Shaw (Edward) & Co.*, [1917] 2 I.R. 367 (K.B. Div., considered *infra*, p. 551, fn. 281.

[239] Cf. *Namlooze Venootschap de Faam* v. *Dorset Manufacturing Co.*, [1949] I.R. 203 (High Ct., Dixon, J. 1948) and *Fibretex Lté* v. *Beleir Ltd.*, 89 I.L.T.R. 141 (Sup. Ct., 1949, aff'g High Ct., Dixon, J., 1949) discussed *infra*, pp. 550-551. It may be argued that public policy considerations affected Hanna, J. in the *Stanhope* case: cf. [1936] Ir. Jur. Rep., at 24.

[240] Cf. *Cheshire & North*, 229, *Dicey & Morris*, 794-800, Mann, *Proper Law and Illegality in Private International Law*, 18 Br. Yrbk of Internat. L. 97, at 107-113 (1937).

[241] 66 I.L.T.R. 33 (High Ct., Meredith, J., 1931).

[242] Cf. *id.*, at 44, and *supra*, p. 520.

"The broad question....is: Will the Courts of Saorstát Éireann enforce contracts which are to be performed by breaking the laws which other countries have found it expedient to make in the interests of good government? Every civilised country has a right to work out the problem of good government within its own territory in its own way — and God knows it is a sufficiently difficult problem. Are our Courts to respect the efforts of such other countries to discharge their duty, or are they to be made the instrument of subverting such efforts? To my mind only one answer is possible to that question. Our Courts will not enforce such contracts except where they have in any case been expressly validated by our legislation.

It is hardly necessary to point out that it was presumably because the plaintiffs knew that the contract which they were seeking to enforce could not be enforced in England, because of the illegal acts to be performed under it, that this action was brought in these Courts, and it is obvious that if actions of this type can be successfully maintained in this country, Dublin will rapidly become the gambler's cockpit of Europe. I see nothing in the Public Charitable Hospitals (Temporary Provisions) Act 1930 to encourage the idea that such a result was intended. Hence, if we desire to be cosmopolitan, let us be so by paying a cosmopolitan regard to the principles of international law."[243]

In this passage, Meredith, J. presents a sound argument against Irish courts hearing actions about contracts *unconnected with Ireland* which are illegal in the country where they are to be performed. But this argument loses some of its force where the proper law is Irish. It should not be overlooked that Meredith, J. was inclined to consider that the proper law was English, and that he held it to be Irish only because both sides assumed that it was so, and because there were "considerations that could be urged"[244] to this effect.

Meredith, J. was satisfied that the 1930 Act contained nothing to validate the contract. Section 3(3) merely legalised the holding of the lottery and did not protect things done even within the State which were otherwise illegal. Meredith, J. considered it "doubtful"[245] whether the Act was intended to have any extra-territorial effect whatever.

Stanhope v. *Hospitals Trust Ltd. (No.2)*[246] is a case of some considerable interest. The plaintiff resided in Durban, where he carried on the business of professional seller of sweepstake tickets. On his own admission[247] this was an illegal activity. He brought an action against the Hospitals Trust, claiming damages for £30,000 for breach of contract and the same sum for negligence. He alleged that he had sent a number of counterfoils to the Hospitals Trust, with the appropriate payments, but that no receipts had been issued and that the counterfoils had not been included in the draw. As a result, he said, the public lost confidence in him and his illegal occupation was destroyed.

In their analysis of the conflicts issues, neither Hanna, J. at trial, nor the Supreme Court on appeal, expressly considered the question of the proper law of contract. Instead they concentrated their attention on the law of the place of performance. Nevertheless, some of the language used to describe this law suggests that the proper law was indeed tacitly taken into consideration.

Hanna, J. directed the jury to find for the defendants. He applied the principle that "a Court of law will not lend its aid to enforce the performance of a contract which appears to have been entered into by both the contracting parties for the express purpose of carrying into effect that which is prohibited by the law of the land".[248]

---

[243] 66 I.L.T.R., at 44.

[244] *Id.*

[245] *Id.*, at 45.

[246] [1936] Ir. Jur. Rep. 25 (Sup. Ct.), rev'g in part [1936] Ir. Jur. Rep. 21 (High Ct., Hanna, J. with jury, 1935). See Dowrick, *supra*, at 510-511.

[247] This aspect of the case is discussed *supra*, pp. 109-110.

[248] [1936] Ir. Jur. Rep., at 23-24.

Furthermore, the damages sought were based on the loss of a trade of a character illegal according to the laws of the country where the performance of the contract on the part of the plaintiff "was undoubtedly to take place".[249]

The Supreme Court reversed in part, and held that there should be a new trial. All the members of the Court were of the view that the contract was one to be performed in the State.[250] FitzGibbon, J. said:

> "The contract was one which, to my mind, was to be performed in Dublin, and to be governed by the law of the place of performance, that is, the law of the Irish Free State, and I can find no evidence that the contract was illegal either by the law of this country or by the law of Natal. It was a contract entirely to be performed in Dublin — completed, possibly, by the posting, by the plaintiff in Natal, of the counterfoils and the appropriate money — but to be carried out in the Irish Free State where it was perfectly legal."[251]

FitzGibbon, J.'s reference to the fact that the contract was "to be governed by the law of the place of performance" indicates that he regarded the proper law of the contract as Irish. Clearly, he rejected the view that the plaintiff's act of completion of the contract by posting the letter in Natal amounted to such "performance" as would merit the application of the law of Natal as the *lex loci solutionis* or even as one of two such *leges*.[252]

On the question of damages, all the members of the Court were agreed that, if the sale of sweepstake tickets was illegal in Natal, the plaintiff could not claim compensation for the destruction of this illegal trade. FitzGibbon, J. and Murnaghan, J. were satisfied that the plantiff's own evidence established the illegality; Kennedy, C.J. was not satisfied that the court should reply on the "casual, haphazard remarks"[253] of the plaintiff, who had no legal expertise.

When we speak of performance being illegal under the *lex loci solutionis,* it should be noted that the performance has to be illegal[254] by the law of the country where it *must,*[255] not *may,*[256] be done. Thus it will not avail a defendant to claim that performance of a contract is illegal in the country where he resides or carries on business,[257] unless this is also the country of the proper law or of the *lex loci solutionis,* or unless public policy prevents enforcement of the contract.

In the *Cripps Warburg*[258] case, D'Arcy, J. did not address the question whether illegality under the *lex loci solutionis,* but not the proper law, might render a contract unenforceable in Ireland. But in that case there was no need to do so since Irish and English law were the only relevant laws and the validity of the transaction was tested under both of these laws as two separate proper laws relating to two separate claims.[259]

---

[249] *Id.,* at 24.

[250] Cf. *id.,* at 26 (*per* Kennedy, C.J.), at 28 (*per* FitzGibbon, J.) and at 29 (*per* Murnaghan, J.).

[251] *Id.,* at 27-28.

[252] Determining what is the *lex loci solutionis* is a notoriously uncertain process and may raise problems of characterisation: *Cheshire & North,* 227-228, *Mauroux* v. *Sociedade Comercial Abel Pereira da Fonseca S.A.R.L.,* [1972] 2 All E.R. 1085, at 1089 (Chy. Div, Hegarry, J.). It is worth noting that under the EEC Convention on the Law Applicable to Contractual Obligations, the Hospitals Trust, and not the plaintiff, would probably have been considered the party effecting the "characteristic performance" of the contract: cf. *infra,* pp. 558-559.

[253] [1936] Ir. Jur. Rep., at 27. Cf. *supra,* pp. 109-110.

[254] Rather than merely difficult or impossible: *Rali Bros* v. *Compania Naviera Sota y Aznar,* [1920] 2 K.B. 287, at 292 (C.A., *per* Lord Sterndale, M.R.), distinguishing *Jacobs* v. *Crédit Lyonnais, supra.*

[255] Cf. *Kahler* v. *Midland Bank Ltd.,* [1950] A.C. 24, at 36 (H.L. (Eng.), *per* Lord Normand, 1949).

[256] Cf. *Jacobs* v. *Crédit Lyonnais, supra..*

[257] Cf. *Dicey & Morris,* 798. See also *Kleinwort Sons & Co.* v. *Ungarische Baumwolle Industrie A/G,* [1939] 2 K.B. 678.

[258] *Supra.*

[259] Cf. pp. 527-529, *supra.*

Illegality under the lex loci contractus

It is now generally accepted that illegality under the *lex loci contractus* is not a sufficient reason for our courts to refuse to enforce a contract otherwise valid.[260] Arbitrary and unjust results would flow from letting such illegality render a contract unenforceable. It is of interest that in *Stanhope*'s case, the question of the place of contracting appears to have been considered largely irrelevant save to the extent that it might throw light on identifying the *lex loci solutionis*.

The role of public policy

We must now consider the final exception to the rule that the proper law of a contract determines its validity. This relates to public policy. Under the Irish internal law of contract, a contract may be invalid as being opposed to public policy.[261] The fact that application of a foreign law would be contrary to Irish public policy is a reason for holding it invalid, not because it offends against the public policy of some foreign law (such as its proper law) but because it offends against *our own*.[262] Fry, J. put the point simply in *Rousillon* v. *Rousillon*:[263]

> "It appears to me....plain on general principles that this Court will not enforce a contract against the public policy of this country, wherever it may be made. It seems to me almost absurd to suppose that the Courts of this country should enforce a contract which they consider to be against public policy, simply because it happens to have been made somewhere else."

Thus a contract, though valid according to the *lex loci contractus* or the proper law, may be void under our law as offending our public policy on such questions as arrangements to facilitate divorce.[264] In *Dalton* v. *Dalton*,[265] O'Hanlon, J. refused

---

[260] The *dictum* to the contrary by Lord Halsbury in *Re Missouri Steamship Co.*, 42 Ch. D. 321, at 336 (C.A., 1889) has been isolated by later decisions: cf. *Vita Food Products Inc.* v. *Unus Shipping Co.*, [1939] A.C. 277, at 296-298 (P.C.). See also *Apicella* v. *Scala*, 66 I.L.T.R. 33, at 38-39 (High Ct., Meredith, J., 1931) (*per* Gavan Duffy, K.C., during argument). The commentators are also opposed to Lord Halsbury's dictum: see *Cheshire & North*, 227, *Dicey & Morris* 790-791, Dowrick, *supra*, at 514, Mann, *Proper Law and Illegality in Private International Law*, 18 Br. Yrbk of Internat. L. 97, at 104 (1937). But cf. *London Finance and Discount Co.* v. *Butler*, [1929] I.R. 90 (High Ct., Hanna, J.), discussed *supra*, pp. 519-520.

[261] See *Clark*, Part IV. In *Purser* v. *Purser*, [1913] 1 I.R. 422 (Ross, J.), aff'd [1913] 1 I.R. 428, Irish spouses had lived for a time in England, the wife there obtaining a protection order against her husband before returning to Ireland, where the spouses resumed cohabitation having entered into an agreement providing for the wife in case of another separation. Ross, J. held that the agreement was not contrary to "the policy of the law", since its dominant purpose had been to put an end to the existing separation. He said (at 424-425):

> "Here it is to be observed that the opinions of Courts on the policy of the law are not constant. They alter in consequence of political and religious change, and they are modified to follow the supposed policy of certain codes of laws, such as the divorce legislation. The domain of morality is not, and has never been in any country, if we except the Jewish theocracy, the same as the domain of State Law. The domain of morality is infinitely wider. It is comprehensive of all the acts and the thoughts of man. Its objects and its sanctions are wholly different. It is possible for a man to be ethically worthless: to be mean, cruel, treacherous, malignant, heartless, and irreligious, and yet he may never have broken any law, civil or criminal.
>
> There are, however, some matters arising in the wide circle of morality to which the State Law must have some regard. There are certain well-recognized cases where the State Law will refuse its aid to enforce agreements apparently just and proper as between the parties, on the ground that they are contrary to what is called the policy of the law."

[262] Cf. *Dicey & Morris*, 801-802.

[263] 14 Ch. D. 351, at 369 (1880).

[264] See, e.g. *Dalton* v. *Dalton*, [1982] I.L.R.M. 418 (High Ct., O'Hanlon, J., 1981), *Hope* v. *Hope*, 8 De G. M. & G. 731, 44 E.R. 572, (1857). For consideration of the policy issues raised by this and similar types of agreement, see Moore, *The Enforceability of Premarital Agreements Contingent Upon Divorce*, 10 Ohio N.L. Rev. 11 (1983).

[265] [1982] I.L.R.M. 418 (Ct., O'Hanlon, J., 1981).

to make a separation agreement an order of the Court (pursuant to section 8 of the Family Law (Maintenance of Spouses and Children) Act 1976, although in all other respects it appeared to be a fair and reasonable one adequately protecting the interests of both the spouses,[266] because the agreement contained a clause to the effect that:

> "[t]he husband and the wife hereby agree to obtain a decree of divorce *a vinculo* and the husband further agrees not to contest any divorce proceedings issued by the wife and husband and wife further acknowledge that they have been living apart since 1 August 1976."

The address given in the agreement for each of the parties was within the State, and O'Hanlon, J. observed that there was "no indication in the agreement or in any of the other documents before the court that the parties or either of them are domiciled elsewhere than in Ireland or intend to adopt a domicile outside Ireland in the future".[267]

It appeared to O'Hanlon, J. that:

> "considerations to public policy require that the court should not lend its support to an agreement provided for the obtaining of a divorce *a vinculo* by a husband and wife, and this may well be the position even if the parties are domiciled elsewhere than in Ireland when the application is made or propose to take up such foreign domicile in the future...
>
> I am of the opinion that to ask the court to make the agreement which has been concluded between the parties in the present case a rule of court is to ask the court to lend its support to a course of conduct which is contrary to public policy within its jurisdiction."[268]

Other contracts which may offend against Irish public policy though valid under their proper law include contracts in restraint of trade,[269] champertous agreements[270] and agreements to stifle a criminal prosecution.[271] Exchange control legislation has been the subject of two reported Irish decisions.[272] In *Namlooze Venootschap de Faam* v. *Dorset Manufacturing Co.*,[273] the plaintiffs, a Dutch firm, supplied goods to the defendants, an Irish firm. The defendants obtained permission, as required by Article 3 of the Emergency Powers (Finance) (No. 7) Order 1941, to export foreign exchange to purchase the goods. However, this permission, which was subject to a time limit, was for the equivalent of £5,419.14s. in Dutch Guilders, whereas the value of the goods was £7,181.11.5d. The defendants paid only the equivalent of £4,038.11.5d.

After the time limit had expired, the plaintiffs issued a summary summons claiming £3,123. An order made under subsequent legislation in 1947 prohibited *any* payment to foreign residents of the plaintiffs' category.

The plaintiffs were unsuccessful. Dixon, J. said:

---

[266] As required by section 8. (The section also requires that the interests of the dependent children (if any) should be adequately protected.) O'Hanlon, J. quoted this part of the section, without comment. The report does contain no suggestion that dependent children were involved in the case.

[267] [1982] I.L.R.M., at 418.

[268] *Id.*, at 419. Cf. *G.* v. *G.*, [1984] I.R. 368 (High Ct., Finlay. P.), discussed *supra,* pp. 308-309.

[269] *Rousillon* v. *Rousillon*, 14 Ch. D. 351 (Fry, J., 1880).

[270] *Grell* v. *Levy*, 16 C.B.(n.s.) 73, 143 E.R. 1052 (1864).

[271] *Kaufman* v. *Gerson*, [1904] 1 K.B. 591 (C.A.). Cf. *Rand* v. *Flynn* [1948] Ir. Jur. Rep. 30 (High Ct., O'Byrne, J., 1947), a case concerning a contract to indemnify a bailsman, where the conflicts aspects were not addressed by the Court.

[272] See Hogan, *Banks and Other Financial Institutions*, ch 13 of P. Ussher ed., *Doing Business in Ireland,* para. 13.06, (1987), Forde, *Contracts that Contravene Exchange Control*, 80 Incorp. L. Soc. of Ir. Gazette 52 (1986).

[273] [1949] I.R. 203 (High Ct., Dixon, J., 1948).

"Whatever the terms of the Court's order, the legal effect of it would be to put the plaintiffs in a position to secure payment of the amount in question and it would thus, even if indirectly, compel the defendants to do an act prohibited by the law for the time being in force. Put thus, I feel that on general principles it would be improper and contrary to public policy for the Courts to give judgment for the plaintiffs on their claim as now framed."[274]

Dixon, J. did not rule out the possibility of the plaintiffs' mounting an action for damages based on the failure by the defendants to use reasonable diligence to obtain or retain the necessary permission, but that was not the case with which he had to deal.

In *Fibretex Lté* v. *Beleir Ltd.*,[275] in the same year, the Supreme Court endorsed Dixon, J.'s approach. The same net point was in issue. The members of the Court were agreed that the action had been prematurely brought, and that the defendants could not legally pay the amount due. As in *Namlooze,* the plaintiffs were held not to be entitled to judgment with a stay of execution. Maguire, C.J. did not exclude the entitlement of a Court to make a declaration as to a plaintiff's entitlement in such circumstances but, since the plaintiff had in fact made no application for such a declaration, it was not necessary to decide the point.

Public policy is less likely to invalidate a foreign contract where the contract has not a close connection with Ireland. In this regard, what is relevant "is in many cases not the character of the foreign contract in the abstract, but the result of its enforcement in the concrete case".[276] The fact that a contract is of a type not known under our law will not of itself be a reason for refusing to enforce it.[277]

Public policy may work so as to result in the *enforcement* of a contract by an Irish court where, under its governing law, the contract is void.[278] This could arise where the foreign rule invalidating the contract is oppressive or discriminatory.

An important aspect of public policy concerns international relations. A contract will be void if it is opposed to Irish interests of State. Thus, a contract likely to jeopardise the friendly relations between Ireland and a foreign friendly country will offend against public policy.[279] This type of contract may be one seeking to defy the exchange control laws of a foreign country, for example, or its penal or revenue laws.[280]

Illegality or unenforceability under Irish statute

A contract that is contrary to a statutory provision in Irish law[281] which is

---

[274] [1949] I.R., at 207. See also *Stockholms Enskilda Bank Aktiebolag* v. *Schering Ltd.*, [1941] 1 K.B. 424, (C.A.), which Dixon, J. regarded as constituting "persuasive authority": [1949] I.R., at 207.

[275] 89 I.L.T.R. 141 (Sup., 1949, aff'g High Ct., Dixon, J., 1947).

[276] *Dicey & Morris,* 803.

[277] *Shahnaz* v. *Rizwan,* [1965] 1 Q.B. 390.

[278] See *Dicey & Morris,* 804, citing *Wolff* v. *Oxholm,* 6 M. & S. 92, 105 E.R. 1177 (1817), *Re Friedrich Krupp A/G,* [1917] 2 Ch. 188 (Younger, J.), *Re Helbert Wagg & Co. Ltd.,* [1956] Ch. 323, at 352, (Upjohn, J., 1955), *Etler* v. *Kertesz,* 26 D.L.R. (2d) 209 (Ont. C.A., 1960).

[279] Cf. *Foster* v. *Driscoll* , [1929] 1 K.B. 470 (C.A., 1928), *Regazzoni* v. *Sethia,* [1956] 2 Q.B. 490 (C.A.). See also *Buchannan Ltd.* v. *McVey,* [1954] I.R. 89, at 99-100 (High Ct., Kingsmill Moore, J., 1950) (aff'd by Sup. Ct., 1951).

[280] Cf. *supra,* pp. 550-551; see also *Dicey & Morris,* 805-806.

[281] Cf. *Keith* v. *Protection Marine Insurance Co. of Paris,* 10 L.R. Ir. 51 (Ex. Div., 1882), where, however, the statutory provision alleged to render the contract void was held not to apply. See also *Ross Bros., Ltd.* v. *Shaw (Edward) & Co.,* [1917] 2 I.R. 367 (K.B. Div.), where the vendor of yarns to be obtained from Belgium was held not to have broken its contract to them since a *Trading with the Enemy Proclamation* prohibited the carrying on of trade with Belgian businesses. *Per* Gibson, J., at 380: "The contracts to be performed as contemplated by custom assumed as a tacit condition that delivery could, as regards our own law, be legally carried out from Belgium. Once Belgium became an enemy territory by reason of German occupation this was impossible." *Per* Pim, J., at 386: "The proclamation made all contracts with countries in the occupation of the enemy null and void. The contract between the defendants and the Belgian millers ceased to exist. In my opinion, any contract dependent upon such void contract, if it had been entered into with knowledge of such dependency, also became null and void. To hold otherwise would be to penalize the defendants here for not attempting to break the law."

intended to apply to the contract cannot be enforced in Ireland. This will be so even where the contract is valid by its proper law. As an example of such statutory provision, section 36 of the Gaming and Lotteries Act 1956[282] provides (in part) that every contract by way of gaming or wagering is void and that no action is to lie for the recovery of any money or thing alleged to be won or to have been paid upon a wager. But, though wagering contracts are void under our law, they are not so under the law in some other countries. Where a right to recover money won under a wagering contract arises under the proper law of the wager, it appears that it may not be enforced here, by reason of section 36 of the 1956 Act.[283]

So also, section 2 of the Family Law Act 1981, which abolishes the action for breach of promise of marriage, provides that no action is to be brought in the State for breach of an agreement to marry one another, "whatever the law applicable to the agreement". Thus, even though the proper law provides for a right of action, no action may be brought here by reason of section 2.[284]

THE EEC CONVENTION ON THE LAW APPLICABLE TO CONTRACTUAL OBLIGATIONS[285]

Introduction

On 19 June 1980 the EEC Convention on the Law Applicable to Contractual

---

[282] See *Clark*, 140ff.

[283] Cf. *Hill* v. *William Hill (Park Lane) Ltd.*, [1949] A.C. 530, at 579 (H.L.(Eng.) *per* Lord Radcliffe). It should be noted that section 36 does not affect *other* rights arising in relation to wagering. Thus, for example, although under our law, it seems that a loan for the purposes of gambling is irrecoverable (*Anthony* v. *Shea*, 86 I.L.T.R. 29 (Circuit Ct., Judge McCarthy, 1951); cf. *Clark*, 142), our courts may nonetheless enforce a right of action for money lent for the purpose of being used by the borrower for gambling where this is valid under its proper law: *Quarrier* v. *Colston*, 1 Ph. 147, 41 E.R. 587 (Lyndhurst, L.C., 1842), *Saxby* v. *Fulton*, [1909] 2 K.B. 208 (C.A., 1909 aff'g. K.B.Div., Bray, J., 1908), distinguishing *Moulis* v. *Owen*, [1907] 1 K.B. 746 (C.A.). In *Moulis* v. *Owen*, the plaintiff made the mistake of suing on the cheque drawn on an English bank, rather than for the money lent in Algiers for gambling purposes, the loan being regarded as valid under French law. The Court of Appeal considered that the contract in respect of the cheque was an English one, thus falling foul of section 1 of the Gaming Act 1835.
    On conflicts aspects of gambling, see generally Anagnost, *Comment: Conflicts—Enforceability of Foreign Gambling Contracts*, 22 U. Miami L. Rev. 853 (1968), *Anon.*, *Comment: Public Policy and Conflict of Laws—Foreign Gambling Debts Collectable in New Jersey*, 27 Rutgers L. Rev. 327 (1974), Davidson, *Note: Illegality and Public Policy in the Conflict of Laws*, 12 How. L.J. 331 (1966).

[284] See also the cases on Irish exchange control legislation, *Namlooze Venootschap de Famm* v. *Dorset Manufacturing Co.*, [1949] I.R. 203 (High Ct., Dixon, J., 1948) and *Fibretex Lté* v. *Beleir Ltd.*, 89 I.L.T.R. 141 (Sup. Ct., 1949, aff. High Ct., Dixon, J., 1949), discussed *supra*, pp. 550-551 and *Boissevain* v. *Weil*, [1950] A.C. 327.

[285] See Gill, *The EEC Convention on the Law Applicable to Contractual Obligations*, 6 J. of the Irish Soc. for Eur. L. 1 (1983), Lagarde, *The European Convention on the Law Applicable to Contractual Obligations: An Apologia*, 22 Va. J. of Internat. L. 91 (1981), Delaume, *The European Convention on the Law Applicable to Contractual Obligations: Why a Convention?*, 22 Virg. J. of Internat. L. 105 (1981), Juenger, *The European Convention on the Law Applicable to Contractual Obligations: Some Critical Observations*, 22 Va. J. of Internat. L. 123 (1981), Cavers, *The Common Market's Draft Conflicts Convention on Obligations: Some Preventive Law Aspects*, 48 S. Calif. L. Rev. 603 (1975), P. North ed., *Contracts Conflicts* (1982), Nadelmann, *Impressionism and Unification of Law: The EEC Draft Convention on the Law Applicable to Contractual and Non-Contractual Obligations*, 24 Amer. J. of Comp. L. 1 (1976), Williams, *The EEC Convention on the Law Applicable to Contractual Obligations*, 35 Int. & Comp. L.Q. 1 (1986), Jaffey, *The English Proper Law Doctrine and the EEC Convention*, 33 Int. & Comp. L.Q. 531 (1984), Weintraub, *How to Choose Law for Contracts, and How Not to: The EEC Convention*, 17 Tex. Internat. L. J. 155 (1982), Lando, *The EEC Draft Convention on the Law Applicable to Contractual and Non-Contractual Obligations*, 38 Rabels Z. 6 (1974), Batiffol, *Projet de Convention CEE sur la loi applicable aux obligations contractuelles*, 11 Rev. Trim. de dr. europ. 181 (1975), O. Lando, B. Hoffman & K. Siehr, eds., *European Private International Law of Obligations* (1975).

Obligations[286] was opened for signature.

The purpose of the Convention is to unify the choice-of-law rules as to contract within the European Community, not merely where the case relates to the Community, and regardless of whether the applicable law under the rules of the Convention is that of a Member State.[287] There is a clear need for the Convention, to prevent forum-shopping,[288] which ironically became even more attractive on account of the Convention on Jurisdiction and Enforcement of Civil and Commercial Judgments.[289] Nine Member States have signed the Convention, which will come into force among ratifying States on the first day of the third month following ratification of the Convention by seven Member States.[290]

The background to the Convention is that it had originally been intended to cover both the law applicable to both contractual and non-contractual obligations, but in 1978 the Brussels Working Group charged with the task decided that it would be better to press ahead with the first element alone, since there was a greater degree of uniformity among Member States on choice-of-law issues in torts.

Scope of the Convention

As has been mentioned, the scope of the Convention is very wide. The rules of the Convention, as a general principle, "apply to contractual obligations in any situation involving a choice between the laws of different countries".[291] Moreover, any law specified by the Convention is to be applied, whether or not it is the law of the Contracting State.[292]

The scope of the expression "contractual obligations" needs some examination. Article 8 (1) provides that the existence and validity of a contract are to be determined by the law which would govern it under the Convention if the contract or term were valid. Thus, if an Irish court has to deal with a promise supported neither by seal nor by consideration, it will refer to the applicable law the question whether a "contractual obligation" is in existence, and be guided by its resolution.[293] The question whether *quasi-contractual* obligations fall within the scope of Article 1 (1) may give rise to some difficulties.[294]

The Convention does not give guidance on the question when, under Article 1 (1), a situation involves a choice between the laws of different countries.

It seems[295] that, where the parties have made a choice that a foreign law should

---

[286] [1980] O.J. L266. The Report on the Convention, by Professor Giuliano of the University of Milan and Professor Lagarde of the University of Paris I, contains a thorough and clear analysis: [1980] O.J.C. 282.

[287] Article 2.

[288] Nadelmann, *Impressionism and Unification of Law: The EEC Draft Convention on the Law Applicable to Contractual and Non-Contractual Obligations,* 24 Amer. J. of Comp. L. 1, at 3 (1976) Juenger, *The European Convention on the Law Applicable to Contractual Obligations: Some Critical Observations,* 22 Va. J. of Internat. L. 123, at 124 (1981), Lando, *The EEC Draft Convention on the Law Applicable to Contractual and Non-Contractual Obligations* 38 Rabels Z. 6, at 7 (1974).

[289] Lagarde, *The European Convention on the Law Applicable to Contractual Obligations: An Apologia,* 22 Va. J. of Internat. L. 91, at 93 (1981).

[290] Article 28. Where a Member State ratifies later, the Convention will enter into force in that State on the first day of the third month following this ratification: Article 29. Of course, there is nothing to prevent a Member State from incorporating into its law the rules of the Convention before it comes into effect, or applying the Convention's choice-of-law rules more widely than Article 1 requires: *Morris & North,* 465.

[291] Article 1 (1).

[292] Article 2. The lack of liaison with non-Member States in the preparation of the Convention has been criticised by Williams, *The EEC Convention on the Law Applicable to Contractual Obligations,* 35 Int. & Comp. L.Q. at 5-6 (1986).

[293] Cf. *Re Bonacina,* [1912] Ch. 394.

[294] Williams, *supra,* at 7, Gill, *supra,* at 4.

[295] Williams, *supra,* at 7.

govern, Article 1 (1) comes into play. Where they have not, "presumably the connection with one or more other countries must be material and not merely fanciful".[296]

Exclusions

There are a number of significant exclusions from the scope of the Convention, specified in Article 1 (2) and (3). These nine[297] exclusions are as follows:

(a) Questions involving the status or legal capacity of national persons, without prejudice to Article 11

Thus questions relating to the validity of marriage, divorce, legitimacy and custody of children[298] fall outside the scope of the Convention.

(b) Contractual obligations relating to:
  —wills and successions,
  —rights in property arising out of matrimonial relationship,
  —rights and duties arising out of a family relationship, parentage, marriage or affinity, including maintenance obligations in respect of children who are not legitimate

The intention here is to exclude from the scope of the Convention "all matters of family law".[299] Family law and commercial law principles do not easily mix, especially in an international context.[300] It is anticipated that most contracts relating to maintenance obligations would fall within the scope of the Hague Convention on the Law Applicable to Maintenance Obligations.[301]

(c) Obligations arising under bills of exchange, cheques and promissory notes and other negotiable instruments to the extent that the obligations under such other negotiable instruments arise out of their negotiable character

The Convention does not attempt to define what characterises a document as a negotiable instrument: this is left to the *lex fori* (including its rules of private international law).[302] As may be seen, the exclusion from the scope of the Convention only applies in relation to obligations arising out of the negotiable character of the instruments. Thus, neither the contracts pursuant to which the instruments are issued nor contracts for their purchase and sale are excluded.[303]

The primary reason for excluding negotiable instruments was to avoid introducing unnecessary complexity into the Convention. The loss is not great for civil law jurisdictions, all of which are parties to the Geneva Conventions on Bills of Exchange (1930)[304] and Cheques (1931).[305] But neither Ireland nor Britain has adopted these Conventions.

(d) Arbitration agreements and agreements on the choice of court

These were excluded after much debate. The majority view was that they covered matters of procedure and judicial administration, which might have endangered

---

[296] *Id.*
[297] The first eight are contained in Article 1 (2); the ninth is Article 1(3).
[298] Cf. the Giuliano-Lagarde Report, para. 3.
[299] Giuliano-Lagarde Report, para. 3.
[300] Cf. Weintraub, *How to Choose Law for Contracts, and How Not to: The EEC Convention,* 17 Tex. Internat. L.J. 155, at 160 (1982).
[301] Williams, *supra,* at 8.
[302] Giuliano-Lagarde Report, para. 4.
[303] *Id.*
[304] Cf. *Rabel,* chs. 58-62.
[305] Cf. *id.,* ch. 63.

ratification of the Convention.[306] Moreover, questions as to the validity and form of jurisdiction agreements are already governed by Article 17 of the Convention on Jurisdiction and Enforcement of Judgments in Civil and Commercial Matters, and the outstanding issues, mainly relating to consent, are unimportant in practice in view of the requirement that the agreements be in writing,[307]

The British would have wished to see arbitration agreements within the scope of the Convention. They argued that an arbitration agreement does not differ from other agreements as regards the contractual aspects, and that in view of the fact that the International Conventions on arbitration had not been ratified by all the Member States, the opportunity to harmonise differing approaches should not be ignored.[308] The French and the Germans in particular opposed the inclusion of arbitration agreements on the basis of the number of conventions in this area should not be multiplied, and on the basis that the procedural and contractual aspects would be difficult to separate.[309] It was agreed that the matter should be excluded from the Convention subject to returning to an examination of the subject once the Convention had been drawn up.

(e) Questions governed by the law of companies and other bodies corporate or unincorporate and the personal liability of officers and members as such for the obligations of the company or body

The reason for this exclusion was that there was no point in trespassing on work already in progress on company law within the European Economic Community.[310] All the complex acts relating to contract, administration and registration, essential for the creation, internal organisation and winding-up of a company or firm, are excluded. But acts or preliminary contracts whose sole purpose is to create obligations between the promoters with a view to forming a company or firm fall within the scope of the Convention.[311]

(f) The question whether an agent is able to bind a principal, or an organ to bind a company or body corporate or unincorporate, to a third party

This exclusion affects only the relationships between the principal and third parties. It does not affect other aspects of agency, including principal-agent and agent-third party relationships.[312] The reason given for the exclusion is that "it is difficult to accept the principle of freedom of contract on this point".[313]

(g) The constitution of trusts and the relationship between settlors, trustees and beneficiaries

Trusts, as understood in common law Member States, thus fall outside the scope of the Convention. But similar institutions in the laws of civil law Member States fall within the provisions of the Convention because they are normally contractual in origin.[314] Where, however, they exhibit the characteristic of a trust as understood in common law, they should be excluded from the Convention.[315]

---

[306] Giuliano-Lagarde Report, para. 5.
[307] *Id.*
[308] *Id.*
[309] *Id.*
[310] *Id.*, para. 6.
[311] *Id.*
[312] *Id.*, para. 7. Williams, *supra*, at 10, notes that where the third party sues the agent for breach of warranty of authority and the agent pleads due authorisation as a defence, the issue is excluded from the scope of the Convention.
[313] Giuliano-Lagarde Report, para. 7.
[314] *Id.*, para. 8.
[315] *Id.*

(h) Evidence and procedure, without prejudice to Article 14

The general principle is clear: evidence and procedure fall outside the scope of the Convention. These matters are governed by the *lex fori* under our conflicts rules.[316]

Article 14 modifies the full force of this exclusion. It provides as follows:

> "(1) The law governing the contract under this Convention applies to the extent that it contains, in the law of contract, rules which raise presumptions of law or determine the burden of proof.
>
> (2) A contract or an act intended to have legal effect may be proved by any mode of proof recognised by the law of the forum or by any of the laws referred to in Article 9 under which that contract or act is formally valid, provided that such mode of proof can be administered by the forum."

In some jurisdictions evidential rules are clearly matters of substance. These will be determined by the law of the contract rather than of the forum. Similarly, a forum's rules as to modes of proof may not have the effect of invalidating a contract formally valid under the terms of Article 9. Thus, *Leroux* v. *Brown*[317] is effectively prevented from operating to defeat a contract that is formally valid under the terms of the Convention.[318]

(i) Contracts of insurance which cover risks situated in the territories of the Member States

This exclusion takes account of work being done in the European Economic Community in the field of insurance.[319]

It is worth noting what is *not* excluded. Article 1 (4) explicitly provides that re-insurance contracts are within the scope of the Convention. These do not raise the same problem as insurance contracts where the protection of the insured person is of major significance.[320] Moreover, contracts of insurance covering risks outside the territories of the Member States manifestly are within the scope of the Convention.

General Rules under the Convention

The central provisions in the Convention for determining the applicable law are Articles 3 (1) and 4 (1). These contain principles which will be largely familiar to Irish and British conflicts lawyers, since they deal with the question of the governing, or proper, law of the contract, whether through the choice of the parties or otherwise. Let us first consider the position where the parties choose the governing law.

Applicable Law Based on Parties' Choice

Article 3 (1) provides as follows:

> "A contract shall be governed by the law[321] chosen by the parties. The choice must be expressed or demonstrated with reasonable certainty by the terms of the contract or the circumstances of the case. By their choice[322] the parties select the law applicable to the whole or a part only of a contract."

---

[316] Cf. *infra*, ch. 34.
[317] 12 C.B. 801, 138 E.R. 1119 (1852).
[318] Cf. Williams, *supra*, at 20-21.
[319] Giuliano-Lagarde Report, para. 10.
[320] *Id.*, para. 11.
[321] "Law" here, and throughout the Convention, means the internal law of the country in question: *renvoi* has no place in the Convention: Article 15. See Giuliano-Lagarde Report, p. 37.
[322] Article 3 (4) provides that the question of the existence and validity of the consent of the parties as to the choice of the applicable law is to be determined by Articles 8, 9 and 11.

Article 3 (1) "simply reaffirms a rule currently embodied in the private international law of all the Member States of the Community and of most other countries".[323]

Article 3 (1) gives the parties a very wide-ranging freedom in choosing the law to govern the contract.[324] This has been welcomed by some commentators[325] as being in harmony with the requirements of contemporary international contracts. On the other hand it has also been stigmatised as "a surrender to the clever manipulation of connecting factors by interested contract draftsmen at the time of their negotiations".[326]

It is to be noted that article 3 (1) applies only where the choice of law is expressed or "demonstrated with reasonable certainty" by the terms of the contract or the circumstances of the case. If neither of these requirements is fulfilled, Article 4 comes into place. This requirement of "reasonable certainty" appears to be more stringent than the test adopted in many English cases,[327] but has the advantage of "preventing attempts to deduce an implied choice from minor indications, the presence of which cannot really be attributed to a real, but unexpressed, choice".[328] Moreover, it avoids "creat[ing] a blur"[329] between Articles 3 and 4.

Article 3 (2) permits the parties at any time to agree to subject the contract to a law other than that which previously governed it.[330] Article 3 (2) further provides that any variation by the parties of the law to be applied made after the conclusion of the contract "shall not prejudice its formal validity under Article 9 or adversely affect the rights of third parties". It seems clear that under Irish law at present, the Court would refuse to give effect to a purported change of the governing law where the purpose was to affect the rights of third parties adversely. Where this is the result, but was not the intention, the position is less certain, since the parties would have complied with the requirements of good faith in making their new selection.

Applicable Law in the Absence of Choice

Among the Member States, the general approach to the problem of determining the governing law in the absence of express choice by the parties has been for the courts to perform this task either on the basis of an inference as to what they "really intended" or (increasingly) on a more frankly objective basis of selection the law with the closest and most real connection with the transaction.[331] An exception is Italy, whose legislation contains detailed specific rules to deal with different categories of contract.

---

[323] Giuliano-Lagarde Report, p. 15. The Report (pp. 15-16) refers to judicial authorities on this question in several of the Member States; so far as Ireland is concerned, it states merely (p. 16) that "Irish law draws its inspiration from the same principles as the English and Scottish legal system". See further Lando, *The EEC Draft Convention on the Law Applicable to Contractual and Non-Contractual Obligations*, 38 Rabels Z. 6, at 12-14 (1974).

[324] Lagarde has observed that Article 3 (1) "is noteworthy because of the extent of freedom it allows the parties. No link is required between the contract and the law selected. Nor is there any normal requirement that the choice be 'bona fide' or 'legal'. It is unlikely, however, that this freedom will have a significant effect, for past legal practice involving conflict of laws does not reveal recourse to fanciful or meaningless choices by the parties. Moreover, other provisions in the Convention prevent fraudulent choices from being made." *The European Convention on the Law Applicable to Contractual Obligations: An Apologia*, 22 Va. J. of Internat. L. 91, 95-96 (1981).

[325] E.g. Williams, *supra*, at 12.

[326] Delaume, *The European Convention on the Law Applicable to Contractual Obligations: Why a Convention?*, 22 Va. J. of Internat. L. 105, at 107 (1981).

[327] See, however, *Amin Rasheed Shipping Corporation* v. *Kuwait Insurance Co.*, [1984] A.C. 50, at 61 (H.L. (Eng.), *per* Lord Diplock, 1983), explained by Williams, *supra*, at 13, fn. 30.

[328] Williams, *supra*, at 13.

[329] Lagarde, *The European Convention on the Law Applicable to Contractual Obligations: An Apologia*, 22 Va. J. of Internat. L. 91, at 97 (1981).

[330] See North, *Varying the Proper Law*, in *Multum Non Multa: Festschrift für Lipstein*, 205 (1980).

[331] Giuliano-Lagarde Report, pp. 19-20.

Article 4 of the Convention deals with this question. Article 4 (1) provides that, to the extent that the law applicable to the contract has not been chosen in accordance with Article 3, the contract is to be governed by the law of the contract with which it is most closely connected.[332]

Thereafter, the Article becomes a good deal more complicated. Its structure is as follows. Paragraph 2 of the Article introduces a presumption that the contract is most closely connected with the country where the party to it, to effect the performance which is characteristic of the contract, resides or (if a business) has its central administration. But this presumption is subject to paragraph 5, which provides that paragraph 2 is not to apply if either (i) the characteristic performance cannot be determined or (ii) it appears from the circumstances as a whole that the contract is more closely connected with another country.[333]

Paragraphs 3 (dealing with contracts involving immoveable property) and 4 (dealing with contracts for the carriage of goods) also minimise the scope of the presumptions provided for in paragraph 2. Moreover, the presumptions specified in paragraphs 3 and 4 are also subject to paragraph 5 to the extent that they must be disregarded if it appears from the circumstances as a whole that the contract is more closely connected with another country.

Let us look a little more closely at these provisions. Article 4 (2) provides as follows:

> "Subject to the provisions of paragraph 5 of this Article, it shall be presumed that the contract is most closely connected with the country where the party who is to effect the performance which is characteristic of the contract has, at the time of the conclusion of the contract, his habitual residence, or, in the case of a body corporate or incorporate, its central administration.[334] However, if the contract is entered into in the course of that party's trade or profession, that country shall be the country in which the principal place of business is situated or, where under the terms of the contract the performance is to be effected through a place of business other than the principal place of business, the country in which that other place of business is situated."

This approach has some obvious advantages. No longer need the court be concerned with such questions as where the contract was concluded or where the act was done.[335] But the important question concerns the notion of "the performance which is characteristic of the contract". What does it mean and how is it to be determined in specific cases?

Where a contract involves the payment of money, the idea is that this payment "is not, of course, the characteristic performance of the contract.[336] It is the performance for which the payment is done, i.e. depending on the type of contract, the delivery of goods, the granting of the right to make use of an item of property, the provision of a service, transport, insurance, banking operations, security, etc.,

---

[332] Article 4 (1) goes on to provide that a severable part of the contract which has a closer connection with another country may, by way of exception, be governed by the law of that other country.

[333] Article 4 (5) contains no indication as to the circumstances which may prompt the Court to disregard the earlier presumption; thus "the judge may feel the need to justify his decision by recourse to the worn-out device of counting relevant connecting factors": Delaume, *The European Convention on the Law Applicable to Contractual Obligations: Why a Convention?*, 22 Va. J. of Internat. L. 105, at 109 (1981).

[334] Cf. the American Law Institute's *Restatement (Second) of Conflict of Laws*, s.188 (1971).

[335] Giuliano-Lagarde Report, p. 21.

[336] See, however, d'Oliveira, *"Characteristic Obligation" in the Draft EEC Obligation Convention*, 25 Amer. J. of Compar. L. 303, at 310-311 (1977): "[T]here are contracts in which the payment of money must be regarded even by unwavering supporters of the doctrine of characteristic performance as typifying the contract. Should rude fortune compel me to pawn my television set, the money 'uncle' gives me will constitute the specific element in the contract of pledge. Another example could be the hire-purchase contract."

which usually constitutes the centre of gravity and the socio-economic function of the contractual transaction."[337]

Of course, not all cases will be so easy:[338] where *both* parties have to perform actions as well as pay money, or where the contract does not involve the payment of money at all, the court may have a difficult task in identifying either party as effecting "*the* performance which is characteristic of the contract".[339] The spectre of collateral contracts and *dépaçage* must loom on the horizon.

Article 4 (3) provides that, notwithstanding paragraph 2, to the extent that the subject matter of the contract is a right in immovable property or a right to use immovable property, it must be presumed[340] that the contract is most closely connected with the country where the immovable property is situated. This harmonises with our existing rules on the question. It is easy to envisage borderline cases involving the sale to Irish residents of holiday villas abroad,[341] where the parties have not specified an applicable law in accordance with Article 3 (1).

Article 4 (4) excludes contracts for the carriage of goods from the presumption in paragraph 2. It goes on to provide that:

"[i]n such a contract if the country in which, at the time the contract is concluded, the carrier has his principal place of business is also the country in which the place of loading or the place of discharge or the principal place of business of the consignor is situated, it shall be presumed that the contract is most closely connected with that country."[342]

Contracts for the carriage of passengers remain subject to the general presumption, when applicable, under Article 4 (2).

The effect of Article 4 (4) is that if, for example, an Irish airline transports goods between Ireland and France, there will be a presumption,[343] in the absence of a choice of law by the parties,[344] that the governing law is Irish. But if an Irish airline transports goods from Britain to France, no presumption would arise under either paragraph 2 or 4 of Article 4, and the Court would have to resolve the question under the general provisions of paragraph 1.[345]

---

[337] Giuliano-Lagarde Report, p. 20. See, however, D'Oliveira, "*Characteristic Obligation" In the Draft EEC Obligation Convention,* 25 Amer. J. of Compar. L. 303, at 328 (1977):
"It is astonishing that a theory that devotes its efforts to comparing the degree to which national economies are involved in given types of transactions, finally enthroning one economy at the expense of the other, should be accepted by an organisation that has as its aim the removal of internal economic frontiers among the participating countries."
D'Oliveira's lucid and provocative analysis of the "characteristic performance" doctrine is well worth studying.

[338] Cf. Juenger, *The European Convention on the Law Applicable to Contractual Obligations: Some Critical Observations,* 22 Va. J. of Internat. L. 123, at 134 (1981): "Paradoxically, although the approach is simplistic, the practical application is far from simple. The more complex is a transaction, the less helpful the criterion becomes."
Also critical is Gill, *The EEC Convention on the Law Applicable to Contractual Obligations,* 6 J. of the Irish Soc. for Eur. L. 1., at 9-10 (1983).

[339] Emphasis added.

[340] Subject, as has been mentioned, to paragraph 5.

[341] Cf. Giuliano-Lagarde Report, p. 21.

[342] For the purposes of paragraph 4, single voyage charter-parties and other contracts the main purpose of which is the carriage of goods, are treated as contracts for the carriage of goods.

[343] Subject, as mentioned, to paragraph. 5.

[344] In practice many contracts for the international carriage of goods will be governed by an express choice of law, referring to international conventions, such as the Hague or Hague-Visby Rules (on carriage of goods by sea) the Warsaw Conventions (carriage by air), CMR (by road) and CIM (by rail): Williams, *supra,* at 16-17.

[345] Giuliano-Lagarde Report, p. 22. See also Lagarde, *The European Convention on the Law Applicable to Contractual Obligations: An Apologia,* 22 Va. J. of Internat. L. 91, at 100 (1981).

Material Validity

Article 8 (1) of the Convention provides that the existence and validity of a contract, or of any term of a contract, is to be determined by the law which would govern it under the Convention if the contract or term were valid. Article 8 (2) modifies this general principle by providing that a party may rely on the law of the country in which he has his habitual residence to establish that he did not consent if it appears from the circumstances that it would not be reasonable to determine the effect of his conduct in accordance with the law specified in Article 8 (1).

The approach adopted here is designed, among other things, to solve the problem of the implications of silence by one party as to the formation of the contract.[346] The solution is a broad, discretionary, one which is a good way of ensuring justice in these cases.[347] The reference to "the circumstances" enables the Court to have regard, not merely to the particular alleged contract from which one party wishes to abstract himself, but also to the previous dealings between the parties. Thus, if an Irish company has a well-established pattern of business with a foreign company, the proper law being that of a country where silence constitutes acceptance, it would be quite unjust for the Irish company to invoke the Irish rule to the contrary. Having regard to the circumstances and exercising its discretion under Article 8 (2), the Court would be able to hold that Article 8 (1) continued to apply.[348]

Formal Validity

The Convention adopts quite a flexible approach to the question of formal validity, giving good effect to the *favor negotii* principle. Where a contract is concluded between persons who are in the same country, it will be formally valid[349] if it satisfies the formal requirements of *either* the law which governs it under the Convention *or* the law of the country where it is concluded.[350] Where the parties are in different countries, the contract will be formally valid if it satisfies the formal requirements of either the law which governs it under the Convention *or* the law of one of those countries.[351]

In either case, where a contract is concluded by an agent, the country in which the agent acts is the relevant country.[352]

Article 9 also deals with an "act intended to have legal effect relating to an existing or contemplated contract". This type of act might be a notice of termination or remission of a debt or a declaration of rescission or repudiation, for example.[353] Such an act will be formally valid if it satisfies the formal requirements of *either* the law which under the Convention governs or would govern the contract *or* the law of the country where the act was done.[354]

Paragraphs 1 and 4 of Article 9 do not apply to consumer contracts,[355] the formal

---

[346] Giuliano-Lagarde Report, p. 28.

[347] Cf. *supra*, pp. 533-535. For consideration of the various approaches canvassed during the preparation of the Convention, see Kühne, *Choice of Law and the Effects of Silence*, in O. Lando, B. Hoffman & K. Siehr eds., *European Private International Law of Obligations*, 121 (1975).

[348] See also Lagarde, *The European Convention on the Law Applicable to Contractual Obligations: An Apologia*, 22 Va. J. of Internat. L. 91, at 101 (1981).

[349] Article 9 does not define what is meant by "formal requirements". It is "nevertheless permissible to consider 'form', for the purposes of Article 9, as including every internal manifestation required of the part of a person expressing the will to be legally bound, and in the absence of which such expression of will would not be legally effective": Giuliano-Lagarde Report, p. 29. As to the relationship between formal requirements, evidence and procedure, cf. Article 14 (2).

[350] Article 9 (1).

[351] Article 9 (2).

[352] Article 9 (3).

[353] Giuliano-Lagarde Report, p. 29.

[354] Article 9 (4).

[355] Article 9 (5).

validity of which is governed by the law of the country in which the consumer has his habitual residence.[356] In view of the social importance of many formal requirements for consumer contracts, where the whole purpose of the formal requirements is to protect the consumer, and put him on notice of the implications of the transaction which he is contemplating, there is much to be said in favour of letting the law of his habitual residence have exclusive control. So far as immoveable property is concerned, a contract the subject matter of which is a right in immoveable property is subject to the mandatory requirements of form of the law of the country where the property is situated if by that law those requirements are imposed irrespective of the country where the contract is concluded and irrespective of the law governing the contract.[357]

Mandatory Rules

The Convention contains important modifications on the application of the proper law. Article 3 (3) provides that where (a) the parties have chosen a foreign law, whether or not accompanied by the choice of a foreign tribunal, and (b) all the other elements relevant to the situation at the time of choice are connected with one country only, the fact that the parties have made this choice is not to prejudice the application of rules of the law of that country which cannot be derogated from by contract (which are referred to as "mandatory rules"). These "mandatory rules" are spelt out in Article 7, which provides as follows:

"(1) When applying under this Convention the law of a country, effect may be given to the mandatory rules of the law of another country with which the situation has a close connection, if and in so far as, under the law of the latter country, those rules must be applied whatever the law applicable to the contract. In considering whether to give effect to these mandatory rules, regard shall be had to their nature and purpose and to the consequences of their application or non-application.
(2) Nothing in this Convention shall restrict the application of the rules of the law of the forum in a situation where they are mandatory irrespective of the law otherwise applicable to the contract."

Article 7 was the most controversial provision of the Convention during the negotiations.[358] Some of its more important features may be noted. First, the "situation" must have "a close connection" with the country whose mandatory rules of law are applied under paragraph 1. Just how close is "close", for this purpose, is a matter for the courts to determine. It seems that the fact that the contract is to be performed in a country or that one party resides or has his main place of business there may be sufficient.[359]

Next it should be noted that paragraph 1 does not *require* the application of the mandatory rules once a close connection has been established. Instead it facilitates their application. In considering whether or not to give them effect, the court must have regard to their nature and purpose and to the consequences of their application or non-application. This involves to some degree the process of "governmental interests" analysis.[360] Finally, it may be noted that Article 22 permits a Contracting

[356] *Id.*
[357] Article 9 (6).
[358] Williams, *supra*, at 23. See also Lagarde, *The European Convention on the Law Applicable to Contractual Obligations: An Apologia,*, 22 Va. J. of Internat. L. 91, at 103 (1981).
[359] Giuliano-Lagarde Report, p. 27.
[360] Lagarde, *The European Convention on the Law Applicable to Contractual Obligations: An Apologia,* 22 Va. J. of Internat. L. 91, at 103 (1981). Cf. Mann, *Contracts: Effect of Mandatory Rules,* ch. 4 of K. Lipstein, ed., *Harmonization of Private International Law by the E.E.C.* at 31 (1978), Delaume, *The European Convention on the Law Applicable to Contractual Obligations: Why a Convention?,* 22 Va. J. of Internat. L. 105, at 113-115, 119 (1981).

State to reserve the right not to apply the provisions of Article 7 (1). Britain exercised this right when signing the Convention.

Article 7 (1) has been subjected to strong criticism. This has concentrated on the uncertainty it will introduce into international trade,[361] in view of the fact that several countries may have "a close connection" with the "situation".[362] Moreover, the discretion given to the court and the uncertain scope of the examination of the "nature and purpose" of rules and the consequences of their application, may lead to unpredictable results.[363] Furthermore, since the provision regarding mandatory rules is not limited to those in existence at the time of the making of the contract, this makes the task of those drafting contracts a dangerous and frustrating one.[364]

So far as Article 7 (2) is concerned, its origins derive from concern among some of the delegations to safeguard the mandatory rules of the forum, notably on cartels, competitions, restrictive practices, consumer protection and rules concerning carriage.[365] Whether the forum is given too much latitude[366] and whether this may encourage forum-shopping are matters on which some fears have been expressed.

Consumer Contracts

Article 5 contains some important modifications to the operation of the applicable law in relation to certain consumer contracts.[367] The Article applies to "a contract the object of which is the supply of goods or services to a person (the consumer) for a purpose which can be regarded as being outside his trade or profession, or a contract for the provision of credit for that object".[368] This definition is intentionally imprecise, to avoid conflict with the various definitions already given in the national legislation.[369]

Paragraph 2 of Article 5 provides that, notwithstanding Article 3, a choice of law made by the parties is not to have the result of depriving the consumer of the protection afforded to him by the mandatory rules of the law of the country in which he has his habitual residence if any one of three conditions is fulfilled.

The *first* of these conditions arises where, in the country of the consumer's habitual residence, the conclusion of the contract was preceded by a specific invitation addressed to him or by advertising,[370] and he had taken in that country all the steps necessary on his part for the conclusion of the contract. Thus, if, for example, an English trader has engaged in door-to door or mail-order selling in Ireland or has

---

[361] Cf. Mann, *supra*, at 36. But see Jackson, *Mandatory Rules and Rules of "Ordre Public"*, ch. 4 of P. North ed., *Contract Conflicts*, at 74-76 (1982).

[362] Delaume, *The European Convention on the Law Applicable to Contractual Obligations: Why a Convention?*, 22 Va. J. of Internat. 1. 105, at 113 (1981).

[363] Delaume, *supra*, at 119. Article 3 (2) offers only a limited avenue of escape since, by the time the mandatory rules come into existence, the parties may no longer be in harmony.

[364] Cf. Gill, *supra*, at 22-23.

[365] Giuliano-Lagarde Report, p. 28.

[366] Cf. Williams, *supra*, at 23-24, 31.

[367] This distinction between ordinary and consumer contracts may be traced to *Ehrenzweig*, 454-458, Ehrenzweig, *Adhesion Contracts on the Conflict of Laws*, 53 Colum. L. Rev. 1072 (1953): cf. Juenger, *The European Convention on Law Applicable to Contractual Obligations: Some Critical Observations*, 22 Va. J. of Internat. L. 123, at 135 (1981). See also Lando, *Consumer Contracts and Party Autonomy in the Conflict of Laws*, 42 Nordisk Tidsskrift for Internat. Ret. 208 (1972), Hartley, *Some Aspects of the Draft Convention from the Point of View of British Law*, in O. Lando, B. Hoffman & K. Siehr eds., *European Private International Law of Obligations*, 105 (1975).

[368] Article 5 (1).

[369] Giuliano-Lagarde Report, p. 23.

[370] Cf. the torts decision, *Bernhard* v. *Harrah's Club*, 16 Cal. 3d 313, 128 Cal. Rept. 215, 546P. 2d 719 (1976), in which the Supreme Court of California accepted that out-of-state advertising may have important choice-of-law implications.

advertised in Irish newspapers or on Irish television, the mandatory rules of Irish law will apply where a consumer habitually resident here buys a product or services from the trader, regardless of any express choice of English, or other foreign, law. But if a person habitually resident here replies to an advertisement in a Canadian publication sold in Ireland, it appears that Article 5 would not apply "unless the advertisement appeared in special editions of the publication intended for European countries. In the latter case the seller will have made a special advertisement intended for the country of the purchaser."[371]

The *second* condition enabling the mandatory rules of law of the country of the consumer's habitual residence to apply is fulfilled where the other party or his agent received the consumer's order in that country. There will, of course, be a considerable overlap between the first and second conditions,[372] but it is quite possible to envisage cases where the order is received in the country of the consumer's habitual residence without having been preceded by any solicitation or advertising there.

The *third* condition is fulfilled where the contract is for the sale of goods[373] and the consumer travelled from the country of his habitual residence to another country and there gave his order, provided that the consumer's journey was arranged by the seller for the purpose of inducing the consumer to buy. This could have special relevance in relation to cross-border shopping expeditions[374] which have periodically been a feature of life in Ireland, especially in the past decade. It should be noted that Article 5 offers protection only where the consumer's journey was *arranged by the seller*, to induce him to buy. Thus, even in cases where a trader from north of the border advertises south of the border, and a consumer habitually resident south of the border is induced to make a purchase at the trader's premises, none of the three conditions of Article 5 will have been fulfilled.

Article 5 (3) provides that, notwithstanding the provisions of Article 4, a contract to which Article 5 applies is, in the absence of choice in accordance with Article 3 to be governed by the law of the country in which the consumer has his habitual residence if it is entered into in the circumstances described in paragraph 2 of Article 5.

Paragraph 4 contains some important exclusions. It provides that Article 5 does not apply to:

(a) a contract of carriage; and
(b) a contract for the supply of services where the services are to be supplied to the consumer exclusively in a country other than in which he has his habitual residence.

Thus, for example, a person habitually resident in Ireland who has an uncomfortable stay at an hotel, on a weekend visit to London, may not invoke the mandatory rules of Irish contract law in his aid even where the hotel has advertised in the Irish papers.[375] But paragraph 5 provides that Article 5 *will* apply to a contract which, for an inclusive price, provides for a combination of travel and accommodation. Thus, package tours are not excluded from the scope of Article 5, and will be subject to the mandatory rules of the law of the consumer's country of habitual residence, provided, of course, the conditions contained in the Article are fulfilled.[376]

---

[371] Giuliano-Lagarde Report, p. 24. Cf. Williams, *supra*, at 24.
[372] Giuliano-Lagarde Report, p. 24.
[373] Note this limitation: unlike the first two conditions, this third condition does not apply to cases involving the supply of services.
[374] Cf. Giuliano-Lagarde Report, p. 24.
[375] Cf. *id.*, p. 24-25.
[376] Cf. *id.*, p. 25.

Individual Employment Contracts

Article 6 contains important provisions for individual contracts of employment, designed to protect the employee. Where the parties have not chosen an applicable law in accordance with Article 3, Article 4 does not apply to individual employment contracts; instead, the contract of employment is governed:

(a) by the law of the country in which the employee habitually carries out his work in performance of the contract, even if he is temporarily employed in another country; or

(b) if the employee does not habitually carry out his work in any one country,[377] by the law of the country in which the place of business through which he was engaged was situated.[378]

Where, however, it appears from the circumstances as a whole that the contract is more closely connected with another country, the contract will be governed by the law of that country.[379]

Where the parties to an employment contract have chosen a law in accordance with Article 3, that choice will be respected, but it is not to have the result of depriving the employee of the protection afforded to him by the mandatory rules of law which would be applicable under Article 6 (2) in the absence of choice.[380] Thus, if the law applicable under Article 6 (2) grants the employee protection greater than that resulting from the law chosen by the parties, the result is not to render the choice of law nugatory: "on the contrary, in this case the law which was chosen continues in principle to be applicable. In so far as the provisions of the law applicable pursuant to paragraph 2 give employees better protection than the chosen law, for example by giving a longer period of notice, these provisions set the provisions of the chosen law aside and are applicable in their place."[381]

It appears that the mandatory rules from which the parties may not derogate extend beyond the provisions relating to the contract of employment itself to include "provisions such as those concerning individual safety and hygiene which are regarded in certain Member States as being provisions of public law".[382] It also appears that, although Article 6 does not affect an employee's trade union with regard to powers deriving from collecting agreements in its own country,[383] it may have a beneficial effect on the employee's rights, since, if the law of the country designated by Article 6 (2) makes a collective agreement binding on the employer, the employee may not be deprived of the protection which the agreement affords him by the choice of law of another State in the individual employment contract.[384]

Public Policy

Article 16 of the Convention follows the well-established precedent of all the Hague Conventions since 1956 in providing that the application of a rule of law of any

---

[377] Or, indeed, where he carries out his work in no country as, for example, where he works on an oil-rig in international waters: *id.* One commentator has criticised the reference to the law of the employer's place of business, on the basis that "the long-range social consequences of improperly protecting a worker's safety or of inadequately compensating his or her injury will be experienced at the employee's habitual residence": Weintraub, *How to Choose for Contracts, and How Not to: The EEC Convention,* 17 Tex. Internat. L.J. 155, at 163 (1982).

[378] Article 6 (2).

[379] *Id.*

[380] Article 6 (1).

[381] Giuliano-Lagarde Report, p. 25.

[382] *Id.*

[383] *Id.*

[384] *Id.*

country specified in the Convention may be refused "only if such application is manifestly incompatible with the public policy *(ordre public)* of the forum".

Scope of the Applicable Law

Article 10 (1) provides a non-exhaustive list of the matters falling within the scope of the law applicable to the contract. It provides as follows:

> "The law applicable to a contract by virtue of Articles 3 to 6 and 12[385] of this convention shall govern in particular:
>
> (a) interpretation;
> (b) performance;
> (c) within the limits of the powers conferred on the court by its procedural law, the consequences of breach, including the assessment of damages in so far as it is governed by rules of law;
> (d) the various ways of extinguishing obligations, and prescription and limitation of actions;
> (e) the consequences of nullity of the contract."

A few words about some of these elements may be called for. So far as interpretation is concerned, no difficulty arises for Irish law. We have seen[386] that, in most cases, the proper law will determine questions of interpretation. In those rare cases where reference to another law may be necessary, the court may always resort to severence under either Article 3 (1) or Article 4 (1).[387]

Questions of assessment of damages and of limitation of actions fall under the heading of procedure in our law. As may be seen, Article 10 (1) subjects them to the applicable law. So far as limitation of actions is concerned, this is surely a good thing, and it may well hasten the inevitable reform of the law on this issue.[388]

Article 10 (2) provides that, in relation to the manner of performance and the steps to be taken in the event of defective performance, regard is to be had to the law of the country in which performance takes place. It does not attempt to define "manner of performance", in view of the lack of a uniform meaning for this concept in the laws of the Member States.[389] Thus, the question must be resolved by the *lex fori*.[390] Among the matters that may fall within the scope of the concept are the rules governing public holidays, the manner in which goods are to be examined and the steps to be taken if they are refused.[391]

It should be noted that Article 10 (2) only requires the Court to "have regard" to the law of the place of performance. The Court is free to apply this law to such extent, if at all, as it considers desirable in doing justice between the parties.[392] This uncertainty is probably worth conceding in the broader interests of justice.

---

[385] Article 12 deals with voluntary assignment: cf. , p. 566.

[386] *Supra* pp. 541-543.

[387] Cf. Williams, *supra*, at 27, 58, who argues reasonably that, in many cases where there is no express choice-of-law clause, the fact that an expression can be given a precise meaning only under a certain law may well lead to the conclusion that there is an implied choice of that law for the purposes of Article 3 (1).

[388] Cf. pp. 639-641, *infra*.

[389] Giuliano-Lagarde Report, p. 33.

[390] Cf. Delaume, *The European Convention on the Law Applicable to Contractual Obligations: Why a Convention?*, 22 Va. J. of Internat. L. 105, at 112 (1981): "As a consequence, inconsistency or contradiction in results becomes possible."

[391] Giuliano-Lagarde Report, p. 33.

[392] *Id.*

Voluntary Assignments

Article 12 contains special provisions dealing with voluntary[393] assignments. It provides as follows:

> " (1) The mutual obligations of assignor and assignee under a voluntary assignment of a right against another person ('the debtor') shall be governed by the law which under this Convention applies to the contract between the assignor and assignee. (2) The law governing the right to which the assignment relates shall determine its assignability, the relationship between the assignee and the debtor, the conditions under which the assignment can be invoked against the debtor and any question whether the debtor's obligations have been discharged."

Subrogation

Article 13 deals with the subrogation of contractual[394] claims. Where a person ("the creditor") has a contractual claim upon another ("the debtor"), and a third person has a duty to satisfy the creditor, or has in fact satisfied the creditor in the discharge of that duty, the law governing the third person's duty to satisfy the creditor determines whether the third person is entitled to exercise against the debtor the rights which the creditor had against the debtor under the law governing their relationship and, if so, whether he may also do so in full or only to a limited extent.[395]

The same rule applies where several persons are subject to the same contractual claim ("co-debtors") and one of them has satisfied the creditor.[396]

---

[393] Assignments by operation of law (such as bankruptcy) do not fall within the scope of Article 12.

[394] Thus, Article 13 has no application to subrogation by operation of law when the debt to be paid has its origin in tort, as, for example, where the insurer succeeds to the rights of the insured against the person causing damage: Giuliano-Lagarde Report, p.35. There is a "total lack of authority" on questions of subrogation in Ireland and England: Gill, *supra*, at 24.

[395] Article 13 (1).

[396] Article 13 (2).

CHAPTER 32

TORTS[1]

Until recently courts in this country and abroad paid little attention to conflicts of law aspects of the law of torts. In the past forty years, however, there has been an explosion of books and articles on the subject. Changes in marketing, technology and lifestyles have undoubtedly contributed to this increasing interest.[2] Drugs that are defective may have been sold in several countries; a defamatory statement made in Washington may be shown on television in Ireland as it takes place; an Irish family may be involved in a traffic accident while on holiday in Spain. Curiously, in spite of the great volume of academic analysis, there has not been a great deal of case law in Ireland and in England[3] on the subject, though there is some evidence that the amount of litigation will increase significantly in the coming decade.

The Competing Theories

Several different theories as to what law should govern liability in tort have been put forward at various times. The three principal theories, which we will examine briefly, are the *lex fori,* the *lex loci delicti* and the proper law of the tort.

The Lex Fori

The *lex fori* was advocated by Savigny as the appropriate law to govern liability in tort. It has had an important position in English law and in the law of Canada, Australia and New Zealand. In Ireland, as we shall see, the position has yet to be finally resolved.

Two main arguments are generally put forward in favour of the *lex fori.* First, it is said that liability in tort is similar to liability in criminal law, where the *lex fori* applies. There is some historical support for this argument. Many torts, such as public nuisance, libel, breach of statutory duty and torts relating primarily to trade disputes, emerged from criminal or quasi-criminal law origins. Moreover, most of the principal crimes — murder, grievous bodily harm, theft, fraud, and extortion, for example — also give rise, in the main, to liability in tort. But there is no direct relationship between crime and tort. For example, a drunken driver who injures no one is guilty of a crime but not a tort, whereas a defamatory statement may give rise to civil liability in circumstances where it would not occasion a sanction under the criminal law.[4]

[1] See generally Hancock, *Torts in the Conflict of Laws* (1942), Stromholm, *Torts in the Conflicts of Laws* (1960), Morse, *Torts in Private International Law* (1978), Cook, ch. 13, Cavers, chs 1, 2, 6, Smith, *Foreign Torts,* ch. 17 of A. Linden ed., *Studies in Canadian Tort Law* (1968), Gill, *The Locus Delicti and Choice of Law in Tort in Irish Private International Law,* 5 I.L.T. (n.s.) 3 (1987), Goode, *Dancing on the Grave of Phillips* v. *Eyre,* 9 Adelaide L. Rev. 345 (1984), Fawcett, *Policy Considerations in Tort Choice of Law,* 47 Modern L. Rev. 650 (1984), Morse, *Choice of Law in Tort: A Comparative Survey,* 32 Am. J. of Comp. L. 51 (1984).
[2] Cf. *Morris,* 301.
[3] Cf. *Id.,* 301-302: "[L]ess than a dozen cases of any significance have been reported in the last hundred years".
[4] Cf. *McMahon & Binchy,* 10.

Moreoever, there is a major difference between the respective functions of criminal law and of tort law. What these functions should be is, of course, a matter for debate,[5] but, in simple terms, criminal law has been perceived as being largely concerned with the punishment and control of immoral, anti-social conduct where the defendant has the requisite *mens rea*. Tort law unquestionably is concerned in part with similar functions, but its goals range far more widely. Some torts are concerned with the adjustment of competing legitimate interests: private nuisance affords an obvious example.[6] Other torts, in their practical operation if not in strict theory, give effect to functions more akin to social welfare than to the attribution of fault. Much of negligence litigation for personal injuries works in this way,[7] and the courts have generally interpreted legislation prescribing safety precautions in factories and mines as imposing liability without fault.[8]

The second principal argument that has been put forward in favour of the *lex fori* as the governing law is that tort law is concerned with matters involving the fundamental public policy of the forum, and that it is therefore not unreasonable that the *lex fori* should be applied. Again there is some truth in the assertion but again it leaves out of consideration far more important factors. Some of the principles of liability in tort do indeed involve the fundamental policy of the forum, but many others do not, any more than principles of contract do.[9] As Cardozo, J. said in a US decision:

> "We are not so provincial as to say that every solution of a problem is wrong because we deal with it otherwise at home."[10]

The Lex Loci Delicti

The view that the *lex loci delicti* should govern liability in tort has much support in European civil law jurisdictions and formerly held sway in the United States.[11] Two principal arguments have been put forward in its favour. The first has a distinctly dated aura, since it is based on the theory of *obligatio* which, as we have seen,[12] has for some time been in disfavour. In a leading decision of its day, *Slater* v. *Mexican National Railway*,[13] Holmes, J. said:

> "The theory of the foreign suit is that although the act complained of was subject to no law having force in the forum, it gave rise to an obligation, an *obligatio*, which, like other obligations, follows the person and may be enforced wherever the person may be found. But as the only source of this obligation is the law of the place of the act, it follows that that law determines not merely the existence of the obligation, but equally determines its extent."

---

[5] Cf. P. Devlin, *The Enforcement of Morals*, chs. 1-2 (1965), H.L.A. Hart, *Law, Liberty and Morality* (1963).

[6] Cf. *McMahon & Binchy*, 479-495, *O'Kane* v. *Campbell*, [1985] I.R. 115 (High Ct., Lynch, J., 1984), *New Imperial & Windsor Hotel Co.* v. *Johnson*, [1912] 1 I.R. 327 (Barton, J.).

[7] Cf. *McMahon & Binchy*, 18-29.

[8] Cf. *Id.*, 288-289.

[9] Cf. *Morris*, 302.

[10] *Loucks* v. *Standard Oil Co. of New York*, 224, N.Y. 99, at 111 120 N.E. 198, at 201 (1918), quoted by Barrington, J., in *Sachs* v. *Standard Bank (Ireland) Ltd*, High Ct., 30 July 1985 (1435P-1983) at p. 12 (a decision not concerning torts). See also Lown, *A Proper Law of Torts in the Conflict of Laws*, 12 Alta. L. Rev. 101, at 124-125 (1974).

[11] See Hancock, *Canadian-American Torts in the Conflict of Laws: The Revival of Policy-Determined Construction Analysis*, 46 Can. Bar Rev. 226, at 231-232 (1968).

[12] *Supra*, pp. 14-15. See further *Morris*, 303, *Cook*, 311-324, Smith, *Foreign Torts*, ch. 17 of A. Linden Ed., *Studies in Canadian Tort Law*, at 566-567 (1968).

[13] 194 U.S. 120, at 126 (1904). Cf. *Loucks* v. *Standard Oil Co. of New York*, 224 N.Y. 99, at 110, 120 N.E. 198, at 200 (1918).

This notion of *obligatio* in relation to tort liability involves a conclusion expressed as a premise. It is not the case that "the only source" of the obligation is the law of the place of the act: that law may or may not be selected but there is nothing inevitable about its application.

The second argument in favour of the *lex loci delicti* is that it enables a person to engage in forward planning: if he knows in advance that the *lex loci delicti* will apply to any tort he commits within a particular country, he can decide either to avoid that country altogether, try not to commit a tort there, or insure himself for any potential liability there.[14] The weakness of this argument, of course, is that it assumes a degree of foresight which may perhaps be attained by a large business organisation but which surely is too much to expect of others who may have dealings with foreign countries. Moreover, determining the place where a tort is committed may involve formidable conceptual difficulties: is it where the defendant's act occurred or where the plaintiff suffered the damage, or should some other criterion be adopted? Finally, the place where the tort is committed may be a matter of chance: a car with a defective axle, on a journey from Dublin to Rome, may break down and injure the driver in any one of four or more countries. If the *lex loci delicti* depends on the place of injury, the arbitrariness of this approach would make it very difficult for a potential defendant to anticipate and provide for in advance.

The proper law of the tort[15]

The third approach as to what should the governing law was proposed by Dr J. C. H. Morris, and has since been adopted by the American Law Institute's *Restatement Second of the Conflict of Laws*. This is the "proper law of the tort".[16] In an article in the Harvard Law Review[17] in 1951, Morris argued that:

> "the matters discussed in a textbook on the domestic law of torts are probably as various, and certainly more heterogeneous, than those discussed in a textbook on the domestic law of contracts. To take a few illustrations only, is it inherently probable that the courts will achieve socially desirable results if they apply the same conflicts rules to liability for automobile negligence, radio defamation, escaping animals, the seduction of women, economic conspiracies, and conversion? The present writer suggests that it is not: the social factors involved differ too fundamentally for that. A proper law approach, intelligently applied, would furnish a much-needed flexibility. It may be conceded that in many, perhaps most, situations there would be no need to look beyond the law of the place of wrong, so long as there is no doubt where the place is. But we ought to have a conflict rule broad and flexible enough to take care of exceptional situations as well as the more normal ones, or else we must formulate an entirely new rule to cope with the exceptional situations. Otherwise the results will begin to offend our common sense."

Morris discussed a number of fact-situations in which the *lex loci delicti* would seem to have no credible claim to govern the question of liability. First he envisaged

---

[14] See Kuratowski, *Torts in Private International Law,* 1 Internat. L.Q. 172, at 188 (1947).

[15] See Morris, *The Proper Law of a Tort,* 64 Harv. L. Rev. 881 (1951). Nygh, *Some Thoughts on the Proper Law of a Tort,* 26 Int. & Comp. L.Q. 932 (1977), Cavers, *The Proper Law of Producers Liability,* 26 Int. & Comp. L.Q. 703 (1977), *Morse,* ch. 10, Lown, *A Proper Law of Torts in the Conflict of Laws,* 12 Alta. L. Rev. 101 (1974), Ehrenzweig, *The Not So "Proper" Law of a Tort: Pandora's Box,* 17 Int. & Comp. L.Q. 1 (1968).

[16] The expression is far from self-explanatory; cf. Nygh, *Some Thoughts on the Proper Law of a Tort,* 26 Int. & Comp. L.Q. 932, at 933 (1977): "In itself the term ... is meaningless. It simply denotes the law applicable to a tort according to the appropriate choice of law rule, and hence begs the question."

[17] Morris, *The Proper Law of a Tort,* 64 Harv. L. Rev. 881, at 884-885 (1951). Morris had first advocated the proper law of a tort in a Note on *M'Elroy* v. *M'Allister,* 1949 S.C. 110 (*Torts in the Conflict of Laws,* 12 Modern L. Rev. 248, at 251-252 (1949)), which received a hostile reception: cf. Gow, *Delict and Private International Law,* 65 L.Q. Rev. 313, at 316-317 (1949).

a co-educational school in the United States organising a summer vacation camp for its students in Quebec, the camp being entirely self-contained and self-supporting, with no other human being within 50 miles. One of the girls may be seduced by one of the boys so that she becomes pregnant; another is bitten by a dog kept in the camp by another boy. Neither incident would have happened but for the negligence of the camp organisers, who are instructors in the school. The girls, the boys and the organisers are all residents in State X, in the United States, where the school is located. Morris asked:

"Does it make sense to say that the question whether the girls or their parents can sue the boys or their parents or the camp organisers in State X 'must' be governed by the law of Quebec, merely because the incidents happened there? To the present writer it does not."[18]

Morris went on to consider the more significant cases of traffic accidents which take place in one country where there are contacts with different States. For example, a traffic accident may occur in France, involving an Irish driver and passenger, on a journey through France to Spain where they intend to have a holiday. French law in such circumstances would appear to have little claim to govern the question of liability in tort. If, to vary the facts, the passenger was English, the question as to what was the "proper law" of the tort could yield a different solution. Morris's point was not that the answer to questions like this was easy; on the contrary, he argued that on occasions it might be very difficult indeed, so difficult that an inflexible rule (such as the application of the *lex loci delicti*) would inevitably yield inappropriate and unjust solutions in some instances.

Another advantage of the proper law approach is that it "would enable the problems to be broken down into smaller groups and thus facilitate a more adequate analysis of the social factors involved".[19] To speak of "liability in tort" as though it were a single uncomplicated notion is misleading. Liability may depend on consideration of several elements. Let us take the example of two office-workers, residents of Cavan, who have too much to drink at a Christmas party organised by their employers in the public house next door to the office, in a town just north of the Border. If one of the office workers offers to drive the other home, and the car crashes in Cavan, killing the passenger, the question of liability will extend beyond the simple matter of whether the defendant had driven negligently: it will be necessary to consider such issues as the nature of the driver's duty of care in the circumstances, the defences of voluntary assumption of risk and contributory negligence, the possible breach of duty by the employers or the publican, the role of vicarious liability, and the range of compensation permitted to the estate of the deceased passenger and to the dependents in relation to the death.

After a review of similar issues,[20] Morris commented:

"It seems extraordinarily unlikely that all these questions can be satisfactorily answered by mechanically applying the law of the place of wrong without reference to the social factors involved, particularly if the wrongful act and the consequential harm occurred in different states, one of which has to be arbitrarily selected as the place of wrong."[21]

Morris concluded his article with a somewhat more debatable argument. He contended that the proper law of the tort theory was not open to one objection which

---

[18] Morris, *supra,* at 885.
[19] *Id.,* at 892.
[20] *Id.,* at 892-893.
[21] *Id.,* at 893.

had been raised to the proper law of the contracts theory, namely, that it produces grave uncertainty in commercial matters.[22] He said:

> "A shipping company or an insurance company may legitimately need to know what law will govern its contracts before it makes them. But a tort is not a consensual transaction. Tort liability is nearly always unexpected. A motorist does not legitimately need to know what law will determine his liability to pay damages if he runs down a pedestrian. His social duty is not to run the pedestrian down; he ought not to be concerned (at least until after the accident) with the questions whether the law imposes on him a strict liability or only a duty of care, or whether his liability is to be governed by the law of State X or the law of State Y. A duty not to cause harm is a good rule socially, though it may not always hold good in the domestic law of torts."[23]

One may dissent from the assertion that tort liability is "nearly always unexpected". This is, of course, true in relation to many (but not all) instances of negligence, but it is clearly not true in relation to such torts as deceit, malicious prosecution, many instances of nuisance, trespass to the person, goods or land, or some torts affecting domestic or economic relations, for example. Moreover, the notion of tortious conduct as involving a "social duty" which need not concern a person until after the accident seems simplistic. To speak of a motorist as having a "social duty" not to drive negligently is surely entirely different from saying that he has a "social duty" not to injure a person without any negligence on his part. Negligence and strict liability raise different questions of moral and social duty, just as do personal and vicarious liability. Finally, the idea of an international common denominator of social duty, even within the context of negligence, may be challenged.[24] Courts in different countries have given various answers to such questions as whether one has a duty not to cause pure economic loss, a duty to rescue or a duty to obtain an informed consent to medical treatment.

As may readily be appreciated, the "proper law of tort" approach has some very great attractions. Above all, it is flexible, allowing the court to apply the law that is most appropriate in the circumstances. This means that the court is not tempted to resort to dubious characterisations and unpalatable exceptions to a general "black letter" rule.[25] Moreover, the proper law approach does not have to concern itself with the problem of identifying the *locus delicti*, since nothing hinges on this question.[26]

But the very advantage of the proper law approach — its flexibility — also presents problems. In abandoning any specific "black letter" rule,[27] it makes the task of the legal adviser an unenviable one, since there is no sure way of knowing which aspect of a particular act will be dominant in any particular court proceedings.

The Judicial Authorities

We must now consider how the law has developed in relation to this subject. As we shall see the story is an unfinished one, in the sense that the Supreme Court has recently expressed dissatisfaction with the approach historically adopted by the courts.

---

[22] Of course, in contract (though not normally in tort), the parties can normally avoid this problem by specifying the proper law: cf. *Boys* v. *Chaplin*, [1971] A.C. 356, at 377-378 (H.L. (Eng.) *per* Lord Hodson) and at 391 (*per* Lord Wilberforce).

[23] Morris, *supra*, at 895.

[24] Cf. Rheinstein, *The Place of Wrong: A Study in the Method of Case Law,* 19 Tulane L. Rev. 4, at 11-13 (1944).

[25] See the English Law Commission Working Paper No. 87 and the Scottish Consultative Memorandum No. 62, *supra,* para. 4.130.

[26] *Id.,* para. 4.131.

[27] Ehrenzweig, *Private International Law, General Part,* 72 (1967) refers to "the 'give-it-up' formulae of the proper law".

We must wait for another day before we can say positively and in full detail what approach the Supreme Court may ultimately favour.

The Rule in Phillips v. Eyre[28]

Up to relatively recently the approach of courts in Ireland and England was to blend the *lex loci delicti* and the *lex fori*. The basis of this approach was a passage in the judgment of Willes, J., in *Phillips* v. *Eyre,*[29] in 1870:

> "As a general rule, in order to found a suit in England, for a wrong alleged to have been committed abroad, two conditions must be fulfilled. First, the wrong must be of such a character that it would have been actionable if committed in England ... Secondly, the act must not have been justifiable by the law of the place where it was done."

The First Limb of the Rule[30]

The first limb of Willes, J.'s rule has been taken to mean that a plaintiff who seeks damages in England for what is actually a tort according to the *lex loci delicti commissi* will not succeed, unless he or she establishes that, if the defendant had done the same act in England, it would have constituted an actionable wrong according to English internal law.

In England, in *The Halley,*[31] a case decided two years before *Phillips* v. *Eyre,* an action was brought in respect of a collision in Belgian waters, caused by the allegedly negligent navigation of the defendants' steamer. The defendants pleaded that the steamer had been under the charge of a pilot whom they were compelled by Belgian law to employ, and that by English internal law of the time (in contrast to Belgian law) they would not be vicariously liable for the pilot's negligence.

The defence succeeded and the plaintiff's action was dismissed. Delivering the judgment of the Judicial Committee of the Privy Council, Selwyn, L.J. said:

> "It is true that in many cases the courts of England inquire into and act upon the law of foreign countries, as in the case of a contract entered into in a foreign country, where, by express reference or by necessary implication, the foreign law is incorporated with the contract, and proof and consideration of the foreign law therefore become necessary to the construction of the contract itself. And as in the case of a collision on an ordinary road in a foreign country, where the rule of the road in force at the place of collision may be a necessary ingredient in the determination of the question by whose fault or negligence the alleged tort was committed. But in these similar cases the English court admits the proof of the foreign law as part of the circumstances attending the execution of the contract, or as one of the facts upon which the existence of the tort or the right to damages may depend, and it then applies and enforces its own law so far as it is applicable to the case thus established; but it is in their Lordships' opinion, alike contrary to principle and to authority to hold that an English court of justice will enforce a foreign municipal law, and will give a remedy in the shape of damages, in respect of an act which, according to its own principles, imposes no liability on the person from whom the damages are claimed."

[28] See Tollefson, *The Rule in Phillips* v. *Eyre,* 4 Alta. L. 36 (1965).
[29] L.R. 6 Q.B. 1, at 28 (1879).
[30] See Hancock, *Torts in the Conflict of Laws: The First Rule in Phillips* v. *Eyre,* 3 U. Toronto L.J. 400 (1940).
[31] L.R. 2 P.C.193 (1868).

This approach has been consistently criticised by the commentators over the years for its unduly parochial nature.[32] It goes much further than the defence of public policy, since it prevents the bringing of any action in tort which is not recognised by the *lex fori*.[33] In this respect it places the victim of a foreign tort in far worse a position than the victim of a breach of a contract governed by a foreign law.[34]

In England the approach encapsulated in the first limb of the rule in *Phillips* v. *Eyre* does not appear to have formed part of the *ratio decidendi* of any case since *The Halley*.[35] In *Chaplin* v. *Boys*,[36] however, the House of Lords gave their unanimous, albeit *obiter*, support to this approach. Lord Pearson said:

> "I am not persuaded that the rule was wrong from the beginning. It has certain advantages and certain disadvantages. The main advantages are, first, that it has a high degree of certainty and, secondly, that it enables an English court to give judgment according to its own ideas of justice. In *The Halley* it would then have seemed unjust to the English court to hold the defendants liable for the fault of a pilot whom they were compelled by the local law to engage and put in charge of their ships ...
>
> Another advantage is that if one Englishman wrongfully injures another in a primitive country or unsettled territory where there is no law of torts, the English courts can give redress. This would be a factor of some importance in 1774, when *Mostyn* v. *Fabrigas* was decided, and even in 1870 when *Phillips* v. *Eyre* was decided, although with the rapid spread of civilisation it has much less importance now."

Lord Wilberforce defended the existing approach, in contrast to that referring to the *lex loci delicti* on the "dubious"[37] ground that to adopt the *lex loci delicti* as the substantive rule would require proof of a foreign law. He admitted that this objection should not be exaggerated but he stressed that:

> "the intrusion of this foreign element would complicate the task of the adviser, who would at least have to consider, to a greater extent than the present rule compels him to, the possible relevance of a foreign law to his client's case."[38]

These reasons, according to McGregor:

> "represent a total negation of any system of conflict of laws and show a predeliction for the sole application of English law, whatever the tort and wherever committed."[39]

---

[32] *Castel*, vol. 2, 615, R. Sharpe, *Interprovincial Product Liability Litigation*, 84 (1982). See also *Grehan* v. *Medical Incorporated and Valley Pines Associates*, [1986] I.L.R.M. 627, at 637 (Sup. Ct., *per* Walsh, J. (for the Court)). But see Ehrenzweig, *The Not So "Proper" Law of a Tort: Pandora's Box*, 17 Int. & Comp. L.Q. 1, at 31-4 (1968). See further *infra*, p. 579.

[33] *Castel*, vol. 2, 615, *Morris*, 307, *Cheshire & North*, 267-268, *Dicey & Morris*, 937, R. Sharpe, *Interprovincial Product Liability Litigation*, 84 (1982), Lown, *A Proper Law of Torts in the Conflict of Laws*, 12 Alta, L. Rev. 101, at 123-125 (1974), Hancock, *Canadian-American Torts in the Conflict of Laws: The Revival of Policy-Determined Construction Analysis*, 46 Can. Bar Rev. 226, at 228-229 (1968). See also *Grehan* v. *Medical Incorporated and Valley Pines Associates*, *supra*, *per* Walsh, J., at 637.

[34] Swan, *New Principles in the Law of Torts: The Conflict of Laws*, [1973] Special Lectures of Law Society of Upper Canada, 505, at 510. See also *Grehan* v. *Medical Incorporated and Valley Pine Associates*, *supra*, *per* Walsh, J., at 637.

[35] English and Scottish Law Commissions' Working Paper No. 87 and Consultative Memorandum No. 62, *supra*, para. 2.8.

[36] [1971] A.C. 356 (H.L.(Eng.), 1969), analysed by North & Webb, *The Effect of Chaplin* v. *Boys*, 19 Int. & Comp. L.Q. 24 (1970), Karsten, *Chaplin* v. *Boys: Another Analysis*, 19 Int. & Comp. L.Q. 35 (1970).

[37] *Castel*, vol. 2, 615.

[38] [1971] A.C., at 389.

[39] McGregor, *The International Accident Problem*, 33 Modern L. Rev. 1, at 5 (1970). See also *Morris*, 307-308. But see Ehrenzweig, *The Not So "Proper" Law of Tort: Pandora's Box*, 17 Int. & Comp. L.Q. 1, at 2-4 (1968).

The essence of the first limb is that, as a general principle, the whole of Irish internal law, is made available to the Irish court in determining whether an action in Ireland founded on a foreign tort is sustainable. Where, however, a question of breach of statutory duty arises, there is no rule requiring the Irish Court to construe the statutory provision as having application to events occurring abroad.[40]

Some commentators[41] have argued that the first limb involves a jurisdictional rather than choice-of-law rule, namely that the wrong must be triable within England. But, as *Dicey & Morris* point out,

> "Willes, J. did not say that the wrong must be actionable by English law; he said it must be of such a character that it would have been actionable if committed in England — a very different proposition. Moreover, he would hardly have cited *The Halley* as his sole authority for this proposition if he had intended to lay down a rule of jurisdiction, since no question of jurisdiction was involved in that case. In *Boys* v. *Chaplin*[42] Lord Wilberforce, who dealt with this matter at some length, was quite explicit that the first rule is a rule for the choice of law and not a jurisdictional rule."[43]

A question that has not yet come before the Irish courts is whether a plaintiff suing in respect of a foreign tort must show, not only that the defendant's conduct would have been actionable if it had occurred here, but also that the right of action *is vested in him or her personally by Irish law*. The issue arose in the Scottish decision of *M'Elroy* v. *M'Allister*.[44] The Court of Session, by a majority, dismissed an action for negligence taken by the executrix of the deceased, who had been killed in a traffic accident in England where according to Scottish law the right of action did not survive the death of the deceased[45] but in English internal law accrued to the executrix.

The decision has been criticised on the basis that "[t]he grounds of actions of reparation vary from system to system and, although they often secure the same practical result in the long run, do so in different ways. To demand precise coincidence in the grounds of action is to impose a burden upon the pursuer which must frequently lead to hardship."[46]

It would, however, be unwise to overstress this line of criticism. After all, the question of the entitlement of the plaintiff to sue goes to the very heart of negligence law. Whether or not negligence is a "term of relation" or one of more general import divided the New York Court of Appeals in what was perhaps the most famous decision[47] in the United States.

The Second Limb of the Rule

As we have seen,[48] the second limb of the rule in *Phillips* v. *Eyre*[49] requires that

---

[40] English and Scottish Law Commissions' Working Paper No. 87 and Consultative Memorandum No. 62, *supra,* at para. 2.12 (footnote references omitted).

[41] Cf. the authorities cited by *Dicey & Morris,* 938.

[42] [1971] A.C. 356, at 385-387. *Dicey & Morris,* 938, refer by way of contrast to Lord Hodson's observations, [1971] A.C., at 373-375, 380.

[43] *Dicey & Morris,* 938.

[44] 1949 S.C. 110, noted by Morris, 12 Modern L. Rev. 248 (1949), Gow, 65 L.Q. Rev. 313 (1949), E. K[ahn], 67 S.A.L.J. 66 (1950).

[45] Cf. *Anton,* 243, fn. 36:
   "If McElroy had survived his accident and himself claimed damages or a 'solatium' for the personal injuries he suffered in the accident, he would presumably have succeeded on proof that such damages are allowed, albeit under a different name, by English law."

[46] *Anton,* 243-244. (The "pursuer" in Scottish law is the "plaintiff" in our law.)

[47] *Palsgraf* v. *Long Island Railroad Co.*, 248 N.Y. 339, 162 N.E. 99 (1928), analysed by Green, *The Palsgraf Case*, 30 Colum. L. Rev. 789 (1930), Cowan, *The Riddle of the Palsgraf Case*, 23 Minn. L. Rev. 46 (1938), Seavey, *Mr Justice Cardozo and the Law of Torts*, 52 Harv. L. Rev. 372 (1939), Prosser, *Palsgraf Revisited*, 52 Mich. L. Rev. 1 (1953).

[48] *Supra,* p. 572.

[49] L.R. 6 Q.B. 1, at 28 (1870).

"the act must not have been justifiable by the law of the place where it was done".
Earlier in his judgment Willes, J. had observed that "an act committed abroad, if
valid and unquestionable by the law of the place, cannot, so far as civil liability
is concerned, be drawn in question elsewhere unless by force of some distinct
exceptional legislation, superadding a liability other than and besides that incident
to the act itself".[50] In *Carr* v. *Fracis Times & Co.*,[51] in 1902, Lord Macnaghten,
virtually repeating the words of Willes, J., said:

> "The act must not have been justifiable by the law of the place where it was
> committed."[52]

What does "justifiable" mean in this context? Was Willes, J. speaking solely in
the context of civil liability,[53] or did his remarks extend to the question of criminal
responsibility or even beyond, to anti-social conduct tolerated by the law?

A decision on this question which resulted in much controversy is that of *Machado*
v. *Fontes*,[54] in 1897. There, the English Court of Appeal held that a publication
in Brazil in respect of which no civil action for libel or otherwise arose under Brazilian
law was none the less actionable for libel in England, because the defendant might
have been criminally prosecuted under Brazilian law in respect of the publication.

Lopes, L.J. interpreted the words "not justifiable" as meaning that "the act relied
on must be one which is innocent in the country where it was committed.[55] Rigby,
L.J. developed further on this theme. In view of the care with which Willes, J. had
prepared the two propositions he enunciated in *Phillips* v. *Eyre*, Rigby, L.J. had
no doubt that the change from "actionable" in the first branch of the Rule to
"justifiable" in the second branch was deliberate. The "innocency of the action
in the foreign country" was, in his view, what was meant by the requirement that
the act be "justifiable", and it was "not really a matter of any importance" what
the nature of the remedy for a wrong in a foreign country might be.

Machado v. *Fontes* provoked a great deal of discussion.[56] Critics argued that it

---

[50] *Id.*, at 28.

[51] [1902] A.C. 176, at 182.

[52] Tollefson, *The Rule in Phillips* v. *Eyre*, 4 Alta. L. Rev., 36, at 36-37 (1965) argues that Willes, J.'s
requirement that the act should not have been "justifiable by the law of the *place where it was done*"
(emphasis added) refers to the *lex loci actus* rather than the *lex loci delicti*, since the only possible
antecedent in the sentence is "act" (rather than "wrong"). However this view has not received the
support of the commentators generally.

[53] The notion of justifiability of one's conduct played a role in the development of actions for trespass
to the person, to goods and to land: see Goodhart & Winfield, *Trespass and Negligence*, 49 L.Q.
Rev. 358 (1933) Gregory, *Trespass to Negligence to Absolute Liability*, 37 Va. L. Rev. 359 (1951),
Roberts, *Negligence: Blackstone to Shaw To? An Intellectual Escapade in a Tory Vein*, 50 Cornell
L.Q. 191 (1964), English Law Commission's Working Paper No. 87 and Scottish Law Commission's
Consultative Memorandum No. 62, para. 2.14.

[54] [1897] 2 Q.B. 231 (C.A.). *Machado* v. *Fontes* was approved by the Supreme Court of Canada in
McLean v. *Pettigrew*, [1945] S.C.R. 62, [1945] 2 D.L.R. 65, where guest passenger legislation
in the *lex loci delicti* would have had the effect of excluding from the scope of the second limb the
negligent driving of a Quebec resident and domiciliary, had not the Court been able to overcome that
hurdle by invoking the offence of driving without due care and attention under Ontario's Highway
Traffic Act. The outcome was surely just on the facts (cf. *Falconbridge*, 820) but the rule would be
capable of causing considerable injustice where Ontario residents and domiciliaries are concerned.
See further Smith, *Foreign Torts*, ch. 17 of A. Linden ed., *Studies in Canadian Tort Law*, at 577
(1968), Read, *What Should Be the Law in Canada Governing Conflict of Laws in Torts?*, 1 Can. Legal
Studies 277, at 297 (1968), Hancock, *Canadian-American Torts in the Conflict of Laws: The Revival
of Policy-Determined Construction Analysis*, 46 Can. Bar Rev. 226, at 243-244 (1968).

[55] [1897] 2 Q.B., at 233.

[56] See *Cheshire*, 7th ed., 1965, 247-248, Hancock, 22 Can. Bar Rev. 853, *Wolff*, 497, Lorenzen, *Tort
Liability and the Conflict of Laws*, 47 L.Q. Rev. 483, at 485-487 (1931), Gutteridge, *A New Approach
to Private International Law*, 6 Camb. L.J. 16, at 20 (1936), Robertson, *The Choice of Law for Tort
Liability in the Conflict of Laws*, 4 Modern L. Rev. 27 (1940), Smith, *Foreign Torts*, ch. 17 of A.
Linden ed., *Studies in Canadian Tort Law*, at 575-577 (1968).

would allow a plaintiff to select a forum where the remedy is more favourable than in the place of the wrong.[57] As against this, Gutteridge, stressing the policy of the forum, observed that it "would be a strange result if an Englishman who in a foreign country publishes a libel concerning another Englishman can thereby save his pocket from the payment of damages".[58] And Smith has argued that one can exaggerate the distinction between criminal and civil law: "the difference, from the victim's point of view, is only a difference of remedy".[59]

In *Boys* v. *Chaplin*,[60] the House of Lords addressed the issue. The effect of that decision appears to be to overrule *Machado* v. *Fontes* and to require, for the purposes of the second limb in *Phillips* v. *Eyre*, that the defendant's conduct be capable of giving rise to civil liability,[61] as between the parties, under the *lex loci delicti*.[62]

Lord Hodson considered that the words "not justifiable" referred only to civil liability. *Machado* v. *Fontes*, in his opinion, was wrong and should be overruled. Lord Guest also accepted that the defendant's conduct "must be actionable ... by the laws of ... the *lex loci delicti*".

Lord Wilberforce gave a more detailed analysis. He said:

"Assuming that, as the basic rule, we continue to require actionability by the *lex fori* subject to some condition as to what the *lex loci delicti* requires, we should, in my opinion, allow a greater and more intelligible force to the *lex loci delicti* than is included in the concept of unjustifiability as normally understood.

The broad principle should surely be that a person should not be permitted to claim in England in respect of a matter for which civil liability does not exist, or is excluded, under the law of the place where the wrong was committed. This non-existence or exclusion may be for a variety of reasons and it would be unwise to attempt a generalisation relevant to the variety of possible wrongs. But in relation to claims for personal injuries one may say that provision of the *lex loci delicti*, denying, or limiting, or qualifying recovery of damages because of some relationship of the defendant to the plaintiff, or in respect of some interest of the plaintiff (such as loss of consortium) or some head of damage (such as pain and suffering) should be given effect to. I can see no case for allowing one resident of Ontario to sue another in the English courts for damages sustained in Ontario as a passenger in the other's car, or one Maltese resident to sue another in the English courts for damages in respect of pain and suffering caused by an accident in Malta. I would, therefore, restate the basic rule of English law with regard to foreign torts as requiring actionability as a tort according to English law, subject to the condition that civil liability in respect of the relevant claim exists as between the actual parties under the law of the foreign country where the act was done."

However, two judges took a different view. Lord Pearson said of *Machado* v. *Fontes*:

"In my opinion, this decision involved a correct interpretation of the Willes formula. The cause of action for the libel was determined by English law, but the defendant would have a defence if he could show that the act complained of was 'justifiable' by the law of the place in which it was committed. It would not be 'justifiable' by that

---

[57] *Cheshire*, 7th ed., 1965, 247-248. See also *Cheshire & North*, 10th ed., 1979, 269; Karsten, *Chaplin* v. *Boys: Another Analysis*, 19 Int. & Comp. L.Q. 35, at 44 (1970). See, however, Crawford, *The "Proper" Law of Delict (A Comment on Boys* v. *Chaplin)*, 85 S.A.L.J. 314, at 317 (1968): "If justice is denied by the *lex loci delicti commissi*, is it unjust that it should be granted under the *lex fori*".

[58] Gutteridge, *A New Approach to Private International Law*, 6 Camb. L.J. 16, at 20 (1936).

[59] Smith, *supra*, at 576. See also Willis, 14 Can. Bar Rev. 1, at 20 (1936), who argues that the defendant "cannot complain if, when he has done something wrong in Brazil, he finds that he must pay for it in England not with incarceration but in cash".

[60] [1971] A.C. 356, analysed by North & Webb, 19 Int. & Comp. L.Q. 24 (1970), Karsten, 19 Int. & Comp. L.Q. 35 (1970).

[61] Not necessarily in tort: liability in contract or quasi-contract, for example, would also appear to suffice.

[62] See further North & Webb, *The Effect of Chaplin* v. *Boys I*, 19 Int. & Comp. L.Q. 24 (1970). English and Scottish Law Commissions' Working Paper No. 87 and Consultative Memorandum No. 62, *supra*, para. 217. See also *Cheshire & North*. 270.

law, if it was a crime by that law. A criminal act would be even less justifiable than a tortious act. There may be an objection to the decision on a different ground, namely, that it may have been permitting a person whose natural forum was a Brazilian court to gain advantages by by-passing his natural forum and suing in the English court ..."

Similarly, Lord Donovan considered that the rule should stay, but that the court should be conscious of the need to reject a case, on the ground of public policy, where there was blatant "forum shopping".

The effect of the "proper law of tort" approach

We must now consider the extent to which the "proper law of tort" approach may have modified the rule in *Phillips* v. *Eyre*. As we have seen,[63] this approach was adopted by the *Restatement Second on Conflict of Laws*. Moreover, in the important decision of *Babcock* v. *Jackson*,[64] the New York Court of Appeals embraced an eclectic approach which included some elements of the proper law approach.[65] Fuld, J. said:

"The 'center of gravity' or 'grouping of contacts' doctrine adopted by this court in conflicts cases involving contracts impresses us as likewise affording the appropriate approach for accommodating the competing interests in tort cases with multi-state contacts. Justice, fairness and 'the best practical result'[66] may best be achieved by giving controlling effect to the law of the jurisdiction which, because of its relationship or contact with the occurrence or the parties, has the greatest concern with the specific issue raised in the litigation. The merit of such a rule is that 'it gives to the place "having the most interest in the problem" paramount control over the legal issues arising out of a particular factual context'[67] and thereby allows the forum to apply "the policy of the jurisdiction most intimately concerned with the outcome of [the] particular litigation."

In *Boys* v. *Chaplin*,[68] the House of Lords considered the doctrine of the proper law of tort, and the *Babcock* decision. The House divided on the question whether the proper law of tort should be accepted into English law. Clearly in favour were Lords Hodson and Wilberforce; clearly against, Lords Guest and Donovan. In the middle was Lord Pearson, whose "diffident language[69] hardly closes the door on the proper law of tort doctrine ..."[70]

Boys v. *Chaplin* left English law in a relatively uncertain state. Some aspects are, however, clear. The first limb of *Phillips* v. *Eyre* remains intact. The second limb also remains, with the words "not justifiable" being interpreted as referring to *civil*

---

[63] *Supra*, p. 569.
[64] 12 N.Y. 2d 473 240 N.Y.S. 2d 743, 191 N.E. 2d 279 (1963), analysed by Cavers, 63 Colum. L. Rev. 1219 (1963), Cheatham, *id.*, at 1229, Currie, *id.*, at 1233, Ehrenzweig, *id.*, at 1243, Leflar, *id.*, at 1247, and Reese, *id.*, at 1251; also by Morris, *The Proper Law of the Tort Again*, 79 L.Q. Rev. 484 (1963), Webb, *Conflict in Conflicts — Vested Rights versus Proper Law: An English Don Reads Babcock*, 9 Villanova L. Rev. 193 (1964). See also Terzian, *The Aftermath of Babcock*, 54 Calif. L. Rev. 1301 (1966).
[65] Cf. Morris, *supra*, at 484: "The Court ... did not actually use the expression 'proper law of the tort' ... but it is quite obvious that this was the theory they had in mind".
[66] Citing *Swift &Co.* v. *Bankers Trust Co.*, 280 N.Y. 135, at 141, 19 N.E. 2d 992, at 995.
[67] Citing *Auten* v. *Auten*, 308 N.Y. 155, at 161, 124 N.E. 2d 99, at 102.
[68] [1971] A.C. 356.
[69] "The new American flexible rule or flexible approach, with its full degree of flexibility, seems — at present at any rate, when the doctrine is of recent origin and further development may be expected — to be lacking in certainty and likely to create or prolong litigation. Nevertheless, it may help the English courts to deal with the danger of 'forum shopping' which is inherent in the English rule": [1971] A.C., at 405.
[70] *Morris*, 314. But see North & Webb, *The Effect of Chaplin* v. *Boys — 2*, 19 Int. & Comp. L.Q. 24, at 25 (1970).

liability (whether tortious, contractual, quasi-contractual or otherwise) rather than to criminal liability. However, the rule in *Phillips* v. *Eyre,* as Willes, J. himself accepted, applies only "as a general rule".[71] In *Boys* v. *Chaplin*[72] Lord Hodson noted that Willes, J. had not said "invariably"; and Lord Wilberforce considered that "[t]he general rule must apply unless clear and satisfying grounds are shown why it should be departed from and what solution, derived from what other rule, should be preferred".[73]

The Irish Revolution

We must now consider what may be described as the "Irish revolution" in choice of law for torts.[74] The dust has yet to settle, and indeed it may properly be said that the battle is not yet over in that only the shadow of the new regime is as yet apparent. But it seems safe to claim that the rule in *Phillips* v. *Eyre* has been routed and that a radically more flexible approach has been preferred.

The cause of this fundamental change is the recent Supreme Court decision of *Grehan* v. *Medical Incorporated and Valley Pines Associates.*[75] The case, as we have seen,[76] was concerned with the question of *locus delicti* in the context of service *ex juris.* As we have also noted, the Supreme Court adopted a flexible approach whereby the court *may* permit service out of the jurisdiction if "*any* significant element has occurred within the jurisdiction"[77] but in deciding whether to do so the court should be under "a heavy burden ... to examine the circumstances of each case ..."[78] The task of the Court was said by Walsh, J. to be:

> "to interpret and to apply the rule in a way designed to ensure that justice and practical common sense prevail. The Court therefore should interpret the rule in the light of a broad policy and in the light of its choice of law implications. If more than one possible interpretation of the rule is available the one which serves to encourage the operation of sensible choice of law rules should be followed rather than one which would tend to frustrate them."[79]

It seems fair to comment that, although these remarks relate to the jurisdictional issue, they strongly suggest that our choice of law rules should themselves be flexibly defined, sensitive to the requirements of the case before the court. It would of course be *possible* to retain the crude mechanisms of the rule in *Phillips* v. *Eyre*; to do so would not *contravene* the broader discretionary approach adopted by the Supreme Court for the purposes of jurisdiction. But it would involve a curious dissonance between jurisdiction and choice of law from which no clear benefits would follow.

Walsh, J. went on to consider, *obiter,* the question of choice of law. He noted that there did not appear to be any reported Irish decision which comprehensively addressed the choice of law issues on tort. He went on to discuss the rule in *Phillips* v. *Eyre* which, he observed, "might appear to have some superficial attractions".[80] In his view the first limb of the rule was:

---

[71] *Phillips* v. *Eyre,* L.R. 6 Q.B. at 28 (1870).

[72] [1971] A.C., at 378.

[73] *Id.,* at 391.

[74] See *Morris,* 316. See also Gill, *The Locus Delicti and Choice of Law in Tort in Irish Private International Law,* 5 I.L.T. (n.s.) 3, at 7 (1987), who says of the recent Supreme Court decision in *Grehan* (discussed immediately hereunder) that, "[i]n terms of its significance, [it] may well be the Irish *Babcock* v. *Jackson*".

[75] [1986] I.L.R.M. 627 (Sup. Ct.).

[76] *Supra,* pp. 151-153.

[77] [1986] I.L.R.M., at 638.

[78] *Id.*

[79] [1986] I.L.R.M., at 637.

[80] *Id.*

"not acceptable notwithstanding the support it received in the British House of Lords in *Chaplin* v. *Boys* because it would close the door of the Court to every action in tort not recognised by Irish law and would require the application of Irish law even though the case had no connection at all with Ireland except that the defendant perhaps took refuge there after the tort was committed. Furthermore it would place the victim of a foreign tort in a far worse position than the victim of a breach of contract governed by foreign law."[81]

So far as the second part of the rule is concerned, Walsh, J. observed that the use of the words "not justifiable" by Willes, J. in *Phillips* v. *Eyre* had been "found to be unsatisfactory because of the ambiguity of the term. In other jurisdictions this branch of the rule has given to difficulties and to some controversial decisions".[82]
Walsh, J. went on:

"The rule in *Phillips* v. *Eyre* has nothing to recommend it because it is capable of producing quite arbitrary decisions and it is a mixture of parochialism and a vehicle for being, in some cases, unduly generous to the plaintiff and, in others, unduly harsh.

In my view, the Irish courts should be sufficiently flexible to be capable of responding to the individual issues presented in each case and to the social and economic dimensions of applying any particular choice of law rule in the proceedings in question."[83]

A brief comment on this short, but vital, passage is in order. There is surely no continuing life in a rule stigmatised by our Supreme Court as having "nothing to recommend it". If *Phillips* v. *Eyre* is dead, what is to replace it? Although Walsh, J. provides no concluded answer to this question, he gives a reasonably clear outline of what this approach should involve. The courts should adopt a "flexible" attitude, responding to "the individual issues": thus, there is no need to select the same choice of law rule to cover all torts[84] or, to resolve the questions of contributory negligence and vicarious liability, for example.[85] Moreover, the courts should have regard to "the social and economic dimensions of applying any particular choice of law in the proceedings in question". This gives the courts a very broad obligation and entitlement to make the choice of law rules responsive to the social and economic environment. If this is not the "proper law" approach, it is as close as makes no difference.

In a stimulating analysis[86] of *Grehan,* Mr. A.V. Gill expresses the view that such a radical departure from current orthodoxies would be "much ... welcomed". But he counsels caution in adopting this interpretation of Walsh, J.'s remarks, in the absence of any formulation by Walsh, J. of a specific alternative choice of law rule to replace that of *Phillips* v. *Eyre.* Moreover, Mr. Gill discerns in two observations of Walsh, J., elsewhere in his judgment, an indication that Walsh, J. continued to understand that a successful Order 11 application would lead to the use of Irish law to determine the substantive issues.

These words of caution are undoubtedly sensible, but they would scarcely give the supporters of the rule in *Phillips* v. *Eyre* much comfort. The central issue in *Grehan* related to jurisdiction rather than choice of law; having indicated his profound disillusion with the rule in *Phillips* v. *Eyre,* it seems that Walsh, J. thought it wise to spell out clearly the new *philosophy* for choice of law, leaving its *specific application* to later decisions. The essence of the "proper law of the tort" is that it is an approach

---

[81] [1986] I.L.R.M., at 637-638.
[82] *Id.,* at 638.
[83] *Id.*
[84] Cf. Lown, *A Proper Law of Torts in the Conflict of Laws,* 12 Alta L. Rev. 101, at 127 (1974).
[85] Cf. Morris, *The Proper Law of a Tort,* 64 Harv. L. Rev. 881, at 892 (1951).
[86] Gill, *supra,* at 7.

rather than a rule or series of rules. It can therefore be argued that Walsh, J. did indeed provide the structure of the new choice of law rule.

As regards Walsh, J.'s observations[87] to which Mr. Gill refers, it must be said that neither of them points unambiguously in the direction of Irish law. In the face of Walsh, J.'s rejection of the rule in *Phillips* v. *Eyre,* expressed in the most unambiguous terms, it would be a bold lawyer who would argue that these observations have any effect in modifying the proposed new approach.

Maritime Torts[88]

Let us examine the conflict of laws aspects of maritime torts. The subject is a complex one, on which there is a dearth of Irish authority. Very briefly the main features of the law are as follows.

Where a tort is committed on the high seas, and is confined to one ship, the law of the flag controls. Collisions between ships appear to be subject to Irish law. The position in relation to other torts involving more than one vessel is less certain.

Where torts are not confined to one ship and they take place in foreign waters, the law of the flag of the ships is irrelevant. For the purposes of the second limb of the rule in *Phillips* v. *Eyre* the *lex loci delicti* is that of the littoral state.[89]

There appears to be no Irish or English authority on the position where the torts are confined to one ship, and take place in foreign waters. It appears that the competition for the title of *lex loci delicti* is between the law of the ships' flag and the law of the littoral state. The English and Scottish Law Commissions consider that the latter, "however unattractive, would appear to be more consistent with the general rule".[90] A Scottish decision[91] supports this approach.

A question of jurisdiction rather than of choice of law arose in *O'Daly* v. *Gulf Oil Terminals (Ireland) Ltd.*[92] In this case, a vessel owned by a French company had exploded when at Whiddy Island. Thirty-seven people died, including the entire crew. In proceedings taken in Ireland by the widow and administrator of a deceased

---

[87] In one of these observations Walsh, J. merely articulates an argument, which he nowhere expressly endorses, and which clearly he does not accept without qualification: "It can be argued that the State in which the injury occurs has a legitimate interest in the application *of its laws* to the victim of the tort..." ([1986] I.L.R.M., at 635; Mr. Gill's emphasis). Of course, even if one accepts the force of the argument, this is entirely consistent with a "proper law" approach. It does not commit the court to apply the law of the place of injury in every case, but rather to give appropriate weight to the interest of that State in having its laws applied. Nor, of course, does it commit the court to apply Irish law. Furthermore, the context of this observation is very much one relating to jurisdiction rather than choice of law. This suggests that the reference to the "laws" of the State of injury embraces its choice of law rules rather than merely the internal law of that State. The other observation mentioned by Mr. Gill presents somewhat more difficulty. Walsh, J. refers to the fact that the plaintiff, who might well have instituted his proceedings in the United States, where the law on products liability would be much more favourable to him, had instead "chosen to have *Irish law* applied in Ireland where he resides..." ([1986] I.L.R.M. at 639; Mr. Gill's emphasis). This *could* mean the Irish internal law (of torts); but in the sentences surrounding this statement, Walsh, J. was clearly addressing the issue of jurisdiction rather than choice of law. It can be argued, therefore, that the reference to "Irish law" includes the choice of law rules of the Irish conflict of laws. In view of what he had to say on the subject of these rules, it seems clear that Walsh, J. was opposed to the automatic application of the Irish internal law, once jurisdiction had been established.

[88] See Winter, *Note: Maritime Torts; The Choice of Law Principles,* 3 Int. & Comp. L.Q. 115 (1954), *Rabel,* vol. 2, Ch. 27.

[89] *The Halley,* L.R. 2 P.C. 193 (P.C. 1868), *The M. Moxham,* 1 P.D. 107 (C.A., 1876), *Carr* v. *Fracis Times & Co.,* [1902] A.C. 176, *The Arum,* [1921] P. 12, *The Waziristan,* [1953] 1 W.L.R. 1446. See further the English Law Commission Working Paper No. 87 and Scottish Law Commission Consultative Memorandum No. 62, *op. cit.,* para. 2.111.

[90] *Op. cit.,* para. 2.112.

[91] *MacKinnon* v. *Iberia Shipping Co. Ltd.,* 1955 S.C. 20.

[92] [1983] I.L.R.M. 163 (High Ct., Barrington, J., 1982).

crew member, the French company contended that the Irish courts had no jurisdiction to try the case on the ground (*inter alia*) that the vessel was a French registered ship which was French territory governed by French law.

Barrington, J. rejected this argument. The French company's task, he noted, was "to show that the fact that a private ship is registered in France and flies the French flag ousts the jurisdiction of the littoral State in whose waters the ship happens to be".[93] But this theory had been "decisively rejected"[94] by the Privy Council, even in the case of a foreign warship, in *Chung Chi Cheung* v. *R.*[95] Lord Atkin, for the Judicial Committee, had said:

> "However the doctrine of extraterritoriality is expressed, it is a fiction, and legal fictions have a tendency to pass beyond their appointed bounds and to harden into dangerous facts. The truth is that the enunciators of the floating island theory have failed to face very obvious possibilities that make the doctrine quite impracticable when tested by the actualities of life on board ship and ashore."[96]

Thus, for example, where a resident of the receiving State committed a crime while on a visit to a ship, and was later arrested on shore, it would be inconceivable that the local courts would be denied jurisdiction. Yet on the "floating island" theory, the crime would have been committed on a portion of foreign territory; " [t]he local court then has no jurisdiction, and this fiction dismisses the offender untried and untriable. For it is a commonplace that a foreign country cannot give territorial jurisdiction by consent."[97]

Barrington, J. said:

> "Lord Atkin was, of course, speaking of a public ship and of the criminal law. I am dealing with a private ship and the law of tort. But the argument in favour of subjecting a private ship to the civil law of the littoral State would appear to be equally strong."[98]

Thus, even if the events of Whiddy could properly be regarded as a tort or civil wrong confined to the vessel, Barrington, J. still regarded the Irish courts as having jurisdiction.

While the case clearly resolved the jurisdictional issue, the question of choice of law, which did not arise for determination in the proceedings, was left in a somewhat uncertain state. Barrington, J. made some observations which appear consistent only with the view that Irish law would play the dominant, if not decisive, role. On conventional choice of law rules, this would be unexceptionable. In the light of the Supreme Court's decision in *Grehan,* and the facts in *O'Daly* v. *Gulf Oil,* no such assumption can automatically be made.

Contributory Negligence[99]

We now must consider the defence of contributory negligence in tort actions. The

[93] [1983] I.L.R.M., at 165.

[94] *Id.*

[95] [1939] A.C. 160 (P.C., 1938).

[96] *Id.,* at 174.

[97] *Id.*

[98] [1983] I.L.R.M., at 366.

[99] See Brownlie & Webb, *Contributory Negligence and the Rule in Phillips* v. *Eyre,* 40 Can. Bar Rev. 79 (1962), North, *Contributory Negligence and the Conflict of Laws,* 16 Int. & Comp. L.Q. 379 (1967), Williams, *Joint Torts and Contributory Negligence,* 339-340 (1951), Morgan, *Choice of Law Governing Proof,* 58 Harv. L. Rev. 153, at 180-191 (1944), Swan, *Tort Liability in the Conflict of Laws: The Case for and an Outline of a New Approach,* 3 U. Br. Colum. L. Rev. 185 (1967), Gerber, *Tort Liability in the Conflict of Laws,* 40 Austr. L.J. 44, 73 (1966), Webb, *Note: Conflict of Laws — Contributory Negligence and the Rule in The Halley,* 44 Can. Bar Rev. 666 (1966), English Law Commission W.P. No. 87 and Scottish Law Commission Consultative Memorandum No. 62, *Private International Law: Choice of Law in Tort and Delicti,* paras. 2.55, 6.15 (1984), Schwartz, ch. 15.

implications for conflicts of law have yet to be fully worked out. The central notion of contributory negligence is that the plaintiff contributed, in part or in full, to his injury or damage by his own negligence or lack of care. Formerly, in Irish law, contributory negligence afforded an absolute defence, regardless of whether the defendant's fault was more serious than that of the plaintiff's.[100]

The Civil Liability Act 1961 has replaced this "all-or-nothing" approach by a system of apportionment of damages. A plaintiff guilty of contributory negligence will have the amount of damages awarded reduced having regard to the respective degrees of fault of the plaintiff and defendant.[101] Fault "is equated to blameworthiness and not to the potency of the causative factors moving from each side".[102]

The general trend in common law countries has been similar to that in Ireland, but important distinctions can arise. Some jurisdictions in the United States have devised modifications to simple apportionment;[103] in a number of countries the courts do indeed have regard to "the potency of the causative factors".[104] The "last clear chance" doctrine, abolished in Ireland in 1961, still has some (albeit fading) vitality in some other countries.[105]

From the standpoint of conflicts of law, these differences can create troublesome problems, which the rule in *Phillips* v. *Eyre* is singularly ill-equipped to handle. The notions of "actionability" and "justifiability" do not easily absorb the concept of comparative degrees of negligence. Nor do they offer clear solutions where contributory negligence continues to afford an absolute defence. There is a danger here of resorting to a semantic solution. It can, for example, be argued that a defendant's admitted negligence is "actionable" even though the particular plaintiff's contributory negligence disentitles him to sue.[106] On the other hand it could be said that, in view of this disentitlement, that which would have been actionable is not so in the particular circumstances.[107] The same difference of views affect the concept of "justifiability".

The important issue of policy, as opposed to semantics, is whether the approach in our domestic law to the defence of contributory negligence should colour the outcome of a foreign case. It may be argued that, if the proper law of the tort is to govern liability, the question of contributory negligence should be determined exclusively by that law. But, as against this, *Grehan* clearly suggests that the proper law approach should respond to individual issues, which could result in the application of a different law to the question of contributory negligence from that applied to the question of the defendant's liability. The issue of denying compensation to careless victims of wrongful conduct is an important one: indeed it may be speculated whether the complete denial of compensation to a plaintiff guilty of contributory negligence, however slight, is so stark and crude a response as to offend against our public policy.

---

[100] Cf. *McMahon & Binchy*, 211-212 (1981). The doctrine of the "last clear chance" mitigated the full force of this rule: *id.*, 212-213.

[101] Section 34(1).

[102] *Kelly* v. *Jameson*, unreported, Sup. Ct., 1 March 1972 (29-1970), *per* Walsh, J., at p. 4. See also *O'Sullivan* v. *Dwyer*, [1971] I.R. 275 (Sup. Ct.), *Carroll* v. *Clare Co. Co.*, [1975] I.R. 221 (Sup. Ct.). Cf. *Daly* v. *Avonmore Creameries, Ltd.*, [1984] I.R. 131, at 148-150 (Sup. Ct., *per* McCarthy, J.).

[103] *Prosser & Keeton*, 473-474.

[104] Cf. *Fleming*, 247 citing XI Int. Encycl. Comp. L. (Torts), ch. 7 s.175 (Honoré) (1973).

[105] Cf. *Fleming*, 250-252.

[106] Cf. *Anderson* v. *Eric Anderson Radio and T.V. Pty. Ltd.*, [1966] Argus L.R. 423, at 424-425 (H. Ct. Austr., *per* Barwick, C.J., 1965).

[107] Cf. *id.*, at 428 (*per* Kitto, J.).

PART VI

FOREIGN JUDGMENTS AND ARBITRATION

CHAPTER 33

RECOGNITION AND ENFORCEMENT OF FOREIGN JUDGMENTS[1] AND ARBITRATIONS

The fact that the world is divided into a number of territorial units having different legal systems gives rise to difficulties as regards enforcement or recognition of judgments. A plaintiff may obtain judgment in a particular country against a defendant but be unable to enforce his judgment against him in that country because the defendant is not resident there and has no assets there against which execution can be levied. The defendant may perhaps be living in Ireland, where he has some or all of his assets. The question will inevitably arise as to the circumstances in which the foreign judgment will be capable of recognition or enforcement here. In this chapter, we will examine the answer to that question.

Enforcement Distinguished from Recognition

A distinction must be drawn at the outset between *enforcement* and *recognition* of a foreign judgment. Enforcement of a foreign judgment is premised on its recognition. On the other hand, a foreign judgment can be recognised without being enforced.

Thus, for example, an Irish court may well *recognise* a foreign divorce, in the sense that the change of the parties' status will be recognised, as well as certain legal *sequelae*, such as the loss of entitlements under the Succession Act 1965.[2] But an Irish court will not enforce the decree of divorce itself, or any part of the decree which cannot be severed from it — an order for costs, for example[3] — as that would be contrary to public policy, in view of the constitutional protection of the Family under Article 41, especially the provisions relating to divorce.[4]

Theoretical Basis for Enforcement and Recognition

What is the underlying principle upon which our courts will recognise and enforce

---

[1] See generally H. Read, *Recognition and Enforcement of Foreign Judgments in the Common Law Units of the British Commonwealth* (1938) F. Piggott, *Foreign Judgments and Jurisdiction* (3rd ed., 1908), Graupner, *Some Recent Aspects of the Recognition and Enforcement of Foreign Judgments in Western Europe,* 12 Int. & Comp. L.Q. 367 (1963), Yntema, *The Enforcement of Foreign Judgments in Anglo-American Law,* 33 Mich. L. Rev. 1129 (1935). Gill, *Jurisdiction and the Enforcement of Foreign Judgments in Ireland,* 4 J. of Irish Soc. for European L. 3, at 17-25 (1980), Exshaw, *The Enforcement of Foreign Judgments in Personam,* 30 Ir. Jur. 1 (1964), de Cock, *Effets et exécution des jugements étrangers,* [1925] — V Recueil des cours 431.

[2] See, e.g. *Re Caffin dec'd; Bank of Ireland Trustee Co.* v. *Caffin,* [1971] I.R. 123 (High Ct., Kenny, J.), *Gaffney* v. *Gaffney,* [1975] I.R. 133 (Sup. Ct.), *T.* v. *T.,* [1983] I.R. 29 (Sup. Ct. 1982, rev'g High Ct., D'Arcy, J., 1981).

[3] See, e.g., *Mayo-Perrott* v. *Mayo-Perrott,* [1958] I.R. 336 (Sup. Ct., 1958, aff'g High Ct., Murnaghan, J., 1955). Contrast *N.M.* v. *E.F.M.,* unreported, High Ct., Hamilton, J. July 1978 (1977-87EMO), *G.* v. *G.* [1984] I.R. 368 (High Ct., Finlay, P.), *Sachs* v. *Standard Chartered Bank (Ireland) Ltd.* as yet unreported, Sup. Ct., 18 July, 1986 (284-1985).

[4] Article 41.3.2° and 3°. See further, *supra,* pp. 271 ff.

the judgment of a foreign tribunal? It used to be considered that the principle was that of comity of courts,[5] whereby our courts would recognise a judgment given by a court of a foreign country if the courts of that country would recognise a judgment of our courts given upon a similar jurisdictional basis. At the base of this approach was the principle of reciprocity.[6] One inconvenient result of the application of this principle is that, if a court itself exercised jurisdiction on an exorbitant basis, it would be bound to recognise the judgments of foreign courts given upon similar exorbitant jurisdictional grounds.[7] Another difficulty is that the comity principle may suggest that the only defence available to a defendant in an action to enforce a foreign judgment is that the foreign court exercised jurisdiction on a basis to which there was no equivalent here. This makes it hard to provide a convincing rationale for the recognised exceptional cases where defences against enforcement of a foreign judgment can prevail.[8]

So the principle of comity was supplanted by the doctrine of obligation.[9] The basis of this approach is that where a Court of competent jurisdiction has adjudged a certain sum to be due from one person to another, a legal obligation arises to pay that sum on which an action of debt to enforce the judgment may be maintained.[10] The classic statement of this doctrine was given by Blackburn J. in *Schibsby* v. *Westenholz*:[11]

"The judgment of a court of competent jurisdiction over the defendant imposes a duty or obligation on him to pay the sum for which the judgment is given, which the courts in this country are bound to enforce."

In *Rainford* v. *Newell—Roberts*,[12] Davitt, P. referred to this passage with approval. In the President's view, the test to be applied was whether the defendant was "under any duty or obligation to comply with the judgment upon which th[e] action [was] brought".[13]

It is worth recalling at this point the debate[14] about the theory of "vested rights" in the development of thought on conflicts of law. This foreign "obligation" of which we now speak may look suspiciously like a vested right. As against this "the resolute

[5] Cf. *M'Donnell* v. *M'Donnell*, [1921] 2 I.R. 148, at 159 (K.B. Div., per Pim, J., dissenting, dissent not affecting this issue, 1920). See also *Dennis* v. *Leinster Paper Co.*, [1901] 2 I.R. 337, at 347 (C.A., *per* FitzGibbon, L.J.), *Geyer* v. *Aguilar*, 7 Term Rep. 681, at 695-696, 101 E.R. 1196, at 1204 (*per* Lord Kenyon, 1798), *Castrique* v. *Imrie*, L.R. 4 H.L. 414, at 439 (*per* Keating, J., 1870). See further *Read*, 52-58.

[6] Kennedy, *Recognition of Judgments in Personam. The Meaning of Reciprocity*, 35 Can. Bar Rev. 123 (1957), Kennedy, *"Reciprocity" in the Recognition of Foreign Judgments: The Implications of Travers* v. *Holley*. 32 Can. Bar Rev. 359 (1954); but cf. Kuhn, *Doctrine of Private International Law in England and American Contrasted with Those of Continental Europe*, 12 Colum. L. Rev. 44, at 47-48 (1912).

[7] But cf. *Gaffney* v. *Gaffney*, [1975] I.R. 133, at 155 (Sup. Ct., *per* Henchy, J.): "The comity of courts under private international law does not require or permit recognition of decisions given, intentionally or unintentionally, in disregard of jurisdictional competence."

[8] Cf. *Piggott*, vol. 1, p. 11, Yntema, *The Enforcement of Foreign Judgments in Anglo-American Law*, 33 Mich. L. Rev. 1129, at 1146 (1935).

[9] *Schibsby* v. *Westenholz*, L.R. 6 Q.B. 155 (1870), *Rainford* v. *Newell-Roberts*, [1962] I.R. 95 (High Ct., Davitt, P., 1961), *Livesley* v. *E. Clemens Horst Co.*, [1924] S.C.R. 605, at 610 (*per* Duff, J.).

[10] *Williams* v. *Jones*, 13 M. & W. 628 at 633, 153 E.R. 262, at 265 (*per* Parke, B., 1845); cited with approval in *M'Donnell* v. *M'Donnell*, [1921] I.R. 148 at 161 (K.B. Div., *per* Molony, C.J., 1920). See also *La Société Anonyme la Chemo-Sérothérapie Belge* v. *Dolan (Dominick A.) & Co. Ltd.*, [1961] I.R. 281, at 287 (High Ct., Teevan, J.). *Maguire* v. *Maguire*, 50 O.L.R. 100, at 103 (App. Div., *per* Middleton, J., 1921).

[11] L.R. 6 Q.B. 155, at 159 (1870).

[12] [1962] I.R. 95, at 104.

[13] *Id.* Davitt, P. also observed (*id.*) that, apart from any question of reciprocity, he was satisfied that "the principle of the comity of Courts is not the one to apply in this matter."

[14] Cf. *supra*, pp. 14-16.

unwillingness on the part of the courts to examine whether the foreign court exercised its jurisdiction properly",[15] the requirement that the foreign court should have had jurisidiction in accordance with Irish rather than foreign rules of conflicts of law and the opportunity for a defendant to avoid liability on grounds (such as fraud or public policy) referable to Irish conflicts of law make it less credible to assert that the Irish courts, in enforcing foreign judgments are merely giving effect to foreign vested rights.[16]

It is also worth noting that the idea of a foreign judgment being based on obligation was derived largely from cases involving actions for debt. It was relatively easy to regard the judgment debtor as owing an "obligation" to the judgement creditor.[17] However, this model is less convincing where the foreign judgment relates to matters of family life, such as divorce,[18] family maintenance[19] or child custody.[20]

Original Cause of Action Not Extinguished

In a domestic Irish case the doctrine of *res judicata* applies, so that, if a person once obtains judgment upon a particular cause of action, that cause of action is extinguished and he may not sue on it again. It is otherwise so far as foreign judgments are concerned.[21] The original cause of action does not merge in the judgment, so a person who has obtained a judgment abroad has a choice of either suing in Ireland on that judgment or suing here on the original cause of action.

This distinction between domestic and foreign judgments is anomalous, particularly in view of the requirement[22] that a foreign judgment must be final and conclusive before it may be enforced here. In *M'Donnell* v. *M'Donnell*[23] Gordon, J. cited with approval Lord Herschell's statement in *Nouvion* v. *Freeman*[24] that, to establish that such a foreign judgment has been pronounced:

"it must be shown that in the Court by which it was pronounced it conclusively, finally, and for ever established the existence of the debt of which it is sought to be made conclusive evidence in this country so as to make it *res judicata* between the parties."

It is scarcely logical[25] to take this approach to foreign judgments, while at the same time allowing the plaintiff to come before our courts and treat the cause of action as one that is not *res judicata* here.

[15] Blom, *The Enforcement of Foreign Judgments in Canada*, 57 Ore. L. Rev. 399, at 425 (1978). See however, *L.B.* v. *H.B.*, [1980] I.L.R.M. 257 (High Ct., Barrington, J.).
[16] Cf. *Dicey & Morris*, 1038, *McLeod*, 582, *Piggott*, vol. 1, pp. 12-13. See also Nussbaum, *Jurisdiction and Foreign Judgments*, 41 Colum. L. Rev. 221, at 235 (1941).
[17] Cf. *supra*, pp. 14-15.
[18] Cf. *supra*, ch. 12.
[19] Cf. Gutteridge, *The International Enforcement of Maintenance Orders*, 2 Int. L.Q. 155, at 156-157 (1948).
[20] Cf. *McLeod*, 582-583.
[21] *La Societé Anonyme la Chemo-Sérothérapie Belge* v. *Dolan (Dominick A.) & Co. Ltd.*, [1961] I.R. 281 (High Ct., Teevan, J., 1960), discussed *infra*, p. 604. See also *Maule* v. *Murray* 7 T.R. 470, 101 E.R. 1081 (1798); *Smith* v. *Nicolls*, 5 Bing. N.C. 208, 132 E.R. 1084 (1839); *Bank of Australasia* v. *Harding*, 9 C.B. 661, 137 E.R. 1052 (1850); *Carl Zeiss Stiftung* v. *Rayner & Keeler Ltd. (No. 2)*, [1967] 1 A.C. 853 (H.L. (Eng.), 1966); *Re Flynn (No. 2)* [1969] 2 Ch. 403 (Buckley, J.), *Edelstyn* v. *Coleman*, 72 I.L.T.R. 142, at 145 (High Ct., O'Byrne, J., 1938), referring to his earlier unreported decision in *Clarke* v. *Cassells Ltd.*, Cf. Gutteridge, *Reciprocity in Regard to Foreign Judgments* 13 Br. Yrbk. of Internat. L. 49, at 61 (1932).
[22] Cf. *infra*, pp. 601 ff.
[23] [1921] 2 I.R. 148, at 153 (K.B. Div., 1920).
[24] 15 A.C. 1, at 9 (1889).
[25] Cf. *Carl Zeiss Stiftung* v. *Rayner and Keeler, Ltd. (No. 2)*, [1967] 1 A.C. 853, at 966 (H.L. (Eng), *per* Lord Wilberforce, 1966).

In any event, it will normally be to the plaintiff's advantage to sue on the foreign judgment rather than on the original cause of action. In the first place this will save him from having to prove his case all over again, with the attendant delay and expense, not to mention the risk of losing. Secondly, the limitation period on the original cause of action may have expired, while that on the action on the foreign judgment has not. As against these considerations, the possibility of recovering an appreciably greater sum in damages in an action in Ireland[26] or of avoiding a partial defence might conceivably outweigh the disadvantages of a new trial in some cases.

Conditions for Recognition and Enforcement of Foreign Judgments

An order of a foreign Court will not be recognised and enforced automatically.[27] Certain conditions have to be fulfilled before a foreign judgment will be regarded by our courts as having created a duty or obligation with which the defendant is bound to comply.

The foreign court must have had "jurisdiction" under Irish conflicts rules

The first, and most fundamental, requirement for maintaining an action on a foreign judgment, *in personam* or *in rem*, is that the judgment must have resulted from an adjudication of a court of competent jurisdiction. This means that the foreign Court must have been a court of competent jurisdiction in relation to the particular defendant according to *Irish* conflicts of law rules, not simply according to the foreign court's own domestic or conflicts rules. A foreign court may have exercised jurisdiction on a basis which by its own law was perfectly valid but, if this basis is unacceptable under Irish conflict of law rules, the judgment will not be recognised or enforced here.

In *Dennis* v. *Leinster Paper Co.*,[28] FitzGibbon, L.J. expressed the position in surely too moderate terms, when he said that:

"no Court can confer jurisdiction on itself merely by deciding wrongly that it has it. The question whether the foreign Court had jursidicion must be decided by the Court in which the foreign judgment is sued upon. I test this question, in this instance, by putting a case. Suppose a small Republic passed an Act of Parliament in these terms − 'Be it enacted that the High Court of Monaco shall have jurisdiction to try and determine all causes of action arising anywhere throughout the world, between subjects of whatever states, provided that the alleged claims are assigned for a nominal consideration to a subject of this Republic, in order that he may sue thereon as attorney for the claimant − Court fees ten per cent on the amount recovered.' All that is necessary to say now is that, in my opinion, there is at least a reasonable prospect that it might be successfully argued in the Court of any foreign country, and certainly in any British Court, that such an enactment could not bind foreigners, and that the comity of nations, and of Courts, would not extend to estop a foreigner from showing, in his own country, that he had a defence upon the merits against a claim upon which a Monaco judgment had been recovered against him in default of appearance."

In the Irish decision of *Rainford* v. *Newell-Roberts*,[29] in 1961, the plaintiffs had obtained judgment in the English High Court on the basis of service out of the jurisdiction against the defendant, a British subject resident in Ireland, for payment of an amount found due on an account of dealings of a medical partnership in England

---

[26] Cf. *infra*, pp. 642-646.

[27] Cf. *Ex parte Fife Banking Co.; In re Little & Little*, 6 Ir. Eq. Rep. 197, at 202 (*per* Mr Commissioner Macan, Ct. of By., 1843): "I have no doubt that the decrees of the Superior Courts of this country are impeachable in this Court; *a multo fortiori*, the decree of a foreign country."

[28] [1901] 2 I.R. 337, at 347 (C.A., *per* Fitzgibbon, L.J.).

[29] [1962] I.R. 95 (High Ct., Davitt, P., 1961), analysed by Exshaw, *The Enforcement of a Foreign Judgment In Personam*, 30 Ir. Jur. 1 (1964).

of which the defendant had been a member. Davitt, P. held that the judgment could not be enforced here on the basis of the defendant's British nationality.[30] The fact that English rules of jurisdiction supported the granting of a judgment was irrelevant.

We must now consider, in turn, recognition and enforcement of judgments *in personam* and judgments *in rem*.

Judgments in personam[31]

We have seen that Irish courts exercise jurisdiction *in personam* based on the presence of the defendant within the jurisdiction,[32] his submission to the jurisdiction or the specific grounds set out in Order 11 of the Rules of the Superior Courts 1986.[33] When it comes to recognising and enforcing foreign *in personam* judgments, our rules, though reflecting much the same approach,[34] are by no means identical.

Let us examine the specific grounds of jurisdiction which our courts have accepted, in respect of the recognition and enforcement *in personam* judgments.

Residence or presence of the defendant

Traditionally the view has been taken that there is jurisdiction where at the date of commencement of the action the defendant was resident or present in the foreign country, so as to have the benefit, and be under the protection, of its laws.[35] No doubts arise in relation to residence, but the position as to mere *temporary presence* in the foreign country is not clear. Irish courts themselves exercise jurisdiction on the basis of mere temporary presence[36] and it might be expected that they would recognise jurisdiction exercised by a foreign court on a similar basis. However, jurisdiction based on mere fleeting presence is exhorbitant.[37] There is also the consideration that our own courts will temper the exhorbitant nature of the jurisdiction in appropriate cases by granting a stay on the ground of vexatiousness or *forum non conveniens*.[38] If our courts are going to recognise foreign judgments given on the basis of mere fleeting presence, how are they going to deal with situations where the foreign court was not the appropriate forum?

---

[30] It is true that Davitt, P. devoted much of his judgment to considering the question of *English* rules of enforcement of foreign judgments, coming to the conclusion (at 104) "with considerable diffidence" that Cheshire was right to reject nationality as a basis of enforcement of foreign judgments. Davitt J. considered this question in such detail, not because it was relevant to English law as the law of the court which granted the judgment sought to be enforced, but because of the light it would throw on Irish conflicts rules as to the enforcement of foreign judgments, wherever granted: cf. [1962] I.R., at 102.

[31] See generally Wortley, *The Enforcement of Claims in Personam in the Conflict of Laws*, Ius et Lex: Festgabe für Gutzwiller 347 (1959), Blom, *The Enforcement of Foreign Judgments in Canada*, 57 Ore. L. Rev. 399, at 409 ff (1978), Clarence Smith, *Personal Jurisdiction*, 2 Int. & Comp. L.Q. 510 (1953), Solomons, *Enforcement of Foreign Judgments: Jurisdiction of Foreign Court*, 25 Int. & Comp. L.Q. 665 (1976), Exshaw, *supra*.

[32] Cf. *supra*, pp. 124-126 where the question as to how short a stay here will ground jurisdiction is analysed.

[33] Cf. *supra*, pp. 132 ff.

[34] See *Rainford* v. *Newell-Roberts*, [1962] I.R. 95, at 100 (High Ct., Davitt, P., 1961), quoting with approval from *Cheshire*, 3rd ed., 1947, pp. 779-780; cf. *Cheshire & North*, 10th ed., 1979, pp. 633-634.

[35] *Rainford* v. *Nowell-Roberts*. [1962] I.R. 95 at 98 (High Ct., Davitt, P., 1961) citing *Dicey*, 1st ed., 1896, rule 80, p. 369. See now *Dicey & Morris* 10th ed., 1980, rule 181. See also the passage from *Cheshire* cited *supra*. And cf. *Edelstyn* v. *Coleman*, 72 I.L.T.R. 142 (High Ct., O'Byrne, J., 1938).

[36] See pp. 124-126, *supra*.

[37] Cf. Dodd, *Jurisdiction in Personal Actions*, 23 Ill L. Rev. 427, at 438 (1929). More generally, see Ehrenzweig, *The Transient Rule of Personal Jurisdiction: The "Power" Myth and Forum Conveniens*, 65 Yale L.J. 289 (1956).

[38] See *supra*, pp. 162 ff.

There is no Irish case where a foreign judgment has been recognised on the basis that the defendant was temporarily present within the foreign jurisdiction.[39] In the English case of *Carrick* v. *Hancock*[40] an English domiciliary appeared in a Swedish court in answer to a writ served on him while on a fleeting visit to Sweden. The English court enforced the judgment given against him by the Swedish court, notwithstanding that the defendant's presence in Sweden was only temporary. However, the case may perhaps be explained[41] on the basis that the defendant submitted to the jurisdiction of the Swedish court and it is not an unequivocal authority for the proposition that mere temporary presence in the foreign jurisdiction will suffice.

For practical purposes, it is only if residence embraces short-term residence that the question arises as to whether a presence within the foreign jurisdiction induced by fraud could afford sufficient grounds for recognition of a judgment based upon it. English decisions[42] suggest that fraud may be a ground for non-recognition. In the United States, the effect of *Restatement*[43] is that if, in the state where the judgment is made it is impeachable for fraud, it should also be impeachable in the state where recognition of the judgment is in question, but that otherwise the judgment should be recognised.

If the defendant is a company, what is the equivalent to residence (or presence) in the foreign jurisdiction? We have already seen[44] that the Irish courts themselves exercise jurisdiction over a company if the company is registered here or has established a place of business here. This jurisdiction stems from the provisions of the Companies Act 1963. At common law the Irish courts exercised jurisdiction over a foreign company if it was present here in the sense of carrying on business here. Similar principles still apply for the purpose of recognition and enforcement of foreign judgments: a company will be regarded as having been within the jurisdiction of a foreign court if it carried on business there so as to render itself amenable to that jurisdiction. In *Dennis* v. *Leinster Paper Co.*,[45] a case dealing with security for costs by a plaintiff seeking to enforce a New York judgment against a public company, the Court of Appeal evinced little enthusiasm for recognising the effectiveness of the judgment where it had been obtained against the managing director of the company who "happened to [be] travelling in New York".[46] Other strong grounds for opposing the enforcement of the judgment were also raised in this case, which, being concerned only with security for costs, did not attempt to determine the substantive question one way or the other. In *Littauer Glove Corporation* v. *F.W. Millington (1920) Ltd.*[47] a director of an English company, while on a visit to New York, was served with a summons against his company. The

---

[39] Gill, *Jurisdiction and the Enforcement of Foreign Judgments in Ireland*, 4 J. of Irish Soc. for European L. 3, at 19 (1980).

[40] 12 Times L.R. 59 Q.B. Div., (Lord Russell of Killowen, C.J., 1895). See also the Canadian decision of *Forbes* v. *Simmons*, 8 Alta. L.R. 87, 7 W.W.R. 97, 20 D.L.R. 100 (Alta. Sup. Ct., Trial Div., Simmons, J., 1914), where the Alberta Court recognised jurisdiction based on the casual presence of the defendant in British Columbia for the purpose of visiting his wife in hospital. Simmons J. said: "If the defendant could succeed on this ground, it would have the effect of curtailing in a considerable degree the well-established doctrine of the supremacy of a state within its own territory". See further *McLean*, 585, Blom, *The Enforcement of Foreign Judgments in Canada*, 57 Ore. L. Rev. 399, at 410-411 (1978).

[41] Cf. *Dicey & Morris*, 1053, *McLean*, 585-586.

[42] *Stein* v. *Valkenhuysen*, E.B. & E. 65, 120 E.R. 431 (1858) and *Watkins* v. *North American Lands, etc., Co.*, 20 Times L.R. 534 (H.L., Eng., 1904).

[43] Section 82, comment f. See further *Leflar* (Revised ed., 1959), 43-44, *Scoles & Hay*, 941-942.

[44] *Supra*, pp. 128-129.

[45] [1901] 2 I.R. 337 (C.A., aff'g K.B. Div., Kenny, J.).

[46] *Id.*, at 345 (*per* Lord Ashbourne, C.).

[47] 44 Times L.R. 746 (K.B. Div., Salter, J., 1928). Cf. *Dennis* v. *Leinster Paper Co.*, [1901] 2 I.R. 337 (C.A., aff'g K.B. Div., Kenny, J.).

company had no place of business in the United States but while in New York the director did occasionally use an office of a customer of his company's. Judgment in default of appearance was given by the New York court against the English company but the English Court declined to enforce the judgment, on the basis that the New York court lacked jurisdiction since the company was not carrying on business in New York. It was said that there must have been some carrying on of business at a definite, and, to some reasonable extent, permanent place[48] within the foreign country. It has also been decided that it is not sufficient if a company merely has an agent in a foreign country with authority to seek customers and elicit orders from them but not to make contracts on behalf of the company.[49]

Submission to the jurisdiction of the foreign court

The court of a foreign country has jurisdiction where a party has, by his own conduct, submitted to that jurisdiction.[50] Submission may occur in several ways.

(i) By appearing as plaintiff in the foreign action[51]

It would clearly be inequitable to allow a person who had himself invoked the jurisdiction of the foreign court by commencing an action as plaintiff or by making a counterclaim to turn around, if the case goes against him, and seek to gainsay that court's jurisdiction.

(ii) By voluntarily appearing to contest the foreign action on the merits[52]

If a defendant voluntarily appeared in the foreign action to contest the case on its merits, then he will clearly be held to have submitted to the foreign court's jurisdiction.[53] He opted to try to obtain a verdict in his own favour and, having essayed his chances in this way, cannot, when the verdict goes against him, deny that the foreign court had jurisdiction at all. This rule applies where the defendant appealed on the merits in the foreign jurisidction after having failed to appear in the hearing at first instance.[54] It also applies where he appeared to contest the jurisdiction but went on to argue the case on its merits.[55]

We must now consider the position where the defendant entered an appearance in the foreign court solely in order to contest the jurisdiction of the foreign court but without contesting the case on its merits. There are no Irish cases directly on this point and the English decisions[56] are unsatisfactory. We have already seen that, where an Irish court's own jurisdiction is concerned,[57] an appearance merely to

---

[48] 44 T.L.R. 746, at 747 (1928).

[49] *Dicey & Morris*, 1054, citing, *inter alia*, *Vogel* v. *Kohnstamm Ltd.*, [1973] Q.B. 133 (Q.B. Div., Ashworth, J., 1971).

[50] *Rainford* v. *Newell-Roberts*, [1962] I.R. 95 at 98, (High Ct., Davitt, P., 1961) and *International Alltex Corporation* v. *Lawler Creations Ltd.*, [1965] I.R. 264 at 268 (High Ct., Kenny, J.), both citing *Dicey*, 1st ed., 1896, p. 369, rule 80, para. 3. See now *Dicey & Morris* 10th ed., 1980, rule 181. See generally, Clarence Smith, *Personal Jurisdiction*, 2 Int. & Comp. L.Q. 510 (1953).

[51] *Rainford* v. *Newell-Roberts*, [1962] I.R. 95, at 98 (High Ct., Davitt, P., 1961) (quoting from *Dicey*), *International Alltex Corporation* v. *Lawler Creations Ltd.*, [1965] I.R. 264, at 268 (High Ct., Kenny, J.). See also *Schibsby* v. *Westenholz*, L.R. 6 Q.B. 155 at 161 (1870), *Burpee* v. *Burpee*, [1929] 3 D.L.R. 18 (B.C. Sup. Ct., McDonald, J.).

[52] *Rainford* v. *Newell-Roberts*, [1962] I.R. 95 at 98 (quoting from *Dicey*), *International Alltex Corporation* v. *Lawler Creations Ltd.*, [1965] I.R. 264 at 268.

[53] *Molony* v. *Gibbons*, 2 Camp. 502, 170 E.R. 1232 (1810); *Guiard* v. *De Clermont*, [1914] 3 K.B. 145 (Lawrence, J.).

[54] *S.A. Consortium General Textiles* v. *Sun and Sand Agencies Ltd.*, [1978] 3 Q.B. (C.A., 1967), *Guiard* v. *De Clermont*, [1914] 3 K.B. 145 (Lawrence, J.).

[55] *Boissière* v. *Brockner & Co.*, 6 Times L.R. 85 (Q.B. Div., Cave, J., 1889), *McFadden* v. *Colville, Ranching Co.* 8 W.W.R. 163 (1915), *Richardson* v. *Allen*, 28 D.L.R. 134 (1916).

[56] Prior to the statutory change brought about by section 33 of the Civil Jurisdiction and Judgments Act 1982: see *Collins*, 143-144.

[57] *Supra*, pp. 129-130.

contest the court's jurisdiction does not constitute a submission to that jurisdiction. It would be reasonable to assume that a similar rule should apply where an Irish court is asked to consider whether a defendant submitted to the jurisdiction of some foreign court. The English authorities tend the other way, however. In *Harris* v. *Taylor*[58] the defendant had been served in England out of the jurisdiction of an Isle of Man court in an action for damages for criminal conversation. A conditional appearance was entered on his behalf in the Isle of Man proceedings to have them set aside on the grounds that the Isle of Man Rules of Court did not allow service out of the jurisdiction, that no cause of action existed in the Isle of Man and that he was not domiciled in and had never been in the Isle of Man. The application to set aside was rejected and judgment was given against the defendant. This judgment was enforced in England, the Court of Appeal holding that the defendant had voluntarily submitted to the jurisdiction of the Manx court. Notwithstanding that the appearance entered had been conditional,[59] once the Manx court had decided that it had jurisdiction, the conditional appearance became unconditional and there was submission.

This decision has been strongly criticised.[60] It was distinguished on rather technical and artificial grounds in *Re Dulles' Settlement (No.2)*[61] which we have already considered in the context of jurisdiction.[62] It was, however, endorsed by the Court of Appeal in *Henry* v. *Geopresco International Ltd.*[63] The plaintiff in the case was resident in Alberta while the defendants were a limited company registered in Jersey and having their head office in London. The plaintiff had been employed by the defendants under contract made in Alberta which contained an arbitration clause. The plaintiff was summarily dismissed by the defendants. He successfully sued them in Alberta, having served them out of the jurisdiction; and he later sought enforcement of the judgment in England. The defendants argued that they had not submitted to the jurisdiction of the Alberta court on the merits of the dispute. They had moved to have service of the writ set aside because the affidavit grounding the application for leave to serve out of the jurisdiction had been defective and because Alberta was not the convenient forum. They had also sought a stay of proceedings on the basis of the arbitration clause. The English Court of Appeal held that the defendants had submitted to the jurisdiction of the Alberta court because they had appeared voluntarily before that court to invite it in its discretion not to exercise the jurisdiction which it undoubtedly had and which the defendants had not questioned. Roskill, L.J. said that the Court was

"not deciding that an appearance *solely* to protest against the jurisdiction is, without more, a voluntary submission. But we do think that the authorities compel this court to say that if such a protest takes the form of or is coupled with what in England would be conditional appearance and an application to set aside an order for service out of the jurisdiction and that application then fails, the entry of that conditional appearance

---

[58] [1915] 2 K.B. 580 (C.A.). See also *Kennedy* v. *Trites*, 10 W.W.R. 412 (B.C. Sup. Ct. Cham., McDonald, J., 1916).
[59] A conditional appearance was described by Bray, J. in the case as "a complete appearance to the action for all purposes subject only to the right reserved by the defendants to apply to set aside the writ or service"; 111 L.T. 564, at 568.
[60] See, e.g. *Cheshire & North*, 638-639.
[61] [1951] Ch. 842 (C.A.). Denning L.J.'s analysis (at 851) is worthy of particular attention. Denning L.J.'s comments in turn were criticised by Roskill L.J., in *Henry* v. *Geopresco International Ltd.*, [1976] Q.B. 726, for addressing an issue not before the Court in the *Dulles* case. But cf. Solomons, *Enforcement of Foreign Judgments: Jurisdiction of Foreign Court*, 25 Int. & Comp. L. Q. 665, at 670 (1976).
[62] *Supra*, p. 130.
[63] [1976] Q.B. 726 (C.A., 1975).

(which then becomes unconditional) is a voluntary submission to the jurisdiction of the foreign court.''[64]

This decision has been criticised because of the over-fine distinctions it draws between a conditional appearance solely to contest the existence of jurisdiction and protesting against the exercise of jurisdiction on a discretionary basis.[65] It is submitted that if a case on this subject were to come before an Irish court, neither *Harris* v. *Taylor*[66] nor *Geopresco* should be followed and that instead submission to the jurisdiction of a foreign court should be held not to have taken place where there was an appearance solely for the purpose of contesting a matter going to the jurisdiction of the foreign court.

This approach may suggest that the defendant is being permitted to impose restrictions on the foreign court's jurisdiction by being entitled to "pick and choose".[67] But on reflection it may be seen that it does not involve any such thing. All that it does is ensure that a defendant so acting will be protected by our conflicts rules, regardless of his fate in the foreign proceedings.

We must now consider the position where the defendant entered an appearance in the foreign court solely in order to protect property of his that was seized or threatened with seizure in the proceedings. Since he could scarcely have completely ignored the proceedings and done nothing, the question arises as to whether his participation designed solely to protect the property may be said to be "voluntary" in any real sense. Fine distinctions have been drawn here too in the English cases:

> "An appearance is voluntary unless it is caused by the fact that property has been already seized by the foreign tribunal, for every appearance which is not made under pressure is a voluntary appearance ... The mere fear that things which may be afterwards carried into the foreign country will be seized is not pressure which will prevent an appearance from being voluntary."[68]

It can be argued that there is no great difference in principle between the two types of case here distinguished. An appearance whose object is to protect property which is about to be subjected to seizure is surely no more voluntary than one to protect property that has already been seized in fact.

A foreign judgment given in default of appearance by the defendant does not count as submission for the purposes of recognition or enforcement. If judgment was given against the defendant in default of appearance but he subsequently moved to have the default judgment set aside, the question of enforcement here depends on whether the application to set the judgment aside was based on jurisdictional grounds only. If this is so, there will have been no submission.[69] If, however, the motion to set aside was based on the merits of the case or a combination of want of jurisdiction and the merits, then there will have been submission.[70]

Let us try to summarise the position from the point of view of a defendant who

---

[64] *Id.*, at 748.
[65] See *Cheshire & North*, 640, Collins, *Harris* v. *Taylor Revived*, 92 L.Q. Rev. 268, at 285-287 (1976); but see Collier, *Casenote*, [1975] Camb. L.J. 219, at 222, and cf. Solomon's attempted reconciliation of the cases: *Enforcement of Foreign Judgments: Jurisdiction of Foreign Court*, 25 Int. & Comp. L.Q. 665, at 673-674 (1976).
[66] *Supra.*
[67] Cf. Carter, 47 Br. Yrbk. of Internat. L. 379, at 379 (1975).
[68] *Voinet* v. *Barrett*, 55 L.J.Q.B. 39, at 41 (1885). See also *De Cosse Brissac* v. *Rathbone* 6 H. & N. 301, 158 E.R. 123 (1861), *Guiard* v. *De Clermont* [1914] 3 K.B. 145 (Lawrence, J.), *Henry* v. *Geopresco International Ltd.*, [1976] Q.B. 726, at 746-747; *Richardson* v. *Allen*, 28 D.L.R. 134 at 144-145 (Alta. Sup. Ct., App. Div., *per* Beck, J., 1916).
[69] *S.A. Consortium General Textiles* v. *Sun & Sand Agencies Ltd.* [1978] Q.B. 279, at 305, 308-309.
[70] *Id.* (C.A., 1967); *Guiard* v. *De Clermont* [1914] 3 K.B. 145 (Lawrence, J.).

has assets in Ireland and who is faced with proceedings in a foreign court which has no jurisdiction over him in an international sense. If he has no assets in the foreign country and is not likely to have assets there in the future, his best course probably is to ignore the foreign proceedings altogether.[71] It that way, his Irish assets will not be in danger because the foreign judgment will not be enforceable here. If he has assets in the foreign jurisdiction concerned as well, then he has to weigh the advantage of ignoring the proceedings altogether, thereby rendering his Irish assets secure, against the disadvantage of running the risk that his foreign assets will be forefeited if the judgment of the foreign court goes against him by default. In weighing this question he will have to bear in mind that even if he appears in the foreign proccedings judgment may still go against him and the result will then be that both sets of assets will be made available for satisfaction of the judgment. This result will follow even if the appearance is only a conditional one. The only circumstance in which a defendant would seem reasonably safe in entering an appearance in the foreign court is where he does so solely in order to protect property of his which has already been seized by the foreign court.

(iii) By having contracted to submit to the jurisdiction of the foreign court[72]

We have already seen[73] that it is common practice in international commercial contracts for the parties to agree that any dispute arising out of the contract is to be litigated before the courts of a particular country or be submitted to arbitration. Where the defendant in a foreign action contracted beforehand that any dispute should be litigated in the courts of the country concerned, and enforcement of the judgment on that action is sought here, he will be held to have submitted to the jurisdiction of the foreign court.

In *International Alltex Corporation* v. *Lawler Creations Ltd.*[74] the plaintiffs, who were incorporated in the State of New York, entered into contracts in Ireland with the defendants, a company registered in Ireland, for the sale of certain cotton goods. The contracts provided for the settlement of disputes by arbitration in New York. When a dispute arose, the plaintiffs took arbitration proceedings in New York; an award made in their favour was later confirmed by an order of the Supreme Court of the State of New York which directed that judgment be entered in favour of the plaintiffs for the amount awarded by the arbitrator. The defendants did not appear in either the arbitration proceedings or the court proceedings in New York though they had received notice of them. The plaintiffs sought enforcement of the New York Supreme Court's judgment in the Irish High Court. Kenny, J. held that the judgment was a confirmation of the award made by the arbitrator and was for the amount awarded by the arbitrator because the award was valid. He held further that, when the defendants submitted to the jurisdiction of the arbitrator in New York, they necessarily submitted to a court order confirming the award of the arbitrator and were bound by a judgment of the court made to confirm and enforce the award.[75]

One matter that has given rise to some controversy is whether the agreement to submit to the foreign jurisdiction must be express or whether an implied submission is sufficient. Part of the difficulty results from some uncertainty of terminology. It is clear that the agreement to submit need not necessarily have been expressed in

---

[71] See Collins, *Harris* v. *Taylor Revived*, 92 L.Q.R. 268, at 287 (1976), Collier, *Casenote*, [1975] Camb. L.J. 219, at 219-220. More generally, see Gill, *Jurisdiction and the Enforcement of Foreign Judgments in Ireland*, 4 J. of Irish Soc. for European L. 3, at 20-22 (1980).

[72] *Rainford* v. *Newell-Roberts* [1962] I.R. 95 at 98 (High Ct., Davitt, P., 1961) (quoting from *Dicey*); *International Alltex Corporation* v. *Lawler* [1965] I.R. 264, at 268 (High Ct., Kenny, J.).

[73] *Supra*, p. 131.

[74] [1965] I.R. 264 (High Ct., Kenny, J.).

[75] *Id.*, at 269-270. See also *Canadian Imperial Bank of Commerce* v. *Kabat*, [1985] N.W.T.R.I. (Sup. Ct., Marshall, J., 1984).

so many words by the defendant: it may have been a tacit agreement arising by clear inference from the conduct of the parties.[76]

In such a case, though the defendant may not have himself said in so many words that he agreed to submit to the jurisdiction, the agreement is "express" as arising by clear inference from his conduct. But will a submission to the jurisdiction of a foreign court be implied where there are no statutes or articles of a company providing for submission but where the defendant has simply entered into, say, a partnership in a foreign country? There is a conflict among the English authorities on this matter. In some cases[77] it has been held that submission will be inferred in these circumstances while in others it has been said or held that it will not.[78] The latter view is preferable because the "assertion that a defendant had submitted by implication to the jurisdiction of a foreign court is all too easily made" and "is clearly open to grae abuse".[79] There is no clear Irish resolution of the matter but such authority as there is seems to be against the concept of implied submission. In *Edelstyn* v. *Coleman*[80] O'Byrne, J.[81] appears to have rejected the argument that the fact that the defendant entered into a contract in a foreign jurisdiction was a submission to that jurisdiction. The brief report of the case makes it difficult, however, to draw any strong conclusions on this question.

It would seem that an agreement to make the law of a particular foreign country the proper law of a contract does not constitute a agreement to submit to the jurisdiction of that court.[82]

Insufficient bases of jurisdiction

We must now consider some grounds which do not afford sufficient bases of jurisdiction for the purposes of recognition and enforcement.

(i) Nationality or allegiance of the defendant

In *Rainford* v. *Newell—Roberts*,[83] in 1961, Davitt P. decided that, under Irish conflicts rules as to enforcement, a foreign court does not have jurisdiction merely because the defendant at the time of the judgment in the action was a subject or national of the foreign country in question. Davitt, P. reviewed a number of English *dicta*[84] to the effect that a foreign court would have jurisdiction in such a case, a

---

[76] Cf. *Copin* v. *Adamson*, L.R. 1 Ex. D. 17 (1875).

[77] *Blohn* v. *Desser*, [1962] 2 Q.B. 116, (Diplock, J., 1916) noted by Lewis, 10 Int. & Comp. L.Q. 910 (1961), Cohn, 11 Int. & Comp. L.Q. 583 (1962), Abel, *id.*, 587, Carter, 38 Br. Yrbk. of Internat. L. 493 (1962), *Sfeir & Co.* v. *National Insurance Co. of New Zealand Ltd.*, [1964] 1 Lloyd's Rep. 330 (Mocatta, J.).

[78] *Sirder Gurdyal Singh* v. *Rajah of Faridkote*, [1894] A.C. 670 at 685-686; *Emanuel* v. *Symon* [1908] 1 K.B. 302, at 305, 313-314; *Vogel* v. *R. & A. Kohnstamm Ltd.*, [1971] 2 All E.R. 1428 noted by Cohn, 21 Int. & Comp. L.Q. 157 (1972). See also *Gyonyor* v. *Sanjenko*, [1971] 5 W.W.R. 381 (Alta. Sup. Ct., Macdonald, J.), *Mattar and Saba* v. *Public Trustee*, [1952] 3 D.L.R. 399 (Alta. Sup. Ct., App. Div.).

[79] Cohn, *Submission to Foreign Jurisdiction*, 21. I.C.L.Q. 157, at 158 (1972).

[80] 72 I.L.T.R. 142 (High Ct., 1938).

[81] Following *Sirdar Gurdyal Singh* v. *Rajah of Faridkote, supra.*

[82] *Dunbee Ltd.* v. *Gilman & Co. (Australia) Pty., Ltd.*, 70 S.R. N.S.W. 219, [1968] 2 Lloyd's Rep. 394. Cf. *Limerick Corporation* v. *Crompton*, [1909] 2 I.R. 120 (K.B. Div., Andrews, J.), considered *supra*, pp. 134-135.

[83] [1962] I.R. 95 (High Ct., Davitt, P., 1961), analysed by Exshaw, *The Enforcement of a Foreign Judgment in Personam*, 30 Ir. Jur. 1 (1964), Jackson, *Note, Foreign Judgments: Nationality and Reciprocity*, 26 Modern L. Rev. 563 (1963).

[84] *General Steam Navigation Co.* v. *Guillow*, 11 M. & W. 877, at 894, *Schibsby* v. *Westenholz*, L.R. 6 Q.B. 155 at 161; *Roussillon* v. *Roussillon* (1880) 14 Ch. Div. 351 at 371; *Emanuel* v. *Symon* [1908] 1 K.B. 302 at 309 and 312; *Harris* v. *Taylor* [1915] 2 K.B. 580 at 591; *Gavin Gibson & Co. Ltd.* v. *Gibson*, [1913] 3 K.B. 379 at 388 (*per* Atkin, J.), *Phillips* v. *Batho*, [1913] 3 K.B. 25 at 29. See also *Douglas* v. *Forrest* (1828) 4 Bing. 686; *Forsyth* v. *Forsyth* [1948] P. 125 at 132. Cf. *In Re Littles*, 10 Ir. Eq. Rep. 275, at 292 (Chy., Brady, L.C., 1847).

proposition which had also been accepted by *Dicey*,[85] *Halsbury, Westlake, Foote* and *Graveson.* Davitt P. preferred the views to the contrary of *Read, Cheshire*[86] and *Wolff.*

Nationality as a basis of a foreign court's jurisdiction has been questioned in a number of English cases[87] over the past twenty five years, and has been subjected to criticism in some Canadian decisions.[88] It is difficult to see why it should have a role in this context in view of the common law's general lack of enthusiasm for nationality as a connecting factor in the conflicts of law.[89]

(ii) Domicile of the defendant

The fact that the defendant is domiciled in Ireland is one of the grounds on which service out of the jurisdiction may be allowed under Order 11 of the Rules of the Superior Courts, 1986. Will jurisdiction exercised by a foreign court on a similar basis be recognised here? In a number of cases the absence of a domicile on the part of the defendant in the foreign country where judgment was given against him has either been pleaded on his behalf or referred to *obiter* in the course of the Irish court's judgment,[91] though no court has gone so far as to state clearly that domicile, in its own right, affords a basis for recognition and enforcement. Since domicile represents a very strong connecting factor between a person and a particular country, it might be thought that it ought to represent a sufficient basis for the jurisdiction of a foreign court. However, as we have seen,[92] the concept of domicile suffers from defects of technicality and artificiality in many instances and a more appropriate connecting factor for jurisdictional purposes would be habitual or ordinary residence. When the E.E.C. Judgments Convention is implemented in Irish law, a judgment of another E.E.C. Contracting State given on the basis of the "domicile" of the defendant in that other Member State will be enforced here: "domicile" for this purpose will normally be determined by the law of that other State, which will usually mean that it will be closer to habitual or ordinary residence than to the traditional common law concept of domicile. At present it would seem that domicile is not of itself a sufficient basis in Irish law for the jurisdiction of a foreign court

---

[85] But abandoned by Morris: cf. *Dicey,* 6th ed., 1949, 356-357 and *Dicey & Morris,* 10th ed., 1980, 1055-1056.

[86] 3rd ed., 1947, pp. 788-789. See now *Cheshire & North,* 10th ed., 1979, pp. 641-642.

[87] *Blohn* v. *Desser* [1962] 2 Q.B. 116, at 123; *Rossano* v. *Manufacturers Life Insurance Co. Ltd.* [1963] 2 Q.B. 352 at 382-383; *Vogel* v. *R. & A. Kohnstamm Ltd.* [1973] Q.B. 133 at 141, all cited by *Dicey & Morris,* 1056.

[88] *Dakota Lumber Co.* v. *Rinderknecht,* 6 Terr. L.R. 210 (C.A., rev'g Wetmore, J., 1905), *Patterson* v. *D'Agostino* 58 D.L.R. (3d) 63 (Niagara S. County Ct., Ont., 1975). See further H. Read, *Recognition and Enforcement of Foreign Judgments in the Common Law Levels of the British Commonwealth,* 151-155 (1938), *McLean,* 595-597, Blom, *The Enforcement of Foreign Judgments in Canada,* 57 Ore. L. Rev 399, at 410 (1978). But see *Fowler* v. *Vail,* 4 O.A.R. 267 (1878) (considered by *Read,* 152-153), and *Marshal* v. *Houghton,* 33 Man. R. 166, [1923] 2 W.W.R. 553 (C.A.), aff'g [1922] 3 W.W.R. 65, 68 D.L.R. 308 (K.B., Dysart, J.).

[89] See pp. 96-98 supra Cf. de Winter, *Nationality or Domicile? The Present State of Affairs,* [1969] — III Recueil des cours 347, at 491-492.

[90] See pp. 96-98 *supra.*

[91] See, for example, *Maubourquet* v. *Wyse,* I.R. 1 C.L. 471 at 484 (Exch., 1867); *Rainford* v. *Nowell-Roberts* [1962] I.R. 95, at 97 (High Ct., Davitt, P., 1961). See also *Turnbull* v. *Walker* 67 L.T. 762, at 769 (1892); *Emanuel* v. *Symon* [1908] 1 K.B. 302, at 308, 314; *Jaffer* v. *Williams* 25 T.L.R. 12, at 13 (1908); *Gavin Gibson & Co.* v. *Gibson* [1913] 3 K.B. 379, at 385. Cf. *Marshall* v. *Houghton* [1923] 2 W.W.R. 553, at 568 (Man. C.A.), where Dannistoun, J.A. said that: "... in respect to judgments as between different self-governing portions of the Empire, the test of nationality or sovereignty being inapplicable, there must be ascertained as a fact the Kingdom, Dominion, or State, to the legislative power of which the defendant owes allegience or obedience, and ..., in determining this point evidence of domicile, and of ordinary residence, may be found conclusive."

[92] *Supra,* ch. 6.

save, of course, in respect of judgments affecting matrimonial status, such as divorce, where domicile plays a most important role.[93]

(iii) Reciprocity[94]

Our courts assume jurisdiction on a discretionary basis over defendants out of the jurisdiction in the cases specified in Order 11 of the Rules of the Superior Courts, 1986.[95] It might be expected, therefore, that judgments of a foreign court exercising jurisdiction on a comparable basis would be enforceable here but this is not so.

In *Edelsteyn* v. *Coleman*,[96] where the defendant, who was resident in the State, had been served out of the jurisdiction of the Northern Ireland court, it was held that an order for service out did not validate a foreign judgment for the purpose of proceedings grounded upon it here. In *Rainford* v. *Newell-Roberts*[97] also it had been sought to make the defendant amenable to the jurisdiction of the English Court by serving him in Ireland, where he was resident. In view of the close similarity between the English Order 11 and ours, Davitt P. had to decide whether the principle of the reciprocity would oblige him to recognise the English judgment. In holding that it would not, he invoked Scrutton, J.'s explanation for the rule in *Phillips* v. *Batho*:[98]

"Under our Order 11, we constantly serve out of the jurisdiction, give judgment against absent foreigners, and enforce that judgment against their property within the jurisidiction. But, when we are asked to enforce the judgment of a foreign Court against an Englishman served in the same way, we decline to do so on the ground that such procedure is contrary to the principles of international law. The reason may be that our English procedure is imposed on us by statute, the justice of which it is useless to question, while the foreign procedure is not imposed and is open to question."

(iv) The cause of action arose in the foreign country

Our courts will not recognise a judgment given on the basis of jurisdiction exercised, against a defendant not otherwise subject to it, by the Courts of the country in which the cause of action arose, or (in cases of contract) by the Courts of the place of performance. This was decided in *Sirdar Gurdyal Singh* v. *Faridkote*,[99] notwithstanding a dictum in *Schibsby* v. *Westenholz*[100] to the effect that, if at the time when the obligation was contracted the defendants were within the foreign country, but left it before the suit was instituted, the laws of that country bound them. In *Edelstyn* v. *Coleman*[101] O'Byrne J. followed the decision in the former case in preference to the *dictum* in the latter and held that a judgment given in Northern Ireland against the defendant who was resident in the State, for damages for breach of a contract made and to be performed in Northern Ireland, would not be enforced.

---

[93] Cf. *supra*, ch. 12.
[94] See Kennedy, *Recognition of Judgments in Personam: The Meaning of Reciprocity*, 35 Can. Bar Rev. 123 (1957) Kennedy, *"Reciprocity" in the Recognition of Foreign Judgments*, 32 Can. Bar Rev. 359 (1957), Gutteridge, *Reciprocity in Regard to Foreign Judgments*, 13 Br. Yrbk. of Internat. L. 49 (1932).
[95] Cf. *supra*, pp. 132-160.
[96] 72 I.L.T.R. 142 (High Ct., O'Byrne, J., 1938).
[97] [1962] I.R. 95 (High Ct., Davitt, P., 1961).
[98] [1913] 3 K.B. 25, at 29. See also the *locus classicus, Schibsby* v. *Westenholz*, L.R. 6 Q.B. 155 (1870), supported by *Turnbull* v. *Walker*, 67 L.T. 767 (1892), *Sharps Commercials Ltd.* v. *Gas Turbines Ltd.*, [1956] N.Z.L.R. 819 (McGregor, J.), *Malaysia — Singapore Airlines Ltd.*, v. *Parker*, [1972] 3 S.A.S.R. 300, at 304 (Bray, C.J.), *Crick* v. *Hennessy*, [1973] W.A.R. 74 (Burt, J., 1972). The weight of authority is not entirely one way, however: cf. *Re Dulles' Settlement (No. 2)*, [1951] Ch. 265, at 851 (C.A., *per* Denning, L.J., *obiter*), *Travers* v. *Holley*, [1953] P. 246, at 257 (C.A., *per* Hodson, L.J.).
[99] [1894] A.C. 670, at 684.
[100] L.R. 6 Q.B. 155, at 161 (*per* Blackburn, J., 1870).
[101] *Supra*.

(v) Possession by the defendant of property in the foreign country

In the nineteenth century there was some support for the view that a foreign country's courts would have jurisdiction *in personam* over the defendant if he had property within that country. In *Maubourquet* v. *Wyse*,[102] in 1867, where enforcement of a French judgment was sought in the Irish court, a demurrer to the defence plea resisiting enforcement was sustained since (among other reasons) the defendant might have "had property in that country at the time the judgment was given ..."[103] However, there is also some Irish authority limiting the scope of this rule. In *In re Littles*[104] an attempt was made to enforce as an *in personam* decree in Ireland against Irish residents a Scottish judgment founded on arrestment of movables *ad jurisdictionem fundandam.*[105] Brady, L.C. held that this was not possible. He noted that the defendants "were not natives of Scotland ... but, they were for some purposes, i.e., to the extent of their funds, amenable"[106] under Scots law. Even under Scots law, it would have been difficult to say that this mode of judgment could be maintained as a personal decree against the defendants. The Lord Chancellor added:

> "In this country at least (unless some other authority be produced) I apprehend that it is clear it cannot. In *Story's Conflicts of Laws;*[107] after stating the mode of proceeding in some States against non-residents by attachment of their property within the jurisdiction, it is laid down that if the defendant has never appeared and contested the suit, it is to all intents and purposes a mere proceeding *in rem,* and not binding on him personally."[108]

In Re Littles is, of course, a decision turning on the question whether a decree was *in personam* or *in rem* but it appears to regard the maximum of potential liability, even on the view that it was *in personam,* as extending no further than the amount of the defendant's funds within the foreign jurisdiction.

In this century, courts have evinced no enthusiasm for this basis of enforcement of *in personam* foreign judgments. In *Emanuel* v. *Symon*[109] it was held that the earlier case of *Becquet* v. *MacCarthy*[110] should not be regarded as "any authority that the mere possession of property locally situate in a foreign country and protected by its laws affords sufficient ground for holding a person bound by the judgment of the tribunals of that country". It is clear that possession of property by the defendant within the foreign jurisdiction does not nowadays found jurisdiction.

Judgment in Rem

The expression "judgment *in rem*" is not confined to judgments in actions *in rem*

---

[102] I.R. 1 C.L. 471 (Exch., 1867).
[103] *Id.,* at 494-495 (*per* Fitzgerald, B.).
[104] 10 Ir. Eq. Rep. 275 (Chy., Brady, L.C., 1847).
[105] See further *Anton,* 106ff.
[106] 10 Ir. Eq. Rep., at 292.
[107] P. 799, para. 549. *Story, id.,* goes on to state:
> "In other words, [such a proceeding] only binds the property seized or attached in the suit to the extent thereof; and it is in no just sense a decree or judgment binding upon him beyond that property. In other countries, it is uniformly so treated and is justly considered as having no extra-territorial force or obligation."
See generally Nadelmann, *Jurisdictionally Improper Fora,* in K. Nadelmann, A. von Mehren & J. Hazard eds. *XXth century Comparative and Conflicts of Law-Legal Essays in Honor of Hessel E. Yntema* 321 (1961), reprinted in K. Nadelmann, *Conflict of Laws: International and Interstate,* 222 (1972).
[108] 10 Ir. Eq. Rep., at 292-293.
[109] [1908] 1 K.B. 302, at 307 (C.A., *per* Lord Alverstone, L.J., 1907). See also *Sirdar Gurdyal Sing* v. *Rajah of Faridkote* [1894] A.C. 670, at 685 (P.C.).
[110] 2 B. & Ad. 951, 109 E.R. 1396 (1831).

but embraces all judgments determining the status of a thing as against the whole world and not merely as between the parties to the action.[111] So, a judgment that vests possession of or property in a thing in a person as against the whole world or that decrees the sale of a thing in satisfaction of a claim against the thing itself is a judgment *in rem*. So also is a judgment that orders property to be sold by way of administration of an estate in bankruptcy or on death. If a judgment consists essentially in an adjudication as to the status of a *person* (e.g. a decree of divorce[112] or nullity[113] or marriage), then it too is a judgment *in rem*.

The question of characterisation may be mentioned briefly. *Read*[114]states:

"Whether a foreign judgment is one *in rem* or *in personam* must be determined as *a fact* by the court in which it is sought to have the judgment recognized regardless of the opinion or view which may have been expressed by the foreign court. This fact is to be arrived at by discovering the effect of the proceeding according to the law of the foreign law district."

Thus the *lex fori* determines the issue in the light of the effect of the foreign proceedings, regardless of how the foreign law characterises this effect.[115]

In some cases it may be difficult to decide whether the foreign judgment was *in rem* or merely created a right *in personam* against the defendant which is capable of being enforced against his property. This distinction may, of course, be vital because, if the judgment was of the latter variety, it could be recognised only if the foreign court had personal jurisdiction in the international sense over the defendant. The complexity of the question is clear from the differences of opinion among the judges in the cases where it has arisen.[116]

Where the subject-matter of the foreign proceedings is moveable or immoveable property, a judgment *in rem* will be recognised or enforced here only if the property was at the time of the proceedings situated[117] in the foreign country concerned. If

[111] See *Fracis Times & Co.* v. *Carr*, 82 L.T. 698 at 701 (1900); *Dollfus Mieg et Compagnie SA* v. *Bank of England* [1949] 1 All E.R. 946 at 957; *Lazarus-Barlow* v. *Regent Estates Co. Ltd.* [1949] 2 All E.R. 118, at 122.

[112] Cf. *Gaffney* v. *Gaffney*, [1975] I.R. 133, at 154 (Sup. Ct., *per* Henchy, J.) and at 156-157 (*per* Griffin, J.). Kenny, J.'s strictures, at trial (*id.*, at 140) are worth recording:

"The expressions *in rem* and *in personam* have been used in relation to the effects of a decree of divorce in some of the English text-books and in the cases decided in the United States of America and Canada on this matter. I think that their use is unfortunate and confuses the discussion. In the Canadian cases the effects *in rem* seem to refer to those of an invalid divorce in so far as the public law is concerned, while the effects *in personam* relate to those between a husband and wife who have been divorced. This was not the sense in which counsel for the defendant used these words. *In rem* seems to me to be a totally inappropriate term to use in relation to the effects of a divorce in so far as the public law and the status of the children of a marriage are concerned. Like most Latin phrases which have been imported into the law, their use in this connection is a substitute for principle and thought."

[113] Cf. *Salvesen* v. *Administrator of Austrian Property* [1927] A.C. 641, at 662 (*per* Lord Dunedin): "[N]either marriage nor the status of marriage is, in the strict sense of the word, *a res,* as that word is used when we speak of a judgment *in rem*. A *res* is a tangible thing within the jurisdiction of the court, such as a ship or other chattel. A metaphysical idea, which is what the status of marriage is, is not strictly a *res*, but it, to borrow a phrase, savours of a *res*, and has all along been treated as such. Now the learned judges make this distinction. They say that in an action of divorce you have to do with a *res*, to wit, the status of marriage, but that in an action of nullity there is no status of marriage to be dealt with, and therefore no *res*. Now it seems to me that celibacy is just as much a status as marriage."

[114] *Read*, 133−134.

[115] Cf. *Jones* v. *Smith*, 56 O.L.R. 550, [1925] 2 D.L.R. 790 (C.A.), where, it is submitted, undue deference was paid to the *lex domicilii's* characterisation.

[116] *Cammell* v. *Sewell* (1858) 3 H. & N. 617; (1860) 5 H. & N. 728; *Castrique* v. *Imrie* (1860) 8 C.B. (N.S.) 1; *sub nom. Imrie* v. *Castrique* (1860) 8 C.B. (N.S.) 405; (1870) L.R. 4 H.L. 414; *The City of Mecca* (1879) 5 P.D. 28; (1881) 6 P.D. 106. See also *In re Littles*, 10 Ir. Eq. Rep. 275 (Ch., Brady, L.C. 1847), discussed *supra*, p. 588.

[117] As to how the *situs* is determined, see *supra*, ch. 19.

the judgment related to title to foreign immovables, then no question of its *enforcement* here could arise − the property is in the foreign jurisdiction and our courts have no effective power over it. So far as *recognition* is concerned, a similar approach is favoured. The courts of the situs of *immoveable* property will be recognised as having sole jurisdiction in an action relating to such property.[118] So, a foreign judgment determining title (under a will or otherwise) to immoveable property situated here will not be recognised,[119] despite the fact that our courts will in some cases determine the validity of wills relating to immovables abroad.[120]

If the foreign judgment *in rem* relates to moveable property, then questions of recognition or enforcement of the judgment may become intermingled with questions of assignment of moveable property. If the foreign judgment operates so as to vest the title to the *res* in the plaintiff, and the plaintiff comes into the Irish courts to assert his title, arising out of that judgment, as against some person within the jurisdiction, he is effect seeking recognition of the judgment as an assignment of the property to him. He is saying "I am owner" rather than "I have a judgment in my favour which I wish to enforce."[121]

In some cases (for example where property is sold by way of administration of deceased person's or a bankrupt's estate), the special rules as to assignment of moveable property will apply.[122] In other cases (for example), where the foreign Court ordered a *res* to be sold in satisfaction of a claim by the plaintiff) the foreign judgment will be recognised only if the *res* was at the time of the action situated within that court's jurisdiction.

This requirement was not satisfied in *McKie* v. *McKie*.[123] The plaintiff's husband bought a prize-winning ticket in the Irish Hospitals Sweepstake. Later she applied for a divorce in California where she and her husband had resided. The Californian Court granted an interlocutory decree dissolving the marriage and determining that the prize money was the community property of the plaintiff and her husband and the Court awarded and assigned it to the plaintiff. The plaintiff then instituted proceedings in the Irish High Court for a declaration that she was entitled to the prize money, an order that the promoters of the Sweepstake should pay to her the sum due and an injunction restraining them from paying the money to any other person. Meredith, J. refused to "render effective the award or assignment by a foreign court of property situate here, and belonging to a person who according to our law is the rightful owner, in exercise of a merely discretionary jurisdiction peculiar to the foreign Court, by which the property can be transferred to a person who only acquires a right or title to it from the order of the Court".[124] The assignment or award of the Californian Court was not a "universal assignment" but simply an adjudication of the Court which it was sought to make effective here.[125] So there was nothing to disturb the application of the general principle[126] that no judgment of a foreign court can have any effect unless the subject−matter of the decision is within the lawful control of the State whose tribunal has pronounced the judgment.[127]

---

[118] *Re Hoyles* [1911] 1 Ch. 179, at 185−186 (C.A., *per* Farwell, L.J., 1910), *Re Trepca Mines Ltd.* [1960] 1 W.L.R. 1273, at 1277 (C.A., *per* Hodson, L.J.).

[119] *Re Hoyles, supra.*

[120] Similarly judgments *in personam* relating to immovables in Ireland will probably not be recognised here (cf. *Duke* v. *Adler,* [1932] S.C.R. 732), even though an Irish court will take jurisdiction over actions *in personam* relating to immovables abroad; cf. *supra,* pp. 403-407.

[121] Cf. *Castrique* v. *Imrie,* L.R. 4 H.L. 414, at 429 (*per* Lord Blackburn, 1870).

[122] See *supra,* ch. 25.

[123] [1933] I.R. 464 (High Ct., Meredith, J.).

[124] *Id.,* at 476.

[125] *Id.,* at 478.

[126] Stated by Blackburn J. in *Castrique* v. *Imrie,* L.R. 4 H.L. 414, at 435 (1870).

[127] [1933] I.R. 464, at 478.

It would appear that an action *in rem* may be taken to enforce a foreign judgment *in rem* relating to ships or their cargo.[128] What constitutes an *in rem* judgment is, as we have seen,[129] a matter on which the Irish, rather than foreign, court has the last word.

Finality and conclusiveness of the foreign judgment

In order to maintain an action on a foreign judgment, it is not sufficient that the judgment be one which results from an adjudication of a Court of competent jurisdiction: it must also be final and conclusive.[130] In *Nouvion* v. *Freeman*[131] Lord Herschell summarised the law on this matter, in a passage that has received support in Irish decisions:

"I think that in order to establish that such a judgment has been pronounced, it must be shown that in the Court by which it was pronounced it conclusively, finally, and for ever established the existence of the debt of which it is sought to be made conclusive evidence in this country, so as to make it *res judicata* between the parties. If it is not conclusive in the same Court which pronounced it, so that notwithstanding such a judgment the existence of the debt may, between the same parties, be afterwards contested in that Court, and upon proper proceedings being taken and such contest being adjudicated upon, it might be declared that there existed no obligation to pay the debt at all, then I do not think that a judgment which is of that character can be regarded as finally and conclusively evidencing the debt, and so entitling the person who has obtained the judgment to claim a decree from our courts for the payment of that debt."

Effect will not, then, be given to a foreign decree which is liable to be abrogated by the same Court which issued it.[132] But a foreign decree need not be final in the sense that it cannot be made the subject of appeal to a higher Court.[133] Once it is final and unalterable in the Court that pronounced it, then the fact that it is subject to appeal or indeed that an appeal is pending, will not render it enforceable here.[134] In such a case however, the Irish court would be most likely to exercise its discretion to grant a stay on execution, pending the outcome of the appeal.[135] Where, however, the effect under the foreign law of lodging an appeal is to stay execution of the judgment, it may be that, in the meantime, the judgment is not actionable here.[136] In *Nouvion* v. *Freeman*[137] the plaintiff took summary or

---

[128] Cf. *The City of Mecca,* 5 P.D. 28 (1879), rev'd on other grounds 6 P.D. 106 (1881), *S.S. Pacific Star* v. *Bank of America National Trust and Savings Association,* [1965] W.A.R. 159 (Full Ct.). See further *Cheshire & North,* 647, *Dicey & Morris,* 1068.

[129] *Supra,* p. 124.

[130] *Nunn* v. *Nunn,* 8 L.R. Ir. 298 (C.A., 1880), aff'g 6 L.R. Ir. 115 (Q.B. Div., 1880), *M'Donnell* v. *M'Donnell* [1921] 2 I.R. 148 (K.B. Div., 1920), *Muldoon* v. *Doyle,* 79 I.L.T.R. 134 (Sup. Ct., 1945, aff'g High Ct., Maguire, P., 1944), *G.* v. *G.* [1984] I.R. 368 (High Ct., Finlay, P.). See further *supra,* pp. 303-307.

[131] 15 App. Cas 1 at 9 (H.L. (Eng.,) 1889), cited with approval in *M'Donnell* v. *M'Donnell* [1921] 2 I.R. 148, by Gordon, J. (in part) at 153 and by Molony, C.J. (in full) at 161 (K.B. Div., 1920). It is for Irish conflict of laws rules to determine, in the light of the evidence as to the effect of a foreign judgment, whether it is or not final and conclusive. The view of the foreign court on this question is not determinative. *Contra Keys* v. *Keys,* [1919] 2 I.R. 160, at 168 (K.B. Div., *per* Gibson, J., 1918);

[132] *Nouvion* v. *Freeman* 15 App. Cas 1, at 13 (H.L. Eng., 1889), cited by Molony, C.J. in *M'Donnell* v. *M'Donnell* [1921] 2 I.R. 148 at 161–162. See also *G.* v. *G.,* [1984] I.R. 368 (High Ct., Finlay, P.

[133] *Nouvion* v. *Freeman,* 15 App. Cas. 1, at 13.

[134] Cf. *Scott* v. *Pilkington* (1862) 2 B. & S.11, *Colt Industries* v. *Sarlie (No.2),* [1966] 1 W.L.R. 1287.

[135] Cf. pp. 164-171, *supra*

[136] Cf. *Cheshire & North,* 651.

[137] 15 App. Cas. 1 (H.L. Eng., 1889). See also *Blohn* v. *Desser,* [1962] 2 Q.B. 116 (Diplock, J., 1961), *Wolff,* 265, *Castel,* vol. 1, 453–454, fn. 161; Cf. Lorenzen, *The Enforcement of American Judgments Abroad,* 2 J. Comp. Leg. (3rd Ser.) 124, at 126 (1920). *Nouvion* v. *Freeman* was distinguished by Maguire, P., in *Muldoon* v. *Doyle,* 79 I.L.T.R. 134, at 138, (High Ct., 1944, aff'g by Sup Ct., 1945). See also *Denman* v. *O'Callaghan,* 31 I.L.T.R. 141 (C.A., 1897).

"executive" proceedings in Spain for the recovery of a debt owing on foot of a sale of land and obtained a "renate" judgment. In such proceedings the defendant is precluded from setting up certain defences, including a denial of validity of the transaction to which the proceedings relate. The unsuccessful party in the executive proceedings may institute ordinary or plenary proceedings in the same court; in these proceedings every available defence may be set up. In the plenary proceedings the "remate" judgment may not be set up as *res judicata* and the plenary judgment supersedes and displaces the "remate" judgment. The House of Lords held that the "remate" was not final and conclusive and could not be enforced.

In Ireland the question of the finality of judgments has raised particular discussion in relation to maintenance orders.[138] These cases are examined in detail in Chapter 14.[139]

There has been some difference of opinion among the authorities as to whether a foreign judgment given in default of appearance is final and conclusive. Where the defendant is entitled as of right to have the default judgment set aside and to have a full hearing on the merits if he applies within a certain period of time, it would seem that it is not final and conclusive as long as that period remains unexpired.[140] However, in a Canadian decision[141] the view was taken that this would, in effect, be to say that the clearer the plaintiff's case the more useless his judgment would be . If the default judgment can only be set aside upon cause being shown by the defendant,[142] then it would appear that the judgment should be regarded as final and conclusive until such a time, if ever, as it is set aside. In an Australian case[143] a foreign separation order, which might upon cause being shown be subsequently altered, varied or discharged, was held to be final and conclusive as long as it remained in force.

In personam judgment must be for definite sum[144]

In *Williams* v. *Jones,* Parke B. said:

> "Where a court of competent jurisdiction has adjudged a certain sum to be due from one person to another, a legal obligation arises to pay that sum on which an action of debt to enforce the judgment may be maintained."[145]

It has also been stated that "the liability of the defendant arises upon an implied contract to pay the amount of the foreign judgment".[146] The amount in question must be a definite sum of money.[147] This includes a final order for costs[148] and a

---

[138] Cf. *M'Donnell* v. *M'Donnell,* [1921] 2 I.R. 148 (K.B. Div., 1920), *G.* v. *G.,* [1984] I.R. 368 (High Ct., Finlay, P.).

[139] *Supra,* pp. 305-309.

[140] *Jeannot* v. *Fuerst* 25 T.L.R. 424, at 425 (1909).

[141] *Boyle* v. *Victoria Yukon Trading Co.* 9 B.C.R. 213 (1909).

[142] Cf. the Rules of the Superior Court 1986, Order 13 (11); and see *Nixon* v. *Loundes,* [1909] 2 I.R. 1 (K.B. Div., 1908).

[143] *Ainslie* v. *Ainslie* 39 C.L.R. 381 (1927).

[144] See *Dicey & Morris,* 1093, *Cheshire & North,* 651.

[145] 13 M. & W. 628, at 633, 153 E.R. 262, at 265 (*per* Parke, B., 1845) quoted in *M'Donnell* v. *M'Donnell* [1921] 2 I.R. 148, at 161 (K.B. Div., *per* Molony, C.J., 1920), and in *Societe Ananyme la Chemo—Serotherapie Belge* v. *Dolan (Dominick A.) & Co. Ltd.,* [1961] I.R. 281, at 287 (High Ct., Teevan, J., 1960), where Parke, B.'s statement appears within a passage from Blackburn, J.'s judgment in *Godard* v. *Gray,* L.R. 6 Q.B. 139 (1870).

[146] *Grant* v. *Easton* 13 Q.B.D. 302, at 303 (1883).

[147] *Sadler* v. *Robins,* 1 Camp. 253 at 256, 170 E.R. 948, at 949 (1808); *M'Donnell* v. *M'Donnell* [1921] 2 I.R. 148.

[148] *Russell* v. *Smyth,* 9 M. & W. 810 (1842); *Boyle* v. *Victoria Yukon Trading Co.,* 9 B.C.R. 213 (Full Ct., 1902).

sum which can be ascertained by a mere arithmetical calculation.[149] It also includes a judgment, not for a definite *single* sum of money, but for *definite sums to be paid periodically* as ordered. An order for the payment of a sum which is subject to the deduction of an amount for costs which has yet to be determined is not enforceable.[150]

If the foreign judgment orders the defendant to do something other than pay a definite sum of money, it is not enforceable. Thus, a decree granting an injunction or specific performance or restitution of a chattel will not be enforced.

The existing rule is an anomalous survival from the days when the forms of action were all important and the appropriate form of action on a foreign judgment was in *indebitatus assumpsit*. It is difficult to see why a foreign judgment of this kind should not be enforced directly. *Wolff*[151] suggests that such a judgment can be recognised as *res judicata*, however, so that, if the plaintiff brings an action claiming damages for non-performance of the obligation established by the original judgment the defendant will probably not be allowed to set up the defence that this judgment was wrong.

Foreign Judgment Cannot Be Examined on Merits

Up to the middle of the last century foreign judgments were regarded as merely *prima facie*, and not conclusive, evidence of the existence of a debt between the parties,[152] so that the merits of the case could be re-examined when a foreign judgment was sued upon. However, it became established that, if the foreign court had jurisdiction in the international sense, the merits of the case could not be re-opened.[153]

The underlying reason for this position is to be found in the maxims *interest rei publicae ut sit finis litium* and *nemo debet bis vexari pro eadem causa* − it is "contrary to principle and expediency for the same questions to be again submitted to a jury in this country".[154] The proper recourse of a party seeking to allege that the foreign judgment was bad for a mistake of fact or of law is to take an appeal in the foreign country concerned. A court in this country cannot act as an appellate court over a judgment given by a foreign court of competent jurisdiction.

A foreign judgment is conclusive despite the fact that there was a defence available to the defendent in the foreign court which he failed to set up. For example, in *Ellis* v. *M'Henry*[155] judgment was given in a Canadian court for a debt against a person who had been made bankrupt in England but who failed to plead his discharge in the bankruptcy as a defence to the Canadian action. An action on the Canadian judgment in England was successful: to allow the defendant to set up the defence he could have pleaded to the original claim would impeach the propriety and correctness of the foreign judgment.[156]

[149] *Beatty* v. *Beatty*, [1924] 1 K.B. 807.
[150] *Sadler* v. *Robins* 1 Camp. 253, 170 E.R. 948 (1808); *Hutton* v. *Dant*, [1924] 1 D.L.R. 401; *Taylor* v. *Begg* [1932] N.Z.L.R. 286.
[151] *Wolff*, 265. See also *Dicey & Morris*, 1093.
[152] *Walker* v. *Witter* 1 Doug. 1 at 5-6 (1778); *Houlditch* v. *Donegal*, 2 Cl. & F. 470, at 477−478, 6 E.R. 1232, at 1234−1235 (1834); cf. the remarks of Lord Plunket, L.C., in the same case; see also *Smith* v. *Nicholls*, 5 Bing. N.C. 208 at 221 (1839), *Otway* v. *Ramsey*, 2 Stra. 1090 (K.B., 1736). See further *Anon.*, *Comment: Reciprocity and the Recognition of Foreign Judgments*, 36 Yale L.J. 542, at 543 (1927).
[153] *Bank of Australasia* v. *Nias*, 16 Q.B. 717 (1851); *De Cosse Brissac* v. *Rathbone*, 6 H. & N. 301 (1861) *Godard* v. *Gray*, L.R. 6 Q.B. 139 (1870); *Vadala* v. *Lawes*, 25 Q.B.D. 310, at 316 (1890). See also *La Societe Anonyme La Chemo−Serotherapie Belge* v. *Dolan (Dominick A.) & Co. Ltd.*, [1961] I.R. 281, *Maubourquet* v. *Wyse*, I.R. 1 C.L. 471, at 490 (Exch., *per* Pigot, C.B., 1867).
[154] *Bank of Australasia* v. *Nias*, 16 Q.B. 717, at 736, 107 E.R. 1055, at 1063 (1851).
[155] L.R. 6 C.P. 228 (1871).
[156] *Id.*, at 238−239. See also *Henderson* v. *Henderson*, 6 Q.B. 288 (1844); *De Cosse Brissac* v. *Rathbone*, *supra*.

In *La Societe Anonyme la Chemo—Serotherapie Belge* v. *Dolan (Dominick A.)* & Co. Ltd.,[157] the plaintiff, a Belgian company, obtained final judgment in Belgium against the defendants, an Irish company, on foot of an agreement to compromise the plaintiff's claim. The claim was for a sum of money which the defendants had undertaken to pay as a royalty on a product in respect of which the plaintiffs had given them the wholesale selling rights in Ireland. The defendants had contested the proceedings in Belgium but, when judgment was given against them there, they did not appeal.

When the plaintiffs sought to enforce the judgment in Ireland, the defendants resisted on the basis that they were entitled to a set—off, for a sum exceeding the amount of the judgment, to compensate them for income tax paid by them in respect of the royalties in Ireland. They argued[158] that, since their original indebtedness to the plaintiffs had not merged in the Belgian judgment, and that as it was thus still open to the plaintiffs to sue the defendents on foot of the original cause of action, the defendants ought not to be precluded from raising all the defences which were open to them to that cause of action, including the defence regarding the income tax payment.

Teevan, J. agreed that the original cause of action survived. This was "so well established that it is not unnecessary to cite authority for the proposition."[159] He also agreed that defences to the original claim similarly survived so far as that claim was concerned. But beyond that, he was unwilling to concur with the defence arguments. He said:

> "The plaintiffs had a choice of two courses of action. They could have sued here on the original claim as it arose under the compromise agreement — using, if they wished, the Belgian judgment as proof of the amount of indebtedness; or they could have sued on the Belgian judgment itself, which they did. As I understand [defence counsel]'s contention it is that, by reason of the distinction between final judgments of our own Courts and those of foreign Courts, the latter are devoid of force save as evidence of the pre—judgment debt. At least, I think, his argument must logically be pushed that far. He says, if the plaintiffs' claim had been simply for the amount due under the compromise agreement, he would have been entitled to deduct the tax; as there is no merger, his right of deduction remains and he can now deduct from the amount of the Belgian judgment — at least from so much of it as is made up of debt.[160]
> This is clearly contrary to authority. That this is so may not appear explicitly from the authorities on which he grounded his arguments, but it follows from them. Otherwise why is it permitted to sue on foreign judgments as themselves causes of action?"[161]

The fact that the foreign court made a mistake as to its own law will not prevent its judgment from being conclusive.[162] Indeed, even the fact that the foreign court made a mistake as to *Irish* law will not avail the defendant.[163] In *Godard* v. *Gray*[164]

---

[157] [1961] I.R. 281 (High Ct., Teevan, J.)

[158] *Id.*, at 283.

[159] *Id.*, at 286.

[160] The judgment also included amounts for costs and interest under Belgian law: [1961] I.R., at 282.

[161] *Id.*, at 286—287.

[162] Cf. *Scott* v. *Pilkington*, 2 B. & S. 11 (1862). See also *Henderson* v. *Henderson supra*. There is some uncertainty as to the position where the defendant, after the foreign judgment has been handed down, discovers new evidence which he could not reasonably have known about beforehand and which shows that the decision was wrong. In *De Cosse Brissac* v. *Rathbone, supra,* such a plea was held bad, but some of the commentators are of the view that this holding can be explained on its special facts and that a plea on these lines should be admitted: see *Dicey & Morris,* 1074—1075, *McLeod.* 601.

[163] Cf. Graveson, *Comparative Aspects of the General Principles of Private International Law,* [1963] — II Recueil des cours 1, at 149.

[164] L.R. 6 Q.B. 139 (1870). See also *Castrique* v. *Imrie,* L.R. 4 H.L. 414 (1870).

a French court, acting on an erroneous view of English law, treated a penalty clause in a charterparty governed by English law as fixing the amount of damages payable in the event of breach. The French judgment was sued upon in England and the defendant pleaded the mistake as to English law. It was held that the defendant could no more set up an excuse that the judgment had proceeded on a mistake as to English law then he could set up as an excuse that there had been a mistake as to the law of some third country incidentally involved or as to any other question of fact.[165]

We must now consider an aspect of this subject on which the judicial authorities are far from clear. Accepting that the foreign court had jurisdiction in the international sense, what should be the effect of showing that it lacked *internal* jurisdiction? For example, if a divorce were obtained by a spouse domiciled in a foreign country, and resident there for six months, that divorce would comply with the jurisdictional requirements, in the international sense,[166] but it would not necessarily comply with the internal jurisdictional requirements of the foreign state — as would be the case where the law of that state required a minimum period of residence of one year and paid no attention to the petitioner's domicile.

The English decisions on this general issue are "at first sight in a state of some confusion",[167] and attempts[168] to reconcile them have proved difficult. Some of the cases[169] appear to support the view that the judgment should be upheld regardless of the lack of jurisdiction under the internal law of the foreign country. The problem with this approach is that it would treat as valid a judgment which had no validity in the foreign country itself and which thus created no rights in the plaintiff.[170]

It is possible to mitigate the full effect of this rule by restricting it to cases where the foreign court had jurisdiction under its internal law but erred in its own rules of procedure,[171] or cases where the judgment, though irregular according to the internal foreign law, was voidable rather than completely null.[172]

Gaffney v. *Gaffney*[173] is a difficult case to interpret in this context. The judgments in the Supreme Court, when considering the question of the English divorce court's jurisdiction, never clearly distinguished between jurisdiction in the international sense and jurisdiction for the purposes of English divorce law. There was an overlap in that domicile would support jurisdiction in both senses, but the husband's (alleged) residence in England could also have supported jurisdiction for the purposes of English divorce law but not for the purposes of jurisdiction in the international sense. Griffin, J.'s quotation[174] of a relevant passage from Lindley, M.R.'s judgment in *Pemberton* v. *Hughes*[175] suggests that Griffin, J. did not dissent from the view that jurisdictional incompetence under the foreign internal law should be ignored; but there is nothing in the remainder of his judgment, or the judgments of the other members of the Court, which throws light on what the position would have been where the English court had jurisdiction in the international sense but not in terms of the requirements of its own divorce law.

[165] L.R. 6 Q.B. at 150 (1870).

[166] Cf. *supra*, pp. 588-589.

[167] *Dicey & Morris*, 1080.

[168] Cf. *Cheshire & North*, 653−655, *Dicey & Morris*, 1080−1081.

[169] Cf. *Pemberton* v. *Hughes*, [1899] 1 Ch. 781, at 791 (C.A., *per* Lindley, L.J.), quoted by Griffin, J., in *Gaffney* v. *Gaffney*, [1975] I.R. 133, at 159−160 (Sup. Ct). See also *Merker* v. *Merker*, [1963]P. 283 (Sir Jocelyn Simon, P., 1962) *Contra, Bater* v. *Bater*, [1906] P. 209, at 232−234 (C.A. *per* Romer, C.J.), *Papadopoulos* v. *Papadopoulas*, [1930] P. 55 (Sir Jocelyn Simon, P., 1970).

[170] *Cheshire & North*, 653−654.

[171] *Id.*, 654, explaining *Pemberton* v. *Hughes, supra*, and *Vanquelin* v. *Bouard*, 15 C.B.N.S. 341, 143 E.R. 817 (1863). This strategy, of course, involves difficult issues of characterisation.

[172] *Read*, 100, explaining *Vanquelin* v. *Bouard, supra*.

[173] [1975] I.R. 133 (Sup. Ct., 1975, aff'g High Ct., Kenny, J., 1973).

[174] *'Id.*, at 158−159.

[175] L.R. 2 P. & D. 435, at 442 (1872).

Estoppel per rem judicatam

To what extent does the doctrine of estoppel *per rem judicatam* apply to a foreign judgment? We have already seen that a foreign judgment is not *res judicata* inasmuch as the original cause of action is not merged in the judgment and extinguished. The plaintiff has the option of either suing on the original cause of action in Ireland or suing on the foreign judgment.[176] But, while this ultimate degree of conclusiveness is denied to foreign judgments, they are otherwise conclusive on the merits. In domestic law there is a rule of evidence whereby an unsuccessful party to litigation is estopped from questioning in any subsequent proceedings the merits of a final decision in that litigation. This species of estoppel is known as estoppel *per rem judicatam* or estoppel by record.[177]

Estoppel *per rem judicatam* applies both to judgments *in personam* and judgments *in rem*, the former being conclusive only as between the parties or their privies, the latter being conclusive as against the whole world.

So far as conflicts of law aspects of estoppel *per rem judicatam* are concerned, a person who successfully defended foreign proceedings where the judgment was final and conclusive and given on the merits, cannot later be sued in Ireland by the same plaintiff on the same cause of action. The plaintiff is estopped from denying the conclusiveness of the judgment. Moreover, where a plaintiff suing abroad has had judgment satisfied there, albeit of an award more modest than he could have obtained in Ireland, he may not later proceed against the same defendant in Ireland in respect of the same injury, looking for further compensation.[178]

Defences Available Against Recognition and Enforcement

The fact that a foreign judgment is regarded as conclusive and unimpeachable as to the merits of the dispute does not mean that a defendant to an action for enforcement of such a judgment is entirely without recourse. We have already seen that he may resist recognition and enforcement on the ground that the foreign court lacked jurisdiction over the subject matter or the parties. There are a number of other defences that he may also raise.

Fraud vitiating the foreign judgment[179]

A purely domestic judgment may be set aside upon the ground of fraud or collusion[180] since it is an abuse of the process of the Court.[181] The jurisdiction to set aside such a judgment does not depend on rules of court[182] but is part of the inherent jurisdiction of the Court.[183] Whether the judgment is by default or consent, or otherwise, is immaterial.[184] Fraud must be clearly alleged and clearly proved.[185] In the clearest of cases, judgment may be set aside on motion; otherwise there should

---

[176] *Carl Zeiss Stiftung* v. *Rayner and Keeler (No.2)*, [1966] 2 All E.R. 536, at 564, citing Spencer Bower on *Res Judicata*, p.3.

[177] Cf. *Cheshire & North*, 656. See, e.g. *Harris* v. *Quine*, L.R. 4 Q.B. 653 (1869).

[178] See *Cheshire & North*, 656.

[179] See Graveson, *Fraud in Foreign Judgments*, 12 Modern L. Rev. 105 (1949).

[180] *Duchess of Kingston's Case* 2 Sm. L.C. (13th ed.) 644, 20 State Tr. 619, [1775–1802] All E.R. Rep. 623; (1776); *McLaffey* v. *McLaffey* [1905] 2 I.R. 292; *Nixon* v. *Loundes* [1909] 2 I.R.1 (K.B. Div., 1908), *Dennis* v. *Leinster Paper Co.*, [1901] 2 I.R. 337, at 340 (K.B. Div., Kenny, J., aff'd by C.A.). See Gordon, *Actions to Set Aside Judgments*, 77 L.Q.R. 358, 533 (1961), and cf. *Denman* v. *O'Callaghan*, 31 I.L.T.R. 141 (C.A., 1897).

[181] *Nixon* v. *Loundes*, [1909] 2 I.R., at 10–11 (K.B. Div., *per* Dodd, J., 1908).

[182] See the Rules of the Superior Courts 1986, Order 13, rule 11, Order 27, rule 14, Order 36, rule 33. Cf. *Fitter & Co.* v. *Tuke*, 40 I.L.T.R. 1 (C.A., 1905).

[183] [1909]2 I.R. at 6 (*per* Gibson, J.).

[184] *Id.*

[185] *Id* at 11 (*per* Dodd, J.)

be an issue to try the question of fraud.[186] The plaintiff must produce evidence of new facts discovered since the former judgment which raise a reasonable probability of the action succeeding.[187] Those facts must be so evidenced and so material as to make it reasonably probable that the action will succeed.[188]

A foreign judgment also may be impeached for fraud. In such circumstances, enforcement of it will be refused in Ireland.[189] The fraud may have been perpetrated by the foreign court itself, as in *Price* v. *Dewhurst*,[190] where some members of a Danish court were shown to have had an interest in the property that was affected by their decision. Normally, of course, the fraud will have been perpetrated upon the foreign court by one or more of the parties.[191]

What sort of evidence is required to invalidate a foreign judgment? Must there, as in the case of domestic judgments, be evidence of new facts discovered since the foreign judgment or may the merits of the foreign judgment be examined by consideration of the same evidence as was given in the foreign court? And is the position different where if the allegation of fraud was considered by the foreign court and rejected by it? Fraud as to the jurisdiction occurred in *Gaffney* v. *Gaffney*[199] where a divorce had been obtained in England on the basis of the common domicile of the spouses there, even though they were in reality domiciled in Ireland at the material time. The husband by means of the threat of physical violence had forced his wife to petition for divorce. The Supreme Court, affirming Kenny, J., held that the divorce decree was ineffective as the English Court had lacked jurisdiction. Henchy, J. said:

> "I fail to see why, although the decree seems good on its face, evidence should not be received to show that its facade conceals a lack of jurisdiction no less detrimental to its validity than if it had been written into the order. To hold otherwise would be to close one's eyes to the available truth and to give effect instead to a spurious divorce which the English court was deluded by sworn misrepresentations into making."[200]

And Griffin, J. said:

> "The decree in the present case was obtained by duress and by fraud going to the point of jurisdiction ... [T]he duress and fraud were those of the husband, but even where a petitioner[201] has obtained a decree in a foreign court which had no jurisdiction

---

[186] *Id.*

[187] *Birch* v. *Birch* [1902] P. 130 at 136 (C.A., *per* Vaughan Williams, J.).

[188] *Id.*, at 136-137.

[189] *Gaffney* v. *Gaffney* [1975] I.R. 133 (Sup. Ct., 1975, aff'g. High Ct., Kenny, J., 1973), *L.B.* v. *H.B.*, [1980] I.L.R.M. 257 (High Ct., Barrington, J.).

[190] 3 Sim. 279, 59 E.R. 111 (Shadwell, V.C., 1837).

[191] Cf. *Gaffney* v. *Gaffney, supra* (fraud on English court, to the knowledge of both parties, brought about by duress exerted by one party over the other).

[192] *Vadala* v. *Lawes* 25 Q.B.D. 310, at 316 (1890).

[193] *Aloulaff* v. *Oppenheimer*, 10 Q.B.D. 295 (1882), *Vadala* v. *Lawes*, 25 Q.B.D. 310 (1890); *Syal* v. *Heyward*, [1948] 2 K.B. 443. See also *Ellerman Lines* v. *Read*, [1928] 2 K.B. 144.

[194] 10 Q.B.D. 295, at 306 (1882).

[195] See *Read*, 272−281; *Castel*, vol 1 488−499.

[196] *Svinskis* v. *Gibson*, [1977] 2 N.Z.L.R. 4 at 10 (C.A.).

[197] *Jacobs* v. *Beaver*, 17 O.L.R. 496 (C.A., 1908).

[198] *Read*, p. 273.

[199] [1975] I.R. 133 (Sup. Ct., 1975, aff'g High Ct., Kenny, J., 1973). See also *Biggar* v. *Biggar*, [1930] 2 D.L.R. 940.

[200] [1975] I.R., at 154−155.

[201] In fact the wife had been the petitioner in the English divorce proceedings, acting under duress imposed by her husband. What Griffin, J. appears to have in mind is a case where there is fraud by the petitioner without any duress being exerted on him or her.

to pronounce it, by deceiving the court into believing it had jurisdiction the Court will treat it as invalid ..."[202]

Some distinctive aspects of the effect of fraud in respect of nullity decrees[203] have been considered earlier. So far as divorce decrees[204] are concerned we have already noted Barrington, J.'s decision on *L.B.* v. *H.B.*,[205] where the parties had presented a factually untrue case to obtain a divorce in France, the country of their domicile. Barrington, J. considered that he should not recognise the divorce decree, not on the basis of fraud, but of a "substantial defeat of justice ..." The decision has implications far wider than the specific context of divorce. It suggests that recognition may be denied to a foreign judgment based on false evidence as to any facts (rather than specifically the question of jurisdiction) where that evidence was knowingly tendered by both, or perhaps one, of the parties.

Foreign judgment contrary to natural or constitutional justice

It is well recognised that foreign decrees contrary to "natural justice"[206] or "substantial justice"[207] may not be recognised here. If a foreign judgment was "obtained in a proceeding conducted in a manner contrary to natural justice then, although it may have been conformable to the law of the country in which it was pronounced, it cannot be legally enforced"[208] in an Irish Court. The precise scope of the defence is not altogether clear. The expression "contrary to natural justice" does not mean that the foreign judgment was merely unjust in the sense of being wrong or mistaken.[209]

The defence may be applicable where there was a failure on the part of the foreign court to observe the maxim *audi alteram partem*. In *Maubourquet* v. *Wyse*,[210] Pigot, C.B. observed that the foundation of this maxim was:

> "laid in the general principles of all jurisprudence which deserves the name. It is a rule of reason and justice, which from very early times the law of England appears to have regarded as of universal application ..."

One type of case where the maxim has been held to have been infringed is where the defendant was not given notice of the action before the foreign court and had not been summoned before it.[211] The maxim *audi alteram partem* may also be

---

[202] [1975] I.R., at 159, citing *Bonaparte* v. *Bonaparte,* [1892] P. 402, and *Middleton* v. *Middleton,* [1967] P. 62 (P.D.A. Div., Cairns, J., 1965).

[203] Cf. *supra,* p. 263.

[204] Cf. *supra,* pp. 282-284.

[205] [1980] I.L.R.M. 257 (High Ct., Barrington, J.).

[206] *Maubourquet* v. *Wyse,* I.R. 1 C.L. 471, at 481 (Exch., *per* Pigot, C.B., 1867) and at 497 (*per* Fitzgerald, B.). See also *Denman* v. *O'Callaghan,* 31, I.L.T.R. 141, at 142 (C.A., *per* Ashbourne, C., 1897).

[207] *Pemberton* v. *Hughes* [1899] 1 Ch. 781 at 790, *per* Lindley, M.R., cited with approval in *Gaffney* v. *Gaffney* [1975] I.R. 133 at 140–141 and 158–159. See also *L.B.* v. *H.B., supra.*

[208] *Maubourquet* v. *Wyse* I.R. 1 C.L. 471, at 481 (Exch., *per* Pigot, C.B. 1867). See also *Dennis* v. *Leinster Paper Co.,* [1901] 2 I.R. 337, at 340–341 (K.B. Div., Kenny, J., aff'd by C.A.).

[209] Cf. *Robinson* v. *Fenner* [1913] 3 K.B. 835 at 842 (Channell, J., 1912):
"It is not enough to say that a decision is very wrong, any more than it is merely to say that it is wrong. It is not enough, therefore, to say that the result works injustice in the particular case, because a wrong decision always does."

[210] I.R. 1 C.L. 471 at 481 (Exch., *per* Pigot C.B., 1867).

[211] *Ferguson* v. *Mahon,* 11 Ad. & El. 179, 113 E.R. 382 (1839) (Irish judgment obtained "behind the back of the defendant" denied recognition in England; Lord Denman considered that "when it appears, as here, that the defendant has never had notice of the proceedings, or been before the Court, it is impossible for us to allow the judgment to be made to the foundation of an action in this country".) See also *Schisby* v. *Westenholz,* L.R. 6 Q.B. 155 (1870), *Shaw* v. *Att. Gen.,* L.R. 2 P. & D. 156 (1870), *Rudd* v. *Rudd,* [1924] P. 72; *Gray* v. *Formosa,* [1963] P. 259; *Lepre* v. *Lepre,* [1965] P. 52; *Macalpine* v. *Macalpine* [1958] P. 35 (P.D.A. Div., Sachs, J., 1957). Cf. *Maubourquet* v. *Wyse,* I.R. 1 C.L. 471 (Ex., 1867), *Cowan* v. *Braidwood,* 1 Man. & G. 882, 133 E.R. 589 (1840). See also Duncan, *Collusive Foreign Divorces — How to Have Your Cake and Eat It.* 3 D.U.L.J. 17, at 19 (1981).

infringed if the defendant, though given adequate notice of the proceedings, was not given a fair hearing at them, as for example where his right to present his case was denied or severely curtailed. But it seems that it is only in a very clear case that a plea to this effect will be allowed. It is clearly not sufficient if the defendant failed to raise a defence in the foreign court which might have been available to him. In *Sims* v. *Thomas*[212] the defendant sought to resist enforcement of a judgment obtained in England upon a bond in which the defendant had joined as one of the sureties. He alleged that no memorial of the bond containing the names of the witnesses to it had been enrolled, with the result that the bond was technically void under a certain English statute. The Irish court considered whether the English judgment was against natural justice and decided that it was not.

Richards, B. said:

> "I assume that the defendant, or some other person for whom he became responsible, got £3000 from the plaintiff, or the person she represents. But, in consequence of an omission or mistake in the names of the witnesses to the memorial, the defendant might have relied on a certain English statute which would have enabled him, perhaps, to keep his money in his pocket, and to defeat the plaintiff in her action. Such a defence was, no doubt, open to him by the law of England; but by that law such a defence must have been put upon the record, and relied on in due season; that was not done; the defendant pretermitted his opportunity of doing so, and the plaintiff obtained a judgment against him. Is that judgment, then, against natural right and justice; or ought we to aid the defendant in his efforts to deprive the plaintiff of the fruits of it when she seeks to enforce it here? In my opinion, we ought not to do so."[213]

The fact that evidence has been excluded in the foreign court pursuant to a rule whereby neither party to the litigation can be called as a witness on his own behalf will not render the foreign judgment contrary to natural justice.[214] Neither will the fact that there was some defect in the evidence before the foreign court if that defect could have been and was brought to light in the foreign proceedings themselves.[215]

We need not here recount[216] the circumstances in which Barrington, J., in *L.B.* v. *H.B.*[217] denied recognition to a French divorce decree on the basis that there had been a "substantial defeat of justice for which the parties, and not the court, b[ore] the responsibility." Suffice it here to note that the exact dimensions of this concept have yet to be filled in. It is difficult to see why it would not also extend to cases involving unilateral fraud by one of the parties as to the grounds presented to the court. Conceivably it could also extend to cases where, without deception by either spouse, vital evidence had been suppressed. At some point, however, our courts are likely to call a halt to extension of this concept on the basis that they are being asked, in effect, to do what they ought not, namely, to become an ultimate court of appeal from the foreign proceedings.

Foreign judgment contrary to public policy

A foreign judgment that is contrary to Irish public policy will be refused recognition and enforcement here. This issue has been examined in detail in Chapter 9.[218]

---

[212] 3 I.L.R. 415 (1841).

[213] *Id.*, at 421.

[214] *Scarpetta* v. *Lowenfeld* 27 T.L.R. 509 (1911). See also *Robinson* v. *Fenner* [1913] 3 K.B. 835 (Channell, J., 1912).

[215] *Jacobson* v. *Frachon* 138 L.T. 386 (C.A., 1927).

[216] Cf. *supra*, pp. 285-286.

[217] *Supra.*

[218] *Supra*, pp. 207-208.

Direct Enforcement of Foreign Judgments by Statute

At common law a foreign judgment can be enforced in Ireland only by bringing an action here on the obligation which it creates. The common law does not allow for direct enforcement by a process of registration or otherwise. However, statute may provide for a simpler, more direct form of enforcement in the case of certain foreign judgments.

Judgments Extension Act 1868 no longer applicable

The Judgments Extension Act 1868 provided for a just such simplified method of enforcement of judgments as between England, Wales, Scotland and Ireland.[219] Under the Act a judgment obtained in one of those countries "for any debt, damages or costs" could be "extended" to one of the other countries by registering in the appropriate court a certificate to the effect that a judgment had been obtained. The registered certificate was of the same force and effect as if the judgment certified by it had been originally obtained in the court in which it was registered.[220] Courts in England[221] and Northern Ireland[222] regarded the 1868 Act as never having applied to the Irish Free State, though the Irish[223] and Scottish[224] courts took a different view. The 1868 Act was eventually repealed by the Courts of Justice Act 1936.[225]

Administration of Justice Act 1920 not applicable

The Administration of Justice Act 1920, which provided for reciprocal enforcement of judgments by registration as between the United Kingdom and Commonwealth counties, has never applied in or to this country.

Maintenance Orders Act 1974

The Maintenance Orders Act 1974, makes provision for the enforcement on a basis of reciprocity of maintenance orders made in the State, in Northern Ireland, England and Wales and Scotland. The Act is "largely modelled"[226] on the provision of the European Convention on Jurisdiction and Enforcement of Judgments

---

[219] See *Anon.*, *The Judgments Extension Act 1868*, 2 Ir. L.T. & Sol. J. 441 (1868), *Anon.*, *Reciprocal Enforcement of Judgments*, 62 I.R. L.T. & Sol. J. 39 (1928), *Anon.*, *Reciprocal Enforcement of Judgments and Decrees, Part I*, 2 N. Ir. L.Q. 189 (1938), *Part II*, 3 N. Ir. L.Q. 91, at 92 (1939), also Articles in 57 Ir. L.T. & Sol. J. 269 (1923), 58 Ir. L.T. & Sol. J. 279 (1924), 59 Ir. L.T. & Col. J. 181 (1925). Decisions considering aspects of the Act, prior to Independence, include *Booth* v. *Egan*, 6 L.R. Ir. 282 (Q.B. Div., 1880), *Johnstone* v. *Bucknall*, [1898] 2 I.R. 499 (Q.B. Div., Gibson, J.), *Boss* v. *O'Connor*, I.R. 9 C.L. 478 (Consol. Cham., 1875), *Part* v. *Scannell*, I.R. 9 C.L. 426 (Com. Pleas, 1875), *Bailey* v. *Welply*, I.R. 4 C.L. 243 (Com. Pleas, 1869) and *Brookes* v. *Harrison*, 6 L.R. (Ir.) 332 (C.A., 1880), aff'g 6 L.R. (Ir.) 85 Ir. 1 (C.A., 1908) aff'g Wylie, J., 1908).
[220] Section 1 of the Act.
[221] *Wakely* v. *Triumph Cycle Co.* [1924] 1 K.B. 214 (C.A., 1923), *Banfield* v. *Chester*, 94 L.J. K.B. 805, 59 I.L.T.R. 118 (C.A., 1925).
[222] *Callan* v. *McKenna*, 63 I.L.T.R. 16 (N.I. High Ct., K.B. Div., Moore, L.C.J. 1928).
[223] *Gieves* v. *O'Conor*, [1924] 2 I.R. 182. And see *Read*, 297. Yntema, *The Enforcement of Foreign Judgments in Anglo-American Law* 33 Mich. L. Rev. 1129, at 1152 (1935).
[224] Cf. *Anton*, 594, *Doohan* v. *National Coal Board*, 1959 S.C. 310, *Harley* v. *Kinnear Moodie & Co.* 1964 S.C. 99.
[225] Section 3, Sch. 1, Pt.1. See *The State (Dowling)* v. *Kingston (No.2)*, [1937] I.R. 699, at 757–758 (Sup. Ct., *per* Meredith, J.) The Scottish decisions referred to at fn. 224 above would appear to have been based on lack of awareness of the repeal effected by the 1936 Act.
It is worth also noting section 180 (1) of the Companies (Consolidation) Act 1908 (repealed by the Companies Act 1963), under which any order made by the Court in England in the winding up of a company could be enforced here "in the same manner in all respects" as if the order had been made by the Irish Court; see further *In re The Bank of Egypt Ltd.*, [1913] 1 I.R. 502 (Barton, J.), and *supra*, pp. 485-486. As to the enforcement of foreign (and, specifically, British) adjudications in respect of bankruptcy, see *supra*, ch. 25.
[226] Terry, *Convention of Accession of Denmark, Ireland and the United Kingdom to the Convention on Jurisdiction and Enforcement of Judgments in Civil and Commercial Matters*, 4 J. of Irish Soc. for Europ. L. 26, at 40 (1980).

in Civil and Commercial Matters.[227] The Act is analysed in detail in the chapter on maintenance obligations.[228]

European Community Judgments

Under Articles 187 and 192 of the E.E.C. Treaty,[229] which are part of the domestic law of the State by virtue of the European Communities Act 1972,[230] judgments of the Court of Justice of the European Communities and decisions of the Council or of the Commission which impose a pecuniary obligation on persons other than the States are enforceable. Enforcement is governed by the rules of civil procedure in force in the State in the territory of which it is carried out.[231] The order for enforcement is appended to the judgment or decision, without formality, other than verification of the authenticity of the decision, by the national authority which the Government of each member State must designate for this purpose.[232] The European Communities (Enforcement of Community Judgments) Regulations 1972[233] designate the Master of the High Court as the national authority for this purpose. On application duly made by the person entitled to enforce a community judgment, the Master must make an order for the enforcement of the Community judgment and append the order of it.[234]

A Community judgment to which an enforcement order has been appended is, for all purposes of execution, of the same force and effect as if the judgment had been a judgment or order given or made by the High Court.[235] Where a sum of money is payable under the Community judgment, the enforcement order must provide that the amount payable is to be such a sum in Irish currency as, on the basis of the rate of exchange prevailing at the date on which the Community judgment was originally given, is equivalent to the sum payable.[236] If the Community judgment has been partly satisfied when enforcement is sought, the enforcement order must be made only in respect of the balance.[237] If the Community judgment is partly or wholly satisfied after the Master has made an enforcement order, he must vary or cancel his order accordingly.[238] Enforcement of a Community judgment may be suspended only by a decision of the European Court of Justice,[239] for the period and on the conditions, if any, stated in the order.[240]

---

[227] Cf. *infra*, pp. 612-616.

[228] *Supra*, pp. 310-317.

[229] See also Articles 180, 159 and 164 of the Euratom Treaty and Articles 44 and 92 of the ECSC Treaty.

[230] Section 2.

[231] Article 192 of the EEC Treaty.

[232] *Id.*

[233] S.T. No. 331 of 1972, made under section 3 of the European Communities Act 1972.

[234] 1972 Regulations, Regulation 4(1).

[235] *Id.*, Regulation 5.

[236] *Id.*, Regulation 4(2).

[237] *Id.*, Regulation 4(3).

[238] *Id.*, Regulation 4(4).

[239] Article 192 of the E.E.C. Treaty.

[240] 1972 Regulations, regulation 6.

EEC Convention on Jurisdiction and the Enforcement of Judgments in Civil and Commercial Matters[241]

This Convention is concerned with judgments in civil and commercial matters[242] of the national Courts of Member States of the E.E.C. The Convention is a "double" one, laying down direct rules as to jurisdiction, which we have already examined.[243] On the assumption that these rules as jurisdiction are properly complied with, the Convention establishes rules for recognition and enforcement which are allowed to take place "virtually automatically".[244] Thus, any defendant who believes that the exercise of jurisidction over him is not permitted by the Convention should, in his own interests, contest the matter by challenging the jurisdiction initially, rather than by standing back and letting the action proceed to judgment, hoping to call the judgment into question when the plaintiff seeks to have it recognised or enforced.[245]

---

[241] For the English and Irish texts of the original Convention of 1968 and the English text of the 1978 Convention of Accession of Denmark, Ireland and the United Kingdom to the 1968 Convention, see the Official Journal of the European Communities, No. L. 304, vol. 21, 30 October 1978, which also contains a consolidated text of the two Conventions. The Irish text of the 1978 Convention is published in *Iris Oifigiúil na glomhphobal Eorpach — Eagrán Speisialta*, 31 Nollaig 1982, which also contains the texts of the Greek Accession Convention. For the Jenard Report on the 1968 Convention and the Schlosser Report on the Convention of Accession, see OJ, C59, Vol. 22 5 March 1979. See, generally, I. Fletcher, *Conflict of Laws and European Community Law, With Special Reference to the Community Conventions on Private International Law*,Ch. 4, esp. at 133–138 (1982), Terry, *Convention of Accession of Denmark, Ireland and the United Kingdom to the Convention on Jurisdiction and Enforcement of Judgments in Civil and Commercial Matters*, 4 J. of Irish Soc. for European L. 26 (1980), Hauschild, *The European Communities Convention of 27 September 1968 on Jurisdiction and Enforcement of Judgments in Civil and Commercial Matters*, 4 J. of Irish Soc. for European L. 43 (1980). Hartley, *The Recognition of Foreign Judgments in England Under the Jurisdiction and Judgments Convention*, in K. Lipstein ed., *Harmonization of Private International Law of the EEC* 103, G. Droz, *Competence Judiciare et Effets des Jugements dans le Marche Commun* (1972), M. Weser, *Convention Communautaire sur la Competence Judiciare et l'Execution des Decisions* (1975), L. Collins, *The Civil Jurisdiction and Judgments Act 1982* chs. 1,2,3,5 (1983), Pointon, *The EEC Convention on the Recognition and Enforcement of Civil and Commercial Judgments and its Implications for English Law*, 1975–2 Legal Issues of European Integration 1, Moloney & Kremlis, *The Brussels Convention on Jurisdiction and the Enforcement of Judgments*, 79 Inc. L. Soc. of Ireland Gaz. 329 (1985), 80 Inc. L. Soc. of Ireland Gaz. 5 (1986).

[242] Article 1 of the Convention. Article 1 provides that the Convention does not apply to four specific matters which could otherwise have fallen within the scope of the words "civil and commercial matters". These are:

> (1) the status or legal capacity of natural persons, rights in property arising out of a matrimonial relationship, (cf. *De Cavel* v. *De Cavel* (No.1), [1979] E.C.R. 1055, [1979] 2 C.M.L.R. 547, *CHW* v. *GJH*, [1982] E.C.R. 1189, [1983] 2 C.M.L.R. 125) wills and succession;
> (2) bankruptcy, proceedings relating to the winding–up of insolvent companies (cf. *Goudain* v. *Nadler*, [1979] E.C.R. 733, [1979] 3 C.M.L.R. 180) or other legal persons, judicial arrangements, compositions and analogous proceedings;
> (3) social security; and
> (4)arbitration.

In these four matters, Irish common law rules will continue to apply. What falls within the scope of the concept of "civil and commercial matters" (apart from these four matters) must be determined by an interpretation independent of the law of either the court giving the original judgment or of the country in which enforcement is sought; instead it "must be interpreted by reference, first, to the objectives and scheme of the Convention and, secondly, to the general principles which stem from the corpus of the national legal systems": *LTU GmbH & Co. K.G.* v. *Eurocontrol*, [1976] E.C.R. 1541, at 1551. The nature of the court charged with the task of hearing the proceedings does not determine whether the matter is or is not a "civil [or] commercial" one for the purpose of the Convention. In the *Eurocontrol* case, it was noted that "Article 1 shows that the concept 'civil and commercial matters' cannot be interpreted solely in the light of the division of jurisdiction between the various types of courts existing in certain States." *Collins*, 19–20 observes that "[t]he Convention will, therefore, cover civil and commercial claims in administrative tribunals [citing the *Jenard Report*, p. 9] and will not include public claims in commercial tribunals [citing *Eurocontrol*]."
See further *supra* p. 182.

[243] See *supra*, pp. 181-191.

[244] *Saunders*, 133.

[245] *Id*. See also Article 28.

There is no danger in contesting the jurisdiction at the initial stage: Article 18 protects the defendant from being held to have consented to the jurisdiction where his appearance was entered "solely to contest the jurisdiction."

The basic recognition and enforcement provisions of the Convention are to the effect that a judgment of a court of one E.E.C. Contracting State is to be given automatic recognition in another Contracting State without any special procedure being required.[246] Article 31 provides that a judgment given in a Contracting State and enforceable there is to be enforced in another Contracting State when, on the application of any interested party, the order for its enforcement has been issued there. If the recognition of a judgment is raised as the principal issue in a dispute, then the simplified procedure for enforcement of judgments that is provided for in the Convention may be applied.[247] Under Article 32, in the case of Ireland, the application is to be submitted to the High Court.

The Convention contains a number of grounds for refusing the application. Article 27 provides that a judgment will not be recognised:

(1) If such recognition is contrary to public policy in the State in which recognition is sought;[248]

(2) Where it was given in default of appearance, if the defendant was not duly served with the document that instituted the proceedings or with an equivalent document[249] in sufficient time to enable him to arrange his defence;[250]

(3) If the judgment is irreconcilable with a judgment given in a dispute between the same parties in the State in which recognition is sought;[251]

(4) If the court of the State in which the judgment was given, in order to arrive at its judgment, has decided a preliminary question concerning the status or legal capacity of natural persons, rights in property arising out of a matrimonial relationship, wills or succession in a way that conflicts with a rule of the private international law of the State in which the recognition is sought, unless the same result would have been reached by the application of the rules of private international law of that State;[252]

(5) If the judgment is irreconcilable with an earlier judgment given in a non—contracting State involving the same parties, provided that this latter judgment fulfills the conditions necessary for its recognition in the State addressed.[253]

Article 28 specifies the four cases in which it is permissible to refuse to recognise a foreign judgment on the ground that the court of the State of origin lacked jurisdiction. These are cases where a judgment conflicts with section 3, 4 or 5 of Title II, or in a case mentioned by Article 59. Section 3 deals with jurisdiction in

---

[246] Article 26(1). Cf. Hartley, *supra*, at 104;

"If the free movement of goods, labour, services, capital etc. are part of the concept of a common market, surely the free movement of judgments should also be regarded as an essential element: its commercial importance is indisputable."

[247] Article 26(2).

[248] Article 27(1). See *Collins*, 107–108.

[249] These words were added by the Accession Convention to harmonise the Convention with Irish and British procedure: see Terry, *Convention of Accession of Denmark, Ireland and the United Kingdom to the Convention on Jurisdiction and Enforcement of Judgments in Civil and Commercial Matters*, 4 J. of Irish Soc. for European L. 26, at 41 (1980). The same change was made to Articles 20 and 46 of the Convention.

[250] Article 27(2), as amended by Article 13(1) of the Convention.

[251] Article 27(3).

[252] Article 27(4).

[253] Article 27(5), added by Article 13(2) of the Convention.

matters relating to insurance; section 4 with jurisdiction in relation to consumer contracts; and section 5 with excessive jurisdiction. Article 59 envisages a situation where a Contracting State may assume, in a convention, an obligation towards a third State not to recognise judgments given in other Contracting States against defendants domiciled or habitually resident in the third State, using rules of exhorbitant jurisdiction.[254]

Article 28(2) provides that, in its examination of the grounds of jurisdiction in any of these four cases, the court or authority to which application is made is bound by the findings of fact on which the court of the State in which the judgment was given based its jurisdiction.[255] As has been pointed out, ''[t]his may of course include a finding on the vital question of the facts relevant to any determinations of the defendant's domicile in the eyes of the *forum,* or, *semble,* even of some other Contracting State''.[256]

Apart from the four cases in which it is permissible to refuse to recognise a judgment based on lack of jurisdiction, the jurisdiction of the court of the State in which the judgment was given may not be reviewed.[257] Moreover, the test of public policy referred to in Article 27(1) may not be applied to the rules relating to jurisdiction.[258]

The cardinal principle underlying the rules for recognition is that under no circumstances may a foreign judgment be reviewed as to its substance.[259]

The Convention provides for a rapid and simple procedure for enforcement[260] of orders.[261] The procedure is based on *ex parte* application.[262] As has been mentioned, application for enforcement must be submitted, in the case of Ireland, to the High Court.[263] The procedure for making the application is governed by the law of the State in which enforcement is sought.[264] The 1986 Bill[265] which sought to give effect to the Convention adopted a procedure involving *ex parte* application to the Master of the High Court similar to that under the Maintenance Orders Act 1974.[266] In any event the decision on an application will have to be given without delay.[267] The party against whom enforcement is sought is not entitled to be heard at this stage.[268] The Convention does not even require that he have been

[254] Cf. *Fletcher,* 119-120, 135.

[255] But the Court in the State in which enforcement is sought ''is not bound by the findings of the original court as to whether the case is within the scope of the Convention'': *Morris,* 133, citing case 29/76 *L.T.U.* v. *Eurocontrol,* [1976] E.C.R. 1541.

[256] *Fletcher,* 135-136.

[257] Article 28(2).

[258] Article 28(3). See *Collins,* 108; cf. *Saunders,* 136.
    ''This .... provision ensures that the potentially elastic notion of public policy cannot be used as a 'long stop' to enable recognition and enforcement to be resisted in cases where the proper course of action which the defendant ought to have pursued was to contest before the foreign court the propriety of its initial assumption of jurisdiction.''

[259] Article 29.

[260] The enforcement procedure is exclusive; an action on the judgment at common law is not permitted. Cf. *De Wolf* v. *Cox,* [1976] E.C.R. 1759, [1979] 2 C.M.L.R. 43, Hartley, (1977) 2 E.L.R. 146.

[261] Provisional or protective orders are enforceable: (Case 143/78 *De Cavel* v. *De Cavel (No. 1),* [1979] E.C.R. 1055); unless they are granted *ex parte* without giving the defendant an opportunity to be heard: Case 123/79 *Denilauler* v. *Couchet Freres,* [1980] E.C.R. 1553.

[262] See Article 31. See *Jenard Report,* p. 47.

[263] Article 32.

[264] Article 33(1).

[265] The *Explanatory and Financial Memorandum* published by the Department of Justice in December, 1986, accompanying the Bill, set out very clearly in paragraphs 19 to 20 how applications for recognition and enforcement would operate.

[266] Cf. *supra,* pp. 311-312.

[267] Article 34(1).

[268] *Id.*

informed of the fact that the application had been made, the intention being "to preserve the element of surprise and to prevent him from removing his assets out of the jurisdiction."[269]

Enforcement may be refused only on one of the grounds for refusal of recognition already referred to above[270] and again the foreign judgment may under no circumstances be reviewed as to its substance.[271]

The defendant[272] may appeal against an enforcement order within a month of being served notice of it[273] or within two months if he is domiciled in a Contracting State other than that in which the decision authorising enforcement was given.[274] The appropriate court in Ireland before which an appeal should be lodged is the High Court.[275] During the time specified for an appeal and until the appeal has been determined, no measures for enforcement "other than protective measures" may be taken against the property of the party against whom enforcement is sought.[276] The High Court may stay the proceedings if an ordinary appeal[277] or, so far as a British judgment is concerned, any form of appeal,[278] has been lodged against a decision authorising enforcement, or the time for lodging the appeal has not expired. A further appeal to the Supreme Court on a point of law is permitted by Article 41.[279]

As regards the enforcement process in general, it is worth noting Article 45 which reflects the Community ethos clearly. It provides that no security, bond or deposit, however described, is to be required of a party who in one Contracting State applies for enforcement of a judgment given in another Contracting State on the ground that he is foreign national or is not domiciled or resident in the State in which enforcement is sought.

One noteworthy feature of the Convention is that the exorbitant bases of jurisdiction in Contracting States, the application of which is prohibited by the Convention as against domiciliaries of E.E.C. Contracting States,[280] will remain available against defendants who are not such domiciliaries; and judgments given against such defendants on such basis of jurisdiction will be enforceable Community-wide under the Convention's simplified enforcement procedure. This has given rise to concern in countries such as Australia and the U.S.A.[281] The Convention enables a Contracting State to enter into a convention with a third country under which judgments given by the courts of other Contracting States on an exorbitant jurisdiction basis would not be enforceable against domiciliaries of the third country.[282]

The Convention entered into force, as between States that have ratified it, on 1 November 1986, which was the first day of the third month following the ratification by all of the original Contracting States and *one* new Contracting State.[283] For a Contracting State ratifying thereafter, the Convention enters into force for that

---

[269] *Morris,* 131.

[270] Article 34(2).

[271] Article 34(3).

[272] A party whose application for enforcement is refused also has a right of appeal: Article 40.

[273] Article 36(1).

[274] Article 36(2).

[275] Article 37.

[276] Article 39(1). Article 39(2) provides that the decision authorising enforcement carries with it the power to proceed to any such protective measures. Thus *Mareva*-type injunctions are not merely permitted but required: *Capelloni & Aquilini* v. *Pelkmans* [1986] I C.M.L.R. 388 (Eur. Ct. of Justice, 1985).

[277] Article 38(1).

[278] Article 38(2).

[279] As amended by Article 20 of the Convention of Accession.

[280] Article 3. See *supra,* p. 182.

[281] See Pryles and Trindade, *The Common Market (E.E.C.) Convention on Jurisdiction and Enforcement of Judgments in Civil and Commercial Matters — Possible Impact upon Australian Citizens,* 42 Aust. L.J. 185, at 192-195 (1974).

[282] Article 59.

[283] Article 39 of the Accession Convention.

Contracting State on the first day of the third month following its ratification.[284] Although the 1986 Bill seeking to give effect to the Convention died with the fall of the last Government, it is probable that a Bill drafted in almost identical terms will shortly be published.

Arbitration[285]

In this section we will examine the conflicts rules in relation to foreign arbitral awards. The topic is of some considerable practical importance, in view of the increasing resort to arbitration as a mechanism for dispute resolution especially in commercial[286] matters.

A foreign arbitral award may be enforced in Ireland in a number of different ways: it may be sued upon in an action at common law or it may be enforced under the Arbitration Act 1954 or the Arbitration Act 1980.

Enforcement at common law

Enforcement by action at common law is always available, whether or not the arbitration award may also be enforced under the 1954[287] or 1980[288] Act. In *International Alltex Corporation* v. *Lawler Creations Ltd.*[289] Kenny, J. cited the following passage from *Cheshire*[290] with approval:

> "A foreign arbitral award is on the same footing as a foreign judgment in the sense that an action to recover the sum awarded may be brought in England. The essentials of success are proof that the parties submitted to arbitration, that the arbitration was conducted in accordance with the submission, and that the award is valid by the law of the country in which it has been made."

The first requirement is that the defendant must have validly submitted to arbitration, as, for example, by having contracted to submit to the jurisdiction of a foreign arbitrator.[291] The validity of any clause in a contract agreeing to submit any disputes to arbitration is governed by the proper law of the contract.[292] Where the parties enter into a contract containing an arbitration clause to cover future disputes that may arise under the contract, there is a strong presumption that the proper law is that of the country where the arbitration is to be held.[293] However, this presumption is rebuttable, since an arbitration clause is only one of a number of circumstances to be considered in determining the proper law of a contract.[294]

---

[284] *Id.* See Terry, *Convention of Accession of Denmark, Ireland and the United Kingdom to the Convention on Jurisdiction and Enforcement of Judgments in Civil and Commercial Matters,* 4 J. of Irish Soc. for European L. 26, at 42 (1980).

[285] See generally C. Schmittohoff ed., *International Commercial Arbitration* (1979), *Symposium — International Commercial Arbitration,* 13 Int'l Law. 209 (1979), *A Symposium on the Enforcement of Foreign Judgments and Arbitral Awards,* 17 Va. J. Int'l L. 729 (1977), Mann, *State Contracts and International Arbitration,* in *Studies in International Law* 56 (1973), J. Wetter, *The International Arbitral Process,* (1979), Ehrenhaft, *Effective International Commercial Arbitration,* 9 L. & Pol'y Int'l Bus. 1191 (1977), *Shareholders and Arbitration Clauses,* 7 Int'l Bus. Law 129 (1979).

[286] It is of interest to note that arbitration has also played a growing role in respect of family disharmony in some countries: see Spencer & Zammitt, *Arbitration : A Proposal for Private Resolution of Disputes Between Divorced or Separated Parents,* [1976] Duke L.J. 911.

[287] Cf. the Arbitration Act 1954, section 59, which preserves the right of enforcement at common law.

[288] Cf. the Arbitration Act 1980, section 11, which also preserves the right of enforcement at common law.

[289] [1965] I.R. 264 at 270. For the facts of the case cf. *supra,* p. 594.

[290] 3rd ed., 1947, p. 768 (see now *Cheshire & North,* 10th ed., 1979, p. 680), citing *Norske Atlas Insurance Co. Ltd.* v. *London General Insurance Co. Ltd.,* 43 T.L.R. 541, at 542 (K.B. Div., MacKinnon, J. 1927).

[291] *International Alltex Corporation* v. *Lawler Creations Ltd.* [1965] I.R. 264, at 269.

[292] *Dalmia Dairy Industries Ltd.* v. *National Bank of Pakistan* [1978] 2 Lloyd's Rep. 223.

[293] *Dicey & Morris,* 1127, citing *Hamlyn* v. *Talisker Distillery* [1894] A.C. 202; *Spurrier* v. *La Cloche,* [1902] A.C. 466; *Norske Atlas Insurance Co. Ltd.* v. *London General Insurance Co. Ltd., supra,* *Tzortzis* v. *Monark Line A/B* [1968] 1 All E.R. 949. See Hirsch, *The Place of Arbitration and the Lex Arbitri,* 34 Arb. J. 43 (1979).

[294] *Dicey & Morris,* 1127, citing *Dalmia Dairy Industries Ltd.* v. *National Bank of Pakistan, supra.*

Where the arbitration agreement relates to a dispute already in existence rather than one that may arise at some time in the future, the law of the country where the arbitration is to be held "is even more likely to be the proper law of the contract, because the arbitration is the sole object of the agreement."[295] The proper law will determine such questions as whether the arbitration agreement has been abrogated by subsequent illegality.[296]

The arbitration must also have been conducted in accordance with the submission. This raises the question of what law is to govern the actual arbitration proceedings themselves (as distinct from the agreement to arbitrate). The parties may, of course, expressly select the law which is to govern the arbitration proceedings. If they fail to make a choice, the arbitration proceedings will "almost certainly"[297] be governed by the law of the place of arbitration as being the place with which the proceedings are most closely connected.[298]

To be enforceable here, the award must be valid by the law governing the arbitration proceedings,[299] which will in most cases be the law of the country in which the arbitration is held.[300] That law will determine such questions as the failure by one party to appoint an arbitrator, and what law the arbitrators are to apply.[301] Once the award is valid by that law, the fact that it would not be in harmony with Irish law — on such a matter as ousting the jurisdiction, for example — will not render it unenforceable.[302]

The award must also be final and conclusive under the law governing the arbitration proceedings.[303] A foreign arbitration award that has been rendered enforceable by a court judgment in the country where it was given may be enforced by an action as a foreign judgment. Thus in *International Alltex Corporation* v. *Lawler Creations Ltd.*,[304] where contracts for the cotton goods by a United States company to an Irish purchaser contained terms specifying[305] that disputes arising from the contracts should be settled by arbitration in New York City in accordance with the rules of the American Arbitration Association, Kenny, J. held that this submission to the jurisdiction of the arbitrator in New York necessarily involved the submission to an order by the Supreme Court of the State of New York confirming the arbitrator's award.[306] On the other hand, a foreign award may be enforced even though it has not been so rendered enforceable by a court judgment in the country where it was given, regardless of whether even if the law of that country requires a court judgment to make the award enforceable.[307]

It appears that a foreign arbitration award, like a foreign judgment, will not be recognised or enforced if the arbitrator had not jurisdiction to make it,[308] or it was obtained by fraud,[309] or its recognition or enforcement would be contrary to public policy,[310] or the arbitration proceedings were contrary to natural justice.[311]

---

[295] *Morris*, 136.
[296] *Compagnie Tunisienne de Navigation S.A.* v. *Compagnie d'Arment Maritime S.A.*, [1971] A.C. 572.
[297] *Morris*, 136.
[298] *James Miller & Partners Ltd.* v. *Whitworth Street Estates (Manchester) Ltd.*, [1970] A.C. 583; *Dalmia Dairy Industries Ltd.* v. *National Bank of Pakistan, supra.*
[299] *Union Nationale des Co-opératives Agricoles et Céréales* v. *R. Catterall & Co. Ltd.* [1959] 2 Q.B. 44.
[300] *Morris*, 137.
[301] *Id.*
[302] *Addison* v. *Brown* [1954] 2 All E.R. 213.
[303] *Dalmia Dairy Industries Ltd.* v. *National Bank of Pakistan, supra*, at 246-250, *Morris*, 137.
[304] [1965] I.R. 264 (High Ct., Kenny, J.).
[305] As one of two options.
[306] Cf. [1965] I.R., at 269-270.
[307] *Union Nationale des Co-opératives Agricoles et Céréales* v. *R. Catterall & Co. Ltd., supra.*
[308] *Kionta Osakeyhtio* v. *Britain and Overseas Trading Co. Ltd.* 1 Lloyd's Rep. 247; *Dalmia Dairy Industries Ltd.* v. *National Bank of Pakistan, supra.*
[309] *Oppenheim & Co.* v. *Mahomed Haneef* [1922] 1 A.C. 482, at 487.
[310] *Hamlyn & Co.* v. *Talisker Distillery* [1894] A.C. 202 at 209, 214; *Dalmia Dairy Industries Ltd.* v. *National Bank of Pakistan, supra* at 267-269, 299-301.
[311] *Dalmia Industries Ltd.* v. *National Bank of Pakistan, supra*, at 269-270.

It has already been mentioned that a foreign arbitration award may be enforced by an action. An alternative method of enforcement may possibly be available under section 41 of the Arbitration Act 1954. This provides that an award on an arbitration agreement may, by leave of the Court, be enforced in the same manner as a judgment or order to the same effect, and that, where leave is so given, judgment may be entered in terms of the award.

Enforcement under the Arbitration Act 1954

Part V of the Arbitration Act 1954 provides for the enforcement of certain foreign arbitration awards. The awards in question are those that are governed by the 1923 Geneva Protocol on Arbitration Clauses[312] or the 1927 Geneva Convention on the Execution of Foreign Arbitral Awards.[313] The award must have been made in pursuance of an arbitration agreement to which the 1923 Protocol applies and between persons who are subject to the jurisdiction[314] of two different States which, on a basis of reciprocity, have been declared by Government order to be parties to the 1927 Convention; the agreement must also have been made in the territory of a State[315] party to the 1927 Convention.[316] The foreign award is enforceable in the State either by action or in the same manner as a domestic award may be enforced by virtue of section 41[317] of the Act.[318] Any foreign award that is enforceable under Part V of the Act must be treated as binding for all purposes on the persons as between whom it was made, and may be relied on by any of them by way of defence, set-off or otherwise in any legal proceedings in the State.[319]

To be enforceable the foreign award must have:

(a) been made in pursuance of an agreement for arbitration which was valid under the law by which it was governed,[320]

(b) been made by the tribunal provided for in the agreement or constituted in manner agreed upon by the parties,

(c) been made in conformity with the law governing the arbitration procedure,

(d) become final in the country in which it was made,[321]

(e) been in respect of a matter which may lawfully be referred to arbitration under the law of the State,

and the enforcement of the award must not be contrary to the public policy or the law of the State.[322]

A foreign award is *not* enforceable if:

(a) the award has been annulled in the country in which it was made, or

(b) the party against whom it is sought to enforce the award was not given notice of the arbitration proceedings in sufficient time to enable him to present his case, or was under some legal incapacity and was not properly represented, *or*

(c) the award does not deal with all the questions referred or contains decisions beyond the scope of the arbitration agreement.[323]

---

[312] See the 1954 Act, First Schedule.
[313] *Id.*, Second Schedule.
[314] The meaning of the expression "subject to the jurisdiction" has given rise to discussion.
[315] It should be noted that this State need not be one in which either party resides or of which either is a citizen.
[316] Section 54(2) of the Act.
[317] Discussed *supra*.
[318] Section 55(1).
[319] Section 55(2) of the Act.
[320] Cf. *Kianta Osakeyhtio* v. *Britain and Overseas Trading Co. Ltd.*, [1954] 1 Lloyd's Rep. 247.
[321] Cf. *Union Nationale des Co-operatives Agricoles* v. *Catterall*, [1959] 2 Q.B. 44. An award is not deemed final if any proceedings for the purposes of contesting the validity of the award are pending in the country in which it was made: section 58 of the Act.
[322] Section 56(1).
[323] Section 56(2).

The party seeking to enforce a foreign award must produce certain specified evidence,[324] including the original award or a duly authenticated copy and evidence proving that the award has become final.

In the next section we will consider the extent to which Part V of the 1954 Act has been superseded by the Arbitration Act 1980.

Enforcement under the Arbitration Act 1980

The Arbitration Act 1980 gives effect to two international Conventions on arbitration. The 1958 New York Convention on the Recognition and Enforcement of Foreign Arbitral Awards[325] and the 1965 Washington Convention on the Settlement of Investment Disputes between States and Nationals of Other States.[326]

The New York Convention was drawn up under the auspices of the United Nations to replace the 1923 Geneva Protocol on Arbitration Clauses and the 1927 Geneva Convention on the Execution of Foreign Arbitral Awards. As we have noted, Part V of the Arbitration Act 1954 gave effect to the earlier Protocol and Convention. It has now been replaced by Part III of the 1980 Act *insofar as arbitration awards emanating from countries that are parties to the New York Convention are concerned.*[327] Part V of the 1954 Act continues to apply in relation to countries that are parties to the Geneva Protocol and Convention but not to the New York Convention.

The overall effect of the 1980 Act is to simplify and extend the scope of enforceable arbitration awards, as well as shifting onto the defendant the burden of resisting enforcement,[328] so that enforcement "can only be refused by the court in very limited circumstances".[329] An award is enforceable as a New York Convention award if it is made, in pursuance of an arbitration agreement in writing,[330] in the territory of a State, other than Ireland, which is party to the Convention.[331] The Act enables the Minister for Foreign Affairs to make an order declaring that any specified State is a party to the Convention and the order is to be evidence that that State is a party to the Convention.[332] It is worth noting that the definition of award under the New York Convention is far less demanding than that under the earlier Protocol and Convention.[333] It is not necessary that the parties be "subject to the

---

[324] Section 57(1).

[325] Cf. the First Schedule to the 1980 Act. See generally G. Gaja, *International Commercial Arbitration: New York Convention* (1978), Sanders, *A Twenty Years' Review of the Convention on the Recognition and Enforcement of Foreign Arbitral Awards*, 13 Int'l Law. 269 (1979), Quigley, *Accession by the United States to the United Nations Conventions on the Recognition and Enforcement of Foreign Arbitral Awards*, 70 Yale L.J. 1049 (1961), Tooboff & Goldstein, *Foreign Arbitral Awards and the 1958 New York Convention: Experience to Date in the U.S. Courts*, 17 Va. J. Int'l L. 469 (1977), Springer, *The United Nations Convention on the Recognition and Enforcement of Foreign Arbitral Awards*, 3 Int'l Law. 320 (1969), Contini, *International Commercial Arbitration: The United Nations Convention on the Recognition and Enforcement of Foreign Arbitral Awards*, 8 Am. J. Compar. L. 283 (1959), Olson, *Note*, 16 Harv. Int. L.J. 705 (1975). Harnick, *Recognition and Enforcement of Foreign Arbitral Awards*, 31 Am. J. Compar. L. 703 (1983), Loftis, *Securing Arbitral Awards: Waiving Immunity under the Sovereign Immunities Act and Ensuring Equitable Remedy by Pre-Award Attachment under the New York Convention*, 9 Suffolk Transnat. L.J. 235 (1985).

[326] Cf. The Second Schedule to the 1980 Act. S.I. No. 195 of 1981 brought Part III of the 1980 Act in relation to the New York Convention into force with effect from 10 August, 1981; S.I. No. 356 of 1980 brought Part IV of the 1980 Act in relation to the Washington Convention into force with effect from 1 January 1981.

[327] Section 10 of the 1980 Act.

[328] *Morris*, 141.

[329] *Cremer GmbH Co.* v. *Co-Operative Molasses Traders Ltd*, [1985] I.L.R.M. 564, at 570 (High Ct., Costello, J. (aff'd by Sup. Ct.)).

[330] Including an agreement contained in an exchange of letters or telegrams: section 2.

[331] Section 6(1) of the 1980 Act.

[332] Section 6(2). Cf. S.I. No. 175 of 1981. See also section 6(3) of the 1980 Act.

[333] See *Morris*, 141.

jurisdiction" of different Contracting States; nor is an arbitration agreement governed by Irish law excluded. Finally, it is worth noting that ratification of the New York Convention has had the incidental effect of enabling Ireland to fulfil the obligation imposed by Article 220 of the E.E.C. Treaty to simplify the formalities relating to the enforcement of arbitration awards throughout the E.E.C.

An award is enforceable either by action or in the same manner as a domestic arbitration award is enforceable by virtue of section 41 of the Arbitration Act 1954. The effect of an enforceable New York Convention award is that it is to be treated as binding for all purposes on the persons between whom it was made and may be relied on by any of them by way of defence, set off or otherwise in any legal proceedings in the State.[334]

As has been mentioned, the burden of proof on the person seeking enforcement of an award is easier than under the earlier Conventions. He must produce the duly authenticated original award or a duly certified copy, and the original arbitration agreement or a duly certified copy, and a certified translation if either of these is in a language other than English or Irish.[335] When he does this the award will be enforced, unless the defendant can establish one or more of the "limited policy grounds"[336] specified on the 1980 Act, which are the only ones on which recognition and enforcement *may* be refused.[337] These are that:

(a) a party to the arbitration agreement was (under the law applicable to him) under some incapacity, *or*

(b) the arbitration agreement was not valid under the law of the country to which the parties subjected it or, failing any indication thereon, under the law of the country where the award was made, *or*

(c) the defendant proves that he was not given proper notice of the appointment of the arbitrator or of the arbitration proceedings or was otherwise unable to present his case, *or*

(d) the award deals with a difference not contemplated by or not falling within the terms of the submission to arbitration or contains decisions on matters

---

The United Nations Convention on the Recognition and Enforcement of Foreign Arbitral Awards, 3 Int'l Law. 320 (1969), Contini, *International Commercial Arbitration: The United Nations Convention on the Recognition and Enforcement of Foreign Arbitral Awards,* 8 Am. J. Compar. L. 283 (1959), Olson, *Note,* 16 Harv. Int. L.J. 705 (1975). Harnick, *Recognition and Enforcement of Foreign Arbitral Awards,* 31 Am. J. Compar. L. 703 (1983), Loftis, *Securing Arbitral Awards: Waiving Immunity under the Sovereign Immunities Act and Ensuring Equitable Remedy by Pre-Award Attachment under the New York Convention,* 9 Suffolk Transnat. L.J. 235 (1985).

[326] Cf. The Second Schedule to the 1980 Act. S.I. No. 195 of 1981 brought Part III of the 1980 Act in relation to the New York Convention into force with effect from 10 August, 1981; S.I. No. 356 of 1980 brought Part IV of the 1980 Act in relation to the Washington Convention into force with effect from 1 January 1981.

[327] Section 10 of the 1980 Act.

[328] *Morris,* 141.

[329] *Cremer GmbH Co.* v. *Co-Operative Molasses Traders Ltd,* [1985] I.L.R.M. 564, at 570 (High Ct., Costello, J. (aff'd by Sup. Ct.)).

[330] Including an agreement contained in an exchange of letters or telegrams: section 2.

[331] Section 6(1) of the 1980 Act.

[332] Section 6(2). Cf. S.I. No. 175 of 1981. See also section 6(3) of the 1980 Act.

[333] See *Morris,* 141.

[334] Section 7(2) of the 1980 Act.

[335] Section 8.

[336] Springer, *supra,* at 323.

[337] Section 9(1). Contrast the defences under section 56(2) of the 1954 Act which give the Court no discretion in the matter.

beyond the scope of the submission to arbitration,[338] *or*

(e) the composition of the arbitral authority or the arbitral procedure was not in accordance with what the parties had agreed or, failing an agreement, with the law of the country where the arbitration took place,[339] *or*

(f) the award has not yet become binding on the parties or has been set aside or suspended by a competent authority of the country in which, or under the law of which, the award was made.[340]

Enforcement of an award may also be refused if the award is in respect of a matter which is not capable of settlement by arbitration under the law of the State, or if it would be contrary to public policy to enforce the award.[341]

The Arbitration Act 1980 also gives effect[342] to the Washington Convention which was drawn up under the aspices of the World Bank to facilitate the settlement of disputes between States (including State agencies) and foreign investors, the object being to stimulate a greater flow of foreign private capital into countries needing it. The Convention provides for the establishment of an International Centre for the Settlement of Investment Disputes, for the setting up of panels of conciliators and arbitrators, for the regulation of conciliation and arbitration proceedings under the Convention and for the enforcement of the pecuniary obligations imposed by an arbitration award. The International Centre has jurisdiction over any legal dispute arising directly out of an investment, between a Contracting State and a national of another Contracting State, which the parties to the dispute consent in writing to submit to the Centre.[343]

The pecuniary obligations imposed by an award of the Centre are, by leave of the High Court, enforceable in the same manner as a judgment order of that Court to the same effect .[344] Where leave is so given, judgment may be entered for the amount due or outstanding under the award.[345] A person applying for enforcement must lodge with his application a copy of the award certified in accordance with[346] the Convention.[347] The Convention provides for a procedure whereby enforcement of an award may be stayed by a Tribunal of the International Centre.[348] If such a stay has been granted in any case before it, the High Court must stay enforcement of the pecuniary obligations imposed by the award and, if an application has been made which might result in such a stay, may stay enforcement of these obligations.[349]

---

[338] Section 9(2)(d). An award containing decisions on matters not submitted to arbitration may, however, be enforced to the extent that it contains decisions on matters which were submitted to arbitration and which can be separated from any decision on matters not submitted: section 9(4). Cf. *Cremer GmbH Co.* v. *Co-Operative Molasses Traders Ltd.*, *supra*, where the Supreme Court held that section 9(2)(d) had no application to a case where the appellants contended that there had been no binding agreement containing an arbitration clause. If matters were as the appellants claimed, said Finlay, C.J. (at 573), then there could be no submission to arbitration and thus no issue as to whether an award dealt with differences not contemplated by, or falling within, the terms of a submission.

[339] Section 9(2)(e). Cf. *Cremer GmbH Co.* v. *Co-Operative Molasses Traders Ltd.*, *supra*, at 573.

[340] Section 9(2).

[341] Section 9(3) of the 1980 Act.

[342] In Part IV.

[343] Article 25 of the Washington Convention.

[344] Section 16(1) of the 1980 Act.

[345] *Id.*

[346] Article 54(2) of the Convention.

[347] Section 16(2) of the 1980 Act.

[348] Articles 50-52 of the Convention.

[349] Section 17 of the 1980 Act.

Staying of Irish proceedings

Under section 12 of the Arbitration Act 1954 the position used to be that a court was required to stay proceedings where there was an arbitration agreement to which the Geneva Protocol on Arbitration Clauses applied unless the court was satisfied that the agreement or arbitration had become inoperative or could not proceed or that there was not in fact any dispute between the parties with regard to the matter agreed to be referred to arbitration. As far as domestic arbitration agreements were concerned, the court might stay proceedings if it was satisfied that there was not sufficient reason why the matter should not be referred to arbitration and that the party against whom proceedings had been instituted was ready and willing to proceed with arbitration.

The Arbitration Act 1980 has made an important change in the position. The effect of the 1980 Act is to put all written[350] arbitration agreements[351] on an equal footing as regards proceedings commenced in breach of them.

Section 5 provides that, if any party to an arbitration agreement commences any proceedings in any court against any other party to such agreement in respect of any matter agreed to be referred to arbitration, any other party to the proceedings may apply to the court to stay the proceedings. The application may be made at any time after an appearance has been entered and before the applicant delivers any pleadings or takes any other steps in the proceedings.[352] Unless the court is satisfied that the arbitration agreement is null and void, inoperative or incapable of being performed or that there is not in fact any dispute between the parties with regard to the matter agreed to be referred to arbitration, it must make an order staying the proceedings.[353] However, the Court does have power to refuse to stay proceedings in relation to domestic arbitration where a question of lack of impartiality on the part of the arbitrator or a question of fraud on the part of any party arises.[354]

---

[350] Cf. section 2(1) of the Act.

[351] Whether domestic or foreign and, in the case of foreign agreements, whether covered by the Geneva Convention and Protocol, the New York Convention, the Washington Convention, or none of these international instruments.

[352] Section 5.

[353] Section 5(1) of the 1980 Act.

[354] Section 5(2) of the 1980 Act, preserving the power of the High Court in this regard under section 39(3) of the 1954 Act.

PART VII

PROCEDURE

CHAPTER 34

SUBSTANCE AND PROCEDURE[1]

Introduction

The distinction between substance and procedure has for long been recognised in the conflict of laws.[2] The distinction is an important one since matters of substance are generally determined by the *lex causae* while matters of procedure are governed by the *lex fori*. The concept of procedure is "a comprehensive one, including process and evidence, methods of execution, rules of limitation affecting the remedy and the course of the court with regard to the kind of relief that can be granted to a suitor".[3]

The rule that matters of procedure should be governed by the *lex fori* is based on considerations of practical necessity. Our judicial administration would descend into chaos if, in a case with a foreign element, the rules of evidence, of pleadings and of execution to be applied were those of a foreign country.[4]

Whether the scope of what is characterised as procedural is too broadly drawn is, however, a separate question which we shall be examining in the course of the chapter.

The objective reality of the distinction between substantive and procedural law has been attacked by several writers,[5] especially those of the realist school, who regard it as artificial and illusory, more in the minds of the judges rather than in the world of experience. More moderately, Cook expresses the issue as follows:

"If we admit that the 'substantive' shades off by imperceptible degrees into the 'procedural', and that the 'line' between them does not 'exist', to be discovered by logic and analysis, but is rather to be drawn so as best to carry out our purpose, we see that our problem resolves itself substantially into this: How far can the court of the forum go in applying the rules taken from the foreign system of law without unduly hindering or inconveniencing itself?"[6]

[1] See generally McClintock, *Distinguishing Substance and Procedure in the Conflict of Laws*, 78 U.Pa. L. Rev. 933 (1930), Twerski & Mayer, *Toward a Pragmatic Solution of Choice-of-Law Problems At the Interface of Substance and Procedure*, 74 Nw. U.L. Rev. 781 (1979), Ailes, *Substance and Procedure in the Conflict of Laws*, 39 Mich. L. Rev. 392 (1941), Castel, *Procedure and the Conflict of Laws*, 16 McGill L.J. 603 (1970).

[2] Ailes, *Substance and Procedure in the Conflict of Laws*, 39 Mich. L. Rev. 392, at 398-399 (1941).

[3] *Livesley* v. *Horst Co.*, [1924] S.C.R. 605, at 608 (*per* Duff, J.), quoted with approval, in *Northern Trust Co.* v. *McLean*, [1926] 3 D.L.R. 93, at 94-95 (Ont. Sup. Ct., App. Div., *per* Hodgins, J.A. (for the Court)). Cf. *Sigurdson* v. *Farrow*, 121 D.L.R. (3d) 183, at 185-189 (Alta. Q.B., Medhurst, J., 1981).

[4] Cf. Beckett, *The Question of Classification ("Qualification") in Private International Law*, 15 Br. Yrbk of Internat. L. 46, at 66 (1934).

[5] See Llewellyn, *The Bramble Bush*, 82-83 (1930); cf. Cook, *An Unpublished Chapter of the Logical and Legal Bases of the Conflict of Laws*, 37 Ill. L. Rev. 418 at 423-424 (1943).

[6] Cook, *"Substance" and "Procedure" in the Conflicts of Laws*, 42 Yale L.J. 1333, at 343-344 (1933). Cf. Weintraub, *The Erie Doctrine and State Conflict of Laws Rules*, 39 Ind. L.J. 228, at 232 (1964). *Yates* v. *Thompson*, 3 Cl. & F. 544 at 577, 6 E.R. 1541, at 1553 (*per* Lord Brougham, 1835).

One of the problems in distinguishing between substance and procedure is that many important rules of law recognised today as ones of substance had their origin in procedural devices.[7] Thus, for example, the rights of the *cestui que trust* and the obligations of the bailee derive from procedural origins. Conversely rules of evidence, such as presumptions and burdens of proof, frequently disguise substantive policies. The doctrine of *res ipsa loquitur*, for example, clearly has important effects on the substance of products liability.[8] Let us now consider a number of matters which, rightly or wrongly, have been characterised as procedural by the courts.

Evidence

As a general principle, questions relating to evidence are governed by the *lex fori*.[9] But it would be wrong to overstress this general principle. We should heed the warning that "... it is not everything that appears in a treatise on the law of evidence that is to be classified as adjective law, but only provisions of a technical or procedural character ..."[10] Of course the troublesome question remains: precisely which rules of evidence are procedural and which are substantive? And what criteria are to guide us in seeking an answer to this question?

Admissibility[11]

Questions as to the admissibility of evidence are determined by the *lex fori*.[12] Thus, documents admissible under the Irish law of evidence may be received in evidence by an Irish court though inadmissible under the *lex causae*.[13]

Though rules of procedure are a matter for the *lex fori*, the *lex fori* can of course have regard to the international dimensions of a case which may require the establishment of specific rules to cover certain foreign cases. In the Northern Ireland case of *King* v. *King*,[14] for example, Andrews, L.C.J. exercised his discretion to permit the reception of an affidavit sworn before a notary public in Manitoba, even though the jurat of the affidavit did not contain a certificate that the notary public knew the deponent or some person named in the jurat who certified his knowledge of the deponent. This defect would almost certainly have been fatal if the affidavit had sworn in Northern Ireland.[15] But the Lord Chief Justice was of opinion that it had occurred in the case before him on account of ignorance of the relevant Rule[16] on the part of the person in Manitoba who had prepared the affidavit. What was involved here was merely the exercise of a judicial discretion within the *lex fori*, rather than the application of a different law to the foreign affidavit.

The courts have drawn a distinction between extrinsic evidence put forward to *interpret* a written document, on the one hand, and extrinsic evidence whose purpose

---

[7] Ailes, *Substance and Procedure in the Conflict of Laws*, 39 Mich. L. Rev. 392, at 402 (1941), quoting Maine's famous remark (*Early Law and Custom*, 389 (1886)): "So great is the ascendency of the Law of Actions in the infancy of Courts of Justice, that substantive law has at first the look of being gradually secreted in the interstices of procedure."

[8] Cf. *Fleming*, 467-468.

[9] *Rev* v. *Griffin*, 4 L.R. (Ir.) 497, at 510 (Cr. Cas. Res., *per* Fitzgerald, B., 1879).

[10] *Mahadervan* v. *Mahadervan*, [1964] P. 233, at 243 (Sir Jocelyn Simon, P.).

[11] See *Dicey & Morris*, 1183-1184, *McLeod*, 220-221, *Castel*, vol. 1, 629-630.

[12] *Yates* v. *Thomson*, 3 Cl. & F. 544, 6 E.R. 1541 (1835), *Bain* v. *Whitehaven and Furness Junction Ry. Co.*, 3 H.L.C.I., 10 E.R. 1 (1850), *Finlay* v. *Finlay*, 31 L.J.P.M.A. 149 (Mat, 1862), *Malo* v. *Clement*, [1943] 4 D.L.R. 773 (Ont. High Ct., Plaxton, J.).

[13] *Dicey & Morris*, 1183, citing *Bristow* v. *Sequeville*, 5 Exch. 275, 155 E.R. 188 (1850).

[14] [1941] Ir. Jur. Rep. 29 (High Ct., K.B. Div. (Mat.), Andrews, L.C.J., 1940). See also *O'Neill* v. *Doran*, I.R. 10 Eq. 187 (V.C. Ct., Chatterton, V.C., 1876), *O'Connor* v. *Bernard*, 4 Ir. Eq. Rep. 689 (Eq. Exch., 1842).

[15] Cf. [1941] Ir. Jur. Rep., at 30-31.

[16] R.S.C. (N.I.) 1936, Or. xxxviii, Rule 14.

is to vary or contradict its terms, on the other.[17] The first kind of case, being a matter of interpretation, is governed by the proper law of the transaction of which the document is a part.[18] The second is simply a matter of evidence, to be determined by the *lex fori*.[19]

The Burden of Proof

In England, it is accepted that "a question as to the onus of proof ... is to be resolved according to the *lex fori*."[20] The burden of proof "represents that degree of certainty which is required by a court as to the facts at issue. As such, its procedural nature is clear."[21] Yet, there is a great deal to be said for treating this question as substantive, since victory in a case can depend on where the burden of proof lies.[22] Clearly the difference between a burden of proof based on the balance of probabilities[23] and one requiring proof beyond a reasonable doubt[24] or other standard of proof[25] may be attributable, in part at least, to substantive policy choices.[26] In this context it may be helpful to distinguish between the *legal* burden of proof and the *evidential* burden of proof. The former concerns "the obligation of a party to meet the requirement of a rule of law that a fact in issue must be proved (or disproved) either by a preponderance of the evidence or beyond reasonable doubt as the case may be."[27] The latter is "the obligation to show, if called upon to do so, that there is sufficient evidence to raise an issue as to the existence or non-existence of a fact in issue, due regard being had to the standard of proof demanded of the party under such obligation."[28] If this distinction is made, it is an attractive proposition that the legal burden of proof should be a matter of substance[29] and the evidential burden of proof a matter of procedure.

In torts litigation, there is authority in the United States[30] which treats as a matter of substance the question of where the burden of proving or disproving contributory negligence lies. The doctrine of *res ipsa loquitur* presents some difficulties. Throughout common law jurisdictions there is much disagreement as to the effect of the doctrine on the burden of proof.[31] On one view, it is merely one species of

---

[17] *Dicey & Morris*, 1183-1184, *Morris*, 455-456.

[18] *St. Pierre* v. *South American Stores Ltd.*, [1937] 3 All E.R. 349 (C.A.).

[19] *Korner* v. *Witkowitzer*, [1950] 2 K.B. 128, at 162-163 (C.A.); affirmed *sub nom. Vitkovice* v. *Korner*, [1951] A.C. 869.

[20] *The "Roberta"*, 58 Ll. L. Rep. 159, at 177 (Langton, J., 1937). See also *In the Estate of Fuld, decd. (No. 3)*, [1968] P., 675, at 696-697 (1965), where Scarman J. considered that an English Probate Court, "if conducting its enquiry *de novo* and not merely giving effect to a probate, or its equivalent, already granted abroad, must in all matters of burden of proof follow scrupulously its own *lex fori*."

[21] *McLeod*, 219.

[22] Cf. *Morris*, 458.

[23] The standard generally applicable in civil proceedings under Irish internal law: cf. *Grimes & Horgan*, 103.

[24] The standard generally applicable in criminal proceedings: cf. *Ryan & Magee*, 358-359, *Sandes*, 178-179, *The People A.G.* v. *Byrne*, [1974] I.R. 1, at 9 (C.C.A., *per* Kenny, J. (for the Court), 1973). *Byrne's* case is noted by Cole, 39 J. of Crim. L. 281 (1975).

[25] As, for example, in proceedings for divorce *a mensa et thoro* where the issue of adultery arises: cf. the Law Reform Commission's *Report on Divorce a Mensa et Thoro, Jactitation of Marriage and the Restitution of Conjugal Rights*, pp. 2-4 (L.R.C. 8-1983).

[26] Cf. *Chadbourn, Levin & Schuchman*, 356-357.

[27] *Cross*, 107.

[28] *Id*. See also *Morse*, 174, and more generally, *Hancock*, 153 ff.

[29] Cf. the *Restatement, Second*, section 134 and the *Hague Convention on the Law Applicable to Products Liability*, Article 8(8). See further *Morse*, 176-178.

[30] *Fitzpatrick* v. *International Ry.*, 252 N.Y. 127, 169 N.E. 112, 68 A.L.R. 801 (1929), *Jarrett* v. *Wabash Ry. Co.*, 57 F. 2d 669 (C.C.A. 2nd Circ. 1932). See *Morse*, 175-176, *Leflar*, 3rd ed., 1977, 248, *Hancock*, 158-159. See also the New York case of *Frummer* v. *Hilton Hotels International, Inc.*, 60 Misc. 2d 840, 304 N.Y.S. 2d 335 (Sup. Ct., 1969), which reached a similar result by means of interests analysis rather than by resorting to substance-procedure characterisation.

[31] See *Fleming*, 296-297, *Prosser & Keeton*, 257-262, *Trindade & Cane*, 350-351, 355-356.

circumstantial evidence, having the effect of ensuring that the plaintiff gets his case to the jury.[32] On another view, where *res ipsa loquitur* applies the defendant will escape liability if he either establishes that he was not negligent or provides a reasonable explanation, equally consistent with negligence and no negligence on his part.[33] On a third view, *res ipsa loquitur* shifts the onus onto the defendant to establish affirmatively that the accident was not caused by his negligence.[34] There is considerable uncertainty, even within particular jurisdictions,[35] as to which view is correct.

So far as the first view is concerned, it seems best to categorise it as procedural.[36] The second and third views have such a potent effect on the burden of proof that they have at least a claim to be treated as raising an issue of substance rather than procedure.[37]

It has been noted[38] that problems may arise where the burden of proof is regarded as procedural in the forum but the *lex causae* considers it substantive: here there would be two conflicting burdens of proof. Conversely, where the burden of proof according to the *lex fori* is regarded as a matter of substance, to be determined by the *lex causae*, but the *lex causae* treats it as procedural, there would theoretically be no law applicable to the burden of proof.[39] One commentator has suggested that, "[i]n the interests of convenience,"[40] the burden of proof should be regarded as procedural in this instance.

Presumptions[41]

Presumptions raise some difficulties in private international law, which have yet to be addressed by the courts. Presumptions are of three kinds. The first is a *presumption of fact*. This permits, but does not require, the trier of fact, on proof of one fact (or state of facts) to find the existence of a presumed fact.[42] Presumptions of fact raise no difficulties in private international law. The second is an *irrebuttable presumption of law*, whereby, on proof of a certain fact (or state of facts), the trier of fact *must* make a particular finding as to another fact of facts.[43] Irish law contains a number of such irrebuttable presumptions of the law,[44] including the presumption that a child under the age of seven has no criminal capacity and the presumption of survivorship.[45]

It is accepted[46] that, for the purposes of conflicts of law, irrebuttable presumptions are rules of substance rather than procedure. Thus, in the English decision *Re Cohn*,[47] where the question of the presumption of survivorship arose in a case where the *lex causae* was German, Uthwatt, J. held that the German rather than the English presumption should govern. He said:

[32] *McMahon & Binchy*, 210.
[33] *Id.*, 209.
[34] *Id.*
[35] *Id.*
[36] Cf. *Id.*, 209-210.
[37] Cf. *Morris*, 179, *Morse*, 178.
[38] By *Morris*, 458, *Dicey & Morris*, 1189, *McLeod*, 219-220.
[39] *Lorenzen*, 134. See also *Morris*, 458.
[40] *McLeod*, 220.
[41] See *Dicey & Morris*, 1189-1190, *Morris*, 458-459, *Cheshire & North*, 700-701, *Wolff*, 227-228, 235-236, 275-276, *McLeod*, 217-219.
[42] *Dicey & Morris*, 1189.
[43] *Id.*
[44] The Constitutional dimension should not be overlooked: cf. *Kelly*, 238-239, Hogan, *Constitutional Law — Judicial Independence and Mandatory Orders*, 5 Dublin U.L.J. (N.S.) 114 (1983).
[45] Succession Act 1965, section 5. See *McGuire*, 24-26.
[46] Cf. *Dicey & Morris*, 1189, *Morris*, 458, *McLeod*, 217. *Cheshire & North*, 700, strike a slightly more cautious note.
[47] [1945] Ch. 5 (Uthwatt, J., 1944). See *Wolff*, 277.

"The mode of proving any fact bearing on survivorship is determined by the *lex fori*. The effect of any fact so proved is for the purpose in hand determined by the law of the domicile. The fact proved in this case is that it is impossible to say whether or not Mrs. Oppenheimer survived Mrs. Cohn. Proof stops there. Section 184 of the Law of Property Act 1925[48] does not come into the picture at all. It is not part of the law of evidence of the *lex fori*, for the section is not directed to helping in the ascertainment of any fact but contains a rule of substantive law directing a certain presumption to be made in all cases affecting the title to property. As a rule of substantive law the section is relevant where title is governed by the law of England. It has no application where title is determined by the law of any other country."[49]

The real difficulties in conflicts of law surround the third type of presumption, the *rebuttable presumption of law*. This arises where, on proof a certain fact (or series of facts), the trier of fact must find that another "presumed" fact exists unless the contrary is proven.[50] Rebuttable presumptions of law include those of marriage,[51] legitimacy,[52] ademption[53] and death[54] as well as those of advancement and resulting trusts,[55] which, though of weakening force, are still of some considerable importance, especially in relation to inter-spousal disputes.[56] The presumptions can best be understood as affecting the burden of proof.[57]

---

[48] Which prescribed the presumption as to survivorship under English law. This statutory provision was drafted more widely than section 5 of our Succession Act 1965, which applies only "for the purposes of distribution of the estate" of any of those deemed to have died simultaneously. See *McGuire*, 25-26.

[49] [1945] Ch., at 7-8.

[50] *Dicey & Morris*, 1189.

[51] See Lee, *Presumption of Valid Marriage in Civil Law*, 76 Ir. Ecc. R. 306 (1951), *Anon.*, *Presumption of Valid Marriage*, 83 Ir. L.T. & Sol. J. 313, 319 (1949), *Mulhern* v. *Clery* [1930] I.R. 649 (Sup. Ct., 1928), *Piers* v. *Piers*, 2 H.L.C. 331, 9 E.R. 1118 (H.L. (Ir), 1849), *In re Darcys Infants*, 11 I.C.L.R. 298 (Com. Pleas, 1860), *In re Estate of M'Loughlin*, 1 L.R. (Ir.) 421 (1878), *Miller* v. *Wheatley*, 28 L.R. Ir. 144 (Q.B. Div., 1891) *Farrell* v. *Maguire*, 3 Ir. L.R. 187 (Q.B., 1841).

[52] See the Law Reform Commission's *Report on Illegitimacy*, pp. 5-6 (L.R.C.4-1982), *Shatter*, 285-288, *Binchy*, 102-109, *S.* v. *S.* [1983] I.R. 68 (High Ct., O'Hanlon, J., 1982), noted by O'Connor, '*The Rule in Russell* v. *Russell*', 1 I.L. Times (n.s.) 76 (1983) and by Binchy, *Marriage, Paternity and Illegitimacy*, 17 Ir. Med. Times No. 6, p. 26 (1983).

[53] See *Wylie*, paras. 3.119-3.120.

[54] See *Anon.*, *Presumptions of Life, Death and Survivorship*, 40 Ir. L.T. & Sol. J. 41, 53, 59 (1905), *Anon.*, *Presumption of Death*, 75 Ir. L. T. & Sol. J. 265 (1941), *Anon. The Presumption of Death Without Issue*, 74 Ir. L.T. & Sol. J. 17 (1940), *Anon.*, *Presumption of Death in the Case of a Holder of a Policy of Life Insurance* 39 Ir. L.T. & Sol. J. 119, 125 (1905), *Pennefather* v. *Pennefather*, I.R. 6 Eq. *In bonis Cooke*, I.R. 5 Eq. 240 (Prob., Warren, J., 1871) 373 (1882) *In re Webb's Estate*, I.R. 5 Eq. 235 (Ch. App., 1871) *M'Mahon* v. *M'Elroy*, I.R. 5 Eq. 1 (V.C.'s Ct., Chatterton, V.C. 1869), *In bonis Inkerman Brown*, 36 I.L.T.R. 173 (K.B. Div. Prob., Andrews, J., 1902), *In bonis Freytag*, 43 I.L.T.R. 116 (K.B. Div. Prob., Bond, J., 1909), *In bonis Atkinson*, I.R. 7 Eq. 219 (Prob. Warren, J., 1873), *In bonis Griffin*, 65 I.L.T.R. 108 (High Ct., Hanna, J., 1931), *O'Hagan* v. *Sun Life Ins. Co. of Canada*, [1932] I.R. 741 (High Ct., O'Byrne, J.), *In re Lavelle; Cassidy* v. *A.G.*, [1940] Ir. Jur. Rep. 8 (High Ct., Gavan Duffy, J., 1939), *In re O'Brien*, [1940] Ir. Jur. Rep. 60 (High Ct., Hanna, J.), *Secretary for War* v. *Booth*, [1901] 2 I.R. 692 (Q.B. Div., 1900), *Estate of Callan deceased; Owens* v. *O'Reilly*, 39 Ir. L.T. & Sol. J. 372 (Chy. Div., Barton, J. 1905), *Thompson's Trusts and Trustee Act*, 39 Ir. L.T. & Sol. J. 372 Chy. Div., Barton, J., 1905), (both cases considered by *Anon.*, 40 Ir. L.T. & Sol. J., at 59-60 (1906)7, *In bonis Connor, Deceased*, 19 L.R. Ir. 261 (Prob. & Mat. Div., Warren, J., 1892), *Mullaly* v. *Walsh*, I.R. 6 C.L. 314 (Q.B., 1872), *Gill* v. *Manly*, 16 I.L.T.R. 57 (Land Com. Litton, Q.C., 1882), *Aylward* v. *Jones*, 18 I.L.T.R. 111 (Land Com., 1884).

[55] Cf. *Wylie*, Paras. 9.044-9.058, 165-171, 261-288, *Binchy*, ch. 7, *Brady, Trusts, Law Reform and the Emancipation of Women*, 6 Dublin U.L.J. 1 (1984).

[56] Cf. *Shatter*, 492-516, Brady, *Trusts, Law Reform, and the Emancipation of Women*, 6 Dublin U.L.J. (n.s.) 1 (1984). As to the application of these presumptions to property in relation to unmarried cohabitation, see *McGill* v. *L.S.*, [1979] I.R. 283 (High Ct., Gannon, J.), *P.* v. *C.*, unreported High Ct., McWilliam, J., 22 February 1980 (1978-1484P), Cooney, *Wives, Mistresses and the Law*, 14 Ir. Jur. (n.s.) 1 (1979), O'Connor, *Indirect Contributions and the Acquisition of a Beneficial Interest in Property*, 2 Ir. L.T. (n.s.) 40 (1984), *Shatter*, 619-622.

[57] *Wolff*, 235.

In the absence of a great deal of case law[58] dealing with how these rebuttable presumptions of law should be characterised, the commentators have suggested a variety of solutions. One would draw a distinction between those rebuttable presumptions of law "which apply only in certain contexts,"[59] on the one hand, and those "which apply in all types of cases,"[60] on the other. The first subcategory would include such presumptions as those of resulting trust, advancement, satisfaction and ademption; the second would comprise presumptions of marriage, legitimacy and death, "which apply (although not always in precisely the same way) to all types of cases".[61] According to this approach, the first subcategory involves presumptions, all of which are "so closely connected with the existence of substantive rights that they ought to be characterised as rules of substance."[62] It is not clear[63] whether presumptions falling within the second subcategory are rules of substance or procedure, but in cases involving presumptions of marriage, the courts have applied the *lex causae* whenever the law was proved,[64] and the most recent English *dictum* on the subject, in *Mahadervan* v. *Mahadervan*,[65] treated such a presumption as a rule of substance.

This approach has not escaped criticism.[66] An alternative approach would eschew any general solution to rebuttable presumptions of law, in favour of an individual investigation of each particular presumption. The presumption of marriage, for example, represents a "strong policy" of the forum."[67] Indeed it may be argued that the *favor matrimonii* principle could justify upholding the validity of a marriage when sustained by a rebuttable presumption in either the *lex fori* or the *lex causae*.[68]

A rebuttable presumption which raises important policy issues is the presumption of legitimacy. In Irish law, in *S.* v. *S.*,[69] O'Hanlon, J. held that the constitutional entitlement of litigants to fair procedures in Court, "equivalent to the concept of 'due process' under the American Constitution...,"[70] required that the presumption of legitimacy should be capable of being rebutted. Thus the rule in *Russell* v. *Russell*,[71] which ran counter to the "paramount public policy"[72] of ascertaining

---

[58] In *Stevenson* v. *Masson*, L.R. 17 Eq. 78 (Bacon, V.C., 1873), the presumption of ademption was treated as a rule of substance. In *Mahadervan* v. *Mahadervan*, [1964] P. 233, at 242-243 (1962), Sir Jocelyn Simon P. treated as a matter of substance a presumption as to the validity of a marriage. Cf. *Reg.* v. *Griffin*, 4 L.R. (Ir.) 497 (Cr. Cas. Res., 1879).

[59] *Dicey & Morris*, 1189.

[60] *Id.*

[61] *Id.*, 1190.

[62] *Id.*, 1189.

[63] *Id.*, 1190.

[64] *Id.*

[65] [1964] P. 233, at 242 (Sir Jocelyn Simon, P.)

[66] Cf. *McLeod* 218:

"It is difficult to see the reason for this breakdown since all of the presumptions have the same purpose or function, i.e., to force a conclusion of fact in the absence of proof to the contrary. Further, it is difficult to see how the learned authors have determined which presumptions belong in which category. All of these rebuttable presumptions of law are merely devices to assist the court in reaching conclusions on which legal rights can be determined, i.e., was there a valid marriage, was the child legitimate, what was the testator's intention. As such, they bear a similarity to simple presumptions of fact. Each of the presumptions deals not with the creating or extinguishing of a right, but with the manner of proving entitlement to the right. On the other hand, irrebuttable presumptions of law determine the existence of a right because the legal conclusion must follow from the application of the presumption. In the case of irrebuttable presumptions of law there can be no 'proof to the contrary'."

[67] *Nygh*, 193, *Ehrenzweig*, 355.

[68] Cf. *Cheshire & North*, 700-701.

[69] [1983] I.R. 68 (High Ct., O'Hanlon, J., 1982).

[70] *Id.*, at 79.

[71] [1924] A.C.687.

[72] [1983] I.R. at 80 (*per* O'Hanlon, J.), adopting the language of Lord Murray, in *Burman* v. *Burman*

truth and doing justice, was held not to have survived the enactment of the 1937 Constitution. It may be argued that, in view of the constitutional dimension to this holding, Irish law would have a strong claim to modify the *lex causae* where the rebuttable presumption of legitimacy under the *lex causae* did not permit compliance with the requirements specified by O'Hanlon, J. Indeed, it may be that an *irrebuttable* presumption of legitimacy under the *lex causae* would be rejected on the grounds of public policy.[73]

Requirement of written evidence[74]

Section 2 of the Statute of Frauds 1695[75] provides that "no action shall be brought" on a number of specified undertakings[76] unless the agreement, or some note or memorandum thereof, is in writing. In *Leroux* v. *Brown*,[77] the English Court of Common Pleas held that an equivalent provision in English legislation was a matter, not of substance, but of procedure, binding all litigants suing in England. The effect was to prevent the enforcement in England of an oral contract whose *lex causae* was French and which was enforceable in France.

Jervis, C.J. observed that the statutory provision

> "does not say, that, unless those requisites are complied with, the contract shall be void, but merely that no action shall be brought upon it: and ... the alternative, 'unless the agreement, or some memorandum or note thereof, shall be writing', — words which are satisfied if there be any written evidence of a previous agreement, — shows that the statute contemplated that the agreement may be good, though not capable of being enforced if not evidenced by writing. This therefore may be a very good agreement, though, for want of a compliance with the requisites of the statute, not enforceable in an English court of justice."[78]

The decision has met with almost universal criticism over the years. The result of the case was that a person who had done everything required by the *lex causae* to render his claim valid and enforceable found that he could not in fact enforce these rights in England. He would "hardly be likely to approve of the view that his substantive rights were unaffected, when in fact they were rendered completely useless to him."[79]

A principal error in *Leroux* v. *Brown* was the assumption that a rule classified

---

1930 S.C. 262, at 271. See Hogan, *Note: Natural and Constitutional Justice — Adieu to Laissez-Faire*, 19 Ir. Jur. (n.s.) 309, at 317-318 (1984).

[73] *Pace Nygh*, 194. Cases where the *lex causae* relates to persons who have no connection with Ireland raise difficult Constitutional questions: cf. *supra*, pp. 25-26.

[74] See *Lorenzen*, ch. 11, *Cook*, 225-233, *Falconbridge*, 94-105, *Dicey & Morris*, 1184-1186, *Morris*, 466-467, *Cheshire & North*, 48-49, 692-693, *Castel*, vol. 1, 630-633, Taintor, *"Universality" in the Conflict of Laws of Contracts*, 1 La. L. Rev. 695, at 713-723 (1939).

[75] 7 Will. III, c. 12, as amended by the Mercantile Law Amendment Act 1856, section 3 and the Landlord and Tenant Law Amendment Act 1860, section 4. See also section 13 of the 1695 Act, substantially repeated in section 4 of the Sale of Goods Act 1893. Cf. *Clark*, 47-57.

[76] Contracts of guarantee, agreements made on consideration of marriage and contracts or sales of lands, and agreements not to be performed within a year. See *Clark*, ch. 4.

[77] 12 C.B. 801, 138 E.R. 1119 (Com. Pleas, 1852).

[78] 12 C.B., at 824, 138 E.R., at 1129.

[79] Beckett, *The Question of Classification ("Qualification") in Private International Law*, 15 Br. Yrbk. of Internat. L. 46, at 70 (1934). With reference to the words "No action shall be brought", Beckett (at 67) observes that:

> "this alone is by no means conclusive. Continental courts have found it necessary, in classifying rules as substance or procedure, entirely to disregard the place in which these rules are to be found in their codes. French courts have found it necessary to classify several provisions of their Code of Procedure as substance, and some provisions of the Civil Code as procedure. It is the real nature of the rule and not the words, or its place in the Code which is relevant."

in one way for internal law purposes must be identically classified in a conflicts context.[80]

Leroux v. *Brown* may be contrasted with a French decision[81] which took the opposite view of provisions in the Civil Code[82] similar to those of the Statute of Frauds.[83] *Leroux* v. *Brown* was doubted by Willes, J.L. on two occasions,[84] but has twice been mentioned with approval, *obiter,* in the House of Lords.[85]

In Ireland, there have been cases[86] before Independence in which the provisions of the Irish Statute of Frauds were applied in respect of contracts with both an Irish and English dimension. The courts did not address the conflicts issue,[87] but this is scarcely surprising in view of the close identity between the respective statutory provisions of the two countries. In the absence of clear precedent, therefore, it is to be hoped that our courts would favour a different approach from that adopted in *Leroux* v. *Brown.*

Witnesses[88]

Whether a witness is competent[89] or compellable "pertains to the method whereby facts are proven and is therefore a matter of procedure,''[90] to be determined exclusively by the *lex fori.* The same rule applies to whether a witness may claim privilege.[91]

Where the question of competence, compellability or privilege depends on the marital status of the person whose testimony is in issue,[92] the status issue must first be determined by the appropriate *lex causae.*[93]

Taking evidence abroad in civil and commercial matters

The normal method of securing the presence of a witness at a trial is by the service on him of a *sub-poena ad testificandum.* To secure documents to be put in evidence, a *sub-poena duces tecum* is served on the person in possession of them, requiring him to produce the documents in court. Service of either type of *sub-poena*[94] is effected by delivering a copy of the *sub-poena* to the intended witness, or person in possession of the documents.[95]

[80] *Rabel,* vol. 1, 56, Bland, *Classification Re-Classified,* 6 Int. & Comp L.Q. 10, at 24 (1957).

[81] *Benton* v. *Horeau,* (1880) 7, *Clunet,* p. 480. See *Lorenzen,* 331-332, 341.

[82] Article 1341.

[83] Cf. Beckett, *The Questions of Classification ("Qualification") in Private International Law,* 15 Br. Yrbk of Internat. L. 46, at 70 (1934). See also the decision of the Superior Court of Delaware, in *Lams* v. *Smith (F.H.) & Co.,* 36 Del. 477, 178 Atl. 651 (1935).

[84] *Williams* v. *Wheeler,* 8 C.B. (N.S.) 299, at 316, 141 E.R. 1181, at 1188 (*per* Willes, J., 1860), *Gibson* v. *Holland,* L.R. 1 C.P. 1, at 8 (*per* Willes, J., 1865).

[85] *Maddison* v. *Alderson,* 8 App. Cas. 467, at 474 (H.L. (Eng.), *per* Lord Selborne 1883) and *Morris* v. *Baron,* [1918] A.C. 1, at 15 (H.L. (Eng.), *per* Lord Haldane, 1917). Article 9 of the Rome Convention restricts the potential scope of *Leroux* v. *Brown:* cf. *supra* p. 556.

[86] *Hopton* v. *M'Carthy,* 10 L.R. Ir. 266 (Q.B. Div., 1882), *Swan* v. *Miller, Son & Torrance Ltd.,* [1919] 1 I.R. 151 (C.A., 1919, rev'g Ross, J., 1918).

[87] In *Hopton* v. *M'Carthy, supra,* at 269, Fitzgerald, J. adverted to the correspondence between the Irish and English statutory provisions but there is nothing in his observation to suggest that the conflicts issue was foremost in his thoughts. See also *Clarke* v. *Gardiner,* 12 I.C.L.R. 472, at 477 (Com. Pleas, *per* Monahan, C.J., 1861).

[88] See *Dicey & Morris,* 1186, *Morris,* 467, *McLeod,* 220.

[89] *Bain* v. *Whitehaven & Furness Junction Ry.,* 3 H.L.C. 1, at 19, 10 E.R. 1, at 8 (*per* Lord Brougham, 1850).

[90] *McLeod,* 220.

[91] *Dicey & Morris,* 1186. See also the *Succession Act 1965,* section 106(2) (qualifications of witnesses necessary for the validity of a testamentary disposition a matter of form); cf. *supra,* p. 434.

[92] Cf. the Law Reform Commission's *Report on Competence and Compellability of Spouses as Witnesses,* ch. 1. (L.R.C. 13-1985).

[93] *Dicey & Morris,* 1186, *McLeod,* 220.

[94] As to which, see generally the Rules of the Superior Courts 1986, Order 39, rules 25-34; Appendix D, Part 1.

[95] *Id.,* rule 33.

If the person on whom it is wished to serve the *sub-poena* is out of the jurisdiction, no *sub-poena* may be issued. Consequently, all that an unwilling witness need do is to go abroad for the duration of the proceedings.[96]

Where documents are outside the jurisdiction, but the person in whose possession they are is within the jurisdiction — on a short visit, for example — it seems that there is power to compel that person to produce those documents.[97] In *Chemical Bank* v. *MacCormack*,[98] it was held, in relation to bankers' books, that there is jurisdiction to make an order compelling an Irish bank to make available for inspection in this country an account in a foreign branch of the bank. However, Carroll, J. decided not to make the order as it would involve "a conflict of jurisdiction, which should be avoided in the interest of the comity of courts."[99]

Although there is no way, through the normal processes, of compelling evidence from persons outside the State, the position where a party who is abroad consents to give evidence or produce documents is somewhat better. The Court may permit the taking of evidence abroad by commission. Moreover, under the long-standing practice of Letters of Request, foreign courts may order the taking of evidence required for proceedings before a court in Ireland.

Let us examine each of these procedures in turn.

Evidence by commission

It appears that the Irish Courts have inherent power to make an order for the examination of witnesses abroad on such terms as they may direct. This power is recognised in the Rules of the Superior Courts 1986,[100] and has for long been exercised.[101] The process is effective only where the witness whose evidence is required is willing to comply with it.

[96] Law Reform Commission, *Report on the Hague Convention on the Taking of Evidence Abroad in Civil or Commercial Matters*, p. 3 (L.R.C. 16-1985). See also *Kent Co. Co.* v. *C.S.*, [1984] I.L.R.M. 292, at 296 (High Ct., Finlay, P., 1983). As to the position before Independence, in relation to witnesses resident in England or Scotland, see *Ross* v. *Burke*, I.R. 6 Eq. 328 (Prob., Warren, J., 1872), *Underwood* v. *Darracott* (No. 2), I.R. 8 Eq. 348 (Sullivan, M.R., 1873), *Bagot* v. *Bagot*, 1 L.R. (Ir.) 1 (Prob., *Potts* v. *Batty* 6 Ir. Jur. (n.s.) 45 (Prob., Keatinge, J., 1860)), *Power* v. *Webber*, I.R. 10 Eq. 188 (V.C. Ct., Chatterton, V.C., 1876), *Dunne* v. *Lewis*, 8 I.C.L.R. liv (Exch., 1859). Cf. *Richardson* v. *Gregory*, 4 I.C.L.R. 248 (Q.B., 1854), where the foreign country in which the witnesses were living is not identified in the report.

[97] L.R.C. 16-1985, p. 3.

[98] [1983] I.L.R.M. 350 (High Ct., Carroll, J.).

[99] [1983] I.L.R.M., at 354. Cf. *In re Synge's Estate*, [1900] 1 I.R. 92 (Ross, J., 1899).

[100] Cf. Order 39, rule 4 of the Rules of the Superior Courts 1986. The Evidence by Commission Act 1859 and Evidence by Commission Act 1885, though not expressly repealed, would not appear to have survived Independence. Cf. *Irish Transport & General Workers Union* v. *Green and Transport & General Workers Union*, [1936] I.R. 471 (High Ct., Meredith, J., 1935), considered *supra*, p. 24

[101] See, e.g., *Carbery Divorce Bill*, [1920] 2 I.R. 345 (H.L.(Ir.) (commission issued by High Court for divorce *a mensa et thoro* permitted to be read in subsequent House of Lords divorce bills as "it appeared that there were no means whereby the attendance of [these witnesses] could be secured at the Bar of the House ... on the second reading, and ... the petitioner was advised that their evidence was essential to establish the truth of the allegations in the Bill": *id.*, at 346." And see *Bagot* v. *Bagot*, 1 L.R. (Ir) 1 (Prob., Warren, J.) 1878), *Walker* v. *Bennett*, I.R. 5 C.L. 366 (Exch., 1871), *Anonymous*, 2 Ir. Ch. Rep. 92 (Cusack Smith, M.R., 1851), *Dunne* v. *Lewis*, 8 I.C.L.R. liv (Exch., 1859), *O'Brien* v. *Carr*, 5 I.C.L.R. 316 (Exch., Greene, B., 1856), *Kirwan* v. *Lindsay*, 2 Ir. Ch. Rep. 23 (Brady, L.C. 1852), *Ex parte Wilkin*, 5 Ir. ch. Rep. 397 (Brady, L.C. 1856), *Druitt* v. *Druitt*, 6 Ir. Ch. Rep. 171 (Chy. App., 1857), *Malley* v. *Malley*, 6 Ir. L. Rep. 154 (Q.B., 1843), *Boyce* v. *Rusboro'*, 2 I.C.L.R. 266 (Q.B. 1852), *Boyce* v. *Rosborough*, 7 I.C.L.R. 17 (Q.B., 1857). Cf *Hutchinson* v. *Cathcart*, 8 Ir. Eq. Rep. 394 (Equity Exch., 1846), where the Irish court declined to order that evidence be taken on commission; it seems that such order, in the circumstances, would have been "a useless expense" (*id.*, at 396, *per* Rogers, counsel, *arguendo*). See generally *Anon.*, *Taking Evidence on Commission*, 98 I.L.T.R. 224, 235 (1964), *Anon.*, *Evidence on Commission*, 84 I.L.T.R. 141, 147 (1950).

The courts are very reluctant to make orders "of a wholesale character"[102] for the taking of evidence on commission: they will do so only in those "necessarily ... very rare"[103] cases where it is "absolutely essential in the interests of justice"[104] that this be done. The illness of a witness who is abroad has on occasion justified an order for taking his evidence on commission. Evidence on commission can also be ordered if a witness has not the financial resources to come here. In *Keane* v. *Hanley,*[105] in 1937, where a will was being challenged in the Irish courts, the Supreme Court held that the evidence of a witness should be taken on commission in California. The witness stated on affidavit that he was employed as a railroad watchman at a wage of a hundred dollars a month, that he had no savings and that his absence from employment would result in his dismissal. The witness stated further that he was unable to afford to travel to Ireland and was not prepared to do so. The plaintiff's entire case rested on the evidence of this witness. The Court considered it "necessary for the purpose of justice" that this evidence be taken on commission.

In *Leonard* v. *Scofield (No. 2),*[106] where a dispute arose about the ownership of prize-money from an Irish Sweep ticket, the plaintiff sought an order that the evidence be taken on commission in New York where his witnesses resided. He claimed that he could not afford to pay their expenses and that most of them would lose their jobs if they had to come to Ireland. Johnston, J. made the requested order in relation to all witnesses save one whose evidence was central to the case since he had been present at the making of the alleged agreement on which the plaintiff's case rested.

Letters of Request

Letters of Request may be issued to the competent judicial authorities in another State requesting the examination of a witness *viva voce* before them or such other person as according to their procedures is competent to take the examination of witnesses.[107] Where an order is made for the issue of a request to examine a witness in a foreign country with which a convention exists, the procedure may be varied;[108] at present no such convention is in force.

The position where Letters of Request are *received* in Ireland from foreign courts is covered by section 1 of the Foreign Tribunals Evidence Act 1856.[109] What usually happens[110] is that letters of request are forwarded by the Embassy of the foreign State to the Department of Foreign Affairs. That Department transmits them

---

[102] *Leonard* v. *Scofield (No. 2),* [1938] Ir. Jur. Rep. 31, at 33 (High Ct., Johnston, J., 1937).

[103] *Id.*

[104] *Id.* In *Neil* v. *Silcock,* 38 I.L.T.R. 5 (C.A., 1903), the Court refused to permit the plaintiff's evidence to be taken on commission in California, where he had gone after the writ had been issued; *per* Walker, L.J. (at 6): "The law is now settled that in the case of a plaintiff a commission will not be granted against the will of the defendant, unless the refusal would amount to an actual denial of justice. Nothing is suggested here, but the question of money which the plaintiff brought on himself by leaving the country." See also *Denny* v. *Denny,* 48 I.L.T.R. 150, at 150 (K.B. Div. (Mat.), Madden, J., 1914), where an application for a commission was refused in relation to two medical witnesses resident in London. Madden, J. observed (at 150) that "....the question of expense is important; but, after all, eminent medical men must obey the orders of the Court. It has been suggested that they would be unwilling witnesses. I confess I am astonished at such an observation; that their evidence would be affected by the circumstances under which they come."

[105] [1938] Ir. Jur. Rep. 16 (Sup. Ct., 1937, varying High Ct., O'Byrne, J., 1937). See also *Maiorana* v. *Graffeo,* unreported, Sup. Ct., 16 January, 1936 (75-1935) (similar facts).

[106] *Supra.*

[107] Cf. Order 39, rule 5(1) and Appendix D, Part 11, forms 1 and 3 of the Rules of the Superior Courts, 1986.

[108] Order 39, rule 5(2) of the Rules of the Superior Courts, 1986.

[109] Section 24 of the Extradition Act 1870 extends to criminal matters the power of the court of a foreign state to obtain evidence in Ireland, in like manner as under the Foreign Tribunals Evidence Act 1856. See further Order 39, Rule 39 of the Rules of the Superior Courts 1986.

[110] Cf. L.R.C. 16-1985, pp. 12ff., and the Foreign Tribunals Evidence Act 1856, section 2. See also *Ex parte Jaffé,* 1 N.I.J.R. 24 (Kenny, J., 1900).

to the Chief State Solicitor who in turn makes the application to a Judge of the High Court, rather than having the agents of the parties to the foreign proceedings take the initiative at this stage. The High Court Judge normally directs that the examination should take place before a District Justice, with questions put by counsel briefed by the Chief State Solicitor.

A witness examined under the Act has "the like right to refuse to answer questions tending to criminate himself, and other questions" as a witness in an ordinary trial.[111] Similarly no person may be compelled to produce any writing or other document that he could not be compelled to produce in an ordinary trial.[112]

There has been little case-law on the subject. In *In re Chomutov Savings Bank*,[113] Murnaghan, J. declined to give effect to a Letter of Request from Czechoslovakia because it was not proved that proceedings had been served on the defendant. Murnaghan, J. stated that the cause of action should be set out in the grounding affidavit so that he could see whether it was a cause of action which could properly be implemented under the Constitution. Further, he held that, if the person to be examined was required to produce documents, these documents should be mentioned in the affidavit. The Supreme Court reversed and made the order sought. Maguire, C.J., who delivered the judgment of the Court, said that the witness's "attitude before the Court and her decision to give evidence or withhold or produce documents is a matter for herself".[114] The Law Reform Commission observe that:

> "[i]t is not clear what was intended by this remark but it seems that the Court may
> have taken the view that objections to a Letter of Request should not be taken until
> the witness appears for examination."[115]

In the later decision of *Hovells* v. *Hovells*,[116] in 1962, the High Court refused a request from a German court to take evidence from an Irish respondent in divorce proceedings on the ground that it would be repugnant to Article 41.3 of the Constitution to grant it. The Supreme Court reversed the decision and granted the order sought.

There have been no recent reported cases on the circumstances in which a Letter of Request will be issued.[117]

Some difficulties attach to this procedure: apart from practical problems in relation to translating foreign languages,[118] the courts of some foreign countries may not permit the examination of witnesses by parties and their lawyers,[119] thus making it impossible to comply with the requirement[120] that witnesses are to be subject to cross-examination and re-examination.

The Foreign Tribunals Evidence Act 1856 has also been the subject of interpretation by the English Courts. A distinction has there been drawn between testimony "in the nature of proof for the purpose of the trial,"[121] which it is permissible to obtain under the Act, and "mere answers to questions on the discovery proceeding designed to lead to a train of inquiry,"[122] which are not permissible. Thus, much of the

---

[111] Section 5.
[112] *Id.*
[113] [1957] I.R. 355 (Sup. Ct., rev'g High Ct., Murnaghan, J.).
[114] *Id.*, at 358.
[115] L.R.C. 16-1985, p. 11.
[116] Irish Times, 1 August 1962, p.5 (Sup. Ct., rev'g High Ct.). See J.M. Kelly, *Fundamental Rights in the Irish Law and Constitution*, 204 (2nd ed., 1967).
[117] L.R.C. 16-1985, p. 8.
[118] *Id.*, pp. 9-10.
[119] *Id.*, p. 9.
[120] Order 38, rule 10 of the Rules of the Superior Courts 1986.
[121] *Radio Corporation of America* v. *Rauland Corporation*, [1956] 1 Q.B. 618, at 646 (Q.B. Div., *per* Devlin, J.).
[122] *Id.*
[122] *Id.*

discovery procedure in the United States would not fall within the scope of the Act.[123] So far as documents are concerned, it has held in *Radio Corporation of America* v. *Rauland Corporation*[124] that, while section 1 of the Act clearly permits orders for production of documents, it does not permit discovery of "indirect material".

Procedure under Conventions

Finally, it should be noted that Order 39, rule 5 (3) of the Rules of the Superior Courts 1986 prescribes the procedure to be used where an Order is made for the examination of a witness or witnesses before the Irish Consular Authority in any foreign country with which a convention in that behalf exists.[125]

Reform of the Law

In 1968, the Hague Conference on Private International Law adopted a Convention on the Taking of Evidence Abroad in Civil or Commercial Matters.[126] The Convention makes provision for the obtaining of evidence on one State pursuant to Letters of Request received from a judicial authority in another State and the taking of evidence in one State by commissioners appointed by courts in another State or by the diplomatic officers or consular agents of that State. The Convention has been ratified by several countries, including Britain.[127]

The Convention seeks a *via media* between the common law approach which allows a great deal of freedom to the parties to the proceedings to arrange for the taking of evidence abroad, and the civil law approach which regards the taking of evidence as a judicial function.[128]

From the standpoint of Irish law, the Convention offers certain advantages:[129] it enables evidence to be taken from an unwilling witness, and it facilitates and clarifies

---

[123] Cf. *id.*, at 649 (*per* Lord Goddard, C.J.), stigmatising pre-trial discovery as "a 'fishing' proceeding which is never allowed in the English courts". For a consideration of Canadian proceedings in respect of this litigation (*Re Radio Corporation of America* v. *Rauland Corporation*, [1956] O.R. 630 (High Ct., Gale, J.)), see Sischy, *Evidence in Aid of Foreign Tribunals*, 1 Osgoode Hall L.J. (No. 2) 49 (1959). See also *Rio Tinto Zinc Corporation* v. *Westinghouse Corporation*, [1978] A.C. 547 (H.L.(Eng.), 1977). In *In re Jahre (Anders)*, [1986] 1 Lloyd's L. Rep. 496, at 515 (C.A., 1985), Kerr, L.J. attempted a definition of the term "fishing":

> "It arises in cases where what is sought is not evidence as such, but information which may lead to a line of enquiry which would disclose evidence. It is the search for material in the hope of being able to raise allegations of fact, as opposed to the elicitation of evidence to support allegations of fact, which have been raised *bona fide* with adequate particularisation."

[124] [1956] 1 Q.B., at 648 (*per* Devlin, J.), explaining *Eccles & Co.* v. *Louisville & Nashville Railroad Co.*, [1912] 1 K.B. 135 (C.A., 1911).

[125] The only bi-lateral convention containing such a provision is the Consular Convention between Ireland and the United States of America 1950, Article 17 of which provides that:

> "a consular officer may, within his district, ... (g) take evidence on behalf of courts of the sending state in a manner permitted under special arrangements on this subject between the High Contracting Parties or otherwise not inconsistent with the laws of the territory."

The Vienna Convention on Consular Relations 1963, to which Ireland is party and which is given the force of law in the State by the Diplomatic Relations and Immunities Act 1967, lists in Article 5 (j) among the functions of a consular post "executing letters rogatory or commissions to take evidence for the courts of the sending State in accordance with international agreements in force, or, in the absence of such international agreements, in any other manner compatible with the laws and regulations of the receiving State."

[126] For commentary on the Convention see the Law Reform Commission's *Report on the Hague Convention on the Taking of Evidence Abroad in Civil or Commercial Matters* (L.R.C. 16-1985). Edwards, *Taking of Evidence Abroad in Civil or Commercial Matters*, 18 Int. & Comp. L.Q. 646 (1969).

[127] Cf. the Evidence (Proceedings in Other Jurisdictions) Act 1975.

[128] Cf. Edwards, *supra*, at 647, *Actes et documents de la Onzième session*, tome IV, *Obtention des preuves à l'étranger*, p. 56 (1970).

[129] Cf. L.R.C. 16-1985, pp. 18-19.

the process for the ordinary litigant. At a time when Ireland is involved in more international trade than a generation ago, and when cheap air transport has led to an increase in international disputes as to child custody,[130] the Convention is likely to be of particular benefit. Where the evidence sought consists of documents, without the need to examine witnesses, the facilities provided by the Convention will again be of great practical help.[131]

The Convention does not appear to hold any dangers since it gives witnesses the cumulative degree of protection against incrimination as exists under the law of the State of origin *and* the law of the State of execution.[132] Moreover, there is no risk of excesses in respect of pre-trial discovery.[133]

The Law Reform Commission in their Sixteenth Report,[134] have recommended that Ireland should ratify the Convention. The Commission consider[135] that the main utility of the Convention will be in cases where prospective witnesses are *unwilling* to travel to Ireland; where they are willing to come here, cost factors will probably continue to dictate that their evidence will be heard here rather than abroad.[136]

Mode of Trial and Nature of Remedy

It "stands to reason"[137] that the *lex fori* should alone determine the mode of trial. So also for the nature of the remedy, "Since remedies are procedural, there is no vested right in a particular remedy for a particular cause of action. The plaintiff must take the remedies available in the forum as he finds them."[138]

So far as the mode of trial is concerned, the *lex fori* determines such matters as how process is to be served[139] and whether the case should be tried by a judge or judge and jury.[140] Rights of appeal,[141] and the method of pronouncing a decree[142] also are matters for the *lex fori*.

So also the nature of the plaintiff's remedy is determined by the *lex fori*, whether or not the *lex fori* provides a more or less extensive remedy than that of the *lex causae*. Thus, for example, if the *lex causae* prescribes merely damages but Irish law provides

---

[130] Cf. *supra*, pp. 332-333.

[131] L.R.C. 16-1985, p. 19.

[132] Article 11. See also Article 10.

[133] Article 23. Cf. L.R.C. 16-1985, pp. 22-23, 34-35, Edwards, *supra*, at 650-651, *Radio Corporation of America* v. *Rauland Corporation, supra, Rio Tinto Zinc Corporation* v. *Westinghouse Electric Corporation, supra*.

[134] *Report on the Hague Convention on the Taking of Evidence Abroad in Civil or Commercial Matters* (L.R.C. 16-1985).

[135] *Id.*, p. 18.

[136] *Id.*

[137] *Morris*, 459. See also *Russell* v. *Kitchen*, 3 I.C.L.R. 613, at 615 (Q.B., *per* Crampton, J., 1854).

[138] *McLean*, 224-225.

[139] *Morris*, 459.

[140] *Id.* See McGregor, *The International Accident Problem*, 33 Modern L. Rev. 1, at 21 (1970), who states that "it can make no difference to this result that it is generally thought that juries are more generous with awards of damages than are judges; no question of principle in relation to quantification is involved here". It is worth noting that fear of high jury awards was a primary motivation for the proposal in the Law Reform (Personal Injuries) Bill 1986 to abolish juries in personal injuries litigation. For criticism of this approach, see B. McMahon, *Judge or Jury?* (1985). The Bill died with the fall of the Government in March, 1987, but the new Government has announced that it will introduce similar legislative proposals.

[141] *Morris*, 459.

[142] Cf. *White* v. *White*, [1947] V.L.R. 434 (Full Ct.): in *Thornton* v. *Thornton*, 65 W.N. (N.S.W.) 87 (1947), a divorce case, Bonney, J. said (at 89):
  "Where the period which Parliament has interposed for the protection of the public [between decree *nisi* and decree absolute] has passed, the suit is ripe for its final stage, namely, the decree absolute, and it seems to me that the method by which the decree is made absolute is a matter which has no bearing upon the rights of the public, and whether such method is strictly laid down by statute, or is provided by rules of Court, or otherwise, it is a matter of procedural law and not substantive law."

also for specific preformance, the Irish court would be free to make a decree for specific performance.[143] In *Lett* v. *Lett*,[144] Fitzgibbon, L.J. quoted from *Fry on Specific Performance:*[145]

> "A contract made abroad may be enforced against a defendant within the jurisdiction of this country, and, as the remedies for breach of a contract are clearly governed by the *lex fori*, it follows that it is no objection to the specific performance in England of a foreign contract that the foreign law might have given no such remedy."

Equally, an Irish court could not make a decree for specific performance or injunction where such a remedy was not available under Irish law, even though the *lex causae* permitted it.[146]

We are speaking here of *judicial* remedies: extra-judicial remedies, such as the right to reject defective goods,[147] are matters of substance, governed by the *lex causae* rather than the *lex fori*.

An interesting question arose in the English case of *Phrantzes* v. *Argenti*,[148] where a Greek woman who had recently married in England claimed a declaration that under Greek law she was entitled to the provision of a dowry by her father, a Greek national resident in England. The amount of the dowry would depend on the wealth and social position of the father and his son-in-law; no dowry was payable where the daughter had committed a fault of such a kind as would disentitle her to inherit from her father.[149] If the father failed to provide a dowry the daughter alone had a right to apply to the court for a decree requiring him to enter into a contract with the husband to provide a dowry. Under Greek law, if the father was abroad, he could be required to enter into the contract before a Greek consul or a foreign notary public.

Lord Parker, C.J. accepted that the obligation of a father to provide a dowry could not be excluded merely because it involved a specific entitlement unknown to English law;[150] but he held against the plaintiff for two reasons. First, the several factors, such as wealth, social position and the question of her possible "fault", involved inquiries and decisions which were "essentially matters for the domestic courts, and matters largely for the discretion of those courts and not our courts".[151] Secondly, the remedy sought was an order condemning the defendant to enter into a contract in a particular form with a person not even party to the proceedings and this presented an insurmountable difficulty since under English law the court could do no more than order payment *to the plaintiff* of the amount found to be appropriate. That "would be to enforce a right which the plaintiff does not possess under Greek law."[152]

As to this second point, the holding seems somewhat narrow. The court apparently

---

[143] *Baschet* v. *London Illustrated Standard Co.*, [1900] 1 Ch. 73, (Kekewich, J., 1899), *Boys* v. *Chaplin*, [1971] A.C. 356, at 394 (H.L. (Eng.) per Lord Pearson) 1969), *Dicey & Morris*, 1177.

[144] [1906] 1 I.R. 618, at 639-640 (C.A.).

[145] *Fry*, 4th ed., p. 52, sections 126-127.

[146] Cf. *Warner Bros Pictures Incorporated* v. *Nelson*, [1937] 1 K.B. 209 (Branson, J., 1936), where (as *Dicey & Morris*, 1177, fn. 15, note) this point was not discussed.

[147] *Morris*, 459.

[148] [1960] 2 Q.B. 19 (Q.B. Div., Lord Parker, C.J.).

[149] *Civil Code*, article 1497.

[150] Distinguishing *In re Macartney, Macfarlane* v. *Macartney*, [1921] 1 Ch. 522 (Astbury, J.) and the New York decision of *De Brimont* v. *Penniman*, 10 Blatch. 436 (1873), where Woodruff, J. held that French law imposing a dowry on a father-in-law to support his son-in-law was local in its nature and operation, being designed to guard against pauperism rather than to confer an internationally enforceable right of action on the son-in-law.

[151] [1960] 2 Q.B., at 35. *Quaere* whether the action for breach of promise prior to its abolition (in England in 1970, in Ireland eleven years later) would not have involved as much judicial discretion in view of the defences available to the defendant.

[152] *Id.*

failed to consider the possibility of applying English law concepts such as trust and agency to get over the small, largely technical, problem relating to the beneficiary of the decree.

Limitation of Actions[153]

Limitation of actions is a subject in relation to which "mechanical characterization has long assumed an important role".[154] Whether the traditional approach would withstand considered critical scrutiny in the light of modern thinking on the subject may be doubted.

According to Irish law, a plaintiff's right to bring an action may be affected in either of two ways by the passage of time:[155] it may be *extinguished* or merely *barred*. In the first case, the plaintiff simply has no further right of action; in the second, however, the theory is that lapse of time deprives the plaintiff of a remedy through legal action but "leaves the right itself intact."[156] This distinction between extinguishing a right and denying a remedy has been criticised by many commentators.[157]

In Irish conflicts of law, the function of characterising a limitation period rests with the *lex fori*. It appears that cases of extinction are treated as a matter of substance and those of barring the plaintiff's action will be treated as a matter of procedure.[158] On this basis, most of Irish limitation periods would seem to be procedural, since they merely bar the plaintiff's remedy. In a relatively small number of cases, however, the statutory provisions,[159] in extinguishing an obligation or the plaintiff's title, appear to be substantive.

Irish courts have yet to consider the question of characterisation in respect of a statutory provision creating a new right but prescribing a special limitation period. Examples include the fatal accidents provisions[160] and the action for contribution.[161]

---

[153] See *Brady & Kerr*, 4-5, Grossman, *Statutes of Limitations and the Conflict of Laws: Modern Analysis*, [1980] Ariz. State L.J. 1, Vernon, *Statutes of Limitations in the Conflict of Laws: Borrowing Statutes*, 32 Rocky MtnL. Rev. 287 (1960), Beckett, The *Question of Classification ("Qualification") in Private International Law*, 15 Br. Yrbk of Internat. L. 46, at 66-69, 75-77 (1934), Ester, *Borrowing Statutes of Limitation and Conflict of Laws*, 15 U. Fla. L. Rev. 33 (1962), R.M.Z., *Comment: Statutes of Limitation: Lex Loci or Lex Fori?*, 4, Va. L. Rev. 299 (1961).

[154] Grossman, *Statute of Limitations and the Conflicts of Laws: Modern Analysis*, [1980] Ariz. State L.J. 1,at 9. Cf. Ester, *Borrowing Statutes of Limitation and Conflict of Laws*,15 U. Fla. L. Rev. 33, at 38 (1962): "The common law rule, hallowed by the *rigor mortis* of precedent , is apparently always applied but frequently lamented." In England, following a Report by the English Law Commission (Law Com. No. 114, Cmnd. 8570, 1982), the law was reformed by the Foreign Limitation Periods Act, 1984. For analysis, see Stone, *Time Limitation in the English Conflict of Laws* [1985] Lloyd's Mar. & Com. L.Q. 497, Carter, *The Foreign Limitation Periods Act 1984*, 101 L.Q. Rev. 68 (1985).

[155] English Law Commission, Working Paper No. 75, *Classification of Limitation in Private International Law*, para. 5 (1980). See further Grossman, *supra*, at 10, fn. 27, Ester, *supra*, at 36-37.

[156] English Law Commission, Working Paper No. 75, *Classification of Limitation in Private International Law*, para. 5 (1980). See further *Brady & Kerr*, 2-3.

[157] See, e.g., Beckett, *The Question of Classification ("Qualification") in Private International Law*, 15 Br. Yrbk of Internat. L. 46, at 67 (1934), Martin, *Statutes of Limitations and Rationality in the Conflict of Laws*, 19 Washburn L.J. 405, at 419-420 (1980). Cf. *Le Roy* v. *Crowninshield*, 15 F. Cas. 362, at 368 (C.C.D. Mass., *per* Justice Story, 1820): "The distinction between a right and a remedy is admitted. But can a right be truly said to exist upon a contract, when all remedy upon it is legally extinguished?".

[158] Cf. *Dicey & Morris*, 1179-1180. See *Huber* v. *Steiner*, Bing. N.C. 202, 132 E.R. 80 (1835), *Hubert* v. *Quine*, L.R. 4 Q.B. 653 (1869), *Black-Clawson International Ltd.* v. *Papierwerke Waldhof-Aschaffenburg A.G.* [1975] A.C. 591 (H.L. (Eng.)).

[159] Cf. e.g. the Statute of Limitations 1957, sections 12(2), 24, 35, 38, 39, 41. See also *M.P.D.* v. *M.D.*, [1981] I.L.R.M. 179 (High Ct., Carroll, J.), holding that section 117(6) of the Succession Act 1965 lays down a strict time limit which bars both the right and the remedy.

[160] Cf. Part IV of the Civil Liability Act 1961, *McMahon & Binchy*, ch. 10. This statutory mechanism traces its origins to *Lord Campbell's Act* of 1846. See generally S. Speiser, *Recovery for Wrongful Death* (2nd ed., 1975), esp. ch. 13.

[161] Cf. the Civil Liability Act 1961, section 31; see *Buckley* v. *Lynch*, [1978] I.R. 6 (High Ct., Finlay, P., 1977).

Authorities in Scotland[162] and the United States[163] suggest that the provision should be treated as substantive. There is much to be said in favour of this approach.[164]

How the rules should work in practice[165]

We must now consider briefly how the rules regarding limitation should work out in practice. The scarcity of case law on some of these questions throughout the common law jurisdictions makes some questions, especially in relation to contract, difficult to resolve with any degree of certainty.

If we assume in our discussion that Irish law is the *lex fori* and New York law the *lex causae*[166] we must first consider the position where the Irish court classifies both its statutory provision and the New York statute of limitations as procedural. In such circumstances it seems clear that Irish law should prevail, since it is the *lex fori*.[167] Thus, a remedy that is no longer available under Irish law may not be preserved though still viable under New York law;[168] conversely, a claim still open under Irish law, but not under New York law, may still be pursued here.[169]

The second case occurs when the Irish court classifies its limitation provision as procedural but regards the New York limitation period as substantive. It is difficult to see why both statutes should not apply in this instance.[170] If this cumulative approach is adopted, the plaintiff's action will expire at the earlier of the two limitation periods. Thus, the *lex fori* would "probably"[171] apply its period of limitation if shorter than that of the *lex causae* on the ground that "it is inconvenient for the *forum* to hear what it considers to be stale claims."[172] Conversely, once the substantive right of action has expired under the *lex causae*, it would seem that the Irish court should dismiss proceedings, though taken within the Irish limitation period, on the ground that "there is simply no right left to be enforced."[173]

The third case occurs where the Irish court classifies both the Irish and the New York statutes of limitation as substantive. In the absence of judicial precedent the outcome of this case is not at all certain. On analogy with *Huber* v. *Steiner*,[174] it can be argued that the expiration of the limitation period under the *lex causae* should kill an action even where the forum's limitation period has not run out. As to the converse position, there is much to be said for sustaining a claim, extinct under the *lex fori*, but still alive under the *lex causae*.[175]

---

[162] *M'Elroy* v. *M'Allister*, 1949 S.C. 110.

[163] Cf. *Scoles & Hay*, 60-61.

[164] See the English Law Commission's Working Paper No. 75, para 8 clause (c); Cf. *Dicey & Morris*, 1180, who would restrict the scope of this exception to cases where the new statutory right of action imposes a shorter period of limitation than that applicable under the general law.

[165] See the English Law Commission's W.P. No. 75, paras. 9-10.

[166] Cf. *id.*, para. 9.

[167] Cf. *id.* See also *Brady & Kerr*, 4, *Dicey & Morris*, 1180.

[168] Cf. *Don* v. *Lippman*, 5 Cl. & Fin, 1, 7 E.R. 303 (1837), *In re Lorillard, Griffiths* v. *Catford*, [1922] 2 Ch. 638, at 645, (*per* Eve, J. (aff'd by C.A.)), *Allard* v. *Charbonneau*, [1953] 2 D.L.R. 442 (Ont. C.A.).

[169] *Bondholders Securities Corporation* v. *Manville*, [1933] 4 D.L.R. 699 (Sask, C.A.), *Carvell* v. *Wallace*, 9 N.S.R. 165 (Sup. Ct., 1873), *Harris* v. *Quine*, L.R. 4 Q.B. 653 (1869), *Huber* v. *Steiner*, 2 Bing. N.C. 202, 132 E.R. 80 (1835), *Société Anonyme Métallurgique de Prayon, Prooz, Belgium* v. *Koppel*, 77 S.J. 800 (Roche, J., 1933), *Williams* v. *Jones*, 13 East 439, 104 E.R. 441 (1811).

[170] Cf. the English Law Commission's W.P. No. 75, para. 8 clause (*b*).

[171] *Dicey & Morris*, 1181.

[172] *Id.*, citing *British Linen Co.* v. *Drummond*, 10 B. & Co. 903, 109 E.R. 683 (1830). In the United States, the judicial authorities are divided on this question: see Wurfel, *Statutes of Limitation in the Conflict of Laws*, 52 N. Car. L. Rev. 489, at 516-517 (1974).

[173] *Dicey & Morris*, 1181; cf. *Black-Clawson International Ltd.* v. *Papierwerke Waldhof-Aschaffenburg A.G.* [1975] A.C. 591 (H.L.(Eng.)).

[174] Bing N.C. 202, 132 E.R. 80 (1835).

[175] *Id.* Cf, the English Law Commission's W.P. No. 75, para. 9. 2.

The final case is where the Irish court classifies its statutory limitation provision as substantive but New York's as procedural. There appears to be no judicial pronouncement on this question in Ireland or in other common law jurisdictions. On one view,[176] surely lacking in practical wisdom, no limitation period would be applied since the Irish limitation period would be irrelevant and the New York period inapplicable in an Irish forum.[177]

The present conflict rules on limitation of actions are unsatisfactory. They encourage forum shopping; they are based on an unreal distinction between right and remedy; and they are increasingly out of harmony with the law in other countries and in the E.E.C.

Lapse of time

It is useful to say a word here about the question of lapse of time. Under Irish law, apart altogether from the provision contained in the *Statute of Limitation 1957,* certain entitlements may be lost though not having been actively pursued. Somewhat similar provisions exist in the laws of most other countries. In the event of a conflict between the *lex fori* and the *lex causae,* it seems that the *lex causae* should prevail.[178]

The Supreme Court decision of *O'Domhnaill* v. *Merrick*[179] casts a shadow on this question, however. The majority there invoked "implied principles of basic fairness of procedures" when dismissing for want of prosecution a case brought within the statutory limitation period by a plaintiff in respect of injuries she had sustained in 1961, when she was three years old. Although he did not express a concluded opinion on the point, Henchy, J. saw merit in the argument that the Statute of Limitations 1957 should be construed so as to be in conformity with article 6(1) of the Convention for the Protection of Human Rights and Fundamental Freedoms (1950), which Ireland had ratified in 1957. Article 6(1) guarantees a fair hearing of civil and criminal proceedings "within a reasonable time".

On one view, the approach favoured in *O'Domhnaill* v. *Merrick* would apply only when Irish law is the *lex causae.* Thus, where the *lex causae* was not Irish, it would not be possible to invoke the Convention, even in respect of a country which has ratified the Convention, unless, through expert evidence, it is established that the Convention has an effect on the law of that country similar to that identified by Henchy, J. with regard to Irish law. On the other hand, it may be argued that the reference to the constitutional dimensions, as well as the emphasis on considerations of natural justice, make it possible that the approach favoured in *O'Domhnaill* v. *Merrick* reflects the public policy of the State, which should override the provisions of a foreign *lex causae.*

---

[176] Supported by a German Supreme Court decision of 1882 (R.G. (4 Jan. 1882) 7 R.G.Z. 21) cited by the English Law Commission, W.P. No. 75, para. 9, fn. 29. The Commission cited more recent German decisions which have refused to follow this case.

[177] Cf. the English Law Commission's W.P. No. 75, para. 9, *Dicey & Morris,* 1181. See also Beckett, *The Question of Classification in Private International Law,* 15 Br. Yearbk. of Internat. L. 46, at 76-77 (1934). One solution would be to follow the suggestion made by *Falconbridge,* 292-293, that the forum should characterise both the foreign statute and the domestic statute for the purpose of determining which of them is applicable within the meaning of the conflict rule of law of the forum relating to limitation of actions. "In an action upon a foreign cause of action the forum should compare the two statutes and if it comes to the conclusion that, notwithstanding differences of wording, the two statutes are intended to perform essentially the same function, it should decide which of the two statutes is subsumed under the conflict rule of the forum." *Id.,* 293. Another solution would be to adopt the approach favoured by most continental European countries that limitation periods are substantive, to be governed by the *lex causae. Id.,* 294.

[178] Cf. *Dicey & Morris,* 1182.

[179] [1984] I.R. 151 (Sup. Ct.).

[180] Cf. *Cheshire & North,* 707.

Damages

Conflict of law aspects of damages involve some difficult conceptual and policy problems. Resolution of these problems has been hindered by the paucity of decisions,[180] and, it must be admitted, the relatively poor quality of judicial analysis in the few cases that considered the subject.

The central difficulty is that, in seeking to unshackle themselves from an over-extensive application of the *lex fori*, the courts have constructed a dubious conceptual criterion which depends on the distinction between *remoteness* of damage, on the one hand, and the *measure* of damages, on the other.[181] As is so often the case in law, a distinction that seems of compelling force in the obvious case may well prove unsatisfactory when it provides cumbersome or unconvincing answers in a wide range of less obvious, but no less important, cases.

Let us first attempt to put the matter in focus. It is clear[182] that the *lex fori* should prevail on such questions as whether damages are by a way of a lump sum, once-and-for-all award (as is the case in Irish law)[183] or by way of periodic payments (as is the case in some Continental countries).[184] If Irish courts were obliged to administer entirely foreign systems of periodic payment, difficulties and confusion could result in some (though scarcely all) cases.

The more difficult question concerns the nature and extent of damages to which the plaintiff should be entitled. There may well be differences between the *lex causae* and *lex fori* as to how damages should be determined. Formerly the tendency was for the *lex fori* to prevail.[185] Commentators criticised the breadth of range of the *lex fori*, which could have the effect of denying rights to which the plaintiff was entitled under the *lex causae* and conferring windfall entitlements where these were not available under the *lex causae*.

To meet the difficulty *Cheshire* proposed[186] that a distinction should be drawn in

---

[181] See *Dicey & Morris*, 1178-1179, *Morris*, 460-461, *Cheshire & North*, 707-710, *Anton*, 549-550, *McLeod*, 225-229, *Castel*, vol. 1, 618-626.

[182] Cf. *Kohnke* v. *Karger* [1951] 2 K.B. 670 (Lynskey, J.), *Boys* v. *Chaplin*, [1971] A.C. 356, at 394 (H.L.(Eng.), *per* Lord Pearson, 1969).

[183] See *McMahon & Binchy*, 563-564.

[184] See Fleming, *Damages: Capital or Rent*, 19 U. Toronto L.J. 295, at 296-299 (1969), McGregor, *The International Accident Problem*, 33 Modern L. Rev. 1, at 21 (1970).

[185] Cf. *Dicey*, 6th ed., 1949, 649-650, *Kohnke* v. *Karger*, [1951] 2 K.B. 670, at 677 (Lynskey, J.).

[186] *Cheshire*, 4th ed., 1952, 659-660. Since Cheshire's argument has prevailed in England (cf. *D'Almeida Aranjo Ltd.* v. *Sir Frederick Becker & Co. Ltd.*, [1953] 2 Q.B. 329 (Q.B.D., Pilcher, J.), *Boys* v. *Chaplin*. [1971] A.C. 356 (H.L.(Eng.) 1969)), it is desirable to quote the relevant passage:

"The truth would appear to be that judicial pronouncements and the statements in textbooks are unintelligible unless two entirely different questions are segregated. In brief, remoteness of liability or remoteness of damage must be distinguished from measure of damages. The rules relating to remoteness indicate what kind of loss actually resulting from the commission of a tort or from a breach of contract is actionable; the rules for the measure of damages show the method by which compensation for an actionable loss is calculated. Damage may be, but damages can never be, too remote. In tort the rule of remoteness established by the *Polemis Case* [[1921] 3 K.B. 560] is that a tortfeasor is responsible for all the direct consequence of his wrongful act, even though they could not reasonably have been anticipated. The analogous rule in contracts, however, is different. The breach of a contract, like the commission of a tort, causes material loss, and it is that loss to which the rule in *Hadley* v. *Baxendale* [9 Exch. 341, 156 E.R. 145 (1854)] applies. In other words, it is impossible to claim monetary compensation in respect even of an admitted loss unless it arose naturally and in the ordinary course of things from breach of contract. But the rule that regulates the measure of damages is the same for contracts as it is for torts. It requires *restitutio in integrum*. In torts compensation must be paid for the whole of the direct loss; in contracts, as *Robinson* v. *Harman* [1 Exch. 850, 154 E.R. 363 (1848)] insists, compensation must be paid for the whole of the natural or foreseeable loss.

Alive to the distinction between remoteness of liability and measure of damages we can now attempt to state the relevant principles of private international law.

the conflict of laws between the remoteness and the measure of damages, respectively. This proposal was enthusiastically, if somewhat uncritically, endorsed by Pilcher, J., in *D'Almeida Aranjo Lda.* v. *Sir Frederick Becker & Co. Ltd.*[187] It subsequently found favour with the House of Lords in *Boys* v. *Chaplin*,[188] where a majority held that the question whether damages were recoverable for pain and suffering[189] was one of remoteness, and thus of substance rather than procedure.

The distinction between remoteness and measure of damages has only rarely been analysed critically by the courts or academic commentators. It causes no particular difficulty in relation to contract, where the distinction in our law between remoteness and measure is well established.[190] So far as tort law is concerned, however, there are conceptual[191] difficulties. The law of negligence has developed in recent years in such a manner that there is no clear conceptual distinction between the issues of duty of care and of remoteness of damage.[192] The borderland between the remoteness and measure of damages in our internal law of torts is a veritable

---

There can be no doubt, at least on principle, that remoteness of liability must be governed by the proper law of the obligation that rests upon the defendant. Not only the existence, but also the extent, of an obligation, whether it springs from a breach of contract or the commission of a wrong, must be determined by the system of law from which it derives its source. The proper law admittedly determines the nature and content of the right created by a contract, and it is clear that the kind of loss for which damages are recoverable upon breach forms part of that contract. Both the nature and the content of a contractual right depend in part upon the question whether certain consequential loss that may ensue if the contract is unperformed will be too remote in the eye of the law. If the proper law determines what constitutes a breach, it is also entitled to determine the consequences of a breach."

[187] [1953] 2 Q.B. 329. Pilcher, J. was "[f]ortified" (id., at 338) by the decision of the Supreme Court of Canada in *Livesley* v. *E. Clemens Horst Co.*, [1924] S.C.R. 605, [1925] 1 D.L.R. 159, though whether this confidence was soundly placed may be debated in view of the fact that in *Livesley* no express support was given to the distinction between remoteness and measure of damages. Indeed Duff, J. used language which would, on its face, be difficult to harmonise with Cheshire's thesis.

[188] [1971] A.C. 356, at 379 (*per* Lord Hodson), at 393 (*per* Lord Wilberforce) and at 394-395 (*per* Lord Pearson. Lord Guest (at 382) and Donovan (at 383) dissented on this point.

[189] Cf. *McMahon & Binchy*, 578 ff.

[190] See *Clark*, ch. 18. Cf. *Boyd* v. *Fitt*, 14 I.C.L.R. 43 (Exch., 1863). See also *Mackenzie* v. *Corballis*, 40 I.L.T.R. 28 (K.B. Div., 1905), where the conflicts dimensions were not explored. It is interesting to find that, in the context of bills of exchange and promissory notes, the courts have classified the measure of damages as a matter of substantive law, and "[n]o one seems ever to have suggested that this should be regarded as a 'matter of procedure' to be governed by the *lex fori*": *Dicey & Morris*, 902, fn. 85. See further *supra*, pp. 492-493. It is also worth noting that, when determining the measure of damages in an action for breach of contract, the court, in applying the *lex fori*, may have regard to the international dimensions of the case on such a question as the differing rates of interest in different countries. Thus in *Parker* v. *Dickie*, 4 L.R. (Ir.) 244 (C.P. Div., 1879), it was accepted that where a solicitor employed to raise money on mortgage for his client who was emigrating to New Zealand failed to send on the money to him, the client could recover damages for interest at the rate applicable in New Zealand during this period of delay.

[191] In practice, the problem has been less pressing. "Traditionally, the issue of damages, within the context of the law of tort has been largely a non-issue in the conflict of laws. Pursuant to the traditional rule in *Phillips* v. *Eyre*, the *lex causae* is the *lex fori*. Accordingly, the *lex fori* applies to all aspects of damage, so that there is no need to characterize 'damages' as substantive or procedural": *McLean*, 227. If the theory of the "proper law of tort" gains support in Irish choice-of-law rules for tort, this position could, however, quickly change. Cf. *supra*, pp. 578-580. See also *Stanhope* v. *Hospitals Trust Ltd. (No. 2)*, [1936] Ir. Jur. Rep. 25 (Sup. Ct.), rev'g in part [1936] Ir. Jur. Rep. 21 (Hanna, J. with jury, 1935), discussed, pp. 645-646.

[192] Cf *Spartan Steel & Alloys Ltd.* v. *Martin*, [1973] Q.B. 27 at 36 (C.A., *per* Lord Denning, M.R.), *McMahon* v. *Binchy*, 193-195. In this context it is useful to contrast the approach adopted by the House of Lords in *Junior Books Ltd.* v. *Veitchi*, [1983] A.C. 520 (H.L. (Sc)) with that favoured by Costello, J. in *Ward* v. *McMaster and Louth Co. Co.*, [1986] I.L.R.M. 43. See further Binchy, *Builders, Defective Houses and Public Authorities: The Old Immunities Crumble*, 4 Ir. L.T. (n.s.) 76, at 77-78 (1986). See also *Hogan & Morgan*, 372-380, *Trindade & Cane*, 380-382, and cf. *Egan (William) & Sons Ltd.* v. *Sisk (John) & Sons Ltd.*, [1986] I.L.R.M. 283 (High Ct., Carroll, J., 1985).

quagmire, in the wake of the recent robust response[193] by the Supreme Court to what it perceived to be overgenerous awards by juries. It is far from easy to say whether the normal maximum of £150,000 for general damages in cases of quadraplegia prescribed by the Supreme Court in *Sinnott* v. *Quinnsworth Ltd.*[194] refers to remoteness or measure.[195] There is a similar doubt regarding the restriction imposed on general damages for victims who are so badly injured as to be rendered not fully aware of their plight.[196] In torts cases, attempting to distinguish between "remoteness" and "measure" presents particular difficulties because tort law, more than contract, is saturated with moral value-judgments and competing social policy goals.[197]

Some other difficulties may be mentioned. Under Irish law, there is a statutory maximum[198] on the amount that may be awarded for mental distress in fatal accidents litigation brought on behalf of dependants. This limit might at first sight appear to be a classic instance of the measure of damages, but on further reflection may be seen to reflect an important policy choice as to the substantive entitlements of dependants in these cases.[199] The selection of £7,500 as the maximum amount is not based on any judgment by the Oireachtas that the suffering of dependants, however close their relationship with the deceased and however many there may be, can properly be measured at no more than £7,500.[200] That sum represents a modest token in the direction of compensation for mental distress, but one so heavily circumscribed, no doubt for good reasons of policy, that it cannot merely be treated as a legislative attempt to prescribe an accurate measure of damages.

---

[193] See *Reddy* v. *Bates*, [1984] I.L.R.M. 197 (Sup. Ct., 1983), *Cooke* v. *Walsh*, [1984] I.L.R.M. 208, at 214ff. (Sup. Ct.), *Sinnott* v. *Quinnsworth Ltd.*, [1984] I.L.R.M. 523 (Sup. Ct.), *Griffiths* v. *Van Raaj*, [1986] I.L.R.M. 582 (Sup. Ct., 1984). In the *Sinnott* case, [1984] I.L.R.M., at 535, McCarthy, J. referred to lawyers and insurers as suffering from "a degree of monetary punch drunkenness that has tended to remove reality from [their] settlements."

[194] Cf. [1984] I.L.R.M. 523, at 532-533 (Sup. Ct., *per* O'Higgins, C.J.; Henchy, Griffin and Hederman, JJ. concurring). See also *id.*, at 535-536 (*per* McCarthy, J.). O'Higgins, C.J. (at 532) expressed the fear that, if too high awards were to continue, "the operation of public policy would be thereby endangered". From the standpoint of conflict of laws, this reference to public policy should be placed in context. The general tenor of the Chief Justice's remarks makes it plain that it was primarily the social and economic impact *in Ireland* of high jury awards which he had in mind. Presumably this consideration would have less force where the defendant (and his insurance company) were foreign.

[195] Cf. McGregor, *The International Accident Problem*, 33 Modern L. Rev. 1, at 25-26 (1970).

[196] This major issue was disposed of briefly by the Supreme Court in *Cooke* v. *Walsh*, [1984] I.L.R.M. 208, at 219 where Griffin, J. (O'Higgins, C.J. Henchy and Hederman, JJ. concurring) considered that damages in these circumstances "should be moderate". In view of the fact that this issue had not been fully debated on the hearing of the appeal, McCarthy J. (at 223) preferred to reserve for further consideration "th[is] very wide question which has been the subject of considerable debate, both in the courts and academically, in the United Kingdom, in Canada and in Australia, and, no doubt, in the United States...." Cf. *Lim Poh Choo* v. *Camden & Islington Area Health Authority*, [1980] A.C. 174 (H.L., 1979), where the House of Lords considered that, if the approach favoured in *H. West & Son Ltd.* v. *Shephard*, [1964] A.C. 326 was to set aside, "it should not be done judicially but legislatively within the context of a comprehensive enactment dealing with all aspects of damage for personal injury": [1980] A.C., at 189.

[197] See Chapman, *Ethical Issues in the Law of Tort*, 20 U.W. Ont. L. Rev. 1 (1982), Williams, *The Aims of the Law of Tort*, 4 Current L. Prob. 137 1851), Fleming, *The Role of Negligence in Modern Tort Law*, 53 Va. L. Rev. 815 (1967), Linden, *Public Law and Private Law: The Frontier from the Perspective of a Tort Lawyer*, 17 Cahiers de Dr. 831 (1976) Linden, *Tort Law as Ombudsman*, 51 Can. Bar Rev. 155 (1973), Linden, *Reconsidering Tort Law as Ombudsman*, in F. Steel & S. Rodgers-Magnet, eds., *Issues in Tort Law*, 1 (1983), Lambert, *Torts in the 80s — An American Perspective*, [1983] Sp. Lectures of L. Soc. of Upper Can. 1.

[198] Civil Liability Act 1961, section 49 (1), as amended by the Courts Act 1981, section 28. See *McMahon & Binchy*, 117-119, Veitch, *Solatium — A Debt Repaid?* 1 Ir. Jur. (N.S.) 35 (1966).

[199] Cf. McGregor, *The International Accident Problem*, 33 Modern L. Rev. 1, at 22 (1970).

[200] The Courts are well aware of this: cf. *McCarthy* v. *Walsh*, [1965] I.R. 246 (Sup. Ct., 1965, rev'g High Ct., Murnaghan, J., 1964), *Dowling* v. *Jedos Ltd.*, unreported, Sup. Ct., 30 March 1977. See further *McMahon & Binchy*, 118-119.

There are other cases where our law has adopted an artificial measure of damages. An example is the amount to be awarded for loss of expectation of life.[201] The very low figure contrasts with the more generous approach in some other countries,[202] as well as, on the other side, the complete denial of this type of compensation by the laws of some other countries.

Yet another example is our approach to the question of taxation and damages.[203] The Supreme Court,[204] reflecting the view of the High Court in earlier decisions,[205] has recently held that "it is the 'take home pay' and not the gross pay"[206] that should be the figure by which loss of earnings should be computed. In some other countries, where there is heavy taxation on the awards, understandably no deduction is made when computing the awards.[207] For our courts to deduct the tax when making the award will result in the assets of the plaintiff being reached twice. It may be argued that our courts should be sensitive to these implications, though it must be admitted that pointing to the problem is easier than specifying the solution. If one moves away from the "safety"[208] of the *lex fori*, there are many competing policies calling for attention, none of which appears to have a clearly pre-eminent claim. Application of the *lex causae*, whether that be determined by the proper law or otherwise, is no guarantee that the result will be fair, so far as these aspects of damages are concerned.

In *Stanhope* v. *Hospitals Trust Ltd. (No. 2)*,[209] the Supreme Court held that the plaintiff, who was engaged furtively in the illegal business of selling sweepstake tickets in Natal, should not be entitled to claim damages in respect of the destruction of this business by reason of the alleged negligence and breach of contract on the part of the defendants. The plaintiff had claimed that the defendant had failed to enter in their draw some counterfoils which he had sent with the appropriate payment. Since the contract was valid under Irish law, which was the proper law and (it would seem[210]) the *lex loci contractus,* the Court, in considering the illegality under the law of Natal, treated this aspect of the plaintiff's claim for damages as a matter of substance. The judgments are not clear on the question whether the Court was dealing with the *measure* or the *remoteness* of damages. Kennedy, C.J. referred to the claim for damages under the "head"[211] of loss of business. This suggests that he considered the issue to be one of the measure of damages. On the other hand, FitzGibbon, J. appeared to regard[212] the claim for breach of contract as being a *separate* claim from the claim for the loss of the plaintiff's trade. To complicate

---

[201] Cf. *McMahon & Binchy*, 581-583.

[202] Cf. *McGregor, supra*, at 22-23.

[203] See Hall, *Taxation of Compensation for Loss of Income*, 73 L.Q. Rev. 212 (1957), *McMahon & Binchy*, 574-576.

[204] *Cooke* v. *Walsh*, [1984] I.L.R.M. 208 (Sup. Ct.).

[205] *Glover* v. *B.L.N. (No. 2)*, [1973] I.R. 432 (High Ct., Kenny, J., 1968), Cf. *Irish Leisure Industries Ltd.* v. *Gaiety Theatre Enterprises Ltd.*, unreported, High Ct., O'Higgins, C.J., 12 February 1975 (1972-2531P).

[206] [1984] I.L.R.M., at 217 (*per* Griffin, J.). See also *Sexton* v. *O'Keeffe* [1966] I.R. 204, at 211 (Sup. Ct., *per* Kingsmill Moore, J., 1964).

[207] Cf. *McGregor, supra*, at 23-24.

[208] *Id.*, at 26.

[209] [1936] Ir. Jur. Rep. 25 (Sup. Ct.), rev'g in part [1936] Ir. Jur. Rep. 21 (Hanna, J. with jury, 1935). The case is discussed in detail, *supra*, pp. 547-548.

[210] Cf. Dowrick, *The Irish Sweep and Irish Law*, 2 Amer. J. of Comp. L. 505, at 508-509 (1953).

[211] [1936] Ir. Jur. Rep., at 26.

[212] Cf. *id.*, at 27-28. If a separate claim was thus in question, one may ask what it might have been. It could be that FitzGibbon, J. had in mind the plaintiff's claim for negligence in connection with the draw. Most probably, under Irish law at that time, the claim would be characterised as one of contract. But if we consider that this is a claim in *tort*, some interesting implications as to choice of law rules arise. Was FitzGibbon, J. applying the *lex loci delicti*, the place of the tort being construed as that where the damage was suffered? Cf. *supra*, pp. 148-149. In the absence of any developed analysis by FitzGibbon, J. it seems futile to speculate further.

matters further, Murnaghan, J. expressed[213] his agreement with the judgment of FitzGibbon, J. but went on the use[214] language indicating that he regarded the issue as relating to the measure of damages, and certainly not as involving an entirely separate claim.

Mareva Injunctions

The term "Mareva injunction"[215] is commonly used to describe injunctions that are granted in order to prevent the defendant from removing assets from the jurisdiction or from disposing of or dealing with them within the jurisdiction in such a way as to frustrate execution under proceedings brought or to be brought by the plaintiff.[216] Formerly, courts of equity were not disposed to grant injunctions to creditors to prevent debtors from disposing of, or otherwise dealing with, their property, unless the creditor had some legal or equitable interest in the property.[217]

In Powerscourt Estates v. *Gallagher,*[218] the plaintiff company sued the defendants on foot of a deed of guarantee. Having obtained an interim injunction, the plaintiff company sought an interlocutory injunction restraining the defendants from disposing of their assets up to the value of the plaintiff company's claim, whether those assets were within or outside the State, so as to defeat the plaintiff company's chances of recovery. The plaintiff company claimed that there were substantial grounds for believing that the defendants would charge their personal assets in such a way that other creditors might obtain fraudulent preference.

The defendants argued that an injunction restraining the disposal of assets could be granted only where a defendant outside the jurisdiction had property within the jurisdiction, or where it was shown that the defendant, because of his foreign nationality or domicile or otherwise, was likely to take his property out of the jurisdiction. This remedy, they said, should not be confused with fraudulent preference in a bankruptcy matter.

McWilliam, J. rejected the defendants' argument. He interpreted "the *Mareva* line of cases"[219] as

"seem[ing] to lead to the conclusion that an injunction may be granted where it appears to the court that dispositions are likely to be made for the purpose of preventing a plaintiff from recovering the amount of his award, as distinct from conducting the normal business or personal affairs of the defendant."[220]

In the later case of *Fleming* v. *Ranks (Ireland) Ltd.,* [221] in 1983, McWilliam J., after a review of the English authorities, was:

[213] [1936] Ir. Jur. Rep., at 28.

[214] *Id.,* at 29.

[215] Cf. *Mareva Compania Naviera S.A.* v. *International Bulkcarries S.A.,* [1975] 2 Ll. Rep. 509. See Powles, chs. 1-6, Gill, *Order XI, "Mareva Injunctions" and the Jurisdiction of the Irish Courts in Private International Law,* 4 Ir. L.T. (n.s.) 70 (1986), Gill, *"Mareva Injunctions" and Foreign Assets,* 4 Ir. L.T. (n.s.) 180 (1986), Harpum, *Commercial Law — Mareva Injunctions in the Irish Courts,* 6 D.U.L.J. 131 (1984), Charleton, *Family Law — Mareva Injunctions,* 4 D.U.L.J. 114 (1982).

[216] *Spry,* 491 (3rd ed., 1984).

[217] *Id.,* citing *Lister & Co.* v. *Stubbs,* 45 Ch.D. 1 (1890), and *Siskina* v. *Distos Compania Naviera S.A.,* [1979] A.C. 210, at 260-261.

[218] [1984] I.L.R.M. 123 (High Ct., McWilliam, J., 1982).

[219] *Id.,* at 126; McWilliams, J. had earlier (*id.*) cited *Third Chandis Corp* v. *Unimarine S.A.,* [1979] 3 W.L.R. 122, *Barclay* v. *Johnson* v. *Yuill,* [1980] 1 W.L.R. 1259, *Rahman* v. *Abu-Taha,* [1980] 1 W.L.R. 1268, *Iraqui M.O.D.* v. *Arcepey Shipping,* [1980] 2 W.L.R. 488, *Z Ltd.* v. *A-Z,* [1982] Q.B. 558 (C.A., 1981). The passage from Megarry V.C.'s judgment in *Barclay Johnson,* cited by McWilliam, J. [1984] I.L.R.M., at 126, falls short of the wide proposition stated in the text above this footnote.

[220] [1984] I.L.R.M., at 126. Harpum, *supra,* at 132-133, considers that a plaintiff should not, in practice, be permitted to elevate himself to a secured creditor by indirectly forcing the defendant to give security for the plaintiff's claim.

[221] [1983] I.L.R.M. 541.

"satisfied that there is jurisdiction to grant such an injunction and that the cases in which it may be granted are not confined to cases in which a defendant in resident outside the State. From the cases cited I would accept that there must be a real risk of the removal or disposal of the defendant's assets, that there must be a danger of default by the defendant, that the plaintiff must show that he has a good arguable case and, weighing the considerations for and against the grant of an injunction, the balance of convenience must be in favour of granting it."[222]

In *Caudron* v. *Air Zaire*,[223] Barr, J. said:

"A *Mareva* injunction is not itself a cause of action, but is merely an ancillary remedy which may enable a plaintiff to 'freeze' an asset which is the property of a defendant and thus ensure its availability to satisfy in whole or in part the amount of the judgment which the plaintiff may obtain against the owner of the asset."

Barr, J. did not accept the argument that a *Mareva* injunction is analogous to a claim *in rem* in the Admiralty jurisdiction and therefore may be regarded as substantive in nature. He was "satisfied that it amounts to no more than ancillary relief which may facilitate a claimant in obtaining satisfaction on foot of [a] monetary judgment obtained by him against the owner of the property which is the subject matter of such an injunction".[234]

Barr, J. approved[225] of the approach favoured by the English Court of Appeal in *Ninemia Maritime Corporation* v. *Trave Schiffahrtsgesellschaft m.b.H. und Co. K.G.*[226] where Kerr, L.J. had expressed the view that:

"the test is whether, on the assumption that the plaintiffs have shown at least 'a good arguable case', the court concludes, on the whole of the evidence then before it, that the refusal of a *Mareva* injunction would involve a real risk that a judgment or award in favour of the plaintiffs would remain unsatisfied."

Parties

We must now consider whether the person sued is the proper defendant in the proceedings.[227] In certain civil law systems a creditor may sue a partner only after he has failed to satisfy his action against the partnership.[228] Under Irish law, a creditor may proceed against a partner without having first to try against the firm or the principal debtor, as the case may be, and without joining them in the proceedings.

There appears to be no reported Irish case dealing with conflicts aspects of the subject. In England it appears that if the *lex causae* excludes liability then this exclusion must be respected by the English courts;[229] but if the *lex causae* imposes liability on the defendant only after satisfaction has been unsuccessfully sought from another party or separate fund, this condition precedent will be treated as a matter of procedure which may be ignored by the English courts.[230]

---

[222] *Id.*, at 545.

[223] [1986] I.L.R.M. 10, at 14 (High Ct., 1985, rev'd by Sup. Ct., 1985).

[224] *Id.*, at 14. See further *supra*, pp. 153-156.

[225] [1986] I.L.R.M., at 16.

[226] [1983] 1 W.L.R. 1412, at 1422.

[227] For consideration of the position of the equitable assignee of a chose in action, see *supra*, pp. 503-504.

[228] *Kuhn*, 85, *Wolff*, 239-240.

[229] *General Steam Navigation Co.* v. *Guillon*, 11 M. & W. 877, 152 E.R. 1061 (1843), *The M. Moxham*, 1 P.D. 107 (C.A., 1876).

[230] *Bullock* v. *Caird*, 10 Q.B. 276 (1875), *Re Doetsch*, [1896] 2 Ch. 836. For criticism, see *Wolff*, 240. Cf. *Cheshire & North* 703, *Dicey & Morris* 1192, *Morris* 465, *Graveson*, 599-600.

Priorities

In some cases the property of a defendant or a deceased person which is available for distribution to creditors or other claimants may not be sufficient to satisfy them all. A question of priorities then arises.

It appears[231] that the *lex fori* governs a limited number of questions relating to priorities:

(*a*) claims of creditors in bankruptcy[232] and winding up of companies;[233]
(*b*) the administration of insolvent estates;[234] *and*
(*c*) claims in Admiralty against ships.[235]

The *lex fori* does not govern other priorities, such as the priority of competing assignments of a debt, which is determined by the proper law of the debt.[236] It seems, too, that the *lex situs* rather than the *lex fori* governs foreign immovables.[237] *Morris* notes that:

"[i]n all the cases in which English law has been applied to decide questions of priorities, the contest has been between claims governed by different laws. In such cases the ground for applying the *lex fori* is not that the procedural convenience of the forum demands this course, but simply that there is no good reason for applying one rather than the other of two conflicting *leges causae*. It is therefore submitted that the priority of competing claims all of which are governed by the same law ought to be determined according to that law."[238]

To this *McLean* has responded that:

"[a]lthough there appears to be much to commend this view, in reason, there is no obvious way to reconcile the different treatment of the competing claims within the conceptual framework."[239]

Execution

The *lex fori* governs the execution of judgments.[240] The principle applies to such questions as whether a debtor may be imprisoned for failure to pay the debt.[241] In *De La Vega* v. *Vianna*,[242] in 1830, a Portuguese defendant resident in England was held to have been properly arrested in England for a debt accrued in Portugal while both the plaintiff (who was Spanish) and defendant had resided in Portugal. At the time of the proceedings, arrest for debt was permitted in England but not in Portugal. Lord Tenterden, C.J., delivering the judgment of the court, said:

"A person suing in this country must take the law as he finds it; he cannot, by virtue

---

[231] Cf. *Morris*, 465, *McLean*, 223.
[232] *Ex parte Melbourn*, 6 Ch. App. 64 (1870), *Re Kloebe*, 28 Ch. D. 175 (Pearson, J., 1884), *Pardo* v. *Bingham*, L.R. 6 Eq. 485 (Lord Romilly, M.R., 1884), *The Colorado*, [1923] P. 102 (C.A.).
[233] Cf. *Forde*, ch. 15, *Keane*, Part 8, *Ussher*, ch. 16.
[234] Cf. *Wylie*, paras. 16.30-16.37.
[235] See *Morris*, 465-466, *Cheshire & North*, 705-706, Price, *Maritime Liens*, 57 L.Q. Rev. 409, (1941), *The Halcyon Isle; Bankers Trust International Ltd.* v. *Todd Shipyards Corporation*, [1981] A.C. 221 (P.C.).
[236] *Morris*, 362-363, 466.
[237] *Norton* v. *Florence Land & Public Works Co.*, 7 Ch. D. 332 (Jessel, M.R., 1877).
[238] *Morris*, 466. See also *Dicey & Morris*, 1193.
[239] *McLean*, 224.
[240] See *Northern Trusts Co.* v. *McLean*, [1926] 3 D.L.R. 93 (Ont. Sup. Ct., App. Div.), *Royal Trust Co.* v. *Kritzwiser*, [1924] 3 D.L.R. 596, at 599 (Sask, C.A., *per* Lamont, J.A. (for the court)). Cf. *Johnstone* v. *Bucknall*, [1898] 2 I.R. 499 (Q.B. Div., Gibson, J.).
[241] Cf. *Delany & Lysaght*, 63, J.M. Kelly, *Fundamental Rights in the Irish Law and Constitution*, 95-97 (2nd ed., 1967), J.M. Kelly, *The Irish Constitution*, 515 (2nd ed., 1984).
[242] 1 B. & Ad. 284, 109 E.R. 792 (1830).

of any regulation in his own country, enjoy greater advantages than other suitors here, and he ought not therefore to be deprived of any superior advantage which the law of this country may confer. He is to have the same rights which all the subjects of this Kingdom are entitled to.''[243]

Conversely, where the *lex fori* prohibits imprisonment for a debt, whether generally or in certain circumstances, the fact that the *lex causae* would permit imprisonment will have no effect. Thus in the Australian case of *Smith* v. *Cotton*,[244] in 1926, Street, C.J. speaking for the majority of the New South Wales Supreme Court, considered that:

> ''[i]t would be an anomalous and an extraordinary state of affairs if a married woman could be imprisoned in [New South Wales] for a debt arising out of a contractual liability incurred in another State, while she should not be imprisoned here in respect of a similar liability if incurred in this State.''

Other matters relating to execution of a judgment properly fall within the scope of the *lex fori*. These include the exigibility of property,[245] whether debts in the hands of third parties can be attached by garnishment,[246] and costs.[247]

Judgments in Foreign Currency

Formerly, in England, a procedural rule applied to the enforcement by action of a foreign-currency obligation, whereby the claim, the judgment and any process of execution in England had to be in sterling;[248] ''the sterling sum for which judgment was given had to be converted from the relevant foreign currency at the rate of exchange obtaining on the day when the obligation became due and payable.''[249] These rules might have had some justification in times when sterling was a reasonably stable currency, but for some years the instability of sterling, coupled with the continuation of these rules, resulted in hardship for either the plaintiff or the defendant in cases where the relative values of sterling and the relevant foreign currency had altered between the time the obligation became due and payable and the time of payment.

After judicial expressions of dissatisfaction, led by Lord Denning, M.R.,[250] the House of Lords in *Milliangos* v. *George Frank (Textiles) Ltd.*[251] in 1975, held that the rules should be changed. Under the new approach, judgment in the relevant foreign currency, and not sterling, was the standard by which the amount to be paid was to be determined. Thus, where the plaintiff claimed in a foreign currency, the

---

[243] 1 B. & Ad. at 288, 109 E.R., at 793.

[244] 27 S.R. (N.S.W.) 41, at 53 (1926). But see *id.*, at 62-64 (*per* Ferguson, J., dissenting).

[245] *Northern Trusts Co.* v. *McLean*, [1926] 3 D.L.R. 93 (Ont. Sup. Ct., App. Div.), *Royal Trust Co.* v. *Kritzwiser*, [1924] 3 D.L.R. 596 (Sask, C.A.).

[246] *Morris*, 466; in accord, *Cheshire & North*, 721, *McLean*, 224.

[247] *Lowden* v. *Accident Insurance Co.*, 43 I.L.T.R. 277 (K.B. Div., 1904).

[248] English Law Commission's Report, *Private International Law: Foreign Money Liabilities*, para. 2.3 (Law Com. No. 124, 1983).

[249] *Id.*, citing *Re United Railways of Havana and Regla Warehouses Ltd.*, [1961] A.C. 1007, *Di Fernando* v. *Simon, Smith & Co. Ltd.*, [1920] 3 K.B. 409, *The Volturno*, [1921] 2 A.C. 544. See further Brand, *Restructuring the U.S. Approach to Judgments on Foreign Currency Liabilities: Building on the English Experience*, 11 Yale J. Int'l L. 139, at 144-147 (1985).

[250] Cf. *The Teh Hu*, [1970] P. 106. See also *Jugoslavenska Oceanska Plovidba* v. *Castle Investment Co. Inc.*, [1974] Q.B. 292, *Schorsch Meier GmbH* v. *Hennin*, [1975] Q.B. 416, Brand, *supra*, at 147-148.

[251] [1976] A.C. 443. See Riordan, *Comment: The Currency of Suit in Actions for Foreign Debts*, 24 McGill L.J. 422 (1978). A very clear review of developments in England, culminating in *Miliangos*, is given by Morris, *English Judgments in Foreign Currency: A ''Procedural'' Revolution*, 41 L. & Contemporary Prob. 44 (1977).

Court should order that the defendant pay the plaintiff either the sum due in the foreign currency or its sterling equivalent at the time of payment, that is, the date of actual payment, or in default, the date at which the court authorised enforcement of the judgment.

The *Miliangos* case left open the question whether the new rule should also apply to actions for damages for breach of contract or tort; Lord Wilberforce stressed that they did not wish to go beyond cases involving money obligations governed by the law of a foreign country "where the money of account and payment is that of that country, or possibly of some other country but not of the United Kingdom."[252] These limitations have been swept away by later decisions, which have held that the *Miliangos* principle applies to contracts governed by English law,[253] and to matters other than debt, including claims for damages for breach of contract,[254] torts[255] and restitution.[256]

In Ireland, the practice formerly appears to have been in accordance with that formerly favoured in England but it seems that the matter was not tested in any case. With the breach from sterling and a similar experience of currency fluctuations in recent years, the argument in favour of a reform on the lines of *Miliangos* and its progeny proved attractive here.

In *Damen & Zonen* v. *O'Shea*,[257] in 1977, McMahon, J. held that a judgment may be given in a foreign currency. The case involved an application for judgment in default of appearance to a summary summons in which the claim was for 14,740.40 Dutch guilders, the price of goods sold and delivered. McMahon, J. noted[258] that there had been no reported decision of an Irish court that a judgment could *not* be given in a foreign currency, but that Irish Courts and court officers had until then followed what was understood to be the common law that judgment could not be given in terms of a foreign currency.

McMahon, J. referred to the *Milliangos*[259] decision, and observed:

"In my view the requirements of international commerce are clearly met by a rule which enables the Court to give judgment in whatever currency the plaintiff is entitled to under the terms of the contract and there is nothing to prevent this Court from adopting the rule which permits justice to be done more effectively."[260]

He saw "no reason in principle why effect should not be given to the terms of a contract securing to the plaintiffs the right to payment in a foreign currency whether the proper law of that contract is Irish law or foreign law."[261] In this context McMahon, J. noted that:

---

[252] *Id.*, at 468.
[253] *Federal Commerce and Navigation Co. Ltd.* v. *Tradax Export S.A.*, [1977] Q.B. 324 (rev'd on other grds, [1978] A.C.1), *Services Europe Atlantique Sud (SAS)* v. *Stockholms Rederiaktiebolag Svea*, [1979] A.C. 685.
[254] *Services Europe Atlantique Sud (SEAS)* v. *Stockholms Rederiaktiebolag Svea, supra.*
[255] *The Despina R* [1979] A.C. 685, *Hoffman* v. *Sofaer*, [1982] 1 W.L.R. 1350. See Knott, *Foreign Currency Judgments in Tort: An Illustration of the Wealth — Time Continuum*, 43 Modern L. Rev. 18 (1980).
[256] *B.P. Exploration Co. (Libya) Ltd.* v. *Hunt (No. 2)*, [1979] 1 W.L.R. 783, at 840-841 (aff'd., [1981] 1 W.L.R. 232 (C.A.), [1982] 2 W.L.R. 253 (H.L.)). The developments in England have not gone unnoticed in the United States: see Brand, *supra*, Lion, *The Need to Retreat from Inflexible Conversion Rules — An Equitable Approach to Judgment in Foreign Currency*, 22 Santa Clara L. Rev. 871 (1982).
[257] Unreported, High Ct., McMahon, J., 25 May 1977 (1977-414).
[258] At p. 1 of the judgment.
[259] *Milliangos* v. *George Frank (Textiles) Ltd.*, [1976] A.C. 443 (H.L.(Eng.), 1975).
[260] Page 3 of McMahon, J.'s judgment.
[261] *Id.*

"[i]n the case of *Barclay's Bank International Ltd.* v. *Levin Brothers (Bradford) Ltd.*,[262] Mocatta J. has held that to obtain judgment expressed in a foreign currency it is not necessary to establish that the proper law of the contract is foreign law and that the passages in the judgments in the House of Lords in the *Miliangos* case which refer to the proper law of the contract merely delimit the extent of that decision but do not preclude a subsequent court from deciding that the right is not confined to contracts the proper law [of] which is foreign law."[263]

The last question arising in the case was the conversion date to be inserted in the judgment of the Court for the purpose of converting the foreign currency into Irish currency. In the *Miliangos* case, as has been mentioned, Lord Wilberforce had held that the proper date was the date of payment, which in England is the date when the Court gives leave to enforce the judgment. McMahon J. noted that such leave is not provided for by our rules of procedure, under which a judgment, once given, is payable immediately without further order. In his opinion the plaintiff was entitled to an order that the defendant should pay him the sum due in Dutch guilders or the Irish currency equivalent at the date when the judgment in default was entered in the office.[264]

In *Northern Bank Ltd* v. *Edwards*,[265] the Supreme Court endorsed *Damen & Zonen* v. *O'Shea*. McCarthy, J. cited *Damen & Zonen* in support of his statement that, where the proper law of the contract for advances was that of Northern Ireland, the plaintiff would have been entitled to judgment that the sum was well charged on lands within the State, expressed in sterling, had it sought this. But a separate question was whether the money charged on the lands should be construed as being in the currency of the State, and McCarthy, J. was satisfied that precedent supported this interpretation. Since the contract was made before Ireland had entered the European Monetary System, the implications for the plaintiff were serious, the Irish currency having appreciably weakened as against sterling in the meanwhile.

---

[262] [1977] Q.B. 270 (Mocatta, J., 1976).
[263] Page 3 of the judgment.
[264] *Id.*, p. 4.
[265] [1984] I.R. 284 (Sup. Ct.).

CHAPTER 35

SECURITY FOR COSTS[1]

In certain circumstances a plaintiff residing outside the jurisdiction may be required to give security for costs. Order 29 of the Rules of the Superior Courts 1986 deals with the question. Rule 1 is of a procedural nature: it provides that "[w]hen a party shall require security for costs from another party", he may apply by notice to the other party for this security, and if the other party does not within forty eight hours undertake to comply with this requirement, the party requiring the security may apply to the Court for an order for security for costs.

Where the court makes an order for security of costs, the amount of the security and the time and manner in which it is to be given and the person (or persons) to whom it is to be given are generally determined by the Master.[2] Where, however, a bond is to be given as security, it must be given to the person requiring the security, and not to an officer of the Court, unless the master directs otherwise;[3] but bonds in matrimonial causes must be given to the Master.[4]

Policy Considerations

The rule that a plaintiff resident abroad may be required to give security for costs was "established by the Judges for the protection of defendants ..."[5] It is a "cardinal principle"[6] that a defendant resident abroad should not be ordered to give security for costs.[7] Why should this be so? The answer is encapsulated in the succinct observation by Andrews, J., in *In the Goods of Twomey Deceased; O'Leary v. Stack:*[8]

> "There is an obvious distinction between the cases of a plaintiff and a defendant. The plaintiff comes into Court; the defendant is brought into Court."

It would be "almost a mockery of justice if a plaintiff, having brought a defendant before a Court, could demand that he should be obliged to give security for the costs

---

[1] See generally *Anon., Security for Costs (The Effect of the Rules of Court 1926)*, 3 Ir. Jur. 19 (1937), *Anon., Orders for Security for Costs: The Measure of Security to be Given*, V.T.H. D[elany], *Security of Costs: The Current Principle*, 24 Ir. Jur. 29 (1958), *Anon., Security for Costs by Plaintiff without the Jurisdiction*, 5 Ir. L.T. & Sol. J. 611 (1871), *Anon., Security for Costs*, 50 Ir. L.T. & Sol. J. 1,7 (1916), *Anon., Security for Costs in the Irish Free State*, 63 Ir. L.T. & Sol. J. 49 (1929), *Anon., Recent Security for Costs Cases*, 79 Ir. L.T. & Sol. J. 115 (1945), *Anon., Some Recent Irish Decisions on Security for Costs*, 88 Ir. L.T. & Sol. J.139, 145 (1954).
[2] Rules of the Superior Courts 1986, Order 29, rule 6.
[3] *Id.*, rule 7.
[4] *Id.*
[5] *White v. Carroll*, I.R. 8 C.L. 296, at 300 (Q.B., *per* Fitzgerald, J., 1874).
[6] *Dicey & Morris*, 1196. See *In the Goods of Twomey Deceased; O'Leary v. Stack*, [1900] 2 I.R. 560 (Q.B. Div. (Prob., Andrews, J.)).
[7] See, however, *Lessee Stewart v. Bartholomew*, 1 Ir. L.R. 377 (Exch. of Pleas, Pennefather, B., 1839).
[8] [1900] 2 I.R. 560, at 565 (Q.B. Div.).

of being allowed to defend himself against the proceedings."[9] On the other hand, there would be a real danger, in the absence of provision for security for costs, that a plaintiff resident abroad could take proceedings here and then return to his own country if the case went against him, leaving the successful defendant the onerous task of pursuing him in a foreign court for his costs.[10]

The rule that only the plaintiff resident abroad may be called on to give security for costs applies even in cases where defendant also resides outside the jurisdiction. The courts consider that "[t]he mischief is precisely the same whether the defendant resides in this country or not. The plaintiff must give security".[11]

Exception to the rule requiring security for costs

An important exception to the rule requiring plaintiffs to give security for costs should be noted at the outset. Section 12 of the Maintenance Orders Act 1974 provides that no security or deposit, however described, may be required from a person seeking enforcement of a maintenance order solely on the ground that he is not residing in the State.[12]

Who is a plaintiff?

If security for costs may be required of plaintiffs resident abroad then, of course, the question of who exactly is a plaintiff becomes one of a considerable importance. In England Order 23 rule 1(3) of the Rules of the Supreme Court provides that references in the rule to a plaintiff and a defendant are to be construed as references to the person (howsoever described on the record) who is in the position of plaintiff or defendant, as the case may be, in the proceedings in question, including a proceeding on a counterclaim.[13]

The Courts "look at the substance of the matter and not merely at the form,"[14] and say "any person who assumes the position of an actor in the proceedings in question is a plaintiff, and any person who is really defending himself against attack is a defendant".[15]

In Ireland there is no equivalent rule in our Rules of the Superior Courts 1986. There have, however, been several cases in which the issue has been clarified.

Administration

In *Wheelan* v. *Irwin*,[16] an administrator with the will annexed of an Irish testator, sought to restrain promoters of a railway company from proceeding with legislation which would have indirectly damaged the value of the estate. The plaintiff was a

---

[9] *Leonard* v. *Scofield*, [1936] I.R. 715, at 718 (High Ct., Johnson, J.). Cf. *Midland Bank Ltd.* v. *Crossley-Cooke*, [1969] I.R. 56, at 62 (Sup. Ct., per Walsh, J.).

[10] See *Redmond* v. *Mooney*, 14 I.C.L.R. *xvii*, at *xix* (Q.B., per Fitzgerald, J., 1862), *In re Beckett*, 5 L.R. Ir. 43, at 44 (*per* Ormsby, J., 1880). See also *Redondo* v. *Chaytor*, 4 Q.B.D. 453, at 457-458 (C.A., *per* Thesiger, L.J. 1879), *Erickson* v. *McFarlane*, 42 O.L.R. 32, at 33 (Middleton, J. (in chambers), 1918).

[11] *Baxter* v. *Morgan*, 6 Taunt 377, at 379, 128 E.R. 1081, at 1081 (*per Curiam*, 1815), quoted with approval by Johnston, J. in *Leonard* v. *Scofield*, [1936] I.R. 715, at 719 (High Ct.) See *also Naamlooze Vennootschap Beleggings Compagnie "Uranus"* v. *Bank of England*, [1948] 1 All E.R. 465 (C.A.).

[12] Cf. *supra*, p. 312. The EEC Judgments Convention (on which the 1974 Act was modelled) adopts the same policy.

[13] Cf. *Dicey & Morris*, 1196.

[14] *Id.*

[15] *Id.*

[16] [1909] 1 I.R. 294 (Meredith, M.R.). See also *Executors Action* v. *Grant*, 12 I.L.R. 358 (Q.B., 1848). cf. *Harwood* v. *Tenison*, 5 Ir. Ch. Rep. 340 (Cusack Smith, M.R., 1856), *Leeson* v. *Leeson*, 4 Ir. Ch. Rep. 28 (Cusack Smith, M.R., 1853), *Loader* v. *Millar*, [1942] Ir. Jur. Rep. 38 (High Ct., Maguire, P.).

New York resident and had no property of his own in Ireland, but there were considerable assets of the testator in Ireland unadministered. Meredith, M.R. ordered security for costs. He said:

> "All the cases in the Chancery Division on this subject which I can recollect were cases in which the plaintiffs rebutted the *prima facie* obligation to give security by showing that they had assets within the jurisdiction available in the event of their being defeated. This is plain; if the plaintiff in this action is suing personally, beyond all doubt he is bound to give security for costs in this action. If he says that he comes in a representative capacity, he is equally bound to give security for costs, unless he proves that there are assets of his testator which the defendant can render available for costs, in the event of the Court awarding costs to the defendant."[17]

The Master of the Rolls rejected[18] the argument that, if the plaintiff lost his case, costs would be awarded against the estate rather than against the plaintiff personally:

> "How can I anticipate the decision of a Court or a Judge as to the costs incurred by an unsuccessful and migratory litigant?"[19]

Wheelan v. *Irwin* was followed by Johnston, J., in *In re Julian; Julian* v. *Goodbody.*[20]

Defendant caveators

A defendant caveator may have an order for security for costs made against him.[21] In *Woods* v. *Byron,*[22] where a police justice from New York State lodged a caveat against the admission of the deceased testator's will to probate, Davitt, J. held that the proper principle to apply was whether the caveat was entered vexatiously or frivolously, or whether the opposition to the will seemed reasonable. He noted that probate actions are somewhat different from common law actions, in that costs do not invariably follow the event.

Probate actions

In *Guion* v. *Heffernan,*[23] a plaintiff in a probate action was required to give security for costs. O'Byrne, J. said:

> "It has been contended on behalf of the plaintiff that she is not, in the circumstances of this action, liable to give security for costs. In support of that contention [counsel] relies on the proposition that where the plaintiff in a probate action merely seeks to have the will proved in solemn form, and is, therefore, in the position of a defendant, he cannot be required to give security for costs. I cannot accept that contention. In the case of *Ward* v. *Skeehan,*[24] .... Andrews, J. held that a defendant caveator may, in a proper case, be ordered to give security for costs. If the defendant caveator, against whom an action is brought, may be required to give security for costs, much more

---

[17] [1909] 1 I.R., at 299.

[18] *Id.*, at 300.

[19] *Id.*

[20] [1936] I.R. 126 (High Ct., Johnston, J.), distinguishing *Rainbow* v. *Kittor,* [1916] 1 Ch. 313 (Sargant, J.).

[21] Cf. *Ward* v. *Skeehan,* [1097] 2 I.R. 1 (Aandrews, J., 1906). Cf. *Lambert* v. *Bassett,* I.R. 11 Eq. 291 (Prob., Warren, J., 1877), *In bonis Flanagan Deceased,* 39 I.L.T.R. 188 (C.A., 1905). See, however, *In the Goods of Twomey; O'Leary* v. *Stack,* [1900] 2 I.R. 560 (Q.B. Div. Prob., Andrews, J.).

[22] [1947] Ir. Jur. Rep. 42 (High Ct., Davitt, J., 1946), See *Anon., Some Recent Irish Decisions on Security for Costs, — Part 2,* 88 Ir. L.T. & Sol. J. 145, at 145-146 (1954).

[23] [1929] I.R. 487 (High Ct., O'Byrne,J., 1928).

[24] [1907] 2 I.R. 1.

so a person who himself brings the action. I have, accordingly, no hesitation in holding that the plaintiff .... may be required to give security for costs."[25]

Nominal plaintiffs

On principle, it would appear that a nominal plaintiff should also be required to give security in appropriate cases. The issue was raised, but not finally resolved, in *Collopy* v. *O'Shaughnessy*.[26] It was there alleged that the female plaintiff had been joined as a nominal plaintiff merely as a strategy to protect her son, the real plaintiff, resident abroad, from having an order for security for costs made against him.

The Court of Appeal, affirming the Exchequer Division, held in the woman's favour on the basis that, on the "very lowest view to be taken of her position,"[27] she was a tenant at will. FitzGibbon C.J. observed:

"Though we cannot say that she was improperly joined as a plaintiff we do not affirm that she necessarily has a good title, nor do we decide that the name of a plaintiff, added merely to prevent a defendant from obtaining security for costs, may not be struck out."[28]

Bankruptcy cases

In *Re Ring, a Bankrupt*,[29] Harrison, J. said:

"In bankruptcy [cases], the Court, at an early stage, takes possession of the bankrupt's property, and any party who is a claimant or creditor is forced to come in and establish that claim, or his title to any portion of that property, and is somewhat more in the position of a Defendant forced into Court to defend his rights than of a Plaintiff instituting proceedings."

Interpleader proceedings

In interpleader proceedings, the Court must try to ascertain who is the real plaintiff, in the sense of being the person who is really responsible for the institution of the litigation;[30] in appropriate cases, he may be required to give security for costs, if he is residing abroad, whether he is named in the interpleader proceedings as plaintiff or defendant. In *Leonard* v. *Scofield*,[31] the plaintiff sued (among others) the Sweepstake Trustees, appointed under the Public Hospitals Act 1933, claiming a declaration that he was entitled to one moiety of a prize of £30,000 won by a ticket

---

[25] [1929] I.R., at 488. Cf. *McNeany* v. *Maguire*, [1923] 2 I.R. 43 (I.F.S. (K.B.Div., Prob.), Dodd, J.), *In the Goods of Twomey, Deceased; O'Learly* v. *Stack*, [1900] 2 I.R. 560 (Q.B. Div., Prob., Andrews, J.).

[26] 6 L.R. Ir. 449 (C.A., 1879). Cf. *Metzenburgh* v. *Chadwick*, 13 Ir. L. R. 59 (Exch. of Pleas, Pennefather, B., 1848), *Contsworth* v. *Willington*, 11 Ir. L.R. 54 (Exch. of Pleas, Pennefather, B., 1847). See also *Salmon* v. *Belfast Alhambra Ltd.*, 37 I.L.T.R. 72 (K.B. Div., Wright, J., 1903) (undischarged bankrupt suing for wrongful dismissal not a nominal plaintiff). In *Clarke* v. *Doolin*, 29 I.L.T.R. 4 (Ch. Div., 1894), Chatterton, V.-C. held that the next friend of an insane person, and thus a nominal plaintiff, was not obliged to give security for costs, even though lacking financial resources.

[27] 6 I.R. Ir., at 454 (*per Ball, C.*).

[28] *Id.*, at 455.

[29] I.R. 3 Eq. 507, at 508 (By., 1869).

[30] Cf. *Dicey & Morris*, 1197.

[31] [1936] I.R. 715 (High Ct., Johnston J.). See also *Belmonte* v. *Aynard*, 4 C.P.D. 221 (C.A., 1879), *In re Milward*, [1900] 1 Ch. 405 (C.A.), discussed in *Leonard* v. *Scofield, supra*, at 720. In a number of English decisions the courts have evinced reluctance to order security against one party but not the other in interpleader proceedings: cf. *Maatschappij Voor Fondsenbezit* v. *Shell Transport & Trading Co.*, [1923] 2 K.B. 166, at 174 (C.A., *per* Bankes, L.J.). *Tudor Furnishers Ltd.* v. *Montague & Son*, [1950] Ch. 113 (Chy. Div., Wynn-Parry, J., 1949).

bearing the name of the defendant, Mary Scofield. Both the plaintiff and Mary Scofield resided in New York.

Pursuant to an order of the Court, the Sweepstake Trustees lodged £15,000 in Court, whereupon they were dismissed from the action. In ordering the plaintiff to give security, Johnston, J. said:

> "Now, in this case the nominal plaintiff is the real plaintiff, he instituted the action in the first instance, and if it had not been commenced the defendant would undoubtedly have been paid the full amount of the prize money."[32]

Co-plaintiffs

We must now consider the question of security for costs where there are co-plaintiffs. In *In bonis Mooney,*[33] Hanna, J. was:

> "of opinion that it is the law, that the ordinary and normal rule is that security for costs will not be ordered against a plaintiff out of the jurisdiction when there is joined with such a plaintiff another *bona fide* plaintiff, or plaintiffs, residing within the jurisdiction; but that the Court can, within its jurisdiction, deal with the plaintiff, or plaintiffs, within the jurisdiction if of opinion that such plaintiff, or plaintiffs, are not real and substantial plaintiffs in the action, or are not entitled to the relief claimed therein, or that they have been joined merely to oust the jurisdiction to order security for costs against the foreign plaintiff."[34]

The quality of the plaintiff's residence

If security for costs is to be ordered where the plaintiff resides out of the jurisdiction, then the question arises as to what kind of "residence" will be required.

Rule 4 of Order 29 provides that a plaintiff ordinarily resident out of the jurisdiction may be ordered to give security for costs though he may be temporarily within the jurisdiction.[35]

The question whether a plaintiff's residence was of sufficient quality to prevent an order for security for costs being made against him arose in *Howard* v. *Howard.*[36] The plaintiff sought to establish his title to the Wicklow estates, and sought an injunction restraining the Earl of Wicklow from receiving the rents and profits from these lands. The plaintiff, born in England, had lived in France for

---

[32] [1936] I.R., at 720.

[33] [1938] I.R. 354, at 358 (High Ct., Hanna, J. 1937).

[34] See also *Collopy* v. *O'Shaughnessy*, 6 L.R. Ir. 449 (C.A., 1879) where there were two plaintiffs, one resident out of the jurisdiction. The Court of Appeal, affirming the Exchequer Division, declined to order the plaintiff out of the jurisdiction to provide security, since it was satisfied that the plaintiff within the jurisdiction was "a substantial plaintiff" (*per* Deasy, L.J. at 454), who had been properly joined in the action. Cf. *Mullan* v. *King*, 31 I.L.T.R. 155 (Q.B., Johnson, J., 1897), *Peppard & Co. Ltd.* v. *Bogoff*, [1962] I.R. 180, at 187 (Sup. Ct., *per* Kingsmill Moore, J., 1957, rev'g High Ct., Dixon, J., 1957), *Personal Service Laundry Ltd.* v. *National Bank Ltd.*, [1964] I.R. 49 (Sup. Ct., 1960), *Houlditch* v. *Stackpoole*, 3 Law Rec. (o.s.) 123 (1830).

[35] Thus many of the older cases, which, to varying degrees, held that temporary presence within the jurisdiction could suffice, no longer have effect. See, e.g. *Redmond* v. *Mooney*, 14 Ir. C.L.R. *xvii* (Q.B., 1862), *Allain* v. *Chambers*, 8 Ir. C.L.R. *vii* (Consol. Cham., Pennefather, B., 1858), *Watson* v. *Porter*, [1907] 2 I.R. 341 (C.A., 1906, rev'g Q.B. Div.), *Conway* v. *Wilson*, 2 Ir. C.L.R. 47 (Q.B., 1851), *Sisson* v. *Cooper*, 4 Ir. L.R. 401 (Com. Pleas, 1842), *O'Neill* v. *O'Neill*, 6 L. Rec. (N.S.) 159 (Eq. Exch. Richards, B., 1838). Cf. *Martin* v. *Russell*, 21 L.R. Ir. 196 (Chatterton, V.C., 1888), *Guion* v. *Heffernon*, [1929] I.R. 487 (High Ct., O'Byrne, J., 1928), *Habgood* v. *Paul*, 8 Ir. C.L.R. xxx (Q.B. Lefroy, C.J. 1859), *Woodley* v. *Woodley*, 3 I.L.R. 86 (Q.B., 1840), distinguished in *Eyre* v. *Baldwin*, 4 I.C.L.R. 270 (Q.B., 1855). It should be noted that sea-faring plaintiffs were for a time treated leniently by the Court: see *Corscaden* v. *Stewart*, 1 I.L.R. 110 (Q.B., 1839), *Conway* v. *Wilson*, 2 Ir. C.L.R. 47 (1851). But cf. *Martin* v. *Russell*, 21 L.R. Ir. 196 (Chatterton, V.-C. 1888).

[36] 30 L.R. Ir. 340 (Q.B. Div., 1892).

twelve years. He worked there as an accountant; his wife, a Parisian, carried on the business of a milliner in a room in a house taken in his name. Before the legal proceedings began, the plaintiff gave up his position as an accountant, surrendered his house (but not the room where his wife carried on business) to his landlord, and attempted to send some of his furniture to Ireland. He became a tenant of a cottage in Monkstown, County Dublin, at a low rent. He begun to think about obtaining employment here as an accountant, journalist or teacher of French. He had no previous business connections with Ireland.

The Court of Queen's Bench, by a majority, held that the petitioner was temporarily rather than ordinarily resident in Ireland. Holmes, J. (of the majority) considered it clear that whether the plaintiff would stay here or not:

> "depends upon circumstances that have not yet developed. If he succeeds in his action he will, no doubt, take up his abode in Shelton Abbey, and have everything handsome about him. If he fails he may obtain in Ireland some employment as remunerate and pleasant as what he had in France; but it is just as likely that he will not. His training, his previous life, his business connexions — all great helps to him in Paris — would be of no assistance here. It is in this uncertainty as regards his future that the solution of the question which we have to determine can be found. Up to a month ago, Paris had been for years his only place of residence and business. He has still a house there in his own name, where his wife is engaged in trade, and in which I understand she and other members of his family are now residing. He has come to this country on speculation, and for the present he has no permanent residence anywhere. If he wins the action, or gets some good employment, he will or may settle here permanently; but until then he can only be regarded as temporarily resident. It would indeed be an anomaly in our law that if some foreign Rothschild were to rent a mansion in Meath for the hunting season, and surround himself there with every material luxury that money can command, he might be obliged, as a condition to suing in this Court, to give security for costs, while a Parisian accountant having all his belongings and connexions in France would be free from this obligation because he holds an empty cottage in Monkstown, for a tenancy determinable in fifteen months, at an annual rent of £12."[37]

Also of the majority, Harrison, J. stated that he did not consider it sufficient for the plaintiff merely to state his intention to remain permanently in Ireland, no matter what might be the result of the proceedings:

> "To enable us to come to a conclusion we must have regard to all the circumstances to the case. If he succeeds it may be assumed he will remain, but if he fails I am not satisfied that he will do so; at all events there is an air of uncertainty in the matter, and I think that this element prevents us treating him as a person permanently residing here."[38]

In *Bull* v. *Wallis & Sons,*[39] the reverse situation arose. The plaintiff, a woman was possessed of considerable property in Cork, where she had a right to reside in her brother's house. She had "merely gone to India for a few months on a

---

[37] *Id.,* at 346-347.

[38] *Id.,* at 369. O'Brien, J.'s dissent (*id.,* at 360) is worth noting. He said of the plaintiff:
"Of course it is open to the Court not to accept his statement. But as to the effect of evidence on the subject, it must be observed that the actual intention alone of the party is sufficient absolutely to determine the question of permanent residence. It requires no experience or confirmation from time. A permanent residence is capable of existing immediately. Though in its nature a question of future conduct, it must be determined at once, and therefore must depend upon intention. Prudence or imprudence, probability or the contrary, or the possibility of change of mind from motives of convenience are merely means of judging whether the intention exists. This renders all evidence more doubtful when applied to what is future or contingent, or may be affected by personal character or varying circumstances, as compared with acts or motives that are already past."

[39] 26 I.L.T.R. 114 (Exch. Div., 1892).

visit".[40] The Court nonetheless ordered her to give security for costs. Palles, C.B. disposed of the issue in a sentence: "A 'right to reside' means nothing; it cannot be taken as having a 'residence' ".[41]

So far as motives for residing abroad are concerned, a distinction appears to be made between what might be called public and private necessity. In *Everard* v. ----- -----[42], in 1839. O'Loghlen, M.R. regarded it as "a settled rule" that an officer in the service of the British Crown, and on duty with his regiment abroad, should not be obliged to give security for costs. In *Clements* v. *Gardiner*,[43] in 1871, O'Brien, J. held that a plaintiff out of the jurisdiction, though engaged on active duty in the service of the British Crown, would be compelled to give security for costs unless it appeared either that his ordinary residence was in Ireland or that he would be in Ireland except for his absence on service. Whether courts today would take a similar view in relation to an Irish soldier on peacekeeping duty abroad is not certain.[44] Nor can we predict what the attitude of the courts would be to cases of pressing private necessity — a man whose contract with a multinational company requires him to work as a geologist in Saudi Arabia for nine months every year, for example, [45] or a person who lives in the Riviera on doctor's orders.

A plaintiff leaving jurisdiction after action brought may have to give security

Where the plaintiff, after the commencement of the action, goes to reside *temporarily* out of the jurisdiction, it appears that security for costs will not be ordered.[46] But where his departure is intended to be *permanent*, the Court may make an order for security for costs.[47]

Possession of property within the jurisdiction

It may happen that a plaintiff, resident outside the jurisdiction, owns substantial property in Ireland. Especially in cases where the property is immovable,[48] this may afford a good reason for not ordering security for costs, since there will be a fund within the jurisdiction against which a successful defendant may seek satisfaction.[49]

Perhaps the clearest test was offered by Bowen, L.J., in *Ebrard* v. *Gassier*,[50] where he said that if the plaintiffs resident abroad desired to escape from their *prima facie* obligation to give security for costs, "they were bound to show that they had substantial property in this country, not of a floating, but of a fixed and permanent nature, which would be available in the event of the defendants being entitled to the costs of the action".

[40] *Id.*, at 115 (*per* counsel for the plaintiff).

[41] *Id.* See also *Habgood* v. *Paul*, 8 I.C.L.R. App. *xxxiii* (Q.B., 1859).

[42] 1 Ir. Eq. Rep. 421 (O'Loughlen, M.R., 1839). Cf. *Long* v. *Tottenham*, 1 Ir. Ch. Rep. 127 (Cusack Smith, M.R., 1850). Older cases also exempted from the obligation to give security for costs consuls, stipendiary magistrates, harbour masters and inspectors of fisheries when they were residing abroad in the course of their duties. *Wynne* v. *Knox*, 14 Ch. Rep. 149, at 150 (1863).

[43] I.R. 6 C.L. 18 (Cons. Cham., O'Brien, J., 1871).

[44] As to the domicile of servicemen, see *supra*, p. 65.

[45] Cf. *Duff* v. *Hore*, *supra*.

[46] *Norris* v. *Duckworth*, 6 Ir. Ch. Rep. 57 (Cusack Smith, M.R., 1856).

[47] *Hodson* v. *M'Queen*, 7 Ir. C.L.R. 288 (Exch., 1857).

[48] In *Clarke* v. *Barber*, 6 Times L.R. 256, at 257 (Q.B. Div., 1890), Denman, J. was reported as saying that "[n]o doubt it was not necessary that it should be land; but it should not be property which could be immediately made away with, or which was embarked in speculative business".

[49] Cf. *In re Apollinaris Co's Trade Marks*, [1891] 1 Ch. 1, at 3 (C.A., *per* Lord Halsbury, L.C., 1890).

[50] 28 Ch. Div. 232, at 234 (C.A., 1884). See also *Kervorkian* v. *Burney (No. 2)*, [1937] 4 All E.R. 468 (C.A.), *Hamburger* v. *Poetting*, 47 L.T. 249, at 249 (Bacon, V.C., 1882). Cf. *Redondo* v. *Chaytor*, 4 Q.B. Div. 453, at 457 (C.A., *per* Thesiger, L.J. 1879), where there was no mention of a requirement that the property within the jurisdiction be substantial.

In Ireland, the courts have been far less enthusiastic than their English counterparts about relieving a plaintiff from the obligation to provide security where he has property within the jurisdiction. In 1824, in *Maxwell* v. *Martin*,[51] the Court of King's Bench declared that "by the practice of this Court the general rule is, that the plaintiff where he is resident abroad, must give security for costs; and his having property in this country does not make any difference". And in *Lord Lucan* v. *Latouche*,[52] McMahon, M.R. said:

"I do not think that the possession of property in the country affords any reasons why a plaintiff residing out of the jurisdiction should not give security for costs."

The issue was brought before the Court of Appeal in 1889, in *Casey* v. *Cork Gas Consumers Co.*[53] The plaintiffs sought damages for injury allegedly caused to their houses in Cork by noxious vapours coming from the defendant's factory. The plaintiffs were resident in Paris. They claimed that they were unable to get tenants for their Cork houses "owing to the stench that constantly proceeds from the gas works, which renders the houses uninhabitable". The defendants argued that the plaintiffs had only an equity of redemption in the premises, having effected a mortgage of them on which a considerable sum remained due.

The Court of Appeal were unanimous that they should continue to adhere to the well-established practice of ordering security even in cases where the plaintiff resident outside the jurisdiction had property within it. Lord Ashbourne, C. said that to accept the plaintiff's argument would involve:

"an entire and complete change in the procedure as it has existed in Ireland for many years; and although a different practice prevails in England, we do not think we should be justified in introducing a change here. Before making any change of such a sweeping character the Judges should be consulted, and asked to frame a new rule."[54]

Fitzgibbon, L.J. observed:

"Here the property is described as 'fee-simple', but it may be subject to any amount of incumbrances, and is not subject to seizure by the sheriff."[55]

And Barry, L.J. considered that it was "a strong thing to be told that there was

---

[51] Fox & Smith, 275, at 276 (1824).

[52] 1 Hogan 448, at 448. In *Fennell* v. *Fitzgerald*, 4 L. Rec. 170 (K.B., 1831), an absentee landlord suing for rent was required to give security for costs, although the land out of which the rent issued was within the jurisdiction. Cf. *Earl of Kingston* v. *Sheehy*, Hayes & Jones 358 (Exch. of Pleas, 1833) where a motion for an order for security for costs against a peer resident out of the jurisdiction was refused. The fact that no attachment could issue against a peer was one reason for refusing the motion. It is of interest, however, that counsel for the Earl of Kingston observed that it was "not pretended that Lord Kingston has not ample property in this country ..." *Id.* In *Lessee Nagle* v. *Power*, 1 Jones 420 (Exch. of Pleas, 1835), the Court refused to make an order for security for costs, the plaintiff consenting to allow the defendant to set off the rent payable to him against any costs that he might become entitled to.
In *Sisson* v. *Cooper*, 4 Ir. L.R. 401 (Com. Pleas, 1842), the Court declined to make an order for security for costs where the plaintiff, resident for some years in Canada, had "considerable property" in and about the city of Dublin. It appears that the true basis of the refusal to make the order was that of the plaintiff's temporary presence within the jurisdiction (a ground no longer applicable: cf. p. 656 *supra*) rather than his possession of property here. In *Loader* v. *Millar*, [1942] Ir. Jur. Rep. 38 (High Ct.) Maguire, P., ordered security for costs where the plaintiff executor, resident in England, had no assets within the jurisdiction, although the deceased's estate included ample assets within the jurisdiction.

[53] 30 L.R. Ir. 713 (C.A., 1889).

[54] *Id.*, at 717.

[55] *Id.*, at 718.

no foundation for the statement that the practice here was different from what it is in England".[56]

In *Bull* v. *Wallis & Sons*,[57] the Court ordered a plaintiff to give security when she was on a temporary visit from Ireland to India, even though she was possessed of "considerable property" in Cork, having there a right of residence in her brother's house, a mortgage on lands owned by the Knights of St. John for £600 and "houses in Main-street..." The Court appeared to attach no weight to this factor.

In *In re Beckett*,[58] Ormsby, J. held that an incumbrancer, as opposed to an owner, of property within the jurisdiction was bound to give security for costs. In *In re M'Allister's Estate*,[59] Monroe, J. followed *In re Beckett*. The petitioner in this case was not an incumbrancer, but claimed title to some of the property mentioned in the petition and sought an order for sale and partition. The property was all in the actual possession of tenants. Monroe, J. ordered the petitioner to give security. He said:

> "The petitioner seeks to sell a property of which she is not in actual possession, and of which [the applicant for security] claims to be in possession .... Whether [the petitioner] can make absolute her conditional order for sale under such circumstances, assuming cause to be shown, I express no opinion at present. The rights, or alleged rights of [the applicant for security], as an owner of the entire premises are assailed; and as he would have no means of recovering his costs against the petitioner in the event of her petition being dismissed, and costs given against her, I must stay all proceedings on this petition, until security for costs be given ..."[60]

In the twentieth century, the Irish courts moved towards a softer approach. In the Supreme Court case of *Heaney* v. *Malocca*,[61] Maguire, C.J. mentioned as a special circumstance depriving the defendant of an order for security a situation "where there is shown to be ample assets within the jurisdiction".

Where the defendant has in his possession goods of the plaintiff worth at least the costs of the proceedings, the Court may decline to order security for costs against the plaintiff.[62]

Plaintiffs resident in Northern Ireland

Rule 2 of Order 29 provides that a defendant "shall not be entitled to an order for security for costs solely on the ground that the plaintiff resides in Northern Ireland". A similar rule has existed in the Northern Ireland Rules[63] since 1936. Prior to its introduction here in 1962, there were calls for a change on these lines in a number of decisions.[64]

The former rule, under the 1905 Rules,[65] had provided that a defendant should not be entitled to an order compelling the plaintiff to give security for costs solely

---

[56] *Id.*, at 719.

[57] 26 I.L.T.R. 114 (Exch. Div.,1892).

[58] 5 L.R. Ir. 43 (1880).

[59] 25 L.R. Ir. 282 (Monroe, J., 1890).

[60] *Id.*, at 283-284.

[61] [1958] I.R. 111, at 115 (Sup. Ct., 1957, rev'g High Ct., Murnaghan, J., 1957).

[62] *Freedland Ltd.* v. *Kelly*, 84 I.L.T. & Sol. J. 65 (Circuit Ct., Judge Connolly, 1950). See further *Anon., Some Recent Irish Decisions on Security for Costs — Part II*, 88 Ir. L.T. & Sol. J. 145, at 146 (1954). See also *Kevorkian* v. *Burney (No. 2)*, [1937] 4 All E.R. 468 (C.A.).

[63] Rules of the Supreme Court (N.I.) 1936, Order *xxix*, rule 2. See *Robinson* v. *McEntee*, 73 I.L.T.R. 53 (N.I.K.B. Div., Andrews, L.C.J., 1939) *Macaura* v. *Smith*, [1939] Ir. Jur. Rep. 46 (N.I.K.B. Div., Andrews, L.C.J.).

[64] *Seth* v. *Menzies*, [1939] I.R. 530, at 533 (High Ct., Maguire P.), *Heany* v. *Malocca*, [1958] I.R. 111, at 115 (Sup. Ct., *per* Maguire, J., 1957).

[65] Rules of the Supreme Court 1905, Order *xxix*, rule 2.

on the ground that the plaintiff resided in England or Scotland. This provision was designed to harmonise with the Judgments Extension Act 1868.[66] After Independence, courts in England[67] and Northern Ireland[68] held that a judgment obtained in the Irish Free State could not be enforced under the 1868 Act. In *Rosenbaum* v. *Hicks,*[69] Pim, J. appears to have taken the same view as to the effect of Independence on the 1868 Act, since he ordered an English Trustee in Bankruptcy to give security for costs, in spite of Order 29, rule 2. The report is far too short to draw any definite conclusion on this question, however, though this inference seems reasonable in view of the fact that counsel for the defence relied strongly on the English case of *Wakely* v. *Triumph Cycle Co.*[70] In *Gremson* v. *Lipman,*[71] the High Court distinguished *Wakely* on the basis that Order 29, rule 2 constituted a definite rule with statutory authority preventing the Court from ordering security for costs on the sole ground of the plaintiff's residence. "So long as [that] Order .... stands", said Sullivan, P., "we are of opinion that we cannot grant such an application as that before us".[72] In *Gieves* v. *O'Connor,*[73] Meredith, J. adopting a robust, purposive, intepretation of the words "in force" in Article 73 of the 1922 Constitution, held that the 1868 Act had continued "in force", in spite of the fact that the Government of Ireland Act 1920 had ceased to have any operation in Southern Ireland on 5 December 1922, the day before the Constitution "sprang into being".[74] In *Perry* v. *Stratham,*[75] the Supreme Court studiously avoided deciding which interpretation was correct.

In 1926, new Rules[76] came into effect. These did not include any equivalent of Order XXIX under the 1905 Rules. In *Evans (Seager) & Co. Ltd.* v. *Farrelly,*[77] the majority[78] of the Supreme Court held that, in view of the English intepretation of the effect of Independence on the 1868 Act, it could not be said that this omission rendered the 1926 Rules incomplete, since there was "actually a solid foundation of reason"[79] for this omission. FitzGibbon, J., dissenting, stressed the fact that Irish courts were no longer bound to have regard to English decisions in framing their own procedure; it seemed to him that the Court was being asked to change its practice, "not because that practice is in any way inconsistent with our Act or rules, but because an English Court has, upon its own construction of our law, altered its practice with reference to ordering security for costs from Irish plaintiffs in English courts".[80]

[66] There had been much uncertainty on this question in the nineteenth century: see *Sayer* v. *Sheehan,* 26 L.R. Ir. 417 (Q.B. Div., Johnson, J., 1890). *Yorke* v. *M'Laughlin,* Ir. R. 8 C.L. 547 (Q.B., 1874), *White* v. *Carroll,* Ir. R. 8 C.L. 296 (Q.B., 1874), *Keegan* v. *Keegan,* 7 L.R. Ir. 101 (Prob., Warren, J., 1881), *Clarke* v. *Croker,* I.R. 8 C.L. 318 (Com. Pleas, 1874), *Corner* v. *Irwin,* I.R. 8 C.L. 504 (Exch., 1874). Cf. *Burke* v. *Irwin,* 41 I.L.T.R. 73 (C.A., 1907).
[67] *Wakely* v. *Triumph Cycle Co.,* [1924] 1 K.B. 214, *Banfield* v. *Chester,* 94 L.J. (K.B.) 805 (C.A., 1925).
[68] *Robinson* v. *M'Entee,* 73 I.L.T.R. 53 (N.I. (K.B. Div., Andrews L.C. J., 1939), *Callan* v. *M'Kenna,* [1929] N.I. 1 (K.B. Div., Moore, L.C.J., 1928).
[69] 58 I.L.T.R. 93 (High Ct., K.B. Div., Pim, J., 1923).
[70] *Supra.*
[71] 58 I.L.T.R. 93 (High Ct., 1924).
[72] *Id.,* at 94.
[73] [1924] 2 I.R. 182 (I.F.S., Meredith, J.).
[74] *Id.,* at 184. Cf. *id.,* at 185:
"Article 73 contemplated a subsequent Adaptation of Enactments Act, and both that Article and the Adaptation of Enactments Act [1922] would be stultified if existing enactments did not remain in force, pending the coming into operation of the Adaptation of Enactments Act.
[75] [1928] I.R. 580, at 582 (Sup. Ct., *per* FitzGibbon, J., for the Court).
[76] Rules of the High Court and Supreme Court 1926.
[77] [1928] I.R. 584 (Sup. Ct., rev'g High Ct., O'Byrne, J.).
[78] Kennedy, C.J. and Murnaghan, J.; FitzGibbon, J. dissenting.
[79] [1928] I.R., at 590 (*per* Kennedy, C.J.).
[80] *Id.,* at 592.

Before the issue could ultimately be resolved by the Supreme Court, the 1868 Act was repealed in 1936.[81]

The court's discretion

The court has a broad discretion when deciding whether or not to order security for costs. This has been stressed in several cases. In *Collins* v. *Doyle*,[82] Finlay, P. (as he then was) observed that, although *prima facie* a defendant establishing a *prima facie* defence to the plaintiff's claim is entitled to an order for security for costs, this "is not an absolute right and the court must exercise a discretion based on the facts of each individual case".

The defendant's affidavit

We must now consider the requirements in relation to the defendant's affidavit. Rule 3 of Order 29 of the Rules of the Superior Courts 1986 provides that:

"[n]o defendant shall be entitled to an order for security for costs by reason of any plaintiff being resident out of the jurisdiction of the Court, unless upon a satisfactory affidavit[83] that such defendant has a defence upon the merits."

If considered in isolation, this rule is ambiguous. It could mean that a defendant shall be entitled to security for costs from a plaintiff resident abroad provided the defendant produces a satisfactory affidavit to establish a defence on the merits. It could, on the other hand, mean that a defendant shall *not* be entitled to security without such affidavit but that the question whether he is in fact entitled must depend on a range of circumstances not addressed by this rule.

In *Cohane* v. *Cohane*,[84] 1968, the Supreme Court favoured the latter interpretation. In this case the trial judge had concluded that because the defendant had produced a satisfactory affidavit, he had no discretion and was required to order security for costs. The Supreme Court reversed. Budd, J.[85] quoted Rule 3 and commented:

"What the Rule says is that an order for security shall not be made in the case of a plaintiff resident out of the jurisdiction unless the defendant files a satisfactory affidavit of merits; it does not say that, if a satisfactory affidavit of merits is filed, security must be given in the case of a plaintiff outside the jurisdiction."[86]

Budd, J. took the view, in the light of precedent, that:

"the court has the right and duty to examine all the circumstances of the case in exercising its discretion even though a defendant *prima facie* is entitled to security where the plaintiff resides outside the jurisdiction and the defendant has filed an affidavit showing that there is a reasonable prospect of a defence being established."[87]

---

[81] Courts of Justice Act 1936, section 3 and First Schedule.

[82] [1982] I.L.R.M. 495, at 496 (High Ct., Finlay P.). Cf. *McNeary* v. *Maguire*, [1923] 2 I.R. 43, at 44 (K.B. Div. (Prob), *per* Dodd, J.). See also *Cohane* v. *Cohane*, [1968] I.R. 176 (Sup. Ct.), *Banco Ambrosiano S.P.A. (in compulsory voluntary liquidation)* v. *Ansbacher & Co. Ltd.*, High Ct., Murphy, J., 19 July 1985 (1984-585P).

[83] Cf. *Hogan* v. *Hogan*, [1924] 2 I.R. 12 (K.B. Div. (I.F.S.), Pim, J., 1923), *Keegan* v. *Keegan*, 7 L.R. Ir. 101 (Prob. Warren, J., 1881), *Tinneny* v. *O'Keefe*, 85 Ir. L.T. & Sol. J. 307 (Circuit Ct., Judge Sheehy, 1951). See further Anon., *Some Recent Irish Decisions on Security for Costs-Part II*, 88 Ir. L.T. & Sol. J. 145, at 145 (1954).

[84] [1968] I.R. 176 (Sup. Ct.).

[85] With whom Ó Dálaigh, C.J., Walsh and FitzGerald, JJ. concurred.

[86] [1968] I.R., at 181.

[87] *Id.*, at 182. See also *Collins* v. *Doyle*, [1982] I.L.R.M. 495, at 496 (High Ct., Finlay, P.), *Bernie* v. *Bernie*, [1959] Ir. Jur. Rep. 78, at 80 (High Ct., Murnaghan, J., 1958), *Banco Ambrosiano S.P.A. (in compulsory voluntary liquidation)* v. *Ansbacher & Co. Ltd.*, High Ct., 19 July 1985, Murphy, J. (1984-585P).

Defendant himself must usually make affidavit

As a general rule the defendant himself must make the affidavit. In *Willans* v. *Patterson*,[88] Richard, B. held that the defendant, rather than his attorney, should make the affidavit, except "under peculiar circumstances".[89] And in *Gardiner* v. *Harris*,[90] in 1881, where the affidavit was made by the defendant's solicitor it was held that "[p]*rima facie,* the affidavit should be made by the party".[91]

In *Banco Ambrosiano S.P.A. (in compulsory voluntary liquidation)* v. *Ansbacher & Co. Ltd.*,[92] in 1985, where again the affidavit had been made by the defendant's solicitor, Murphy, J. referred to *Gardiner* v. *Harris* and said:

> "It is well settled law in this jurisdiction that *prima facie* an affidavit [supporting a motion for security for costs] should be sworn by the defendant himself .... The failure to have the affidavit sworn by the defendant himself would have been sufficient grounds for refusing the order, although perhaps in other circumstances it might have been appropriate to stand over the matter to afford the defendant an opportunity of correcting the defect."[93]

Since, however, the affidavit's shortcomings were "of a more fundamental nature"[94] this possibility did not arise.

The affidavit must be a satisfactory one

As we have seen, Rule 3 of Order 29 of the Rules of the Superior Courts 1986 requires the defendant to present "a satisfactory" affidavit that he or she has a defence on the merits. What does "satisfactory" mean here? The courts have frequently stressed that the notion should be interpreted objectively. In *Walter* v. *Atkinson*,[95] Fitzgibbon, L.J. said:

> "I agree with [counsel for the defendant] that when a party comes in to get security he is not bound to prove his defence; but still, 'a satisfactory affidavit' must mean an affidavit that satisfies the Court of something. It appears to me that when a defendant applies for security for costs, he must not merely swear that he has a defence on the merits .... but that he must give some evidence to satisfy the Court that there is a reasonable prospect of his establishing some more or less specific or ascertainable defence."

In *Power* v. *Irish Civil Service (Permanent) Building Society*,[96] FitzGerald, J.

---

[88] 8 Ir. C.L.R. *xxix* (Consol. Cham., Richards, B., 1858).

[89] *Id.*, at *xxix* (adopting argument of counsel for plaintiff).

[90] 8 L.R. Ir. 352 (C.P. Div., 1881).

[91] 8 L.R. Ir., at 353 (*per* Morris, C.J.). See however, *Perpetual Trustee Co. Ltd.* v. *Bolger,* 67 I.L.T.R. 259 (High Ct., O'Byrne, J., 1933), where the affidavit was sworn by the defendant's solicitors without objection; and cf. *Clarke* v. *Dickson,* 8 I.L.R. 410 (Com. Pleas, 1846), where Doherty, C.J. denied that "as a general rule" the fact that the affidavit was sworn by the defendant's attorney would afford a ground for objection. He considered that the authorities cited, *Jacobson* v. *Carr,* 1 Cr. & D. 107 (Q.B., 1837) and *Hennahy* v. *Hutchins,* (cited in *Stewart's Law Forms,* 344), "rather show that no such rule exists".

[92] High Ct., 19 July 1985 (1984-585P).

[93] Page 3 of the judgment.

[94] *Id.*

[95] [1895] 1 I.R. 246, at 249 (C.A., 1894). See also *id.* (*per* Walker, C.), and *id.*, at 250 (*per* Barry, L.J.), and cf. *Dennis* v. *Leinster Paper Co.,* [1901] 2 I.R. 337 (C.A.), *Ashworth* v. *White,* I.R. 5 C.L. 520 (Q.B., 1871), *Gardiner* v. *Harris,* 8 L.R. Ir. 352 (C.P. Div., 1881), *Caldwell* v. *Kilworth,* 9 I.C.L.R. App. *vii* (Q.B., Hayes, J., 1959), *Perpetual Trustee Co. Ltd.* v. *Bolger,* 67 I.L.T.R. 259 (High Ct., O'Byrne, J., 1933), *Birch* v. *Purtill,* [1936] I.R. 122 (High Ct., O'Byrne, J.), *Seth* v. *Menzies,* [1939] I.R. 530 (High Ct., Maguire, P.).

[96] [1968] I.R. 158, at 164-165 (Sup. Ct). See also *id.*, at 163 (*per* Walsh, J.) and at 159-161 (*per* Ó Dálaigh, C.J. dissenting). In this case, the majority upheld a bald assertion by the defendants that they had a defence on the merits because the plaintiff's failure to furnish any details of alleged wrongdoing left them with no other option.

was of the opinion that the assessment of whether an affidavit is satisfactory or not:

> "must be made with due regard to the nature of the action, the facts pleaded in the
> statement of claim and the cause of action, or causes of action, therein pleaded. The
> purpose of the proviso to the Rule is to ensure that a defendant who has no defence,
> or who is not prepared to swear on oath that he has a defence, shall not be permitted
> to restrain a plaintiff from proceeding with his claim unfettered by delay or the lodgment
> of security. Before ordering security to be given, the court has to be satisfied that the
> defendant has a statable defence to the action and that consequently there is an issue
> to be tried."

In *Banco Ambrosiano S.P.A. (in compulsory voluntary liquidation)* v. *Ansbacher
& Co. Ltd.*,[97] in 1985, the plaintiffs alleged that money in a bank account in Nassau
had been unlawfully transferred from it and that, through a series of further unlawful
dealings, part of these moneys, amounting to around thirty million dollars, had been
lodged with the first named defendants. Another defendant sought security for costs
against the plaintiff.

Murphy, J. declined to grant security, since the affidavit did not offer sufficient
evidence to satisfy the Court that that defendant had a reasonable prospect of
establishing a defence: Murphy, J. commented: "Not only may one describe the
affidavit as containing hearsay evidence but it is to some extent hearsay upon
hearsay."[98] Moreover, the affidavit did not challenge or deal with the allegation
that the moneys had originated from the account in Nassau or that they had been
dealt within the manner alleged by the plaintiff. From the affidavit it would be
impossible to know whether the defendant seeking security for costs was going to
make the case that the moneys in the account with the first named defendant had
the origin claimed by the plaintiff or had a totally different origin, or whether it
was his contention that the intervening transactions affected the title of the plaintiffs
to those moneys.[99]

In these circumstances it seemed to Murphy, J. that the affidavit offered little
evidence to satisfy him that there was a defence or that the defendant had a reasonable
prospect of establishing a defence.[100]

Murphy, J. emphasised that he was in no way casting doubt on the fact that the
defendant seeking security for costs might have, and had indeed pleaded, a fully
and comprehensive defence. He added:

> "Defendants are under no obligation to put their defence on affidavit. It is only for
> the purpose of obtaining an order for security for costs that a defendant must put in
> a satisfactory affidavit showing the defence he proposes to make."[101]

Level at which security for costs should be set

Although there has been some judicial support[102] for the view that security for
costs should be set at a level that is likely to meet the costs to which the defendant
will be put in defending the action, the better view seems to be that all must depend
on the circumstances of the case. In the Supreme Court case of *Thalle* v. *Soares*[103]

---

[97] High Ct., 19 July 1985 (1984-585P).
[98] Page 4 of the judgment.
[99] *Id.*
[100] Cf. *Power* v. *Irish Civil Service Building Society* [1968] I.R. 158, at 159-160 (Sup. Ct. *per* Ó Dálaigh,
C.J.). As has been mentioned, Ó Dálaigh, C.J. was dissenting but, in Murphy, J.'s view, there was
"no reason to doubt that his comments in relation to this aspect of the matter represented the views
of the entire Court": p. 3 of the judgment.
[101] Page 4 of the judgment.
[102] Cf. e.g. *Gibson* v. *Goleman*, [1950] I.R. 50, at 55 (High Ct., Dixon, J.).
[103] [1957] I.R. 182, at 193 (Sup. Ct., 1954).

Kingsmill Moore, J., speaking for the Court, pointed out that those who drafted the rule in respect of security for costs had carefully avoided giving any indication as to a measure by which the amount of security was to be gauged. It seemed to him that they and their successors had:

> "left everything at large, realising that the considerations which arise when the amount of security has to be fixed are so varied and so numerous as to render dangerous any striving after precise direction. Security for costs must be so fixed as to advance the ends of justice and not to hinder them. If the amount is too small a plaintiff with a speculative or even dishonest case may be able to force a defendant into an unfavourable settlement by the threat of expensive litigation whose costs may be irrecoverable: if too large a defendant may be able to defeat an honest and substantial claim because the plaintiff cannot find the necessary security. Somewhere between Scylla and Charybdis a way has to be found but there can be no Admiralty chart, no succinct sailing directions."

Kingsmill Moore, J. could find only one case[104] where security had been ordered for the full amount of estimated costs. His own experience of the practice which had prevailed in Ireland "from 1919 until recent years"[105] was that it was customary to require as security an amount not more than about a third of the costs likely to be incurred by the defendant. The Court must be careful, he said, "not to fix a sum which will shut out the plaintiff from such rights as he may have".[106]

The poverty of a plaintiff as a special circumstance

In a number of cases, the plaintiff's poverty has been invoked by one or other party as a factor to influence the court in coming to its conclusion as to whether to order security for costs. The present position was succinctly stated by Finlay, P. (as he then was), in *Collins* v. *Doyle*[107]

> "Poverty on the part of the plaintiff making it impossible for him to comply with an order for security for costs is not, even when *prima facie* established, of itself, automatically a reason for refusing the order."

In *Flynn* v. *Eivers*,[108] Casey, J. declined to order security for costs where the plaintiff contended that he was so poor that an order against him would deprive him of the chance of continuing with proceedings. The plaintiff was a labourer from County Longford who, for the previous six years, had been working in Nottingham, contributing the greater part of his earnings in supporting his wife and family.[109] Casey, J. accepted[110] that the general question of whether to grant security for costs was a matter in which he had a discretion. He refused to grant security, being "satisfied that, having regard to the financial circumstances of the plaintiff, to make

---

[104] *Massey* v. *Allen*, 12 Ch. D. 807 (1879). See V. T. H. D[elany], 24 Ir. Jur. 28 (1958).

[105] [1957] I.R. at 194.

[106] *Id.*

[107] [1982] I.L.R.M. 495, at 496 (High Ct., Finlay, P.). See also *Browne* v. *Redmond*, II Ir. C.L.R. xxvi (Q.B., 1861), *Kennedy* v. *Keane*, [1901] 2 I.R. 640 (Q.B. Div., Kenny, J., 1900), *Graham* v. *Wray*, 35 I.L.T.R. 237 (C.A., 1901) *Jones* v. *Evans*, 35 I.L.T.R. 237n (C.A., 1901), *Heaney* v. *Malocca*, [1958] I.R. 111 (Sup. Ct., 1957, rev'g High Ct., Murnaghan, J., 1957), *Cohane* v. *Cohane*, [1968] I.R. 176 (Sup. Ct.), *Peppard & Co. Ltd.* v. *Bogoff*, [1962] I.R. 180 (Sup. Ct., 1957, rev'g High Ct., Dixon, J., 1957), *Yorke* v. *M'Loughlin*, I.R. 8 C.L. 547 (Q.B., 1874), *Watson* v. *Porter*, 41 I.L.T.R. 17 (C.A., 1906).

[108] 86 I.L.T.R. 85 (reported *sub nom. Flynn* v. *Rivers*).

[109] The defendant had alleged in his affidavit that the plaintiff had placed his family in industrial schools. The report is not clear as to the actual whereabouts of the wife.

[110] 86 I.L.T.R., at 85.

an order for security for costs would be tantamount to a judicial determination of the action".[111]

This approach was roundly criticised by the Supreme Court in *Heaney* v. *Malocca*.[112] In *Heaney* v. *Malocca*, the plaintiff, a resident of Newry, was injured when she fell down stairs in the defendant's restaurant in Dundalk. Her action for negligence based on the allegedly dangerous state of non-repair of the stairs was met by a motion by the defendant for security of costs. An affidavit supporting the motion stated that, from an engineer's report furnished in respect of the stairs, it was believed that the defendant had a good defence on the merits.

In her replying affidavit, the plaintiff stated that she was a widow with six children, that her sole income was ten pounds per week, and that she used almost all of this in feeding and clothing the children and in paying the rent. On this account, she stated, she was unable to furnish any security for costs, and she asked the Court to exercise its discretion in her favour.

Murnaghan, J. held in favour of the plaintiff, following Casey, J.'s judgment in *Flynn* v. *Eivers;*[113] but the Supreme Court reversed. Maguire, C.J. said:

"In *Flynn* v. *Eivers,* Mr. Justice Casey did not consider any circumstances other than the poverty of the plaintiff and refused to make the order on the ground that to do so would be tantamount to a judicial determination of the action. In my opinion this goes too far.

Mr. Justice Murnaghan is correct in saying that the position is that *prima facie* a defendant is entitled to an order for security for costs where the plaintiff resides outside the jurisdiction. In order to deprive him of this right some special circumstance must be shown, e.g. that there is no defence to the action ....[114] or where there [are] shown to be ample assets within the jurisdiction. There may be other circumstances which would justify the exercise of the Court's discretion in favour of the plaintiff. Here it is suggested by the defendant, on the report of an engineer, that she has a good defence to the action. In view of this and no other circumstances being shown to justify its being refused the application should have been granted."[115]

Maguire, J., concurring, considered that:

"mere poverty is not in itself a sufficient ground either for refusing or granting an order for security for costs.[116] The facts of each case have to be considered fully in order that the discretion of the judge may be properly exercised."[117]

Plaintiff's poverty attributable to defendant's wrong

Sometimes the plaintiff claims that his or her poverty was brought about by the defendant's wrong. This factor may be taken into consideration by the Court in deciding whether or not to order security. In *Collins* v. *Doyle,*[118] Finlay, P. said:

"Amongst the matters to which a court may have regard in exercising a discretion against ordering security is if a *prima facie* case has been made by the plaintiff to the effect that his inability to give security flows from the wrong committed by the defendant."

[111] *Id.,* at 86.
[112] [1958] I.R. 111 (Sup. Ct., 1957, rev'g High Ct., Murnaghan, J. 1957).
[113] 86 I.L.T.R. 85 (reported *sub nom. Flynn* v. *Rivers*).
[114] Citing *Perpetual Trustee Co.* v. *Bolger,* 67 I.L.T.R. 259 (1933), and *Birch* v. *Purtill,* [1936] I.R. 122.
[115] [1958] I.R., at 114-115.
[116] Citing *Graham* v. *Wray,* 35 I.L.T.R. 237 (C.A., 1901). See also *M'Caffney* v. *Brennan,* 10 I.C.L.R. 159 (Exch., Pigot, C.B. 1860) and *Browne* v. *Redmond,* 11 I.C.L.R. xxvi (Q.B., 1861).
[117] [1958] I.R., at 115. See also *Brooke* v. *Kavanagh,* 21 L.R. Ir. 474 (C.A., 1889).
[118] [1982] I.L.R.M., at 496. See also *Duffy* v. *Joyce,* 25 L.R. Ir. 42, at 44 (Porter, M.R., 1890).

Finlay, P. went on to say:

"In this application the case made by the plaintiff on his affidavit precisely is that his inability to give security for costs arises from an inability to earn caused by the defendant's wrong.

Although I accept the disapproval expressed by the Supreme Court in *Heaney* v. *Malocca* of the decision in *Flynn* v. *Rivers* holding poverty in effect to be an absolute answer to an application for security I am impressed by the apparent injustice of requiring a person who cannot provide security to do so when his inability may flow from the wrong of the defendant. In general it would appear to me that the principle underlying a defendant's right to security for costs must be that he should not suffer from an inability to recover the cost of successfully defending the claim arising from the fact that the unsuccessful plaintiff resides and has his assets outside the jurisdiction of the court. Such a principle does not seem to me to justify giving to a defendant an adventitious protection against the claim of a plaintiff whom he may have impoverished, by reason of the place of residence of that plaintiff which is on the individual facts irrelevant to the reality of recovering costs.

I am therefore satisfied I must exercise my discretion by refusing this application."[119]

Peppard & Co. Ltd. v. *Bogoff*[120] is a Supreme Court decision concerned with the question of security for costs[121] in relation to the first plaintiff, a limited company registered in Ireland, without assets and not carrying on business here. The Supreme Court, reversing Dixon, J., held that security for costs should not be ordered.

On the question of the plaintiff's poverty, the court noted that the plaintiff's argument was that the defendants had conspired to transfer the business of the plaintiff company elsewhere. Kingsmill-Moore, J. said:

"If this be the case — and on an application for security for costs a Court cannot try the merits — to order security would be to allow the defendants to defeat an action by reason of an impecuniosity which they have themselves wrongfully and deliberately produced, a result which a Court would strive to avoid."[122]

In *Cohane* v. *Cohane*,[123] the plaintiff sued her husband on foot of a separation agreement made in New York in accordance with the laws of that state. The defendant, who had obtained a Mexican divorce and had remarried, was living in Ireland. He had failed to pay certain sums of money to his wife, in breach of the agreement.

[119] *Id.*

[120] [1962] I.R. 180 (Sup. Ct., 1957, rev'g High Ct., Dixon, J., 1957).

[121] Under section 278 of the Companies (Consolidation) Act 1908. See now the Companies Act 1963, section 390. Cf. Doolan, *The Insolvent Company and Security for Costs*, 4 Ir. L.T. (n.s.) 218 (1986). It has been said that the same considerations and principles as to security for costs in this context apply to companies "are equally applicable to litigation between individuals": *Banco Ambrosiano S.P.A. (in compulsory voluntary Liquidation)* v. *Ansbacher & Co. Ltd.*, High Ct., Murphy, J., 1985, at p. 2 (1984-585). In accord are *Cohane* v. *Cohane*, [1968] I.R. 176, at 190-191 (Sup. Ct., *per* Budd, J.) and *Peppard & Co. Ltd.* v. *Bogoff*, supra. In *Gibson* v. *Coleman*, [1950] I.R. 50, at 54 (High Ct.), Dixon, J. observed that:
"[t]he basic difficulty is the same in each case namely, the unlikelihood of the defendant recovering his costs."
But see *Thalle* v. *Soares* [1957] I.R. 182, at 192 (Sup. Ct., *per* Kingsmill Moore, J. (for the Court 1954)).

[122] [1962] I.R., at 187. See also *Irish Commercial Society Ltd.* v. *Plunkett*, High Ct., Costello, J., 29 November 1985 (1984-2277P:) *S.E.E. Co. Ltd.* v. *Public Lighting Services Ltd. and Petit Jean (U.K.) Ltd.*, Sup. Ct., 12 May, 1986. *O'Toole (Jack) Ltd.* v. *Mac Eoin Kelly Associates*, (Sup. Ct., 24 July 1986, aff'g High Ct., Barr, J.,10 February 1986 (1984-6051P); Doolan, *The Insolvent Company and Security for Costs*, 4 Ir. L.T. (n.s.) 218 (1986).

[123] [1968] I.R.,at 182.

The defendant sought security for costs, and the High Court granted the order, considering itself bound to do so once the defendant had submitted a satisfactory affidavit specifying a defence on the merits. That defence was wide-ranging.[124]

On appeal, the Supreme Court held that there was a discretion to refuse to order security for costs in spite of the production of a satisfactory affidavit. The Supreme Court declined to make the order on the ground primarily that the plaintiff's poverty had been brought about by the defendant's breach of his obligations to her.

In *Scanlan* v. *Abbey Service Garage*,[125] in 1964, the Supreme Court held that where the defendant's conduct had resulted in the plaintiff's impoverishment, no order for security for costs should be made in the circumstances of the case. The brief report of the case states that it was held that "the order sought was discretionary. The matters relied upon by the defendants as constituting special circumstances arose directly as a consequence of the injuries which the [plaintiff] suffered in the collision. It would be unfair and inconsistent to allow the defendants to rely on these circumstances as constituting special circumstances."[126]

Delay and waiver

In some circumstances the defendant by his delay or inaction may be held to have disentitled himself to obtain an order for security for costs.[127] It would be unfair on a plaintiff if the defendant could hold in reserve an application for security for costs indefinitely and, having led the plaintiff to belief that it would not be used, produce this weapon at the last moment.[128] The court will have regard to all the circumstances, including the length of the delay and the extent to which either party has led the other party into holding back from pressing their claim or defence, as the case may be.

---

[124] Briefly it included the arguments that a contract for a future possible separation was contrary to public policy as tending to encourage infidelity, and that an agreement encouraging the possibility of divorce was contrary to public policy and to the provision of the Constitution, especially Article 41.

[125] 98 I.L.T. & Sol. J. 464 (Sup. Ct., 1964).

[126] *Id.*, at 465. For consideration of the position where security for costs is sought against an appellant Cf. *Midland Bank Ltd.* v. *Crossley-Cooke*, [1969] I.R. 56, at 61-62 (Sup. Ct., *per* Walsh, J.).

[127] There have been several cases in which this question has arisen: see, e.g. *Bush* v. *Curran*, 9 Ir. C.L.R. *xxx* (Q.B., 1859), *Duffy* v. *Joyce*, 25 L.R. Ir. 42 (Porter, M.R., 1890), *Heil* v. *Lazenby*, 12 L.R. Ir. 75 (Q.B. Div., 1883), *Watson* v. *Pim*, 2 Ir. Eq. Rep. 26 (O'Loghlen M.R., 1839), *Charlesworth* v. *Clayton*, 10 L.R. Ir. 357 (Ex. Div., Andrews, J. 1882), *Taylor* v. *Low*, 3 Ir. C.L. Rep. 223 (Q.B., 1854), *Tellett* v. *Lalor*, 10 L.R. Ir. 357 (Ex. Div., 1882), *Leckham* v. *Gresham*, 2 Ir. C.L.R. 139 (Exch., 1852), *Freel* v. *Trant*,11 Ir. Eq. Rep. 278 (Cusack Smith, M.R., 1847), *United General Life Assurance Co.* v. *Beale*, 8 Ir. C.L.R. *xxx* (Consol. Cham., Crampton, J., 1858), *Hogan* v. *Hogan (No. 2)*, [1924] 2 I.R. 14 (K.B. Div. (I.F.S.), Dodd, J., 1923), *Jack* v. *Noble*, 17 I.C.L.R. 381 (1867), *Beausang* v. *Condon*, 13 I.C.L.R. app. *xxxvii* (Exch., 1862), *Guido* v. *Grainger*, Ir. R. 8 C.L. 113 (Q.B., 1874), *Samuelson* v. *Andrews*, Ir. R. 3 C.L. 575 (Com. Pleas, 1868), *Lynch* v. *Clarkin*, 33 I.L.T.R.157 (C.A., 1899), *Burke* v. *Grt. Southern & Western Ry.*, 36 I.L.T.R. 51 (C.A., 1902), *Dongan & Titterington Ltd.* v. *Economical Housing Co.*, 41 I.L.T.R. 57 (C.A., 1907), *Clarke* v. *Dickson*, 8 Ir. L.R. 161 (Com. Pleas, 1846), *Watson* v. *Chadwick*, 8 Ir. L.R. 291 (Exch. of Pleas, 1845), *Clarke* v. *Riordan*, 9 I.C.L.R. App. *xxiv* (Exch., Pigot, C.B., 1859), *Stewart* v. *Ballance*, 10 I.C.L.R. App. 1 (Exch., Pigot, C.B., 1860), *Leeson* v. *Leeson*, 4 Ir. Ch. Rep. 28 (Cusack Smith, M.R., 1853), *Bentley* v. *Robinson*, 4 Ir. Ch. Rep. 37 (Cusack Smith, M.R.,1853), *Parke* v. *Parke*, 1 I.C.L.R. 632 (Monahan, C.J., 1851), *Taylor* v. *Low*, 3 I.C.L.R.223 (Lefroy, C.J., 1854), *Leckham* v. *Gresham*, 2 I.C.L.R. 139 (Pigot, C.B., 1852), *Bateman* v. *Sneyd*, 2 I.C.L.R. 376 (Monahan, C.J., 1852). *Long* v. *Tottenham*, 1 Ir. Ch. Rep. 127 (Cusack Smith, M.R., 1850), *Long* v. *Long*, 1 Ir. Ch. Rep. 618 (Cusack Smith, M.R., 1851); see also the Supreme Court case of *S.E.E. Co. Ltd.* v. *Public Lighting Services Ltd.* Sup. Ct., 12 May 1986, a decision in relation to section 390 of the Companies Act 1963 (as to which cf. *supra*, p. 667), noted by Doolan, *The Insolvent Company and Security For Costs*, 4 Ir. L.T. (N.S.) 218 (1986).

[128] Cf. *Dongan & Titterington Ltd.* v. *Economical Housing Co.*, 41 I.L.T.R. 57, at 57 (C.A., *per* FitzGibbon, L.J. 1907).

Variation of amount of security for costs

In *Levison* v. *Hodges,*[129] it was held that the Court had power, after security for costs had already been ordered, to order further security to be given, where the defendant's attorney swore that the costs out of pocket already exceeded the original security. Jackson, J. considered that:

".... we should violate the foundation on which the practice rests, if we did not hold that it was competent for us to enlarge the security, if such an enlargement should become necessary in future stages of the proceedings; for the necessary consequence of holding that no such enlargement could be made would be that the officer would, in every case, give the outside measure of security, which would, of course, be prejudicial to, and entail difficulties upon, the suitor himself, who was out of the jurisdiction."[130]

Role of appellate court

In *Dennis* v. *Leinster Paper Co.,*[131] a decision of the Court of Appeal in 1901, Lord Ashbourne, C. said:

"The Court of Appeal is very slow to review, much more to set aside, an order made by a Judge of the Court below in the exercise of his discretion unless we are satisfied that there was a miscarriage of justice or some serious misconception of law or fact."

Fitzgibbon, C.J. added that the trial judge:

"had only to determine whether the defendants' affidavit that they had a defence on the merits was 'satisfactory' and upon such a point the opinion of the primary Court ought to be almost, if not quite, conclusive."[132]

And Holmes, L.J. said:

"If there is any case in which an appellate Court ought to be cautious in dealing with an order of a Court of First Instance, it is where it directs a litigant to give security for costs. The grounds on which discretion ought to be exercised on such applications are so well understood by the Judges who are in the habit of hearing them, that it would be presumptuous to interfere with these orders unless where it is shown that there has been some error in legal principle."[333]

[129] 8 Ir. L.R. 112 (Com. Pleas, 1846).
[130] *Id.,* at 113.
[131] [1901] 2 I.R. 337, at 344 (C.A.). As to the right to appeal against an order of the Master, see *Murray* v. *Laverty & Sons,* 40 I.L.T.R. 131 (K.B. Div., 1905).
[132] [1901] 2 I.R., at 345-346.
[133] *Id.,* at 349.

INDEX

A

Act of Bankruptcy: see *Bankruptcy*
Action
 breach of promise, for, abolished, 532, 552
 classification of cause of: see
  Characterisation
 damages: see *Damages*
 evidence: see *Evidence*
 in personam, 124-160, 589-598; see also
  Judgment in Personam
 in rem, 160-162, 598-601; see also
  Actions in Rem: Jurisdiction
  Over
 jurisdiction: see *Jurisdiction*
 limitation periods, 639-641
 restitution of conjugal rights, action for,
  297-300
Actions in Rem; Jurisdiction Over
 admiralty jurisdiction, 161, 162, 174, 177
 arrest of property, 160-162
 cargo, 160-162
 generally, 160-162
 judgment *in rem* distinguished, 161
 meaning of action *in rem*, 160-161
 procedure, 162
 release of property, 162
 ship, action against, 161, 174-177
 stay of action, 162
Administration of Estates
 "ancillary" grant, 456-459
 assets, recovery of, 458
 choice of law, 458-459
 effect of Irish grant, 457-458
 executor *de son tort*, 458
 foreign administrator acting in Ireland
  without Irish grant, 459-460
 generally, 453-461
 historical background, 453-454
 Irish courts, jurisdiction of, 453-475
 lex fori governs, 458
 person to whom grant is made, 455-457
 "principal" administration, 456-457
 separate wills, 454-455
Admiralty
 arrest of property, 162
 cargo, 162
 generally, 161-162
 jurisdiction, 161-162
 procedure, 162
 release of property, 162
 salvage of cargo or freight, EEC Judgments
  Convention and ... 188

 ship, action against, 161, 162, 174-177
 sovereign immunity, 174-177
 stay of action, 162
Adoption
 choice of law, 371
 comparative aspects, 368-369
 domicile-based test for recognition, 373-374
 effects, 374-375
 eligibility under Irish law, 371
 foreign adoption, recognition of, 372-374;
  see also *Hague Convention on
  Adoptions (1964)*
 generally, 368-380
 Hague Convention on Adoptions (1964),
  376; see also *Hague Convention on
  Adoptions (1964)*
 historical aspects, 368-369
 jurisdiction, 370-371
 legitimated child, 371
 reciprocity principle, 373
 reform proposals, 375-376
 Review Committee on Adoption Services,
  proposals of, 375-376
 succession entitlements, 375
Affiliation Proceedings
 choice of law, 319
 generally, 310-320
 jurisdiction, 317-319
 Maintenance Orders Act 1974, 310-317; see
  also *Maintenance Orders Act
  1974*
 recognition of foreign orders, 319-320
Agobard, Bishop, 6
Air Carriage
 jurisdiction, 160
 marriage celebrated on aircraft, 267
 situs of civil aircraft, 398
 will made on plane, 433
Alien Enemy, 171-172; see also *Ineligible
  Parties*
Ambassador
 diplomatic immunity, 178-180
 domicile, 66
 Foreign Marriages Act 1892, functions
  under, 231
Analytical Jurisprudence, 29
Annulment: see *Hague Convention on
  Marriage (1978), Jurisdiction in
  Proceedings for Nullity of
  Marriage, Marriage Validity
  and Recognition of Foreign
  Nullity Decrees*

Appearance
default of, judgment in, 602, 609-669
foreign action, in, constitutes submission,
592-595
Appointment, Power of: see *Power of
Appointment*
Arbitration
Arbitration Act 1954, enforcement under,
618-619
Arbitration Act 1980, 618-619
common law, enforcement of, 616-618
finality and conclusiveness, 617
generally, 159, 616-622
jurisdiction, 159
proper law, 616-617
staying of Irish proceedings, 612-622
Arrest, in Admiralty, 162
Assignment on Marriage, 414-428; see also
Family Property
Assignment of Choses in Action: see *Choses
in Action, Assignment of*
Assumed Jurisdiction: see *Service out of
the Jurisdiction*
Attachment
lex situs governs, 499

B

Baldus, 6
Bankruptcy
acts of bankruptcy, 463-464
administration, 480
certificate of conformity, 480-481
discharge, 480-481
EEC Judgments Convention does not extend
to, 182, 612
foreign adjudication, effect of, in Ireland,
478-480
generally, 24, 462-481
Independence, effect of, on rules as to
vesting, 469-471
jurisdiction of the Irish courts, 463-465
mutual aid, 471-477
mutual enforcement, 477-478
Northern Ireland, 475-476
objects of bankruptcy legislation, 463
"other British courts", 476-477
vesting under order of English court, 468-471
vesting under order of Irish court, 465-468
Bartolus, 7
Beale, 14-15
Beckett, 29
Bigamy
capacity to marry, 231-232
foreign law, proof of, 115-116
Bills of Exchange, 487-493; see also
Negotiable Instruments
Bona Vacantia, 429-430
*Breach of Promise of Marriage, Action for
Abolished,* 532, 552
"British Possessions", former, 385
Burden of Proof
domicile, change of, 74-75
generally, 627-628

C

Canon Law
administration of estates, 453-454
expert evidence as to, 107
foreign law, whether, 118-120
marriage, 223-228
Capacity
contract, to: see *Contractual
Capacity*
family property, 424-426
immovables, to take and transfer, 409-411
legatee, of, 431
marry, to, 231-240, 246-247
mental: see *Mental Incompetency*
negotiable instruments, 488
testator, of, 430-431
Carriage
air, by: see *Air Carriage*
maritime torts, 581-582
sea, by, 145-147, 160
Cavers, 19-21
Characterisation
bona vacantia, 429-430
commorientes, 434, 627-628
damages, 642-646
domicile, 49, 50
evidential presumptions, 629-631
formal requirements, 631-632
generally, 27-30
immovables, interests in, 392-393
insolvency, 476
jus regale, 429-430
limitation of actions, 639-641
marriage, 28-30
property, 390-400; see also *Property,*
substance and procedure, 625-626
Charitable Trusts, 507-508, 511-512
Chattels
chattels real, 393
situs, how determined, 398
transfer of, 494-500; see also *Choses in
Possession, Transfer of*
Child: see *Minor*
Choses in Action, Assignment of
capacity, 502-503
competing assignments, 503-504
essentials, 503
formalities, 503
garnishment, 505
generally, 501-505
lex domicilii of creditor, 501
lex loci actus, 502
lex situs, 501-502
priorities, 503-504
proper law of the debt, 502
shares, 504-505
Choses in Possession, Transfer of
attachment of movables, 499
donatio mortis causa, 500
generally, 494, 500
goods *in transitu,* 499
gift, 500

Irish decisions, 496-499
lex domicilii, 494, 500
lex loci actus, 495
lex situs, 495
proper law of the transfer, 496
Classification: see *Characterisation*
Comity Doctrine, 13-14, 586
Common Law Marriage, 228-231, 246
Commorientes, 434, 628-629
Companies
  central management and control, 482-484
  creditors, equality among, 486
  dissolved company, 485
  domicile, 484
  dual residence, whether possible, 483-484
  EEC Judgments Convention and, 190
  incorporation, company domiciled in country
    of, 484
  generally, 482-486
  implicit revivification, theory of, 485
  "one man" company, 482-483
  nationality, 484
  "real centre of management" and
    nationality, 484
  residence, 482-484
  winding up, 485-486
Confiscation, 204; see also *Expropriatory
    Legislation*
Conflict of Laws
  history, 3-21
  is part of Irish law, 3-24
  objectives, 4
Conjugal Rights: see *Restitution of
    Conjugal Rights*
Construction: see *Interpretation*
Consul, 180-181, 231, 636
*Consular Convention Between
    Ireland and the United States
    of America (1950)*, 636
Contract
  absence of choice of proper law by parties,
    526-530
  acceptance, 533-535; see also *Offer and
    Acceptance*
  "bona fide" choice, meaning of, 521-522
  breach of promise, actions for, prohibited,
    regardless of proper law, 532
  capacity, 539-541; see also
    Contractual Capacity
  cause, civil law concept of, 537
  choice of governing law by parties, 521-526
  consent, lack of, 535-537
  consideration, 537, 553
  contract made in one country to be
    performed in another, 530-531
  contractual documents, form of, raising
    inference as to choice of proper law, 525
  currency, 526, 542-543
  discharge, 543-544
  duress, 535-537
  essential validity, 544-545
  exchange control, 208, 550-551
  formal validity, 537-539; see also *Formal
    Validity of Contract*
  fraud, 535-537

frustration, 543
generally, 517-566
hire purchase agreement, 533
illegality, 545-552; see also *Illegality
    of Contract*
incorporation contrasted, 523-524
inferred choice of proper law, 524-526
international sale of goods, contract for,
    532-533
interpretation, 541-543
lex fori sometimes applied, 531-532
lex loci solutionis and performance,
    543-544
misrepresentation, 535-537
mistake, 535-537
non-disclosure, 535-537
  non est factum, 535-537
novation, 543
objective approach, 522-523, 526-527
offer, 533-535; see also *Offer and
    Acceptance*
performance, 543-544
proper law, doctrine of, 518-533: see
    Proper Law of Contract
"putative proper law", 534-535
residence of parties, 525, 530
Rome Convention, 517, 518, 552-566: see
    *EEC Convention of the Law
    Applicable to Contractual
    Obligations*
sale of goods, 532-533
statutory exceptions to application of proper
    law, 525, 532-533
subject matter of contract, nature and
    location of, 525, 529-530
subjective approach, 522-523, 526-527
supply of service, contract for, 533
undue inference, 535-537
Contractual Capacity
  age of majority, 540
  drunkenness, 540
  generally, 539-541
  insanity, 540
  lex loci contractus, 540-541
  lex domicilii, 539-540
  proper law, 541
  residence of defendant, 541
Contributory Negligence, 582, 627
Conventions
  Consular Convention between Ireland and the
    United States of America (1950), 636
  Council of Europe Convention on Child
    Custody, 345-347
  EEC Convention on the Law Applicable to
    Contractual Obligations: see *EEC
    Convention on the Law
    Applicable to Contractual
    Obligations*
  EEC Judgments Convention: see
    Judgments Convention
  Geneva Convention on Arbitral Awards
    619-620
  Hague Convention on Adoptions: see
    *Hague Convention on
    Adoptions (1964)*

Hague Convention on the Celebration of Marriages (1902), 226

Hague Convention on the Form of Wills (1961), 433-434

Hague Convention on International Child Abduction, 339-343

Hague Convention on Marriage (1978), 266-268

Hague Convention on Recognition of Divorces and Legal Separations (1970), 292-293

Hague Convention on the Taking of Evidence Abroad in Civil or Commercial Matters (1968), 636-637

New York Convention on the Recognition and Enforcement of Foreign Arbitral Awards (1958), 619-620

Vienna Convention on Consular Relations (1963), 180

Vienna Convention on Diplomatic Relations (1963), 180

Washington Convention on the Settlement of Investment Disputes between States and Nationals of other States (1965), 619-620

Council of Europe
privileges and immunities of, 180

Council of Europe Convention on Child Custody, 343-345

Curator, Foreign, 386-387

Currency
foreign, judgment in, 649-651
interpretation of contract, 526, 542-543

Currie, 16-19, 21

Customs Cooperation Council
privileges and immunities of, 181

D

Damages
expectation of life, damages for loss of, 645
fatal accidents, 644
generally, 637-638, 642-646
illegal business, 645-646
measure, 642-646
mental distress, 644
recent limitations on jury awards, 644
remoteness, 642-646
taxation, whether to be taken into account in assessing damages, 645
unawareness of injury, 644

D'Argentré, 7-8

Declarations
by persons ignorant of exact meaning of domicile, 69-70
context in which made, 67-68
conduct must be consistent with, 68-69
death, as to apprehended place of, 72
domicile, as to, 66-72
earlier declarations, evidence of, 67
failure to make, 72
"home", references to, 71-72
legal advice, made on, 70-71

Death
administration of estates, 453-461; see also

Administration of Estates
commorientes, 434, 628-629
fatal accidents litigation, 639-640, 644
presumption as to, 629
succession on, 27-28, 429-452; see also *Succession*

Debt
assignment of, 501-505
bankruptcy, 462-481; see also *Bankruptcy*
currency of; see *Currency*
garnishment, 505
novation, 544
situs of, 398-399

Declaration of Legitimacy
affidavit, procedural requirements as to, 356
applicants, permitted, 356
Attorney-General must be respondent, 356
collusion, 356
effect of declaration, 356
fraud, 356
generally, 355-357
jurisdictional aspects, 356-357
petition, procedural requirements as to, 356
proleptic domicile, 356-357
illegitimacy, order declaring, may not be made, 357

Declaration as to Legitimation
applicants, permitted, 366-367
Attorney-General must be respondent, 367
collusion, 367
effect of declaration, 367
fraud, 367
generally, 366-367
jurisdictional aspects, 367
procedural aspects, 367

Deportation, Domicile of Person Subject to, 54-55

• *Diplomatic Immunity*
commencement of immunity, 180
consular immunity, 180-181
Council of Europe, privileges and immunities of, 180
Customs Cooperation Council, privileges and immunities of, 181
"diplomatic agent" defined, 178
European Communities, privileges and immunities of, 181
evidence, diplomatic agent not obliged to give, 179
execution against diplomatic agent not generally permitted, 178-179
failure to claim privilege, 181
family members of diplomatic agent, 179
generally, 178-181
head of mission, 178
household of diplomatic agent, 179
official duties, actions performed within, 179
Organisation for Economic Cooperation and Development, privileges and immunities of, 180-181
premises of mission, 178
private residence of diplomatic agent, 178
professional or commercial activity, 179

real action relating to private immovable
property, 178
succession, action relating to, 179
termination of immunity, 180
United Nations, privileges and immunities of,
180
waiver of consular immunity, 180
waiver of diplomatic immunity, 179-180
Divorce
ancillary orders, 289-292
Channel Islands, 283
Constitution, effect of, 271-280
domicile and, 60, 270-278, 281-284
domicile of dependency of married women,
278
duress, 286-287
England and Wales, 283
estoppel by conduct, 287-289
estoppel by record, 287-288
fraud, 284
generally, 30, 269-293
grounds other than domicile, 278-280
Hague Convention on Recognition of
Divorces and Legal Separations (1970),
292-293
Isle of Man, 283
maintenance, 289-292
natural or constitutional justice, failure to
comply with, 285-286
non-recognition, grounds for, 284-287
Northern Ireland, 278, 283
position before 1937, 269-270
"real and substantial connection" test,
278-280
recognition of foreign divorce, 269-293
reform proposals, 293
Scotland, 283
statutory changes, 281-284
Divorce A Mensa Et Thoro
choice of law, 296
domicile, 295
generally, 51, 294-297
historical background, 294
jurisdiction, 294-296
matrimonial home of spouses, 295
recognition of foreign decrees, 296-297
residence, 294-296
Domicile
abandonment of domicile of choice: see
Domicile of Choice
abandonment of domicile of origin: see
Domicile of Origin
area of, 47-49
child: see *Domicile of Child*
choice, domicile of: see *Domicile of
Choice*
depencency, domicile of: see *Domicile of
Dependency*
determined according to Irish law, 50
divorce and, 269-284
federation, 47, 49-50
foundling, 83-83
generally, 45-96
Ireland, Northern, domicile in, 47-49
Ireland, Republic of, domicile in, 47-49

legality of transaction contingent on domicile
in one of two countries, 51-53
lex domicilii: see *Lex Domicilii*
lex fori and, 49, 50
married women: see *Domicile of
Married Women*
meaning of, 45-46
mentall ill person: see *Domicile of
Mentally Ill Persons*
minor: see *Domicile of Minors*
origin, domicile of: see *Domicile of
Origin*
residence: see *Residence, Ordinary
Residence*
single conception theory, 50-51
territorial boundaries, change in, 47-49
Domicile of Choice
abandonment of, 72-74
acquisition of, 53-60
armed forces, members of, 65
business, relevance of place of, 58-60
compulsion, effect on, 61-66
declarations: see *Declarations*
diplomats, 66
direct evidence as to intention, 66-72
intention, 55-60, 66-72
meaning of, 46
medical necessity, 61-64
prisoners, 64-65
residence, 53-54
soldier, 65
weight of intention required, 55-58
Domicile of Dependency
married women, former domicile of
dependency of: see *Domicile of
Married Women*
meaning of, 46
mentally ill persons, domicile of: see
*Domicile of Mentally Ill
Persons*
minors, domicile of: see *Domicile of
Minors*
Domicile of Married Women
abolition of domicile of dependency, 78-79
dependency, former domicile of, 46, 77-82
divorce and, 278, 281-283
generally, 46, 77-82
judicial analysis of, 79-82
rationale for former domicile of dependency,
77-78
Domicile of Mentally Ill Persons
adults, 93-94
children, 93-95
father's domicile, effect of, 93-94
generally, 93-96
history of, 93-95
reform proposals, 95-96
Domicile of Minors
adopted child, of, 84-85
change of, 85-89
death of both parents, 89-90
death of father, after, 83, 89-90
death of mother, after, 90
father's domicile, effect of, 83, 85-89
foundling, 83-84

generally, 46, 82
"home", meaning of, 87-89
illegitimate child, of, 83, 85, 89
joint custody, 89
legitimate child, of, 83, 85
legitimated child, of, 83
"living apart", meaning of, 87-88
majority, domicile on attaining, 91
marriage, effect of, 90
mentally disabled minors, 93-96
mother's domicile, effect of, 83, 85-89
parents living apart, 85-89
policy considerations, 92
statutory changes, 82-83, 84, 87-91
termination of domicile of dependency,
    90-91
widowed mother, legitimate child of, 85,
    89
Domicile of Origin
abandonment of, 74-75
generally, 74-77
meaning of, 46
reform, proposals for, 75-77
revival of, 73, 76-77
Donatio Mortis Causa, 500
Donee of Power, 449-452
Donor of Power, 449-452
Dowry
Breach of promise, action for, abolished,
    532, 542
characterisation, 638-639
lex fori and, 638-639
marriage settlements, 414-428
Dumoulin, 7-8
Duress
contract and, 535, 537
divorce obtained under, 286-287
domicile of prisoner, 64-65
marriage, validity of, and, 240-242,
    247-248
ordinary residence under, 101-103
residence under, 54-55
Dutch School, 8-9

E

Election, Doctrine of, 439
Embassy: see *Ambassador, Diplomatic
    Immunity*
Enemy: see *Alien Enemy, Ineligible Parties*
Endorsement of Negotiable Instrument, 489;
    see also *Negotiable Instrument*
Enforcement of Judgment
generally, 589-591; see also *Judgment in
    Personam, Judgment in Rem*
EEC Judgments Convention, under, 614-615;
    see also *Judgments Convention*
Equity
immovables, jurisdiction over, and, 403-407
Estoppel
divorce, recognition of, and, 289
judgment, recognition of, and, 606
European Communities
generally, 22
Judgments Convention, 182-192; see also

Judgments Convention
privileges and immunities of, 182
Rome Convention, 517-518, 552-566; see
    also *EEC Convention on the Law
    Applicable to Contractual
    Obligations*
*EEC Convention on the Law Applicable to
    Contractual Obligations*
absence of choice, applicable law in,
    557-559
advertising, 562-563
agent's power to bind principal, 555
applicable law, scope of, 565
arbitration agreements, 554-555
bills of exchange, 554
breach, consequences of, 565
carriage of goods, 559, 565
carriage of passengers, 559
characteristic performance, 558-559
cheques, 554
choice of court, agreements on, 554-555
co-debtors, 566
companies, questions governing, 555
consideration, 553
consumer contracts, 560-561, 562-563
creditor, satisfaction of, 566
cross-border shopping expedition, 563
damages, assessment of, 565
employment contract, 564
evidence and procedure, 556
exclusions, 553-555
extinguishing obligations, 565
formal validity, 560
generally, 517-518, 552-566
immovable property, presumption as to
    contract in respect of, 559
insurance contracts covering risks situated
    in territories of Member States, 556
interpretation, 565
legal capacity, question involving, 554
limitation of actions, 565
maintenance obligations, 554
mandatory rules, 561-563
material validity, 560
negotiable instruments, 554
nullity of contract, consequences of, 565
parties' choice, applicable law based on,
    556
performance, 565
prescription, 565
presumptions as to applicable law, 558
promissory notes, 554
public policy, 564-565
purpose, 553
quasi-contractual obligation, 553
rights and duties arising out of family
    relationship, parentage, marriage or
    affinity, 554
rights in property arising out of
    matrimonial relationship, 554
scope, 553-556
status, question involving, 554
subrogation, 556
successions, contractual obligations
    relating to, 554

trustees, sellors and beneficiaries,
relationship between, 555
trusts, constitutions of, 555
unincorporated bodies, questions
governing, 555
voluntary assignments, 566
wills, contractual obligations relating to,
554
EEC Judgments Convention: see
Judgments Convention
Evidence
abroad, taking evidence, in civil and
commercial matters, 632-637: see also
Taking Evidence Abroad
ademption, presumption of, 629-630
admissibility, 626
advancement, presumption of, 629-630
burden of proof, 627-629
compellability of witness, 632
competence of witness, 632
contradiction of terms of document,
626-627
constitutional dimension, 630-631
death, presumption of, 629-630
generally, 626-637
interpretation of document, 626-627
irrebuttable presumption of law, 626
legitimacy, presumption of, 629-631
marriage, presumption of, 629-631
presumption, 628-631
privilege, entitlement of witness to claim,
632
rebuttable presumption, 629-631
res ipsa loquitur, 627-628
resulting trust, 629-630
Statute of Frauds, 631-632
witnesses, 632
written evidence, requirement of, 631-323
Exchange Control, 208, 550-551
Exclusion of a Foreign Law
anti-trust legislation, 207
expropriatory legislation, 204-207; see
also *Exproprietary
Legislation*
foreign penal laws, 192-197; see also
Penal Laws
foreign revenue laws, 198-204; see also
Revue Laws
generally, 192-208
import and export regulations, 207
"penal" discriminatory rules, 197
price control regulations, 207
public laws, 207
public policy, foreign laws repugnant to
Irish, 207-208; see also *Public
Policy*
Executor: see *Administration of Estates*
Expectation of Life, Damages for Loss of, 645
Expropriatory Legislation
confiscation of property, 204
constitutional aspects, 206-207
de facto government, 207
de jure government, 207
Foreign Affairs, Minister for, role of in

relation to recognition of foreign
government, 207
generally, 204-207
nationalisation of property, 204
nationals of foreign state, 204
property situated outside territory of
expropriating state, 204-206
recognition of foreign government, 207
requisition of property, 204
revenue claims, relationship with, 205-206
Extinction of Cause of Action, 639-641
Extra-Judicial Divorce, 274

F

Family Property
ante-nuptial contract, where made,
420-422
ante-nuptial contract, where none, 416-421
capacity, 424-426
domicile, relevance of, 416-418, 424-426
deferred community of property, 424
essential validity, 426
formal validity, 426-427
generally, 414-428
immovables, 422
interpretation, 423, 427
Married Women's Status Act 1957,
section 12, proceedings under, 427-428
mutability, 418-420
policy considerations, 415-416
proper law, 423-424
separation of property, 414-416, 422
validity, 423
Fatal Accidents Litigation, 644
Federation, Domicile and, 47, 49-50
Feudalism, 6
Fiduciary Relationship
jurisdiction as to immovables and,
403-407
Foreign Affiliation Order, Recognition of,
319-320
Foreign Adoption, Recognition of, 372-374;
see also *Hague Convention on
Adoptions (1964)*
Foreign Arbitrations
Arbitration Act 1954, enforcement under,
618-619
Arbitration Act 1980, enforcement under,
619-621
common law, enforcement at, 616-618
finality and conclusiveness of award, 617
fraud, 617
generally, 616-622
Geneva Convention on the Execution of
Foreign Arbitral Awards, 619-620
Geneva Protocol on Arbitration Clauses
(1923), 619-620
jurisdiction of arbitrator, lack of, 617
New York Convention (1958), 619-620
public policy, 617
stay of Irish proceedings, 621-622
Washington Convention (1965), 619, 622
Foreign Bill of Exchange, 488, 490

Foreign Curator, 386-387
Foreign Currency, Judgment in, 649-651
Foreign Judgment
    Administration of Justice Act 1920 not
        applicable, 610
    appearance, foreign judgment in default
        of, 602
    assignment, relationship with, 600
    cargo, judgment as to, 601
    characterisation of judgment, 599
    conditions for recognition and
        enforcement, 588-601
    constitutional judgment, foreign judgment
        contrary to, 608-609
    defences against recognition and
        enforcement, 606-609
    definite sum, foreign judgment must be
        for, 602-603
    direct enforcement of foreign judgments
        by statute, 610-611
    EEC Convention on Jurisdiction and the
        Enforcement of Judgments in Civil and
        Commercial Matters, 612-616; see also
        Judgments Convention
    enforcement distinguished from
        recognition, 585
    estoppel *per rem judicatam,* 606
European Community judgment, 611
    finality of foreign judgment, 601-602
    foreign court must have had
        ''jurisdiction'' under Irish conflicts
        rules, 588-589
    fraud vitiating foreign judgment, 606-608
    generally, 585-615
    Judgments Extension Act 1868 no longer
        applicable, 610
    judgments *in personam,* 589-598; see also
        JUDGMENT *In Personam*
    judgment *in rem,* 598-601
    Maintenance orders 304-317, 610-611
    merits, foreign judgment cannot be
        examined on, 603-606
    mistake as to law made by foreign court,
        604-605
    Natural justice, foreign judgment contrary
        to, 608-609
    original cause of action not extinguished,
        586-587
    public policy, foreign judgment contrary
        to, 609
    theoretical basis for enforcement and
        recognition, 584-586
    ship, judgment as to, 601
Foreign Law, Ascertainment of: see *Proof
    of Foreign Law*
Foreign Law, Exclusion of: see *Exclusion
    of a Foreign Law*
Foreign Nullity Decree, Recognition of,
    255-260; see also *Recognition of
    Foreign Nullity Decrees*
Foreign Immovable, see 391-407; see also
    Movables and Immovables: Jurisdiction Over
Foreign Legitimation, Recognition of,
    357-364; see also *Legitimation*

Foreign Maintenance Order, Recognition of,
    304-317; see also *Maintenance Entitlements,
    Maintenance Orders Act 1974*
Foreign Sovereign, 173-178; see also
    Sovereign Immunity
Formal Validity of Contract
    exceptional cases, 538-539
    generally, 537-539
    lex fori, 538-539
    lex loci contractus, 537-538
    local law, reliance on, 538
    marriage, of ... 218-231, 246; see also
        Marriage Validity
    proper law, 538
    public policy, 538-539
    Statute of Frauds, 539
    substance-procedure characterisation, 539
Forum Non Conveniens, 164-168; see also
    Stay of Proceedings
Foundling, Domicile of, 83-84
Fraud
    divorce, non-recognition of, on account
        of, 284
    foreign judgment, non-recognition on
        account of, 606-608
    foreign nullity decree obtained and,   263
    jurisdiction over immovables and, 405-407
    marriage, consent to, 240-242, 247-248
Frustration of Contract, 543

G

Gaming, 552
Garnishment, 505
*Geneva Convention on the Execution of
    Foreign Arbitral Awards* (1927), 619-620
*Geneva Protocol on Arbitration Clauses
    (1923),* 619-620
Gift, 500
Glossators, 6
Guardian, 321-346; see further *Minor*

H

Habitual Residence
    definition, proposed statutory, 99-100
    domicile, comparison with, 98-99
    generally, 45, 98-100
    intention, role of, 98-100
    meaning, 98-99
    minors, 99
    reform proposals, 99-100
    spouse, habitual residence of, 99-100
    transient life style, 99
Hague Convention on Adoptions (1964)
    adopted child, requirements as to, 378
    adoptive parent or parents, requirements
        as to, 377-378
    adults, adoption of, excluded, 378
    choice of law, 378
    generally, 376-380
    incidents and effects excluded, 377

interest of the child, 379
"internal" adoptions excluded, 377
limits of, 377
public policy, 379-380
recognition, 379
single adopting parent, 377
Hague Convention on International Child Abduction, 339-343
Hague Convention on Marriage (1978), 266-268
Hague Convention on Recognition of Divorces and Legal Separations (1970), 292-293
Hague Convention on the Celebration of Marriages (1902), 226
Hague Convention on the Form of Wills (1961), 433-434
Hague Convention on the Taking of Evidence Abroad in Civil or Commercial Matters (1968), 636-637
High Seas
marriage celebrated on, 231
tort committed on, 581
Hire Purchase
proper law, exception to application of, 533
Historical Background
D'Argentré, 7-8
Cavers, 19-21
comity doctrine, 13-14
Currie, 16-19, 21
Dumoulin, 7-8
Dutch School, 8-9
feudalism, 6
generally, 3-21
Greece, 4-5
Huber, 8-9, 12, 13
Ireland, development of conflict of laws in, 22-26
local law theory, 15-16
Mancini, 11-12
Reese, 19
renvoi, development of doctrine of, 38-44
Rome, 4-5
von Savigny, 11-12, 15
Statistist, 6-7
Story, 9, 12-13
territorialist approach, 12-13
vested rights theory, 14-15
Voet, 8-9
Home
capacity to marry, and law of matrimonial, 232-235
declaration referring to, and domicile of choice, 71-72
domicile of child and, 87-90
family property and intended family home, 418
Huber, 8-9, 12, 13, 521
Husband and Wife
divorce, 269-293; see also *Divorce*
divorce *a mensa et thoro*, 294-297; see also *Divorce a Mensa et Thoro*
family property, 414-428; see laos *Family Property*

marriage validity, 218-250; see also *Marriage Validity*
restitution of conjugal rights, action for, 250-260; see also *Jurisdiction in Proceedings for Nullity of Marriage*

I

Illegal Residence, 54-55, 101-103
Illegality of Contract
breach of promise, action for, prohibited, 552
Champtertons agreement, 550
divorce, contract facilitating, 549-550
exchange control legislation, 550-551
Gaming and Lotteries Act 1956, 552
generally, 545-552
international relations, 551
Irish statute, under, 551-552
lex loci contractus, under, 549
lex loci solutionis, under, 546-548
maintenance, 549-550
penal laws, foreign, 551
proper law, under, 545-546
prosecution, agreement to stifle, 550
public policy, 549-552
restraint of trade, 550
revenue laws, foreign, 551
State, interests of, contract opposed to, 551
wagering contract, 552
Illegitimacy: see *Legitimacy, Legitimation*
Immovables: Jurisdiction over
Admiralty jurisdiction, 407
contract concerning foreign land, 404-405
exceptions to exclusion of jurisdiction, 403-407
exclusion of jurisdiction, 402-407
fiduciary relationship, 406-407
fraud, 405-406
generally, 401-407
historical background, 401
maritime lien, 407
personal obligation to plaintiff, action founded on, 403-404
possession of land abroad, disputes as to, 402-407
question affecting foreign land arising incidentally in Irish proceedings, 407
sovereign immunity, 177
trespass to, 402-407
title to land abroad, disputes as to, 402-407
Immovables
capacity to take and transfer immovables, 409-411
choice-of-law, 408-413
contract relating to immovables, 412-413
EEC Convention on the Law Applicable to Contractual Obligations; presumption as to contract in respect of, 559
equity, jurisdiction over immovables and 403-407
essential validity of transfer, 411

family property, 422; see also *Family
  Property*
formalities, 411
fiduciary relationship, jurisdiction as to
  immovables and 403-407
generally, 408-413
in rem, judgment, 598-601
Judgments Convention and, 190
jurisdiction over, 401-407; see also
  Immovables, Jurisdiction Over
lex situs controls, 408-409
lex situs, meaning of, 409
succession, intestate, and, 429-430; see
  also *Succession*
trusts of, 512-513
Immunity: see *Diplomatic Immunity, Sovereign
  Immunity*
Impotence, 242-246, 248; see also *Marriage
  Validity*
"*Incidental Question*", *The*
  capacity to marry and, 33-34
  definition of, 31
  eclectic approach, 32
  generally, 31-34
  judicial analysis, 33-34
  lex causae and, 32
  lex domicilii and, 31
  lex fori and, 31, 32
  principal question, how distinguished, 34
Indorsement of Negotiable Instruments, 489;
  see also *Negotiable Instruments*
Ineligible Parties
  alien enemy, who is, 171-172
  alien friend, who is, 171
  carrying on business in enemy State, 172
  generally, 171-172
  naturalised citizen, 171-172
  surreptitious entry into the jurisdiction,
    172
Infant: see *Minor*
Inheritance: see *Succession*
Injunction
  jurisdiction of Irish Court, 153-156
  restraining litigation abroad, 163, 164,
    170-172
Inland Bill of Exchange, 489
In Rem Actions: see *Actions in Rem:
  Jurisdiction over*
Insanity: see *Mental Incompetency*
Insolvency: see *Bankruptcy, Companies*
Insurance Contract
  Judgments Convention and, 189
  Judgments Convention on the Law
    Applicable to Contractual Obligations;
    contracts covering risks situated in
    territories of Member States, 556
  where broken, 145
  where made, 141
Intended Matrimonial Home
  capacity to marry and, 232-235
  family property and, 418
Interpleader Proceedings, 159
Interpretation
  contract, 541-543

family settlement, 423, 427
legitimacy, 354-355
negotiable instrument, 488-489
trust, 510, 512
will, 442-447
Intestate Succession, 429-430; see also
Succession
Invalid, Domicile of, 61-64
Ireland
  conflict of laws and, 22-26
  northern: see *Northern Ireland*
Isle of Man, Divorce Obtained in, 283

J

Joinder of Parties
  procedure, 647
  service out of the jurisdiction, 157-159
Judgments Convention
  appearance, judgment in default of, 613
  automatic recognition of judgments,
    general principle of, 612-613
  bankruptcy, Convention does not extend
    to, 182, 612
  branch, agency or other establishment,
    dispute arising out of operation of, 186-187
  choice of jurisdiction agreement, 190-191
  company matters, 190
  constructive trusts, 188
  consumer contracts, 189
  contract; defendant may be sued in place
    of performance of obligation in
    question, 184-185
  "contract"; how characterised, 184
  damages, civil claim for, based on act
    giving rise to criminal proceedings,
    186
  delict; defendant may be sued at place where
    harmful event occurred, 186
  dissolution of company, 200
  domicile of defendant the basis of general
    jurisdiction, 183
  domicile, meaning of, for purposes of
    Convention, 183
  earlier judgment, irreconcilability with,
    613
  enforcement procedure, 614-615
  exclusive jurisdiction, 189-191
  exorbitant jurisdiction, prohibition of,
    182-183
  generally, 181-191, 612-616
  habitual residence, 183
  history of, 181-182
  immovable property, 190
  implementation of, 182
  implied trusts, 188
  in rem, rights, in immovable property,
    190
  Insurance, contracts of, 189
  jurisdiction, rules as to, 183-191, 613-614
  legal capacity, preliminary question as to,
    613
  legislation required, 182
  maintenance, defendant may be sued in

place where maintenance creditor is domicile or habitually resident, 185-186

maintenance, proceedings ancilliary to proceedings concerning status of person, 185-186

maritime lien, 188-189

matrimonial property rights, preliminary question as to, 613

non-recognition or non-enforcement of judgment, grounds for, 612-613

"obligation"; meaning of, 185

ordinary residence, 183

place of performance of contract, how determined, 185

public policy, 613-614

quasi-delict; defendant may be sued at place where harmful event occurred, 186

ratification of, 182

restitution, civil action for, based on act giving rise to criminal proceedings, 186

review as to substance not permitted, 614

salvage of cargo or freight, 188

seat of company, 190

security for costs, limitation on, 615

service on defendant, lack of due, 613

ship, 188-189

special jurisdictional rules, 183-189

status, preliminary question as to, 613

succession, preliminary question as to, 613

temporary presence, jurisdiction based on is exorbitant, 182-183

tenancies of immovable property, 190

transition provision as to jurisdiction based on agreement then contract is to be followed by Irish law, 184

trust, 187-188

Judgment In Personam

cause of action arising in foreign country not sufficient basis of jurisdiction, 597

comity doctrine no longer applies, 586

contract to submit to jurisdiction of foreign court, 594-595

domicile of defendant not apparently sufficient basis of jurisdiction, 596-597

estoppel, 606

fraud, 606-608

insufficient bases of jurisdiction, 595-598

nationality of defendant not sufficient basis of jurisdiction, 595-596

plaintiff, appearance as, in foreign court, 591

possession by defendant of property in foreign country not sufficient basis of jurisdiction, 598

presence of defendant, 589-591

reciprocity not sufficient basis of jurisdiction, 597

recognition and enforcement of, generally, 589-598

residence of defendant, 589

submission to jurisdiction of foreign court, 591-595

voluntary appearance to contest foreign action on merits, 591-594

Judgment In Rem, 598-601

Judicial Notice of Foreign Law, 105; see further *Proof of Foreign Law*

Jurisdiction: see also *Service Out of the Jurisdiction*

assumed jurisdiction, 132-160

diplomatic immunity, 178-181

exempt parties, 173-182; see also *Sovereign Immunity* and *Diplomatic Immunity*

fleeting presence, 125

foreign sovereign states, 173-178: see also *Sovereign Immunity*

generally, 123-191

immovables, jurisdiction over, 401-407

ineligible parties: see *Ineligible Parties*

In personam, actions, 124-160

In rem, actions: see *Actions in Rem: Jurisdiction Over*

nationality of plaintiff not basis for, 131-132, 160-162

personal presence, jurisdiction based on, 124-126

submission: see *Submission*

service of summons: see *Service of Summons*

service out of the jurisdiction: see *Service out of the Jurisdiction*

stay of proceedings: see *Stay of Proceedings*

temporary presence, 125

trick, presence obtained by, 125-126

Jurisdiction in Proceedings for Nullity of Marriage

domicile and void marriages, 250-251

domicile and voidable marriages, 253-254

generally, 250-255

place of celebration and void marriages, 252-253

reform proposals, 255

residence and void marriages, 251-252

residence and voidable marriages, 254-255

void and voidable marriages, distinction between, 250

void marriages, 250-253

voidable marriages, 253-255

Jury, Lex Fori, Determines Whether There Should be, 637

Land

immovables, 391-398; see also *Immovables*

in fee, 393

interest in land held on trust for sale, 397

jurisdiction in relation to foreign land, 401-407

leasehold, 393

mortgagee's interest in land, 396-397

questions affecting foreign land, arising incidentally in Irish proceedings, 407

Settled Land Act 1882, capital moneys arising under 393-396

L

Legal Separation: see *Divorce A Mensa Et Thoro, Hague Convention on Recognition of Divorces and Legal Separations (1970)*
Legitimacy
  constructionist approach, 354-355
  declaration of legitimacy, 355-356; see also *Declaration of Legitimacy*
  generally, 347-357
  father's domicile, 351-352
  Irish law, rules as to legitimacy in, 347
  lex domicilii, role of, 350-354
  lex fori, role of, 348-350
  marriage, relevance of, 347-350
  mother's domicile, 352
  parent, law of one, conferring legitimate status, 352-353
  parents' domicile, 352
  status of, 349-350
  succession, 354-355
  title contrasted with status, 349-350
  void marriage, child of, 347
  voidable marriage, child of, 347
Legitimation
  common law, legitimation at, 357-360
  declaration as to, 366-367; see also *Declaration as to Legitimation*
  domicile and, 52-53
  foreign statute, legitimation by, 363-364
  generally, 357-367
  history of, 357
  per subsequens matrimonium, 357-362
  property, 361
  recognition, legitimation by, 362-363
  succession, 368-369
Lex Causae
  characterisation and, 32
  damages and, 642-646
  execution of judgment and, 642-649
  extra-judicial remedies governed by, 618
  generally, 29
  "Incidental Question", the, and *lex causae*, 32
  irrebuttable presumptions and, 628-629
  lapse of time, 641
  limitation of actions and, 639-641
  mode of trial and, 637-638
  partner, whether must be joined in proceedings, 647
  rebuttable presumptions and, 629-631
  witness, competence and compellability of, 632
  written evidence, requirement of, and, 631-632
Lex Domicilii
  domicile: see *Domicile*
  renvoi and, 35-44
Lex Fori

damages, governed by, 642-646
divorce *a mensa et thoro*, choice of law
domicile, characterisation of, by *lex fori*, 31, 32
evidence, 626-637; see also *Evidence*
execution of judgments, 648-649
foreign currency, judgments in, 649-651
generally, 28-30
governs procedure, 625-631
illegal residence, denial of benefits in relation to, 54-55
"Incidental Question", the, and the *lex fori*, 31, 32
injunctions, 646-647
lapse of time, 641
legitimacy, 348-350
limitation of actions, 639-641
marriage and, 241-243, 245-246, 249
mode of trial, governed by, 637
nature of remedy governed by, 637-639
parties to proceedings, 647
priorities, 648
restitution of conjugal rights, choice of law, 300
torts, 567-568
Lex Loci Actus
  chose in action, assignment of, 502
  chose in possession, transfer of, 495
Lex Loci Celebrationis
  formalities for marriage, 28, 219-227; see also *Marriage Validity*
  formation, 28
  marriage and, 28
  polygamy and, 213
Lex Loci Delicti, 568-569
Lex Patriae
  renvoi and, 36-37, 38-44
  nationality and, 96-98; see also *Nationality*
Lex Situs
  categorisation of property, 392
  chose in action, assignment of, 501-502
  chose in possession, assignment of, 495
  construction of testamentary disposition, 445-447
  EEC Judgments Convention and, 200
  essential validity of testamentary, disposition and, 434
  formalities relating to wills and, 432
  generally governs contracts relating to immovables, 412-413
  governs immovables, 408-411
  intestate succession and, 430
  meaning of, 44, 408
  power by appointment, 450-458
  priorities and, 648
  statutory entitlements, 435-441
  succession and, 401, 430, 431, 432-434
  testamentary capacity and, 431
  trust of immovable, 512-513
  renvoi and, 44
  revocation of by destruction of will, 448
Limitation of Actions, 639-641
Lis Alibi Pendens: see *Stay of Proceedings*
Local Law Theory, 15-16

M

Maintenance Entitlements
affiliation proceedings: see *Affiliation Proceedings*
choice of law, 302-303
common law, recognition and enforcement at, 303-309
divisible divorce, 303-304
enforcement of foreign orders, 304-317
finality and conclusiveness by order, 305-309
generally, 289-292, 301-320
jurisdiction, 302
Maintenance Orders Act 1974: see *Maintenance Orders Act 1974*
Maintenance Orders (Facilities for Enforcement) Act 1920, 309-310
policy considerations, 301-302
recognition of foreign orders, 304-317
Maintenance Orders Act 1974
affiliation order falls within definition of "maintenance order", 310-311
enforcement of District Court, 314-315
enforcement of maintenance order made in reciprocating jurisdiction, 311-313
evidence, taking of, 317
generally, 310-317, 610-611
"maintenance order" defined, 310-311
maintenance orders made in the State, 315-317
non-recognition, grounds for, 313-314
partial enforcement, 314
public policy, 313-314
revocation, 315, 316
security for costs, prohibition or orders for, 314
variation, 315, 316
Mancini, 11, 12
Mansfield, Lord, 9, 518-519
Maritime Torts, 580-581
Marriage Validity; see also *Jurisdiction in Proceedings for Nullity of Marriage, Recognition of Foreign Nullity Decrees*
age, minimum, proposal in respect of, 247
ancillary orders in nullity proceedings, proposal in relation to, 249
capacity to marry, 231-240, 246-247
common law marriage, 228-231, 246
consent to marry, 33-34, 52, 240-242, 247
divorce, capacity to marry after, 236-240, 247
dual domicile test, 232-235, 246-247
duress, 241-242
exceptions to application of *lex loci celebrationis*, 228-231, 246
exceptions to general rule as to capacity to marry, 235-240
Foreign Marriages Act 1892, 231, 246
foreign nullity decrees, recognition of: see *Recognition of Foreign Nullity Decrees*
formal validity, 218-231, 246
generally, 218-250

grounds for annulment unknown to forum, 248-249
habitual residence as proposed test for capacity to marry and for consent issues, 247-248
Hague Convention on Marriage (1978), 266-268
high seas, marriage celebrated on, 231
impotence, 242-246, 248
incapacity under *lex loci celebrationis* where this is *lex fori* also, 236
"incidental question", the, 33-34
"intended matrimonial home" test, 232-235
lex loci celebrationis prevails over personal law, 227
lex loci celebrationis, role of, in relation to formal validity, 28, 219-223, 246
Lourdes marriages, 223-227
mistake as to nature of ceremony, 242
nullity proceedings, jurisdiction: see *Jurisdiction in Proceedings for Nullity of Marriage*
parental consent requirements, proposals in respect of, 247
post-nuptial matters as grounds for annulment, 248
potentially polygamous marriage, 230-231
qualities of spouse, mistake as to, 242
reform proposals, 246-250
refusal to consummate marriage, proposals in rspect of, 248
renvoi and *lex loci celebrationis*, 227-228
retrospective invalidity legislation, 227
"sham marriage", 242
Sottomayor v De Barros (No. 2), rule in, 235-236
void and voidable marriages, distinction between, 249
Married Women, Domicile of: see *Domicile of Married Women*
Matrimonial Causes
divorce, 269-293; see also *Divorce*
divorce *a mensa et thoro*, 294-297; see also *Divorce A Mensa Et Thoro*
maintenance entitlements, 289-291 301-320; see also *Maintenance Entitlements*
nullity of marriage, 218-268; see also *Hague Convention on Marriage (1978), Jurisdiction in Proceedings for Nullity of Marriage, Marriage Validity, Polygamy and Recognition of Foreign Nullity Decrees*
restitution of conjugal rights
Matrimonial Home: see *Home*
Matrimonial Property Regimes, 414-428; see also *Family Property*
Mental Distress, Compensation for, 644
Mental Incompetency
"British possessions", former, 385

committee, appointment of, 381-382
domicile, 382-383
domicile: see *Domicile of Mentally Ill Persons*
English courts, 383-384
foreign committee, 386-387
foreign court, jurisdiction of, 386
foreign curator, 386-387
generally, 381-387
habitual residence, 98-100
historical aspects, 381
presence within the State, 382
President of High Court, jurisdiction of, 381-385
property situated abroad, 383
Registrar of Wards of Court, 381
removal abroad of mentally incompetent person, 385-386
Scottish courts, 383, 384
termination of wardship, 386
Merger, Doctrine of, and Foreign Judgments, 587-588
Minister for Foreign Affairs, Certificate as to Recognition of Sovereign Authority, 177-178
Minor
abduction, offence of, 346
applicable law, 323
domicile of: see *Domicile of Minors*
domicile of minor, 325-326; see also *Domicile of Minors*
Constitution, role of, 321-322, 334-339, 341
Council of Europe Convention, 343-345
education, foreign, 330-332
foreign guardians, 327-330
fund in court, 328-329
generally, 321-346
Guardianship of Infants Act 1964, 322
habitual residence of minor, 99, 325
Hague Convention on International Child Abduction, 339-342
international child abduction, 332-346
jurisdiction, 323-327
minors taken abroad, 330, 345-346
movable property within the State, 328-329
national law, the, 334-339
nationality of minor, 323-324
offences, 321-346
ordinary residence of minor, 101, 324-325
presence of minor within the State, 326-327
proposed removal of minor abroad, 330-332
reform proposals, 343, 345-346
security for costs not permitted under Hague Convention, 342
Mistake
contract, vitiated by, 535-537
marriage, validity of, affected by, 242
Mode of Trial, Lex Fori Determines, 637
Monogamy
"breakdown of marriage", 211-212

divorce on demand, 212
generally, 211-217
marriage, meaning of, 211
permanence of marriage, 211-212
Mortgagee's Interest in Land, How Characterised, 396-398
Movables; see also *Choses in Possession, Transfer of, Choses in Action, Assignment of, Negotiable Instrument*
characterisation of, 391-392
chattels real, 391
construction of wills, 442-445
essential validity as to wills, 434-435
family property, 414-428
formalities as to wills, 432-434
interests in land held on trust for sale not movables, 397-398
intestate succession, 429-430
mortgagee's interest in land, 396-397
personalty, not identical with, 392
power of appointment exercisable by will, 449-452
revocation by destruction of will, 448
situs of, 398-400
statutory entitlements, 435-441
succession to testamentary succession, capacity, 430-431

N

Natural Justice
foreign divorce decree contrary to, 285-286
foreign judgment contrary to, 608-609
foreign nullity decree contrary to, 263
Nationalisation, 204; see also *Expropriatory Legislation*
Nationality
America, Central, 97
America, South, 97
Austria, 96
Belgium, 96
clarity of concept, 97
dual, 97
emigration and, 97-98
emigrés, 98
evasion of state policy, prevention of, 97
France, 96
generally, 96-98
history, 96-98
immigrant tradition, countries with, 97-99
Luxembourg, 96
Mancini and, 11-12, 96
multiple, 97
Netherlands, 96
Statelessness, 97
Negligence, 567, 569, 571, 582; see also *Contributory Negligence*
Negotiable Instrument
capacity, 488
damages, measure of, 492-493
dishonour, 490-491
exchange, rate of, 491-492
formal validity, 487-488
generally, 487-493

Independence, effect of, 487-488
indorsement, 487
interpretation, 488-489
meaning of, 487
negotiability, 487
payment, date of, 492
presentment, 490-491
transfer, 490
"United Kingdom", how to be
  interpreted, 487-488
validity, 488-489
New York Convention on the Recognition and
  Enforcement of Foreign Arbitral
  Awards (1958), 619-620
Northern Ireland
  bankruptcy, 475-476
  constitutional developments, 22-25
  contract, 531
  divorce, 278, 283
  divorce *a mensa et thoro*, 295
  domicile, 47-49
  Judgments Extension Act 1868, 610, 660-661
  jurisdiction, 143, 158-159
  lex loci celebrationis, 244
  Maintenance Orders Act 1974, 310-317,
    610-611
  malicious injury, 148
  mental incompetency, 384
  negotiable instrument, 487-488
  residence as basis of jurisdiction in
    proceedings for nullity of void
    marriage, 251-252
  security for costs, 660-662
Novation, 544
Nullity of Marriage: see *Hague*
  Convention on Marriage
  (1978), Jurisdiction in
  Proceedings for Nullity of
  Marriage, Marriage
  Validity, Polygamy and
  Recognition of Foreign
  Nullity Decrees

O

Obligation
  contract: see *Contract*
  doctrine of, in relation to the recognition
    of judgments, 586-587
  EEC Convention: see *EEC*
    Convention on the Law
    Applicable to Contractual
    Obligations
  quasi-contract: see *Quasi-Contract*
  tort, 568-569
Offer and Acceptance
  generally, 139-141, 533-535
  lex fori, 534
  lex loci contractus, 533-534
  "putative proper law", 534-535
Ordinary Residence
  casual residence distinguished, 101
  child, 101
  continuity, required degree of, 101
  country, ordinary residence in more than
    one, 101
  deportation order, effect on, 101-103
  generally, 101-103
  illegal entrant, 101-103
  meaning, 101-103
  parents living apart, effect on child's
    ordinary residence, 101
  prisoner, 101-103
  "residence" relation to, 101
  voluntariness, 101-103
Organisation for Economic Cooperation and
  Development
  privileges and imunities of, 180-181
Origin, Domicile of: see *Domicile of Origin*

P

Parent: see *Minor*
Partner, Service of, 127
Partial Renvoi, 36
Penal Laws
  adequacy of rationale, 193
  basis of exclusion, 192-193
  compensation, orders for, in criminal
    proceedings, 195
  contempt of court, 195-197
  crimes, 193
  generally, 192-197
  "penal" discriminatory rules, 197
  private remedy, 194-195
  public nuisance, damages for, 195
  punitive damages, 195
  remedial statutory provisions, 194-195
  violation of statute, 194
  what constitutes a "penal law", 193-197
Perpetuities, Rule Against, 441-442
Personal Representative: see *Administration of*
  Estates
Personalty: see *Movables*
Polygamy
  cultural background, 213
  divorce *a mensa et thoro*, 215
  fatal accidents litigation, 216
  generally, 212-217
  initially monogamous marriage, 214
  legitimacy, 217
  lex domicilii, role of, 213, 215
  lex loci celebrationis, role of, 213
  maintenance obligations, 215-216
  Married Women's Status Act 1957, rights
    under, 216
  matrimonial relief, demand of, 214-217
  polygamous marriage, meaning of,
    212-213
  potentially polygamous marriage, 213-214
  public policy, 215
  succession entitlements, 216
Post-Glossators, 6-7
Power of Appointment
  capacity, 450
  construction, 451
  essential validity, 450-451
  formalities, 450
  generally, 449-452

nature of, 449
revocation, 451-452
will, power exercised by, 449
Preliminary Question: see *"Incidental Question", The*
Presumption
  ademption, of, 629-630
  advancement, of, 629-630
  commorientes, 434, 628-629
  constitutional dimension, 630-631
  death, of, 629-630
  fact, of, 628
  generally, 628-631
  rebuttable, of law, 629-631
  legitimacy, of, 629-631
  marriage, of, 629-630
  resulting trust and, 629-630
Prisoner
  domicile of, 64-65
  ordinary residence of, 101-103
Private International Law: see *Conflict of Laws*
Probate: see *Administration of Estates*
Procedure: see *Substance and Procedure*
Promise of Marriage, Action for Breach of, Abolished, 532, 552
Proof of Foreign Law
  academic knowledge of foreign law as basis of expertise, 107
  admission as to foreign law, 112
  ambassador as expert, 108
  banker as expert, 108
  bankruptcy, proof of foreign law as to, 117
  "best evidence" rule, 108
  canon law, expert witness on, 107
  canon law, whether foreign law, 118-120
  determination of foreign law without proof, 112-113
  documentary material, 110-111
  embassy official as expert, 108
  expert evidence, 105-110
  expert, qualifications for being, 106-110
  fact, proof of foreign law a question of, 104-105
  failure to prove foreign law, 112-118
  familiarity with foreign law does not itself constitute expertise, 108
  former practitioner as expert, 107
  generally, 104-120
  Irish cases where foreign law was not proved, 114-118
  Irish law applied when foreign law not proved, 113
  judicial notice, 105
  legal practitioner, foreign, as expert, 106-108
  marriage, proof of foreign law as to, 115-117
  merchant as expert, 108
  mode of proof, 105-110
  necessity for proof, 105
  non-lawyer as expert, 108
  plaintiff's evidence, effect of, 109-110
  presumption as to foreign law's identity

  with Irish law, 113
  statutory material, 110-111, 113
  uncontradicted evidence, 108, 111
  unduly relaxed approach to proof occasionally adopted, 108, 110
Provinces, Domicile and, 47
Proper Law of Contract
  absence of choice of proper law by parties, 526-530
  "bona fide" choice, meaning of, 521-522
  breach of promise, actions for, prohibited, regardless of proper law, 56
  capacity to contract, 541
  choice of governing law by parties, 521-526
  contract made in one country to be performed in another, 530-531
  contractual documents, form of, raising inference as to choice of proper law, 515
  currency in which payment to be made, 526
  generally, 518-533
  hire-purchase agreement, 533
  incorporation contrasted, 523-524
  inferred choice of proper law, 524-526
  international sale of goods, contract for, 532-533
  lex fori sometimes applied, 531-532
  lex loci contractus formerly preferred, 519-520
  lex loci contractus no longer the test, 520-521
  Lord Mansfield's role, 518-519
  minimum degree of connection between contract and chosen law, 522
  modern approach, 521-533
  objective approach, 522-523, 526-527
  origins of doctrine, 518-519
  "putative proper law", 536-537
  residence of parties, 525, 530
  sale of goods, 532-533
  statutory exceptions to application of proper law, 532-533
  subject matter of contract, nature and location of, 525, 523-530
  subjective approach, 522-523, 526-527
  supply of service, contract for, 533
Property
  bill of exchange, *situs* of, 399
  capital moneys arising under the Settled Land Act 1882, 393-396
  characterisation of, 391-400
  chattels, 393, 398, 494-500
  choses in action, 501-505; see also *Choses in Action, Assignment of*
  chose in action, *situs* of, 398-399
  choses in possession, 494-500; see also *Choses in Possession, Transfer of*
  immovable property, characterisation of, 402: see also *Immovables*
  interests in immovables, 392-393
  interests in land held on trust for sale, 397-398
  land, 391-392, 397-398

land, *situs* of, 398
lex situs, role of, 392
mortgagee's interest in land, 396-397
movables and immovables distinguished, 391-400
personalty, 392
realty, 392
share, *situs* of, 399
shares, 399, 504-505
simple contract debt, *situs* of, 398-399
situs, how determined, 398-400
specialty debt, *situs* of, 398-399
trust for sale, interest in land held on, 397-398
unadministered estate, *situs* of interests in, 400
Public Policy
contract and, 538-539
economic context, 208
exchange control regulations, 208, 550-551
generally, 207-208
foreign laws repugnant to Irish public policy, 207-208
justice, fundamental conception of, 208
natural justice foreign judgment contrary to, 208
polygamous marriages and, 215

Q

Quasi-Contract
EEC Convention on the Law Applicable to Contractual Obligations and, 184, 553
jurisdiction, 141-142

R

Recognition
adoption, of foreign, 372-374; see also *Adoption*
arbitration, of foreign: see *Foreign Arbitrations*
judgment, of foreign: see *Foreign Judgments*
legitimation, by, 362-363
nullity decrees: see *Recognition of Foreign Nullity Decrees*
Recognition and Enforcement of Foreign Arbitrations: see *Foreign Arbitrations*
Recognition and Enforcement of Foreign Judgments: see *Foreign Judgments*
Recognition of Foreign Nullity Decrees
ancillary relief, 264
capacity to marry after foreign nullity decree, 264
common domicile, decree obtained in country of, 256-257
common domicile, decree recognised in country of, 259
common residence, 260-261
domicile, 256-260
domicile of one party, 257-259
domicile of one party, decree recognised as

valid in country of, 260
effects of foreign nullity decree, 263-264
fraud, decree obtained by, not recognised, 263
generally, 255-265
grounds for withholding recognition, 262-263
habitual residence, 261
natural justice, decree not recognised if contrary to, 363
non-recognition of foreign decree, 265
place of celebration, 262
public policy, decree not recognised if contrary to, 262
"real and substantial connection" test, 261
reciprocity, 261
reform proposals, 265
residence, 260-261
residence of one party, 261
"substantial justice", decree not recognised if contrary to, 262
Reese, 19
Remedy
damages, 637-638, 642-646
defective goods, right to reject, 638
dowry, 638-639
entitlement unknown to Irish law, 638-639
extra-judicial, 638
judicial, 637-638
lex causae, role of, 638
lex fori, role of, 637-638
specific performance, 638
Remoteness of Damage, 642-646
Renvoi
chattels, transfer of, 44
common law and, 38-44
contract, 44
desistement theory, 36
"foreign court" approach, 36-37
generally, 35-44
historical development of doctrine, 38-44
lex situs, 44
meaning of, 35-38
partial renvoi, 36
remission, 36
social factors, 38
transmission, 36
Requisition, 204; see also *Expropriatory Legislation*
Reservation of Title, 44, 496-498
Residence
abandonment of domicile of choice and, 72
domicile and, 53-55
habitual residence: see *Habitual Residence*
"home", meaning of, in relation to domicile of minors, 87-89
illegal, 54-55, 101-103
joint custody, domicile of minors and, 89
"living apart", parents who are, 87-88
ordinary residence: see *Ordinary Residence*
Res Ipsa Loquitur, 627-628
Restitution of Conjugal Rights
choice of law, 300

constitutional uncertainty as to, 297
generally, 297-300
grounds for, 297-298
jurisdiction, 298-300
nature of proceedings, 297-298
recognition of foreign decrees, 300
Revenue Laws
bankruptcy, 202-203
costs in divorce proceedings, 198
extradition, 203-204
generally, 198-204
hospital expenses, claim for, 198
legal aid, 198
municipal rates, 198
non-enforcement does not imply non-
recognition, 201-202
policy basis on non-enforceability rule,
198-201
rationale of non-enforceability rule
questioned, 200-201
revenue debt, what constitutes, 198
state health insurance scheme, 198
Revival of Domicile of Origin, 73, 76-77
Revocation of Will
characterisation, 449
destruction of will, 448
generally, 447-449
later will of codicil, 447-448
power of appointment, 451-452
subsequent marriage, 448-449
will made in contemplation of subsequent
marriage, 449
Roman Law
conflict of laws, role in development of, 4-5
Roman Empire, fall of, 5
Statutists, 6-7
Rome Convention: see *EEC Convention on the
Law Applicable to Contractual
Obligations*

S

Sale of Goods
consumer contracts, 560-561, 562-563
international contract law, 532-533, 558-559
proper law, exception to application of,
532-533
Saliceto, 7
Savigny, von, 10-11, 15
Sea
admiralty: see *Admiralty*
arrest of property, 162
cargo, 162
maritime torts, 580-581
marriage at, 230
situs of, 398
will made on ship, 433
Security for Costs
administration, 653-654
affidavit of defendant, 662-664
bankruptcy proceedings, 655
co-plaintiffs, 656
defendant caveator, 654
defendant's wrong contributing to plaintiff's

poverty, 656-669
delay, 669
discretion of the Court, 662
exception to rule, 653
generally, 652-669
interpleader proceedings, 655-656
level at which costs should be set, 664-665
Maintenance Orders Act 1974, no
requirement for security for costs under,
653
nominal plaintiff, 655
Northern Ireland, plaintiff resident in,
660-662
plaintiff leaving jurisdiction, 658
"plaintiff", who is, 653-656
policy considerations, 652-653
poverty of plaintiff, 665-669
probate action, 654-655
property, possession of, within jurisdiction,
658-660
residence, quality of plaintiff's, 656-658
"satisfactory" affidavit, meaning of,
663-664
waiver, 669
Separation: see *Divorce a Mensa et Thoro*
Separation Agreement, 549-550
Service of Summons
companies, service on, 128-129
delivery of copy of summons, 126
evasion of, 127
generally, 125-129
modes of, 125-129
partners, service on, 127
personal service, 126
solicitor, service on, 126
substituted service, 126-127
Service out of the Jurisdiction
air, carriage by, proceeding in relation to,
160
arbitration, enforcement of award, 159
arbitration held or to be held within
jurisdiction, 159
act affecting land within jurisdiction,
136-137
administration of personal estate where
deceased domiciled within jurisdiction,
138
affidavit, supporting, 135-136
agent, contract made by or through, 142
annulment of contract, 139-147
carriers, 145-147
comparative cost and convenience of
proceeding in Ireland or elsewhere,
133-134
construction of acts, deeds, wills contracts,
obligations or liabilities affecting land
within jurisdiction, 136-137
contract, 134-135
contract affecting land within jurisdiction,
136-137
contract governed by Irish law, 143
contract made within the jurisdiction,
139-142
damages or other relief for breach of
contract, 139-147

deeds affecting land within jurisdiction,
136-137
discretionary nature of order, 132
dissolution of contract, 139-147
domicile of dependent as basis of
jurisdiction, 138
elective approach in relation to tort,
151-153
enforcement of contract, 139-147
England, defendant resident in, 134
ex parte motion for, 135-136
forum conveniens, 134; see also *Forum
Conveniens*
generally, 132-160
hereditaments situate within jurisdiction,
136-137
impossibility of performance of part of
contract which ought to have been
performed within jurisdiction, 144-147
injunction, 153-156
interpleader proceeding, 159
Irish developments in relation to tort,
151-153
land situate within the jurisdiction, action
concerns, 136
"last event" approach in relation to tort,
148-149
liability affecting land within jurisdiction,
136-137
Mareva injunction, 153-156
mortgage of personal property situate within
jurisdiction, 160
necessary or proper party to action,
157-159
no order for service out of jurisdiction
unless case falls within Order 11, 133
Northern Ireland, defendant resident in, 134
obligation affecting land within jurisdiction,
136-137
Order 12, 133-160
ordinary residence of defendant as basis of
jurisdiction, 138
"place of acting" approach in relation to
tort, 149
"postal rule" in relation to contracts,
140-141
procedure, 135-136
proceedings elsewhere, relevance of, 134;
see also *Stay of Proceedings*
quasi-contract, 141-142
"real and substantial" connection approach
in relation to tort, 150
rectification, setting aside or enforcement of
acts, deeds, wills, contracts, obligations
or liabilities affecting land within
jurisdiction, 136-137
rescission of contract, 139-147
Scotland, defendant resident in, 134
ship registered under *Mercantile Marine Act
1955*, proceeding relating to, 160
small demands, 134
statutory claim for recovery of expenses,
137
"substance of the cause of action"
approach in relation to tort, 149-150

testimony, perpetuation of, relating to land
within the jurisdiction, 136
tort committed within jurisdiction, action
founded on, 147-153
town rates, claim for, 137, 142
trade mark, ownership of, 160
trusts of written instrument, execution of,
138
unsound mind, person of, domiciled in or
citizen of Ireland, 159
value of claim or property affected,
133-134
Settlement: see *Family Property*
Shares
assignment intended to bind company, 504
parties between, effect of transfer as, 504-505
situs of, 399, 504
transfer of, 504-505
Ship
action against, 161-162, 174-177
admiralty: see *Admiralty*
arrest of property, 162
cargo, 162
maritime torts, 581-582
marriage on, 231
situs of, 398
will made on, 535
Situs
bill of exchange, 399
chose in action 398-399
land, 398
how determined, 398-400
share, 399
simple contract debt, 398-399
specialty debt, 398-399
unadministered estate, interests in, 400
Soldier, Domicile of, 65
Sovereign Immunity
admiralty proceedings, 173-177
agent, 175-177
chattels, 174-177
choses in action, 177
commercial purposes, 174-177
counterclaim, 174
Foreign Affairs, role of Minister for, as to
recognition of sovereign authority,
177-178
generally, 173-178
immovables within the jurisdiction, 177
proprietary interest, 175, 176-177
public use, ships employed for, 174
recognition of sovereign authority, 177-178
requisitioned vessels, 174, 176
ships, 174-177
trust fund or property within the
jurisdiction, 177
voluntary submission, 173-174
Statutists, 6-7
Stay of Proceedings
exclusive jurisdiction of foreign forum, 163
foreign forum, choice of, 163-164
forum non-conveniens, 163-168
generally, 162-171
judicial discretion, 164-168
"natural" forum, 166-168

oppressiveness and vexatiousness of action, 165-166
restraining foreign proceedings, 169
staying proceedings within the jurisdiction, 168-169
Story, 9, 12-13
Submission
  agreement to submit to jurisdiction, 131
  foreign sovereign, submission by, 173-174
  generally, 129-131
  interlocutory relief, seeking, 130-131
  plaintiff, commencing action as, 130
  solicitor, instructing, to accept service, 129
  unconditional appearance, 129-130
Substance and Procedure
  Admiralty, claim in, against ship, 648
  administration of insolvent estate, 648
  characterisation of limitation provision, 639
  characterisation of matter as one of substance or procedure, 625-626
  creditor in bankruptcy or winding-up, 648
  damages, 637-639; see also *Damages*
  dowry, 638-639
  evidence, 626-631; see also *Evidence*
  execution of judgments, 648-649
  foreign currency, judgment in, 649-651
  generally, 625-651
  historical background, 626
  injunction, 646-647
  jury trial, 637
  lapse of time, 641
  limitation of actions, 639-641
  Mareva injunction, 153-156, 646-647
  measure of damages, 642-646
  parties, 647
  priorities, 648
  remedy, nature of, 637-639
  remoteness of damage, 642-646
  specific performance, 637-638
  trial, mode of, 637
Succession
  aircraft, testamentary disposition made on, 433
  bona vacantia, 429-430
  capacity, 430-431
  charities, rules as to, 442
  construction, 442-447
  essential validity of will, 434-435
  formalities, 432-434
  generally, 27-28, 429-452
  Hague Convention on the Form of Wills (1961), 433-434
  immovables, intestate succession regarding, 430
  intestate succession, 429-430
  jus regale, 429-430
  "legal right" of surviving spouse, 435-441
  Lord Kingsdown's Act 1861, 432
  movables, intestate succession regarding, 429-430
  power of appointment, 449-452; see also *Power of Appointment*
  renvoi and, 38-44
  revocation, 447-449, 451-452; see also *Revocation of Will*

rule against perpetuities, 441-442
section 117 applications, 435-439
statutory entitlements, 435-441
Succession Act 1965, Part VIII, 433-434
testamentary succession, 430-452
ultimus heres, State succeeding as, 429-430
vessel, testamentary disposition made on, 433
wills: see *Wills*

T

Taking Evidence Abroad
  commission, evidence by, 633-634
  documents, production of, 632-633
  generally, 632-637
  letters of request, 633, 634-636
  public policy, 635
  reform proposals, 636-637
  sub-poena ad testificandum, 632-634
  sub-poena duces tecum, 632-634
Territorial Boundaries, Change In, and Domicile, 47-49
Territorialist Approach, 12-13
Torts
  contributory negligence, 581-582
  damages: see *Damages*
  fatal accidents litigation, 644
  generally, 147-153, 567-582
  lex fori, 567-568
  lex loci delicti, 568-569
  mental distress, 644
  maritime torts, 580-581
  Phillips v Eyre, the Rule in, 572-577
  proper law of the tort, 569-571, 577-580
  theories, 567-571
  unawareness of injury, 644
Trade Disputes, 24
Trade Mark, 160
Trespass, Jurisdiction in Action for, 147-153, 401-403
Transfer of Choses in Possession: see *Choses in Possession, Transfer of*
Trial, Mode of, Lex Fori Determines, 637
Trust
  administration, 510-512
  construction, 510, 513
  charitable, 507-508, 511, 512
  cy-près, 512
  generally, 506-513
  historical aspects, 506
  immovables, trusts of, 512-513
  lex situs, role of, 512-513
  marriage settlement, 509
  movables, trusts of, 507-512
  restraint on alienation of beneficial interest, 510
  testamentary, 507-508

U

United Nations
  privileges and immunities of, 180

V

Venue, Doctrine of, 401
Vested Rights Theory, 14-15
*Vienna Convention on Consular Relations
    (1963)*, 180
*Vienna Convention on Diplomatic Relations
    (1961)*, 178-180; see also *Diplomatic
    Immunity*
Voet, 8-9
Voidable Marriages
  domicile as basis for nullity jurisdiction,
    253-254
  generally, 253-255
  reform proposals, 249, 255
  residence as basis for nullity jurisdiction,
    254, 255
  void marriages distinguished, 249, 250
Void Marriages
  domicile as basis of nullity jurisdiction,
    250-251
  generally, 250-253
  place of celebration as basis of nullity
    jurisdiction, 252-253
  reform proposals, 249, 255
  residence as basis of nullity jurisdiction,
    251-252
  voidable marriages, distinguished, 249, 250

W

Wager, 552
*Washington Convention on the Settlement of
    Investment Disputes Between States and
    Nationals of Other States (1965)*, 622
Wills
  aircraft, made on, 433
  construction, 442-447
  formal validity of, 38-41
  generally, 27-28
  lex domicilii and, 38-44
  renvoi and, 38-44
  ship, made on, 433
Winding-up, 485-486
Witness
  compellability, 632
  competence, 632
  evidence: see *Evidence*
  evidence abroad, taking, 632-637
  expert, as to foreign law, 106-111; see also
    Proof of Foreign Law
  privilege, 632